James Lyon

Born and raised in Australia, James has had a long fascination with America which started with the *Mickey Mouse Club,* developed with *Zorro* and *The Lone Ranger,* and matured with *Citizen Kane* and *Chinatown.* A social scientist by training, and a sceptic by nature, he has spent the last seven years working for Lonely Planet, as an editor, researcher, and writer. He has seen much of California as a budget traveler, ski-bum, and used-car buyer, either by himself, or with his wife, Pauline, and more recently with their two young sons. His favorite parts of California include the Anza-Borrego Desert, the Golden Gate Bridge, the High Sierra, and of course Disneyland.

Tony Wheeler

Tony was born in England but grew up in Pakistan, the Bahamas, and the USA. He returned to England to do a degree in engineering at Warwick University, worked as an automotive design engineer, returned to university to complete an MBA in London, then dropped out on the Asian overland trail with his wife Maureen. They've been traveling ever since, having set up Lonely Planet Publications in the mid-'70s. Travel for the Wheelers is considerably enlived by their daughter Tashi and their son Kieran.

Marisa Gierlich

Born in Hermosa Beach, California, Marisa grew up with the beach as her backyard and the Pacific Ocean as her playground. Thanks to adventurous parents she started traveling at age six. While getting her degree in English from UC Berkeley she wrote guides to France, Sweden, Sicily, Rome, and Alaska for the *Berkeley Guides,* then headed 'out west' to write the Montana chapter of Lonely Planet's *Rocky Mountain States.* Her ultimate goals in life are to surf the perfect wave and attain unsurpassed complete perfect enlightenment.

Nancy Keller

Born and raised in Northern California, Nancy worked in the alternative press for several years, doing every aspect of newspaper work from editorial and reporting to delivering the papers. She returned to university to earn an MA in journalism, graduating in 1986. Since then she's been traveling and writing in Mexico, Israel, Egypt, Europe, various South Pacific islands, New Zealand, and Central America. Despite all the movement, she still calls Forestville home, and says one of the best things about working on this book was that she got to stay home for a while. Nancy is author or co-author of several LP books including *Rarotonga & the Cook Islands, New Zealand, Mexico,* and *Central America on a shoestring;* upcoming projects include updates of *Central America* and *Guatemala, Belize & Yucatán.*

John Gottberg

John was working as news and graphics editor for the *Los Angeles Times* travel section when he and LP publisher Tony Wheeler first discussed the *Los Angeles city guide* and this book. Previously, he had earned BA degrees from the universities of Oregon and Washington, spent a year in Hawaii on an Asian Studies fellowship, and worked his way around the world as a musician in New Zealand, a chef in Australia, a ski instructor in France, a bartender in Amsterdam, and a carpenter in Sweden. During meanderings through Asia in the mid-'70s, he used the first edition of Tony's *Southeast Asia on a shoestring.* In the 1980s, John was managing editor for APA Publications' *Insight Guides* in Singapore. He now lives in Boise, Idaho, and is a contributing editor to *International Living* magazine.

From the Authors

James Lyon Many people in tourist offices, national parks offices, libraries, and travel agencies, provided information, encouragement, and helpful advice, and I am grateful for their efforts and their professionalism. Special thanks to the Opie family of San Diego who were so hospitable and helpful, and to the staff at LP's Oakland office who produced this book despite the shortcomings of the authors. Thanks to the *Southwest* author, Rob Rachowiecki, for use of his research and information. Finally, thanks to my family – to Mike and Bennie who put up with the tedium of travel, enthused at the unexpected, and deflated the hype; and always to Pauline, my research assistant, administrator, wife, and muse.

Tony Wheeler I left my heart in San Francisco after spending a year and a half there in the mid-'80s. I've been a regular returnee ever since and I could happily move back tomorrow. So exploring the Bay Area in detail was a real labor of love, but

California
& Nevada

a lonely planet travel survival kit

James Lyon
Tony Wheeler
Marisa Gierlich
Nancy Keller
John Gottberg

California & Nevada

1st edition

Published by
Lonely Planet Publications
Head Office: PO Box 617, Hawthorn, Vic 3122, Australia
Branches: 150 Linden St, Oakland, CA 94607, USA
              10a Spring Place, London NW5 3BH, UK
              1 rue du Dahomey, 75011 Paris, France

Printed by
Colorcraft Ltd, Hong Kong

Photographs by
Cover photo: Harold Sund (Image Bank), Giant sequoia, Sequoia National Park
Title page: Nancy Keller, Death Valley, California
California title page: James Lyon, San Diego, California
Nevada title page: Dave Houser, Las Vegas, Nevada

Published
May 1996

National Library of Australia Cataloguing in Publication Data

California & Nevada.

1st ed.
Includes index.
ISBN 0 86442 335 7.

1. California – Guidebooks. 2. Nevada – Guidebooks.
I. Lyon, James. (Series: Lonely Planet travel survival kit).

917.930433

text & maps © Lonely Planet 1996
photos © photographers as indicated 1996
climate charts compiled from information supplied by Patrick J Tyson, © Patrick J Tyson, 1996

it's too big, too varied, and too complex a conglomeration of cities for one person to even dream of coming to grips with. Fortunately the enthusiastic band of hard-living Lonely Planeteers at our office in beautiful downtown Oakland (some of them real honest-to-God native Californians) fanned out to add an insider's perspective to my outsider's viewpoint. Particular thanks to these staffers for graciously revealing all their favorite restaurants, bars, rumors, and odd-ball places . . . well, almost all.

Marisa Gierlich First of all, many thanks to coordinating author James Lyon for his lengthy and very helpful suggestions.

Thanks to my dad for sharing his knowledge of the San Bernardino Mountains with me, and to my mom for being a stellar travel partner throughout Orange County and Santa Barbara. Hooray for the diamond lanes! Thanks to both for providing the state's best accommodations, totally free.

Dick and Virginia Nall were helpful in Laguna Beach research, as were Jaimie and Bonnie – thanks a heap! Thanks to Cassidy Schmidt for providing a place to rest in the Gold Country, and to Chris Emery for his expertise on rafting the American River. Thanks to George and Donna Lee for wonderful accommodation and information in Lake Tahoe. Kathy Dent was a great campground guide and fun campfire partner (Mariah too!). Mike Pontrelli was a wonderful host in June Lake – thanks for the gourmet meals and writing space. Many thanks to Jason Blantz for his thoughtful recommendations and directions to interesting places in the Eastern Sierra. Hope you can come along next time Jason! Thanks to Anne Newton and Scott and Jen Levin for showing me around Santa Barbara, and to the Smathers for kind hospitality and information about Ventura and Oxnard. And infinite thanks to Paul, who explored the Central Coast with me, handled all our wedding logistics while I was doing research in the Sierras, and became my lifetime partner (August 4, 1995) while I was writing this book. You're the best!

Nancy Keller Greatest thanks to the many people at the LP USA office who worked on this book – to the editors, who are magicians of the highest order and an author's best friend; to Caroline Liou and Eric Kettunen, LP USA's 'author liaison' people who have always been helpful, understanding, and supportive beyond any reasonable expectation; and to James Lyon, coordinating author of this book, for the same. Thanks also to Tom Brosnahan and Tony Wheeler, who gave me the opportunities that allowed me to transform from a Sonoma County journalist to an international author.

Great thanks to Karen Bridge of Healdsburg Travel, who helped me gather information for the Getting There and Away and Getting Around chapters, and to the many people who were helpful as I traveled throughout Northern California doing the research for this book. It would take many pages to name them all; people in virtually every little chamber of commerce, visitors center, and ranger station were helpful, kind, and enthusiastic about the project, in the face of collectively millions of questions.

Special thanks to Betty Browne of the Alpenrose Hostel in Mt Shasta, who exposed me to many interesting aspects of the Mt Shasta area, and to the interesting people I met there.

Thanks also the people at home in Forestville whose warm friendship kept the fire burning in my heart through two Russian River floods and many long, challenging days and nights at the typewriter in my cozy little room out in the forest, as I wrote my parts of this book. Special thanks to Trish Bagley, Roon Searcy, Jerry Hoy, Joe Leary, Katy Ha, Mother FM Holloway and the Greater Power House COGIC, and to Rudy Edwards.

I would like to dedicate my part of this book to Rudy Edwards, my 20-year friend, and to Richard Lansdell, a free spirit and my friend for 25 years, who went to a better world on December 24, 1995. God bless you Ricky. See you the next time.

John Gottberg Thanks to the convention & visitors bureaus of Los Angeles, Santa Monica, Pasadena, Orange County, and Long Beach; to the public relations firms Blaze Company, Burks Hamner, Victoria King, Murphy/O'Brien, and Steve Valentine; and especially to fellow writer-photographers Jeff Fellenzer, Bret Lundberg, Dave and Andrea Peevers, and Michael Stinson for their continued assistance and support.

From the Publisher

For the breadth, depth, and accuracy of this guidebook Lonely Planet thanks coordinating taskmistress Laini Taylor, senior troubleshooter Carolyn Hubbard, chief hairsplitters Michelle Gagne, Tom Downs, and Caroline Liou, and mercurial whipping boy Don Gates. Many thanks also to Marisa Gierlich, Greg Mills, and Eric Kettunen for eleventh-hour research and alacrity.

Map production was overseen by Alex Guilbert, and realized by himself, Paul Clifton, Hayden Foell, Beca Lafore, Cyndy Johnsen, Chris Salcedo, Scott Summers, and freelancers Scott Noren, Blake Summers, and Mark Williams. Hugh D'Andrade, Hayden, Mark Butler, and JR Swanson were the illustrators. Chris Carlsson, Heather Harrison, Don, Laini, and Tom sneaked in a few relevant sidebars, and Jen Morris and Scott Stampfli each added a favorite site or two of their own. Richard Wilson and Hugh were responsible for layout, and 'Mr Renaissance' D'Andrade also designed the cover. Scott Summers remains the all-high potentate of production.

And finally, kudos to Lonely Planet's noble Accounting, Marketing, Sales, and Warehouse staff members, who toil behind the scenes to keep these books in print, and whose praise we sing in just appreciation.

This Book

This 1st edition was produced at Lonely Planet's stately US office. An LP veteran, James was the coordinating author and wrote San Diego, California Deserts, and all of Nevada; Tony covered the San Francisco Bay Area, Wine Country, and Monterey Peninsula; Nancy wrote Northern Mountains, North Coast, and portions of the Sacramento Valley; John wrote most of LA; and Marisa gave us Gold Country, the San Joaquin Valley, the Sierra Nevada, Orange County, and parts of the Sacramento Valley, Central Coast, and Los Angeles.

Warning & Request

Things change – prices go up, schedules change, good places go bad, and bad places go bankrupt – nothing stays the same. So if you find things better or worse, recently opened or long since closed, please write and tell us and help make the next edition better.

Your letters will be used to help update future editions and, where possible, important changes will also be included as a Stop Press section in reprints.

We greatly appreciate all information that is sent to us by travelers. Back at Lonely Planet we employ a hard-working readers' letters team to sort through the many letters we receive. The best ones will be rewarded with a free copy of the next edition or another Lonely Planet guide if you prefer. We give away lots of books, but, unfortunately, not every letter/postcard receives one.

Contents

Map Legend

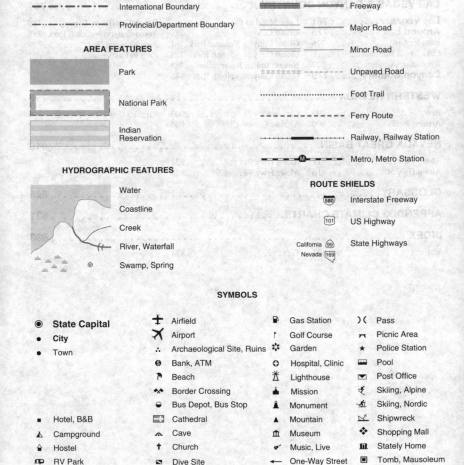

BOUNDARIES

International Boundary

Provincial/Department Boundary

AREA FEATURES

Park

National Park

Indian
Reservation

HYDROGRAPHIC FEATURES

Water

Coastline

Creek

River, Waterfall

Swamp, Spring

ROUTES

Freeway

Major Road

Minor Road

Unpaved Road

Foot Trail

Ferry Route

Railway, Railway Station

Metro, Metro Station

ROUTE SHIELDS

580 Interstate Freeway

101 US Highway

California 99
Nevada 169   State Highways

SYMBOLS

◉ **State Capital**
● **City**
● Town

■ Hotel, B&B
▲ Campground
⌂ Hostel
⊞ RV Park
▼ Restaurant
▮ Bar (Place to Drink)
▰ Cafe

✦ Airfield
✈ Airport
∴ Archaeological Site, Ruins
§ Bank, ATM
⚐ Beach
✦✦ Border Crossing
⊖ Bus Depot, Bus Stop
⊞ Cathedral
⌒ Cave
† Church
⬮ Dive Site
⚑ Embassy
⚓ Fishing, Fish Hatchery
⋈ Foot Bridge

⛽ Gas Station
⛳ Golf Course
❖ Garden
⊕ Hospital, Clinic
⚱ Lighthouse
♠ Mission
⚐ Monument
▲ Mountain
🏛 Museum
♪ Music, Live
← One-Way Street
⚎ Observatory
Ⓟ Parking
♠ Park

)(Pass
⚘ Picnic Area
★ Police Station
⚏ Pool
✉ Post Office
⛷ Skiing, Alpine
⛷ Skiing, Nordic
⚓ Shipwreck
❖ Shopping Mall
🏛 Stately Home
▣ Tomb, Mausoleum
⚑ Trailhead
⚜ Winery
🐘 Zoo

Note: not all symbols displayed above appear in this book.

Introduction

In 1510, the Spanish novelist Montalvo described a mythical golden island, rich beyond all dreams, ruled by the beautiful virgin Queen Calafia – California had its name and its image 30 years before Europeans discovered it. At that time, half of North America's indigenous population was living peacefully along the West Coast and the inland hills, finding all that they needed in the sea and the forests. The early Spanish explorers were unimpressed, and it was 200 years before the first Spanish missions gave California its architectural motif, and another 100 years before wealthy Californio cattle barons pioneered the leisurely outdoor lifestyle.

California's frenetic energy dates from the 1849 Gold Rush and its admission to the Union in 1850. From that day to this, people have brought their dreams to California, where optimism is a religion, opportunity is an article of faith, and reality can be made to order. The movie industry found that California had every location it wanted, from sand dunes to snow fields. Entertainment became an industry, Hollywood became the dream factory of the world, and the image of the California lifestyle became its most successful product. However, it's also a place where problems emerge, and where solutions are tested – Los Angeles may have been the first city to experience serious air pollution from motor vehicles, but it was also a pioneer in emission controls.

Nowadays visitors come to California not so much for its history, but to gain a glimpse of the future. Trends may not all start here, but they catch on first and fastest here – from supermarkets to snowboards, personal computers to health-food pizzas, vanity license plates to plastic credit cards. This is where the world looks to see which way-out fad will be next year's mainstream fashion.

For the traveler, California has every-thing. Accommodations range from free campsites to luxury suites, and the eating options run from fast-food takeaways to gourmet restaurants with celebrity chefs. The cities have music, art, nightlife, and every luxury and frivolity that can be imagined. Suburban life centers on the shopping mall, where the business of buying and selling has been raised from a necessity to an art form, and where shopping is a major leisure activity. Beaches, forests, mountains, deserts, rivers, and islands cater to every conceivable outdoor pursuit, from scuba diving to ice climbing, bird watching to triathlon. And because every pastime is an industry in California, this is the best place to see the very latest in windsurfing, mountain biking, bungee jumping, in-line skating, or whatever else you're into.

In California nobody needs to feel like a tourist, because no race, accent, or national origin is out of place here. Californians may not distinguish between a visitor and an immigrant – they assume that anyone who visits for more than a few days will want to stay for life. Every visitor will find California at least somewhat familiar – it's just like on TV, only more so. Meanwhile, it's the Californians who act like tourists: from the surf at Mission Beach to the ski slopes of Squaw Valley, they're here to enjoy themselves, seriously.

Nevada is a state of its own, with a long historical tie with California, and a long history of entertaining Californians – but it's more Wild West than West Coast. When you've had enough of the hype and commercialism of California, come across the border and see hype and commercialism reach its ultimate conclusion in the glitter of Las Vegas. Then get back to nature in a vast expanse of uncrowded mountain ranges, deserts, and lakes, and take a detour to Arizona's Grand Canyon and the national parks of southern Utah.

Only 150 years ago, California was the

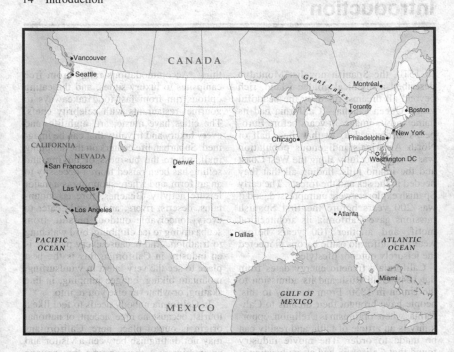

last outpost of European settlement, on the very edge of the known world, much less accessible than Africa or the Amazon. Now it's one of the most accessible places on earth, easy and convenient for travel, and surprisingly economical if you can restrict your spending to the necessities. It has a scale, a diversity, and a richness that is reflected in its landscapes, its people, its food, and its mythology – it's the place where everything is possible. There may be other visions of the future, but at the moment, California is the most user-friendly, and the most fun.

Facts for the Visitor

PLANNING
When to Go

Anytime is a good time to visit California – there's always something to enjoy. The best time depends on what you want to do: hiking, canoeing, whitewater rafting, and many other warm-weather outdoor activities can be enjoyed in the summer, spring, and fall; skiing is good in the mountains in winter and early spring. Beaches are scenic all year, but the water tends to be cold in Northern California where swimming is only good for a month or so. In Southern California, swimming is good for quite a few months, but surfers and divers still use wet suits. Whale watchers like winter, when the California gray whales migrate down the coast from Alaska.

You'll see wildflowers blooming everywhere in spring and summer; trees, orchards, and vineyards changing colors in autumn; while winter weather is beautiful in the desert areas. Urban attractions – museums, music and cultural performances, cafes and restaurants, zoos and aquariums, and so on – are enjoyable year round. Many of the most scenic mountain areas, national forests, and parks are, however, inaccessible in winter because of heavy snow.

California has a wide variety of climatic zones, so you need to consider individual towns and regions, rather than the area as a whole. Check the Climate sections in the Facts about California and Facts about Nevada chapters.

Nevada has a higher mean elevation than California and its weather tends to be more extreme. If you're just going to hit the casinos in Las Vegas and Reno, anytime is fine, but the Great Basin can be bitterly cold in winter and some of the most scenic areas are closed. Summers are hot, but bearable, while late spring and early fall are probably the best times.

Days are long in the middle of summer, when the sun can set somewhere after 9 pm and the balmy evenings linger, and short in the middle of winter, when the sun can go down as early as 4:30 pm, abruptly plunging everything into darkness before the rush hour commuters have even gotten off work.

School holidays are from early June to the beginning of September and around Christmas and Easter. Memorial Day weekend and Labor Day weekend mark the beginning and end of the 'official' summer tourist seasons. This is the busiest season for tourism, and prices are higher. Visiting California just before or just after the summer school holidays enables you to take advantage of some brilliant weather and also avoid the tourist rush.

What to Bring

Anything you can think of, you can buy in California, from an alarm clock to a zoom lens. Don't bring too much, because you'll probably want to buy more things when you arrive. An old travel adage is probably excellent advice here – bring half the things you think you'll need, and twice the money,

Dress is generally casual in public places. Men will only need a jacket and tie for the fanciest restaurants, or if they're doing business. Trouser suits are acceptable business attire for women, except in the most conservative industries, like banking, where a skirt is often required. When packing clothing, be sure to choose things that will enable you to dress in layers. There's a lot of variation in climate throughout the region, and any one day can present many changes; even hot days can soon be followed by chilly nights.

You'll need warm clothes in winter; winters are much warmer in the south than in the north, but cold, rainy weather can catch you anywhere, anytime in winter. You must be prepared for snow in the mountains in winter.

For very hot weather, you'll need a hat, sunscreen, and some light, loose clothing and pants. A water bottle and sunglasses are also essential. In addition, in the desert long-sleeved light clothing and long pants will aid in protection from sun and windburn, and help retain moisture.

A sleeping bag is a good idea if you'll be using hostels. You can bring a tent, but rentals are usually available as well near outdoors areas. Basic utensils like a cup, bowl, and spoon allow you to have cereal and a drink for a light breakfast, and they're useful with kids. Some travelers bring a small immersion heater and a cup to heat up water for instant coffee or soup in their room.

Even so, if you forget something, don't worry about it. You can easily get everything you need (and many things you don't need) fairly inexpensively in California.

Maps

Members of the American Automobile Association (AAA) can receive excellent state road maps from their local AAA office. In addition to sheet maps of California and of Nevada & Utah, there are more detailed maps covering smaller areas, including the major metropolitan and recreation areas. They don't publish a list of their maps – you have to tell them where you're going, and they give you the maps they think you'll need. Maps are available to non-members for around $3 to $4.

Visitors centers and chambers of commerce often have quite good local maps free or at a low cost. In Nevada, visitors centers give out a good color map of the state produced by the Department of Transportation. National park entrance stations or visitors centers will give you a free color map after you pay the entrance fee. USFS ranger stations sell maps of the various national forests for around $4 each.

Hikers and backpackers can purchase topographical maps from the US Geological Survey (USGS) Map & Book Sales (headquartered in Denver, Colorado – but the store in Menlo Park, California, is the West's regional location). A list of maps is available upon request. Many camping stores, travel bookstores, and national park visitors centers and USFS ranger stations sell USGS maps of their immediate area. The maps most useful for hikers are the 1:62,500 scale (approximately one inch to one mile).

Most convenience stores and gas stations sell sheet maps of the local area, which are typically detailed, accurate, and complete with an index of street names. Publishers include Rand McNally, Gousha, and USA Maps Inc, and they all charge around $2.50 for a big color map.

Atlases Visitors spending a significant amount of time in the region should try to acquire the appropriate state volume of the DeLorme Atlas & Gazetteer mapping series, which contain detailed topographic and highway maps at a scale of 1:150,000 as well as very helpful listings of campgrounds, historic sites, parks, natural features, and even scenic drives. Readily available in good bookstores, these are especially useful off the main highways and cost about $20 each.

The basic Rand McNally Road Atlas covers all of the USA and Canada, and is convenient to use in the car. For the best coverage of urban areas, get the appropriate Thomas Brothers Guide, in a handy spiral bound book format, for around $20.

TOURIST OFFICES
Local Tourist Offices

The California Division of Tourism (☎ 800-862-2543), PO Box 1499, Sacramento, CA 95812-1499, mails out a useful free information packet for visitors and answers most questions about travel in California.

The Nevada Commission on Tourism (☎ 702-687-4322) is even more helpful in providing information. Tourism is a big part of the Nevada economy, and the commission will send you free books and maps covering the whole state and listing just about every hotel, RV park, annual event, and attraction.

Many towns have a visitors center, which will typically have tons of brochures and local information. The staff are usually helpful and well informed. In other towns, the visitors center function is performed by the local chamber of commerce; however they often close on weekends and only provide information about member establishments, and this may exclude the very cheapest places to stay and eat.

Tourist Offices Abroad
US embassies will often have tourist information (see US embassies). The United States Travel & Tourism Administration (USTTA) has the following offices abroad:

Australia
Level 59, MLC Centre, King & Castlereagh Sts, Sydney, NSW 2001 (☎ (2) 233-4666)
Canada
480 University Ave, Suite 602, Toronto, Ontario, M5G 1V2 (☎ (416) 595-5082)
1253 McGill College Ave, Suite 328, Montreal, Quebec H3B 2Y5 (☎ (514) 861-5040)
1095 West Pender St, Vancouver, BC VBE 2M6 (☎ (604) 685-1930)
France
2 Ave Gabriel, 75382 Paris Cedex OB (☎ (1) 42.60.00.66)
Germany
Platenstrasse 1, 60320 Frankfurt (☎ (69) 95-67-90-0)
Italy
Via Principe Amedeo 2/10, 20121 Milano (☎ (2) 2900-2657)
Japan
Kokusai Building, 3-1-1 Marunouchi, Chiyoda-ku, Tokyo 100 (☎ (3) 3212-2124)
Mexico
Edificio Plaza Comermex, 402, Blvd M Avila Camacho No 1, Colonia Polanco Chapultepec, 11560 Mexico, DF (☎ (5) 520-3010)
UK
24 Grosvenor Square, London, England W1A 1AE (☎ (0171) 495-4466)

VISAS & DOCUMENTS
All foreign visitors (other than Canadians) must bring their passport. US citizens and Canadians may want a passport as well, in the event they're tempted to extend their travels into Mexico. All visitors should bring their driver's license and any health-insurance or travel-insurance cards.

You'll need a picture ID to show that you are over 21 to buy alcohol or gain admission to bars or clubs. A good idea is to make a photocopy of your passport and international ID to carry around instead of the original. There's nothing worse than losing your identity on a trip.

Canadians must have proper proof of Canadian citizenship, such as a citizenship card with photo ID or a passport. Visitors from other countries must have a valid passport and most visitors also require a US visa.

Visas
Apart from Canadians, and those entering under the visa-waiver program (see below), all foreign visitors will need to obtain a visa from a US consulate or embassy. In most countries the process can be done by mail, or through a travel agent.

Your passport should be valid for at least six months longer than your intended stay in the USA and you'll need to submit a recent photo (37 x 37 mm) with the application. Documents of financial stability and/or guarantees from a US resident are sometimes required, particularly for those from Third World countries.

Visa applicants may be required to 'demonstrate binding obligations' that will ensure their return back home. Because of this requirement, those planning to travel through other countries before arriving in the USA are generally better off applying for their US visa while they are still in their home country – rather than while on the road.

The most common visa is a Non-Immigrant Visitors Visa, B1 for business purposes, B2 for tourism or visiting friends and relatives. A visitors visa is good for one or five years with multiple entries, and it specifically prohibits the visitor from taking paid employment in the USA. The validity period depends on what country you're from. The length of time you'll be allowed to stay in the USA is ultimately determined by US immigration authorities

HIV & Entering the USA

Everyone entering the USA who is not a US citizen is subject to the authority of the Immigration & Naturalization Service (INS). The INS can keep someone from entering or staying in the USA by excluding or deporting them. This is especially relevant to travellers with HIV (Human Immunodeficiency Virus). Though being HIV-positive is not grounds for deportation, it is a 'ground of exclusion' and the INS can invoke this rule and refuse to admit visitors to the country.

Although the INS doesn't test people for HIV at the point of entry into the USA, they may try to exclude anyone who answers yes to this question on the non-immigrant visa application form: 'Have you ever been afflicted with a communicable disease of public health significance?' INS officials may also stop people if they seem sick, are carrying AIDS/HIV medicine or, sadly, if the officer happens to think the person looks gay, though sexual orientation is not legally a ground of exclusion. A visitor may be deported if the INS later finds that they have HIV but did not declare it. Being HIV-positive is not a 'ground for deportation,' but failing to provide correct information on the visa application is.

If you do have HIV, but can prove to consular officials you are the spouse, parent, or child of a US citizen or legal permanent resident (green-card holder), you are exempt from the exclusionary law.

It is imperative that visitors know and assert their rights. Immigrants and visitors who may face exclusion should discuss their rights and options with a trained immigration advocate within the USA before applying for a visa. For legal immigration information and referrals to immigration advocates, contact The National Immigration Project of the National Lawyers Guild (☎ 617-227-9727), 14 Beacon St, Suite 506, Boston, MA 02108; or Immigrant HIV Assistance Project, Bar Association of San Francisco (☎ 415-267-0795), 685 Market St, Suite 700, San Francisco, CA 94105. ■

at the port of entry. If you're coming to the USA to work or study, you will probably need a different type of visa, and the company or institution which you're going to should make the arrangements. Allow six months in advance for processing the application.

Entering the USA If you have a non-US passport, with a visa, you must complete an Arrival/Departure Record (form I-94) before you front up to the immigration desk. It's usually handed out on the plane, along with the customs declaration. It's a rather badly designed form, and lots of people take more than one attempt to get it right. Qantas suggests you start at the last question, and work upwards. Answers should be written *below* the questions. For question 12, 'Address While in the United States,' give the address of the location where you will spend the first night. Complete the Departure Record too (the lower part of the form), giving exactly the same answers for questions 14 to 17 as for questions 1 to 4.

The immigration area has smiling pictures of the president welcoming you to the USA, but there's usually a line at the immigration desk, and the staff of the Immigration & Naturalization Service (INS) can be less than welcoming. Their main concern is to exclude those who are likely to work illegally or overstay, so visitors will be asked about their plans, and perhaps about whether they have sufficient funds for their stay. If they think you're OK, a six-month entry is usually approved, even if you say you only want to enter for a few weeks.

It's a good idea to be able to list an itinerary which will account for the period for which you ask to be admitted, and to be able to show you have $300 or $400 for every week of your intended stay. These days, a couple of major credit cards will go a long way towards establishing 'sufficient funds.' Don't make too much of having friends, relatives, or business contacts in the USA – the INS official may decide that this will make you more likely to overstay.

Visa-Waiver Program Citizens of certain countries may enter the USA without a US visa, for stays of 90 days or less, under the reciprocal visa-waiver program. Currently these countries are the UK, New Zealand, Japan, Italy, Spain, Austria, the Netherlands, Belgium, Switzerland, France, Germany, Norway, Denmark, Sweden, Finland, Iceland, San Marino, Andorra, Luxembourg, Liechtenstein, and Monaco. Under this program you must have a round trip ticket that is non-refundable in the USA and you will not be allowed to extend your stay beyond 90 days.

Visa Extensions & Re-Entry If you want, need, or hope to stay in the USA longer than the date stamped on your passport, go to the local INS office (or call ☎ 800-755-0777, or look in the local white pages telephone directory under US Government) *before* the stamped date to apply for an extension. Anytime after that will usually lead to an unamusing conversation with an INS official who will assume you want to work illegally. If you find yourself in that situation, it's a good idea to bring a US citizen with you to vouch for your character. It's also a good idea to have some verification that you have enough money to support yourself.

Alternatively, cross the border into Mexico, and apply for another period of entry when you come back. US officials don't usually collect the Departure Record cards from your passport when you leave at a land border, so they may not notice if you've overstayed by a couple of days. Returning to the USA, you go through the same procedure as when you entered the USA for the first time, so be ready with your proposed itinerary, and evidence of sufficient funds. If you try this border hopping more than once, to get a third six-month period of entry, you may find the INS very strict. Generally it seems that they are reluctant to let you stay more than a year.

Travel Insurance
No matter how you're traveling, make sure you take out travel insurance. This should cover you not only for medical expenses and luggage theft or loss, but also for unavoidable cancellation or delays in your travel arrangements, and everyone should be covered for the worst possible case, such as an accident that requires hospital treatment and a flight home. Coverage depends on your insurance and type of ticket, so ask both your insurer and your ticket-issuing agency to explain the finer points. STA Travel offers a variety of travel insurance options at reasonable prices. Ticket loss is also covered by travel insurance. Make sure you have a separate record of all your ticket details – or better still, a photocopy of it. Also make a copy of your policy, in case the original is lost.

Buy travel insurance as early as possible. If you buy it the week before you fly, you may find, for instance, that you're not covered for delays to your flight caused by strikes or other industrial action that may have been in force before you took out the insurance.

If you're planning to travel a long time, the insurance may seem very expensive – but if you can't afford it, you certainly won't be able to afford a medical emergency in the USA.

International Driving Permit
An International Driving Permit is a useful accessory for foreign visitors in the USA. Local traffic police are more likely to accept it as valid identification than an unfamiliar document from another country. Your national automobile association can provide one for a small fee. They're usually valid for one year.

Hostel Card
Most hostels in the USA are members of Hostelling International/American Youth Hostel (HI/AYH), which is affiliated with the International Youth Hostel Federation (IYHF). You can purchase membership on the spot when checking in, although it's probably advisable to purchase it before

you leave home. Most hostels allow non-members to stay, but charge a few dollars more.

Student & Youth Cards

If you're a student, get an international student ID or bring along a school or university ID card to take advantage of the discounts available to students.

Seniors' Cards

All people over the age of 65 get discounts throughout the USA. All you need is ID with proof of age should you be carded. There are organizations such as AARP (see Senior Travelers) that offer membership cards for further discounts.

Automobile Association Cards

The American Automobile Association (AAA) is extremely useful, even if you'll only be driving a little (there are frequently AAA discounts at accommodations), so don't forget your card if you're a member, or a member of an affiliated group.

EMBASSIES
US Embassies Abroad

US diplomatic offices abroad include the following:

Australia
    US Embassy: 21 Moonah Place, Yarralumla ACT 2600 (☎ (6) 270 5000)
    Consulate Level 59 MLC Center 19-29 Martin Place, Sydney NSW 2000 (☎ (2) 9373 9200)
    Consulate: 553 St Kilda Rd, Melbourne (☎ 9526 5900) There are also consulates in Perth and Brisbane.
Austria
    Boltzmanngasse 16, A-1091, Vienna (☎ (1) 313-39)
Belgium
    Blvd du Régent 27, B-1000, Brussels (☎ (2) 513 38 30)
Canada
    US Embassy: 100 Wellington St, Ottawa, Ontario 1P 5T1 (☎ (613) 238-5335)
    US Consulate-General: 1095 West Pender St, Vancouver, BC V6E 2M6 (☎ (604) 685-1930)

US Consulate-General: 1155 rue St-Alexandre, Montreal, Quebec (☎ (514) 398-9695) There are also consulates in Toronto, Calgary, and Halifax.
Denmark
    Dag Hammarskjolds Allé 24, Copenhagen (☎ 31 42 31 44)
Finland
    Itainen Puistotie 14A, Helsinki (☎ (0) 171-931)
France
    US Embassy, 2 rue Saint Florentin, 75001 Paris (☎ (1) 42.96.12.02)
    There are also consulates in Bordeaux, Lyon, Marseille, Nice, Strasbourg, and Toulouse.
Germany
    Deichmanns Aue 29, 53179 Bonn (☎ (228) 33 91)
India
    Shanti Path, Chanakyapuri 110021, New Delhi (☎ (11) 60-0651)
Ireland
    42 Elgin Rd, Ballsbridge, Dublin (☎ (1) 687 122)
Israel
    71 Hayarkon St, Tel Aviv (☎ (3) 517-4338)
Japan
    1-10-5 Akasaka Chome, Minato-ku, Tokyo (☎ (3) 224-5000)
Mexico
    Paseo de la Reforma 305, Cuauhtémoc, 06500 Mexico City (☎ (5) 211-00-42)
Netherlands
    US Embassy: Lange Voorhout 102, 2514 EJ The Hague (☎ (70) 310 92 09)
    US Consulate: Museumplein 19, 1071 DJ Amsterdam (☎ (20) 310 9209)
New Zealand
    29 Fitzherbert Terrace, Thorndon, Wellington (☎ (4) 722 068)
Norway
    Drammensvein 18, Oslo (☎ (22) 44 85 50)
Singapore
    30 Hill St, Singapore 0617 (☎ 338-0251)
South Africa
    877 Pretorius St, Box 9536, Pretoria 0001 (☎ (12) 342-1048)
Spain
    Calle Serrano 75, 28006 Madrid (☎ (1) 577 4000)
Sweden
    Strandvagen 101, S-115 89 Stockholm (☎ (8) 783 5300)
Switzerland
    Jubilaumsstrasse 93, 3005 Berne (☎ (31) 357 70 11)

UK
US Embassy, 5 Upper Grosvenor St, London
W1 (☎ (0171) 499 9000)
US Consulate-General, 3 Regent Terrace,
Edinburgh EH7 5BW (☎ (31) 556 8315)
US Consulate-General, Queens House,
Belfast BT1 6EQ (☎ (232) 328 239)

Foreign Embassies in the USA
Most nations have an embassy in Washington, DC – to find the telephone number, call Washington, DC information (☎ 202-555-1212). Many countries have consulates in the major cities of California (see the San Francisco, Los Angeles, and San Diego chapters). Mexico has consulates in the big cities, and also in Calexico, Fresno, Sacramento, San Bernadino, and San Jose.

CUSTOMS
US customs allows each person over the age of 21 to bring one liter of liquor and 200 cigarettes duty-free into the USA. US citizens are allowed to import, duty-free, $400 worth of gifts from abroad while non-US citizens are allowed to bring in $100 worth. Should you be carrying more than $10,000 in cash, traveler's checks, money orders, and the like, you need to declare the excess amount. There is no legal restriction on the amount which may be imported, but undeclared sums in excess of $10,000 may be subject to confiscation.

Any fruit, vegetables, or other food or plant material should be declared when you arrive by air, or left in the bins in the arrival area. If you enter California by road, you will be asked to surrender fruit or vegetables at roadside agriculture inspection stations. This is aimed at preventing the spread of pests and plant diseases into California's rich agricultural areas.

MONEY
The US dollar is divided into 100 cents (¢). Coins come in denominations of 1¢ (penny), 5¢ (nickel), 10¢ (dime), 25¢ (quarter), and the seldom seen 50¢ (half dollar). Quarters are the most commonly used coins in vending machines and parking meters, so it's handy to have a stash of

them. Notes, commonly called bills, come in $1, $2, $5, $10, $20, $50, and $100 denominations – $2 bills are rare, but perfectly legal. There is also a $1 coin that the government has tried unsuccessfully to bring into mass circulation; you may get them as change from ticket and stamp machines. Be aware that they look similar to quarters.

Costs
The cost of travel in California and Nevada depends a great deal on the degree of comfort you require. Generally it's more expensive to travel alone, and moving around a lot costs more than having longer stays in fewer places. The main expenses are transportation, accommodations, food, and the cost of sightseeing and entertainment.

Transportation The best way to get around is by car, except in a few central city areas, like San Francisco and Las Vegas. Car rental is available in most towns of any size. Rates can be as cheap as $100 a week for a compact or sub-compact, at off-peak rates. More often, though, rentals begin around $130 for a week. Liability insurance, if you are not already covered by a credit card or personal insurance policy, is usually another $7 a day, and collision insurance for the car itself may be another $9. Gas (ie gasoline, petrol) is cheap, ranging from about $1.05 to $1.50 for a US gallon, depending on the location and grade of fuel. Remote places charge the highest prices – as much as $2 for a gallon, so fill up in towns.

If you'll be in California more than about three months, it may be worth buying a car, which will change your cost structure a little. For more information on rentals and purchasing a car, see the Getting Around chapter.

Intercity buses are inexpensive – Los Angeles to San Francisco can be as little as $30 on a special Greyhound fare. Trains are more expensive than buses, but there can be cheap roundtrip deals. The cost of flying varies greatly, but cheap tickets are available, and can be even less than the bus fare (See Getting There & Away and Getting Around).

Accommodations The cheapest option is camping, which will usually cost a minimum of around $5 for a basic site in campgrounds on public land. Developed campgrounds, public or private, charge around $12 for a tent site if there are hot showers and other facilities available. An RV site, with power and water hookups, will be up to around $20. Camping is not really an option unless you have a car, which offsets some of the savings.

Youth hostels affiliated with HI/AYH cost around $12 for a bunk bed in a dorm room. Independent travelers hostels are becoming more common, and charge about the same. Cheap and basic motels are also a good deal for a couple of budget travelers, at about $30 for a double room in cheap motel strips. Single rooms are not much cheaper, and a room for a family or two couples won't cost much more.

Travelers looking for more than a basic room can find very comfortable mid-range accommodations for $50 to $70 a double in most places, and some towns have luxury hotels with rooms for more than $100. Any place near a beach, national park, or major attraction will be relatively expensive in the tourist season. B&Bs are not for budget travelers; they start at about $50 for a double, but most are in the $60 to $100 range. There is more information about accommodations later on in this chapter.

Food & Drink Basic food items and prepackaged meals are cheap, so if you're staying in one place for more than a few days, and you have minimal kitchen facilities, you could prepare your own meals for as little as $5 for two. At the cheapest fast-food restaurants you can get a large hamburger, soft drink, and French fries for about $3 or $4. Many towns have all-you-can-eat restaurants where the starving budget traveler can fill up for about $5. For a little more money, Mexican or Chinese restaurants offer great meals for under $10,

and a large pizza – enough for two – can be had for $10 and up. Tax and tips add to the cost of eating out, so budget a minimum of around $5 for breakfast, $7 for lunch, and $12 for dinner. At better restaurants, you can eat very well for under $25 per person, including a beer or a glass of wine. In first-class restaurants you can easily spend $100 on dinner for two. More details on food are given later in this chapter.

A 12-oz bottle of domestic beer can range from $1.50 to $4.00 in a bar or restaurant. A six-pack of domestic beers costs $3 to $5 in the supermarket, while a six-pack of soft drinks is around $3, depending on the brand. A cup of coffee is usually $1.

Sightseeing & Entertainment Many of the best and most interesting things to see and do cost nothing – like walking across the Golden Gate Bridge, enjoying the view from Big Sur, checking the scene at Venice Beach, or browsing in a big shopping mall. But California is consumer country, and most things will cost money sooner or later. Small museums may charge as little as $2, but $3 to $6 is more common. Bigger, or more commercial attractions cost more, eg $7 to see the California Academy of Sciences; $13 for the San Diego Zoo, $28 for Sea World, and $31 for Disneyland. Entrance into national parks, historical sites, etc costs $3 to $10 a vehicle (irrespective of whether there are six people or just a driver), usually good for multiple entries over seven days. First-run movies are usually $7, but you can sometimes pay $2 in budget theaters showing movies that have been out for a few months.

It's easy to spend lots of money in California – there are just so many tempting shops, restaurants, attractions, and activities. Venice Beach may be free, but if you rent a bike or in-line skates, buy a hot dog and a Coke, and see some irresistible souvenir, your cheap afternoon can easily cost $50. Traveling on a super-tight budget can be frustrating, even depressing, if you just can't afford to enjoy the place.

Extras In hotels, beware of grossly inflated charges for some services, especially telephones and laundry. To avoid unpleasant surprises, ask about these before you incur any expenses.

Traveler's Checks
If you plan to carry traveler's checks, buy them in US dollars. Restaurants, hotels, and most stores accept US dollar traveler's checks as if they were cash, so you'll never have to exchange them at a bank or pay an exchange fee.

ATMs
Most banks have automated teller machines (ATMs), which are usually open 24 hours a day. There are various ATM networks and most banks are affiliated with several. Some of the most common are Cirrus, Plus, Star Systems, and Interlink. You can also find ATMs at most airports, large grocery stores, shopping malls and in a growing number of convenience stores.

For a small charge, you can withdraw cash from an ATM using a credit card or a charge card. Credit cards usually have a 2% fee with a $2 minimum and you must first have established a Personal Identification Number (PIN), but using bank cards linked to a personal checking account is usually far cheaper. Check with your bank or credit card company for exact information.

Credit & Debit Cards
Major credit and charge cards are almost universally accepted by hotels, restaurants, gas stations, shops, and larger grocery stores. Many recreational and tourist activities accept credit cards, and most car rental agencies insist on them. The most commonly accepted cards are Visa, MasterCard, and American Express. Discover and Diners Club cards are also accepted by a fair number of businesses.

Ticket buying services won't reserve tickets over the phone unless you offer a credit card number. Even if you loathe credit cards and prefer to rely on traveler's checks and ATMs, it's a good idea to carry one (best bets are Visa or MasterCard) for emergencies.

Unlike a credit card, a debit card deducts payment directly from the user's bank account. Instead of an interest rate, users are charged a minimal fee for the transaction. Be sure to check with your bank to confirm that your debit card will be accepted in California and Nevada. For telephone numbers to call in case your card is lost or stolen, see the Emergency section.

International Transfers
Money can be wired to and from the main branches of most banks, as well as through Western Union and American Express, but check the charges for the service. A better option may be to have someone add funds to your credit card, which you can then get a cash advance against.

Tipping
Tipping is expected in restaurants where you are served at your table and better hotels, as well as by taxi drivers, hairdressers, and baggage carriers. Serving staff in restaurants are paid less than minimum wage and rely upon tips for their livelihoods. Tip 15% unless the service is terrible (in which case a complaint to the manager is warranted) or 20% if the service is great. Never tip in fast-food, take-out, or buffet-style restaurants where you serve yourself.

Taxi drivers expect 10% and hairdressers get 15% if their service is satisfactory. Baggage carriers (skycaps in airports, bellboys in hotels) receive $1 for the first bag and 50¢ for each additional bag carried. In budget hotels (where there aren't bellboys anyway) tips are not expected. In luxury hotels, tipping can reach irritating proportions – doormen, bellboys, parking attendants, and chambermaids are all tipped at least $1 for each service performed. However, simply saying 'thank you' to an attendant who merely opens the door when you could just as easily have done it yourself is OK.

Special Deals

The USA is probably the most promotion-oriented society on earth. Everything has an angle and with a little detective work and a lot of gumption, the traveler stands to find some worthwhile bargains.

Off-season hotel prices, for example, are frequently negotiable. 'You know, I'd love to stay at your fine establishment, but Joe Bob's Hotel down the street is much cheaper.' Be confident, but don't be rude. Indicate the amount you would be prepared to pay – 'Do you have any rooms under $30?' is a good way to ask.

Visitors centers and chambers of commerce usually have lots of brochures, often with discount coupons for local attractions, restaurants, and accommodations. You'll find similar brochures in motel lobbies. Free tourist information publications often have discount coupons. Sunday newspapers typically have discount coupons for local supermarkets and advertising circulars for sales at department stores. Coupon books for local merchants can be purchased at independent bookshops; they're usually on display at the front counter. Supermarkets also run specials on tickets for local attractions, especially 'family' attractions, like amusement parks, or professional sporting events (usually baseball). If there is skiing within a two-hour drive, cheap lift tickets are often available at supermarkets as well.

Don't get too excited about all these coupons – there's usually a catch. 'Free Pizza' can mean something like a free version of their smallest, cheapest pizza, for a party of four, with purchase of another pizza of equal or greater value; offer not valid after 5 pm or on weekends; tax and gratuity not included. But $2 off the admission price of an attraction you wanted to see anyway is not to be sneezed at.

If you plan to rent a car, rental agencies sometimes offer discounts in tandem with national motel chains. Since the deregulation of the US airline industry, airlines have been jockeying to provide the most appealing premiums for potential flyers. If you belong to any frequent-flyer programs, be sure to ask what discounts they entitle you to.

Taxes

Almost everything you pay for in the USA is taxed. Occasionally, the tax is included in the advertised price (eg, plane tickets, gas, drinks in a bar, and entrance tickets for museums or theaters). Restaurant meals and drinks, accommodations, and most other purchases are taxed, and this is added to the advertised cost.

Basic state sales taxes are 7.25% in California and 6.75% in Nevada (7% in Clark County). For meals, rooms, and other purchases, there are state plus local (city or county) taxes added on to lodging, restaurant, and car rental bills. This means that as you move around California and Nevada, you'll pay different taxes in every town. The prices given in this book do not include taxes.

Currency Exchange

Most banks will exchange cash or traveler's checks in major foreign currencies, though banks in outlying areas don't do so very often, and it may take them some time. It's probably less of a hassle to exchange foreign currency in larger cities. Additionally, Thomas Cook, American Express, and exchange windows in airports offer exchange (although you'll get a better rate at a bank).

At press time, exchange rates were:

Australia	A$1	=	$0.74
Canada	C$1	=	$0.74
Germany	DM1	=	$0.75
Hong Kong	HK$10	=	$1.34
Japan	¥100	=	$1.17
New Zealand	NZ$1	=	$0.69
UK	UK£1	=	$1.64

POST & TELECOMMUNICATIONS

Postal Rates

Postage rates increase every few years. The next increase is expected in 1997, when postage rates will probably go up by about 10%. Currently, rates for 1st-class mail within the USA are 32¢ for letters up to one ounce (23¢ for each additional ounce) and 20¢ for postcards.

International airmail rates (except Canada and Mexico) are 60¢ for a half-ounce letter, 95¢ for a one-ounce letter and 39¢ for each additional half ounce. International postcard rates are 40¢. Letters to Canada are 46¢ for a one-ounce letter, 23¢ for each additional ounce and 30¢ for a postcard. Letters to Mexico are 35¢ for a half-ounce letter, 45¢ for a one-ounce letter and 30¢ for a postcard. Aerogrammes are 45¢.

The cost for parcels airmailed anywhere within the USA is $3 for two pounds or less, increasing by $1 per pound up to $6 for five pounds. For heavier items, rates differ according to the distance mailed. Books, periodicals, and computer disks can be sent by a cheaper 4th-class rate.

Sending Mail

If you have the correct postage, you can drop your mail into any blue mail box. These are found at many convenient locations including shopping centers, airports, and street corners. The times of the next mail pickup are written on the inside of the lid of the mail box. This sign also indicates the location of the nearest mail box with later or more frequent pickup.

If you need to buy stamps or weigh your mail, go to the nearest post office. In addition, larger towns have branch post offices and post office centers in some supermarkets and drugstores. For the address of the nearest office, call the main post office listed under Postal Service in the US Government section in the white pages of the telephone directory.

Usually, post offices in main towns are open weekdays from 8 am to 5 pm and on Saturday 8 am to 3 pm, but it all depends on the branch. The major cities have a 24-hour Express Mail service (at a higher cost) in the city's main post office.

Receiving Mail

You can have mail sent to you care of General Delivery at any post office that has its own zip (postal) code. It's best to have your intended date of arrival (if the sender knows it) clearly marked on the envelope. Mail is usually held for 10 days before it's returned to the sender. You'll need picture ID to collect general delivery mail. Alternatively, have mail sent to the local representative of American Express or Thomas Cook, provide mail service for their clients.

Telephone

All phone numbers within the USA consist of a three-digit area code followed by a seven-digit local number. If you are calling locally, just dial the seven-digit number. If you are calling long distance, dial 1 + the three-digit area code + the seven-digit number.

If you're calling from abroad, the international country code for the USA is 1.

The 800 and 888 area codes are designated for toll-free numbers within the USA and sometimes from Canada as well. These calls, including calls to toll-free area code information, are free.

The 900 area code is designated for calls for which the caller pays at a premium rate. They have a reputation of being sleazy operations – a smorgasbord of phone sex at $2.99 a minute is one of many offerings.

Many businesses use letters instead of numbers for their telephone numbers in an attempt to make it snappy and memorable (like the airline: 800-2FLY-AWA – watch for other examples of this emerging art form). Sometimes it is difficult to read the letters on the number pad. If you can't read the letters, here they are: 1 doesn't get any; 2 – ABC, 3 – DEF, 4 – GHI, 5 – JKL, 6 – MNO, 7 – PRS, 8 – TUV, 9 – WXY. Sorry, no Qs or Zs.

Directory Assistance Directory assistance can be reached locally by dialing ☎ 411. For assistance outside your area code, dial 1 + the three-digit area code of the place you want to call + 555-1212, though this does carry a charge of around 75¢. For example, to obtain directory assistance for San Francisco, dial 1 + 415 + 555-1212. Area codes for places outside the region are listed in telephone directories – which of course, have local listings in the white pages and commercial listings by category in the yellow pages, and are free to use.

Hotel Phones Many hotels (especially the more expensive ones) add a service charge of 50¢ to $1 for each local call made from a room phone and they also have hefty surcharges for long-distance calls.

Pay Phones Public pay phones, which can be found in most lobbies, are always cheaper. Local calls usually cost 20¢ at Pacific Bell pay phones, although occasional private phones may charge more. You can pump in quarters, use a credit card, or make collect calls from pay phones.

Phone Cards A new long distance alternative is phone debit cards, which allow purchasers to pay in advance, with access through a toll-free 800 number. In amounts of $5, $10, $20, and $50, these are available from vending machines in airports, hotels, convenience stores, and other tourist centers. When using credit cards to place your call, be aware of people watching you, especially in public places like airports. Thieves will memorize numbers and use them to make large numbers of international calls.

Rates Long-distance rates vary depending on the destination and which telephone company you use – call the operator (☎ 0) for rate information. Don't ask the operator to put your call through, however, because operator-assisted calls are much more expensive than direct-dial calls. Generally, nights (11 pm to 8 am) and all day Saturday and Sunday are the cheapest times to call (60% discount). Evenings (Sunday to Friday 5 to 11 pm) are mid-priced (35% discount). Day calls (weekdays 8 am to 5 pm) are full-priced calls within the USA.

International Calls To make an international call direct, dial ☎ 011, then the country code, followed by the area code and the phone number. You may need to wait as long as 45 seconds for the ringing to start. International rates vary depending on the time of day and the destination. For example, the cheapest rates from California to London, England, are between 5 pm and 6 am, whilst when calling Melbourne, Australia, the cheapest rates are from 2 am to 1 pm, California time. Again, rates vary depending on the telephone company used and the destination. Call the operator (☎ 0) for rates. The first minute is always more expensive than additional minutes.

Fax, Telegram & Email
Fax machines are easy to find in the USA, at shipping companies like Mail Boxes, Etc, photocopy services, and hotel business service centers, but be prepared to pay high prices (over $1 a page). Telegrams can be sent from Western Union (☎ 800-325-6000). Email is quickly becoming a preferred method of communication; however, unless you have a laptop and modem that can be plugged into a telephone socket, it's difficult to get on-line. Hotel business service centers may provide connections, and trendy restaurants and cafes sometimes offer internet service as well.

BOOKS
There are a vast number of books on just about every aspect of California, and guides to the most esoteric activities. If you want to find out about Art Deco architecture, killer roller coasters, or the gay rodeo circuit, one of the many excellent bookstores or libraries will be able to help you. National park offices and museums can have excellent selections of specialized books and maps, and if they are government-run institutions, you will save about 7% because they don't charge sales tax.

Guidebooks
Most of the main guidebook publishers have guides to California, or to Californian cities. The AAA tour books, free to members and affiliates, have good editions on specific parts of the states, like the desert areas, or Lake Tahoe, as well as guides to the main cities and to California

& Nevada. Some specialized guidebooks for specific activities, like hiking and skiing, are listed in the Outdoor Activities chapter. Other guides to local areas may be mentioned in the sections under those places.

Field Guides

A variety of books will help you identify Californian plants and animals, tell you where you can see them and give you insight into their biology.

The Peterson Field Guide Series has almost 40 excellent books including *Mammals* by William H Burt and Richard P Grossenheider (3rd ed, 1976), *Western Birds* by Roger Tory Peterson (3rd ed, 1990), *Western Reptiles & Amphibians* by Robert C Stebbins (1985), *Western Butter-flies* by Tilden & Smith and *Southwestern & Texas Wildflowers* by Niehaus, Ripper & Savage.

There are numerous other field guides. The series of *Audubon Society Field Guides* (Knopf) covers birds, plants, and animals, arranged by color using photos – a departure from the standard field guides, which are arranged in biological sequence. The Audubon Society Nature Guide *Deserts* by James A MacMahon (Knopf, 1985) gives a fine overview of the Southwestern deserts as well as being a field guide to the most important plants and animals of these regions. The *Golden Field Guide* series (Western Publishing Company) is known for its simple approach and is often preferred by beginners. The National Geographic Society's *Field Guide to the Birds of North America* (2nd ed, 1987) is well-done and one of the most detailed.

History & Culture

For an overall history of California, try *California: an Interpretive History*, by Walton Bean. A history of the USA will help you get an understanding of California in context, because California does have a particular place in the national history and the national psyche. For a more social history, read some of the fictional works set

in California at various periods (see Literature in the Facts about California chapter). To get a picture of the first European settlements, look at some of the following works descriptions by early visitors and residents.

One of the first travelers to record his impressions of California was Richard Henry Dana, whose visits to California in 1835, during the Mexican rancho period, are recounted in *Two Years Before the Mast*. He found the Californios idle and thriftless, and spending far more on their dress than they should: it's a good read, and widely available. Dana Point, south of LA, is named for the author.

Nevada – A History (1977), by Robert Laxalt, is somewhat idiosyncratic, but an entertaining history of the silver state. Another easy-to-follow history is *The Nevada Adventure*, by James Hulse (University of Nevada Press, 1972).

Several well-known writers have taken their pens to Las Vegas. The famously titled *Fear & Loathing in Las Vegas* (1971) is mostly about Hunter S Thompson's reactions to a wide variety of drugs, but you may have similar reactions to the city itself.

Environment

The *Cadillac Desert: The American West and Its Disappearing Water* by Marc Reisner (Penguin, 1986), is a thorough account of how the exploding populations of Western states have exploited and argued over every drop of available water. It's equally relevant to Nevada.

A combination travel book and geological text, *Basin and Range* by John McPhee (1981) is based around a drive across Nevada and Utah on I-80, and is a recommended read.

Native Americans

The best introduction for the serious student is the 20-volume *Handbook of North American Indians* (Smithsonian Institution). The volumes that cover this region are *Volume 8: California* edited by Robert Heizer (1978), and *Volume 11: Great Basin* edited by Warren L D'Azevedo (1986).

Another authoritative text is *The California Indians* by R F Heizer & M A Whipple.

MEDIA

The USA has a wide spectrum of newspapers, magazines, and book publishers, both nationally and regionally.

Radio and TV also support a wide variety of news programs, though most of the reporting tends to center on the USA.

Newspapers & Magazines

There are over 1500 daily newspapers published in the USA. The newspaper with the highest circulation is *Wall Street Journal* followed by *USA Today*, *New York Times*, and *Los Angeles Times*, which are all available in major cities. Besides the *Los Angeles Times*, California's most widely-read newspapers are the *San Francisco Chronicle* and the *San Diego Union*. These newspapers' Sunday editions have supplements listing the coming week's events in arts and entertainment.

Most other cities have a local daily newspaper. These papers are worth looking at to get an idea of the local issues in the areas you visit – bridge congestion in the Bay area; salination in the Imperial Valley; or gambling revenues in Reno.

Newspapers such as *SF Weekly*, the *Bay Area Guardian*, *LA Weekly*, and *San Diego Reader* are usually independent and have well-written stories concerning local and national news, and current entertainment listings including restaurant and theater reviews.

Radio

All rental cars have car radios. Most stations have a range of less than 100 miles, so you'll have to keep changing stations as you drive. In the southern parts of California, Mexican stations can easily be picked up, but they're hard to distinguish from the US stations broadcasting in Spanish. In and near major cities, there's a wide variety of music and entertainment. In rural areas, be prepared for a predominance of country & western music, Christian programming, local news, and 'talk radio.'

There are many talk radio stations, especially on AM. They can be entertaining, but don't believe most of what you hear; as Bill Watterson's cartoon character Calvin describes the philosophy of the talk show broadcaster: 'I'll spout simplistic opinions for hours on end, ridicule anyone who disagrees with me, and generally foster divisiveness, cynicism, and a lower level of public dialog!'

National Public Radio (NPR) features a more level-headed approach to news, discussion, and music. NPR normally broadcasts on the lower end of the FM band.

TV

Even the cheapest motel rooms have a color TV set, though sometimes they don't work very well. They receive the local affiliates of the five networks which dominate American broadcast television – ABC, CBS, NBC, FOX, and PBS. PBS, the Public Broadcasting System, is noncommercial, and has a quite good news service, and some thoughtful current affairs programming – check the Newshour with Jim Lehrer. Other PBS programs feature educational shows, classical music and theater, and quite a few BBC productions.

Better motels boast TV with access to cable stations, usually ESPN (all sports), CNN (all news), the Weather Channel (you guessed it), and HBO (movies). With a couple of shopping channels, music video channels, and the odd TV evangelist, it's quite common to have 20 or more programs to choose from, and absolutely nothing worth watching. Pay-per-view events or movies are pretty hard to access without realizing you are going to be charged for the service – and usually only better hotels carry the service. Check with the front desk if you're unsure.

PHOTOGRAPHY & VIDEO

Film & Equipment

Print film is widely available at supermarkets and discount drugstores. For processing, drugstores are usually good, inexpensive places. If it's dropped off by noon, you can usually pick it up the next day. A roll of 35 mm 100 ASA color film with 24 exposures will cost about $6 to get processed.

If you want your pictures right away, you can find one-hour processing services in the yellow pages under Photo Processing, but be prepared to pay dearly. Slide film isn't so widely available, but still easy to find in larger stores, photography shops, and around major tourist attractions.

Film can be damaged by excessive heat, so don't leave your camera and film in the car on a hot day, or leave your camera on the dashboard.

It's worth carrying a spare battery for your camera to avoid disappointment when your camera dies in the middle of nowhere. Bring a haze or ultraviolet filter, as much for protection as for effect. If you're buying a new camera for your trip do so several weeks before you leave and practice using it.

Technique

Proverbially sunny California offers plenty of light for photography, especially in the southern and desert areas. When sunlight is strong, and the sun is high in the sky, photographs tend to emphasize shadows and wash out highlights. It's best to take your pictures during the early morning and the late afternoon, when light is softer and the sun is low in the sky.

A polarizing filter can also help to provide more contrast when photographing in strong light, especially at high altitudes, in the snow and in deserts. The filter can make sky, cloud, and water look much more dramatic.

In forests you'll find that light levels are surprisingly low, and a fast film, or an infill flash may be helpful. The often foggy conditions on the California coast are frustrating for photographers, but do present some opportunities for atmospheric shots. Look for interesting shapes emerging from the mist, and bracket the exposures over several F-stops.

Video

Blank tapes for your video camera are available at most big shopping centers. Though American pre-recorded video tapes may use a system not compatible with equipment in other countries, blank tapes will be formatted as you record on them, according to the system used by the camera.

Etiquette

Californians tend to be deferential around photographers, and will make a point of not walking in front of your camera, even if you want them to. No one seems to mind being photographed in the context of an overall scene, but if you want a close-up shot, you should ask first. Then the problem is to have the subject look natural. Native Americans on reservations may prefer not to be photographed, or they may ask for a payment.

Airport Security

All passengers on flights have to pass their luggage through X-ray machines. Technology as it is today doesn't jeopardize lower-speed film. If you're paranoid, carry your film and cameras in an accessible, visible way, and ask the security staff to check them visually.

TIME

California and Nevada are on Pacific Standard Time, which is eight hours behind Greenwich mean time; it is three hours behind Eastern Standard Time (New York, Florida), two hours behind Central Standard Time (Illinois, Texas), one hour behind Mountain Time (Colorado, Arizona), one hour ahead of Alaska time and two or three hours ahead of Hawaii time. When it is 3 pm in New York, it is noon in San Francisco.

Like the rest of the USA, California and Nevada observe Daylight Saving Time in the summer. The clock is moved forward one hour on the first weekend in April and moved back again on the last weekend in October. Since the entire USA (with the exception of Hawaii) does this, the time differences remain constant within the USA, but they may create an hour of difference in relation to other countries (who may also observe their own daylight savings hours).

ELECTRICITY

The entire USA uses 110 V and 60 cycles and the plugs have two (flat) or three (two flat, one round) pins. Plugs with three pins don't fit into a two-hole socket, but adapters are easy to buy. Two-pin plugs, especially ones with equal dimensions, can easily slip out of the socket. Should this happen a quick remedy is to stretch the prongs apart a bit for a tighter fit.

WEIGHTS & MEASURES

Distances are in feet, yards, and miles. Dry weights are in ounces, pounds, and tons. Gasoline is dispensed by the US gallon, which is about 20% less than the Imperial gallon. US pints and quarts are also 20% less than Imperial ones.

The most significant exception to the use of Imperial measures is the wine industry, whose standard size is 750 ml, but the labels of canned and liquid supermarket foods usually list both English measures and their metric equivalents. There is a conversion chart at the back of the book.

LAUNDRY

There are self-service, coin-operated laundries in most towns, some motels, and many campgrounds. Washing a load costs about $1 and drying it another $1. Coin-operated vending machines sell single-wash size packages of detergent but it's usually cheaper to pick up a small box at the supermarket. Some laundries have attendants who will wash, dry, and fold your clothes for you for an additional charge. To find a laundry, look under Laundries in the yellow pages of the phone directory. Dry cleaners are also listed under Laundries or Cleaners.

WASTE & RECYCLING

The consumer society generates vast amounts of packaging, but the waste disposal industry is very efficient too. Littering is frowned upon by most Americans, and travelers should show respect for the places they are visiting. Both states have anti-littering laws, and can impose hefty fines on offenders. There are trash bins everywhere you're likely to need them, and they are cleared regularly. There are a few dirty neighborhoods, but in general, highways, parks, and urban areas in California and Nevada are remarkably clean and free of rubbish.

You'll find recycling centers in the larger towns. Materials accepted are usually plastic and glass bottles, aluminum and tin cans, and newspapers. Some campgrounds and a few roadside rest areas also have recycling bins next to the trash bins, so look out for those. Perhaps better than recycling is to reduce your use of throwaway products. Many gas stations and convenience stores sell large plastic insulated cups with lids which are inexpensive and ideal for hot and cold drinks. You can usually save a few cents by using your cup to buy drinks.

When hiking and camping in the wilderness, take out everything you bring in – this includes *any* kind of garbage you may create. See the Outdoor Activities chapter for more on low impact camping.

HEALTH

Generally speaking, the USA is a healthy place to visit. There are no prevalent diseases or risks associated with traveling here, and the country is well-served by hospitals. However, because of the high cost of health care, international travelers should take out comprehensive travel insurance before they leave. If you're from a country with a national health insurance scheme, you should find out whether this will cover you for the cost of any health care you may need in the USA. It probably won't.

Also, if you should fall ill in the USA, avoid going to emergency rooms. Although these are often the easiest places to go for treatment, they are also incredibly expensive. Many city hospitals have 'urgent care clinics,' which are designed to deal with walk-in clients with less than catastrophic injuries and illnesses. You'll pay a lot less for treatment at these clinics. If you know someone in the area, consider asking them to ring their doctor: often private doctors are willing to examine foreign visitors as a courtesy to their regular patients, but a fee, often around $100, may still be applied.

Predeparture Preparations

Make sure you're healthy before you start traveling. If you are embarking on a long trip, make sure your teeth are in good shape. If you wear glasses, take a spare pair and your prescription. You can get new spectacles made up quickly and competently for as little as $100, depending on the prescription and frame you choose. If you require a particular medication, take an adequate supply and bring a prescription in case you lose your supply. Diabetics should contact their physician before traveling.

Immunizations

Vaccinations provide protection against diseases you might meet along the way, and some shots must be had four weeks in advance of departure.

Currently yellow fever is the only vaccine required to enter the USA from an infected area. Your doctor may recommend booster shots against other diseases before you travel, though they are not required by law. The period of protection offered by vaccinations differs widely and some are contraindicated if you are pregnant.

Health Insurance

A travel insurance policy to cover medical problems is absolutely essential in the USA, where some hospitals may refuse care without evidence of insurance. There are a wide variety of policies and your travel agent will have recommendations. A good travel insurance policy will also cover you against theft or loss of luggage, public liability, and for the cost of unavoidable changes or cancellation. Policies handled by STA Travel or other student travel organizations are usually good value. Some policies offer lower and higher medical expenses options, but the higher one is chiefly for countries like the USA with extremely high medical costs. Check the small print.

- Some policies specifically exclude 'dangerous activities' like scuba diving, motorcycling, and even trekking. If these activities are on your agenda avoid this sort of policy.
- You may prefer a policy which pays doctors or hospitals directly, rather than your having to pay first and claim later. If you have to claim later, keep all documentation. Some policies ask you to call back (reverse charges) to a center in your home country for an immediate assessment of your problem.
- Check whether the policy covers ambulance fees or an emergency flight home. If you have to stretch out you will need two seats and somebody has to pay for it!

Medical Kit It's useful to carry a small, straightforward medical kit. This should include:

- Aspirin, acetaminophen, or panadol, for pain or fever
- Antihistamine (such as Benadryl), which is useful as a decongestant for colds, and to ease the itch from allergies, insect bites or stings, or to help prevent motion sickness
- Antibiotics, which are useful for traveling off the beaten track, but they must be prescribed and you should carry the prescription with you
- Kaolin preparation (Pepto-Bismol), for stomach upsets
- Antiseptic, Betadine, mercurochrome, and antibiotic powder or similar 'dry' spray, for cuts and grazes
- Calamine lotion, to ease irritation from bites or stings
- Bandages, for minor injuries
- Scissors, tweezers, and a thermometer (airlines prohibit mercury thermometers)
- Insect repellent, sunscreen lotion, lip balm, and water purification tablets.

Note Antibiotics are specific to the infections they can treat. Ideally they should be administered only under medical supervision and never taken indiscriminately. They are only available under medical prescription in the USA. Take only the recommended dose at the prescribed intervals and continue using it for the prescribed period, even if symptoms disappear earlier. Stop immediately if there are any serious reactions and don't use the antibiotic at all if you are unsure if you have the correct one.

Basic Rules

Care in what you eat and drink is the most important health rule; stomach upsets are the most likely travel health problem (between 30% and 50% of travelers in a two-week stay experience this) but the majority of these upsets will be minor. American standards of cleanliness in places serving food and drink are very high.

Tap water in California is perfectly safe to drink, though it may smell or taste of chlorine. It may also contain some bacteria to which your gut may not be quite accustomed, at least for the first few days. Bottled drinking water is widely available.

In hot climates make sure you drink enough water – don't rely on feeling thirsty to indicate when you should drink. Not needing to urinate or very dark yellow urine is a danger sign. Always carry a water bottle with you on long trips.

Everyday Health

Normal body temperature is 98.6°F or 37°C; more than 2°C or 4°F higher indicates a 'high' fever. The normal adult pulse rate is 60 to 80 per minute (children 80 to 100, babies 100 to 140). You should know how to take a temperature and a pulse rate.

Respiration (breathing) rate is also an indicator of illness. Count the number of breaths per minute: between 12 and 20 is normal for adults and older children (up to 30 for younger children, 40 for babies). People with a high fever or serious respiratory illness (like pneumonia) breathe more quickly than normal. More than 40 shallow breaths a minute usually means pneumonia.

Travel & Climate Related Problems

Motion Sickness Eating lightly before and during a trip will reduce the chances of motion sickness. If you are prone to motion sickness, try to find a place that minimizes disturbance, for example, near the wing on aircraft, near the center on buses. Fresh air usually helps, while reading or cigarette smoke doesn't. Commercial anti-motion sickness preparations, which can cause drowsiness, have to be taken before the trip

commences; when you're feeling sick it's too late. Ginger, a natural preventative, is available in capsule form.

Jet Lag Jet lag is experienced when a person travels by air across more than three time zones (each time zone usually represents a one-hour time difference). It occurs because many of the functions of the human body are regulated by internal 24-hour cycles called circadian rhythms. When we travel long distances rapidly, our bodies take time to adjust to the 'new time' of our destination, and we may experience fatigue, disorientation, insomnia, anxiety, impaired concentration, and loss of appetite. These effects will usually be gone within three days of arrival, but there are ways of minimizing the impact of jet lag:

- Rest for a couple of days prior to departure; try to avoid late nights and last-minute dashes for traveler's checks, passport, etc.
- Try to select flight schedules that minimize sleep deprivation; arriving in the early evening means you can go to sleep soon after you arrive. For very long flights, try to organize a stopover.
- Avoid excessive eating (which bloats the stomach) and alcohol (which causes dehydration) during the flight. Instead, drink plenty of noncarbonated, nonalcoholic drinks such as fruit juice or water.
- Avoid smoking, as this reduces the amount of oxygen in the airplane cabin even further and causes greater fatigue.
- Make yourself comfortable by wearing loose-fitting clothes and perhaps bringing an eye mask and ear plugs to help you sleep.

Sunburn In the desert or at high altitude you can get sunburned surprisingly quickly, even through cloud cover. Use a sunscreen and take extra care to cover areas not normally exposed to sun. A wide-brim hat is the most basic protection, and you should also use zinc cream or some other lotion with a sun protection factor (SPF) of 24 or more for your nose and lips. Calamine lotion and Noxema provide some relief from mild sunburn.

Heat Exhaustion Dehydration or salt deficiency can cause heat exhaustion. Take time to acclimatize to high temperatures and make sure that you get enough liquids. Salt deficiency is characterized by fatigue, lethargy, headaches, giddiness, and muscle cramps. Salt tablets may help. Vomiting or diarrhea can also deplete your liquid and salt levels. Anhydrotic heat exhaustion, caused by the inability to sweat, is quite rare, but unlike the other forms of heat exhaustion it is likely to strike people who have been in a hot climate for some time, rather than newcomers. Again, always carry – and use – a water bottle on long trips.

Heat Stroke Long, continuous periods of exposure to high temperatures can leave you vulnerable to this serious, sometimes fatal, condition, which occurs when the body's heat-regulating mechanism breaks down and body temperature rises to dangerous levels. Avoid excessive alcohol intake or strenuous activity when you first arrive in a hot climate.

Symptoms include feeling unwell, lack of perspiration, and a high body temperature of 102°F to 105° F (39°C to 41°C). Hospitalization is essential for extreme cases, but meanwhile get out of the sun, remove clothing, cover with a wet sheet or towel, and fan continually.

Hypothermia Changeable weather at high altitudes can leave you vulnerable to exposure: after dark, temperatures in the mountains or desert can drop from balmy to below freezing, while a sudden soaking and high winds can lower your body temperature too rapidly. If possible, avoid traveling alone; partners are more likely to avoid hypothermia successfully. If you must travel alone, especially when hiking, be sure someone knows your route and when you expect to return.

Seek shelter when bad weather is unavoidable. Woolen clothing, or synthetics which retain warmth when wet, are superior to cotton. A quality sleeping bag is a worthwhile investment, although goose down loses much of its insulating qualities when wet. Carry high-energy, easily digestible snacks like chocolate or dried fruit.

Get hypothermia victims out of the wind or rain, remove their clothing if it's wet and replace it with dry, warm clothing. Give them hot liquids – not alcohol – and high-calorie, easily digestible food. In advanced stages it may be necessary to place victims in warm sleeping bags and get in with them. Do not rub victims but place them near a fire or, if possible, in a warm (not hot) bath.

Altitude Sickness Acute Mountain Sickness (AMS) occurs at high altitude and can be fatal. It's most unlikely at elevations less than 10,000 or 11,000 feet, so it will only concern those who are hiking or climbing in the High Sierra. In the thinner atmosphere of the high mountains, lack of oxygen causes many individuals to suffer headaches, nausea, shortness of breath, physical weakness, and other symptoms which can lead to very serious consequences, especially if combined with heat exhaustion, sunburn, or hypothermia.

Most people recover within a few hours or days. If the symptoms persist it is imperative to descend to lower elevations. For mild cases, everyday painkillers such as aspirin will relieve symptoms until the body adapts. Avoid smoking, drinking alcohol, eating heavily, or exercising strenuously. It is always wise to sleep at a lower altitude than the greatest height reached during the day. A number of other measures can prevent or minimize AMS:

- Ascend slowly – take frequent rest days, spending two to three nights for each climb of 3000 feet (1000 meters). If you reach a high altitude by trekking, acclimatization takes place gradually and you are less likely to be affected than if you fly direct.
- Drink extra fluids. The mountain air is dry and cold and you lose moisture as you breathe.
- Eat light, high-carbohydrate meals for more energy.
- Avoid alcohol, which may increase the risk of dehydration.
- Avoid sedatives.

Infectious Diseases

Diarrhea A change of water, food, or climate can all cause the runs; diarrhea caused by contaminated food or water is more serious, but unlikely in the USA. Despite all your precautions you may still have a mild bout of travelers' diarrhea from exotic food or drink. Dehydration is the main danger with any diarrhea, particularly for children where dehydration can occur quite quickly. Fluid replacement remains the mainstay of management. Weak black tea with a little sugar, soda water, or soft drinks diluted 50% with water are all good. With severe diarrhea a rehydrating solution is necessary to replace minerals and salts.

Giardiasis Commonly known as giardia, and sometimes 'Beaver Fever,' this intestinal parasite is present in contaminated water. Giardia has even contaminated apparently pristine rushing streams in the backcountry.

Symptoms are stomach cramps, nausea, a bloated stomach, watery, foul-smelling diarrhea, and frequent gas. Giardia can appear several weeks after exposure; symptoms may disappear for a few days and then return, a pattern which may continue. If you think you have it, see a doctor: antibiotics are useless.

Hepatitis Hepatitis is a general term for inflammation of the liver. There are many causes of this condition: poor sanitation, contact with infected blood products, drugs, alcohol, and contact with an infected person are but a few. The symptoms are fever, chills, headache, fatigue, feelings of weakness, and aches and pains, followed by loss of appetite, nausea, vomiting, abdominal pain, dark urine, light colored feces, and jaundiced skin, and the whites of the eyes may turn yellow. Viral hepatitis is an infection of the liver, which can have several unpleasant symptoms, or no symptoms at all, with the infected person not knowing that they have the disease. The discovery of new strains has led to a virtual alphabet soup, with hepatitis A, B, C, D, E,

and a rumored G. Hep C, D, E, and G are fairly rare.

Tetanus Tetanus is difficult to treat but is preventable with immunization. Tetanus occurs when a wound becomes infected by a germ which lives in the feces of animals or people, so clean all cuts, punctures or animal bites.

Sexually Transmitted Diseases Sexual contact with an infected partner spreads these diseases. While only abstinence is 100% preventative, using condoms is also effective. Gonorrhoea and syphilis are the most common of these diseases; sores, blisters or rashes around the genitals, discharges or pain when urinating are common symptoms. Symptoms may be less marked or not observed at all in women. The treatment of gonorrhoea and syphilis is by antibiotics. Herpes, however, has no known cure. Don't be shy about going to the hospital to get any symptoms checked.

HIV/AIDS Any exposure to blood, blood products, or bodily fluids may put the individual at risk. Infection can come from practicing unprotected sex or sharing contaminated needles. Apart from abstinence, the most effective preventative is always to practice safe sex using condoms. It is impossible to detect a person's HIV status without a blood test.

HIV/AIDS can also be spread through infected blood transfusions; most developing countries cannot afford to screen blood for transfusions, though the blood supply in the USA is now well screened. It can also be spread if needles are re-used for acupuncture, tattooing, or body piercing.

A good resource for help and information is the US Center of Disease Control AIDS hotline (☎ 800-343-2347). AIDS support groups are listed in the front of phone books.

Cuts, Bites & Stings

Cuts & Scratches Skin punctures can easily become infected in hot climates and may be difficult to heal. Treat any cut with an antiseptic such as Betadine. Where possible avoid bandages and Band-aids, which can keep wounds wet.

Bites & Stings Bee and wasp stings are usually painful rather than dangerous. Calamine lotion will give relief, and ice packs will reduce the pain and swelling. Some spiders have poisonous bites – avoid using bare hands to turn over rocks or large pieces of wood.

First Aid In the case of snake bite, avoid slashing and sucking the wound, avoid tight tourniquets (a light constricting band above the bite can help), avoid ice, keep the affected area below the level of the heart and move it as little as possible. Do not ingest alcohol or any drugs. Stay calm and get to a medical facility as soon as possible.

In the case of spiders and scorpions, there are no special first-aid techniques, but you should call Poison Control (in the front of the phone book or ask the operator) for advice. Use ice on minor bites, but visit a doctor if an unusual reaction develops.

If you are hiking a long way from the nearest phone or other help, and you are bitten or stung, you should hike out and get help, particularly in the case of snake and spider bites. Often, reactions are delayed for up to 12 hours and you can hike out before then. For more information on some of these bugs and reptiles see Dangers & Annoyances later in this chapter.

Ticks Ticks are a parasitic arachnid that may be present in brush, forest and grasslands, where hikers often get them on their legs or in their boots. The adults suck blood from hosts by burying their head into skin, but are often found unattached and can simply be brushed off. However, if one has attached itself to you, pulling it off and leaving the head in the skin increases the likelihood of infection or disease such as Rocky Mountain spotted fever or Lyme disease.

Always check your body for ticks after walking through a high-grass or thickly-forested area. If you do find a tick on you,

induce it to let go by rubbing on oil, alcohol, or petroleum jelly, or press it with a very hot object like a match or a cigarette. The tick should back out and can then be disposed of. If you get sick in the next couple of weeks, consult a doctor.

WOMEN TRAVELERS

Women often face different situations when traveling than men do. If you are a woman traveler, especially a woman traveling alone, maintain a little extra awareness of your surroundings. People are generally friendly and happy to help travelers. The following suggestions should reduce or eliminate the chances of problems, but the best advice is to trust your instincts.

In general, you might want to ask for advice at your hotel or telephone the visitors center if you are unsure which areas are considered unsafe, especially when making room reservations. Tourist maps can sometimes be deceiving, compressing areas that are not tourist attractions and making the distances look shorter than they are.

Avoiding vulnerable situations and conducting yourself in a common-sense manner will help you to avoid most problems. You're more vulnerable if you've been drinking or using drugs than if you're sober; and you're more vulnerable alone than if you're with company. If you don't want company, most men will respect a firm but polite 'no thank you.'

Don't pick up hitchhikers if driving alone. At night avoid getting out of your car to flag down help; turn on your hazard lights and wait for the police to arrive. Leaving the hood open is a sign that you need help.

Many women protect themselves with a whistle, mace, cayenne pepper spray, or some self-defense training. If you decide to purchase a spray, contact a police station to find out about regulations and training classes. Laws regarding sprays vary from state to state, so be informed based on your destination. It is a federal felony to carry defensive sprays on airplanes.

The headquarters for the National Organization for Women (NOW, ☎ 202-331-0066), 1000 16th St NW, Suite 700, Washington, DC 20036, is a good resource for information and can refer you to state and local chapters. Planned Parenthood (☎ 212-541-7800), 810 7th Ave, New York, NY 10019, can refer you to clinics throughout the country and offer advice on medical issues. Check the yellow pages under Women's Organizations & Services for local resources.

GAY & LESBIAN TRAVELERS

By far the most established gay communities are in the major cities of California, where gay men and women can live their lives openly. With the nation's largest gay population residing in San Francisco, Californians have become tolerant in all but the smallest towns. In Nevada, it is much harder to be open about sexual preferences, and gays can be prosecuted for open displays of affection. Gay travelers should be *especially* careful in rural areas – holding hands might get you bashed.

Apart from the Castro district of San Francisco, there are established gay communities in the Hillcrest suburb in San Diego, West Hollywood in LA, and in Palm Springs/Cathedral City. All these places have gay and alternative newspapers that list what's happening and provide phone numbers of local organizations.

With AIDS as a constant and harsh reality, California's gay communities are becoming strong advocates of safe sex and anti-AIDS campaigns. Single-sex marriages are also increasingly popular, though not yet recognized by the state.

A couple of good national guidebooks are *The Women's Traveler*, providing listings for lesbians, and *Damron's Address Book* for men, both published by the Damron Company (☎ 415-255-0404, 800-462-6654), PO Box 422458, San Francisco, CA 94142-2458. Ferrari's *Places for Women* and *Places for Men* are also useful, as are guides to specific cities like *Betty & Pansy's Severe Queer Reviews* to San Francisco, New York City, and Washington,

DC. These can be found at any good bookstore.

Another good resource is the Gay Yellow Pages (☎ 212-674-0120), PO Box 533, Village Station, NY 10014-0533, which has national as well as regional editions.

For people with online capabilities America Online (AOL) hosts the Gay & Lesbian Community Forum. This is also the online home of National Gay/Lesbian Task Force (NGLTF), Gay and Lesbian Alliance Against Defamation (GLAAD), Parents-Friends of Lesbians and Gays (P-FLAG), and other regional, state, and national organizations. Michelle Quirk, host of AOL's Gay & Lesbian Community Forum, can be contacted at quirk@aol.com.

National resource numbers include the National AIDS/HIV Hotline (☎ 800-342 2437), the National Gay/Lesbian Task Force (☎ 202-332-6483 in Washington, DC) and the Lambda Legal Defense Fund (☎ 212-995-8585 in New York City, 213-937-2727 in Los Angeles).

DISABLED TRAVELERS

Travel within the USA is becoming easier for people with disabilities, and California is as good as its gets. The more populous the area, the greater the likelihood of facilities for the disabled, so it's important to call ahead to see what is available. The biggest favor you can do yourself is to plan ahead.

The Americans with Disabilities Act (ADA) requires that all public buildings (including hotels, restaurants, theaters, and museums) be wheelchair accessible. Buses and trains must have wheelchair lifts and telephone companies are required to provide relay operators (available via TTY numbers) for the hearing impaired. Many banks now provide ATM instructions in Braille and you will find audible crossing signals as well as dropped curbs at most intersections.

Larger private and chain hotels have suites for disabled guests, with Hilton, Hyatt, and Embassy Suites being the most reliable. Car rental agencies such as Budget, Hertz, and Enterprise offer hand-controlled vehicles and vans with wheelchair lifts at no extra charge, but you must reserve them well in advance. Wheelers (☎ 800-456-1371), a subdivision of Avis, specializes in such vehicles.

All major airlines, Greyhound buses, and Amtrak trains will allow service animals like guide dogs to accompany passengers and will frequently sell two-for-one packages when attendants of disabled passengers are required. (Amtrak also offers a 15% discount with 72 hours advanced notice.) Airlines must accept wheelchairs as checked baggage and have an onboard chair available, though some advance notice may be required on smaller aircraft. Airlines will also provide assistance for connecting, boarding, and deplaning flights – just ask for assistance when making your reservation. American Airlines is said to have an especially well-trained staff.

Most national and state parks and recreation areas have paved or boardwalk-style nature trails. Blind or permanently disabled US residents can get a Golden Access Passport for free admission to all national parks (available at park entrances). Contact the Outdoors Disabled Foundation (☎ 312-927-6834) for recommended destinations and stores where you can find adventurous attendants and travel partners.

There are a number of organizations and tour providers that specialize in the needs of disabled travelers:

Access
The Foundation for Accessibility by the Disabled, PO Box 356, Malverne, NY 11565 (☎ 516-887-5798)
Information Center for Individuals with Disabilities
Call or write for their free listings and travel advice. Fort Point Place, 1st Floor, 27-43 Wormwood St, Boston, MA 02210 (☎ 617-727-5540, TTY 345-9743, 800-248-3737)
Mobility International USA
Advises disabled travelers on mobility issues. It also runs an exchange program. PO Box 3551, Eugene, OR 97403 (☎ 503-343-1284)
Moss Rehabilitation Hospital's Travel Information Service

1200 W Tabor Road, Philadelphia, PA 19141-3099 (☎ 215-456-9600, TTY 456-9602)
SATH
Society for the Advancement of Travel for the Handicapped, 347 Fifth Ave No 610, New York, NY 10016 (☎ 212-447-7284)
Twin Peaks Press
Publishes several handbooks for disabled travelers. PO Box 129, Vancouver, WA 98666 (☎ 202-694-2462, 800-637-2256)
Handicapped Travel Newsletter
This nonprofit publication has good information on US government legislation and traveling around the world. Subscriptions are $10 annually. PO Drawer 269, Athens, TX 75751 (☎/fax 903-677-1260)
The Center for Independent Living
Has counseling and information services. 2539 Telegraph Ave, Berkeley, CA 94705 (☎ 510-841-4776)
Travel Industry Disabled Exchange
A subscription news and information service. 5435 Donna Ave, Tarzana, CA 91356 (☎ 818-343-6339)

SENIOR TRAVELERS

When myriad 'senior' discounts begin to apply, the prospect of rediscovering the USA elicits a magnetic draw for foreigners and the native-born alike. Though the age where the benefits begin varies with the attraction, travelers age 50 years and up can expect to receive cut rates and benefits unknown to (and the envy of) their younger fellows. Be sure to inquire about such rates at hotels, museums, and restaurants.

Visitors to national parks and campgrounds can cut costs greatly by using the Golden Age Passport, a card that allows US citizens over 62 (and those traveling in the same car) free admission nationwide and a 50% reduction on camping fees. You can apply in person for any of these at any national park or regional office of the USFS or NPS or call ☎ 800-280-2267 for information and ordering.

National advocacy groups that can help in planning your travels include the following:

American Association of Retired Persons
The AARP is an advocacy group for Ameri-

cans 50 years and older and is a good resource for travel bargains. A one-year membership is available to US residents for $8. 601 E St NW, Washington, DC 20049 (☎ 800-227-7737)

Elderhostel
Elderhostel is a nonprofit organization that offers seniors the opportunity to attend academic college courses throughout the USA and Canada. The programs last one to three weeks and include meals and accommodations, and are open to people 55 years and older and their companions. 75 Federal St, Boston, MA 02110-1941 (☎ 617-426-8056)

Grand Circle Travel
This organization offers escorted tours and travel information in a variety of formats and distributes a free useful booklet, *Going Abroad: 101 Tips for Mature Travelers*. 347 Congress St, Boston, MA 02210 (☎ 617-350-7500, fax 350-6206)

National Council of Senior Citizens
Membership (you needn't be a US citizen to apply) to this group gives access to added Medicare insurance, a mail-order prescription service, and a variety of discount information and travel-related advice. Fees are $13/30/150 for one year/three years/lifetime. 1331 F St NW, Washington, DC 20004 (☎ 202-347-8800)

TRAVEL WITH CHILDREN

For information on enjoying travel with the young ones, read *Travel with Children* (1995) by Lonely Planet co-founder Maureen Wheeler.

USEFUL ORGANIZATIONS
American Automobile Association

The AAA, with offices in all major cities and many smaller towns, provides emergency roadside service in the event of an accident, breakdown, or locking your keys in the car. Service is free within a given radius of the nearest service center, and they will tow your car to a mechanic if they can't fix it. The nationwide toll-free roadside assistance number is ☎ 800-222-4357, 800-AAA-HELP.

AAA also provides great travel information, free road maps and guide books, and sells American Express traveler's checks without commission. The AAA membership card will often get you discounts for accommodations, car rental, and admission charges. If you plan a lot of motoring – even in a rental car, it is usually worth joining the AAA specially – it costs $56 for the first year, and $39 for subsequent years.

Members of foreign affiliates, like the Automobile Association in the UK, are entitled to the same services if they bring their membership cards and/or a letter of introduction.

National Park Service & US Forest Service

Most federally-owned lands are managed by either the National Park Service (NPS) or the US Forest Service (USFS).

National parks most often surround spectacular natural features and cover hundreds of sq miles. National park campground reservations and some information can be obtained by calling Destinet (☎ 800-365-2267), their reservations specialists. You can also write to the National Park Service Public Inquiry, Department of the Interior, 18th and C Sts NW, Washington, DC 20013. The California National Parks office (☎ 415-556-0560) is at Fort Mason, Bldg 201, Bay and Franklin Sts, San Francisco, CA 94123. Contact individual parks for specific information.

Information about national forests can be obtained from ranger stations which are listed in the text. National forest campground and reservation information can also be obtained by calling ☎ 800-280-2267. General information about federal lands is available from the Fish & Wildlife Service and the Bureau of Land Management (see below) and from the following agencies:

National Forests Pacific-Southwest Region
US Forest Service, 630 Sansome St, San Francisco, CA 94111 (☎ 415-705-2874)

National Forests Intermountain Region
Covers Nevada. 324 25th St, Ogden, UT 84401 (☎ 801-629-8600)

Golden Passports Golden Age Passports are free and allow permanent US residents 62 years and older unlimited entry to all sites in the national park system, with discounts on camping and other fees.

Golden Access Passports offer the same to US residents who are medically blind or permanently disabled.

Golden Eagle Passports cost $25 annually and offer one-year entry into national parks to the holder and accompanying guests. You can apply in person for any of these at any national park or regional office of the USFS or NPS or call ☎ 800-280-2267 for information and ordering.

Bureau of Land Management
The BLM manages public use of federal lands. They offer no-frills camping, often in untouched settings. Each state has a regional office in the state capital. Look in the white pages under US Government, or call the Federal Information Directory (☎ 800-726-4995).

US Fish & Wildlife Service
Each state has a few regional USFWS offices that provide information about viewing local wildlife. Their locations can be found in the white pages phone directory under the Department of the Interior – US Government or you can call the Federal Information Directory (☎ 800-726-4995).

California State Parks
State parks are usually small, and protect a specific natural or historical feature. There are 275 state parks in California, managed by the Department of Parks & Recreation (☎ 916-653-6995), Box 942896, Sacramento, CA 94296.

State Fish & Game Departments
State government Fish & Game Departments are responsible for hunting and fishing regulations. Information about seasons, licenses, and other regulations is available from:

California Department of Fish & Game
1416 9th St, Sacramento, CA 95814 (☎ 916-653-7664)
Nevada Department of Wildlife
1100 Valley Rd, Reno, NV 89512 (☎ 702-688-1500)

DANGERS & ANNOYANCES
Road accidents are probably the greatest single risk of injury – see the Getting Around chapter for more information on driving.

Otherwise, California and Nevada are not dangerous places, but there are some things to beware of. There is some risk of violent crime, but it is mostly confined to well-defined areas. Wildlife presents some potential dangers, which are not a big threat, but you should be aware of them. Then there's the earthquakes.

See the California Deserts chapter for some advice on minimizing the risks of desert travel, and the Sierra Nevada chapter for advice on wilderness safety.

Crime
The good news is that tourists will rarely get tricked, cheated, or conned simply because they're tourists. The bad news is that violent crime is a problem for tourists as well as locals, especially in the cities. Gang violence is a serious inner-city issue, notably in areas of Oakland, South San Francisco, and parts of Bakersfield, Modesto, and Stockton, and parts of LA like Compton, Watts, and South Central. Avoid these neighborhoods, especially after dark.

If you find yourself in a neighborhood where you would rather not be, do your best to look confident and sure of yourself, don't stop every few minutes to look at that useless map. Hail a taxi and get out of there if you can. Don't abandon a bright street for a darker one. If you're accosted by a mugger, there's no 100% recommended policy, but handing over whatever he wants is much better than getting knifed or shot. Have something to hand over: it's a good idea not to carry too much cash or valuables, but it can be a very bad idea to carry nothing. Drugged or otherwise crazed muggers are not too happy to find their victims are penniless.

Carry your money (and only the money you'll need for that day) somewhere inside your clothing (in a money belt, a bra, or your socks) rather than in a handbag or an outside pocket. Stash the money in several places. Most hotels and hostels provide safekeeping, so you can leave your money, passport and other valuables with them. Hide, or don't wear, any valuable jewelry.

Always lock cars and put valuables out of sight, whether leaving the car for a few minutes or longer, and whether you are in towns or in the remote backcountry. Rent a car with a lockable trunk. If your car is bumped from behind, it is best to keep going to a well-lit area, service station, or even a police station.

Be aware of your surroundings and who may be watching you. Avoid walking dimly lit streets at night, particularly if you are alone. Walk purposefully. Exercise particular caution in large parking lots or parking structures at night. Try to use ATM machines only in well-trafficked areas.

In hotels, don't leave valuables lying around your room. Use safety deposit boxes or at least place valuables in a locked bag. Don't open your door to strangers – check the peephole or call the front desk if unexpected people are trying to enter.

Panhandlers & Homeless

You're likely to bump into beggars on the streets of many Californian communities. They're usually called panhandlers, transients, indigents, or bums, and they are generally harmless. Aggressive or threatening requests for money occur occasionally, but this 'panhassling' is more of an annoyance than a danger.

The official advice is 'don't encourage them,' you're only going to make visitors an easy mark and concentrate more homeless panhandlers in tourist-heavy areas. If you want to contribute towards a solution, you might consider a donation to a charity which cares for the urban poor.

Many of the homeless suffer from medical or psychiatric problems, and their behavior can be decidedly weird. Some are suffering from the effects of alcohol or drug abuse. At least a proportion of the homeless resist any institutional help, and may be genuinely free spirits in the American hobo tradition. Certainly, the presence of beggars on the streets of wealthy communities is often rationalized by the belief that 'they choose to be there, and they could get a home if they wanted to,' though this often defies credibility.

Panhandlers can have some style too. They probably need it, because even panhandling can be a competitive business in California. Many are very polite, and suggest you have a nice day even if you don't give them money. Often they have witty signs like: 'residentially challenged,' 'non-aggressive panhandler,' and 'Let's be honest, I need a beer.'

Earthquakes

San Francisco had the Big One in 1906, followed 83 years later by the not-quite-so-Big One in 1989. In 1994 it was Los Angeles' turn, when a 6.6-magnitude quake damaged buildings, collapsed freeways, and caused a dozen deaths. Most of California is earthquake prone, and though you'd be unlucky to experience a bad quake on a short visit, it's inevitable that they will occur from time to time. Public consciousness of earthquakes is quite high, and detailed earthquake precautions are listed in the front of phone books. Every home is supposed to have an emergency kit ready all the time, with fresh water, flashlight, radio, batteries, and a few days supply of canned food.

The main danger during a really big quake is being hit by something falling, whether it's falling debris or furniture falling over. If you're indoors hit the floor and if possible get under something, like a strong table for example. Don't rush outside, you may be hit by falling glass or building debris. If you're outside then move away from buildings, trees, power lines, or anything else that might fall or shower debris on you. If you're in a car, stop if it is safe, but not under bridges or overpasses or in tunnels.

Wildlife Big & Small

Drivers should watch for stock on highways, especially in the deserts and Nevada's range country. Areas are signed as Open Range or with the silhouette of a cow, or something to that effect. Hitting a steer at 55 mph will total your car, kill the animal, and might kill you as well.

There are snakes, spiders, scorpions, and other venomous creatures in the region, but fatalities are very rare. This is partly because these animals tend to avoid humans, and partly because their venom is designed to kill small animals rather than big ones. The descriptions below are largely for interest, but note that most of these venomous animals are found in urban as well as rural areas. If you are bitten or stung by one of these small critters, refer to the Health section under Cuts, Bites & Stings. Some larger animals could cause serious injury or death, but you would have to be foolish and unlucky to be attacked.

Bears Bears are attracted to campgrounds where they may find accessible food in bags, tents, cars, or (Yogi's favorite) picnic baskets. They may rip tents and break car windows, and scratch, bite, or maul people who obstruct them. Never feed bears (or any other wildlife), and ensure that food and nice-smelling stuff like deodorant is kept in a bear-resistant container, well away from your tent. See the Outdoor Dangers & Annoyances sidebar in the Sierra Nevada chapter for more advice.

Mountain Lions These beautiful creatures, also called cougars or pumas, have been known to attack humans. There was one fatal attack in 1994 which received much publicity. They're most common in the lower western Sierra, and the mountains and forests east of Los Angeles and San Diego, especially in areas with lots of deer. Rangers recommend to stay calm if you meet a lion, hold your ground, try to appear large by raising your arms or grabbing a stick, and if the lion gets aggressive or attacks, fight back, shout, and throw objects at it.

Gila Monsters This is one of only two venomous lizards in the world, occasionally found in the deserts of California and

Nevada. It's large and slow with a bizarre, multicolored, beaded appearance, and it can reach two feet in length. Although a bite could be fatal, it's very hard to get bitten: you pretty much have to pick the monster up and force-feed it your finger. There have been no fatalities in the last several years. Gila monsters are legally protected and should not be handled.

Snakes When hiking, watch where you are stepping, particularly on hot summer afternoons and evenings when **rattlesnakes** like to bask in the middle of the trail. They are also often active at night. There are many species of rattler, most easily identified by the 'rattle' of scales at the tip of the tail. These emit a rapid rattling sound when the snake is disturbed. Most rattlesnakes have roughly diamond-shaped patterns along their backs and vary in length from two to six feet. If you are bitten, you will experience rapid swelling, very severe pain and possible temporary paralysis, but rarely do victims die. Antivenin is available in most hospitals. Seek medical help; if possible bring the dead snake for identification. Don't attempt to catch the snake if there is even a remote possibility of being bitten again.

Scorpions Scorpions spend their days under rocks or woodpiles, so use caution when around these. The long stinger curving up and around the back is characteristic of these animals. The stings can be very painful but are almost never fatal; again, small children are at highest risk.

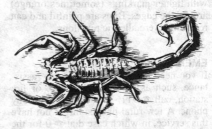

There are more than 70 species of scorpions in North America.

Fear not the male black widow – it doesn't bite.
It's the female's venom that is poisonous.

Spiders The most dangerous spider in the area is the **black widow**, a species that has gained notoriety because the venomous female eats her mate after sex. The female has a small, round body marked with a red hourglass shape under its abdomen. She makes very messy webs, so avoid these, as the widow will bite if harassed. Bites are very painful but rarely fatal, except in young children. Antivenin is available.

The large (up to six inches in diameter) and hairy **tarantula** looks much worse than it is – it bites very rarely and then usually when it is roughly handled. The bite is not very serious, although it is temporarily quite painful.

Other Creatures Centipedes bite occasionally, resulting in a painfully inflamed wound that lasts for about a day. Some local ants may also give painful stings. Conenose bugs (also called kissing or assassin bugs) are from one-half to one inch long and have elongated heads. The winged bodies are oval and brown or black with lighter markings (sometimes orange) around the edges. Bites are painful and can result in severe allergic reactions.

EMERGENCY
If you need any kind of emergency assistance, such as police, ambulance, or fire station, call ☎ 911. This is free from any phone. A few rural phones might not have this service, in which case dial ☎ 0 for the operator and ask for emergency assistance – it's still free.

Credit Card Numbers
If you lose your credit cards or they get stolen contact the company immediately. Following are toll-free numbers for the main credit cards. Contact your bank if you lose your ATM card.

Visa   ☎ 800-336-8472
MasterCard   ☎ 800-826-2181
American Express ☎ 800-528-4800,
                         800-221-7282 for
                         traveler's checks
Discover   ☎ 800-347-2683
Diners Club   ☎ 800-234-6377

LEGAL MATTERS
If you are stopped by the police for any reason, bear in mind that there is no system of paying fines on the spot. For traffic offenses, the police officer will explain your options to you. Attempting to pay the fine to the officer is frowned upon at best and may lead to a charge of bribery to compound your troubles. Should the officer decide that you should pay up front, he or she can exercise their authority and take you directly to the magistrate instead of allowing you the usual 30-day period to pay the fine.

If you are arrested for more serious offenses, you are allowed to remain silent and are presumed innocent until proven guilty. There is no legal reason to speak to a police officer if you don't wish. All persons who are arrested are legally allowed (and given) the right to make one phone call. If you don't have a lawyer or family member to help you, call your embassy. The police will give you the number upon request.

Driving
Speed limits are 55 or 65 mph on interstates and freeways unless otherwise posted. Speed limits on other highways are 55 mph or less, and in cities can vary from 25 to 45 mph. Seat belts must be worn, children must have proper seats and restraints, and motorcyclists must wear helmets. Stiff fines, jail time, and other penalties can be incurred for driving under the

influence of alcohol or drugs. See the Getting Around chapter for more on driving.

Drinking

The legal drinking age is 21 and you can be asked for a photo ID to prove your age. Being 'carded' is standard practice in many places – it may be a pain if you're in your 20s, but it's nice to be carded after you turn 30.

Drugs

In California, possession of under one ounce of marijuana is a misdemeanor, and though it is punishable by up to one year in jail, a fine is more likely. Possession of any other drug, including cocaine, ecstasy, LSD, heroin, hashish, or more than an ounce of weed is a felony, punishable by lengthy jail sentences, depending on the circumstances. Conviction of any drug offense is grounds for deportation of a foreigner. Drug laws in Nevada are generally stricter on soft drugs, and more strictly enforced.

BUSINESS HOURS

Generally speaking, business hours are weekdays from 9 am to 5 pm, and this includes banks and post offices. A few banks are open on Saturdays from 9 am to 2 pm. Post offices are sometimes open on Saturday morning.

In most cities and large towns, a few supermarkets, restaurants, and gas stations will be open 24 hours a day. Shops are usually open Monday to Saturday from 9 or 10 am to 5 or 6 pm, but often open until 9 pm in shopping malls. Sunday hours are noon to 5 pm.

PUBLIC HOLIDAYS

National public holidays are celebrated throughout the USA. Banks, schools, and government offices (including post offices) are closed and transportation, museums, and other services are on a Sunday schedule. Holidays falling on a Sunday are usually observed on the following Monday.

January
>   *New Year's Day*, January 1
>   *Martin Luther King, Jr Day* – held on the third Monday of the month it celebrates this civil rights leader's birthday (January 15, 1929)

February
>   *Presidents' Day* – held on the third Monday of the month, it celebrates the birthdays of Abraham Lincoln (February 12, 1809) and George Washington (February 22, 1732)

March/April
>   *Easter* – observed the first Sunday after a full moon in March or April

May
>   *Memorial Day* – held on the last Monday in the month, it honors the war dead (and is also the unofficial first day of the summer tourist season)

July
>   *Independence Day* – the 4th of July, celebrates the adoption of the Declaration of Independence on that day in 1776; parades, fireworks displays, and a huge variety of other events are held throughout the country

September
>   *Labor Day* – held on the first Monday of the month, it honors working people (and is also the unofficial end of the summer tourist season)

October
>   *Columbus Day* – held on the second Monday of the month, it commemorates the landing of Christopher Columbus in the Bahamas on October 12, 1492. Though it is a federal holiday, many Native Americans do not consider this day a cause for celebration.

November
>   *Veterans Day* – November 11, honors war veterans
>   *Thanksgiving* – held on the fourth Thursday of the month, it's a day of giving thanks for the bounty of America and is traditionally celebrated with a big family dinner, usually turkey and fall harvest vegetables

December
>   *Christmas Day* – December 25

CULTURAL EVENTS

The USA is always ready to call a day an event. Retailers remind the masses of coming events with huge advertising binges running for months before the actual day. Some of these are also public holidays (see above) and therefore banks, schools, and government buildings are closed.

California's rich mixture of cultures means there's almost unlimited variety in its events. In the urban centers there are celebrations for everything from Chinese New Year, to St Patrick's Day, to Mexico's Cinco de Mayo. 'Carnaval,' a spinoff of Mardi Gras, is celebrated in San Francisco not in the days just before Lent, but in June.

January
Chinese New Year – begins at the end of January or the beginning of February and lasts two weeks. The first day is celebrated with parades, firecrackers, fireworks, and lots of food. The biggest celebrations are in San Francisco and Los Angeles.
Vietnamese New Year or Tet – at about the same time, is a big celebration in San Jose

February
Valentine's Day – February 14. No one knows why St Valentine is associated with romance in the USA but this is the day of roses, sappy greeting cards, and packed restaurants. Some people wear red and give out 'Be My Valentine' candies.

March
St Patrick's Day – March 17. The patron saint of Ireland is honored by all those who feel the Irish in their blood. Everyone wears green (or you can get pinched), stores sell green bread, bars serve green beer, and towns and cities put on frolicking parades of marching bands and community groups.

April
Easter Those who observe the holiday may go to church, paint eggs, eat chocolate eggs, or any mixture of the above. Travel during this weekend is usually expensive and crowded. Good Friday is not observed as a holiday.
Passover – celebrated either in March or April, depending on the Jewish calendar. Families get together to honor persecuted forebears, partake in the symbolic seder dinner and eat unleavened bread.

May
Cinco de Mayo – May 5. Celebrates the day the Mexicans wiped out the French army in 1862. Big celebrations are in San Diego, San Jose, Los Angeles, Oceanside, Calexico, and anywhere else with a Mexican population.
Mothers Day – held on the third Sunday of the month with lots of cards, flowers, and busy restaurants

June
Fathers Day – third Sunday, same idea, different parent.
Juneteenth – June 17. A few communities in California celebrate the emancipation of African-American slaves on this day

July
Independence Day – more commonly called 4th of July. Lots of flags are flown, barbecues abound, parades storm the streets of many towns, fireworks litter the air and ground.

October
Halloween – October 31. Kids and adults dress in costumes. In safer neighborhoods, children go 'trick-or-treating' for candy. San Francisco has both a gala 'Exotic/Erotic Ball' and the Castro district has a well-known evening street festival – come in costume.

November
Day of the Dead – observed in areas with Mexican communities on November 2. This is a day for families to honor dead relatives, and make breads and sweets resembling skeletons, skulls and such.
Election Day – held on the second Tuesday of the month. This is the chance for US citizens to perform their patriotic duty and vote.
Thanksgiving – held on the last Thursday of the month. The most important family gathering is celebrated with a bounty of food and football games on TV and parades in New York City and Pasadena. The following day is the busiest shopping day of the year.

December
Christmas – Christmas Eve is as much of an event as the day itself with church services, caroling in the streets, people cruising neighborhoods looking for the best light displays, and stores full of procrastinators
Kwanzaa – held from December 26 to 31. This seven-day African-American celebration gives thanks to the harvest.
Hanukkah – Eight days in December, according to the Jewish calendar; also called, 'The Feast of Lights'
New Year's Eve – December 31. People celebrate with little tradition other than dressing up and drinking champagne. The following day people stay home to nurse their hangovers and watch college football.

SPECIAL EVENTS
Apart from national holidays and cultural events, there are many local celebrations, sporting events, art festivals, county fairs, car shows, Native American powwows, and so on, unique to California and Nevada.

Most of these are annual, usually scheduled for a weekend at about the same time every year. In addition, there may be some one-off occasions, like the 50th anniversary of Steinbeck's *Cannery Row*, which was commemorated with a whole series of performances, seminars, and ceremonies in Monterey.

Rural events usually include all the amusements of small town life. Each county has an annual fair, where competitions are held for everything from prize pigs to apple pie, and they also put forth music, arts & crafts, rodeos, and carnival rides.

Only a selection of the events is given here – for more information, see the geographical entries.

California

For a complete, current list, with exact dates and one-off events, contact the California Division of Tourism (☎ 800-862-2543), PO Box 1499, Sacramento, CA 95812-1499, and ask for the *Golden California Special Events* booklet.

January
    Tournament of Roses January 1, the famous Rose Bowl Parade, and Rose Bowl football game, Pasadena
    Tex Cushion Memorial Sled Dog Race early January, at Mammoth Lakes
    Santa Cruz Fungus Festival mid-January, display of edible and poisonous mushrooms
    San Diego Marathon late January

February
    Festival of Whales early February to early March, the annual whale migration is celebrated in Dana Point and elsewhere
    California Farm Equipment Show early February, this huge exhibition of agricultural technology takes place in Tulare
    National Date Festival mid to late February, combines a county fair with a celebration of the date industry in Indio, plus camel and ostrich races
    African-American Cultural Heritage Parade & Expo mid-February, features African music, artifacts, and food in Riverside
    Pacific Orchid Exposition late February, the San Francisco Orchid Society hosts this great flower show

March
    Desert Circuit Horse Show 1st week of March, thousands come to Palm Springs for international show jumping
    Snowfest early March, a winter carnival in Truckee and around Lake Tahoe
    Celtic Faire mid-March, lots of Scottish, Irish, Cornish, and Welsh stuff in Sonora
    Return of the Swallows around March 22, the swallows return to the Mission of San Juan Capistrano, celebrated with dances and a parade
    Viva el Mariachi late March, mariachis march in Fresno
    Shasta Dixieland Jazz Festival last weekend of March, jazz bands congregate in Redding

April
    Calico Hullabaloo early April, in the rebuilt mining town of Calico, the highlight is the World Tobacco Spitting Competition
    Long Beach Grand Prix early April, a major Indy car race in the streets of Long Beach
    Red Bluff Rodeo mid-April, one of the biggest in the country
    Cherry Blossom Festival mid-April, a Japanese community event in San Francisco
    Stockton Asparagus Festival 3rd weekend in April
    Coronado Flower Show late April, a large horticultural show in well-cultivated Coronado
    Ramona Pageant three weeks from late April to early May, portraying mission Indian life, in Hemet
    San Francisco International Film Festival, late April to early May

May
    Stanford Pow Wow mid-May, a big intertribal gathering in Palo Alto
    Calaveras County Fair & Jumping Frog Jubilee mid-May, a classic county fair, with a famous frog jumping contest, in Angels Camp
    Bay to Breakers 3rd Sunday in May, over 100,000 Bay Area joggers
    Tehachapi Wind Fair late May, has lots of exhibits on alternative energy, plus kites, gliders, and sky-diving
    Feats of Clay, late May to mid-June, fine contemporary ceramic art exhibit, in Lincoln
    Sacramento Jazz Jubilee late May, one of the biggest 'trad' and Dixieland jazz festivals
    Carnaval, late May, San Francisco's huge bash, with floats and street entertainment

June
    Merced West Coast Antique Fly-In early June air show with old and home-built aircraft

Scottish Highland Games early June, kilts and cabers converge on Modesto

Push Rods Car Show mid-June, features a 'show 'n' shine' of street hot rods, in Bakersfield

Indian Fair mid-June, Native American festival in San Diego

Tour of Nevada City Bicycle Classic mid-June, a race through the streets of this historic town

Gay Freedom Day Parade, late June, attracts thousands of people to San Francisco

Christopher Street West Gay & Lesbian Pride Festival late June, a big gay event in West Hollywood

Mid-Summer Scandinavian Festival around June 22, a Scandinavian solstice celebration in Ferndale

Indian Hill Pow Wow late June gathering of many tribes, with Indian dances, crafts, and foods, in Tehachapi

July

4th of July is celebrated in most Californian communities, and there aren't many other events in early July

Orange County Fair for three weeks starting mid-month, lots of exhibits and entertainment

Blues & Art On Polk mid-July, blues, art, and food festival in San Francisco

California Rodeo late July, a big prize-money event on the circuit, in Salinas

US Open Surfing Competition late July, at Huntington Beach

Volksfest late July, a Volkswagen fest in Lakeport

Gilroy Garlic Festival late July, lots of garlic food and jokes, in Gilroy

US Open Sandcastle Contest late July, sand sculpture becomes an art and a competition, on Imperial Beach in San Diego

August

Old Spanish Days Fiesta early August, the biggest of several ethnic festivals in Santa Barbara

Indian Fair Days early August, Native American food, crafts, and dances, in North Fork

Nisei Week Japanese Festival one week, early August, Japanese parades, dancing, and martial arts, in Los Angeles

Historic Automobile Races late August, vintage vehicle racing and displays, in Monterey

African Marketplace & Cultural Faire three weekends in late August and early September, African food, art, and entertainment, in Los Angeles

California State Fair mid-August to early September, in Sacramento

September

Annual Scottish Gathering of the Clans Labor Day weekend, big on bagpipes, dancing, and haggis, in Pleasanton

Monterey Grand Prix early September, last Indy race of the season

Los Angeles County Fair runs for most of the month, rodeos, carnival attractions, and music, in Pomona

San Diego Street Scene early September, food and music fest in the streets of the Gaslamp Quarter

Monterey Jazz Festival mid-September, long-running, big-name festival of traditional and modern styles

Watts Towers Jazz Festival late September, features jazz, gospel, R&B, and other African-American sounds, in the shadow of the Watts Towers on the edge of downtown LA

National Yo-Yo Championships last weekend in September, see the world's best yo-yo-ists perform in Chico

Oktoberfest throughout September and October, lots of places celebrate German heritage and their taste for beer

October

California Avocado Festival very early in October, see the world's largest guacamole in Carpintera

Nascar October Classic mid-October, a big Nascar race in Bakersfield

Beyond the Boundaries late October, festival of art, sport, and culture by and for those with physical and mental disabilities, in San Luis Obispo

Halloween late October, all sorts of costume parades and parties, with some of the most outrageous in San Francisco and West Hollywood

November

All Hallows Day, All Saints Day & Day of the Dead, on October 31, and November 1 and 2, Mexican communities everywhere celebrate the dead

Village Faire early November, large street fair in Carlsbad

Death Valley Fall Festival & 49er Encampment, in Shoshone and Furnace Creek, feature fiddlers, barbecues, and backcountry caravans recalling the history of early immigrants

Christmas Tree Lighting end of November, many communities kick off the Christmas season by lighting up a large tree in a public place

December

Christmas festivities occur all month across the state – some of the more unusual or interesting include:

Victorian Christmas, hay rides, chestnut roasts, craft stalls, Father Christmases and period festivities in Nevada City

Truckers Christmas Convoy early December, parade and display of big rigs in Christmas decorations – put a manger on your Mack truck and bring it to Eureka

Christmas Boat Parade mid-December, hundreds of brightly lit boats float past Newport Beach

Russian Heritage Christmas late December, Babushka comes to the Russian River, at Guerneville

New Year's Eve on Pine Square, a big street party with light show and fireworks, at Long Beach

Nevada

Las Vegas has more special events than the rest of the state put together. Apart from the many gaming tournaments, there are lots of trade fairs and industry expositions using the city's extensive conference facilities. Reno also has some big events, while the towns in Nevada's backcountry feature county fairs, rodeos, powwows, and off-road car and motorbike racing. Call the Nevada Commission on Tourism (☎ 702-687-4322) for a complete list with exact dates.

January

Consumer Electronics Show, the biggest trade show of the year at the Las Vegas Convention Center

Cowboy Poetry Gathering late January, features poetry, music, art, yodeling, drinking, and other manifestations of cowboy culture, in Elko

March

St Patrick's Day March 17, celebrated with a big parade in Las Vegas

May

Helldorado Days Rodeo & Western Festival the Wild West comes to Las Vegas

Snow Mountain Pow Wow Las Vegas

June

Cowboy Music Gathering another festival of cowboy culture in Elko

Reno Rodeo mid-June, one of the biggest rodeos in the country

Stewart Indian Museum Pow Wow early June, in Carson City

Best in the Desert Motorcycle Race early June, near Ely

July

National Basque Festival July 4, big Basque festival featuring lots of food and dance, in Elko

All Indian Rodeo & Stampede Indian Days Pow Wow late July, in Fallon

August

Hot August Nights early August, parades of '50s cars and concerts of '50s music, in Reno

Delamar 250 Off-Road Race mid-August, at Pioche

Nevada State Fair late August, rides, games, and livestock events at the Reno Fairgrounds

September

National Championship Air Races mid-September, the world's longest-running airshow happens at the Reno airport

Camel Races mid-September, camel races and celebrations in Virginia City

Las Vegas Jaycees State Fair late September to early October

October

Great Fallon Air Show late October, in Fallon

December

National Finals Rodeo early December, Las Vegas

WORK

Unemployment has risen in California, and there are plenty of applicants, legal and otherwise, for even the most menial and poorly paid jobs. Seasonal work is possible in national parks, ski areas, and other tourist sites; for information, contact park concessionaires or local chambers of commerce.

If you are a foreigner in the USA with a standard non-immigrant visitors visa, you are expressly forbidden to take paid work in the USA, and will probably be deported if you're caught working illegally. Legislation passed in the 1980s makes it an offense to employ an illegal worker, so there is a requirement on employers to establish the bona fides of their employees. Thus, it's much tougher for a foreigner to get work than it used to be.

For foreigners to work legally, they need to apply for a work visa before they leave home, and they're not easy to get. A J-1 visa, for exchange visitors, is issued mostly to young people for work in summer camps, or a H-2B visa which you get when being sponsored by a US employer. The latter is not easy to obtain since the employer has to prove that no US citizen or permanent resident is available to do the job.

ACCOMMODATIONS

California's accommodations scene is remarkably bland. Campsites exist as glorified parking lots in all but the most remote areas, and hotels and motels are owned by multinational corporations who specialize in sterility. Hostels are increasingly an alternative for budget travelers. Any town with a population over 1000 will have some type of lodging, but chances are it will be in a cookie-cutter motel room with a price tag of $45.

You must be willing to drive great distances (past hordes of freeway exit motel clusters) to experience the best accommodations California has to offer – campsites nestled in the redwoods, inns which cling to the rocky central coast, and elegant B&Bs perched upon golden hillsides of the Napa Valley.

Camping

While you'll find loads of campgrounds in California (over 800 at last count), few provide a back-to-nature experience. And unless you travel in spring or fall, there will be plenty of other people sharing the experience.

Tenters will find the best camping on the north coast, in the Sierra, and in the deserts. The higher and more northerly areas may be too cold for camping in winter, and the deserts may be too hot in summer. Facilities at backcountry campgrounds range from pit toilets, pumped water, and fire grates, to a flat spot with a sign telling you that this is indeed a campground. State park campgrounds cost $7 to $11 and include potable water, picnic tables, and fire pits;

flush toilets and electricity are rare. A state park campground price schedule is available free from California Department of Parks & Recreation, PO Box 942896, Sacramento, CA 94296-0001.

National park campgrounds are generally more spiffy than others, with flush toilets and access to hot showers. Prices are usually $14, with walk-in sites (for backpackers and cyclists) for $3. Reservations for state and national park campgrounds are made through Destinet (☎ 800-365-2267). Dispersed camping in undeveloped sites is allowed on BLM land with a fire permit (available free at ranger stations).

California's private campgrounds offer hot showers, laundry facilities, a store (often equipped with the ultimate camp accessory – an espresso machine), and often a pool or volleyball courts. These places usually cater to the recreational vehicle (RV) crowd, with dump stations and spacious RV sites for about $25, which have hookups for power (110v) and water. Tenters are usually herded together on a strip of grass which may or may not be shaded and is usually not secluded. Tent sites normally have a picnic table and fire pit and cost $11 to $18 per night for two people; pets and extra people cost around $2 each. For information on California's private campgrounds, contact the California Travel Parks Association (☎ 916-885-1624), PO Box 5648, Auburn, CA 95604.

Kampgrounds of America (KOA) is the largest and most visible chain of private kampgrounds, perched at many a freeway exit near the outskirts of town. In addition to the above mentioned amenities, KOAs have Kamping Kabins which sleep up to four people and kost $29 a night. You provide your own blanket/sleeping bag and share the kampground bathrooms. Regular kampsites are around $27 with hookups, $17 without. For a free list of KOAs, kontact KOA (☎ 406-248-7444), PO Box 30558, Billings, MT 59114.

Hostels

Hostelling International The 'official' youth hostels in the USA are affiliated with

Gas, Food, Lodging

When coming into a city on the highway you will notice signs that say 'Gas Food Lodging' followed by something like 'Next Three Exits.' Don't assume these exits will lead you directly into the city center – they won't. You'll end up amid strips of chain motels, fast-food restaurants, and gas stations with small grocery stores. If you have no intention of staying in town, but would rather catch a few hours' sleep and head out early on the road, these establishments provide cheap accommodations and food and a bit of true Americana. ∎

Hostelling International/American Youth Hostels (HI/AYH), which is a member of the International Youth Hostel Federation. California has about 30 HI/AYH hostels, well-located in the large cities, or in remote picturesque settings. People with their own cars should make it a point to stay at Point Montara or Pigeon Point hostels, in converted lighthouses perched high above the Pacific (see geographical heading for details).

HI/AYH publishes a guide which lists all of their hostels in North America. It's available for $7 from hostels, most bookstores, and the *HI/AYH Golden Gate Council* (☎ 415-863-9939), 425 Divisadero St No 307, San Francisco, CA 94117. Places with HI/AYH hostels include:

North coast
　Redwoods National Park
　Arcata
　Leggett
Northern mountains
　Mt Shasta
Sacramento
San Francisco Bay Area
　San Francisco (2)
　Point Reyes National Seashore
　Marin Headlands
　Los Altos
　San Jose
Central coast
　Santa Cruz
　Pigeon Point
　Point Montara
　San Luis Obispo
　Santa Barbara
Southern California
　Hollywood (3)
　Santa Monica
　Venice Beach (3)
　San Pedro
　Fullerton (near Disneyland)
　San Diego (2)

Beds are $7 to $14 per person, per night for HI/AYH members, and usually $3 more for non-members. Memberships cost $25 per year, and are available at most hostels, Council Travel agencies, and from the HI/AYH Golden Gate Council. There are no age restrictions on membership.

Basic facilities include dormitory-style rooms (though private rooms are sometimes available), shared single-sex bathrooms, equipped kitchens, and a common room with TV, games, and reading material. Most hostels close during the day and have a midnight curfew, though these rules fluctuate from place to place.

Reservations can be made with a credit card by calling the hostel between 7 and 10 am or 5 and 10 pm, but will only be held until 10 pm of the night you plan to arrive (if you don't show up, they can't give the bed to someone else, and you are still charged for one night's stay). If you call in the morning to reserve a bed for that same night, no credit card is needed.

Independent Hostels There's a growing number of independent hostels which provide basic dormitory accommodations to low-budget travelers, and the occasional private double room for couples. The quality of these hostels varies quite a bit, but bathrooms are usually shared, and most have a kitchen, laundry, notice board, and TV. Sometimes a light breakfast is included. Some of them put on a cheap evening meal, throw regular parties for the guests, arrange local tours, pick up guests at transportation hubs, and generally give young travelers what they want. They don't usually have curfews. Dormitory beds cost about $10 to $12 a night. A private room costs from about $20 for two people.

Often these hostels will say that they only accept international travelers, basically to keep out destitute locals. In fact, they will usually take Americans if they look like they will fit in with the other guests – a passport, HI/AYH card, or international plane ticket will help establish your traveler credentials.

Motels

Motel rooms are often priced by the number of beds, rather than the number of occupants. A room with a double- or queen-size bed will often cost the same for one or two people, while a room with two beds will cost more. Many rooms have two double beds, which are good for families if your kids will share a bed. Many motels advertise that 'kids stay free,' though you will have to pay extra for a baby cot or a 'rollaway' (portable bed).

Chain Motels The majority of California's motels are affiliated with well-publicized national chains, and clusters of these establishments huddle together around freeway exits. Most have a central phone number, answering 24 hours, but it is only for reservations and may not have any detailed information about an individual property. Each chain has a booklet which lists all of their locations with the address, facilities, and phone number of each one. The reservation numbers of some of the best known chains are:

Motel 6
   ☎ 505-891-6161
E-Z 8 Motels
   ☎ 800-326-6835
Days Inn
   ☎ 800-329-7466, 800-DAYS-INN
Travelodge
   ☎ 800-255-3035
Econo Lodge, Rodeway Inn
   ☎ 800-424-4777
Super 8 Motel
   ☎ 800-800-8000
Comfort Inn, Sleep Inn
   ☎ 800-221-2222
Best Western
   ☎ 800-528 1234
Howard Johnson
   ☎ 800- 446-4656, 800-I-GO-HOJO

Some chains are cheaper than others, and the price also depends on the location and the season. Motel 6 or E-Z 8 are usually the cheapest of the chains in a given area, while Best Western and Howard Johnson are on the high end. The price of a Motel 6 is a fair index of the cost of accommodations in a town. For more information on price, see Costs, in this chapter.

While the chain motels are not too exciting, they are reliably clean, and the rooms will have a private bathroom, heating, air conditioning, and usually cable television. Other amenities might include a swimming pool, coin laundry, and phones with free local calls.

Independent Motels Independently owned motels ('mom 'n pop' places) are usually found in the same area as chain motels, and are a bit less standardized in their prices and facilities. The cheapest ones will cost a few dollars less than the Motel 6 (ask for discounts when paying cash), though they tend to be more worn than their spiffy corporate counterparts. But many independent motels are well-run, friendly, and the rooms will always have a private bathroom, television, and sometimes a telephone. Often they are owned by East Indian families who take pride in their business and keep the facilities especially clean.

Houseboating

An alternative to land-based accommodations are fully-equipped, fully-operational houseboats that tour the lakes and river deltas of California and Nevada. You'll have all the necessities, including hot water, linens, and cooking facilities- and thanks to the climate in these states you can usually count on sunny skies, calm waters, and warm weather to enhance fishing, sunning, swimming, and lake touring.

Renting a boat for a weekend or a week is typically cost effective for groups of more than three. Houseboats can sleep up to 16 and as few as six, but it's recommended that you rent a boat that holds two more than are in your party since quarters can be cramped. Summer is the high season, but during low and shoulder seasons the chance for rain spoiling outdoor fun is greater.

Most companies have a minimum of three nights for a rental, with the best values for a week-long rental, and don't forget discounts (around 20%) for accompanying smaller boats. For a 10-person houseboat, low season/high season rates average around $800/1500 for a weekend rental, and $1100/1700 for a week-long stay. Accordingly, rates are higher for larger boats and less for smaller and the only way to get the best deal is to be thorough when inquiring about amenities (ice chests/refrigerators, air conditioner, stereo, TV, waterslide?), exactly how many nights are counted in a 'weekend' and a 'week' (it varies) and what accompanying discounts can be had.

Forever Resorts Houseboat Rentals operates on Lake Mojave and Lake Mead both on the Arizona/Nevada border; and on the Sacramento River Delta, California. PO Box 52038, Phoenix, AZ 85072 (☎ 602-968-5646, 800-255-5561)

Funtime-Fulltime/Bidwell Marina rents on Lake Oroville, California. 801 Bidwell Canyon Rd, Oroville, CA 95966 (☎ 916-589-3165)

Herman and Helen's Marina rents on the Sacramento River Delta, California. Venice Island Ferry, Stockton, CA 95219 (☎ 800-676-4841)

Aramark operates on Lake Powell, between Arizona and Utah. Lake Powell, UT (☎ 800-528-6154)

Seven Crown Resorts rents on Lake Mead, Lake Mojave, Lake Shasta, California; and the California Delta. PO Box 16247, Irvine, CA 92713-0068 (☎ 800-752-9669)

Shasta Lake Houseboat Information Line will get you in touch with a suitable marina based on your needs. Lake Shasta, CA (☎ 800-874-2782) ■

Hotels

These differ from motels in that they do not surround a car park, and usually have some sort of a lobby. California's hotels tend to be either very expensive or very seedy, without much in between.

The good ones have amenities like in-house restaurants and bars, swimming pools, fitness centers, and room service. In California – especially in Wine Country, the north coast, and around LA and Palm Springs – look for the fabled 'spa' feature which could include mineral baths, mud baths, and hot springs or may simply be beauty outposts that provide facials and footrubs. When you see or hear 'spa,' ask the hotel exactly what that includes and what services are included in the price of a room.

Most hotels are national chains, with central 24-hour reservation numbers. Prices at these places range from $89 to $139 per night for a double room.

Radisson	☎ 800-333-3333
Hyatt	☎ 800-233-1234
Holiday Inn	☎ 800-465-4329
Marriott	☎ 800-228-9290
Sheraton	☎ 800-325-3535

At the opposite end of the spectrum are old hotels which double as transient rooming houses and are usually near train and bus stations in downtown areas, or the less-than-desirable parts of large cities, though these hotels are not usually dangerous themselves. The cheapest of them will have shared bathroom and toilet facilities. Watch out for dishonest desk clerks who try to convince tourists that their hotel is the only place to stay for miles around – this is hardly ever the case. So don't pay more than $30 for a scummy looking hotel just because it's near the train station.

In historic towns or districts in cities, old hotels are sometimes restored to their original period and outfitted with goodies like modern plumbing, television, and telephones. These can be nice, atmospheric places to stay, but they will cost more than a motel with equivalent standards.

B&Bs

While California's bed and breakfasts (B&Bs) range from restored mansions in the middle of town to rustic cabins surrounded by nothing but trees, they all offer the same sort of deal – a private room (bathrooms may or may not be private), hot breakfast, and personal atmosphere. Prices range from $55 to $185 per night for a double room, so this is not a low-budget option. Sometimes proprietors charge per person rather than per room, so be sure you know the correct rate before getting settled.

B&Bs tend to be frequented by people with comfortable budgets – rather than hard-core traveling types. If a substantial breakfast holds you through the day, consider the price of a B&B to include some of your food expenses for the next day. Sometimes the price is not much higher than a motel plus a big breakfast, and the B&B might serve tea and cookies in the afternoon.

For a list of California's B&Bs, contact *B&B International* (☎ 415-696-1690, 800-872-4500, fax 415-696-1699), PO Box 282910, San Francisco, CA 94128-2910. This organization also plans B&B itineraries for the Napa Valley, Mendocino, Yosemite, and Santa Barbara areas.

Resorts & Lodges

Luxury resorts have so much to do that often they are destinations in themselves. They are very expensive and only a few are mentioned in the text.

Ski resorts usually have a central reservations hotline to fill their full range of accommodations, from motel rooms to condos. They might charge up to $200 or so per night/per bed in mid-winter, and drop prices to less than half in the snowless summer.

Lodges are often in highly-touristed rural areas and are rustic looking but usually quite comfortable inside. Restaurants are on the premises and tour services are often available. National park lodges are not cheap, with most rooms going for close to $100 for a double during the high season, but they can be your only option if you want to stay inside the park without camping. Therefore many lodges are fully booked months in advance during the summer.

FOOD

California's dining scene is as diverse as its population. It is possible to eat Mexican *huevos rancheros* for breakfast, a Thai curry for lunch, and Indian thali for dinner – without venturing out of one neighborhood. Of course this is primarily true in big cities, but even small towns are likely to have at least one Mexican restaurant and one Chinese place. For those without an adventurous palate, the standard American fare is served at diners, coffeeshops, and fast-food chains and is never too far away. Pizza, commonly regarded as an American specialty, is also around everywhere.

Grocery Stores

California's climate is very conducive to picnicking, and you'll find many delis, markets, and cafes which stock all the necessary items from pre-made salads to single-serving bottles of wine. In the Central Valley, roadside fruit stands sell locally grown, seasonal produce and a variety of dried fruits and nuts for ridiculously low prices.

Health food stores and natural foods markets (California's equivalent to New York delis) usually carry organic produce, food in bulk (where you pay by the pound), and a deli section with sandwiches, burritos, and beverages including smoothies (a blend of fruit, juice, and sometimes yogurt) – always fresh, healthy, and tasty. Health food stores tend to be more expensive than supermarkets because of the high cost of organic ingredients which are farmed on a small and intensive scale.

Real shoestringers will want to stick to supermarkets like Safeway, Vons, Lucky, or Albertson's, which have very competitive prices and are found everywhere. These stores are often open 24 hours and have salad bars, delis, and bakeries. You could easily get enough for two meals for two people for around $10 – the problem is getting smaller quantities, or keeping food for a few meals.

Fast-Food Chains
Not particularly exciting or healthy, fast-food chains are cheap, reliable stand-bys for just about any meal and will usually have clean bathrooms. In many ways they are characteristically Californian – efficient, convenient, colorful, and close to the freeway.

For hamburgers, the main choices are McDonalds, Burger King, Carl's Jr (only in California), and Wendy's. Unique to California is the venerable In-N-Out Burger, which has a brief menu, but die-hard followers will travel 50 miles out of the way to find one.

Jack-in-the-Box, also unique to the Western states, ventures beyond burgers with tacos and burritos. Taco Bell has really cheap (and actually pretty good) quasi-Mexican food, though often lacks a place to sit indoors. Del Taco, another Western chain and Taco Bell's main rival, costs a dollar or two more and has a larger selection of non-Mexican items, and more dishes with vegetables.

Pizza Hut, Straw Hat, and Round Table are the most common pizza parlor chains, and require a bit more time and money than other fast-food places. One of the best aspects of pizza parlors is their entertainment value – most are stocked with video games, small rides, and even show old Laurel and Hardy movies. Domino's Pizza place has delivery or pick up only; they don't have tables. Crispy thin-crust pizza with unique ingredients and not so much grease is available at California Pizza Kitchen, a chain started in California, and usually found in malls.

Eating Out
Breakfast Big breakfasts are an affordable way to fill yourself up, provided you can stomach large quantities of greasy food before noon. A breakfast of pancakes, eggs, and sausage or a hearty omelet costs around $4.50, and usually includes *homefries* (diced potatoes fried with onions, bell-peppers, or spices) or *hashbrowns* (shredded potatoes fried to a golden brown), toast, and 'bottomless cups' (unlimited refills) of coffee. You get a choice of how your eggs are cooked – scrambled, sunnyside up, over easy (flipped, but with a runny yolk), or over hard (flipped with a hard yolk). Typically the good-value breakfast special is on from about 6 to 11 am. *Denny's* and *IHOP* (International House of Pancakes) are restaurant chains which serve decent breakfasts and are usually open 24 hours a day.

Lunch Usually served from 11:30 am to 2 pm, lunch is often the best value meal. Prices may be one-third less than the dinner menu, though the food and portions are identical. For a bustling, energetic lunch scene, head to the business district of any city – like San Francisco's Financial District – where the number of suit-clad business people is an indication of the best or cheapest places to eat.

Dinner In large cities, many restaurants offer 'early-bird specials' which feature a complete meal (usually the menu is limited) for around $5, between 4 and 6 pm. Spending a few dollars on drinks during 'Happy Hour' (usually between 4 and 7 pm) will often get you free appetizers which can be anything from a bowl of peanuts to a hot buffet; sports bars and bars in large hotel chains such as the Hyatt, Red Lion, and Holiday Inns have the best deals. People tend to eat early, and many restaurants are closed or deserted by 10 pm.

Tax & Tipping Tipping is left to your discretion and should reflect the quality of service given, but is normally about 15%. Therefore: when looking at menus, remember to add 25% to advertised prices when you're served at your table. Fast-food restaurants offer counter service; it's a good value since tipping is not expected. For more on this see Costs in this chapter.

California Cuisine

A gourmet movement in the mid-1980s, led by Alice Waters of Berkeley's Chez Panisse restaurant, Wolfgang Puck of LA's Spago, and Nancy Waters of San Francisco's Boulevard, established a definable California cuisine which revolves around fresh, seasonal ingredients, unusual combinations, and artistic presentation. It's basically the local version of French *nouvelle cuisine*. Low-fat recipes and cooking methods are a big part of California cuisine, but by no means define it. Typical entrees might include angel-hair pasta with sun dried tomatoes, garlic, and fresh basil; or braised chicken with sesame-ginger soy sauce on a bed of wilted greens, accompanied by a California Chardonnay, of course. The main problem with this kind of food is that, although it is often a feast for the eyes, it may leave you $20 poorer and still hungry.

Eating American Style

A standard American diner or restaurant meal has all the ingredients of a healthy diet, but often served in quantities way in excess of what a healthy person needs. Food is frequently flavored with salt and seasoning, served with sauce, and may be fried, or deep fried, in oil or fat. The service is prompt: the server hands out menus and takes your drinks order; if you haven't decided on your meal by the time the waitress is back with drinks, she will return every two minutes until you make up your mind.

Salad is usually served first, and comes with a choice of dressings. There's also soup, or 'appetizers' like fried potato skins with cheese, barbecued chicken wings, or garlic bread. Starters like this will finish many people. If you're not a big eater, it's quite OK to order salad and/or an appetizer, and nothing else.

The main dish is called the entree, and it's usually big on meat: beef, chicken, or fish. These usually come with a starch (rice or potatoes) and a vegetable. When visiting a hamburger joint, often the choices are given cute names – you can get the Bay Burger, Mountain Burger, or Border Burger depending on location. Sandwich shops do much the same with varied ingredients. Usually burgers and sandwiches will come with a pile of French-fried potatoes, and will cost between $3 and $7 – tonier restaurants charge more, but don't necessarily serve a bigger or better burger or sandwich.

If you have room left, there's always dessert. Try fudge cake, cheese cake, carrot cake, key-lime pie, peach pie, apple pie, mud pie, or death by chocolate. If you want it with ice cream, that's a la mode. If you want the ice cream without the pie, try a sundae or a banana split.

Coffee comes regular or de-caf. It's usually good, and the 'bottomless cup' means free refills. But as soon as you stop asking for refills, the waitress will ask if there's anything more she can get you, and this is your cue to leave the table to the next customer. American restaurants rely on rapid turnover, and their staff rely on tips – the more customers, the more income. If you can't finish your dinner, they'll be happy to give you the leftovers in a doggie bag, even if you don't have a dog. Don't be embarrassed – they're used to it. ■

Seafood

Fish and shellfish are great in California, especially along the coast. In Northern California, Dungeness crab is in-season from November to March. Here, seafood restaurants serve traditional dishes like clam chowder, *cioppino* (a tomato based stew full of crab, clams, white fish, and seasoned with wine and herbs), and usually have northern waters' fresh salmon. South of San Francisco, seafood takes on a Mexican flare and may be served as fish tacos, or Vera Cruz style (cooked with tomatoes, peppers, and onions and served over rice). In most seafood restaurants, however, there is the option of plain old grilled, sautéed, or fried fish served with rice or potatoes and a salad. Prices are typically in the $7 to $14 range. For the best prices, and often the best quality (though choices might be limited to fish & chips or fried clams), hunt out fish markets that have a deli counter, or look for small stands on the end of a pier.

Ethnic Food

You'll find just about every type of international food in California – Italian, Peruvian, Cambodian – you name it, but the two most common types are Mexican and Chinese.

Mexican Food from south of the border is a staple of many a Californian's diet, and until you've eaten *carnitas* (pork) or fish tacos washed down by a Pacifico, you have not experienced California culture. Chain restaurants like Chevy's (unique to California) and Taco Bell serve Americanized Mexican food – good for the faint of stomach. *Taquerias* are, strictly speaking, little places serving tacos, but they are cheap and good. The further south you travel in California, the better and more frequent Mexican restaurants become.

For the real thing, you have to find a place with red vinyl booths, Mexican music blaring on the radio, and fake flowers hung on the wall. Here you will get authentic *enchiladas* (chicken, beef, or cheese wrapped in a corn tortilla and covered with red or green sauce and cheese), *tacos* (a corn or flour tortilla filled with beef or chicken, cheese, lettuce, and salsa), *tamales* (cornmeal *masa* stuffed usually with meat, sometimes not), and *huevos rancheros* (a corn tortilla topped with fried eggs and red ranchero sauce), all of which come with chips, salsa, rice, and beans. A *burrito* (a flour tortilla filled with beans, rice, and meat or vegetables), is not authentically Mexican but very tasty, filling, and cheap.

Most Mexican food contains substantial amounts of cheese and lard. For healthier versions, look for places serving whole pinto or black beans instead of the typical fried ones and ask to leave off the cheese, guacamole, and sour cream.

Chinese With the largest Chinese population, San Francisco's Chinese restaurants range from hole-in-the wall joints where the menu is scribbled (in Chinese characters) on a paper place mat, to posh restaurants with live lobster tanks and pink tablecloths: this is repeated all over the state. Most Chinese restaurants offer the standard sweet and sour, moo-shu (eaten with little rice pancakes), and kung-pao (made with peanuts and spicy chilies) dishes, and can easily accommodate vegetarians. As a rule, Hunan and Szechwan food tends to be spicier than Mandarin food. Dim sum is a Chinese brunch where they bring small dishes of meat or bean filled buns, pot stickers (fried, filled dumplings), rice balls, and other sweet and savory pastries around on carts and you point to what you want then pay according to the number of plates you've accumulated at the end – a really fun way to eat!

Pacific Rim The newest trend in upscale California restaurants (especially in Los Angeles and San Francisco) is Pacific Rim or Cal-Asian cooking. The focus here is on ingredients and seasonings, with cooking methods similar to Chinese and Japanese food. Meats and fish are seasoned with unlikely combinations of turmeric, cilantro (fresh coriander), ginger, garlic, chili paste, and fresh fruit juices (usually citrus), and served with Asian staples like rice, sweet potatoes, or buckwheat *udon* noodles. Appetizers are often the most interesting things on the menu, ranging from grilled portobello mushrooms, to pounded rice wrapped in seaweed, to mustard-spiked crab cakes. Don't hesitate to order several of these things and make it your meal. Sweet California wine, like a Riesling or Gewurtztraminer, is recommended to cool the spiciness.

Wolfgang Puck, the father of the movement, dominates the scene with his *Chinois on Main* in Santa Monica, and *Postrio* in San Francisco. *Rockenwagner*, in Santa Monica, and *California Fats* in Sacramento are also recommended.

Tapas Tapas bars (not to be confused with 'topless bars') are making waves among California's young, hip, party crowd, especially in Los Angeles and San Francisco. Tapas are traditionally Spanish appetizers-small plates of food you eat while standing at a bar. The California version is about the same (with more vegetarian options), though you usually order from a menu and are served at a table. Typical offerings include sautéed mushrooms, fried calamari, plantains and soupy black beans, and *tortilla* (frittata with potatoes and onions), costing $4 to $7.

DRINKS
Nonalcoholic
Most restaurants provide customers with free ice water – tap water is safe to drink. All the usual soft drinks are available, although you may be asked if you'll drink Coke instead of Pepsi and vice versa. 'Lemonade' is a lemon-sugar-ice water mix – if you want the clear, fizzy stuff that the British call lemonade, ask for Sprite or 7-Up. Some US soft drinks may be unfamiliar – Dr Pepper is some sort of sarsaparilla; Mountain Dew is a yellow liquid very high in sugar and caffeine.

For the ultimate low calorie, caffeine-free soft drink, ask for club soda (ie soda water), or mineral water. Fancy French brands, like Vittel and Evian, are popular among yuppies, but the local product, Calistoga, from the small spa town in Northern California, is also trendy and just as good.

Many restaurants offer milk, including low-fat varieties. You can often get fresh-squeezed orange juice at better restaurants, but packaged juices are more common.

Coffee is served much more often than tea, usually with a choice of regular or 'decaf.' Drinkers of English-style tea will be disappointed. Tea is usually a cup of hot water with a tea bag next to it – milk is not normally added, but a slice of lemon often is. Iced tea, with sugar and lemon, is available in cans as a soft drink.

Alcoholic
Beer The big name brands of domestic beer are available everywhere, though some locals as well as visitors find them lacking in taste. To order beer, you must specify the type you want. If you just ask for a beer, you will get a rapid-fire list of every brand on the market. Many California restaurants can serve only wine and beer.

Sometimes there are lesser known local brews from microbrewries or 'brewpubs,' in which various beers are brewed on the premises, and you can get a dozen different types on tap. Supermarkets and big liquor stores can stock a bewildering variety of imported beers, which are more expensive, but may be more to your taste.

Beer sold in the USA has a lower alcohol content than the beer in most other countries, which may be why many visitors find it bland. Imported beers must conform to the same restriction on alcohol content, and are often specially made for export to the USA. If you're particularly fond of Fosters, Heineken, or Moosehead at home, you may be disappointed to find that it has been wimped down for the American market. For example, the Fosters Lager sold in the USA is actually made in Canada, and doesn't taste much like the Fosters sold in Australia at all.

Note that 'lite' beer means lower in calories (90 instead of 180), but not lower in alcohol. But it brings up the question: is there such a thing as 'light' beer?

Wine California produces excellent varietal wines, and some very affordable generic wines which are an excellent value for the tippler on a tight budget. The first wine making dates from the Spanish mission period, when grapes were grown to make sacramental wines, but the industry is now very sophisticated, and its best wines are respected the world over.

While grapes are grown in most of the fertile areas of the state, it is the Napa and Sonoma Valleys north of San Francisco which produce the very best wine (see the Wine Country chapter). Californian white wines include Fumé Blanc, Riesling, Gewurztraminer, Chenin Blanc, Zinfandel, and the most popular, Chardonnay. Reds include Pinot Noir, Merlot, Beaujolais, Cabernet Sauvignon, and Zinfandel. A reasonable bottle of red or white from the Central Valley or Southern California vineyards can be bought for $6 to $10. At a good discount liquor store or supermarket, you can get something quite drinkable for $3 to $6.

If you want to taste the best California wines, look for those which are labeled as 'produced and bottled by' a Sonoma or Napa Valley winery. This means that at least 85% of the grapes were grown in that area, and 75% were fermented by the vintner who bottled the wine. The Sonoma Valley Chardonnay is probably the best California white, while Napa Valley Cabernet Sauvignon is probably the best red. Zinfandel is the most distinctively California wine, and is available as both a red and a white. Sparking wines of the region are easily measuring up to French champagne, at much more reasonable prices.

Spirits All bars have a big range of 'hard liquor:' gin, brandy, rum, vodka, whiskey, etc invariably served with lots of ice ('on the rocks') unless you ask for 'straight up.' If you ask for whiskey you'll get American whiskey, which is called bourbon if it's

made in Kentucky (eg Jim Beam), or whiskey if it's not (eg Jack Daniels). If you want Scotch whiskey, ask for Scotch.

Other typically local types of firewater come from south of the border. Tequila, from Mexico, is popular in drinks like the Margarita, or the Tequila Sunrise. The American taste for cocktails originated during Prohibition, when lots of flavorful mixers were used to disguise the taste of bathtub gin. These days there are thousands of named cocktail recipes, and many bars will have their own special concoction, usually with a fancy or a funny name, like the Screaming Orgasm, or the Butterball.

ENTERTAINMENT
Movies
Nearly every town, and just about every shopping mall in California, has a movie theater. Movie listings can be found in local papers under the entertainment section. The average ticket price is $7, with discounts usually offered for films showing before 6 pm. Look for two-for-one or half-price tickets on Monday or Tuesday night.

In larger cities you'll find small, independent theaters which show alternative, classic, and foreign films. In any theater, popcorn, candy, and soda concessions can end up costing twice as much as your ticket if you're not careful!

Concerts
Big-name performers from Madonna to Tom Jones usually make the same California route: the San Diego Sports Arena; Los Angeles Coliseum, Hollywood Bowl, or Greek Theater; San Francisco Peninsula's Shoreline Theater or Oakland's Coliseum; and Cal Expo in Sacramento. Anything at the Hollywood Bowl, on a warm summer night with a picnic and bottle of wine, is bound to be memorable. Los Angeles and San Francisco have many other venues where you can hear anything from Ukrainian folk music to punk rock every night of the week.

San Francisco also has some good medium-size venues like The Fillmore, The Warfield, and the Great American Music

Hall. Oakland has the best jazz and blues spots, namely Kimball's East and Yoshi's. Tickets to big-name shows cost around $30, while those at smaller venues range from $2 to $20.

Theater

Los Angeles is California's undisputed theater capital, launching many plays and musicals that go on to gain international acclaim. A big reason for this is the abundance of talent hanging around Hollywood waiting for a big break. Actors and actresses who have already 'made it' also like to perform live theater to hone their skills. Most musicals are performed at the Shubert Theater, Ahmanson, or Dorothy Chandler Pavilion (see the Los Angeles chapter).

San Diego has an excellent reputation for theater, with venues including the Simon Edison Center, the Repertory Theater in Horton Plaza, and the La Jolla Playhouse at UCSD. It's close enough to LA to be accessible to the Hollywood pool of actors, directors, and designers.

While San Francisco doesn't share the same talent pool, its theater productions are

---

Event Tickets

The Ticketmaster agency essentially has a monopoly on selling tickets in advance for concerts and sporting events. The rock band Pearl Jam tried a boycott in 1995 by holding concerts at non-Ticketmaster venues – such as polo fields and racetracks – and selling tickets through independent agencies. The public supported the boycott idea but had a hard time buying tickets, making the whole thing a bit of a flop. BASS is the Bay Area equivalent, with outlets in mainstream record stores such as Tower Records.

These agencies usually charge $3 more than face value per ticket. 'Scalpers' buy and sell tickets in front of performance venues at the time of the event. This practice is illegal and there's no guarantee that the tickets you're buying are authentic. ∎

---

conceptually strong. Fringy and avant-garde adaptations are excellent here, though not always for the faint-hearted. In the East Bay, the Orinda Shakespeare Festival does consistently outstanding productions in an outdoor setting from May to October.

Ticket prices vary according to the size and notoriety of a production. Most theaters offer 'rush' or 'student rush' tickets, available for reduced prices a few hours before the performance; there are no reservations or guarantees with these tickets, but they are generally excellent seats.

Symphony & Opera

San Francisco and Los Angeles both have outstanding symphonies under the direction of new young charismatic conductors Michael Tilson Thomas and Esa-Pekka Salonen, respectively. Tilson Thomas's premiere performance was a daring piece by a local artist – sure sign that he intends to stir up the repertoire a bit. Salonen, a dashing Scandinavian, is currently considered one of the finest conductors in the world and has strong public support. San Francisco performances are at Davies Symphony Hall, where even bad seats are pretty good. Tickets at both start at around $35.

The Berkeley Symphony, conducted by Kent Nagano who also directs the opera in Lyon, France, is said to be world-class but their performances are very sporadic (only about four per year). They perform at Zellerbach Hall on the UC Berkeley campus. The San Diego and San Jose symphonies are also very good, but in a totally different class.

In Los Angeles, the Los Angeles Music Center Opera performs, and many noteworthy opera productions pass through the city as well. San Francisco Opera's performances range from mediocre to quite good. Unless you spend at least $75 on a ticket (or have good luck getting a last-minute rush seat), you're basically guaranteed a bad seat. The San Diego opera has a season from January to May in the Civic Theater, and reasonable seats are affordable.

Spectator Sports

Including the pre-season, the National Football League (NFL) football season runs from August to mid-January, Major League Baseball (MLB) baseball from March to October, National Basketball Association (NBA) basketball from November to April, and National Hockey League (NHL) hockey from October to April.

If you're into sports, California is the perfect place in the USA to visit with possibly more professional teams than any other state. California has three NFL teams: the San Diego Chargers, San Francisco 49ers, and Oakland Raiders; five MLB teams: the LA Dodgers, California (Anaheim) Angels, San Diego Padres, San Francisco Giants, and Oakland A's; three NBA teams: the Sacramento Kings, LA Lakers, and Golden State (Oakland) Warriors; and two NHL teams: the LA Kings and San Jose Sharks.

You can usually buy tickets from scalpers or at the stadium on the day of the game. Games can be sold out (especially 49ers, Lakers, and Kings games) so it's best to call ahead.

College sports events are also fun to attend, especially if there is a strong rivalry between schools (for example UCLA vs USC or Stanford vs UC, Berkeley). This goes for just about any sport from soccer to ultimate Frisbee.

Beach volleyball is becoming more popular each year. Beach towns in the South Bay (see the Los Angeles chapter) host several professional tournaments each summer, with the Hermosa Open and Manhattan Open being the most important. Entrance is free. Volleyball's equivalent to baseball's 'seventh inning stretch' or football's 'halftime show' is jumping in the ocean and grabbing a beer.

THINGS TO BUY

California is a major agricultural producer, so some distinctively Californian purchases might be almonds, dried fruit, dates, and wine. The best place to pick up fruit and nuts is at road side stands in the San Joaquin Valley (along I-5, I-80, or small side roads) or Hadley's Orchards in Palm Springs or North County San Diego. The Napa and Sonoma Valleys produce the best wines, and you can enjoy tasting and buying directly from the winery, though most well-known wines are actually less expensive at liquor stores. Even common California wines such as Robert Mondavi, Fetzer, and Beaulieu Vineyards, available at most grocery stores for around $5 a bottle, fetch outrageous sums abroad.

California's diverse communities also offer some interesting things to buy. San Francisco's Chinatown has Chinese bookstores, and apothecaries that carry ginger and ginseng products said to promote long life and vitality. You can also get interesting green and black teas for very good prices. Los Angeles' Olivera St and Old Town San Diego have traditional Mexican crafts such as leather shoes and belts, candles, and embroidered fabrics. For better prices and assured authenticity, you might prefer to go down to the border town of Tijuana for the day. For an array of imported goods – from Guatemalan jackets to Indian temple incense – head to Berkeley's Telegraph Ave or Venice Beach.

The sheer variety and quantity of consumer goods, in the USA generally and California particularly, is staggering to many visitors. Some things are just fantastic in their frivolity. If you come around Halloween, look at the huge selection of masks and costumes. At Christmas, be overwhelmed by decorations and Yuletide junk. At any time, be impressed with the wit and cleverness displayed in things like greeting cards, bumper stickers, fridge magnets, and T-shirts. Also interesting are the many highly specialized shops, with incredible stocks of such esoteric items as high performance kites, reproduction road signs, hunting knives, and Harley Davidson belt buckles. At a Disney shop or a Warner Brothers shop you can get all sorts of fun stuff emblazoned with your favorite cartoon character. If you're into movie memorabilia, old posters, or books about movies, you'll find plenty in LA.

Not only is there variety, but prices of most consumer goods are lower in the USA than just about anywhere else. If you're really looking for bargains, check the following:

Factory Outlets Usually clumped together near a freeway exit on the outskirts of a big city, these strip malls have designer clothes, shoes, housewares, and other products at discounted prices. The stuff is usually damaged, irregular, or leftover from the previous season and thus can't be sold in stores. Some outlets (also called 'warehouses') cut costs by employing few workers and omitting things like dressing rooms, racks, and mirrors; at these places you basically serve yourself.

Thrift Shops & Garage Sales One person's trash is another person's treasure. Thrift shops and used clothing stores are really popular now, with the '70s/grunge look in fashion. At *Aardvark's* and *Buffalo Exchange*, in LA and the Bay Area, you can find leather jackets, bell bottoms, used Levis, Hawaiian shirts, plaid flannels, and flower-print dresses for under $20. Old-fashioned thrift stores, usually run by a church or charity (for example the Salvation Army or Goodwill) have everything from salt & pepper shakers to bicycles and record players.

When people clean out their garage and can't bring themselves to throw out the junk they uncover, they put price tags on it, scatter it across the lawn, and hope some other foolish soul will find a use for it. Some people spend every Saturday driving from sale to sale, starting at 7 am to get the 'good stuff' before it's gone. While you can occasionally find good bargains, the quality of stuff is totally hit or miss. Good people-watching is guaranteed. Look in the newspaper classified ads for times and locations.

Outdoor Activities

California is the only place in the USA where you can surf in the morning and ski in the afternoon, or go from the lowest to the highest point in the lower 48 states in one weekend. This chapter explores some of the many alternatives in both Nevada and California, ranging from near universals like hiking and backpacking to more esoteric, specialized pursuits like surfing and hot-air ballooning. Though each pursuit has specialized gear shops (usually the best source for local information), Recreational Equipment Incorporated (REI) co-op stores are excellent for all-around outdoor needs. The knowledgeable staff sells everything from carabiners to wool socks to stoves to kayak paddles, and rents out tents, skis, stoves, bikes, and kayaks.

HIKING & BACKPACKING

There is perhaps no better way to appreciate the beauty of California – its secluded beaches, rugged coast, lofty glacial peaks, and peaceful dense forests – than on foot and on the trail. Taking a few days' (or even a few hours') break from the highway to explore the great outdoors can refresh road-weary travelers and give them a heightened appreciation of the scenery which goes whizzing past day after day. Some travelers will experience one good hike and decide to plan the rest of their trip around wilderness or hiking areas.

With California's and Nevada's diverse landscape it is possible to experience coastal, desert, mountain, and foothill scenery in a pristine state, protected as part of national park or wilderness land.

Treading Lightly

Backcountry areas are composed of fragile environments and cannot support an inundation of human activity, especially insensitive and careless activity. A good suggestion is to treat the backcountry like you would your own backyard.

A new code of backcountry ethics is evolving to deal with the growing numbers of people in the wilderness. Most conservation organizations and hikers' manuals have their own set of backcountry codes, all of which outline the same important principles: minimizing the impact on the land, leaving no trace and taking nothing but photographs and memories. Above all, stay on the main trail, stay on the main trail, and, lastly, even if it means walking through mud or crossing a patch of snow, *stay on the main trail*.

National Parks

Unless you have a few days to get into the backcountry of a national park, or are visiting during non-tourist season (before Memorial Day and after Labor Day), expect hiking in national parks to be crowded.

Travelers with little hiking experience will appreciate the well-marked and well-maintained trails in national parks, often with restroom facilities at either end and interpretive displays along the way. The trails give access to the parks' natural features, and usually show up on NPS maps as nature trails or self-guided interpretive trails. These hikes are usually no longer than two miles.

Hikers seeking true wilderness away from heavy foot traffic should avoid national parks and try less-celebrated wilderness areas and mountain ranges. Most national parks require overnight hikers to carry backcountry permits, available from visitors centers or ranger stations, which must be obtained 24 hours in advance and require you to follow a specific itinerary. While this system reduces the chance of people getting lost in the backcountry and limits the number of people using one area at any given time, it may detract from the sense of space and freedom hiking can give. Yosemite National Park has a route of

High Sierra Camps for people who enjoy backpacking without carrying a heavy load.

Wilderness Areas

About 49% of California land is public, managed by the NPS, USFS, and BLM. Most designated wilderness areas are on USFS land; the BLM wilderness areas can be among the best in terms of sheer solitude.

The 1964 Wilderness Act, the first major act of Congress to set aside large, roadless, federally-administered areas, defines wilderness as:

An area where the earth and its community of life are untrammeled by man, where man himself is a visitor who does not remain… It is a region which contains no permanent human inhabitants, no possibility for motorized travel, and is spacious enough so that a traveler crossing it by foot or horse must have the experience of sleeping out of doors.

Wilderness areas in California offer excellent hiking and backpacking opportunities. Most wilderness areas do not require permits for hiking and backpacking and often have no developed campsites. Some of the most hikable USFS wilderness areas are the Desolation, Ansel Adams, and John Muir (all in the Sierra Nevada).

Wilderness Camping Camping in undeveloped areas is rewarding for its peacefulness, but presents special concerns. Take care to ensure that the area you choose can comfortably support your presence and leave the surroundings in better condition than on arrival. The following list of guidelines should help.

- Camp below the timberline, since alpine areas are generally more fragile. Good campsites are found, not made. Altering a site shouldn't be necessary.
- Camp at least 200 feet (70 adult steps) away from the nearest lake, river, or stream.
- Bury human waste in cat holes dug six to eight inches deep, at least 200 feet from water, camp or trails. The salt and minerals in urine attract deer; use a tent-bottle (funnel attachments are available for women) if you are prone to middle-of-the-night calls by Mother Nature. Camouflage the cat hole when finished.
- Use soaps and detergents sparingly or not at all, and never allow these things to enter streams or lakes. When washing yourself (a backcountry luxury, not necessity), lather up (with biodegradable soap) and rinse yourself with cans of water 200 feet away from your water source. Scatter dish water after removing all food particles.
- Carry a lightweight stove for cooking and use a lantern instead of a campfire.
- If a fire is allowed and appropriate, dig out the native topsoil and build a fire in the hole. Gather sticks no larger than an adult's wrist from the ground. Do not snap branches off live, dead, or downed trees. Pour wastewater from meals around the perimeter of the campfire to prevent the fire from spreading, and thoroughly douse it before leaving or going to bed.
- Burn cans to get rid of their odor, then remove them from the ashes and pack them out.
- Pack out what you pack in, including all trash – yours *and* others'.

Safety

The major forces to be reckoned with while hiking and camping are the weather (which is uncontrollable) and your own frame of mind. Be prepared for unpredictable weather – you may go to bed under a clear sky and wake up to two feet of snow, even in mid-August. Afternoon thunderstorms are very common in the Sierra Nevada. Carry a rain jacket and light pair of long underwear at all times; in spring and fall, take this precaution even on short afternoon hikes. Backpackers should have a packliner (heavy-duty garbage bags work well), a full set of rain gear and food that does not require cooking. A positive attitude is helpful in any situation. If a hot shower, comfortable mattress, and clean clothes are essential to your well-being, don't head out into the wilderness for five days – stick to day hikes.

Highest safety measures suggest never hiking alone, but solo travelers should not be discouraged, especially if they value solitude. The important thing is to always let someone know where you are going and how long you plan to be gone. Use sign-in boards at trailheads or ranger stations.

Pacific Crest Trail

A truly amazing thing about the West Coast of the USA is that you can walk from Mexico to Canada, across the entire expanse of California, Oregon, and Washington, almost without setting foot off national park or national forest lands. Simply follow the Pacific Crest Trail (PCT). This 2638-mile trail passes through 24 national forests, 7 national parks, 33 designated wilderness areas, and 6 state parks, always following as closely as possible the crest of the Sierra Nevada Range in California and the Cascade Range in Oregon and Washington, at an average elevation of 5000 feet.

To hike the trail in its entirety, at a good clip of 15 miles a day, would take nearly half a year; the California portion about four months. But you don't have to undertake such a dramatic, cross-state trek to take advantage of the PCT. Day or weekend hikers can plan short trips on many accessible segments of the trail.

Many of California's most spectacular wilderness areas are traversed by the PCT, from Anza-Borrego Desert State Park in the very south, through Sequoia and Yosemite National Parks, Lake Tahoe, and Lassen National Volcanic Park.

The Pacific Crest Trail Association, headquartered in California, can provide detailed information on the trail, as well as addresses for regional USFS and wilderness area offices, tips on long and short-distance backpacking trips, weather conditions, and which areas require wilderness permits. Call them at ☎ 800-817-2243, or write to 5325 Elkhorn Blvd, Suite 256, Sacramento, CA 95842. ■

Travelers looking for hiking companions can inquire or post notices at ranger stations, outdoors stores, campgrounds, and youth hostels.

Fording rivers and streams is another potentially dangerous but often necessary part of being on the trail. In national parks and along maintained trails in national forests, bridges usually cross large bodies of water (this is not the case in designated wilderness areas, where bridges are taboo). Upon reaching a river, unclip all of your pack straps – your pack is expendable, you are not. Avoid crossing barefoot – river cobbles will suck body heat right out of your feet, numbing them and making it impossible to navigate. Bring a pair of lightweight canvas sneakers to avoid sloshing around in wet boots for the rest of your hike.

Although cold water will make you want to cross as quickly as possible, don't rush things: take small steps, watch where you are stepping and keep your balance. Using a staff for balance is helpful, but don't rely on it to support all your weight. Don't enter water higher than mid-thigh; once higher than that your body gives the current a large mass to work against.

If you get wet, wring your clothes out immediately, wipe off all the excess water on your body and hair and put on any dry clothes you (or your partner) might have. Synthetic fabrics and wool retain heat when they get wet, but cotton does not.

People with little hiking or backpacking experience should not attempt to do too much, too soon, or they might end up being non-hikers for the wrong reasons. Know your limitations, know the route you are going to take and pace yourself accordingly. Remember, there is absolutely nothing wrong with turning back or not going as far as you originally planned.

What to Bring

Equipment The following is meant to be a general guideline for backpackers, not an 'if-I-have-everything-here-I'll-be-fine' checklist. Know yourself and what special things you may need on the trail; consider the area and climatic conditions you will be traveling in. This list is inadequate for snow country or winter.

• Boots – light to medium weight are recommended for day hikes, while sturdy boots are necessary for extended trips with a heavy pack. Most importantly they should be well broken in and have a good heel. Waterproof boots are preferable.

- Alternative footwear – thongs or sandals or running shoes for wearing around camp and canvas sneakers for crossing streams.
- Socks – heavy polypropylene or wool will stay warm even if they get wet. Frequent changes during the day reduce the chance of blisters, but are usually impractical.
- Subdued colors are recommended, but if hiking during hunting season, blaze orange is a necessity.
- Shorts, light shirt – for everyday wear; remember that heavy cotton takes a long time to dry and is very cold when wet.
- Long-sleeve shirt – light cotton, wool, or polypropylene. A button-down front makes layering easy and can be left open when the weather is hot and your arms need protection from the sun.
- Long pants – heavy denim jeans take forever to dry. Sturdy cotton or canvas pants are good for trekking through brush, and cotton or nylon sweats are comfortable to wear around camp. Long underwear with shorts over them is the perfect combo – warm but not cumbersome – for trail hiking where there is not much brush.
- Wool or polypropylene or polar fleece sweater or pullover – essential in chilly or cold weather.
- Rain gear – light, breathable, and waterproof is the ideal combination. If nothing else is available, use heavy-duty trash bags to cover you and your packs.
- Hat – wool or polypropylene is best for cold weather, while a cotton hat with a brim is good for sun protection. About 80% of body heat escapes through the top of the head. Keep your head (and neck) warm to reduce the chances of hypothermia.
- Bandanna or handkerchief – good for a runny nose, dirty face, unmanageable hair, picnic lunch, and flag (especially a red one).
- Small towel – one which is indestructible and will dry quickly.
- First Aid Kit – should include self-adhesive bandages, disinfectant, antibiotic salve or cream, gauze, small scissors, and tweezers.
- Knife, fork, spoon, and mug – a double-layer plastic mug with a lid is best. A mug acts as eating and drinking receptacle, mixing bowl and wash basin; the handle protects you from getting burned. Bring an extra cup if you like to eat and drink simultaneously.
- Pots and pans – aluminum cook sets are best, but any sturdy one-quart pot is sufficient. True gourmands who want more than pasta, soup, and freeze-dried food will need a skillet or frying pan. A pot scrubber is helpful for removing stubborn oatmeal, especially when using cold water and no soap.
- Stove – lightweight and easy to operate is ideal. Most outdoors stores rent propane or butane stoves; test the stove before you head out, even cook a meal on it, to familiarize yourself with any quirks it may have.
- Water purifier – optional but really nice to have; water can be purified by boiling for at least 10 minutes.
- Matches or lighter – waterproof matches are good and having several lighters on hand is smart.
- Candle or lantern – candles are easy to operate, but do not stay lit when they are dropped or wet and can be hazardous inside a tent. Outdoors stores rent lanterns; test it before you hit the trail.
- Flashlight – each person should have his or her own and be sure its batteries have plenty of life left in them.
- Sleeping bag – goose-down bags are warm and lightweight, but worthless if they get wet; most outdoors stores rent synthetic bags.
- Sleeping pad – this is strictly a personal preference. Use a sweater or sleeping bag sack stuffed with clothes as a pillow.
- Tent – make sure it is waterproof, or has a waterproof cover, and know how to put it up *before* you reach camp. Remember that your packs will be sharing the tent with you.
- Camera and binoculars – extra film and waterproof film canisters (sealable plastic bags work well).
- Compass and maps – each person should have his/her own.
- Eyeglasses – contact-lens wearers should always bring a back-up set.
- Sundries – toilet paper, small sealable plastic bags, insect repellent, sun screen, lip balm, unscented moisturizing cream, moleskin for foot blisters, dental floss (burnable and good when there is no water for brushing), sunglasses, deck of cards, pen or pencil and paper or notebook, books, and nature guides.

Food Keeping your energy up is important, but so is keeping your pack light. Backpackers tend to eat a substantial breakfast and dinner and snack heavily in between. There is no need to be excessive. If you pack loads of food you'll probably use it, but if you have just enough you will probably not miss anything.

Some basic staples are: packaged instant

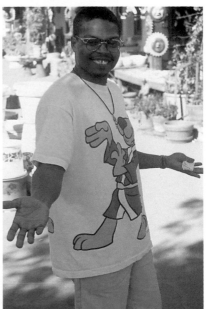

Earthquakes? Pollution? Traffic jams?. . . but it's *sunny!*

The family that sprays together. . .

. . . strays together.

oatmeal, bread (the denser the better), rice or pasta, instant soup or ramen noodles, dehydrated meat (jerky), dried fruit, energy bars, chocolate, trail mix, and peanut butter or honey or jam (in plastic jars or squeeze bottles).

Books
There are quite a few good how-to and where-to books on the market, usually found in outdoors stores, or bookstores' Sports & Recreation or Outdoors sections. Chris Camden's *Backpacker's Handbook* (Camden, Maine: Ragged Mountain Press, 1992) is a beefy collection of tips for the trail. More candid is *A Hiker's Companion* (Seattle: The Mountaineers, 1992), written by Cindy Ross and Todd Gladfelter, who hiked 12,000 miles before sitting down to write. *How to Shit in the Woods* (Berkeley: Ten Speed Press, 1994) is Kathleen Meyer's explicit, comic, and useful manual on toilet training in the wilderness.

The best California-specific guides are published by the Wilderness Press (Berkeley, CA) which does *The John Muir Trail*, *The Pacific Crest Trail*, *Sierra North*, *Lassen Volcanic National Park*, and *Yosemite*, and The Mountaineers (Seattle, WA) whose repertoire includes *California's Central Sierra & Coast Range*, *Best Day Hikes of the California Northwest*, and *The West Coast Trail*.

Maps
A good map is essential for any hiking trip. NPS and USFS ranger stations usually stock topographical maps that cost $2 to $6. In the absence of a ranger station, try the local stationary or hardware store.

Longer hikes require two types of maps: USGS Quadrangles and US Department of Agriculture-Forest Service maps. To order a map index and price list, contact the US Geological Survey, PO Box 25286, Denver, CO 80225. For general information on maps, see also the Facts for the Visitor chapter; for information regarding maps of specific forests, wilderness areas, or national parks, see the appropriate geographic entry.

Getting There & Away
Often getting to the backcountry can be a trying tangle of switchback roads and unmarked forest service roads. For this reason it is recommended that you obtain a topographical map and a USFS map of the area you intend to traverse.

Ski lifts and gondolas offer a boost for getting high into the wilderness and are often starting points for trails, notably around Lake Tahoe and Mammoth Mountain.

BICYCLING & MOUNTAIN BIKING
Bike-friendly cities where you can ditch the car and ride to museums and other attractions on a network of routes include Santa Barbara, Santa Cruz, Davis, and parts of San Diego and Los Angeles. Amtrak allows four bikes on the first car of every train on a first-come, first-served basis. For information contact the Amtrak Bike Program (☎ 800-660-4287).

Marin County (specifically Mt Tamalpais) claims to be the birthplace of mountain biking. California's current MTB mecca, however, is Mammoth Mountain, home to the annual Kamikazee World Cup Downhill Race – one of the fastest races on the circuit (held in early July). Mammoth's mountain bike park (☎ 619-934-0606) has a slalom course and Obstacle Area plus miles' worth of steep dirt just begging for fat tires.

Multi-day bike tours – from Death Valley blossom rides to Napa Valley wine tasting trips – are available through Backroads (☎ 510-527-1555, 800-245-3874), 1516 5th St, Berkeley, CA 94710. Southern Yosemite Mountain Guides (☎ 415-309-3153), PO Box 301, Bass Lake, CA 93604, offers gnarly mountain bike rides in the Sierra Nevada.

Information
Bike shops are the best place to find out about the local cycle scene. *California Bicyclist* magazine, available at most bike shops, is the definitive resource. They publish monthly Northern California and Southern California editions with a

Slanging through the Outdoors

après ski – the after-ski social scene at lodges, restaurants, bars and clubs

backcountry skiing – refers to either walk-in extreme alpine skiing or cross-country skiing beyond marked trails; carries risks of avalanche and getting lost

bumps – moguls

buy it – or **bite it** or **biff** – to crash as in 'He bought it;' 'He bit it;' 'He totally biffed.'

catch air – also **get air** – on any jump, from a mogul to a skateboard half-pipe, to put a lot of space (air) between the ground and yourself

chopped up – soft powder snow that is no longer pristine

chute – a narrow ski run sided by rock or trees

cross-country – also known as Nordic skiing or ski touring

demos – high-end rental skis. One often 'demos' a pair of skis before buying them

double – two-person chair lift

dumping – a heavy snow: 'Squaw really got a dumping last night.'

extreme skiing – expert skiing over very steep, varied terrain often out of bounds of the regular ski area

half-pipe – for skateboarders, this is literally a concrete bowl used by boarders to skate up the sides – now commonly made of snow at downhill areas for snowboarders

heli-skiing – extreme skiing in which skiers are helicoptered to the top of a mountain and ski their way back to base

hot dog – to perform dangerous acts: 'She was hot dogging down the hill;' or the performer: 'The dude taking those moguls is such a hot dog.'

peak bagger – one who climbs a mountain only to be able to claim he or she has reached the summit or peak

performance – a higher quality rental ski or mountain bike than the shop's basic package; in the case of skis they're not as high quality as demos

portage – to carry a kayak or canoe over land avoiding an impassable stretch of river or

regional calendar of events, and the annual *Pedalers' Guide* which lists California's cycling clubs. *City Sports* is another popular magazine which also devotes space to running and swimming.

Members of the national League of American Bicyclists (LAB, ☎ 410-539-3399, 800-288-2453), 190 W Ostend St, Suite 120, Baltimore, MD 21230, may transport their bikes for free on selected airlines and obtain a list of hospitality homes in each state that offer simple accommodations to touring cyclists. The LAB also publishes an annual *Almanac* that lists contacts in each state, along with information about bicycle routes and special events. Bicycle tourists will also want to get a copy of the *Cyclosource*

Catalog listing books and maps and *The Cyclist's Yellow Pages*, a trip-planning resource, both published by Adventure Cycling Association (☎ 406-721-1776), 150 E Pine St, Missoula, MT 59802.

Kimberly Grob's *Best Bike Rides in California* (Old Saybrook, CT: Globe Pequot Press, 1995) is a concise, user-friendly guide to mountain bike trails and touring routes.

Maps of Lake Tahoe/Gold Country, North San Francisco Bay/Sacramento, San Francisco Peninsula/ Santa Cruz Mountains, and South San Francisco Bay/ Monterey Bay Area, are available from Krebs Cycle Products, PO Box 7337, Santa Cruz, CA 95061. Descriptions of off-road bike trails in national forests are generally from one body of water to another. Sometimes refers to the foot path or trail used for those purposes

put-in – riverside where rafters or canoers can put in their boats

quad – four-person chair lift

schuss – ski straight down the fall line, no turns

shredder – person who cuts up the mountain with expert snowboard technique

self-register – this is a sheet at the head of a backcountry hiking trail where you will sign in your destination and how long you plan to be in the wilderness. It's very important for safety.

Sierra cement – typically heavy, wet snow common in the Sierra Nevada

ski bums – die-hard skiers who would sell their mother for a lift ticket, often working at resorts, hotels, restaurants in ski towns throughout the West

slalom – smoothly carved parallel turns

snowcat skiing – extreme skiing, where skiers are driven by snowcat to a remote area to ski their way back to base

soaring – an air tour given by specialists in gliders, engine-less aircraft

suspension bike – a mountain bike with shocks on the front fork to ease bumps and jarring

telemarking – a downhill turn performed on cross-country skis, in which the skier's heel is not attached to the ski, and the outside ski slides forward of the inside ski

walking the dog – a slow mountain biker: 'Joe was holding up the rest of us; he was really walking the dog.'

whitewater rafting – also known as tubing, river rafting, river running or to 'shooting the rapids'

x-c skiing – usually a written abbreviation of cross-country skiing

yard sale – when a person leaves a multitude of clothing behind after a devastating downhill ski fall, such as hat, gloves, skis, and poles, scattered along the face of the run ■

available by contacting the forest supervisor's office in the area. DeLorme publishes a topographic *Atlas & Gazetteer* for each state. These are good tools for planning trail rides.

Laws and Regulations

Throughout California, bikes are restricted from entering designated wilderness areas and national park trails, but may otherwise ride on national forest and BLM single-track trails. Trail etiquette requires that cyclists yield to other users. Helmets should always be worn to reduce the risk of head injury, but they are not mandated by law. National parks require that all riders under 18 years wear a helmet.

SKIING

The Sierra Nevada, Lake Tahoe in particular, is home to California's most popular ski destinations. High mountains and reliable snow conditions have attracted investors and multi-million-dollar ski resorts, equipped with the latest in chair lift technology, snow-grooming systems, and facilities. Along with the big-name places like Squaw Valley USA, are small operations with a handful of lifts and cheaper ticket prices good for beginners and families. Another pocket of ski slopes is around Big Bear, in the mountains east of Los Angeles.

In addition to downhill skiing and snowboarding, there are ample opportunities for cross-country and backcountry skiing, especially in the eastern Sierra. The USFS often maintains summer hiking trails as cross-country ski trails during the winter, offering great opportunities to experience areas that teem with people in the summer. Some resorts specialize in cross-country skiing and offer weekend or week-long packages that include lodging, meals, and equipment rentals. Some downhill areas (for example Kirkwood and Northstar-at-Tahoe) also have cross-country areas, and in the winter golf courses often have terrain suited to beginners.

Ski areas are often well-equipped with places to stay, places to eat, shops, entertainment venues, child-care facilities (both on and off the mountain), and transportation. In fact, it is possible to stay a week at some of the bigger places without ever leaving the slopes.

Usually ski areas have at least one comfortable base lodge with a rental office, ski shop, and lockers. There are also cafeterias and lounges or bars, where non-skiers, tired skiers, or cold skiers can relax in warmth in front of a bay window looking out onto the scene outside. You do not have to buy a lift ticket or trail pass or pay to enjoy the base lodge. One thing is guaranteed – you can save at least $5 a day by buying food at a grocery store and packing your own lunch. Use lockers and you won't have to tote your food around and worry about falling on your sandwich.

Books

In *Skiing America* (Hampstead, New Hampshire: World Leisure Corporation, 1994), Charles Leocha has compiled facts and figures about all of America's big ski resorts. *Ski* and *Skiing* are both year-round, widely available magazines, featuring travel articles, how-to advice, and equipment tests; try to get a copy of the October or November issues for general information.

Snow Country magazine ranks ski areas throughout the USA on the basis of categories including terrain, ski school, night life, lodging, and dining.

Downhill Skiing

Downhill skiing is a way of life for some people. You will find genuine ski bums who do what they can to survive and pass the time during the summer while they wait for the first flakes to fall. Then when the lifts open, usually around Thanksgiving weekend, they either get a job on the slopes, which provides them with a free season pass, or a job in a restaurant, which frees the daylight hours for skiing.

Around Lake Tahoe you can schuss all day on the slopes and spend the evening watching casino shows, drinking free cocktails, and trying to win back the price of that expensive lift ticket. Mammoth has a rollicking après-ski scene where people party as hard as they ski. The areas near Los Angeles are popular with day trippers which means traffic to and from the slopes (especially Friday and Sunday evenings) is often horrendous.

At major ski areas, lift tickets cost $35 to $45 for a full day and $17 to $30 for a half-day which usually starts at 1 pm. Three-day or week-long lift passes are usually more economical, especially if they do not need to be used on consecutive days. Equipment rentals are available at or near even the smallest ski areas, though renting equipment in a nearby town can be cheaper if you have the capacity to transport it to the slopes; basic rentals, including skis, boots, and poles, cost from $12 a day.

Visitors planning on taking lessons should rent equipment on the mountain since the price of a lesson, around $22 for a half-day, usually includes equipment rentals, with no discount for having your own gear. Children's ski schools are popular places to stash the kids for a day, offering lessons, day-care facilities, and providing lunch for around $35 per child.

Cross-Country Skiing

Cross-country or Nordic skiing offers a chance to get exercise, experience natural beauty at close quarters, and save a few dollars by not buying a downhill lift ticket. Trail passes at cross-country resorts, where they groom tracks and trails, usually cost $12 to $17; skiing in the backcountry is free.

Royal Gorge, near Lake Tahoe, is North America's largest cross-country ski resort and a mecca for enthusiasts. National parks, notably Yosemite and Kings Canyon, close their roads during the winter and maintain cross-country trails into the parks' interiors. Possibly the most delightful cross-country experience is staying at a remote lodge where you wake up to a hearty breakfast, ski all day, and return to a homemade dinner, hot tub, and roaring fire. Rock Creek Resort (in the eastern Sierra), Tioga Pass Resort (near Yosemite National Park), and Montecito-Sequoia Lodge (at Kings Canyon/Sequoia National Park) are some favorites. Sierra Ski Touring (☎ 702-782-3047), PO Box 176, Gardnerville, NV 89410, offers one- to seven-day ski tours in the High Sierra including snow camping and telemark instruction.

Snowboarding

This sport has recently swept the nation's ski culture and taken on a following of its own. Growing legions of snowboarders are seen on California slopes, eschewing the difficult-to-master art of downhill skiing for the more natural maneuvering by standing sideways, strapped to a four-foot board with outside edges. Baggy pants and funky hats have replaced more traditional ski garb and as a rule, snowboarders love powder snow, hate moguls and ice, and need an older sibling's ID to get into bars at night.

While no ski mountain has yet declared

A popular joke among skiers: How does a snowboarder introduce him/herself to a skier?
'Sorry dude!'

itself a snowboard-only area, more and more ski mountains are developing half-pipes and renting the necessary equipment in ski shops. There are now four magazines dedicated entirely to snowboarding, which is four more than there were two years ago.

ROCK CLIMBING & MOUNTAINEERING

People don't just come to California to surf. The granite monoliths and glacial peaks of the Sierra Nevada and singular volcanic domes of the Cascades entice the world's best climbers and mountaineers. El Capitan and Half Dome in Yosemite National Park are both legendary climbs up the face of sheer granite walls. Joshua Tree National Monument is also popular with rock climbers, especially for those who value technique and finesse more than magnitude. The peaks of Mt Shasta, Lassen Peak, and Mt Ritter (all above 13,000 feet) are impressive mountaineering destinations, and Mt Whitney, the highest in the USA at 14,494 feet, has a mountaineers' route that is a 'perfect balance of fun and challenge' according to the owner of the Whitney Portal store who has made the ascent over 50 times.

Recently, rock climbers have subordinated the idea of reaching summits to testing their skills on varied routes on difficult terrain, with the achievement of a summit either secondary or unimportant; the technique of climbing is the important matter.

Climbing and mountaineering are demanding activities requiring top physical condition, an understanding of the composition of various rock types and their hazards, other hazards of the high country, and familiarity with a variety of equipment, including ropes, chocks, bolts, carabiners, and harnesses. Many climbers prefer granite, like that found in the Sierra, because of its strength and frequent handholds, but some climbers prefer limestone for a challenge. Some sedimentary rock is suitable for climbing, but crumbling volcanic rock can be very difficult.

Climbers and mountaineers categorize

routes on a scale of one to five; Class 1 is hiking, while Class 2 involves climbing on unstable materials like talus and may require use of the hands for keeping balance, especially with a heavy pack. Class 3 places the climber in dangerous situations, involving exposed terrain (the Sierra Club uses the example of a staircase on a high building without handholds – scary but not difficult), with the likely consequences of a fall being a broken limb.

Class 4 involves steep rock, smaller holds, and great exposure, with obligatory use of ropes and knowledge of knots and techniques like belaying and rappelling; the consequences of falling are death rather than injury. Class 5 divides into a dozen or more subcategories based on degree of difficulty and requires advanced techniques, including proficiency with rope.

The Access Fund, PO Box 67A25, Los Angeles, CA 90067, is a nonprofit organization working to keep climbing areas open to the public by purchasing or negotiating access to key sites.

Safety

Climbing is potentially a hazardous activity, though serious accidents are more spectacular than frequent; driving to the climbing site can be more dangerous than the climb itself. Nevertheless, climbers should be aware of hazards which can contribute to falls and very serious injury or death.

Weather is an important factor, as rain makes rock slippery and lightning can strike an exposed climber; hypothermia is an additional concern. In dry weather, lack of water can lead to dehydration.

Minimum Impact

Many climbers are now following guidelines similar to those established for hikers to preserve the resource on which their sport relies. These include concentrating impact in high-use areas by using established roads, trails, and routes for access; dispersing use in pristine areas and avoiding the creation of new trails; refraining from creating or enhancing handholds; and

eschewing the placement of bolts wherever possible. Climbers should also take special caution to respect archaeological and cultural resources, such as rock art, and refrain from climbing in such areas.

Books

A good summary of general introductory material on climbing is available in Steve Roper's *The Climbing Guide to the High Sierra* (San Francisco: Sierra Club Books). *The Climbers Guide to Tahoe Rock* (Evergreen, CO: Chockstone Press, 1991) is a technical climber's source book for the Lake Tahoe area.

For historical background on climbing and mountaineering in the USA, consult Chris Jones's *Climbing in North America* (Berkeley: University of California Press, 1976).

Climbing Schools

Travelers wishing to acquire climbing skills can do so at several schools and guide services throughout the region. For the most comprehensive instruction available in outdoor skills, offering college and university credit, contact the National Outdoor Leadership School (NOLS, ☎ 307-332-6973), 288 Main St, Lander, WY 82520.

Alpine Skills International (☎ 916-426-9108), PO Box 8, Lake Norden, CA 95724, whose base camp is on Donner Pass near Lake Tahoe, conducts seminars in rock climbing, mountaineering, snow and ice climbing, backcountry skiing, and avalanche survival. Their trips are a great way to break into the mountaineering scene. Seminars are conducted from the hut, where you do a series of day trips, and on the trail; there are offerings for all skill levels. Less of a commitment are classes available through the University of California's recreation department, Cal Adventures (☎ 510-642-4000). These are taught on a simulated rock wall on the Berkeley campus, with the option of a second class on a real rock.

The Yosemite Mountaineering School (☎ 209-372-1244 September to May, 209-372-1335 June to August), headquartered in Yosemite National Park, has daily beginner and intermediate classes ($65) and world-class guides that lead instructional trips up some of the park's star routes.

RIDING & PACK TRIPS

Horseback riding is especially popular in the mountains, where it allows access to high alpine scenery with relatively little effort. On 'spot trips' an outfitter carries your gear (and you, if desired) to a chosen destination and leaves you to hike out or picks you up days or weeks later. Most outfitters also offer full-service trips, where they provide everything from meals to tents to naturalist guides. Spot trips cost about $125 per person, while full-service trips usually cost that much per day. Some of the best outfitters are in the eastern Sierra.

More casual riders will find rides expensive, as visitors during the short summer tourist season end up paying for the cost of feeding these hay burners over the winter: rates for recreational riding start around $15 per hour or $25 for two hours, though the hourly rate falls rapidly thereafter and full-day trips usually cost around $75 with a guide. Experienced riders may want to let the owners know, or else you may be saddled with an excessively docile stable nag.

RIVER RAFTING & KAYAKING

California offers a myriad of alternatives for one of the most exhilarating outdoor activities possible: whitewater rafting. Commercial outfitters provide whitewater experiences ranging from short, inexpensive morning or afternoon trips to overnights and multi-day expeditions; those on NPS, USFS, and BLM lands operate under permits from the appropriate agency, but individuals and groups with their own equipment do not need permits. Those not ready for whitewater excitement can try more sedate float or tube trips.

Whitewater trips take place in either large rafts seating a dozen or more people, or smaller rafts seating half a dozen; the latter are more interesting and exciting because the ride over the rapids can be rougher and because everyone participates in rowing. Most outfitters also rent whitewater kayaks and canoes which require more skill and maneuvering; instruction is usually provided.

While whitewater trips are not without danger, and it's not unusual for participants to fall out of the raft in rough water, but serious injuries are rare and a huge majority of trips are without incident. All participants must wear US Coast Guard-approved life jackets, and even non-swimmers are welcome. All trips have at least one river guide trained in lifesaving techniques.

River Rankings

Class I – easy
 The river ranges from flatwater to occasional series of mild rapids.
Class II – medium
 The river has frequent stretches of rapids with waves up to three feet high and easy chutes, ledges, and falls. The best route is easy to identify and the entire river can be run in open canoes.
Class III – difficult
 The rivers feature numerous rapids with high, irregular waves and difficult chutes and falls that often require scouting. They are for experienced paddlers who either use kayaks and rafts or have a spray cover for their canoe.
Class IV – very difficult
 Rivers with long stretches of irregular waves, powerful back eddies, and even constricted canyons. Scouting is mandatory and rescues can be difficult in many places. Suitable in rafts or whitewater kayaks with paddlers equipped with helmets.
Class V – extremely difficult
 Rivers with continuous violent rapids,

powerful rollers, and high, unavoidable waves and haystacks. These rivers are only for whitewater kayaks and paddlers who are proficient in the Eskimo roll.

Class VI – highest level of difficulty
These rivers are rarely run except by highly experienced kayakers under ideal conditions.

Wild & Scenic Rivers

Congressional legislation establishes certain criteria for the preservation of rivers with outstanding natural qualities; many of these are the best places for whitewater rafting and canoeing. Wild rivers are, simply speaking, free-flowing and remote, while scenic rivers enjoy relatively natural surroundings and are free of impoundment, but have better access by road. Recreational rivers are more developed and usually have roads close by.

Organized Trips

The most popular destination is the South Fork of the American River. Operators, concentrated in the small town of Coloma (see the Gold Country chapter), run half-day trips and multi-day adventures which include meals and camp accommodations. Half-day options are usually more action-packed and economical than full-day trips, though overnighters are the most fun. Half-day trips cost $40 to $70, full-day trips around $90, and two-day trips usually start at $180.

OARS (☎ 209-736-4677), PO Box 67, Angels Camp, CA 95222, runs whitewater rafting and kayak trips on the American, Kern, Tuolumne, and Mokulumne Rivers. Through the University of California recreation department, Cal Adventures (☎ 510-

---

Surfspeak

Much of the general California slang comes from Southern California surfer speak. And a lot of surfspeak goes way beyond the act of surfing. Here's a very small sample. See the book *Surfinary* (Ten Speed Press) for more in-depth coverage.

all over – really excited about something. 'I'm all over that party tonight, dude.'
ankle slappers – tiny waves that aren't worth surfing

beached – so stuffed with grunts one is unable to surf
beard – veteran surfer
boardhead – ardent surfer
body womp – riding waves on stomach; 'body boarding,' or 'body surfing'
burly – very cold outside
butter – women; also 'biddies'

Casper – person without a suntan; from 'Casper the Friendly Ghost'
clean peeler – the ideal wave

decoy – a non-surfer

free it up – come on and tell me

gel – calm down; similar to 'chill'
Green Room – inside the tube
grommet – disciple of a soul surfer; surfing novice ('gremlin'); or surf groupie ('dismo')
grunts – food: 'Let's grab some grunts.'

hair ball – a big wave that is surfable; also 'grinder'
hollow wave – wave with a steep face and small barrel
hondo – tourist

insane – totally great: 'Look at those insane waves.'

kneebangers – long baggy shorts worn by surfers

latronic – adios, see ya later: 'Latronic, dude.'

macker – a huge wave that is often too big to handle: also 'green monster'

642-4000) offers economical raft and kayak trips on the American and Klamath Rivers.

SEA KAYAKING

This quiet, unobtrusive sport allows you to visit unexplored islands and stretches of coast and view marine life at close range. Sea kayaks, which hold one or two people, are larger and more stable than whitewater boats, making them safer and easier to navigate. They also have storage capacity so you can take them on overnight or even week-long trips. Imagine paddling to a secluded beach on one of the Channel Islands and setting up camp for a week!

The most popular destinations are the Channel Islands, off the central coast, and Catalina Island further south. These places are good overnight destinations for experi-enced kayakers. Day trips are also rewarding, especially in areas where you are likely to see seals and sea lions, such as Tomales Bay, Monterey Bay, and San Luis Obispo Bay (notably north of Cayucos).

Island Packers (☎ 805-642-7688, 642-1393), 1867 Spinnaker Drive, Ventura, CA 93001, provide guided trips to the Channel Islands. For instruction, equipment rental, and a list of regional guides, contact California Canoe & Kayak (☎ 510-893-7833), 409 Water St, Oakland, CA 94607. Average prices are $50 to $60 per day, $350 to $450 for a week including food.

SURFING

Invented by the Pacific Islanders, made popular by Duke Kahanamoku in Hawaii in the 1920s, and brought to California in

---

meat wave – a vehicle filled with surfers

nip factor – how cold it is outside
nipple rash – when body boarding rubs your nipples raw
nuch – short for 'not much.' 'Hey, wussup?' 'Nuch.'

quimby – jerk, loser

raw – excellent: 'Hey, you've got some raw moves, man.'

schmeg – the crap of the world
scrut – eat maximum quantities of grunts; also 'haken,' 'pig out'
sharking – surfing
skank – raunchy girl
stoked – totally intense feeling you did something awesome, like when you ran out of a barrel
soul surfer – a surfer who surfs for the feel not the look. A soul surfer wouldn't explain to a non-surfer why he surfs because he knows you wouldn't understand. 'Those who understand cannot explain, those who explain do not understand.'
styling – surfing really well; also 'killing it'

tubular – literally, surfing in a tube; alternately, anything that is most excellent

veg – to sit around and do nothing. Alternatively, to 'veg out'

wall – when the entire wave breaks at the same time. One can't ride walls without getting 'worked.'
wag – an idiotic male personage. Also a 'Gilligan' (from TV show *Gilligan's Island*) or a 'Barney' (from Barney Rubble on *The Flintstones*).
weeded – crushed by a wave: also 'worked,' 'biffed,' 'toaded,' 'lunched,' 'pounded,' or 'prosecuted'
wicked – very cool

Yar! – way cool. 'Yar! Excellent ride, dude.'

zipper – a fast-breaking wave ■

1951, surfing is California's signature sport. It has imbued a look, language, and way of life that is 'typically' Californian: laid-back, easy-going, and totally dedicated to sun and sea.

California's 'big three' surf spots are Rincon, Malibu, and Trestles, all of them point breaks (where swells peak up into steep waves as they encounter a shelf-like point) known for consistently clean, glassy, big waves. Beginner and intermediate surfers should be content to watch the action at these places (which also get very crowded). The best place to learn surfing is at beach breaks or long, shallow bays where waves are small and rolling. San Onofre and San Diego's Tourmaline are good beginner spots. And although long boards are heavy and unwieldy compared to the short boards most commonly used, they are easier to balance on and less likely to 'pearl' (when the tip of the board takes a dive). Morey Doyle boards, made of spongy foam, are the ultimate beginner's tool.

You'll find surfboard rental stands on just about every beach from San Diego to Santa Barbara. Rentals cost around $8 per hour and lessons, which are much less common, cost about $10.

Northern California has its own surf scene, with colder water, bigger waves, and an abundance of sharks. Made popular when professional surfer Mark Foo died there in 1994, Mavericks (near Half Moon Bay) has waves that rival Hawaii's. Humbolt County grows its own crop of big-wave surfers right along with its marijuana plants.

WINDSURFING

Though you can put-in at any beach or public boat launch, there are few places that rent windsurfing equipment, making it necessary for serious boarders to have their own. Beginners and casual boarders will find relatively calm conditions and rental facilities at San Diego's Mission Bay, Marina Del Rey in Los Angeles, and the Berkeley Marina. California's premiere windsurfing locales include the San Fran-

cisco Bay, Rio Vista in the Sacramento River delta, and Lopez Lake, just east of San Luis Obispo. Lake Tahoe also gets decent wind, though the water is quite cold from October to June.

SCUBA DIVING & SNORKELING

To get into the depths of California's waters, you must be certified. This requires 28 hours of classroom and pool experience and one open-water dive – usually an investment of several months and several hundred dollars. For a list of instructors and dive schools, contact the National Association for Underwater Instruction (NAUI, ☎ 714-621-5801, 800-553-6284), PO Box 14650, Montclair, CA 91763.

Quick one- to three-day courses can get you into shallow waters to see the underwater world. This is especially satisfying in places like La Jolla, Monterey, and Catalina Islands where kelp beds house a rich marine environment close to the surface. Local dive shops are the best resources for equipment, guides, and instructors. *Scuba Diving* and *Sport Diver* are widely available magazines dedicated entirely to underwater pursuits.

If you don't have the time, money, or desire to dive deep, you can often rent a snorkel, mask, and fins for under $10 an hour. In touristy spots such as Avalon (on Catalina Island), Morro Bay, and Santa Barbara, people set up equipment rentals along the beach from the back of a van or truck.

FISHING

California's native fish populations have been devastated by indiscriminate planting of introduced species, overfishing, and water pollution. Logging and overgrazing on the north coast have caused stream banks to erode and temperatures to rise above habitable levels. Overfishing by commercial fishermen, a long-time threat to California's salmon population, is extreme along the north coast, though valiant efforts have been made in curbing the devastation. It is recommended not to eat fish from water near urban areas, like

Santa Monica and the San Francisco Bay, more than three times per week; pregnant women should avoid it altogether.

The *good* news is that some fish are alive and well and waiting to be caught. The Klamath, Eel, Trinity, and Pit Rivers are excellent for trout, as are Lake Shasta and Whiskeytown Reservoir. Deep-sea fishing for salmon, halibut, yellowfin, and marlin is popular along the central coast (for example Monterey and Morro Bay) and around San Diego.

A California State Fishing license, good for freshwater and saltwater fishing, costs $23 and is good from January 1 to December 31. Licenses are available at most sporting goods stores or Department of Fish & Game offices.

CAVING
Experienced spelunkers can explore caves in several areas of limestone bedrock, mostly but not exclusively in the Sierra Nevada foothills. Several cave areas are open to casual visitors for guided tours, without need of equipment or experience: California Caverns and Mercer Caverns in the Gold Country, Boyden Cavern and Crystal Cave in Kings Canyon/Sequoia National Park, and Lehman Caves in Great Basin National Park, eastern Nevada.

Because of the delicate and tightly circumscribed subterranean environments, cavers must make special efforts to respect the ecosystem and its inhabitants by leaving no trace of human presence, avoiding contact with sensitive formations, and refraining from disturbing bats and other animals. Cavers should also travel in groups, with a minimum of three persons. Hazards associated with caving include poisonous gases and dangerous spores.

The National Speleological Society (☎ 205-852-1300), Cave Ave, Huntsville, AL 35801, offers a comprehensive list of explorable caves organized by state.

GOLF
Recent decades have seen a proliferation of golf courses throughout California – in many ways an unfortunate development that wastes colossal amounts of water for irrigation in a very arid region. Even many small towns have 9- or 18-hole courses open to the public at reasonable prices, while the more established resorts have deluxe courses with very high greens fees. California's concentration of courses are ironically where there is the least water: Palm Springs, Palm Desert, and San Diego. The state's premiere courses are probably Pebble Beach and Spyglass Hill, both on the central coast near Monterey.

BUNGEE JUMPING
The activity has its ups and downs, as small operators with a construction crane can spring up anywhere to offer elasticized aerobics at local fairs or roadside amusement sites. One of the most scenic drops is from a free-standing platform atop the ski slopes at Squaw Valley USA, near Lake Tahoe.

HOT-AIR BALLOONING
Floating above California in a wicker 'gondola' has its attractions, given the scenery, but it's not cheap at the relatively few locations that offer it commercially. Most flights leave at dawn and go 1000 to 2000 feet above the ground. The most popular spot is the Wine Country, where most operators offer fancy gondola treats like champagne, local wine, and cheese. One-hour flights cost $125 to $165. Other spots where ballooning is popular are San Diego's North County and around Palm Springs.

SKY DIVING
If jumping out of a plane and falling at a speed of 150 miles per hour before opening your chute 3000 feet above the ground sounds fun, then you should head to Perris Valley in southeastern California. At the Perris Valley Skydiving School (☎ 909-657-1664, 800-832-8818), 2091 Goetz Rd, Perris, CA 92570, you can go from the classroom to the sky in half an hour with an instructor, or in six hours if you want to go solo. The only requirements are being over 18 years of age, under 215 pounds, and watching the instructional video that

includes a lawyer telling you that the sky-diving school is not responsible for any accidents.

These trips are more for the adrenaline rush than the scenery, since Perris Valley is as ugly from the air as it is from the ground.

Getting There & Away

Whether coming from elsewhere in the USA or from abroad, the fastest way to get to California is by plane. The main gateway airports, for domestic and international flights, are Los Angeles (LAX) and San Francisco (SFO). Domestic flights go to many other centers, of which the busiest are San Diego and Las Vegas, Nevada. There are excellent highways connecting California with the rest of North America, and quite good train and bus services, but it's still a long way to other major population centers.

Within the USA

AIR

The best advice if you're thinking of flying between California and Nevada and the rest of the USA is to start out by visiting a good travel agent, who will have all the up-to-the-minute details on fares, routes, discounts, and so on. All of these change practically daily.

Two of the most reputable discount travel agents in the USA are STA Travel and Council Travel. Both sell the International Student Identity Card (ISIC) and specialize in student travel, with special discount fares for students and for anyone age 26 and under, but anyone is welcome to use their services. STA (☎ 800-777-0112) has offices in California in San Francisco, Berkeley, Los Angeles, and Santa Monica, with others around the USA in Boston, Cambridge, New York, and Philadelphia. Council Travel (☎ 800-226-8624) has 39 offices around the USA including, in California, offices in Berkeley, Davis, La Jolla, Long Beach, Los Angeles, Palo Alto, San Diego, San Francisco, and Santa Barbara.

Special fares are sometimes available through discount travel agents. Check the ads in the Sunday travel sections of the larger newspapers such as the *Los Angeles Times*, the *San Francisco Chronicle*, the *New York Times*, and the *Chicago Tribune*.

There are many ways of getting cheaper fares than the standard economy fares. Advance-purchase options often give a series of graduated discounts for purchasing your ticket 7, 14, or 21 days in advance, with the biggest savings on a 21-day advance purchase; this is a common system but it varies for different airlines and routes.

Choosing carefully the day and time of travel is another way to save money; the same flight might cost you much less if you go on a weekend as opposed to a weekday, or if you take a night flight, for example. Some airlines offer companion fares that are practically a two-for-the-price-of-one discount from the full coach fare; if more than one person is flying, be sure to investigate companion fare options.

Choosing certain routes can also give you big savings; although there are hundreds of air routes making it possible to fly almost anywhere in the USA, often the ticket prices are lower on the major 'air highways.' Flying between the East and West Coasts, check charter flights in addition to the regular airlines; travel agents will have information on both. Often you can get good deals on flights to/from New York and Chicago from both San Francisco and Los Angeles, and between Los Angeles and Miami. Some especially attractive fares when we were asking included New York-San Francisco, New York-Los Angeles and Miami-Los Angeles flights for around $300 roundtrip, and Chicago-San Francisco or Chicago-Los Angeles flights for around $200.

Airlines often have 'price wars,' lowering their prices drastically to compete when one airline declares a special promotion. Price wars usually don't last long – only a few days – so if you hear of a price war and want to get the special price, don't delay. One travel agent advised us that price wars can happen every three or four weeks, and recommended that travelers check back once a week or so before buying their ticket, if time permits, to see if a price war or special discount comes up.

Don't forget package tours, in which airfare is combined with other features such as hotels, sightseeing tours, or rental cars. These are sometimes a good deal; see Tours further on in this section. Packages will typically go to a major tourist destination like Disneyland or Las Vegas.

Major US Domestic Airlines
Major domestic airlines include:

Alaska Airlines	☎ 800-426-0333
America West	☎ 800-235-9292
American	☎ 800-433-7300
Continental	☎ 800-525-0280
Delta	☎ 800-221-1212
Hawaiian Airlines	☎ 800-367-5320
Northwest	☎ 800-225-2525
Southwest	☎ 800-531-5601
TWA	☎ 800-892-4141
United	☎ 800-241-6522

Visit USA Passes
Almost all domestic carriers offer Visit USA passes to non-US citizens. The passes are actually a book of coupons – each coupon equals a flight. The following airlines are representative of the kind of deals available, but it's a good idea to ask your travel agent about other airlines that offer the service.

Continental Airlines' Visit USA pass can be purchased in conjunction with an international airline ticket anywhere outside the USA except Canada and Mexico. All travel must be completed within 60 days of the first flight to the USA or 81 days after arrival in the USA. You must have your trip planned out in order to purchase the coupons. If you decide to change destinations once in the USA, you will be fined $50. High-season prices are $479 for three (minimum purchase) and $769 for eight (maximum purchase).

Northwest offers the same deal, but gives you the option of flying standby.

American Airlines uses the same coupon structure and also sells the passes outside of the USA, excluding Canada and Mexico, in conjunction with an international ticket. You must know where you want to go on your first flight and stick to that schedule or be penalized. You must also reserve flights one day in advance, and if a coupon only takes you halfway to your destination, you will have to buy the remaining ticket at full price.

Delta has two different systems for travelers coming across the Atlantic. Visit USA gives travelers a discount, but you need to have your itinerary mapped out to take advantage of this. The other option is Discover America, in which a traveler buys coupons good for standby travel anywhere in the continental USA. One flight equals one coupon. Only two transcontinental flights are allowed – Delta prefers that your travels follow some sort of circular pattern. Four coupons cost about $550, 10 cost $1250. Children's fares are about $40 less. In order to purchase coupons, the trans-Atlantic flight must be paid in advance.

When flying standby, call the airline a day or two before the flight and make a 'standby reservation.' This way you get priority over all the others who just appear and hope to get on the flight the same day.

Getting Bumped
Airlines try to guarantee themselves consistently full planes by overbooking and counting on some passengers not showing up. This usually involves 'bumping' passengers off full flights. Getting bumped can be a nuisance because you have to wait around for the next flight, but if you have a day's leeway, you can really take advantage of the system.

When you check in at the airline counter, ask if they will need volunteers to be bumped, and ask what the compensation will be. Depending on the desirability of the flight, this can range from a $200 voucher toward your next flight to a fully paid roundtrip ticket. Be sure to try and confirm a later flight so you don't get stuck in the airport on standby. If you have to spend the night, airlines frequently foot the hotel bill for their bumpees. All in all, it can be a great deal, and many people plan their trips with a day to spare in order to try for a free ticket that will cover their next trip.

However, be aware that, due to this same system, being just a little late for boarding could get you bumped with none of these benefits.

LAND
Bus

Greyhound (☎ 800-231-2222) has a network of routes covering most of the USA; several regional bus lines also operate in connection with the Greyhound network. See the Getting Around chapter for details on reservations, discounts, travel passes, etc. If you don't have your own vehicle, Greyhound is about the cheapest way of traveling the USA. Sample one-way rates from Los Angeles are: Las Vegas $39, Seattle $61, Denver $97, Chicago $124, and New York City $134; from San Francisco: Las Vegas $54, Seattle, $46, Denver $102, Chicago $124, and New York City $136.

The 'alternative' bus line, Green Tortoise (☎ 415-956-7500, 800-867-8647), offers 10- to 14-day trips across the USA between San Francisco and New York and Boston, operating in summer from May to September. The Green Tortoise is very different from Greyhound, providing not only transport but also a sort of home-on-wheels, with foam mattress bunks, communal food and cooking, and stops for hiking, swimming, whitewater rafting, visits to national and state parks, camping, and cookouts. It costs more and takes longer than Greyhound; for example, Greyhound will get you from San Francisco to New York for $129 one way in about three days; by Green Tortoise the trip will take 10 days at a cost of $279 plus $71 food fund, or 14 days at $349 plus $81 food fund, depending on when you go.

Green Tortoise also operates a weekly north-south route between Los Angeles and San Francisco connecting with another, twice-weekly route between San Francisco and Seattle; this trip has fewer recreational stops, making it from San Francisco to Seattle in about 24 hours. You can catch either the cross-country or the north-south bus at many points along the way; phone for information or to request a brochure.

Train

Amtrak (☎ 800-872-7245) has an extensive rail system throughout the USA. The trains are comfortable, with dining and lounge cars on long-distance routes. Reservations can be made anytime from 11 months in advance to the day of departure; it's a good idea to reserve as far in advance as you can, since space on most trains is limited, and this gives you the best chance at getting a discount fare.

The *Southwest Chief* has daily service between Chicago and Los Angeles via Kansas City, Missouri; Albuquerque, New Mexico; Flagstaff, Arizona; and Kingman, Arizona. The *Desert Wind* runs daily between Chicago and Los Angeles via Denver, Colorado; Salt Lake City, Utah; and Las Vegas, Nevada. There are also daily *California Zephyr* trains between Salt Lake City and Oakland. The *Sunset Limited* train runs three times a week on the southern route from Los Angeles through Phoenix, Arizona; Tucson, Arizona; and El Paso, Texas to New Orleans, Louisiana. The *Coast Starlite* goes up the West Coast, from Los Angeles to Oakland (with shuttle connections to San Francisco, up to Portland, and to Seattle). Los Angeles to Oakland costs $75 one way, and is often more expensive than a flight.

A variety of one-way, roundtrip, and touring fares are available, with discounts for seniors age 62 and over, children age 2 to 15, military, and disabled travelers. Fares vary according to type of seating; you can travel in coach seats or in various types of sleeping compartments. Low-season fares are offered on all tickets from early January to mid-June and from late August to mid-December. Ask about the All-Aboard Pass if you want to make several stops. Amtrak also offers a variety of all-inclusive holiday tour packages.

Car

Much of the advice on driving in the Getting Around chapter also applies for driving longer distances to/from other parts of the USA; see that chapter for details.

Drive-Away Cars One option for longer trips is a 'drive-away car:' vehicle transport companies always need drivers to move cars from one place to another.

To be a driver you must be over 21 and be able to present a valid driver's license, personal references, and a $200 to $300 cash deposit which is refunded upon safe delivery of the car; some companies also require a print-out of your driving record to show that you are a safe driver, or a major credit card, or three forms of ID. You pay nothing for the use of the car, they pay you nothing to drive it; they do pay the insurance, and you pay for the fuel you use (usually they start you off with a full tank).

You must present the car to its destination at a specified time, but you do get a chance to stop off and do some sightseeing along the way; usually the time allotted for making the trip works out to require about six hours of driving per day. Between California and the East Coast, for example, you're allowed around 8 to 10 days.

Depending where you want to go, there may or may not be cars available at the time you want to go; probably it's easiest to find a car needing to be transported from the West to the East Coast, or vice versa, rather than points in between, but anything is possible. Phone a week or two ahead of when you want to travel, to give them time to match you with a car.

Drive-away car companies are listed in the yellow pages under Automobile Transporters & Drive-Away Companies; they include A AAAdvantage Auto Transport (☎ 800-480-1733), A Anthony's Drive-away Truckaway (☎ 800-779-5368), A-A Auto Transport & Driveaway (☎ 800-466-6935), A-1 Auto Movers (☎ 800-606-2006), Auto Driveaway (☎ 800-869-1489),

Contranz (☎ 800-862-9999), and National Auto Transport (☎ 800-225-9611).

TOURS

Package tours, which may include airfare, accommodations, and other features such as ground transport, tickets to major attractions, sightseeing tours, and so on, can work out to be more economical than if you purchased each element separately, and more convenient. Most airlines have packages for popular destinations. A reliable source of information are major international travel agents like Thomas Cook and American Express. Probably those of most interest to the general traveler are coach tours that visit national parks and guest ranch excursions.

Green Tortoise (see Bus) offers a number of tours to various parts of the USA and further afield, south into Mexico and Central America, north into Alaska. Their USA tours, all roundtrips departing from San Francisco, include a 16-day National Parks Loop tour, a nine-day Desert Loop of the Southwest tour, a nine-day Grand Canyon tour, plus other tours within California (see the Getting Around chapter).

Trek America (☎ 908-362-9198, 800-221-0596, fax 362-9313), PO Box 470, Blairstown, NJ 07825, offers roundtrip camping tours of different areas of the country. In England, contact Trek House (☎ 869-38777, fax 338846), The Bullring, Deddington, Banbury, Oxon OX15 0TT. These tours last from one to nine weeks and are designed for small, international groups (13 maximum) between the ages of 18 and 38. Tour prices vary by season, July to September begin the highest. Tours cost about $1000 for a 10-day trip to about $3500 for a nine-week journey around the country.

Similar deals are available from Suntreks (☎ 707-523-1800, 800-292-9696, fax 523-1911), Sun Plaza, 77 W 3rd St, Santa Rosa, CA 95401. Suntreks also has an office in Australia (☎ 02 281-8000, fax 02 281-2722), 62 Mary St, Surry Hills, Sydney NSW 2010. Their tours attract predominantly young international travelers, although there is no age limit. Prices range from about $1600 for the three-week trek to $4500 for their 13-week around-America treks.

Road Runner USA/Canada (☎ 800-873-5872), 6762A Centinela Ave, Culver City, CA 90230, organizes one- and two-week treks in conjunction with Hostelling International to different parts of the USA. They also have offices in England (☎ 892-542010), PO Box 105, Kelly House, Warwich Rd, Tunbridge Wells, Kent TN1 1ZN, and in Australia (☎ 02 299-8844), Wholsesale Pty Ltd, 8th Floor, 350 Kent St, Sydney NSW 2000.

To/From Abroad

AIR
Airports
Los Angeles International Airport (LAX, ☎ 310-646-5252) and San Francisco International Airport (SFO, ☎ 415-876-7809) are both serviced by most all major airlines. See the Los Angeles and San Francisco chapters for specifics. Any international flight will wind up in one of these two airports, but for domestic travelers (as well as those coming from Mexico and Canada) there are a number of convenient, mid-size airports like Oakland, San Jose, John Wayne, and Burbank that are close to the big cities but much less hectic than the international airports. These are also often served by regional discount airlines like Southwest.

Major International Airlines
Major international airlines serving the USA include:

Air Canada	☎ 800-776-3000
Air France	☎ 800-237-2747
Air New Zealand	☎ 800-262-1234
American Airlines	☎ 800-433-7300
British Airways	☎ 800-247-9297
Canadian Airlines	☎ 800-426-7000
Continental Airlines	☎ 800-525-0280
Delta Air Lines	☎ 800-221-1212
Japan Air Lines	☎ 800-525-3663
KLM	☎ 800-374-7747
Northwest Airlines	☎ 800-447-4747
Qantas Airways	☎ 800-227-4500
TWA	☎ 800-221-2000
United Airlines	☎ 800-241-6522
USAir	☎ 800-428-4322
Virgin Atlantic	☎ 800-862-8621

Arriving in the USA
Even if you are continuing immediately to another city, the first airport that you land in is where you must carry out immigration and customs formalities. Even if your luggage is checked from, say, London to Phoenix, you will still have to take it through customs if you first land in Chicago. Passengers from the Pacific Rim might go through immigration and customs in Honolulu, if their flight stops there on the way to California.

Passengers aboard the airplane are given standard immigration and customs forms to fill out. After the plane lands, you'll first go through immigration. There are two lines: one is for US citizens and residents, and the other is for nonresidents. After immigration, you collect your baggage and then pass through customs. If you have nothing to declare, you'll probably clear customs quickly and without a luggage search, but don't count on it. For details on customs allowances, and the procedure for foreigners entering the USA, see the Facts for the Visitor chapter.

If your flight is continuing to another city, or you have a connecting flight, it is your responsibility to get your bags to the right place. Normally, there are airline counters just outside the customs area that will help you. The airport will also have a Travelers Aid desk, phones, car rentals, and other facilities.

Baggage & Other Restrictions
On most domestic and international flights you are limited to two checked bags, or three if you don't have a carry-on. There could be a charge if you bring more or if the size of the bags exceeds the airline's limits. It's best to check with the individual airline if you are worried about this.

Air Travel Glossary

Air Shuttles – these are short domestic flights between major cities in which you can buy a ticket right at the gate at the time of the flight. This very often operates in conjunction with ticketless travel – and means you should arrive early at the gate to assure yourself a seat and travel without extra baggage.

Apex – Apex, or 'advance purchase excursion' is a discounted ticket that must be paid for in advance. There are penalties if you wish to change it.

Bucket Shop – An unbonded travel agency specializing in discounted airline tickets.

Bumping – Just because you have a confirmed seat doesn't mean you're going to get on the plane – see the Getting Bumped section.

Cancellation Penalties – If you must cancel or change an Apex ticket there are often heavy penalties involved, but insurance can sometimes be taken out against these penalties. Some airlines impose penalties on regular tickets as well, particularly against 'no show' passengers.

Check In – Airlines ask you to check in a certain time ahead of the flight departure (usually two hours on international flights). If you fail to check in on time and the flight is overbooked the airline can cancel your booking and give your seat to somebody else.

Confirmation – Having a ticket written out with the flight and date you want doesn't mean you have a seat until the agent has checked with the airline that your status is 'OK' or confirmed. Meanwhile you could just be 'on request.'

Direct Flight – Rather than nonstop, these flights have brief layovers at intermediate cities on long domestic flights; for example a one-hour 'stop' in Chicago on a New York-San Francisco flight. While better than changing planes, this still adds a considerable amount of time to your flight, but may save you money.

Discounted Tickets – There are two types of discounted fares – officially discounted (see Promotional Fares) and unofficially discounted. The lowest prices often impose drawbacks like flying with unpopular airlines, inconvenient schedules, or unpleasant routes and connections. A discounted ticket can save you other things than money – you may be able to pay Apex prices without the associated Apex advance booking and other requirements. Discounted tickets only exist when there is fierce competition.

Full Fares – Airlines traditionally offer 1st class (coded F), business class (coded J) and economy class (coded Y) tickets. These days there are so many promotional and discounted fares available from the regular economy class that few passengers pay full economy fare.

Lost Tickets – If you lose your airline ticket an airline will usually treat it like a travelers' check and, after inquiries, issue you with another one. Legally, however, an airline is entitled to treat it like cash and if you lose it then it's gone forever. Take good care of your tickets.

No Shows – No shows are passengers who fail to show up for their flight. Full-fare passengers who fail to turn up are sometimes entitled to travel on a later flight. The rest of us are penalized (see Cancellation Penalties).

Nonstop Flights – the most ideal way to fly is not to change planes or stop at all along the way, this is only called 'nonstop' and is often confused with flying direct. Nonstop is becoming harder to come by on longer flights, and therefore pricier.

On Request – An unconfirmed booking for a flight; see Confirmation.

Open Jaws – A return ticket where you fly to one place but return from another. If available this can save you backtracking to your arrival point.

Overbooking – Airlines hate to fly empty seats and since every flight has some passengers who fail to show up they often book more passengers than they have seats. Usually the excess passengers balance those who fail to show up but occasionally somebody gets bumped. If this happens guess who it's most likely to be? The passengers who check in late.

Promotional Fares – Officially discounted fares like Apex fares which are available from travel agents or direct from the airline.

Reconfirmation – At least 72 hours prior to departure time of an onward or return flight you must contact the airline and 'reconfirm' that you intend to be on the flight. If you don't do this the airline can delete your name from the passenger list and you could lose your seat. You don't have to reconfirm the first flight on your itinerary or if your stopover is less than 72 hours. It doesn't hurt to reconfirm more than once.

Restrictions – Discounted tickets often have various restrictions on them – advance purchase is the most usual one (see Apex). Others are restrictions on the minimum and maximum period you must be away, such as a minimum of 14 days or a maximum of one year. See Cancellation Penalties.

Standby – A discounted ticket where you only fly if there is a seat free at the last moment. Standby fares are usually only available on domestic routes.

Ticketless Travel – a new method used by low-fare domestic airlines where you buy tickets over the phone or through an agent, and pick up the boarding pass at the gate with picture identification. It's a very convenient and inexpensive way to travel, unless you have luggage to check – then you wait in a baggage check line *and* the boarding gate line – or are late for the flight, in which case you could end up bumped. Try to go with only carry-ons for these flights.

Tickets Out – An entry requirement for many countries is that you have an onward or return ticket, in other words, a ticket out of the country. If you're not sure what you intend to do next, the easiest solution is to buy the cheapest onward ticket to a neighboring country or a ticket from a reliable airline which can later be refunded if you do not use it.

Transferred Tickets – Airline tickets cannot be transferred from one person to another. Travelers sometimes try to sell the return half of their ticket, but officials can ask you to prove that you are the person named on the ticket. This is unlikely to happen on domestic flights, but on an international flight tickets may be compared with passports.

Travel Agencies – Travel agencies vary widely and you should use one that suits your needs. Some simply handle tours, while full-service agencies handle everything from tours and tickets to car rental and hotel bookings. A good one will do all these things and can save you a lot of money but if all you want is a ticket at the lowest possible price, then you really need an agency specializing in discounted tickets. A discount ticket agency, however, may not be useful for things like hotel bookings.

Travel Periods – Some officially discounted fares, Apex fares in particular, vary with the time of year. There is often a low (off-peak) season and a high (peak) season. Sometimes there's an intermediate or shoulder season as well. At peak times, when everyone wants to fly, all discounted fares may be higher or there may simply be no discounted tickets available. Usually the fare depends on your outward flight – if you depart in the high season and return in the low season, you pay the high-season fare. ■

On some international flights the luggage allowance is based on weight, not numbers; again, check with the airline.

If your luggage is delayed upon arrival (which is rare), some airlines will give a cash advance to purchase necessities. If sporting equipment is misplaced, the airline may pay for rentals. Should the luggage be lost, it is important to submit a claim. The airline doesn't have to pay the full amount of the claim, rather they can estimate the value of your lost items. It may take them anywhere from six weeks to three months to process the claim and pay you.

Smoking Smoking is prohibited on all flights within the USA. Many international flights are following suit, so if it matters to you, call and find out. Incidentally, the restriction applies to the passenger cabin and the lavatories but not the cockpit. Many airports in the USA also restrict smoking, but they compensate by having 'smoking rooms.'

Illegal Items Items that are illegal to take on a plane, either checked or as carry-on, include aerosols of polishes, waxes, etc; tear gas and pepper spray; camp stoves with fuel; and divers' tanks that are full. Matches should not be checked.

Air Travelers with Special Needs

If you have special needs of any sort – a broken leg, dietary restrictions, dependence on a wheelchair, responsibility for a baby, fear of flying – you should let the airline know as soon as possible so that they can make arrangements accordingly. It may also be worth ringing round the airlines before you make your booking to find out how they can handle your particular needs. You should remind them when you reconfirm your booking (at least 72 hours before departure) and again when you check in at the airport.

Airports and airlines can be surprisingly helpful, but they do need advance warning. Most international airports can provide escorts from check-in desk to plane where needed, and there should be ramps, lifts, accessible toilets, and reachable phones. Aircraft toilets, on the other hand, are likely to present a problem; travelers should discuss this with the airline at an early stage and, if necessary, with their doctor.

Guide dogs for the blind will often have to travel in a specially pressurized baggage compartment with other animals, away from their owner, though smaller guide dogs may be admitted to the cabin. Guide dogs are not subject to quarantine as long as they have proof of being vaccinated against rabies.

Deaf travelers can ask for airport and in-flight announcements to be written down for them.

Children under two travel for 10% of the standard fare (or free, on some airlines), as long as they don't occupy a seat. (They don't get a baggage allowance either.) 'Skycots' should be provided by the airline if requested in advance; these will take a child weighing up to about 22 pounds. Children between 2 and 12 can usually occupy a seat for half to two-thirds of the full fare, and do get a baggage allowance. Strollers can often be taken on as hand luggage.

Buying Tickets

Numerous airlines fly to the USA, and a variety of fares are available; in addition to a straightforward roundtrip ticket, it can also be part of a Round-the-World ticket or Circle Pacific fare. It pays to do a bit of research and shop around first. You might start by perusing travel sections of magazines like *Time Out* and *TNT* in the UK, or the Saturday editions of newspapers like the *Sydney Morning Herald* and *The Age* in Australia. Ads in these publications offer cheap fares, but don't be surprised if they happen to be sold out when you contact the agents: they're usually low-season fares on obscure airlines with conditions attached.

Start shopping for a ticket early – some of the cheapest tickets must be bought months in advance, and some popular flights sell out early. Talk to other recent travelers – they may be able to stop you from making some of the same old mistakes. Look at the ads in newspapers and magazines, consult reference books, and watch for special offers.

Note that high season in the USA is mid-June to mid-September (summer) and the one week before and after Christmas. The best rates for travel to and in the USA are found November through March.

Call travel agents for bargains (airlines can supply information on routes and timetables; however, except at times of fare wars, they do not supply the cheapest tickets). Airlines often have competitive low-season, student, and senior citizens' fares, but they often have complicated conditions and catches. Find out the fare, the route, the duration of the journey, and any restrictions on the ticket.

Cheap tickets are available in two distinct categories: official and unofficial. Official ones have a variety of names including advance-purchase fares, budget fares, Apex, and super-Apex. Unofficial tickets are simply discounted tickets that the airlines release through selected travel agents (not through airline offices). The cheapest tickets are often non refundable and require an extra fee for changing your flight (usually $50). Many insurance policies will cover this loss if you have to change your flight for emergency reasons. Return (roundtrip) tickets usually work out cheaper than two one-way fares – often *much* cheaper.

Use the fares quoted in this book as a guide only. They are approximate and based on the rates advertised by travel agents and airlines at press time. Quoted airfares do not necessarily constitute a recommendation for the carrier.

If traveling from the UK, you will probably find that the cheapest flights are being advertised by obscure bucket shops whose names haven't yet reached the telephone directory. Many such firms are honest and solvent, but there are a few rogues who will take your money and disappear, to reopen elsewhere a month or two later under a new name. If you feel suspicious about a firm,

don't give them all the money at once – leave a deposit of 20% or so and pay the balance on receiving the ticket. If they insist on cash in advance, go elsewhere. And once you have the ticket, ring the airline to confirm that you are booked on the flight.

You may decide to pay more than the rock-bottom fare by opting for the safety of a better-known travel agent. Established firms like STA Travel, which has offices worldwide, Council Travel in the USA or Travel CUTS in Canada offer good prices to most destinations.

Once you have your ticket, make a copy of it, and keep the copy separate from the original ticket. This will help you get a replacement if the ticket is lost or stolen.

Remember to buy travel insurance as early as possible.

Round-the-World Tickets
Round-the-World (RTW) tickets have become very popular in the last few years. Airline RTW tickets are often real bargains and can work out to be no more expensive or even cheaper than an ordinary return ticket.

The official airline RTW tickets are usually put together by a combination of two airlines, and permit you to fly anywhere you want on their route systems as long as you do not backtrack. Other restrictions are that you must usually book the first sector in advance and cancellation penalties apply. There may be restrictions on the number of stops permitted, and tickets are usually valid from 90 days up to a year. An alternative type of RTW ticket is one put together by a travel agent using a combination of discounted tickets.

Although most airlines restrict the number of sectors that can be flown within the USA and Canada to four, and some airlines black out a few heavily traveled routes (like Honolulu to Tokyo), stopovers are otherwise generally unlimited. In most cases a 14-day advance purchase is required. After the ticket is purchased, dates can be changed without penalty and tickets can be rewritten to add or delete stops for $50 each.

The majority of RTW tickets restrict you to just two airlines. US Air, British Airways, and Qantas Airways offer a RTW ticket called the Global Explorer that allows you to combine routes on all three airlines to a total of 28,500 miles for US$2999 or A$2499 to A$3099.

Qantas also flies in conjunction with Delta Air Lines, Northwest Airlines, Canadian Airlines, Air France, and KLM. Qantas RTW tickets, with any of the aforementioned partner airlines, cost US$3247 or A$3199.

Canadian Airlines offers numerous RTW combinations, such as with Philippine Airlines for C$2790 that could include Manila, Dubai, Pakistan, and Europe; another with KLM that could include Cairo, Bombay, Delhi, and Amsterdam for C$3149; and a third with South African Airways that could include Australia and Africa for C$3499.

Many other airlines also offer RTW tickets. Continental Airlines, for example, links up with either Malaysia Airlines, Singapore Airlines, or Thai Airways for US$2570. TWA's lowest priced RTW, linking up with Korean Air, costs US$2087 and allows stops in Honolulu, Seoul, Tel Aviv, Amsterdam, and Paris or London.

Circle Pacific Tickets

Circle Pacific tickets use a combination of airlines to circle the Pacific – combining Australia, New Zealand, North America, and Asia. Rather than simply flying from point A to point B, these tickets allow you to swing through much of the Pacific Rim and eastern Asia taking in a variety of destinations – as long as you keep traveling in the same circular direction. As with RTW tickets there are advance-purchase restrictions and limits on how many stopovers you can take. These fares are likely to be around 15% cheaper than RTW tickets.

Circle Pacific routes essentially have the same fares: A$2899 when purchased in Australia, US$2449 when purchased in the USA, and C$3309 when purchased in Canada. They include four stopovers with the option of adding additional stops at US$50 each. There's a 14-day advance-purchase requirement, a 25% cancellation penalty and a maximum stay of six months. There are also higher business class and 1st-class fares. Departure and airport-use taxes, which will vary with the itinerary, are additional.

Qantas Airways offers Circle Pacific routes in partnership with Delta Air Lines, Japan Air Lines, Northwest Airlines, or Continental Airlines. In the off-season, the Australian winter, Qantas occasionally offers hefty discounts on tickets that use it as the primary carrier.

United Airlines flies in conjunction with Cathay Pacific, Qantas, Ansett, Malaysia Airlines, or British Airways. Canadian Airlines has Circle Pacific fares from Vancouver that include, in one combination or another, virtually all Pacific Rim destinations. Canadian's partners include Qantas, Air New Zealand, Singapore, Garuda, Cathay Pacific, or Malaysia Airlines.

To/From Canada

Travel CUTS has offices in all major cities. The *Toronto Globe & Mail* and *Vancouver Sun* carry travel agents' ads; the magazine *Great Expeditions* (PO Box 8000-411, Abbotsford, BC V2S 6H1) is also useful.

There are daily flights to San Francisco and Los Angeles from Vancouver and Toronto, and many smaller Canadian cities have connections as well. A one-way flight between Los Angeles and Vancouver is around US$288.

To/From the UK & Ireland

Check the ads in magazines like *Time Out*, plus the Sunday papers and *Exchange & Mart*. Also check the free magazines widely available in London – start by looking outside the main railway stations.

Most British travel agents are registered with the ABTA (Association of British Travel Agents). If you have paid for your flight to an ABTA-registered agent who then goes out of business, ABTA will guarantee a refund or an alternative. Unregistered bucket shops are riskier but sometimes cheaper.

London is arguably the world's headquarters for bucket shops, which are well advertised and can usually beat published airline fares. Two good, reliable agents for cheap tickets in the UK are Trailfinders (☎ 0171-938-3366), 46 Earls Court Rd, London W8 6EJ, and STA Travel (☎ 0171-937-9962), 74 Old Brompton Rd, London SW7. Trailfinders produces a lavishly illustrated brochure including air fare details.

Virgin Atlantic has a roundtrip high-season fares from London to New York for £368 with a 21-day advance purchase to £508 with a seven-day advance purchase, and to Los Angeles for £568 with 21-day advance purchase.

The Globetrotters Club (BCM Roving, London WC1N 3XX) publishes a newsletter called *Globe* that covers obscure destinations and can help you find traveling companions.

To/From Continental Europe

If you are planning to remain on the West Coast, it is definitely worth flying straight there: you can save hours of flight time and airport dawdling. Flights from London, Copenhagen, and Amsterdam fly non-stop into Los Angeles. San Francisco has direct links to Paris. There are also some direct flights from Europe to Las Vegas.

The main airlines between Europe and the Western USA are British Airways, United, KLM, and Lufthansa. Fares fluctuate wildly, but are usually FF3550 to FF5290 roundtrip between Paris and Los Angeles, NF1385 to NF1690 Amsterdam-Los Angeles, DM1449 to DM 1749 Frankfurt-Los Angeles, in high season.

In Amsterdam, NBBS is a popular travel agent. In Paris Transalpino and Council Travel are popular agencies. The newsletter *Farang* (La Rue 8 á 4261 Braives, Belgium) deals with exotic destinations, as does the magazine *Aventure du Bout du Monde* (116 rue de Javel, 75015 Paris, France).

Virgin Atlantic flights from Paris to New York are substantially cheaper; a ticket

with seven-day advance purchase ranges from FF3790 to FF4530.

To/From Australia & New Zealand

In Australia and New Zealand, STA Travel and Flight Centres International are major dealers in cheap air fares; check the travel agents' ads in the yellow pages and call around.

Qantas flies to Los Angeles from Sydney, Melbourne (via Sydney or Auckland), and Cairns. United flies to San Francisco from Sydney and Auckland and also flies to Los Angeles.

The cheapest tickets have a 21-day advance-purchase requirement, a minimum stay of seven days and a maximum stay of 60 days. Qantas flies from Melbourne or Sydney to Los Angeles for A$1470 in the low season and A$1820 in the high season. Qantas flights from Cairns to Los Angeles cost A$1579 in the low season and A$1919 in the high season. Flying with Air New Zealand is slightly cheaper, and both Qantas and Air New Zealand offer tickets with longer stays or stopovers, but you pay more. Full-time students can save A$80 to A$140 on roundtrip fares to the USA.

Roundtrip flights from Auckland to Los Angeles on Qantas cost NZ$1720 in the low season. (This is the quoted student fare.)

To/From Asia

Hong Kong is the discount plane ticket capital of the region, but its bucket shops can be unreliable. Ask the advice of other travelers before buying a ticket. STA Travel, which is dependable, has branches in Hong Kong, Tokyo, Singapore, Bangkok, and Kuala Lumpur. Many flights to the USA go via Honolulu, Hawaii.

To/From Japan United Airlines has three flights a day to Honolulu from Tokyo with connections to Los Angeles and San Francisco. Northwest and Japan Air Lines also have daily direct flights to the West Coast from Tokyo; Japan Air Lines also flies to Honolulu from Osaka, Nagoya, Fukuoka, and Sapporo.

To/From Southeast Asia There are numerous airlines flying to the USA from Southeast Asia; bucket shops in places like Bangkok and Singapore should be able to come up with the best deals. Tickets to the US West Coast often allow a free stopover in Honolulu.

Northwest Airlines flies to Honolulu from Hong Kong, Bangkok, Manila, Seoul, and Singapore, with connections to the West Coast. Korean Air and Philippine Airlines also have flights from a number of Southeast Asian cities to Honolulu, with onward connections.

To/From Mexico
There are regular flights from San Francisco and Los Angeles to the major cities and tourist destinations in Mexico. At times (depending on prices and exchange rates), it can be substantially cheaper to fly to major Mexican cities from Tijuana, than from the Southern California airports in Los Angeles or even San Diego. Tijuana is the northernmost Mexican city, just south of San Diego, and only a couple of hours by bus from Los Angeles.

To/From Central & South America
There are many direct flights from Los Angeles to Central and South America, and others going via Miami or Houston. Check the international flag-carrier airlines of the countries you want to connect to (Aerolineas Argentinas, LANChile, Varig, etc), as well as US airlines like United and American.

LAND
If you're driving into California from Mexico and Canada, don't forget the vehicle's registration papers, liability insurance, and your home driver's license. Canadian and Mexican driver's licenses are accepted, but an international driver's permit is a good idea.

LEAVING THE USA
You should check in for international flights two hours early. During check-in procedures, you will be asked questions about whether you packed your own bags, whether anyone else has had access to them since you packed them and whether you have received any parcels to carry. These questions are for security reasons.

Departure Taxes
Airport taxes are normally included in the cost of tickets bought in the USA, and even tickets purchased abroad usually have this included. There's a $6 airport departure tax on all passengers bound for a foreign destination, and a $6.50 North American Free Trade Agreement (NAFTA) tax on all passengers entering the USA from a foreign country, both added to the purchase price of your air ticket.

WARNING
This chapter is particularly vulnerable to change – prices for international travel are volatile, routes are introduced and cancelled, schedules change, rules are amended, special deals come and go. Airlines and governments seem to take a perverse pleasure in making price structures and regulations as complicated as possible and you should check directly with the airline or travel agent to make sure you understand how a fare (and ticket you may buy) works.

In addition, the travel industry is highly competitive and there are many lurks and perks. The upshot of this is that you should get opinions, quotes, and advice from as many airlines and trael agents as possible before you part with your hard-earned cash. The details given in this chapter should be regarded only as pointers and cannot be any substitute for your own careful, up-to-date research.

Getting Around

AIR

Flying can be a convenient way of getting around California and Nevada, especially if time is limited. Depending where you're flying to/from, how far in advance you buy your ticket and a few other factors, flying is sometimes not much more expensive than making the same trip by bus, train, or rental car.

The major airports in the California/Nevada region are the San Francisco and Los Angeles international airports. If you're flying to/from other countries or the rest of the USA, you'll probably use one of these.

For flying within the region, there are a number of smaller airports. These include Sacramento, Oakland, San Jose, Burbank, Ontario, Orange County, San Diego, Las Vegas, and Reno; even smaller ones include Eureka, Chico, Santa Rosa, Santa Barbara, Long Beach, and Palm Springs. Additional tiny airports are mentioned in the regional

chapters. Often it costs much more to fly to the small airports than to the larger ones, but not always. The route between San Francisco and Los Angeles is probably one of the most heavily traveled air routes in the USA.

The best advice if you're thinking of air travel is to visit a good travel agent, who will have up-to-the-minute computerized information on fares, routes, discounts, price wars, special promotions, and so on. See the Getting There & Away chapter for information on STA and Council Travel, the two agencies specializing in student and youth travel.

A number of routes have especially frequent and convenient service, with airplanes taking off every 45 minutes to 1½ hours; these routes include San Francisco-Los Angeles (SF-LA), SF-Burbank, SF-Orange County, SF-San Diego, SF-Reno, Oakland-LA and LA-Las Vegas. It's

RICK GERHARTER

possible to just show up at the airport, buy your ticket and hop on, but the airlines recommend you make reservations to guarantee you a seat; buying your ticket in advance usually gets you a lower fare, too. See the Getting There & Away chapter for more about advance purchase and other types of discount fares – much of the same advice applies, whether you're flying a route within California and Nevada or within the rest of the USA.

Here are some of the main airlines serving California & Nevada:

America West	☎ 800-235-9292
American	☎ 800-433-7300
Continental	☎ 800-525-0280
Delta	☎ 800-221-1212
MarkAir	☎ 800-627-5247
Northwest	☎ 800-225-2525
Reno Air	☎ 800-736-6247
Southwest	☎ 800-435-9792
United	☎ 800-241-6522
USAir	☎ 800-428-4322

BUS
Greyhound
Greyhound (☎ 800-231-2222) is the major long-distance bus company in California and Nevada, with routes extending throughout the USA and into Canada. A number of other bus lines connect with the Greyhound system. Dozens of smaller bus companies provide regional bus services, and there are also local bus services within towns, cities, or counties.

You can buy a Greyhound ticket as late as 15 minutes before departure, but they will only fill the number of seats on the bus – no standing allowed. It's not a bad idea to buy your ticket in advance, if possible, to assure you of a seat. Sometimes buying your ticket in advance makes it cheaper – a recent promotion offered a one-way ticket to ride anywhere in California for $29, if the ticket was purchased three days in advance, a considerable savings for long-distance trips. More frequently, discounts are available only if you purchase your ticket 21 days in advance of travel.

A Greyhound Ameripass allows you unlimited travel anywhere in the Grey-

hound system for 7 days for $250, 15 days for $350, or 30 days for $550 (fares are subject to change).

Green Tortoise
This is an alternative bus line and tour company (☎ 415-956-7500, 800-867-8647). The buses, with seats knocked out and replaced by bunks with foam mattresses, cover several regular routes in California, as well as trips further afield (see the Getting There & Away chapter). Their north-south route operates once a week between San Francisco and Los Angeles, twice a week between San Francisco and Seattle; you can join the bus at any of several scheduled stopping points along the way.

TRAIN
Amtrak (☎ 800-872-7245) has an extensive rail-and-bus system throughout California, with 'Amtrak Thruway' buses providing convenient connections to/from the rail network to rural towns, Yosemite National Park, and a couple of routes crossing Nevada. See the Getting There & Away chapter for advice on reservations, off-peak fare periods, and more. See below under Tours for details on Amtrak's 'Focus on California' nine-day tour.

CAR & MOTORCYCLE
Driving is probably the easiest, cheapest, and best way to get around California and Nevada; having your own wheels enables you to go wherever you want, whenever you want, giving you the freedom to explore many places that are inconvenient or impossible to reach by public transport. Distances tend to be long, public transport not always convenient, and hitchhiking slow or risky, so most Californians get around by car. With a car it's feasible to carry camping and cooking gear and a cooler, and some of the cost of the car can be offset by savings in accommodations and food.

Three north-south routes traverse California. Highway 1, known as the Pacific Coast Hwy, is the slowest and curviest but also most scenic route, hugging the coast, passing by sandy beaches and clinging to rugged cliffs that drop steeply into the ocean. Highway 101, hugging the coast together with Hwy 1 for some sections and running the lengths of lovely valleys just inland from the Coastal Range for much of its distance, is also scenic, though not as spectacular as the Pacific Coast Hwy. Interstate 5, the fastest but least scenic and most boring route, traverses the flat San Joaquin Valley and heads up the center of the state into Oregon.

Major east-west highways include I-80, heading northeast from San Francisco through Reno and on to Salt Lake City; I-15, heading northeast out of Los Angeles through Las Vegas and on to Salt Lake City; I-40, heading east from Barstow to Flagstaff, Arizona and on to Albuquerque, New Mexico; I-10, heading east from Los Angeles to Phoenix, Arizona; and I-8, heading east from San Diego to Tucson, Arizona.

Rental Cars

Renting a car is a good value if you want to get around California and Nevada, especially with more than one person to share the costs. Prices vary widely so shop around, and be sure to ask for the best rate – discounts may be offered for renting on weekends, for three days, by the week, month, or even for renting it in one place and returning it to another if the company needs to move cars in that direction. Car rental is cheaper in big cities, especially LA. It makes sense to rent a car there, rather than taking buses or trains to a rural center, then paying a higher rate for a car for a shorter period.

Compare the total cost, including insurance and mileage; one company may charge a little less for the car, but a little more for the insurance. Also estimate the distance you'll be driving; an 'unlimited mileage' plan works out more economically than a 'cost-per-mile' plan if you'll be driving long distances, and increasingly unlimited mileage is found only in urban areas. If you'll be needing the vehicle for

several weeks, leasing may be cheaper than renting. See the Getting There & Away chapter for information on 'drive-away' cars.

Rental companies require that you have a major credit card, that you be at least 25 years old (21 in some cases), and that you have a valid driver's license (your home license will do). Some credit cards offer automatic insurance when you use them to pay for travel; check with your credit card about this, as it can save you having to pay the extra insurance cost. It can be worth it to get one of these kinds of cards if you'll be renting a car, as insurance can add around an extra $10 per day to the cost of the car. Your regular liability car insurance may also cover you driving a rental car – check with your insurance company before you leave home.

Think about whether you want to rent a car and return it to the same place you got it, or get a 'one-way' rental and return it to a different place. While local rental car companies may have only one or two offices, the larger companies have many offices throughout California, Nevada, and the rest of the USA. Be sure to ask if there is a drop-off charge, and if the price of the car is different for a one-way rental. Sometimes a hefty drop-off charge makes one-way rentals impractical, but sometimes there is no extra charge.

The major nationwide rental car companies are:

Alamo	☎ 800-327-9633
Avis	☎ 800-831-2847
Budget	☎ 800-527-0700
Dollar	☎ 800-800-4000
Enterprise	☎ 800-325-8007
Hertz	☎ 800-654-3131
National	☎ 800-328-4567
Thrifty	☎ 800-367-2277

Rent-A-Wreck (☎ 800-421-7253) offers older vehicles at cheaper prices. There are also thousands of smaller local companies, which sometimes offer cheaper prices. RVs can also be rented; look in the yellow pages under Recreational Vehicles – Renting & Leasing.

Buying a Vehicle

If you'll be driving in North America for more than about two or three months, you may want to consider buying. For periods of less than two months, it would probably be cheaper, and certainly less hassle, to rent a car.

Cars bought at a dealer cost more, but may come with warranties and/or financing options. Buying from an individual is usually cheaper; look in the newspaper classified ads or special ad publications for used vehicles. Check the Blue Book for the average value of the model and year of vehicle you're considering, and have it checked out by a mechanic or diagnostic service before you buy. AAA may be helpful. Bargaining when buying a used car – offering less than the asking price and then reaching a compromise price – is standard practice.

If you buy from a dealer, the dealer will submit the required forms to the DMV for the car's registration to be transferred into your name. If you buy from an individual, you (the buyer) must register the vehicle with the DMV within 10 days of purchase. To register the vehicle you will need the bill of sale, the title to the car (the 'pink slip'), proof of insurance or other financial responsibility, and a state smog certificate; California law specifies that every vehicle made in 1966 or thereafter must pass a state smog inspection before it can be registered. It is the seller's responsibility to see that it passes; be sure you don't buy a car that won't pass the inspection, or you may face some costly repairs to bring it up to standard before you can register and legally drive it.

Rules of the Road

Visitors to California and Nevada over 18 years of age can drive using their driver's license from their home state or country, as long as that license remains valid. Visitors from 16 to 18 years old can drive on their home driver's license provided they obtain a Nonresident Minor's Certificate from the Department of Motor Vehicles (DMV) within 10 days of arrival in California.

The *California Driver Handbook* explains everything you need to know about driving in California; you can pick one up free from any DMV office. This easy illustrated booklet contains all the rules of the road and it's a good idea to read it. Nevada's driving rules are basically the same as California's.

Driving in California is the same as in the rest of the USA, with a few local quirks. California has a seat belt law – you must buckle up. Whether you are a driver or a passenger, you can be given a citation and fine if you don't use your safety belt, which should have both lap and shoulder sections. Children under four years old, or those weighing less than 40 pounds, must ride in approved child safety seats.

Financial Responsibility Every driver or owner of a motor vehicle must 'maintain financial responsibility;' the easiest way to do this is to be covered by insurance. California law specifies a fixed minimum amount of liability insurance, to protect the health and property of others in case of an accident. If you are involved in any type of accident, regardless of fault – if someone bumps into your car in a parking lot, for example – and you don't have insurance, penalties are severe; in addition to financial penalties, your driver's license will be suspended for one year. If you are coming from another country or even another state, check to see if your home insurance will cover you in California; many out-of-state insurance companies are not authorized to operate in California. See the Rental Car section for details on insurance when you rent a car.

Speed Limits The speed limit is 65 mph on the interstate highways in designated rural areas, 55 mph on all other highways. You can drive five mph over the limit without much likelihood of being pulled over, but if you're doing 10 mph over the limit, you'll be caught sooner or later. The limit is 25 mph in cities and towns, with posted speed limits for various other types of roads. Watch for school zones which can be as low as 15 mph during school hours –

these limits are strictly enforced, and fines can be hefty.

Littering California has an aggressive campaign against littering. If you are seen throwing anything from a vehicle onto the roadway – bottles, cans, trash, a lighted cigarette, or anything else – the law states that you must be fined $1000, and you may also be forced to pick up whatever you discarded. Littering convictions are shown on your driving record the same as other driving violations. Keep any trash with you inside the vehicle until you get to a place to discard it.

Parking Penalties are particularly severe for unauthorized parking in a zone reserved for those with special disability license plates or parking placards, designated by a blue curb or a blue sign with a wheelchair figure either mounted or painted on the ground. The fine could be, let's say, $10 for parking in a no-parking zone marked with a red curb, but $300 for parking in a blue-curb zone.

Curbs are confusingly color coded for parking restriction; the different colors are:

red	no parking or even stopping
yellow	30-minute maximum for vehicles with commercial plates, 7 am to 6 pm.
green	10-minute parking zone from 9 am to 6 pm
white	five-minute parking zone for adjacent businesses only
blue	disabled parking only; proper identification required.

Driving Under the Influence Penalties are severe for DUI – driving under the influence of alcohol and/or drugs. If police have any reason to suspect you may have been drinking, they will demand that you take a test to determine the level of alcohol in your body. You have the right to choose a breath test, a urine test, or a blood test, but you do not have the right to refuse to be tested; refusing to be tested is treated the same as taking the test and failing it, and carries the same penalties, except for a longer period of suspension of your driver's license (one year).

The legal limits of alcohol in your body for driving are well below the level of 'drunkenness;' you don't have to be 'drunk' to be breaking the law. If you are found to have a blood alcohol concentration of 0.08% or more (0.01% if you are under 21 years old), you can be required to serve 48 hours to six months in jail, pay $390 to $1000 in fines, and have your driver's license suspended for four months to a year. If you own the car in which you were driving, the state can impound it for 30 days – and make you pay for the storage. All of these are for a first offense – penalties for subsequent offenses are even more severe.

DUI's are completely avoidable when a 'designated driver,' one in a group who will consume no alcohol or drugs, and be responsible for transporting the entire group safely, is decided upon at the beginning of the evening. Bars and restaurants usually offer free non-alcoholic drinks or other incentives to the designated driver.

It is also illegal to carry 'open containers' of alcohol in a vehicle, even in the passenger section, even if they are empty. Containers that are full and sealed may be carried, but if they have ever been opened they must be stored in the trunk.

AAA Membership

If you'll be doing much driving, whether in your own vehicle, someone else's, or a rental, membership in the California State Automobile Association (AAA; called 'triple A') is an excellent thing to have. Having a AAA card entitles you to free 24-hour roadside emergency service anywhere in the USA, including a few gallons of gas to get you going again if you run out, basic mechanical help, and free towing to the nearest mechanic. They also offer free maps and travel planning advice, a free tour book and other travel literature, give advice on how to buy a used car, sell reasonable car insurance, and have travel agency services and many other benefits. AAA offices are found throughout California, Nevada, and the rest of the USA; membership costs $56 the first year, $39 per year thereafter. If you are a member of an automobile association in another country, check to see if your membership entitles you to reciprocal rights in the USA; it probably does. Call ☎ 800-874-7532 for membership details.

Car Sharing

If you're looking for someone to ride along to share the cost of fuel, ask around or put a notice up in hostels, check the ride boards at universities, or even check the newspaper classified ads. Hostels can be especially good places to find riders, not only for long trips but also for sharing the cost to rent a car for local day trips. Expenses that would be monumental for one person suddenly become manageable if you can find three or four other people to split the cost.

Recreational Vehicles

You'll see many RVs in California, in all sizes up to giant-size models that are like houses on wheels. Campgrounds with full hookups are found almost everywhere. RVs are more expensive than cars to rent or buy, and they're bulky and not as economical to drive, but they solve all your transport, accommodation, and cooking needs in one go.

Motorcycles

To operate a motorcycle or moped you must have a special motorcycle license; separate licenses are issued for driving a motorcycle or moped with an engine size of 149cc or less, a motorcycle with an engine size of 150cc or more, and a motorcycle with three wheels or one with an attached sidecar.

A *Motorcycle Driver Supplement* booklet, a supplement to the *California Driver Handbook*, giving all the rules of the road for motorcyclists, may be picked up free from any DMV office. The law specifies that all drivers and passengers of motorcycles and mopeds, including children, must wear a securely fastened safety helmet. Motorcycles of less than 150cc engine size may not be driven on freeways.

BICYCLE

Bicycling makes it possible to see the countryside at a slower, more intimate pace than is possible with motorized transport; it's non-polluting, inexpensive, and you'll get some great exercise into the bargain, as well as having your own transport for getting around once you reach your destination.

Bicycles can be rented by the hour, day, week, or month. They can be bought new at sporting goods stores, discount warehouse stores, or used at flea markets and often from notice boards at hostels; you could also check the newspaper classified ads. Prices vary drastically depending on what you get.

A number of books are available on cycling and route planning in California and Nevada, some suggesting local rides, others routes for long-distance trips, still others places for off-road biking. Some of these are mentioned in the Outdoor Activities chapter; many others, including many specializing in local areas, can be found in local bookstores. Several organizations can help you with route planning, including Bikecentennial (☎ 406-721-1776), PO Box 8308-P, Missoula, MT 59807, a nationwide bicyclists' club.

You can bicycle anywhere except on freeways, where signs at on-ramps specify that no bicycles, motor-driven cycles (mopeds with less than 150cc engines) or pedestrians may pass beyond a certain point. You can cycle on parts of the coastal Hwy 1, but beware of treacherous curves and narrow roadways. Cycling is more enjoyable on the less-traveled roads; sometimes parallel or frontage roads enable you to basically follow the major highways without actually being on them.

If you plan a long bicycling trip and get tired of pedaling, or if you want to avoid the hilliest spots or bad weather, you can always take your bike along on public transport. Greyhound will carry bicycles as luggage for $10 provided they are boxed; Green Tortoise does the same, but prefers them unboxed. Amtrak will carry bicycles as checked baggage for a $10 fee, and they provide free bicycle boxes. Some airlines will carry boxed bicycles as 'sporting equipment' for no additional cost. You can also send your bike as freight on any of these services.

Safety In some parts of California there is a law that bicyclists must wear a safety helmet. Although at this writing it is not yet a state-wide law, it's moving in that direction. Get in the habit of wearing a safety helmet, or risk a citation – not to mention serious and needless injury should you have an upset. A headlight and reflectors are requirements everywhere for riding at night, and reflective and/or bright clothing is a good idea, too. Carry water with you, and a repair kit in case you have a flat tire or other problem.

Using a heavy duty bicycle lock is essential, as bicycle theft is a big business. Some locks come with insurance against bicycle theft, and it's worth the investment – Citadel and Kryptonite are two such companies, and there are others. Etch your driver's license number or other ID onto the frame of your bike and register it with the police – most police stations have etching equipment available for this purpose and it takes only a few minutes to do.

HITCHHIKING
Hitchhiking is never entirely safe and we don't recommend it. Travelers who decide to hitch should understand that they are taking a small but potentially serious risk. However, some people do choose to hitch, and the advice that follows should help to make their journeys as safe as possible.

There have been so many incidents of violence, sexual harassment, rape, and other types of trouble that now people are much more reluctant to pick up hitchhikers, and to hitch. Hitching may be easier in more laid-back parts of rural Northern California, where the old hippie ethic may still exist in some places – however it's very rural and chances of getting stranded are high. You must use extreme caution everywhere, both when hitchhiking and when picking up hitchhikers.

Women should never hitchhike alone; even women in pairs are not completely safe. Some women hitchhikers accept rides only from other women, or if there are women or children in the car. Drivers may be more reluctant to pick men up, so most likely a man and woman together have the best chance of getting a ride and of being safe hitching.

The usual common-sense hitching rules apply. Stand where you can be easily seen, and where drivers can pull over easily and safely. You can hitchhike on roads and highways, but not on freeways, where you must stand on the on-ramp, somewhere in front of the white sign stating that pedestrians are prohibited beyond this point. If someone is already hitching there, let them get a ride first, or position yourself some distance ahead of them, so they'll be spotted by drivers first. Drivers may not stop if it looks like there's a crowd of hitchhikers.

Be alert and cautious when accepting a ride, and discern which rides not to take. Avoid not only crazy or intoxicated drivers, but also rides that will drop you at a terrible spot to continue your journey. Use your instincts and don't get into a car if it seems suspicious for any reason, or even for no reason. You can always wait for another ride, but once you're in a car it might not be so easy to get out again.

BOAT
Boating is a way to get around in a few parts of California, notably to Catalina Island in southern California. On San Francisco Bay, ferry routes operate between San Francisco and Sausalito, Tiburon, Larkspur, Oakland, Alameda, and Vallejo. Details are given in the appropriate sections. Some small ferries and water taxis operate on San Diego Bay and Mission Bay.

LOCAL TRANSPORT
Airport Transport
Airport shuttle buses provide convenient transport to/from the major airports. To the San Francisco International and Oakland airports there are airport shuttles serving

areas as far away as Santa Rosa in the north and Gilroy in the south; to the Los Angeles International Airport there are airport shuttles serving destinations as far away as Santa Barbara. These far-flung services usually pick up and drop off passengers hourly at designated bus stops; door-to-door airport shuttle services operate within the larger cities. Look for airport shuttle services under Airport Transportation Service or Buses in the yellow pages.

Bus

Most cities and larger towns have local bus systems, sometimes providing service only within the town or city, sometimes ranging farther afield to connect several towns in a regional area, or to provide transport from smaller towns to the larger towns nearby. These services are mentioned in the geographical chapters.

Train

Bay Area Rapid Transit (BART) is an underground (and underwater) train network around the San Francisco Bay Area. The *Coaster* commuter trains operate along the coast from Oceanside to downtown San Diego.

Other local trains, some of them historic, operate primarily as tourist attractions. Notable among these are the *Skunk Train* between Willits and Fort Bragg, the *Northcoast Daylight* between Willits and Eureka, the *Blue Goose* from Yreka to Montague, the *Napa Valley Wine Train* between Napa and St Helena, the *Roaring Camp* and *Big Trees Narrow-Gauge Railroads* from Felton up to the summit of Bear Mountain or into Santa Cruz, the *Mother Lode Cannon Ball* operating from Jamestown, the *Sacramento Southern Railroad* from Sacramento to Hood, and the Campo Railroad Museum's 16-mile excursion in rugged country near the Mexican border. In

Nevada, there are short tourist railway rides in Carson City, Virginia City, and Ely.

Taxi

Taxis are metered. While taxis are a comparatively expensive form of transport, they are great for certain occasions, such as coming home late at night in a major city. If you don't spot a taxi cruising, you can phone for one; look under Taxi in the yellow pages.

TOURS

Tours run the gamut from whitewater rafting through remote wilderness areas to sightseeing tours of major tourist attractions in the urban centers. Whether you go on a long-distance tour lasting several days or a local sightseeing tour of a few hours, a theme tour – wine tasting, horseback riding, bird watching and nature, rafting, or what have you – tours can often make an easy way to get around and do things, especially if time is limited. Travel agents and tourist offices have bundles of information and brochures about tours; specific tours are also mentioned throughout this book.

Amtrak offers a nine-day guided 'Focus on California' tour by train departing from San Francisco, heading up through the Wine Country and Sacramento to Lake Tahoe, curving down through Yosemite National Park to Monterey, then heading down the coast through Carmel, Big Sur, past Hearst Castle, through Santa Maria, Solvang, Santa Barbara, and Malibu, ending up at Los Angeles. It can be booked through travel agents or directly with Amtrak.

Green Tortoise offers several roundtrip bus tours departing from San Francisco. Within California there's a six-day Northern California Redwoods and Parks Loop and a three-day tour of Yosemite and the eastern Sierra Nevada; longer tours are mentioned in the Getting There & Away chapter.

Cruising the Castro, San Francisco

Mariachis, Los Angeles

The great, bustling Doo Dah Parade, Pasadena

Networking, California style

JOHN ZEGART

Let's hope he plants two.

NANCY KELLER
Seagull – the beachgoer's nemesis

CHRIS SALCEDO
Roam with a view – Mt Tam is a hiker's paradise

WAYNE BERNHARDSON
Yucca flowers are best sniffed from a distance.

NANCY KELLER
Tule reeds, Modoc National Wildlife Refuge

California

Facts about California

HISTORY

It's generally accepted that the first people to inhabit America came from east Asia, over a land bridge to Alaska across what is now the Bering Strait. This land bridge was related to recurrent Ice Ages, during which the sea level was lower. There is some disagreement about the time at which migrations took place – the estimates range from as early as 35,000 years ago, to somewhere between 12,000 and 13,000 years ago. The oldest undisputed evidence of human occupation in any part of the Americas is from about 12,000 years ago.

There is room for dissent about the whole land bridge theory. For one thing, there is no evidence of a progression in the age of artifacts and remains from North to South America, which one would expect if the Americas were populated by a land migration from Alaska to southern Patagonia. Other finds are believed to be older than the date of the land bridge, though these are disputed. A skull found at Del Mar, in southern California, was initially dated at 48,000 years old – about 13,000 years before the earliest estimates for the land bridge. Most controversial are the chipped stones found at the Calico Early Man Site, claimed to be artifacts around 200,000 years old. This would place them among the oldest archaeological finds anywhere in the world, and force a re-think of all the accepted ideas about human evolution and distribution.

Prehistory

Stone tools found at sites in the Bakersfield area have been dated to around 12,000 to 8000 years ago – about the same period as the early stone points discovered in Clovis, New Mexico. Many other sites across the state have yielded evidence of people from around 8000 to 4000 years ago, from large middens of sea shells along the coast, to campfire sites in the mountains.

Some of the most interesting archaeological remains are the numerous rock art sites, dating from 3000 to 500 years ago. There are over 1000 of these in California, and they give some idea of the cultural diversity of the indigenous populations, with five identifiable styles of pictographs (where the design is painted on with one or more colors) and five styles of petroglyphs (where the design is pecked, chipped or abraded onto the rock). Many of the sites are closed to the public, or access is restricted in the interests of preservation. Three areas where rock art can be seen are the Chaw' Se Indian Grinding Rocks State Park, in the Gold Country; Little Petroglyph Canyon, north of Ridgecrest (contact the Maturango Museum there); and the Chumash Painted Cave, near Santa Barbara.

Where rock art depicts identifiable animal and human forms, it gives clues to the lifestyle of the various groups. Petroglyphs from the southeastern part of the state depict the hunting of animals like deer and bighorn sheep, and are in the same style as rock art from the Great Basin in Nevada. Chumash pictographs from the coast near Santa Barbara show marine animals, and indicate that the sea was an important source of food. *Morteros*, or grinding holes, are often found at the same sites as rock art. These bowl-shaped depressions in flat rocks were used to grind acorns and other seeds into flour.

California's Indians

The archaeological evidence, combined with accounts from the early European visitors, and later ethnographic research, give quite a clear picture of the Indians at the time of European contact. There were several major language families, over 20 language groups, with more than 100 dialects, spread over all the habitable parts of the state. Their total numbers were probably between 150,000 and 300,000, though some recent estimates run considerably higher. This doesn't sound like many, but it is estimated that over half of the Native American population of what is now continental USA lived in the area of modern California at the time the Spanish arrived. They lived in small groups and villages, in many cases shifting with the seasons from the valleys and the coast up to the mountains. The largest villages of which there are traces, in the Central Valley, are reckoned to have had 1500 to 2000 residents.

Acorn meal was the dietary staple, supplemented by small game, such as rabbits and deer, and fish and shellfish along the coast. Many other plants were used for food and fiber. There were some earthenware pots, fish nets, bows, arrows, and spears with chipped stone points, but the most highly developed craft was basket making. The baskets were woven with local grasses and plant fibers, decorated with attractive geometric designs, and many were so tightly woven that they would hold water – examples can be seen in many museums. There was some trade between the groups, especially between coastal and inland people, but generally they did not interact much. In most cases a village would have no common language with its neighbors. Conflict between the groups was almost nonexistent, and they had no class of warriors and no tradition of warfare, at least until the Europeans arrived.

Several museums have good exhibits on Native American archaeology and anthropology, like the Hearst Museum at UC Berkeley, the Museum of Man in San Diego, and the Gene Autry Western Heritage Museum in Los Angeles.

European Discovery

Following the conquest of Mexico, the Spanish were exploring the limits of their new empire. There was much fanciful speculation about a golden island beyond the West Coast, and California was actually named before it was discovered, after a mythical island in a Spanish novel. The southern tip of California was settled by Spaniards in 1535, but it was not until 1539 that an exploration by Francisco de Ulloa established that it was on a peninsula rather than an island. The peninsula became known as Baja (lower) California, and the coast to the north was called Alta (upper) California.

Juan Rodríguez Cabrillo, a Portuguese explorer and retired conquistador, was engaged by the Spanish government to lead an expedition up the West Coast and find the fabled land of gold and spices that many still hoped for. He was also to find the equally mythical Strait of Anian, an imagined sea route between the Pacific and the Atlantic – the Spanish version of the Northwest Passage. In 1542, Cabrillo's ships sailed into San Diego Harbor (which he named San Miguel), and his crew became the first Europeans to see mainland California. The ships sat out a storm in the harbor, then followed the coast north, pausing to check out some of the islands around Catalina. On one of these, Cabrillo fell ill, died, and was buried. The expedition continued north as far as Oregon, then returned to Mexico with charts and descriptions of the coast, but no evidence of a sea route to the Atlantic, no cities of gold, and no islands of spice. The authorities were unimpressed, and showed no interest in California for 60 years.

At that time Spanish ships began to ply the Pacific, carrying Mexican silver to the Philippines to trade for the exotic goods of Asia. These Manila galleons often took a northerly route back to the Americas to catch the westerly winds, and they sometimes struck land on the California coast. The galleons were also harassed by English pirates, including Sir Francis Drake, who sailed up the California coast in 1579. He missed the entrance to San Francisco Bay, but pulled in near Point Reyes (at what is now Drake's Bay), to repair his ship, which was literally bursting with the weight of plundered Spanish silver. He claimed the land for Queen Elizabeth, and named it Nova Albion (New England), then left for other adventures. (He wrote that he left a

CALIFORNIA

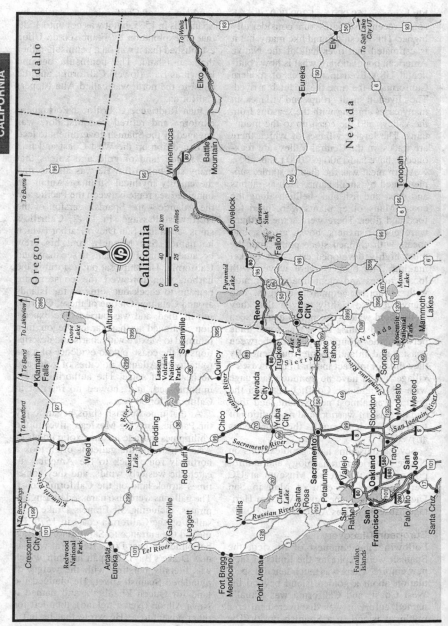

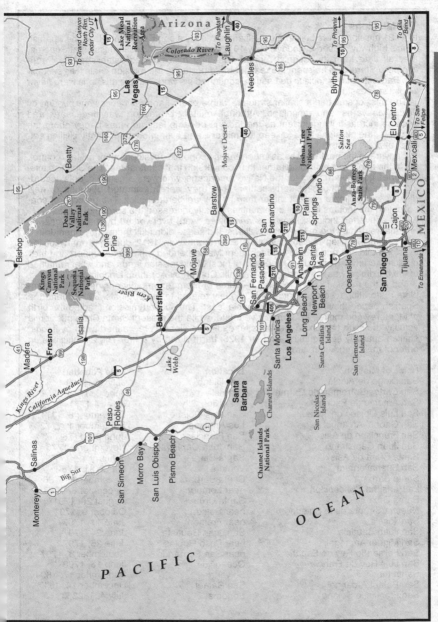

CALIFORNIA

The Missions

In all 21 missions were built in Alta California, mostly along El Camino Réal, the Spanish 'king's highway,' traced by today's Hwy 101. Except for the Mexican mission at Sonoma, they all date from the Spanish period. The first mission was established by Padre Junípero Serra, and he spent the rest of his life nurturing the mission chain. His successor, Padre Fermin Francisco de Lasuén, continued his work, but the missions were never wholly successful.

The missions all had a similar structure with a church and residences surrounded by fields, vineyards, and ranchland. Although military protection was necessary, and became increasingly important as the Indians became less and less happy about the intruders, the missions tried to keep the military, and even more importantly civilian settlers, at arms length.

Converting the heathen was as important as economic development or military control, but in the end it was extinction rather than conversion that came about. The Spanish missionaries had little respect for the Native Americans, who were a gentle people according to the descriptions of early settlers, but they were decimated because of new diseases and simple neglect rather than by any deliberate policy. The process of consolidating the Indians in small communities greatly increased the spread of disease.

The converted Indians, known as *neophytes*, were overworked by the missionaries and maltreated by the military and civilians. If disease didn't kill them, they often drifted away from the alien missions. A severe earthquake in 1812 damaged many of the mission buildings and in 1834 independent Mexico ended their state support and they gradually crumbled into ruin. Ownership of most of the mission lands, and what remained of the buildings, was returned to the Catholic Church by Abraham Lincoln.

Today the missions are a mixed lot – some of them remarkably original, others complete restorations, some of them only vaguely related to the originals. Even during the Spanish period they had been a moveable feast. The second mission marked the birth of Monterey and moved to Carmel a year later while the present Santa Clara mission is actually the sixth church on the fifth site; earlier versions were washed away by floods, shaken apart by earthquakes, and, in 1926, burnt down by a fire. The 21 missions, in order of their foundation, are:

Name of Mission	Location	Date Founded
San Diego de Alcalá	San Diego	July 16, 1769
San Carlos Borromeo de Carmelo	Carmel	June 3, 1770
San Antonio de Padua	near King City	July 14 1771
San Luis Obispo de Tolosa	San Luis Obispo	September 8, 1771
San Gabriel Arcangel	Los Angeles	September 1, 1772
San Francisco de Asis	San Francisco	June 29, 1776
San Juan Capistrano	San Juan Capistrano	November 1 1776
Santa Clara de Asis	Santa Clara	January 12, 1777
San Buenaventura	Ventura	March 31, 1782
Santa Barbara	Santa Barbara	December 4, 1786
La Purísima Concepción	near Lompoc	December 8, 1787
Santa Cruz	Santa Cruz	August 28, 1791
Nuestra Señora de la Soledad	near Soledad	October 9, 1791
San Jose	near Fremont	June 11, 1797
San Juan Bautista	San Juan Bautista	June 24, 1797
San Miguel Arcangel	near Paso Robles	June 25, 1797
San Fernando Rey de España	near San Fernando	September 8, 1797
San Luis Rey de Francia	Oceanside	June 13, 1798
Santa Ines	Solvang	September 17, 1804
San Rafael Arcangel	San Rafael	December 14, 1817
San Francisco Solano	Sonoma	July 4, 1823 ■

brass plate nailed to a post recording his visit. A plate was supposedly found there in 1937, and is now in the Bancroft Library at UC Berkeley – it is probably a fake.)

The Spanish decided they needed to secure some ports on the Pacific coast, and sent Sebastian Vizcaino to find them. Vizcaino was a better salesman than he was a leader and navigator, and his first expedition was a disaster that didn't get past Baja California. In his second attempt, in 1602, he rediscovered the harbor at San Diego, and gave it its present name. Contrary to his orders, he renamed many of the features of the coast, and made glowing reports of the value of his 'discoveries,' in particular Monterey harbor. Perhaps no one believed Vizcaino's reports, because they were pigeonholed for 160 years as Spain continued to ignore its remotest territory.

The Mission Period

As Russian ships came to California's coast in search of sea otter pelts, and British trappers and explorers were spreading throughout the West, the Spanish government finally decided it was time for some permanent settlement. Also, the church was anxious to start missionary work among the Indians. California was to be settled by a combination of Catholic missions and military *presidios*. The Indian converts would live in the mission, learn trade and agricultural skills, and ultimately establish *pueblos* that would be like little Spanish towns. The first colonizing expedition, the 'Sacred Expedition,' was a major undertaking, with land based parties and supply ships converging on San Diego in 1769 – only half of the original 300 settlers made it that far. Padre Junípero Serra stayed in San Diego to set up the first mission, while Gaspar de Portola continued north with instructions to form a second outpost at Monterey.

Portola went right past Monterey, as he didn't see anything like the fine protected harbor that Vizcaino had described. His party continued north until they were stopped at a large bay, later named San

San Francisco de Solano (1823)

San Rafael Arcangel (1817)

San Francisco de Asis (Mission Dolores -1776)

Santa Clara de Asis (1777)

San Jose de Guadalupe (1797)

Santa Cruz (1791)

San Carlos Borromeo de Carmelo (1770)

San Juan Bautista (1797)

Nuestra Señora de la Soledad (1791)

San Antonio de Padua (1771)

San Miguel Arcangel (1797)

El Camino Real

San Luis Obispo de Tolosa (1771)

California Missions

0   40   80 km
0   25   50 miles

La Purisima Concepcion (1787)

Santa Ines (1804)

Santa Barbara (1786)

San Buenaventura (1782)

San Fernando Rey de España (1797)

San Gabriel Arcangel (1772)

San Juan Capistrano (1776)

El Camino Real

San Luis Rey de Francia (1798)

San Diego de Alcala (1769)

PACIFIC OCEAN

CALIFORNIA

Francisco. Returning disappointed to San Diego, he found Serra's party desperately awaiting an overdue supply ship, and with not one Indian convert after eight months of missionary activity. They were on the point of abandoning the expedition, but after a day of prayer, the supply ship arrived just in time. Portola returned north to the unpromising site of Monterey, and though he realized its shortcomings, he dutifully established the second presidio and mission there, as he had been ordered.

Four presidios were established, at San Diego (1769), Monterey (1770), Santa Barbara (1782), and San Francisco (1776), to protect the missions and deter foreign intruders. In fact, these garrisons created more threats than they deterred, as the soldiers aroused hostility by raiding the Indian camps to rape and kidnap women. Not only were the presidios militarily weak, but their weakness was well known to rival powers, and did nothing to strengthen Spain's claims to Vancouver Island or Oregon.

With the Indians decimated by disease, an attempt was made to build up the pueblos in California with soldier families and civilians from Mexico. The first group came overland from Sonora, led by Juan Bautista de Anza on the route he pioneered across the southern desert. They settled on the San Francisco peninsula in 1776, where they found good grass. They named the place 'Yerba Buena,' though their first crops failed in the sandy soil and salty air. Other civilian pueblos were established at San Jose (1777) and Los Angeles (1781), but they attracted few settlers from Mexico, and those that came were neither farmers who could cultivate the land, nor soldiers who could defend it.

The missions were more successful at agriculture, and by 1800 they were growing grapes, fruit, and wheat, raising cattle, and supplying enough food for themselves and the presidios. During the Mexican War of Independence, from 1810 to 1821, supplies from Mexico were cut off completely, and Alta California was, of necessity, self-sufficient. But as a way of colonizing the wilds of California, and converting the natives to Christianity, the mission period was an abject failure. The Spanish population remained small, the missions achieved little better than mere survival, foreign intruders were not greatly deterred, and more Indians died than were converted. Conflict between Spanish and Indians persisted, with a major revolt in Santa Barbara as late as 1824.

The Rancho Period

When Mexico became independent of Spain in 1821, the new government regarded the church with mistrust, and sought new ways to make California a profitable possession. In 1833 the missions were secularized. Mission lands were appropriated, and divided between the mission Indians and new settlers, who were encouraged to come to California with the promise of land grants. Within two years, some 12 million acres of land were given out in over 700 land grants. Few Indians held onto their land, as they fell victim to conniving landholders and corrupt administrators, while huge tracts of land – *ranchos* – were acquired by a small number of powerful *rancheros*.

The ranchos were the focal points of a pastoral society that produced huge numbers of cattle, but little else. Though much money was made selling tallow and hide to the ships that plied this trade, most of it was spent on importing all manner of goods from outside. There was no diversification of agriculture, and no development of industry, infrastructure, or commerce. Trade with outsiders had been prohibited by the Spanish, but grew out of control during Mexican rule, with American traders buying the hides, and selling every necessity and luxury that could be produced on the East Coast and shipped around Cape Horn.

The society itself was almost feudal. The landholding elite, called *Californios*, dressed in fine cloths, rode fine horses, and entertained lavishly, but were basically uneducated and lived in ranch houses without running water, sewerage, or

CALIFORNIA

wooden floors. Most of the work was done by *mestizos*, born of European and Indian parents, while the Indians were almost totally marginalized.

American interest in California increased on two levels. At the official level, driven by a belief in the 'Manifest Destiny' of the USA to control all the territory across to the Pacific, various offers were made to purchase Alta California from the Mexican government. At the unofficial level, American explorers, trappers, traders, whalers, settlers, and opportunists entered California and seized on many of the prospects for profit that the Californios ignored in favor of ranching. Some of the Americans who started businesses became Catholics, married locals, and assimilated into Californio society. One American, Richard Henry Dana, author of *Two Years Before the Mast* (1840), worked on a ship in the hide trade in the 1830s and wrote disparagingly of Californians as 'an idle and thriftless people who can make nothing for themselves.'

Other intruders were Russian hunters of sea-otter pelts, who had actually established a fort just north of San Francisco in 1812 (the area is still known as the Russian River). Trappers from the Hudson's Bay Company had reached the Sacramento Valley in the 1820s, and the British government had offered to buy California in exchange for unpaid debts. When frontiersman Jedediah Smith turned up in San Diego in 1827, the Mexican authorities were alarmed to discover that the route from the east was not impassable. Another frontiersman, Kit Carson, pioneered an immigrant route across the Sierra Nevada to Los Angeles. One interloper whose name was linked to California's destiny was John Sutter, an expatriate Swiss who, in 1839, persuaded the governor to grant him 50,000 acres in the Sacramento Valley. It happened that his ranch was at the western end of another trail, over the Truckee Pass, on which the first American wagon trundled into California in 1841, and which the ill-fated Donner Party followed in 1846.

The Bear Flag Republic

American settlers in California became increasingly discontented with the ineffectual and remote government from Mexico City. While the USA made proposals to buy the territory from Mexico, some settlers in northern California plotted a more direct approach, thinking that if they revolted, the USA would surely send troops to assist them. When the USA annexed Texas, in 1845, the Mexican government ordered all the foreigners to leave California. Though the authorities didn't, and probably couldn't, enforce this decree, it certainly increased the discontent of the American settlers.

A few months later, Captain John Frémont, the explorer and map-maker, arrived in California with 68 soldiers from the Corps of Topographical Engineers. Emboldened by Fremont's presence, the rebels seized the town of Sonoma, hoisted an improvised flag with a crudely drawn bear, and proclaimed California the 'Bear Flag Republic.' It was one of the shortest lived republics in history, but the bear, and the words 'California Republic' still survive on the state flag.

The Mexican-American War

In May 1846, the USA declared war on Mexico, and US forces quickly occupied all the presidios and imposed martial law. Some Californios took to the hills, but those who remained in the towns experienced an oppressive occupation. In September the Californios revolted. The Californio lancers, with their knowledge of the countryside and their skills on horseback, actually defeated the Americans in small battles near Los Angeles, in the Salinas Valley, and at San Pasqual. Their victories were short lived – the Americans had reinforcements arriving by ship while the Californios were on their own.

In any case, it was all a side-show. The war was really won and lost in mainland Mexico, with Americans taking the important cities of Monterrey, Veracruz, and ultimately, in 1847, Mexico City itself. In these circumstances, the Mexicans had little choice but to cede much of their northern territory to the USA. The Treaty of Guadalupe Hidalgo, signed on February 2, 1848, turned over California to the USA, along with most of New Mexico and Arizona. An interesting feature of this treaty was that it guaranteed the rights of Mexican citizens living in areas taken over by the USA. Many Mexicans feel that this provision still entitles them to live and work in those states, regardless of their country of birth. They joke that Mexicans are now re-occupying the lost lands, one person at a time.

Gold

By an amazing coincidence, gold was discovered in northern California within days of the treaty with Mexico being signed. The owner of the land where it was found, John Sutter (remember him?), managed to keep the discovery quiet for a few months without realizing that Mexico was in the process of signing away a gold mine. Though gold deposits had been found earlier in California, neither the Mexican government nor the rancheros had shown much interest in mining ventures.

With a characteristically Californian blend of hype and enthusiasm, the gold discovery transformed the new American outpost. When Mexican rule ended, the population was about 14,000 (including 6000 Indians). In 1848 and '49, over 90,000 people from other parts of the USA, and all over the world, rushed to California, and the state population boomed by 565%. The growth and wealth stimulated every aspect of life, from agriculture and banking, to construction and journalism. Hills were stripped bare, erosion wiped out vegetation, streams silted up, and mercury washed down to San Francisco Bay. San Francisco became a hotbed of gambling, prostitution, drink, and chicanery.

Ostensibly under military rule, Califor-

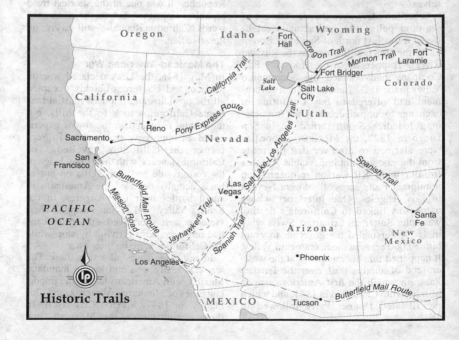

Historic Trails

nia had little effective government at all. The currency was a mixture of gold slugs, debased coinage, and foreign cash, the main law was 'miners law,' and land ownership was uncertain. The rancheros still claimed title to most of California's usable lands, while thousands of new immigrants were squatting on sites, as homesteaders on untitled lands, in the expectation that they would be able to claim a 160-acre lot for $200. In 1850, California was admitted to the union as a non-slave state – nationally it was part of a compromise that balanced the slave and non-slave states in the senate. Locally, there were thoughts of making two states, with slavery in southern California – but the first task was to sort out the ownership of land.

A congressional commission was sent to California to adjudicate the land claims. Landholders were required to prove their claims with documents and witnesses, and many could not do so. Their lands were then available for settlement or purchase by new arrivals. It was hardly fair to the rancheros, whose land rights had been guaranteed in the treaty of Guadalupe Hidalgo, but it permitted an explosive growth of agriculture, industry, and commerce, not to mention real estate speculation, which has been a major sport ever since. By 1860 the population reached 380,000, and the easy gold had all been taken. The Indians suffered badly from this growth, and despite armed resistance that continued into the 1870s, they were displaced from most of their traditional lands, confined to reservations, and their numbers greatly diminished.

The second boom for California came with the discovery of the Comstock silver lode in 1860, though the lode was actually over the border in what would soon become Nevada. Exploiting the lode required deep-mining techniques, which meant companies, stocks, trading, and speculation. San Francisco made more money out of stocks than Nevada did out of mining – mansions sprouted on Nob Hill, and Californian businessmen became renowned for their audacity – *not* their scruples.

The Transcontinental Railroad

Railroad building was a mania in mid-19th-century America, and was made extra profitable by capitalizing on real estate deals along the route. Though essentially private projects, railroads were often subsidized with cash and land grants by governments, and towns offered inducements to the railroad companies to ensure that they would be connected to the new line.

The transcontinental railroad was simple in conception, vast in scale, and revolutionary in its impact. The tracks were laid simultaneously from the east and the west, meeting in the middle of Utah in 1869. The track going east from Sacramento was the work of the Central Pacific Railroad and thousands of Chinese laborers. The company had great political influence, and gained substantial subsidies and land grants along the route – one of its principals, Leland Stanford, became State Governor in 1863, and it was all legal because the company lawyer was also a judge of the state supreme court.

The new railroad meant that the trip from New York to San Francisco could be done in four or five comfortable days, rather than two arduous months. It also opened eastern markets to Californian agricultural products, and facilitated the import of eastern goods to California. The construction and the completion of the project caused a surge in growth, with the population increasing by 47% during the 1860s, and another 54% in the 1870s. The Civil War (1861-65) provided an impetus for local industry as the normal flow of eastern goods had slowed. Agriculture diversified, with new crops, including oranges, being grown for export. Californian real estate developers and 'boosters' promoted the state, and investment flooded in, as well as immigrants, particularly from states devastated by the Civil War.

Inevitably the boom was followed by a bust in the mid-1870s. Speculation had raised land prices to levels no farmer or immigrant could afford, the railroad brought in products that undersold the goods made in California, and some 15,000

Chinese workers, no longer needed for rail construction, flooded the labor market. There was a period of labor unrest, which culminated in anti-Chinese laws, and a reformed state constitution in 1879.

Industry & Agriculture

It took big bribes to bring a branch line to Los Angeles in 1876, but in 1885, a new Atchison, Topeka & Santa Fe Railroad directly linked Los Angeles across the Arizona desert to the East Coast and broke the power of the Central Pacific monopoly. The competition between the railroads greatly reduced the cost of transport, and led to a more diverse development across the state, particularly in southern California and the San Joaquin Valley.

Much of the land granted to the railroads was sold in big lots to speculators, who also acquired, with the help of corrupt politicians and administrators, much of the farm land that was released for new settlement. Much of the state's agricultural land became consolidated as large holdings in the hands of a small number of city-based landlords, establishing the pattern of big, industrial scale 'agribusiness' rather than small family farms. These big businesses were well placed to provide the substantial investment, and the political connections, required to bring irrigation water to the farmland. They also established a need for cheap farm workers, commonly met by poor immigrants and minorities, even today.

In the absence of coal, iron ore, or abundant water, heavy industry was slow to develop. The discovery of oil in the Los Angeles area in 1892 was a boon in itself, and stimulated the development of petroleum processing and chemical industries.

The 20th Century

The population, wealth, and importance of California has grown dramatically throughout the 20th century. The big San Francisco earthquake and fire of 1906 destroyed most of the city, but it was barely a hiccup in the state's development – population increased by 60% in the decade to 1910. The revolu-tionary years in Mexico, from 1910 to 1921, saw a huge influx from south of the border, reestablishing the Hispanic heritage that had been almost totally extinguished by American dominance. The Panama Canal, completed in 1914, made bulk shipping feasible between East and West Coasts.

During the 1920s, the population grew by a mammoth 66%, the highest growth rate since the Gold Rush. The Great Depression saw another wave of immigrants, this time from the impoverished states of the dust bowl. Outbreaks of social and labor unrest led to a rapid growth of the Democratic party. Some of the Depression-era public works projects had lasting benefits, great and small, from San Francisco's Bay Bridge to the restoration of mission buildings.

WWII had a major impact on California, and not just from the influx of military and defense workers, and the development of new industries. As elsewhere, women were co-opted into war work, and proved themselves in a range of traditionally male jobs. Anti-Asian sentiments re-surfaced, and many Japanese-Americans were interned, while more Mexicans came in to fill labor shortages. Many of the service people who passed through California actually liked the place so much that they returned to settle after the war. In the 1940s the population grew by 53%; and in the 1950s, by another 49%.

Throughout this century, a number of aspects of Californian life have emerged as recurring themes.

Water The development of California, especially southern California and the agricultural industries, has always been heavily dependent on the supply of water. One of the first big projects was the aqueduct to bring water from northern California down to the Central Valley and Los Angeles area. In the early 1900s, the Los Angeles aqueduct was built, taking water from the Owens Valley in the Eastern Sierra and channeling hundreds of miles to the West Coast. California also claims a large share of the water from the Colorado River, which is dammed in several places and its waters diverted to the agricultural areas of the Imperial Valley, Coachella Valley, and the cities of southern California. The capacity of these schemes has been expanded throughout the 20th century, to the point where they're now close to extracting the maximum available water from all of them.

All these projects have major environmental and political implications, from the drying up of wetlands and habitats in the Sacramento River delta to salination in the Imperial Valley. The channeling of water from north to south causes some resentment in northern California – 75% of the water comes from northern California, but 75% of it is used in the south, much of it in areas that are natural deserts. Conservationists have taken Los Angeles water authorities to court over the depletion of lakes and streams in the eastern Sierra, and won significant concessions. California's share of the Colorado River water is being contested by the burgeoning states of the Southwest sunbelt, whose own needs are increasing rapidly.

Growth, Immigration & Minorities California has been in a state of demographic and economic growth ever since it was admitted to the union, and much of the growth has been contributed by immigration. The result is a richly multicultural society, but one in which race relations have often been strained.

Immigrants from racial minorities are typically welcomed in times of rapid growth, but have often been rejected when times get tough. Thus, Chinese railway workers were sought after in the 1860s but victimized in the 1870s. The Webb Alien Land Law of 1913 prevented some Asian minorities from owning land. Impoverished Midwestern farm workers were turned away at the state line in the 1930s. During WWII, 93,000 people of Japanese extraction were interned. Black Americans came in large numbers to take jobs in the postwar boom, but often became unemployed when the economy took a downturn. Predomi-

nantly black suburbs of Los Angeles were the scene of violent outbursts, notably in 1965, 1979, and 1992. Mexican and other Latin American workers do most of the farm labor and domestic work in the state, but in 1994, in the face of increasing unemployment and state-government deficits, California voted for Proposition 187, which would deny illegal immigrants access to state government services, including schools and hospitals.

Quite apart from any question of racism, the wisdom of further immigration and growth is now a pertinent question. The urban areas of California are pressing limits in terms of traffic congestion, air pollution, water supply, and available land for housing. It is also becoming clear that excessive growth may destroy the very features that make the state so attractive – many Californians are genuinely concerned that beaches are becoming too crowded, national parks are being damaged by the sheer number of visitors, and the enjoyment of outdoor activities is being diminished by their popularity. California's growth seems to be both unstoppable and unsustainable.

The Military Despite the fact that it has never been the scene of a major conflict, California must be one of the most militarized places on earth. During and after WWI, aircraft industries were established by Douglas and the Lockheed brothers in Los Angeles, and by Curtiss in San Diego. Following the bombing of Pearl Harbor, the headquarters of the US Pacific fleet moved to San Diego, and has remained there ever since. The big Camp Pendleton Marine Corps base was established south of Orange County, and the Colorado desert became (temporarily) one of the biggest military training grounds in history. Shipbuilding started in San Francisco, while aircraft plants in Los Angeles turned out planes by the thousands, and the movie industry turned to producing films and propaganda pieces.

After WWII, the state retained a sophisticated slice of the military-industrial complex, with some very high-tech Cold War industries, from avionics and missile manufacturing, to helicopter and nuclear submarine maintenance. Military activities include recruit training for the Marine Corps, advanced training for Navy jet fighter pilots, submarine bases, aircraft testing facilities, several Air Force bases, weapons and gunnery ranges, and home ports for the US Navy.

The military is a source of not just jobs, but of high-quality, high-income jobs, and 1990s cutbacks in military spending have hit the state hard. While the military played a big part in establishing the manufacturing industry in California and bringing in much of its research & development base, it has not been easy to convert military industries to the production of goods for export or domestic consumption.

'The Industry' The establishment of the movie industry in California started around 1910, as producers sought conditions for year-round filming. Not only has 'The Industry' become a major employer in Los Angeles, but has done a lot to promote California's image throughout the country and the world. As film, and later TV, became the predominant media of the 20th century, California moved to center stage in the world of popular culture.

Social Change Unconstrained by the burden of traditions, bankrolled by affluence, and promoted by its pervasive media, California has become a leader in new attitudes and social movements – it is a national and international trendsetter. As early as the 1930s, Hollywood was promoting fashions and fads for the middle classes, even as strikes and social unrest rocked San Francisco and Steinbeck articulated a new concern for the welfare and worth of common people. As California became engulfed in postwar, 1950s affluence, the 'Beat' movement reacted against the banality and conformism of suburban life, turning to coffeehouses for jazz, philosophy, poetry, and pot.

When the postwar baby boomers hit their late teens, many took up where the Beat Generation left off, rejecting their parents' values, doing drugs, dropping out, and screwing around in a mass display of adolescent rebellion that climaxed, but didn't conclude, with the San Francisco 'Summer of Love' in 1967. Though the hippie 'counterculture' was an international phenomenon, California was at the leading edge of its music, its psychedelic art, and its new libertarianism. Sex, drugs, and rock 'n' roll went down big on the West Coast.

New Left politics, the anti-Vietnam War movement, and Black Liberation were forced onto the political agenda, and flower power and give-peace-a-chance politics seemed instantly naive. The 1968 assassination of Robert Kennedy in Los Angeles, the sometimes violent repression of demonstrations, as at Berkeley in 1968, and the death of a spectator at a Rolling Stones concert all served to strip the era of its innocence.

Though the hippie era is long over, it spawned a number of social movements in which California is still a leader. The Gay Pride movement started in San Francisco, and it is still the most openly, exuberantly gay city in the world. AIDS has dimmed the spark somewhat, and now San Francisco is a leader in care and treatment of the disease. California was way ahead in environmentalism, too – the Sierra Club was founded here in 1892 by John Muir, and is still an active and effective environmental lobby group. Though California has a serious air-pollution problem, it also leads the world in vehicle emission controls and environmental legislation.

As a contribution to the yuppie values of the 1980s, southern California gave the world Ronald Reagan and Reaganomics, while northern California contributed Michael Milkin, the junk-bond king. Now California is right at the forefront of the healthy lifestyle, New-Age '90s, with more aerobic classes and actualization workshops than you can shake your totem at. Leisure activities like in-line skating, snowboarding, and mountain biking are industries in California. Be careful what you laugh at – from hot tubs to soyburgers, California's flavor of the month will probably be the world trend next year.

GEOGRAPHY

The third-largest state after Alaska and Texas, California is roughly the size of Sweden, covering about 157,000 sq miles. It is bordered by Oregon in the north, Mexico in the south, Nevada and Arizona in the east, and the 700-mile Pacific coast to the west. The northern edge of California is at the same latitude as New York or Rome, and the southern edge is at the same latitude as Savannah, Georgia or Tel Aviv. Mountain ranges and water, or lack of it, create the state's prominent geographic regions.

Coast The Coastal Range runs along most of the coast, with gentle foothills in the east, and rocky cliffs that plunge straight into the Pacific on the west. San Francisco Bay divides the range roughly in half: the North Coast, famous for its coast redwoods, is sparsely populated and very foggy; the Central Coast, from San Francisco to Ventura, has a milder climate, more sandy beaches, and many more inhabitants, mostly around Santa Barbara.

Three-quarters of the way down the state, the Coastal Range is joined to the Sierras by a series of mountains called the Transverse Ranges. These mountains, mostly around 5000 feet high, divide the state into southern and northern California. To the south, the Los Angeles Basin directly fronts the ocean, bordered by a series of mountains that extend into Mexico. These mountains, once consistently visible from sea, are often shrouded by a thick layer of smog from the state's most inhabited region. San Diego, on the edge of this plateau, is about 120 miles south, next to the Mexican border.

Sierra Nevada & Northern Mountains
The prominent Sierra Nevada stretches 400 miles along California's eastern border and joins the southern end of the Cascade Range just north of Lake Tahoe. While the two ranges appear to form an almost continuous line, they contain very different geology: the Sierra Nevada is a westward-tilted fault block with glacier-carved valleys, while the Cascade Range is a chain of distinct volcanic peaks.

Peaks in the Sierra Nevada are higher at the southern end, culminating with 14,494-foot Mt Whitney – the highest in the continental USA. The Cascade Range, which extends to Oregon and Washington, is dominated by Mt Lassen (10,457 feet) and Mt Shasta (14,162 feet). East of the Cascades, on the Oregon border, sits the sparsely populated Modoc Plateau. West of the Cascades, the rugged Klamath Mountains have been carved by the unruly Klamath and Trinity Rivers.

The Sierra's western foothills, from 2000 to 5000 feet, were the site of the 1849 Gold Rush, and destination of California's famous '49ers.'

Central Valley Between the Sierra Nevada and the Coastal Range lies California's Central Valley, a fertile 430-mile-long region that leads the country in cotton, peach, almond, and grape production. The Central Valley comprises two river valley systems – the Sacramento Valley in the north, and the San Joaquin Valley in the south. The two meet at the Sacramento Delta and flow west to the Pacific via San Francisco Bay.

Deserts The Mojave Desert spreads north and east of Los Angeles, south of the Sierra, and east into Nevada. South of the Mojave, and east of the coastal range, the low desert includes the Imperial and Coachella Valleys, now heavily irrigated farmland, and the Salton Sea. East of the Sierra Nevada, Owens Valley and Death Valley are on the edge of the Great Basin of Nevada and Utah.

CLIMATE
California has a great diversity of climates. There is a lot of variation of climate between the warmer south and the cooler north. San Francisco is famous for its fog.

CALIFORNIA

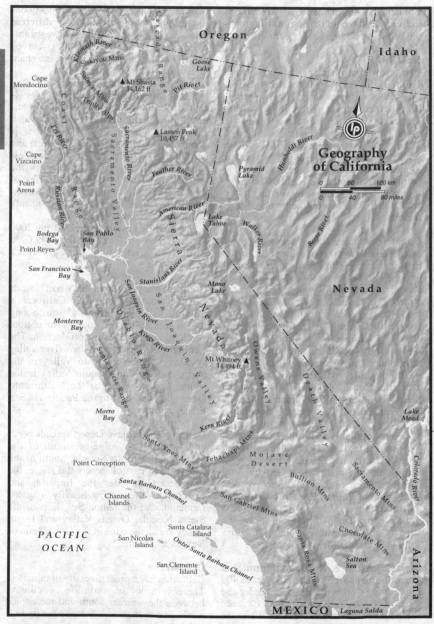

Geography
of California

'The morning fog may chill the air, I don't care, my heart waits there . . . ' sang Tony Bennett, and it's true – a typical weather forecast for San Francisco, at any time of year, as indeed for most of the north coast, is 'fog night and morning, burning off by mid-day.' Fog along the coast is especially noticeable in summer, when hot inland temperatures cause a mist to rise from the cooler ocean waters offshore. The south coast is warmer year round, mild in winter, not too hot in summer, but still subject to marine fogs.

The mountainous eastern part of the state, at a much higher elevation, is pleasant in summer and gets snow in winter; snow usually occurs only at higher elevations.

The San Joaquin and Sacramento River valleys are extremely hot in summer. In the winter, these valleys tend to be cool and foggy, with a type of fog known as tule fog, which hugs the ground and is so thick that you can't see through it. Be extremely careful if you're driving through tule fog; every year it causes chain-reaction traffic accidents where long lines of cars crash into each other.

The deserts, especially the low desert and Death Valley, are extremely hot in summer, often recording the highest temperatures in the country, but warm, dry, and extremely pleasant in winter. The Mojave is higher and not quite so hot in summer; cool to cold in the winter.

Nights can be chilly in most of the state, for most of the year. Be sure to have a sweater with you at any time of year. See the climate charts in the appendix for information on average temperatures.

ENVIRONMENT

According to the *1991-1992 Green Index*, California is ranked number one for environmental policies but 19th for its overall environmental conditions. Though conditions are on a general upswing due to the cooperation of environmentalists with farmers and irrigators, and the work of politicians, California still faces complex and catastrophic problems, most of which have to do with people. It's not just the number of people or the rate of growth, it's the level of consumption and affluence – so many products, so much waste, and so much leisure time.

California's population grew 26% from 1980 to 1990, and is projected to reach upwards of 38 million by 2010. Roughly half of these people live in the southern fifth of the state, in a desert environment that does not naturally support human life. Water is 'imported' from mountains in the north, fossil fuels are tapped for energy, wetlands and deserts are paved and built upon, freeways connect residential to work areas (often an hour's drive apart), and people rely more heavily on automobiles.

Overgrazing and logging on the north coast threaten fish (namely coho salmon and steelhead trout) populations which, being at the base of the food chain, affects all wildlife. Ozone creeps high into the Sierra, making its seemingly pristine lakes vulnerable to acid rain and snowmelt and damaging over 60% of its pine trees. Housing developments in the Central Valley are causing farmlands to vanish and wildlife habitats to dwindle so much that deer and mountain lions are becoming part of the urban landscape. Farming brings up a whole different set of issues dealing with pesticides, water rights (80% of California's water goes to farmers), and, because most farm workers are Hispanic, social justice.

Air Pollution Travelers will probably notice poor air quality more than any other problem. Southern California is the only place in the USA whose air quality is defined, by an act of Congress, as 'extremely' threatening. Federal health-based air quality standards are exceeded more than 200 days a year, and the ozone standard is also violated frequently. A thick orange-brown haze sits above the Los Angeles Basin, obliterating views of the surrounding mountains. Breathing can become difficult by late afternoon (especially if you're involved in athletic activity) and people often complain of stinging or runny eyes (it's especially bad if you wear contact lenses).

Despite this grim picture, there are reasons to be hopeful. The Air Resources Board, created in 1968, oversees 14 air quality control regions that must meet ever more stringent Environmental Protection Agency (EPA) standards. The Natural Resources Defense Council (NRDC) recently completed a plan to reduce emissions by 20% by the year 2000, 40% by 2010. With these combined efforts, plus the addition of carpool lanes to most freeways, southern California's air quality has improved considerably in the past five years. An ingenious solution in northern California is the Bay Area Vehicle Buyback Coalition, which buys cars made before 1972, when the first emissions standards were set, and puts them in the junk yard.

Wilderness Preservation Monterey Bay and the Channel Islands are now National Marine Sanctuaries and much of the state's desert region, including Death Valley and the Mojave Desert, are protected under the California Deserts Protection Act. The more land under National Park jurisdiction (whose main goal is to protect and preserve) instead of National Forest (which favors timber and farm industry) or Bureau of Land Management (often called the Bureau of Logging and Mining) jurisdiction, the better.

Environmental organizations such as The Sierra Club, Friends of the Rivers, the Nature Conservancy, Save San Francisco Bay Association, Klamath Forest Alliance, and Monterey's Save Our Shores, have made great efforts on behalf of California's environment.

Water From 1987 to 1993, California experienced one of its worst droughts in history, with precipitation ranging between 61% and 90% below normal. As a result, the state has made revolutionary progress in cutting back on water use. Water suppliers signed a conservation agreement with environmental groups requiring water utilities to adopt 16 'best management practices' for conservation, including offering rebates on low-flush toilets and providing free water audits to those who implement the practices with the most force. The Department of Water Resources set up a water bank that bought surplus water and sold it to those with shortages. Meanwhile, some cities began to reuse wastewater and several coastal communities developed desalinization systems to remove salt from sea water.

California's most controversial water issue deals with the transfer of water from the northern to southern part of the state. The Bureau of Reclamation's Central Valley Project, built in the 1930s, dams most of California's major rivers to provide irrigation and hydroelectric power to the Los Angeles area which, though basically a desert, supports over half the state's population. See the sidebar on Mono Lake in the Sierra Nevada chapter for more information.

Toxic discharge, primarily from pesticides used in irrigation, is also a serious water issue. With the San Joaquin and Sacramento Valleys the most fertile in the USA, crop revenues have long been more important than environmental protection.

Waste California produces the most solid waste, per capita, in the USA. Its 365 municipal landfills are pushing capacity, making environmental planners increasingly worried about what to do with the phenomenal amount of waste produced each year. Much of the problem lies in the state's affluence – so many products – and concurrent lack of funds for environmental education. Corporate offenders often choose to pay exorbitant fines rather than clean up their acts, though increases in fines have risen enough in the past few years that this is becoming less common.

Energy On the flip side of the waste problem, California gets continually high marks on its 'environmental report card' for Integrated Resource Planning (IRP) practices. Southern California Edison, California's largest utility companies, began a positive trend in 1978 when they offered incentives to industrial and residential customers for installing more efficient equipment. The program has proved to be very effective in reducing emissions. Unfortunately, California still produces the second-largest amount of toxic gas emissions in the USA, largely due to the population's automobile dependence.

FLORA & FAUNA

California has just about every type of ecosystem in existence, from deserts to forests to wetlands to high alpine zones. Flora and fauna varies accordingly, though some things are common throughout the state, namely oak trees, mule and black-tailed deer, squirrels, Steller's jays, and LBBs (little brown birds). Of special note are the superlative trees in the state, including the world's tallest (coast redwood), largest (sequoia), and oldest (bristlecone pine).

Coast

Flora Coastal ecosystems range from very wet in the north, to very dry in the south. The Coastal Range runs along most of California's coastline, its west side plunging straight into the sea and its eastern side rolling gently toward the Central Valley. The north end of the range has stands of coast redwoods, giant beauties with spongy red bark, flat needles, and olive-size cones. The lush forest floor surrounding these trees supports sword ferns, redwood sorrel, and other plants.

South of Humbolt County, where annual precipitation is considerably less, plant life is less specialized. Along the central coast, you'll find Monterey cypress and Monterey pine, which look like they are being blown over even when it's not windy. They both have thick, rough, grayish bark, long-reaching branches clustered at their tops, and long needles. Inland, extending from the east side of the Coastal Range to the western foothills of the Sierra Nevada, you'll find California black oak, with broad

The Life of a Threatened Fish

Examining the life of a steelhead trout or coho salmon, both 'indicator' fish whose survival or decline tell of the environment's health, gives a good overall picture of California's environmental challenges. A fish's natural life cycle is to hatch in a river, swim out to sea, and return to its home waters to spawn and die. Sounds simple, right? Not for a California fish.

First of all, to get downstream they must pass over dams built in the 1930s as part of the Bureau of Reclamation's Central Valley Project, meant to turn southern California into a breadbasket (all of California's major rivers are dammed at least once). If the fish makes it past the dam into the San Joaquin-Sacramento Delta, it then faces the danger of being sucked southward by massive pumps that transport Delta waters to farmers in the Central Valley and urban populations. If it makes it past the pumps into San Francisco Bay, the state's main holding tank for southbound water, it has to deal with pollution caused by pesticides, industry, and urban run-off. With the Bay now a fraction of its original size, pollution's impact is magnified.

Say the fish finally makes it out the Golden Gate. Now it has to be smart enough to avoid the nets of commercial fishermen, who have long overfished the waters off the north coast, and strong enough to withstand the underwater noise pollution caused by tankers and military flights. Apparently this type of pollution, which disrupts mating procedures, is one of the major threats to California's whale population.

When it's time to head back upstream, the fish has to hope that logging hasn't stripped the stream of its shade, causing river temperatures to rise to a lethal level, and that grazing hasn't eroded the river stream banks and blocked the way home. The final triumph is if the fish's redd (like a crib) is still intact (undisturbed by logging, mining, or grazing) and can hold future generations. ∎

fingery leaves (bristly at the ends) and gray-black bark. The smooth, shiny acorns from these trees were a staple for California Indians.

Further south, past Santa Barbara, is a much more arid region. In the mountains surrounding the Los Angeles Basin you'll find Canyon live oak, with holly-like evergreen leaves and fuzzy acorns; aromatic California laurel, with long slender leaves that turn purple; and Eastwood and Cuyamaca manzanita, tree-like shrubs with intensely red bark and small berries. The Torrey pine, a species adapted to sparse rainfall and sandy, stony soils, is another rare tree; the last mainland stands are near San Diego.

Fauna The coast offers many chances to see California's *Pinnipedia* ('feather feet'), including northern elephant and harbor seals, California sea lions (which have ears), and sea otters. The best place to see these friendly creatures, which like to bask in the sun, is from Point Lobos State Reserve to Santa Barbara and at the La Jolla children's pool. San Miguel, one of the Channel Islands, has the largest pinniped population in the world. Año Nuevo State Reserve on the San Francisco Peninsula is a major elephant seal breeding ground.

California gray whales are often visible off the coast from December to March when they head to warm waters in Mexico. Once in a while you'll see them breaching, but usually you can just spot the spray from their fluke and part of their back or tail. Good whale watching points are Point Reyes, Eureka, Fort Bragg, Bodega Bay (north of San Francisco), Davenport Landing (near Santa Cruz), Point Loma, and Dana Point. Companies in Monterey, Santa Barbara, Morro Bay, and San Diego offer whale-watching excursions.

Bottle-nosed dolphins and porpoise swim quite close to shore in groups called 'pods.' They can be seen year round from Morro Bay to Mexico. One of the oddest creatures off the coast are flying fish, often seen between the southern coast and Catalina Island.

California brown pelicans, indigenous to the Channel Islands, were threatened with extinction because the insecticide DDT from Ventura County farms was contaminating the fish on which the pelicans fed. Eating the poisoned fish caused thinning in the pelican's egg shells, so few eggs survived long enough to hatch. DDT was banned several years ago and the pelican population is on the rise.

Other coastal birds include gulls and grebes, terns, cormorants, sandpipers, and cute little sanderlings that like to chase waves from the shore. The California Condor, a black and white bird with a 9- to 10-foot wing span, has long been one of the state's most endangered animals. Currently there are three pair living in the wild in the San Rafael Mountains near Santa Barbara.

Sierra Nevada

Flora The Sierra Nevada has three distinct zones: dry western foothills covered with oak and chaparral; conifer forests from about 2000 to 8000 feet; and a high-alpine zone above 8000 feet, where a lack of humus and alluvial deposit supports tundra-like expanses of moss and lichen. Wildflowers such as bright red Indian paintbrush, purplish-blue broadleaf lupine, yellow-orange common monkeyflower, and deep purple bowl-tubed iris bloom in alpine meadows from April to June (depending on the season). Recommended reading is the *Sierra Club Naturalist's Guide* (Sierra Club Books, 1979), by Stephen Whitney; ranger stations and visitor centers also provide good information (usually a display and brochure) pertaining to specific areas.

The diversity of plant and animal life within the Sierra's conifer forests (on its western side) make them the most interesting. This is where the Giant sequoias stand, in isolated groves within the boundaries of Yosemite, Kings Canyon, and Sequoia National Parks. With their enormous bodies, red shaggy bark, and small, tight pine cones, these are unique to California and an absolute 'must-see.' Also within the conifer forests are incense cedar, with bark like a sequoia and leaves like a juniper bush; lodgepole and ponderosa pine, both with medium-sized pine cones, golden-brown bark that resembles a jig-saw puzzle, and long, spindly needles; sugar pine, with large oblong cones and branches that cluster toward the top of the tree; and red and white fir, noticeable for their dense cylindrical cones, short needles, and branches that start quite close to the ground.

Broad-leafed trees in the Sierra, found mostly near water, include Pacific dogwood, whose greenish-white flowers bloom in late May; shimmery quaking aspen, with large circular leaves that turn butter-yellow in the fall; black cottonwood, which have small white flowers that shed a fibrous fluff in the wind (enough of this on the ground makes it look like there's snow); and white alder, which resembles a cottonwood with its round, pointed leaves but has reddish bark and small cones instead of flowers.

Fauna Environmental factors that vary according to elevation – notably precipitation (snowfall) and food availability – essentially determine where animals live in the Sierra. For example, gray squirrels, common throughout the lower ranges, can't survive the winters above 7000 feet. Nor can valley pocket gophers or Swainson's

thrushes, though their ecological counterparts, mountain pocket gophers and hermit thrushes, do fine at higher elevations.

Some creatures, however, survive by migrating within the range according to season. These include mule deer, with sharp hooves and large mule-like ears (bucks grow antlers each year), bighorn sheep, and birds such as Steller's jays, hummingbirds, and woodpeckers. High in the Sierra you'll find yellow-bellied marmots (essentially large ground squirrels) and several kinds of chipmunks that look like tiny squirrels with slender tails and stripes running down their backs.

Black bears are plentiful from 3000 to about 8000 feet. They are small as bears go, weighing around 300 pounds or more, and are omniverous, eating berries, nuts, roots, grasses, insects, eggs, small mammals, fish, and carrion.

Central Valley

Flora Called the 'most fertile valley in the world,' the heavily irrigated Central Valley supports domesticated crops such as apricots, grapes, peaches, almonds, walnuts, and cotton. North of Sacramento, wetlands irrigated by the Sacramento River are used to grow rice.

Fauna Mountain lions have become more aggressive recently, as housing developments have encroached on their habitat. Their presence is especially an issue where they threaten livestock and (in two fatal incidents in 1994) people.

Also threatened by Central Valley development are ducks, geese, and osprey, pintails, egrets, and other waterfowl that depend on the Pacific Flyway for their annual migration. One of four major bird freeways in North America, the Flyway extends north-south through most of the valley, with the main lay-over points in the Delta and north of Sacramento.

Deserts

Flora Though the word 'desert' conjures up images of vast expanses of nothingness, there is a subtle beauty about California's

The backwards-flying hummingbird, almost life-size

Coyotes actually prefer livestock, rodents, and garbage to roadrunners.

deserts that intensifies the longer you're there. Most plants have adapted to the arid climate with thin, spiny leaves that resist moisture loss (and deter grazing animals) and seed/flowering mechanisms that kick into full gear during the brief moisture period.

Perhaps the most conspicuous and familiar desert flower is the bright orange California poppy, the state flower, which blooms in March and April. There's a fantastic display of these in the California Poppy Reserve in Antelope Valley, directly north of LA.

More cactus-like are the creosote, a small bush that has small, hard leaves with a waxy feel and a distinctive smell; the spiky ocotillo shrub, with its extended cane-like branches (which may seem dead) that sprout leaves after a rainfall, and produce bright red-orange flowers in spring; and catclaw, an acacia species with small, sharp, hooked spikes, which scratch you or grab your clothing if you brush past – hence the nickname 'wait-a-minute bush.'

Desert cacti are probably the most intriguing forms of life out here. At first glance the cholla cactus appears so furry and soft that one variety is actually known as teddy-bear cactus. But the fur actually consists of extremely sharp, barbed spines that can bury themselves in skin at the slightest touch. Viewed from a safe distance, chollas show a delightful variety of shapes, and a delicate pale gold color, especially when the light is behind them and each branch is surrounded by a luminous halo. They produce a bright yellow flower in the spring.

Like something from a Dr Seuss book, Joshua trees are a type of yucca, and are related to the lily. They're found in much of the Mojave desert, not just in Joshua Tree National Park, and were named by immigrant Mormons, who saw them as Joshua, welcoming them to the promised land. Almost as widespread are prickly pear, a flat cactus that produces showy flowers ranging in color from pink and magenta to yellow and orange. The smoke tree, a small, fine-leafed tree with a smoky blue color, is said to indicate the presence of underground water.

Known widely from its presence in Western movies, tumbleweed is actually an import from Eastern Europe. These annuals, which grow quickly to become a ball of tough branches attached to the ground by a single stem, uproot and tumble across the desert in the summer wind. The Washingtonia palm is the only native variety of the trees that are almost emblematic of southern California. They grow naturally in desert oases, and produce stalks of small black berries that are quite tasty.

Irrigated by Colorado River water, the Coachella Valley supports date, citrus, and grape crops, while the Imperial Valley has winter vegetables, cotton, and fruit.

Fauna Most desert wildlife is nocturnal, rarely visible during the day. Roadrunners, little gray birds with long, straight tails and a poof of feathers on top of their heads, are quite visible on the side of the road. So are desert tortoises, whose slow pace has landed them on the Endangered Species list because they're often victim to car tires. Other desert inhabitants, all very cute but extremely shy, are the reddish kit fox, bob cat (who has no tail), coyote (who walks with its hind legs slightly to the left of his front legs), jackrabbit, kangaroo rat, and a variety of snakes, lizards, and spiders.

The Salton Sea, a stop-over for migratory birds, is an excellent place for birdwatching.

NATIONAL & STATE PARKS

With 75% of California's population inhabiting only 1% of the state's land, there is plenty of terrain not yet under concrete or asphalt. Some of California's more famous 'wilderness' areas, notably Yosemite National Park and the Lake Tahoe area, are no longer wild, but their scenery remains awe-inspiring. Lesser-known areas, especially in the northern part of the state, contain mountains, rivers, and canyons that go relatively unvisited for most of the year.

California has 17 areas that are part of the National Park System, administered by the National Park Service under the US Department of the Interior, and 270 units designated as State Parks and run by the California State Park System. California's 18 National Forests are run by the United States Forest Service (USFS), which is part of the United States Department of Agriculture (USDA). While all of these designations tend to make one's head spin, they are really only important at an administrative level.

State Parks

California's State Park System divides its land into three separate categories: State Parks (SP), State Beaches (SB), and State Recreation Areas (SRA). The primary designation between categories is related to resource values and occurs between State Parks and State Recreation Areas.

In a State Park, there are valuable resources whose protection is the park's priority; many State Parks include reserves or preserves set aside to protect endangered plants, animals, and habitats.

In a State Recreation Area – often an artificial lake or reservoir – recreation is considered the primary resource. While both offer camping and have access roads, State Parks have fewer roads open to vehicular traffic and are more strict about campfires and water use.

State Beaches are basically State Parks by the sea.

Hearst San Simeon State Historical Monument (Hearst Castle) is a historical site in the state park system. The majority of California State Parks are concentrated along Hwy 1, on the North and Central Coasts.

National Parks & Monuments

California's National Parks contain some of the most spectacular and worthwhile scenery in the state. Recently Death Valley, Joshua Tree, and the Channel Islands were 'upgraded' from National Monument to National Park status. Although in practice a National Monument is equivalent to a National Park, the term 'National Park' is more widely recognized and accepted as an important region, so the government often changes a National Monument to a National Park to symbolize an area's importance or need of protection.

Yosemite This is California's, and one of America's, most famous and visited parks, known for its solid granite monoliths and numerous waterfalls.

Kings Canyon & Sequoia National Parks Run as one unit, these parks are famous for giant sequoia trees (found no where else in the world), the deepest canyon in North America, and excellent hiking.

Death Valley An enigmatically beautiful landscape of salt pillars and sun cracked flats rimmed by dramatic peaks.

Joshua Tree National Park Known for its Joshua trees and Mojave yuccas, this is a rock climbers mecca.

Channel Islands The northern five of a seven-island chain, these islands, off the coast of Santa Barbara, are prized for their underwater life and population of seals, sea lions, and sea otters.

Point Reyes National Seashore This is a birder's paradise, famous for its many species of shorebirds, and often shrouded in fog.

Redwood National Park Here stand the giant coast redwoods, in the same family as giant sequoias, the tallest trees in the world.

Lava Beds National Monument Just below the Oregon border, this area is full of volcanic formations.

Mt Lassen Volcanic National Park Shaped by the same igneous intrusion that formed Lava Beds, Mt Lassen is considered an active volcano, though quiet since 1916.

The parks are open year round and offer a totally different experience in the off-season, especially Yosemite, Sequoia/Kings Canyon, and Mt Lassen, which get snow.

Death Valley and Joshua Tree are best visited October to April, before the thermostat starts soaring above the 100° F mark.

Many people feel that Yosemite is best between September and May, when crowds are at a minimum and when, in deep winter, it is blanketed with snow. Of course, hiking and camping are reduced during those months. Information for all the parks is available from the Western Region Information Center (☎ 415-556-0560), NPS, Fort Mason Bldg 201, San Francisco, CA 94123.

National Forests
Many of the forests contain designated wilderness areas in which motorized vehicles and bicycles are prohibited, and hikers are required to obtain a permit for any overnight stay. The concentration of these is along the Sierra Crest, accessible via the Eastern Sierra, Yosemite, and Kings Canyon/Sequoia National Parks.

Maps ($3 each) and information are available from the USDA Forest Service (☎ 415-705-2874), 630 Sansome St, San Francisco, CA 94111. The National Reservation System (☎ 800-280-2267) is open Monday to Friday from 8 am to 5 pm, weekends from 9 am to 2 pm.

GOVERNMENT
The USA has a republican form of government, which is popularly defined as government 'of the people, by the people and for the people.' The US Constitution, passed in 1789 and amended 26 times since, provides the fundamental laws for the running of the national government and the relations between the national and state governments.

US citizens over the age of 18 are eligible to vote (criminals may lose this right, depending on their crime). Elections are hotly contested, and politicians and parties spend many millions of dollars on political campaigns that can become acrimonious. Despite this, barely half of the eligible voters cast a ballot in most state and federal elections.

There are two main political parties – the Republicans (called the GOP for Grand Old Party) and the Democrats. Independent politicians occasionally provide a third choice. Other parties do exist, but they are too small to play a significant part in government. Traditionally, Republicans are conservative, and Democrats are liberal, though there is a range of positions in each party – some southern Democrats can be very conservative. Often, the President and his Cabinet are of one party, while the Congress may have a majority of the opposing party.

In so far as generalizations can be made, Republicans favor cutting taxes, shrinking nationally funded (federal) programs of health care, education, and welfare, as well as minimizing or eliminating national funding for items such as arts programs and abortion. Republicans believe such programs are better handled at the state level. Democrats prefer higher taxation and more federal funding of these programs. Republicans support spending a larger proportion of the federal budget on the military than do Democrats.

National Government

The national legislature is made up of the bicameral Congress – the Senate and the House of Representatives. The Senate has two senators from each of the 50 states, while the 435-member House has one or more members from each state, depending on the state's population. Senators are elected for six years, and representatives are elected for two.

The judicial branch is headed by the Supreme Court, which consists of nine justices who are appointed for life by the President and approved by the Senate.

The executive branch consists of the President, elected for a four-year term, the Cabinet, and various assistants. The 14 members of the President's Cabinet are each appointed by the President but must be approved by the Senate. The President has the power to veto laws passed by Congress, although a law can still be passed if two-thirds of the members vote for it the second time, overriding the President's veto.

The President is chosen by an Electoral College consisting of a number of individual electors from each state equivalent to its number of senators and representatives, who vote in accordance with the popular vote within their state. To be elected, the

Democrats and Republicans dance the political twist.

President must obtain a majority of 270 of the total 538 electoral votes (the District of Columbia has no voting representatives in Congress, but nevertheless has three electoral votes). The President may serve only two terms. The 104th Congress (1995 to 1997), has a Republican majority in both houses, the first time they have had such a majority since WWII.

State Government

Each of the 50 states has its own government, run along similar lines to the national government. The head of the executive branch of state government is the governor, and California's the bicameral legislature consists of a 40-member senate, and an 80-member general assembly, elected for four-year terms in California.

National (federal) laws apply to all states, although there are often conflicts between federal and state interests. States can have different laws about driving, drugs, alcohol use, and taxes, which are discussed in Facts for the Visitor.

Traditionally, northern California is Democrat while southern California is Republican, and conservative Republican at that. In the 1992 election, the state elected a Republican governor.

There are 58 counties in the state, many of which include one or more incorporated cities.

ECONOMY
US Economy

The USA has a GNP of $6,350 billion, making it the largest national economy on earth. However, the national debt, mostly accumulated by overspending during the '80s, stands at a rough $4,350 billion, and it keeps growing because of interest payments and an annual trade deficit of $254 billion.

The distribution of income is unequal, with the lowest 20% of income earners receiving 4.4% of national income, while the top 5% receive 17.6%. Whole areas of the USA are wealthier than others, and within a city the standard of living can vary considerably from neighborhood to neighborhood. In fact, income in the USA is much more equally distributed than in most countries, particularly developing countries, because of the large and affluent middle class. Inequality looks bad in the USA because many of the poor are highly visible, and the general standard of living is so high, but statistics show that countries like France, Argentina, Thailand, and Mexico, have much higher levels of inequality.

The USA has a progressive income tax scale, with the poorest paying around 15% of personal earnings and the richest fifth paying around 40%. A median income earner would pay around 20% of earnings, but sales taxes of around 10% are added to the cost of nearly every item.

California Economy

With an extremely large and diverse economy, California has the largest state income in the USA. If California were a country, its gross national product (GNP) would be about the eighth largest in the world (1990 – $650 billion per annum) – a bit larger than Canada or China, and a bit smaller than France or Britain.

Agricultural output is the highest of any state, with around eight million acres of irrigated farmland, producing cattle, cotton, dairy products, wine grapes, fruit, vegetables, grain, and more. Farming is a highly mechanized corporate industry, aptly described as agribusiness, with huge investment in land, and a workforce of poorly paid, mostly Hispanic farm laborers. California's marijuana crop is probably worth close to a billion dollars a year, unofficially of course. Forestry is still big, despite conservationists' efforts to preserve more of the state's 17 million acres of public and private forests. Fishing has declined as boats have had to go further and work harder for fewer fish.

A good deal of secondary industry is based on the processing of primary products, including fish packing, fruit and vegetable canning and packaging, wine making, petroleum processing, and timber milling. Not well endowed with resources for heavy industry, California has success-

fully concentrated on the manufacture of aircraft, aerospace components, electronics, computers, and hi-tech consumer goods. The construction industry, civil engineering, and military hardware are all huge and highly developed industries.

Nevertheless, California is post-industrial in the range of its tertiary industries – banking, finance, education, research & development, computer software, TV, movies, tourism, corporate services, and so on. Real estate remains a big business – in some places it seems like every second property is on the market. California has always made a big industry out of selling itself.

Though mining was at one time California's greatest industry, it now has a minor place in the economy, with most of the gold gone and the oil reserves depleted. Today's mining is of more prosaic minerals, like sand, cement, gravel, borates, and natural gas.

California's economic problems include its share of the national debt, quite a high level of inequality, unemployment around 9%, increasing dependence on imported oil, and the loss of many valuable defense contracts and bases. Nonetheless, it remains one of the wealthiest economies anywhere, with a GNP per head of over $22,000 per year, and a material standard of living that is the envy of much of the world. Most visitors will be impressed by the evidence of public prosperity – the road system, parks, museums, and public buildings.

Even more striking is the apparent private wealth – it seems like almost every one has a brand new car, nice clothes, the latest in leisure equipment, and plenty to spend on restaurants, shopping, and entertainment. Of course, a lot of this is charged up on plastic, but what the heck – they're still buying, and the economic wheels keep turning, even if the debt is getting bigger.

POPULATION & PEOPLE

With a population of 29,558,000 counted in the 1990 census, and an estimated 1993 population of 31,211,000, California is the most populous state in the USA; if it were a separate nation it would be the 30th most populous nation in the world. With 190.4 people per sq mile, it ranks 11th in population density out of the 50 states. Well over 90% of the population lives in urban areas, though, so there are plenty of wide-open spaces. The median age is 32.8 years.

According to the 1990 census, California's largest cities are Los Angeles (3,485,398), San Diego (1,110,549), San Jose (782,248), San Francisco (723,959), Long Beach (429,433), Sacramento (369,365), Fresno (354,202), Santa Ana (293,742) and Anaheim (266,406).

If you consider not just the populations within the city limits, but the greater metropolitan areas (including the suburbs), the populations of the cities are much larger. In terms of metropolitan areas, Los Angeles, with a population of 13,470,900, ranks second in the USA only to New York (population is 18,053,800); the San Francisco metropolitan area (population 5,953,100)

comes in fourth in the USA (after Chicago), while San Diego's metropolitan population of 2,285,000 ranks 19th in the USA; Sacramento, with 1,336,500 people, ranks 28th.

California's racial mixture is 60.8% white, 23.7% Hispanic, 6.5% black, and 9.0% Asian and 'other' races; the 'other' races include Native Americans (American Indians), who comprise around 0.8%. Foreign-born people make up 15% of the state's population; about 30% of the USA's immigrants live in California. Of these, immigrants from Mexico are the largest group, followed by immigrants from the Philippines, China, Vietnam, Korea, Iran, El Salvador, India, Taiwan, Hong Kong, Laos, Cambodia, Thailand, Guatemala, UK, Canada, Japan, Nicaragua, Peru, Afghanistan, Germany, Pakistan (in that order) and many other countries as well. This makes for a lot of diversity in language, religion, and every other element of culture, especially in the urban areas, where many immigrants live.

California's population figures tell an interesting story of continual increase, starting right off with the Gold Rush in 1848-49, when the '49ers' caused a 565% increase in the recorded population in just two years, even before statehood was declared in 1850.

ARTS

California is blessed (or cursed, depending on who you talk to) with two cities with two of the most dynamic cultural scenes that you could hope to find anywhere. San Francisco's liberalism and humanistic tradition have made it a publishing center second only to New York and writers have been flocking to the *Sturm-und-Drang* of Northern California's coast for inspiration for years. Jazz, opera, public theater, and splendid museums make San Francisco a very livable city

To the south lies the city that entertainment built, Los Angeles. Actors, and those who would like to think themselves as such, have given the restaurants of Los Angeles a formidable army of hopeful

California Population (Historic)

Year	Population	% of Increase	% of US Population
1848	14,000 (est)	N/A	–
1850	93,000	565%	0.4%
1860	380,000	309%	1.2%
1870	560,000	47%	1.4%
1880	865,000	54%	1.7%
1890	1,213,000	40%	1.9%
1900	1,485,000	22%	2.0%
1910	2,378,000	60%	2.6%
1920	3,427,000	44%	3.2%
1930	5,677,000	66%	4.6%
1940	6,950,000	22%	5.2%
1950	10,643,000	53%	7.0%
1960	15,863,000	49%	8.8%
1970	20,039,000	26%	9.8%
1980	23,780,000	19%	10.5%
1990	29,558,000	24%	11.6%
1991	30,321,000	2.6%	12.1%
1992	30,982,000	2.2%	12.2%
1993	31,552,000	1.8%	12.3%

sources used: 1993 *California Almanac*

waiters, always waiting for the big break. Los Angelenos enjoy the spoils of all the wealth generated by the folks who live up in the hills in the form of several world class museums and a cinema scene whose variety is unparalleled anywhere.

Music

Throughout the 20th century, California has been a mecca for musical talent, whether native or imported.

Ranchero Driving through the Central Valley, turn on your radio and flip through the stations for a while – when you hear something like a polka except with lyrics in Spanish, you've hit a Ranchero station. Ranchero is a music popular in the rural agricultural areas throughout California – indeed throughout the West all the way to Texas (anywhere there's a sizable Mexican-American rural population). German settlers brought polka with them to the Southwest, where it merged with the indigenous Spanish-influenced dance music. It can be a fun alternative to the usual Top 40 blather.

Jazz In the 1940s, jazz arrived in California. It was while holding a nightly gig in Hollywood that Charlie Parker was offered a seven-month engagement in Camarillo State Hospital's drug rehabilitation ward. Looking back on that experience, he later recorded 'Relaxing at Camarillo' for LA's Dial label. Many great jazzmen were born in Los Angeles: Dexter Gordon, Charles Mingus, and Art Pepper among them.

In the '50s, Cool Jazz was born with artists such as Pepper, Dave Brubeck, Vince Guaraldi, Buddy Collette, Gerry Mulligan, Chet Baker, and Shelly Manne performing under the Pacific's relaxing influence. At clubs such as Shelly's Manne-Hole in Hollywood, the Lighthouse at Hermosa Beach, and Bimbo's 365 Club and the Blackhawk up in North Beach, San Francisco, they created a soothing, harmonically sophisticated style of jazz that took the edge off the East Coast-oriented bop scene.

Jazz is appealing to a new generation with groove-heavy Acid Jazz and acts such as the bop-edged Charlie Hunter Trio and Spearhead, who combine activist-inspired verse with a backdrop of Free Jazz. Swing has also made a huge comeback, replete with athletic jitterbugging and zoot suits.

Rhythm & Blues From the '40s through the '60s, South Central LA was home to a number of outstanding nightclubs presenting blues, R&B, jazz, and soul. Watts churned out vocal groups in the doo-wop tradition, including the Penguins, who first recorded 'Earth Angel' for LA's Doo-Tone records. A juke joint crawl in the mid-'50s would likely have included T-Bone Walker, Amos Milburn, or Charles Brown.

At the hub of a thriving Watts musical scene, Johnny Otis brought many forms of music to the public's attention with his popular Johnny Otis Orchestra – featuring Little Esther Phillips – and his record label, DIG. Starting in the early '60s, Sam Cooke performed hit after hit and ran his SAR record label, attracting soul and gospel talent from around the country to Los Angeles. (Johnny Otis still occasionally plays in a grocery he owns in the tiny Sonoma County town of Sebastopol.)

Seminal bluesman John Lee Hooker can still be seen cruising his hometown of Oakland in a large domestic automobile, whose license plate reads, 'Da Hook.'

Rock & Roll Though rock & roll was from the beginning recorded in California, the first homegrown talent to make it big in the '50s was Richie Valens, whose 'La Bamba' was a rockified traditional Mexican folksong. In the early '60s, LA's beaches and suburbs were treated to a highly popular style of rock & roll called surf music, of which the Beach Boys are the best known. They combined easy-to-enjoy rock & roll rhythms, innovative use of harmonies, and young California themes – cars, girls, and surf. They played down the beach themes in the late '60s, and pioneered the use of advanced studio recording techniques, especially for their big 1966 hit 'Good

Vibrations.' Dick Dale and Jan & Dean were also local talents. In the mid-'60s, a group of UCLA students – among them the 'lizard king,' Jim Morrison – formed The Doors, who grooved the Sunset Strip for half a decade.

Meanwhile, San Francisco had begun a heady ferment that was the beginning of the psychedelic revolution. Apart from big-name acts like the Grateful Dead and Jefferson Airplane, Bay Area bands like Janis Joplin's Big Brother & the Holding Company, Sly & the Family Stone, and Credence Clearwater Revival were key players in defining the era's sound. Carlos Santana formed the band Santana during the late '60s, and succeeded in blending Latin American rhythm with rock & roll. Master promoter Bill Graham, often referred to as the 'Godfather of San Francisco Rock,' used these groups to revolutionize the way popular music is presented and by doing so set the stage for a new era of world-class entertainers.

In direct revolt against the love-bead status quo the singular Frank Zappa, with his band the Mothers of Invention, began his indescribable career with the album *Freak Out* in the mid-'60s. The Mothers' satire took on all comers, be it conservative war hawks, or mind-numbed hippies. In 1969 at the Altamont Speedway, about 60 miles from San Francisco, security men (actually Hell's Angels) murdered a concert goer at a Rolling Stones concert. Some claim that this unfortunate incident marked the end of the hippie era.

About this time, Tom Waits began haunting the smaller clubs of LA with a voice rusted over from bottom-shelf bourbon and filterless cigarettes. Waits brought to the world music built on sounds dragged out from a tin pan alley junkyard, influenced by the varied likes of Louis Armstrong, Kurt Weill, and Harry Partch.

The late '70's and early '80's brought the young and sick out to hear California's brand of punk. California Punk grew up around (of all things) skateboard culture. Early on, LA punks were listening to the Punk-a-Billy stylings of X. Though not strictly punk, X's combination of Exene Cervenka and John Doe's vocals over the rockabilly guitar licks of Billy Zoom created an original, decidedly Angeleno sound that simply blew the doors off the local punk scene. For a more pronounced punk sound, Black Flag led the way with the rants of singer Henry Rollins.

In the mid-'80s, Los Lobos emerged from East LA with a Mexican-influenced rock sound that crossed racial boundaries around the country. Out of Downey came Dave and Phil Alvin and the Blasters, whose rockabilly revival continues today in such clubs as the Brown Derby and the Mint. Also bred locally, the Red Hot Chili Peppers exploded on the national scene in the late-'80s with a highly-charged, funk-punk sound.

San Francisco (whose now-defunct Winterland Ballroom was the scene of the Sex Pistols' final concert) produced the Avengers and the Dead Kennedys. Jello Biafra, the lead singer of the DK's, ran for mayor in the mid-'80s. One of his better remembered campaign promises was to require San Francisco's police force to dress in clown suits while patrolling the city streets.

Current Bay Area acts that have reached prominence include Primus, Chris Isaak, 4-Non Blondes, and punk revivalists Green Day.

Rap The area stretching from South Central LA on down to Long Beach is the local rap hotbed, producing such artists as Snoop Doggy Dog and NWA, whose album *Straight Outta Compton* might best represent LA's rap scene, as well as offer insight from some of the city's most popular artists. The north country has also produced some noteworthy acts with less edge such as Digital Underground (whose Tupac Shakur has established himself as an artist in his own right), the ribald Too Short, and the brooding Disposable Heroes of Hip-hopcrasy.

Classical Music & Concerts The big cities all have symphony orchestras and opera and concert venues. See the relevant chapters for details. Open-air concerts are a pleasant feature of music performances in Southern California, with the Los Angeles Philharmonic Orchestra performing its 'symphonies under the stars' at the Hollywood Bowl.

Dance
In the 1950s, many dance styles originated on Hollywood stages, at beach parties, and in Los Angeles night clubs. The 'shag' and 'swim,' both Gidget-type teeny bopper dances that involve profuse arm and hip swinging, are said to have come from the surf scene on beaches southwest of Los Angeles. Currently 'line dancing' (where people stand shoulder to shoulder executing choreographed moves in unison) is popular in funk and hip-hop clubs and country and western bars. You'll also find line dancing at wedding receptions, senior citizen centers, and fashionable clubs in San Francisco and Los Angeles.

Always into health and alternative activities, Californians have also begun to experiment with dance as a healing art. Spinning oneself into a higher consciousness is thought to free the 'inner self,' and dances used in healing or purification ceremonies by indigenous cultures are adopted to help people get in touch with their 'universal tribal and indigenous roots' (promotional flyer from the Berkeley Festival of Dance). You're most likely to find such dance classes in the Bay Area, Santa Cruz, and Big Sur.

Clubs Santa Monica, Hollywood, and San Francisco have the concentration of dance clubs, with a few good spots in San Diego and Fresno's Tower District. The club scene ranges from polished Hollywood spots like House of Blues and Society, to grunt-sweat-don't-care-what-you-look-like places such as The Pink in Santa Monica and Nikki's in San Francisco. A cover charge (what you must pay to enter) can be free to $10, with prices being higher on weekends. Some places have free entrance but a two drink minimum, or charge half price before 9 pm (most clubs don't 'happen' until after 10 pm). Each club has its own musical style, but Hip-hop, House, and Techno are the most popular. Dancing alone or in groups is quite acceptable.

San Francisco and Los Angeles have some good Latino night clubs that have nightly salsa dancing. Usually about half the crowd is Latino, and dance skills vary from nearly professional to 'how in the heck do you do this?' Some clubs are strictly salsa, but most have a good mix throughout the week then concentrate on salsa on the weekend.

Ballet While the San Francisco Ballet tours internationally and generally gets rave reviews, many San Franciscans are of the opinion that it is overrated and overpriced, and prefer the Oakland Ballet. The biggest difference between the two is that San Francisco's does interesting contemporary pieces while Oakland's productions are very traditional. Zellerbach Hall, on the UC Berkeley campus, occasionally gets international ballet and contemporary dance companies. The New York-based Jose Limon Dance Foundation recently launched an ensemble in San Jose; performances are usually at the University Theater (☎ 408-924-4555).

Performers like Martha Graham, Alvin Ailey, and Bella Lewitzky got their start in Los Angeles. The best source for information on LA's performances is the Dance Resource Center of Greater Los Angeles (☎ 213-227-9162). Two venues have regular dance performances scheduled: LA Contemporary Exhibitions (LACE, ☎ 213-957-1777), 6922 Hollywood Blvd, Hollywood, and Highways Performance Space (☎ 310-453-1755), 1651 18th St, Santa Monica. The annual production of *The Nutcracker Suite* at the Shrine Auditorium is outstanding.

Art
The earliest California artists were of course the Indians who used pigment to make spiritual and communicative paintings on rocks and caves, often as part of

shamanistic rituals intended to ensure successful hunting. While most tribes had their own decorative style, the Chumash are considered the most artistic because of the whimsical designs and bright colors they used. Chumash Painted Cave, near Santa Barbara, is a good example.

Early Landscape Artists California's first landscape painters were essentially tourists who recorded California's gentle light and natural landscape in their works. Many such artists were trained cartographers, accompanying Spanish explorers to record images of Alta California. An impressive reproduction of a scene painted by the artist who accompanied Sebastian Vizcaino adorns the walls of the Santa Barbara Courthouse.

In the 1850s, California's population increased with easterners coming west to seek fortune in the gold mines. Gold Rush pursuits often proved futile, so artists fell back on painting skills to make a living. Thomas Hill and German immigrant Albert Bierstadt were the two most famous Gold Rush-era artists. Travels to Yosemite, Death Valley, and the giant sequoia groves supplied most of their subject matter. Bierstadt voiced the general sentiment of early painters in writing that California 'holds land and light that can not be found in such quality nor quantity anywhere else.' As California's popularity grew, Currier & Ives sent landscape artists such as Thomas A Ayers and Charles Nahl to do lithographs of California scenes, which they sold in mail order catalogs. While most of this work is in the Library of Congress in Washington, DC, there are a few pieces at the Haggin Museum in Stockton and at the Oakland Museum.

The High Provincials As California's population grew, artists with East Coast and European training came to California specifically to paint. Known as High Provincials (referring to their 'high-brow' training and conviction of California as 'the' place to paint), these artists centered themselves in San Francisco, Los Angeles,

Carmel, Santa Barbara, and Laguna Beach. They were also known as the Southern Californians for geographic reasons. William Chase, often regarded as the finest art teacher of the late-19th century, paid a visit to California in 1896 and praised California's light and landscape, thus fortifying the state's popularity.

Guy Rose was the first California native to gain international recognition as an artist. He lived in Giverny for one year studying with Claude Monet and, upon returning in 1914, introduced Impressionism to California artists. This ushered in the era of painting out-of-doors, to which California was already conducive. Desert and seascapes were favorite subject matter, and eucalyptus trees appeared in so many paintings that California artists were often called the Eucalyptus School.

The best place to see these works are in the galleries of Carmel and Laguna Beach, which still survive as artist communities though they've been overrun with tourism. Laguna Beach's annual Pageant of the Masters and Sawdust Festival is one of California's largest arts festivals.

Modern Art California's debut into the national art scene, previously confined to New York and Chicago, was in 1940 when Man Ray moved to Los Angeles. Man Ray brought Surrealism and Dadaism, both well suited to California's off-the-wall, rebellious lifestyle, to the West Coast and spurred artists to venture away from traditionalism. Artists began to explore texture and shadow, intensified by California's light, and bright colors to capture California's atmosphere.

In the '40s and '50s, California art reflected the strong Abstract Expressionist movement in New York. Then in 1951, San Francisco artists David Park submitted a painting of a woman's figure to a competition, signifying the first move away from Abstract Expressionism. Elmer Bischoff soon followed Park's lead, and together they revitalized the exploration of painting figures which came to be known as the Bay Area Figurative Art Movement. The large following included Richard Diebenkorn, who eventually took his interpretation of space and light to a more abstract level.

This is also when Asian art began influencing California artists, especially in Los Angeles where Asian and California artists shared work and ideas. Sam Francis, famous for his abstract landscapes, multicolored spatterings, and Zen-influenced paintings where bands of color surround a large blank canvas, played a key part in this Cal-Asian movement with an open-door gallery in Santa Monica. His Japanese wife, an accomplished artist herself, helped connect Japanese art dealers and aspiring California artists. A Japanese Pavilion at the LA County Museum of Art (LACMA) brings California and Japanese movements together according to genre.

Pop Art In the Bay Area, as artists rejected the rigid, contrived categories of stylized art, an art that could not be defined as 'art' according to previous movements emerged. This 'funk art,' as it came to be known, incorporated everyday objects – lampshades, sea shells, cigarettes – into elaborate sculptures and pieces of bricolage. At the same time, Los Angeles saw the development of the 'Light and Space' movement, which also resisted the over-commodification of art, in the work of James Turrell and Robert Irwin.

In the 1960s, California artists were caught up in the nation's growing chaos and confusion. With Vietnam and the growth of freeways, California art turned remarkably disillusioned and dark. Romantic landscapes portraying California as the land of opportunity turned to 'freeway scapes' showing smog and overcrowding, with much allusion to the lost or tempered American Dream. Wayne Thiebaud's pop interpretations of freeways and city streets are strong examples. San Francisco, with Haight-Ashbury as a focal point, saw a huge output of psychedelic work by poster and album cover artists such as Rick Griffin, Stanley Mouse, and Allen Kelley. R Crumb and his art in Zap Comix

(remember 'Keep on truckin'?) was also very influential in this movement.

Where to See It The best places to see early California landscapes are the Oakland Museum, the Haggin Museum in Stockton, the Crocker Art Museum in Sacramento, and independent galleries in Laguna Beach (Orange County).

California's most progressive art comes out of Los Angeles, with the Los Angeles Museum of Contemporary Art (MOCA) and its Temporary Contemporary, in a converted warehouse in Little Tokyo, producing the most avant-garde shows in the state. The San Francisco Museum of Modern Art (SFMOMA), housed in a controversial modern structure by Swiss architect Mario Botta, has a substantial if conservative permanent collection. Across the Bay, the UC Berkeley Art Museum is a bit hit-or-miss, but often has excellent contemporary exhibits. The San Diego Museum of Contemporary Art (one downtown and one in La Jolla) shows mostly European works.

For fine art, the Los Angeles County Museum of Art (LACMA) and the Asian Art Museum and the MH de Young Museum, in San Francisco, have large and varied permanent collections and get world class traveling exhibits. San Francisco's Palace of the Legion of Honor, in Lincoln Park, has an important collection of European work.

Funk and pop art pieces grace many a poster shop in San Francisco, mostly on Haight St. Los Angeles' Watts Towers are perhaps the most famous and accessible pieces of folk bricolage.

Architecture

California's architecture is a jumble of styles, uses a hodgepodge of materials, and reflects various degrees of quality and care. In essence, it is as diverse as the state's population.

Spanish-Mexican Period When Spain launched exploratory expeditions to Alta California in the 1770s, the 'Laws of the Indies' served as a blueprint for mission

CALIFORNIA

San Diego is a great place to see Mission Style architecture.

development. The missions, in addition to being near rancherias, waterways, and the sea, had to be built around a courtyard where a garden and kitchen could be kept, with houses for livestock and horses nearby. Building materials reflected what the natives and padres found on hand: adobe, limestone, and grass.

Though the missions themselves crumbled into disrepair as the padres' influence waned, the building style was practical for California's climate. Patrons of California's ranchos adopted the style, eventually known as California Rancho or Rancho Adobe, and used it when building headquarters for their enormous properties. There are outstanding examples of adobes in Old Town in San Diego and Santa Barbara.

Victorians With the 1849 Gold Rush and California's statehood, architecture became Americanized almost immediately. As people arrived and accrued great fortunes, they built in a style familiar to them. With few trained architects on the scene and a general labor shortage, new buildings were often constructed using prefabricated structures ordered by mail from England, China, and Australia. This is when Victorians became popular, especially in San Francisco and on the North Coast. California's upper class built grand Victorian mansions (such as the Carson Mansion in Eureka, Governor's Mansion in Sacramento, and Meux Home in Fresno) to keep up with East Coast fashion that reflected the style popular during the reign of Queen Victoria. Soon smaller, less detailed versions were being produced in great quantities. Their bulging 'bay' windows were good for San Francisco's hills, as they allow views of more than the neighbors walls, and prefabricated construction made them cheap.

Spanish & Mission Revival After this rejection of its Hispanic Heritage during the Victorian period, romantic enthusiasm for California Missions was revived thanks to writings by Helen Hunt Jackson. Construction of Leland Stanford, Jr University in Palo Alto, and the arrival of William Templeton Johnson and Irving Gill on the architectural scene fortified this trend. Architects began to build in Mission Revival Style, using courtyards, arched entryways, long covered porches, and fountains. At the same time, architects built in the Spanish Colonial Revival Style, with two-story structures and open balconies. The two styles were frequently intertwined.

Former Santa Fe (now Amtrak) railroad stations throughout the state reflect this style, with outstanding examples in Stockton, Davis, Los Angeles, San Juan Capistrano, and San Diego.

California Bungalow In the 1890s, Willis Polk, Bernard Maybeck, and John Galen Howard arrived in California – the most influential group in what could be considered 'California Architecture.' Working mostly in the Bay Area, these architects consciously responded to California's climate and developing lifestyle. The

California Bungalow, a one-story wood structure with overhanging gables and a large porch, allowed indoor-outdoor living and quick, inexpensive construction. Whole neighborhoods of Bungalows sprang up at the end of WWI during LA's oil boom.

Arts & Crafts The Arts & Crafts movement, started and brought to an art by Bernard Maybeck, Greene & Greene, and Julia Morgan, was a decorative style incorporated into both California Bungalows and Mission Revival styles. Buildings from this movement combine various indigenous styles – Japanese, Spanish, English – with handcrafted details – carved wood, stained glass, sculpted tile – to make some of California's most beautiful buildings, including Bernard Maybeck's First Church of Christ Science (1906) in Berkeley; the Greenes' Gamble House (1908) in Pasadena; the Hollyhock House (1921), a collaboration of Frank Lloyd Wright and Rudolph Schindler, in Los Angeles; and Irving Gill's Marston House (1905) in San Diego. William Wurster, who started with rigid Classical buildings and softened under the Arts & Crafts influence, is one of California's most prolific architects whose work is mostly in Stockton and the Bay Area.

Classical Revival & Eclectic During the rise of Arts & Crafts, big-name architects also felt compelled to prove themselves in established architecture realms, which were building in the Classical Revival Style. Thus most of California's monumental buildings, especially courthouses, civic auditoriums, museums, and exposition spaces, reflect stylized European and East Coast training. Examples of this include San Francisco's Civic Center and Palace of Fine Arts, and the California Quadrangle in San Diego's Balboa Park, all of which were built for Panama-Pacific Expositions celebrating the opening of the Panama Canal in 1915.

The best example of California Eclectic, where basically anything goes, is William Randolph Hearst's house at San Simeon (Hearst Castle) – a mixture of Gothic, Moorish, and Spanish Romanesque – which Julia Morgan described as 'giving the client what he wants.'

Postwar Architecture After WWII, a large and comfortable middle class demanded 'modern' affordable family housing en mass. Freeways and parking lots influenced public planning, and suburban neighborhoods grew to facilitate the commuters' lifestyles. Inexpensive materials, prefabricated walls, cabinets and fixtures, and standardized floor plans allowed preplanned neighborhoods to be built quickly and cheaply. Tract housing developments, still spreading like wildfire over southeastern California, now surround most major cities. Shopping malls and strip malls (several stores surrounding a parking lot) have taken the life out of most downtowns and spread it over miles of boulevards. Fresno is probably the best example of this decentralization.

Post Modernism In response to this bland, mass produced architecture (which does, however, meet people's needs), important architects have become more reactive and strong. In LA, where Frank Gehry is reigning guru, contemporary structures still respond to California's climate and light, but with minimalist tendencies and emphasis on space and color. California's, and especially Los Angeles' modern architecture, described by Aaron Betsky (architectural curator of the San Francisco Museum of Modern Art), 'at its best does not look like building, but is an abstract interruption of the city, a piece of technology honed for living, or a self-consciously vivid set for modern living.' Concentrations of this avant-garde are in the Oakland Hills, which was almost completely leveled by fire in 1989, and in various pockets of Los Angeles (especially Santa Monica and Venice Beach).

Of course, California's free and easy style has allowed for zany structures influenced by nothing but whim and imagination. Often dubbed California Roadside Vernacular, these buildings usually have onomatopoetic character: a hot-dog stand shaped like a hot dog, a donut shop with a huge donut on the roof, a production studio shaped like a pair of binoculars, an Orange Julius stand in the form of (what else?) a giant navel orange. Southern California has the market on these.

Literature

The name California began its life as a literary device, coming from an imaginary kingdom that was featured in one of 1510's bestsellers, *Las sergas de Esplandian*. Perhaps California's 20th century took its cue from this auspicious beginning, because some of the brightest lights in 20th century American literature have made California their home.

The Gold Rush Era to the '20s Mark Twain came west to work in Carson City, Nevada, but was almost immediately enticed to Virginia City, and edited a newspaper there during the frenzied rush to the Comstock Lode. He penned mine company promotional pieces as a lucrative sideline, and wrote about pioneering life at the silver mines in *Roughing It* (1872). It covers his stagecoach journey to the West, mining days, and his experience of an earthquake. More of Twain's tales from the Gold Rush are recounted in *The Celebrated Jumping Frogs of Calaveras County & Other Stories*. Another pioneering visitor to the Bay Area, Scottish-born Robert Louis Stevenson, lived briefly in Monterey and San Francisco and honeymooned by an abandoned silver mine in nearby Calistoga. The stay led to his book *The Silverado Squatters* (1872). Professional hell-raiser Jack London was San Francisco-born and Oakland-bred. London turned out a massive volume of writings including his own suitably fictionalized story under the title *Martin Eden* (1909).

California increasingly received attention from writers with its rise to prominence in the early part of this century. One of the first novels to look at California's prosperity critically was Upton Sinclair's *Oil!* (1927), a work of muckraking historical fiction with socialist overtones.

The Modern Era Arguably the most influential author to emerge from California was John Steinbeck. Steinbeck turned attention from the two metropolises to the farms of the Central Valley and the down and out of Monterey County. The first of his California novels was *Tortilla Flat* (1935), which dealt with the Mexican American community of Monterey. His most overtly political novel, *In Dubious Battle* (1936), told a grim story of a violent fruit pickers' strike. The classic portrayal of Monterey is his *Cannery Row* (1945), a description of the working class in and around Monterey's cannery district. Another writer who tried to capture life in rural California was William Saroyan, who wrote extensively of the Armenian immigrant community of Fresno where he grew up.

Eugene O'Neill took his 1936 Nobel prize money and transplanted to the sleepy suburban village of Danville on the cusp of the Central Valley near San Francisco. He wrote the plays the *The Ice Man Cometh* and *Long Day's Journey Into Night* there.

LA's image as a tough, vulgar town started to emerge in the '30s and the '40s with John Fante's *Ask the Dust* (1939), a tour of Depression-era Los Angeles. The fame and fortune fantasies of struggling writer Arturo Bandini jar violently against the grim reality of LA's dusty downtown streets, where 'the smell of gasoline makes the sight of palm trees seem sad.' Aldous Huxley's novel *After Many a Summer Dies the Swan* (1939) is a fine and ironic work based on the life of newspaper magnate William Randolph Hearst (as was Orson Welles' film *Citizen Kane*). Nathanael West's *The Day of the Locust* (1939) is one of the best – and most cynical – novels about Hollywood ever written. Every paragraph seems to place one shrewd observation upon another, which strangely, for this city that so steadfastly insists on revising itself, still holds true more than a half century later. Two other novels that make sharply critical observations about the early years of Hollywood are F Scott Fitzgerald's final work, *The Last Tycoon* (1940), and Budd Schulberg's *What Makes Sammy Run?* (1941). Evelyn Waugh's *The Loved One* (1948), on the other hand, takes a humorous look at the funeral trade in Hollywood.

Poet-playwright Kenneth Rexroth began his San Francisco tenure of literary domination with his first collection entitled *In What Hour* (1940). Rexroth, also an influential critic, was instrumental in jump-starting the careers of several Bay Area artists, notably those of the Beat Generation.

The Pulps In the '30s, San Francisco and Los Angeles became the twin capitals of the pulp detective novel. Dashiell Hammett's Sam Spade *(The Maltese Falcon*; 1930) and Nick and Nora Charles *(The Thin Man*; 1932) plied their trade in San Francisco, while Raymond Chandler's Philip Marlowe *(The Big Sleep*; 1939) found trouble in the hills of Los Angeles. Both authors' books are populated with troubled characters riding the tide of evil forces that seem to govern the metropolis – before they sink to the bottom. Hammett made San Francisco's fog a sinister side character in his books, while Chandler played on differences between the haves and the have-nots in sunny LA. Latter-day practitioners of the art include Jim Thompson *(The Grifters*; 1963), Elmore Leonard *(Get Shorty*; 1990), and Walter Mosley *(White Butterfly*; 1990).

The Beats After the chaos of WWII, the Beat Generation engaged a new style of writing: short, sharp, and alive. They made their home in San Francisco and their bible was Jack Kerouac's *On the Road* (1957), a pseudo-documentary in 'spontaneous prose.' Allen Ginsberg was their premier poet and his *Howl & Other Poems* (1956) their angry anthem. A writer himself, Lawrence Ferlinghetti became the Beats' patron and publisher and today their era lives on at his City Lights Bookshop, still churning out the hipsters after 40 years in North Beach. With the Beats came a sort of *glasnost* that spread to other art forms, notably standup comedy. This was the first time in the USA that comedians began to ruthlessly explore the underbelly of American experience. Lenny Bruce, Lord Buckley, Mort Sahl, Bob Newhart, and Jonathan Winters were in the vanguard of the new comedy.

The '60s San Francisco dominated the literary scene in California during the '60s. Essayist Joan Didion captures a '60s sense of upheaval in *Slouching Towards Bethlehem* (1968), giving a caustic look at flower power and the Haight-Ashbury. Tom Wolfe also puts '60s San Francisco in perspective with *The Kandy-Kolored Tangerine Flake Streamlined Baby* (1965) and *The Electric Kool-Aid Acid Test* (1968). The latter blends the Grateful Dead, the Hell's Angels, and Ken Kesey's band of Merry Pranksters, who began their acid-laced 'magic bus' journey in Santa Cruz. A precursor to the spirit of the era, Kesey's own *One Flew Over the Cuckoo's Nest* (1962) pits a free-thinking individual against a stifling authority, drawing from his experiences at a local psychiatric ward for its setting.

Richard Brautigan's curious novels haven't aged too well but were a major cult in their time. *Trout Fishing in America* (1967) is one of the best. East Bay writer Philip K Dick is chiefly remembered for his science fiction, notably *Do Androids Dream of Electric Sheep?* (1968), which under the title *Blade Runner* became a classic sci-fi film. Dick's *The Man in the High Castle* (1962) envisions a Japanese-dominated San Francisco after Japan and Germany have won WWII, dividing the USA between them. Frank Herbert of the *Dune* series fame was also a local during these years, as was Thomas Pynchon, whose *The Crying of Lot 49* (1966) takes place in 1960s Berkeley (Pynchon is purported to live in the Los Angeles working class suburb of San Pedro) .

Charles Bukowski's idiosyncratic (and some would say drunken) poetry and prose depicted the earthier side of working class life in rusty old San Pedro.

The Hangover – the '70s & Beyond The bloated excess of '70s California became a favorite target for writers. Hunter S Thompson began his savage exploration of the collapse of the hippie dream with *Hell's Angels* (1970) and went on to chronicle its death throws throughout the decade. *The Great Shark Hunt* (1974) is a collection of some of his more acidic (pharmaceutical and otherwise) essays. *Generation of Swine* (1990) is a collection of columns Thompson wrote during a stint at the *San Francisco Examiner*.

1970 was bumper year for novels about LA. Terry Southern's *Blue Movie* concerns the decadent side of Hollywood; Joan Didion's *Play It as It Lays* looks at Los Angelenos with a dry, not-too-kind wit; *Post Office*, by poet-novelist Charles Bukowski, captures the down-and-out side of downtown; and *Chicano*, by Richard Vasquez, takes a dramatic look at the Hispanic Barrio of East LA. LA's cocaine-addled '80s got the treatment in Bret Easton Ellis' *Less than Zero* (1985).

No writer watched San Francisco's gay fraternity emerge from the closet with clearer vision than Armistead Maupin with his *Tales of the City* series. Starting, like the best Victorian potboilers, as newspaper serials in 1979 they became a smash hit collection of literary soap operas, light as a feather but great to read and a clear as day recreation of the heady days of pre-AIDS excess. *Tales of the City, Further Tales of the City, More Tales of the City, Babycakes*, and *Significant Others* bring that period back to life and the TV series was equally delightful. The late Randy Shilts, local author of *And the Band Played On* (1987), a moving account of the early years of AIDS awareness, also wrote for the *Examiner* and *Chronicle*.

Contemporary Writers The West Coast has always attracted artists and writers, and today the California literary community is stronger than ever, with many prominent writers making their homes here, including Alice Walker, Pulitzer Prize-winning author of *The Color Purple*; Amy Tan, author of *The Joy Luck Club*; Chilean novelist Isabel Allende, author of *The House of Spirits*; romance novelist Danielle Steele (with a new novel seemingly every other month); Anne Lamott; Post-modernist Kathy Acker; Dorothy Alison; Maxine Hong Kingston; Elmore Leonard; Walter Mosely; Pico Iyer; and James Ellroy.

The list of California writers would not be complete without mentioning Wallace Stegner, whose prize-winning novels and nonfiction qualify him as one of the great writers of the American West. Stegner died in 1993, but his legacy lives on at the prestigious Stanford University, whose Creative Writing Program is named after him.

There's an impressive group of poets as well. The poet laureate of the USA, Robert Hass, author of the collections *Human Wishes* and *20th Century Pleasures*, is a professor at the University of California, Berkeley. Polish Nobel laureate Czeslaw Milosz also teaches at Berkeley, and the two have teamed up on translations of Milosz' poetry.

Film
California culture is unique in that the state's primary art form, film, is also a major export – and it's a medium with a powerful presence in the lives of not only Americans, but people throughout the world. Consequently, images of California are distributed far beyond the state's boundaries, and ultimately reflect back on the state itself. Hardly anyone can come to California without some cinematic reference to the place, and many who have settled here make every effort to live up to the hype.

LA in particular has turned the camera inward incessantly, and as a result, it's probably the most self aware city in the world. Perhaps the greatest film about Los Angeles is *Chinatown* (1974). Directed by Roman Polanski and starring Jack Nicholson and Faye Dunaway, this is the story of LA's early-20th century water wars. Robert Towne's brilliant screenplay deftly deals with the shrewd deceptions that helped make Los Angeles what it is today.

Blade Runner (1982) is a sci-fi thriller directed by Ridley Scott and starring Harrison Ford, Rutger Hauer, and Sean Young. The film projects modern Los Angeles into the 21st century, with newer buildings reaching further into the sky – icy fortresses contrasting starkly with chaotic, neglected streets.

John Singleton's *Boyz N the Hood* (1991), starring Cuba Gooding, Jr, offers a major reality check: maybe this is what it's really like to come of age as a black teen in today's inner city. Meanwhile, Lawrence Kazdan's *Grand Canyon* (1991), starring Danny Glover and Kevin Kline, presents a glimmer of hope as black and white families cope with the sobering realities of racial tensions in modern LA. *My Family – Mi Familia* (1994) is a multi-generational epic of the trials and tribulations of a Mexican-American family in East LA during the first half of the 20th century. The films of Hollywood's latest wunderkind, Quentin Tarantino, are self-consciously influenced by Noir classics, Westerns, and Hong Kong thrillers and prominently feature modern-day Los Angeles. *Pulp Fiction* (1994), both written and directed by Tarantino, is a humorous and ironic view of LA from the bottom up. For all of its action, the film is quite realistically stuck much of the time in cars cruising LA's streets.

In *LA Story* (1991), comedian Steve Martin parodies the city that he calls home. Just about every aspect of LA life – from traffic to earthquakes – gets the irreverent Martin treatment.

Billy Wilder's *Sunset Boulevard* (1950), starring Gloria Swanson and William Holden, is a fascinating study of the way in which Hollywood discards its aged stars. The Paramount lot and Schwab's Drugstore are two of its many local settings.

A much more contemporary comment on Hollywood is Robert Altman's *The Player*,

released in 1992. Starring Tim Robbins and Fred Ward, this is a classic satire on the movie-making machinery, featuring dozens of cameos by the very actors and actresses being spoofed.

San Francisco has made a great backdrop for an amazing number of movies. Almost everything in the Hollywood lexicon from comedies to sci fi have used the 'City by the Bay' as a stage. A number of big production companies are based in the Bay Area, including Francis Ford Coppola's Zoetrope and, most famously, in Marin County, George Lucas' LucasFilm and Industrial Light & Magic, the high-tech company that produces the computer-generated special effects for Hollywood's biggest releases.

The first big San Francisco movie was, of course, Clark Gable's *San Francisco* (1936), which relives the 1906 quake. *The Joy Luck Club* (1993), the film of Amy Tan's best selling book, explores China old and China new, anchored in the city's Chinatown. Remarkably no American film company or TV network had the nerve to make a movie out of Armistead Maupin's long running gay soap opera *Tales of the City*; it took Britain's Channel 4 to bring it to the small screen in 1993.

The hit film *The Graduate* (1967), set in status-hungry middle-class California, is notable for Dustin Hoffman's unique ability to get to Berkeley by crossing the Bay Bridge in the San Francisco direction – his red Alfa Romeo simply looks better on the top deck.

We've all hurtled up and down San Francisco's streets with Steve McQueen in *Bullit*, the 1968 thriller that served as the benchmark for a good car chase ever since, but Clint Eastwood's Dirty Harry character also found San Francisco familiar territory. The highly questionable cop started his film career there with the 1971 *Dirty Harry*.

Alfred Hitchcock's movies often made use of San Francisco locales. 1958's *Vertigo* starred Kim Novak and James Stewart and wandered all over San Francisco with lengthy pauses at the Palace of

Human Potential, Self-Realization & Actualization

Rivaling religion in California is the 'human potential' industry, with adherents who put big stock in deep, long, loving looks, and demand 'integrity' and 'space' in their 'primary relationships.' Their vocabulary, let's call it psychobabble, is an amalgam of jargon from Humanistic Psychology to religion, and has started to become part of mainstream language – a lot of people now 'need their space,' and say 'I hear you.'

If you want to get 'deep' and 'meaningful' in your travel experience on the West Coast, plug into the fascinating network of 'facilitators,' 'seminars,' 'trainings,' and 'multilevel marketing schemes' that will bring you closer to your 'inner child,' 'true self,' and your 'soul purpose.' Just remember to act earnest, take everything at face value, and keep your wallet close to your side – you may be asked to display your 'prosperity consciousness.' You might find the following phrases useful and validating:

actualize
to manifest one's infinite potential

affirmations
lies you tell yourself until you believe them

Are you okay with that?
Does that mesh with your higher purpose and the rantings of your inner child?

channeling
1. wisdom from people with incredible imaginations and a penchant for Elizabethan theatrics   2. the New Age's answer to speaking in tongues

A Course in Miracles
Christianity with a New Age spin

EST
Erhard Seminar Training. Also known as Zen for the Masses. A human potential process named after former used-car salesman, Werner Erhard. Features long-winded lectures and a major league sales spiel. Now known as 'The Forum' or 'Landmark Education.'

higher self
your in-tune, in-touch, spiritually together self just waiting to be accessed if you only buy the speaker's book

I honor that
as in 'I respect what you're saying.' Probably the most annoying of all psychobabble. The key here, as with most psychobabble, is to have an air of hushed earnest authenticity and seriousness about your delivery.

I need my space
room to think, breathe or cheat on your spouse

I have problems with that
your action or point of view violates a carefully worked out, ironclad, and rather PC view I have of the world

issues
1. deep psychological difficulties best resolved through hugely overpriced workshops or therapy, eg 'It appears you have issues with your father.' 2. a very effective come-on used by facilitators and therapists across the USA

male bonding
homoerotic drumming for straight men

newage
pseudo-spiritual garbage. Rhymes with 'sewage.'

past life regression
you and 10,000 other people were Cleopatra in a past life

share
a psychobabbler speaks. 'I'd like to share something with the group.'

Thank you for sharing.
a way for a facilitator to get the last word in after someone's share

victim
all psychobabblers have been victims at one time or another ■

the Legion of Honor and at Fort Point. Those pesky feathered fiends made nuisances of themselves just north of San Francisco in 1963's *The Birds*.

Of course the classic San Francisco private eye was Dashiell Hammett's Sam Spade. His screen double, Humphrey Bogart, appeared in *The Maltese Falcon* (1941), a classic murder mystery.

The Wild One (1954) was one of the first movies to exploit the 'rebellious youth' theme: Marlon Brando leads a motorcycle gang that invades a town in rural California.

For a taste of life in a small Central Valley town (Modesto to be exact) on a June night in '62, check George Lucas' tribute to cruising, *American Graffiti* (1973). For a glimpse at the Malibu surf scene at about the same time, *Big Wednesday* (1978) is worth a rental (although it was actually filmed in Santa Barbara). Santa Cruz became the haunt of Generation X vampires in the *Lost Boys* (1978).

Billy Wilder's classic Marilyn Monroe comedy *Some Like It Hot* (1959) elegantly captures in black & white all the splendor of San Diego's Hotel del Coronado. The schmaltzy *Pretty Woman* (1990) stars Julie Roberts as the luckiest hooker in LA – but it's filmed partly in San Diego.

Martin Mull's *The Serial* is a cutting satire of the feel-good New Age ethos of '70s Marin County (1980). The Gold Rush is portrayed from very different perspectives in two films. *Paint Your Wagon* (1969) is a bloated musical featuring the chilling vocal talents of Clint Eastwood and Lee Marvin as prospectors in the Mother Lode. Rent this film at your own peril. *1000 Pieces of Gold* (1992) is a small, subdued, independently produced film telling the story of a Chinese woman sold into servitude to a Mother Lode brothel, who manages to become a woman of independent means.

RELIGION

Like the rest of the USA, California is primarily Christian; 45% of Californians are Protestant, 25% are Roman Catholic, 5% are Jewish, and 7% are of other faiths; 18% express no sectarian preference. Still, only 9% say they are not at all religious; 22% describe themselves as very religious, 47% as fairly religious, and 22% as slightly religious.

Within the ranks of Protestants are many different sects, ranging from staid conservative denominations to evangelical 'born-again' Pentecostals. Though they are claimed by only 7% of the population, the 'other' religions probably represented every other religion on earth; the large numbers of Californians with roots in countries around the world means that California has sizable numbers of Muslims, Hindus, Buddhists, Sikhs, Baha'is, and every other religion you can think of. Mosques, temples, synagogues, and other religious centers are found throughout California, especially in the larger population centers where most of the immigrants or people with foreign backgrounds live.

Of course, as 'the land of the fruits and the nuts,' California is also home to a number of unusual religious persuasions, from gay churches to faith healers to idealistic utopian communities. California has always had utopian religious communities tucked away in isolated places, and it still does.

LANGUAGE

According to a 1990 census, 31.5% of Californians over five years old speak a language other than English at home. Still, American English predominates on the streets and in places of business. You're most likely to hear foreign languages in the ethnic communities of the big cities, though rural areas in Southern California and the Central Valley are increasingly Hispanic while those in northern California are increasingly Asian.

Visitors to the major national parks will often find introductory brochures printed in Spanish, German, French, or Japanese.

Pronunciation

Californians tend to speak casually, leaving the endings off words, skipping syllables, and running words together. *Yeah*, *mmmhmm*, and *uh-huh* mean 'yes,' while *uh-uh* and *hmmhm* mean 'no.' Look for a nod or shake of the head to confirm: nod is 'yes,' shake is 'no.' Dirty is pronounced 'dirdy,' 'Do you want to?' is 'dyawana,' 'I don't know' is 'Idunno,' 'all right' 'awright,' and 'what is up?' (as in 'what is going on?') comes out as simply 'sup?'

Greetings & Civilities

Greetings are fairly uncomplicated with the standard 'hello,' 'hi,' 'good morning,' 'good afternoon,' 'how are you?,' the more colloquial 'hey,' 'hey there,' and 'howdy' among the options. There's more variety with a farewell, including 'bye,' 'goodbye,' 'bye-bye,' 'see ya,' 'take it easy,' 'later,' 'take care,' 'don't work too hard,' and the ubiquitous 'have a nice day.'

While Americans run short on 'please,' they say 'thank you' after almost anything. You'll hear 'excuse me' instead of 'sorry.' In a conversation, the listener will interject *mm-hmmm* or *uh-huh* frequently to let the speaker know they're paying attention and want them to go on. It's a much more enthusiastic style than the judgment-reserving *mmm*. For some talkers, the enthusiastic uh-huhs aren't enough, and they will pepper their speech with 'y'know' or 'you hear what I'm saying?,' which is not a strictly literal question.

So-Cal Speak

California's most recognized dialect, the style presented in songs and movies, comes from the beaches and shopping malls of Southern California. This casual talk is usually called 'surfer' or 'valley' talk (as in San Fernando Valley), though the two are very similar. While it may be hard to believe that people do talk this way, it's like totally true. Check it out, dude.

The most common zones (places) to scope out (observe) this lingo (language) are on So-Cal (Southern California) beaches, especially where there is killer (good) wave action (surf) and a mellow scene (ambience). This kind of rap (talk) doesn't necessarily reflect the speaker's intelligence or level of education as much as where he/she has been hangin' (as in hanging around).

Killer, *bitchin*, *awesome*, *sweet*, *stylin'*, and *stellar* basically mean 'really good.' *Bunk*, *nappy*, *shitty*, and *slack* mean 'really bad,' and *hairy* means scary. *Gnarly* and *insane* can mean anything extreme, just like *totally* or *hella* put before a word makes its meaning more significant (for example gnarly or insane waves might be totally killer, totally hairy or totally bunk). *Vibes* are feelings or indications you get from a person or place, and can be good, bad, or *weird* (strange). A *dude* can be male or female, and is often precluded by *hey*, the common term for 'hi.' To *cruise* means 'to go,' by foot, car, bike, or skateboard. *All right* and *right on* are confirmations that you and whoever you're speaking with are *on the same wavelength* (have similar understanding).

Lots of sub-communities based on common work and leisure interests generate new words and usages at an incredible rate. Californian language is not constrained by tradition.

Ethnic Languages

Though foreign language speakers are not common in most tourist areas, California's ethnic diversity is represented in the languages of ethnic communities and neighborhoods across the state. Los Angeles, San Francisco, and most San Joaquin Valley towns have neighborhoods where Spanish, Chinese, Japanese, Vietnamese, Korean, or Cambodian is the dominant language.

Street signs, billboards, and menus in San Francisco's Chinatown are mostly in Chinese characters without English translation. In Southern California, towns and geographical features have Spanish names – Santa Barbara, San Diego, La Mesa, El Cajon – but these reflect early history rather than current demography. The many Spanish names of suburban streets reflect the desire of developers to come up with something more exotic than Main St, or 5th Ave. Wouldn't you rather live in Via de la Valle than Valley Road?

San Francisco

• *pop 753,400* ☎ *415*

Visually spectacular, historically colorful, and a regular trendsetter in everything from flower power to gay liberation, San Francisco consistently tops the polls as America's favorite city.

The city's irresistible attraction starts with the way it looks. Streets soar up and plunge down the steep hills, framing spectacular views and hiding quiet little pockets within the urban chaos. In the background there's always the Bay, crossed by not one but two of the world's best known bridges. What's more, San Francisco is a city of multiple disguises; sure there's a booming downtown business center, but there are also a host of micro cities. San Francisco's colorful, crowded, and frenetic Chinatown jostle up against ritzy Union Square, and quickly fades to the bars, cafes, and restaurants of North Beach, the Beat center of the '50s. That blends into Fisherman's Wharf, the raucous tourist center and jumping-off point for Alcatraz. There's also the Latino enclave of the Mission, the gay epicenter of the Castro, the club scene in SoMa, reminders of the flower power era in the Haight-Ashbury, and the much-loved Golden Gate Park.

Of course, there's much more to do than simply eye the scenery. San Francisco has to be one of the world's great eating centers with everything from Mexican and Asian cheap eats to stylish restaurants serving the city's cutting edge California cuisine. After dark the city's theaters, clubs, and bars are relaxed and welcoming. Add to that fantastic shopping and lots of outdoor activities and you've got San Francisco: it's quite a city.

HISTORY

San Francisco is a new city. Though the Miwok and Ohlone Indians inhabited the area, it was less than 250 years ago that the first European eyes were set on the Bay, by the overland party of Gaspar de Portola who was establishing a string of missions throughout Alta California for the Spanish. Mistaking the Bay for the previously identified bay at Point Reyes, to the north, his party turned back to Monterey. The Spanish didn't return until 1775, when Juan Manuel de Ayala sailed into the Bay, the first European to enter what was later nicknamed the 'Golden Gate.' The following year the presidio was built just above the Golden Gate, and Mission Dolores was established three miles south in the heart of today's Mission district.

Victory in the Mexican-American War ceded the land to the USA in 1846 – excellent timing, because gold was discovered in the Sierra Nevada two years later and the population of the newly renamed San Francisco exploded from 500 to 25,000 within a year. Aside from a transport and supply center, the booming city provided other essential services to miners, chiefly banking and R&R.

Notorious during the latter half of the 1800s as a world-class hotbed of murder and mayhem, the area that now engulfs the northeastern edge of the Financial District was a labyrinth of casinos and cat houses, saloons and cabarets, opium dens and distilleries, catering to vices of every sort. After the 'Big One,' the 1906 earthquake and fire that leveled half of San Francisco, much of the red-light district was destroyed, and the city sought to prevent it from being rebuilt. However, it wasn't until 1917 that a federal decree closed the brothels once and for all and laid to rest the city's most sordid period.

The Big One gave San Francisco an opportunity to rebuild the city, and frantic years of city planning and construction followed. By the time the Depression hit in the 1930s, San Francisco had regenerated itself into a cutting edge modern city, hosting the Panama-Pacific Exposition in

1915 to flaunt its stylish new image. San Francisco still suffered through the Great Depression and, like other cities, gigantic public works projects were one of the attempts to yank the economy out of the doldrums. The Bay Area certainly got its money's worth from these 1930s projects; the Bay Bridge of 1936 and the Golden Gate Bridge of 1937 are still magnificent symbols of the city.

During WWII the Bay Area became a major launching pad for military operations in the Pacific and gigantic shipyards soon sprang up around the Bay, boosting the population to the highest it's ever been (more than 775,000).

The decades that follow are marked by the prominence of colorful subcultures: the Beats spearheaded '50s counterculture and the hippies followed in the '60s. If marijuana was the drug of choice for the '50s then LSD was the '60s trip. Long hair and the new wave of rock music were adopted from England, and when 20,000 people congregated in Golden Gate Park for a free concert in 1967 the 'Summer of Love' kicked off and 'flower power' and 'free love' became San Francisco passwords. After a decade of realignments and upheavals the '70s were comparatively relaxed. The hippies had led a sexual revolution but it was a predominantly heterosexual one; a homosexual one followed in the '70s as San Francisco's gays stepped decisively out of the closet and slammed the door shut behind them. Gay Pride became a rallying call, and the previously underground homosexual community 'came out' in all its glory.

By the '80s and '90s San Francisco had cemented its reputation as the most liberal and tolerant of cities, a mecca for alternative lifestyles and a place for everyone.

ORIENTATION

The city of San Francisco is a compact area, covering the tip of a 30-mile-long peninsula with the Pacific Ocean on one side and the San Francisco Bay on the other. The city can be neatly divided into three sections. The central part resembles a slice of pie, with Van Ness Ave and Market St marking the two sides and the Embarcadero the rounded edge of the pie. Squeezed into this compact slice are the Union Square area, the Financial District, the Civic Center area, Chinatown, North Beach, Nob Hill, Russian Hill, and Fisherman's Wharf.

To the south of Market St lies SoMa, an upwardly mobile warehouse zone. SoMa fades into the Mission, the city's Latino

The Beat Generation

From the days of the Gold Rush, San Francisco has always been a freewheeling city. Artists, musicians, and writers often sang its praises in them, but it wasn't until the mid-1950s that national attention was first focused on 'the City' as the birthplace of a scene of its own. When Jack Kerouac and Allen Ginsberg, upstart students at Columbia University, fled the indifference of New York City and joined forces with the San Francisco Renaissance, a poets' movement begun by poet and literary critic Kenneth Rexroth, the Beat Generation was given a voice. They engaged in a new style of writing – short, sharp, and alive. Their bible was Kerouac's *On the Road* (1957), and Ginsberg's *Howl* (1956) was their angry anthem. A writer himself, Lawrence Ferlinghetti became the Beats' patron and publisher and today their era lives on at his City Lights Bookstore, still churning out the hipsters after 40 years in North Beach.

The Beats spoke of a life unbound by social conventions, motivated by spontaneous creativity rather than greed and ambition. Even the term 'beat' (associated with the rhythm of bongo drums that were a common element to their poetry readings) was taken from the jazz-speak of the day meaning a state of finished exhaustion and alluding to the supreme happiness preached in the Beatitudes of Jesus. The term *beatnik* came along later; created, it is claimed, by *San Francisco Chronicle* columnist Herb Caen fusing the 'far out' Beats with the just-launched Sputnik satellite. ∎

The 49-Mile Drive

Make some stops along the way and the 49-Mile Drive could take you all day. Devised for the 1939-40 Treasure Island Exposition, the drive covers almost all the city's highlights. Although it's well signposted with instantly recognizable seagull signs, a map and an alert navigator are still a good idea. Pick up a map at the visitors center – it traces the route. ∎

---

quarter, and then the Castro, the city's gay quarter.

The third and final part of the city is also physically the largest – the long sweep from Van Ness Ave all the way to the Pacific Ocean. It's a varied area encompassing upscale neighborhoods like the Marina and Pacific Heights, less pricey zones like the Richmond and Sunset districts, as well as areas with a flavor all their own, such as Japantown and the Haight-Ashbury. The city's three great park lands – the Presidio, Lincoln Park, and Golden Gate Park – are also in this area.

See Getting Around at the end of the chapter for public transportation options for each neighborhood.

Maps

Good quality maps of San Francisco are available from bookstores but giveaway maps from a variety of sources are generally adequate for most visitors. Rent-a-car firms have heaps of maps but the best of the free maps is the *San Francisco Street Map & Visitor Guide,* available at many of the city's hotels. If you're going to be exploring the city by public transportation, the Muni *Street & Transit Map* is a smart $2 investment. Get a copy at the Visitors Information Center or any large bookstore. The Rand McNally Map Store (☎ 777-3131), 595 Market St at 2nd, is a good place to pick up maps.

For convenience, nothing beats the *Streetwise San Francisco* map, close to pocket size yet still legible, and laminated for durability. Several detailed street atlases

to the Bay Area are put out by Thomas Bros Maps; you can pick one up at their store (☎ 981-7520), 550 Jackson St at Columbus, or at just about any bookstore.

INFORMATION
Tourist Offices

In the heart of the city, a stone's throw from Union Square and right by the most popular cable car turnaround, the San Francisco Visitors Information Center (☎ 391-2000) is at the lower level of Hallidie Plaza at Market and Powell. The center is open weekdays from 9 am to 5:30 pm, Saturday from 9 am to 3 pm, and Sunday from 10 am to 2 pm.

The center has a 24-hour phone service offering recorded 'what's on' information. It operates in English (☎ 391-2001), French (☎ 391-2003), German (☎ 391-2004), Spanish (☎ 391-2122), and Japanese (☎ 391-2101).

Foreign Consulates

Plenty of countries have consulate representation in San Francisco. What government wouldn't want a home away in this city? Here's a list of different Consulate-Generals:

Australia
    1 Bush St (☎ 362-6160)
Denmark
    Suite 1440, 601 Montgomery St (☎ 391-0100)
Finland
    333 Bush St (☎ 772-6649)
France
    540 Bush St (☎ 397-4330)
Germany
    1960 Jackson St (☎ 775-1061)
Ireland
    655 Montgomery St (☎ 392-4214)
Israel
    456 Montgomery St (☎ 398-8885)
Italy
    2590 Webster St (☎ 931-4924)
Japan
    50 Fremont St (☎ 777-3533)
Netherlands
    1 Maritime Plaza (☎ 981-6454)
New Zealand
    1 Maritime Plaza, Suite 700 (☎ 399-1455)

Norway
    20 California St (☎ 986-0766)
Sweden
    120 Montgomery St (☎ 788-2631)
Switzerland
    456 Montgomery St (☎ 788-2272)
UK
    1 Sansome St (☎ 981-3030)

Money

San Francisco International Airport has a currency exchange office at the Bank of America International Terminal branch and in Boarding Area D; hours are 7 am to 11 pm.

American Express card holders can obtain cash advances from Amex Travel Services offices (there are five in San Francisco; look for American Express in the white pages).

Post & Telecommunications

The main San Francisco post office (☎ 441-8329) is the Civic Center Post Office, 101 Hyde St Mail can be sent to you here marked c/o General Delivery, San Francisco, CA 94142, USA. Post offices are generally open weekdays 9 am to 5 pm and Saturday 9 am to 1 pm. There's a post office (☎ 956-3570) in the basement of Macy's on Union Square, open Monday to Saturday from 10 am to 5:30 pm and Sunday 11 am to 5 pm. Public phones cost 20¢ for local calls, more if you're calling to the East Bay.

Travel Agencies

Good travel agents include STA Travel (☎ 391-8407), 51 Grant Ave, and Council Travel (☎ 421-3473), 530 Bush St, or (☎ 566-6222), 919 Irving St.

Bookstores

Many city bookstores are open late, often every night of the week. Borders (☎ 399-1633) is a huge and glossy bookstore with a cafe on the northwest corner of Union Square. A Clean Well Lighted Place for Books (☎ 441-6670), 601 Van Ness Ave in Opera Plaza near the Civic Center, is a good place to hear author readings. The Booksmith (☎ 863-8688), 1644 Haight St,

is a general bookstore in the most ungeneral of neighborhoods.

Green Apple Books (☎ 387-2272), 506 Clement St, between 6th and 7th in the Richmond district, is one of the best bookstores in the city.

San Francisco's most famous bookstore, City Lights (☎ 362-8193), 261 Columbus Ave, North Beach, was the first paperbacks-only bookshop in the USA and has always been at the cutting edge of writing and literature. It was the center of the Beats in the '50s and is still owned by its founder, poet Lawrence Ferlinghetti. It's a wonderful place to book browse late at night – the poetry room upstairs has hands down the best selection anywhere.

Rand McNally (☎ 777-3131), 595 Market St at 2nd, has a superb selection of travel books and maps. On the other side of the Financial District, Thomas Bros Books & Maps (☎ 981-7520), 550 Jackson St in Jackson Square, also specializes in travel and maps. A Different Light Bookstore (☎ 431-0891), 489 Castro St in the Castro, is America's largest gay and lesbian bookseller.

Newspapers

The Bay Area's number-one daily, the *San Francisco Chronicle*, is definitely not one of the USA's great newspapers. It's supplemented by the evening *San Francisco Examiner*. On Sundays they get together to produce the *San Francisco Examiner-Chronicle*, which includes the popular 'pink section' entertainment supplement.

A journalistic highlight is the amazing assortment of free papers. The leaders in this field are the *San Francisco Bay Guardian* and the *SF Weekly* both with intelligent coverage of local events and politics plus superb restaurant, film, and other arts reviews. They also have extremely colorful personal ads.

Harold Newsstand (☎ 441-2665), 524 Geary St, has the best choice of out-of-town newspapers in the city. Cafe de la Presse (☎ 398-2680), 328 Grant Ave, has European papers and magazines. Both places are near Union Square.

CALIFORNIA

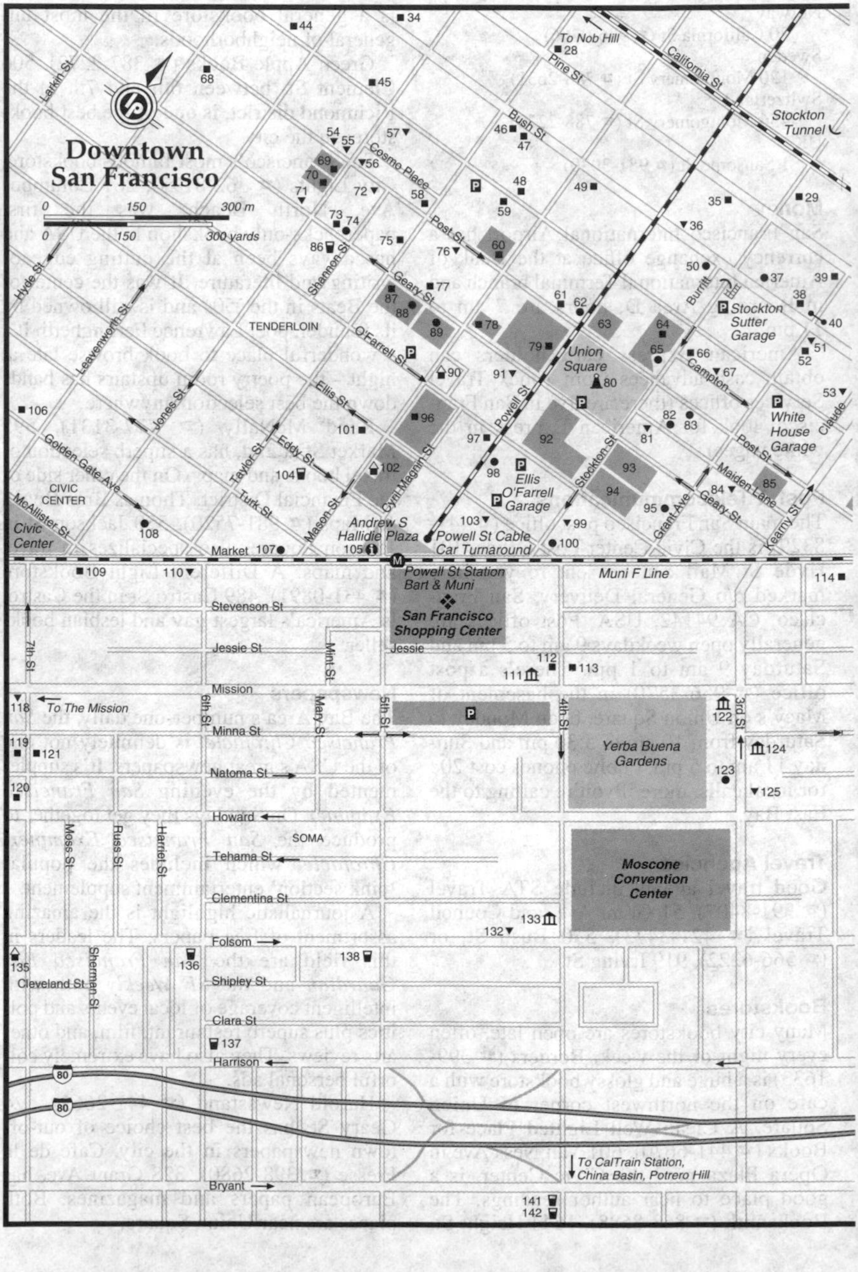
Downtown San Francisco
0 150 300 m
0 150 300 yards
CALIFORNIA
To Nob Hill
California St
Pine St
Bush St
Stockton Tunnel
Larkin St
Cosmo Place
Post St
Geary St
O'Farrell St
Ellis St
Eddy St
Turk St
Golden Gate Ave
McAllister St
Hyde St
Leavenworth St
Jones St
Taylor St
Shannon St
Mason St
Cyril Magnin St
Powell St
Stockton St
Grant Ave
Kearny St
Claude
Burritt
Campton
Maiden Lane
TENDERLOIN
CIVIC CENTER
Civic Center
Union Square
Stockton Sutter Garage
White House Garage
Ellis O'Farrell Garage
Andrew S Hallidie Plaza
Powell St Cable Car Turnaround
Market
Powell St Station Bart & Muni
Muni F Line
San Francisco Shopping Center
Stevenson St
Jessie St
Jessie
Mint St
Mission
Mary St
5th St
4th St
3rd St
6th St
7th St
To The Mission
Minna St
Natoma St
Howard
SOMA
Tehama St
Clementina St
Folsom
Shipley St
Cleveland St
Clara St
Harrison
Bryant
Moss St
Russ St
Harriet St
Sherman St
Yerba Buena Gardens
Moscone Convention Center
80
To CalTrain Station, China Basin, Potrero Hill
34 44 28 68 45 54 55 57 46 47 69 56 70 71 72 58 48 49 59 35 29 73 74 75 86 36 60 76 50 37 39 77 87 88 61 62 38 89 78 63 64 40 79 65 66 51 52 90 91 80 67 53 106 96 82 83 101 97 92 81 102 104 98 93 85 84 94 108 103 99 95 107 105 100 109 110 114 112 113 111 118 122 119 121 124 123 120 125 133 132 135 136 138 137 141 142

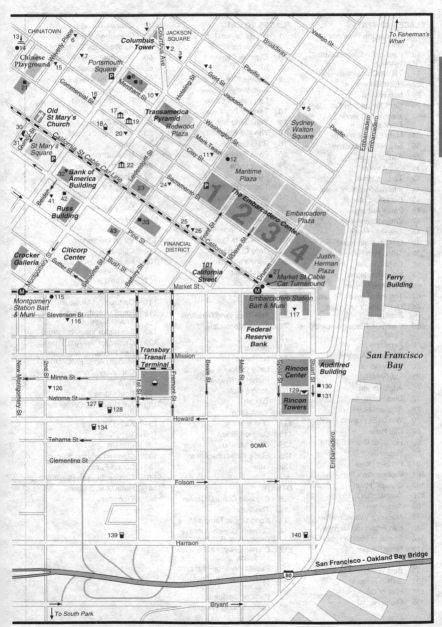

CHINATOWN

To Fisherman's Wharf

Columbus Tower

JACKSON SQUARE

Broadway

Vallejo St

13
14
6
Whitfield Place
Chinese Playground
15
7
Portsmouth Square
8
9
Merchant St
10
21
Commercial St
16

2
3
Columbus Ave
Jackson St
4
Gold St
Pacific

Pacific

5
Sydney Walton Square

Embarcadero
Embarcadero

Old St Mary's Church
30
31
Quincy St
St Mary's Square
California St Cable Car Line
17
18
19
20
Transamerica Pyramid
Redwood Walton Plaza
Hotaling St
Washington St
Mark Twain
Clay St
11
12
Maritime Plaza

Bank of America Building
32
41
42
Belden
Russ Building
22
23
24
Leidesdorff St
Sacramento St
Front St
Davis St
P
The Embarcadero Center
1
2
3
4
Embarcadero Plaza

43
33
Pine St
25
26
California St
FINANCIAL DISTRICT
Embarcadero Plaza

Crocker Galleria
Citicorp Center
Montgomery St
Sutter St
Sansome St
Bush St
Battery St
101 California Street
Drumm
27
Market St Cable Car Turnaround
Justin Herman Plaza
Ferry Building

Market St

M
Montgomery Station Bart & Muni
115
Stevenson St
116

M
Embarcadero Station Bart & Muni
117
Federal Reserve Bank

San Francisco Bay

New Montgomery St
2nd St
Minna St
126
Natoma St
127
128
1st St
Fremont St
Mission
Beale St
Main St
Spear St
Stuart St
Rincon Center
Audiffred Building
129
130
131
Rincon Towers

134
Howard

Tehama St
Clementina St
SOMA
Folsom

139
140
Harrison

San Francisco - Oakland Bay Bridge

80

Bryant

To South Park

CALIFORNIA

PLACES TO STAY

9 Holiday Inn Financial District
18 Pacific Tradewinds Guest House
21 YMCA Chinatown
27 Hyatt Regency
28 Nob Hill Inn
29 Ritz-Carlton San Francisco
33 Mandarin Oriental San Francisco
34 Mary Elizabeth Inn
35 Nob Hill Lambourne
38 Astoria Hotel
39 Grant Plaza
42 Temple Hotel
44 International York Hotel
45 Beresford Manor
46 Petite Auberge
47 White Swan Inn
48 Sheehan Hotel
49 Golden Gate Hotel
52 Triton Hotel
58 Dakota Hotel
59 Beresford Hotel
60 Pan Pacific Hotel
61 The Inn at Union Square
64 Grand Hyatt on Union Square
66 Campton Place Kempinski Hotel
68 Pensione
69 Beresford Arms Hotel
70 Brady Acres
73 Savoy Hotel
75 Adelaide Inn
77 Diva Hotel
78 Raphael Hotel
79 Westin St Francis Hotel
87 Clift Hotel
90 Hostel at Union Square
96 Hotel Nikko
97 Herbert Hotel
101 Globetrotters Inn
102 Olympic Hotel
106 Central YMCA Hotel
109 Aida Hotel
112 Mosser's Victorian Hotel
113 San Francisco Marriott
114 Sheraton Palace Hotel
119 Hotel Britton
120 Best Western Carriage Inn
121 Best Western Americana
130 Griffon Hotel
131 Harbor Court Hotel
135 Globe Hostel

PLACES TO EAT

1 House of Nan King
2 Cornucopia
3 Cypress Club
4 Bix
5 Square One
6 Sam Wo's
7 Empress of China
10 Tommy Toy's
11 Yank Sing
15 The Pot Sticker
16 R&G Lounge
20 Palio Paninoteca
24 Sol y Luna
25 Aqua
26 Tadich Grill
31 Lotus Garden
32 Carnelian Room
36 Masa's
41 Belden Place Restaurants
51 Cafe de la Presse
53 Cafe Claude
54 Burma's House
55 Borobudur
56 Thai Stick
57 Fleur de Lys
67 Anjou
71 Ten Thousand Buddhas
72 China Moon Cafe
76 Postrio
81 Mocca
84 Nosheria
91 Lefty O'Doul's
99 Planet Hollywood
103 John's Grill
110 Tu Lan
116 Yank Sing
117 One Market
118 Cafe do Brasil
125 Caffe Museo
126 Eddie Rickenbacker's
132 Lulu

OTHER

8 Chinese Cultural Center
12 The Punchline
13 Kong Chow Temple
14 Chinese Consolidated Benevolent Building
17 Chinese Historical Society Museum
19 Pacific Heritage Museum
22 Wells Fargo History Museum
23 Bank of California
30 Ching Chung Temple
37 Council Travel
40 Chinatown Gate
43 Pacific Stock Exchange
50 Maltese Falcon Plaque
62 Borders Bookstore
63 Saks Fifth Avenue
65 Children's Fountain
74 Harold Newstand
80 Dewey Monument
82 Circle Gallery
83 American Express
85 Gump's
86 Blue Lamp
88 Curran Theatre
89 Geary Theatre
92 Macy's West
93 Neiman - Marcus
94 Macy's East
95 STA Travel
98 Books Inc.
100 Virgin Megastore
104 Club 181
105 Hallidie Plaza & Visitor Information
107 Warfield
108 Hollywood Billiards
111 Cartoon Art Museum
115 Rand McNally Map & Travel Store
122 Center for the Arts Forum
123 Center for the Arts Theater
124 San Francisco Museum of Modern Art (SFMOMA)
127 Caribbean Zone
128 DV8
129 Post Office
133 Ansel Adams Center for Photography
134 Kate O'Brien's
136 1015 Club
137 End Up
138 Covered Wagon Saloon
139 Sound Factory
140 Gordon Biersch Brewery
141 Hotel Utah Saloon
142 Trocadero

CALIFORNIA

Laundry

To liven up the drudgery of wash day, try Brain Wash (☎ 255-4866), 1122 Folsom St, where you can hang out in the cafe while you wait for your clothes. At the corner of Golden Gate Park, Wash Club (☎ 681-9274), 520 Frederick St at Stanyan, offers shoe repair, photo developing, TV, and video games in addition to washers and dryers and a dry-cleaning service.

Medical Services

Check the yellow pages under 'Physicians & Surgeons' or 'Clinics' to find a doctor. In real emergencies call ☎ 911 for an ambulance. In that case you're not going to be too worried about where you end up, but San Francisco General Hospital (☎ 206-8000), 1001 Potrero Ave, has an emergency room. For women's health issues, Planned Parenthood has clinics at (☎ 441-5454), 815 Eddy, and (☎ 765-6905) 222 Front St.

Dentists can be found by calling the Dental Information Service (☎ 398-0618).

UNION SQUARE

San Francisco's downtown tourist center, Union Square, is surrounded on all sides by pricey hotels, airline offices, and classy shops including the city's prime department stores. The center of the square is dominated by the 97-foot-high **Dewey Monument**, erected in 1903. Among the buildings flanking the square is the 1904 **St Francis Hotel**, which features in many Dashiell Hammett novels, notably *The Maltese Falcon*. In the Grand Hyatt plaza on Stockton St, sculptor Ruth Asawa's bronze **Children's Fountain** portrays San Francisco's history in intricate detail.

On the east side of the square, **Maiden Lane** is crowded with pricey salons and boutiques. This lane had a previous incarnation very much at odds with its present upscale image. Before the 1906 earthquake it was Morton St, lined with bordellos and known as one of the bawdiest dives in a city renowned for racy living. During the rebuilding, the city fathers endowed it with its hopeful new name and cleaned up its image to match. The 1949 **Circle Gallery** (☎ 982-2100), 140 Maiden Lane, is the only Frank Lloyd Wright building in the city and its spiral walkway marks it as Wright's practice run for his later Guggenheim Museum in New York City.

San Francisco's compact **Theater District** lies immediately southwest of the square, crumbling from there into the porn and prostitution quarters of the dismal Tenderloin. A few blocks north of Union Square, Burritt St is a tiny alley off Bush St, just a few steps west of Stockton. On the wall look for a plaque announcing that:

On approximately this spot, Miles Archer, partner of Sam Spade, was done in by Brigid O'Shaughnessy.

'Done in' fictionally, of course, in the pages of *The Maltese Falcon*.

CIVIC CENTER

The compact Civic Center area is a study in contrasts, where the city's architectural and cultural aspirations collide head on with its human problems. Separating City Hall and the Opera House from downtown are the grubby blocks of the **Tenderloin**, San Francisco's red-light district, and the city's pressing homeless problem has come to roost in Civic Center Plaza itself.

The 1906 disaster destroyed the earlier city hall which was replaced in 1915 with the present Beaux Arts-style **City Hall** (☎ 554-4000), at 400 Van Ness Ave. Modeled after St Peter's Basilica in Vatican City, the dome is actually higher than the US Capitol in Washington, DC. A major seismic retrofit is underway following the 1989 earthquake, and City Hall will be closed to the public for several years to come.

Across from City Hall, the **War Memorial Opera House** (☎ 864-3330), 301 Van Ness Ave, built in 1932, is the site for performances by the city's acclaimed opera and ballet companies. The formal peace treaty between the USA and Japan after WWII was signed here in 1951. Adjacent to it is the **Veteran's Building**, 401 Van Ness Ave, housing the Herbst Theater (☎ 392-4400). It's a near double to the

Opera House. The United Nations charter was signed here in 1945. Cross McAllister St to the 1986 **State Building**, that mirrors the curved frontage of **Louise M Davies Symphony Hall** (☎ 431-5400), one block south.

SOMA

SoMa, as the South of Market area is known, is a combination of office buildings spilling out of the Financial District, fancy condominiums popping up along the Embarcadero near the Bay Bridge, a busy tourist and convention precinct around

Yerba Buena Gardens, and the late night entertainment scene along Folsom St.

The **Yerba Buena Gardens** (☎ 541-0312), is the open-air public center of SoMa. The complex includes the **Center for the Arts** (☎ 978-2787), with galleries and short-term exhibits, and a theater for performances. The center is open Tuesday to Sunday, 11 am to 6 pm. Entry is $3/2.50. Linked to the gardens by a bridge across Howard St is the **George R Moscone Convention Center** (☎ 267-6400), the city's main exhibition area.

In 1995 the new **San Francisco**

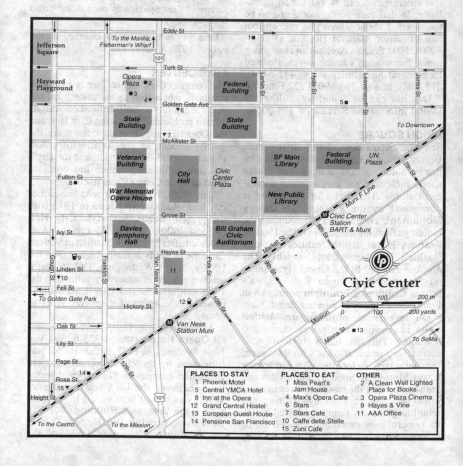

PLACES TO STAY
1 Phoenix Motel
5 Central YMCA Hotel
8 Inn at the Opera
12 Grand Central Hostel
13 European Guest House
14 Pensione San Francisco

PLACES TO EAT
1 Miss Pearl's
    Jam House
4 Max's Opera Cafe
6 Stars
7 Stars Cafe
10 Caffe delle Stelle
15 Zuni Cafe

OTHER
2 A Clean Well Lighted
    Place for Books
3 Opera Plaza Cinema
9 Hayes & Vine
11 AAA Office

Museum of Modern Art (SFMOMA, ☎ 357-4000), designed by Swiss architect Mario Botta, opened directly across from the Yerba Buena Gardens, and the city's modern art collection finally had a worthy home. The museum is at 151 3rd St and is open Tuesday to Sunday, 11 am to 6 pm; Thursday until 9 pm. Entry is $7/3.50.

The **Ansel Adams Center for Photography** (☎ 495-7000), 250 4th St, is dedicated to photography as art, with particular reference to Ansel Adams; it's open Tuesday to Sunday, 11 am to 5 pm. Entry is $4. The **Cartoon Art Museum** (☎ 227-8666), 814 Mission St, features constantly changing exhibits of cartoon art. It's open Wednesday to Friday from 11 am to 5 pm, Saturday from 10 am to 5 pm, and Sunday from 1 to 5 pm. Admission is $3.50.

The luxurious **Palace Hotel** opened in 1875 as the most opulent hotel in the city. Along the way, it killed its creator, William Ralston, who was driven to bankruptcy and a heart attack by financial pressures. It burned down in the post-earthquake fire in 1906 and was reopened in 1909, snazzier than ever. Afternoon tea in the leafy Garden Court is the place to contemplate the 1991 renovation which cost over $100 million. A drink in the Pied Piper Bar, with its huge 1909 Maxfield Parrish painting, *Pied Piper*, is another prime relaxing spot.

The USS *Jeremiah O'Brien* (☎ 441-3101), the sole surviving WWII Liberty Ship in complete and working order, is on display at Pier 32. It had an illustrious history including 11 voyages as part of the D-Day landings at Normandy. On board you can explore the crew area and bridge, and investigate the engine room. The ship is open weekdays from 9 am to 3 pm, weekends from 9 am to 4 pm. Entry is $5/2.

FINANCIAL DISTRICT

The city's tall buildings are densely concentrated in the blocks from Union Square to the Bay. This is the city's banking center, an important factor since this has been San Francisco's core business ever since banks started to appear in the 1850s to handle the state's gold rush fortunes. It's a frantically busy area during the day with taxis, power-dressing business people, and suicidal bike messengers all competing for street space. Come dark it's a different animal; apart from a handful of restaurants and bars, the district is serenely quiet.

Visiting the Financial District is essentially an architectural experience. The completion of the **Bank of America building** in 1969 ushered in a new era for San Francisco's previously low-rise skyline. Not only was the 52-story, 761-foot building at 555 California St much higher than any earlier building, but its red South Dakota granite construction looked very different from the city's consistent pale coloring.

The bank's founder, AP Giannini, established the Bank of Italy in 1904, focusing on small businesses and farmers in the Italian community. When disaster struck the city in 1906, he trucked out his bank's assets ahead of the advancing flames and as a result, his was the first bank back in business after the disaster and he never looked back. He formed the Bank of America in the '30s, and by 1948 it was the largest bank in the country.

San Francisco's highest building at 853 feet, the **Transamerica Pyramid**, 600 Montgomery St, was completed in 1972, and though it was initially reviled, it quickly became a modern symbol of the city. The Transamerica Center includes a half-acre stand of redwood trees in Redwood Plaza where lunchtime concerts take placeon Fridays from May through September.

After the Transamerica Pyramid, the cylindrical tower at **101 California St** is probably the most instantly recognizable of the city's tall buildings. The Gothic 1928 **Russ Building**, 253 Montgomery St, was the tallest in the city from its creation until 1964.

Other buildings of note in the district include the 1930 **Pacific Stock Exchange** at 301 Pine St, and the 1908 **Bank of California building** at 400 California St, fronted by Corinthian columns and housing the Museum of Money of the American West (☎ 765-0400) in its basement. The

CALIFORNIA

Emperor Norton

Emperor Norton I was born Joshua Abraham Norton in 1819 and came to San Francisco as a young man, where he made a fortune off the city's boomtown economy. In 1852 he lost everything in a business gamble and never recovered. After eight years of increasing poverty he seems to have snapped, at least in one key respect: he declared himself the Emperor of the United States, and within a month added the title Protector of Mexico.

Norton spent the next 20 years of his life becoming an icon and widely loved mascot of San Francisco, living an oddly dignified life and causing no one any harm. He never appeared without his uniform with its bulky epaulets, a plumed hat, and a sword at his hip. He issued his own scrip in 50¢, $5, and $10 denominations and though it became mainly a collector's item, it was good-naturedly accepted by many shopkeepers. Among the many decrees he made as emperor, such as that to dissolve the republican form of government in the USA, was his famous injunction against the use of the word 'Frisco':

COURTESY THE
BANCROFT LIBRARY

Whoever after due and proper warning shall be heard to utter the abominable word 'Frisco,' which has no linguistic or other warrant, shall be deemed guilty of a High Misdemeanor, and shall pay into the Imperial Treasury as penalty the sum of $25.

After his death in 1880, thousands attended his funeral. He now rests in Colma Cemetery under a prominent headstone unambiguously affirming his status in death, as in life, as 'Emperor of the United States & Protector of Mexico.' ■

Wells Fargo History Museum (☎ 396-2619), 420 Montgomery St, tells the story of Wells Fargo Bank, the company founded in 1852 to provide banking and stagecoach delivery services to miners and businesses throughout the West.

The waterfront **Embarcadero**, once the busiest area of the city, was killed first by the two Bay bridges, which ended the ferry boat era, and then by the death of the old-style wharves, superseded by the container ship era. Completed in 1898, the **Ferry Building** at the bottom of California and Market Sts, had its heyday in the 1920s and '30s up until the completion of the bridges.

Four skyscrapers mark the huge **Embarcadero Center** between Sacramento and Clay Sts, starting on Embarcadero at the Park Hyatt and Justin Herman Plaza, a popular lunch spot for Financial District suits and ending at Battery and the Old Federal Reserve Building. At the base of the four buildings (Embarcadero 1 to 4) is a mix of shops and restaurants, and a post office.

CHINATOWN

The most densely packed pocket of the city, and perhaps the most colorful, there's no missing Chinatown. There are no essential sights – no single place in Chinatown which any San Francisco visitor absolutely *must* see. However, it's a great place for casual wandering and for soaking up the atmosphere and stumbling across interesting little corners and alleys as you go. Packed with shops and restaurants, Grant Ave has had a colorful history from its inception as Calle de la Fundacion, the main street of a Mexican village of Yerba Buena. Renamed Dupont St, or Du Pon Gai to the Chinese, it became synonomous with brothels, gambling dives, opium dens, and brawling *tongs* (Chinese gangs). It was renamed after president and Civil WAr general Ulysses S Grant in the year of his death in 1885. Once you get off touristy Grant Ave look for Chinese apothecary shops and colorful overhanging balconies, and listen to the continuing background noise of the Chinese language which, linguists claim, is impossible to whisper.

The most colorful time to visit is during the Chinese New Year in late January/early February, with a parade and fireworks and other festivities, but the day-to-day bustle of Chinatown is reason enough to visit anytime.

Chinatown visits usually begin at the dragon-studded **Chinatown Gate** at the Bush St entrance to Grant Ave. The Taoist **Ching Chung Temple** (☎ 433-2623) at 532 Grant Ave is open daily. At the intersection with California St is **Old St Mary's Church** (☎ 986-4388); its 90-foot tower was the tallest building in the city when it was completed in 1854 and was the first Roman Catholic cathedral on the West Coast. **St Mary's Square**, off California St, is one of few large open spaces in Chinatown. When Chinatown was cleaned up in the late 19th century, the brothels, gambling dens, and bars from all over the area were concentrated here and then burned down in the aftermath of the 1906 earthquake.

Also of interest is the **Kong Chow Temple** (☎ 434-2513), above the post office at 855 Stockton St, which claims perhaps the oldest Chinese altar in the USA. The **Chinese Consolidated Benevolent Building**, at 843 Stockton St, looks even more temple-like and was the former home of the Six Companies, the Chinese organization that used to bring Chinese laborers to California and later fought for Chinese legal rights.

For a good idea of off-the-main-street Chinatown, duck into colorful **Waverly Place**, between Grant and Stockton, with its many open balconies and upstairs temples. **Ross Alley** is another picturesque lane; known at one time as Gau Leuie Sung Hong or Old Spanish Alley, it was wall-to-wall gambling dens and brothels in the late 1870s. This is a favorite of moviemakers, featured in films like *Big Trouble in Little China*. At 56 Ross Alley the signless **Golden Gate Cookie Company** (☎ 781-3956) turns out fortune cookies ('sexy' fortunes are their specialty).

Portsmouth Square, at Kearny and Washington Sts, is another open space in Chinatown. It was originally the plaza for the Mexican settlement of Yerba Buena, and its name comes from John B Montgomery's sloop, the *Portsmouth*. Montgomery arrived in 1846 to claim the city for the USA and a plaque commemorates that it was here that the Stars and Stripes was first raised in San Francisco.

A trio of museums provides cultural information on the Chinese community: the **Chinese Cultural Center** (☎ 986-1822) in the Holiday Inn at 750 Kearny St acroos from Portsmouth Square; the **Chinese Historical Society Museum** (☎ 391-1188) at 650 Commercial St; and the **Pacific Heritage Museum** (☎ 399-1124), 608 Commercial St.

NORTH BEACH

North Beach started as the city's Italian quarter and their heritage lives on in the restaurants, bars, and lively nightlife. The Beats took over in the '50s and added cafes, jazz clubs, and the City Lights Bookstore to the mix. Today it's one of the liveliest parts of the city after dark and a great place for a cheap meal, a cold beer, or a strong cup of coffee.

Start from the Transamerica Pyramid and stroll up Columbus Ave. The green **Columbus Tower** of 1905 at the corner of Kearny St was bought and restored by filmmaker Francis Ford Coppola in 1970. The block from Pacific Ave to Broadway can lay claim to being the literary heart of the city. A coffee at **Vesuvio Cafe** is sure to spark any literary hound into finding their way to the shelves of **City Lights Bookstore**, just across Jack Kerouac St. City Lights was founded in 1953 by poet Lawrence Ferlinghetti, who still owns it, and has always been a center for cutting edge books and poetry. At the junction of Columbus, Broadway, and Grant Sts there's another historic San Francisco cultural site. The **Condor Bistro** is a very bland replacement for the old Condor Club where, as a plaque solemnly announces, silicon-enhanced Carol Doda first went topless on June 19, 1964 and bottomless on September 3, 1969.

The **Museum of North Beach** (☎ 391-6210), 1435 Stockton St, in the Eureka Bank mezzanine, has photographs and memorabilia tracing the history of this colorful area in the late-19th and early-20th centuries.

The 1924 **Sts Peter & Paul Church** (☎ 421-0809), 666 Filbert St, overlooks Washington Square. It's the largest Catholic church in San Francisco and each October the Santa Maria del Lume (patron saint of fishermen) procession makes its way down Columbus Ave to Fisherman's Wharf to bless the fishing fleet.

Atop Telegraph Hill the 210-foot **Coit Tower** is one of San Francisco's prime landmarks. It was built in 1934, financed by San Francisco eccentric Lillie Hitchcock Coit. A rebel against strait-laced Victorianism, Ms Coit often dressed as a man to gamble in North Beach, wore short skirts to go ice skating, sneaked away on a men's camping trip, and harbored a life-long passion for a good fire. In 1863 the 15-year-old Lillie was adopted as the mascot of the Knickerbocker Hose Company No 5 and it's said she 'rarely missed a blaze.'

Inside the tower is a superb series of Rivera-style murals of San Franciscans at work painted by 25 local artists as part of a '30s WPA project. The tower (☎ 362-0808) is open daily from 10 am to 7:30 pm. The ride to the top costs $3. If you're on foot,

take the wooden Filbert Steps which lead down past the picturesque cottages of Darrell Place and Napier Lane to Levi's Plaza and the Embarcadero.

RUSSIAN HILL
West of North Beach are the roller-coaster streets of Russian Hill, with some of the city's prime real estate as well as the famous **Lombard St** switchback. This stretch of street, the 1000 block, wiggles down the hillside to win the accolade of 'the world's crookedest street,' notching up ten turns as it goes. At one time, the crooked block was just as straight as any other, but with a 27% incline it was too steep for cars to manage, so in 1922 the curves were added. It's not only a spectacular slalom but also a pretty one when the whole block is dense with hydrangea blooms.

The top of Russian Hill is so steep that not all the roads manage to surmount it, making way for pocket-size patches of green – affording some incredible views of the city below – like **Ina Coolbrith Park** on Taylor and steep stairways like **Macondray Lane** between Leavenworth and Taylor, the Barbary Lane of Armistead Maupin's *Tales of the City*. Another lane of literary interest is Russell Place where, at No 29, Jack Kerouac drafted *On the Road* and several other works while living with Neal and Carolyn Cassady in 1952.

At 800 Chestnut St, the **San Francisco Art Institute** (☎ 771-7020) is renowned for its fine Diego Rivera Gallery with a wonderful example of the Mexican artist's famous murals from 1931. The Institute's cloisters and courtyards date from 1926 with a 1970 addition. There is a cafe, and fine views over the Bay from the terraces. The galleries are open Tuesday to Saturday, 10 am to 5 pm.

For Russian Hill hangouts and stores head to **Polk St** which slopes down to Ghiradelli Square.

NOB HILL
Nob Hill is a classy district perched atop one of the city's famous hills. It's been that

Cable Cars

The Transamerica Pyramid and the Golden Gate Bridge make fine city symbols but San Francisco has another much older icon, the beloved cable car. Cable cars were conceived by English mining engineer Andrew Hallidie as a replacement for the horse-driven trams that found the city's steep streets difficult and dangerous.

From Hallidie's first experimental line on Clay St in 1873, cable cars quickly caught on and by 1890 there were eight operators, 500 cable cars, and a route network of over 100 miles. By the turn of the century, the system was already past its heyday and shrinking in the face of newfangled electric streetcars. The 1906 earthquake was a disaster for the cable car system, but the death knell sounded in January 1947 when the mayor announced the last lines would be replaced by bus services. He hadn't reckoned with Friedel Klussmann's 'Citizens Committee to Save the Cable Cars,' and a groundswell of public support which reprieved the Powell St lines.

San Franciscans may have saved the system from politicians and accountants but saving it from old age became a new problem as derailments and runaways became increasingly frequent occurrences. In 1979, a six-month shutdown for a million dollars' worth of repairs was just a Band-aid solution and in 1982 the system was finally closed for a $60 million complete overhaul. The rebuilt system, which reopened in 1984, consists of 40 cars on three lines covering a total of 12 miles. That may be a pale shadow of its heyday but the cable cars are an enormously popular tourist attraction and much loved by San Franciscans. ■

way ever since the arrival of cable cars in the 1870s made the 338-foot summit accessible. The elite moved in and promptly built the most opulent mansions in the city. Mark Hopkins and Collis P Huntington were the builders who, with financiers Charles Crocker and Leland Stanford, made fortunes from the Central Pacific Railroad. Stanford, Huntington, and Hopkins have given their names to Nob Hill hotels – The Huntington, Mark Hopkins, and Stanford Court. Crocker's name is applied to a bank, and Stanford went on to become the Governor of California and found Stanford University. The Fairmont was built by the daughter of silver magnate James Grantham Fair.

Besides hotels, there's **Grace Cathedral** (☎ 776-6611), 1051 Taylor St. The bronze doors are casts of Ghiberti's Gates of Paradise in the Baptistry in Florence, Italy and the magnificent Rose Window was made in Chartres, France in 1964. Also of note is the Keith Haring Altarpiece, *The Life of Christ*, dedicated in 1995 by the AIDS Memorial Chapel Project, and meditational labyrinths, copies of those found in Chartres, both inside and outside.

The **Cable Car Barn & Museum** (☎ 474-1887), 1201 Mason St, is the power plant that tows all the cable cars, it's the garage where the cable cars park at night, and it's a museum displaying, among other things, inventor Andrew Hallidie's prototype.

FISHERMAN'S WHARF

All serious guides to San Francisco are required by city ordinance to denounce Fisherman's Wharf as a tasteless, tacky tourist trap. Well it is, but it's certainly fun. The fishermen have almost all disappeared;

now this tourist epicenter is packed with shopping centers, hokey museums, and countless accommodations.

If there's a single focus for the Fisherman's Wharf tourist crush, it's undoubtedly **Pier 39**, a remodeled working pier with a host of restaurants, a huge collection of shops appealing to every conceivable touristic buying impulse, a pretty Venetian carousel for the kids, and the Center Stage for street entertainers. Around 1990, California **sea lions** began to haul out on a section of the walkways beside Pier 39. Today the takeover has been complete, and

hundreds of sea lions bask in the sun, woofing noisily.

There are other shopping centers recycled from factories and industrial zones in the area: Ghirardelli Square, once home to its namesake San Francisco chocolatier (there are still two Ghirardelli shops in the square); and the Cannery, the old Del Monte fruit canning factory. On the 3rd floor of the Cannery, the **Museum of the City of San Francisco** (☎ 928-0289) tells the story of the city with, hardly surprisingly, particular emphasis on the earthquakes of 1906 and 1989. It's open

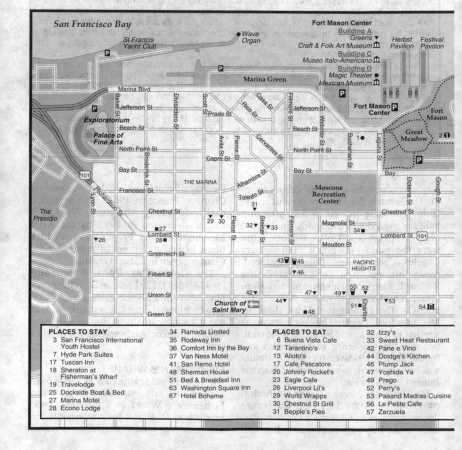

PLACES TO STAY
3 San Francisco International Youth Hostel
7 Hyde Park Suites
17 Tuscan Inn
18 Sheraton at Fisherman's Wharf
19 Travelodge
25 Dockside Boat & Bed
27 Marina Motel
28 Econo Lodge
34 Ramada Limited
35 Rodeway Inn
36 Comfort Inn by the Bay
37 Van Ness Motel
41 San Remo Hotel
48 Sherman House
51 Bed & Breakfast Inn
63 Washington Square Inn
67 Hotel Boheme

PLACES TO EAT
6 Buena Vista Cafe
12 Tarantino's
13 Alioto's
17 Cafe Pescatore
20 Johnny Rocket's
23 Eagle Cafe
25 Liverpool Lil's
29 World Wrapps
30 Chestnut St Grill
31 Bepple's Pies
32 Izzy's
33 Sweet Heat Restaurant
42 Pane e Vino
44 Doidge's Kitchen
46 Plump Jack
47 Yoshida Ya
49 Prego
52 Perry's
53 Pasand Madras Cuisine
56 Le Petite Cafe
57 Zarzuela

Wednesday to Sunday from 10 am to 4 pm and is free.

If carnival attractions are your thing, you can savor the delights of the **Wax Museum** (☎ 800-439-4305), the **Medieval Dungeon**, where you can thrill to repellent ancient tortures, or the **Ripley's Believe It or Not! Museum** (☎ 771-6188), all lined up along Jefferson St.

Despite all its tackiness, Fisherman's Wharf does host a number of legitimate attractions, especially for maritime history buffs. Overlooking Aquatic Park, the **San Francisco National Maritime Museum**

(☎ 556-8177) recounts the Bay Area's nautical history with a fine collection of ship models. It's open daily from 10 am to 5 pm, and entry is free. Five classic ships are moored at the **Hyde St Historic Ships Pier** (☎ 556-3002) including the *Balclutha*, an 1886 iron hull square-rigger. The collection is open May to mid-September from 10 am to 6 pm and mid-September to April from 9:30 am to 5 pm. Entry is $2/1.

The USS *Pampanito* (☎ 929-0202) at Pier 45 is a WWII US Navy submarine built in 1943. It made six Pacific patrols during the last years of the war and sunk six

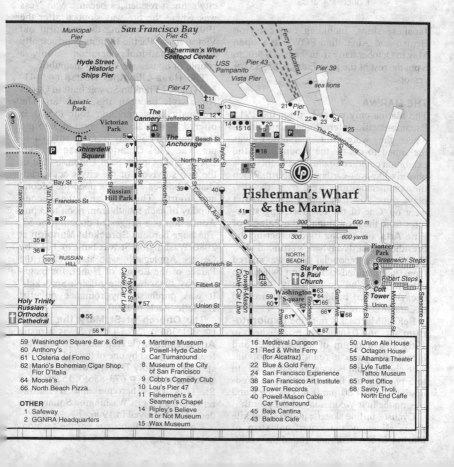

59 Washington Square Bar & Grill	4 Maritime Museum	16 Medieval Dungeon
60 Anthony's	5 Powell-Hyde Cable	21 Red & White Ferry
61 L'Osteria del Forno	Car Turnaround	(for Alcatraz)
62 Mario's Bohemian Cigar Shop,	7 Museum of the City	22 Blue & Gold Ferry
Fior D'Italia	of San Francisco	24 San Francisco Experience
64 Moose's	9 Cobb's Comedy Club	38 San Francisco Art Institute
66 North Beach Pizza	10 Lou's Pier 47	39 Tower Records
	11 Fishermen's &	40 Powell-Mason Cable
OTHER	Seamen's Chapel	Car Turnaround
1 Safeway	14 Ripley's Believe	45 Baja Cantina
2 GGNRA Headquarters	It or Not Museum	43 Balboa Cafe
	15 Wax Museum	

50 Union Ale House
54 Octagon House
55 Alhambra Theater
58 Lyle Tuttle
Tattoo Museum
65 Post Office
68 Savoy Tivoli,
North End Caffe

Sleeping sea lions captivate hundreds of tourists at Pier 39.

Japanese ships, including two carrying British and Australian POWs. It's open May to October daily from 9 am to 8 pm; to 6 pm the rest of the year. Entry is $5, $3 for seniors.

THE MARINA
The Marina only popped up for the 1915 Panama-Pacific International Exposition, when the waterfront marshland was reclaimed to create the grounds for the exhibition commemorating San Francisco's phoenix-like post-earthquake rebirth. When the commemorations were over, the displays came down and the Marina district went up. One of the few surviving structures from the Exposition is the **Palace of Fine Arts**, off Marina Blvd bordering the Presidio. Bernard Maybeck's artificial classical ruin was so popular that it was spared from its intended demolition when the exhibition closed. In the early '60s, the decaying stucco building was resurrected in durable concrete.

Behind Maybeck's ruin, the **Exploratorium** (☎ 561-0360) was established in 1969 as a museum of art, science, and human perception; it's enormously popular with children and is open daily from 10 am to 5 pm, to 6 pm in summer and on Wednesdays until 9:30 pm. Entry is $9/5 and free on the first Wednesday of the month.

Cyclists, in-line skaters, joggers, and kite flyers all enjoy the waterfront strip of **Marina Green**. Continue round the yachting marina to find the curious **Wave Organ** at the tip of the breakwater.

Adjoining the Aquatic Park, **Fort Mason** (☎ 979-3010) was a Spanish and then US military fort. Most of the buildings were handed over for civilian use in the 1970s and now house a colorful mix of galleries, museums, theaters, and the city's finest vegetarian restaurant, Greens (see Places to Eat).

PACIFIC HEIGHTS
This wealthy hilltop area has many of the city's finest residences because Van·Ness was where the fire was stopped after the 1906 quake. Inspecting the beautiful old Victorians of Pacific Heights is principally a wander-and-look operation – only a couple of houses are open to the public.

The **Haas-Lilienthal House** (☎ 441-3004), 2007 Franklin St, was built in Queen Anne style between 1882 and '86. The tediously slow one-hour tour ($5/3) is offered Wednesday from noon to 3:15 pm (last tour) and Sunday from 11 am to 4:15 pm. The 1861 **Octagon House** (☎ 441-7512), 2645 Gough St at Union, is one of the two survivors of the city's octagonal-shaped houses craze. It's open the second and fourth Thursday and the second Sunday of each month from noon to 3 pm. Admission is a suggested donation of $3. The huge baroque **Spreckels Mansion** at 2080 Washington St was built in 1912 by George Applegarth, who also created the Palace of the Legion of Honor, for mega-wealthy sugar magnate Adolph Spreckels. It was purchased by romance novelist Danielle Steele in 1990.

The **Church of St Mary the Virgin** (☎ 921-3665), 2325 Union St, is a rustic Arts & Crafts-style creation of 1891 with a fountain still fed by one of the old farmland springs. The **Holy Trinity Russian Orthodox Cathedral** (☎ 673-8565), 1520 Green St, is a 1909 baroque and Byzantine replacement for its Washington Square predecessor destroyed in 1906.

Union and Fillmore Sts are the fashionable shopping and restaurant enclaves.

JAPANTOWN

Just to the south of Fillmore St is the cultural center of Japantown.

There have been Japanese in San Francisco since the 1860s and today only a tiny portion of them live in the compact Japantown area. Known as Nihonmachi in Japanese, the area only developed after the 1906 earthquake but the WWII internment of Japanese and Japanese-Americans was a major setback. Many former residents were unable to reclaim their homes after the war.

The three shopping plazas of the **Japan Center** opened in 1968 around Peace Plaza with its five-story Peace Pagoda, and are packed with Japanese restaurants and shops.

Japanese-style communal baths come to San Francisco at the **Kabuki Hot Spring** (☎ 922-6000), 1750 Geary Blvd, open weekdays from 10 am to 10 pm and weekends from 9 am to 10 pm. They're open to men Monday, Tuesday, Thursday, and Saturday and to women Wednesday, Friday, and Sunday. You can enjoy the baths, sauna, steam room, and traditional Amma/Shiatsu massage; call ☎ 922-6002 for massage appointments.

St Mary's Cathedral (☎ 567-2020), 1111 Gough St at Geary Blvd, a couple of blocks east of Fillmore St is the city's third St Mary's and is a slightly more modern in its architecture.

HAIGHT-ASHBURY

Just east of Golden Gate Park the Haight-Ashbury area, locally known simply as 'the Haight,' is chiefly famed as the epicenter of San Francisco's brief fling as the city of love and home of flower power in 1966-67.

There was no single event that shaped the scene, but several forces seem to have been catalysts. In 1964, Ken Kesey took his acid-drenched voyage across the USA, chronicled by Tom Wolfe in *The Electric Kool-Aid Acid Test*. The Grateful Dead (then called The Warlocks) were establishing the era's sound, and promotion genius Bill Graham 'dropped out' to produce theater with the politically radical San Francisco Mime Troupe. Other revolutionaries, like the anarchist Diggers, maintained that money, like church and state, was dead, and proved their point by providing meals ('free because it's yours') at their famous Digger Feeds. By 1966 the area was attracting hundreds of new pilgrims a day. In January of that year Kesey's psychedelic Trips Festival – anticipating the Human Be-In, one year later – laid the path for the Summer of Love.

It proved to be a brief, if glowing, heyday. By late '67 drug overdoses and incidences of violence were increasing among the hippies, gawkers, media, and police. The Haight is still a colorful area, but despite the throngs of tie-dyed stragglers, the Summer of Love is just a dreamlike memory. The street sign at the corner of Haight and Ashbury is about the only icon of the times that remains unchanged, but the Haight is still a great place to wander. Start at the Golden Gate Park end, wander up Haight St, dive into a few strange shops, stop for a cheap meal and a cup of strong coffee – that's what it's all about. Deadheads should pass by **710 Ashbury St**, the onetime communal home of the Grateful Dead.

East of Haight-Ashbury, the **Lower Haight** is a colorful few blocks of grungy clubs and bars, and a few blocks south, tiny **Cole Valley** is a more upscale version with cafes, restaurants, and shops.

THE CASTRO & NOE VALLEY

The compact Castro is the gay center of San Francisco, and is one of the city's best neighborhoods for strolling, watching the streetlife, stopping for a coffee, shopping, getting a body piercing, or having a leisurely lunch. The magnificent **Castro Theater** (see Entertainment) is the highlight of Castro St and the center for the annual Gay & Lesbian Film Festival. **Harvey Milk Plaza**, at the Muni station at the intersection of Market and Castro, is dedicated to the unofficial 'mayor of Castro,' killed along with Mayor Moscone in 1978.

The Castro's magnificent memorial to the swath AIDS has cut through the gay community is the AIDS Memorial Quilt. Each of the over 25,000 individually crafted, six-feet by three-feet panels commemorates an AIDS victim. The **Names Project Gallery** (☎ 863-1966) at 2362 Market St recounts the quilt's ongoing creation and its travels, most remarkably a display of panels in Washington, DC seen by over half a million people.

Continue south along Castro or Noe Sts and you'll come to **Noe Valley**, another of San Francisco's wonderful small neighborhoods. The mix of Victorian homes, upscale restaurants and coffeehouses, and eclectic shops gives it a villagey feel; 24th St is the main drag.

THE MISSION

The Mission is one of the oldest parts of the city, a Spanish-speaking enclave, and a great place for a cheap meal. The heart of the district stretches east-west, between Dolores and South Van Ness, and north-south, between 16th and 25th Sts. Valencia

---

Gay San Francisco

From its earliest days as a seaport, through the riotous Gold Rush years to the present, San Francisco has been a liberal city with a tradition of tolerance for alternative lifestyles. It was here, appropriately enough, that a gay community began to form during WWII and its aftermath. San Francisco served as a gateway to the Pacific, with arriving and departing naval fleets mooring at the harbor. When the armed forces conducted purges and dishonorably discharged scores of gay servicemen, it was in San Francisco that they found themselves. Unwilling to head home, many stayed, forming the foundation of the world's largest and strongest gay community.

In the early '50s, a chapter of the Mattachine Society, the first serious homosexual rights organization in the USA, sprang up in San Francisco, and in 1955 the Daughters of Bilitis (DOB), the nation's first lesbian organization, was founded in San Francisco. These were the beginnings of what is known as the homophile movement, a non-confrontational, non-conformist gay movement that distanced itself from bar culture.

During the 1959 mayoral campaign, challenger Russell Wolden accused incumbent mayor George Christopher of turning San Francisco into 'the national headquarters of the organized homosexuals in the United States.' Christopher was reelected, but was not about to be accused of being soft on queers. He responded with a massive police crackdown of gay male cruising areas, raids which resulted in a public blacklist of gay citizens.

Resistance to this persecution did not come out of the homophile movement but in the bars, and one in particular, the Black Cat, dubbed by Allen Ginsberg as 'the greatest gay bar in America.' Jose Sarria, a drag performer at the Black Cat, ran for city supervisor in 1961, becoming the first openly gay person to run for public office in the USA.

The age of tolerance had not yet arrived, however. In 1965 a dance sponsored by the Council on Religion & the Homosexual was raided by the police, and everyone in attendance was arrested and photographed. The city was outraged and even the media denounced the behavior of the police. This event helped to turn the tide in the city's perception of the gay community. The crackdown on gay bars stopped, and a gay person was appointed to sit on the police community relations board.

With the 1977 election of gay activist Harvey Milk to the Board of Supervisors, recognition of the gay rights movement reached a new peak, but the euphoria was to be short-lived. The following year, Milk and Mayor George Moscone were assassinated by Dan White, an avowedly anti-gay former police officer.

Their deaths marked the beginning of the end of the heyday, the opulence of which further faded when the first cases of AIDS – at the time known as GRID, Gay-Related Immune Deficiency – were reported in San Francisco in 1981. From these events a new era of information and protection was born. The rainbow banners and lavender triangles, signifying the community's pride and resilience, are as common today as they were 20 years ago but the extravagance of the '70s now resurfaces mainly at the Castro and Folsom St Fairs and the annual Gay & Lesbian Freedom Day parade. ■

CALIFORNIA

The Castro & the Mission

0   200   400 m
0   200   400 yards

PLACES TO STAY
4 Perramont Hotel
5 Twin Peaks Hotel
10 Beck's Motor Lodge
32 Dolores Park Inn
38 Black Stallion B&B

PLACES TO EAT
1 Woodward's Garden
6 Amazing Grace
8 La Mediterranee
11 Pastaio

12 Cafe Picaro
13 Ti Couz
17 Pozole
19 Cafe Macondo
21 Truly Mediterranean
22 Puerto Alegre
23 Taquería La Cumbre
24 Cafe Istanbul
34 Orphan Andy's
34 Hot 'n' Hunky
35 Patio Cafe
39 La Rondalla

BARS & CAFES
2 Jumpin' Java
3 Cafe du Nord
7 Red Dora's Bearded Lady
   Cafe & Gallery
9 Cafe Flore
15 The Detour
16 The Cafe,
   The Gauntlet
25 Esta Noche
26 Castro Station
27 Phoenix Club

30 Twin Peaks Tavern
33 Elbo Room

OTHER
14 Names Project Gallery
18 Josie's Cabaret & Juice Joint
20 The Roxie
28 A Different Light Bookstore
29 Castro Theater
36 Miguel Hidalgo Statue
37 Women's Building, Dovre Club

and Mission are the two main streets for shops and restaurants.

The district takes its name from the **Mission Dolores** (☎ 621-8203) at Dolores and 16th Sts, the sixth mission to be founded by Father Junipero Serra for the Spanish. Its site was consecrated on June 29, 1776 and a temporary structure was erected, so this oldest building in San Francisco can claim to be five days older than the USA. The permanent building was constructed in 1782 by Franciscan monks, with Native American labor. Today the humble mission building is overshadowed by the adjoining basilica, built in 1913. The mis-

sion is open daily from 9 am to 4 pm, and admission is $1. **Dolores Park**, a couple of blocks south, is a popular spot on sunny days.

The other prime Mission attraction is its hundreds of colorful **murals**, depicting everything from San Francisco's labor history to Central American independence struggles, the women's movement, and local streetlife. One of the most amazing examples of mural art is on the **Women's Building** at 3543 18th St between Valencia and Guerrero where the paintings of heroic or oppressed women swirl dramatically from the sidewalk to the very top of the building. Narrow **Balmy Alley** between Treat and Harrison off 24th St, is lined from end to end with murals.

GOLDEN GATE PARK

San Francisco's biggest park stretches almost halfway across the six-mile-wide peninsula. An 1870 competition to design the park was won by 24-year-old William Hammond Hall, who devised a way to reclaim the windswept sand dunes. In 1871 he commenced the task of turning 1017 acres of dunes into the largest developed park in the world, and by the 1880s the park had become the city's most popular attraction. John McLaren took over the park's management 1887 and administered the park for the next 56 years, until he died at the age of 97. Park information (☎ 666-7200) is available from McLaren Lodge at the entrance to the park.

The **Conservatory of Flowers** (☎ 666-7200), the oldest building in the park, was brought from Ireland for a millionaire's estate, but the millionaire died before it could be built and it went up instead in Golden Gate Park in 1878. It houses a steamy collection of tropical flora. It's open daily from 9 am to 5 pm and entry is $2.50.

The **California Academy of Sciences** (☎ 750-7145) is a large natural history museum with a variety of child-pleasing exhibits including the Steinhart Aquarium and the Morrison Planetarium. It's open daily from 10 am to 5 pm (9 am to 6 pm from July 4 to Labor Day) and entry is $7/4.

The **MH de Young Memorial Museum** (☎ 863-3330) has a fine collection of American art as well as exhibits from Africa, Oceania, and the Americas. The adjacent **Asian Art Museum** (☎ 668-8921) houses the Avery Brundage Collection and other superb art from the Middle East, the Indian subcontinent, Southeast Asia, Tibet, China, Korea, and Japan. Both are open Tuesday to Sunday from 10 am to 5 pm and entry is $5/2.

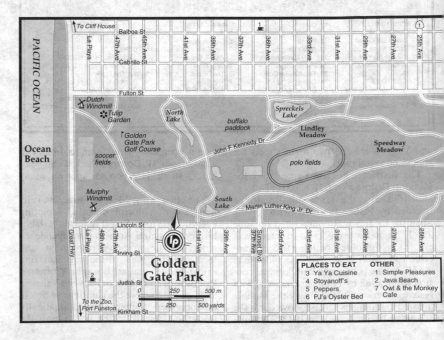

PLACES TO EAT	OTHER
3 Ya Ya Cuisine	1 Simple Pleasures
4 Stoyanoff's	2 Java Beach
5 Peppers	7 Owl & the Monkey
6 PJ's Oyster Bed	Cafe

The popular **Japanese Tea Garden** (☎ 666-7200) features a pagoda, gates, bridges, a variety of statues, and a nice little tea house where you can enjoy green tea and fortune cookies for $2. It's claimed fortune cookies were actually invented here, back in 1909. The gardens are open daily in summer from 9 am to 6:30 pm and in winter from 8:30 am to 6 pm. Entry is $2/1.

The **Strybing Arboretum & Botanical Gardens** (☎ 661-1316) encompasses a number of smaller gardens within its 70 acres, including the Garden of Fragrance, the California Collection of Native Plants, and the Japanese Moon-Viewing Garden. Free tours of the Arboretum take place every day.

The park is packed with sporting facilities including 7½ miles of bicycle trails, many miles of jogging trails, 12 miles of horse riding trails, an archery range, baseball and softball diamonds, fly-casting pools, a cramped nine-hole golf course,

lawn bowling greens, horseshoe pitching and petanque courts, four soccer fields, and 21 tennis courts. Rowboats, pedal boats, and electric boats can be rented (☎ 752-0347) on Stow Lake for around $10 to $13 an hour. See Activities to find out where to rent bicycles and in-line skates. On Sundays some roads in the park are closed to traffic, allowing sports enthusiasts to buzz around.

THE PRESIDIO

The Presidio has had a long military history. In the Spanish era it was established in 1776 as the site of the first fort, or presidio, and was linked with the religious center of Mission Dolores, three miles to the south, by the Divisadero; the modern street follows that old route. Under American rule, Fort Point was built at the start of the 1861-65 Civil War to guard the entrance to the Bay, but never saw battle or cannon fire and was abandoned in 1900. The Presidio's military role ends in 1996 with the comple-

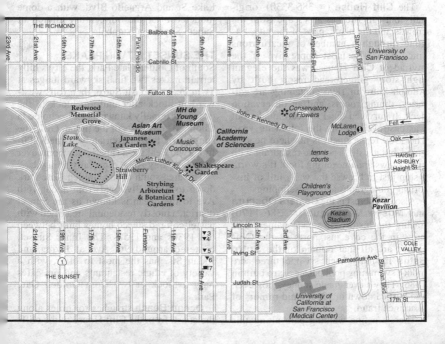

tion of a three-year changeover to a National Park.

Housed in a Civil War-era hospital building, the **Presidio Museum** (☎ 556-0865), at Funston Ave and Lincoln Blvd, documents the history of California and the West Coast with a military emphasis. Along the ocean side of the peninsula is **Baker Beach**, the most picturesque of the city's beaches with craggy rock formations backed up against cliffs. Due to the cold water and currents, it's not much of a swimming beach, but it is popular with sunbathers, with or without the swimsuit.

THE RICHMOND
Bordered by the green park land of the Presidio to the north and Golden Gate Park to the south, the uniform rectangles of the Richmond district stretch all the way to the ocean. The restaurants and bookshops along busy Clement St make up the heart of the area, and also the heart of New Chinatown.

The **Cliff House** (☎ 386-3330), originally built in 1863 as an escape from the crowds and the hectic pace of the city, has gone through a number of incarnations since then. The most impressive of the myriad of Cliff Houses was the elegant eight-story gingerbread resort built by Adolph Sutro in 1896 containing art galleries, dining rooms, and an observation deck. It survived the 1906 earthquake but was destroyed by fire the following year. The 1909 replacement is nowhere near as grand, but it's still a popular restaurant with great views and unexciting food. It's worth a stop just to browse the walls full of historical photographs and newsclippings.

Also of interest is the **Camera Obscura** and **Musée Mécanique** (☎ 386-1170) tracing the history of arcade games. The ruins in the cove just north of the Cliff House are all that remain of the **Sutro Baths**, the magnificent six-pool three-acre indoor swimming pool palace Sutro built in 1886. They never made money, however, and burned down in 1966, amid rumors of insurance fraud.

There's a fine walking path along this surprisingly rugged stretch of coast from the Cliff House to Lands End where there are terrific views across the Golden Gate. It starts by the remains of Sutro Baths and passes through **Lincoln Park**, which was established by Golden Gate park-keeper John McLaren. Within the park is the **California Palace of the Legion of Honor** (☎ 863-3330), one of San Francisco's premier art museums, with a world-class collection of medieval to 20th-century European art. It was originally designed for the 1915 Panama-Pacific Exposition as a replica of the Palais de la Légion d'Honneur in Paris, and Alma Spreckels hired architect George Applegarth to erect a permanent version. It's open Tuesday to Sunday from 10 am to 5 pm; entry is $6, children are free.

Two interesting churches are in the area: the Russian Orthodox **Holy Virgin Cathedral** (☎ 221-3255), 6210 Geary Blvd, with its golden onion domes, and the 1925 Jewish **Temple Emanu-El** (☎ 751-2535), Lake St and Arguello Blvd, with a dome modeled after the 6th-century church of Sancta Sophia in Istanbul.

THE SUNSET & TWIN PEAKS
South of Golden Gate Park, the city's hilly terrain makes two final skyward lunges at Twin Peaks and Mt Sutro, then rolls westward in block after uniform block to the ocean. Originally known as El Pecho de la Chola, 'The Breasts of the Indian Girl,' the summit of the appropriately named 900-foot Twin Peaks is a superb viewpoint over the whole Bay Area, especially at night.

The area south of the Golden Gate Park down to Sloat Blvd and from about 16th Ave to the ocean is known as the Sunset district, a mostly residential area filled with pastel-colored stucco homes built between the 1930s and 1950s. The Inner Sunset, centered around 9th Ave at Irving and Judah Sts, has the most to offer, with a variety of ethnic restaurants and fun cafes only a block or two from Golden Gate Park.

Ocean Beach stretches for miles along the coast, from the Cliff House to the cliffs

TONY WHEELER

Jaywalker's last glance

TONY WHEELER

It's not an ashtray, it's SFMOMA!

TONY WHEELER

Vesuvio, where the Beats go on

TONY WHEELER

Public art in the Mission

Mural by Juana Alicia, *Alto Al Fuego/Cease Fire*, ©1988.

TONY WHEELER

North Beach at night

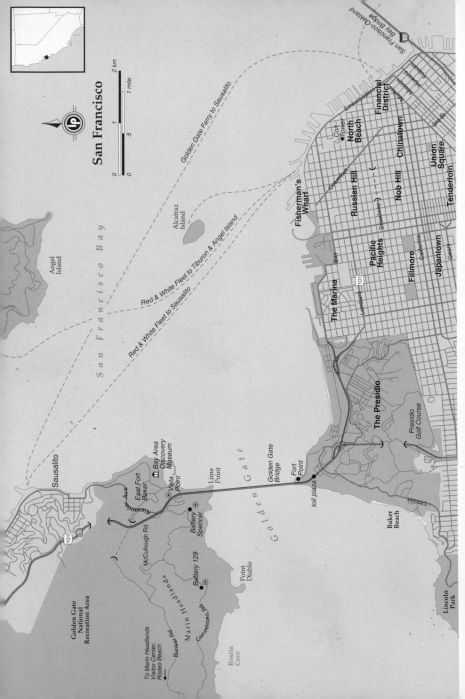

TONY WHEELER
Self expression in 'Bezerkeley'

TONY WHEELER
Marin mailboxes, Muir Beach

TONY WHEELER
Point Reyes Lighthouse

TONY WHEELER
Carmel Mission

TONY WHEELER
Old St Hilary's Church, Tiburon

of Fort Funston. On sunny days you'll find a classic California beach scene, packed with sunbathers, surfers, and picnickers. Unfortunately, sunny days are few and far between.

The **San Francisco Zoo** (☎ 753-7061), Sloat Blvd and 45th Ave, is open daily from 10 am to 5 pm. Entry is $7/3, and free on the first Wednesday of the month. A mile south, **Fort Funston** is a beautiful windswept area of cliffs, trails, and beach and a great place to spend an afternoon hang-gliding or, more likely, watching the hang-gliders float above the cliffs.

THE BAY

The San Francisco Bay is the largest on the California coast, stretching about 60 miles in length and up to 12 miles in width. It's fed by the Sacramento and San Joaquin Rivers, mingling with the sea through the Golden Gate. It is, however, very shallow, averaging only six to 10 feet in depth at low tide!

Commenced in January 1933 and opened in May 1937, the beautiful **Golden Gate Bridge** (☎ 921-5858) links San Francisco with Marin County and, despite competition from modern constructions like the Transamerica Pyramid, remains the symbol of the city. The bridge, designed by Joseph B Strauss who built over 400 bridges in his career, is nearly two miles in length with a main span of 4200 feet. At the time of its completion, it was the longest suspension bridge in the world. Its name comes from the Golden Gate entrance to the harbor, but could just as easily have come from the 'international orange' paint scheme. Painting the bridge is a never-ending job and a team of 25 painters add another 1000 golden gallons every week. A prime starting point for a bridge inspection is the Fort Point Lookout (☎ 556-1693), on Marine Drive at the southern end of the bridge. On weekends pedestrians can walk the bridge on the city side, while bicyclists zoom along on the ocean side. During the week, all merge on the city side. Cars pay a $3 toll for southbound travel (Marin to San Francisco).

Longer and older, but less picturesque, the **Bay Bridge** was built between April 1933 and November 1936 and is just over six miles long. The 1989 earthquake revealed that it was not 100% earthquake proof when a 50-foot top deck piece of the Yerba Buena-Oakland section slumped on to the lower deck, killing a motorist. There's a $1 toll for westbound travel

From 1933 to 1963 the rocky island in the middle of San Francisco Bay was the most famous prison in the USA. The 12-acre **Alcatraz**, also known as 'the Rock,' was escape-proof, and though several inmates got themselves off the island, none were known to reach land alive. It's only 1½ miles from the island to the mainland but they're 1½ very cold miles and swept by the Bay's often ferocious currents, not to mention the occasional shark. After its closure, the island was more or less forgotten for six years and then taken over by Native Americans who conducted a protest sit-in from 1969 to 1971. Red & White Ferries (☎ 546-2896 for information, 546-2700 for tickets) runs to the island from Pier 41 and tickets must be booked in advance. Tickets can also be booked through Ticketron (☎ 392-7469). The tour points out the cells occupied by famous residents like Al Capone, 'Machine Gun' Kelly, and Robert Stroud, the 'birdman of Alcatraz.'

ACTIVITIES

San Franciscans are an energetic lot and there are plenty of opportunities to burn calories even within the city limits.

Bicycling

The mountain bike *was* invented in Marin County, and Golden Gate Park and the Presidio have great cycling potential. You can bike across the Golden Gate Bridge to the Headlands or transport your bike up to Mt Tam, the Bay Area's supreme mountain biking challenge (see the San Francisco Bay Area chapter). Around the city there are 'bike route' signs pointing the way to different parks. The routes usually manage to avoid the most suicidal of hills. If you're under 18 it's the law to wear a helmet, and

it's the law for all to have a light when pedalling at night. And of course, always carry a good lock.

For rentals, try the Avenue Cyclery (☎ 387-3155), 756 Stanyan St, right by Golden Gate Park in the Haight-Ashbury. Nearby is the Start to Finish Biking Shop (☎ 221-7211), 672 Stanyan St, and there are two other Start to Finish shops: at 2530 Lombard St (☎ 202-9830) in the Marina district, and at 599 2nd St at Brannan (☎ 243-8812) in SoMa. American Bicycle Rental (☎ 931-0234), 2715 Hyde St, is at Fisherman's Wharf.

Golf
There are three public golf courses in San Francisco: Harding Park (☎ 664-4690) at Harding and Skyline Blvds near Lake Merced; Lincoln Park course (☎ 750-4653), 34th Ave and Clement St; and a nine-hole course at Golden Gate Park (☎ 751-8987) near the beach at the Fulton St and 47th Ave entrance. Exciting news for golfers: in the summer of 1995, the Presidio Golf Course (☎ 561-4653), near the Presidio's Arguello Gate, opened to the public for the first time after a century of exclusive use by US military personnel. Book far in advance.

Running & Skating
Marina Green has a 2½-mile jogging track and fitness course and there are many running paths through Golden Gate Park. The Presidio is another great park running area with plenty of routes from the Marina right past the Golden Gate Bridge to Baker Beach.

In-line skating is very popular in Golden Gate Park; you can rent skates at Skates on Haight (☎ 752-8376), 1818 Haight St, and cruise directly into the park.

Tennis
There are free public tennis courts all over San Francisco. The courts at Mission Dolores Park are popular; for others, call San Francisco Recreation & Park Department (☎ 753-7001). The 21 courts in Golden Gate Park charge a fee.

Sailing & Windsurfing
Any view over the bay, dotted with sails, shows this is prime sailing country. It's tricky territory, though, and only for experienced sailors. Sailing Education Adventures (☎ 775-8779) in Fort Mason offers sailing lessons and social events. Spinnaker Sailing (☎ 543-7333) also offers lessons and charters boats.

The Bay also has great windsurfing, but it is not kind to beginners. The San Francisco School of Windsurfing (☎ 753-3235) offers lessons on Lake Merced and at Candlestick Park. For more experienced board sailors, Crissy Field, in the shadow of the Golden Gate Bridge, is a world-class sailing spot. A good place to watch is Fort Point, right under the Golden Gate Bridge.

Surfing
Ocean Beach is one of the most challenging and exhausting places to surf in Cali-

fornia, especially in winter when the powerful, cold swells can reach 12 feet or more. There are no lifeguards and you should never surf alone or without at least a three-mm full-length wetsuit. For a recorded message of the latest surfing conditions at Ocean Beach call Wise Surfing at ☎ 665-9473. Go to Fort Point to watch surfers battle the waves under the Golden Gate Bridge.

ORGANIZED WALKING TOURS

Walking tours are a great way to get intimate with the city; if you don't have the energy, Gray Lines (☎ 558-9400) runs horribly fake-looking motorized cable cars around the city.

San Francisco lays out a rich feast for those keen on doing their sightseeing on foot. The visitor information center caters to walkers with an excellent line of walking-tour leaflets to Chinatown, Fisherman's Wharf, North Beach, Pacific Heights, and Union Square.

Helen's Walk Tours (☎ 510-524-4544) offers a variety of walks from two hours for $20 to a 3½-hour grand tour for $40. San Francisco Strolls (☎ 282-7924) also offer lots of possibilities including a Brothel Stroll and a Barbary Coast Stroll; these 2½-hour perambulations cost $20. The Friends of the San Francisco Public Library (☎ 557-4266) offer an eclectic variety of free (donations accepted) walking tours led by savvy local historians.

Chinatown is a walker's favorite, of course, and you can tag along on a Chinese Heritage Walk (Saturday afternoon, $15) or a Chinese Culinary Walk & Luncheon (Friday morning, $30) from the Chinese Culture Center (☎ 986-1822). Or, take a Chinatown Adventure Tour with the Wok Wiz (☎ 355-9657) for $25 or $35 with lunch. The Mission District Mural Walk (☎ 285-2287) points out, of course, the Mission's murals. Want the inside line on San Francisco's gay mecca, the Castro? Then try Cruisin' the Castro (☎ 550-8110, preferably 5 to 8 pm) with local resident Trevor Hailey; her Tuesday to Saturday morning, 3½-hour walk costs $30 includ-

ing brunch. Keen to relive the Summer of Love? Join a Flower Power Haight-Ashbury Walking Tour (☎ 221-8442) to find the site of the Human Be-In, the Drugstore Cafe, and the Grateful Dead's house. The two-hour walk takes place Tuesday and Saturday mornings and costs $15.

SPECIAL EVENTS

Street Fairs Pretty much every neighborhood in San Francisco hosts a street fair on the main 'strip' during the year, most landing in summer. Some of the most popular are the Folsom St Fair in late September (the most 'alternative' fair), and the Castro St Fair in early October. For arts & crafts mixed with blues or jazz, there's the Polk St Fair and the Fillmore St Fair, both in the summer months. North Beach hosts a Columbus Day Fair, and Haight St goes all out in June for their fair.

Chinese New Year Late January or early February. The Golden Dragon Parade, led by a 75-foot long dragon, is the highlight of the New Year festivities. Check with the Chinatown Chamber of Commerce (☎ 982-3000), 730 Sacramento St, for details.

SF International Film Festival Two weeks in April. The country's oldest film festival is concentrated at the Kabuki cinema in Japantown with films also at other Bay Area cinemas. Phone ☎ 929-5000 for details.

Bay to Breakers Third Sunday in May. Over 100,000 Bay Area joggers (many in crazy costumes) make their way from the Bay (the Embarcadero) to Breakers (the Pacific Ocean). Phone ☎ 808-5000, ext 2222, or contact the *San Francisco Examiner* (☎ 777-2424) for details and entry forms.

Carnaval Memorial Day weekend. If Rio and New Orleans can have a carnaval why not San Francisco? Lots of music and dancing in the streets of the Mission. Phone ☎ 826-1401 for details.

Gay Events June is a celebratory month for San Francisco's gay community, with the **Gay & Lesbian Film Festival** playing at the Castro Theater and **Gay Pride Week** leading up to the last Sunday in June, when the often outrageous **Gay Freedom Day Parade** is held. The evening before the parade is the **Pink Saturday** party on Castro St. Up to a half of a million people congregate down Market St for the city's biggest annual parade, followed by a huge party and fair at the City Hall.

Cable Car Bell-Ringing Championship Late June/early July. Cable car drivers compete to be the loudest or most tuneful bell ringer. Phone ☎ 923-6202 for details.

San Francisco Shakespeare Festival Free performances are given of a different play each year, starting Labor Day weekend in Golden Gate Park and other Bay Area parks. Phone ☎ 666-2222 for details.

San Francisco Blues Festival Late September. For two days bands and some blues legends jam out the blues on Fort Mason's Great Meadow. Phone ☎ 510-762-2277 (BASS tickets) for details.

San Francisco Jazz Festival Mid to late October. Catch jazz performances throughout the city; call ☎ 788-7353 for details.

Halloween October 31. The most crazed night of the year, with hundreds of thousands of costumed revelers taking to the streets, particularly Castro St. The **Exotic-Erotic Halloween Ball** (☎ 567-2255) at the Concourse Exhibition Center is one of the highlights.

PLACES TO STAY

Deciding where you're going to stay in San Francisco is a two-part process: where do you want to stay and what do you want to stay in? The decisions are interrelated: if you want a romantic B&B, you won't end up in the Financial District, and if you want a luxury hotel, chances are you'll wind up on Nob Hill or around Union Square. The following section is divided first by type of accommodations and then further by neighborhood.

Hostels & an RV Park

San Francisco has a surprising number of backpacker hostels. Hosteling International (HI) has two locations. The large, well equipped *Hostel at Union Square* (☎ 788-5604) is at 312 Mason St, a stone's throw from **Union Square**. The cost is $15 in peak season. The second HI hostel, the *San Francisco International Hostel* (☎ 771-7277) is in Building 240 at **Fort Mason** near Fisherman's Wharf. Nightly cost is $15 and $6.50 for kids; there's a 1 am curfew.

Globetrotters Inn (☎ 346-5786), 225 Ellis St at Mason in the Union Square/Tenderloin area, costs $12 per night or $75 a week. In the fuzzy zone where **Chinatown** fades into the Financial District, the *Pacific Tradewinds Guest House* (☎ 433-7970), 680 Sacramento St, is the smallest of the city hostels and rates are $14 or seven nights for the price of six (if paid in advance). Move over towards **North Beach** and the medium-size *Green Tortoise Hostel* (☎ 834-1000) at 494 Broadway has beds in dorms for $14 or some single and double rooms. Near the **Civic Center** the *Grand Central Hostel* (☎ 703-9988), 1412 Market St, is one of the city's largest with beds for $12 or singles/doubles at $20/30.

There are three hostels in **SoMa**, two small and one large, great for nightclubbers yet generally pretty quiet. The big one is the *Globe Hostel* (☎ 431-0540), at 10 Hallam Place; the hostel is actually right on Folsom between 7th and 8th but the entrance is on this small side street. It's for 'international travelers' only but US citizens with passports may talk their way in. The cost is $12 to $15 a bed. Right across the road is the *San Francisco International Student Center* (☎ 487-1463), 1188 Folsom St at $12 a night. The *European Guest House* (☎ 861-6634) is at 761 Minna St, an alley that runs parallel to Mission, between 8th and 9th Sts. Nightly cost in the summer is $14.

The *San Francisco RV Park* (☎ 986-8730, 800-548-2425), 250 King St, is between 3rd and 4th Sts, three blocks south of I-80 and right by the CalTrain Station. There are 200 full hookup spaces to park your RV for $34 a night, all conveniences included.

Union Square
Parking can get pricey in this area, so if the hotel you are staying in doesn't provide parking, try the parking garage at 123 O'Farrell St (☎ 986-4800) (6 pm to 8 am for $5) or by the day at the garage at 5th and Mission (☎ 982-8522), that charges $12 for 24 hours.

Bottom End The area to the west of Union Square has San Francisco's greatest density of hotels. The cheapest of the decent places, ranging from $30 to $50 a night, include the *Adelaide Inn* (☎ 441-2261), 5 Isadora Duncan Court; the *Herbert Hotel* (☎ 362-1600), 161 Powell St; and the *Olympic Hotel* (☎ 982-5010), 140 Mason St.

A step up from those at $50 to $80 are: the *Dakota Hotel* (☎ 931-7475), 606 Post St, with a TV, microwave, and refrigerator in every room; *Brady Acres* (☎ 929-8033, 800-627-2396), at 649 Jones St, where each room has a private bathroom and mini-kitchen; Victorian-style *Pensione International* (☎ 775-3344), at 875 Post St; the *Sheehan Hotel* (☎ 775-6500, 800-848-1529), 620 Sutter St, with fitness facilities and an indoor swimming pool; the *Beresford Manor* (☎ 673-3330, 800-533-6533), 860 Sutter St, which specializes in long-term accommodations for foreign students; and the *Golden Gate Hotel* (☎ 392-3702), 775 Bush St.

For women only, the *Mary Elizabeth Inn* (☎ 673-6768), 1040 Bush St, is $45 a day including two meals, and has a weekly rate of $147.

Middle You'll find some charismatic mid-priced hotels in the $95 to $125 range: the older *Raphael Hotel* (☎ 986-2000, 800-821-5343), at 386 Geary St, claims to be

San Francisco's 'elegant little hotel;' the *Diva Hotel* (☎ 885-0200, 800-553-1900) is cleanly modern in the glass, chrome, and black enamel style; *The Inn at Union Square* (☎ 397-3510, 800-288-4346), 440 Post St, has elegantly old-fashioned rooms and suites, continental breakfast, afternoon tea, and wine; the Art Deco *York Hotel* (☎ 885-6800), 940 Sutter St is a rather elegant establishment which was used for the stairway scenes in Hitchcock's *Vertigo*; and the *Savoy Hotel* (☎ 441-2700), 580 Geary St, is an excellent value with a homey style and afternoon tea and sherry. The *Beresford Arms Hotel* (☎ 673-2600, 800-533-6533), 701 Post St, is a well-kept older hotel with some very spacious rooms, some of them with kitchens, as is its sister establishment, the *Beresford Hotel* (☎ 673-9900, 800-533-6533) at 635 Sutter St.

A step up in price, the *White Swan Inn* (☎ 775-1755), 845 Bush St, and the *Petite Auberge* (☎ 928-6000), 863 Bush St, are somewhere between hotel and B&B with romantic decor and rooms at $145 to $165. The *Triton Hotel* (☎ 394-0500, 800-433-6611), 342 Grant Ave, is notable for its 140 exotically designed guestrooms. Complimentary morning coffee and evening wine is served in the lobby and the popular Cafe de la Presse and Aïoli restaurant are part of the hotel. Rooms range from $105 to $175.

Top End Rooms at the luxury hotels typically start out at $170 to $190 and rise to $275; suites are significantly more. The *Westin St Francis Hotel* (☎ 397-7000, 800-228-3000), 335 Powell St occupying the entire west side of Union Square, is one of the city's most famous hotels. The *Grand Hyatt on Union Square* (☎ 398-1234, 800-233-1234) is on the north side of the square at 345 Stockton St.

The *Campton Place Kempinski Hotel* (☎ 781-5555), 340 Stockton St, is a small and serene hotel which makes a special effort to appeal to businesswomen, and the *Clift Hotel* (☎ 775-4700, 800-437-4824), 495 Geary St at Taylor, is known for its stand-out service. *Hotel Nikko* (☎ 394-1111), 222 Mason St is a very modern establishment with a Japanese flavor. The *Pan Pacific Hotel* (☎ 771-8600, 800-327-8585), 500 Post St, has 330 stylish rooms.

Civic Center & Tenderloin

The *Central YMCA Hotel* (☎ 885-0460), 220 Golden Gate Ave at Leavenworth, is on the Tenderloin side of the Civic Center, but it offers simple, clean rooms with shared bathroom facilities for $28/38. At 601 Eddy St and Larkin, the *Phoenix Motel* (☎ 776-1380) is not the place to consider a stroll around at night, but this recycled motel is a wonderful fantasy, complete with a Miami or Waikiki beach atmosphere, the popular Caribbean restaurant Miss Pearl's Jam House, and two great movie collections – one featuring San Francisco, the other 'rock band on the road' movies (visiting bands are known to stay here). Free parking and a continental breakfast make the rooms, at $89 to $99, a great value.

The *Inn at the Opera* (☎ 863-8400, 800-325-2708), 333 Fulton St at Franklin, is right behind the Opera House and used to be the place where visiting opera singers stayed. Now it's a small boutique hotel with 48 rooms from $125 to $200.

SoMa

Bottom End The *Hotel Britton* (☎ 621-7001), 112 7th St, and *Mosser's Victorian Hotel* (☎ 986-4400, 800-227-3804), 54 4th St off Market, both have rooms in the $50 to $70 range. The *Aida Hotel* (☎ 863-4141, 800-863-2432) at 1087 Market St is neat and tidy and an excellent value at $30/35 with private bathrooms. The *Pensione San Francisco* (☎ 864-1271), 1668 Market St, is a pleasant little place with rooms with shared bath at $42 to $55, including continental breakfast.

Middle The *Best Western Americania* (☎ 626-0200, 800-444-5816), 121 7th St, and the *Best Western Carriage Inn* (☎ 552-8600, 800-444-5817), 140 7th St, are standard motels with free parking and swimming pools. Prices are $70 to $120.

Down by the Embarcadero Center, the *Griffon Hotel* (☎ 495-2100, 800-321-

2201), 155 Steuart St and the *Harbor Court Hotel* (☎ 882-1300, 800-346-0555), 165 Steuart St have more character in addition to their waterfront locations. Rates range between $145 and $175

Top End One of San Francisco's most famous and elegant hotels, the *Sheraton Palace Hotel* (☎ 392-8600, 800-325-3535), 2 New Montgomery St at Market, was the ultimate in luxury when it opened in 1875. The central Garden Court is worth seeing even if you're not staying here. Basic rooms are $235 to $315. The *San Francisco Marriott* (☎ 896-1600), at 55 4th St, is big and brash with 1500 rooms at $150 on weekdays and $215 to $240 on weekends.

Financial District

The *Temple Hotel* (☎ 781-2565), 469 Pine St is about the only affordable hotel in the district. Rooms are $30/35 for singles/doubles without bath, $40/45 with bath.

On the other end of the scale, the *Mandarin Oriental San Francisco* (☎ 885-0999, 800-622-0404), 222 Sansome St, has 158 rooms from the 38th to 48th floors of the third-highest building in the city. The views are spectacular and the rooms cost $275 to $395. The *Hyatt Regency* (☎ 788-1234, 800-233-1234), 5 Embarcadero Center, is probably San Francisco's most architecturally memorable hotel with its backward leaning 20-story atrium. The 800 rooms cost $195 to $245.

Chinatown

The *YMCA Chinatown* (☎ 982-4412), 855 Sacramento St, only takes men and requires reservations; rooms are $28/38 with the seventh night free. The female alternative is the *Gum Moon Women's Residence* (☎ 421-8827), 940 Washington St at Stockton, with rooms at $20 to $25.

The *Grant Plaza* (☎ 434-3883, 800-472-6899), 465 Grant Ave, and the *Astoria Hotel* (☎ 434-8889), 510 Bush St, have the real Chinatown feel, with rooms around $40.

The *Holiday Inn Financial District* (☎ 433-6600), 750 Kearny St, also known at the Holiday Inn Chinatown, is one of the city's least favorite architectural creations and has rooms at $120 to $170.

North Beach

The *Washington Square Inn* (☎ 981-4220, 800-388-0220), 1660 Stockton St, has 15 rooms ranging from $85 to $180. There's also a newly refurbished, absolutely grand small hotel in the heart of North Beach, *Hotel Bohème* (☎ 433-9111), 444 Columbus Ave. The decor is heavy into that gangster-era/Naked Lunch/Beat Generation chic – very American, very stylized, and, at $95 to $115, cheaper than most hotels in the area.

Nob Hill

Nob Hill is topped by four of the city's oldest and classiest hotels, but there are a pair of mid-range ones, too. The *Nob Hill Lambourne* (☎ 433-2287, 800-275-8466), 725 Pine St, is best described as a boutique business hotel. The rooms each have a computer, fax, and voice mail facilities, and cost from $125 for standard rooms to $199. The *Nob Hill Inn* (☎ 673-6080), 1000 Pine St at Taylor, is a pleasant 21-room hotel with prices from $90 to $200.

Nob Hill's seductively smooth, old-school hotels are the *Fairmont Hotel* (☎ 772-5000, 800-527-4727), 950 Mason St; the *Huntington Hotel* (☎ 474-5400) at 1075 California St; the *Stouffer Stanford Court Hotel* (☎ 989-3500, 800-622-0957), 905 California St; and the *Mark Hopkins Inter-Continental* (☎ 392-3434, 800-327-0200), at 999 California St. Rooms typically cost between $170 and $300, depending on the degree of opulence. Even if you can't afford to stay, the cocktail lounges are worth a stop: try the Fairmont's New Orleans Room for jazz and martinis, and the Tonga Room for tropical cocktails and a half-hourly thunder shower. The Mark Hopkins' Top of the Mark lounge is renowned for its superb views.

The *Ritz-Carlton San Francisco* (☎ 296-7465), 600 Stockton St at California, is in a palace-like 1909 building; rooms start at $240 and head up towards the stratosphere.

Fisherman's Wharf

Fisherman's Wharf is overrun with standard tourist motels like the *Travelodge* (☎ 392-6700), 250 Beach St and the *Sheraton at Fisherman's Wharf* (☎ 362-5500), at 2500 Mason St. There's also a Marriott, a Holiday Inn, a Howard Johnson, a Hyatt, and a Ramada. Call their toll free numbers for information.

There are some places that break out of the cookie cutter mold, like the pleasantly old-fashioned *San Remo Hotel* (☎ 776-8688, 800-352-7366), at 2237 Mason St. Singles are $35 to $55 and doubles are $55 to $75. The *Tuscan Inn* (☎ 561-1100, 800-648-4246), 425 Northpoint St, is a luxurious hotel with complimentary wine in the afternoon and prices from $120 to $145. *Hyde Park Suites* (☎ 771-0200), 2655 Hyde St, has suites with full kitchens at $165 to $190.

Pier 39 has an unusual variation on the B&B theme: *Dockside Boat & Bed* (☎ 392-5526) has a number of boats moored in the marina where you can have a double room for the night for $95 to $225 on weekdays and $125 to $275 on weekends.

The Marina

This is the real motel quarter of San Francisco. Lombard St is packed wall-to-wall with motels, gas stations, and fast fooderies. There's the *Marina Motel* (☎ 921-9406, 800-346-6118), 2576 Lombard St; an *Econo Lodge* (☎ 921-2505), at No 2505, with a swimming pool; a *Ramada Limited* (☎ 775-8116), at No 1940; and the *Rodeway Inn* (☎ 673-0691), at No 1450. All have rooms at less than $50. The *Van Ness Motel* (☎ 776-3220, 800-422-0372), at 2850 Van Ness Ave between Lombard and Chestnut, has a quieter location.

Turn down Van Ness Ave to find more motels, generally at slightly higher prices. They include the *Comfort Inn by the Bay* (☎ 928-5000, 800-424-6423), 2775 Van Ness Ave, which has rooms from $70 to $130.

Pacific Heights

Pacific Heights has a scattering of pleasant places. The *Bed & Breakfast Inn* (☎ 921-9784), at 4 Charlton Court, is nicely furnished with some quite romantic rooms for $70 to $90 without bath, $115 to $140 with bath. A block south of Union St at 2160 Green St, *Sherman House* (☎ 563-3600) is one of the most luxurious small hotels in the city with just 14 rooms in an elegant 1876 building; they charge from $250 to a whopping $825 a night. The *Mansions Hotel* (☎ 929-9444), 2220 Sacramento St, is a curious place, resolutely old-fashioned with a resident ghost, and pricey rooms at $130 to $350. There's also an excellent breakfast.

Japantown

The *Best Western Miyako Inn* (☎ 921-4000), 1800 Sutter St, on the corner of Buchanan, adds Japanese trimmings to the Best Western formula with rooms at $81/91. At the eastern end of the Japan Center complex, the larger and more expensive *Miyako Hotel* (☎ 922-3200), 1625 Post St, is a deluxe hotel designed with shoji screens on the windows and deep Japanese bathtubs in the bathrooms at $120 to $150 for singles and $150 to $170 for doubles.

The *Queen Anne Hotel* (☎ 441-2828, 800-227-3970), 1590 Sutter St, is one of the most elegant B&Bs in the city, a fine 1890 building with 49 rooms and suites ranging from $99 to $275. A continental breakfast is included, as well as sherry and cookies in the afternoon.

Haight-Ashbury

The *Metro Hotel* (☎ 861-5364), 319 Divisadero St in the Lower Haight, offers cheap and clean rooms with bath from $45 to $55. The *Stanyan Park Hotel* (☎ 751-1000), 750 Stanyan St, is right by Golden Gate Park, in a fine old Victorian building with rooms from $78 to $96.

The *Red Victorian B&B* (☎ 864-1978), 1665 Haight St, offers a wonderful opportunity to relive the Summer of Love. Choose from the Flower Child Room, the Sunshine Room, the Rainbow Room, the Peace Room, or even the Summer of Love Room. Rates for two people range from $76 to $200. Other B&Bs in the Haight area include the *Victorian Inn on the Park* (☎ 931-1830, 800-435-1967), 301 Lyon St at Fell, on the north side of the Panhandle, and *Spencer House* (☎ 626-9205), 1080 Haight St, a superb 1887 Queen Anne Victorian mansion just east of Buena Vista Park. Both go for about $100 to $160.

Alamo Square, north of Lower Haight towards Japantown, is famous for its Victorians. The *Alamo Square Inn* (☎ 922-2055), 719 Scott St, occupies a pair of Victorian mansions with rooms at $85 to $135. The *Archbishop's Mansion* (☎ 563-7872), 1000 Fulton St on Alamo Square, was indeed built, back in 1904, for the city's archbishop. Rooms with private bathrooms are $120 to $200.

The Castro

The *Twin Peaks Hotel* (☎ 621-9467), 2160 Market St, and the *Perramont Hotel* (☎ 863-3222), 2162 Market St, are basic and cheap at $35 to $50. *Beck's Motor Lodge* (☎ 621-8212), 2222 Market St, is a bland motel with 57 rooms at $77 to $99.

A couple of places cater to same-sex couples. The *Black Stallion* (☎ 863-0131), 635 Castro St, is a black-painted Victorian offering clothing-optional accommodations to gay men; rates are around $75. *House O' Chicks* (☎ 861-9849), 2162 15th St, offers cozy accommodations for lesbians.

The Mission

The *Inn San Francisco* (☎ 641-0188), 943 South Van Ness Ave, is one of the nicest B&Bs around, housed in a fine old 1872 mansion. Rooms range from $75 to $195; deluxe rooms include hot tub, spa, or fireplace. There's also an outdoor hot tub and a rooftop sundeck.

The *Dolores Park Inn* (☎ 861-9335), 3641 17th St at Dolores, is a small B&B between the Mission Dolores and Mission Dolores Park with doubles from $75 to $160 and a pleasant garden.

Near the Airport

Right at the airport, beside Hwy 101, the *San Francisco Airport Hilton* (☎ 589-0770) has 530 rooms at $140 to $180.

Millbrae, just south of the airport, has a half dozen places, several of them with rooms in the $50 to $70 range, including the *Clarion Hotel* (☎ 692-6363, 800-391-9644), at 401 East Millbrae Ave. South San Francisco, just north of the airport, has plenty more including a Best Western and a Days Inn. There's *Crown Sterling Suites* (☎ 589-3400), at 250 Gateway Blvd, with 313 rooms at $93.

PLACES TO EAT

With more restaurants per capita than any other city in the USA, San Francisco can conjure up just about every cuisine known to the world. Go to Chinatown for Chinese, North Beach for Italian, the Mission for Mexican and Latin American, and Japantown for sushi bars, but don't stop there. Around the city there's Afghan, Burmese, Cambodian, Creole, Cajun, Ethiopian, Filipino, French, Greek, Indian, Korean, Lebanese, Moroccan, Spanish, Thai, Turkish, and more, including the Bay Area's own invention: California cuisine, where *fresh*, *light*, and *creative* are the key words.

Union Square

There are plenty of cheap, unremarkable places to get a quick meal around Union Square, but don't settle for those. *Mocca* (☎ 956-1188), and *Nosheria* (☎ 398-3557) on Maiden Lane, do fancy sandwiches, and

Cafe de la Presse, across from the Chinatown Gate, (☎ 398-2680) includes an international selection of magazines and books with breakfast dishes and sandwiches and burgers in the $7.50 to $9 range. The *San Francisco Health Food Store* (☎ 392-8477), 333 Sutter St, serves some of the best shakes ($3) around at an old-fashioned soda counter.

South of Union Square at 63 Ellis St, *John's Grill* (☎ 986-3274) has been operating since 1908 and plays up its Dashiell Hammett connections. Just a few steps from Union Square at 333 Geary St, *Lefty O'Doul's* (☎ 982-8900) does big, cheap meals like spaghetti with meat sauce, salad, and bread. *Ten Thousand Buddhas* (☎ 928-2178), 610 Geary St at Jones, prepares vegetarian Chinese-Buddhist food. Looking for the latest Hard Rock copycat? Check out the overzealous *Planet Hollywood* (☎ 421-7827) at 2 Stockton St, on the corner of Market St. There's loud music and cinema paraphernalia for tourists who really wish they were in Los Angeles but got stuck up north.

A little pricier, the cozy little *Cafe Claude* (☎ 392-3505), 7 Claude Lane, between Sutter and Bush just west of Kearny, is a little bistro with the mandatory snide French waiters and excellent French onion soup. *Anjou* (☎ 392-5373), 44 Campton Place, is another small bistro.

Three of the city's most renowned (and expensive) restaurants are around Union Square. *Postrio* (☎ 776-7825), 545 Post St, is one of the city's prime exponents of

International Post St

The two blocks of Post St from Taylor to Leavenworth, starting just three blocks west of Union Square, have an interesting enclave of Asian restaurants. The *China Moon Cafe* (☎ 775-4789), 639 Post St, is a modern, distinctly untraditional Chinese restaurant which tackles Chinese food with a wholly modern perspective, in an equally modern-looking space.

The *Thai Stick* (☎ 928-7730), 698 Post St, on the corner of Jones, cooks up good basic Thai food. Cross Taylor St to find the moderately-priced Indonesia restaurant *Borobudur* (☎ 775-1512), 700 Post St, named after the famous Javanese Buddhist temple. There's also *Burma's House* (☎ 775-1156), 720 Post St, one of the city's handful of Burmese restaurants. Not that Burma has the world's most interesting cuisine but how often do you get to try it? ■

California cuisine, as dreamed up by Wolfgang Puck. *Masa's* (☎ 989-7154), 648 Bush St, and *Fleur de Lys* (☎ 673-7779), 777 Sutter St, are both internationally known French restaurants run by celebrity chefs (Julian Serrano and Hubert Kelly, respectively).

Civic Center

The Civic Center is a curious zone where San Francisco at its glossiest gets entangled with San Francisco at its worst, and the restaurants in the area are an equally curious blend: McDonald's and the famous Stars are almost side by side. *Stars* (☎ 861-7827) has entrances at 150 Redwood Alley and 555 Golden Gate Ave. This is one of San Francisco's cutting-edge dining establishments, owned by celebrity chef Jeremiah Tower. It's a big, relaxed, stylish place; a block away, at 500 Van Ness Ave, *Stars Cafe* provides similar food at lower prices.

At the glossy *Max's Opera Cafe* (☎ 771-7301), 601 Van Ness Ave, the food is basic American, the clientele mainly of the opera/symphony/ballet set, and the wait-staff sings for you!

Just west of the Civic Center in **Hayes Valley**, *Caffe Delle Stelle* (☎ 252-1110), 395 Hayes St at Gough, is a reasonably priced, always-packed trattoria with simple decor, and delicious food. *Zuni Cafe* (☎ 552-2522), 1658 Market St, does southwestern food with a distinctly Californian touch and has an ample oyster-bar menu. Service wavers from good to negligent, but it's relentlessly trendy and a great place to see and be seen.

Miss Pearl's Jam House (☎ 775-5267), in the Phoenix Motel at 601 Eddy St, brings Caribbean rhythms to the **Tenderloin**. The restaurant is fun and the food is delicious. *Brother Juniper's Restaurant* (☎ 771-8929), 1065 Sutter St near Larkin, is one of the best breakfast spots in the city, with great fresh breads and hearty organic food. It's open for lunch and dinner but closed on Sunday. The muralled *Tommy's Joynt* (☎ 775-4216), at the corner of Van Ness and Geary, has reasonably priced soups, stews, sandwiches, and an amazing variety of beers from all over the world.

SoMa

SoMa is becoming more and more popular as a place to eat with restaurants popping up around Yerba Buena Gardens and the neighborhood becoming increasingly artsy.

Topping the hip list is *Lulu* (☎ 495-5775), 816 Folsom St at 4th, a modern, spacious restaurant specializing in grilled California-style dishes. *Julie's Supper Club* (☎ 861-0707), 1123 Folsom St, has an interesting menu, unusual decor, and live jazz on weekends. At 570 4th St, *Fringale* (☎ 543-0573) is a popular Basque bistro, crowded and noisy and a surprisingly good value. Very south of Market in China Basin is *42°* (☎ 777-5558), 235 16th St at Illinois, serving tasty and diverse Mediterranean cuisine on the haute healthy side, with live jazz. The hard-to-find *Mission Rock Resort* (☎ 621-5538), at 817 China Basin at Mariposa, is the place for a waterfront breakfast or lunch.

For something a bit easier on the budget, *Hamburger Mary's* (☎ 626-5767), 1582 Folsom St, is a long-time late-night hangout with great burgers. *Eddie Rickenbacker's* (☎ 543-3498), at 133 2nd St, also does burgers, and the decor is as important as the food – you'll see a biplane, motorcycles and a model train set suspended from the ceiling. *Icon Byte Bar & Grill* (☎ 861-2983) at the corner of 9th and Folsom Sts, features some eclectic local artwork. If you get a drink or a meal you can log onto their one computer and send email to your friends. *¡Wa-Ha-Ka!* (☎ 861-1410), at 1489 Folsom St at 11th, has reasonable Mexican food and stays open late for between-club munch attacks. For great Vietnamese food at ridiculously low prices, brave a dismal neighborhood to find *Tu Lan* (☎ 626-0927), 8 6th St at Market.

For dim sum, *Yank Sing* (☎ 541-4949), at 49 Stevenson Place, is just off Market St, between 1st and 2nd Sts. In the curiously London-like little patch of green just south of I-80, the *South Park Cafe* (☎ 495-7275), 108 South Park, has a very French flavor,

Teatime

Remarkably, despite the coffee craze, tea has also had a resurgence in San Francisco, and a number of the ritziest hotels put on equally ritzy afternoon teas. The *Garden Court* (☎ 546-5011), in the Palace Hotel, 2 New Montgomery St at Market, may well be the ritziest; the full English experience, served Wednesday to Sunday from 2 to 4:30 pm, costs $15.95. The garden setting alone, complete with chandeliers and a glass ceiling, makes it worth considering.

On Union Square, or more correctly above Union Square, the *Rotunda* (☎ 362-4777), in the Neiman-Marcus department store, 150 Stockton St, does afternoon tea from 3 to 5 pm. Cross the square to the *Compass Rose* at the St Francis Hotel (☎ 774-0167), 335 Powell St, where tea is served, with musical accompaniment, from 3 to 5 pm. Close to the square, the *Campton Place Kempinski Hotel* (☎ 781-5555), 340 Stockton St, puts out the cucumber sandwiches from 2:30 to 4:30 pm.

The very ritzy *Ritz-Carlton* (☎ 296-7465), 600 Stockton St, also does very traditional English-style afternoon teas though often with some unusual variations. A classical pianist adds to the mood. Also on Nob Hill, the *Lower Lounge* at the Mark Hopkins Inter-Continental (☎ 392-3434), 999 California St, presents a pleasantly old-fashioned teatime (fruit cake and scones, of course) from 2:30 to 5:30 pm. Ditto at the *Fairmont Hotel* (☎ 772-5000), 950 Mason St, where $14.50 buys enough sandwiches, pastries, and cookies to feed two.

Finally, for an open-air tea, travel west to the *Japanese Tea Garden* (☎ 752-1171) in Golden Gate Park. This is the cheapest tea you'll find at just $2 including fortune cookies, although you'll also have to pay $2 to enter the gardens. They're open daily in summer from 9 am to 6:30 pm and in winter from 8:30 am to 5:30 pm. ■

---

terrific French fries, and reasonable prices. The *Delancey Street Restaurant* (☎ 512-5179), 600 Embarcadero, serves an interesting menu combining Mexican, Thai, Caribbean, and Cajun influences.

At *Ruby's* (☎ 541-0795), at 489 3rd St, you can't miss the huge tomato hanging out front. Inside there's big sandwiches and knockout pizzas. The new SFMOMA on 3rd St opposite Yerba Buena Gardens has the very Californian and overpriced *Caffe Museo* (☎ 357-4500), and right in the gardens there's a branch of the popular *Pasqua* coffee bars. *Cafe do Brasil* (☎ 626-6432), 104 7th St, is a good place for breakfast or for a meal of Brazilian-style tapas.

Financial District

This is where bankers, lawyers, and other professionals wine and dine their clients, and the restaurants tend to reflect their desire to impress. A favorite place for business lunches, the string of restaurants on Belden Lane between Bush and Pine near Kearny includes the excellent Italian *Cafe Tiramisu* (☎ 421-7044), the Mediterranean

Cafe 52 (☎ 433-5200), *Vic's Place* (☎ 981-5222), and *Cafe Bastille* (☎ 986-5673), with excellent French dishes. *Palio Paninoteca* (☎ 362-6900), 505 Montgomery St, serves excellent coffee and focaccia sandwiches.

Local food buffs claim *Yank Sing* (☎ 781-1111), 427 Battery St, has the best dim sum this side of Hong Kong, and *Harbor Village* (☎ 781-8833), 4 Embarcadero Center, gives it a run for its money. *Tommy Toy's* (☎ 397-4888), 655 Montgomery St, manages to bring a French flavor to Chinese cuisine. The service is excellent and the prices sky-high.

At 240 California St, the clubby but charming *Tadich Grill* (☎ 391-1849) is the oldest restaurant in San Francisco, and serves fabulous Mediterranean-style seafood. Along the Embarcadero, *Fog City Diner* (☎ 982-2000) looks like a traditional diner viewed through rose-colored glasses. It's pricey but the food is excellent and there's a wide variety of wines by the glass.

The very 'in' seafood restaurant *Aqua* (☎ 956-9662), 252 California St, is cool and modern with pricey, contemporary French and American dishes. More reasonably priced, *Sol y Luna* (☎ 296-8696), 475 Sacramento St, is a Spanish *tapas* restaurant with salsa dancing after dinner hours.

You can rub shoulders with the high fliers at the sky-high *Carnelian Room* (☎ 433-7500), on the 52nd floor of the Bank of America Building, 555 California St. Men are required to wear a jacket. It's open for cocktails from 4 pm, dinner from 6 pm, and Sunday brunch at 10 am. The *Cypress Club* (☎ 296-8555), 500 Jackson St, looks like it was designed by an architect moonlighting as a cartoonist – the prices are definitely steep but thankfully the food is as good as the design is weird. Nearby *Bix* (☎ 433-6300), at 56 Gold St in Jackson Square, is a very popular and very luxurious place.

Two other chic establishments, *Splendido* (☎ 986-3222), on the Promenade Level of 4 Embarcadero Center, and *Square One* (☎ 788 1110), 190 Pacific Ave are creative, imaginative, and, naturally, expensive. Chef Bradley Ogden's *One Market* (☎ 777-5577) at 1 Market St offers a fresh, seasonal menu of nouveau 'American cuisine' and a fine wine list, accompanied by jazz piano in the evenings.

Chinatown

Not surprisingly, Chinatown is packed with Chinese restaurants from tiny hole-in-the-wall places with cheap eats, to cavernous but equally economical dim sum houses, to pricey restaurants serving the latest Chinese haute cuisine.

Feng Haung Pastry Shop (☎ 421-7885), 761 Jackson St, and *Garden Bakery* (☎ 397-5838), 777 Jackson St, offer traditional Chinese pastries and hot tea. Inexpensive Chinese restaurants include the always packed *House of Nanking* (☎ 421-1429), 919 Kearny St, and the *R&G Lounge* (☎ 982-7877), 631 Kearny St. *The Pot Sticker* (☎ 397-9985), 150 Waverley Place, serves some of the best pot stickers in the city. *Sam Wo's* (☎ 982-0596), at 813 Washington St was a favorite of the Beat writers, but it was the rudeness of the

waiters rather than the quality of the food that made it so popular! A great place to satisfy late-night munchies, it's open until 7 am.

The *Lotus Garden* (☎ 397-0707), upstairs at 532 Grant Ave, is a Chinese vegetarian restaurant with a Taoist temple above it. *Brandy Ho's* (☎ 788-7527) at 217 Columbus Ave serves spicy food from the Hunan region.

The *Empress of China* (☎ 434-1345), 838 Grant Ave, is a complete contrast to Chinatown's cheap dives. If you want Chinese food at its best, then this is a place to try.

North Beach

North Beach is *the* neighborhood for choice Italian food and drinks, from an espresso to kick-start your morning to a plate of pasta to satisfy late-night hunger pangs. For breakfast or a snack, start with *Cornucopia* (☎ 398-1511), at 14 Columbus Ave or the *Stella Pastry* (☎ 986-2914) at 446 Columbus Ave.

Pizza and pasta are, of course, North Beach specialties and *North Beach Pizza* (☎ 433-2444), 1499 Grant Ave, is one of the best-known pizzerias in the city. They have a second branch *North Beach Pizza Too* two blocks south at 1310 Grant Ave. *L'Osteria del Forno* (☎ 982-1124), 519 Columbus Ave, is a tiny place run by two Italian women who make wonderful handmade raviolis and pizzas. *Basta Pasta* (☎ 434-2248), 1268 Grant Ave, is a long-running, reasonably priced pasta restaurant. The *Stinking Rose* (☎ 781-7673), 325 Columbus Ave, proclaims itself as a 'garlic restaurant' although it does admit to serving some food with its garlic. At *Anthony's* (☎ 391-4488), 1701 Powell St, pasta meets seafood, at excellent prices.

Mario's Bohemian Cigar Store (☎ 362-0536), 566 Columbus Ave, is an inexpensive cafe/bar/restaurant that looks out onto Washington Square and serves focaccia sandwiches and tiramisu. Washington Square also has two of San Francisco's prime power-lunching restaurants: the *Washington Square Bar & Grill* (☎ 982-8123), 1707 Powell St, which has been around forever, and *Moose's* (☎ 989-7800), 1652 Stockton St, with a great people-watching view and good food. Also on the square, the *Fior D'Italia* (☎ 986-1886), 601 Union St, claims to be the oldest Italian restaurant in the entire country.

Zax (☎ 563-6266), 2330 Taylor St near Columbus, is a California bistro serving its cosmopolitan crowd stupendous food from a small but inventive menu.

Nob Hill & Russian Hill

At 1517 Polk St, between California and Sacramento, the *Swan Oyster Depot* (☎ 673-1101) serves beer, clam chowder, shrimp cocktails and sourdough bread for one of the best cheap meals in the city. They close at 5:30 pm and all day Sunday. *Hard Rock Cafe* (☎ 885-1699), 1699 Van Ness Ave at Sacramento, can be raucously noisy and over-energetic but it's open until all hours and the food (burgers, fries, shakes) is not a bad value. Getting a bit fancier, right in the heart of Nob Hill, *Hyde Street Bistro* (☎ 441-7778), 1521 Hyde St, has a seasonal menu based on Austrian and northern Italian cuisine at decent prices. *I Fratelli* (☎ 474-8240), 1896 Hyde St, has

CALIFORNIA

Dim Sum

For the cautious newcomer tasting unknown cuisines, *dim sum* is one of the easiest possible introductions. San Francisco rivals Hong Kong in dim sum restaurants, which are also known as *yum cha* or 'drink tea,' because they originated from tea houses. Chinese businessmen used to spend so many hours in tea houses – they virtually served as extensions of their offices – that the tea houses began serving snacks and lunch. Waiters roll carts among the crowds of hungry diners; on the carts are the dim sum, small individual plates of delicacies, many of them cooked in pastry. You simply select the plates you like from the passing carts. Traditionally the bill was tabulated by counting the number of empty plates on the table, but they generally keep better track now. A group is really required to tackle dim sum since you want to try as many different dishes as possible.

The *New Asia* (☎ 391-6666), 772 Pacific Ave, is a typical, big, open, noisy dim sum place with all the architectural style of an aircraft hangar. Some of the city's most popular dim sum eateries are not in Chinatown. Head towards the Financial District to find *Yank Sing*, just on the other side of the Transamerica Pyramid, or towards the Embarcadero to *Harbor Village*. There's a second *Yank Sing* in SoMa. See the appropriate sections for more details.

Jackson St between Grant and Stockton is home to several dim sum factories that offer take-out dim sum for about 40¢ a piece. *Yung Kee Rice Noodle Co*, 732 Jackson St, is popular with the locals. Check out the buns steaming in the back of this cramped and narrow store and ask the staff to show you what types of fillings the different buns contain. Other factories include *Delicious Dim Sum* (☎ 781-0721), 752 Jackson St, and *House of Dim Sum* (☎ 399-0888), 735 Jackson St. ■

large portions of wonderful Italian fare, Chianti, and a very friendly atmosphere. *Zarzuela* (☎ 346-0800), 2000 Hyde St at Union, is an authentic Spanish tapas place where the prices are reasonable but the dishes a bit skimpy.

The casual *Le Petit Cafe* (☎ 776-5356), 2164 Larkin St at Green, has great breakfasts of fresh-squeezed orange juice, scones, eggs, and French toast.

Fisherman's Wharf
Fresh seafood is a Fisherman's Wharf specialty, from the takeaway food stalls to expensive waterfront restaurants, although better quality can be found in other parts of the city. If you're here during the mid-November to June crab season, enjoy Dungeness crab and sourdough bread – about as San Franciscan as you can get. Try *Alioto's* (☎ 673-0183), 8 Fisherman's Wharf, or *Tarantino's* (☎ 775-5600), 206 Jefferson St, both with great views and entrees from $13 to $20. At Ghirardelli Square, *McCormick & Kuleto's* (☎ 929-1730) has an extensive seafood menu. *Cafe Pescatore* (☎ 561-1111), 2455 Mason St in the Tuscan Inn, is an excellent restaurant noted for its seafood, pasta, and pizza.

For landlubbers there's the half-a-century old *Eagle Cafe* (☎ 433-3689) on Pier 39 – a basic diner with nice views; at night it's just a bar. The *Buena Vista Cafe* (☎ 474-5044), 2765 Hyde St, and the '50s-style diner *Johnny Rocket's* (☎ 693-9120), 81 Jefferson St, also turn out burgers and fries.

The Marina & Fort Mason
Chestnut St is the restaurant locus of the Marina. The pleasant *Chestnut St Grill* (☎ 922-5558), 2231 Chestnut St, has a huge choice of sandwiches and burgers. *World Wrapps* (☎ 563-9727), 2257 Chestnut St, takes the idea of burritos one step further, wrapping tortillas around a choice of international ingredients, from Thai chicken to curried vegetables. *Bepple's Pies* (☎ 931-6226), 2142 Chestnut St, serves sandwiches and tempting dessert pies until late at night. *Sweet Heat Restau-*

rant (☎ 474-9191), 3324 Steiner St, fixes innovative and healthy Californian/Mexican food at reasonable prices.

If you're looking for a hearty meal, *Izzy's* (☎ 563-0487), 3345 Steiner St, is the place to go for steak, chops, and seafood. Over at Fort Mason is *Greens* (☎ 771-6222), Building A, one of the city's best-known vegetarian restaurants.

At 2942 Lyon St, at the main gate to the Presidio and within walking distance to the Palace of Fine Arts, *Liverpool Lil's* (☎ 921-6664) is a small neighborhood dive with reasonable prices, a seafood and burgers menu, and an English pub-style atmosphere.

Pacific Heights
Perry's (☎ 922-9022), 1944 Union St, has a crowded bar and good burgers and salads. *Doidge's Kitchen* (☎ 921-2149), 2217 Union St, is another Pacific Heights institution, although here the main feature is breakfast and lunch; it's not cheap but the food is great.

Prego (☎ 563-3305), 2000 Union St, is a modern, mid-priced Italian restaurant with a popular bar. *Pasand Madras Cuisine* (☎ 922-4498), 1875 Union St, manages to combine jazz and Indian food.

Yoshida Ya (☎ 346-3431), 2909 Webster St just off Union, is pleasant-looking but pricey, specializing in tempura and yakitori. *Pane e Vino* (☎ 346-2111), 3011 Steiner St, has an open kitchen and excellent pasta dishes.

Plump Jack (☎ 563-4755), 3127 Fillmore St, has reasonably priced burgers, sandwiches, and pastas at lunchtime in elegant yet friendly bistro surroundings. At night they serve more sophisticated fare with an emphasis on seafood and a superb wine-by-the-glass list.

Japantown & the Fillmore
The three interconnected shopping centers of Japan Center- the Tasamak Plaza, Kintetsu Restaurant Mall, and the Kinokuniya Building – are packed with restaurants, particularly the Kintetsu Mall.

Floating sushi bars like *Isobune* (☎ 563-

1030), at 1737 Post St in the Kintetsu Mall, are very popular in Japan but slightly unusual here. It's fun and cheap and the sushi is delicious. Also in the Kintetsu Mall, *Mifune* (☎ 922-0337), offers popular Japanese dishes, particularly noodles, at moderate prices.

Sanppo (☎ 346-3486), 1702 Post St, is a down-home, cheap Japanese restaurant. In the Kinokuniya Building at 1582 Webster St, *Isuzu* (☎ 922-2290), is a more upscale restaurant specializing in seafood.

Much more expensive Japantown restaurants include the pricey *Elka Restaurant* (☎ 922-7788) in the Miyako Hotel at 1625 Post St, which blends Pacific Rim cooking styles. *Benihana of Tokyo* (☎ 563-4844), 1737 Post St, in the Kintetsu Mall, is a large chain restaurant where the chefs prepare your food at the table.

The restaurant stretch of Fillmore St, between Sutter and Jackson Sts just north of Japantown, blends Japanese restaurants with other cuisines. The popular *Jackson Fillmore* (☎ 346-5288), 2506 Fillmore St at Jackson St, is set in an old-fashioned diner and serves fine southern Italian food at reasonable prices. The *Elite Cafe* (☎ 346-8668), 2049 Fillmore St, is an informal and extremely popular Cajun and Creole seafood restaurant. *Pacific Heights Bar & Grill* (☎ 567-3337), 2001 Fillmore St, is a neighborhood restaurant with California cuisine and a great oyster bar. *Osome* (☎ 346-2311), 1923 Fillmore St, has some of the best Japanese food in the city.

Haight-Ashbury

The '60s may be long gone but the Haight is still a youth zone and the emphasis here is definitely on cheap eats, in a decidedly hip setting.

You can start your day with great bagels at *Holey Bagel* (☎ 626-9111), 1206 Masonic Ave, or have a more complete breakfast at a number of restaurants: the Lower Haight's *Spaghetti Western* (☎ 864-8461), 576 Haight St; *Kate's Kitchen* (☎ 626-3984), 471 Haight St; and the *Squat & Gobble Cafe* (☎ 487-0551), 237 Fillmore St all serve big hearty meals. *Zazie*

(☎ 564-5332), 941 Cole St in Cole Valley, is known for gingerbread pancakes, hefty omlettes, and lattes served in big ceramic bowls.

Later, fill up on spicy Cajun and Creole vittles at the *Crescent City Cafe* (☎ 863-1374), 1418 Haight St, or satisfy carnivorous instincts at the *Pork Store Cafe* (☎ 864-6981), 1451 Haight St. *All You Knead* (☎ 552-4550), 1466 Haight St, is very much part of the Haight-Ashbury scene and is open from breakfast until late with a vigorously healthy menu.

There are numerous unique eating experiences to be had in the Haight. *Kan Zaman* (☎ 751-9656), 1793 Haight St, does Middle Eastern food in a funky Arabian nights kind of place with cushion-on-the-floor seating. Enjoy a hookah pipe ($7) after the meal. *Cha Cha Cha* (☎ 386-7670), 1801 Haight St is a very crowded, colorful place with excellent Caribbean-influenced tapas (try the fried plantains with black beans) and sangria. At *Massawa* (☎ 621-4129), 1538 Haight St, you eat Eritrean/Ethiopian food with your fingers, especially fun with a group.

Two blocks south of Haight St, at 775 Frederick St by Golden Gate Park, *Ganges* (☎ 661-7290) is a terrific Indian vegetarian restaurant, but it's closed on Sunday and Monday. In the Lower Haight is *Thep Phanom* (☎ 431-2526), 400 Waller St, hailed as one of San Francisco's best Thai restaurants.

The Castro & Noe Valley

The Castro's most popular pastime is people-watching so, naturally, the most popular restaurants tend to be ones with good vantage points. Heading the list is *Cafe Flore* (☎ 621-8579), 2298 Market St, a popular coffeehouse with a large outside patio that is packed on sunny days. At the gourmet grocery/deli *Harvest Ranch Market* (☎ 626-0805), 2285 Market St at 16th, there are no tables, but outdoor sidewalk benches provide a resting spot while you indulge in their amazing assortment of sandwiches, sushi, fresh produce, vegan baked goods, salads, and much more.

The *Patio Cafe* (☎ 621-4640), 531 Castro St between 18th and 19th, has a big, noisy, covered patio tucked away in the back. *Hot 'n' Hunky* (☎ 621-6365), 4039 18th St, just off Castro, is a strong contender in the 'best burger in San Francisco' contest.

Pozole (☎ 626-2666), 2337 Market St, feels a bit like a hallucination with its pink walls and religious art, but it's hip and therefore the burritos tend to cost a few dollars more than the norm. If you want to sample Middle Eastern eats, try the popular and excellent *La Méditerranée* (☎ 431-7210), at 288 Noe St *Orphan Andy's* (☎ 864-9795), 3991 17th St, a Castro institution, is a popular burger-and-fries diner open 24 hours.

In nearby Noe Valley, *Firefly* (☎ 821-7652), 4288 24th St at Douglass, advertises 'home cooking with no ethnic boundaries.' The shrimp and scallop potstickers are delicious! It's upscale but affordable. *Tom Peasant Pies* (☎ 642-1316), 4108 24th St, makes an assortment of sweet and savory tarts, a great light snack.

The Mission
While the Mission doesn't offer a wide choice of 'fine dining,' for a cheap, filling, and often surprisingly high-quality meal it's hard to beat.

Restaurants – Latino
The junction of 16th and Valencia is a hot restaurant corner in the Mission with more than ten interesting restaurants within one block. *Taquería La Cumbre* (☎ 863-8205), 515 Valencia St, and *Puerto Alegre* (☎ 626-2922), 546 Valencia St, are cheap, excellent Mexican eateries. *La Taquería* (☎ 285-7117), 2889 Mission St, just south of the 24th St BART, claims to be the Mission's original taquería. There are no surprises but it's a neighborhood standby. The extremely popular *Cafe Macondo* (☎ 863-6517), 3159 16th St, decked out with comfortable couches and tables with reading lamps, serves strong coffee and some Central American dishes.

La Rondalla (☎ 647-7474), 901 Valencia St at 20th, is brave enough to escape from the standard tacos and enchiladas to tackle more adventurous Mexican fare. A mariachi band performs in the evening. At *El Nuevo Frutilandia* (☎ 648-2958), 3077 24th St, they serve up huge Cuban and Puerto Rican meals, accompanied by guitar music on the weekend.

Restaurants – Rest of the World
In that restaurant-packed block of 16th at Valencia, *Pastaio* (☎ 255-2440), 3182 16th St, is a cozy little pizzeria, and *Ti Couz* (☎ 252-7373), 3108 16th St, turns out a huge variety of sweet ($2 to $5) and savory ($3 to $8) crepes. *Truly Mediterranean* (☎ 252-7482), 3109 16th St, serves terrific shwarmas, falafels, and other eastern Mediterranean delicacies, including many vegetarian dishes. *Cafe Picaro* (☎ 431-4089), 3120 16th St, is a colorful, Spanish tapas restaurant. Another place for tapas ($4 to $5) is the tasty, popular *Esperpento* (☎ 282-8867), at 3295 22nd St, just off Valencia.

Cafe Istanbul (☎ 863-8854), 525 Valencia St, pumps out ultra-strong Turkish coffee and filling Middle Eastern dishes. *Pauline's Pizza* (☎ 552-2050), 260 Valencia St, makes great gourmet pizzas heavy with imaginative toppings. At the northern edge of the Mission, just off Market St, *Amazing Grace* (☎ 626-6411), 216 Church St, is a cafeteria-style vegetarian restaurant with a great salad bar.

Not all of the Mission's dining possibilities are necessarily cheap. *Le Trou* (☎ 550-8169), 1007 Guerrero St, is a traditional French restaurant with a three-course fixed price menu. Across the road, *Flying Saucer* (☎ 641-9955), 1000 Guerrero St, is a tiny restaurant that serves sophisticated and innovative cuisine amid its off-the-wall decor. *Woodward's Garden* (☎ 621-7122), 1700 Mission St, is an intimate and unpretentious place with delicious Californian cuisine.

The Richmond
The inner Richmond, on the east side of Park Presidio Blvd (Hwy 1), has become 'New Chinatown' with a slew of Chinese

and other Asian restaurants. Clement St, east of Park Presidio Blvd and again between 20th and 25th Sts, has a wide selection.

More than a few sushi enthusiasts have proclaimed *Kabuto* (☎ 752-5652), 5116 Geary Blvd, the best sushi bar in the city. It's closed Monday and Tuesday and can be crowded on weekends but is open late. *Angkor Wat* (☎ 221-7887), 4217 Geary Blvd, has terrific Cambodian food. *Tommy's Mexican Restaurant* (☎ 387-4747), 5929 Geary Blvd, specializes in Yucatán cuisine.

The best known Thai restaurant in the area, *Khan Toke Thai House* (☎ 668-6654), 5937 Geary Blvd, has a romantic but casual atmosphere; wear loose-fitting clothing and make sure there are no holes in your socks, as you'll be asked to remove your shoes and sit at low tables. *Le Soleil* (☎ 668-4848), 133 Clement St between 2nd and 3rd Aves, is an outstanding Vietnamese restaurant.

The *Cliff House* (☎ 386-3330), 1090 Point Lobos Ave, is known for its colorful history and great views (if you can snag a window seat) but not for the food, which consists of ordinary sandwiches and burgers from $8. Just in back of the Cliff House, you can get the same superb views, and a peek at the foundations of the Sutro Baths, from *Louis' Restaurant* (☎ 387-6330), 902 Point Lobos Ave, where the burgers are only $5.50.

The Sunset

South of Golden Gate Park, the Sunset district also has a large collection of budget ethnic eating places, particularly along Irving Ave from 5th all the way to 25th. The star of the inner Sunset is *PJ's Oyster Bed* (☎ 566-7775), 737 Irving St, a Cajun/Creole seafood restaurant and fish market.

There's also a concentration of middle-range restaurants along 9th Ave between Lincoln and Irving. *Ya Ya Cuisine* (☎ 566-6966), 1220 9th Ave, is perhaps the only place in the world where you can get Iranian-Californian food. Just down the block, *Stoyanoff's* (☎ 664-3664), 1240 9th

Ave, serves some of the best Greek food in the city. *Peppers* (☎ 566-7678), 1290 9th Ave, is a tiny Mexican restaurant known for its fresh ingredients and mesquite-grilled meat.

ENTERTAINMENT

San Francisco's nightlife doesn't hinge on huge, hyper-fashionable nightclubs but rather on its eclectic bars, hopping dance clubs, and cutting-edge concert spaces. There are a number of theater venues, a renowned opera house, a symphony, and a ballet company. Sporting events are also important.

The *San Francisco Chronicle* has fairly extensive movie and theater listings and the Sunday 'pink section' is really complete. The city's most extensive run-down on entertainment possibilities is found in the free weeklies: the *San Francisco Bay Guardian* and the *SF Weekly*. For tickets to the theater, the big music acts and other shows call BASS (☎ 510-762-2277) or go to their outlets at The Wherehouse or Tower Records stores. TIX Bay Area (☎ 433-7827) at 251 Stockton St in Union Square sells half-price tickets to musical

---

Go to Church
The *Glide Memorial United Methodist Church* (☎ 771-6300), 330 Ellis St, puts on an all-inclusive service featuring a bumpin' gospel choir and an acid-casualty slide show. *St Mary's Cathedral* (☎ 567-2020), 1111 Gough St at Geary, near Japantown, has free concerts every Sunday at 3:30 pm.

On Wednesdays at 6 pm and Sundays at 11:45 am, *St John's African Orthodox Church* (☎ 621-4054), 351 Divisadero at Oak, popularly known as the 'Church of St John Coltrane,' holds its services in a converted storefront hung with Byzantine-style paintings of the jazz master with his sax in one hand and holy scriptures in the other. Lovers of jazz and Jesus pack the place and music reaches a devotional high as the entire congregation jams to Coltrane's *A Love Supreme* and other religious tunes. ■

performances, opera, dance, and theater. The booth is open Tuesday to Thursday from 11 am to 6 pm and Friday and Saturday from 11 am to 7 pm. They take cash only and charge a $1 service fee.

Coffeehouses

San Francisco may not quite rival Seattle – the USA's coffee capital – but caffeine enthusiasts will not be disappointed. Apart from individual outlets the city also has a number of coffeehouse chains. The Seattle chain *Starbucks* has several locations – the coffee is good but the staff takes itself a little too seriously. *Peets* is a Bay Area institution with really strong java and less snooty service. Some others are *Spinelli*, *Pasqua*, and *Royal Grounds*.

Coffeehouses sometimes straddle several categories: they may be bar and restaurant as much as a cafe. The following listings are essentially cafes where you go to sip coffee and sit around – reading, doodling, watching the world go by, or simply daydreaming.

Union Square & Civic Center *Cafe de la Presse* (☎ 398-2680), 352 Grant Ave across from the Chinatown Gate, is a popular, European-style cafe with an international selection of newspapers and magazines.

Two of downtown's coolest casual hangouts are in Hayes Valley, near the Civic Center. At funky little *Momi Toby's Revolution Cafe* (☎ 626-1508), 528 Laguna St, there are magazines, a piano, and even an Etch 'n Sketch to play with. *Mad Magda's Russian Tea Room & Cafe* (☎ 864-7654), 579 Hayes St, has a psychic on duty at all times ($13 for a sitting).

North Beach It's the North Beach cafes that really give the neighborhood its laid-back, European character. To nurse a coffee in leisure day or night, Grant Ave is the ideal cafe thoroughfare.

Long-time cafe fanatics report that *Caffe Trieste* (☎ 392-6739), 601 Vallejo St at Grant, is the best spot in the city for engaging in intellectual conversation. Other good places to try include the popular little *North End Caffe* (☎ 956-3350), 1402 Grant Ave, and *Gathering Caffe* (☎ 433-4247), 1326 Grant Ave, which often features jazz. The large, inviting *Savoy Tivoli* (☎ 362-7023), 1434 Grant Ave, is as much a bar as a cafe, as is *Vesuvio Cafe* (☎ 362-3370), 255 Columbus Ave, former hangout of the Beats.

Haight-Ashbury This neighborhood overflows with comfortable cafes where you can enjoy a strong coffee while watching the entertaining street action. The *People's Cafe* (☎ 553-8842), 1419 Haight St, and *Cafe Paradiso* (☎ 221-5244), 1725 Haight St both serve quality coffee and snacks. *Blue Front* (☎ 252-5917), 1430 Haight St, serves coffee until late at night and often has live music.

Lower Haight offers its youthful, cafe-bound residents a host of possibilities, particularly as a late-night alternative to bars. The sprawling *Horse Shoe* (☎ 626-8852), 556 Haight St attracts the laid-back slacker crowd. It's open until 1 am nightly and is crowded with people who look like they'll still be there at 1 am the next day. *Cafe International* (☎ 552-7390), 508 Haight St, draws a quieter, more introspective clientele.

The Castro The Castro has a number of the coffee chain outlets, like Spinelli on Castro St and Pasqua on 18th, but *Cafe Flore* (☎ 621-8579), 2298 Market St, has an outdoor patio and really capitalizes on the chic Castro ambience. Not known as 'Cafe Hairdo' for nothing, this is the number one beauty-flaunting spot in the neighborhood. Or, for less attitude, go to the low-key *Jumpin' Java* (☎ 431-5282), 139 Noe St, between 14th and 15th.

The Mission The Mission may be best known for its huge selection of Latino restaurants but it's also got a weird and wonderful collection of coffee bars. The very popular *Cafe La Boheme* (☎ 285-4122), 3318 24th St, turns out a huge variety of coffees. *Muddy's* (☎ 647-7994), 1304 Valencia at 24th St, is a large, cluttered cafe littered with newspapers, and chess and backgammon games for patrons. *Red Dora's Bearded Lady Cafe & Gallery* (☎ 626-2805), 485 14th St near Guerrero, is a lesbian coffeehouse that doubles as a gallery, and hosts various readings and events on weekend evenings.

The Richmond & the Sunset At the very end of Muni's N-Judah line, *Java Beach* (☎ 665-5282) is the local hangout for surfers, beachcombers, and other sun lovers, with outdoor tables right across from the beach. The homey and old-fashioned *Owl & the Monkey Cafe* (☎ 665-4840), 1336 9th Ave, has a garden patio and puts on a diverse mix of live acoustic music, as well as open-mic poetry readings. Across the park in the Richmond, *Simple Pleasures* (☎ 387-4022), 3434 Balboa St, is a funky, cluttered cafe with a garage-sale furniture collection and live music.

Bars & Clubs
Union Square The best place to have a drink around Union Square is in the ritzy hotel lounges. Start at the warmly atmospheric *Compass Rose* (☎ 774-0167), in the St Francis Hotel, one of the city's most romantic and historic bars. The Clift Hotel's Art Deco *Redwood Room* (☎ 775-4700), 496 Geary St at Taylor, is open to midnight every night except Friday and Saturday, when there's live jazz until 1 am. The *Starlight Roof* at the Sir Francis Drake Hotel (☎ 392-7755), 450 Powell St, just off Union Square, has wonderful views. Just across Market St in SoMa, the opulent Palace Hotel (☎ 392-8600), has the *Pied Piper Bar*, with its huge 1909 Maxfield Parrish painting, the *Pied Piper*, but the nearby airy *Garden Court* is an even nicer place for a drink.

Civic Center & the Tenderloin Devotees of the grape must check out *Hayes & Vine* (☎ 626-5301), 377 Hayes St, a beautiful, sophisticated wine bar with a selection of international wines.

Despite its questionable Tenderloin

Pool & Billiards
Eager to catch up on your misspent youth? San Francisco's pool-hall possibilities include *Chalkers* (☎ 512-0450), 1 Rincon Center, 101 Spear St at Mission. This civilized pool parlor even offers 'informal instruction from a roving pro.' *Hollywood Billiards* (☎ 252-9643), 61 Golden Gate St, is not in the nicest part of the Tenderloin, but there are no less than 37 billiard tables and a full bar. It's open 24 hours from Wednesday through Saturday. In the upper Haight, *Park Bowl* (☎ 752-2366), 1855 Haight St, is a grungy old-fashioned bowling alley with a billiards room.
There's free pool every day from 3 to 7 pm at the popular *Paradise Lounge* (☎ 861-6908), 1501 Folsom St in SoMa. You can combine pool with jazz at *Cafe du Nord* (☎ 861-5018), 2170 Market St in the Castro, or at *Elbo Room* (☎ 552-7788), 647 Valencia St in the Mission. ■

address *Club 181* (☎ 673-8181), 181 Eddy St at Taylor, is a slick supper club and nightclub with some of the hottest jazz in town. The *Edinburgh Castle* (☎ 885-4074), 950 Geary St, has a big selection of British beers on tap. If you have a hankering for a Tartan Bitter and a game of darts, this is the place.

SoMa San Francisco's hip South of Market district, with the greatest concentration of bars and clubs in the city, is definitely the place to go for late-night entertainment. The SoMa dance and live music clubs are scattered along Folsom and 11th Sts.

Bars The Bay Bridge sails right over the top of the *Gordon Biersch Brewery* (☎ 243-8246), 2 Harrison St, an immensely popular after-work gathering place for the suit set. In the Folsom St nightclub strip *Kate O'Brien's* (☎ 882-7240), 579 Howard St, is a comfortable Irish pub. On 11th St is *20 Tank Brewery* (☎ 255-9455), 316 11th St, a microbrewery bar popular for sinking a few between clubs. *The Eagle* (☎ 626-0880) at 12th and Harrison is the quintessential leather bar, and a good place to find out about leather happenings.

Live Music SoMa is a prime hunting ground for blues and jazz, particularly for 'new jazz.' *Julie's Supper Club* (☎ 861-0707), 1123 Folsom St at 7th, is a bustling restaurant with live blues and jazz on Friday and Saturday night. *Eleven* (☎ 431-3337), 374 11th St at Harrison, and *330 Ritch* (☎ 541-9574), at 330 Ritch St, also combine food and jazz; Eleven does Italian, 330 Ritch, tapas. The two-story *Up & Down Club* (☎ 626-2388), 1151 Folsom St between 7th and 8th, is a hip spot to hear local jazz bands and is open Monday to Saturday.

The *Hotel Utah Saloon* (☎ 421-8308), 500 4th St at Bryant, and the *Covered Wagon Saloon* (☎ 974-1585), 911 Folsom St at 5th, are bars that host bands several nights a week. You can also dance at the fashionable *Cat's Grill & Alley Club* (☎ 431-3332), 1190 Folsom St near 8th. The decor is surreal, and they also serve tapas until late. *Slim's* (☎ 621-3330), 333 11th St, is an authentic R&B club partly owned by '70s rock star Boz Scaggs; an impressive group of artists pass through – check the *Bay Guardian* for listings.

Right on the corner of 11th at 1501 Folsom St is the *Paradise Lounge* (☎ 861-6906), a noisy, crowded, youthful hangout. There may be as many as five different shows on some nights, ranging from rock to jazz to poetry readings. You'll know *Holy Cow* (☎ 621-6087), 1535 Folsom St, by the life-size plastic cow suspended over the sidewalk. A young SoMa crowd flocks here nightly and the music is mainstream.

Dance Clubs Nightclubbing in SoMa requires some local, underground knowledge, as trendy clubs constantly fade in and out. To find out what's going on, check the weekly *Bay Guardian* Calendar section.

Towards the bay end of Howard St, *DV8* (☎ 777-1419), 55 Natoma St, boasts four floors of music, drinking, and dancing until 4 am from Thursday to Sunday in an urban derelict zone. Next door, *The Caribbean*

Zone (☎ 541-9465), 55 Natoma St, is someone's fantasy of a tropical getaway in SoMa. Tables are tucked amid lagoons waterfalls, and you can climb upstairs into the hull of a crashed airplane or dance to reggae amid the fern fronds downstairs.

The *DNA Lounge* (☎ 626-1409), 375 11th, is a big, mass-market dance club open every night until 4 am with DJs or live bands. The crowd at the *Trocadero* (☎ 495-6620), 520 4th St between Bryant and Brannan, varies with the theme for the evening. Once a week is 'Bondage a Go-Go,' a soft-core S&M party. The dance floor is as big as a roller rink, and the disco balls were salvaged from an old Rolling Stones tour. The *Sound Factory* (☎ 543-1300), 525 Harrison, is the amusement park of dance clubs, with 15,000 sq feet of dance space in many rooms on many levels. *Ten15* (☎ 431-1200) at 1015 Folsom, is another biggie with a fluctuating music menu depending on the DJs.

The *End Up* (☎ 543-7700), 995 Harrison St at 6th, underneath the freeway, is one of the most popular dance clubs in the city, particularly on its gay and lesbian nights. *The Stud* (☎ 863-6623), 399 9th St at Harrison, is another gay and lesbian dance club.

Financial District The 52nd-floor *Carnelian Room* (☎ 433-7500), atop the Bank of America Building, 555 California St, has the best views in the city. The circular bar at *Equinox* (☎ 788-1234), at the top of the bayfront Hyatt Regency Hotel, rotates the full 360°, showing off San Francisco from every conceivable angle.

Nob Hill Topping the list of Nob Hill bars is the *Top of the Mark* (☎ 392-3434), the rooftop bar atop the Mark Hopkins Hotel, at 999 California St. Ride the glass elevator to the *Oak Room* in the Fairmont Hotel (☎ 772-5000), down an $8 bottle of beer, dig the view, visit the free hors d'oeuvres table often, and remember to tip big. The Fairmont's *Tonga Room* is wacky fun and definitely worth seeing, although the drinks are expensive. Hurricanes blow through the artificial lagoon every half hour. The *New Orleans Room*, also in the Fairmont, is one of the city's best jazz venues.

North Beach The *Vesuvio Cafe* (☎ 362-3370), 255 Columbus Ave, looks across Jack Kerouac St to City Lights Bookstore. Vesuvio's history as a Beat hangout may make it a tourist attraction but it continues to be a popular neighborhood bar. Two other historic bars sit directly across Columbus Ave. *Tosca Cafe* (☎ 391-1244, 986-9651), 242 Columbus Ave, is as famous for its people-watching opportunities as it is for the arias that emanate from the all-opera jukebox. Local literati are known to unwind here in the red vinyl diner booths. Next door, across the tiny Adler Plaza, is the dark, cavernous *Specs'* (☎ 421-4112), also known as the 'Adler Museum,' with an amusing hodgepodge of memorabilia plastered on the walls and ceiling.

A block south, at 155 Columbus Ave, the *San Francisco Brewing Company* (☎ 434-3344) is a modern establishment with a microbrewery turning out its own beer on the premises. There's live music several nights a week. Finally, or more correctly firstly, there's the *Saloon* (☎ 989-7666), 1232 Grant Ave, just above Columbus. This worn-looking old bar was one of only two buildings in North Beach to survive the 1906 fire – the owners say it's been standing since 1861. Blues and '60s rock names often perform here.

Fisherman's Wharf Try an Irish coffee at the *Buena Vista Cafe* (☎ 474-5044), 2765 Hyde St – they claim to have introduced it to San Francisco.

On Pier 39, the *Eagle Cafe* (☎ 433-3689) is an authentic old bar that especially stands out amidst the hokey Wharf madness. *Lou's Pier 47* (☎ 771-0377), 300 Jefferson St, features real blues seven nights a week.

Pacific Heights Pacific Heights is famous as singles' bar territory. *Perry's* (☎ 922-9022), 1944 Union St, is the number-one

cruising spot and is featured in Armistead Maupin's *Tales of the City* novels as the archetypal San Francisco 'breeder' bar. The *Pierce St Annex* (☎ 567-1400), 3138 Fillmore St, has an equally strong reputation. You'll find 21 different beers on tap at the hugely popular and noisy *Union Ale House* (☎ 921-0300), 1980 Union St.

One of the city's most infamous yuppie cruising spots is the intersection of Fillmore and Greenwich Sts, which was known as 'the Triangle' until one of the trio of bars closed down. The *Balboa Cafe* (☎ 921-3944) and the *Baja Cantina* (☎ 885-2252) are still there, as are the hordes of tipsy suburban singles.

Japantown & the Fillmore *Jack's Bar* (☎ 567-3227), 1601 Fillmore St, has been a popular blues hangout since the 1930s. There's live jazz or blues every night and it's open until 2 am. Big with the just graduated crowd, *Frankie's Bohemian Cafe* (☎ 621-4725), 1862 Divisadero at Pine, is an eclectic bar/cafe.

Haight-Ashbury In keeping up with its eclectic roots, the Haight-Ashbury boasts a collection of varied bars and clubs.

The *Persian Aub Zam Zam* (☎ 861-2545), 1633 Haight St, has achieved cult status namely due to Bruno, the ornery bartender, who, on some nights, will only serve martinis, and then only if you ask nicely. If you feel like donning the '40s outfit you just bought at one of the Haight's slew of vintage stores, head to the distinctly retro *Club Deluxe* (☎ 552-6949), 1511 Haight St, where the crowd dresses the part, enjoying the swing and big band tunes. *Club Boomerang* (☎ 387-2996), 1840 Haight St is a small, crowded venue where up-and-coming bands perform.

If you're tired of the Upper Haight bustle of tie-dyed panhandlers and just want to relax to some smooth jazz or feel-good surfabilly, head to the *Kezar Bar & Restaurant* (☎ 681-7678), 900 Cole St at Carl where you can down a big burger with a cool martini.

In the Lower Haight at the three blocks

of Haight St between Pierce and Webster, there's a jumping enclave of noisy bars where young crowds pass the evening hours. The appropriately dark *Midtown Bar* (☎ 558-8019), 582 Haight St, starts to fill up early in the evening and throbs with action throughout the night. Across the street are two post-industrial bars, *Noc Noc* (☎ 861-5811), at 557 Haight St, and *Toronado* (☎ 863-2276), at 547 Haight St. How do you recognize a post-industrial bar? Well, Noc Noc, with its space-age, curving metal bar and light fixtures, is the place where the spaceship crew from *Alien* hang out when they're earthside.

Head back across Haight St to the *Mad Dog in the Fog* (☎ 626-7279), at 530 Haight St, a popular British-style pub with dart boards, soccer on TV, and a young, heavy-drinking crowd. *The Top* (☎ 864-7386), at 424 Haight St, and *Nickie's* (☎ 621-6508), at 460 Haight St, are two noisy, hopping joints packed most nights of the week.

The Castro Cruising the Castro is a time-honored activity for the city's large gay community. The *Twin Peaks Tavern* (☎ 864-9470), 401 Castro St at Market St, pioneered large bay windows so the patrons could watch the passing scene. *The Detour* (☎ 861-6053), 2348 Market St, offers great drink bargains, with $1 beers and shots on Sunday, and the longest happy hour around from 2 to 8 pm. *The Cafe* (☎ 861-3846), 2367 Market St, has a large deck overlook-

ing Market St, an outdoor garden patio, and a pool table. Other bars include *Castro Station* (☎ 626-7220), 456 Castro St, and the *Phoenix Club* (☎ 552-6827), 482 Castro St.

As far as straight/mixed bars go, the '30s-style *Cafe du Nord* (☎ 861-5016), 2170 Market St at Sanchez, is a former speakeasy that combines jazz and West Coast blues at its best. Tuesday is Latin music night, with free salsa dancing lessons at 9 pm.

The Mission The Mission's bars are, like most everything else about the Mission, an eclectic, funky mix. *El Rio* (☎ 282-3325), 3158 Mission St, is a large, cheerful bar and dance club. The always-packed *Elbo Room* (☎ 552-7788), 647 Valencia St, is dominated by a long bar (serving cheap drinks) and pool tables, and a dance floor and stage upstairs, where many of San Francisco's new jazz bands get their start. *Slow Club* (☎ 241-9390), 2501 Mariposa St, is a hip and mellow hang-out with a dimly lit restaurant and a bar tucked away in back.

At the crowded 16th and Valencia St junction, *Esta Noche* (☎ 861-5757), 3079 16th St, is a Latino gay bar. *Zeitgeist* (☎ 255-7505), 199 Valencia St, is the 'in' spot for bikers – from bicycle messengers to motorcyclists. *Dalva* (☎ 252-7740), 3121 16th St, serves spicy glasses of sangria. Across the street, *Kilowatt* (☎ 861-2595), 3160 16th St, is a new hot venue for local bands.

Gay & Lesbian Nightlife

San Francisco's gay nightlife scene extends beyond the Castro's borders and a number of mainstream clubs feature a weekly gay and lesbian night. On Sundays, the *Covered Wagon Saloon* hosts its 'Muffdive' night for women only. *Club Townsend* (☎ 974-6020), 177 Townsend St at 3rd and the *End Up* (☎ 543-7700), 995 Harrison St at 5th feature gay and lesbian dance nights on different evenings of the week. To zero in on the current hotspot, your best bet is to ask around at some of the established Castro bars and cafes.

A *Different Light Bookstore* (☎ 431-0891) at 489 Castro St is a veritable fountain of information and an excellent place to find out about the night's happenings. Pick up the free gay papers, the *Bay Area Reporter* and the biweekly *San Francisco Bay Times* for bar and club listings. *On-Q* and *Odyssey* magazines are also good bets. A terrific and fun-to-read source of information is *Betty & Pansy's Severe Queer Review of San Francisco*, available at A Different Light. ■

CALIFORNIA

At the base of Potrero Hill, the aptly-named *Bottom of the Hill* (☎ 626-4455, 621-4455 for show information), 1233 17th St, presents live music seven nights a week – it's one of the hottest venues for up-and-coming bands. They also have a patio.

The Richmond *The Plough & the Stars* (☎ 751-1122), 116 Clement St, takes top honors as one of the most popular Irish bars in the city with cheap beers and occasional live bands.

Concert Venues

The *Fillmore Auditorium* (☎ 346-6000), 1805 Geary Blvd at Fillmore, is back in action with a broad range of live music from big-name rock bands to wild punk gigs. In keeping with the tradition Bill Graham began in the '60s, free apples and psychedelic posters are handed out to everyone attending a concert.

The stylish, old bordello-turned-concert hall, the *Great American Music Hall* (☎ 885-0750), 859 O'Farrell St, between Polk and Larkin, puts on a true mix of acts from acoustic folk to African rhythm to rock & roll. The *Warfield* (☎ 775-7722), 982 Market St, between 5th and 6th, near the Civic Center, hosts headliners and up-and-coming local groups. Most huge concerts are usually held outside San Francisco at the *Oakland Coliseum*, the *Shoreline Amphitheater* in Mountain View, or a number of other stadium-size venues.

Comedy & Cabaret

A number of bars occasionally feature comedy nights, but for the real thing, San Francisco has two immensely popular comedy clubs: The *Punchline* (☎ 397-

4337) at 444 Battery St in Maritime Plaza in the heart of the Financial District and *Cobb's Comedy Club* (☎ 928-4320), 2801 Leavenworth St, in the Cannery at Fisherman's Wharf.

At *Finocchio's* (☎ 982-9388), 506 Broadway in North Beach, female impersonators engage in a 'been-there, seen-that' type of comedy routine. In the Castro, *Josie's Cabaret & Juice Joint* (☎ 861-7933), 3583 16th St, puts on gay and lesbian comedy and cabaret performances nightly, and has a great backyard patio for balmy afternoons.

Cinema

Forget those modern multi-screen theaters – San Francisco boasts a bunch of great, old, single-screen dinosaur theaters. The Bay Area is a terrific region for moviegoers with wonderful old cinemas, discerning local film buffs, and lots of foreign and art house venues.

Topping the list for cinemas where the building is as interesting as the film is undoubtedly the *Castro Theatre* (☎ 621-6120), 429 Castro St just off Market. A magnificent Wurlitzer organ rises out of the stage and the theater has as much plush velvet, Grecian columns, and fake plants as any vintage cinema buff can take.

In business since 1913, the *Clay Theater* (☎ 346-1123), 2261 Fillmore St at Clay, is the longest continuously operating cinema in the city. It still looks magnificent, if a little careworn.

The *Roxie* (☎ 863-1087), 3117 16th St at Valencia, in the Mission, screens an adventurous, eclectic selection of films; the *Lumière* (☎ 885-3200), 1572 California St near Polk, shows a mix of art house films and new releases; the Art Deco *Balboa* (☎ 221-8184), 3630 Balboa St, in the Richmond district, has been operating since 1926 and screens new releases; and the *Alhambra* (☎ 775-2137), 2330 Polk St at Union in Russian Hill is a general release cinema but looks fantastic.

At the small *Red Vic* (☎ 668-3994), 1727 Haight St in the Haight-Ashbury, you can see rare cult films and other interesting oldies. The *Casting Couch* (☎ 986-7001), 950 Battery St near Levi's Plaza and the Embarcadero, is a tiny theater with luxury loveseat couches seating just 46 people. Gourmet snacks are delivered to your seat; admission is $8.50. The *San Francisco Cinematheque* (☎ 978-2787) is in the Center for the Arts, 701 Mission St in Yerba Buena Gardens.

The better multiplex cinemas include the eight-screen *Kabuki 8 Theater* (☎ 931-9800), 1881 Post St in Japantown, the towering glass-and-steel *Galaxy* (☎ 474-8700), 1285 Sutter St and Van Ness Ave, and *Opera Plaza* (☎ 771-0102), 601 Van Ness Ave.

The city hosts the San Francisco Film Festival (☎ 931-3456) in April (mainly at the Kabuki) and the Lesbian & Gay Film Festival in June (at the Castro Theatre).

Performing Arts

Theater San Francisco is not a cutting-edge city for theater, but it has one major company, the American Conservatory Theater (ACT, ☎ 749-2228), which puts on performances at a number of theaters, including the Geary Theater and the Stage Door Theater. The big spectacular shows – like the Andrew Lloyd-Webber musicals – play at the *Curran Theatre* (☎ 474-3800), 445 Geary St, between Mason and Taylor.

Many of the jokes will go straight over non-San Franciscans' heads, but *Beach Blanket Babylon* at *Club Fugazi* (☎ 421-4222), 678 Green St in North Beach, is San Francisco's longest-running comedy extravaganza, now into its third decade and still packing them in (over 21 years of age, except at matinees, please!).

There are many small theater spaces like *The Marsh* (641-0235), 1062 Valencia St, around the city that host experimental shows, and plenty of active small theaters doing alternative pieces. Check the *Bay Guardian* for current listings.

Classical Music The *San Francisco Symphony* performs September to May in the Davies Symphony Hall (☎ 431-5400), Van Ness Ave at Grove St. The *San Francisco*

Conservatory of Music (☎ 759-3475) puts on a variety of performances at Hellman Hall, 1201 Ortega Ave at 19th.

Opera The acclaimed *San Francisco Opera* performs from early September to mid-December at the War Memorial Opera House (☎ 864-3330), 301 Van Ness Ave at Grove St.

Dance The *San Francisco Ballet* (☎ 703-9400), the oldest ballet company in the USA, performs at the opera house or at the Center for the Arts Theater (☎ 978-2787), 700 Howard St at 3rd, in the Yerba Buena Gardens in SoMa.

Spectator Sports

San Francisco's NFL team, the *San Francisco 49ers* (☎ 468-2249), has been a regular Super Bowl champion, while the National League baseball team the *San Francisco Giants* (☎ 467-8000) has slugged its way into the hearts of local fans. Both teams play at the cold and windy Candlestick Park, south of the city. Sporting event tickets are available through BASS (☎ 510-762-2277). Ticket brokers, who sometimes charge astronomical prices, include Just Tix (☎ 510-838-0193) and Mr Ticket (☎ 292-7328).

THINGS TO BUY

San Francisco's shopping, like its nightlife, is best when the words 'small,' 'odd,' and 'eccentric' come in to play. Sure, there are big department stores and an international selection of name brand boutiques, but the oddities of the Castro, Haight-Ashbury, or Pacific Heights are a lot more fun.

Antiques & Art

The Jackson Square area, a small enclave at the borderland between the Financial District and North Beach, is one of the city's prime shopping areas for antiques. The Jackson Square Art & Antique Dealers Association (☎ 296-8150), 414 Jackson St, is an umbrella organization for 25 of these dealers.

Naughty San Francisco

There's a strong 'adults only' market in San Francisco, ranging from harmless 'sexy' fortune cookies to the most bizarre fringes of avant garde porn. There are even rumors of a vampire cult (actually a role-playing game hip with the Goth crowd) that meets in abandoned warehouses; the city's premiere game store, Gamescape (☎ 621-4263), 333 Divisadero, *might* be able to give you details.

In the heart of the Mission there's a shop providing means for adult entertainment. Good Vibrations (☎ 974-8980), 1210 Valencia St, specializes in vibrators of all types and sizes, as well as other paraphernalia. This tasteful sex shop has sex toys, books, and videos. If you're into the leather subculture, do your shopping in the Castro and SoMa. Image Leather (☎ 621-7551), 2199 Market St, is a hard-core leather and fetish gear shop; descend into the 'dungeon' where there's a . . . well, a museum of sorts.

For naughty edibles, the Cake Gallery (☎ 861-2253), 290 9th St in SoMa, bakes X-rated cakes. They've got a photo album of their most questionable comestibles. The *Golden Gate Cookie Company* (☎ 781-3956), 56 Ross Alley in Chinatown, makes fortune cookies – they specialize in 'sexy' fortunes!

And while strip joints may be on their way out, at the *Nob Hill Cinema* (☎ 781-9468), 729 Bush St, near Powell, you can still see 'big nude men' perform. The entry fee is $20; phone inquiries elicit an amazing recorded message about what you're going to see. At the *O'Farrell Theater* (☎ 776-6686), at 895 O'Farrell St it's lots of nude dancing women.

The O'Farrell Theater has had a colorful history even for an x-rated spot. The Mitchell Brothers learned their craft at the San Francisco State University's film department and struck it lucky in 1972 when Marilyn Chambers, the star of their first big-budget porn flick, *Behind the Green Door*, simultaneously managed to become the picture-of-innocence loving mother on a million Ivory Snow detergent boxes. Her soapbox career was quickly terminated but neither Marilyn nor the Mitchell brothers looked back. Until 1991 that is, when one Mitchell brother shot and killed the other one. Sentenced to six years for voluntary manslaughter, he's currently out on a half-million dollars' bail while the appeals go through. ■

Streets going west out of Union Square are home to many galleries. On Geary St you'll find a run of galleries on the south side of the street between Powell and Mason; one of the better is Caldwell Snyder (☎ 296-7896) at 357 Geary. Others include the Nevska Gallery (☎ 392-4932), right next door, focusing on Russian art, and Galerie Adrienne (☎ 288-6575) with a modern mix.

In the vicinity of SFMOMA, South of Market, are some great galleries that give a decent perspective on the alternative San Francisco art scene. Among the many are Acme Gallery (☎ 896-2263) at 667 Howard St, and 111 Minna St Gallery (☎ 974-1719) with a small coffee bar.

Bicycles

Bicycle stores to try include Start to Finish (☎ 202-9830), 2530 Lombard St in the Marina, and (☎ 243-8812), at 599 2nd St at Brannan in SoMa. They rent and repair bicycles and will ship overseas. Avenue Cyclery (☎ 387-3155), 756 Stanyan St, by Golden Gate Park in the Haight-Ashbury, and City Cycle (☎ 346-2242), 3001 Steiner St in Pacific Heights, are other stores to try.

Cameras & Photography

Adolph Gasser (☎ 495-3852), 181 2nd St, south of Market, has a huge range of new and used photographic and video equipment, and also processes film. Downtown, Brooks Camera (☎ 392-1900), 45 Kearny St, sells new cameras and does repairs and rentals, as does Camera Boutique (☎ 982-4946), 342 Kearny St.

For cheap film and developing, call ☎ 334-2020 for the nearest Walgreens Drugs. For quickie one-hour jobs, Fox Photo and Ritz Camera each have several local labs with a decent selection of films. Check the yellow pages for locations.

Food & Drink

There's a Saturday farmers' market, from 8:30 am to 2:30 pm, at the Embarcadero by the Ferry Plaza Building, offering locally grown and organic produce, fresh baked breads, and other local items.

If you don't leave San Francisco with an appreciation for **sourdough bread** you haven't tried enough. Boudin Bakery (☎ 928-1849), 156 Jefferson St, Fisherman's Wharf, is still the best place for classic sourdough. There's another Boudin in the basement of the Macy's in Union Square (☎ 296-4740), one in Ghirardelli Square (☎ 928-7404), and a number of others throughout the city.

Ghirardelli, of course, is the name in **chocolate**. You can find Ghirardelli treats all over the city and beyond, but to make an experience of it, go to their stores in the namesake square: Ghirardelli's Premium Chocolates (☎ 474-3938) sells ice cream and fountain drinks, and Ghirardelli Too (☎ 474-1414) has gifts, espresso, and frozen yogurt. Both are usually open past 9 pm. If you want to buy their chocolate bars head to Walgreens where you can get them for much cheaper.

For overseas visitors, taking back a couple bottles of Napa or Sonoma Valley **wine** is a great idea. The Napa Valley Winery Exchange (☎ 771-2887), 415 Taylor St, downtown, has small production and specialist wines. Plump Jack Wines (☎ 346-9870) at 3201 Fillmore can give you excellent recommendations. Trader Joe's (☎ 863-1292), 555 9th St, and Cost Plus (☎ 928-6200), 2552 Taylor St, both have excellent deals.

Music

For a huge selection of CDs and great prices go by Tower Records. There are a few outlets around the city including Tower Outlet (☎ 957-9660), 660 3rd St in the SoMa outlet zone, but Tower Records (☎ 885-0500), Columbus Ave and Bay, close to Fisherman's Wharf, is one of the best.

For used records, CDs, and tapes try Rough Trade Absolute Music (☎ 543-7091), 695 3rd St, best known for launching punk and alternative music in the '70s and '80s, both on indie labels and its own.

And, of course, the largest music store in the world has opened its doors in San Francisco, the Virgin Megastore (☎ 397-4525), 2 Stockton St at Market, complete with listening stations and a cafe.

Outdoor Gear

Many of these stores sell not only clothing but the necessaries for outdoor adventure, including travel guides. They can give good advice, and have bulletin boards full of information.

The North Face (☎ 433-3223), 180 Post St, has a good selection of high-quality outdoor and adventure travel gear. Try their factory outlet store in SoMa (☎ 626-6444), 1325 Howard St, for discounted styles. Patagonia (☎ 771-2050), 770 North Point, Fisherman's Wharf, is another respected name in outdoor gear. Eddie Bauer (☎ 986-7600), 220 Post St, has three floors of outdoor equipment and clothing.

Piercings & Tattoos

Getting a pin through it is a San Francisco specialty; numerous specialist body piercers will pierce parts of your body that go way beyond those mundane ears. Piercing specialists start with The Gauntlet (☎ 431-3133), 2377 Market St at Castro. In the Haight-Ashbury there's Anubis Warpus (☎ 431-2218), 1525 Haight St, and in the Lower Haight, Body Manipulations (☎ 621-0408), 254 Fillmore St.

Tattoos are what you need to go with your piercings and the Lyle Tuttle (☎ 775-4991) tattoo parlor, at 841 Columbus Ave in North Beach, also has a small tattoo museum.

Where to Shop

Union Square San Francisco's downtown shopping concentrates around Union Square and nearby Market St. Macy's (☎ 397-3333), Neiman-Marcus (☎ 362-3900), and Saks Fifth Avenue (☎ 986-4300) make up the square's trio of plush department stores. Two blocks down

Powell St from the square, the stylish San Francisco Shopping Center (☎ 495-5656), 865 Market St, contains Nordstrom (☎ 243-8500) and many smaller shops. In the surrounding streets you'll find the fashion world well represented by the likes of Chanel, Ralph Lauren, Gianni Versace, Emporio Armani, and Gucci. Gump's (☎ 982-1616), 135 Post St, is a San Francisco institution, half museum and half home furnishings store.

SoMa The big deal in SoMa is outlet shopping. Yerba Buena Square (☎ 974-5136), 899 Howard St at 5th, and the 660 Center (☎ 227-0464), 660 3rd St at Townsend, both house a variety of outlet operations and are open daily. The Esprit Factory Outlet (☎ 957-2550), 499 Illinois St at 16th, Potrero Hill, is a big warehouse with 30% to 50% discounts on Esprit apparel.

Chinatown Only Fisherman's Wharf rivals Chinatown for sheer quantity of tourist junk. If you want a cheap souvenir then you've come to the right place. Explore the back streets and alleys and you'll find all sorts of less-touristy goods like bargain-priced dishes and bowls or weird herbal pharmaceuticals.

Haight-Ashbury The Haight has a fine collection of strange shops. It's particularly good for music, especially older and second hand records, and used clothing, though it also has its share of pricey shops. 683 Haight St (☎ 861-1311) has '60s rock & roll memorabilia, and Comic Relief (☎ 552-9010) at 1597 Haight St is the place for off-the-wall comic books.

Fisherman's Wharf If you really need a San Francisco souvenir, you'll find what you're looking for at one or all of Fisherman's Wharf's shopping centers: Pier 39, The Cannery, Ghirardelli Square, and the Anchorage.

Union St & the Marina Union St in Pacific Height's 'Cow Hollow' is dotted with interesting boutiques, antique stores, and trendy little galleries. Only a few blocks down towards the Bay is Chestnut St in the Marina, an equally upscale little enclave tending toward the twenty-something crowd.

The Castro & Noe Valley Just south of Market St, and barely off the new F Muni line, four blocks of Castro St are the center of the busy neighborhood, housing numerous shops and restaurants. For fun, check out Cliff's Variety (☎ 431-5365), 479 Castro St, where you can find anything from Play-Doh to that three-penny nail you need to hang your SFMOMA poster.

Follow Castro south, over a hill, and below lies Noe Valley. 24th St is the main shopping street. This haven is for those looking to get away from the tourist throng and browse a thoroughly San Francisco street with the usual fine selection of art and clothes, coffee and books.

GETTING THERE & AWAY
Air
San Francisco International Airport (SFO) is the major airport in the Bay Area. International flights arrive and depart from here, but travelers from other US (particularly West Coast) cities may find cheaper flights into Oakland International Airport across the Bay, a hub for discount airlines like Southwest.

SFO (☎ 876-7809) is on the Peninsula, 14 miles south of downtown off Hwy 101. The North Terminal is where American, Canadian, and United Airlines are based; the South Terminal, home to Air Canada, Alaska Airlines, America West, Continental, Delta, Southwest, TWA, and USAir; and the International Terminal is where you'll find all international airlines (except for the Canadian ones), plus the international services of Alaska Airlines, Delta, Northwest, and United.

Information booths (white courtesy phone ☎ 7-0018) on the lower level of all three terminals operate daily from 8 am to midnight. Travelers' Aid information booths on the upper level operate daily from 9 am to 9 pm.

Bus

The Transbay bus terminal (☎ 495-1575), 425 Mission St at 1st St in SoMa, is the major bus depot in San Francisco. If you're heading out to neighboring communities you can take AC Transit (☎ 510-839-2882) buses to the East Bay, Golden Gate Transit (☎ 332-6600) buses north to Marin and Sonoma Counties, SamTrans (☎ 800-660-4287) buses south to Palo Alto and along the Pacific coast, and Santa Clara Transit (☎ (408) 321-2300) buses to go south beyond Palo Alto and to San Jose.

Greyhound has multiple buses daily to Los Angeles ($35 one way, $69 roundtrip) and other destinations, and Green Tortoise (☎ 956-7500), 494 Broadway at Kearny, is always a fun alternative. It's $30 to Los Angeles.

Train

CalTrain (☎ 800-660-4287) operates down the Peninsula, linking San Francisco with Palo Alto (Stanford University) and San Jose. The Amtrak terminal is at Jack London Square in Oakland. A free shuttle bus

---

Negotiating the Neighborhoods

If you're planning on getting around on public transit, you really should pick up a free Muni map at the visitors center. Some of the most important Muni routes for visitors include:

No 5 Fulton Along Market, McAllister, and Fulton Sts along the north side of Golden Gate Park all the way to the ocean.

No 7 Haight From the Ferry Building along Market and Haight Sts, through Haight-Ashbury, to the southeast corner of Golden Gate Park; daytime only.

No 14 Mission Along Mission St through SoMa and the Mission district.

No 15 3rd St From 3rd St in SoMa, through the Financial District on Kearny St, through North Beach on Columbus Ave, then along Powell St to the Fisherman's Wharf area.

No 18 46th Ave Palace of the Legion of Honor to Sutro Baths along the western edge of Golden Gate Park on the Great Hwy, past San Francisco Zoo and Lake Merced.

No 22 Fillmore From Potrero Hill, through the Mission along Fillmore St, past Japantown to Pacific Heights and the Marina.

No 24 Divisadero Through Noe Valley, along Castro St then Divisadero to Pacific Heights.

No 26 Valencia Through the historic areas of the Mission, along Valencia St to Market and Polk, and through SoMa along Mission St.

No 28 19th Ave From Fort Mason to the Golden Gate Bridge toll plaza and on through the Presidio, Richmond District, Golden Gate Park and south through the Sunset district all the way to Daly City BART.

No 30 Stockton From the CalTrain Station in SoMa, along 3rd and Market Sts, then on Stockton St through Chinatown, and Columbus Ave through North Beach to Fisherman's Wharf, Fort Mason, and the Palace of Fine Arts.

No 32 Embarcadero From the CalTrain Station along the Embarcadero, past the Ferry Building to Fisherman's Wharf.

No 37 Corbett A winding route from the Haight-Ashbury via Buena Vista Park to Twin Peaks.

No 38 Geary From the Transbay bus terminal along Market St and then Geary Blvd all the way to the Cliff House at the ocean.

No 71 Haight-Noriega Along Market and Haight Sts, through the Haight-Ashbury, along the south side of Golden Gate Park and then down to Noriega St through the Outer Sunset to the ocean. ■

connects with the CalTrain station and with the Ferry Building on the Embarcadero.

GETTING AROUND
To/From the Airports
SFO The airport operates a ground transportation information hotline (☎ 800-736-2008), weekdays 7:30 am to 5 pm.

SamTrans (☎ 800-660-4287) express bus No 3X ($1) takes 20 minutes to reach the Daly City BART station from where you can ride the BART to San Francisco. The SamTrans 7F express service ($2) to the Transbay terminal takes half an hour but no baggage is allowed; the 7B bus ($1) does allow baggage but it's an all-stop service, taking about an hour.

Or take the free CalTrain (☎ 800-660-4287) shuttle on its nine-minute ride to the Millbrae CalTrain station. From there you can ride the CalTrain north to San Francisco.

Airport transport buses include the SFO Airporter (☎ 495-8404, 800-532-8405 in Northern California only), which drops off at major hotels in three city zones. Fares are $8 one way, $15 roundtrip.

A shuttle is a minibus service operating either to specific locations or on request. They typically cost $9 to $11 one way. Super Shuttle (☎ 558-8500), Lorrie's (☎ 334-9000) and Quake City (☎ 255-4899) are a few.

Oakland International Airport Travelers arriving in Oakland can catch the $2 shuttle bus from the airport to the Coliseum BART station and the Daly City BART train to San Francisco. Super Shuttle (☎ 510-268-8700) operates door-to-door service to destinations in the East Bay and San Francisco for $12 to $21.

Public Transportation
Muni San Francisco's principal public transport system is Muni (Municipal Transit Agency, ☎ 673-6864) which operates bus lines, streetcars, and cable cars. A free Muni Timetable is available from the visitors center, and there is a detailed *Street & Transit Map* that costs $2. Standard

---

Cable Car Routes
California St This route runs straight up California St from the Embarcadero Terminal at Market St through the Financial District and Chinatown then up Nob Hill before dropping down to Van Ness. There are great views of the Bay during the climb up (or drop down) Nob Hill.

Powell-Mason From the Hallidie Plaza terminal at the junction of Market and Powell Sts the cable car climbs up Powell St past Union Square before descending down Mason, Columbus, and Taylor towards Fisherman's Wharf.

Powell-Hyde This route follows a similar pattern to the Powell-Mason line but follows Jackson St for five blocks and then turns down Hyde St to terminate at Aquatic Park, near Fisherman's Wharf. Along Hyde St it crosses the top of curvy Lombard St. ∎

Muni fares for buses or streetcars is $1; children and seniors (65 +) pay 35¢. Cable car fares are $2. A Muni Passport, available in one-day ($6), three-day ($10), or seven-day ($15) versions, allows unlimited travel on all Muni transport including cable cars. A cheaper Weekly Pass costs $9 and allows bus and railway travel and discounts on cable car trips.

BART The Bay Area Rapid Transit system (BART, ☎ 788-2278) is a subway system linking San Francisco with the East Bay. There are four BART lines, with Daly City, Richmond, North Concord/Martinez, and Fremont as the extremities of the service. In the city, the route runs beneath Market St; the Powell St station is the most convenient to Union Square. A monthly Muni Fast Pass ($35, also includes all Muni and CalTrain services) covers BART travel within San Francisco.

Car & Motorcycle
A car is the last thing you want in downtown San Francisco – it's a two-part nightmare of negotiating the hills and parking,

not to mention traffic. Remember, on hill streets (with a grade as little as 3%) you must 'curb wheels' so that they ride up against the curb – there are daunting fines for failing to do so.

The American Automobile Association (AAA, ☎ 565-2012) has an office at 150 Van Ness Ave.

Parking Some of the cheaper downtown parking garages are at 123 O'Farrell St (6 pm to 8 am for $5) or at 5th and Mission Sts (24 hours for $12). The parking garage under Portsmouth Square in Chinatown is very reasonably priced for shorter stops, and ditto the St Mary's Square Garage on California St near Grant. The multi-story parking garage at Sutter and Stockton Sts, just north of Union Square, is also a good value.

Car Rentals All the big rent-a-car operators can be found in San Francisco, particularly at the airports. The downtown offices are: Alamo (☎ 882-9440), 687 Folsom St; Avis (☎ 885-5011), 675 Post St; Budget (☎ 928-7864), 321 Mason St; Dollar (☎ 771-5300), 364 O'Farrell St; Hertz (☎ 771-2200), 433 Mason St; and Thrifty (☎ 788-8111), 520 Mason St.

Want to rent something flashy? Sunbelt Car Rental (☎ 771-9191) rents convertibles, BMWs, Corvettes, Jaguars, Mustangs, and 4-wheel drives. A motorcycle? Dubbelju (☎ 495-2774) has BMWs and Harleys.

Taxi
If you need to call a cab, some of the major companies are City Cab (☎ 468-7200), De Soto Cab (☎ 673-1414), and Yellow Cab (☎ 626-2345).

Bicycle
For most visitors bicycles will not be an ideal way of getting around the city – there's too much traffic and all those hills are fearsome – but the Bay Area is a great place for recreational bike riding. A bike is the ideal way to explore the Presidio, Golden Gate Park, or to travel across the Golden Gate Bridge to Marin County. See the Activities section for more information. Bicycles are allowed on BART but only on the last car of the train. Call BART for regulations on hours and how to get a free permit.

Ferry
There are three major ferry operators in San Francisco. **Blue & Gold Ferries** (☎ 510-522-3300) runs the Alameda-Oakland Ferry from Pier 39 at Fisherman's Wharf via the Ferry Building to Alameda and Oakland. **Golden Gate Ferry** (☎ 332-6600) has regular service from the Ferry Building to Larkspur and Sausalito in Marin County. **Red & White Fleet** has services to Sausalito, Tiburon, and Angel Island in Marin County, from Pier 41 and Pier 43½ at Fisherman's Wharf. Red & White also operates a daily San Francisco City Tour and a Golden Gate Bridge Cruise, as well as the only Alcatraz service.

San Francisco Bay Area

Marin County

☎ *415*

If there's a part of the Bay Area that consciously tries to live up to the California dream it's Marin (muh-RIN) County. Just a short drive across the Golden Gate Bridge from San Francisco, Marin is wealthy, laid back, and right in tune with every trend that comes by, from hot tubs to mountain biking to designer pizzas. But Marin's reputation for the highest standard of living in the state doesn't tell the whole story. Its breathtaking views of San Francisco across the Bay, abundance of hiking and biking trails, and great climate make it definitely worth the trip. What brings visitors to Marin is the splendor of Mt Tamalpais (Mt Tam), Muir Woods, and the wild Pacific coastline, as well as the charm of its well-kept artsy communities, such as waterfront Sausalito and woodsy Mill Valley.

Orientation

There are two important routes through Marin: busy Hwy 101 spears straight north through Marin while quiet Hwy 1 winds its way up the sparsely populated coast. Sir Francis Drake Blvd is the thoroughfare that cuts across west Marin from Hwy 101 to the ocean. Highway 1 intersects with Hwy 101 at Mill Valley. If you want to visit the coast, tank up before starting out on Hwy 1 – there are no gas stations from Mill Valley all the way north to Bolinas or Point Reyes Station.

From the East Bay, Hwy 580 comes in over the Richmond-San Rafael bridge ($1 toll for westbound traffic) to meet 101 at Larkspur.

Information

The Marin County Convention & Visitors Bureau (☎ 472-7470) in the Civic Center building in San Rafael, handles tourist information for the entire county. Information is also readily available from visitors centers in Sausalito, Tiburon, and Mill Valley and other city chambers of commerce. There are park visitors centers in the Mt Tam, Muir Woods, and Point Reyes parks while Marin Headlands is part of the Golden Gate National Recreation Area.

Free publications include *Marin County Visitor*, a semiannual tourism guide, and *Coastal Traveler*, which covers the Marin coast and further north. The *Pacific Sun* is a free weekly newspaper that details events and goings-on throughout Marin, and the *Independent Journal* is Marin's daily paper.

For accommodations, the B&B Exchange of Marin (☎ 485-1971) makes bookings throughout Marin at anything from fancy B&Bs to Sausalito houseboats.

San Francisco
Bay Area Locator

Getting There & Away

Buses and ferries will get you *to* Marin, but only a car will get you *around* conveniently, so if you want to explore, renting a car in San Francisco is advisable. Of course, you can also bike it.

Bus Golden Gate Transit (☎ 332-6600) operates numerous buses from San Francisco across the Golden Gate Bridge and around Marin County. Greyhound buses depart from San Francisco to the San Rafael depot twice daily; it's $5 one way.

Gray Line (☎ 558-9400) bus tours from San Francisco depart the Transbay terminal at 9 am and 1:30 pm daily and make a 3½-hour circuit of Marin including visits to Sausalito and Muir Woods for $28/14; reservations are required.

Ferry Golden Gate Ferries (☎ 332-6600) operates from the San Francisco Ferry Building to Sausalito and Larkspur Landing, hourly from 6 am to 9 pm on weekdays. The Red & White Fleet (☎ 546-2628) provides ferry service from Pier 43½ at Fisherman's Wharf in San Francisco to Sausalito and Tiburon.

Getting Around

The Golden Gate Transit buses will get you from place to place around suburban Marin fairly effectively although getting to Mt Tamalpais, Muir Woods and along the coast is not so easy. It's best to drive. Bicycles are also a great way to get around, with many bicycle trails in western Marin and around Mt Tamalpais. Wheel Escapes (☎ 332-0218), in Sausalito at 30 Liberty St, rents bikes $5 per hour or $21 for the day. Mike's Bicycle Center (☎ 454-3747) at 1601 4th St, San Rafael, offers a large selection of rentals.

MARIN HEADLANDS

One would think that the prime waterfront land lining the Golden Gate entrance to the Bay would be stacked with expensive condominium developments, but it's strikingly pristine. On the San Francisco side the Presidio and Lincoln Park are protected areas, and on the Marin side, the Headlands are maintained by the Golden Gate National Recreation Area (GGNRA). These rolling coastal hills are the vantage point for the most spectacular views of San Francisco, as well as having a number of interesting attractions.

Marin County

```
0        3        6 km
0    2        4 miles
```

MMWD = Marin Municipal Water District Watershed
GGNRA = Golden Gate National Recreation Area

CALIFORNIA

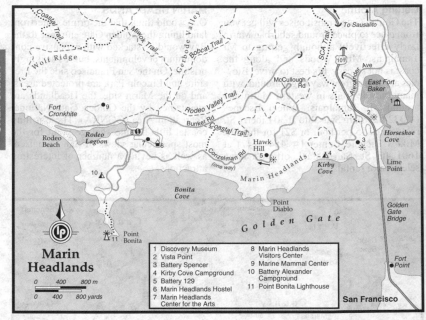

Marin
Headlands

0   400   800 m
0   400   800 yards

1 Discovery Museum
2 Vista Point
3 Battery Spencer
4 Kirby Cove Campground
5 Battery 129
6 Marin Headlands Hostel
7 Marin Headlands
   Center for the Arts
8 Marin Headlands
   Visitors Center
9 Marine Mammal Center
10 Battery Alexander
   Campground
11 Point Bonita Lighthouse

San Francisco

The Army has much to do with the area being as it is today. For over a century they controlled the area for its strategic position, and though they never saw much in the way of enemy attack, they did serve to fend off the hungry developers. After the Army vacated these hills, Representative Philip Burton and concerned citizens were able to create the GGNRA.

Orientation & Information
Heading north across the Golden Gate Bridge, exit at Alexander Ave, the first exit, and avoid Fort Baker, the tourist-ridden coach-tour stopping place on the east side of the highway. Dip left under the highway instead, and head out west for the expansive views and hiking trailheads. Conzelman Rd heads up into the hills, where it eventually forks: Conzelman continues west and McCullough heads inland to join Bunker Rd toward Rodeo Beach and the Marine Mammal Center.

Information is available from the GGNRA (☎ 556-0560) or the Marin Headlands Visitors Center (☎ 331-1540) at Fort Barry on Bunker Rd near Rodeo Lagoon.

Things to See & Do
Fort Baker is generally a mob scene to avoid, but the **Discovery Museum** (☎ 332-7674) within is a first-rate children's museum housed in converted military barracks. From arts & crafts to construction and biology to photography, everything is hands on. Kids love it and grown-ups will too.

A quarter mile up Conzelman Rd from the highway you'll reach **Battery Spencer**. Dating back to the Spanish-American War, this site encompasses a short trail that leads to a towering view of the Golden Gate Bridge and the city beyond. Continue up Conzelman Rd to **Hawk Hill**. From late summer to early fall, thousands of migrating birds of prey can be seen soaring on the

CHRIS SALCEDO

Rodeo Beach in the Marin Headlands

updrafts along the cliffs. There are several trails in this area and you can explore the remains of the never-completed Battery 129.

Heading west the road becomes a one-lane steep descent hanging above Bonita Cove. When the road forks, head left to Battery Mendell and yet another sparkling view of San Francisco. **Point Bonita Lighthouse**, built in 1877, is accessible by trail and two footbridges from this point. It is open Saturday and Sunday afternoons. The loop road continues down to Rodeo Lagoon and Rodeo Beach.

Duck, egrets, and brown pelicans gather at **Rodeo Lagoon** throughout the summer months. The beach is easily accessible and a pleasant place to enjoy the rugged Pacific. There are picnic sites available and trails that lead up into the hills. In the vicinity, the **Marin Headlands Center for the Arts** is a refurbished barracks converted to artists workspaces and conference facilities. The **Marine Mammal Center** (☎ 289-7325), on the north side of the lagoon, cares for injured and orphaned sea creatures, rehabilitating them before releasing them to the wild. It's open daily from 10 am to 4 pm; admission is free, but donations are requested.

The parking area at the very end of Bunker Rd is also the trailhead for the **Coastal Trail**, a great hiking route that meanders inland and then back out to the coast to the north at Muir Beach.

Places to Stay
Camping is available within the headlands.

Permits are required and are available at the Marin Headlands Visitors Center. For information call ☎ 331-1540. The HI *Marin Headlands Hostel* (☎ 331-2777) is also near the visitors center; it's $11 per night, open all year round.

Getting There & Away
On weekends and holidays you can take Muni Bus No 76 from San Francisco.

SAUSALITO
• *pop 7000*
Sausalito, Spanish for 'little grove of willows,' is the first town you encounter after crossing the Golden Gate Bridge from

---

An Energetic Marin Roundtrip
Got energy to burn and want a real Bay Area experience? From San Francisco, walk across the Golden Gate Bridge to the Marin Headlands and continue down to Sausalito (about four miles, altogether). If it's a summer weekend you may actually overtake cars stuck in the traffic jam inching their way into town. Wander the shops and waterfront then take Golden Gate Transit bus No 10 to Tiburon ($1.25). (You can lunch in either Tiburon or Sausalito.) Take the ferry across from Tiburon to Angel Island ($5 roundtrip), rent a bicycle ($25 all day), and ride around the island. Then take the Red & White Ferry from Tiburon back to San Francisco ($5.50) and ride the cable car back to downtown ($2). Total cost: $13.75 in fares plus $25 if you rent a bicycle. ■

San Francisco. Once a small seafaring center populated by fisherfolk, the tiny bayside community is now fiercely expensive and fashionable, a tourist haven with a curious mix of junky souvenir shops and costly galleries and boutiques. The crowds get dense and the parking impossible, but there's no denying Sausalito's beauty, stretched along the water's edge with uninterrupted views of San Francisco and Angel Island. It makes a great day out from San Francisco and the ferry connection is a fun alternative to the parking problems. If you're feeling fit you can also walk there, across the Golden Gate Bridge, through Sausalito's luxurious hillside real estate, and into downtown.

Sausalito has had a varied and interesting history, having begun as a 19,000-acre land grant to an army captain in 1838. When it became the terminus of the railway line down the Pacific coast, it entered a new stage as a busy lumber port with a racy and colorful waterfront noted for its freewheeling bars and bordellos. WWII brought dramatic changes when Sausalito became the site of Marinship, a huge shipbuilding yard that turned out 15 Liberty Ships, 16 oilers, and 62 tankers. At its hard-working peak of efficiency the yard turned out a completed ship every 13 days and built one tanker start-to-finish in just 33 days. After the war a new bohemian period began, with a resident artists' colony living in 'arks,' houseboats moored along the bayside.

Orientation & Information

Commercial Sausalito is essentially one street, the waterfront Bridgeway Blvd. Humboldt Park and the Ferry Terminal mark the town center. Continue past the center and the Village Fair shopping center to the old Marinship site, now a cluster of yacht marinas around Liberty Ship Way. The visitors center (☎ 332-0505), upstairs in the Village Fair on Bridgeway, is open Tuesday to Sunday from 11:30 am to 4 pm and has a small exhibit of Sausalito's history.

Things to See & Do

While Sausalito's most potent attraction is its bayside setting, with sailboats silhouetted against the shimmering image of the city across the water, there is also some exploring to be done in town.

The visitors center provides a walking guide booklet to make wandering the Sausalito waterfront more interesting. The **Plaza de Viña Del Mar Park**, near the ferry terminus, has a fountain flanked by 14-foot-tall elephant statues recycled from the 1915 Panama-Pacific Exposition in Golden Gate Park. Opposite Johnson St, toward the Bay Model, **Ark Row** has a number of arks, houseboats that were once common on the Bay. The first arks were made in the 1880s and there are still several hundred in Sausalito.

The Army Corps of Engineers' **Bay Model** Visitor Center (☎ 332-3871) is housed in one of the old Marinship warehouses, at 2100 Bridgeway. The US Army built the model in 1954 to study the complex water flows of the Bay. The center also has interesting displays on the remarkable story of Marinship. The center is open in summer, Tuesday to Sunday, from 9 am to 4 pm; in winter, Tuesday to Saturday, from 9 am to 4 pm.

Outside are two historic ships; phone ☎ 556-3002 to book tours. Tours of the *Wapama*, a 1915 wooden steam schooner looking for all the world like Noah's Ark, are on Saturday at 11 am. Tours of the *Hercules*, a 1907 steam tug, are on Saturday at 12:30 pm.

If you're interested in shopping, check out the Village Fair (☎ 332-1092), 777 Bridgeway, which features a collection of shops and boutiques. There's also an endless selection of tourist shops that sell postcards, T-shirts, and souvenirs all along Bridgeway.

Places to Stay

Accommodation options in Sausalito's trio of Victorian-era hotels are limited and expensive. The *Sausalito Hotel* (☎ 332-4900) at 16 El Portal St and Bridgeway is close to the ferry terminus in the center of Sausalito. Closed for remodeling at press time, it's slated to reopen in summer of

1996; call ahead. The charming and historic *Casa Madrona* (☎ 332-0502, 800-288-0502) at 801 Bridgeway plays its romantic image to the hilt; the 32 rooms are so individual that they each have a name. Prices range from around $125 to $200, more for the single suite. The *Alta Mira Continental Hotel* (☎ 332-1350) at 125 Buckley Ave, is a block back from Bridgeway Blvd, overlooking the town center and the Bay. Rooms are $70 for a queen and up to $170 for suites with private sundeck and view of the Bay.

Places to Eat

Bridgeway is packed with lots of cafes, all catering to tourists. Though you'll find the best selection on Bridgeway, you won't find the best prices. Another option is to go where the locals go on Caledonia St.

Bridgeway Burgers (☎ 332-9471), 737 Bridgeway, turns out burgers from $4.15; take them across the road to the waterside. Orderly lines are ensured by a sign suggesting that customers 'Please form a line to your right' in 10 different languages. One of them translates as: 'You go stay rite brah.' You can get the same burgers, at slightly higher prices, in *Paterson's* (☎ 332-1264), the pub next door at No 739.

Caffé Tutti (☎ 332-0211) at 12 El Portal St, by the Sausalito Hotel, produces sandwiches, pizza, and pasta dishes and a wide variety of coffees. *Café Sausalito* (☎ 332-6579) on the 4th floor of Village Fair at 777 Bridgeway Blvd has great views over the bay. The *Waterfront Café* (☎ 332-5625), on Liberty Ship Way at the marina south of the Bay Model, is a good place to sit and watch the boats with a coffee and a big $4 sandwich. Catch up on the European scene with espresso drinks and pastries at *Cafe Trieste* (☎ 332-7770), 1000 Bridgeway.

A short distance north of the busy central area, and one block back from Bridgeway, Caledonia St has a collection of cheaper eating places in a neat little clump between Johnson and Pine. Try *Café Soleil* (☎ 331-9355) at No 37 for a caffeine hit. *Gatsbys* (☎ 332-4500) at No 39 serves up deep-dish pizza and is a good place for a beer, for lunch Friday to Sunday, or dinners any night. Then there's the *Stuffed Croissant* (☎ 332-7103) at No 43 for sandwiches, and *Arawan* (☎ 332-0882) at No 47 for Thai food (main courses under $10). If you're a sushi lover, *Sushi Ran* (☎ 332-3620) at No 107 serves delicious Japanese cuisine. It's always crowded, so make reservations for dinner or eat at the sushi bar.

Getting There & Away

Driving to Sausalito from San Francisco, take the Alexander Ave exit, the first exit after the Golden Gate Bridge, and follow the signs into Sausalito. There are three municipal parking lots (with meters) north of the town square at Bridgeway and El Portal. Parking meters run daily from 8 am to 6 pm.

The ferry is a fun alternative for getting to Sausalito. Golden Gate Ferry (☎ 332-6600) operates to and from the San Francisco Ferry Building for $4.25/3.20 one way. The ferries operate up to 10 times daily on weekdays and the trip takes 30 minutes. The Red & White Fleet (☎ 546-2896) operates to and from Pier 43½ at Fisherman's Wharf up to six times daily weekdays, seven times on weekends and costs $5.50/2.75. You can bring bicycles on the ferries.

Golden Gate Transit bus Nos 10, 20, and 50 daily, No 2 during commuter hours, and No 63 on weekends, run to Sausalito from San Francisco for $2. Bus No 10 runs from Sausalito via Mill Valley to Tiburon about every half hour weekdays, every hour on weekends for $1.25.

Getting Around

Wheel Escapes (☎ 332-0218) at 30 Liberty Ship Way rents bikes from $5 an hour, $21 a day. Battens & Boards (☎ 332-0212) on Bridgeway Blvd at Pine St rents bikes at $7.50 and $23.

TIBURON
• *pop 8000*

Tiburon – the name comes from the Spanish *Punta de Tiburon* or 'Shark Point' – is a pricey bayside community which, much

CALIFORNIA

like Sausalito, is noted for its gorgeous views. It's connected by ferry with downtown San Francisco and is also the jumping-off point for nearby Angel Island.

Orientation & Information

Tiburon rests on a peninsula pointing out into the center of the Bay. The central part of town is comprised of Tiburon Blvd with Juanita Lane and charming Main St arcing off. Main St is also known as Ark Row, where the old bayside houseboats have taken root on dry land and metamorphosed into classy shops and boutiques. Visitor information is available from the Tiburon Peninsula Chamber of Commerce (☎ 435-5633) at 96B Main St.

Things to See & Do

Browse as you stroll past the shops on Main St, grab a bite to eat, take the ferry to Angel Island, and you've seen Tiburon. There are great views over the town from the hillside **Old St Hilary's Church** (☎ 435-1853), a fine 1888 example of carpenter gothic. It's open April to October, Wednesday and Sunday from 1 to 4 pm. Back toward Hwy 101 the **Richardson Bay Audubon Center** (☎ 388-2524), 376 Greenwood Beach Rd, is home to a wide variety of waterbirds. The center is open Wednesday to Sunday from 9 am to 5 pm and entry is $1. Nature walks take place on Sundays at 9 am and 1 pm.

Wine aficionados can enjoy free wine sampling at **Windsor Vineyards** (☎ 435-3113), 72 Main St. This small California winery has a selection of over 40 wines to choose from. What better gift idea to bring back from the Bay Area than California wine with a personalized label? It's open daily Sunday through Thursday from 10 am to 6 pm; Friday and Saturday from 10 am to 7 pm.

Places to Stay

The *Tiburon Lodge* (☎ 435-3133, 800-842-8766) at 1651 Tiburon Blvd is about all Tiburon has to offer by way of places to stay. It's modern and classy with regular rooms at $105 to $125 for most of the year,

rising to $125 to $150 from May through September.

Places to Eat

Sam's Anchor Cafe (☎ 435-4527) at 27 Main St is a popular local hangout with an unbeatable view. On a sunny day there may be a long wait for tables on the deck. Sandwiches are $6.25 to $10. Stop by for lunch and soak in the sun, or have a daiquiri or drink and lounge on the deck overlooking the Bay. Right next to Sam's is the *Sweden House Café* (☎ 435-9767) at 35 Main St. Also right on the waterfront is *Guaymas* (☎ 435-6300) at 5 Main St, an authentic and very popular Mexican restaurant with a great outdoor dining area and entrees around $10 to $12.

Over on Tiburon Blvd there's the *New Morning Café* (☎ 435-4315) at No 1696 and *Verde Guardino* (☎ 435-6464) in the Point Tiburon Plaza.

Getting There & Away

From northbound Hwy 101, take the turnoff marked Tiburon, onto Tiburon Blvd (also known as Hwy 131) until you hit Main St.

Ferries dock right in front of the Guaymas restaurant on Main St. The Red & White Fleet (☎ 546-2896) connects with Pier 43½ at Fisherman's Wharf. The one-way fare is $5.50/2.75 and you can bring bicycles on the ferry. Ferries connect regularly to nearby Angel Island.

Golden Gate Transit bus No 10 runs from San Francisco ($2.50) and Sausalito ($1.25) via Mill Valley to Tiburon about every half hour weekdays and every hour on weekends. During the weekday commute time bus No 8 runs direct between San Francisco and Tiburon.

ANGEL ISLAND

Angel Island State Park (☎ 435-1915), the 750-acre island just a few minutes by ferry from Tiburon, is a popular place for walking, biking, and picnics and offers fine views across the Bay. It's had a varied history as a military base and as an immigration station.

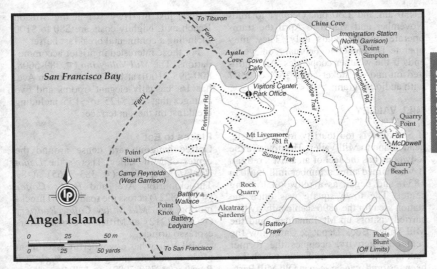

CALIFORNIA

There are 12 miles of roads and trails around the island including a hike (no bikes) to the summit of 781-foot Mt Livermore and a five-mile perimeter trail that offers a 360° panorama of the Bay. In Ayala Cove, the sheltered harbor on the Tiburon side of the island, a small beach backs up to grassy picnic lawns fringed by forest. A number of historical buildings are also found on the island: Camp Reynolds, on the western side, was built as a US Army defense post in 1863 during the Civil War. Fort McDowell, on the eastern side, was built in 1898 during the Spanish-American War. The Immigration Station operated from 1910 to 1940 but this 'Ellis Island of the West' was an even less welcoming place than its New York counterpart. During WWII the barracks became an internment camp for Japanese Americans. The Immigration Station is open on weekends and holidays from 11 am to 3:30 pm. Guided tours of Camp Reynolds and of the East Garrison Chapel and Guard House at Fort McDowell run the same hours. A more recent military presence is the Nike Missile site, intended to bring down Russian nuclear bombers bound for San Francisco but only in operation from 1955 to 1963.

Places to Stay & Eat

You can camp on the island at one of nine small campsites for $9 in the peak season, $7 in the off season. Reservations are made through Destinet. The *Cove Café* (☎ 435-0358) at Ayala Cove has food, sandwiches, and picnic supplies.

Getting There & Away

The Angel Island-Tiburon Ferry (☎ 435-2131) from Tiburon costs $5/3, another $1 to bring a bicycle. Services are daily in summer, less frequent after September 5.

Red & White Ferry (☎ 546-2896) operates to the island from Pier 43½ at Fisherman's Wharf but only on weekends and only twice each day. The roundtrip costs $9/4.50. Blue & Gold Ferry (☎ 705-5444) operates from Pier 39 and the Ferry Building via Angel Island to Vallejo.

Getting Around

Bicycles can be rented at Ayala Cove on the island for $10 an hour or $25 for the day. Roller skates, in-line skates, and skateboards are not allowed. Tram tours (☎ 897-0715) around the island operate May to September, weekends hourly from 10:30 am to 3:30 pm; weekdays at 10:30 and

11:30 am and 1:30 pm. October to mid-November and March to April the trams operate on weekends only. They may operate December to February on weekends if the weather cooperates. An unlimited on-and-off ticket costs $5/4 or $9/7 with audio program.

MILL VALLEY
• *pop 14,000*

If Sausalito is too touristy for your taste, head inland to Mill Valley. This town in the redwoods has the feel of an artist's retreat. It was named after a lumber mill built in 1834, and began as a redwood logging center. The town square was once the station area for the 1896 scenic railway that carried visitors up Mt Tamalpais, and the Mill Valley Book Depot & Café, now the center of activity, occupies the former station. The historic mill site, which has been restored, can be seen at Old Mill Park.

Information
In Mill Valley visitor information is available from the Chamber of Commerce (☎ 388-9700) at 85 Throckmorton Ave. It's open Monday to Friday from 11 am to 1 pm and 1:30 to 4 pm.

Things to See & Do
Many hikers and mountain bikers enjoy stopping in Mill Valley on their way up to Mt Tam. Mill Valley is best enjoyed by foot, strolling around Miller Ave and down Throckmorton. Shopping enthusiasts will be pleased to find a collection of antique stores and beautiful home furnishing stores. If you're looking for a creative alternative check out the **Handmade Ceramic Studio** at 401 Strawberry Village (☎ 388-8668) where 'You paint it, we fire it, it's yours.'

Places to Stay
As you travel further into Marin, you'll find Best Westerns, Travelodges, and Holiday Inns clustered close to Hwy 101. The *Holiday Inn Express* (☎ 332-5700, 800-258-3894) is just four miles north of the Golden Gate at 160 Shoreline Hwy, Mill Valley, just off Hwy 101 at the Stinson Beach exit. Nightly costs are $80 to $100 including a continental breakfast buffet.

For those interested in pricier accommodations, The *Mill Valley Inn* (☎ 389-6608, 800-595-2100), at 165 Throckmorton Ave, has 16 'casually elegant' rooms and two cottages that run $125 to $155 including breakfast on the sun terrace.

Places to Eat
Coffee hangouts are dense around the center of Mill Valley. There's the *Depot Bookstore & Café* (☎ 383-2665) at 87 Throckmorton Ave, and *Peet's Coffee* (☎ 381-8227) across the road at 88 Throckmorton Ave. *Mill Valley Coffee Roastery* (☎ 383-2912) at Miller Ave also offers espresso drinks.

Mill Valley has a wonderful assortment of cheap eats and dining choices. *High Tech Burrito* (☎ 388-7002) at 118 Strawberry Village, the shopping center on Hwy 101 in Mill Valley, turns out extremely popular Marin-style (read: healthy) burritos. For hearty sandwiches, salads, and gourmet take-out try *Picnic* (☎ 380-8886) at 610 Strawberry Village. *Phyllis' Giant Burgers* (☎ 381-5116) at 72 E Blithedale, makes Marin's premier burgers. *Mama's Royal Café* (☎ 388-3261) at 387 Miller Ave is a laid-back '60s style diner. Stock up on sandwiches and picnic goodies on your way up to Mt Tam at *Whole Foods Market* (☎ 381-1200) at 414 Miller.

For fine dining, try the *Buckeye Roadhouse* (☎ 331-2600), at 15 Shoreline Hwy, which offers excellent food from a versatile menu of barbecued chicken, linguine with clams, and grilled items. Entrees range from $14 to $25. No doubt about it, the best Thai food in Marin can be found at *Thep Lela* (☎ 383-3444) in the Strawberry Village. *Jenny Low's Chinese Kitchen* (☎ 388-8868), 38 Miller Ave, does delicious, inventive nouveau Chinese. You might want to call ahead as this is a popular place and it can get really busy. There's good Italian food at stylish *Piazza D'Angelo* (☎ 388-2000) at 22 Miller Ave, and another popular Mill Valley restaurant is

Avenue Grill (☎ 388-6003) at 44 E Blithedale Ave.

Entertainment
Sweetwater (☎ 388-2820), 153 Throckmorton Ave, is Marin's finest spot for live music. Bonnie Raitt, Clarence Clemons, and local Bay Area musicians have performed at this jazz/blues venue. You never know who will show up!

Getting There & Away
From Hwy 101, take the Hwy 1 exit just past Sausalito. Follow Miller Ave all the way into the Mill Valley plaza, the center of town. From San Francisco, Golden Gate Transit bus No 10 runs to Mill Valley ($2) via Sausalito and continues to Tiburon.

SIR FRANCIS DRAKE BLVD
Clustered around Hwy 101 and Sir Francis Drake Blvd are the small inland towns of Corte Madera, Larkspur, Kentfield, Ross, San Anselmo, and Fairfax. On weekends mountain bikers flock to Ross, Kentfield, and San Anselmo on their way up to the trails around Phoenix Lake.

Further out on Sir Francis Drake Blvd, Forest Knolls and Lagunitas are excellent stop-overs en route to the coast.

Corte Madera and Larkspur are situated on either side of Hwy 101. In downtown Larkspur, charming Magnolia Ave is a fun place for window-shopping, or you can explore the redwoods in nearby Madrone Canyon. Stop by Book Passage (☎ 927-0960), 51 Tamal Vista Blvd in the Market Place in Corte Madera, for excellent coffee, pastries, and deli meals in one of the best bookstores in California – their travel section is especially good, and there is nightly entertainment in the form of author events and slide shows. On the east side of the freeway the hulking mass of San Quentin State Penitentiary squats above the water, proving that in the Bay Area, even maximum security prisoners get pretty good views.

San Anselmo is noted for its fine selection of antique shops along San Anselmo Ave and beyond. Fairfax is another sleepy little town with a hippie feel to it. Stroll down Broadway Blvd and Bolinas Rd and you'll find an array of cafes and whole food stores. For the ultimate Fairfax experience, stop by the *Juice Joynt*, 63 Broadway, for fruit smoothies. If you're lucky, the owner will give you an astrology chart reading as he blends your custom made drink.

Places to Stay
The *Best Western Corte Madera Inn* (☎ 924-1502) is adjacent to Hwy 101 at 1815 Redwood Hwy, Corte Madera. There are 110 rooms around a pleasant garden and pool; rooms cost $80 to $105. Round the corner the *Madera Village Inn* (☎ 924-3608, 800-362-3372) at 45 Tamal Vista Blvd has rooms and suites with kitchen facilities from $59 to $109.

Places to Eat
Housed in an old-style Victorian tucked away in a redwood canyon, the *Lark Creek Inn* (☎ 924-7766), 234 Magnolia Ave, is one of the best dining experiences in all of Marin. Chef Bradley Ogden brings a creative flair to American food – a four star dining experience. *Marin Joes* (☎ 924-2081) at 1585 Casa Buena Drive in Corte Madera is one of Marin's oldest restaurants and remains a favorite for locals. This timeless Italian restaurant cooks up great steaks, hamburgers, and Caesar salads. You won't find goat cheese or sundried tomatoes here! Be prepared to wait though, as it's always crowded. At the Market Place, 51 Tamal Vista Blvd, the *Savannah Grill* (☎ 924-6774) is a very Californian restaurant: a little heart beside a menu item (typically $10 to $13) indicates that, in true Marin fashion, it's been judged good for you.

There are several restaurants and cafes worthy of a stop inbound or outbound from Point Reyes in Lagunitas and Forest Knolls. *Two Birds Cafe* at 6921 Sir Francis Drake (☎ 488-9952) serves up hearty breakfasts, lunches, and gourmet country dinners ($8 to $13 for dinner specialties). *Le Printemps* (☎ 488-9500) at 7303 Sir Francis Drake in nearby Lagunitas is a charming French cafe with a daily selection of soups, salads, and pasta.

Entertainment
If you're into microbreweries, *Marin Brewing Company* (☎ 461-4677), 1809 Larkspur Landing Circle, is arguably the best in the whole Bay Area. The house-brewed beer bears names like San Quentin Break-Out Stout and Mt Tam Pale Ale, and the food is pretty good, too. It's something of a pickup scene.

Getting There & Away
GGT bus No 20 connects to Corte Madera, Larkspur, and San Anselmo. Various other services including Nos 30 and 40 go via Corte Madera and on up Hwy 101. There are more services during the weekday commute times.

The Golden Gate Ferry (☎ 332-6600) service from the Ferry Building in San Francisco to Larkspur Landing takes 50 minutes and operates up to 13 times daily on weekdays ($2.50/1.90), six times on weekends ($4.25/3.20). You can bring bicycles on the ferry.

SAN RAFAEL
• *pop 48,000*
San Rafael, the largest town in Marin, is more down to earth and less Marin-like than other Marin centers and consequently is largely ignored. Just north of the town Lucas Valley Rd heads off west to Point Reyes Station, passing *Star Wars* creator George Lucas' Skywalker Ranch movie center.

Orientation
Fourth St is the main drag in town, and it's lined with cafes and shops; if you follow it west out of downtown, it meets Sir Francis Drake Blvd out to the coast.

Mission San Rafael Arcangel
The Mission San Rafael Arcangel (☎ 456-3016) was founded in 1817, the penultimate Californian mission, and in 1833 it was the first to be secularized. The remains of the abandoned mission were torn down

in 1870 so the present mission building is completely new, built in 1949 following what little was known about the short-lived original. The mission is at 1104 5th Ave at A St and the chapel is open daily while the mission museum is open Monday to Saturday from 11 am to 4 pm; Sunday from 10 am to 4 pm.

Marin County Civic Center
The Civic Center (☎ 499-7407) complex blends into the hills just east of Hwy 101, two miles north of central San Rafael. This was the only government building Frank Lloyd Wright ever built and there's an information kiosk in the entry lobby if you want to find out more. The complex is open Monday to Friday from 8 am to 5 pm.

China Camp State Park
From Hwy 101 take the North San Pedro exit and continue three miles east from San Rafael to China Camp State Park (☎ 456-0766). At the park's entrance you'll find the abandoned remains of a Chinese fishing village and the small China Camp Museum. There were once many such small Chinese shrimp fishing encampments around the San Francisco Bay.

McNears Beach & Park
McNear's Beach (☎ 499-7816) may not be the most popular beach in Marin, but it has the best weather. On the Bay and protected from the dense fog and wind that haunts the coast, McNear's also boasts a swimming pool. Follow North San Pedro Rd from Hwy 101 in San Rafael. There's a $2 drive-in fee.

Places to Stay
The camp sites at the *China Camp State Park* (☎ 456-0766) cost $15 a night. Call Destinet for reservations in high season, April to October.

In downtown San Rafael, motels are once again the order of the day. The *San Rafael Inn* (☎ 454-9470, 800-442-9470) is at 865 E Francisco Blvd and has rooms at $40 to $60. The small *Panama Hotel* (☎ 457-3993) at 4 Bayview St is a hotel with some history and style. Rooms range from $50, with shared bath, and $90 to $110 for rooms with private bath.

Places to Eat
San Rafael hosts a plethora of ethnic possibilities; satisfy your sushi cravings at *Kamikaze* (☎ 457-6776) in Montecito shopping center; enjoy Chinese food at *Pier 6* (☎ 457-1733) at 1559 4th St; great Thai at *My Thai Restaurant* (☎ 456-4455) at 1230 4th St. The *Rice Table* (☎ 456-1808) at 617 4th St serves up Indonesian food in a casual setting. For authentic Mexican food, try *Las Camelias* (☎ 453-5850) at 912 Lincoln Ave. *Salute* (☎ 453-7596) at 706 3rd St is open for lunch, dinner, or drinks, with a variety of fresh pasta and pizza. One of Marin's best vegetarian restaurants is *Milly's* (☎ 459-1601), 1613 4th St. It's closed on Mondays.

Entertainment
The *Pacific Tap & Grill* (☎ 457-9711) at 812 4th St is the place to go for a cold microbrewery beer in San Rafael. *New George's* (☎ 457-8424), 842 4th St, is good for up-and-coming bands and dancing.

Getting There & Away
Numerous Golden Gate Transit buses operate between San Francisco and the San Rafael Transit Center at 3rd and Hetherton. Bus No 40 is the only service that takes bicycles across the Golden Gate Bridge.

MT TAMALPAIS STATE PARK
Standing guard over Marin County, majestic Mt Tamalpais (Mt Tam, 2571 feet) has breathtaking 360° views of ocean, Bay, city, and hills rolling into the distance. Over 200 miles of hiking and biking trails wind around the mountain, and deer, fox, bobcat, and even, it is said, the occasional mountain lion dwell in the forests and dells.

Mt Tam was a sacred place to the coastal Miwok Indians thousands of years before the arrival of Europeans and American settlers. By the late-19th century, San Franciscans were escaping the bustle of the city

Getting Ready to Hike
With its 6400 sprawling acres of redwood canyons, grasslands, and endless trails, Mt Tam may seem daunting to the first-time visitor. Whether you're a hard-core mountain biker or hiker, there are plenty of guides to help you make the best of your time. Some of the best are:

- *Tamalpais Trails* by Barry Spitz; a handy guide with detailed maps and trails for anyone interested in exploring the wonders of Mt Tam.
- *Bay Area Mountain Bike Trails* by Conrad J Boisvert; lists 45 bike rides in the Bay Area, giving distances, skill levels, riding times, and mile markers.
- *The Marin Mountain Bike Guide* by Armor Todd; lists trips and trails of some of the best hiking/biking spots in Marin.
- *Mt Tam: A Hiking, Running & Nature Guide* and *Hiking Marin: Great Hikes in Marin County* by Don & Kay Marin; with maps, rating charts, and descriptions about when it's best to go.
- *Rambler's Guide to the Trails of Mt Tamalpais* by Olmsted & Bros Map Co; a detailed map with descriptions of the trails.

If you're serious about getting some hiking in you'll probably want to buy some books and maps. One of the best places to look is Book Passage (☎ 927-0960) in Corte Madera. Another option is to latch onto a group who really know what they're doing: the Sierra Club. The Sierra Club leads free hikes of varying difficulty (up to a grueling annual 31-mile ordeal) every Saturday and Sunday. Call ☎ 776-2211, ext 6884 for recorded information. The hikes are led by local hikers who know the mountain like the backs of their hands – in many cases they blazed the original trails! It's a good way to meet people, and the best possible way to meet the mountain. ∎

CALIFORNIA

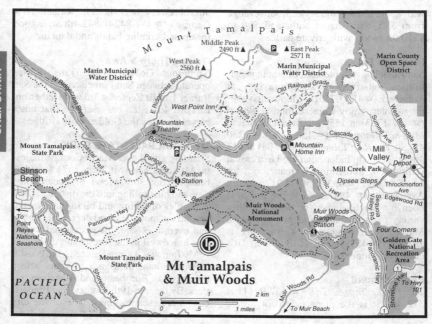

Mt Tamalpais & Muir Woods

with all-day outings on the mountain, and in 1896 'The World's Crookedest Railroad' was completed from Mill Valley to the summit. The railroad was closed in 1930 and today the Old Railroad Grade is one of the most popular and scenic hiking and biking paths on the mountain.

Mt Tamalpais State Park was formed in 1928 of land purchased by naturalist William Kent (who also donated the land that became Muir Woods National Monument in 1907); it now encompasses 6300 acres of wilds. The rich, natural beauty of Mt Tam and the surrounding area is inspiring – especially considering that it lies within an hour's drive from one of the state's largest metropolitan areas.

Orientation & Information
Panoramic Hwy climbs from Mill Valley through the park to Stinson Beach. Pantoll Station (☎ 388-2070), 801 Panoramic Hwy, is the park headquarters; pick up a map for $1 at the station.

Driving from Pantoll Station it's four miles to East Peak summit – take Pantoll Rd and then Ridgecrest Blvd to the top. Parking is $5 and a 10-minute hike leads to the very top and the best views.

Hiking
Pantoll is an excellent place to start a hike. The Steep Ravine Trail follows a wooded creek to the coast (about two miles each way), or, for a longer hike to Stinson Beach it connects with the Dipsea Trail; you can return via the Matt Davis Trail for a good loop. The Matt Davis Trail continues on beyond Pantoll to wrap gently around the mountain, with wonderful views.

The seven-mile Dipsea Trail from Mill Valley climbs right over the coastal range and down to Stinson Beach, cutting through a corner of Muir Woods. The trail starts at Old Mill Park, right in downtown Mill Valley, with a climb up 676 steps in three separate flights. Having surmounted Windy Gap at 760 feet the trail then tumbles down Suicide Hill and clambers right back up Dynamite Hill and Cardiac (where do they get these names!) to reach Lone Tree at 1350 feet. From there it's pretty much downhill apart from short ascents at Insult Hill and Steep Ravine.

Biking
Bikers must stay on fire roads (and off the single-track trails) and keep speeds under 15 mph. The rangers take these rules seriously – even using radar guns on the weekends – and a ticket can result in a $250 fine.

The most popular ride is the Old Railroad Grade, which starts in Mill Valley and climbs to the West Point Inn about 2000 feet above the town. The grade begins near the end of E Blithdale Rd and can also be caught by climbing the steeper, paved Summit Rd out of town which connects with the grade after a 1000-foot climb. It takes about an hour to reach the West Point Inn from Mill Valley, and from there it's either an easy half-hour ride to the summit, a direct return to Mill Valley, or, for a longer ride, a half-hour down to Muir Woods or the coast via Pantoll Station along the Old Stage fire road. However,

both of these options will require more climbing to return to Mill Valley.

From just west of Pantoll Station bikers can either take the Deer Park fire road through giant redwoods and leading to the main entrance of Muir Woods, or the Coastal fire road with breathtaking views of the coast before joining Hwy 1 two miles north of Muir Beach. Either option requires a return to Mill Valley via Frank Valley/Muir Woods Rd, which climbs steadily (800 feet) to Panoramic Hwy and then becomes Sequoia Valley Rd as it drops toward Mill Valley. A left turn on Wildomar and two right turns at Mill Creek Park leads to the center of Mill Valley at the Depot Bookstore.

Places to Stay
There are 16 family campsites at Pantoll Station; there are no RV hookups, but RVs can park in the lower lot for one night only. Steep Ravine features six campsites and cabins; see Stinson Beach, below.

For a romantic escape the *Mountain Home Inn* (☎ 381-9000) at 810 Panoramic Hwy, Mill Valley on the way up Mt Tam, has great views, 10 rooms, and costs $131 to $239, including breakfast. It's also a superb spot for lunch.

Getting There & Away
Muir Woods is just 12 miles north of the Golden Gate Bridge via Hwy 101 and Hwy 1. On weekends Golden Gate Transit bus No 63 from San Francisco stops along the Panoramic Highway at Mountain Home Inn and Pantoll Station.

MUIR WOODS NATIONAL MONUMENT
The slopes of Mt Tam were once carpeted in mighty redwoods but now Muir Woods is the only remnant. President Theodore Roosevelt made it a national monument in 1908 and named it after Sierra Club founder John Muir. The 550-acre reserve, surrounded on all sides by Mt Tam State Park, is the closest redwood stand to San Francisco so it can get very crowded, although the tour buses don't arrive too

---

Birth of the Mountain Bike
Marin is the birthplace of the legendary mountain bike. In 1974 native Californian and bicycle racer Gary Fisher dreamt up a balloon-tire bike that could carry him through the wilderness. Unlike the bicycles born out of the early 1960s, nicknamed 'clunkers,' Fisher's invention was the first of its kind to have thumb shifters, triple crank, motorcycle brake levers, and extra-long crank arms.

In 1980, Fisher and a friend started up their company called Mountain Bikes and the new Fisher Off-Road Racing Team won event after event at the national and state level. The Gary Fisher Bicycle Company was born shortly after. 'Some follow convention, others choose to leave it in the dust,' is the company's motto. Today, Fisher can still be found on Mt Tam road-testing every bike the company creates. ■

early or stay too late. Muir Woods National Monument is open from 8 am to sunset.

Muir Woods is just 12 miles north of the Golden Gate Bridge via Hwy 101 and Hwy 1. The main entrance is on Muir Woods Rd; turn off Panoramic Hwy at Four Corners and follow the signs. There's a ranger station (☎ 388-2595) and a crowded parking area. For an easy walk, try the one-mile Main Trail Loop, which leads alongside Redwood Creek to the 1000-year-old trees at Cathedral Grove and returns via Bohemian Grove, where the tallest tree in the park stands 254 feet high.

You can also walk down into Muir Woods by following trails from the Panoramic Hwy like the Bootjack Trail from the Bootjack picnic area, or the Ben Johnson Trail from the Pantoll campground.

THE COAST
Muir Beach
Muir Beach is the nearest north coast beach town to San Francisco but it's much quieter than Stinson Beach, five miles further north. Note the amazing roadside lineup of mail boxes at the Muir Beach junction of Highway 1. Just north of Muir Beach there are superb views up and down the coast from the Muir Beach Overlook. From the concrete lookouts watch was kept for invading Japanese ships during WWII.

At the beach junction the very English looking *Pelican Inn* (☎ 383-6000) has a popular bar and restaurant and rooms for $143 to $165. Green Gulch Farm & Zen Center (☎ 383-3134) at 1601 Shoreline Highway is in the hills above Muir Beach and has a Buddhist retreat, Sunday morning meditation sessions, and study programs. At the center's *Lindisfarne Guest House* (☎ 383-3134) there are 12 rooms around a central atrium, built in the Japanese fashion without nails. Singles are $55 to $70, doubles $90 to $105, including buffet-style vegetarian meals.

Stinson Beach
Stretching for three miles, Stinson Beach is the most popular beach along Hwy 1. Despite its freezing waters and frequently overcast skies, it still draws crowds of surfers, hikers, and Sunday drivers, especially on weekends. There are a couple of cafes and breakfast spots and a number of motels and B&Bs, most of them along Hwy 1 through town. Less than a mile south of Stinson Beach is the popular **Red Rocks nudist beach**.

Stinson Beach Park Information is ☎ 868-0942; for updated weather information call ☎ 868-1922.

Things to See & Do If you're tired of the beach, the town of Stinson Beach has a small selection of galleries and shops. The Stinson Beach Art Center Gallery (☎ 868-0553) at 3448 Shoreline Hwy showcases works by Marin County artists. Across the street at No 3445 the Claudia Chapline Gallery (☎ 868-2308) houses a collection of contemporary paintings, drawings, and crafts by Marin artists. There's also a sculpture garden.

Stocked with nature guides, travel books, and bestsellers, Stinson Beach Books (☎ 868-0700) at No 3455 is open daily from 10:30 am to 5:30 pm.

On the hillside beside the Bolinas Lagoon the **Audubon Canyon Ranch** (☎ 868-9244) is a major nesting ground for great blue herons and great egrets. Visitors can observe them in the trees from the other side of the narrow canyon. The ranch is open mid-March to mid-July, weekends from 10 am to 4 pm.

Places to Stay At 3416 Hwy 1, the *Stinson Beach Motel* (☎ 868-1712) is a simple older motel with rooms at $50. Right next door at 1 Belvedere Ave, *Redwoods Haus B&B* (☎ 868-1034) has a 'zimmer frei' sign, which indicates just how many Europeans come along this road. Done up in a rather over-fussy English style, it costs $55 to $75. Back from the highway at 37 Belvedere Ave, is the bigger *Casa del Mar Inn* (☎ 868-2124) with rates from $100 to $210. The *Sandpiper Motel* (☎ 868-1632) is closer to the beach, near the Parkside Café at 1 Marine Way, and has a variety of studios and cabins for $45. The

Ocean Court Motel (☎ 868-0212) provides oceanview rooms. Located a block off Route 1 at 18 Arenal Ave on a quiet side street all rooms have private bath and kitchen facilities.

A mile south of Stinson Beach is the *Steep Ravine Environmental Campground* (☎ 456-5218) with campsites and 10 rustic cabins with wood stoves on a coastal bluff. Nightly cost is $30.

Places to Eat At 3458 Shoreline Hwy the *Sand Dollar Restaurant* (☎ 868-0434) is a nice local bar and restaurant with entrees at $10 to $14. Right across the road at No 3465 is the *Stinson Beach Grill* (☎ 868-2002). Off the highway down toward the beach the popular *Parkside Café* (☎ 868-1272) at 43 Arenal offers hearty breakfasts as well as soups, salads, and a variety of fish dishes. In winter it's closed on Tuesdays and Wednesdays.

Getting There & Away By car it's not much over half an hour from San Francisco via the winding Shoreline Hwy through Muir Beach or via the equally winding Panoramic Hwy. During summer the heavy beach traffic can cause lots of delays.

On weekends Golden Gate Transit bus No 63 runs to Stinson Beach, as well as three services a day all the way from San Francisco ($3.50) and four more just from Marin City. Service is less frequent during the winter months.

Richard Brautigan

In the 1960s and '70s Richard Brautigan built up a huge cult following for his wonderfully surreal novels. He was described as 'a master of American black absurdism' by the London *Financial Times*. Born in 1935 in the Pacific Northwest he lived and wrote in San Francisco a series of delightfully crazy books like *Trout Fishing in America*, *Willard & His Bowling Trophies*, *Sombrero Fallout*, and *The Hawkline Monster*. In 1985 he committed suicide in Bolinas. ∎

Bolinas

If a corner of Haight-Ashbury managed to reincarnate after the '60s then it probably came back as Bolinas, a pretty little place just far enough from San Francisco to make a good day out. Bolinas has often been accused of being in a 'time-warp.' In fact, this sleepy little village became famous for its disappearing direction signs, removed by local residents intent on hiding away from the outside world as it passed by on Hwy 1. Though the town of Bolinas may prove difficult to find at times, the fabulous vistas for bird-watching, unspoiled beaches, and serene environment makes Bolinas well worth the effort.

Bolinas has one of the few gas stations along the coast: northbound the next ones are at the Olema Ranch Campground and at Point Reyes Station, southbound you have to go all the way to Mill Valley. The free monthly *Pacific Coastal Post* gives an interesting perspective on the world, as seen from Bolinas.

Things to See & Do The **Point Reyes Bird Observatory** located on Mesa Rd (☎ 868-0655) is where bird banding and netting demonstrations are made on weekends from 6 am to noon. There's a visitors center and nature trail. Beyond the observatory you can continue to the Palomarin car park and follow walking trails right into the park. It's only three miles past Bass and Pelican Lakes to the Alamere Falls at Wildcat Beach or a fine 15-mile loop takes walkers on to the Wildcat Camp, up the Glen Trail to the Ridge Trail and back along that trail to the starting point.

The **Bolinas Museum** (☎ 868-0330) at 48 Wharf Rd has changing exhibits on the art and history of coastal Marin. It's open Thursday from 5 to 7 pm and Friday to Sunday from 1 to 5 pm. The tidal pools at the **Duxbury Reef Nature Reserve**, round the end from Duxbury Point, feature starfish, anemones, and other rockpool creatures.

Places to Stay Although Bolinas residents are famously unenthusiastic about

CALIFORNIA

outsiders there are a couple of low-key accommodation possibilities. At the bend at 41 Wharf Rd *Smiley's Schooner Lagoon* (☎ 868-1311) has five motel-style rooms in the back at $60 on weekdays, $70 on weekends. Just off Wharf Rd at 15 Brighton Ave the *Grand Hotel* (☎ 868-1757) is very ungrand looking with two rooms sharing a common bathroom and kitchen, costing $44 for the first night and $33 on subsequent nights.

The *Blue Heron Inn* (☎ 868-1102) at 11 Wharf Rd has a couple of pretty rooms at $90 a night, including breakfast across the road at the Shop Café. There are several other small B&Bs in town including *Sharon House* (☎ 868-1641) at 65 Horseshoe Hill Rd and *Elfriede's Beach Haus* (☎ 868-9778) at 59 Brighton Ave.

Places to Eat On Wharf Rd *Smiley's Schooner Lagoon* is the popular drinking hole in town and also has food. Across the road at 46 Wharf Rd the *Shop Café* (☎ 868-9984) has burgers, sandwiches, Mexican food, and wine by the glass. *Bolinas Bakery & Cafe* (☎ 868-0211) at 20 Wharf Rd is an all organic flour bakery with a variety of breads, pastries, and homemade pies.

Getting There & Away By car follow Hwy 1 north from Stinson Beach and immediately past the end of the Bolinas Lagoon and the Audubon Canyon Ranch is the turn-off to Bolinas. It's unsignposted since this is where Bolinas signs are removed. There's no public transport past Stinson Beach.

You can also get to Bolinas from Sir Francis Drake Blvd as it winds its way from Fairfax into Lagunitas and Forest Knolls.

Point Reyes National Seashore
Divided from the mainland by Tomales Bay, the triangular peninsula of Point Reyes National Seashore comprises 110 sq miles of long fog-swept beaches, lagoons, rough-hewn rock formations, and forested cliffs. Extensive inland and coastal hiking trails and four hike-in camping areas make this a perfect destination for wilderness seekers, despite the damage caused by a 1995 fire that consumed some 13,000 acres when campers failed to extinguish an illegal fire.

The westernmost point of the peninsula, the Point Reyes Headlands, is crowned by the Point Reyes Lighthouse, the best spot in

---

Sir Francis Drake
Did the English explorer land at Drake's Beach in 1579? We're unlikely to ever know for sure but it's fairly certain he did put in somewhere around the San Francisco Bay Area, and Point Reyes is probably the best candidate for the site. Drake was an extraordinary character: a self-made man, fearless, resourceful, clever, ruthless, and very lucky. In 1577 he set off from England in a fleet of five small ships. His mission was exploration and adventure, to be financed by what could best be described as piracy, with the hated Spanish the intended victims.

In 1579 the *Golden Hind* was alone off the California coast. Two of the ships, brought only to carry supplies, had been abandoned. The third ship had sunk with all hands during the rounding of Cape Horn and the fourth had lost contact and turned back to England. There had been rich pickings at the expense of the hapless Spanish but the *Golden Hind* was in sorry shape. Somewhere along the coast Drake put in to a sheltered bay and careened his ship; ran it aground at high tide and tipped it on its side to repair its ravaged hull. He stayed there for five weeks, trading with the local Indians and exploring inland where one of his crew noted that the land was much more welcoming than it appeared from the sea. Eventually Drake sailed off on a trip that would carry him right around the world and bring him back to England as a phenomenally wealthy and famous explorer. He cemented his fame by helping defeat the Spanish Armada in 1588. Was Point Reyes the *Nova Albion* or 'New England' he claimed for the queen? It may well have been. ∎

the Bay Area for whale watching. To the north a long strand of beach stretches for miles. To the south is Drakes Bay, with Drakes Estero and Limantour Estero Reserve branching off into saltwater lagoons.

There are three small Point Reyes towns but Olema and Point Reyes Station are just outside the park boundaries; only Inverness is actually in the park. The weather at Point Reyes is very changeable and even hot summer days can suddenly give way to dense fog followed by high winds. Winter days can be cold and wet but hikers should be prepared for the worst at any time of year.

Orientation Four vehicle roads lead into the park. Limantour Rd from Olema or Pt Reyes Station runs via the HI Point Reyes Hostel to Limantour Beach. Beyond Inverness the road along Tomales Bay splits in two. Pierce Point Rd runs north to McLures Beach and Pierce Point Ranch, from where the Tomales Point Trail takes hikers all the way to the north of the park. Sir Francis Drake Blvd runs south to Point Reyes Beach and Point Reyes itself with a branch off to Drakes Beach.

Information The Bear Valley Visitors Center (☎ 663-1092) is the park headquarters with a great deal of park information and interesting park displays plus the fascinating earthquake trail introducing visitors to the actual epicenter of the 1906 Big One. It's open Monday to Friday from 9 am to 5 pm; Saturday and Sunday from 8 am to 5 pm. There are additional visitors centers at the Point Reyes Lighthouse (☎ 669-1534), open Thursday to Monday from 10 am to 5 pm; and at the Ken Patrick Center (☎ 669-1250), open weekends and holidays from 10 am to noon and 12:30 to 5 pm, at Drakes Beach.

Things to See & Do Olema advertises itself as the epicenter of the 1906 earthquake that devastated San Francisco. The 0.7-mile long **Earthquake Trail** at the nearby Bear Valley Visitors Center offers a graphic portrayal of a big quake's power. At one point the trail passes a fence the western half of which shifted 16 feet north. Also from the visitors center a half-mile trail leads to Kule Loklo, a reproduction of a **Miwok village**. The Miwoks were the Native American tribe who used to live along this coast.

From the car park at the termination of the Sir Francis Drake Blvd, a short walk leads to the small visitors center and the pathway *down* to the **Point Reyes Lighthouse**. It leads down because the lighthouse is 300 feet below the top of the 600-foot-high headland, so that its light will shine out below the fog which often blankets Point Reyes. This is a wild and ferocious spot, rated as the windiest point along the West Coast. The French Fresnel lens in the lighthouse is original, dating from 1870. On a clear day the view extends out to the Farallon Islands and all the way south to San Francisco. This is a prime spot for whale watching. The lighthouse is open Thursday to Monday from 10 am to 4:30 pm.

Heading to the top of the peninsula, Pierce Point Rd splits right from Sir Francis Drake Blvd. Tomales Bay State Park and Marshall Beach offer calm waters for canoeing and birding in Tomales Bay. There are beaches, picnic sites, and trails at these areas. Further down the road, Kehoe Beach and McClures Beach are a stark contrast to the calm waters of Tomales Bay. This long strand of fog-laden and windswept beach stretches for miles. At low tide on calmer days the tide pools are a good place to explore, but be cautious as pounding surf and strong currents are always present. Do not swim in these waters.

Gray Whales

Gray whales may be spotted at various points along the California coast, and the Point Reyes Lighthouse is a superb viewpoint to spot these huge creatures on their annual 6000-mile migration. During the summer the whales feed in the Arctic waters between Alaska and Russian Siberia. Around October they start to move south down the Pacific coast of Canada and the USA to the sheltered lagoons in the Gulf of California by the Mexican state of Baja California.

The whales, led by the pregnant cows, pass Point Reyes in December and January. They're followed by pods of females and courting males, usually in groups of three to five, and then by the younger whales. The whales usually spend about two months around Baja California during which time the pregnant whales give birth to calves 15 or 16 feet long and weighing 2000 to 2500 pounds. The new born whales put on 200 pounds a day and in February the reverse trip begins.

Gray whales live up to 50 years and grow to 50 feet in length and weigh up to 45 tons. Spotting whales is a simple combination of patience and being there at the right time. Spouting, the exhalation of moist, warm air, is usually the first sign that a whale's about. A series of spouts, about 15 seconds apart, may be followed by a sight of the creature's tail as it dives down. If you're lucky you may see whales 'spy hopping' (sticking their heads out of the water to look around) or even 'breaching' (leaping clear out of the water). Bring binoculars as the whales are typically a quarter to a half mile out to sea, though they're closer to shore on the southbound leg of the journey.

Bay & Delta Charters (☎ 332-6811) runs all-day, naturalist-led whale-watching expeditions on weekends during both migration seasons. They depart from Sausalito for the Farallon Islands, 28 miles outside the Golden Gate. It's $59 per person and reservations are required. ■

Bicycles are prohibited within the actual wilderness area of the park but there are still over 35 miles of excellent **mountain biking** trails. Walkers should be adequately prepared for unexpected weather changes, bring drinking water, and stick to the trails. Poison oak and dangerously crumbling cliff edges await those who wander off the trails.

Places to Stay The HI *Point Reyes Hostel* (☎ 663-8811) is about 1½ miles from Limantour Beach and six miles from the visitors center, just off Limantour Rd. Nightly costs are $10 and there's a family room and kitchen facilities but bring food as the nearest supplies are in Point Reyes Station.

There are no drive-in camping sites in the Point Reyes reserve but there are four hike-in campgrounds with pit toilets. Free permits must be obtained from the Bear Valley Visitors Center. Outside of the reserve the *Olema Ranch Campground* (☎ 663-8001, 800-655-2267) has RV hookups ($24), tent sites, and a wide range of facilities. Full hookups and tent sites are $16, with an extra $2.50 for each additional person after two. Less expensive and much more inviting is the not-too-distant *Samuel P Taylor Park*, just seven miles east of Point Reyes on Sir Francis Drake Blvd. This 2600-acre park provides 60 secluded creekside campsites in redwood groves. Nightly cost is $14; reserve through Destinet.

Point Reyes Station and Inverness have a surprising number of small B&Bs and a number of booking agencies. Try B&B Cottages of Point Reyes (☎ 663-9445), Coastal Lodging (☎ 485-2678, 663-1351), which also has B&Bs in Bolinas, or Inns of Marin (☎ 663-2000, 800-887-2880).

Places to Eat Right in the center of Point Reyes Station the *Bovine Bakery* (☎ 663-9420) on Main St is the local meeting place for a breakfast coffee or muffin. It's closed Mondays. The *Station House Cafe* (☎ 663-1515), at the other end of Main St, is a favorite local eating place. It's closed Tuesdays.

Inverness stretches along the side of Tomales Bay and offers pizza and pasta at the *Gray Whale Pizza* (☎ 669-1244) or, of all things, Czech food at *Vladimir's Restaurant* (☎ 669-1021). The *Knave of Hearts* (☎ 663-1236), 12301 Sir Francis Drake Blvd, is a bakery offering delectable pastries and pies made by the spirited owner and chef. A hot cup of soup will warm you up before you begin your journey. In the same building is *Perry's* (☎ 663-1491), the place to get sandwiches and other supplies for the reserve. Half way from Inverness to the Point Reyes Lighthouse look for the sign to the *Johnson's Drakes Bay Oysters* (☎ 669-1149) where oysters are sold, Tuesday to Sunday, 8 am to 4 pm, fresh from the farm and at well below city prices.

Getting There & Away By car Point Reyes can be reached via the winding coastal Highway 1 or by Sir Francis Drake Blvd through San Anselmo and Fairfax.

Golden Gate Transit bus No 24 runs weekdays between Inverness, Point Reyes Station, and San Francisco ($4) in the *very early* morning and back in the evening. On weekends bus No 65 ($2.50) runs to and from the San Rafael Transit Center twice each day.

Getting Around Bikes can be rented from Trail Head Rentals in Olema (☎ 663-1958) at Hwy 1 and Bear Valley Rd. You can rent by the hour ($7), or by the day ($20).

The East Bay

☎ *510*

Linking San Francisco to the East Bay, the double-decker Bay Bridge may not star on as many postcards as the Golden Gate but it's longer and much busier. Gritty Oakland and opinionated Berkeley dominate the East Bay while suburbs sprawl north all the way to the Wine Country and south all the way to San Jose. Barely five miles inland a range of hills pops up to hem the East Bay conurbation with miles of surprisingly pristine park land. Across the range are more dormitory suburbs and towering Mt Diablo, the highest peak in the Bay Area. The East Bay was originally known as the Contra Costa or 'opposite coast,' a name still applied to one of the East Bay counties.

OAKLAND
• *pop 380,000*

Poor Oakland, victim of one of this century's truly memorable put downs, has been searching for a 'there' ever since native daughter Gertrude Stein announced 'There is no *there* there.' Oakland has always languished in San Francisco's shadow, but it has enough attractions to justify a foray across the Bay. It's a city of remarkable racial and economic diversity encompassing a busy harbor, a frenetic Chinatown, the popular shops and restaurants of Piedmont and College Aves, and the vast Regional Parks along the hills. Oakland is also well known for its enduring progressive jazz and blues scene.

History
Oakland grew from Mexican ranch land to become a small town in the 1850s, linked by a ferry service with San Francisco. The Gold Rush pushed Oakland along but the city's real takeoff came with the

CALIFORNIA

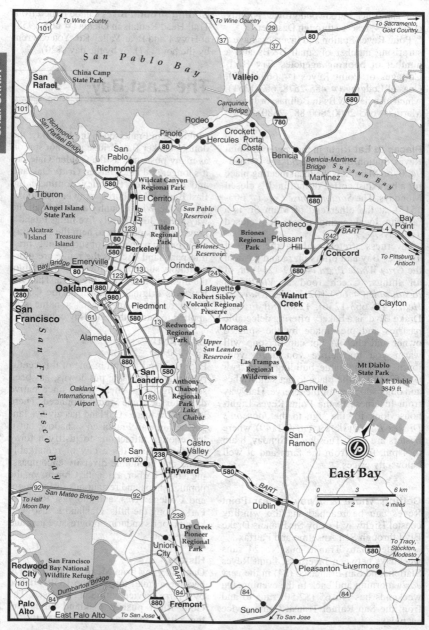

completion of the Transcontinental Railway in 1869. As the western terminus of the line, Oakland rapidly became a major industrial and business center. The completion of the San Francisco-Oakland Bay Bridge in 1936 provided another boost to the city and in recent years, as San Francisco's importance as a shipping port has dwindled and died, Oakland has grown to become a major container port.

Unfortunately, while parts of Oakland have thrived other parts have declined and to many people the name has become synonymous with urban decay, drug trafficking, and gang warfare. It's certainly true that there are parts of Oakland which are best avoided but much of the city is surprisingly livable, helped by a climate that manages to be just as pleasant as San Francisco's at its best, while sidestepping the cold and foggy days which are San Francisco at its worst.

Orientation

Oakland is a long, slender city, and its suburbs – ranging from the down-and-out to the over-the-top – reach far beyond where tourists are likely to find themselves. In general, real estate values rise with the altitude, so the further you go east, into the hills, the nicer the neighborhoods become. West Oakland is heavily industrial but with housing projects and dreary residential pockets, and South Oakland is somewhere to avoid exiting the freeway. Interstate 880 traces the edge of the Bay and I-580 parallels it about 1½ miles inland.

Broadway is the backbone of downtown Oakland, running from Jack London Square at the waterfront north to upscale Piedmont and Rockridge. Telegraph Ave branches off Broadway at 15th St, and will take you straight to Berkeley. There are BART stations on Broadway at 12th and 19th Sts. To reach Lake Merritt, take Grand Ave east from Broadway.

Information

There's an Oakland Convention & Visitors Bureau (☎ 839-9000, 800-262-5526), Suite 200, 1000 Broadway, and some information is also available from the kiosk at the Jack London Square car park by the big Barnes & Noble bookstore (☎ 272-0120). Other Oakland bookstores include Walden Pond (☎ 832-4438) at 3316 Grand Ave, with a good selection of used and new books. If you're interested in African American literature or history, check out the Marcus Bookstore (☎ 652-2344), 3900 Martin Luther King, Jr Way.

The *Oakland Tribune* is Oakland's daily newspaper although it's often in financial difficulties. De Lauer's Super Newsstand (☎ 451-6157), 1310 Broadway, has a huge selection of US and international papers and magazines.

Information on the East Bay's surprisingly large number of parks including the excellent Regional Parks booklet can be obtained from the East Bay Regional Parks District (☎ 562-7275) at 2950 Peralta Oaks Court.

The Black Panthers

The '60s may have brought flowers and love to San Francisco but it brought revolution to the East Bay – to the campus in Berkeley, to the streets in Oakland. The Black Panther Party was founded in 1966 in Oakland by Huey Newton and Bobby Seale and developed a manifesto calling for the exemption of blacks from the laws of 'white America,' the release of all blacks from jails, and the payment of 'compensation' for 'white American' oppression. The party's violent image prompted an equally violent police reaction and there were a number of spectacular shootouts between Panthers and police. Eldridge Cleaver, Minister of Information for the party and author of *Soul on Ice*, skipped bail in 1968 after one confrontation and spent several years in Cuba and Algeria. The Black Panthers faded out in the '70s and Huey Newton was killed in a 1989 West Oakland drug squabble. Eldridge Cleaver has since gone on to become a recycling entrepreneur. ■

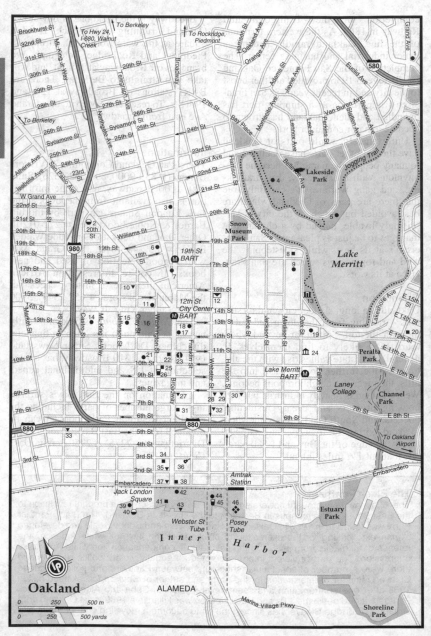

PLACES TO STAY		35	Dolma's Deli	17	De Lauer's Super
8	Lake Merritt Hotel	37	Overland House Bar & Grill		Newsstand
20	Lakeside Motel	43	Scott's	18	Alameda County
22	Parc Oakland Hotel				Courthouse
25	Washington Inn	**OTHER**		19	Tribune Tower
31	Oakland Travelodge	1	Grand Lake Theater	21	Oakland Convention
34	Best Western Thunderbird	2	Greyhound Bus Station		Center
	Inn	3	Paramount Theater	23	Convention & Visitors
38	Jack London Inn	4	Children's Fairyland		Bureau
41	Waterfront Plaza Hotel	5	Sailboat Clubhouse	24	Oakland Museum
		6	Fox Oakland Theater	26	Pacific Coast Brewing
PLACES TO EAT		7	Cathedral Building		Company
10	Calaca	9	Scottish Rite Temple	36	Merchant's
27	Battam Bang	11	City Hall	39	USS Potomac
28	Sun Hongkong	12	Main Post Office	40	Ferry Terminal
29	Nan Yang	13	Camron-Stanford House	42	Barnes & Noble
30	Phnom Penh	14	Preservation Park	44	London's Yukon Cabin
32	Vi's	15	Federal Building	45	First & Last Chance Saloon
33	Gingerbread House	16	City Center	46	Jack London Village

Downtown Oakland

The pedestrianized **City Center** forms the heart of downtown Oakland, with the twin towers of the Federal Building as a backdrop. A block to the east at 13th and Franklin Sts, the 1923 **Oakland Tribune Tower** is a very visible Oakland icon but unfortunately you cannot go up it since the '89 quake. Just west of the City Center is **Preservation Park** (☎ 874-7580), at the junction of 13th St and Martin Luther King, Jr Way. The 16 restored Victorian houses date from 1870 to 1910 and were collected from all over Oakland and brought back to be resurrected within a stone's throw of the downtown center. Tours can be arranged by calling ☎ 238-3234.

The 1914 **City Hall** at 14th and Washington is immediately north of the City Center while a couple of blocks south is the **Victorian Row** of Old Oakland. These two rows of houses along 9th St date from the 1860s to 1880s. On the east side of Broadway, Oakland's **Chinatown** centers around Franklin and Webster Sts. It's a much less touristy but equally authentic version of the one across the Bay – the restaurants are just as good and often lower in price.

North of the center Telegraph Ave angles off Broadway and heads toward Berkeley. In the angle stands the flatiron **Cathedral Building** of 1913. Continue up Broadway to the **Paramount Movie Theater** (☎ 465-6400), at 2025 Broadway and 21st. This wonderful 1931 Art Deco movie theater is home to the Oakland Ballet and the Oakland East Bay Symphony. Tours are usually available on the first and third Saturdays of the month at 10 am and cost $1. Oakland has some other memorable movie palaces – the 3500-seat 1928 **Fox Oakland Theater** at Telegraph and 19th, once the largest cinema west of Chicago, now stands empty and unused. The equally massive **Grand Lake Theater** on Grand Ave and Lake Park Ave, plays first-run movies.

Jack London Square

Oakland has roundly ignored Gertrude Stein, a wealthy stockbroker's daughter after all, but rough-edged Jack London has been much more to local tastes and the waterfront where he once raised hell now bears his name. It's been a tough project to convert a decaying industrial area into a tourist zone of restaurants and shops but the huge Barnes & Noble bookstore at the waterfront end of Broadway is finally providing a focus.

Restaurants are the main attraction but there are several historic reminders of the local author. It's said that Jack was a regular visitor to the 1880 **Heinhold's First & Last Chance Saloon**, maintained in all its period glory. Next to the saloon is **London's Yukon cabin** and if ever a building looked out of place it's this one. Dumping a shabby little log cabin into the middle of a carpark is not a recipe for conjuring up the tough days on the far north goldfields. Still, if Jack ever wandered back he could probably make a better fortune scraping the coins off the cabin floor than he ever did from gold prospecting. In Jack London Village, a waterfront shopping center at the square, the **Jack London Museum** (☎ 451-8218) has a variety of exhibits about the author. It's open Tuesday to Saturday from 10:30 am to 6 pm and Sunday from 11:30 am to 6 pm; a $1 donation is requested.

Jack London Village also has the **Ebony Museum** (☎ 763-0745), which displays African and African-American art; a $1 donation is welcome. The USS *Potomac* (☎ 839-7533), Franklin D Roosevelt's 'floating White House,' is moored by the ferry wharf. It's open from 1 to 4 pm, Wednesdays and Sundays, entry is $5. Free boat tours of the container **Port of Oakland** (☎ 272-1200) operate in the spring and summer.

Jack London Square is the site for a variety of shows, displays, and events throughout the year plus a busy farmer's market every Sunday. The new Amtrak Oakland Station, which is also the terminus for San Francisco, opened at Jack London Square in late 1995.

Lake Merritt

Oakland's visual centerpiece is Lake Merritt, created in 1869 by damming an arm of the Oakland estuary. It was the first

---

London & Stein

Neither of Oakland's famous writers was actually born in Oakland, and they were as different as West Oakland from the Oakland hills. Gertrude Stein, the daughter of a wealthy stockbroker, was born in 1874 in Pennsylvania, then lived in Vienna and Paris before coming to Oakland for her school years. After college she moved to Paris where she lived until her death just after the end of WWII. Stein was famous mainly for being famous, and she courted and encouraged many of the seminal artists and writers of her era, most notably Picasso and Hemingway. Her attempts to emulate cubist art in her writing ensured she would be an unread writer and her best known book is probably *The Autobiography of Alice B Toklas*, which is actually her own autobiography, not that of her long term partner.

Born in San Francisco in 1876, Jack London's mother was a spiritualist, and his father, who soon deserted them, was an Irish astrologer. London began to turn his life into an adventure story while still a teenager, poaching oysters in the San Francisco Bay with his own boat the *Razzle Dazzle*, working on a ship to Japan, riding freight trains around the USA as a hobo, and enthusiastically embracing socialism. Self-educated, he entered the University of California, Berkeley but soon quit to join the 1897 Klondike Gold Rush. Back from Alaska, and still broke, he threw himself into writing with spectacular energy, turning out everything from songs to horror stories. His first book, *The Son of the Wolf*, was published in 1900 and for the next 16 years he averaged three books a year! His writing was often slapdash but the energy was undeniable. London soon became the highest paid writer in the USA but he burnt through the cash even faster. In 1910 he turned to farming at Glen Ellen in the Sonoma Valley (see the Wine Country chapter) and in 1916 died in somewhat mysterious circumstances, officially from kidney disease but quite possibly a drug-overdose suicide.

Oakland remembers its writers in quite different ways. Roustabout Jack has a whole waterfront neighborhood at Jack London Square, complete with his First & Last Chance bar, his Klondike Gold Rush hut, and a Jack London Museum. Less fondly remembered Gertrude simply has an abstract statue of *There*. It's there, right in the City Center at Broadway and 13th in downtown Oakland. ■

national wildlife refuge in the USA, and teems with migratory waterfowl. The lake is connected to the sea, so its 155 acres are saltwater. A popular 3.2-mile jogging track encircles the lake while Lakeside Park, at the northern end of the lake, includes **Children's Fairyland** (☎ 238-6876), opened in 1950 and said to have been an inspiration for Disneyland. Like other Bay Area parks, Lake Merritt is fine for a daytime visit but not so good at night.

Boats can be rented at the Sailboat Clubhouse at the north side of the lake Monday to Friday, 10:30 am to 4 pm, Saturday and Sunday to 5 pm. Hourly charges are $6 for canoes or rowboats, $6 to $12 for sailboats although for the latter you must be able to prove you're a competent sailor. The sternwheeler *Merritt Queen* (☎ 444-3807) paddles around the lake on Saturdays and Sundays from 11 am to 3 pm, later in summer. Half-hour trips cost $1.50/75¢.

In the late-19th century Lake Merritt was lined with fine homes but a century later there is just a sole survivor: the **Camron-Stanford House** (☎ 835-1976) at 1418 Lakeside Drive. It was taken over by the city administration in 1907, and from 1910 until the new museum opened in 1967 it functioned as the city museum. Low-key tours of some of the rooms take place Wednesdays from 11 am to 4 pm and Sundays from 1 to 5 pm at a cost of $4/2. The best aspect of the house, however, is simply its wonderful lakeside setting and the hint it gives of how Oakland would have looked in its Victorian heyday.

Other interesting buildings around the lake include the fine old **Lake Merritt Hotel**, 1800 Madison St, the imposing 1908 **Scottish Rite Temple** on Lakeside Drive, and the 1935 **Alameda County Courthouse** at 12th and Oak Sts, which makes a fine backdrop from the roof garden of the Oakland Museum.

Oakland Museum
Opened in 1967 the Oakland Museum (☎ 238-3401), at 11th and Oak Sts near Lake Merritt, is a very rare creation, a piece of '60s raw concrete brutalism that actually

seems to work. It's not an easy museum to find your way around as the various display areas are totally separate but the effort is worthwhile.

Starting at the top from the Oak St entrance the Gallery of California Art has an eclectic collection that juxtaposes new with old, modern with traditional, paintings with sculpture, furniture with photographs. Below it is the Cowell Hall of California History with a jam-packed display of artifacts from the California story including gems like the highly polished steam fire pump of 1898, which the Oakland fire department took across the Bay to help fight the post-quake fire in 1906. A series of displays glimpse unique aspects of California life such as the beach culture, the car culture, the suburbs culture, the movie culture, and even the flower power era of Haight-Ashbury in the '60s. Finally the Hall of California Ecology has a variety of displays conjuring up the state's varied natural history including some dramatic stuffed wildlife tableaux.

There's a cafe and a museum store and the museum is open Wednesday to Saturday from 10 am to 5 pm; Sunday, noon to 7 pm. Entry is $4/2 and there's a moderately priced car park in the building.

North Oakland
Following Broadway north out of downtown, the strip of car dealerships is no indication of the high-rent neighborhoods lying just ahead. The small city of **Piedmont**, the East Bay's richest, is an oasis in the middle of Oakland – its main drag, Piedmont Ave, branches off Broadway and has wall-to-wall antique stores, coffeehouses, fine restaurants, and hot tub spas.

Rockridge is one of the East Bay's most coveted addresses, big with UC Berkeley graduate students in particular. The main street, College Ave, blends into Berkeley, and the whole length of it is lined with eclectic shops, and lots of pubs and cafes.

The Hills
The further east you go from downtown, the more convoluted the streets become,

winding through exclusive hillside communities like Montclair before reaching the ridgeline, where a series of parks edge the hills. The area around the junctions of Hwys 13 and 24 was the site for the disastrous October 1991 firestorm that killed 26 people and destroyed over 3000 houses. The houses have mostly been rebuilt but the vegetation is intentionally much sparser, as nobody wants a replay of the blaze.

The **Robert Sibley Volcanic Regional Preserve** is the northernmost of the parks; there are great views over the Bay Area from the 1761-foot Round Top Peak, an old volcano cone. Grizzly Peak Blvd runs north along the hilltops to Tilden Regional Park overlooking Berkeley while Skyline Blvd runs south through **Redwood Regional Park** and **Anthony Chabot Regional Park**. At **Joaquin Miller Park**, adjacent to Redwood Regional, you can see the cabin, known as The Abbey (or 'the Abby' in his simplified spelling), of Sierra poet Joaquin Miller; AC Transit bus Nos 46 and 64 will take you there from downtown.

Below Joaquin Miller Park at 4766 Lincoln Ave, just west of Hwy 13, stands the **Oakland Mormon Temple & Visitors' Center** (☎ 531-1475) where free guided tours of the outer temple and grounds are given 9 am to 9 pm daily. You can't actually enter the temple but if you want to find out more about this all-American religion a trip here could save the longer trek to Salt Lake City. A stone's thrown down Lincoln Ave is the Byzantine-looking **Greek Orthodox Church of the Ascension** (☎ 531-3400), 4700 Lincoln Ave, with icons painted on its gold-anodized dome.

Further south is the **Oakland Zoo** (☎ 632-9525), 9777 Golf Links Rd. It has the usual gang of zoo animals and is open 10 am to 4 pm daily, weather permitting. Admission is $5/3, plus $3 to park. **Dunsmuir House** (☎ 562-3232) at 2960 Peralta Oaks Court is a fine old mansion with surrounding gardens. Tours operate April through September, Wednesday at noon and 1 pm, and the first and third Sunday of

each month at noon, 1, and 2 pm. Entry is $4/3.

South Oakland

South Oakland goes on and on, one numbered block after another, before finally blending into San Leandro. The **Oakland Coliseum** beside the I-880 is home to the Oakland A's baseball team and the Golden State Warriors basketball team.

At the bayside Oakland International Airport the **Western Aerospace Museum** (☎ 638-7100) is at 8280 Boeing St. Turn off the airport entrance road northbound onto Doolittle Drive and watch for the aircraft. The museum's collection includes a Lockheed Electra (like the one Amelia Earhart disappeared in back in 1937) and a Harrier jump jet (like the one Arnie Schwarzenegger shot at the bad guys with in *True Lies*). Pride of place goes to the huge four-engined British Short Solent flying boat. The museum is open Wednesday to Sunday from 10 am to 4 pm and entry is $3 for adults, free for kids. An internal inspection of the Solent costs another $2.

Places to Stay

Oakland is no competition for San Francisco when it comes to accommodations – the only possibilities for a cheap night here are places you'd really prefer not to know about, and the convenient BART service makes a visit from San Francisco an easy alternative to staying in the East Bay.

Camping There are eight RV spaces and 23 tent sites at *Anthony Chabot Regional Park* (☎ 635-0135), as well as 10 walk-in sites. It's a good spot if you're car camping and want to spend a few nights in the Bay Area (as San Francisco offers no tent camping at all). Rates are $13 per night; it's a few miles south of Oakland off I-580.

Downtown The *Oakland Travelodge* (☎ 451-6316, 800-832-5885) on the corner of Broadway and 7th is conveniently central, only six blocks from the 12th St BART station and a stone's throw from Chinatown. Featureless but large rooms equipped with cooking facilities, are $55/65. Much cheaper (initially at least) beds can be found right across Broadway from the Travelodge. It's the jail division of the police department; get caught DUI (Driving Under the Influence) in Oakland and you could score a free night here.

Close to Lake Merritt the *Lakeside Motel* (☎ 444-4949) at 122 E 12th St start at $30 a night. The wonderful old *Lake Merritt Hotel* (☎ 832-2300, 800-933-4683) overlooks the lake from its prime position at 1800 Madison St. This stately 1927 hotel has big suite-like rooms with separate kitchen/dining areas. Breakfast is included and can be enjoyed in the glassed-in dining room overlooking the lake. Nightly cost ranges from $89 to $159 and if you have to stay in Oakland this is a fine place to do it.

The *Marriott Parc Oakland Hotel* (☎ 451-4000, 800-338-1338) is a deluxe hotel at 1001 Broadway, joined on to the Oakland Convention Center. There is nearly 500 rooms with nightly costs from $105 to $150. Across 10th St is the smaller *Washington Inn* (☎ 452-1776) at 495 10th St at $90/100 including continental breakfast.

Near Jack London Square the *Jack London Inn* (☎ 444-2032) at 444 Embarcadero West is clean and cheap with rooms at just $35 to $40 a night. The *Best Western Thunderbird Inn* (☎ 452-4565, 800-633-5973) at 233 Broadway at 3rd provides regular motel accommodations and a swimming pool for $65 a night. Right on the waterfront, at the end of Broadway, the *Waterfront Plaza Hotel* (☎ 836-3800) at 10 Washington St is more expensive at $140 to $155, dropping to $100 to $110 on Fridays and Saturdays.

Like Pier 39 in San Francisco, Jack London Square has an unusual variation on the B&B theme. *Dockside Bed & Boat* (☎ 444-5858, 800-436-2574) at 77 Jack London Square has a number of boats moored in the square's marina where you can have a double room for the night for $95 to $225 weekdays, $125 to $275 weekends.

Oakland Airport There is a cluster of hotels in South Oakland, beside the I-880 freeway or on the short Hegenberger Rd axis between the Oakland Coliseum and Oakland Airport. They include a *Motel 6* (☎ 638-1180); the *Days Inn – Oakland Airport* (☎ 568-1880, 800-448-3297); the *Oakland Airport Hilton* (☎ 635-5000, 800-445-8667); and the *Holiday Inn Oakland International Airport* (☎ 562-5311, 800-465-4329).

Places to Eat

Downtown & Chinatown The glossy City Center development has a collection of popular lunchtime spots, particularly good when the sun is shining and you can eat outside. They include the excellent little Japanese snack bar *Genji* (☎ 839-2808). *Calaca* (☎ 444-6995), up the street at 1615 Clay St, serves *very creative* entrees that can best be described as Mexican/Cajun ... *sort of*. Alligator tacos and oyster gumbo share the menu with more traditional, always delicious, burritos and salads. It's open for lunch only, 11 am to 2 pm, weekdays.

Oakland's Chinatown may be less picturesque than San Francisco's but it's just as busy and provides equally tasty and economical dining opportunities in places like *Nan Yang* (☎ 465-6924), 301 8th St, which is essentially Chinese but has a distinctly Burmese flavor. Sit upstairs at the *Sun Hongkong Restaurant* (☎ 465-1940), 389 8th St. It has great seafood, and at $5 to $6 a plate it's also cheap. *Phnom Penh* (☎ 893-3825) at 251 8th St and *Battam Bang* (☎ 839-8815) at 850 Broadway both take you to China via Cambodia. Battam Bang's eggplant in lime sauce is a taste treat. For Vietnamese, you can't go wrong with spring rolls and pho from *Vi's Restaurant* (☎ 835-8375), 724 Webster St, a neighborhood favorite serving the freshest, largest servings in the brightest, cleanest dining room.

Jack London Square *Dolma's Deli* (☎ 839-1951) at 201 Broadway does great falafel sandwiches. The *Happy Belly Deli*

& *Café* (☎ 835-0446) in Jack London Village turns out big, tasty sandwiches and has outdoor tables on a flower-filled deck. The *Overland House Bar & Grill* (☎ 268-9222) at 101 Broadway on the corner of Embarcadero is a popular spot for lunch or dinner or just for a drink at the bar.

Down at the waterfront *Scott's* (☎ 444-3456) at 2 Broadway is an upscale and rather pricey seafood restaurant with views over the water. *Shenanigan's* (☎ 839-8333) in Jack London Village offers steak and seafood and a good bar with views across to San Francisco. Finally, West Oakland also boasts Oakland's most eye-catching restaurant: there's no way you can miss the bright pink gingerbread exterior of *TJ's Gingerbread House* (☎ 444-7373) at 741 5th St on the corner of Brush St. Creole cooking is on offer Tuesday to Saturday.

Lake Merritt If you're at all hungry in Oakland, don't even read the rest of this section – just go to *Spettro* (☎ 465-8320), 3355 Lakeshore Ave. You won't find this caliber of creative cuisine and first-rate service for these prices anywhere else. To do it right, order a couple of appetizers (the Veracruz shrimp cocktail with avocado and the Thai mussels are amazing) then move on to Caesar salad and a gourmet pizza. They're only open for dinner, but the same folks run a lunch place, Calaca, downtown.

North Oakland Piedmont eating places include *Gaylords* (☎ 547-5184) at 4150 Piedmont on the corner of 41st, a popular breakfast and coffee spot. At 3853 Piedmont Ave the *Bay Wolf Restaurant* (☎ 655-6004) is Oakland's ritzy contribution to California cuisine. And *Barney's Gourmet Hamburgers* (☎ 655-7180) at 4162 Piedmont Ave is Oakland's contribution to anyone's search for a great burger. Huge servings of french fries, homemade soups, chicken burgers, and an outdoor patio add to the attraction. There are other Barney's at 5819 College Ave (☎ 601-0444) in Rockridge and in Berkeley.

College Ave has a number of other popular restaurants. *Zachary's Pizza* (☎ 655-6385) at No 5801, wins the Best Pizza in the Bay Area award virtually every year for their Chicago-style pizzas stuffed with fresh ingredients like spinach and chicken; there's always a line out the door, so anticipate your hunger and get there early. *Cactus Taqueria* (☎ 547-1305) at No 5525 is a good place for big, cheap burritos, and *Gaucho's* (☎ 652-3665), No 5478, does gourmet French-Mex with a New Orleans twist; try the grilled lamb burrito. Tiny *Creme de la Creme* (☎ 420-8822) at No 5362 is a romantic little champagne-brunch type of place with rich French food and claustrophobic charm.

Directly across from BART at 5655 College Ave is *Oliveto's* (☎ 547-5356), where the beautiful people sit at little tables and sip coffee or wine. Upstairs is a very good restaurant specializing in Northern Italian cuisine. Next to Oliveto's is the Market Square, with a selection of excellent gourmet food shops where you can put your own meal together.

The East Bay has a number of excellent Ethiopian restaurants; try *Asmara* (☎ 547-5100) at 5020 Telegraph for an authentic introduction to this East African cuisine.

Momma's Royale (☎ 547-7600), 4012 Broadway, is a dingy diner with hipsters coming out of the woodwork for heaping tasty weekend breakfasts. All the freebie zines and weeklies imaginable line the entrance – you'll need them for the wait!

Entertainment

Coffeehouses East Bay coffee specialist *Peet's* can be found at 4050 Piedmont Ave (☎ 655-3228) in Piedmont and at 3258 Lakeshore Ave (☎ 832-6761) by Lake Merritt. Also by the lake at 3363 Grand Ave, *The Coffee Mill* (☎ 465-4224) is the oldest coffeehouse in Oakland, with outdoor seating and an open poetry reading on Thursdays at 7 pm.

Cinemas & Theater The Oakland Symphony and Oakland Ballet perform at the Art Deco *Paramount Theater* (☎ 465-6400) at 2025 Broadway; they don't play movies here very often, but when they do, it's an experience. They don't make movie palaces like the huge *Grand Lake Theatre* (☎ 452-3556) at 3200 Grand Ave anymore. Unfortunately, they only play big Hollywood releases, though if you *have* to see the latest Stallone flick, you ought to see it here. There's also a huge multiplex cinema at Jack London Square.

Bars For a historic drink head to the tiny *First & Last Chance Saloon* (☎ 839-6761) at Jack London Square, where the teenage Jack London is said to have hung out in the 1890s. The *Pacific Coast Brewing Company* (☎ 836-2739) brews its own interesting beers (all with whaling names) at 906 Washington St between 9th and 10th Sts.

If you're in the mood for a pre-karaoke-machine sing along, try the quaintly bizarre *Alley* (☎ 444-8505) at 3325 Grand Ave near Lake Merritt. You'll find whiskey-voiced Rod Dibble at a grand piano surrounded with stools – grab a laminated songbook and wait for the microphone to come around.

Rockridge bars are still twenty-something-oriented, but without the frat boys and the fake ID crowd you find closer to the Berkeley campus. On College Ave you'll find the *E-Line Ale House* (☎ 547-8786), No 5612, a great pub a stone's throw from the BART station (they have lots of microbrews on tap and serve snacks like mashed potatoes); *Paradise Bar & Grill* (☎ 652-8540), No 5356, with jazz on weekends; and *Bill McNally's* (☎ 654-9463), which brings Oakland's Irish diaspora to No 5352. Just down the street at No 5515 is *The Hut* (☎ 653-2565), where the tragically hip congregate for billiards.

In Piedmont, *Cato's Ale House* (☎ 655-3349), 3891 Piedmont Ave, offers a bounty of beers on tap and decent pub food.

Live Music There are free jazz and pop concerts in Jack London Square every Thursday evening during the summer. If you're looking for more of a bar setting, *Merchant's* (☎ 465-8032), tucked in a warehouse at 3rd and Franklin Sts, is a seedy dive featuring up-and-coming alter-native rock bands on Friday and Saturday nights, cheap drinks, and minimal cover. People making a pilgrimage to the legendary *Stork Club* (☎ 444-6174), 380 12th St, should be forewarned that the musical selection is rather 'challenging.' This is not your ordinary honky tonk – this is where the post-punk offspring of Joseph Bueys and John Cage get together and confuse the hell out of local truckers and other innocent bystanders.

Eli's Mile High Club (☎ 655-6661) at 3629 Martin Luther King, Jr Way is a renowned blues center with music Wednesday to Sunday and a $4 to $8 cover charge. It's the kind of dive where you'd expect great, gritty blues to be generated.

The tiny *5th Amendment* (☎ 832-3242) at 3255 Lakeshore Drive offers blues in an intimate setting, and *The Serenader* (☎ 832-2644), just around the corner at 504 Lake Park Ave, does the same but with an outdoor patio.

Yoshi's (☎ 652-9200) at 6030 Claremont Ave manages to combine jazz and Japanese food in a big 300-seat club. Yoshi's will be moving at the end of '96, so be sure to call ahead to find out the new location. Jazz also features at the famous *Kimball's East* (☎ 658-2555) at 5800 Shellmound St in Emeryville, where big names headline. Downstairs at *Kimball's Carnival* the music takes on a Latin/Caribbean flavor.

Spectator Sports The American League Oakland A's baseball team (☎ 638-4900), the NBA Golden State Warriors basketball team (☎ 638-6300), and the NFL Raiders football team (☎ 800-949-2626), newly returned from a 13-year stint in Los Angeles, play at the Oakland Coliseum (☎ 639-7700). It's on Hegenberger Rd by I-880, near Oakland Airport and the Coliseum BART Station. The A's stadium is a much cozier place than frigid Candlestick Park across the Bay.

You can book tickets for football, baseball, or basketball games through BASS (☎ 762-2277, 415-776-1999). Bleacher seats for A's games are around $5 and have a good view. More expensive seats range from $11 to $20. For most baseball games it's no problem to just turn up and save the BASS booking fee. Tickets to see the Warriors play are another story – book as far ahead as possible with BASS or call the Warriors direct for advice. If you can get them tickets are typically in the $20 to $30 range.

Getting There & Away
You can arrive in Oakland by air, bus, Amtrak train, BART or even ferry. From San Francisco by car you cross the Bay Bridge and then enter Oakland by I-580 or I-980.

Air Oakland International Airport is almost directly across the Bay from San Francisco Airport. Arriving or departing the Bay Area through this less crowded alternative can make good sense, especially since the discount airlines like Southwest and Morris Air use Oakland Airport, not San Francisco. They're in Terminal 2, and all the other airlines operate out of Terminal 1.

BART The modern Bay Area Rapid Transit (BART) service (☎ 465-2278) connects Oakland with San Francisco via the Daly City line, Berkeley via the Richmond line, Walnut Creek via the North Concord/Martinez line, and Lake Merritt and cities south on the Fremont line. The Rockridge stop is along the North Concord/Martinez line. The regular one-way downtown San Francisco to downtown Oakland fare is $1.75 and takes less than 15 minutes. A BART-to-Bus transfer ticket available from white AC Transit machines near the exit costs 60¢/35¢.

Bus Alameda County or AC Transit (☎ 839-2882, 800-559-4636) operates a Transbay bus service westbound (to San Francisco) and eastbound (to Oakland) that costs $2.20/1.25. There are a host of AC Transit services between Oakland and Berkeley.

Greyhound operates direct from Oakland to Vallejo, San Francisco, San Jose, Santa Rosa, and Sacramento (the San Francisco

terminal has a lot more direct-service options). The Greyhound Bus Station is at 2103 San Pablo Ave.

Train Amtrak trains operate up and down the coast through Oakland, which is also the terminus for San Francisco. There's a connecting bus service across the Bay. The new Amtrak Station is located at Jack London Square.

Ferry Slowest and most expensive but undoubtedly the most enjoyable way of traveling between San Francisco and Oakland is by ferry. The huge container cranes hovering threateningly above the Oakland docks are said to have inspired the Imperial Walkers George Lucas dreamed up for *The Empire Strikes Back*. The Alameda/Oakland Ferry (☎ 522-3300) operates from San Francisco's Pier 39 to the San Francisco Ferry Building (15 minutes), Alameda (20 minutes), and Jack London Square in Oakland (10 minutes). There are up to 12 services a day weekdays, six to eight weekends. The one-way fare for adults/children is $3.75/1.50. Tickets are purchased on board the ferry. You can get a free transfer between the ferry and AC Transit buses or MUNI bus and rail services or transfer to cable cars for $1.

Getting Around
To/From the Airport A taxi to downtown Oakland costs about $15, across the Bay to San Francisco count on $50. There are shuttle buses to the Coliseum BART Station every 10 minutes for $2/50¢. They run Monday to Saturday from 6 am to midnight; Sunday from 9 am to midnight. AC Transit Bus No 58 operates between Oakland Airport and Jack London Square (via the Coliseum BART Station) – local fare is $1.10.

There are numerous scheduled and door-to-door bus services. Bay Area Shuttle (☎ 800-871-7781) goes to major hotels in Oakland, Emeryville, and Berkeley every half hour for $12. SuperShuttle (☎ 268-8700) operates door-to-door to Oakland and San Francisco destinations for $12 to

$21. To destinations further afield, down the Peninsula or South Bay, fares go up to $45.

Local Transport AC Transit (☎ 839-2882) has a comprehensive bus network around the East Bay, particularly between Oakland and Berkeley. See Berkeley for some Oakland-Berkeley services. There's lots of short-term free car parking around Jack London Square. Bikes can be rented from Carl's Bikes (☎ 835-8763) at 2416 Telegraph Ave and from Cycle Sports (☎ 444-7900) at 3241 Grand Ave.

BERKELEY
• *pop 140,000*

Berkeley – also known as 'Bezerkely,' 'the People's Republic of Berkeley,' and 'the only city in America with its own foreign policy' – is dominated by the huge Berkeley campus of the University of California. Erstwhile seat of radical student politics, Berkeley has mellowed since its '60s heyday, but is still a mecca of liberalism and the bizarre. Here, students study as hard as they play, with the many coffeehouses accommodating library overflow; mohawked urban urchins beg money 'for beer or dog food;' and there are enough Nobel laureates about to necessitate Nobel-only parking spaces! Add to the mix street vendors, gawkers, pot-legalization activists, the down-and-out homeless, and a cast of street personalities with names like 'Hate Man,' 'Rare,' and 'Rick Star,' and you'll begin to get a sense of Berkeley. It's the kind of place where the T-shirts for sale

CALIFORNIA

Subverting the Dominant Paradigm

Berkeley students have always been passionate about their beliefs. As far back as the 1930s, student activists were rallying against social injustice and human rights violations, but it wasn't until the '60s that the city became famous – or, to many, notorious – as the nation's premier *domestic* battleground.

By 1964, students had already been vocalizing their opposition to such events as President Kennedy's Bay of Pigs invasion and Senator McCarthy's 'House Un-American Activities Committee' hearings. But on September 30 when a peaceful sit-in at Sproul Hall was disrupted by police, the revolution began to gain momentum. Freedom of speech and anti-Vietnam War sentiment were the focal issues, and over the next five years UC Regents (administration) and then-governor Ronald Reagan led a harsh campaign of violent anti-protest reprisal that involved arrests in the thousands, veritable armies of riot police, multiple tear gas assaults, and even a 17-day-long occupation by the National Guard.

The spring of 1969 was the height of the turmoil, and an unlikely symbol emerged at the heart of it: People's Park. In April, a derelict plot of land belonging to the university was dubbed 'Power to the People Park' and hundreds of hippies came armed with trees and flowers to create a center for their counterculture. In May, shortly after the land was consecrated by the Berkeley Free Church, the university seized the land, erecting fences overnight. In the resulting riots, hundreds were injured and one man was killed by stray gunfire. Both students and faculty were so horrified by the behavior of the administration and police that they voted overwhelmingly to tear the fence down. It didn't come down until 1972, and the administration persists to this day in making periodic claims to the land. Community sentiment still runs high and it seems that, though the park is now little more than a needle-littered wasteland and a crashpad for the homeless, the passionate idealism of its inception will not easily be forgotten.

Headline-makers in more recent years include 'the Naked Guy,' a student who tried, unsuccessfully, to have Berkeley named a 'clothing optional' campus (and became a common sight strolling to class in nothing but his backpack and sandals), and Rosebud d'Onofrio, a 19-year-old homeless People's Park activist who broke into the UC Chancellor's home with a machete and was gunned down by police, sparking riots and looting all along Telegraph Ave. ■

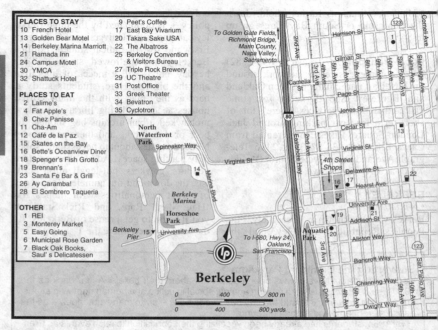

PLACES TO STAY
10 French Hotel
13 Golden Bear Motel
14 Berkeley Marina Marriott
21 Ramada Inn
24 Campus Motel
30 YMCA
32 Shattuck Hotel

PLACES TO EAT
2 Lalime's
4 Fat Apple's
8 Chez Panisse
11 Cha-Am
12 Café de la Paz
15 Skates on the Bay
16 Bette's Oceanview Diner
18 Spenger's Fish Grotto
23 Santa Fe Bar & Grill
26 Ay Caramba!
28 El Sombrero Taqueria

OTHER
1 REI
3 Monterey Market
5 Easy Going
6 Municipal Rose Garden
7 Black Oak Books,
   Saul's Delicatessen

9 Peet's Coffee
17 East Bay Vivarium
20 Takara Sake USA
22 The Albatross
25 Berkeley Convention
   & Visitors Bureau
27 Triple Rock Brewery
29 UC Theatre
31 Post Office
33 Greek Theater
34 Bevatron
35 Cyclotron

To Golden Gate Fields,
Richmond Bridge,
Marin County,
Napa Valley,
Sacramento

North
Waterfront
Park
Spinnaker Way

4th Street
Shops

Virginia St

Berkeley
Marina

Horseshoe
Park

Berkeley
Pier

University Ave

To I-580, Hwy 24,
Oakland,
San Francisco

Aquatic
Park

Berkeley

on the street don't read 'I [heart] Berkeley' but rather 'Subvert the dominant paradigm' – and people do.

But the student sector isn't all there is to Berkeley. The city reaches all the way from the Bay to the crest of the East Bay hills at Tilden Park, where a pretty little lake and some terrific hiking and biking trails will make you forget the city is only a few minutes away. There are also a number of neighborhoods with distinct personalities all brimming with restaurants and the ubiquitous Berkeley coffeehouses and bookstores.

Orientation

Interstate 80 borders the western edge of Berkeley, next to the Marina; from here University Ave is a straight shot all the way to the heart of the city, the university campus.

Shattuck Ave crosses University Ave one block before campus; to the north on Shat-

tuck is the 'Gourmet Ghetto,' and to the south the BART station and all of Berkeley's big movie theaters.

The only difficulty in navigating Berkeley is the one-way streets in the Southside (Telegraph Ave) area. To get to Telegraph, just turn right when University hits campus, and then right on Durant Ave. There's also a pay-parking structure on Durant just before Telegraph, probably your best bet because all the streets are metered – and dreadfully well enforced.

Information

The Berkeley Convention & Visitors Bureau (☎ 549-7040) is at 1834 University Ave and is open Monday to Friday from 9 am to 5 pm. A visitor hotline provides selectable recorded information 24 hours a day at ☎ 549-8710.

A map of the Berkeley campus can be obtained from the visitors center (☎ 642-5215) at 101 University Hall, 2200 Univer-

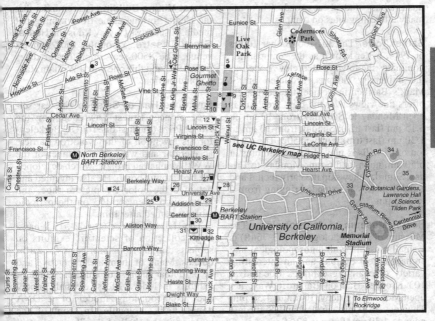

see UC Berkeley map

sity Ave, at the junction with Oxford St, or from the Information Center (☎ 642-4636) in the student union building on Sproul Plaza, by the Telegraph Ave/Bancroft Way junction. Free two-hour tours of the campus depart from the 101 University Hall center on Monday, Wednesday, and Friday at 10 am and 1 pm.

Berkeley Cares (☎ 845-4629) works to alleviate the problems of the homeless in Berkeley. They promise to make good use of any donations.

Newspapers The *Daily Californian*, now known as the 'not-quite-every-other-daily Cal' due to diminished funds, is a student-produced giveaway newspaper with listings of campus events. Other interesting free papers include the weekly *Express* and *The East Bay Monthly*. Whelan's Smoke Shop on Bancroft Way at Telegraph has an international newspaper and magazine selection. Ditto for the excellent magazine selection at Cody's.

University of California, Berkeley

There are nine campuses of the University of California and the Berkeley campus is the oldest college in the state and second in size only to UCLA in Los Angeles. The decision to found the college here was made in 1866, when the campus area was ranchland and the only settlement was tiny Ocean View, where the 4th St shops and restaurants now congregate. The first students arrived in 1873 and the college has never looked back. Today there are more than 30,000 students, more than 1000 professors, and more Nobel laureates than you could point a particle accelerator at.

From Telegraph Ave, the tightly packed campus is entered via Sproul Plaza and the Sather Gate, the center for people watching and soapbox oration. From Center St, near the BART station at the west end of the campus, you can follow the south fork of Strawberry Creek to the plaza and gate. The Student Union building (where to shop for Cal paraphernalia) is on the plaza, so this is a busy student crossroads. There are many interesting sites on campus.

Sather Tower The 307-foot Sather Tower of 1914, better known as the 'campanile,' dominates the town of Berkeley as well as the university campus. Modeled on St Mark's Basilica in Venice, the campanile offers fine views over the Bay Area and is open Monday to Saturday from 10 am to 3:15 pm (last trip); Sunday from 10 am to 1:30 pm (last trip). Entry is 50¢. The carillon of 61 bells is played for 10 minutes at 6:50 am, noon, and 6 pm, Monday to Friday. Saturday they skip the early recital and Sunday there's an extended ringing from 2 to 2:45 pm.

Hearst Museum of Anthropology The Museum of Anthropology (☎ 643-7648) is a small museum with anthropological and archaeological exhibits and an interesting variety of changing exhibits. Located at 103 Kroeber Hall on Bancroft Way, it's open Monday to Friday, 10 am to 4:30 pm; Thursday to 9 pm; Friday and Saturday, noon to 4:30 pm. Entry is $2/50¢.

Other Central Campus Buildings The **South Hall**, just southwest of the Sather Tower, is the oldest building on the campus, dating back to its 1873 foundation. The **Museum of Paleontology** is in the wonderfully ornate Life Sciences Building (☎ 642-1821). The extensive fossil collection was originally established in 1860 and includes skeletons of a duck-billed, herbivorous parasaurolophus; a dolphin-like icthyosaur; and a marine plesiosaur. There's also an earthquake recorder and other exhibits.

In the administration rooms of the **Bancroft Library**, showcases display the surprisingly small gold nugget that sparked the 1849 Gold Rush along with other items of Californian history. There are also some displays in the adjacent **Doe Library**. The Hearst name pops up regularly around the campus although Phoebe Apperson Hearst, mother of William Randolph Hearst, was the main benefactor. The elegant little 1907

Hearst Mining Building is a reminder that the Hearst fortune came from mining not media. Just across Gayley Rd is the **Hearst Greek Theatre**, a popular rock concert venue. The 8500-seat amphitheater dates from 1903 and this one was a William Randolph donation.

Lawrence Hall of Science Nuclear science pioneer Ernest Lawrence won the Nobel Prize (the first one for UC Berkeley) for his invention of the cyclotron particle accelerator and was a key member of the WWII Manhattan Project, which developed the first atomic bomb. He also invented and patented the color-TV picture tube, and lawrencium, element 103 on the periodic table, is named after him.

The Hall of Science (☎ 642-5132) has a huge collection of scientific exhibits on subjects ranging from laser beams to earthquakes. Many of them are interactive and of particular interest to children. Outdoor exhibits include a life-size whale model and a 60-foot-long model of a DNA double-helix molecule. In front of the building is the shell of the 75-ton electromagnet which was the key element in Lawrence's first cyclotron. Amazingly the cyclotron itself had a diameter of just 27.5 inches; today they're studying quarks with a particle accelerator 15 miles across!

The Hall of Science is on Centennial Drive below Grizzly Peak Blvd in the Berkeley Hills above the main campus and has fine views over the Bay. AC Transit bus Nos 8 and 65 run up there and your transfer ticket gives a $1 discount on the entry price. The UC Berkeley Hill Service Shuttle from the Hearst Mining Circle also runs there. The center is open daily from 10 am to 5 pm and entry is $6/4. There's also the Discovery Corner Store and a snack bar.

Botanical Garden The university's botanical garden (☎ 642-3343) is on Centennial Drive at Strawberry Canyon, on the way up to the Lawrence Hall of Science and can also be reached by the UC shuttle bus, but not the AC Transit services. With over

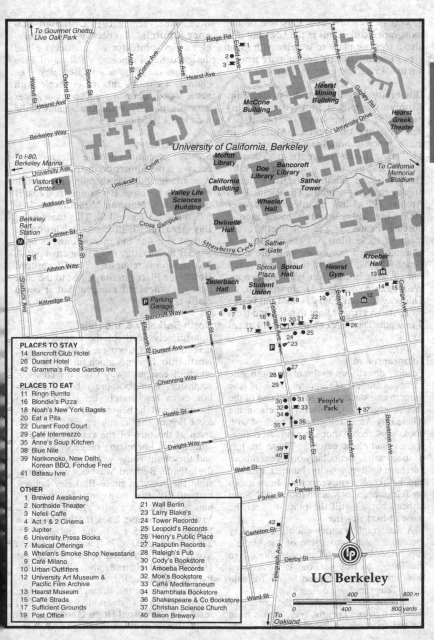

To Gourmet Ghetto,
Live Oak Park

Ridge Rd

Euclid Ave

Hearst Ave

McCone
Building

Hearst
Mining
Building

Hearst
Greek
Theater

University Drive

University of California, Berkeley

Moffitt
Library

Doe
Library

Bancroft
Library

Sather
Tower

California
Building

To California
Memorial
Stadium

Valley Life
Sciences
Building

Wheeler
Hall

To I-80,
Berkeley Marina
University Ave

Visitors
Center

Addison St

Dwinelle
Hall

Berkeley
Bart
Station

Center St

Cross Campus

Strawberry Creek

Sather
Gate

Kroeber
Hall

Fulton St

Allston Way

Sproul
Plaza

Sproul
Hall

Hearst
Gym

Zellerbach
Hall

Student
Union

Kittredge St

Parking
Garage

Bancroft Way

Dana St

Ellsworth St

Telegraph Ave

Bowditch St

College Ave

Durant Ave

Channing Way

Haste St

People's
Park

Dwight Way

Regent St

Hillegass Ave

Benvenue Ave

Blake St

Parker St

Carleton St

Derby St

Ward St

To
Oakland

UC Berkeley

PLACES TO STAY
14 Bancroft Club Hotel
26 Durant Hotel
42 Gramma's Rose Garden Inn

PLACES TO EAT
11 Bingo Burrito
16 Blondie's Pizza
18 Noah's New York Bagels
20 Eat a Pita
22 Durant Food Court
29 Café Intermezzo
35 Anne's Soup Kitchen
38 Blue Nile
39 Norikonoko, New Delhi,
     Korean BBQ, Fondue Fred
41 Bateau Ivre

OTHER
1   Brewed Awakening
2   Northside Theater
3   Nefeli Caffe
4   Act 1 & 2 Cinema
5   Jupiter
6   University Press Books
7   Musical Offerings
8   Whelan's Smoke Shop Newsstand
9   Café Milano
10 Urban Outfitters
12 University Art Museum &
     Pacific Film Archive
13 Hearst Museum
15 Caffé Strada
17 Sufficient Grounds
19 Post Office

21 Wall Berlin
24 Larry Blake's
24 Tower Records
25 Leopold's Records
26 Henry's Public Place
27 Rasputin Records
28 Raleigh's Pub
30 Cody's Bookstore
31 Amoeba Records
32 Moe's Bookstore
33 Caffé Mediterraneum
34 Shambhala Bookstore
36 Shakespeare & Co Bookstore
37 Christian Science Church
40 Bison Brewery

0   400   800 m
0   400   800 yards

13,000 species of plants it is one of the most varied collections in the USA but it is also a pleasant place to wander with great views over the Bay. It's open daily from 9 am to 4:45 pm and entry is free.

University Art Museum & Pacific Film Archive Completed in 1970 the multi-mezzanine Art Museum (☎ 642-0808) manages, like the Oakland Museum, to make concrete brutalism look attractive. The six galleries range from Asian to modern and include a gallery of work by Hans Hofmann. Additionally, five galleries display changing exhibits. The Pacific Film Archive (PFA) has a collection of over 7000 films and a schedule based around obscure themes; you're not likely to see many of these films anywhere else. The museum has a bookstore and the Café Grace. The Art Museum is just outside the campus at 2626 Bancroft Way and is open Wednesday to Sunday, 11 am to 5 pm, on Thursday to 9 pm. Entry is $6/4 but is free on Thursdays from 11 am to noon and from 5 to 9 pm. The PFA entrance is on Durant Ave.

Telegraph Ave
Leading directly up to the main south gate of the campus, Telegraph Ave is the numero uno student hangout and one of the most energetic and colorful streets in the whole Bay Area. Telegraph is packed with bookshops, record shops, boutiques, coffee-houses, and cheap eateries. There are lots of street stalls, particularly on weekends, to purchase tie-dye, jewelry, bumper stickers, and the like. Recent years have been tough on Telegraph, which often looks a bit down at heel, but it's still the place to feel the pulse of Berkeley life.

A Telegraph wander should definitely include a foray into some of the street's superb bookstores and music stores. See the Things to Buy section. It's estimated there are over one million books for sale along Telegraph!

Just east of Telegraph, at the corner of Bowditch St and Dwight Way, across from the sad spectacle of People's Park, stands Bernard Maybeck's 1910 **Christian Science Church**. Maybeck was UC Berkeley's first professor of architecture and designed San Francisco's Palace of Fine Arts plus many homes in Berkeley. The church, a curious mix of concrete with rustic wood, is open for Sunday services but tours run only on the first Sunday of the month at 12:15 pm.

South Berkeley
South of the campus and the Telegraph Ave enclave is the **Elmwood** district of College Ave, another popular shopping precinct. It eventually becomes Rockridge. Just east is the **Judah L Magnes Museum** (☎ 549-6950) at 2911 Russell St. This museum of Bay Area Jewish life, art, and history is housed in a fine old mansion and is open Sunday to Thursday from 10 am to 4 pm. A $3 donation is requested. The **Claremont Hotel** (see Places to Stay), just to the east, isn't a Disneyland escapee, but it could easily be.

North Berkeley & the Hills
Immediately north of the campus is the neighborhood known as, you guessed it, **Northside**. It seems much further than the width of campus away from the chaos of southside, with its more subdued coffee-houses, a few stately brick schools of theology, and the beginnings of the magnificent homes that climb up into the hills. Even at the turn of the century Berkeley attracted an interesting range of residents and they built some wonderful houses on the hillside. Bernard Maybeck was responsible for many of these Berkeley houses, particularly his own and his family's houses at the La Loma Ave and Buena Vista Way junction. Look for the **Maybeck houses** at 1515 La Loma and at 2704, 2711, 2733, 2751, 2754, and 2780 Buena Vista. Other interesting houses include the 1914 **Rowell House**, above Codornices Park at Tamalpais Rd.

Euclid Ave is the center of Northside; follow it up a few steep blocks and you'll reach the **Municipal Rose Garden**, a lush amphitheater of roses looking out over the

Bay. Adjacent to it is **Codornices Park**, and higher up the hillside is **La Loma Park**. Codornices Creek flows down through this series of parks.

To the west, the area known as the 'Gourmet Ghetto' is centered around Shattuck Ave and Walnut St. There's shopping, books, and coffee, of course, but food is the main attraction, with **Chez Panisse** the most famous restaurant in the Bay Area, as well as the cooperatively owned Cheese Board and its little pizza shop, plus the original Peet's Coffee. **Live Oak Park** is just north along Walnut St. Even further north, Shattuck Ave passes through a tunnel and becomes **Solano Ave**, yet another wonderful street for strolling, eating, etc.

Tilden Regional Park
Berkeley starts at the Bay and ends in the hills where Tilden Regional Park looks down over the Bay Area. The 2065-acre park has over 30 miles of walking and horseback-riding trails or you can swim in Lake Anza for $2/1. Other attractions in this popular local park include a superb 1906 carousel and a wonderful miniature steam train line that operates Saturday and Sunday from 11 am to 6 pm, plus summer weekdays, noon to 5 pm. There's also a children's farm, a botanic garden, a golf course, and the Environmental Education Center (open Tuesday to Sunday, 10 am to 5 pm). A hiking trailhead at the uppermost of the steam trains parking lots forks out into several terrific trails with views of the Bay – a great place to watch the sunset.

AC Transit bus No 67 runs to Tilden Park from the Berkeley BART Station, No 10 from the El Cerrito BART Station.

West Berkeley
Berkeley divides neatly into the flatlands and the hills. San Pablo Ave, the prefreeway main road up the East Bay, is the dividing line through the flatlands although these days even the low rent industrial and warehouse area west of San Pablo is moving upscale. The **4th St area**, a colorful little enclave of restaurants and shops, is

the oldest part of Berkeley. The small settlement of Ocean View that once stood here was all there was prior to the decision to found the campus.

At 708 Addison St, south of University Ave and by the railway tracks, the Japanese-owned **Takara Sake USA** (☎ 540-8250) is America's largest sake brewery and is open for tastings from noon to 6 pm.

Berkeley Marina
The Marina was built on reclaimed land, starting in 1936 as a WPA project and extending through the '40s and '50s before a halt to further reclamation was called in 1962. The pier jutting out from the Marina has much older origins. It was originally built in the 1870s and replaced by a ferry pier in 1920, well before the Bay Bridge was built. At one time the pier extended three miles out into the shallow Bay in order to reach the 13-foot-deep water the ferries needed to dock. Of course the Bay shoreline was much further inland at that time, the Eastshore Freeway (I-80/580) was built in the 1930s about 1000 feet out into the Bay and the land between the freeway and the shoreline was reclaimed. Berkeley ferry services ended in 1936 and part of the pier has since been rebuilt although crumbling fragments of the old wooden pier stretch much further out into the Bay. AC Transit bus No 51 runs to the marina from downtown Berkeley.

The mile-long Berkeley Aquatic Park lake, fed by tidegates under the highway, is a reminder of that old shoreline, roughly delineated by the old Santa Fe railroad line. The lake is popular with migrating waterfowl, despite its freeway proximity. There are plans afoot to create a bayshore park extending from Emeryville all the way to Richmond.

Places to Stay
Berkeley is not a great place for cheap accommodations; if economy is the aim then San Francisco is a better bet. Berkeley accommodations can be found by the Bay,

along University Ave from the Bay to the campus or around the campus itself. More information on places to stay in Berkeley can be obtained 24 hours a day from the Convention & Visitors Bureau visitor hotline at ☎ 549-8710, ext 102.

Bay to Berkeley The *Berkeley Marina Marriott* (☎ 548-7920, 800-228-9290) at 200 Marina Blvd is Berkeley's biggest and glossiest hotel. It's nicely situated on the waterfront with great views across the Bay and although it's some distance from almost everything else in Berkeley there's a free shuttle to BART. The 373 rooms cost from $130 to $140 weekdays, cheaper on weekends.

University Ave, which runs from the Bay straight to the university, is dotted with motels from dirt cheap to medium range. One of the largest of these motels is the 110 room *Ramada Inn* (☎ 849-1121, 800-272-6232), between the Bay and San Pablo at 920 University Ave, where rooms cost $59/65. Typical of cheaper University Ave motels is the no frills but well kept 23 room *Campus Motel* (☎ 841-3844) at 1619 University Ave, where rooms are around $50. There are a number of others nearby. The *Golden Bear Motel* (☎ 525-6770) at 1620 San Pablo Ave is a slightly better class motel, though not in a great area, with rooms at $45.

Right in the Gourmet Ghetto the 18-room *French Hotel* (☎ 548-9930) at 1538 Shattuck Ave is a modern building with very straightforward rooms at $85 single or double. There's a popular café downstairs. In the center of downtown Berkeley the *Shattuck Hotel* (☎ 845-7300, 800-742-8882) is a larger and older hotel with 175 rooms at $70/80 including continental breakfast. It's just off Shattuck, close to BART, at 2086 Allston Way.

There's no youth hostel in Berkeley, or elsewhere in the East Bay for that matter, but there is the *YMCA* (☎ 848-6800) at 2001 Allston Way, in the heart of downtown Berkeley. Cubicle-like singles with shared bathroom facilities are $25 and there's a gym and swimming pool.

Around the Campus Directly across the road from the campus at 2680 Bancroft Way the *Bancroft Club Hotel* (☎ 549-1000, 800-549-1002) has 22 rooms, all non-smoking, at $59 to $69 during the week, $89 to $99 on Friday and Saturday. Formerly the College Women's Club the cost includes breakfast at the adjacent Caffé Strada. Only a block back from the campus the *Durant Hotel* (☎ 845-8981, 800-238-7268) at 2600 Durant is a larger 140-room hotel with a popular bar. Nightly costs are from $75 to $90.

There are several B&Bs in the campus area. *Gramma's Rose Garden Inn* (☎ 549-2145) has 40 comfortable although rather variable rooms, all with attached bathroom, in two older and three newer buildings at 2740 Telegraph Ave. If you can put up with the appalling name nightly costs are $85 in the main house, $110 to $150 in the other buildings. That includes a less-than-special breakfast, wine in the evenings, and coffee or tea at any time. Other B&Bs are much smaller, like the four room *Elmwood House* (☎ 540-5123), a turn-of-the-century building at 2609 College Ave. Two rooms share a bathroom and cost $65, the other two are $75 and $90. Add $10 for a one night stay, subtract $10 for single rate.

South of the campus it's hard to miss Berkeley's most visible hotel, the fantasyland *Claremont Hotel* (☎ 843-3000, 800-551-7266) on Ashby Ave and Domingo. Built in 1914, in part to lure day trippers across from San Francisco, the chateau-like construction is now a resort hotel with rooms at $165 to $224 and all sorts of packages starting from a room for one weekend night for $149 or $179.

Places to Eat

Telegraph by the campus and Shattuck and University Ave in the Berkeley 'downtown' are the main places for a meal but all the many neighborhoods have their own pockets of restaurants and cafes.

Telegraph Ave & Southside Telegraph Ave is the place for cheap eats and snacks, with a number of quality restaurants as well. Don't be discouraged by the rude, purple-haired, pierced-faced counter help you'll encounter at most places; locals joke that there must be a 'Telegraph Ave Employment Agency' dedicated to finding the most disrespectful possible staff for any restaurant or shop on the strip.

Telegraph institutions start with *Blondie's Pizza* (☎ 548-1129) at No 2340 which has been turning out heavy duty pizza by the slice ($1.50 to $3), quite probably from the very day UC Berkeley opened for business. *Noah's New York Bagels* (☎ 849-9951) at No 2344 is the place for bagels, and *Café Intermezzo* (☎ 849-1128), No 2475, has the biggest sandwiches (on fresh bread) and salads.

At 2511 Durant Ave, *Eat a Pita* (☎ 841-6482) turns out great gyros, schwarma, and hummus to eat there or take away. A little further down Durant there's an international food court with an array of cheap ethnic joints, and a donut shop. For burritos, *Bingo Burrito* (☎ 704-8018) in the YWCA building on the corner of Bancroft and Bowditch has outdoor patios and a fresh salsa bar.

Ann's Soup Kitchen (☎ 548-8885) at 2498 Telegraph also combines quality and quantity with low prices for soups, salads, and sandwiches. It's also a popular breakfast joint with pancakes, eggs, etc.

Blue Nile (☎ 540-6777), 2525 Telegraph Ave, is one of the Bay Area's most popular Ethiopian restaurants with low prices (entrees at $6.50 to $7.50) and pleasantly friendly service that goes well with a very friendly cuisine. You sit in private booths hung with bead curtains and share the dishes that are placed in the middle of the table and scooped up with the pancake-like Ethiopian bread known as *injera*. Their honey wine is delicious. A block further down is *Bateau Ivre* (☎ 849-1100), 2629 Telegraph, a classy French restaurant also good for beer, wine, coffee, and/or snacks.

At 2556 Telegraph there's another small enclave of interesting ethnic restaurants like the friendly little Japanese *Norikonoko* (☎ 548-1274) with meals at $6 to $11. It's closed Tuesdays. Alternatively there's

Indian food at *New Delhi* (☎ 486-0477), Korean at the *Korean BBQ* (☎ 548-2525), and even Swiss fondue at *Fondue Fred* (☎ 549-0850).

Shattuck & University Aves Shattuck's 'Gourmet Ghetto' has sprung up around Alice Waters' Chez Panisse. She can claim to have invented California cuisine – a sort of West Coast interpretation of French cuisine nouvelle and *Chez Panisse* at 1517 Shattuck Ave is one of the best-known restaurants in America. There's a formal downstairs restaurant (☎ 548-5525) that offers one fixed three- or four-course menu each night. There's no choice, that night's selection is what you get. And it is not cheap, varying from $35 per person on a three-course night up to $65 for a four-course meal on Friday or Saturday, plus tax, drinks, and a 15% service charge of course. Reservations are absolutely required. Upstairs a more relaxed café section (☎ 548-5049) has starters at $5 to $9, entrees at $14 to $16.

Also in the neighborhood are two wonderful Thai restaurants, right next door to each other in converted Victorian homes. *Cha-Am* (☎ 848-9664), 1543 Shattuck Ave, is a favorite.

The *Santa Fe Bar & Grill* (☎ 841-4740) at 1310 University Ave, well down toward San Pablo serves stylish food in what used to be a train depot on the old Santa Fe Railway line.

Most other Shattuck and University Ave places are much more down to earth. 1950s-style *Original Mel's Diner* (☎ 540-6351) at 2240 Shattuck Ave does burgers and shakes till midnight every night. *Party Sushi* (☎ 841-1776) is a small, bright, lively restaurant and take-out at 1776 Shattuck Ave.

Ay Caramba! (☎ 843-1298) at 1901 University Ave does great low priced Mexican food, cafeteria-style. Like Blondie's on Telegraph it's been around long enough to qualify as a Berkeley institution. *El Sombrero Taqueria* (☎ 843-1311) at 2101 University Ave is a bigger, more restaurant-like Mexican restaurant on the corner of Shattuck. The flavor is still Spanish at *Café de la Paz* (☎ 843-0662) at 1600 Shattuck Ave for tapas and other Latin dishes.

At *Fat Apple's* (☎ 526-2260), 1346 Martin Luther King, Jr Way at Rose, there's almost always a line waiting to get in. The food is straightforward, from burgers to BLTs to apple pie, but always well prepared at this deservedly popular Berkeley mainstay.

College Ave, 4th St & Other Locations

For curry fans *India Pavilion* (☎ 841-6871) at 2914 College Ave has a lunchtime buffet for $5.95. *La Mediterraneé* (☎ 540-7773) at 2936 College Ave is a bright place with a distinctly Berkeley flavor and a primarily Lebanese menu. The meals are filling and the sampler plate at $10 per person (minimum two) is great value. It's closed on Sundays.

Fourth St, on the 'wrong' side of San Pablo toward the waterfront, has an interesting little enclave of shops and restaurants. *Brennan's* (☎ 841-0960), on 4th St on the south side of University Ave is a cavernous straightforward bar with cafeteria-style food. A Mexican and a Chinese restaurant share the same car park. *Spenger's Fish Grotto* (☎ 845-7771) at 1919 4th St, just north of University, is a Bay Area institution, a huge place turning out excellent seafood. Also in this 4th St restaurant ghetto is *Bette's Oceanview Diner* (☎ 644-3230) at 1807 4th St, with honest food and a local reputation for having kicked out a would-be diner for reading *Playboy*.

Gilman St, running east from San Pablo, has several interesting places in a suburban setting. *Lalime's* (☎ 527-9838) at 1329 Gilman St near the BART line has great food and a nightly prix fixe three-course menu at $17 to $26 and a three-course wine selection to go with it at $9 to $13. At 1277 Gilman, on the other side of the BART overpass, *Toot Sweets* (☎ 526-0610) is a local institution, a small bakery with a handful of counter stools and a couple of tables outside offering tea, coffee, and

some of the best muffins and other baked goodies in the whole Bay Area.

Solano Ave, on the northern edge of Berkeley, has restaurants like the Mediterranean-influenced *Rivoli's* (☎ 526-2542) at No 1539 or pizza specialist *Zachary's* (☎ 525-5950) at No 1853 and coffee bars like *Café del Sol* (☎ 525-4927) at No 1742. On the bayside at the Berkeley Marina *Skates on the Bay* (☎ 549-1900) has great views across the Bay to San Francisco.

Grocery Stores & Markets Gourmet Ghetto residents don't have to eat out as there are top class ingredients to go with the cookbooks. On Gilman St, midway between San Pablo and Shattuck, the *Monterey Market* is the place for fresh vegetables and fruit. There's a *Farmer's Market* on Haste St and Telegraph Ave from mid-May to December on Sundays. *Andronico's Park & Shop* is a gourmet supermarket at 1550 Shattuck Ave and Cedar and at Telegraph and Parker. *Saul's Delicatessen* (☎ 848-3354) at 1475 Shattuck Ave is Berkeley's premier deli and does fine sandwiches. For great bread there are a couple of branches of *Acme Bread Co* in Berkeley, one of them at 1601 San Pablo Ave, while for cheese where else but the *Cheese Board* at 1504 Shattuck Ave. Their *Cheese Board Pizza Collective* a few doors down at No 1512 makes superb pizzas. Finally, for fine teas and coffees *Peet's* at 2124 Vine St is where the chain started.

Entertainment

Coffeehouses Berkeley is absolutely crawling with coffeehouses. The most popular are: *Caffé Strada* (☎ 843-5282) at 2300 College Ave and Bancroft, with a tree-shaded patio; *Café Milano* (☎ 644-3100) 2522 Bancroft Way near Telegraph, with a sky-lit loft; *Wall Berlin* (☎ 540-8449) at 2517, proclaiming itself a 'kaffeebeerhaus,' with the strongest java around; and the cafe at the *International House* (☎ 642-9932) at Bancroft and Piedmont Aves, where the university's foreign students hang out. Down at the end of the main Telegraph strip is *Caffé Mediterraneum* (☎ 549-

1128), No 2475, which has been around forever and attracts an older crowd, including, rumor has it, poet Allen Ginsberg now and again. It's a big, two level place with a good salad bar, great coffee, and lots of cakes.

Coffee isn't restricted to the Telegraph Ave area. *Brewed Awakening* (☎ 540-8865) at 1807 Euclid Ave is a popular Northside coffee bar and breakfast spot. In the Elmwood district of College Ave *Espresso Roma* (☎ 644-3773) at No 2960 is a big, busy coffee bar with unusual sandwiches at $5 to $6. *Café Panini* (☎ 849-0405) in the Trumpetvine Court at 2115 Allston Way, just off Shattuck, is another popular place for a coffee break. *Café Ariel* (☎ 845-4300) at 1600 Shattuck Ave at Cedar has a great outdoor patio or try the stylish *Bel Forno* 644-1601) at 1400 Shattuck. Lots of places can lay claim to being the birthplace of the Bay Area's coffee mania but *Peet's* (☎ 841-0564) at 2124 Vine, in the Gourmet Ghetto, was certainly one of the first. Also on Northside, *Nefeli Caffe* (☎ 841-6374), 1854 Euclid Ave, is a little Greek coffeehouse that serves light meals.

Bars & Live Music Close to the campus *Henry's Publick House* (☎ 845-8981) at 2600 Durant in the Durant Hotel tries to look like an olde English pub, but unfortunately is overrun by raucous frat boys. *Larry Blake's* (☎ 848-0886) at 2367 Telegraph Ave is noisy and busy with regular live music, blues a specialty. It's got bars on three levels; the music is downstairs, and there's a cover charge. *Raleigh's Pub* (☎ 848-8652) at 2438 Telegraph Ave is a little more relaxed with a wide selection of beers on tap and a patio in back. Further along, the *Bison Brewing Company* (☎ 841-7734) at 2598 Telegraph Ave has microbrewery beers and live music on weekends with a small cover charge. All these places also have food. A ways out towards the Bay on San Pablo Ave is *The Albatross* (☎ 849-4714), the oldest pub in Berkeley. The owner maintains that 'all the waitresses have college degrees and anyone behind the bar has a doctorate. We don't tolerate stupidity here.' There's a fireplace, lots of dart boards, a popcorn machine, and deep, comfy booths.

The music ranges from Irish folk to jazz to blues and alternative rock at the *Starry Plough* (☎ 841-2082) at 3101 Shattuck Ave. The cover charge is typically about $5, and sometimes they give free Irish dancing lessons. *Jupiter* (☎ 843-1761) at 2181 Shattuck near the BART Station has a wide range of microbrews on tap, the best outdoor beer garden in the Bay Area, and live music, jazz on some nights. Microbrew is also the specialty at *Triple Rock Brewery* (☎ 843-2739) at 1920 Shattuck Ave, where they make their own. Down towards the Bay *Brennan's* (see Places to Eat) on 4th St is a cavernous and most 'un-Berkeley' place for food or a drink.

Other Performance Spaces *Ashkenaz* (☎ 525-5054) at 1317 San Pablo Ave puts on a wide variety of live performances from jazz to zydeco to a whole range of world music. *La Peña Cultural Center* (☎ 849-2568) at 3105 Shattuck Ave has live music, comedy, theater, poetry, and a myriad of other performances with a Latin American flavor. Entry costs are in the $5 to $10 range. There's folk, sometimes with a twist, always with coffee, at *Freight & Salvage* (☎ 548-1761) at 1111 Addison St near San Pablo. Cover charges are in the $8 to $15 bracket.

The *Berkeley Repertory Theater* (☎ 845-4700) at 2025 Addison St is very highly respected and does a range of classical and modern theater. A wide variety of international performers take to the stage at *Zellerbach Hall* (☎ 642-9988) on the campus; at the architecturally notable *Julia Morgan Theater* (☎ 584-5946) at 2640 College Ave; and at the *Maybeck Recital Hall* (☎ 848-3228) at 1537 Euclid Ave. Big outdoor concerts are put on at the 8500-seat *Hearst Greek Theater* on the campus. The Cal Performances Ticket Office at Zellerbach Hall handles ticketing for performances on campus. There's lots of free student theater during the school year;

check flyers around campus and the *Daily Californian* for current productions.

Cinemas Berkeley has plenty of cinemas and lots of art house places in particular. The University Art Museum's *Pacific Film Archive* (☎ 642-1124) at 2621 Durant Ave near the campus has nightly classic film shows. The *UC Theater* (☎ 843-6267) at 2036 University Ave is a Berkeley institution with different films every night and weekly midnight performances of *Rocky Horror Picture Show* and *Reservoir Dogs*.

Other cinemas are largely clustered around Shattuck Ave, near the BART station. They include *Act 1 & 2* (☎ 548-7200) at 2128 Center St and the *UA Cinema* (☎ 843-1487) at 2274 Shattuck Ave. The *Northside Theater* (☎ 841-6000) is indeed on the northside of the campus at 1828 Euclid Ave. The *Oaks Theater* (☎ 526-1836) is at 1875 Solano Ave.

Spectator Sports Sporting venues in Berkeley include the 76,000 seat Memorial Stadium of 1923, where the November Big Game takes place, a football clash between Berkeley and Stanford. Call ☎ 800-462-3277 for ticket information on the UC Berkeley teams. Football tickets are easier to get than basketball tickets, which are often sold out far in advance.

Things to Buy
Bookstores The whole Bay Area is well endowed with bookstores but Berkeley is especially book-rich. A steady stream of visiting authors talk about their books at a number of these shops.

Cody's (☎ 845-7852) at 2454 Telegraph Ave is not just one of the best Bay Area bookstores; it's a great bookshop by any standards. There are regular visiting authors and Cody's was a pioneer of the practice of posting mini-reviews and reading suggestions from the bookshop staff. Cody's is open daily from 10 am to 10 pm. Telegraph Ave also has Moe's (☎ 849-2087) at No 2476 with a multi-level mix of new and second-hand books. It's open Sunday to Thursday from 10 am to 11

pm, Friday and Saturday from 10 am to midnight. Across the road at No 2499 is Shakespeare & Company (☎ 841-8916), where the emphasis is on second-hand books. It's open daily from 10:30 am to 9:45 pm. Shambhala (☎ 848-8443) at 2482 Telegraph Ave is where Berkeley meets the mystic east. Across from campus on Bancroft Way is University Press Books (☎ 548-0585), which specializes in books from university presses.

In the Gourmet Ghetto, Black Oak (☎ 486-0698) at 1491 Shattuck has new books and a tasteful selection of second-hand titles. It's so relaxed they even provide chairs for dedicated browsers and visiting authors are a regular feature. Black Oak is open daily from 10 am to 10 pm. At 2352 Shattuck there's a good example of the Barnes & Noble superstore (☎ 644-0861). It's open daily from 9 am to 11 pm. Pegasus (☎ 525-6888) at 1855 Solano is principally second-hand but has some new books and also sells records. It's open Sunday to Thursday from 10 am to 10 pm; Friday and Saturday from 10 am to 10:45 pm. Avenue Books (☎ 549-3532), 2904 College Ave in Elmwood, is a good general bookstore.

Berkeley also has a number of specialist outlets like Easy Going (☎ 843-3533) at 1385 Shattuck Ave at Rose, a long-running travel bookshop that backs up its excellent book selection with a wide variety of bags and other travel gear and has regular speakers. For architecture and building books try the Builder's Booksource (☎ 845-6874) at 1817 4th St.

Music Telegraph Ave is the record center of Berkeley as well as the book center. Tower Records (☎ 841-0101) at 2510 Durant is big, mainstream, and very price competitive. Down at 2585 Telegraph Ave at Parker is Tower Classical (☎ 849-2500) for classical music; Musical Offerings (☎ 849-0211) on Bancroft is a cafe and classical CD store. Rasputin Records (☎ 848-9004), at Telegraph and Channing, is a huge multi-story emporium of new and used music. Amoeba (☎ 549-1125) at 2455

Telegraph Ave also mixes new with used and has the best selection of vinyl LPs, remember them? Finally Leopold's (☎ 848-2015) at 2518 Durant Ave is the specialist for non-mainstream rock & roll, jazz, world music, and the like.

Other Shops Although there are Nature Company (☎ 524-9052) outlets worldwide the company was born in Berkeley so the store on 4th St at Hearst is worth a visit. With all the environmental consciousness blowing around Berkeley it's hardly surprising there's so much outdoor interest and North Face (☎ 526-3530) equipment is actually based in Berkeley at 1238 5th St. You can also find Royal Robbins (☎ 527-1961) at 841 Gilman and there's a huge REI (☎ 527-4140) branch at 1338 San Pablo Ave with everything from mountain bikes to kayaks as well as shoes, clothing, and all manner of outdoor equipment. Whole Earth Access (☎ 845-3000) at 2990 7th St, just off I-80 at the Ashby exit, has clothing, furniture, electronics, and all sorts of whole-earth-style stuff.

There are all sorts of other shops around Berkeley from the weird to the wonderful. The ACCI Gallery (☎ 843-2527) at 1652 Shattuck has interesting art displays and all sorts of strange local crafts. Annapurna (☎ 841-6187) at 2416 Telegraph Ave is a genuine 'head' shop. Street vendors sell all sorts of unusual things, particularly on weekends. At 1827-C 5th St, near the Marina, the East Bay Vivarium (☎ 841-1400) proudly boasts the 'largest selection of reptiles in the West.' Boas as big as palm trees share the warehouse/store with iguanas, tarantulas, scorpions, and a giant Madagascar hissing cockroach or two. For lovers of things that slither and creep, this place is not to be missed.

Getting There & Away
With your own motorized wheels you can approach Berkeley from San Francisco by taking the Bay Bridge and then following I-80 or Hwy 24, depending which side of Berkeley you want to arrive on.

Bus AC Transit (☎ 839-2882, 800-559-4636) has bus services between San Francisco and Berkeley. They take 30 minutes and operate over 40 times a day weekdays; the fare is $2.50/1.25 westbound (to San Francisco) and $2.50/1 eastbound (to Berkeley).

AC Transit buses between Berkeley and downtown Oakland include the No 15 between downtown Oakland and downtown Berkeley, the No 40, which operates straight along Telegraph Ave between the two centers, and the No 51, which operates Alameda-Oakland-Berkeley Campus-Berkeley Marina.

BART The main Berkeley BART station (☎ 465-2278) is on Shattuck, right in the center, and there are two other BART stops in the town. The fare to or from Oakland is 90¢, to or from San Francisco it's $2.10. A BART-to-Bus transfer ticket available for white AC Transit machines near the exit costs 60¢/35¢.

Getting Around
Berkeley TRiP (Transit, Ride sharing & Parking, ☎ 644-7665) has all sorts of public transport information as well as suggestions for alternative travel and car pool info. Their Commute Store is at 2033 Center St near the BART Station.

AC Transit operates public buses in Berkeley, see Getting There & Away. UC Transit Operations (☎ 642-5149) operates connecting services on to the campus. The UC Berkeley Shuttle Service runs from Center St and Shattuck Ave in downtown Berkeley to Hearst Mining Circle on Campus. From there the Hill Service Shuttle runs Centennial Drive to the higher parts of the campus for 50¢.

Bikes can be rented in Berkeley from Missing Link (☎ 843-4763) at 1961 Shattuck Ave (they also sell new bikes across the street); Solano Ave Cyclery (☎ 524-1094) at 1554 Solano Ave; and Square Wheels, Inc (☎ 549-8350), 2135 University Ave.

Car parking can be tough around the campus area although the Sather Gate parking garage, between Durant Ave and Channing Way, just off Telegraph, offers free parking for the first half hour. The parking situation is better in the evenings and on weekends when many of the university lots, reserved for university staff during working hours, are open to the public for a flat $3.

BEYOND THE HILLS

Head east from San Francisco on I-80 and you sail across the Bay Bridge, skim past Oakland and Berkeley on Hwy 24, plunge into the Caldecott Tunnel and emerge the other side of the Berkeley hills in suburbia. The tunnel doesn't just bring an attitude adjustment, it also heralds a climatic exchange. This side of the range is fog free, hotter in summer and colder in winter. BART runs through the hills to Walnut Creek, Pleasant Hill, and Concord and BART Express Buses (☎ 676-2278) connect to Danville, Dublin, Livermore, and other centers. BART-to-bus transfer tickets for County Connection buses (☎ 676-7500) cost just 25¢.

Briones Regional Park

Briones (☎ 562-7275) is a 3500-acre park situated smack in the middle of suburbia next to the affluent village of Lafayette. Geared toward hikers, there's over 20 miles of well maintained, uncrowded trails (some of which wind through a working cattle ranch – don't worry, they're nice cows) with spectacular views of the Diablo valley below. There's also reservable camping and picnic sites.

Briones' claim to fame is the massive concentration of newts (a bit like salamanders) that populate it during the cool, wet fall months when rain-fed freshwater ponds appear almost as if by magic. From Oakland, take Hwy 24 east through the Caldecott Tunnel to the Orinda exit. Turn left onto Camino Pablo (it will become San Pablo Dam Rd) and follow it to Bear Creek Rd, then turn right. You will see the sign for Briones on the right.

Danville

• pop 31,000

The Spielbergian town of Danville looks like the archetype of the perfect upper-middle-class Californian suburb. Each house with 2.3 shiny new cars in the driveway and 2.3 smiling kids roller blading past the neatly trimmed lawns, where the automatic sprinklers come on at precisely 7:15 each morning. Danville has the home of playwright Eugene O'Neill, an amazing auto museum, and sits in the shadow of Mt Diablo.

Tao House O'Neill built Tao House with his 1936 Nobel prize money and wrote *The Iceman Cometh, Long Day's Journey into Night,* and some of his other late works here. Free tours (☎ 838-0249) operate Wednesday to Sunday from 10 am and 12:30 pm, but they must be booked in advance because you have to be picked up by a bus from downtown Danville, as the neighbors don't want to share car parking space with a tourist attraction!

Blackhawk Museums At the corner of Crow Canyon Rd and Camino Tassajara, five miles from the Sycamore Valley Rd exit on I-680, is Blackhawk Plaza, a somewhat bizarre shopping center with definite upscale pretensions. Car dealer turned real estate magnate Kenneth Behring developed Blackhawk and built the two museums (☎ 736-2280) here for the University of California. The **UC Berkeley Museum** has paleontology displays from the university collection including a mastodon skeleton unearthed nearby. Changing exhibits supplement this permanent one.

The adjoining **Behring Auto Museum** must be one of the world's most luxurious car museums, a fitting showcase for a collection of cars that were expensive even when they were brand new. Nothing here is mundane: the Ferraris are rare ones, the Bugatti collection is amazing (French Bugattis were the Ferraris of the 1920s and '30s) but like British aristocracy much of the collection sports double-barreled names: Rolls-Royce, Talbot-Lago, Hispano-

Suiza, Isotta Fraschini, Pierce-Arrow. When you've visited the museum don't miss the car showroom in the adjacent shopping plaza, just in case you'd like to take one home.

The museums are open Tuesday to Sunday from 10 am to 5 pm; Wednesday 10 am to 9 pm. In summer they also open on Monday. Combined entry to the two museums is $7/4.

Getting There & Away
From San Francisco, I-80 takes you across the Bay Bridge and Hwy 24 goes through the Caldecott Tunnel out to Walnut Creek where you merge with I-680 to Danville. BART Express buses run from the Pleasant Hill BART Station to Danville and Dublin.

Mt Diablo
Towering behind Danville is 3849-foot Mt Diablo, easily the highest peak in the Bay Area and over 1000 feet higher than Marin's Mt Tam. Perched on the edge of the Central Valley, on a clear day (early on a winter morning for the clearest weather) the views can be amazing: out to the Farallon Islands beyond the Bay to the west, in to the Sierras to the east. There's a $5 entry charge to Mt Diablo State Park (☎ 837-2525), which can be approached from Walnut Creek or Danville. There's a park office at the junction of the two entry roads from where a winding road climbs up to close to the summit. There are 50 miles of hiking trails (and lots of poison oak off the trails), three campgrounds (reservations through Destinet), fine views, and, in summer, very hot weather. Park wildlife includes deer, foxes, coyotes, bobcats, and even mountain lions.

Dublin, Livermore & Altamont
South of Danville the I-680 and I-580 cross at Dublin. The I-580 runs east from Dublin toward the LA bound I-5 passing Livermore where the University of California's **Lawrence Livermore Laboratories** are an R&D center for nuclear weapons research. This was also the center for Reagan's star war fantasies. There's a visitors

center (☎ 422-6408) two miles south of the I-580 on Greenville Rd, open Monday to Friday from 9 am to 4:30 pm.

The Bay Area bids farewell to departing visitors with a final high-tech sight. The consistently windy **Altamont Pass** is dotted with an eerie collection of power-generating wind fans; this wind farm is a pioneering site for the turning of a stiff breeze into kilowatts. The remains of the old **Altamont Speedway** stands at the junction where I-580 bends south and I-205 continues east. The film *Gimme Shelter* tells the story of the disastrous 1969 Rolling Stones concert at the speedway, which brought flower power and the Woodstock era to a crashing end.

SAN PABLO & SUISUN BAYS
It's easy to forget that there are more bays to the north of the San Francisco Bay. The San Rafael Bridge, linking Contra Costa County with Marin, is the dividing line between the San Francisco Bay and the San Pablo Bay. In turn the narrow Carquinez Straits leads to the Suisun Bay and then the Sacramento River. North of Berkeley is Richmond, home to the gargantuan WWII Kaiser Shipyards and now an equally enormous oil refinery. The Richmond BART Station is adjacent to the Amtrak station if you're taking a train north or east.

The towns along the Carquinez Straits had a brief boom in the Gold Rush era but the gradual outward crawl of the Bay Area suburbs is threatening to wake them from their long ghost town slumbers. Port Costa was once the southern terminus for huge railway ferries which shuttled across from Benicia on the northern side of the strait. BART Express Buses (☎ 510-676-2278) connect to Martinez and other centers. BART-to-bus transfer tickets for County Connection buses (☎ 510-676-7500) cost just 50¢.

Vallejo
• *pop 109,000* ☎ 707
For one week in 1852 Vallejo was going to become the California state capital, then the legislature changed their mind. It did

become the first US naval station on the West Coast and the **Vallejo Navy & Historical Museum** (☎ 643-0077) at 734 Marin St tells the navy story. It's open Tuesday to Friday, 10 am to 4:30 pm and entry is $1.50.

One of the Bay Area's larger tourist attractions **Marine World Africa USA** (☎ 643-6722) has sharks, killer whales, dolphins, seals, sea lions (that's the Marine World), camels, chimpanzees (Africa), plus elephants and tigers (from Asia so really that should be tagged on the title). Recently dinosaurs (not live unfortunately) have been added to the show. The park is on Marine World Parkway, five miles north of Vallejo, 30 miles northeast of San Francisco, and just 10 miles south of the Napa Valley. In summer it's open daily, 9:30 am to 6:30 pm; the rest of the year, Wednesday to Sunday, 9:30 am to 5 pm. Entry is $26/18.

Monday to Saturday visitors can take the BART (☎ 415-992-2278) to Richmond from where shuttle buses run to the park. Blue & Gold Fleet (☎ 415-705-5444) operates ferries from San Francisco's Pier 41 at Fisherman's Wharf to Vallejo for $13 roundtrip. Amtrak and Gray Line (☎ 415-558-7300) also go there. Vallejo Transit (☎ 800-640-2877) operates BARTlink buses for $2 from the El Cerrito Del Norte BART Station to Vallejo.

Benicia
• *pop 24,000 ☎ 707*

For a short time after the 1849 Gold Rush Benicia was a port to rival San Francisco and for one year from February 1853 to February 1854 it was the state capital. Only some fine old buildings hint at that lost glory. The town was founded in 1847 by Robert Semple, leader of the 'Bear Flag Revolt,' (see Sonoma in the Wine Country chapter) and Mariano Guadalupe Vallejo, the Mexican leader whom he had overthrown in that revolt just one year earlier. The chamber of commerce (☎ 745-2120) is at 601 1st St and they have a walking-tour leaflet.

The 1852 **Old State Capitol** (☎ 745-

3385) at 1st and W G Sts is now a museum, open Thursday to Monday, 10 am to 5 pm. Entry is $3, which includes the only other building open to the public, the adjacent 1840s **Fischer-Hanlon House** (☎ 745-3385) at 117 W G St. There are, however, many interesting old houses around town including a number which were built on the East Coast and shipped around the Horn. The rectory of St Paul's Episcopal Church at 122 E J St started life in Connecticut in 1790 and was dismantled and shipped to Benicia in 1868. Today Benicia is having a modest revival as a relaxed arts and crafts center.

Benicia Transit (☎ 745-0815) operates buses from the Pleasant Hill BART station to Benicia.

Martinez
• *pop 32,000 ☎ 510*

North of Walnut Creek, sleepy Martinez has the **John Muir National Historic Site** (☎ 228-8860) where the pioneering conservationist and Sierra Club founder lived from 1890 until his death in 1914. The house was built by his father-in-law in 1882 and for visitors expecting something in tune with Muir's hearty outdoors image it can be a surprise and disappointment since it reflects his in-laws' tastes and lifestyle more than his own. The grounds include the 1844 Martinez Adobe, part of the ranch on which the house was built. The house is two miles south of Martinez at 4292 Alhambra Ave and is open Wednesday to Sunday from 10 am to 4:30 pm and entry is $2.

Martinez was the birthplace of baseball slugger Joe DiMaggio, 'joltin' Joe' who married Marilyn Monroe. From Concord, at the end of the BART line, BART Express bus services (☎ 676-2278) connect to Martinez.

The Peninsula

San Francisco is the tip of a 30-mile-long peninsula, sandwiched between the Pacific

Ocean to the west and the San Francisco Bay to the east. Interstate 280 is the dividing line between the densely populated South Bay area and the rugged and remarkably lightly populated Pacific coast.

San Francisco – with all its style, attitude, and edge – disappears almost as soon as you get on Hwy 101. City gives way to suburbia and it's continuous right down to San Jose and beyond. Down Hwy 101 there's actually little reason to pause once you leave San Francisco – Candlestick Park and San Francisco Airport pass by, but Palo Alto and Stanford University are the first real reason to stop. The alternative I-280 has a couple of places of interest en route to Palo Alto.

Highway 1 runs down the Pacific coast via Half Moon Bay and a string of interesting beaches to Santa Cruz. Highway 101 runs down the other side of the San Francisco Peninsula to Santa Clara from where Hwy 17 makes its way across to Santa Cruz. These two important routes can be combined into an interesting loop or extended to the Monterey Peninsula.

SAN FRANCISCO TO PALO ALTO
☎ 415

Colma & Crystal Springs Lake
With its sweeping bends, I-280 is a much more elegant highway than gritty, crowded 101. Just beyond Daly City is Colma, the graveyard of San Francisco ever since cemeteries were banned within the city limits. Notables buried here include sculptor Benjamino Bufano, gunslinger Wyatt Earp, and jeans inventor Levi Strauss. There's also a bizarre pet cemetery. Get a cemetery tour leaflet from the Colma Town Hall (☎ 997-8300), 1198 El Camino Réal at Serramonte Blvd.

Crystal Springs is one of the San Andreas fault lakes, a city reservoir. It was from the hilltops between the lake and coast that Spanish explorers first looked down on San Francisco Bay. Today the view is over suburbs and the airport.

Filoli
Filoli (☎ 364-2880) is a superb country

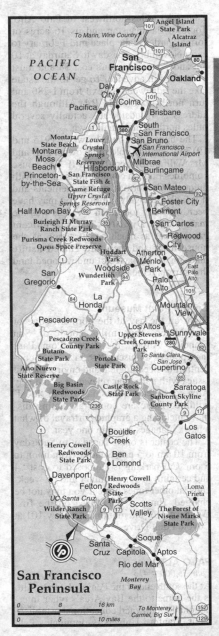

San Francisco Peninsula

estate, 10 miles northwest of Palo Alto. Tours of the mansion and its 16 acres of formal gardens take place mid-February to early November, Tuesday to Saturday at 10 am and 1 pm. The tours cost $8 and must be booked in advance. To get to the estate take the Edgewood Rd exit from I-280 and turn north up Cañada Rd. Although the address is Woodside it's actually several miles north of that small town.

The house was built between 1915 and 1917 by wealthy gold mine owners Mr and Mrs William Bowers Bourn II. The house combines English country house style with uniquely Californian design elements and if it looks strangely familiar you may have been watching too much TV: this was the mansion in *Dynasty*. The magnificent gardens are as much an attraction as the house itself and there are guided nature hikes on the 620 acres of undeveloped land that surround the estate.

Coyote Point Museum

Right on the bay at the northern edge of San Mateo, four miles south of San Francisco Airport, the Coyote Point Park incorporates a museum (☎ 342-7755) concentrating on ecological and environmental issues with particular relevance to the Bay Area ecosystem and a small zoo of 'local' wildlife. There are some fascinating displays including a graphic portrayal of what a hawk manages to eat in one year.

The center is open Tuesday to Saturday from 10 am to 5 pm; Sunday from noon to 5 pm. Car parking is supposed to cost $4 and certainly will in summer and on weekends, at other times of year you may not be charged. Entry is $3/1, free on the first Wednesday of the month. Exit Hwy 101 at Coyote Point Drive.

PALO ALTO
• *pop 56,000* ☎ *415*
At the south end of the Peninsula, Palo Alto is the home to the Bay Area's other internationally renowned educational establishment. Stanford University dominates Palo

Alto in the same way the town of Berkeley revolves around its campus. But Palo Alto is a glossier, more affluent-looking place and the university isn't the only focus – this is also a major high-tech center on the northern fringe of Silicon Valley and home to companies like Hewlett-Packard.

Orientation & Information
Palo Alto and adjacent Menlo Park are bordered by Hwy 101 on the north side and I-280 on the south. In between it's bisected by El Camino Réal, which also divides the town from the campus. University Ave is the main street of Palo Alto and continues, with a name change to Palm Drive, straight into the heart of the campus. The extensive Stanford Shopping Center is on El Camino Réal just north of the campus. The tall *(alto)* tree *(palo)* which gave the town its name is beside the San Francisquito Creek where the railway line crosses it just north of the town center. Approach East Palo Alto, on the east side of Hwy 101, with caution; it's a world away from affluent Palo Alto.

The chamber of commerce (☎ 324-3121) at 325 Forest Ave is open Monday to Friday from 9 am to noon and 1 to 5 pm. The free *Palo Alto Weekly* paper comes out twice weekly. *Metro*, a free paper for the whole Santa Clara Valley, is packed with entertainment information. Palo Alto has a great deal of public art – murals and sculptures – dotted around the town. Pick up a copy of *The Art of Palo Alto Site Map* and go looking for 'Nun Flying Paper Airplane' (at 440 University Ave), one of the slightly surreal collection of Greg Brown murals.

Bookstores Like any good university town Stanford has plenty of bookstores. Stacey's (☎ 326-0681) is a good general bookshop right downtown at 219 University Ave. Away from downtown Kepler's Bookshop (☎ 324-4321) at 1010 El Camino Réal in Menlo Park is a bright, modern bookshop with a very popular adjacent café. The area's premier travel bookshop is Phileas Fogg's (☎ 327-1754) in the Stanford Shopping Center.

Stanford University

Leland Stanford was one of San Francisco's robber barons, but when the Stanfords' only child died of typhoid during a European tour in 1884 the Stanfords decided to build a university in his memory. Stanford University opened in 1891, just two years before Leland Stanford's death, but the university grew to become a prestigious and wealthy institution. The campus was built on the site of the Stanfords' farm and as a result Stanford is still known as 'the farm.' Since the farm was used for horse stock breeding it has also provoked ribald comments from Berkeley jokers about what 'studs' the Stanford men are.

Campus Orientation & Information

From downtown Palo Alto, University Ave spears straight into the heart of the spacious campus, becoming Palm Drive when it crosses El Camino Real, ending at the oval in front of the central campus buildings around the Main Quad. The Stanford University Information Booth (☎ 723-2560) is in the Memorial Hall, right in front of Hoover Tower, just east of the Main Quad. It's open daily from 10 am to 4 pm. Despite its size, parking on the campus can be a real pain in the ass. Bring change but if you can't find one of the limited supply of parking meters get an all day parking permit from the Information Booth for $4 in the blue lots (convenient) or $1 in the yellow (not so convenient). There are cafeterias in the Tresidder Union, south of the Main Quad.

Around the Campus

Free one-hour walking tours of the campus depart from the Information Booth daily at 11 am and 3:15 pm. Five Auguste Rodin *Burghers of Calais* bronze sculptures mark the entrance to the Main Quad, an open plaza where the original 12 campus buildings, in a mix of Romanesque and Mission Revival Styles, were joined by the **Memorial Church** in 1903. The church, with its beautiful mosaic-tiled frontage, stained glass windows, and organ with 7777 pipes, was

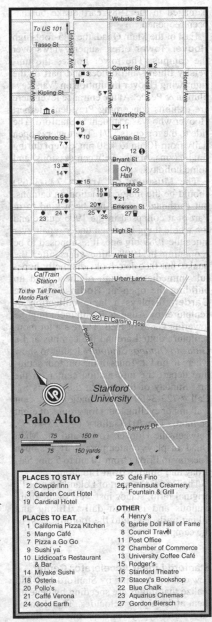

PLACES TO STAY
2 Cowper Inn
3 Garden Court Hotel
19 Cardinal Hotel

PLACES TO EAT
1 California Pizza Kitchen
5 Mango Café
7 Pizza a Go Go
9 Sushi ya
10 Liddicoat's Restaurant & Bar
14 Miyake Sushi
18 Osteria
20 Pollo's
21 Caffé Verona
24 Good Earth
25 Café Fino
26 Peninsula Creamery Fountain & Grill

OTHER
4 Henry's
6 Barbie Doll Hall of Fame
8 Council Travel
11 Post Office
12 Chamber of Commerce
13 University Coffee Café
15 Rodger's
16 Stanford Theatre
17 Stacey's Bookshop
22 Blue Chalk
23 Aquarius Cinemas
27 Gordon Biersch

damaged in the 1989 earthquake but has been reopened.

East of the Main Quad, the 285-foot-high **Hoover Tower** offers superb views over the campus. The tower houses the university library and offices and part of the right-wing Hoover Institution on War, Revolution & Peace. At the entrance level there are exhibits concerning President Herbert Hoover who was a student at Stanford. The ride to the top costs $2/1. The tower is open daily from 10 am to 4:30 pm, except during final exams, breaks between sessions, and some holidays.

The **Museum of Art** (☎ 723-3469) should be the major attraction on campus, but earthquakes have not been kind to it. Part of it collapsed in the 1906 quake and the whole thing has been under repair ever since the 1989 big one. It's supposed to be reopening in 1998, nine years after the quake, but that date looks distinctly hopeful. Immediately south of the closed up building the open-air **Rodin Sculpture Garden** displays a large collection of sculptures by Auguste Rodin including the towering Gates of Hell. There's a lot more sculpture dotted around the campus and a *Guide to Outdoor Sculpture* leaflet to show where to find it. Tours of the outdoor sculpture depart the information center on the first Sunday of the month; the cost is $2. Call ☎ 723-3469 for information on docent walking or cycling tours for groups of eight or more. The **Art Gallery** (☎ 723-4177), between the Hoover Tower and the Main Quad, displays contemporary art. It's open Tuesday to Friday from 10 am to 5 pm; Saturday and Sunday from 1 to 5 pm.

The **Red Barn**, part of Leland Stanford's original farm, stands just west of the main campus and is open daily. Hiking and biking trails lead into the foothills west of the campus.

Stanford Linear Accelerator Center

Few drivers speeding by Stanford on I-280 realize that things are speeding by beneath them at far higher velocities. The elementary particle physics department's linear accelerator goes right under the freeway. Positrons hurtle down a straight two-mile path in an accelerator beam tube (or *linac*) that is only four-inches in diameter on their way to high speed impacts at the other end of the tube. Opened in 1961, experiments at SLAC proved that the protons and neutrons that make up the atomic nucleus are made of even more fundamental particles called *quarks*. Chalk up a Nobel Prize for that discovery.

Later a *storage ring* was tagged on to the end of the *linac*, so that positrons and electrons and could be streamed in, traveling in opposite directions at close to the speed of light. The resulting collisions revealed the existence of the *psi* (made up of a *quark* and an *antiquark)* and of a new type of *quark*, charmingly named a *charm*. That was good enough for another Nobel Prize.

These experiments do more than turn up more and more atomic particles to affix weird names to. Scientists at SLAC are hard at work probing the fundamental forces that created the universe or experimenting with the creation of X-ray lasers and visitors are welcome to have a peek. Tours operate several times a week, usually at 9 am or 1 pm. The tours are free but advance reservations must be made by calling ☎ 926-2204. The SLAC is west of the campus at 2575 Sand Hill Rd, east of I-280.

Barbie Doll Hall of Fame

Barbie, that ageless icon, and her associated friends pop up in over 15,000 incarnations from Barbie as a nun to Ken (totally killing his wimpy image) in his Desert Storm camouflage fatigues. There's also a varied assortment of Barbie equipment including her stretch limousine, her windsurfer, her catamaran, her motorcycle, her horse, her mountain bike, and so on. Plus, of course, Barbie's myriad outfits over the years, not forgetting her extensive range of rather risque lingerie, presumably all presents from Ken. The museum (☎ 326-5841) is at 433 Waverly St and is open Tuesday to Saturday from 1:30 to 4:30 pm; Saturday also 10 am to noon. Entry is $4, no reductions for younger Barbie enthusiasts.

Places to Stay

The HI *Hidden Villa* (☎ 949-8648) hostel is at 26870 Moody Rd in the Los Altos Hills two miles west of I-280. Nightly cost is $9 for HI members, $12 for others, but the hostel is closed from June through August. It's in a great location, close to many hiking trails, but don't plan to get there by public transport.

For cheap accommodations in Palo Alto or adjacent Menlo Park, try the motels along El Camino Réal. Just north of the campus in Menlo Park the *Best Western Riviera Motor Lodge* (☎ 321-8772, 800-632-7255) at 15 El Camino Réal has rooms at $65 to $75. Continue a block further to the cheaper *Stanford Arms* (☎ 325-1428) at 115 El Camino Réal at $40 to $50.

South of the campus in Palo Alto the *Coronet Motel* (☎ 326-1081) at 2455 El Camino Réal is just north of Page Mill Rd, as close as you'll get to campus on this side. It can be a bit noisy but at $40 to $50 it's great value. There's quite a collection of cheaper motels with rooms between $40 and $70 a bit further out, including the *Townhouse Inn* (☎ 493-4492) at No 4164; the *Sky Ranch Inn* (☎ 493-7221, 800-255-4759) at No 4234; the *Country Inn* (☎ 948-9154) at No 4345; and, of course, a *Motel 6* (☎ 949-0833) at No 4301. The *Super 8 Motel* (☎ 493-9085, 800-800-8000) at 3200 El Camino Réal, two miles south of the campus, has a pool and rooms at $50 to $65.

Escape from El Camino Réal to downtown Palo Alto, where the resolutely old-fashioned *Cardinal Hotel* (☎ 323-5101) has a terrific central location at 235 Hamilton Ave. Once the finest address in town, it still has style. Rooms with shared bathroom cost $45 to $60, rooms with attached bathroom cost from $65. The B&B *Cowper Inn* (☎ 327-4475) at 705 Cowper St is close to the downtown center with 14 rooms, two without attached bathroom for about $60, the rest with from $100. Right in the center, just off University Ave, the *Garden Court*

Hotel (☎ 322-9000, 800-824-9028) is at 520 Cowper St and in this elegant smaller hotel the 61 rooms are arrayed around a courtyard and cost from $190 to $240.

Places to Eat

In a few compact blocks of downtown Palo Alto every food requirement a university population could conjure up is satisfied.

Founded in 1923 but looking as if yesterday was the opening day, the wonderfully authentic *Peninsula Creamery Fountain & Grill* (☎ 323-3131) at 566 Emerson St and Hamilton looks superb. The $3.25 milkshakes are particularly renowned and it's open for breakfast, lunch, and dinner until 10, 11 pm, or midnight depending on the night.

From a morning muffin to a late night coffee *Caffé Verona* (☎ 326-9942) at 236 Hamilton Ave packs them in. At 271 University Ave the *University Coffee Café* (☎ 322-5301) combines coffee with microbrewery beer and wine and some great sandwiches in an obviously appealing package. *Rodger's* (☎ 324-4228) at 250 University at Ramona also conjures up university-strength coffee and keeps it coming until late at night. Leave Palo Alto for the excellent *Café Borrone* (☎ 327-0830), right next to the equally excellent Kepler's Bookshop at 1010 El Camino Réal in Menlo Park.

Pollo's (☎ 473-0212) at 543 Emerson St offers cheap, cheerful, and filling Tex-Mex food in a very bright setting; eat well for $4. Or head to *Liddicoat's Restaurants & Bar*, a cheap-eats food center at 340 University Ave where Greek, Indian, Mexican, Chinese, and burgers are all on offer, with a bar to boot. The establishments are open Monday to Saturday from 10 am to 8 pm. Some of them also open on Sunday to 6 pm. *Pizza a Go Go* (☎ 322-8100) at 335 University Ave is the local pizzeria of choice. Upscale pizzas are the order of the day at *California Pizza Kitchen* (☎ 323-7332) at 531 Cowper St, one of the chain.

The *Mango Café* (☎ 325-3229) at 435 Hamilton Ave brings the flavors of Jamaica and Trinidad & Tobago to suburban Palo

Alto, quite a feat. Entrees are a bargain at $5 to $9. Shift to Japan where the window display alone is worth the price of entry at *Miyake Sushi* (☎ 323-9449), 261 University Ave. Once inside the prices are surprisingly reasonable. Or there's the excellent *Sushi-ya* (☎ 322-0330) at 380 University Ave. At the *Good Earth* (☎ 321-9449), 185 University Ave at Emerson, the menu is an amazingly international creation stretching from burgers to Mexican to Cajun to Malaysian.

Osteria (☎ 328-5700) at 247 Hamilton Ave and Ramona cooks up Italian food from Tuscany. This stylish and very popular restaurant has pasta dishes around $9, entrees around $12. White tablecloths are also the order of the day at *Café Fino* (☎ 326-6082) at 544 Emerson St, which manages to combine stylishness with an almost mannered old-fashioned feel. The menu features pizza and pasta as well as entrees.

Entertainment
Blue Chalk (☎ 326-1020) at 630 Ramona St is a multi-level restaurant (Cajun food), bar, and pool hall where the green felt tables have mysteriously changed to blue. It's very popular. Microbrewed beer is the drink of choice at *Gordon Biersch* (☎ 327-4475) at 604 Emerson St. *Henry's* (☎ 326-5680) at 482 University Ave is a 'NY Style' bar and restaurant.

If you're young (very young on the nights for 14- to 17-year-olds) you can rock & roll at *The Edge* (☎ 324-3343) at 260 California Ave, southeast of the campus. Entry charges are usually around $8. Check *Metro* for other places for music.

The *Stanford Theatre* (☎ 324-3700) at 221 University Ave matches Hollywood classics to its 'mighty' Wurlitzer organ. Round the corner is *Aquarius Cinemas* (☎ 327-3240) at 430 Emerson St.

Getting There & Away
Palo Alto is about 30 miles south of San Francisco, 15 miles north of San Jose. The CalTrain (☎ 800-660-4287) San Francisco-San Jose-Gilroy service runs via Menlo Park, Palo Alto, and Stanford. There are about 30 trains a day on weekdays, 12 on Saturdays. San Francisco to Palo Alto takes about an hour for $3.25. Palo Alto to San Jose takes another half hour for $2.25. The CalTrain Station is beside Alma St, just north of University Ave.

SamTrans (☎ 800-660-4287) bus routes No 7F and 16F operate between San Francisco and Palo Alto up to 40 times daily on weekdays. The fare for the one hour, 20 minute trip is $2. Santa Clara Transportation Agency (☎ 800-894-9908) shuttles buses around Palo Alto and all over the Santa Clara Valley. You can zip between Palo Alto and San Jose on the No 300 express service ($2.25, weekdays only) or on the slower No 22 ($1.10). The Transit Center by the CalTrain Station is the place to find buses.

Getting Around
The free Marguerite shuttle links the Stanford campus with the SLAC during the day, with the CalTrain station at commute hours, and with the Stanford Shopping Center and downtown Palo Alto at midday. There's free two-hour car parking all over town or you can park all day for 50¢ at the CalTrain station. See the Stanford section for suggestions on campus parking.

The Bike Connection (☎ 424-8034) at 2086 El Camino Réal, to the southeast of the campus, rents bikes for $20 a day. There's a network of bicycle routes around the town.

AROUND PALO ALTO
☎ 415

NASA-Ames Research & Moffett Field
Moffett Field is right beside Hwy 101, a few miles south of Palo Alto. The NASA-Ames Research Center (☎ 604-6497) at the north side of the field conducted specialized research into hyper-velocity flight, and its gigantic wind tunnel is still used for advanced aerospace research. Turn off Hwy 101 at the Moffett Field exit and turn left immediately in front of the main gate to reach the visitors center. A one-third scale model of a space shuttle fronts the center,

Apple Computers

Apple was the archetypal Silicon Valley company, a business that came from nowhere and ignored all the business school theories that big companies were unassailable. Actually Apple didn't come from nowhere, it came from Steven Jobs' parents garage where, in 1976, Jobs and UC Berkeley dropout Stephen Wozniak created the Apple I. Both were working for Hewlett-Packard at the time and were members of the Homebrew Computer Club, a Palo Alto meeting place for computer enthusiasts. Wozniak was the creator, Jobs the salesman, and the Apple I was little more than a circuit board but within a year Apple was an incorporated company and the 1977 Apple II was a real microcomputer with a keyboard, screen, and many of the features computer users are so familiar with today.

In 1978 Apple moved to Cupertino, where it's still headquartered today. By 1980 the company had gone public and by 1982, just six years from that first garage circuit board, Apple had a billion dollar turnover. Wozniak and Jobs both left Apple in 1985 and although Apple is just one of many personal computer manufacturers today, its uniquely user-friendly operation has ensured its survival. ∎

along with a U2 spy plane and other aerospace hardware. Inside are various exhibits about NASA and the work conducted at the center. The center is open Monday to Friday from 8 am to 4:30 pm and entry is free.

Much more interesting than a visit to the center is a tour of the actual research center. These are also free but must be booked at least two weeks in advance by calling ☎ 604-6274. The two-hour tour involves a two-mile walk and may include visits to the wind tunnel, flight simulation facilities, or the centrifuge.

Until recently most of Moffett Field was used by the US Navy but from Hwy 101 the hangar on the field looks as if it was designed for a Zeppelin, which is pretty close to the truth. In the 1930s the US Navy had two 785-foot-long dirigibles, the USS *Akron* and the USS *Macon*. Filled with helium (an inert gas, unlike the explosive hydrogen that brought down the *Hindenberg*) these craft were like flying aircraft carriers with five fighter planes that could be launched and retrieved while in flight. In 1933, just eight days before the 1100-foot-long hangar was to be dedicated, the *Akron* crashed in a storm off New Jersey, killing 73 crew members including Rear Admiral Moffett, the navy's lighter-than-air visionary. In 1935, in a near identical disaster, the *Macon* crashed into the sea off Big Sur. There's a model of the *Macon*, without a single word of explanation, in the NASA-Ames displays but the Maritime Museum in Monterey has information about the crash and the recent discovery of the wreckage.

Silicon Valley

Don't look for Silicon Valley on the map – it doesn't exist. Silicon is the basic element used to make the silicon chips that form the basis of modern micro-computers and since the Santa Clara Valley – stretching from Palo Alto down through Mountain View, Sunnyvale, Cupertino, and Santa Clara to San Jose – is thought of as the birthplace of the micro-computer, it's been dubbed 'Silicon Valley.' Not only does it not exist on the map, but the Silicon Valley is pretty hard to define even at ground level. The Santa Clara Valley is wide, flat, and distinctly un-valley-like and the towns in the valley are essentially a string of shopping centers and industrial parks, linked by a maze of freeways. It's hard to imagine that even after WWII this was still a wide expanse of orchards and farms.

There's very little to 'see' in Silicon Valley; the cutting edge computer companies are secretive and not keen on factory tours. Their anonymous-looking buildings – expanses of black glass are an architectural favorite – hint at their attitude. The Tech Museum in San Jose gives some of the valley's technological flavor and since the computer business is famed for its garage start-ups, enthusiasts may want to drive by

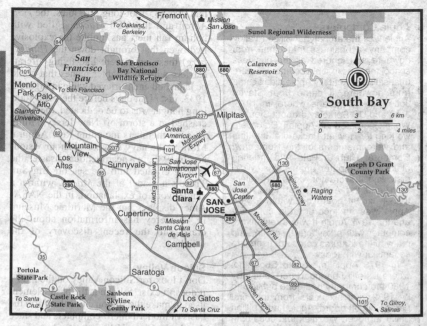

367 Addison Ave, just five blocks south of University Ave in downtown Palo Alto, to see the garage where William Hewlett and David Packard started computer giant Hewlett-Packard.

SAN JOSE
• *pop 835,500* ☎ *408*

A flat, sprawling city with more than a hint of Los Angeles in its makeup, San Jose, the 11th largest city in the country, and the third safest, is the capital of Silicon Valley. San Jose is no competition for San Francisco for visitors but when it comes to money and growth it's the Bay Area king. It has grown astonishingly fast in the past 30 years and its population now exceeds San Francisco's. Founded in 1777 as El Pueblo de San Jose this is California's oldest Spanish civilian settlement. The city had a brief period as the state capital from 1849 until 1851 but it was too small and the capital was shifted to Sacramento.

Orientation
Downtown San Jose is at the junction of Hwy 87 and I-280. Highway 101 and I-880 complete the box. San Jose State University is just east of downtown, Santa Clara University is eight miles northwest and close to San Jose International Airport.

Information
The helpful Convention & Visitors Bureau (☎ 283-8833) has its main office on the 10th floor, 333 W San Carlos St, just west of the center. It's open Monday to Friday from 8 am to 5 pm. There's also a desk in the Convention Center, open daily from 8 am to 5:30 pm. *Metro* is the free Santa Clara Valley newspaper. The San Jose Events Hotline (☎ 295-2265) will tell you what's happening and where.

Tech Museum
Correctly titled the Technology Museum of Innovation (☎ 279-7150) this is exactly the sort of museum you would expect to work

CALIFORNIA

well in Silicon Valley and it does. Exhibits include everything from high-tech bicycles to fascinating displays on the production of silicon chips. There are numerous interactive displays including a host of robotic exhibits, even an artistic robot that will have a go at sketching your portrait. The 'audiokinetic' sculpture in its high glass case outside the museum sets the technologically creative but fun-loving tone for this small but excellent museum. The museum is at 145 W San Carlos St across from the Convention Center. It's open Tuesday to Sunday from 10 am to 5 pm and entry is $6/4.

Children's Discovery Museum
A tech museum for kids, the Discovery Museum (☎ 279-7150) at 180 Woz Way is open Tuesday to Saturday from 10 am to 5 pm, Sunday from noon to 5 pm. Entry is $6/4.

Peralta Adobe & Fallon House
These very different houses (☎ 993-8182) are across the road from each other with a visitors center at 175 W St John St at San Pedro. The Peralta Adobe dates from 1797 and is the last survivor from the original Spanish pueblo, which at that time would have stretched from here to around the Fairmont Hotel by Plaza Park. The building is an example of a Californian adobe structure at its most basic and the two rooms have been furnished as they might have been during their occupation by the Gonzales and Peralta families. Luis-María Peralta came to the Bay Area as a 16 year old and died an American citizen and a millionaire, the owner of a large chunk of the East Bay.

Across the road the Fallon house shows how quickly things changed. Thomas Fallon married the daughter of an important Mexican landowner, built this fine house in 1854-55, and went on to become mayor of San Jose. Tours of the houses take place Wednesday to Sunday from 11 am to 4:30 pm. The cost is $6/3.

San Jose Museum of Art
The city's excellent art gallery (☎ 294-

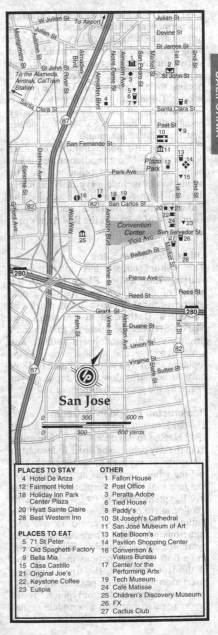

PLACES TO STAY
4   Hotel De Anza
12 Fairmont Hotel
18 Holiday Inn Park
    Center Plaza
20 Hyatt Sainte Claire
28 Best Western Inn

PLACES TO EAT
5   71 St Peter
7   Old Spaghetti Factory
9   Bella Mia
15 Casa Castillo
21 Original Joe's
22 Keystone Coffee
23 Eulipia

OTHER
1   Fallon House
2   Post Office
3   Peralta Adobe
6   Tied House
8   Paddy's
10 St Joseph's Cathedral
11 San José Museum of Art
13 Katie Bloom's
14 Pavilion Shopping Center
16 Convention &
    Vistors Bureau
17 Center for the
    Performing Arts
19 Tech Museum
24 Café Matisse
25 Children's Discovery Museum
26 FX
27 Cactus Club

2787) at 110 S Market St at San Fernando has permanent exhibitions and a variety of imaginative changing exhibits. The modern wing was added in 1991 to a building that started life as the post office in 1892, was damaged by the 1906 earthquake, and became the art gallery in 1933. The gallery is open Tuesday to Friday from 9 am to 6 pm, Saturday 10 am to 4 pm, and Sunday noon to 4 pm. Entry is $5/3 but free on the first Thursday of the month.

The city also has a number of other private and public art galleries and many public sculptures and other works. The public works include a typically minutely detailed Ruth Asawa bronze outside the Federal Building on 1st St and the usual assortment of works by the Bay Area's prolific Benjamino Bufano.

Other Downtown Sites

The visitors bureau has an *Historical Walking Tour* leaflet. **Plaza Park** in the center of downtown San Jose is a part of the original Spanish town plaza. **St Joséph's Cathedral** at Fernando and Market Sts was the pueblo's first church; originally built in adobe in 1803 it was replaced by a second adobe church in 1845, replaced again by a wooden church in 1869 only to be burnt down and replaced yet again, by the present building, in 1875.

Rosicrucian Egyptian Museum

The Rosicrucian Order has a large center at 1342 Naglee Ave and Park, about five miles from the city center. The order is devoted to the study of mysticism and metaphysics and the whole center has an Egypt-meets-San Jose look. The centerpiece is the extensive Egyptian Museum (☎ 947-3636) with a collection of pharaonic artifacts including statues, jewelry, household items, and numerous mummies. There are models of pyramids, tombs, temples, funeral boats, and a host of reproductions including one of the Rosetta Stone, the triple language inscription which made possible the translation of Egyptian hieroglyphics. Tours depart regularly around a complete reproduction of a nobleman's subterranean tomb

chamber. The museum is open daily from 9 am to 5 pm and entry is $6/3.50. There's a small shop in the museum building and the larger Alexandria shop with a coffee bar in the park grounds.

The complex also has one of the oldest planetariums in the USA. Call ☎ 947-3635 for show times. Entry is $4/3.

San Jose Historical Museum

The San Jose Historical Museum (☎ 287-2290), three miles southeast of the center at 1600 Senter Rd in Kelley Park, has an interesting collection of historic buildings brought from all over San Jose. The centerpiece of the museum is a half-scale replica of the 237-foot-high 1881 Electric Light Tower. The original tower was a pioneering attempt at street lighting, intended to illuminate the entire town center. It was a complete failure but, lights or not, was left standing as a central landmark until it toppled over in 1915. In the shadow of the tower is a replica of San Jose native Amadeo Giannini's 1909 Bank of Italy. This was the first branch outside San Francisco of the banking chain that eventually became the Bank of America.

Other buildings include a hotel, an 1888 Chinese temple, a post office, and a variety of houses. The Trolley Restoration Barn restores historic trolley cars to operate on San Jose's light-rail line. The trolleys are also run on the park's own short line. The museum is open Monday to Friday from 10 am to 4:30 pm; Saturday and Sunday from noon to 4:30 pm. Entry is $4/2.

Kelley Park also features a Japanese Friendship Tea Garden and Happy Hollow Park & Zoo.

Winchester Mystery House

The real mystery here is how anybody managed to build such a ridiculous house; a hodgepodge of silly little rooms all jammed together like a child's build-a-house game. Sarah Winchester inherited the Winchester Rifle fortune and, so it is surmised, spent the rest of her life building this sprawling mansion because the spirits of those killed by her husband's guns told her to do so.

These days the NRA would soon have her convinced that guns never killed anybody and, conscience salved, a competent architect could be called in.

The house (☎ 247-2101) is 10 miles west of central San Jose on Winchester Blvd, just north of the I-280. It's open daily, from 9 am (9:30 am November through February) with the last tour departing at 4, 4:30, or 5 pm depending on the month and day except from mid-June through Labor Day when the last tour departs at 8 pm. Entry is $12.50/6.50, which includes a one-hour tour of the house, a self-guided tour of the gardens and grounds, and entry to a guns and rifles exhibit. Sure it's an appalling tourist trap but it's kind of fun.

A free shuttle bus service connects with major San Jose hotels; call ☎ 247-2000 for information.

Places to Stay

There are several RV parks near the city and campsites in Mt Madonna County Park and Joseph D Grant County Park

Sanborn Park HI Hostel (☎ 741-0166) is 12 miles west of San Jose at 15808 Sanborn Rd in the redwood forest of Sanborn County Park near Saratoga. There are beds for 39, some private rooms, and the nightly cost is $8.50 for members, $10.50 for others (under 18 half price). Check-in is at 5 pm. Getting there by public transport involves several changes of bus. Bring food as the nearest shops and restaurants are four miles away in Saratoga.

There are lots of motels along The Alameda (take Santa Clara St west; it becomes The Alameda) from downtown out to Santa Clara University. They include the *Comfort Inn Airport South* (☎ 453-1100) at 2118 The Alameda with rooms at $60 to $65 and the *Arena Hotel* (☎ 294-6500) at 817 The Alameda with rooms from $70 to $110.

Downtown, the *Best Western Inn* (☎ 298-3500, 800-528-1234) is at 455 S 2nd St and also has a 1st St entrance. It's a straightforward Best Western motel but with a conveniently central location. Rooms are $60 and there's a pool. Also right in the center the

Holiday Inn Park Center Plaza (☎ 998-0400) at 282 Almaden Blvd is right by the Convention Center and has rooms for $76.

There's a selection of more expensive places in the city center. The Art Deco *Hotel De Anza* (☎ 286-1000, 800-843-3700), 233 W Santa Clara St, has been totally restored with prices to match its plush comforts. Old or not, this is Silicon Valley so every room has three phones, dedicated data lines and fax ports, and not only a TV and VCR but another TV in the bathroom! Rooms are $130 to $175.

Other possibilities include the *Hyatt Sainte Claire* (☎ 295-2000, 800-824-6835) at 302 S Market St, on the corner of W San Carlos and across from the Convention Center. Rooms are $80 to $150. The luxurious *Fairmont Hotel* (☎ 998-1900) is at 170 S Market St, right on Plaza Park, and has rooms from $140 to $220 during the week, dropping to $90 on Friday and Saturday nights. North of the center *Hensley House* (☎ 298-3537) at 456 N 3rd St has B&B accommodations from $75 to $125.

Places to Eat

There are plenty of places to choose from along S 1st St and on San Pedro St by San Pedro Square. Mexican restaurants can be found along S 1st St and along E Santa Clara St. There's a string of Vietnamese restaurants along E Santa Clara St from 4th to 12th Sts. Japanese restaurants are concentrated in Japantown, north of the center around Jackson St and the intersections with 4th, 5th, and 6th Sts.

At 301 S 1st St, on the corner with W San Carlos, *Original Joe's* (☎ 292-7030) does stock standard Italian dishes for an appreciative audience. A little further north *Casa Castillo* (☎ 971-8132) at No 200 turns out honest Mexican food in a marginally more formal than usual setting. Try *Keystone Coffee* (☎ 292-4698) at No 321 for a breakfast muffin to go with the coffee.

San Pedro Square is just about continuous restaurants, bars, and cafes. *Tied House* (☎ 295-2739) at 65 N San Pedro St is a microbrewery with beer at $1.90 a half pint, $3 a pint, and a standard burgers-and-the-like menu. The *Old Spaghetti Factory* (☎ 288-7488) at 51 N San Pedro St offers standard pasta fare, typically at $5 to $7 for entrees.

More expensive places include *Eulipia* (☎ 280-6161) at 374 S 1st St – the name comes from a jazz record called *The Return of the 5000-Pound Man*. The restaurant was a San Jose pioneer of California cuisine and does an appetizer-entree-dessert prix fixe menu at $25. Further up at 58 S 1st St is *Bella Mia* (☎ 280-1993), a very popular Italian restaurant. At 71 N San Pedro St, *71 St Peter* (☎ 971-8523) is a pleasant little place with an interesting Mediterranean menu.

Entertainment
Coffee and beer can be found along S 1st St where *Café Matisse* (☎ 298-7788) at No 371 offers poetry to go with the caffeine.

For some reason San Jose seems to attract English and Irish pubs. *Katie Bloom's* (☎ 294-4408) at 150 S 1st St in the Pavilion Shopping Center and *Paddy's* (☎ 293-1118) at 31 E Santa Clara St are of the Irish variety. The *Tied House* (see Places to Eat above) is also worth trying.

On S 1st St *F/X* (☎ 298-9796) at No 400 and the *Cactus Club* (☎ 280-0885), across the road at No 417, are popular live music venues. S 1st St has a number of cinemas like *Studio Theater* (☎ 292-5811) at No 396 or *Camera One* (☎ 294-3800) at No 366; *Camera Three* (☎ 998-3300) is at 288 S 2nd St.

San Jose has a repertory theater, an opera company, a ballet company, and a symphony. Sports teams include the National Hockey League's San Jose Sharks.

Getting There & Away
'Do you know the way to San Jose' Dionne Warwick warbled sweetly in the Burt Bacharach hit. Well, San Jose is right at the bottom end of the San Francisco Bay, about 40 miles from Oakland (by I-880) or San Francisco (by Hwy 101 or I-280). Although I-280 is slightly longer it's usually quicker than 101, which typically takes about 1½ hours. On the East Bay side, I-880 runs

between Oakland and San Jose while I-680 come in from Dublin. There's a ride board at the San Jose State Student Union.

Air San Jose International Airport (☎ 277-4759), at the junction of Hwy 101 and I-880, collects the 'international' label for flights to Canada and Mexico. There are two terminals with American, Reno Air, and Southwest using Terminal A; Alaska, Delta, Mexicana, Northwest, TWA, United, USAir, and others using Terminal C.

Bus, Train & BART The quickest and most convenient connection between San Jose and San Francisco is the one-hour, 20-minute CalTrain (☎ 800-660-4287) service for $4.50. There are more than 40 departures a day; every 15 minutes during rush hour to every hour at other times. The Cal-Train Station is at 65 Cahill St just south of The Alameda. You can get to the station from central San Jose on bus No 64 for $1.10 or for the same fare the Light Rail (see Getting Around) will take you to the Tamien CalTrain Station, south of the center.

Apart from Greyhound there are no direct San Jose-San Francisco buses; the best bus option costs $2.85 and takes No 22 from San Jose to Stanford and then 7F from Stanford to San Francisco.

By bus and BART, take Express Bus No 180 to the Fremont BART station ($1.75) from where BART will take you all the way to Oakland, Berkeley, or across to San Francisco (about $2.50). There's also the Peerless Bus (☎ 986-0156) to Oakland. Greyhound (☎ 295-4151) at 70 S Almaden Ave in Santa Clara, operates to San Francisco ($5) and Los Angeles ($29).

The Cahill St CalTrain Station is also the Amtrak station and San Jose is on the Oakland-Los Angeles route.

Getting Around
To/From the Airport As the constant roar of jets overhead proves, San Jose International Airport is very close to downtown. A taxi between the airport and downtown costs about $12. Every 10 minutes the free

Light Rail Shuttle bus runs from both terminals to the Metro Airport Light Rail station from where you can ride the San Jose Light Rail to downtown for just $1.10. The VIP Airport Shuttle (☎ 378-8847) offers door-to-door bus service for $12 to $15 to most Silicon Valley destinations.

Public Transport The San Jose Light Rail system (☎ 321-2300) runs 20 miles north-south from the city center, as far as Almaden and Santa Teresa in the south and via the Civic Center, Airport, and Great America to Old Ironsides in the north. Fares on this modern trolley system are $1.10/55¢ for a two-hour pass. A Day Pass costs $2.20/1.10 and also allows use of the bus system. A Super Day Pass for $3.50 also includes express buses.

If the city has the funds available it also runs a number of historic trolley cars, one of them all the way from Melbourne, Australia. They date from 1903 to 1928 and operate along the central five-block 'transit mall' and north as far as the Civic Center. These vintage vehicles run, weather permitting, every 20 minutes weekdays from 9 am to 3:30 pm; weekends from 11 am to 6 pm. Fare on the historic trolleys is just 50¢ but the regular passes are also valid.

Santa Clara County Transportation Agency (TA) buses (☎ 321-2300, 800-894-9908) run all over Silicon Valley. Regular fares are the same as for the Light Rail (see above). Express buses cost $1.75, Super Express buses are $2.25.

AROUND SAN JOSE
Mission San Jose de Guadalupe
Founded in 1797 about 15 miles east of El Camino Réal, this was the 14th mission in the chain and its large Indian population and fertile agricultural lands made it one of the most successful. The major earthquake of 1868 virtually leveled the mission church of 1809 and it was replaced by a wooden church. In 1979 the wooden church was sold and moved to San Mateo; the adobe church seen today is a reasonably faithful reconstruction of the 1809 church.

It was completed in 1985 and represents the mission church as it would have been around 1833 to 1840. A statue of St Bonaventure, in a side altar, dates from around 1808 and survived the 1868 earthquake. The adjacent living quarters, now housing a small mission museum, are original.

The mission (☎ 510 657-1797) is at 43300 Mission Blvd in Fremont, at the foot of Mission Peak Regional Preserve. From I-880 or I-680 take the Mission Blvd exit to Washington Blvd. The museum and mission are open daily from 10 am to 5 pm and a $2 donation is suggested.

Mission Santa Clara de Asis
The eighth mission in California is eight miles from downtown San Jose on the Santa Clara University campus in Santa Clara. The mission started life in 1777 on the Guadalupe River but floods, earthquakes, and fires have forced regular rebuilds. Floods forced the first move, the second site was only temporary, the fourth church, a substantial adobe construction, was finished in 1784 but an earthquake in 1818 forced the move to the present site. That church, the fifth, was completed in 1822 but in 1926 it burnt down so the present church, an enlarged version of the 1822 church completed in 1928, is the sixth church on the fifth site!

Many of the roof tiles came from the earlier buildings and the church is fronted by a wooden cross from the original mission of 1777 but the only remains from the 1822 mission are a nearby adobe wall and an adobe building. The first college in California was opened at the mission in 1851. It grew to become Santa Clara University and the mission church is now the college chapel.

Across the old mission plaza the **De Saisset Museum** (☎ 554-4528) houses art and history collections and a California History Collection. The museum is open Tuesday to Sunday from 11 am to 4 pm. Santa Clara University is within walking distance of the Santa Clara CalTrain Station.

Raging Waters

This water theme park (☎ 270-8000) features slides, pools, and other watery thrills. It's at Tully and White Rds, 13 miles east of the center at Lake Cunningham. It's open May to September and the admission is $18.95/14.95.

Great America

On Hwy 101 at Great America Parkway in Santa Clara, Paramount's Great America (☎ 988-1776) is an amusement park that throws you into rides recreating various Paramount movies including *Top Gun*, *Days of Thunder*, and *Star Trek* adventures. June through August the park is open daily; in spring and fall it opens weekends and holidays. The entry price of $27.95/13.95 includes all rides.

SAN FRANCISCO TO HALF MOON BAY

☎ 415

One of the real surprises of San Francisco is how fast the urban landscape disappears, north or south along the remarkably wild and undeveloped coast. It's about 70 miles from San Francisco to Santa Cruz and the coast road, winding Hwy 1, passes by beach after beach, many of them unseen from the highway, many of them washed by wild and unpredictable surf, all of them more suitable for sunbathing than swimming because the water is always cold. A couple of terrific HI hostels, at Point Montara (22 miles from San Francisco) and Pigeon Point (36 miles) make this an interesting route for cyclists. There's no access charge to the state beaches along the coast but car parking usually costs $5.

Getting There & Away

SamTrans Bus No 1L (and 1C during commute hours) operates from the Daly City BART Station down the coast to Half Moon Bay. Buses No 90H (Monday to Saturday) and 96C (limited service) go from Montara down the coast to Half Moon Bay from where the 90H goes across the Peninsula to Hillsdale Shopping Center in San Mateo while the 96C continues down the coast via San Gregorio, Pescadero, and Año Nuevo to Waddell Creek. Phone ☎ 800-660-4287 for bus information.

Pacifica & Devil's Slide

Pacifica and Point San Pedro, 15 miles from downtown San Francisco, signal the end of the urban sprawl. Periodically the point also marks the end of Hwy 1 as the Devil's Slide, an unstable cliff area just a mile to the south, sometimes does just that after winter storms. Rebuilding and repairs always seem to be delayed by arguments between developers and conservationists about just what should be done about this problem stretch in the long term. A circuitous bypass is usually cobbled together when the Slide lives up to its name.

Collecting a suntan or catching a wave are the attractions at **Rockaway Beach** and the more popular **Pacifica State Beach**.

Gray Whale Cove to Miramar Beach

Just south of Point San Pedro is **Gray Whale Cove State Beach**, one of the coast's popular 'clothing optional' beaches. There's a bus stop with steps down to the beach and a car park. Montara State Beach is just a half mile south. From **Montara**, 22 miles from San Francisco, trails climb up from the Martini Creek parking lot into the **McNee Ranch State Park**.

Point Montara Lighthouse HI Hostel (☎ 728-7177) on Hwy 1 and 16th St started life as a fog station in 1875. The hostel is adjacent to the current lighthouse, which dates from 1928. This very popular hostel has a living room, kitchen facilities, even an outdoor hot tub and international clientele. Dorm beds cost $11 for HI members, $14 for others; there are a couple of private rooms at the normal rate per person plus a $10 room charge. In summer reservations are usually essential, especially on weekends. The SamTrans bus driver will let you off close to the hostel if you ask. Montara has a number of B&Bs at lower price levels than Half Moon Bay. They include *Farallone Inn* (☎ 728-8200, 800-350-9777) at 1410 Main St and *Goose & Turrets* (☎ 728-5451) at 835 George St.

South of the lighthouse the *Fitzgerald Marine Reserve* at Moss Beach is an extensive area of natural tidal pools, exposed at low tide. Moss Beach has places to eat: The *Moss Beach Distillery* (☎ 728-5595) at Beach Way and Ocean Blvd sits on a cliff and claims to be haunted by the 'Blue Lady,' who wanders the cliffs awaiting the return of her piano-playing lover. South of Pillar Point, fishing boats bring in their catch at the Pillar Point Harbor, some of which gets cooked up in seafront restaurants at Princeton-by-the-Sea, like the *Shorebird* (☎ 728-5541), 390 Capistrano Rd, which is popular. South again is **Miramar**, just two miles north of Half Moon Bay, one of the most popular surfing breaks along the coast. The *Harbor View Inn* (☎ 726-2329) at 51 Alhambra Ave is at El Granada, close to Pillar Point Harbor, and has rooms at $60 to $70.

HALF MOON BAY
• *pop 9000* ☎ 415

The main town between San Francisco (28 miles north) and Santa Cruz (40 miles south), and just across the Santa Cruz Mountains from San Jose (43 miles east), Half Moon Bay developed as a beach escape from the big city back in the Victorian era. The long stretches of beach still attract weekenders and there are a host of rather upscale B&Bs. Main St, with shops, cafes, and restaurants, is the main drag. Visitor information is available at The Caboose (☎ 726-5202), 225 S Cabrillo Hwy, which is Hwy 1, and the Half Moon Bay Coastside Chamber of Commerce (☎ 726-8380), 520 Kelly Ave.

Pumpkins are a major crop around Half Moon Bay and the pre-Halloween harvest is celebrated in an annual **Pumpkin Festival**. Brew-Ha-Ha is a June beerfest, the Bluegrass Festival brings music in September, and there are a host of other festivals

and celebrations through the year. Inland there are trails through Purissima Creek Redwoods for cyclists and walkers. To rent a sailboat, try Half Moon Bay Sailing Center (☎ 728-8621); $25 an hour, $135 for the day, with a $200 deposit.

Overnighting at Half Moon Bay can be very cheap or rather expensive. The cheap options are the spartan campsites at the *Half Moon Bay State Beach* (☎ 726-8820), just west of the town. Nightly cost is $12 and the site is probably a little too close to the town for comfort. Stuck here, you're neither in town nor out of it. The *Ramada Limited* (☎ 726-9700, 800-272-6232) at 3020 Cabrillo Hwy has rooms at $55 to $85, which is about as low as prices go in Half Moon Bay.

San Benito House (☎ 726-3425) at 356 Main St is one of the more moderately priced Half Moon Bay B&Bs. The *Old Thyme Inn* (☎ 726-1616), 779 Main St, is in a Queen Anne Victorian, circa 1899; very 'cute.'

Cameron's Restaurant & Inn (☎ 726-5705), 1410 S Cabrillo Hwy, is an English-style pub in a century-old building, with a large selection of beers and a range of food. There are three rooms upstairs, scant in luxuries but priced at $50 weeknights and $60 weekends. For a cheap meal, Half Moon Bay is as rampant with taquerias as the rest of California; *Three Amigos* (☎ 726-6080), 200 N Cabrillo Hwy, is the best.

HALF MOON BAY TO SANTA CRUZ
☎ 415

More beaches lie south of Half Moon Bay, starting with San Gregorio State Beach, 10 miles to the south. There's a clothing-optional stretch to the north but the beach can get so chilly only polar bears would find the idea appealing. Pomponio and Pescadero State Beaches follow down the coast to the pleasant little town of Pescadero. Bird watchers enjoy the Pescadero Marsh Reserve where guided walks take place on weekends year round. A mid-August weekend hosts the annual **Pesca-**

dero **Arts & Fun Fest** with live music, arts & crafts, and food.

Nine miles east of San Gregorio State Beach on Hwy 84, *Applejacks Inn* roadhouse offers backyard barbecue, Harleys, and a whole lot of local color, 'Easy Rider' style. If you've come looking for the grizzly side of Americana, look no further. There's live music on Saturday nights.

The *Pescadero Creekside Barn* (☎ 879-1046), offers lodging for two in downtown Pescadero (call for directions). On weekends there's a two-night minimum, for $175. Located above a small art gallery, amenities include a fireplace, clawfoot tub, rustic decor, and beautiful views.

The HI *Pigeon Point Lighthouse Hostel* (☎ 879-0633) at Pigeon Point, five miles south of Pescadero, uses the old lighthouse keeper's quarters and features an outdoor hot tub. It's such a pleasant place that it's hardly surprising that in summer it's usually essential to make advance reservations. Beds in the four dorms are $11 for HI members, $14 for others. There are also some private rooms for an additional $10. The 110-foot lighthouse, one of the tallest in America, was built in 1872.

Inland, large stretches of the hills are protected in a patchwork of parks which, just like the coast, remain remarkably untouched despite the huge urban popula-

tions only a few miles to the north and east. The drive east on Hwy 84 through La Honda to Palo Alto winds through impressive stands of trees. The tiny township of **La Honda** is surrounded by four parks offering lots of opportunities for hiking or mountain biking and a number of campgrounds. The redwood forest of **Butano State Park** is one of these interesting reserves, and Big Basin Redwoods State Park is even more impressive.

Big Basin Redwoods State Park (☎ 408-338-6132) encompasses 25 sq miles of the largest redwoods in the Southern Coastal Mountain Range, as well as rivers and streams, wildlife, and many miles of hiking trails. The old-growth forests contain stands of fir, cedar, bay, madrone, and oak. Big Basin is California's first state park, signed into law in 1902 after a heated battle between local conservationists and logging interests. Many of the redwoods here are over 1500 years old.

There are 115 tent/RV sites ($14 to $16), 32 walk-in sites (secluded in a thick redwood grove at Wastahi Campground), and 36 tent cabins with wood-burning stoves ($32). Reserve through Destinet.

Año Nuevo State Reserve

A visit to the elephant seal colony on Año

Elephant Seals

Elephant seals follow a precise calendar: between September and November young seals and the yearlings, who left the beach earlier in the year, return and take up residence. In November and December the adult males return and start the ritual struggles to assert superiority; only the largest, strongest, and most aggressive 'alpha' males will be able to gather a harem. From December through February the adult females will arrive, pregnant from last year's beach activities, give birth to their pups and, about a month later, mate with the dominant males, hulking brutes weighing up to three tons!

At birth an elephant seal pup weighs about 80 pounds and, while being fed by its mother, puts on about seven pounds a day! A month's solid feeding will bring its weight up to about 300 pounds but at around this time, usually in March, the females depart, abandoning their offspring on the beach. For the next two to three months the young seals, now known as 'weaners,' lounge around in groups known as 'pods,' gradually learning to swim, first in the rivers and tidal pools, then in the sea. Finally they too depart, having lost 20 to 30% of their weight during this prolonged fast. By April the last young seals have left but during April and May the adult females return to molt. They depart and the beach is empty until July and August when the adult males also return to molt. Then in September the juvenile seals start to return, and the cycle begins again. ■

Nuevo Beach is a wonderful experience but at the mid-winter peak season you must plan well ahead. The beach is five miles south of Pigeon Point, 27 miles north of Santa Cruz.

Elephant seals were just as fearless two centuries ago as they are today, but unfortunately, club-toting seal trappers were not in the same seal-friendly category as camera-toting tourists. Between 1800 and 1850 the elephant seal was driven to the edge of extinction. Only a handful survived around the Guadalupe Islands off the Mexican state of Baja California. With substitutes for seal oil and more recent conservationist attitudes, the elephant seal made a comeback, reappearing on the Southern California coast from around 1920. In 1955 they returned to Año Nuevo beach and today the beach is home to 3000 or more in the peak season.

The peak season is during the mating and birthing time, and from December 15 to the end of March visitors are only allowed on heavily booked guided tours. For the peak of the peak season, mid-January to mid-February, it's recommended you book eight weeks ahead! Although the park office (☎ 415-879-0227) can advise on your chances of getting a place, bookings can only be made through Destinet. The tour costs $4 per person, plus $4 for parking. From the ranger station it's a three-mile roundtrip walk to the beach and the visit takes 2½ hours. If you haven't booked, bad weather can sometimes lead to last minute cancellations. The rest of the year, from April 1 to December 15, there are no tour requirements. From mid-January to late-February SamTrans has weekend bus runs ($10) to the reserve from San Mateo, but you must reserve by mail weeks in advance – call ☎ 800-660-4287 for a payment form.

SANTA CRUZ
• *pop 50,000 ☎ 408*

Santa Cruz is a popular weekend escape from San Francisco with some fine beaches, a wonderfully old fashioned boardwalk amusement park, and a big student population at the University of California to ensure lots of nightlife and entertainment. Santa Cruz has managed to retain a slightly uncommercial feel; there are no big hotels and traces of the '60s linger. This was, after all, where Ken Kesey launched his notorious '60s activities and Neil Young still lives in the hills backing the coast.

Collapsing freeways in Oakland and fires raging through the Marina grabbed the '89 Loma Prieta earthquake headlines but per capita it was Santa Cruz, close to the epicenter, which really suffered. Pacific Ave Mall was decimated, a number of people were killed by collapsing buildings, and reconstruction and empty lots continue to this day. Watsonville, 17 miles southeast, was even closer to the epicenter.

Orientation & Information
Santa Cruz stretches for a long way along the coast, blending into Capitola, a slightly lower key beach resort. It's 70 miles south of San Francisco by Hwy 1 down the coast, by I-280 and twisting Hwy 9 or, fastest, by I-280 then Hwy 17. It's 35 miles west of San Jose by winding Hwy 17 and 40 miles north of Monterey by Hwy 1. Santa Cruz itself can be a little confusing with roads winding up and downhill and disappearing then reappearing as they cross the San Lorenzo River. Pacific Ave is the main street of downtown Santa Cruz, with Front St one block east. The University of California campus is about 2½ miles northwest of the center.

The Visitor Information Center (☎ 425-1234) at 701 Front St is open Monday to Saturday from 9 am to 5 pm; Sunday from 10 am to 4 pm. In the summer there's an information kiosk on Ocean St between Water St and Soquel Ave. It's open daily from 10 am to 6 pm. *Metro Santa Cruz* is the town's free newspaper. Bookshops include the big Bookshop Santa Cruz (☎ 423-0900) at 1520 Pacific Ave, the new and secondhand Logos (☎ 427-5100) at 1117 Pacific Ave, and the New Age (smell of patchouli in the air) Gateway Books

CALIFORNIA

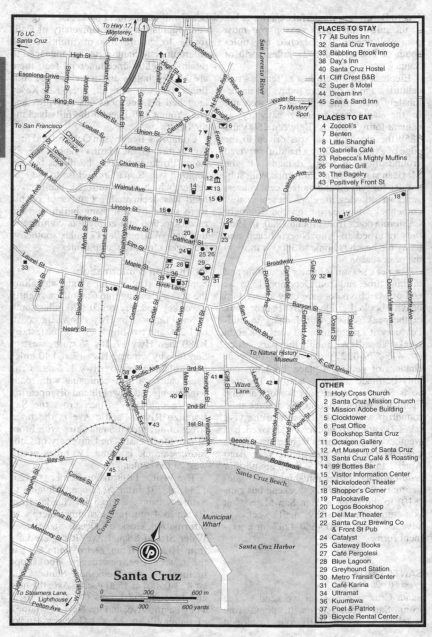

To Hwy 17, Monterey, San Jose

PLACES TO STAY
17 All Suites Inn
32 Santa Cruz Travelodge
33 Babbling Brook Inn
38 Day's Inn
40 Santa Cruz Hostel
41 Cliff Crest B&B
42 Super 8 Motel
44 Dream Inn
45 Sea & Sand Inn

PLACES TO EAT
4 Zoccoli's
7 Benten
8 Little Shanghai
10 Gabriella Café
23 Rebecca's Mighty Muffins
26 Pontiac Grill
35 The Bagelry
43 Positively Front St

OTHER
1 Holy Cross Church
2 Santa Cruz Mission Church
3 Mission Adobe Building
5 Clocktower
6 Post Office
9 Bookshop Santa Cruz
11 Octagon Gallery
12 Art Museum of Santa Cruz
13 Santa Cruz Café & Roasting
14 99 Bottles Bar
15 Visitor Information Center
16 Nickelodeon Theater
18 Shopper's Corner
19 Palookaville
20 Logos Bookshop
21 Del Mar Theater
22 Santa Cruz Brewing Co
     & Front St Pub
24 Catalyst
25 Gateway Books
27 Café Pergolesi
28 Blue Lagoon
29 Greyhound Station
30 Metro Transit Center
31 Café Karina
34 Ultramat
36 Kuumbwa
37 Poet & Patriot
39 Bicycle Rental Center

Santa Cruz

0   300   600 m
0   300   600 yards

(☎ 429-9600) at Pacific Ave and Cathcart. Ultramat (☎ 426-9274) is a laundry at 501 Laurel St at Washington.

Boardwalk

The 1906 Boardwalk (☎ 423-5590) is the oldest beachfront amusement park on the West Coast with the half-mile-long 1923 Giant Dipper, a 'woody' rollercoaster, and the 1911 Looff carousel – both national historic landmarks. The Boardwalk is only open weekends and some holidays during the winter (in December it's not open on weekends) but in June, July, and August it's open daily. Rides cost from $1.50 up to $2.50 and $3 for the properly scary ones or $17.95 in summer, $10.25 in winter, for an unlimited rides ticket. The adjacent 1907 **Coconut Grove** still hosts big acts in its ornate Grand Ballroom but the Big Band era was its heyday.

Mission Santa Cruz

The 'Mission of the Holy Cross' has always been a rather sorry affair although it did give the town its name. Founded in 1791, the 12th of the Californian missions, Santa Cruz was isolated from the comings and goings along El Camino Réal and had an uneconomically small Ohlone Indian population. Missions needed Indians to Christianize and to do the hard work. Worse, the mission was too close to a Spanish settlement – sad experience had proven that settlements and missions did not mix. The mission fell apart after secularization, the mission church simply disappeared, and today the Holy Cross Church on High St stands on the original site. At the corner of High and Emmet Sts the mission church was rebuilt in 1932 as a half size replica of the original.

Mission Plaza is just across Water St from the north end of Pacific Ave but the only original construction is the adobe building on School St. The mission church (☎ 426-5686) is open daily from 9 am to 5 pm, the gift shop from 2:30 to 4:30 pm. The adobe building is open in summer, Thursday to Sunday from 10 am to 4 pm; in winter, Thursday and Friday from 10 am to 3 pm; Saturday and Sunday from 11 am to 4 pm.

Museums & Art Galleries

The **Art Museum of Santa Cruz County** (☎ 429-1964), 705 Front St, is open Tuesday to Sunday from 11 am to 4 pm; Thursday to 8 pm. Entry is $3/free. The adjacent **Octagon Gallery** houses temporary exhibits.

The **Santa Cruz City Museum of Natural History** (☎ 429-3773) is at 1305 E Cliff Drive, close to the waterfront but on the east side of the San Lorenzo River. A gray whale figure fronts the museum and inside displays include the fossil skeleton of a huge sea cow from 10 to 12 million years ago, a local relative of the still extant dugong of Australasia or manatee of the Caribbean. It's open Tuesday to Friday from 10 am to 5 pm; Saturday and Sunday from 1 to 5 pm. Entry is $2/50¢. Like Pacific Grove on the Monterey Peninsula, Santa Cruz is an overwintering center for monarch butterflies (see Pacific Grove). From October to March they can be seen on trees behind the Natural History Museum and also at Natural Bridges State Beach.

The **Surfing Museum** (☎ 429-3429) at Lighthouse Point, W Cliff Drive, overlooks Steamer's Lane, the most popular surfing break at Santa Cruz. The museum is open Thursday to Monday from noon to 4 pm, and entry is free. The Santa Cruz Surfing Club was founded in 1936 and there's a surfer statue at the end of Pelton Ave to mark the event.

University of California, Santa Cruz

Established in 1965, the University of California, Santa Cruz has 10,000 students and a fine campus dotted with interesting buildings and fine stands of redwood trees in the hills above the town. Campus buildings include two galleries, a renowned arboretum, and a number of buildings from the Cowell Ranch of the 1860s, on which the campus was built.

The university's **Long Marine Laboratory & Aquarium** (☎ 459-4308) at 100 Shaffer on the west side of town has a col-

New-Age Santa Cruz

One of Santa Cruz's more New-Agey characteristics is its proclivity for natural health and healing facilities. For organic fruits and vegetables, and spices and flowers of all varieties you'd be hard pressed to find better shopping than at the weekly Farmers' Market, every Wednesday from roughly 2 to 6 pm on Lincoln St between Pacific and Cedar. Follow the scent of patchouli. Stapleton's (☎ 425-5888) at 415 River St offers a good selection of fresh organic and dried foods and Shopper's Corner at Soquel and Branciforte is a great mom 'n pop neighborhood market with a good meat selection and hundreds of wines to choose from. Vitamins and goodness in bulk reside at The Food Bin/Herb Room (☎ 423-5526), 1130 Mission St at Laurel.

If hunting and gathering leaves you feeling groggy, unwind in the private hot tubs at The Well Within (☎ 458-9355), 112 Elm St, where each blissfully tranquil room overlooks a Japanese-style bamboo garden. Rates are $6.50 per person before 6 pm, evenings and rooms with saunas are more. Or, for a more enlightened outing, Kiva Retreat House (☎ 429-1142) at 702 Water St has several outdoor hot tubs, a cold plunge, and a sauna within a 'clothing optional' garden setting, $10 for the whole day, and they're open to midnight. Private tubs are available at $15 an hour. Both establishments also provide massage therapy in a strictly non-sexual atmosphere with rates beginning at $30 per ½ hour session. Check also the postings in most local cafes and bookshops for private practitioners, many of whose rates vary on a sliding scale.

It's no surprise that Santa Cruz teems with faith healers and spiritualists of every variety. The good news is their acceptance has also left room for an abundance of non-traditional health practitioners. See the local telephone directory for acupuncturists, herbalists, homeopathists, or just to have your essential oils changed and your chakras realigned. ■

lection of aquarium tanks and a blue whale skeleton. It's open Tuesday to Sunday from 1 to 4 pm. A $2 donation is suggested.

Natural Bridges State Beach

Just north of Santa Cruz, at the end of W Cliff Drive, there's a good beach, interesting tidal pools, and trees where monarch butterflies congregate. What there isn't is a natural bridge, which washed away a few years ago.

Railways

The arrival of the Southern Pacific Railway put Victorian-era Santa Cruz on the tourist map and although there are no railway connections to the town today there are two train rides (☎ 335-4400). The town's railway history started with a freight line built in 1875 from the wharf seven miles up the San Lorenzo River Canyon to Felton. The spectacular route and the Big Trees redwood grove near Felton soon attracted tourists as well as freight. In 1880 a narrow gauge line across the Santa Cruz Mountains linked San Francisco, Oakland, and San Jose to bring visitors to Felton and then down to the beach. In 1940 a severe storm washed out the line from the Bay Area to Felton and it was never repaired. The short Santa Cruz-Felton line reverted to freight use.

In 1985 passenger services restarted as the **Santa Cruz, Big Trees & Pacific Railway**. The short, but slow and scenic, trip between the boardwalk and Roaring Camp, outside Felton, takes two hours. In spring and fall the trains operate weekends and holidays; from mid-June to early September they operate daily. There are two roundtrips daily and the return cost is $14/10.50.

From Roaring Camp, a recreation of an 1880s logging town, you can take the second railway trip on the narrow-gauge steam locomotives of the **Roaring Camp & Big Trees Railroad**. The 1¼-hour roundtrip to the Big Trees redwood stand costs $12.50/9. This route operates weekends and holidays year round, daily in summer.

At the turn of the century Santa Cruz potentially had another railway link to San Francisco. The Ocean Shore Railroad planned to build a line down the coast but it was plagued by the difficult and unstable terrain (just as Hwy 1 is today) and it never consisted of more than random stretches connected by ferry services. The 1906 earthquake finished it off.

Mystery Spot
This fine old-fashioned tourist trap has probably scarcely changed from the day it opened in the 1940s. On the steeply sloping hillside compasses point crazily, mysterious forces push you around, balls roll uphill and buildings lean at silly angles. It's open daily from 9:30 am to 5 pm, and this good, clean, harmless fun costs $4/2 including a yellow bumper sticker. The Mystery Spot (☎ 423-8897) is on Branciforte Drive, take Market St out of Santa Cruz, under Hwy 1 and up into the hills.

Activities
The north side of Monterey Bay is warmer than the south, which is cooled in summer by the upwelling waters from the Monterey Canyon. As a result, beach activities are much more feasible at Santa Cruz than at Monterey. **Surfing** is also popular with Steamer's Lane the most popular break. Pleasure Point Beach, on E Cliff Drive toward Capitola, and Manresa State Beach, beyond Capitola, are other favorites. Equipment can be rented from Go Skate (☎ 425-8578) at 601 Beach St or from Freeline Design (☎ 476-2950) at 821 41st Ave. Want to learn to surf? Richard Schmidt (☎ 423-0928) guarantees you'll be standing and surfing the first day out. A first time two-hour group lesson costs $70, a private lesson is $50 an hour, all equipment included.

Kayak Connection (☎ 479-1121) at 413 Lake Ave rents kayaks. Whale watching trips also depart from the pier, 2½ to three hours, $16/12. Dive with Ocean Odyssey (☎ 475-3483) at 2345 S Rodeo Gulch Rd.

On dry land **bicycling** is enormously popular with many interesting rides up into

the hills that back the town. Henry Cowell Redwoods State Park is a particularly popular getaway or try the W Cliff Drive coast ride from the wharf to Natural Bridges State Beach.

Places to Stay
If economy is important, Santa Cruz is a much better deal than nearby Monterey. The beach resort has camping sites in the vicinity, a youth hostel, a vast range of predominantly cheaper motels, and a handful of pricier B&Bs and a few more expensive motels. Remarkably there are none of the big hotels you might expect at such a popular beach and surprisingly little beach-front construction.

Camping There are camp sites in the mountains or on the beach. Phone Destinet for reservations in the *Big Basin Redwood State Park* at Boulder Creek, the *Henry Cowell Redwood State Park* at Felton, the *New Brighton State Beach Park* at Capitola, the *Seacliff State Beach Park* at Aptos, the *Sunset State Beach Park* at Watsonville and other state parks. The *Santa Cruz KOA Kampground* (☎ 722-0551) is in Watsonville near the beach.

Hostels The HI *Santa Cruz Hostel* (☎ 423-8304) at 315 Main St is just two blocks from the beach and the wharf or five blocks from downtown. This very pleasant hostel has a great location with beds at $12 to $14 and an 11 pm curfew.

Motels Recommending motels at Santa Cruz is a fairly hopeless task – there are so many and they're so unmemorable! Prices are variable, due to proximity to the beach, whether it's a weekday (cheaper) or weekend (pricier), and season. On a dull, midweek day in winter many motels will have signs offering rooms for as little as $25. On a summer weekend that same room might fetch up toward $100.

There are many motels along Hwy 1, or Mission Rd as it's known within the town limits. For a few minutes drive to the beach you'll get more room for less money. Other good hunting grounds are on the streets running back from Beach St and the Boardwalk, where some real dives can be found; or along Ocean St on the other side of the San Lorenzo River and along Riverside Ave on both sides of the river.

Day's Inn (☎ 423-8564) at 325 Pacific Ave is an absolutely standard motel in the no-man's land between downtown and the waterfront although the walk to the wharf is only a couple of blocks. Rooms drop as low as $38 in the low season, and climb to $68 to $98 in high season. Other standard motels close to the beach include the *Super 8 Motel* (☎ 426-3707, 800-800-8000) at 338 Riverside Ave with rooms from $36 to $98 in the off season, from $58 to $135 in season.

Across the river from downtown the *Best Western All Suites Inn* (☎ 458-9898, 800-528-1234) is at 500 Ocean St on the corner with Soquel Drive. All the rooms are suites and costs range from $50 to $150 in the off season, from $75 to $160 in season. Or there's the *Santa Cruz Travelodge* (☎ 426-2300, 800-578-7878) at 525 Ocean St. Prices here can drop to $50 to $80 in the off season, or climb to $60 to $115 in season.

If 'location, location, location' are the three key definers of real estate value then *Sea & Sand Inn* (☎ 427-3400) at 201 W Cliff Drive deserves its higher prices. The neat and tidy motel is right on the cliff edge and every room looks across the bay to the wharf. Rates here are variable between summer and winter, weekends and weekdays. Standard rooms can drop as low as $75 or climb as high as $125 and larger rooms can go up to $190, including a continental breakfast. The only 'big' hotel at Santa Cruz is the adjacent *Dream Inn* (☎ 426-4330, 800-662-3838) at 175 W Cliff Drive. There are 160 rooms, all with ocean views, plus pool, sauna, and restaurant and bar. Rooms cost $135 to $225 in the high season, dropping to $75 to $145 in the low season.

B&Bs include *Cliff Crest* (☎ 427-2609) at 407 Cliff St, close to the beach and boardwalk. The five rooms in this attractive Victorian mansion range from $85 to $135.

Or try *Babbling Brook Inn* (☎ 427-2437), not quite so conveniently located at 1025 Laurel St but with very attractive rooms and a garden complete with a stream and waterfall. Prices for the 12 rooms range from $85 to $150.

Places to Eat
Start the day at *Rebecca's Mighty Muffins* (☎ 429-1940) at 514A Front St, for great muffins in more than 30 varieties. The *Bagelry* (☎ 429-8049) at 320A Cedar St on the corner with Maple is another popular breakfast spot.

For cheap eats, pizzerias and Mexican restaurants are scattered all over Santa Cruz or there are burger-style alternatives like *Positively Front St* (☎ 426-1944) at 44 Front St, just a half block from the wharf. Pasta and pizza also feature on their menu. *Pontiac Grill* (☎ 427-2290) at 429 Front St and Cathcart is an authentic looking modern interpretation of a '50s diner with burgers at $4 to $5. *Little Shanghai* (☎ 458-2460) at 1010 Cedar St and Locust is a cheap, simple, and very popular Chinese restaurant.

The *Gabriella Café* (☎ 457-1677), 910 Cedar St, is a nice little candelit restaurant with an interesting menu featuring pastas at $8 to $10 and entrees at $13 to $15. At *Benten* (☎ 425-7079) at 1541 Pacific Ave, arriving customers are met with a chorus of *irasshaimase!* (welcome!), which would pass muster in any Tokyo robatayaki. They have great benten boxes and the *moochi* ice cream is fabulous. *Memphis Minnie's* (☎ 429-6464) at 1415 Santa Cruz cooks up seafood Cajun style. *Zoccoli's Pasta House* (☎ 423-1717) at 2017 N Pacific Ave is a popular Italian restaurant, closed on Mondays.

You can drive right out on the pier where a number of seafood restaurants including, right at the end, the *Dolphin* (☎ 426-5830), a straightforward diner-style restaurant with good views and entrees at $8 to $10.

Entertainment
The student population may account for the heavy concentration of coffee bars purvey-

ing cupfuls of strong caffeine. *Café Pergolesi* (☎ 426-1775) at 418 Cedar St at Elm is a very popular, very studenty coffee bar with a balcony overlooking the street and good coffee and great cakes and pies. *Georgiana's Café* (☎ 427-9900) is a popular retreat in the Bookshop Santa Cruz, 1522 Pacific Ave. *Santa Cruz Café & Roasting* (☎ 459-0100) at 1330 Pacific Ave also brews strong coffee. *Café Karina* (☎ 454-9547) at 418 Front St combines coffee with entertainment including poetry readings and music.

Santa Cruz's large student population is also reflected in the many pubs, bars, and night spots. The *Santa Cruz Brewing Co & Front St Pub* (☎ 429-8838) at 516 Front St has a microbrewery with beers at $2.25 and $3 plus a burgers and sandwich style menu. The *Poet & Patriot* (☎ 426-8620), on Cedar Sq, squeezed between Cedar St and Pacific Ave, aims for the English pub style. Or there's the *99 Bottles Bar* (☎ 459-9999), just a nice place for a beer at 104 Walnut Ave.

Kuumbwa (☎ 427-2227) on Cedar Sq at 320-2 Cedar St is a pleasant little bar and dance center with a neon sign announcing 'Jazz.' Jazz is indeed the main theme but some nights it can be anything from hippie rock onwards. *Palookaville* (☎ 454-0600) at 1133 Pacific Ave is another mixed venue with a wide variety of entertainment. There's a cluster of night spots along Pacific Ave between Maple and Cathcart, opposite the Metro Center including the very popular *Catalyst* (☎ 423-1336) at No 1011 and *Blue Lagoon* (☎ 423-7117), popular with gays at No 923.

Other places around Santa Cruz include *Moe's Alley* (☎ 479-1854) at 1535 Commercial Way for blues, and *Live Soup* (☎ 458-3461) at 1602 Ocean St for another variable list of performers.

For movies head to the *Del Mar Theater* (☎ 425-0616) at 1124 Pacific Ave or *Nickelodeon* (☎ 426-7500) at Lincoln and Cedar Sts.

Getting There & Away
Greyhound (☎ 423-1800), 425 Front St, operates the San Francisco-Santa Cruz-Monterey-Santa Barbara-Los Angeles route twice a day in each direction. Fares are San Francisco $12, Monterey $8.50, Los Angeles $46. Peerless Stages operate Santa Cruz-San Jose-Hayward-Oakland four times a day. Fares are San Jose $5.50, Oakland $12.50.

Weekdays, Hwy 17 Express Bus Services take just over an hour to San Jose. Inquire at the Metro Center about where to pick it up. Connections from the CalTrain/Amtrak station in San Jose take 45 minutes and cost $5. Monterey-Salinas Transit bus No 28 connects to Salinas via Castroville, No 29 via Prunedale. The Santa Cruz Airporter (☎ 423-1214, 800-497-4997) operates to San Jose and San Francisco Airports.

Getting Around
In summer the Beach Shuttle connects town and beach. Santa Cruz Metropolitan Transit (☎ 425-8600) operates from the Metro Center at 920 Pacific Ave. Metro's *Headways* is the local public transport newspaper. One-way trips are $1, a day pass costs $3. Useful services include No 3 to Natural Bridges State Beach; No 35 to Felton and on up to Ben Lomond and Boulder Creek; No 40 to Davenport and the north coast beaches; No 41 to Bonny Doon; and No 69 straight to the Capitola Transit Center.

The Bicycle Rental Center (☎ 426-8687) at 415 Pacific Ave rents bikes for $25 a day. You can take bikes on many of the local bus services.

On summer weekends parking near the boardwalk can be difficult and it may be better to park downtown and take the shuttle bus.

SAN JUAN BAUTISTA
• *pop 2000 ☎ 408*
In this pleasantly sleepy semi-ghost town, California's 15th mission, fronted by the only original Spanish plaza in the state, is precariously perched right on the edge of the San Andreas Fault! The critical scenes in Hitchcock's *Vertigo* take place at the

mission. San Juan Bautista is on Hwy 156, about two miles east of Hwy 101 between San Jose and Salinas on the way to Monterey.

The Mission

The mission (☎ 623-4528) was founded in 1797 and construction of the church started fitfully in 1803. The interior, completed in 1816, was painted by an American sailor who jumped ship in Monterey and may well have been the first US resident of California. The church was built with three aisles but at some point the outer aisles were walled off and the 1906 earthquake brought the outer walls down. They were not repaired until the 1970s when the inner archways were opened up to make this the largest of California's mission churches. The bell tower was also added at that time. The footprints of bears and coyotes can be seen on the red tiled floor, the animals probably walked across the tiles as they were hardening, a reminder of what a rugged and wild place California was two centuries ago. The mission church is open daily from 9:30 am to 4:30 pm and a $1 donation is requested.

In the Spanish era the area had a large Indian population and over 4000 of them are buried in the old cemetery beside the northeast wall of the mission. The ridge along the north side of the church is the actual line of the San Andreas fault. North of the cemetery a section of the old El Camino Réal, the 'King's Highway', can be seen. This Spanish road, built to link the missions, was the first road in the state and in many places Hwy 101 still follows its route.

The Plaza & the Town

The buildings around the expansive old Spanish plaza are part of the State Historic Park, which is open daily from 10 am to 4:30 pm; entry is $2/1. The **Plaza Hotel** started life as a single-story adobe in 1814 and was enlarged and converted into a hotel

in 1858; in its time it was a very popular overnight stagecoach halt. The adjacent **Castro House** was built for José Maria Castro, who led a successful 1836 revolt against the unpopular Governor Juan Gutiérrez and repeated the performance in 1843 when Governor Micheltorena was usurped and deported. In 1848 the house was bought by the Breen family, survivors of the ill-fated Donner Party, which was stranded for 111 days in the Sierra Nevadas during the extraordinarily severe winter of 1846. The Breens made a quick gold rush fortune in 1848 and the house remained with the family until 1933.

Angelo Zanetta, owner of the Plaza Hotel, built Plaza Hall across the square in 1868. He hoped would become the county courthouse, but San Juan Bautista was passed over as the county seat. The large blacksmith shop and the Plaza Stable of about 1861 hint at San Juan in its heyday when as many as 11 stagecoaches a day passed through, many of them on the busy San Francisco-Los Angeles route. The completion of the railway in 1876 bypassed San Juan Bautista and the town became a sleepy backwater.

Away from the plaza, today's small town looks almost frozen in time and there are many attractive old buildings and a string of restaurants and cafes along 3rd St. The town has a couple of motels.

AROUND SAN JUAN BAUTISTA
☎ 408

Gilroy, 14 miles north of San Juan Bautista by Hwy 101 at the southern end of the Santa Clara Valley, claims to be the Garlic Capital of the World and celebrates this achievement every July with an annual Garlic Festival (☎ 842-1625). **Castroville**, 15 miles southwest where Hwy 156 meets Hwy 1, is also a World Capital but this time it's for artichokes! In fact, nine out of 10 US artichokes come from Castroville and yes, there's an annual Artichoke Festival in September (☎ 633-3402).

Wine Country

☎ 707

Only about 5% of California wine comes from San Francisco's 'Wine Country,' the parallel Sonoma and Napa Valleys. Most California wine comes from the irrigated Central Valley but that's the bulk stuff, California plonk ordinaire. The Wine Country is where the state's high-quality wine originates and is an easy day trip from San Francisco, but an overnight stay will give you a much better taste of the vineyards. There are plenty of restaurants and accommodations to tempt you to linger, however tourism is just as important as wine production, so summer weekends can get decidedly crowded.

The early Spanish and Mexican settlers produced some wine but Hungarian Count Agoston Haraszthy started the modern wine business when he bought land in the Sonoma Valley in 1857. By the late 1860s there were already 50 vintners in the Napa Valley. Later in the century things started to go bad, a double assault from cheap imports and the arrival of the deadly root louse *phylloxera*, fresh from devastating the vineyards of Europe. The wine business was still stumbling from these attacks when Prohibition delivered the knock-out in 1919. Remarkably, a handful of wineries continued in business, producing sacramental wine! Prohibition ended in 1933, but it was not until the 1960s that wine production really got back into high gear. Beating French wines in a blind tasting in Paris in 1976 put the Napa Valley on the international wine map, and it's never looked back.

Spring and fall are the best times to visit. Summers tend to be hot and dusty as well as crowded. Fall combines fine weather with the grape harvest and the 'crush,' when the wine making season gets underway with the pressing of the grapes. However, wine isn't all these valleys have to offer; there's Spanish and Mexican his-tory in Sonoma, lots of activities, mud baths and spas at Calistoga, literary connections with two important writers, and cartoon connections with two popular cartoonists.

Wine Tasting

These days few Napa Valley wineries offer free tastings; if you want to sample the wines you'll have to pay, usually around $3 for three varieties. In the Sonoma Valley, on the other hand, free tastings are still the rule rather than the exception. In any case, you don't want to do *too* much tasting, visiting six wineries in a day is usually quite enough; some say that three or four are better numbers. Wineries will generally have their wines on sale, and tasting followed by buying a bottle to go with a long, leisurely picnic lunch is a fine way to approach the valley. Don't come to the wineries looking for bargains, the wines are usually on sale at full retail price and can often be found cheaper at liquor shops and supermarkets. Of course wines from some of the smaller boutique wineries, as well as special vintages or reserves, will only be available from the wineries themselves or from a very restricted list of outlets.

There are literally hundreds of wineries in the valleys so those mentioned in this chapter are just a tempting taste of some of the largest and best known and some of the quirkier and more interesting smaller places. At some wineries facilities for visitors consist of little more than a tasting room. Others may have displays, museums, art galleries, and do-it-yourself or guided tours of the wine making process.

Wine Country whites include Fume Blanc, Riesling, Gewurztraminer, Chenin Blanc, and the premier California Chardonnay. Reds include Pinot Noir, Merlot, and Beaujolais; the robust Cabernet Sauvignon is probably the premier California red but the peppery Zinfandel is the really unique California red.

Gliders & Hot-Air Balloons

When you get tired of the valleys at ground level you can look down on it from above either on glider flights from Calistoga or on the very popular balloon trips.

Glider flights cost $80 to $110 for one, or $110 to $150 for two, and are operated by Calistoga Gliders (☎ 942-5000) from the Gliderport at 1546 Lincoln Ave, right in downtown Calistoga.

Hot-air balloon flights are operated by a host of specialists in the Napa and Sonoma Valleys, many of them in Yountville. Balloon flights are usually made early in the morning (around 7 am), when the air is coolest. Balloon flights usually include a champagne breakfast after you land and typically cost around $165; remember to make reservations. Some operators make two flights so you have an opportunity to ride on one flight and follow in the pursuit vehicle on the other.

In Yountville call Above the West (☎ 800-627-7259), Adventures Aloft (☎ 255-8688), Balloon Aviation (☎ 252-7067, 800-367-6272), or Napa Valley Balloons (☎ 944-0228, 800-253-2224). In Santa

Rosa there's Air Flambuoyant (☎ 838-8500, 800-456-4711), in Rutheford call the Bonaventura Balloon Company (☎ 944-2822, 800-359-6272), and in Calistoga try Once in a Lifetime Balloon (☎ 942-6541).

Bicycling

Bicycling around the Wine Country is a favorite, although it's best to stick to the quieter back roads – take the Silverado Trail rather than Hwy 29 through the Napa Valley and Arnold Drive rather than Hwy 12 through the Sonoma Valley. Both valleys are fairly flat and cycle friendly but you'd better have your low gear abilities tuned up if you want to ride from one valley to the other, particularly by the testing Oakville Grade between Oakville and Glen Ellen.

Bicycles, if transported in a box, can be brought up to the Wine Country on Greyhound buses for $10. Golden Gate Transit will only take bicycles on route No 40; this will take you across the Golden Gate Bridge as far as San Rafael, beyond that you're on your own.

There are bicycle rental agencies in a number of Wine Country towns. Getaway Bicycle Tours (☎ 942-0332) in Calistoga does half-day downhill trips ($49 including bike) and 25- to 30-mile all-day trips ($79 including bike and picnic lunch).

Hiking

Though it's not the number one activity, there are places to take some time out amid the landscape. Robert Louis Stevenson State Park is undeveloped, and has a five-mile dusty trail to the top of Mt St Helena (4343 feet), where on a good day there are excellent views. There are longer trails in developed Bothe-Napa Valley State Park (☎ 942-4575) which charges $5 per car, but the 12 miles of trails run along a perennial stream. In Sonoma, check out the trails at some of the wineries.

Getting There & Away

The Friday evening rush hour from 3 to 7 pm may be an exception, but at more reasonable times the Wine Country is just an

---

S-A-L-E

Finding those four favorite letters in the city might often be a hunt, but here there are outlet malls offering manufacturers' direct discounts on premium labels. In Napa, take the 1st St exit west from Hwy 29 to get to Factory Stores Drive, where you'll find over 40 outlet stores including Timberland, J Crew, and Cole-Haan. In St Helena, you'll see the mall on the west side of Hwy 29 about a mile north of town. This is a smaller center with eight outlet stores, including Donna Karan and Movado.

In Yountville, wade through the 40 touristy retail shops of the Vintage 1870 center (☎ 944-2451) on Washington St to find art, pottery, and wine in a few choice spots. A walk up and down the three blocks of Main St (Hwy 29) and a few side roads in St Helena will reward shoppers and gawkers alike. In the city of Sonoma, shops abound around the main plaza – look for wine, cheese, and bread as well as arts & crafts, tobacco, and cookware. ■

---

hour's drive north via Hwy 101 through Marin County or I-80 through the East Bay. The best way to explore the valleys is by car, although don't do too much tasting if you're the driver.

Public transport can get you to the valleys although it's not the ideal way of working your way around the wineries. Greyhound has services right up the Napa Valley to Calistoga ($4 one way) twice daily via Oakland, Vallejo, Oakville, and St Helena. Call for services north past Calistoga and to Sonoma. Napa Valley Transit (☎ 707-255-7631, 800-696-6445) runs up the Napa Valley from the Vallejo BARTlink bus stop to Calistoga. Six buses run daily from Monday to Saturday. Fares range from $1 to $2.50.

Golden Gate Transit (☎ 415-332-6600, 707-544-1323) has buses from San Francisco to Sonoma and up the valley as far as Agua Caliente (No 90) and to Santa Rosa via Petaluma (Nos 71, 72, 74, 75, 80). Sonoma County Transit (☎ 707-576-7433,

800-345-7433) has local services up the Sonoma Valley.

Amtrak goes to Martinez (south of Vallejo) and a connecting bus runs to the main Napa Valley centers.

Tours from San Francisco are operated by Gray Lines (☎ 415-558-9400), their daily $42/21 tour departs from the Transbay Terminal at 9 am, returns nine hours later, and includes visits to three wineries either in Sonoma or Napa with complimentary wine tasting and a stop to shop and lunch on your own.

Napa Valley

The Napa Valley lies further inland, is the longer of the two valleys at around 30 miles, and has more wineries. Napa, at the southern end of the valley, is the major town but is of little interest. Better places for a pause are St Helena and, at the top of the valley, Calistoga – a name famous for mineral water rather than wine. Two roads run north-south along the valley, Hwy 29 and the quieter and more scenic Silverado Trail, just a mile or two east.

NAPA VALLEY WINERIES

There are over 200 wineries in the Napa Valley but many of them are either small operations without the personnel to welcome visitors or they simply don't want them. Most wineries are open for tasting every day, usually from 10 or 11 am to 4 or 4:30 pm. Call ahead if you'd like a tour, which usually depart at set hours or require a reservation.

Beaulieu Beaulieu, French for 'beautiful view' and named after an area in France, was founded in 1900 by a French immigrant and is now one of the larger Napa Valley wineries. Tastings are free, although premium wines are $4. 1960 St Helena Hwy, Rutherford (☎ 963-2411).

Beringer Beringer is fronted by the fine 1883 Rhine House, there are tours every

half hour and free tastings in the old bottling room. Tastings of the classier wines cost $2 or $3. Beringer was founded by German brothers Jacob and Frederick Beringer in 1876 and is the oldest continuously operating winery in the valley. It survived Prohibition by manufacturing sacramental and medicinal wines. Extensive tunnels, where the wines are aged at constant temperature, burrow into the hill behind the winery. 2000 Main St, St Helena (☎ 963-4812).

Château Montelena At the north end of the valley, Château Montelena has a beautiful lake with Japanese-style bridges and pavilions and there is a popular picnic site, although permission must be requested in advance. There's a $5 tasting fee and a fine stone chateau. 1429 Tubbs Lane, Calistoga (☎ 942-5105).

Clos Pegase This is another winery where architecture, art and wine form an alliance, no doubt blessed by money! Interesting sculptures dot the grounds of the 1987 Michael Graves-designed buildings, and modern art graces the visitors center, making the place a must-see. There are tours at 11 am and 2 pm and open tasting for $3 daily from 9 am to 5 pm. 1060 Dunaweal Lane, Calistoga (☎ 942-4981).

Domaine Chandon French champagne maker Moët et Chandon now has several 'new world' wineries where they make 'sparkling wine' (rather than champagne since the French insist that champagne is only champagne when it comes from the Champagne district of France). The winery has interesting displays, an informative tour, an exquisite restaurant and patio (see Yountville Places to Eat), and tastings for $3 to $5. California Drive, Yountville (☎ 944-2280).

Grgich Hills Cellar Pronounced girr-gich, this unpretentious tasting room (free on weekdays, $2 on weekends – but you keep the glass) may be small, but these may be the wines with which you compare all the rest. Tours are by appointment. 1829 St Helena Hwy, Rutherford (☎ 963-2784).

Hess Collection Wine and art merge in this decidedly top-end winery with a wonderfully expensive art gallery spread over three floors. The flaming typewriter is a favorite piece but there are works by Francis Bacon and other international artists. The winery is about equidistant between the Napa and Sonoma Valleys. Wine tasting costs $2.50. 4411 Redwood Rd, Napa (☎ 255-1144).

Robert Mondavi This is a big, commercial winery with a Mission-looking design fronted by a Benjamino Bufano statue, but it puts on an informative tour on the wine making process. A tasting costs $2 to $4 although if you take the tour you're rewarded with a free tasting. Reservations are required for the longer three- to four-hour 'In-Depth Tours.' Hwy 29, Oakville (☎ 226-1395).

Stag's Leap It was a Stag's Leap Cabernet Sauvignon that bested the French back in 1976 and they continue to produce exceptional wines. 5766 Silverado Trail, Napa (☎ 944-2020).

St Supéry The historic 1882 Atkinson House fronts the modern winery with some of the most innovative and interactive displays in the valley, including interesting explanations of wine colors and aromas. There's a self-guided tour and a $2.50 'lifetime' tasting fee; keep your card, you can come back for another slurp. 8440 St Helena Hwy, Rutherford (☎ 963-4507).

Sterling Vineyards The gimmick here is a gondola ride which carries you to the hilltop winery with good views across the valley. Wines here are known for their quality; the winery is architecturally interesting as well. A $6/3 ticket to ride includes a tour and the tasting fee, and there's a reduced price on weekdays for AAA members. 1111 Dunaweal Lane, Calistoga (☎ 942-3344).

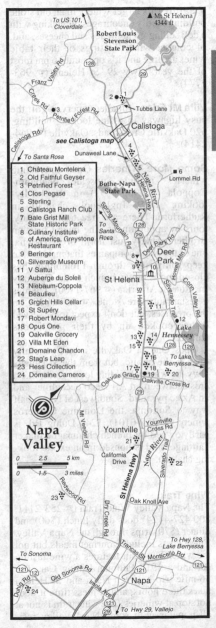

1 Château Montelena
2 Old Faithful Geyser
3 Petrified Forest
4 Clos Pegase
5 Sterling
6 Calistoga Ranch Club
7 Bale Grist Mill
   State Historic Park
8 Culinary Institute
   of America, Greystone
   Restaurant
9 Beringer
10 Silverado Museum
11 V Sattui
12 Auberge du Soleil
13 Niebaum-Coppola
14 Beaulieu
15 Grgich Hills Cellar
16 St Supéry
17 Robert Mondavi
18 Opus One
19 Oakville Grocery
20 Villa Mt Eden
21 Domaine Chandon
22 Stag's Leap
23 Hess Collection
24 Domaine Carneros

V Sattui This larger winery in an old stone building loudly encourages picnicking with a deli selling great breads and cheeses, and, of course, wine. Tastings of their table wines are free and it's open until 6 pm most of the year. Hwy 29, St Helena (☎ 963-7774).

Villa Mt Eden a smaller winery, it's off the busy highway in a fine looking building. 620 Oakville Crossroads, Oakville (☎ 944-2414).

Some More Wineries Other interesting wineries include upscale Niebaum-Coppola (☎ 963-9099) in the lordly-looking 1879 Inglenook chateau in Rutherford. There are free tastings daily, tours by appointment. The huge Christian Brothers winery just north of St Helena, one of the Napa companies that managed to keep going right through Prohibition, has closed and is now a branch of the Culinary Institute of America (☎ 967-1100). There is a restaurant (Greystone, ☎ 967-1010) on the premises, but don't expect to be served dishes cooked up by their prestigious students.

Opus One in Oakville is not generally open to the public, but from the St Helena Hwy the winery building looks great, like a cross between an Art Deco oceanliner and an Aztec pyramid. Southwest of Napa, half way to Sonoma, the Domaine Carneros winery (☎ 257-0101), 1240 Duhig Rd, is partly owned by French champagne maker Taittinger and is housed in an exotic looking chateau.

Wine Train
The Napa Valley Wine Train (☎ 253-2111, 800-427-4124) does daily lunch ($60) and dinner ($70) trips through the Napa Valley. These costs include gourmet meals but not the wine. The train features a wine tasting car and a 1917 Pullman Dining Car. The 36-mile trip between Napa and St Helena takes three hours, and at press time it does not stop at wineries. The wine train is not at all popular with some Napa Valley residents and wineries. You may see 'No Wine Train' signs posted along the way.

NAPA
• *pop 64,000* ☎ 707

Napa may be the main town of the valley, but there's little reason to pause in this dull center. There are more charming towns with a wider variety of restaurants and more attractive places to stay further up the valley. Napa had a brief history as a river port before railways enticed the traffic away. There are a number of interesting old buildings around town and the visitors bureau has a walking tour leaflet.

Orientation & Information
Napa is sandwiched between the Silverado

An Affair to Remember

The Wine Country has surely garnered an excellent worldwide reputation not only for its grapes and wineries, but also for fostering extraordinary culinary talent. Often, a visit includes that once-in-a-lifetime dining experience. The following are top-class restaurants that provide consistently great food (accompanied by the perfect wine) and are raved about by reviewers and patrons alike. A good way to try the experience *and* economize is to show up for lunch, but call first. This is just a list; for details see Places to Eat under each destination. As usual, expect to pay top dollar, have reservations and dress accordingly.

La Boucane	Napa
Auberge du Soleil	
* Restaurant*	Rutherford
Brava Terrace	St Helena
Catahoula	Calistoga
Domaine Chandon	Yountville
John Ash & Co	Santa Rosa
French Laundry	Yountville
Mustards Grill	between
	Yountville and
	Oakville
Ristorante Tra Vigne	St Helena
Stars Oakville Cafe	Oakville
Terra	St Helena
Trilogy	St Helena ■

Trail and Hwy 29, but coming from San Francisco stick to Hwy 29 until you see the downtown exit sign (turning off on the Silverado Trail into Napa just shows that Napa has plenty of suburbs). Coming north on I-80, the fastest route to Hwy 29 is via Hwy 37, which avoids the downtrodden town of Vallejo.

The main street through Napa is 1st St. In the downtown shopping center the Napa Valley Visitors Bureau (☎ 226-7459) at 1310 Napa Town Center, right off 1st St, is the biggest and most active information center in the valley. It's open daily, 9 am to 5 pm and they will make room reservations.

Bicycling
Napa Valley Cyclery (☎ 255-3377) at 4080 Byway East just off Hwy 29 rents bicycles at $22 to $28 a day. They also offer one way rentals, for an extra $25 you can ride to Calistoga where they will pick you up and return you and the bike to Napa.

Places to Stay
The *Travelodge* (☎ 226-1871) at the corner of 2nd and Coombs Sts is centrally located but otherwise just a dull standard motel. Rooms are $69 on weekends, $49 during the week, down to $39 with coupons.

The *Silverado Motel* (☎ 253-0892) at 500 Silverado Trail is southeast of the town center on Hwy 121 and rooms cost less than $40 with discount coupons but usually they're in the $40 to $50 bracket. The *Napa Valley Budget Inn* (☎ 257-6111) at 3380 Solano Ave is just west of Hwy 29, off Redwood Rd. The motel has a pool and rooms usually at $66/75 a single/double, higher on weekends.

Places to Eat
Downtown Joes (☎ 258-2337), 902 Main St, on the riverbank, right at the end of 2nd St, incorporates a microbrewery and restaurant and operates from breakfast to dinner. Right across the junction is *PJ's Café* (☎ 224-0607), 1001 2nd St, a standard diner offering honest and straightforward food including burgers, sandwiches, pastas, and pizzas.

The *Napa Valley Coffee Roasting Co.* (☎ 224-2233), at 948 Main St on the corner with 1st St, is a good breakfast spot in a historic building. In the heart of the shopping center by Napa's funny clocktower are two popular Mexican places: *Taqueria Tres Hermanos* (☎ 224-6062) at 1122 1st St, and *Don Perico Restaurant* (☎ 252-4707) at 1025 1st St.

For elegant meals, make reservations at *Bistro Don Giovanni* (☎ 224-3300), 4110 St Helena Hwy, serving lunch and dinner ($13) with daily specials. The *Foothill Cafe* (☎ 252-6178), 2766 Old Sonoma Rd (in the J&B Shopping Center), is a casual respite from the glamour of other Napa attractions, and offers reasonably-priced dinner entrees Wednesday through Sunday. *La Boucane* (☎ 253-1177), 1778 2nd St, gets high marks for its French cuisine when money isn't an issue but is closed on Sundays and in January.

Getting There & Around
See the introductory Wine Country Getting There & Away section for information on Greyhound buses originating in San Francisco, and on Napa Valley Transit buses from the Vallejo BARTlink bus stop.

The Valley Intracity Neighborhood Express (VINE, ☎ 800-696-6445) operates buses around Napa.

YOUNTVILLE & AROUND
☎ 707

About a third of the way up the valley Yountville is a stone's throw off Hwy 29 and just north on the highway are Oakville and Rutherford. There are a handful of places to stay and plenty of restaurants but otherwise St Helena and Calistoga, further north, make better bases. Vintage 1870 is Yountville's rather twee shopping center and across Washington St there's a visitors center (☎ 944-0904).

Places to Stay
There is camping on the shores of Lake Berryessa at the private *Lake Berryessa Marina Resort* (☎ 996-2161), 5800 Knoxville Rd. Seventy sites for tenters ($13) and

about 50 with hookups for RVs ($21) are complemented by a full-service marina and an array of facilities. It's open year round, and reservations are recommended in summer. To get there take Hwy 128 (Sage Canyon Rd) about 11 miles east from Rutherford, and go north (left) on Berryessa Knoxville Rd for nine miles.

Otherwise, Yountville is a pricey place to stay. The *Napa Valley Lodge* (☎ 944-2468) at 2230 Madison St has 55 rooms from around $130 to $200 and there is a host of B&Bs.

Places to Eat

To grab a bite for a picnic, stop by the *Oakville Grocery Co* (☎ 944-8802), 7856 St Helena Hwy, just north of Yountville in the tiny settlement of Oakville, which is possibly the best gourmet deli in the two valleys.

Since all of the places mentioned below are favorites, you'll probably want to phone up for reservations. The extremely popular *Diner* (☎ 944-2626) at 6476 Washington St proclaims that it has 'legendary food;' it's standard diner food with Mexican additions. Next door is another branch of the popular California chain of *Piatti* (☎ 944-2070) Italian restaurants, and *Compadres* (☎ 944-2406) at 6539 Washington St by the Vintage 1870 center has 'Western food with a Mexican accent.'

The *Stars Oakville Café* (☎ 944-8905), right on Hwy 29 next to the Oakville Grocery Co, is a branch of the renowned San Francisco restaurant and offers outdoor dining. Between Yountville and Oakville is *Mustards Grill* (☎ 944-2424), 7399 St Helena Hwy, which consistently gets rave reviews for food and service. A treat is *Domaine Chandon* (☎ 944-2892), 1 California Drive (off Hwy 29), Yountville. Patio dining is offered, and jackets are required at dinner, but most agree that the effort is well worth the price. It's closed in January.

Another on the high end of elegant is *French Laundry* (☎ 944-2380), 6640 Washington St, Yountville. A leisurely meal will be your event for the evening, and a prix-fixe menu ($28 or $36 lunch and $57 or $70 dinner) is offered. Most auspicious is the *Auberge du Soleil Restaurant* (☎ 963-1211, 800-348-5406), at the same location as the top-end resort, 180 Rutherford Hill Rd in Rutherford. Possibly the most regal restaurant in the area, Auberge du Soleil also deigns to serve breakfast and asks that you not wear shorts after 6 pm.

ST HELENA
• *pop 5000* ☎ *707*

Highway 29, running right through St Helena, is also called Main St in town, and can get uncomfortably busy on summer weekends. There are lots of interesting old buildings to walk around and plenty of restaurants. There is a visitors center (☎ 963-4456) at 1080 Main St. For bicycling around, St Helena Cyclery (☎ 963-7736) at 1156 Main St rents bikes for $25 a day.

Silverado Museum

In 1880 Robert Louis Stevenson, at that time sick, penniless and unknown (though soon to be wealthy and world famous), stayed in an abandoned bunkhouse at the old Silverado Mine near Mt St Helena with his new wife Fanny Osbourne. His novel, *The Silverado Squatters*, is based on his time there. The Silverado Museum has a fascinating collection of memorabilia relating to this attractive and intriguing writer.

The museum (☎ 963-3757), at 1490 Library Lane, is open Tuesday to Sunday, noon to 4 pm; entry is free. To get to Library Lane turn east off Hwy 29, at the Adams St traffic lights and cross the railway tracks. The adjacent library building houses the Napa Valley Wine Library.

Napa Valley Museum

In Vintage Hall at 473 Main St the Napa Valley Museum (☎ 963-7411) has exhibits on the story of the valley. It's open weekdays, 9 am to 4 pm, weekends 11 am to 3 pm; entry is $2.

Places to Stay

See the Calistoga section for information on camping at Bothe-Napa Valley State

Park, midway between St Helena and Calistoga.

The *El Bonita Motel* (☎ 963-3216) at 195 Main St has rooms from $65 to $110 in the peak season, down to $46 to $89 in the off season. Right in the center of town the *Hotel St Helena* (☎ 963-4388) at 1309 Main St dates from 1881 and has 18 rooms (some with private bathrooms) from $130/77 to $180/112 high season/low season, and suites at $250/160. The *Harvest Inn* (☎ 963-9463, 800-950-8466) is at 1 Main St and offers 54 rooms in an English Tudor-style building. There are two pools, lots of luxuries and prices from $100 to over $300.

Places to Eat
The *Model Bakery* (☎ 963-8192) at 1357 Main St serves great scones, muffins and coffee. It's closed on Monday. *Gillwoods Café* (☎ 963-1788) at 1313 Main St is a straightforward diner. *Armadillo's* (☎ 963-8082) at 1304 Main St, right across from the Hotel St Helena, is a very bright and colorful Mexican restaurant.

St Helena has some interesting places for a classy meal, but remember to make reservations. *Pairs Parkside Cafe* (☎ 963-7566), at 1420 Main St, is a small, but light and airy place for a civilized lunch or dinner at a good price – some call it '*the* find in the Wine Country.' On the southern edge of town *Ristorante Tra Vigne* (☎ 963-4444) at 1050 Charter Oak Ave, right on Main St, is a stylish Italian restaurant with a reputation for some of the best food in the valley. Pizzas are $8 to $10, pasta dishes $10 to $12, entrees $15 to $16. *Trilogy* (☎ 963-5507) at 1234 Main St, right in town, has a

$32 prix fixe menu ($48 with wine). It's closed Monday.

Terra (☎ 963-8931), 1345 Railroad Ave, serves up excellent meals and may be a 'must eat;' it's closed Tuesday. Try also the lauded bistro *Brava Terrace* (☎ 963-9300), 3010 St Helena Hwy. It's closed in January.

Getting There & Away
See the introductory Wine Country Getting There & Away section for information on Greyhound and Napa Valley Transit buses up the valley. The Napa Valley Transit buses run six times a day from Monday to Saturday.

CALISTOGA
• *pop 4500* ☎ *707*
'I'll have a Calistoga' is a familiar phrase in California; the name is now synonymous with bottled water. The town is probably the most attractive of the Napa settlements with plenty of places to stay and eat. The City Hall on Washington St was built in 1902 as the Bedlam Opera House. The 1868 Railroad Depot on Lincoln Ave closed down in 1929 and now houses shops and restaurants.

Not only mineral water bubbles up from below, Calistoga's hot springs have spawned a collection of spas where you can indulge in the local specialty of hot mud baths. It's said the town's curious name came from tongue-tied Sam Brannan, who founded the town in 1859 with the heartfelt belief that it would emulate the New York spa town of Saratoga and become the 'Calistoga of Sarafornia.'

Sam Brannan
Born in Maine in 1819, Sam Brannan was a larger-than-life character who roamed the US working in printing and newspapers before heading to California in 1845 to found a Mormon colony. His passion for religious pioneering quickly faded and in 1847 he founded San Francisco's first newspaper, and in 1848 made the dramatic declaration that gold had been discovered at Coloma, sparking the Gold Rush. The healthy properties of Calistoga's spas and springs were his next discovery but towards the end of his colorful life his luck ran out and he died, penniless, in 1888. ∎

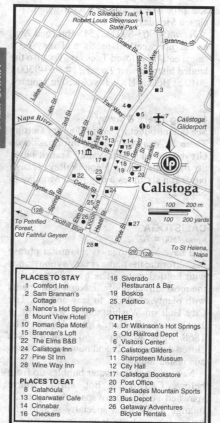

Calistoga

PLACES TO STAY
1 Comfort Inn
2 Sam Brannan's Cottage
3 Nance's Hot Springs
4 Mount View Hotel
10 Roman Spa Motel
15 Brannan's Loft
22 The Elms B&B
24 Calistoga Inn
27 Pine St Inn
28 Wine Way Inn

PLACES TO EAT
8 Catahoula
13 Clearwater Cafe
14 Cinnabar
16 Checkers

18 Siverado Restaurant & Bar
19 Boskos
25 Pacifico

OTHER
4 Dr Wilkinson's Hot Springs
5 Old Railroad Depot
6 Visitors Center
7 Calistoga Gliders
11 Sharpsteen Museum
12 City Hall
17 Calistoga Bookstore
20 Post Office
21 Palisades Mountain Sports
23 Bus Depot
26 Getaway Adventures Bicycle Rentals

Orientation & Information

Calistoga's shops and restaurants are strung along Lincoln Ave, stretching from Hwy 29 across to the Silverado Trail. The Chamber of Commerce Visitors Center (☎ 942-6333), at 1458 Lincoln Ave behind the Old Depot, is open daily, 10 am to 5 pm. Calistoga Bookstore (☎ 942-4123) at 1343 Lincoln Ave has a wide variety of books. Calistoga has a varied selection of festivals through the year including a terrific 4th of July Silverado Parade.

Spas & Mud

Basking up to your neck in a tub full of mud is all the go in Calistoga. The town has a collection of hot spring spas and mud bath emporiums where you can be buried in hot mud and emerge much better for the experience. Mud bath packages take about an hour and cost from around $40. You start with 10 to 12 minutes semi-submerged in hot mud, followed by a shower, then a 15 to 20 minute soak in a hot mineral water bathtub. An optional steam bath and a cooling towel wrap follows. The treatment can be extended to include a massage, pushing the cost up to $65 and beyond. Baths can be taken solo or, in some establishments, as couples. Variations can include thin mud *fango* baths, herbal wraps, seaweed baths, and all sorts of exotic massages. Discount coupons are sometimes available from the visitors center. Calistoga spa centers include:

Calistoga Spa Hot Springs
    1006 Washington St (☎ 942-6269)
Golden Haven Hot Springs
    1713 Lake St (☎ 942-6793)
Lincoln Ave Spa
    1339 Lincoln Ave (☎ 942-5296)
Dr Wilkinson's Hot Springs
    1507 Lincoln Ave (☎ 942-4636)
Nance's Hot Springs
    1614 Lincoln Ave (☎ 942-6211)

Shoestringers looking for non-commercial and lower priced spas can find them further afield. Ask the Sonoma Valley Visitors Bureau (☎ 707-996-1090) and the Santa Rosa Visitors Bureau (☎ 707-577-8674, 800-404-7673) for spas in their area.

Harbin Hot Springs (☎ 987-2477, 800-622-2477) is about four miles beyond Middletown, which in turn is 12 miles directly north of Calistoga, beyond the Robert Louis Stevenson State Park (see below). Run by the Heart Consciousness Church it offers all the usual spa stuff in their 'clothes optional' pools, and a vegetarian restaurant open limited hours. Dorm accommodations run from $23 to $35 and you must bring your own linen. No-frills camping facilities are also available.

West of St Helena is **White Sulphur Springs** (☎ 963-8588) offering mineral pools and a full-service spa in a serene, wooded setting complete with hiking trails and a main lodge. Their accommodations can be shared rustic rooms 'summer-camp style' for $70 to $140, or private cabins for $115 to $145 – a bargain for the experience.

Sharpsteen Museum

Created by an ex-Disney animator, the Sharpsteen Museum (☎ 942-5911) has a collection of dioramas showing scenes from the town's colorful history. A restored cottage from Brannan's original Calistoga resort is part of the museum which is at 1311 Washington St. (The only Brannan cottage still at its original site is at 106 Wapoo Ave.) It's open April to October daily, 10 am to 4 pm; and November to March daily, noon to 4 pm. Entry is free.

Bicycling

Getaway Adventures (☎ 942-0332), at 1117 Lincoln Ave, rents bicycles for $25 a day. Bikes can also be rented from Palisades Mountain Sports (☎ 942-9687) at 1330B Gerrard, behind the post office on Washington St.

Places to Stay

Camping & Cabins You can camp at the *Napa County Fairgrounds* (☎ 942-5111) at 1435 Oak St a few blocks north of the center of town, or at the *Bothe-Napa Valley State Park* (☎ 942-4575, Destinet 800-444-7275) three miles south on Hwy 29. The Bothe-Napa Valley site has a popular swimming pool. A tent site for two is less than $15 at either campground.

Economizers can head south via the Silverado Trail to the *Calistoga Ranch Club* (☎ 942-6565) at 580 Lommel Rd. The 167-acre grounds have tent sites at $19, cabins for four at $45, airstream trailers for five at $89, and there's a swimming pool. Or head 2½ miles north on the Petrified Forest Rd to the *Triple-S-Ranch* (☎ 942-6730) at 4600 Mt Home Ranch Rd where cabins cost $59 and there's a swimming pool. The ranch is closed January to the end of March.

Motels & Hotels Right in the center of town, the *Calistoga Inn* (☎ 942-4101) at 1250 Lincoln Ave is a historic hotel with 18 simple double rooms with shared bathrooms. Rooms cost $60 to $70 on weekends, $50 on weekdays.

Mount View Hotel (☎ 942-6877) at 1457 Lincoln Ave combines historic style with modern facilities including a spa (mud baths for two) and swimming pool. Regular rooms range from $85 to $125. Just north of the town center at 1865 Lincoln Ave the *Comfort Inn* (☎ 942-9400) is a larger motel with rooms as low as $65 on an off-season weekday, and up to $105 on a high-season weekend.

Several places combine spas with accommodations including the *Roman Spa Motel* (☎ 942-4441) at 1300 Washington St where there are spas, whirlpools, saunas and mud baths to go with the rooms which drop as low as $60 and climb as high as $130. Rooms at *Nance's Hot Springs*

Finding B&Bs

Prices at Wine Country B&Bs vary by season and day of the week. Despite higher prices on weekends and two-night minimums at many places it can still be difficult to find a room at peak times, so book ahead. The valleys have motels and other more mundane accommodations but B&Bs are the prime attraction. Well, it's romantic, isn't it? Most of the following associations track room availability and can give you information on the B&Bs they represent:

B&B International
　PO Box 282910, San Francisco, CA
　94128-2910 (☎ 415-696-1690, 800-
　872-4500; fax 415-696-1699)
B&B Inns of Napa Valley
　(☎ 707-944-4444)
Napa Valley Tourist Bureau
　(☎ 707-944-1558, 258-1957)
Napa Valley Reservations Unlimited
　(☎ 707-252-1985, 800-251-6272)
B&B Association of Sonoma Valley
　(☎ 707-938-9513, 800-969-4667)
B&B Inns of Sonoma Valley
　(☎ 707-996-4667, 800-284-6677) ■

(☎ 942-6211), 1614 Lincoln Ave all have kitchenettes and cost $55 midwinter and $75 in summer. A couple of blocks back from Lincoln Ave, the motel-like *Pine Street Inn* (☎ 942-6829) at 1202 Pine St has mud baths, seaweed body wraps and other Calistoga specialties. Rooms with small kitchens are $85 to $95.

B&Bs There are lots of B&Bs in Calistoga, call the visitors center if these are booked. *Brannan's Loft* (☎ 963-2181) at 1436 Lincoln Ave has just four rooms, ranging from $75 to $125. Close to the center of town *The Elms B&B* (☎ 942-9476, 800-235-4316) at 1300 Cedar St has seven comfortable and well-equipped rooms from $120 off season to $170 midseason. The *Wine Way Inn* (☎ 942-0680, 800-572-0679) is at 1019 Foothill Blvd (Hwy 29), and has six rooms at $80 to $130. The *Sam Brannan Cottage B&B* (☎ 942-4200), at 109 Wapoo Ave, is on the National Register of Historic Places and was recently restored. Rooms run from $99 to $156.

Places to Eat

Lincoln Ave has plenty of dining possibilities starting at the Hwy 29 end with *Pacifico* (☎ 942-4400), with excellent Mexican food at No 1237. Across the road the *Calistoga Inn* (☎ 942-4101) at No 1250 has microbrews from the Napa Valley Brewing Company and good California cuisine. Continue to *Boskos* (☎ 942-9088), a popular pizzeria and pasta specialist at No 1360 and the adjacent *Silverado Restaurant & Bar* (☎ 942-6725) at No 1374.

Checkers (☎ 942-9300) at No 1414 is a very popular gourmet pizza place, part of a very small pizzeria chain, the other half of the chain is in Santa Rosa. Next there's *Cinnabar* (☎ 942-6989) at No 1440 and, across the road, the *Clearwater Café* (☎ 942-9777) at No 1403 serves good, basic food.

The food at *Catahoula* (☎ 942-2275), at 1457 Lincoln Ave in the Mount View Hotel, is hearty Cajun fare but the style is certainly California. The best seats are those at the bar, where you can watch owner-chef Jan Birnbaum perform in instant communication with the rest of the kitchen via rock-star headphone. Catahoula is closed on Tuesdays.

Getting There & Away

The Napa Valley Transit buses run six times a day and cost $2.50 to other end of the valley. Greyhound also services Calistoga. See the introductory Wine Country Getting There & Away section for details.

BALE GRIST MILL STATE HISTORIC PARK

Part of the Bale Grist Mill State Historic Park (☎ 707-963-2236), is the 36-foot wheel which ground the local farmers' grain to flour and dates from 1846. There are good picnicking opportunities here, and a mile-long hiking trail to the adjacent Bothe-Napa Valley State Park.

The mill and park are visible from Hwy 29, midway between St Helena and Calistoga, and is open daily, 10 am to 5 pm. Entry is $2/1. Early in October the living history festival, Old Mill Days, is celebrated here.

OLD FAITHFUL GEYSER

Featured in *National Geographic* in 1948, Calistoga's slightly smaller version of Yellowstone's Old Faithful spouts off on a fairly regular 50-minute cycle, shooting boiling water 60 feet into the air. The geyser (☎ 707-942-6463) is about two miles north of town at 1299 Tubbs Lane and is open in summer daily, 9 am to 6 pm; in winter to 5 pm. Entry is $5/2 and local newspapers often have discount coupons.

PETRIFIED FOREST

Three million years ago a volcanic eruption at Mt St Helena blew down a stand of redwood trees between Calistoga and Santa Rosa. The trees all fell in the same direction, pointing away from the center of the blast and were covered in ash and mud. Over the millennia the trunks of these mighty trees were petrified or turned into stone and gradually the overlay eroded away to expose the trunks. The first stumps were discovered in 1870 and a monument marks the visit to the petrified forest by Robert Louis Stevenson in 1880. He described his visit in *The Silverado Squatters*. The forest (☎ 707-942-6667) is at 4100 Petrified Forest Rd, west off Hwy 128 1½ miles north of town, and is open in summer daily, 10 am to 6 pm; in winter to 5 pm. Entry is $3/1.

ROBERT LOUIS STEVENSON STATE PARK

The long-extinct volcano cone of Mt St Helena closes off the end of the valley, eight miles north of Calistoga in the undeveloped state park (☎ 707-942-4575). It's a tiring five-mile climb to the peak's 4343-foot summit but clear weather will reward walkers with superb views. The park includes the site of the old Silverado Mine where Stevenson honeymooned in 1880. Entrance is at the end of Hwy 29, and it's free.

Sonoma Valley

On the westward side of the hills, which separate the two Wine Country valleys, Sonoma Valley is about 15 miles in length. It's lower key than Napa, with fewer wineries and less commercialism. It's sometimes known as the Valley of the Moon from a Native American legend and Jack London story. Sonoma, at the southern end of the valley is surrounded by wineries and has a fascinating Spanish and Mexican history. Santa Rosa, at the northern end of the valley, is more the 'big city metropolis.'

SONOMA VALLEY WINERIES

The wine's just as good as Napa Valley's but the wineries are less crowded and, happily, free tastings are still the norm. In contrast to the 200-plus Napa wineries there are only 30 or so here. If you don't have a car Sonoma makes a good base as there are several wineries within easy bicycling distance of the town center.

Benziger On the road up to Jack London Park, this interesting and very educational winery includes a do-it-yourself walk by the grapevines and tractor/trailer tours of the whole winery. Interesting art exhibits include a display of wine label artwork and there's a picnic area. 1883 London Ranch Rd, Glen Ellen (☎ 935-3000).

Buena Vista The historic winery dates back to 1857 and the pioneering Hungarian vintner Count Agoston Haraszthy. There's a fine old building with art, and paid tastings upstairs, free tastings downstairs. There's also a picnic area. This is the largest winery in the Carneros Valley – which stretches east-west between the southern Napa and Sonoma Valleys. 18000 Old Winery Rd (☎ 938-1266, 800-926-1266).

Chateau St Jean There's a short self-guided tour of this winery, noted for its whites and its pleasant grounds with a picnic area. 8555 Sonoma Hwy, Kenwood – at the northern end of the valley (☎ 833-4134).

Gundlach-Bundschu One of Sonoma Valley's oldest wineries, Gundlach-Bundschu was founded by a Bavarian immigrant in 1858. Although grapes continued to be grown on the property right through Prohibition, wine production did

CALIFORNIA

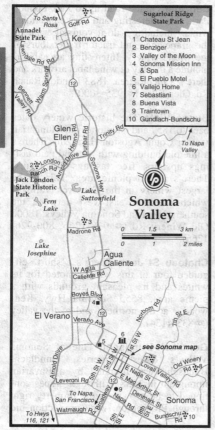

1 Chateau St Jean
2 Benziger
3 Valley of the Moon
4 Sonoma Mission Inn & Spa
5 El Pueblo Motel
6 Vallejo Home
7 Sebastiani
8 Buena Vista
9 Traintown
10 Gundlach-Bundschu

Sonoma Valley

0   1.5   3 km
0   1   2 miles

see Sonoma map

not recommence until 1973. The winery is reached by a very winding road and has a lake, hiking trail, and picnic area. 2000 Denmark St, Sonoma (☎ 938-5277).

Sebastiani There are regular tours in this venerable old winery. Italian immigrant Samuele Sebastiani bought the winery building in 1904. 389 4th St E, Sonoma (☎ 938-5532).

Valley of the Moon This small, pleasantly relaxed little winery is well out of the mainstream and just far enough off busy Hwy 12

to escape the traffic. 777 Madrone Rd, Glen Ellen (☎ 996-6941).

SONOMA
• pop 8000 ☎ 707

Sonoma's green and shady plaza loudly proclaims the town's Mexican heritage and there are a number of interesting buildings from that era. Sonoma was, believe it or not, the site of a second American revolution, this time against the Mexicans. In 1846 California was an uneasy place, Mexico had neither the resources nor the energy to effectively manage far flung centers like Sonoma, and the growing number of American settlers was leading to increased tension. Colonel Mariano Guadalupe Vallejo, the retired Mexican commander, had actually suggested that an American takeover was in the best interests of the region, but on June 14, 1846, the matter was taken out of his hands when the lightly guarded Sonoma presidio was taken over by a band of American frontiersmen.

Poor Vallejo was bundled off to imprisonment in Sacramento but the Bear Flag Revolt was short lived. Only a month later the Mexican-American War broke out, California was taken over and the Independent Republic of California joined the United States. The abortive revolt did, however, give California its state flag and that's why the flag proclaims 'Republic of California:' for that short period this patch of Northern California was indeed an independent country.

Vallejo, whose name pops up all over the town, was soon back in Sonoma and continued to play a major role in the development of the region. He was elected to the first state senate in 1850 and was mayor of Sonoma from 1852 to 1860. Unfortunately for Vallejo, although he was the owner of more than 273 sq miles of prime California real estate at the time of the Bear Flag Revolt, his fortune gradually drained away and he spent his later years writing a five volume *History of California*.

Orientation & Information
The spacious old plaza, laid out by General

Vallejo in 1834, decisively marks the center of Sonoma with hotels, restaurants, shops, and other facilities arranged around it. The very helpful Sonoma Valley Visitors' Bureau (☎ 996-1090) on the east side of the plaza at 453 1st St E is open in summer daily, 9 am to 7 pm; in winter daily, 9 am to 5 pm. It displays an accommodations list with prices, a helpful idea. They also have a walking tour leaflet to the town's many interesting buildings.

Sonoma has celebrations, cook-offs, concerts, and wine auctions taking place throughout the year. There's even a Hooker Party (honoring General Hooker, of course). Check with the visitors bureau for details.

Sonoma State Historic Park

The mission, the nearby Sonoma Barracks and the Vallejo Home are all part of the Sonoma State Historic Park (☎ 938-1519). The buildings are open daily, 10 am to 5 pm and combined entry to all three is $2/1.

Mission San Francisco Solano de Sonoma The 21st and final California mission and the only one built during the Mexican period (the rest were all founded by the Spanish), the Sonoma mission was built in 1823, in part to forestall the Russian colony on the coast at Fort Ross from moving inland. After secularization in 1834 the mission served as Sonoma's parish church until 1881 when the church building was sold. Although the original mission church is gone, it was replaced by a chapel built in 1840-41. Five rooms of the original mission remain and the dining room displays a collection of 61 paintings of the missions, all done between 1903 and 1905, showing them at that time. The mission is on E Spain St, at the northeast corner of the plaza.

Sonoma Barracks Built by Vallejo between 1836 and 1840 the adobe barracks are on E Spain St overlooking the plaza. They housed Mexican troops, then became American military quarters before starting a long and varied civilian life. Now a

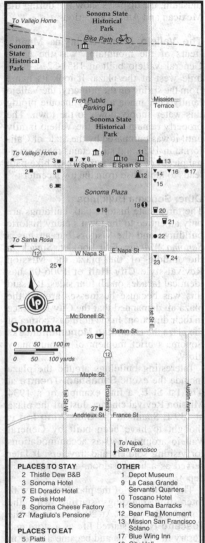

Sonoma

PLACES TO STAY	OTHER
2 Thistle Dew B&B	1 Depot Museum
3 Sonoma Hotel	9 La Casa Grande
5 El Dorado Hotel	Servants' Quarters
7 Swiss Hotel	10 Toscano Hotel
8 Sonoma Cheese Factory	11 Sonoma Barracks
27 Magliulo's Pensione	12 Bear Flag Monument
	13 Mission San Francisco
PLACES TO EAT	Solano
5 Piatti	17 Blue Wing Inn
6 Coffee Garden Cafe	18 City Hall
14 Old Sonoma	19 Visitors Bureau
Creamery & Cafe	20 Wine Exchange
15 Zino's Ristorante	of Sonoma
16 La Casa	21 Murphy's Irish Pub
23 Della Santina's	22 Sebastiani Theatre
24 Eastside Oyster Bar & Grill	26 Post Office
25 Feed Store Cafe & Bakery	

museum, the displays show life during the Mexican and American periods.

The Vallejo Home Lachryma Montis, 'tears of the mountain,' was the home General Vallejo built in 1851-52, a half-mile west of the plaza. It took its name from the spring on the property; the Vallejo family later made a handy income piping this water supply down to the town. The property remained with the Vallejo family until it was purchased by the State of California in 1933 and still retains many original pieces of Vallejo furniture. A bike path leads to the house from the town center.

Other Sonoma Buildings

The three state historic park buildings are only an entree to the town's many historic buildings and the visitors bureau has a *Sonoma Walking Tour* booklet. Smack in the middle of the plaza the Mission Revival-style **City Hall** of 1906-08 has identical facades on all four sides. It's said this was because businesses around the plaza all demanded that the City Hall face in their direction! In the northeast corner of the plaza the **Bear Flag Monument** marks Sonoma's brief moment of revolutionary glory.

Interesting buildings around the plaza include the exotic **Sebastiani Theatre** at 476 1st St E, a fine example of a 1934 Mission Revival cinema. Just off the plaza at 139 E Spain St, the **Blue Wing Inn** is thought to have been built by General Vallejo around 1840 as accommodations for visiting soldiers and travelers. It later served as a hotel, saloon, and stagecoach depot.

The north side of the plaza is lined with interesting buildings starting with the Sonoma Barracks. At 20 E Spain St the **Toscano Hotel** started life as a store and library in the 1850s and became a hotel in 1886. Tours take place on weekends from 1 to 4 pm and Monday from 11 am to 1 pm. Vallejo's first Sonoma home, **La Casa Grande**, was built around 1835 on this side of the plaza but most of it burned down in 1867. The imposing house had a three-

story tower and 11 of Vallejo's children were born there. Casa Grande had a variety of uses after the Vallejo family moved to their new home but only the servants' quarters, where the general's Native American servants were housed, remains today.

You can see traditional Sonoma Jack cheese being made in the Art Moderne **Sonoma Cheese Factory** at 2 W Spain St. The adobe **Swiss Hotel** at 18 W Spain St started as a home for Salvador Vallejo in the late 1830s and became a hotel in the 1880s, which it continues to be today. On the west side of the plaza at 415 1st St W the **Salvador Vallejo Adobe** was also built by General Vallejo's brother between 1836 and 1846. It now houses the popular Coffee Garden Café.

Depot Museum

North of the plaza in Depot Park, the Depot Museum (☎ 938-9765) has historic exhibits and art. The museum building has had a checkered history. In the 1880s a railway line ran along Spain St to the plaza: the depot building was constructed on the north side and the railway company gradually took over most of the plaza until public protests forced their move to Depot Park. The railway closed down in 1917, but when the old building was being converted into the museum it burned down and the current building is a 1978 replica of the original. A bicycle track now follows the route the train once took through town. It's open Wednesday to Sunday, 1 to 4:30 pm.

Traintown

At Traintown (☎ 938-3912), one mile south of the plaza on Broadway, a miniature steam engine makes 20-minute trips for $2.80/1.90. The train operates October to

May, Friday through Sunday, 10:30 am to 5 pm; June to September it runs daily, 10:30 am to 5 pm.

Bicycling

Sonoma Valley Cyclery (☎ 935-3377) at 20079 Broadway rents bicycles for $22 to $28 a day. Bikes can also be rented from the Good Time Bicycle Company (☎ 938-0453) at 18503 Hwy 12, north of the center towards Santa Rosa.

Places to Stay

Camping The nearest campground to Sonoma is the *Sugarloaf Ridge State Park* just north of Kenwood at 2605 Adobe Canyon Rd where sites cost $15 per night. As with other state park campsites, reservations are made by phoning Destinet (☎ 800-444-7275). There's the *Petaluma KOA* (☎ 763-1492) close to Hwy 101 with reservable, year-round sites for around $23, and lakeside camping ($11) at *Spring Lake Regional Park* (☎ 539-8082) in Santa Rosa open mid-May to mid-September.

Hotels & Motels The *El Pueblo Motel* (☎ 996-3651), one mile west of the town center at 896 W Napa St, is about as cheap as it comes in Sonoma. They offer standard motel rooms at $57 to $70. *Magliulo's Pensione* (☎ 996-1031) is at 691 Broadway, a short distance south of the plaza, and has rooms at $77 to $88 and a fine restaurant. The *Best Western Sonoma Valley Inn* (☎ 938-9200) at 550 2nd St W is just a block west of the plaza and has rooms at a pricey $154 on summer weekends, falling to $100 to $110 off-season weekends and summer weekdays and down to $80 on off-season weekdays.

There are a number of stylish older hotels right on the plaza. The fine old *Swiss Hotel* (☎ 938-2884) at 18 W Spain St on the north side of the plaza has just five pleasantly elegant rooms, all different and all with wavy floors and walls to show just what a historic place it is. Rooms at the front look out over the plaza. General Vallejo constructed the building in 1850 and it has been the Swiss Hotel since 1909.

In summer rooms cost $120 to $160 on weekends, $110 to $130 during the week. Prices include breakfast, and drop by $20 to $40 in the winter. The *Sonoma Hotel* (☎ 996-2996, 800-468-6016) at 110 W Spain St, right on the northwest corner of the plaza, has rooms with shared bathroom at $75 and $85, with attached bathroom at $115 and $120. The *El Dorado Hotel* (☎ 996-3030, 800-289-3031), at 405 1st St W, costs as much as $135 to $145 on summer weekends, and as little as $85 to $90 on winter weekdays. The rooms have balconies, there's a pool, and breakfast is included in the price.

The *Sonoma Mission Inn & Spa* (☎ 938-9000, 800-862-4945 in California, 800-358-9022 outside California), on Hwy 12, charges perhaps too much for their small, elegant rooms, though you receive complimentary use of their Olympic-size pool and the 'fitness paladium.' In summer, rooms cost $225 to $350; off-season rates are $185 to $325. However, the spa there is well worth the dough.

B&Bs B&Bs in town include the *Thistle Dew B&B* (☎ 800-382-7895) just west of the plaza at 171 W Spain St with six rooms at $100 to $135. East of the plaza the very pleasant *Victorian Gardens Inn* (☎ 996-5339) at 316 E Napa St has four rooms at $79 to $139. The old house dates from 1870 and has a swimming pool.

Places to Eat

If you're stocking up for a Sonoma Valley picnic, *Good to Go* (☎ 938-0301) at 603 Broadway next to the post office, has everything you'll need for gourmet takeout. Or try the *Sonoma Cheese Factory* (☎ 996-1931) at 2 W Spain St and get your bread from the *Sonoma French Bakery* at 470 E Spain St (closed Sunday and Monday), both on the plaza.

The *Coffee Garden Café* (☎ 996-6645) at 415-421 1st St W by the plaza is housed in a historic adobe building with a pretty garden in the rear. They make good coffee and snacks and have a leaflet on the building's colorful history. The Mission Revival-style *Old Sonoma Creamery & Café* (☎ 938-2938) at 400 1st St E at the northeast corner of the plaza is an old fashioned cafe, ice cream parlor, deli, and even wine bar. They've been making ice cream here since 1930. The *Feed Store Cafe & Bakery* (☎ 938-2122), 529 1st St W, opens at 7 am with inexpensive and very tasty food.

Della Santina's (☎ 935-0576) at 101 E Napa St at the southeast corner of the plaza is a small restaurant cooking up very well prepared recipes from the Tuscany region of Italy. At 420 1st St E on the east side of the plaza *Zino's* (☎ 996-4466) is a touristy and very popular but also very friendly place with main courses at $12 to $15 and 48 (count 'em!) wines by the glass. Italian food gets a third go at *Piatti* (☎ 996-2351) at 405 1st St W in the El Dorado Hotel.

Given Sonoma's solid Mexican origins it's surprising that Italian restaurants are so plentiful (there are others around town) and Mexican ones so rare. The balance is slightly righted with *La Casa* (☎ 996-3406) at 121 E Spain St, a popular restaurant just east of the plaza and right across from the Mission. The *Eastside Oyster Bar & Grill* (☎ 939-1266) at 133 E Napa St, serves oysters on the half shell as well as daily wild game specials in addition to a California cuisine menu.

The General's Daughter (☎ 938-4004), 400 W Spain St at the foot of 4th St W, serves excellent cuisine on the affordable side.

The Grille at the Sonoma Mission Inn & Spa, Hwy 12 at Boyes Blvd, gets raves from travel magazine writers, but for the pricey experience, you're better off trying one of the other top-end Wine Country restaurants (see the sidebar above for a selection). Or try the less expensive *Big Three Cafe* (☎ 938-9000 ext 415), in the same location, where entrees are around $12.

Entertainment

All that running around valley wineries can be saved with a single trip to the *Wine Exchange of Sonoma* (☎ 938-1794) at 452 1st St E on the plaza where a changing variety of wines are available for tasting every day for $1, or by the glass for $3.50 or $4.50.

Murphy's Irish Pub (☎ 935-0660), down a laneway off the plaza at 464 1st St E, has a variety of beers, pub food including fish & chips, a dart board and patio seating. The *Sebastiana Theater* (☎ 996-2020) at 476 1st St E has first run films and live performances.

Getting There & Away

Golden Gate Transit bus No 90 operates San Francisco-San Rafael-Sonoma ($4.50, one way) twice daily northbound and three times southbound. Sonoma County Transit (☎ 707-576-7433, 800-345-7433) has local services up the valley. Greyhound has flag-stop service from Napa to Sonoma, and up the Sonoma Valley to Santa Rosa and beyond.

JACK LONDON STATE HISTORIC PARK

Napa Valley has Robert Louis Stevenson, Sonoma has Jack London, and this park traces the last years of his short life. Shuffling occupations from Oakland fisherman to Alaskan gold prospector to Pacific yachtsman, as well as, of course, novelist on the side, London finished by taking up farming. He bought Beauty Ranch in 1905 and moved there permanently in 1910; today he would have been called an organic farmer. With his wife Charmian he lived and wrote in a small cottage while his huge mansion, Wolf House, was being built, but on the eve of its completion in 1913 it burned down. The cause was never determined but it was most probably arson; staunchly socialist London certainly had enemies. The disaster was a devastating blow and although he toyed with the idea of rebuilding he died in 1916, before it got underway.

After his death Charmian built the House of Happy Walls which is now preserved as a Jack London museum. It's a half-mile walk from there to the remains of Wolf House, passing London's grave along the way. Other walking paths wind around the farm to the cottage where he lived and worked. Trails, some of them open to mountain bikes, also lead further into the park. Renowned thickets of poison oak await those who wander off the trails. Jack London State Historic Park (☎ 707-938-5216) is off Hwy 12, past the small settlement of Glen Ellen and is free and open daily, 10 am to 5 pm, in summer to 7 pm. Parking is $5. The House of Happy Walls museum is open daily, 10 am to 5 pm.

SANTA ROSA
• *pop 113,000* ☎ *707*

Two cartoonists and a horticulturist are Santa Rosa's claim to fame. The sprawling town is the major population center of the wine district and offers cheaper accommodations than the touristy wine centers, but otherwise there's not a lot of reason to hang around. The Sonoma County Harvest Fair (☎ 545-4200) runs from late July to early August, a busy but excellent time to stop by.

Orientation & Information
The Santa Rosa Visitors Bureau (☎ 577-8674, 800-404-7673) at 637 1st St is open weekdays 9 am to 5 pm; weekends 10 am to 2 pm; longer hours in summer. The main shopping street is three blocks north along 4th St which abruptly ends at Hwy 101 but re-emerges on the other side in the historic Railway Square area. Two of the town's three attractions are walking distance south of the town center but the third, the Snoopy Gallery, is 2½ miles north.

There are a number of downtown parking lots with free parking for the first 1½ hours.

Luther Burbank Home & Gardens
At the corner of Santa Rosa and Sonoma Aves the pioneering horticulturist's home and garden was where he developed many of his hybrid species. The garden (☎ 524-5445) is free; tours of the house operate April through October, from Wednesday to Sunday, every half hour from 10 am to 3:30 pm for $2.

Ripley Museum
At 492 Sonoma Ave, in Julliard Park across Santa Rosa Ave from the Luther Burbank Home & Garden, the Ripley's Believe It or Not Memorial Museum (☎ 524-5233) is dedicated to Robert Ripley, the Santa Rosa cartoonist, who spent his life tracking down oddities to publish in his syndicated 'Believe It or Not!' column. The feature first appeared in 1918 and continues today, long after Ripley's death in 1949. Appropriately the museum is housed in one of his oddities, a church built entirely from a single redwood tree. The museum is open April through October, Wednesday to Sunday, 10:30 am to 3:30 pm. Entry is $1.50/75¢.

Snoopy's Gallery
Cartoonist Charles Schulz is a long term Santa Rosa resident and his Peanuts cartoon strip can claim to have added 'security blanket' to the dictionary. The gallery has an awesome collection of Peanuts paraphernalia while the mezzanine level recounts the story of the cartoon's worldwide success. Snoopy's Gallery (☎ 546-3385) is at 1667 W Steele Lane beside the Redwood Empire Ice Arena (☎ 546-7147), 2½ miles north of the town center, off Hwy 101. It's open Monday to Saturday, 10 am to 6 pm; Sunday to 5 pm.

Places to Stay
Camping There are sites for $14 at *Spring Lake Regional Park* (☎ 539-8092) off Montgomery on Summerfield Drive, adjacent to Annadel State Park. See the Sonoma section for the Sugarloaf Ridge State Park at Kenwood.

Hotels & Motels The *Astro Motel* (☎ 545-8555) is at 323 Santa Rosa Ave beside Julliard Park and very close to the downtown center. This plain and simple motel claims to offer the lowest prices in town, as low as $28/32 for singles/doubles weekdays in the off season.

The large *Days Inn* (☎ 573-9000, 800-354-7672), at 175 Railroad St just off 3rd St west of Hwy 101 and on the edge of

Railroad Square, has a swimming pool and rooms for $65/75 off season, which rises to a precious $90/100 in summer.

The historic *Hotel La Rose* (☎ 579-3200) is at 308 Wilson St, just across from the railway depot in the Railroad Square area. Rooms are $50 to $65 off season or $65 to $75 in the high season. Suites cost more, but can be a bargain on off-season week-nights. South of Railroad Square there's *Pygmalion House* (☎ 526-3407) at 331 Orange St, a B&B with rooms at $60 to $70 in an 1880s Victorian house. An easy way to check availability at numerous B&Bs is to call B&B Inns of Sonoma County (☎ 433-4667), but they can't book for you.

Places to Eat

Almost any appetite can be satisfied down-town along 4th St where there are also a number of bookshops, some of them with their own coffee bars. The caffeine urge can also be satisfied at *Wolf Caffe* (☎ 546-9653) on the corner of Mendocino Ave, or at the very popular *Sonoma Coffee Company* (☎ 573-8022) further west at 521 4th St.

Checkers (☎ 578-4000) at No 523 is a sister restaurant to the popular Calistoga pizza and pasta specialist. *Caffe Portofino* at 535 4th St, is a bustling and entertaining dinner stop, with entrees at around $10. Across the road is the big and bright Mexican *Cantina* (☎ 523-3663) at No 500. *Fourth St Bistro* (☎ 526-2225) at 645 4th St

offers 'Mediterranean rim' cuisine and a particular vegetarian tilt.

Highway 101 then chops 4th St off but it reappears on the other side of the freeway in the historic Railway Square area. Here you'll find the popular *Taqueria Fonseca's* (☎ 576-0131) at No 117 while across the road *Omelette Express* (☎ 525-1690) at No 112 also pulls 'em in.

As a Railway Square finale the much pricier *Mixx* (☎ 573-1344), at 135 4th St on the corner with Davis St, has a very eclec-tic menu and stays open reasonably late. Farther away, *John Ash & Co* (☎ 527-7687), 4330 Barnes Rd in the Vintner's Inn, is also pricey but is often raved about; some say it's overrated. For the same meal at less expense, dine on the patio or at the bar from the *Vinyard Cafe* menu. It's closed on Monday. At *Lisa Hemenway's* (☎ 526-5111), 714 Village Court there will be jokes about the location (it's in the very '70s Village Court Mall), but certainly not about the wine, nor the expressive menu.

Getting There & Away

Golden Gate Transit (☎ 415-332-6600, 707-544-1323) has buses from San Fran-cisco via Petaluma (Nos 71, 72, 74, 75 and 80) for $4.50. Sonoma County Transit (☎ 707-576-7433, 800-345-7433) has local services up the Sonoma Valley. Greyhound has services to Santa Rosa and further north from Napa to Sonoma and up the Sonoma Valley and from San Francisco via Petaluma.

Sacramento Valley

Heading north from Sacramento, the northern reaches of the Central Valley are like the rest of the valley – flat, agricultural, very hot in summer, often with low-lying tule fog in winter. While this chapter follows Hwys 70 and 99 through the valley, there is overlap with the Gold Country. Along the route you'll find some delightful places to visit, from sleepy mining towns to vibrant, youthful university towns.

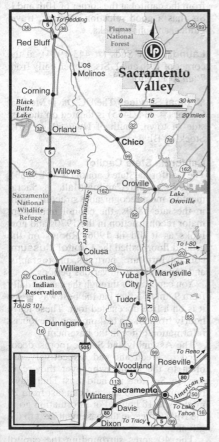

SACRAMENTO
• *pop 385,000* ☎ 916

Sacramento, California's capital, is as conservative and uninteresting as the gray suits and square haircuts donned by its politicians. Its skyline, impressive from afar, sprang up in the 1980s at the expense of street level businesses. Though bustling on weekdays, the downtown empties out after sunset and feels like a ghost town on weekends.

As the capital, however, Sacramento has some redeeming sites and a stable economy, aided by the Port of Sacramento (the second largest export harbor in the US), California State University Sacramento (known for its business school), and satellite medical facilities of the University of California, Davis, known as one of the top ranked medical schools in the US. People required to spend some time in the capital city will find just compensation in good restaurants, and museums.

History

In 1839, Swiss immigrant John Sutter arrived in California and proposed to build an outpost north of San Francisco for the Mexican government. The government gave Sutter 76 sq miles of land around the confluence of the American and Sacramento Rivers where, with the aid of local Miwok tribes, Sutter built an adobe fort, planted crops, and ran cattle. As the only outpost between San Francisco and Vancouver, Sutter's Fort became a bastion of security and general rendezvous. When James Marshall discovered gold in the tailrace of Sutter's lumber mill near Coloma in 1848, hundreds of thousands of people flocked to California – most of whom traveled through Sutter's Fort. Sam Brannan built several structures west of the fort, along the Sacramento River, to benefit from the new influx of miners. Sutter gave his

CALIFORNIA

fort to his son who christened the newly sprung town 'Sacramento.'

Though plagued by fires and flood, the riverfront settlement prospered and became the state capital in 1850.

Orientation

Sacramento sits at the confluence of the Sacramento and American Rivers, roughly half way between San Francisco and Lake Tahoe.

Interstate 5 runs along the western edge of downtown between the city and the Sacramento River, and becomes Hwy 99 when it leaves town to the north. Interstate 80 goes west to San Francisco and northeast to Reno by way of Donner Pass and north Lake Tahoe. The I-80 Business route (Bus 80) cuts through downtown. Highway 50 branches off Bus 80 towards Placerville and South Lake Tahoe.

Downtown, numbered streets run north-south, with 3rd St as the main thoroughfare going south (one-way), and 5th St as the main thoroughfare going north (one way); lettered streets run east-west, with Capitol Ave (also called Capitol Mall) replacing M St.

Information

Sacramento's main Visitor Information Center (☎ 442-7644) is in Old Sacramento at 1104 Front St, and is open daily from 9 am to 5 pm. The Convention & Visitor's Bureau (☎ 264-7777), 1421 K St, has bus schedules and information on current events. It is open weekdays from 8 am to 5 pm.

The *Sacramento Bee*, the local daily newspaper, maintains an automated local information line (☎ 552-5252) covering weather, events, and museum hours.

Money There is a concentration of banks downtown on J St, near the Downtown Plaza Mall. Regular banking hours are weekdays 9 am to 6 pm. The American Express office (☎ 441-1780), 515 L St, is open on weekdays 9 am to 5 pm.

Post & Telecommunications The main post office (☎ 263-7181) is at 2000 Royal Oaks Drive, though most transactions can be handled at the small branch in the visitors center in Old Sacramento, open daily from 9 am to 5 pm.

For fax transactions, Kinko's Copies (☎ 731-4012) at 4765 J St, is open 24 hours.

Bookstores The best selection of Sacramento and California history books is in the gift shop of the capitol, open daily from 9 am to 6 pm.

The *Avid Reader* (☎ 443-7323), across from the capitol at the corner of 10th and L Sts, has a good selection of maps, travel guides, and photo books.

Laundry City Suds (☎ 443-1914), at the corner of 19th and L Sts, is open daily from 7 am to 11 pm.

Medical Services The UC Davis Medical Center (☎ 734-2455) is located on the east side of town, south of Hwy 50, at 2315 Stockton Blvd.

California State Capitol

The California State Capitol (☎ 324-0333), at 10th St and Capitol Mall, is Sacramento's most recognizable structure. Built in the late 1800s, the capitol underwent major reconstruction in the 1970s and now looks as it did in 1906. Rooms on the ground floor, called the **Capitol Museum**, contain furniture, portraits, photographs, and documents from various periods.

You can wander through the capitol daily from 9 am to 5 pm, but the best way to see it is on a free docent-led tour. These leave hourly from 10 am to 4 pm from the tourist information office in the basement.

The Assembly and Senate rooms, decorated in green and red respectively, are open to the public whenever they're in session. Sessions are held most Thursdays, beginning at 9:30 am, and can last from 20 minutes to 18 hours. For information go to the Bills Office, in the basement next to the gift shop.

The 40 acres surrounding the capitol

make up the **Capitol Park**, with trees from all over the world – a nice place to picnic or escape summer's heat. In the east end is a powerful and somewhat graphic Vietnam War memorial.

Old Sacramento

Once a bustling river port filled with hopeful gold seekers, Old Sacramento (Old Sac) contains California's largest concentration of buildings on the National Register of Historic Places – now candy stores, T-shirt shops, and restaurants. Besides the California Railroad Museum (see below), Old Sac's best feature is its riverfront setting. The *Spirit of Sacramento*, an 1842 paddlewheeler, makes one-hour narrated tours of the Sacramento River worth the $10 ticket. The boat leaves from the L St dock next to the visitor center every hour in summer. For information call ☎ 552-2933 or 800-433-0263.

At Old Sac's north end, near where the notorious 'Big Four' – Leland Stanford, Mark Hopkins, JP Huntington, and Charles Crocker – masterminded fundraising campaigns and track-laying strategies for the first transcontinental railroad, is the excellent **California State Railroad Museum** (☎ 552-5252 ext 7245). Its collection of locomotives, freight and passenger cars, toy models, and memorabilia took 14 years to acquire and is well displayed.

Tickets costs $5, and include entrance to the restored Central Pacific Passenger Depot, across the plaza from the museum entrance. Both are open daily, 9 am to 5 pm.

Next door to the railroad museum is the **Discovery Museum (Sacramento Museum of Science & Technology)** (☎ 264-5057), with hands-on exhibits and a good display of Gold Rush-era artifacts. The museum is open May to September from 10 am to 5 pm, October to April noon to 5 pm (closed Mondays), and costs $3.50.

CALIFORNIA

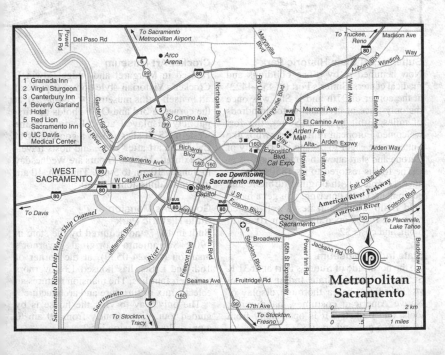

Metropolitan Sacramento

1 Granada Inn
2 Virgin Sturgeon
3 Canterbury Inn
4 Beverly Garland Hotel
5 Red Lion Sacramento Inn
6 UC Davis Medical Center

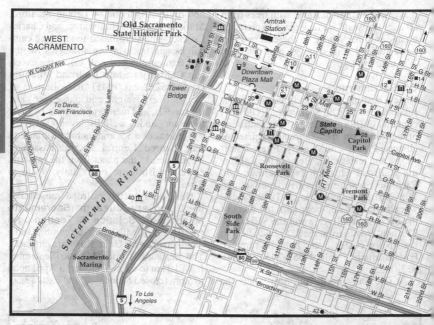

Sutter's Fort State Historic Park

Now hemmed in by office buildings and medical centers, Sutter's Fort (☎ 455-4422) at the corner of 27th and L Sts, was once the only trace of civilization for hundreds of miles. Built by John Sutter, the fort welcomed European immigrants who, like Sutter, were eager to escape the rigidity of Europe and start anew in America.

The fort is restored to its 1850s appearance, complete with original furniture and equipment. Upon entering, you get a hand-held radio which narrates a self-guided tour. The fort is open daily from 10 am to 5 pm, and costs $2.

State Indian Museum

On the north side of Sutter's Fort at 2631 K St, the California State Indian Museum (☎ 324-0971), has a thorough display of Native American costumes, handicrafts, tools, and basketry. It is open daily from 10 am to 5 pm, and costs $2.

Crocker Art Museum

Housed in Margaret and Judge Edwin B Crocker's Victorian-style home – a piece of art in itself – this museum (☎ 264-5423), at the corner of 3rd and O Sts, holds the first publicly displayed art collection in the western US. It also houses a good show of California art after 1945, and hosts traveling exhibits. Museum hours are Wednesday to Sunday 10 am to 5 pm, Thursday 10 am to 9 pm. Admission is $4.50.

Governor's Mansion State Historic Park

Built in 1877 and acquired by the state in 1906, Sacramento's original governor's mansion (☎ 324-0539), at the corner of 16th and L Sts, has housed 13 governors and their families. The mansion features an eclectic mix of furniture and architecture.

The only way to visit the house is by guided tour, given hourly from 10 am to 4 pm daily. Admission is $2.

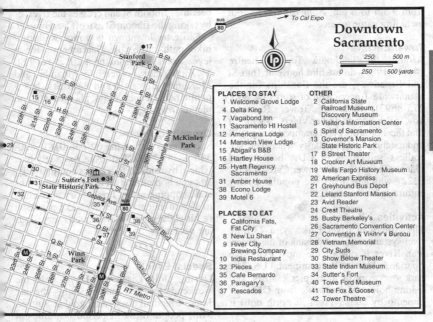

CALIFORNIA

Downtown
Sacramento

0   250   500 m
0   250   500 yards

To Cal Expo

PLACES TO STAY
1 Welcome Grove Lodge
4 Delta King
7 Vagabond Inn
11 Sacramento HI Hostel
12 Americana Lodge
14 Mansion View Lodge
15 Abigail's B&B
16 Hartley House
25 Hyatt Regency
   Sacramento
31 Amber House
38 Econo Lodge
39 Motel 6

PLACES TO EAT
6 California Fats,
   Fat City
8 New Lu Shan
9 River City
   Brewing Company
10 India Restaurant
32 Pieces
35 Cafe Bernardo
36 Paragary's
37 Pescados

OTHER
2 California State
   Railroad Museum,
   Discovery Museum
3 Visitor's Information Center
5 Spirit of Sacramento
13 Governor's Mansion
   State Historic Park
17 B Street Theater
18 Crooker Art Museum
19 Wells Fargo History Museum
20 American Express
21 Greyhound Bus Depot
22 Leland Stanford Mansion
23 Avid Reader
24 Crest Theatre
25 Busby Berkeley's
26 Sacramento Convention Center
27 Convention & Visitor's Bureau
28 Vietnam Memorial
29 City Suds
30 Show Below Theater
33 State Indian Museum
34 Sutter's Fort
40 Towe Ford Museum
41 The Fox & Goose
42 Tower Theatre

Leland Stanford Mansion

This mansion at 8th and N Sts was built in 1859 by Leland Stanford, one of the railroad industry's 'Big Four.' Under constant restoration, the mansion can be visited by tour on Tuesdays, Thursdays, and Saturdays for $2. This tour is unique in that it reveals flood-damaged floors and ceilings, and odd things found in the walls during restoration. Call ☎ 324-0575 for tour times.

Towe Ford Museum

The 157 beautifully restored Ford cars and trucks housed in the Towe Ford Museum (☎ 442-6802), south of I-80 at 2200 Front St, is enough to make any car enthusiast drool. Next door, the gift shop has a large collection of automobile memorabilia and picture books. Both are open daily from 9 am to 6 pm. Admission is $5.

Wells Fargo History Museum

Located in the Wells Fargo Center at 400 Capitol Mall, the museum (☎ 440-4161) has a collection of original documents, photographs, and lithographs from Sacramento's early days. Naturally, the museum's theme is Wells Fargo's 'instrumental role in settling the West' – from the first messenger's trip across the Sierras in 1852. The museum is open weekdays from 9 am to 5 pm and is free.

Cal Expo

Site of the California State Fair (held every summer), Cal Expo, east of I-80 from the Cal Expo exit, has 700 acres of exhibit facilities in constant use for everything from the California Bridal Fair to the Motor World USA convention. For current events call ☎ 263-3000.

Also at Cal Expo is **Waterworld USA & Paradise Island Family Fun Center** (☎ 924-0555), a tangle of waterslides, bumper cars, miniature golf courses, and carnival games. The park is open daily from 9 am to 6 pm. Admission is $8, not including game tokens.

Tower Enclave

Around the landmark Tower Theatre (☎ 443-1982), an art-film house at 16th St and Broadway, are the flagships for the nationwide Tower chain of stores (☎ 800-275-8693), including Tower Records, Tower Books, and Tower Video. You might find the stores ugly and cramped, but you'll understand their popularity when you see endless selections of CDs, books, and videos. There's even a Tower Cafe (☎ 441-0222) which reflects the popular coffee culture in Sacramento.

Activities

The American River Parkway, a 23-mile river system on the north bank of the American River is one of the most extensive riparian habitats in the continental US. The park's network of trails, picnic areas, and fishing holes are accessible from Old Sacramento by taking Front St north until it

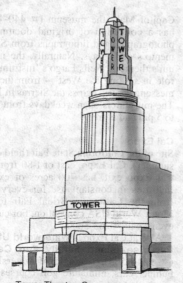
Tower Theatre, Sacramento

becomes Jiboom St and crosses the river, or by taking the Jiboom St exit off I-5/Hwy 99.

Close to downtown is a nice walk/run/bike path along the Sacramento River levee, accessible from the north end of J St. McKinley Park, bordered by Alhambra and McKinley Blvds, H and 33rd Sts, has a public pool, tennis courts, playground, and picnic areas.

Organized Tours

Sacramento Gray Line (☎ 648-0181, 800-356-9838), 2600 North Ave, has a city tour which, by running four buses continuously, lets you hop off and on at major attractions and shopping areas. Prices vary according to season, but are generally $25 per person (a bit cheaper in the winter). Reservations are necessary.

Special Events

During Gold Discovery Days, held the weekend closest to January 28th – the day James Marshall discovered gold at Sutter's Mill, people dress in period costumes at Sutter's Fort State Historic Park and set to making barrels, pounding iron, and baking bread.

The Sacramento Jazz Jubilee (☎ 372-5277), held the last weekend in May, attracts big names from all over the US. Venues are widespread, but music usually ends up spilling over into the streets.

In mid-June, the California Railroad Festival (☎ 445-7387) takes place at the Railroad Museum in Old Sac, where old locomotives roll out for the occasion.

The California State Fair is held at Cal Expo from mid-August to mid-September, and includes a rodeo, agriculture displays, arts, crafts, food vendors, rides, carnival games, and live music.

Winterfest, Sacramento's way of dealing with oppressive winter skies, is a six-week event from the third weekend of November until the weekend following New Year's Day. Events include parades and street performances, and an outdoor ice skating rink is set up downtown. For information call ☎ 442-8575.

Places to Stay – bottom end

Camping & Hostel Sacramento's *KOA* (☎ 371-6771) campground, 3951 Lake Rd W, near the W Capitol Ave exit off I-80 in West Sacramento, has a few grassy tent sites for $18, and RV sites for $23. Amenities include a pool, store, and laundry.

The brand new *Sacramento HI Hostel* (☎ 443-1691), 900 H St, in a restored 1885 Victorian, is walking distance to the capitol, Old Sac, and the train station. There are eight dorm rooms and two private rooms with a total of 70 beds, a nice common area, kitchen facilities, and laundry room. Beds are $10 per night, or $12 for non-HI/AYH members. The hostel attracts an international crowd and makes a good place to find rides to San Francisco and Lake Tahoe. Office hours are daily from 7:30 to 9:30 am and 5 to 10 pm.

Motels Most chain motels are north of downtown off the I-80 Cal Expo exit. Closer to downtown off the J St exit, near Sacramento's medical facilities, are *Motel 6* (☎ 457-0777), 1415 30th St, and *Econo Lodge* (☎ 454-4400), 1319 30th St, which both charge around $32/40 a single/double.

One of Sacramento's nicest budget motels, the *Americana Lodge* (☎ 444-3980), 818 15th St, is centrally located, has clean, fresh rooms for $35/38, and a small pool. Nearby, the *Mansion View Lodge* (☎ 443-6631), 711 16th St, has comparable rooms for $38/42.

Sacramento's concentration of cheap, independent motels is in West Sacramento along W Capitol Ave – a depressing strip, best avoided by solo travelers after dark. Rooms cost $25 to $35 and are generally clean, but may have carpet, beds, and plumbing that are older than you are. The nicest place is the *Welcome Grove Lodge* (☎ 371-8526), 600 W Capitol Ave, with quiet rooms for $31.

At the very west end, the *Granada Inn* (☎ 372-2780), 4751 W Capitol Ave, is part of a small chain of 'truckers' motels.' It has newly decorated but noisy rooms for $36/38, and a 24-hour coffeeshop next door.

Places to Stay – middle

Sacramento's mid-level accommodations cater to business people. Weekend rates are usually $20 to $30 cheaper than those listed below. Most accommodations offer free airport shuttle service, and are near places to eat.

The *Vagabond Inn* (☎ 446-1481), 909 3rd St, is within walking distance to most attractions. It has a heated pool and rooms for $68/73.

Near Cal Expo and the Arden Fair shopping mall, the *Beverly Garland Hotel* (☎ 929-7900), 1780 Tribute Rd, has a restaurant, spa and fitness center, and rooms which cost $74. In the same area, the *Canterbury Inn* (☎ 927-0927), 1900 Canterbury Rd, is a good value with rooms for $55/65, and an outdoor pool and spa.

Places to Stay – top end

Hotels Besides being a novelty, the *Delta King* (☎ 444-5464, 800-825-5464), housed in the *Spirit of Sacramento* paddlewheeler docked at the L St landing in Old Sac, has an unbeatable location. State rooms – which are small compared to similarly priced hotel rooms – cost $99 to $140.

Across from the capitol and convention center, the *Hyatt Regency Sacramento* (☎ 443-1234), 1209 L St, caters to guests who wear suits. Rooms cost $80 to $110, and amenities include a pool, spa, fitness center, and two restaurants.

Near Cal Expo, the *Red Lion's Sacramento Inn* (☎ 922-8041), 1401 Arden Way, has Sacramento's most deluxe accommodations, with a resort-like layout including indoor and outdoor pools, a spa, fitness center, several restaurants, and a nightclub with live music and dancing. Rooms start at $140.

B&Bs Sacramento's B&Bs are in a residential neighborhood north of the capitol, within walking distance of downtown. Prices include a full breakfast. *Abigail's* (☎ 800-858-1568), 2120 G St, has five rooms, each with a private bathroom, patio, and hot tub for $95 to $165.

Nearby, the Arts & Crafts-style *Hartley*

House (☎ 447-7829, 800-831-5806), at the corner of 22nd and G St, has rooms with large windows, private bath, TV, and telephone for $95 to $165.

Sacramento's best known B&B is the *Amber House* (☎ 444-8085, 800-755-6526), 1315 22nd St, which has a nice porch swing, rooms with private bath, TV, VCR, and telephone (some have in-room Jacuzzis) for $95 to $200.

Places to Eat

There are basically two types of places to eat in Sacramento: yuppified cafes open weekdays for lunch, and nice restaurants where dinner costs around $20 per person. Budget travelers should make lunch their main meal, or go to a nice restaurant for dinner and consider it the evening's entertainment.

Pieces, 1309 21st St, sells pizza by the slice ($1.50) and is open late. *Cafe Bernardo* (☎ 443-1180), 2726 Capitol Ave, has a good atmosphere and excellent, inexpensive food. The Thai chicken salad ($6), portobello mushroom burger ($5), and chicken pot pie ($5) are house specialties. *Pescados* (☎ 452-7237), 2801 P St, has great fish tacos for $1.50 each ($4 for two tacos, rice and beans), and 'Beach Blanket Bingo' decor.

There is an all-you-can-eat Chinese buffet at *New Lu Shan* (☎ 444-2543), 403 J St, which costs $5 for lunch and $7 for dinner.

Sacramento's only East Indian restaurant is *India Restaurant* (☎ 448-9046), 729 J St, whose spicy food is expensive for dinner but reasonable for lunch.

In an old barge on the north bank of the American River, the *Virgin Sturgeon* (☎ 921-2694),1577 Garden Hwy (west of I-5), is the locals' favorite for seafood ($8 to $14), barbecued ribs ($7), and Cuban black beans and rice ($5). The outside patio gets crowded with boaters drinking Bloody Marys on summer weekends.

The Fat and Paragary families both have several restaurants and a name synonymous with 'good food.' *California Fats* (☎ 441-7966), 1015 Front St in Old Sacramento,

---

Farmers' Markets

Look to buy excellent quality farm-fresh produce, homemade foods and herbs and spices, as well as fresh flowers at these collections of vendors. Check out Denio's Roseville Farmers' Market & Auction (☎ 782-2704) a less-direct market (the guys behind the counter don't actually raise the produce) Saturdays through Wednesdays year round. In summer, the Roosevelt Park Market, at the corner of 9th and P Sts, runs June through October on Tuesday mornings, and the Thursday Night Market at the K St Mall runs May through September. In nearby Davis, the Davis Farmers' Market, which is held in Central Park (between C and B Sts) Wednesdays from 2 to 7 pm and Saturdays 7 am to noon, is a good place to sample locally grown produce. ■

---

has pizzas, seafood, and grilled items with a California-Asian twist. Rock shrimp and mushroom pasta ($12) and potstickers with dipping sauces ($8) are house specialties.

Next door, but joined at the kitchen, *Fat City* (☎ 446-6768), 1001 Front St, has Old Sacramento ambiance and a straightforward selection of grilled meats and fish, sandwiches, salads, and pastas for $8 to $16.

Paragary's (☎ 456-5121), 2726 N St at the corner of 27th, is the epitome of good taste – white tablecloths, wood paneling, large pieces of colorful art, a great wine list and quality pasta, meat, and fish for $8 to $15.

The trendy *River City Brewing Company* (☎ 447-2739), in the Downtown Plaza near the K St entrance, serves nouvelle cuisine with Thai, Southwest and Italian influences. The blue-cheese burger ($8), grilled chicken breast with black bean sauce ($12), and smoked mozzarella pizza ($10) are all good. Beer costs $3 a pint.

Entertainment

Pick up a copy of the *Sacramento News & Review*, available at cafes, restaurants and music stores, for a list of current happenings around town.

Cinema The *Crest Theater* (☎ 442-7378), 1013 K St, shows classic, foreign, and alternative films in its old theater, new releases in its recently renovated auditorium.

Bars & Clubs With five clubs – including a tropical beach bar, country & western dance hall, and comedy club – under one roof, *America Live!* (☎ 447-5483), in the Downtown Plaza shopping mall, is basically an after-dark department store. Also in the Downtown Plaza, the *River City Brewing Company* (see Places to Eat) has a yuppified chic-industrial setting and good microbrews.

Busby Berkeley's (☎ 443-1234), on the top floor of the Hyatt Regency at 1209 L St, has a great view and happy hour from 5 to 6 pm. Tucked away in a residential neighborhood, *The Fox & Goose* (☎ 443-8825), 1001 R St, has live music (usually blues or reggae) Wednesday to Sunday nights after 9 pm.

The *Cattle Club* (☎ 386-0390), 7042 Folsom Blvd, has an excellent local live rock scene that does its best not to fit Sacramento's square mold. The *Crest Theater* (see above) hosts live bands.

Performing Arts The *Community Center Theater*, in the Sacramento Convention Center, is home to Sacramento's Opera, Ballet, Symphony and most big-name entertainers who come to town. For ticket information call the box office (☎ 264-5181), in the theater lobby at 1301 L St.

The intimate *B Street Theater* (☎ 443-5300), 2711 B St, hosts off-Broadway plays of contemporary playwrights, while the *Show Below Theater* (☎ 446-2787), in the basement of an old Victorian at the corner of 22nd and L Sts, has obscure dramas and comedies.

Spectator Sports The Kings, Sacramento's professional basketball team, plays home games at the *Arco Arena* from November to May. Every game in the Kings' history has been sold out, but there are often tickets available at the arena box office right before game time. Tickets cost $12 to $45. For schedule information call ☎ 928-3650.

Getting There & Away

Air The small but busy Sacramento Metropolitan Airport (☎ 648-0700), 15 miles north of downtown off I-5, is serviced by Alaska, America West, American, Delta, Southwest, Horizon Air, Northwest, United, and TWA.

Bus Greyhound (☎ 482-4993, 444-7270), at the corner of 7th and L Sts, goes to San Francisco ($9) every hour on the half hour from 6:30 am to 6:30 pm. Seven buses daily leave for Los Angeles ($35).

Train Sacramento's Amtrak Passenger Depot is between downtown and Old Sac at 4th and I Sts. Trains leave daily for Chicago, Seattle, Los Angeles, and San Diego; ticket prices depend on availability. Trains to San Francisco ($14) leave three times daily.

Getting Around

To/From the Airport Numerous shuttle services connect Sacramento's airport to downtown ($9), West Sacramento ($20), and Davis ($20). There are complimentary phones in the airport terminals, and an information booth in front of terminal 6. Shuttles pick up from the median curb in front of the restaurant building.

Taxi service to get downtown is about $24 for one to four people.

Bus Sacramento Regional Transit buses run daily from 5 am to 10 pm and cost $1.25 for a one-hour ride including one transfer. Sacramento's light rail system (also run by Regional Transit) stops along K St, but is mostly used for the commute to outlying communities. For route and schedule information call ☎ 321-2877.

Car Most car rental agencies have booths at the airport in the car rental terminal (serviced by a free shuttle from the main airport terminals). These include Alamo (☎ 646-6020), Avis (☎ 922-6501), Budget (☎ 922-7316), Hertz (☎ 927-3882) and National (☎ 568-2415).

Companies not at the airport tend to be a bit cheaper. These include Enterprise (☎ 446-6444), Senator Ford (☎ 392-4225), and Thrifty (☎ 447-2847), each of which will arrange a pick-up and/or drop-off at the airport, bus or train station.

Taxi Service is regulated and costs $2.80 for the first mile and $2.20 for each additional mile. Camelia City Cab Company (☎ 381-6868), and Yellow Cab (☎ 444-2222) are Sacramento's two main companies. The Hyatt Regency on L St always has a surplus of cabs.

DAVIS
• *pop 46,000 ☎ 916*

Davis is primarily a college town centering around the University of California, Davis (UCD), one of the top schools in the US for medicine and agriculture. The student population supports a good, slightly alternative cafe and pub scene during the week, but heads to Tahoe or San Francisco on weekends, leaving the town as boring as its landscape (Davis' only hill is a bridge over the railroad tracks). The conservative year-round population lets out a big sigh of relief each spring when classes end.

Orientation
Interstate 80 skirts the south edge of town, with the Davis/Olive St exit giving the easiest access to downtown, via Richards Blvd and 1st St . Lettered streets run north-south, and numbered streets run east-west. The main thoroughfares are B, F, and G Sts, and E 8th St.

UCD lies southwest of downtown, bordered by A St, 1st St, and Russell Blvd. The campus's main entrances are from I-80 via Old Davis Rd, or from downtown via 3rd St.

Information
Davis' small chamber of commerce and visitors center (☎ 756-5160), 228 B St, has a good city map for $1.50, a dining and lodging guide, and schedules for regional transportation (including Amtrak). For information about current events, check the bulletin boards in cafes, bookshops, and campus buildings.

For books, the *Avid Reader* (☎ 758-4040), 617 2nd St, has a good selection and is open until 11 pm; while *Bogey's Books* (☎ 757-6127), 733 E St, deals in used and out-of-print books. The campus bookstore (☎ 752-2580), in the student union, has a large selection and UCD souvenirs. Just outside the door is a rideboard where students who need or are willing to give rides (usually to the Bay Area) post notices.

Things to See & Do
The Davis Art Association publishes a small brochure (available at the chamber of commerce) with information about art in public spaces. The one-room, nonprofit **Pence Gallery** (☎ 758-3370), 212 D St, has exhibits of contemporary California art, and frequent lectures. It is open Tuesday to Saturday from noon to 4 pm, and is free.

Free **UCD campus tours** are available weekends at 10 am and 1 pm, and on weekdays by appointment. For information call ☎ 752-8111, or stop by the Buehler Alumni & Visitors Center on Old Davis Rd. Campus maps are available at the visitors center, and at all campus entrances.

From May to August, the Davis Summerfest features food vendors, street performers and live bands from 5:30 to 8:30 pm on Wednesday nights.

Places to Stay
Reservations are imperative in May and September.

Motels The *Davis Motel* (☎ 756-0910), on the south side of I-80 at 1111 Richards Blvd, is the only motel in Davis that is not downtown. They have a pool, and rooms with microwaves and refrigerators for $42/56 a single/double.

Rooms at the *Econo Lodge* (☎ 756-1040, 800-424-4777), 221 D St, are a little old but include a refrigerator, small microwave, and coffee maker for $46/52.

Directly across from UCD's east entrance, the *Aggie Inn* (☎ 756-0352), 245 1st St, has homey rooms for $62/66, free coffee and pastries, and an outdoor spa. Also near the campus, the *Best Western University Lodge* (☎ 756-7890, 800-528-1234), 123 B St at the corner of 2nd St, has nice rooms for $59/65.

The *Ramada Inn* (☎ 753-3600), 110 F St, has a small pool and rooms for $59/65.

B&Bs The *Davis Bed 'n' Breakfast Inn* (☎ 753-9611), 422 A St, has an old-fashioned living room and cozy rooms with private baths for $55.

A block away at 304 A St, the *University Inn Bed and Breakfast* (☎ 800-756-8648) has complimentary fruit, chocolates, and coffee, and rooms with private baths for $50 to $65.

Places to Eat
Davis' student population demands cheap, convenient food and coffee by the gallons. At the corner of 3rd and A Sts is a concentration of cheap restaurants, including a taqueria, middle eastern restaurant, and grilled sandwich shop.

Osaka Sushi (☎ 758-2288), 630 G St, has sushi to rival San Francisco's best, and excellent sashimi, tempura, and teriyaki dinners for $8 to $14.

The small, casual *Crepe Bistro* (☎ 753-2575), set back from the street in a shopping center at 234 E St, has sweet and savory crepes for around $5 and big salads for $4 to $7.

Sudwerk (☎ 758-8700), south of the freeway at 2001 2nd St, is a German brewery that serves home-brewed beer, bratwurst and sauerkraut, burgers, and large salads for around $10.

Getting There & Away
Bus Yolobus (☎ 800-371-2877) runs between Davis and Sacramento 10 times daily and costs $1.50 one-way. Buses leave from the UCD Memorial Union on the corner of 5th St and Howard Way.

Unitrans (☎ 752-2877) has double-decker red buses which shuttle people around the UCD campus for 50¢. Buses stop at blue and white ASUCD signs, and run weekdays 7:30 am to 5 pm.

Train Davis' Amtrak station (☎ 758-4220) is at the corner of 2nd and H St, on the southern edge of downtown. Seven eastbound trains go to Sacramento ($7) and Reno, Nevada ($11), and seven westbound trains go to San Francisco ($14) daily.

YUBA CITY & MARYSVILLE
• *pops 27,437 & 12,324* ☎ *916*
These twin cities are joined by two bridges spanning the Feather River and basically function as one: Yuba City provides shopping malls, automotive stores, and fast food restaurants, while Marysville entertains tourists with its historic downtown, Victorian-style architecture, and concentration of Chinese history. Due to floods caused by early mining practices, Marysville is entirely surrounded by levees, making its business district compact.

These towns are also part of the Northern Mines section of Gold Country.

History
As the head of the Feather River, Marysville boomed during the Gold Rush when nearly all people and supplies destined for the northern mines passed through her gates. A large Chinese population settled to work in the mines, and remained in Marysville to work on the railroad when it pushed through in the early 1900s.

In 1841, John Sutter established Hock Farm, the first large-scale agricultural project in Northern California, just south of present day Yuba City. Its proximity to Marysville's port made it an agricultural trade center. The rich and elite built their houses in Yuba City (along 2nd St), giving the town great political sway, and in 1899 Yuba City became the seat of Sutter County.

Orientation & Information

Highway 99 runs north-south along Yuba City's western edge. Highway 20 runs east-west through Yuba City as Colusa Ave (the main thoroughfare), crosses the Feather River Bridge, and runs into Marysville as 10th St.

Yuba City's historic district lies south of Hwy 20 along Plumas Ave and 2nd St. The heart of Marysville's central business and historic district is between 1st and 5th, and B and E Sts.

The best place to pick up brochures and walking-tour maps is at the Mary Aaron Museum (☎ 743-1004), 704 D St, in Marysville, open Tuesday to Saturday from 1:30 to 4:30 pm. The Best Western, 1001 Clark Ave at the corner of Hwy 20 in Yuba City, also has maps and brochures and is open 24 hours.

Marysville's main post office is at the corner of 4th and C Sts, right across from Wells Fargo Bank.

Things to See

The **Community Memorial Museum of Sutter County** (☎ 741-7141), 1333 Butte House Rd, Yuba City, chronicles Sutter County history from the Maidu Indians to present-day farmers, and has some amusing 1850s photographs. It's free and open Tuesday to Friday from 9 am to 5 pm, on weekends noon to 4 pm.

South of central Yuba City on 2nd St, are the 1899 Sutter County Courthouse, Hall of Records, and graceful houses which reflect Victorian, Italianate, and Classical architecture. Julia Morgan (of Hearst Castle fame) designed the Kline-Smith House at 364 2nd St.

The **Mary Aaron Museum** (☎ 743-1004), housed in a 1855 Gothic Revival brick structure at 704 D St, Marysville, has local history exhibits, including artifacts and photographs from Marysville's Chinese community. The 150-year-old dragon costume used each year in Marys-

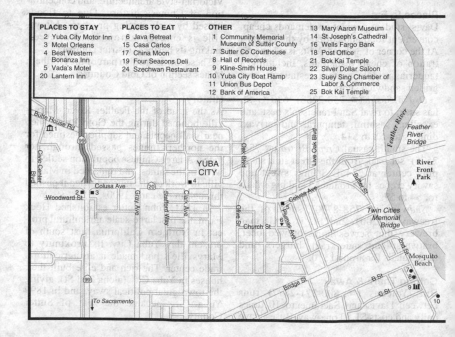

PLACES TO STAY	PLACES TO EAT	OTHER	
2 Yuba City Motor Inn	6 Java Retreat	1 Community Memorial	13 Mary Aaron Museum
3 Motel Orleans	15 Casa Carlos	Museum of Sutter County	14 St Joseph's Cathedral
4 Best Western	17 China Moon	7 Sutter Co Courthouse	16 Wells Fargo Bank
Bonanza Inn	19 Four Seasons Deli	8 Hall of Records	18 Post Office
5 Vada's Motel	24 Szechwan Restaurant	9 Kline-Smith House	21 Bok Kai Temple
20 Lantern Inn		10 Yuba City Boat Ramp	22 Silver Dollar Saloon
		11 Union Bus Depot	23 Suey Sing Chamber of
		12 Bank of America	Labor & Commerce
			25 Bok Kai Temple

ville's Bok Kai Festival is outstanding. One block east is St Joseph's Cathedral, built in 1855.

At the southern end of B, C, and D Sts is Marysville's **Chinatown** – the largest, most active, and best preserved in the Gold Country. The Suey Sing Chamber of Labor & Commerce, 305 1st St, is still the community hub and the Buddhist Church is the central place of worship. The **Bok Kai Temple**, at the southern end of D St behind the Silver Dollar Saloon, is the only temple dedicated to *Bok Eye* (the water god) in California. The temple is only open on Bomb Day (the first Sunday in March), at the end of the two-day Bok Kai Festival.

Places to Stay

Accommodations are concentrated along Hwys 99 and 20 in Yuba City. *Motel Orleans* (☎ 674-1592), at the junction of Hwys 99 and 20, has an outdoor pool and modern rooms for $32/37. Across Hwy 99,

the *Yuba City Motor Inn* (☎ 674-4000), has a spa, pool, nice lobby, and rooms for $63/75. *Vada's Motel* (☎ 671-1151), 545 Colusa Ave, has budget rooms for $30/38.

In Marysville, the *Lantern Inn* (☎ 742-6946), is at the busy corner of 1st and E Sts, walking distance to downtown. Rooms cost $42/45.

Places to Eat

For good coffee, sandwiches, and salads, try the arty *Java Retreat*, 728 Plumas St in Yuba City, open from 6 am until late.

Casa Carlos (☎ 742-7793), 413 6th St, serves big Mexican dinners for $7 to $9, and lethal pitchers of margaritas for $4.50. The *Szechwan Restaurant* (☎ 743-0660), 223 1st St, has a reputation for serving the most authentic Chinese food in Marysville, while *China Moon* is more elegant. Prices are around $4 for lunch, and $6 to $8 for dinner, at both places.

The *Four Seasons Deli* (☎ 743-8221), 423 B St, is a popular spot for sandwiches, soups, and salads.

The *Silver Dollar Saloon* (☎ 642-9020), at the corner of D and 1st Sts, serves Marysville's best steaks, barbecued chicken, and ribs – not recommended for vegetarians. Prices are $6 to $14. The bar came around Cape Horn in the 1850s and is laden with silver. Live country bands stir up a crowd on Friday and Saturday nights.

Getting There & Away

Greyhound buses leave from Marysville's Union Bus Station at 905 5th St, and go to Sacramento five times daily for $9 and San Francisco twice daily for $20.

Amtrak has two trains and three buses daily which go to Sacramento for $13, and San Francisco for $28.

OROVILLE
• *pop 12,300* ☎ 916

The town's biggest claim to fame is the Oroville Dam, nine miles northeast of town, whose construction in the 1960s created Lake Oroville. Besides the dam and the recreational opportunities afforded by the Lake Oroville State Recreation Area,

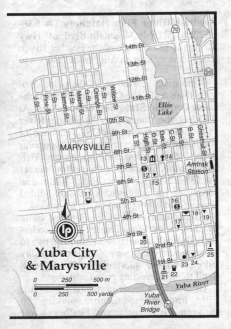

Yuba City & Marysville

Joss Houses

'Joss,' which in pidgin English means 'deity,' is a corruption of the Portuguese word *deos* which early navigators applied to idols they found in the East Indies. Joss Houses were the principle places of worship for Chinese miners, and often the only public symbol of Chinese culture in mining towns.

The exterior of a Joss House was usually very simple, while the interior was decorated with rich and symbolic ornamentation. The principle images represented were the 'God of Sombre Heavens,' 'God of War,' 'God of Medicine,' and 'God of Wealth,' combining characteristics of Buddhism, Taoism, and Confucianism. Men came to the Joss House to ask special favors of a god, or to offer prayers and supplication.

The rituals required to 'talk' with a god were very formalized. A man entered the Joss House, made a bow with clasped hands, lit the appropriate candles and incense, knelt on a mat, and called the god by name three times. He then took two semi-oval blocks of wood called 'Yum Yeung Puey' and tossed them into the air. If both blocks landed in the same position it was an unfavorable omen. If one block faced up and the other faced down, it meant that the god had to be persuaded. The worshipper then knocked his head on the ground three times, offered his petition, and took a cylindrical pot of numbered bamboo slips and shook the pot until one of them fell out. The priest or Joss House keeper checked the number, and looked up the omen in an ancient text. The priest then beat drums and rang the Joss House bells while the worshipper burned paper money as final payment. At last the fortune was told.

The Bok Kai Temple in Marysville, only open once a year during the Bok Kai Festival, is the only remaining Joss House in the Gold Country. Nevada City's Firehouse No 1 Museum has a reconstructed altar from an 1860s Joss House, and a good collection of related Chinese relics. ■

Oroville is basically a service town for the surrounding area, with its cattle ranches and olive, nut and citrus orchards.

The Oroville Ranger Station, La Porte Ranger District (☎ 534-6500) at 875 Mitchell Ave is open weekdays, 8 am to 4:30 pm, with maps and information for the Plumas National Forest.

For current road conditions, especially if you'll be heading up into the mountains in winter, phone ☎ 800-427-7623.

Things to See & Do

The **Chinese Temple** (☎ 538-2496) at 1500 Broderick St was built in 1863 to serve Oroville's Chinese community, which was the second largest in California after San Francisco's. Tours of the temple and grounds are given Wednesday to Friday from 11 am to 3 pm, Sunday noon to 3 pm (closed December 15 to January 31). You can see Chinook salmon jumping the fish ladder during their annual migration from September to November at the

Feather River Fish Hatchery (☎ 538-2222) at 5 Table Mountain Blvd, off Hwy 70 on the north bank of the Feather River. The hatchery is open daily from 7:30 am to 4 pm.

Nine miles northeast of Oroville, Oroville Dam and Lake Oroville are part of the **Lake Oroville State Recreation Area**. At 770 feet, this dam across the Feather River is the tallest dam in the USA, and one of the highest dams ever built. It's a popular place for recreation. Pick up the free *Visitor's Guide*, available at the visitors center (☎ 538-2219), 917 Kelly Ridge Rd, and in Oroville, for suggestions on self-guided driving and hiking tours in the area.

Hiking trails include the **Feather Falls Trail** to the 640-foot Feather Falls (moderately difficult, seven miles roundtrip, two to three hours each way – a good all-day hike), and the quarter-mile **Bald Rock Trail** to an interesting rock formation.

Highway 70 heads northeast from Oroville into the mountains, snaking up through the magnificent Feather River

Canyon. During autumn the leaves change colors, making this a most scenic drive.

Special Events

Held for one week in May, Feather Fiesta Days, celebrates the discovery of gold at Bidwell Bar on the Feather River in 1848. Bidwell Bar is now submerged by the lake, but townsfolk gather on the shore in period costume to celebrate their history.

Places to Stay & Eat

The Lake Oroville Visitors Center has maps and details of USFS campgrounds, including Bidwell Canyon Campground; make reservations through Destinet.

Houseboats can be rented at Bidwell Canyon Marina (☎ 589-3165, 800-637-1767) on the south end of the lake, or at the Lime Saddle Marina (☎ 800-834-7517) on the west branch of the Feather River. Both places also rent boats for getting to those boat-in campgrounds.

Feather River Blvd, which runs along the east side of Hwy 70 is the 'motel row,' with chain motels in the $30 to $50 range.

Jean Pratt's Riverside B&B (☎ 533-1413) at 45 Cabana Drive is in a secluded spot on the west bank of the Feather River just off Oro Dam Blvd. Rooms and suites range from $53 to $95. Overlooking the lake, the *Lake Oroville B&B* (☎ 589-0700) at 240 Sunday Drive, Berry Creek, has six rooms at $65 to $110.

The *Cornucopia Restaurant & Pie Shop*, on Montgomery St on the east side of Hwy 70, is open 24 hours, as is *Jerry's Restaurant* a few blocks south on Feather River Blvd.

Getting There & Away

Greyhound buses heading north and south

Ishi

In the early morning of August 29, 1911, a frantic barking of dogs woke the butchers sleeping inside a slaughterhouse outside of Oroville. When they came out, they found their dogs holding a man at bay – an Indian clad only in a loincloth, who was starving, exhausted, afraid, and spoke no English.

They called the sheriff, who took the man to the jail until something could be decided. Newspapers declared a 'wild man' had been discovered, and people thronged in, hoping to see him. Local Indians came and tried to communicate with him in Maidu and Wintu, but to no avail – his language was different from those of the surrounding tribes.

Anthropologists from the University of California, Berkeley, Professors Kroeber and Waterman, read the accounts in the news; Waterman took the train to Oroville and, using lists of vocabulary words of the Yana Indians who had once lived in this region, discovered that the man belonged to the Yahi, the southernmost tribe of the Yanas, that until this man showed up had been believed to be extinct.

Waterman took 'Ishi', meaning 'man' in his own language, to the museum at the university, where he was cared for and brought back to health. Ishi spent his remaining years there, telling the anthropologists his life story and teaching them his tribal language, lore, and ways.

Ishi's tribe had been virtually exterminated by settlers before Ishi was born; when he was a child, around 1870, there were only about 12 or 15 Yahis left, hiding in remote areas in the foothills east of Red Bluff. Ishi, his mother, his sister, and an old man were all that were left of the Yahi by 1908. In that year the others died and Ishi was left alone. On March 25, 1916 Ishi died of tuberculosis at the university hospital, and the Yahi disappeared forever.

The book *Ishi in Two Worlds: A Biography of the Last Wild Indian in North America* by Theodora Kroeber, tells Ishi's story. While in Oroville you can drive to the site of the slaughterhouse where he was found but all that remains is a monument by the side of the road. Part of the Lassen National Forest in the foothills east of Red Bluff, including Deer Creek and other areas where Ishi and the Yahis lived, is now called the Ishi Wilderness. If you go to Berkeley, you can also see the exhibit on Ishi at the university museum. ∎

stop at the Budget Inn at 580 Oro Dam Blvd, a couple of blocks east of Hwy 70. Tickets are sold at the hotel office from 10 am to 6 pm daily. Butte County Transit (☎ 534-9999, 800-822-8145) operates a bus to the Kelly Ridge area of Lake Oroville.

CHICO
• pop 47,000 ☎ 916

Chico is a university town, which means you'll find a vibrant youthful feel and more going on than you'd expect from its size. Chico was founded in 1860 by John Bidwell, who came to California in 1841 and proceeded to make himself one of its most illustrious early pioneers. In the late 1840s he purchased 40 sq miles here, called the Rancho del Arroyo Chico. In 1868, after a term as a California congressman in Washington, DC, he married Annie Ellicott Kennedy, daughter of a prominent Washington official, and they moved to the new mansion he had built, now the Bidwell

John & Annie Bidwell

John Bidwell, founder of Chico, was one of California's most prominent pioneers. Born in New York in 1819, he left home to attend school in Ohio, continued west to Missouri, and on to the then-Mexican province of Alta California. In spring of 1841, several years before the Gold Rush, he organized the first overland wagon train to California, which arrived safely in November, 1841.

Soon after arriving, Bidwell began working for John Sutter. He later supported the Bear Flag Revolt in 1846 and served in the Mexican-American War, attaining the rank of general. After the war he returned to Sutter's Fort and was present when James Marshall discovered gold there in January, 1848. Bidwell carried the news to San Francisco, setting off the California Gold Rush.

Later in 1848, Bidwell discovered gold at Bidwell Bar on the middle fork of the Feather River, now submerged beneath Lake Oroville. The following year he began purchasing the land that he loved the most out of all he had seen in California, the 26,000-acre Rancho del Arroyo Chico. California agriculture was still in an experimental stage at the time, and Bidwell became one of its most ardent enthusiasts, importing and experimenting with a great variety of plants, animals, and farming techniques.

Entering politics, he was elected first to the state assembly, then to the state senate, and then, in 1865, the year the Civil War ended, to the US House of Representatives in Washington DC. In Washington he came into contact with the Kennedy family, most notably their eldest daughter Annie, whom he came to love 'more than all the world beside.' Annie, 20 years his junior, refused his proposal of marriage and Bidwell returned to California in March, 1867 where he turned his attention to getting his ranch organized, planting crops and trees, and renewing work on the mansion that is now the Bidwell Mansion State Historic Park – hoping to attract Annie to come to California and become his wife.

The two wrote long, impassioned letters to one another for many months, wherein he agreed not to pester her about love or marriage in exchange for her continued friendship. Then on October 7, 1867, she wrote to him a historic letter. It begins, 'Perhaps the contents of this note will surprise you, perhaps not,' and in it she agrees to marry him, leave her home in Washington, and live on his ranch in Chico.

They were married in Washington in April, 1868, and returned to Chico in May. They lived a long and happy life here, though they never had children. The Bidwells were very busy in the highest political and social circles of the growing state and they were benefactors to many charitable causes.

Annie and John both loved the growing town of Chico, which John had laid out near their mansion. After John died in 1900, Annie gave their favorite part of all their lands, the land near upper Chico Creek, to the city for a park; this is Bidwell Park today. Annie remained at the mansion in Chico until her death in 1918, continuing in the public service. The Bidwells are still beloved figures in Chico. ■

CALIFORNIA

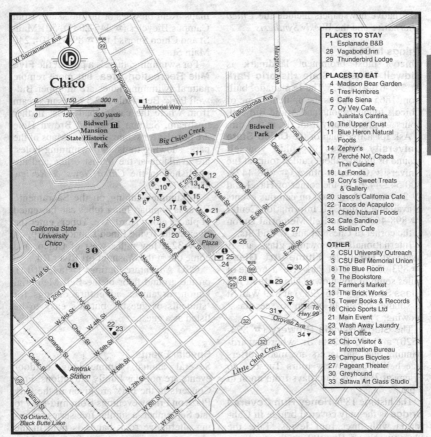

Chico

PLACES TO STAY
1 Esplanade B&B
28 Vagabond Inn
29 Thunderbird Lodge

PLACES TO EAT
4 Madison Bear Garden
5 Tres Hombres
6 Caffe Siena
7 Oy Vey Cafe,
    Juanita's Cantina
10 The Upper Crust
11 Blue Heron Natural
    Foods
14 Zephyr's
17 Perché No!, Chada
    Thai Cuisine
18 La Fonda
19 Cory's Sweet Treats
    & Gallery
20 Jasco's California Cafe
22 Tacos de Acapulco
31 Chico Natural Foods
32 Cafe Sandino
34 Sicilian Cafe

OTHER
2 CSU University Outreach
3 CSU Bell Memorial Union
8 The Blue Room
9 The Bookstore
12 Farmer's Market
13 The Brick Works
15 Tower Books & Records
16 Chico Sports Ltd
21 Main Event
23 Wash Away Laundry
24 Post Office
25 Chico Visitor &
    Information Bureau
26 Campus Bicycles
27 Pageant Theater
30 Greyhound
33 Satava Art Glass Studio

Mansion State Historic Park. After John died in 1900, Annie continued as a philanthropist there until her death in 1918.

Downtown Chico is flat, relatively compact, and easy to get around – just look for the compass directions on the streets to figure out if you are east or west. The Esplanade and Main St divide east and west addresses.

Orientation & Information
The Chico Visitor & Information Bureau (☎ 891-5556) is at 500 Main St. It offers free maps, plenty of information on things to do, and a monthly calendar of events.

The AAA (☎ 891-8601) at 2221 Forest Ave, near Hwy 99, is open weekdays from 8:30 am to 5 pm.

From mid-May to late September the weather is very hot, with 110°F days cooling off to the 80s or 90s at night.

The Bookstore, 118 Main St, has millions of quality used books. Tower Books & Records at 211 Main St is open every day from 9 am to midnight, making browsing a popular nighttime activity in Chico.

Pick up a copy of the excellent free weekly newspaper, the *Chico News & Review*, to find out what's happening around town; it comes out every Thursday.

Alternative newspapers include the *Chico Alternative* and the *Weekly Synthesis*.

Things to See

Chico's most prominent landmark is **Bidwell Mansion State Historic Park** (☎ 345-6144) at 525 The Esplanade, built from 1865 to 1868 as the opulent home of Chico's founders John and Annie Bidwell. Tours are given hourly from 10 am to 4 pm.

Ask for a free map of the **Chico State University** campus to guide yourself around or inquire about guided tours at the University Outreach office (☎ 898-4428, 800-542-4426) on the corner of Hazel and W 2nd Sts. Information on campus events is available at the CSU Information Center (☎ 898-4636) in the Bell Memorial Union at the corner of Chestnut and W 2nd Sts.

Internationally renowned glass art is made at **Orient & Flume Art Glass** (☎ 893-0373) at 2161 Park Ave, a couple of miles south of downtown. The **Satava Art Glass Studio** (☎ 345-7985) at 819 Wall St is smaller but is an option to see glass-blowing.

The **Sierra Nevada Brewery** (☎ 893-3520) at 1075 E 20th St, where award-winning ales and lagers are made, offers free half-hour brewery tours Tuesday to Friday at 2:30 pm, Saturdays from noon to 3 pm.

The historic 1894 **Honey Run Covered Bridge** is the only covered bridge in California with three roof levels. Take the Skyway exit off Hwy 99 on the southern outskirts of Chico, head east about a mile, turn left onto Honey Run-Humbug Rd, and the bridge is five miles along.

Activities

The extensive **Bidwell Park** stretches 10 miles northwest along Chico Creek, starting from downtown. In 1937 *The Adventures of Robin Hood* was filmed here; parts of *Gone With the Wind* were filmed here in 1938, and in 1950 *The Red Badge of Courage* was shot here. In the park, the **Chico Creek Nature Center** (☎ 891-4671), about two miles east of downtown, offers nature exhibits and events, and park

maps. Rent bicycles or in-line skates from Campus Bicycles (☎ 345-2081), 501 Main St and Chico Sports Ltd (☎ 894-1110), 240 Main St.

For swimming, there's a pool at the **Five Mile Recreation Area**, but more remote natural swimming holes are in upper Bidwell Park: Bear Hole is 2.5 miles upstream from where the paved road ends; further upstream, Salmon Hole and Brown Hole are popular for skinny-dipping. Maps of the park, showing trails and swimming holes, are available at the tourist office and are published in the *Chico News & Review Visitor Guide*.

In summer, tubing on the Sacramento River is popular; inner tubes can be rented at places along Nord Ave. Tubers enter the river at the Irvine Finch Launch Ramp, on Hwy 32 a few miles west of Chico, and come out at the Washout off River Rd.

CSU Adventure Outings (☎ 898-4011), on the ground floor of the Bell Memorial Union, organizes adventure outings for 'students or guests,' but it's easy to be listed as a guest.

Special Events

Several annual summer-long outdoor events are popular family attractions. Free Concerts in the Park are given in the City Plaza on Friday evenings from mid-May to late September; a similar free series featuring alternative rock bands is held in the plaza on Tuesday evenings from late May to late October. Shakespeare in the Park (☎ 891-4081) at Cedar Grove in lower Bidwell Park runs from mid-July to the end of August.

Places to Stay

Camping The Woodson Bridge State Recreation Area (☎ 916-839-2112, 800-444-7275) about 25 miles north on Hwy 99, then west towards Corning, has a pleasant campground with tent and RV sites on the riverbank for $12 per night. Black Butte Lake (☎ 916-865-4781) about a 35-minute drive west from Chico past Orland is another option.

Motels & Hotels Good-value motels are found in three convenient areas in Chico: downtown, on The Esplanade, and beside Hwy 99 at the Cohasset Rd exit. This is a campus town though – graduation and homecoming ceremonies can fill up hotels and raise the price. Downtown motels include the *Thunderbird Lodge* (☎ 343-7911), 715 Main St with singles/doubles at $35/40, and the similarly priced *Vagabond Inn* (☎ 895-1323), 630 Main St. The *Rio Lindo Motel* (☎ 342-7555), 2324 The Esplanade, is a good deal at $28/31. The quiet and secure *Safari Motel* (☎ 343-3201) at 2352 The Esplanade, charges $37/39. The *Holiday Inn* (☎ 345-2491, 800-310-2491), 685 Manzanita Court, is the largest and fanciest hotel in Chico, with a restaurant, bar, dancing on weekends, and rooms at $72. There are cheaper chain hotels along this strip as well.

B&Bs The *Esplanade B&B* (☎ 345-8084) at 620 The Esplanade, opposite the Bidwell Mansion, has six rooms from $45 to $65.

In an attractive almond orchard near town, *Johnson's Country Inn* (☎ 345-7829) at 3935 Morehead Ave, has four rooms from $80 to $125. *Palms of Chico* (☎ 343-6868) at 1525 Dayton, on a 40-acre organic farm about a mile southwest of town, has five rooms at $75/85.

Places to Eat
Natural food supermarkets include *Chico Natural Foods* at 818 Main St and *Blue Heron Natural Foods* at 256 E 1st St at the corner of Wall St. An outdoor *Farmers' Market* is held in the city parking lot at the corner of Wall and E 2nd Sts on Saturdays from 7:30 am to 1 pm year round; from June to September it's held again on Wednesdays from 5:30 to 8:30 pm.

For a 'down home' breakfast, *Kalico Kitchen* at 2396 The Esplanade serves ample portions of good inexpensive food with fast, friendly service, and air conditioning. *Cory's Sweet Treats & Gallery* at 230 W 3rd St is a popular breakfast and Sunday brunch spot; it's closed Monday. The *Upper Crust* at 130 Main St has fine

baked goods and light meals. There's live music on Thursday, Friday, and Saturday nights. The *Oy Vey Cafe* at 146 2nd St, open every day from 7 am to 3 pm, features bagels baked on the premises. Across the street, *Perchè No!* has Belgian waffles, Italian gelato, and espresso. *Chada Thai Cuisine* at 117-B W 2nd St serves authentic vegetarian Thai food for lunch and dinner every day except Sunday.

A Chico favorite, *Jasco's California Cafe* upstairs in the Phoenix Building on the corner of Broadway and W 3rd St, serves excellent California-style food, gourmet pizza, and good lunch specials.

Gashouse Pizza, a 'living legend,' has two branches: one at 2359 The Esplanade and the original, smaller pizzeria, in a former gas station at 1444 Park Ave on the corner of E 15th St. The *Sicilian Cafe* at 1020 Main St, is famous for its superb family-style Italian dinners. For fondues, try *Rubino's Cafe* at 2626 Cohasset Rd, three miles from downtown across Hwy 99.

Juanita's Cantina at 126 W 2nd St has tasty organic Mexican food and live music every night. Other inexpensive Mexican fare can be found at *Cafe Sandino*, 817 Main St and at *Tacos de Acapulco*, 429 Ivy St at W 5th St, which is popular with students. *La Fonda*, at the corner of Salem and W 2nd Sts has an inexpensive taco and tostada bar with unlimited trips. *Tres Hombres* at 100 Broadway is good fun for drinking and people-watching, and stays open until 2 am.

Top-end *Zephyr's* (☎ 895-1328) at 192 E 3rd St has a simple atmosphere but it's famous for its gourmet food. It's open for lunch Tuesday to Friday, dinner Tuesday to Saturday, and sometimes for Sunday brunch.

Entertainment
The *Madison Bear Garden* at 316 W 2nd St, on the corner of Salem St, is a fun restaurant/saloon popular with college students. There's dancing on Thursday, Friday, and Saturday nights, and nightly drink specials. *La Salle's* at 229 Broadway is another weekend dance spot for young

people, while the *Brick Works* at the corner of Wall and E 2nd Sts draws a slightly older crowd. The *Sierra Nevada Taproom & Restaurant*, featuring ales and lagers, at the Sierra Nevada Brewery, 1075 E 20th St, is a popular bar/restaurant open Tuesday to Saturday from 11 am to 11 pm, Sunday from 10 am to 2 pm,

Country music reigns at the *Jolly Fox* at 2601 The Esplanade, just north of East Ave, with a live dance band Wednesday, Friday, and Saturday nights, a casino and card room.

The *Main Event* at 319 Main St and the *Blue Room* at 139 W 1st St are bars with live music on weekends. For live music in a coffeehouse atmosphere, check out *Upper Crust* and *Caffe Siena*; *Juanita's Cantina* also has live music (see Places to Eat).

For theater, concerts, art exhibits, and other cultural events at the CSU campus, contact the CSU box office (☎ 898-5791) or the CSU Information Center (☎ 898-4636) in the Bell Memorial Union.

The *Pageant Theatre* (☎ 343-0663) at 351 E 6th St, screens international and 'alternative' films; Monday is bargain night.

Getting There & Away

The Chico airport is small and flights expensive; so if you must fly, head to Sacramento instead.

The Greyhound depot (☎ 343-8266) is at 717 Wall St. Four buses heading north and south depart daily. Butte County Transit (☎ 916-534-9999) has buses to Paradise, Oroville, and Gridley every day except Sunday. Amtrak has a station at the corner of W 5th and Orange Sts. It's unattended but the schedule for train and Amtrak Thruway bus connections is posted on the wall. Tickets can be purchased at travel agencies. Notices from people offering or seeking shared rides are posted on the ride board in the Bell Memorial Union building, on the CSU campus near the corner of W 2nd St and Chestnut St.

Rental car companies in town include Enterprise Rental Cars (☎ 899-1188) at 2267 The Esplanade and Northstate Auto Rentals (☎ 342-9637) at 196 Humboldt Ave. There are more companies at the airport.

RED BLUFF

• *pop 13,000 ☎ 916*

Red Bluff is a small, relaxing town where Victorian-era homes line quiet, shady, tree-lined streets and ice-cream socials and rodeos bring the community together. Because it's at the junction of I-5 and Hwy 99, many people pass through, and it's a convenient base for visits to Lassen Volcanic National Park (see the Northern Mountains chapter).

Orientation & Information

Most of the town is on the west bank of the Sacramento River, on the west side of I-5. The town's main intersection is the corner of Antelope Blvd and Main St. The historic Victorian neighborhood is in the blocks west of Main St. Many motels, fast-food places and 24-hour gas stations and restaurants serving drive-through travelers are on Antelope Blvd near the junction of I-5.

Main St has many other services including the chamber of commerce (☎ 527-6220, 800-655-6255) at 100 Main St. The post office is on the corner of Jefferson and Walnut Sts. Launderland is at 259-D S Main St; D&S E-Z Wash is in the Holiday Market shopping center at the corner of Antelope Blvd and Chestnut Ave.

Things to See & Do

The chamber of commerce has a free brochure for a self-guided tour of the Victorian homes and there are many antique stores both on and off Main St. The **Kelly-Griggs House Museum** (☎ 527-1129) at 311 Washington St, a classical Victorian home with period furnishings and exhibits, is open for tours Thursday to Sunday from 2 to 5 pm in summer, to 4 pm in winter.

On a beautiful bluff overlooking the Sacramento River the **William B Ide Adobe State Historic Park** (☎ 529-8599) at 21659 Adobe Rd preserves the original adobe home and grounds of pioneer William B Ide who came to California with his wife and children in 1845, 'fought' in the 1846 Bear Flag Revolt at Sonoma to win California's independence from Mexico, and was named president of the short-lived California Republic until California came under the protection of the US. To get there, turn east from Main St onto Adobe Rd about a mile north of downtown and go about another mile, following the signs.

The **Red Bluff Lake Recreation Area** has hiking trails, bicycle paths, boat ramps, a wildlife viewing area. The **Tehama-Colusa Fish Facility & Salmon Viewing Plaza** (☎ 527-3043) on Sale Lane at the Diversion Dam has year-round educational displays on Chinook salmon and steelhead trout, both of which migrate up the Sacramento River to spawn. The fish are most abundant from September to December.

Rafting on the Sacramento River is popular in summer. Rafts can be rented at Jelly's Ferry (☎ 527-3016), 21785 Bend Ferry Rd, a few miles north of town.

Places to Stay
The *Sycamore Grove Camping Area* (☎ 246-5313) in the Red Bluff Lake Recreation Area, is a quiet, attractive USFS campground; spaces are $10 per night, first come, first grabbed. The *Bend RV Park* (☎ 527-6289), is on the Sacramento River about four miles north of Red Bluff. Tent/RV sites are $11/18, with cheaper weekly and monthly rates. Take the Jellys Ferry Rd exit from I-5, four miles north of Red Bluff, and head east 2.5 miles, following the signs.

Most hotels are along Antelope Blvd and Main St. *King's Lodge* (☎ 527-6020, 800-426-5655) at 38 Antelope Blvd, is an attractive motel with singles/doubles at $30/37. The *Sky Terrace Motel* (☎ 527-4145) at 99 Main St has rooms at $24/29 and cheaper weekly rates, and the *Lamplighter Lodge* (☎ 527-1150) at 210 S Main St, with rooms at $35/42.

A few Victorian homes have been turned into B&Bs, including the *Jeter Victorian Inn B&B* (☎ 527-7574) at 1107 Jefferson St with five rooms from $65 to $140. In the countryside near town, *Bed, Breakfast & Barn* (☎ 527-7769) at 25185 66th Ave charges $60 to $98.

Places to Eat
Marie's Family Restaurant, 604 Main St at the corner of Antelope Blvd has a salad bar and plenty of good selections. *The Feedbag* at 200 S Main St is popular with locals and is famous for its giant flapjacks at breakfast. *Collectibles & Delectables* at 521 Walnut St, three blocks west of Main St features great coffee and interesting baked goods. The *Green Barn* on the corner of Antelope Blvd and Chestnut Ave is a long-established family restaurant popular with both locals and travelers. *Wild Bill's Rib-Steakhouse & Saloon* at 500 Riverside Way, just off Antelope Blvd and one block east of Main St, has a beautiful dining room and deck overlooking the river. There are plenty of other selections aside from ribs and steaks, and they have 'ribs to go' from 4 to 10 pm.

For Mexican, try *Francisco's Mexican Restaurant*, 480 Antelope Blvd in the Holiday Market shopping center, or *La Comida* at 360 S Main St.

Getting There & Away
Greyhound (☎ 527-0434) heads north and south on I-5 stopping at Foster Freeze, 1060 Main St at the corner of Union St.

Mt Lassen Motor Transit (☎ 916-529-2722) operates a mail-and-passenger bus from Red Bluff to Susanville and back every day except Sunday. It departs from the Foster Freeze at 8 am, arriving in Susanville at 1 pm, with stops along the way at Mineral (for Lassen Volcanic National Park), Chester, and Westwood. The bus departs Susanville at 1:30 pm for the return trip.

Gold Country

California's 'Gold Country,' also known as the 'Mother Lode Country,' extends 300 miles along (aptly numbered) Hwy 49 through the western Sierra Nevada foothills. Besides beautiful scenery and an abundance of outdoor recreation opportunities, the area has a wealth of restored mining towns and unrestored 'ghost towns' which match Hollywood images of the Old West. Most tourists pass straight through the Gold Country en route to the Sierra Nevada and Lake Tahoe or, inversely, the coast; so this part of California is relatively untouristed and very slow-paced.

Many foothills residents are refugees from the San Francisco or Sacramento rat race.

History
The Gold Rush started when James Marshall was inspecting the lumber mill he was building for John Sutter near present-day Coloma. He saw a fleck of gold in the mill's tailrace water and pulled out a gold nugget 'roughly half the size of a pea.' Marshall consulted Sutter, who tested the gold chunk by methods described in an encyclopedia, and the two men found the piece to be of high-quality gold. Sutter, however, wanted to finish his mill and thus made an agreement with his workers (most of whom were Mormons) that they could keep all of the gold they found in their spare time if they kept working. Nevertheless, by the time the mill was complete gold seekers were trickling into the area.

Sam Brannan came to Coloma a few months after Marshall's discovery to investigate the rumors. After finding six ounces of gold in one afternoon, he was convinced that there was money to be made. Brannan went back to San Francisco and bought every piece of mining equipment in the area – from handkerchiefs to shovels. He then alerted the newspapers and paraded the streets, gold dust in hand, proclaiming:

'There's gold in the Sierra foothills!' When gold seekers sought equipment for their adventure, Brannan sold them goods at a 100% mark-up and was a rich man by the time the first rush even began.

The first true rush was from San Francisco to the Sierra Nevada foothills in the spring of 1848. During this wave, men found gold so easily that they thought nothing of spending (or gambling) all they had in one night. News spread to Oregon,

304

South America, and the East Coast, and by the end of 1848, over 30,000 people had come. By '49, the real Gold Rush was on when 60,000 more people migrated to California to find the 'Mother Lode.'

The Mother Lode refers to the huge load of gold people believed they would find in the Sierra Nevada foothills, based purely on hopeful conjecture. Highway 49 is numbered in reference to the year the big rush to this area occured; it runs along the Sierra foothills where the mines were located. The supposed Mother Lode was never found and, according to geologists, does not and cannot exist because of the way gold occurs in rock formations.

Getting the Gold

California gold exists in two kinds of deposits: lode, where gold quartz is buried deep in the ground; and placer, which originated in lodes but has been moved over the centuries by erosion and weathering. Mining techniques depend on the fact that gold is heavier than the gravel, dirt, sand, etc surrounding it and will settle to the bottom of a receptacle while other debris is washed away.

Already separated from its earthen bed, and usually washed to stream and river bottoms, placer gold is the easiest to get. Miners plunge a pan into a stream bed, swirl gravel and sand around, and let the gold settle to the bottom while the other stuff splashes over the sides. This 'panning' was the most popular technique in early California mining.

To process larger amounts of gravel, miners used sluice boxes – long rectangular boxes outfitted with tin riffles and sieves. Dirt was shoveled into the box and the stream passed over it, washing dirt away and catching gold dust in the riffles. Sometimes gaspowered dredges vacuumed the bottom of a river or stream, depositing the debris into large sluice boxes manned by several people. Dredges are still used in mining, visible in remote areas along river banks.

To get to lode deposits, miners go far into the earth, into the 'hardrock' surrounding quartz gold. The labor and equipment required for hardrock mining is so great that most hardrock mines are owned by large companies such as the famous Anaconda Company which mined Montana, Nevada, and California, or wealthy families such as the Bournes who operated Grass Valley's Empire Mine. This type of mining blasts a vertical or inclined tunnel into the earth and sends miners down, via elevators or railroad cars which also brought the ore to the surface. The ore was then put through a stamp mill which crushed the rock fine enough to be sluiced.

Until it was banned in 1884 (see Malakoff Diggins State Historic Park), hydraulic mining was also used to mine lodes. Water cannons blasted entire hillsides away and miners sluiced the mud and debris that came washing down.

Other Mining Terms

arastra – a round, shallow pool with a turn-style in the middle to which several large boulders and a donkey's harness was attached; gold-bearing rocks were placed in the pool with a small amount of water, and as the donkey walked, the boulders crushed the rocks to fine gravel which was then panned or sluiced.

dredge – a gas-power pump used for vacuuming the sand a gravel a the bottom of a stream or river; it usually had a spout to deposit the debris into a sluice box.

ore – pieces of rock, usually about the size of a grapefruit, containing gold.

stamp mill – a large metal or wood frame from which hung several 'stamps,' long metal rods with solid cylinders at the end; cranks operated by water or horse power brought the stamps to the top of the frame, usually at various intervals, then let them fall with full weight to the surface below, where ore was placed.

tailings – the leftover debris from a sluice box. ■

Due to Marshall's find, most people headed straight for Coloma. Thus the Northern Mines (or Northern Diggins) along the Yuba, Feather, Bear, and American Rivers, held the first real settlements with Sacramento and Marysville as their gateways. As people realized that the topography and geology of the Consumes, Calaveras, Stanislaus, and Tuolumne Rivers was similar, they started exploring the southern foothills and found equally rich deposits. These Southern Mines were originally reached via Stockton.

Northern Mines

The Northern Mines, from Nevada City to Placerville, are some of the most picturesque in the Gold Country – perched on mountain sides, entrenched in canyons, and bordered by the Tahoe National Forest. Interstate 80, which connects Sacramento,

Lake Tahoe, and Reno, Nevada, offers easy access to most of them, though Hwy 49 is more scenic.

NEVADA CITY
• *pop 2855* ☎ *916*

Cute as a Victorian button and better preserved, Nevada City is a charming tourist town with artistic roots. As a key hub for the stagecoach lines passing the Sierra Nevada summit and Yuba River gold camps, Nevada City established itself around 1850, and by 1851 boasted the area's first playhouse.

A post-Gold Rush rush occurred in the 1970s when hippies from the Bay Area moved to Nevada City for a peaceful life among trees and kindred spirits. Now the hillside town has friendly New Agers and outdoors types, as well as old timers who still carry gun racks in their pick-up trucks.

Orientation
Nevada City's streets, often crammed with

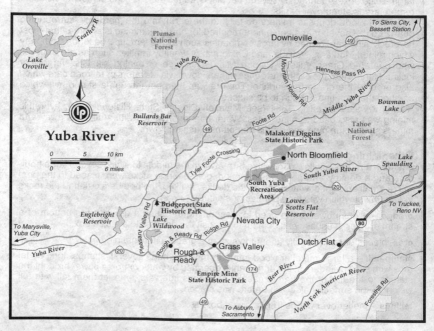

CALIFORNIA

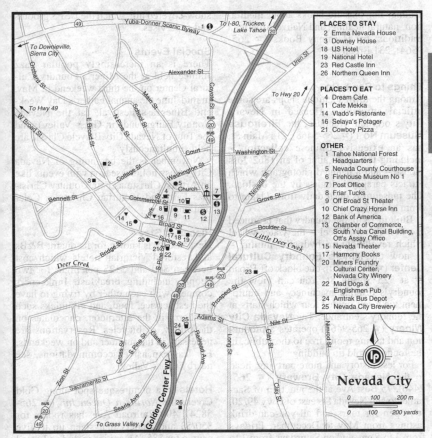

PLACES TO STAY
2 Emma Nevada House
3 Downey House
18 US Hotel
19 National Hotel
23 Red Castle Inn
26 Northern Queen Inn

PLACES TO EAT
4 Dream Cafe
11 Cafe Mekka
14 Vlado's Ristorante
16 Selaya's Potager
21 Cowboy Pizza

OTHER
1 Tahoe National Forest
   Headquarters
5 Nevada County Courthouse
6 Firehouse Museum No 1
7 Post Office
8 Friar Tucks
9 Off Broad St Theater
10 Chief Crazy Horse Inn
12 Bank of America
13 Chamber of Commerce,
   South Yuba Canal Building,
   Ott's Assay Office
15 Nevada Theater
17 Harmony Books
20 Miners Foundry
   Cultural Center,
   Nevada City Winery
22 Mad Dogs &
   Englishmen Pub
24 Amtrak Bus Depot
25 Nevada City Brewery

Nevada City

0   100   200 m
0   100   200 yards

pedestrians and horse-drawn carriages, are best navigated on foot. Broad St is the main thoroughfare where businesses are concentrated; it's easily reached by the Broad St exit off Hwy 49/20, the main highway which passes by to the east. Turn east from the exit; there is a four-hour parking lot (free) here; the bridge accross the highway has a pedestrian lane. Nevada City is about 150 miles from San Francisco.

Information
The chamber of commerce (☎ 265-2692, 800-655-6569), 132 Main St at the east end of Commercial St, has an immaculate

public toilet and barrage of brochures on recreation, lodging, restaurants, and entertainment. It's in Ott's Assay Office, where James J Ott assayed the first ore samples from Nevada's Comstock Load.

The Tahoe National Forest USFS Headquarters (☎ 265-4531), on Hwy 49 at the north end of Coyote St, is a good resource for information about backcountry trips. A topographical map of the entire Tahoe National Forest is posted in front of the office and is open weekdays from 8 am to 5 pm.

Firehouse Museum No 1 (see below) has the best selection of local history books around. For obscure books about meditation, natural healing, and Native American traditions, try Harmony Books (☎ 265-9564), 231 Broad St.

Things to See & Do

Among the town's antique shops are some official attractions. Housed in Nevada City's original firehouse, the **Firehouse Museum No 1** (☎ 265-5468), 214 Main St, has an extensive Chinese collection – including the entire altar of an 1862 Joss House – and a haunted photograph which attracts parapsychologists by the busload. The museum is open daily from 11 am to 4 pm and is free.

Built in 1856, the foundry that produced the first Pelton Wheel – the water wheel which revolutionized hydraulic mining – is now the **Miners Foundry Cultural Center** (☎ 265-5040), one block off Broad St at 325 Spring St. You can view the foundry's original machinery and equipment via a self-guided tour which starts at the foundry's entrance. The **Nevada City Winery** (☎ 265-9463) operates a production and tasting room, free to the public, in the foundry's old tin building.

For less history and more partying, head to the **Nevada City Brewery** (☎ 265-2446), 75 Bost Ave at the junction of Sacramento and Nevada Sts east of Hwy 49/20. It's open for tours and all-you-can-drink tastings from May to December, Fridays from 3 to 5 pm, and on Saturdays from 1 to 5 pm.

About 5½ miles north of Nevada City on Hwy 49 is a trailhead for the **Independence Trail** which extends along the old Excelsior Canal; the west branch offers a four mile loop to Jones Bar Rd and passes several good swimming holes. One mile further north on Hwy 49 is an access point for the South Fork of the Yuba River, good for swimming and fishing.

During the winter there are designated Sno Park and Snowplay areas along Hwy 49, at Bassetts Station and Yuba Pass. You pay a fee (usually $3, sometimes $6) to park near an open area, usually close to a snow-covered hill, which the USFS grooms and supervises.

Special Events

There is an increasingly popular Jazz Jubilee held at the Miner's Foundry Cultural Center on the third weekend in May. In mid-June the annual Father's Day Weekend Bluegrass Festival, (at the Nevada County Fairgrounds in Grass Valley), and the Tour of Nevada City Bicycle Classic are held simultaneously.

November is the beginning of Nevada City's busy holiday season with events like an Artists' Christmas Fair, Country Christmas Fair, and Victorian Christmas Celebration.

Places to Stay

Nevada City is known for its quaint B&Bs and restored Victorian hotels which cost between $60 and $125 per night for two people, including breakfast. Innkeepers compete with each other by trying to have the best service, food, and gimmicks such as sherry in the afternoon, chocolates on the pillow, or bicycles. Reservations are necessary in the summer and on weekends. For less expensive accommodations, see nearby Grass Valley.

Hotels In a picturesque spot along Gold Creek, the *Northern Queen Inn* (☎ 265-5824), 400 Railroad Ave, has rooms for $50/53 and chalets that sleep up to five people for $85. Amenities include a heated pool, spa, and restaurant.

In the heart of Nevada City, the *National Hotel* (☎ 265-4551), 211 Broad St, is the oldest continuously operating hotel west of the Rocky Mountains. Interiors match the building's 1850s construction. Singles/doubles cost $68/74.

A few doors down, the *US Hotel* (☎ 265-7999) has five rooms, each with a private parlor, for $64 to $78, including a continental breakfast.

B&Bs East of Hwy 49 on a hill overlooking downtown, *The Red Castle Inn* (☎ 265-5135), 109 Prospect St, has beautiful grounds, a buffet breakfast, and seven rooms for $70 to $140.

Closer to town, the *Emma Nevada House* (☎ 265-4415, 800-916-3662), 528 E Broad St, is in the childhood home of opera singer Emma Nevada. It has a hot tub and six rooms for $100 to $150, including a full breakfast. A few doors down, the *Downey House* (☎ 265-2815, 800-258-2815), 517 W Broad St, has southwest decor, nice gardens and has rooms for $60 to $95 midweek, $75 to $100 on weekends.

Places to Eat

Nevada City's cafes and delis serve tasty and affordable food. Around the corner from Selaya's Potager at 320 Broad St, *Selaya's Potager Gourmet Food to Go* (☎ 265-0558), has vegetable salads, cold chicken and pasta dishes, and inventive sandwiches for $3 to $5. Entrees in the restaurant cost $8 to $15.

The *Dream Cafe* (☎ 265-5282), 316 Commercial St, is a grungy New Age hang out that serves good coffee and espresso. Hot breakfasts and homemade soups cost around $3. More chic is *Cafe Mekka* (☎ 478-1517), whose couches, drapes, and free-standing walls attract an eclectically hip crowd. Wonderful baked goods cost $2 to $5. Both cafes have live acoustic music on weekends, and Cafe Mekka hosts an open drum circle on Thursday nights.

People wait in line to eat at *Cowboy Pizza* (☎ 265-2334), 315 Spring St, where specials include curry vegetable and Popeye pizza, both around $15 for a large (closed Monday and Tuesday).

For a hearty Italian meal among locals, try *Vlado's Ristorante* (☎ 265-2831), 423 Broad St. All dinners include antipasto, bread, salad, vegetables, and pasta and cost $10 to $15.

Earthsong (☎ 265-9392), south of downtown on Argall Way, is a popular vegetarian/health food restaurant with Mexican, Chinese, and Indian dishes for around $7.

Entertainment

The *Mad Dogs & Englishmen Pub* (☎ 265-8173), 211 Spring St, serves microbrews and wine to Nevada City's outdoorsy crowd, and has live entertainment on weekends. For a night among serious – but friendly – drinkers and pool sharks, try the *Chief Crazy Horse Inn* (☎ 265-9933), 203 Commercial St. One block away but worlds apart, *Friar Tucks* (☎ 265-9030), 111 Pine St, is a cozy wine bar with a 30-something crowd and live music on the weekends.

The *Magic Theater* (☎ 265-8262), south of downtown at 107 Argall Way, shows foreign and art films for $2 (Monday to Thursday), or $4 (Friday to Sunday).

The Foothill Theatre Company (☎ 265-9320) stages performances in the 1865 brick *Nevada Theater* at 401 Broad St. More intimate, the *Off Broadstreet Theater* (☎ 265-8686), 305 Commercial St, is a 'dessert theater' which presents mostly adult comedies.

Getting There & Around

Amtrak runs two buses daily (both in the morning) between Nevada City/Grass Valley and Sacramento ($20). The bus stops at the Express Mart store, 301 Sacramento St at its junction with Hwy 49. Eastbound travelers must go via Sacramento.

The Gold Country Stage (☎ 916-477-0103) has routes traveling the three miles between Grass Valley and Nevada City ($1 per ride, $2 for an all-day pass). In Nevada City it stops at the corner of Broad and Coyote Sts; in Grass Valley in front of the post office on W Main St.

GRASS VALLEY
• *pop 9048* ☎ *916*

Grass Valley is where Nevada City's locals buy groceries, service their cars, and get their pets groomed. Its historic business district, while still intact, is dwarfed by a concentration of mini malls, gas stations, and fast food restaurants, which sprung up when building codes were tossed aside in the name of progress. The Empire Mine and Powerhouse Museum are two of the area's most noteworthy attractions. Grass Valley offers cheap accommodations and

CALIFORNIA

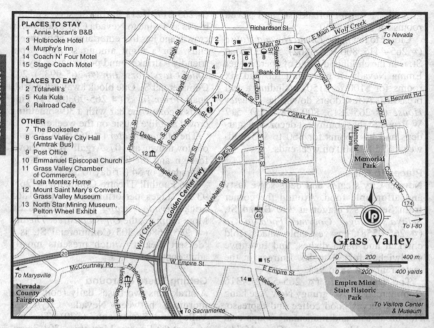

PLACES TO STAY
1 Annie Horan's B&B
3 Holbrooke Hotel
4 Murphy's Inn
14 Coach N' Four Motel
15 Stage Coach Motel

PLACES TO EAT
2 Tofanelli's
5 Kula Kula
6 Railroad Cafe

OTHER
7 The Bookseller
8 Grass Valley City Hall
   (Amtrak Bus)
9 Post Office
10 Emmanuel Episcopal Church
11 Grass Valley Chamber
   of Commerce,
   Lola Montez Home
12 Mount Saint Mary's Convent,
   Grass Valley Museum
13 North Star Mining Museum,
   Pelton Wheel Exhibit

Grass Valley

less expensive antiques than its neighboring towns.

History

In 1851 George Knight followed a wayward cow to the slope of Gold Hill and stubbed his toe on a piece of gold-filled quartz. Rumor of the find spread quickly, and within three years Grass Valley had a population of 3000.

Grass Valley's mines – notably George Bourne's Empire Mine – were among the first shaft mines in California, and showed California mine owners and investors that, with promotion of a company's stock and the use of large scale operations, there were big bucks to be made in quartz mining. This was the first mining company to sell stock. Because of the labor needed in the Empire Mine, Grass Valley was bigger than Los Angeles and San Diego in the 1860s and the largest and longest-lasting mining town in California.

Orientation

Grass Valley is three miles south of Nevada City on Hwy 49; both lie immediately west of the freeway.

Grass Valley's main thoroughfares are Mill St and W Main St (the heart of the historic business district), and E Main St which goes north to the shopping centers and mini malls, continues north as the Nevada City Hwy, and on into Nevada City as Sacramento St. S Auburn St divides E and W Empire St.

Empire Mine State Historic Park

Situated atop 367 miles of mine shafts, which, from 1850 to 1956, produced six million ounces of gold (about two billion modern dollars' worth), Empire Mine State Historic Park is the Gold Country's best preserved quartz mining operation – worth a half-day's exploration. The large mine yard contains headframes, stamp mills, water wheels, and pulleys, and is surrounded by the company offices – all made of wasterock.

The visitors center and museum, well-marked at the park entrance on the right hand side of E Empire St when traveling east, shows a worthwhile movie and offers free ranger-led tours every hour. If you miss the tour, be sure to see the color-coded mine system model in the room adjacent to the visitors center. Next to the largest head-frame in the mine yard is a stairway that leads 40 feet down into the main mine shaft.

On the other side of the visitors center, are stately buildings which belonged to the Bourne family, under whose ownership the Empire Mine truly prospered. You can visit the elegant country club, English manor home, gardener's house, and rose garden on a docent-led tour; check the visitors center for the day's schedule.

Hiking trails begin near the old stamp mill in the mine yard, and pass abandoned mines and equipment. A trail map is available at the visitors center. The park and visitors center (☎ 273-8522), two miles east of Grass Valley via the Empire St exit off Hwy 49, is open daily from 9 am to 5 pm. Admission is $5.

North Star Mining Museum
Housed in the North Star Mine's stone powerhouse on the west bank of Deer Creek, at Mill St's south end, this museum (☎ 273-4255) has a quality collection of Pelton water wheels – and their proto-types – mining equipment, and artifacts. A few shady, creek-side tables behind the museum make nice picnic spots. The museum is open May to September daily, from 9 am to 4 pm. Admission is by donation.

Church St
The south end of Church St is dominated by Mt St Mary's Convent, built in 1863 to house Irish nuns who cared for children orphaned from mining accidents. Within the convent are St Joseph's Chapel and the Grass Valley Museum (☎ 272-4725) which is open weekdays from 10 am to

Grass Valley's Lola Montez
Lola Montez was the 19th century equivalent to Madonna – beautiful, glamorous, and just a bit controversial. Born in Ireland, she took to London's stages as a Spanish dancer, where she won the heart of Germany's Ludwig I who bestowed on her the title of Countess of Landsfelt. During a student revolution against the king in 1848, Lola was found sitting in a window drinking champagne, a maneuver that resulted in her exodus from Germany.

After dabbling in Paris with comrades George Sand and Victor Hugo, Lola – who was now over 30 and loosing some zeal – moved to America where less sophisticated audiences still applauded her sensual dances and exotic beauty. Always longing to be the center of attention, she moved from New York to Boston to Philadelphia, and finally to California where she was assured a captive audience. By 1853, however, San Francisco and Sacramento already had their share of glamorous entertainers, so Lola went on to settle in Grass Valley, a rough and tumble mining town that accepted her with open arms.

Lola stirred controversy by wearing low-cut dresses, smoking Cuban cigars, keeping two grizzly cubs as pets, and serving champagne and imported whiskey at her European-style 'salons.' Considered heaven by the miners and hell by miners' wives, Lola was Grass Valley's most famous citizen until the Australian gold rush drew her south to untainted audiences. Her former home, now the chamber of commerce, is still a Grass Valley landmark. ■

5 pm, and on weekends from 11 am to 4 pm (free). Also on Church St is the **Emmanuel Episcopal Church** which, as the second oldest Episcopal church in California, has continuously served its parish since 1858.

Special Events
As home to the Nevada County Fairgrounds, Grass Valley hosts most of the area's large events, including the Sierra Festival of the Arts in late May, the annual

CALIFORNIA

Father's Day Weekend Bluegrass Festival in June, and the week-long Nevada County Fair in mid-August. For a current schedule and event information, call ☎ 273-6217.

Places to Stay

Motels & Hotels The *Stage Coach Motel* (☎ 272-3701), 405 S Auburn, has rooms for $30 Monday to Thursday and $35 on weekends. The *Coach N' Four Motel* (☎ 273-8009), 628 S Auburn St, has rooms from $36 to $45 depending on how many days you stay.

Two miles south of Grass Valley on Hwy 49, the *Golden Chain Motel* (☎ 273-7279) has four acres of woods, a picnic area, and heated pool. Rooms cost $42/48 a single/double and are noisy unless you ask for one away from the highway.

The *Best Western Gold Country Inn* (☎ 273-1393), about two miles north of downtown, east off Hwy 49/20's Brunswick exit at 11972 Sutton Way, has a pool, spa, and rooms for $53/65, including coffee and pastries in the morning.

The *Holbrooke Hotel* (☎ 273-1353), 212 W Main St, has been in continuous use since 1852, and has Mark Twain's signature in the hotel register.

B&Bs *Annie Horan's* (☎ 272-2418), at 415 W Main St, prides itself on its 1874 furnishings and architecture. Rooms cost $80 to $120 on Friday and Saturday and $65 to $95 midweek. *Murphy's Inn* (☎ 273-6873), 318 Neal St, has eight Victorian-style rooms which cost $75 to $135, and very welcoming owners.

Places to Eat

Tofanelli's (☎ 272-1468), 302 W Main St, has simple decor, friendly service, and reliably good food (especially breakfast). At the *Railroad Cafe* (☎ 274-2233), 111 W Main St, model trains circle above the small, unassuming dining room where breakfast and lunch are served until 4 pm daily. *Kula Kula* (☎ 274-229), 207 W Main St, serves outstanding Japanese food for under $10 ($5 for lunch), and has live piano music on Saturday night.

Getting There & Away

Amtrak buses going to/from Sacramento stop three times daily at Grass Valley City Hall, 125 E Main St.

ROUGH & READY

Named after president Zachary Taylor, Rough & Ready is five miles west of Hwy 49 on Rough and Ready Hwy which bypasses Grass Valley and drops south to Hwy 20 – a scenic route between Nevada City and Marysville. The town absolutely swells during the last weekend in June

---

The Cornish Pastie

Though the mines are long closed, Grass Valley folks still love their Cornish pasties (pronounced PAST-eez), pastry pockets stuffed with meat and potatoes and resembling turnovers or Italian calzones. Introduced by tin miners from Cornwall, England, pasties were inexpensive and easy to make, and traveled well in a miner's lunch pail. In fact, a three-level lunch pail was invented around the pastie: the bottom level held hot tea which kept the pasties on the 2nd level warm; sweets and tobacco took up the 3rd level.

Although Grass Valley's pastie shops advertise 'original ingredients' and '100-year-old recipes,' you probably wouldn't want to eat a true 1850s pastie, made with bacon grease, salted beef, and months-old potatoes. Today's versions are usually made with vegetable shortening, and filled with everything from apples to broccoli and turkey.

Ask any older woman in the area where you can get the best pastie around, and she'll inevitably answer 'in my kitchen,' however should you not get invited, a reliable place to sample a pastie is at *Marshall's Pasties* (☎ 916-272-2844), 203 Mill St. It has a cramped counter downstairs and a few well-worn tables upstairs. Thanks to modern technology, Marshall's now uses a microwave to warm up their 100-year-old recipe. ■

when thousands of people come to participate in the Rough & Ready Secession Day Chili Cook-Off.

BRIDGEPORT STATE HISTORIC PARK

Bridgeport State Historic Park, six miles north of Hwy 20 on Pleasant Valley Rd, is about one-third history lesson and two-thirds recreation opportunity. The historical highlight is the Bridgeport Bridge, the longest covered bridge in the USA, built in 1862 as part of toll road between the northern gold mines and Nevada's Comstock Lode. During the summer, Bridgeport is a favorite point for jumping into the South Fork of the Yuba River which slows and pools among rocks and sandy beaches. The Englebright Reservoir, one mile south by foot trail, has several undeveloped campsites.

MALAKOFF DIGGINS
STATE HISTORIC PARK

The world's first water cannons – designed specifically for hydraulic mining – cut a 200-foot canyon through Tertiary bedrock to unearth rich veins of gold. Rubble washed down from the hillsides, and the tailings dropped back into the South and Middle Forks of the Yuba River – eventually creating a problem when the waste reached the flat Sacramento Valley floor: by the 1860s, 20-foot mud glaciers blocked the rivers and caused severe flooding each spring during the Sierra's snowmelt. After a year of heated courtroom (and bar room) debate between farmers and miners, the worst hydraulic mining practices were prohibited, making hydraulicking impossible. North Bloomfield, the small mining community at the center of Malakoff's operation, went bankrupt and dormant.

The process left behind red stratified cliffs and gigantic mounds of tailings which make for great hiking and exploring. Most of North Bloomfield's structures are restored to their original condition, and house a few operating stores. The **Malakoff Mine State Historic Park Headquarters & Museum** (☎ 916-265-2740) shows an interesting movie and sells literature and

maps. Admission to the park, including the museum, costs $5 per vehicle.

The park has primitive campsites, three developed *campgrounds*, and four rental cabins (converted old miner's cabins), plus many picnic areas and a network of hiking trails.

To reach the park, take Hwy 49 11 miles north of Nevada City and turn east (right) on Tyler Foote Rd which goes northeast for 17 miles to the park entrance. The road crosses a 5000-foot pass and hits washboard gravel just before the park entrance; a four-wheel drive vehicle is often necessary during the winter. Call the park headquarters for road information.

YUBA RIVER

The northernmost segment of Hwy 49 follows the tempestuous Yuba River through remote pine forests. **Downieville**, the area's hub, is a sleepy town which was once a notoriously rough and tumble place: its first justice of the peace was also the local saloon keeper.

Thirteen miles north of Downieville, **Sierra City** looks much like other abandoned Gold Country towns but was scorched in a 1940s fire, making it quite photogenic. **Basset Station**, lies on the Pacific Crest Trail near the Sierra's Gold Lakes Region – a popular spot for hiking, fishing, and camping.

AUBURN
• *pop 10,592* ☎ *916*

In 1856, trains began operating from Sacramento to Folsom, and Auburn started its own minor railroad which eventually became part of Central Pacific's transcontinental route. Interstate 80 follows this route, making Auburn one of the most visited towns in the Gold Country. While other Gold Country towns are more picturesque and less developed, you can explore Auburn in a couple of hours and never venture far from the freeway.

The little communities around Auburn, notably Penryn, Foresthill, and Dutch Flat, make good excuses to get off the highway and into the trees, especially on Wednesday and weekend afternoons when their folksy museums are open. Get details from the Auburn Area Chamber of Commerce.

Orientation & Information

Lincoln Way and High St, the main thoroughfares which connect old town and downtown, form an 'X' whose juncture is downtown's main intersection. People conduct business in 'uptown' Auburn – a series of generic strip malls north of town along Hwy 49 – but 'downtown' and 'old town' contain Auburn's not-too-glitzy antique stores, neon-signed bars, and good restaurants.

Housed in the old Auburn railroad depot at the north end of Lincoln Way, the Auburn Area Chamber of Commerce (☎ 885-5616, 800-433-7575), has museum, lodging, and dining guides, and is open weekdays 9 am to 5 pm.

Things to See & Do

Auburn's best history displays are at the **Placer County Museum** (☎ 889-6500), on the 1st floor of the stately Placer County Courthouse (the building you see from the freeway). The museum is open Tuesday to Sunday from 10 am to 4 pm for $1. The courthouse is open daily from 8 am to 5 pm. More educational and less polished is the **Gold Country Museum** (☎ 889-4134), towards the back of the fairgrounds on High St, open Tuesday to Friday from 10 am to 3:30 pm, and on weekends 11 am to 4 pm ($1). Also at the fairgrounds is a large **farmers' market**, held Saturdays from 9 am to around 3 pm.

Built in 1851 as the Traveler's Rest Hotel, the **Bernhard Museum Complex** (☎ 889-4156), 291 Auburn-Folsom Rd (at the south end of High St), is now a museum that displays the typical life of a 19th century farm family, including the requisite winery and carriage house. Tours leave hourly ($1); closed Monday.

The **North American Indian Annex** (☎ 889-6500), attached to Auburn's Civic Center, has a worthwhile collection of artifacts which can be viewed weekdays by appointment.

Special Events

Most of Auburn's (and Placer County's) big events take place at the Gold Country Fairgrounds on High St, just south of old town via Sacramento St.

In April, Auburn's Wild West Stampede (a semi-pro rodeo) precedes the less testosterone-driven Antique Doll Show. Also in April is the American River Endurance Ride, a 50-mile equestrian event which ends in Auburn.

The last weekend in May attracts fiddlers, dancers, and a large partying crowd to the Gold N' Fiddle Festival. For information call ☎ 888-8682.

In mid-August, the 100-mile Tevis Cup Western States Trail Ride ends in Auburn and is celebrated with parades, music, and a horse show. The Gold Country Fair is held the first weekend in September, and the Antique Street Fair is in mid-October.

Places to Stay & Eat

The only motel in downtown Auburn is the *Elmwood Motel* (☎ 885-5186), 588 High St, with an outdoor pool and adequately clean rooms for $32/41 a single/double.

At the north end of Lincoln Way, three miles north of downtown, the *Best Western Golden Key* (☎ 885-8611) has a heated pool and rooms for $60. Nearby, the *Country Squire Inn* (☎ 885-7025) has a pool, hot tub, and rooms for $41/47.

Alongside I-80 on Auburn Ravine Rd are a few motels, including the *Auburn Inn* (☎ 885-1800, 800-272-1444) which has a spa, pool, and rooms for $60/64, and the small *Foothills Motel* (☎ 885-8444) with a pool, hot tub, friendly owners, and rooms for $42/48.

Old town Auburn has good restaurants, while downtown is a coffeeshop hub where you can dine on grilled-cheese sandwiches and coleslaw with the over-60 crowd.

Awful Annies (☎ 888-9857), a local favorite in old town at 160 Sacramento St, serves breakfast and lunch indoors or outdoors on a deck. *Cafe Delicias* (☎ 885-2050), 1591 Lincoln Way in old town, is the best place for Mexican food.

Try *Bootleggers* (☎ 889-2229) for a

splurge. It's housed in Auburn's original city hall at 210 Washington St. Prices are $8 to $18 for lunch and dinner.

Getting There & Away
Amtrak buses to Sacramento ($13) leave four times daily from the bus shelter at 403 Grass Valley Hwy (Hwy 49), directly across from the Thrifty shopping center. Tickets are bought on board.

COLOMA
☎ 916

Originally known for its proximity to Sutter's Mill (the first gold discovery site), Coloma is now equally famous for its whitewater rafting. Situated on the North Fork of the American River, about 11 miles north of Placerville, all that makes up the 'town' is the Marshall Gold Discovery State Historic Park and a few choice campgrounds and businesses along Hwy 49. The Coloma Deli (☎ 622-1122), on Hwy 49, acts as Coloma's general store, tourist information center, and general year-round rendezvous.

Marshall Gold Discovery State Historic Park
The North Fork of the American River and Hwy 49 run right through Marshall Gold Discovery State Historic Park, about two miles south of the Coloma Deli. Though you can see most of the park by just driving through, its hiking trails, restored buildings, and replica of Sutter's Mill warrant a few hours out of the car. The State Park Visitors Information Center & Museum (☎ 622-3470) shows a worthwhile movie and has a good mining exhibit.

You can make a loop tour by car up to the James Marshall Memorial statue and grave sight, or hike up the monument trail which passes old mining equipment and some nice picnic areas. The visitors center and the picnic area across from the mill reconstruction have interpretive trail maps.

Try panning for gold on the river's east bank, just across the bridge from the mill replica. Pans are available from the visitors center, and demonstrations are given most weekends from May to September.

The park is open daily from 8 am to sunset, while the visitor center is open from 8 am to 4:30 pm (May to September until 6 pm). Admission is $5, which is collected at the museum. If, however, you don't go to the museum, payment is not enforced.

Whitewater Rafting
The American River offers some of California's most accessible whitewater rafting. Accessibility means crowds on most weekends, but it also means a wide choice of trips and outfitters. The Coloma Deli is a good place to find out about river conditions and trip availability.

Half-day trips usually start upstream at Chile Bar and take out near Marshall Gold Discovery State Historic Park. Full-day trips put in at the Coloma Bridge and take out at Salmon Falls, near Folsom Lake. The half-day options start in Class III water and are action-packed to the end (full-day trips

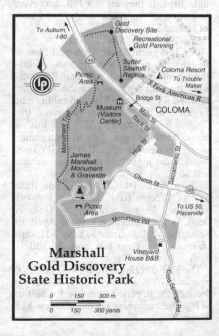

Marshall Gold Discovery State Historic Park

start out slowly then build up to Class III as a climax). The full-day trips include lunch which, with the bigger companies, is often a gourmet affair. Recommended for their meticulous equipment, knowledgeable guides, and tasty food, *Whitewater Connection* (☎ 800-336-7238) has half-day trips for $69/$79 weekday/weekend, full-day trips for $89/$99, and two-day trips for $189/219. Cheaper operators offer no-frills service.

A free and fun pastime is watching people navigate the Trouble Maker rapid, upstream from the bridge next to Sutter's Mill in the state park.

Across from the Coloma Deli is the Coloma Club – a bar, restaurant, and hangout alive with guides and river rats when the water is high.

Places to Stay & Eat
Most rafting companies own private campgrounds, open to their guests who do overnight trips. If they are not full, however, they often let those who do day trips stay for around $10.

The *American River Resort* (☎ 622-6700), just south of the state park, has a playground, pond, farm animals, swimming pool, restaurant, and bar. Reservations are necessary only in the summer. Tent and RV sites cost $28, and cabins rent for $100 to $125. Across the river, the *Coloma Resort* (☎ 621-2267) gets just as crowded but has more space at each campsite (fewer trees though). Tent and RV sites cost $27 per night, and two-person cabins cost $63.

Camp Lotus (☎ 622-8672), one mile west of Coloma (take the Lotus turn-off from Hwy 49, just south of the Coloma Deli), is for tenters only from April to November. Sites, from $15 to $21, are grassy, showers are hot, and the toilets flush.

The *Vineyard House B&B* (☎ 622-2217), built in 1870 as a winery estate, has rooms decorated with period furniture for $80 to $110. The restaurant serves a fancy $15 dinner.

PLACERVILLE
• *pop 8355* ☎ *916*
'Old Hangtown,' as Placerville is fondly known, has always relied on passing traffic for its livelihood. Originally it was a destination for gold seekers who reached California along the South Fork of the American River. In 1857 the first stage coach to cross the Sierra Nevada between California and Nevada's Carson Valley linked Placerville with the nation's first transcontinental stage route. Today, Placerville is a gas and food stop for people traveling between Sacramento and South Lake Tahoe on Hwy 50. An hour's stop reveals a bustling and well-preserved downtown, and colorful regional museum.

History
Called 'Dry Diggings' through the summer of 1848, Placerville was the second sizable gold camp to develop after Coloma. In 1849, five men charged with robbery and attempted murder were brought to a makeshift miner's court. When the acting judge (supposedly a saloon keeper) asked the population what to do with the culprits, someone shouted 'Hang them!' The men were taken to a tree on Main St and hung right then and there, turning Dry Diggins into Hangtown. The town became Placerville as placer mining became increasingly reliable and miners' families started moving in.

Orientation & Information
Main St, the heart of downtown Placerville, runs parallel to Hwy 50 between Canal St and Cedar Ravine Rd. Mini malls and fast food chains lie at both ends of Main St, but are concentrated towards the east end of town.

The El Dorado County Chamber of Commerce (☎ 621-5885, 800-457-6279), 542 Main St, has information concerning Gold Country and the Lake Tahoe area, and is open weekdays from 9 am to 6 pm. The Wine Smith (☎ 622-0516), 346 Main St, sells a good recreation guide to El Dorado County for $1. Banks, several good bookstores, and a post office are on Main St.

Things to See & Do

Most buildings along main street date back to the 1850s, including the **El Dorado County Courthouse**, and **Placerville Hardware**, 441 Main St, the oldest continuously operating hardware store west of the Mississippi River. An old photograph in front of the store shows early Placerville and the hangman's tree.

The **Soda Factory Museum** (☎ 626-0773), housed in the Fountain & Tallman Soda Works Building at 524 Main St, has a small collection of old soda factory relics and Placerville photographs. The museum is open on weekends from noon to 4 pm.

The **El Dorado County Historical Museum** (☎ 621-5865), on the El Dorado County Fairgrounds west of downtown Placerville (exit north on Placerville Drive from Hwy 50), is an extensive complex of restored buildings, mining equipment, and recreated businesses. It's open Wednesday to Sunday from 10 am to 4 pm and is free.

In early October, the **Dixieland Jazz Jubilee** attracts big-name musicians from all over the country. Call ☎ 621-5885 for more information.

Places to Stay

The *Placerville KOA* (☎ 676-2267), six miles west of Placerville on Hwy 50 (exit north on Shingle Springs Drive), sits on 18 acres of land and has a store, laundry, pool, etc. Tent sites are pretty well shaded, though not very grassy, and cost $17. Hookups cost $25.

In downtown Placerville, the *Cary House Hotel* (☎ 622-4271), 300 Main St, has newly restored rooms that slightly resemble their bordello history for $41/52. Ask for a room in back to avoid street noise.

The large pink *Combellack-Blair House B&B* (☎ 622-3764), two blocks south of Main St at 3059 Cedar Ravine Rd, has three Victorian style rooms for $90 to $100. The *Chichester-McKee House B&B* (☎ 626-1882, 800-831-4008), north of Hwy 50 at 800 Spring St (Hwy 49), charges $75 per night for two people, $100 for three people.

Places to Eat

Fast food chains – well marked and highly visible from Hwy 50 – abound in Placerville, but 'real' food is found downtown.

Sweetie Pies (☎ 642-0128), 577 Main St, is a good place for lunch and baked goods. *Lil' Mama D Carlo's* (☎ 626-1612), 482 Main St, serves homemade ravioli and cannelloni for under $10. For Mexican food, *La Casa Grande* (☎ 626-5454), 251 Main St, is popular with the locals, though the atmosphere – and salsa – at *Tortilla Flats* (☎ 626-0101), 564 Main St, is nicer. Prices are comparable – around $6 for most items.

Entertainment

The *Empire Theater* (☎ 626-7735), 432 Main St, shows current Hollywood films for $5.50.

Placerville's bars are akin to watering holes in the midwest: they open at 6 am, get a yearly cleaning on Christmas, and are great for soaking up local color. Side by side on Main St, the *Hangman's Tree*, *Liar's Bench*, and *Gil's Bar* are good for catching the ol' Hangtown scene.

Getting There & Away

Amtrak has three buses daily to Sacramento ($7). The bus stop is in front of the Buttercup Pantry Restaurant, just south of Hwy 50 at the corner of Pacific and Main Sts.

Tickets to Sacramento on Greyhound, which also has three buses daily, cost $8.50 one way. The Greyhound station is at 1750 Broadway. It's closed Saturday afternoon and Sunday.

AROUND PLACERVILLE
Apple Hill

In 1860, a miner planted a Rhode Island greening apple tree on the Larsens' property and began the prolific Apple Hill. The miner's Rhode Island greening still stands (a major gimmick for the Larsens), and is now flanked by granny smiths, pippins, red and yellow delicious, fujis from Japan, and braeburns from New Zealand. Apple growers sell directly to the public, usually from September to around Christmas.

A decent map of Apple Hill is available at the Apple Hill Visitors Center in the Camino Hotel, near the Camino exit off Hwy 50. For a condensed Apple Hill tour, take the Camino exit north onto Barkley Rd until it becomes Larsen Drive, and follow Larsen Drive (which will become Cable and then Mace Rd) until it meets Pony Express Trail back beside Hwy 50. White signs emblazoned with bright red apples mark connecting side roads and byways.

Favorite stops are Larsen's Apple Barn, 2461 Larsen Drive; Boa Vista Orchards, 2952 Carson Rd; High Hill Ranch, just off Carson Rd at 2901 High Hill Rd; Bolsters Hilltop Ranch, 2000 Larsen Drive; and Argyres Orchard, 4220 N Canyon Rd.

El Dorado County Farm Trails

The El Dorado County Farm Trails Association tries to 'keep small farming alive in a rural lifestyle that stands at the doorstep of urban development' (from a promotional flier). One of their more visible efforts is a 100-mile route marked with blue, red, and yellow El Dorado County Farm Trails signs indicating that the adjacent farm sells directly to the public and welcomes visitors. Maps and information are available at the El Dorado County Chamber of Commerce in Placerville, or by calling the El Dorado County Farm Trails Association at ☎ 621-4772.

Wineries

El Dorado County wines are becoming increasingly popular. Most wineries are open year round and offer tastings on the weekends. During Passport Weekends, held in March and April, one 'passport' gets you into seven wineries that offer special tastings and tours. Contact the El Dorado Winery Association, PO Box 1614, Placerville, CA 95667, or try the chamber of commerce in Placerville (☎ 621-5885, 800-457-6279). Some wineries to look out for are Lava Cap Winery (☎ 621-0175), 2221 Fruitridge Rd; Madrona Vineyards (☎ 644-5948), just north of Carson Rd on High Hill Rd; and Boeger Winery (☎ 622-8094) at 1709 Carson Rd.

Southern Mines

The Southern Mines extend from Placerville south to Mariposa, and are bordered by the Stanislaus National Forest in the northeast and Yosemite National Park in the southeast. Placerville is about a two hours' drive from San Francisco. Towns between Placerville and Mariposa are generally 40 minutes apart; Mariposa is about six hours from LA.

AMADOR CITY
• *pop 153* ☎ 209

Two miles west of Sutter Creek, Amador City is proud of its status as the smallest incorporated township in California. Once home to the Keystone Mine – one of the most prolific gold producers in California – the town lay deserted from the mine's closure until the 1950s when a family from Sacramento bought the dilapidated buildings and converted them into antique shops. Now there are half a dozen antique and collectibles shops and an excellent birders store in town, and rumors that a museum dedicated to the women of the Gold Country will open in 1996.

Stop by the Imperial Hotel to pick up a walking tour map. Behind Amador City's old firehouse (the building with a bright red garage door and bell tower in front), is a stone arastra once used to grind gold-laced quartz. Rocks were placed in the pit and crushed by iron balls pulled by donkeys. The rubble was then panned for the gold which broke loose in the process. The arastra still works, and is put to use during the Jose Amador Fiesta, which takes place

---

Miners' Law
At the peak of the Gold Rush, gold was found regularly enough to eliminate crime, and what crime did occur was dealt with by 'miners' law,' such as tying a man to a tree stark naked in the middle of mosquito season. ∎

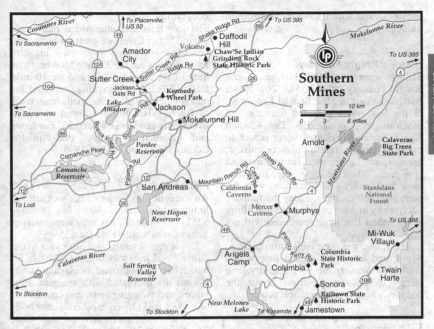

in late April. With Spanish dancing and music, demonstrations of gold mining techniques, and arts & crafts booths set up, the festival makes an entertaining half-day.

Places to Stay & Eat

The *Imperial Hotel* (☎ 267-9172, 800-242-5594) serves gourmet dinners in an elegant dining room for around $20 per person, including wine. Rooms, decorated with antiques, cost $60 on weeknights, $75 weekends and holidays, including breakfast.

Housed in the old Keystone Mining Company offices, the *Mine House Inn* (☎ 267-5900, 800-646-3473) has seven rooms with original decor for $50 to $70 weeknights, $65 to $90 weekends and holidays, and include breakfast.

SUTTER CREEK
• *pop 1200 ☎ 209*

In its prime, Sutter Creek was the Gold Country's main foundry center, with three foundries operating in 1873. Now it's one of the Gold Country's most endearing towns.

Its raised, arcaded sidewalks and high-balconied buildings are free from any modern architecture. Espresso bars, boutiques, and B&Bs are the only reminders that time isn't stuck in the 1890s.

Orientation & Information

Highway 49, called Main St within the city limits, is the backbone of Sutter Creek's business district.

For information and a walking tour map, stop by the Sutter Creek Visitors Center (☎ 800-400-0305), housed in the Historic Knight Foundry on Eureka St, three blocks east of Main St. The Bubble Gum Bookstore (☎ 267-5680), 59 Main St, has an excellent selection of history books – including many small ones written by locals – and Gold Country maps and guides.

Historic Knight Foundry

Still in operation after 120 years, the Knight Foundry (☎ 267-5543, 267-1449), two blocks east of Main St at 81 Eureka St, is the last water powered foundry and machine shop in the US. The 42-inch Knight water wheel uses water power to operate large cranes, planers, drills, presses, and lathes, used for making cast iron parts. When the mines were in operation, the foundry's biggest orders were for pans and rock crushers. Today the foundry survives by making custom parts and filling small orders that large operations will not take.

The foundry is open daily from 9 am to 4 pm, and has a self-guided tour which costs $1. Workers are very friendly, and happy to answer questions about the foundry's history and technical process.

Bicycling

The low hills and uncrowded backroads around Sutter Creek are great for bicycling, provided you have your own bicycle. Favorite trips are the 33-mile loop between Sutter Creek and Jackson, and the 10-mile Daffodil Hill tour – a springtime ritual for many. Uncrowded, scenic roads branch off of Buena Vista Rd, southwest of Sutter Creek between Hwys 88 and 12. For maps and information contact the Amador County Bike Club (☎ 223-3890).

Places to Stay

An exception to Sutter Creek's expensive lodging scene, the *Bellotti Inn* (☎ 267-5211), 53 Main St, has musty rooms atop Sutter Creek's oldest bar for $35/45.

Loyal guests return year after year to the *Sutter Creek Inn* (☎ 267-5606), 75 Main St, which has 18 rooms and an elegant parlor. Rooms are decorated with antiques, fireplaces, and swinging beds, and cost $55 to $88 ($88 to $115 on weekends and holidays). Reservations are advised. Next door, *The Foxes* (☎ 267-5882), 77 Main St, has seven plush rooms with televisions, designer furniture, and bathrobes. Prices are $110 to $140.

Housed in a beautiful Craftsman-style home one block east of Main St, the *Picture Rock Inn* (☎ 267-5500, 800-399-2389), 55 Eureka St, has rooms for $90 to $105.

Places to Eat

Sutter Creek's coffeehouses serve hearty sandwiches and baked goods. The local favorite is *Back Roads* (☎ 267-0440), just off Main St at 74-A Main St, which has a lively atmosphere and serves big sandwiches and hot lunch specials for around $5. *Fat Pats* (☎ 267-5983), at the corner of Main and Hanford Sts, has a sterile atmosphere, but they bake their own bread and serve a salad with their $5 sandwiches.

Ruby's Cafe (☎ 267-0566), 15 Eureka St, has excellent burgers, pasta, and vegetarian items for under $10, plus live music on weekends (closed Monday and Tuesday).

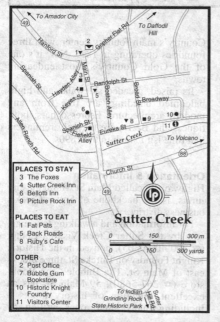

PLACES TO STAY
3 The Foxes
4 Sutter Creek Inn
6 Bellotti Inn
9 Picture Rock Inn

PLACES TO EAT
1 Fat Pats
5 Back Roads
8 Ruby's Cafe

OTHER
2 Post Office
7 Bubble Gum
    Bookstore
10 Historic Knight
    Foundry
11 Visitors Center

Sutter Creek

0   150   300 m
0   150   300 yards

CHAW'SE INDIAN GRINDING ROCK STATE HISTORIC PARK

Sacred ground for the local Miwok Indians, this state park contains a limestone outcropping covered with petroglyphs – 363 originals and a few modern additions – and mortar holes called *chaw'Ses* used for grinding acorns into meal. The 1185 holes are the most on any one rock in California.

Adjacent to the rock are replica Miwok structures and the **Regional Indian Museum** (☎ 209-296-7488) which has educational displays about Northern Miwok culture and gives free tours of the park on weekends. Big Time Days, a traditional Miwok festival held the fourth weekend in September, is well worth visiting.

The park *campground* has 21 sites with stoves, tables, and restrooms (no showers). Sites are first come, first served and cost $6. To get there from Sutter Creek, take Ridge Rd to the east.

DAFFODIL HILL

Between mid-March and mid-April, Daffodil Hill, 14 miles east of Sutter Creek on Shake Ridge Rd (from the north end of Main St), is blanketed with over 300,000 daffodils. The McLaughlin family has owned the hilltop farm since 1887, and keeps hyacinth, tulips, violets, lilacs, and the occasional peacock amongst the daffodils. The hill is open daily when the flowers are in bloom.

VOLCANO

Volcano, 14 miles east of Sutter Creek on Sutter Creek Rd, is the most complete, unrestored mining town in the Gold Country. Miners named the town for its encircling hills, though its early days were explosive with dance halls, saloons, and bordellos.

Volcano had the first astronomical observation site, private law school, and library in California. The St George Hotel, on Main St, is the only business still in operation. The Wells Fargo office, Odd Fellows and Masonic Halls, jail, and brewery are vacant but still in pretty good shape.

AMADOR, PARDEE & CAMANCHE LAKES

Southwest of Sutter Creek, the Mokelumne River feeds Amador Lake, Pardee Lake, and Camanche Reservoir. Pardee Lake, open February to November, is exclusively a fishing lake, while the other two – especially Camanche – are popular for jetskiing, water-skiing, and windsurfing. Bass and sunfish are the most common fish in the lakes, though Camanche also has trout and Kokanee salmon. The one major access route is Buena Vista Rd, between Hwy 88 and Hwy 12. The lakes are about two hours from the Bay Area, but most traffic is from Sacramento, and local areas. You can get the obligatory fishing license and tackle, rent boats, and launch boats at any of the resorts listed below.

Camanche Southshore Resort (☎ 209-763-5178), on Camanche Parkway just north of Hwy 12, has shady tent sites for $14, RV hookups for $18, and cottages for $75. At the other end of the reservoir but owned by the same people, the *Camanche Northshore Resort* (☎ 209-763-5121) has identical prices, but more partiers and less shade; it also has motel rooms for $35. *Lake Amador Resort* (☎ 209-274-4739), three miles south of Hwy 88 on Jackson Valley Rd, has tent sites for $15, and caters to anglers.

JACKSON

• *pop 3545* ☎ 209

From 1860 to 1920, when the Kennedy and Eureka Mines were in full swing, Jackson was the area's primary entertainment center, known for its saloons, gambling halls, and bordellos (the Bank of America stands on the site of 'Pinky's Temple'). Businesses geared towards tourism now occupy these historic structures, while Jackson supports a large service industry, located in strip malls on the fringes of town.

Jackson's accommodations are the most affordable in the area. The *Visitors Guide to Amador County* lists things to see and do in the area, and is available from the chamber of commerce (☎ 223-0350), at the junction

CALIFORNIA

of Hwys 49 and 88, open weekdays from 9 am to 5 pm.

Amador County Museum

The museum (☎ 223-6386), two blocks north of Main St at 225 Church St, contains general Gold Country history displays, a good collection of old phonographs and musical instruments, and several closets worth of antique clothes. Highlights include a 1908 baseball uniform and a stealth .32-caliber cane. (The judge who owned the house in which the museum is located had his cane outfitted with a .32 caliber gun, the nozzel housed in the end of the cane and the trigger in its handle.) The museum is open Wednesday to Sunday from 10 am to 4 pm and charges a $1 admission.

Kennedy Wheel Park

North of downtown Jackson, this park contains two 58-foot diameter wheels that resemble small carnival rides. In 1912, the state legislature forbade mining operations to dump tailings into rivers because of the flooding it caused in the Sacramento Valley. The Kennedy Mines' engineers built four of the wheels to convey tailings over two low hills into an impounding dam by way of gravity flumes. One wheel still stands erect and another lies on the ground. Be sure to climb to the top of the hill behind the wheels to see the dam.

Places to Stay & Eat

Jackson's small, inexpensive motels are on the outskirts of town near Hwys 49 and 88. The *Amador Motel* (☎ 223-0970), 12408 Kennedy Flat Rd, has a small garden, outdoor pool, and 10 rooms for $37/45 a single/double. The *Jackson Holiday Lodge* (☎ 223-0486), a half mile west of downtown on Hwy 49/88, has an outdoor pool and spacious rooms and cottages for $37/42. Half-way between Jackson and Sutter Creek on Hwy 49, the Spanish-style *El Campo Casa Resort Motel* (☎ 223-0100) has a nice courtyard, outdoor pool, and rooms for $37/56.

Mel & Faye's Drive-In (☎ 223-0853), at the junction of Hwys 49 and 88, is a local institution and favorite stop for travelers. Breakfast begins at 5 am, though Mel's is best known for $3 burgers served in paper-lined baskets with mounds of French fries. *Theresa's Restaurant* (☎ 223-1786), has been dishing up four-course Italian dinners for three generations. Meals cost around $11 per person.

MOKELUMNE HILL

Mokelumne Hill, known locally as 'Moke Hill,' was first settled by French trappers in the early 1840s. When gold was discovered in 1848, Moke Hill became the principal mining town of Calaveras County and the county seat from 1853 to 1856. Now Moke Hill is a good place to see historic buildings without the common barrage of antique stores and gift shops.

Hotel Leger (☎ 209-286-1401), 8304 Main St, has a classic bar (established in 1851) with a pot-belly stove, ceiling fans, and marble tables. Its Thursday night calamari dinners and Saturday afternoon live bands attract large crowds. Worn but peaceful rooms cost $55/75.

SAN ANDREAS

• *pop 2115* ☎ *209*

As the seat of Calaveras County, San Andreas has utilitarian businesses concentrated on Hwy 49. The old town, north of Hwy 49 along N Main St, is noteworthy for its county courthouse with an art gallery, restored jail and jailyard (where Black Bart, the famous highway bandit, awaited trial), and the **Calaveras County Museum** which has one of the area's best history displays. The museum is open daily from 10 am to 4 pm and costs $1.

In Cave City, nine miles east of San Andreas, are the spectacular **California Caverns** (☎ 736-2708) which John Muir described as 'graceful flowing folds deeply placated like stiff silken drapery.' Regular tours take two hours and cost $3 per person. For $60, the same company's Wild Cave Expedition tours take four hours and include some serious spelunking. The caverns are open daily mid-May to mid-October.

Homey rooms at *Bonnie's Inn* (☎ 754-3212), on Hwy 49 towards the west end of town, cost $42/48 during the week, $52/68 on weekends. Across Hwy 49, *The Robin's Nest* (☎ 754-1076), has rooms for $55 to $95, including breakfast.

ANGELS CAMP
☎ 209

Founded by George Angel in 1849, Angel's Camp was a service center for surrounding gravel and quartz mines. Hard rock mining peaked in the 1890s, when 200 stamp mills ran around the clock. Remains of the last mine are visible in Utica Park, at the west end of Main St. The **Angel's Camp Museum** (☎ 736-2963), 753 S Main St, documents the area's mining heyday with photographs, relics, and three acres of old equipment.

Thanks to Mark Twain's short story 'The Celebrated Jumping Frog of Calaveras County,' Angels Camp has smiling frogs painted on the sidewalk along Main St. The International Frog Jump Competition is held the third weekend in May, and Mark Twain Days are celebrated on 4th of July weekend.

The Calaveras Lodging & Visitors Association (☎ 736-0049, 800-225-3764), 1211 S Main St, is a good place to get brochures and maps.

Places to Stay & Eat
The *Angels Camp KOA* (☎ 736-0149) is two miles south of downtown at 3069 Hwy 49. The *Jumping Frog Motel* (☎ 736-2191), at the corner of Main and Church Sts, has friendly young owners and simple rooms surrounding a courtyard for $35/46. Further east on Main St, the new *Angels Inn Motel* (☎ 736-4242), has a pool and uninteresting rooms for $55.

La Hacienda Restaurant (☎ 736-6711), 15 S Main St, is the favorite for chile rellenos, enchiladas, and tostadas. Dinners are around $8, lunches are around $6.

Mark Twain's presence is still strongly felt in Calaveras county.

MURPHYS
• *pop 1517* ☎ 209

With a main street that looks like a cross between a Norman Rockwell painting and a Jimmy Stewart Western, Murphys is endearing, quaint, charming, and a favorite destination of people from Sacramento and San Francisco. It is named for Daniel and John Murphy who set up a trading post and mining operation on Murphy Creek in conjunction with the local Maidu Indians in the early 1840s.

Orientation & Information
Murphys Stage Stop (☎ 728-2200), 416 Main St, is a bookstore with an extensive California history room. *The Harbinger*, a monthly paper, lists events, activities, and services. Murphys' unofficial but efficient visitor information center is the Murphys Realty Office (☎ 728-3408), at the east end of town, open daily from 8 am to 6 pm.

The work of *E Clampus Vitus*, an organization that tended to miners' widows and orphans, is documented on the 'Wall of

Relative Ovation,' a mural at the end of Main St.

Mercer Caverns

These caves were discovered in 1885 by Walter Mercer who, after a long day of gold prospecting, tried to find some water to quench his thirst, but found a cool stream of air coming out of the ground instead.

Mercer Caverns (☎ 728-2101) are one mile north of Murphys via a well-marked road from the east end of Main St. A 45-minute guided tour takes you past enormous stalactites, stalagmites, and vaulted chambers with names like 'Chinese Meat Market' and 'Organ Loft.' They're open October to May daily, from 11 am to 4 pm, and June to August daily, from 9 am to 5 pm. Admission is $3.

Wineries

The Calaveras Wine Association publishes a list of local wineries, available at Murphys Realty. Big Trees Carriage Company (☎ 728-2602) offers a $30, three-hour tour which includes wine tasting, a gourmet picnic, and a historical tour of Murphys.

Activities

The Stanislaus River, known as 'the Stan,' is now often submerged by the New Melones Reservoir's backwater. The river is still great for swimming, and in drought years offers exciting rafting. Parrots Ferry Rd, east from Hwy 49, crosses the Stan and passes two river access points before it reaches Columbia State Historic Park.

Nearby is the trailhead for the Natural Bridge Trail, a three-mile trail which winds through the river canyon past two large natural bridges and some grottos.

The Outdoor Adventure River Specialists (OARS, ☎ 209-736-4677, 800-446-7238), makes daily rafting runs through a Stanislaus River canyon for $90 per person including lunch.

Places to Stay & Eat

All the accommodations in Murphys are expensive B&Bs. Check nearby Arnold for less-expensive alternatives.

Known as Murphys Hotel, the *Murphys Historic Hotel & Lodge* (☎ 728-3444, 800-532-7684) is touted as the best place to stay and eat locally. The historic rooms cost $110; modern rooms are $70/90; a continental breakfast is included. The dining room is known for its cinnamon rolls ($2.50) and serves standard lunch fare for $6 to $10, and dinner specialties like prime rib, fresh salmon, and herb-crusted chicken for $9 to $18. Reservations are a good idea.

The *Redbud Inn* (☎ 728-8533, 800-827-8533), directly across Main St from the Murphys Hotel, has 13 rooms (most have a fireplace, balcony, and hot tub) for $90 to $125 including a full breakfast. The *Dunbar House 1880 Bed & Breakfast* (☎ 728-2897, 800-225-3764), on the east end of Main St, has a beautiful garden and four antique-laden rooms for $125 a night.

The best place for coffee and sophisticated food is *Grounds* (☎ 728-8663), 402 Main St. They serve breakfast and lunch daily, and dinner on Friday and Saturday nights. House specialties include a breakfast burrito ($6), chicken Caesar salad ($7), and grilled eggplant sandwich ($5). *Sun China* (☎ 728-1294), 386 Main St, serves cheap but unexciting food (closed Mondays).

ARNOLD
☎ 209

About 18 miles northeast of Murphys on Hwy 4, Arnold is a small community which survives on tourist traffic from Caliveras Big Trees State Park, just two miles away. Accommodations here are more affordable than in Murphys. The *Arnold Timberline Lodge* (☎ 795-7666), the only place that gets cable TV, has old but clean rooms with fireplaces for $49/55. *Ebbetts Pass Lodge Motel* (☎ 795-1563) has raggedy rooms, with new bathrooms, facing the highway at $37/49. Rooms off the highway cost $51/56. The *Tamarack Pines Inn* (☎ 753-2080) has the newest facilities in the area and cross-country ski trails from their back yard; double rooms are $70, kitchenettes that sleep four are $90.

Mr B's Diner (☎ 795-0601) has good,

solid, economical all-American food and a friendly atmosphere.

CALAVERAS BIG TREES STATE PARK

This park, 20 miles northeast of Murphys on the western slope of the Sierra Nevada at about 5000 foot elevation, is a great place to hike and camp among giant sequoia trees. Though small and undeveloped, it is easy to access and not too crowded.

It has two giant sequoia groves, 6000 acres of pine forest, and the Stanislaus River and Beaver Creek which offer good trout fishing and great swimming. During the winter, the North Grove stays open for snow-camping and cross-country skiing.

North Grove

The North Grove Campground is the park entrance, where the visitors center, ranger station (☎ 209-795-2334), and main parking lots are. Less crowded is the Oak Hollow Campground, nine miles further on.

The **North Grove Big Trees Trail**, a one-mile self-guided loop, begins next to the visitors center and winds along the forest floor past the Big Stump and Mother of the Forest trees. A four-mile trail climbs out of the North Grove, crosses a ridge, and descends 1500 feet to the Stanislaus River (to avoid the strenuous return climb, park your car at the river and hitch back to the North Grove).

South Grove

Not accessible by car, and devoid of any picnic areas or campgrounds, the South Grove is a designated nature preserve and contains the park's most remote reaches. From the Beaver Creek picnic area follow the nine-mile **South Grove Trail** on foot. You don't have to hike the whole thing to have a memorable experience!

COLUMBIA

• *pop 1799* ☎ *209*

Known as the 'Gem of the Southern Mines,' Columbia is now a State Historic Park with four blocks of delightfully preserved 1850s buildings. Concessionaires wear period costumes and sell old fashioned products, and the blacksmith and shoemaker use traditional methods. A horse-drawn carriage is the only vehicle allowed on the streets.

Columbia's early prospectors panned dirt which they scraped from between limestone outcroppings (visible at both ends of Main St). Encouraged by small finds, they eventually employed hydraulic methods. Remains of the flume rest behind the buildings on the south end of Main St.

The Columbia Docent Association and Museum (☎ 532-4301), at the corner of Main and State Sts, has history exhibits. For a brochure about the park, stop by the Columbia Park Ranger Station (☎ 532-0150), on Parrots Ferry Rd between Broadway and Washington St.

Places to Stay & Eat

Established in 1856, the *City Hotel* (☎ 532-1479), on Main St, has restored rooms for $70 to $90. The hotel restaurant is run by students of Columbia College's Hospitality Management Program, and serves some of the best food in the Gold Country. The four-course menu changes daily, and costs $28 per person.

Owned and operated by the City Hotel, the *Fallon Hotel* (☎ 532-1470), established in 1857, has 'petite rooms' for $55, balcony rooms for $75 to $90, and serves a continental breakfast.

Just outside the park, on the road to Sonora, is the *Columbia Inn* (☎ 533-0446) with rooms for $32/38 per single/double.

Entertainment

The *Fallon Hotel Theater* (☎ 532-4644) stages contemporary productions – usually musicals – of notable quality. Shows run year round Thursday to Sunday, and tickets cost $15 to $22.

SONORA

• *pop 4153* ☎ *209*

Settled by miners from Sonora, Mexico, this town was, in its heyday, a cosmopolitan center with Spanish plazas, elaborate

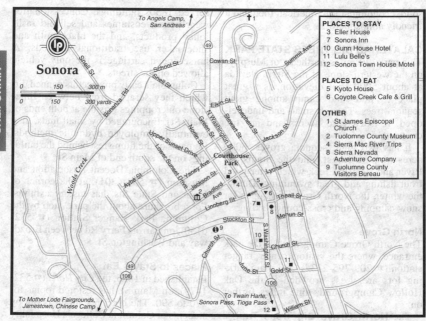

Sonora

To Angels Camp,
San Andreas

PLACES TO STAY
3 Eller House
7 Sonora Inn
10 Gunn House Hotel
11 Lulu Belle's
12 Sonora Town House Motel

PLACES TO EAT
5 Kyoto House
6 Coyote Creek Cafe & Grill

OTHER
1 St James Episcopal
  Church
2 Tuolumne County Museum
4 Sierra Mac River Trips
8 Sierra Nevada
  Adventure Company
9 Tuolumne County
  Visitors Bureau

To Mother Lode Fairgrounds,
Jamestown, Chinese Camp

To Twain Harte,
Sonora Pass, Tioga Pass

---

saloons, and the Southern Mines' largest concentration of gamblers, drunkards, and gold. Still bustling as the Tuolumne County seat and a thoroughfare for Yosemite National Park travelers, Sonora has a conservative population and wealth of outdoors enthusiasts. New Agers from the surrounding hills bring good vegetarian restaurants and alternative entertainment to Sonora's historic downtown.

Orientation & Information
Sonora Pass (Hwy 108) and Tioga Pass (Hwy 120) cross the Sierra Nevada east of Sonora (see the Sierra Nevada chapter).

Downtown Sonora centers around the T-shaped intersection of Washington and Stockton Sts, with Washington being the main thoroughfare. Businesses on Washington St include banks, bookstores, and antique shops. The Tuolumne County Visitors Bureau (☎ 533-4420, 800-446-1333), 55 W Stockton St, is open Monday to Thursday from 9 am to 5 pm, and on Fridays and weekends until 6 pm.

Stop by the Sierra Nevada Adventure Company (☎ 532-5621), 173 S Washington St, for maps, equipment, and friendly advice on where to climb, hike, and fish.

Things to See
Housed in the former Tuolumne County Jail, the **Tuolumne County Museum** (☎ 532-1317), 158 W Bradford Ave two blocks west of Washington St, has Gold Rush photographs, guns, antiques, and clothing. It's free and open daily.

Residential neighborhoods, off the north end of Washington St, are lined with beautifully restored Victorian houses. **St James Episcopal Church**, a local landmark built in 1858, is now simply called the 'Red Church.'

In late September, the Tuolumne County Wild West Film Festival, at the Mother Lode Fairgrounds east of Stockton St on Southgate Drive, features a rodeo, street fair, and outdoor screenings of classic westerns. For information call the visitors center.

Whitewater Rafting
The Tuolumne River is known for its class IV rapids and its population of golden eagles and red-tailed hawks. The Stanislaus River is more accessible and heavily traveled. Sierra Mac River Trips Inc (☎ 532-1327, 800-457-2580), 19 W Bradford Ave, PO Box 366, Sonora, CA 95370, has a good reputation. Also recommended by locals, Zephyr Whitewater Expeditions (☎ 800-431-3636) runs trips on the Kings, Merced, Stanislaus, and American Rivers. Half-day trips start at about $65. Week-long expeditions cost around $500.

Places to Stay
Motels The *Sonora Town House Motel* (☎ 532-3633), 350 S Washington St, has a pool, hot tub, and modern rooms for $55/60, $65/70 in summer. Ask for a room away from Washington St to avoid traffic noise.

Rooms in the *Gunn House Hotel* (☎ 532-3421), 286 S Washington St, cost $45/55 including a continental breakfast.

An institution since 1896, the historic *Sonora Inn* (☎ 532-2400), 160 S Washington St, has a variety of rooms – about half are in a motel addition behind the original hotel – for $55 to $105.

East of downtown, just past the McDonald's and Taco Bell on Hwy 108, the *Aladdin Motor Inn* (☎ 533-4971, 800-696-3969) has standard rooms for $38/42 including a continental breakfast. Across the highway, the *Best Western Sonora Oaks Motor Hotel* (☎ 533-4400), has rooms for $55/62.

B&Bs The *Eller House* (☎ 532-0420), 56 W Bradford Ave, is a charming Victorian surrounded by gardens with rooms for $55 to $85. Overlooking downtown, *Lulu Belle's* (☎ 533-3455, 800-538-3455), at 85 Gold St, has Southern grace and charm, California-style. Rooms cost $80 to $90 and include a full breakfast.

Places to Eat
Sonora's restaurants are concentrated along S Washington St, downtown. The *Coyote Creek Cafe & Grill* (☎ 532-9115), 177 S Washington, has hearty, healthy food with a Southwestern twist, and vegetarian dishes; prices run $6 to $11. Upstairs at 145 S Washington St, *Kyoto House* (☎ 532-2625) has excellent sushi for around $7 (closed Monday).

Open 24 hours, the *Sonora Inn Cafe* (☎ 532-2400), in the Sonora Inn at 160 S Washington, has basic breakfasts, burgers, and sandwiches.

TWAIN HARTE
Eleven miles northeast of Sonora on Hwy 108, Twain Harte is a woodsy resort town with flower lined streets and a proliferation of antique shops. Twain Harte was established in 1924 as an overnight, food, and fuel stop between Lake Tahoe and Yosemite Valley, and is named after authors Mark Twain and Bret Harte, who briefly lived here.

JAMESTOWN
☎ 209
Just south of the junction of Hwys 49 and 108, Jamestown (affectionately called 'Jimtown') was the site of three major booms. The first was caused by Tuolumne County's first gold strike in 1848, the second came with the arrival of the railroad in 1897, and the third occurred in the 1920s when Jamestown became construction headquarters for dams on the Stanislaus and Tuolumne Rivers. Its various growth spurts have left a varied collection of brick, stone, and adobe structures which now house shops, cafes, and bookstores. The National Hotel (☎ 984-3446, 800-894-3446), 77 Main St, is a good place to pick up information.

Railtown 1897 State Historic Park
This area (☎ 984-3953), south of Main St on 5th Ave, has a 26-acre collection of trains and railroad equipment and was the backdrop for the film *High Noon*. Guided

tours, included in the $3 admission fee, are given daily from 9:30 am to 4:30 pm.

Train rides on the Mother Lode Cannon Ball, a narrow-guage railroad once used to transport ore, lumber, and miners to and from the mines, make a one-hour loop through the forest, past old mines and equipment. It runs March to November for $9.

CHINESE CAMP

Chinese Camp, 10 miles south of Sonora on Hwy 49, once had an all-Chinese population of about 5000. The 'Trees of Heaven,' a thick growth of pines which hide many of the old structures, were originally brought by the Chinese. Few buildings have been restored, making Chinese Camp one of the better ghost towns around. In the spring, the surrounding hills bloom with wildflowers and almond blossoms. There is a small branch of the Tuolumne County Visitors Bureau (☎ 984-4636) in the old general store at the corner of Hwy 49 and Main St, open in summer daily.

Northern Mountains

Natural beauty is definitely the attraction here. This chapter contains some of California's most beautiful features, including majestic Mt Shasta, Shasta Lake, and many other beautiful, clean lakes surrounded by mountain forests, Lassen Volcanic National Monument, Lava Beds National Monument, and others. But there are plenty of places mentioned in this chapter that even most native Californians will never see, thinking them too remote. The relaxed, uncrowded nature of tourism up here makes it especially enjoyable – and you can find all the services you need, without competing for them with thousands of other visitors.

Mt Shasta Area

☎ 916

You'll probably never forget your first glimpse of Mt Shasta. Naturalist and Sierra Club founder John Muir, of the first time he saw Mt Shasta, exclaimed: 'When I first caught sight of it I was 50 miles away and afoot, alone, and weary. Yet all my blood turned to wine, and I have not been weary since.'

Many people are attracted to the mountain for its reputed spiritual qualities; others are attracted simply for its beauty and its fine recreational possibilities. Camping, hiking, skiing, soaking in hot springs, mountain biking, and simply scenic driving are all popular activities on the mountain.

The **Shasta-Trinity National Forest** is a 2.1 million-acre forest extending in patches from the Six Rivers National Forest in the west all the way to the Modoc National Forest in the east. Within the forest are some of northern California's prime recreational attractions including Trinity/Clair Engle Lake, Whiskeytown Lake, Lewiston Lake, Shasta Lake, and Mt Shasta. It also includes Trinity Alps Wilderness, Mt Shasta Wilderness, Castle Crags Wilderness, Chanchelulla Wilderness, and part of Yolla Bolly-Middle Eel Wilderness. A 154-mile section of the Pacific Crest Trail passes through the forest, as do the nine-mile Sisson-Callahan National Recreation Trail and the eight-mile South Fork National Recreation Trail.

The Shasta-Trinity National Forests Supervisor's Office at 2400 Washington Ave in Redding (☎ 246-5222) has information about the entire forest and is a good reference on mountain activities. The Mt Shasta Visitors Bureau puts out a free pamphlet, *Things to See & Do*, which is also a fine place to look for recreation suggestions.

MT SHASTA – THE TOWN
• *pop 3500* • *elev 3561 feet*

The pleasant town of Mt Shasta is dwarfed by its namesake mountain, which towers 10,600 feet above it. When European fur trappers arrived in the area in the 1820s they found several small Indian tribes including the Shasta, Karuk, Klamath, Modoc, Wintu, and Pit Indians. By 1851, hordes of gold rush miners had arrived, disrupting the Indians' traditional livelihoods. The railroad ushered in a booming lumber industry and since the town was surrounded by many 'dry' lumber towns, Mt Shasta became a bawdy, good-time town for the lumberjacks.

Originally called Strawberry Valley for the abundant wild strawberries that grew here, the town was renamed Sisson, after its principal landowner, postmaster, and innkeeper, then given the name Mt Shasta in the 1920s. Today, 'new age' residents have replaced the lumberjacks.

With plenty of good places to stay and eat, and a quiet and friendly atmosphere, the town makes an excellent base for exploring the area's many natural wonders.

The busiest times for visiting Mt Shasta are from Memorial Day through Labor Day, and on weekends during the ski season, from around late-November through April.

Orientation & Information

Orienting yourself is a snap, with Mt Shasta towering above you on the east side and the Eddy Mountains on the west. The town center is a few blocks east of I-5, 60 miles north of Redding; take the Central Mt Shasta exit and head east toward the mountain. This puts you on Lake St, one of the town's principal streets. A few blocks east you will come to the town's busiest inter-

section, where Lake St meets Mt Shasta Blvd; this is Mt Shasta's 'main drag.'

Tourist Offices The Mt Shasta Visitors Center (☎ 926-4865, 800-926-4865), 300 Pine St on the corner of Lake St, one block west of Mt Shasta Blvd, has plenty of information on the town and the surrounding area. They also offer several free publications about recreation in Siskiyou County and the vicinity.

The Mt Shasta Ranger District Office (☎ 926-4511), 204 W Alma St, 1½ blocks west of Mt Shasta Blvd, has maps, information, permits, suggestions, good advice,

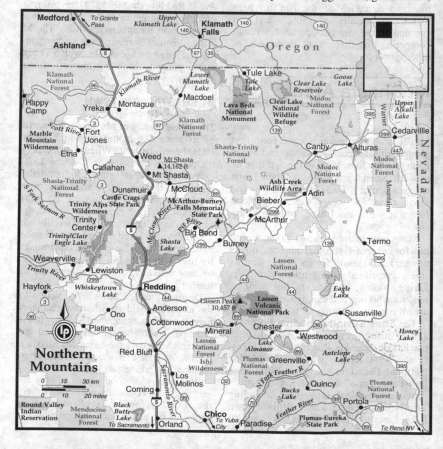

Northern Mountains

and everything else you need for exploring the Shasta-Trinity area. The AAA office (☎ 842-4416), 111B W Lake St, is beside the gas station on the southwest corner of Mt Shasta Blvd and Lake St.

Bookstores Several bookshops carry interesting selections of books about Mt Shasta, from its geology to its folklore. Check out the 'new age' *Golden Bough Bookstore* (☎ 926-3228), 219 N Mt Shasta Blvd; *Wings Bookstore* (☎ 926-3041), 226 N Mt Shasta Blvd; and *Village Books* (☎ 926-1678), 320 N Mt Shasta Blvd. The Sisson Museum also has a good selection of books.

Things to See & Do

Most of Mt Shasta's attractions are in the surrounding area, but the town has a few places worth visiting, too. In the beautiful 26-acre **City Park,** on Nixon Rd about a mile north of the town center, the headwaters of the **Sacramento River** gurgle up from the ground in a large, cool spring. The park also contains hiking trails, picnic and sports areas, a gazebo, and children's playgrounds.

The **Sisson Museum** (☎ 926-5508) and the **Mt Shasta Fish Hatchery** (☎ 926-2215) are side by side at 1 Old Stage Rd, half a mile west of I-5. The museum features exhibits on the geology and history of the town and the mountain. The hatchery has large ponds where you can see and feed several types of trout.

Fifth Season Sports (☎ 926-3606), 300 N Mt Shasta Blvd at Lake St, rents mountain climbing gear, camping and backpacking gear, mountain bikes, skis, snowshoes, and more. The House of Ski (☎ 926-2359), 1208 Everitt Memorial Hwy, on the road up the mountain, also rents sporting gear.

Places to Stay

Camping A few blocks north of the center of town, *Mt Shasta KOA* (☎ 926-4029, 800-736-3617), 900 N Mt Shasta Blvd (off E Hinckley St), is an attractive campground charging $19.50 for tents, $22 to $27 for

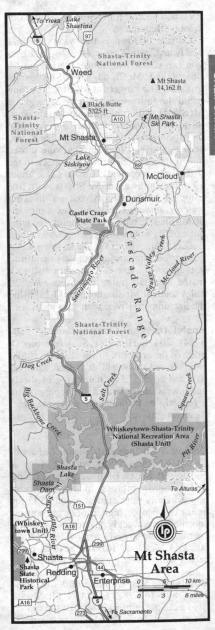

CALIFORNIA

RVs, and $32/40 for cabins; ask about off-season discounts.

Outside of town is the waterside *Lake Siskiyou Camp-Resort* (☎ 926-2618), or you can check with ranger stations in Mt Shasta and McCloud for USFS campgrounds. The rangers at Mt Shasta recommend the following: *McBride Springs,* on Mt Shasta, with running water, no showers, pit toilets ($6/site); *Panther Springs,* also on Mt Shasta, with a Wintu Indian sacred springs above it (the springs were closed due to an avalanche in 1995 so check to see if it's been reopened); *Castle Lake,* about 13 miles southwest of Mt Shasta, with free camping for tents only, but no drinking water; *Gumboot Lake,* 15 miles southwest of Mt Shasta, with free camping for tents only, purify your own drinking water; *Toad Lake,* 15 miles from Mt Shasta town, not a designated campground but very beautiful, you go down a gravel road and must walk in the last half-mile; and *Sims Flat,* 20 miles south of Mt Shasta just off I-5, beside the Sacramento River, with sites at $8.

Hostel *Alpenrose Cottage Hostel* (☎ 926-6724), 204 E Hinckley St a few blocks north of the center of town, attracts visitors from around the world. It's clean, open all day, and costs $13 including use of sheets and towels. Betty Brown, the proprietor, is a fountain of information about the area. Reservations are recommended but no membership card is required.

Cabins & Cottages *Mt Shasta Cabins & Cottages* (☎ 926-5396), with an office at 500 S Mt Shasta Blvd, rents everything from studio cottages to four-bedroom houses. Daily rates start at around $45 for one or two people, higher for larger houses, and there are weekly and off-season discounts. *Strawberry Court* (☎ 926-4704), 305 Old McCloud Rd, has several brick cabins with private garages for $46/50.

Motels The *Shasta Lodge Motel* (☎ 926-2815, 800-742-7821), 724 N Mt Shasta Blvd a couple of blocks north of the center, is a pleasant, basic motel with newly renovated rooms ($29/32) and a friendly atmosphere.

Several other decent motels are spread out along S Mt Shasta Blvd. Most have pools and hot tubs, and charge around $40 to $50 in the summer. Try *Travel Inn* (☎ 926-4617), *Alpine Lodge Motel* (☎ 926-3145), *Mountain Air Lodge & Ski House* (☎ 926-3411), or *Evergreen Lodge* (☎ 926-2143).

A fancier motel, the *Strawberry Valley Inn* (☎ 926-2052), 1142 S Mt Shasta Blvd, has rooms at $50/60 including a breakfast buffet, wine or beer in the evening, a garden, and a terrace with a view of the mountain. The *Tree House Best Western Motor Inn* (☎ 926-3101), I-5 and Lake St, charges $60/70.

B&Bs & Resorts *Ward's Big Foot Ranch* (☎ 926-5170, 800-926-1272), 1530 Hill Rd, is a delightful B&B on a farm with large, beautiful grounds and two rooms at $65 and $75. The *Wagon Creek Inn* (☎ 926-0838, 800-995-9260), 1239 Woodland Park Drive at Old Stage Rd, is a log cabin lodge with rooms at $65 and $75. *Mt Shasta Resort* (☎ 926-3030), 1000 Siskiyou Lake St, is the poshest place to stay, with a golf course, a fine restaurant/lounge, and all the amenities. One-bedroom chalets are $95 to $115, two-bedroom chalets are $115 to $155.

Places to Eat
The *Bagel Cafe & Bakery,* 105 E Alma St just east of Mt Shasta Blvd, has plenty of healthy selections and is a pleasant place to hang out. The *Shasta Mountain Bakery,* 315 N Mt Shasta Blvd, has all kinds of baked goods, including sourdough.

Wendie's Italian Restaurant, 610 S Mt Shasta Blvd, is great for a simple, hearty homestyle breakfast, lunch, or dinner. Another good Italian dinner house is *Mike & Tony's,* 501 S Mt Shasta Blvd, and also worthwhile is *Piedmont Restaurant,* 1200 S Mt Shasta Blvd.

A popular hangout, *Willy's Bavarian Kitchen,* 107 Chestnut St at Mt Shasta Blvd, serves German food with vegetarian options, and has a small beer garden with a view of the mountain. *King Wah's Lamplighter Restaurant,* 903 S Mt Shasta Blvd, specializes in Cantonese cuisine and thick-cut steaks.

Critics and locals alike rave about *Bellissimo* (☎ 926-4461), 104-A W Lake St, with its unusual international cuisine. Reservations are a good idea. *Serge's* (☎ 926-1276), 531 Chestnut St, one block east of Mt Shasta Blvd, serves fine French cuisine with creative variations; there's seating indoors or on the mountain-view terrace.

For Mexican meals, try up-market *Lalo's* at 520 N Mt Shasta Blvd, or, on the opposite end of the economic spectrum, *Poncho & Lefkowitz,* 310 W Lake St, serving up homestyle Mexican food and gourmet hot dogs from a trailer in the Payless parking lot, with tables out under a tent.

Cervelli's Market, 625 S Mt Shasta Blvd, boasts 'the best deli sandwiches in town.' Natural foods markets are *Berryvale Natural Foods Grocery,* 305 S Mt Shasta Blvd, next to the post office, and the *Mountain Song Natural Foods Market* in the Mt Shasta Shopping Center off W Lake St.

Entertainment
The *Vet's Club Bar,* 406 N Mt Shasta Blvd, has live music (mostly rock 'n' roll) and dancing on Thursday, Friday, and Saturday nights. The *Bagel Cafe & Bakery* (see Places to Eat) also has live acoustic music on weekends.

Getting There & Away
Greyhound buses on I-5 do not pull into Mt Shasta, but they will if you telephone to request a stop. If you want to travel south, phone the Greyhound office in Weed (☎ 938-4454); if you want to travel north, call the office in Redding (☎ 241-2531). The bus will stop at the corner of W Lake St and Morgan Ave, but only during the daytime. Reservations can be made by calling 800-231-2222.

The STAGE bus (☎ 842-8295, 800-247-8243) includes Mt Shasta in its local route serving McCloud, Dunsmuir, Mt Shasta, Weed, Yreka, and Montague; other buses connect at Yreka for Fort Jones, Greenview, Etna, Klamath River, and out to Happy Camp. Telephone for pick-up at least two hours ahead.

In winter, the CHP's recorded report (☎ 842-4438) gives weather and road conditions (roads closed, chains required, etc) for all Siskiyou County roads.

MT SHASTA – THE MOUNTAIN
• *elev 14,162 feet*
'Lonely as God, white as a winter moon' wrote Joaquin Miller of Mt Shasta in *Life Among the Modocs.* Dominating the landscape for 50 miles around and visible for over 100 miles around many parts of northern California and southern Oregon, Mt Shasta is the most notable feature in this part of northern California. Though not California's highest mountain – it ranks sixth highest – it seems especially magnificent because it rises up alone on the landscape, unrivaled by other mountains.

Mt Shasta is part of the vast Cascade volcanic chain that includes Lassen Peak to the south and others north to Canada. Though some sources say Mt Shasta is extinct, others note the presence of thermal hot springs and say it may simply be dormant; smoke was seen puffing out of the crater on the summit in the 1850s, though the last eruption was probably a few hundred years ago. The mountain has two cones – the main cone has a crater about 200 yards across, and the younger, shorter cone on the western flank, called Shastina, has a crater about half a mile wide.

Of course the primary attraction is the mountain itself. Hiking, mountain biking, climbing, cross-country and downhill skiing, and snowshoeing, as well as plain old sightseeing, are all popular activities on the mountain, with a number of hiking trails providing recreation for all types of visitors. The mountain is classified as a wilderness area and any time you set foot on it, whether for hiking, climbing, camping, or whatever, you must obtain a free permit from the Mt Shasta ranger station and a free campfire permit if you plan on going camping. The ranger station sells topographical maps of the mountain and will advise you on current conditions.

Driving

You can drive up the mountain for a fine view at any time of year. The Everitt Memorial Hwy goes up to 7900 feet; to get on it, simply head east on Lake St from downtown Mt Shasta and keep on going. The Mt Shasta ranger station offers a free map for a round-the-mountain driving tour starting at Mt Shasta and finishing at Weed; this may be possible only in late summer, depending on how much snowfall there's been that winter.

Hiking

A steep, treeless, black volcanic cone on the north side of the town of Mt Shasta, **Black Butte** rises almost 3000 feet over the town. A 2½-mile trail to the top is steep and rocky in many places, and as there is neither shade nor water on the trail, heat can be a problem when climbing in summer. Allow two to five hours or more for a roundtrip hike; wear good hiking shoes and bring plenty of drinking water. The ranger station has a pamphlet about the climb.

Rangers can also direct you to access points along the **Pacific Crest Trail** – of which there are many – including points at Gumboot Lake, Deadfall Lake, Toad Lake, and Castle Crags State Park. Two easy sections the rangers recommend are the relatively flat, four-mile trail to **Deadfall Lake**, and the two-mile section from Gumboot Lake to **Seven Lakes Basin**.

Or try the nine-mile **Sisson-Callahan National Recreation Trail**, a historic trail established in the mid-1800s by prospectors, trappers, and cattlemen to connect the mining town of Callahan with the town of Sisson, now called Mt Shasta.

Climbing

Climbing to the summit is best done in summer from around May to August. How long it takes to climb up the mountain and back depends on many factors including the route selected, the physical condition of

the climbers, weather conditions, and more. Though the roundtrip can conceivably be done in one day with eight to 12 hours of solid hiking, it's best to allow at least two days for the climb, spending a night on the mountain. Though the hiking distance to the summit is only around six miles, it makes a vertical climb of over 7000 feet, so acclimatizing to the elevation is important. You'll need crampons, an ice ax, and a helmet, all of which can be rented locally. Rockslides and unpredictable weather can be hazardous, so novices

---

The Strange Legends of Mt Shasta

Mt Shasta has been inspiring legends since long before Europeans arrived on the scene. Local Indians had their own legends about the mountain, some remarkably similar to more modern occult legends. Several of these modern legends are – to say the least – a bit unusual, but there are those who believe in them. One legend has it that a race of Lemurians – refugees from the 'lost continent' of Lemuria, now submerged beneath the Pacific Ocean – live inside the mountain. Variations on the theme say that a race of 'little people,' invisible people, or a mystic brotherhood, live inside the mountain. GW Ballard, founder of Mt Shasta's St Germain Foundation (also known as 'I AM'), claims to have had a mystical meeting with his namesake saint on the mountain in the summer of 1930.

Many believe Mt Shasta is a center or magnet for spiritual energy, or that a vortex of spiritual energy is formed by the triangle of Mt Shasta, Mt Eddy, and Castle Crags. Many of these spirit-conscious people live or visit here because they believe their own spiritual powers are increased near Mt Shasta. Still others say that whatever your particular characteristics, they will be intensified by the mountain's energy – be it for good or for ill. And then, of course, there are plenty of people who think that all this spiritual stuff is a bunch of nonsense! ■

should contact the ranger station for a list of available guides.

Mt Shasta Ski Park

On the south slope of Mt Shasta, off Hwy 89 heading towards McCloud, the Mt Shasta Ski Park (☎ 926-8610, snow reports 926-8686) is open in winter for skiing and snowboarding, usually from around late-November to April, depending on snowfall. The park has an 1100-foot vertical drop and 22 Alpine runs; rentals, instruction, and weekly specials are all available.

The ski park is also open in summer, from around late-June to early-September, for scenic chairlift rides and an educational exhibit on volcanoes. Mountain bikers can take the chairlift up and come whooshing back down. Summer hours are Wednesday to Sunday from 10 am to 4 pm.

The Lakes

Near Mt Shasta are a number of beautiful mountain lakes including **Lake Siskiyou**, the largest, 2.5 miles southwest of Mt Shasta. Stop at **Box Canyon Dam** for a view into the picturesque 200-foot-deep canyon. Another 10 miles up in the mountains is **Castle Lake**, a pristine site surrounded by granite formations and pine forest. Swimming, fishing, picnicking, and free camping are popular here in summer; in winter, people ice-skate on the lake. **Lake Shastina**, about 15 miles north of Mt Shasta, is another nearby beauty.

The Mt Shasta ranger station distributes a pamphlet, *Alpine Lakes of the Mt Shasta Ranger District,* with details on 50 nearby lakes, some accessible only by dirt roads or hiking trails – great for getting away from it all. You can camp beside any of the lakes, as long as you get a free campfire permit from the ranger station and set up your camp at least 200 feet from the water.

DUNSMUIR

• *pop 2170* • *elev 2300 feet*

Eight miles south of Mt Shasta, six miles north of Castle Crags State Park, and nestled into the forested Sacramento River Canyon, the picturesque town of Dunsmuir

is known for its pristine scenery and good fishing. Dunsmuir hit the national news in July 1991 when six train cars derailed and fell into the river, one of them spilling a toxic chemical into the water killing fish and wildlife. The chemical was rendered harmless, but it took awhile for the river's ecosystem to get back to normal. The river is clean once again, and the fish are back.

The Dunsmuir Chamber of Commerce (☎ 235-2177), 4841 Dunsmuir Ave, has free maps, walking guide pamphlets, and information about the town.

Things to See & Do

The peaceful **Dunsmuir City Park** beside the Sacramento River is worth visiting; go around behind the steam engine near the north side of the chamber of commerce, and follow the winding road until you reach the park. On the way is the **Alexander Dunsmuir Fountain,** which coal baron Dunsmuir gave to the town in exchange for naming it after him.

Dunsmuir has two beautiful waterfalls worth visiting. **Hedge Creek Falls** is just a five-minute walk from a lovely little botanical garden on Dunsmuir Ave. In the garden, look for the viewpoint overlooking the river. A five-minute walk upstream on a forest trail brings you to the falls. **Moss-brae Falls** is larger and more spectacular. Turn west from Dunsmuir Ave onto Scarlett Way, passing under an archway marked 'Shasta Retreat.' Park by the railroad tracks and walk upstream along the tracks, which run beside the river, for about half an hour until you reach a railroad bridge built in 1901. Shortly before reaching the bridge, walk down a little path through the trees to the river and the falls. NOTE: Be *extremely careful* of trains as you walk the tracks – the river's sound can make it impossible to hear trains coming. Two trains passed us in half an hour when we did this walk, and we never heard either of them, just looked up and saw they were upon us. So watch out!

Places to Stay

Certainly the most unusual place to stay in Dunsmuir is in a vintage railroad caboose at the *Railroad Park Resort* (☎ 235-4440, 800-974-7245), 100 Railroad Park Rd, one mile south of town (take the Railroad Park exit off I-5). A caboose or a cabin costs $60/65 ($10 cheaper in winter). There's also a campground with tent/RV sites at $13/18. *Cave Springs Resort* (☎ 235-2721), 4727 Dunsmuir Ave, overlooking the Sacramento River, has motel rooms from $37 to $49, cabins with kitchens from $31 to $45, mobile homes from $49 to $60, and RV spaces at $14 (no tents). Weekly rates are cheaper. The *Oak Tree Inn* (☎ 235-2884), 6604 Dunsmuir Ave, on the south end of town, is another comfortable, relaxed lodging in a beautiful setting; regular rooms are $42, with larger suites available. Several other motels along Dunsmuir Ave are in the $40 to $50 range.

The *Dunsmuir B&B Inn* (☎ 235-4543), 5423 Dunsmuir Ave, comes highly recommended by travelers. You can cook in the kitchen or barbecue in the yard, and use the outdoor spa pool. The four guest rooms, all with private bath, are $50 to $60.

Places to Eat

Shelby's, 5843 Dunsmuir Ave, is Dunsmuir's most popular eatery, with a friendly small town atmosphere, delicious food, and interesting, unusual selections on the menu for all meals. It's open Wednesday to Saturday from 7 am to 8 pm, Sunday to Tuesday 7 am to 2 pm.

Red's Cajun Cookin', 6000 Dunsmuir Ave, is a great find – locals and visitors alike love this place, with its friendly owners and authentic Cajun and Creole food. It's open Tuesday to Saturday, 11:30 am to 9 pm.

The *Railroad Park Resort* (see Places to Stay) offers dining in vintage railroad dining cars – a little more expensive, but definitely something different.

Getting There & Away

Greyhound stops at a bus stop on Dunsmuir Ave, near Spruce St. The closest depots are in Weed (19 miles north) and Redding (52 miles south). See the Mt Shasta section for details on how to arrange stops. The STAGE bus serves Dunsmuir, Mt Shasta, and other local destinations; see the Mt Shasta section for specifics.

The Amtrak station at 5750 Sacramento Ave, one block east of Dunsmuir Ave, is the only train stop in Siskiyou County – the north-south *Coast Starlight* train stops here. Buy tickets at local travel agencies or from the conductor aboard the train, but call to make a reservation.

CASTLE CRAGS STATE PARK

Dominated by magnificent granite crags, Castle Crags State Park is just off I-5, six miles south of Dunsmuir. The crags are similar to the granite formations of Yosemite National Park and the eastern Sierra, and Castle Dome here resembles Yosemite's famous Half Dome.

Hiking trails include the gentle one-mile Indian Creek Nature Trail, the mile-long moderately strenuous Root Creek Trail, the strenuous 2.7-mile Crags Trail/Indian Springs Trail, and seven miles of the Pacific Crest Trail, passing through the park at the base of the crags. There's fishing in the Sacramento River at the picnic and camping area on the opposite side of I-5.

The office at the park entrance (☎ 235-2684) is open daily and has all the information you could want about the park.

Camping

Camping is allowed only at designated camping sites within the park. Camping sites are open all year, even in winter when there is snow. Destinet takes reservations from mid-May to mid-September; the rest of the year it's first-come, first-served. The sites have running water and hot showers, but no hookups. Cost is $14 per night. Or you can camp for free in the Shasta-Trinity National Forest surrounding the park; you must have a campfire permit, issued free at park offices.

Across the highway in Castella, the small, quiet *Cragview Valley Park* (☎ 235-0081) has tent sites at $10 and RV sites with/without hookups at $15/12. Also across the highway, the state park's riverside Picnic Area has camping at $14 per night.

THE LAKES
Shasta Lake

About 15 minutes north of Redding on I-5 is Shasta Lake, one of California's most beautiful lakes and the largest reservoir in California. It is a popular place, with hikes and campgrounds around the lake, and just about anything that floats on the water.

The Shasta Lake Information Center (☎ 275-1589, 800-474-2782) has free pamphlets with maps and details on hiking trails, fishing, and boating around the lake. From I-5, take the Mountaingate Wonderland Blvd exit, 10 miles north of Redding, and turn right on Holiday Rd. At the south end of Shasta Lake, the magnificent **Shasta Dam** is the second most massive dam in the USA. Its 487-foot spillway is the largest manmade waterfall in the world – three times higher than Niagara Falls. The dam was built from 1938 to 1945; Woody Guthrie wrote *This Land is Your Land* while he was here working on the dam. Free tours are given every day departing from the Shasta Dam Visitors Center (☎ 275-4463).

Lake Shasta Caverns (☎ 238-2341, 800-795-2283) is a network of limestone and marble caves. Tours operate every day and include a boat ride across Lake Shasta to get to the caves; tours are $12 for all ages. The tour lasts around two hours, with one hour inside the caves. Bring a sweater, as the temperature inside the caves is 58°F year round. Take the Shasta Caverns Rd exit from I-5, about 20 minutes north of Redding, and follow the signs.

Places to Stay The USFS operates campgrounds around the lake, some accessible by road, others accessible only by boat, all at $11 to $14 per site. Some of the most scenic are *Ellery Creek, Hirz Bay, McCloud Bridge, Moore Creek,* and *Pine Point.* All are open from April to September and are available on a first-come, first-served basis. Plenty of commercial campgrounds surround the lake, including the *Antlers RV Park & Campground* (☎ 800-642-6849), *Holiday Harbor* (☎ 800-776-2628), and *Lakehead Campground & RV Park* (☎ 238-2671). Camping outside organized campgrounds requires a campfire permit, available free from the information center or from any USFS office.

Houseboats and other boats can be rented from the multitude of marinas, including *Antlers Resort & Marina* (☎ 800-238-3924), *Jones Valley Resort* (☎ 800-223-7950), *Shasta Marina* (☎ 238-2284), and the *Silverthorn Resort Marina* (☎ 275-1571, 800-332-3044). If you do want to rent a houseboat, reserve one as far in advance as possible – many are booked a full year in advance, especially for the summer months.

Whiskeytown Lake

Eight miles west of Redding, Whiskeytown Lake is a pleasant lake that takes its name from the mining town beneath its waters. When the lake was created by the construction of a 282-foot dam, old Whiskeytown was swallowed up. It's an active spot for everything from water skiing to gold panning. Boats can be rented at Oak Bottom Marina, just off Hwy 299.

The Whiskeytown Visitors Center (☎ 246-1225), on the south end of the lake just off Hwy 299 offers free maps of the Whiskeytown Unit and advice on all recreational activities. There's free camping at the *Brandy Creek Campground,* in a grove of trees beside the lake, on a first-come, first-served basis for self-contained RVs only (no tents). The *Oak Bottom Campground* is in a more open setting, allows both tent and RV camping, and accepts reservations through Destinet.

Lewiston Lake

26 miles west of Redding, Lewiston (population 1500) is an attractive, tiny remnant of a town that makes a pleasant rest stop. It's right beside the Trinity River, where there's a campground and good fishing below the bridge. About 1½ miles north, Lewiston Lake is little but it's a peaceful alternative to the other lakes in the area, due to the 10

mph speed limit. The lake is kept at a constant level, providing a fine habitat for fish (especially rainbow, brook, and brown trout) and waterfowl, with a number of migrating bird species – you may see ospreys and bald eagles fishing in the early evening.

Several USFS and commercial campgrounds are spaced around the lake, all around $8 per night. There's also the *Lakeview Terrace Resort* (☎ 778-3803) with cabins, camping, and boat rental. In town, the *Lewiston Inn,* built in 1899, is no longer a functioning hotel but it's a bar-restaurant-hangout with a lot of character. It's open Wednesday to Sunday, with the bar opening at 3 pm and the restaurant at 6 pm. A few doors away is the *Old Lewiston Bridge RV Resort* (☎ 778-3894, 800-922-1924), which offers tent and RV camping beside the river bridge.

Trinity/Clair Engle Lake
Just north of Lewiston Lake, Trinity Lake (sometimes called Clair Engle Lake) is California's third-largest man-made lake and attracts multitudes of people for swimming, fishing, and any number of watersports. The west side of the lake has most of the campgrounds, RV parks, motels, boat rentals, and restaurants. The east side of the lake is quieter, with more secluded campgrounds, some accessible only by boat. The ranger station in Weaverville has information on USFS campgrounds.

REDDING
• *pop 70,000* • *elev 560 feet*
At the north end of the Sacramento Valley, ringed by mountain ranges on three sides, Redding is a rather unremarkable town but many travelers spend a few days here, as it makes a convenient base for day trips to many attractive places including Lassen Volcanic National Park, Lake Shasta, the Shasta Caverns caves, Whiskeytown Lake, the Shasta State Historic Park, Lewiston, Weaverville, and many other worthwhile destinations.

Orientation & Information
Downtown Redding is bordered by the Sacramento River on the north and east sides; its major thoroughfares are Pine and Market Sts. The I-5 Cypress St exit and Hilltop Drive, east of I-5, are where standard hotels and fast-food joints can be found.

The Redding Convention and Visitors' Bureau (☎ 225-4100, 800-874-7562) is at 777 Auditorium Drive. The Shasta-Trinity National Forest Headquarters (☎ 246-5222, recorded information 246-5338, camping reservations ☎ 800-280-2267), 2400 Washington St off Park Marina Drive, has maps and permits for this and all seven national forests in northern California. It's open most of the year Monday to Friday from 7:30 am to 4:30 pm and until 5 pm in summer.

Things to See & Do
Just north of downtown, across the river, is the attractive **Caldwell Park** with two fine museums, the Redding Museum of Art & History (☎ 243-8801) and the Carter House Natural Science Museum (☎ 225-4125), plus a swimming pool, and the head of the Sacramento River Trail, great for hiking and bicycling. The **Old City Hall Arts Center** (☎ 241-7320), 1313 Market St, one block north of the Downtown Mall, features changing art exhibits in the old city hall building. The tourist office publishes a free pamphlet for three self-guided tours of Redding's historic architecture.

Six miles west of Redding on Hwy 299, **Shasta State Historic Park** preserves the ruins of the Gold Rush mining town of **Shasta** (not to be confused with the above-mentioned town of Mt Shasta), including an old courthouse that is now a museum. When the gold rush was at its height, everything and everyone had to pass through Shasta. But when the railroad bypassed it to set up in Poverty Flat, poor Shasta lost its luster.

In the summer people go **rafting** and **canoeing** on the Sacramento River. Park Marina Water Sports (☎ 246-8388), 2515 Park Marina Drive, rents rafts and canoes

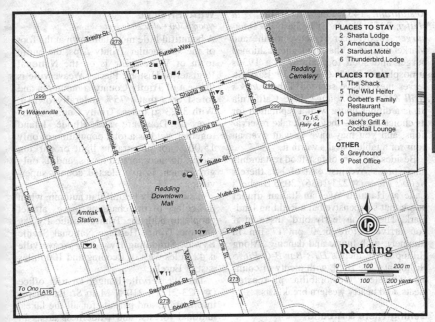

PLACES TO STAY
2 Shasta Lodge
3 Americana Lodge
4 Stardust Motel
6 Thunderbird Lodge

PLACES TO EAT
1 The Shack
5 The Wild Heifer
7 Corbett's Family
  Restaurant
10 Damburger
11 Jack's Grill &
  Cocktail Lounge

OTHER
8 Greyhound
9 Post Office

Redding

for a 12-mile trip down the river, including a shuttle service to bring you back again. Alpine Outfitters (☎ 221-7333, 24-hour snow report ☎ 221-7669), 950 Hilltop Drive, rents recreational equipment for every season.

Places to Stay
Downtown, the *Thunderbird Lodge* (☎ 243-5422), 1350 Pine St, is a homey, friendly motel charging $30/35. Nearby are the *Stardust Motel* (☎ 241-6121), 1200 Pine St, with rooms for $28/32, and the *Shasta Lodge* (☎ 243-6133), 1245 Pine St, with rooms at $28/31. The *Americana Lodge* (☎ 241-7020), 1250 Pine St, has rooms at $28/32, some with cooking facilities. The *River Inn Motor Hotel* (☎ 241-9500, 800-995-4341), 1835 Park Marina Drive, near the Sacramento River, is an attractive motel with many amenities; rates are $42/48.

A couple of 'motel rows' are near I-5 on the south end of town. On Bechelli Lane, just west of the freeway near the Cypress Ave exit, are a couple of clean, economical

motels: the *Motel 6* (☎ 221-0562, 800-440-6000), 2385 Bechelli Lane, with quiet rooms facing away from the highway for $36/42, and the *Colony Inn* (☎ 223-1935, 800-354-5222), 2731 Bechelli Lane, with rooms for $34/38. On the east side of the freeway, hilltop Drive has a number of larger, more up-market hotels and motels.

Redding's B&B (☎ 222-2494) at 1094 Palisades Ave also has three pleasant rooms for $27 to $37 single, $65 to $75 double. *Palisades Paradise* (☎ 223-5305, 800-382-4649), 1200 Palisades Ave, has two rooms for $60 and $75. Both of these places are on a bluff overlooking the Sacramento River, and have outdoor hot tubs. The more elegant Victorian *Tiffany House B&B Inn* (☎ 244-3225), 1510 Barabara Rd, has two rooms and one separate cottage for $75 to $125, singles $10 less.

Places to Eat
Downtown, try the locally popular *The Shack*, 1325 Eureka Way, *Corbett's Family*

Restaurant, 1455 Pine St, or the *Wild Heifer,* 1177 Shasta St at East St. *Damburger,* 1320 Placer St between Pine and Market Sts, is a charming, old-fashioned burger and soda fountain with a 1930s atmosphere. *Buz's Crab,* 2159 East St, serves inexpensive seafood dishes. *Jack's Grill & Cocktail Lounge,* 1743 California St, is a dinner house with a reputation for its choice steaks – they don't take reservations, and you may have to wait over an hour for a table, but it's worth it.

Besides the bevy of fast-food restaurants on Cypress Ave just east of I-5, there's *Nello's Place* (☎ 223-1636), 3055 Bechelli Lane at Hartnell Ave, an Italian dinner house that's expensive but a Redding landmark. There's an 'early bird' discount if you arrive before 6:30 pm (7 pm in summer), with music and dancing. Along Hilltop Drive there's *DJ's Bar-B-Q Pit,* 5 Hilltop at Lake Blvd, with plenty of country & western memorabilia, pit-roasted meats, and hearty western breakfasts.

Getting There & Around
The Greyhound station (☎ 241-2531), 1321 Butte St at Pine St, is open 24 hours a day in summer, 4:30 am to 4:30 pm the rest of the year. Buy tickets for Amtrak on the train or at a travel agency. The station is at 1620 Yuba St, one block west of the downtown mall.

The Redding Area Bus Authority (RABA, ☎ 241-2877) has 11 city routes plus express routes to Burney and Shingletown. Buses operate Monday to Friday from 6:30 am to 6:30 pm, Saturday 9:30 am to 6:30 pm, with no service on Sundays.

TRINITY SCENIC BYWAY
Heading west from Redding, Hwy 299, known as the Trinity Scenic Byway, winds through beautiful, rugged mountain scenery for 150 miles to reach Arcata, on the coast near Eureka. Along the way it passes along the winding Trinity River and through the Shasta-Trinity and Six Rivers National Forests, past Whiskeytown Lake and historic towns including Shasta and Weaverville.

WEAVERVILLE
• *pop 3500* • *elev 2045 feet*
A beautiful little mountain town at the foot of the spectacular Trinity Alps, the entire town of Weaverville is on the National Register of Historic Places. Weaverville is the seat of Trinity County, a mountain and forest area that's 75% federally owned. With 3223 sq miles, Trinity County is the size of Delaware and Rhode Island together, yet has a total population of only 15,000, not one traffic light or parking meter, no incorporated towns, and its only government is five elected county supervisors.

It's especially beautiful in autumn, when the colors of the changing leaves attract people to both the Trinity Scenic Byway and the Trinity Heritage National Scenic Byway. Straddling Hwy 299, Weaverville is 42 miles west of Redding and 100 miles east of Eureka.

The Weaverville Ranger District office (☎ 623-2121), 210 N Main St, has maps, information, and permits for all the lakes, national forests, and wilderness areas in and near Trinity County, with photos and details of all the hiking trails (length, difficulty, etc), camping areas, recreation, and so on. The Trinity County Chamber of Commerce (☎ 623-6101, 800-421-7259) is at 317 Main St.

Things to See & Do
You can spend some very pleasant hours just strolling around the historic town, visiting the art galleries, crafts shops, museums, and historic places. Plaques on the outsides of the buildings tell when they were built and what they were. **Joss House State Historic Park** (☎ 623-5284), in the center of town, is the oldest Chinese temple in California; its ornate altar, sent from China, is over 3000 years old. The **Weaverville Drug Store** at 219 Main St, 'California's Oldest Living Pharmacy,' was established in 1853 and is a living museum as well as a functioning pharmacy. Free pamphlets for the Trinity Scenic Byway and the Trinity Heritage National Scenic Byway (see below) self-guided driving

tours are available at the chamber of commerce and the ranger station.

A **farmers' market** is held from June to October on Saturday mornings from 9 am to noon in the parking lot of the Weaverville Community Service District building at 716 Main St.

Places to Stay

The ranger station has great information on USFS campgrounds; two they recommend are *Bridge Camp* on Stewarts Fork Creek and the larger *Tannery Gulch Campground* on Trinity Lake, with a boat ramp, swimming, and fishing. Reservations can be made through Destinet. The *Weaverville Hotel* (☎ 623-3121), in the center of town at 203 Main St, is a charming, 1861 hotel, that's old-fashioned, comfortable, and well cared for. The seven rooms, all with private bath or shower, are $32 including free tea or coffee in the morning. Reception is below the hotel, at Brady's Sport Shop. On the west end of town, the *Red Hill Motel* (☎ 623-4331) is a quiet, pleasant place with 14 rustic cabins at $30/35, higher with kitchens or for family units. It's on Red Hill Rd just off Main St, a block from the center of town and opposite the ranger station. Several other motels are on Hwy 299, on the east side of town.

Places to Eat

Along Main St try the *Pacific Brewery Restaurant & Bar,* 401 Main St, *Mustard Seed Cafe,* 252 Main St, or *La Casita,* downstairs, serving Mexican food. Just off Main St, behind the Gold Rush Jewelers, the *Gooseberry Cafe* on Center St is worth looking for; it has a great atmosphere and delicious organic foods all made from scratch. *La Grange Cafe,* 315 N Main St, has vegetarian dishes and a friendly local atmosphere – if the weather's nice, sit out on the patio. You can find places that tend to stay open later along Nugget Lane, on the east end of town, including *Sawmill Saloon,* a bar with pool tables that serves lunch and dinner.

Mountain Marketplace, in the center of town, is a natural foods grocery store with a juice bar and vegetarian deli.

Getting There & Away

A local bus makes a Monday-to-Friday Weaverville-Lewiston loop via Hwy 299 and Hwy 3; another local bus runs between Weaverville and Hayfork (☎ 623-5438 for details).

TRINITY HERITAGE NATIONAL SCENIC BYWAY

This 111-mile scenic drive starts by leaving **Weaverville** on Hwy 3, goes over the 9025-foot **Mt Eddy,** and finally meets I-5 just north of **Weed.** You can do all, or only part of the tour; it takes all day to do the whole thing. The part north of Coffee Creek is made impassable by snow in winter. There are good places to stop for a picnic or hike – the route intersects various hiking trails including the historic **Sisson-Callahan National Recreation Trail** and the **Pacific Crest Trail,** which you can take south from the road for three miles of easy grade for a pleasant day hike to the **Deadfall Lakes Basin.**

A free USFS pamphlet details the route and the stops along the way; it's available at any of the ranger stations or tourist offices in the area.

McCLOUD

• *pop 1600* • *elev 3238 feet*

McCloud, a tiny historic mill town, is at the foot of the south slope of Mt Shasta, on the north side of Hwy 89, nine miles east of I-5. The Ranger District office (☎ 964-2184), two blocks east of the town, has plenty of information on camping and outdoor recreation in the area. **Lake McCloud,** nine miles south of town on Squaw Valley Rd, is a beautiful, small, peaceful lake good for swimming and picnicking. The **McCloud River Loop,** a six-mile dirt road drive along the Upper McCloud River, begins at Fowlers Camp, 5½ miles east of McCloud, and emerges onto Hwy 89 11 miles east of town. You'll see some waterfalls, a riparian wildlife habitat for bird-watching in Bigelow Meadow, and a hiking trail. The drive can easily be done by vehicle or bicycle.

Hiking is good in the area, with several fine trails, including the **Squaw Valley Creek Trail,** an easy five-mile loop south of town in the beautiful Squaw Valley, with swimming, fishing, and picnicking along the way. Other hiking trails in the area include the short **Ah-Di-Na Nature Trail** and a portion of the **Pacific Crest Trail,** both accessible from the Ah-Di-Na campground. Ask the ranger station for a free pamphlet outlining the route and directions to trailheads.

Saunter down here to see some square dancing events at **McCloud Dance Country** (☎ 964-2252), a 1906 dance hall on the corner of Broadway and Pine. Open dances are held every Friday and Saturday evening, with rounds at 7:30 pm and squares starting at 8 pm.

Fishing is popular on Lake McCloud, the Upper McCloud River (stocked with trout), on Squaw Valley Creek, and various other places; Ah-Di-Na is popular for fly-fishing.

Places to Stay
Camping There's camping nearby at several USFS campgrounds, including the popular *Fowler's Camp*; the ranger station has details. Six miles south of town on the road to Lake McCloud, *Friday's Retreat* (☎ 964-2878, 529-0698) in the beautiful Squaw Valley, with forest, meadows and the Squaw Valley Creek. Tent/RV sites are $10/15, with weekly discounts.

B&Bs McCloud is a very small town but it has a number of fine B&Bs. Largest and probably the most notable is the *McCloud B&B Hotel* (☎ 964-2822, 800-964-2823), 408 Main St, in the center of the tiny town. A registered historic landmark, the 1916 grand hotel was lovingly restored to a luxurious standard and opened amid great hoopla in May 1995. Spacious rooms are $68 to $88, suites $120 to $130, with a variety of discounts.

The *Stoney Brook Inn* (☎ 964-2300, 800-369-6118), 309 W Colombero, is a peaceful 'new age'-style B&B with a hot tub and sauna, therapeutic massage, an organic vegetarian restaurant, a Native American sweat lodge, and a variety of accommodations including rooms with shared bath at $28/40, rooms with private bath at $36/50, and fully-equipped kitchen suites at $55 to $70, all with weekly rates available offseason. Non-guests can use the hot tub and sauna for $5.

Not right in town, but near it, the *McCloud Guest House* (☎ 964-3160), 606 W Colombero Drive, is an elegantly restored 1907 country mansion with five guest rooms from $75 to $90, a large grounds, and a locally famous restaurant.

Places to Eat
Besides the restaurants in the above B&Bs, try the simple little *McCloud Soda Shoppe & Cafe* in the Old Mercantile Building at 245 Main St, an old-fashioned, all-American cafe and soda fountain.

McARTHUR-BURNEY FALLS MEMORIAL STATE PARK
This state park about 40 miles east of McCloud on Hwy 89 holds the beautiful McArthur-Burney Falls, Lake Britton, and a number of fine hiking trails, picnic, and camping areas. Fed by a spring, the falls run with the same amount of water and at the same temperature (48°F) all year round; clear, lava-filtered water comes surging not only over the edge of the falls, but also right through the rocks of the waterfall's face. There's a lookout point beside the parking lot, with hiking trails going up and down the creek from the falls. A nature trail heading downstream brings you to Lake Britton. Other trails include a section of the Pacific Crest Trail, a trail to Lake Britton Dam and Rock Creek, and another trail to Baum Lake and the Crystal Lake Hatchery.

About 10 miles northeast of McArthur-Burney Falls is **Ahjumawi Lava Springs State Park,** an area known for its beautiful rivers and lava flows. It stays pristine because it can only be reached by boat. The rangers at McArthur-Burney Falls can supply information.

Camping in the park costs $14 per site (with hot showers), $12 in winter; day use is $5 per vehicle. The park (☎ 335-2777) is open all year, with camping even when there's snow on the ground.

BIG BEND HOT SPRINGS
If soaking in a hot spring in an idyllic mountain setting is your idea of bliss, then this is your place. Big Bend Hot Springs (☎ 337-6680) is a tattered old resort, now maintained by a private community. The locals are a bit trippy, but everyone is sociable and the focus is on the 'healing waters.'

The temperatures of the three main soaking tubs are controlled by the mixing of 180°F natural spring water and the chilly waters of the Pit River. These rock-and-concrete tubs are terraced above a bend in the river, where a wooden deck connects them and a trail leads down to the Pit. The outdoor setting is very peaceful and is especially soothing if you've been camping or traveling.

Also on the property (follow the dirt road) is a natural series of riverside pools – in some cases holes – in which hot water cools as it flows toward the river. These pockets are a perfect spot for a steaming soak next to the snow-fed mountain river.

Clothing is optional and no alcohol is allowed on the property. Access to the springs costs $8 a day; $9 per car per night for camping (they have eight or nine sites for car/tent camping that are so-so).

Places to Stay
A great place to camp if you use the hot springs is at *Deadlun Campground* beside the Iron Canyon Reservoir, only six miles from Big Bend. Camps are set beside the reservoir in a thick pine and cedar forest. Here you'll find good trout fishing and numerous trails, peaks, and creeks within walking distance. Deadlun takes no reservations, has no fees, nor any piped water, so bring your own for drinking and cooking. There are 15 sites for tents or motor homes. Follow Big Bend Rd through town and continue north for 2.1 miles, then turn left on Rd 38N11 and drive 3.3 miles to the

reservoir. Turn right and go 1.5 miles to Deadlun Campground.

Getting There & Away
From Redding drive 37 miles east on Hwy 299 to Big Bend Rd, then 16 miles north to the little village of Big Bend. Turn west on Hot Springs Rd (just before the general store). At the end of the road and up the hill is a dirt parking area. Here you will see the wooden-cabin 'office' – inquire inside about using the springs.

ASH CREEK WILDLIFE AREA
In a remote area further east along Hwy 299 near the junction of Hwy 139, the Ash Creek Wildlife Area is one of the most remote of California's wildlife areas. The **Big Swamp,** about 3000 acres of natural wetlands, provides a protected habitat for dozens of species of birds as well as for antelope and deer. Maps and information are available at the Department of Fish & Game office in Bieber (☎ 294-5824), on Hwy 299.

WEED
• *pop 3000* • *elev 3467 feet*
Nine miles north of Mt Shasta on I-5, at the junction of Hwy 95, Weed is a nondescript, working-class town, hard-hit by the recession of lumber milling. Several little motels, restaurants, and gas stations on Weed Blvd, running parallel to I-5. Try the *Townhouse Motel* (☎ 938-4431), 157 S Weed Blvd, for $28/33, or the *Y Motel* (☎ 938-4481), 90 N Weed Blvd, with slightly cheaper rooms and a family restaurant.

STEWART MINERAL SPRINGS
In the mountains west of Weed, Stewart Mineral Springs (☎ 938-2222, 800-322-9223), 4617 Stewart Springs Rd, is known for its healing spring waters. It was founded in 1875 by Henry Stewart, after he was brought here by Indians on the point of death and attributed his healing to the healthful properties of the mineral waters, said to draw toxins out of the body. You soak in mineral water in small individual

rooms with clawfoot tubs, alternating with runs to the sauna down the hall; cost is $15 per day, or $12 if you're spending the night.

Other features include massage, body wraps, Native American sweat lodge purifications, a meditation room, a sunbathing deck, and various lodgings including camping ($10), tepees ($15), dorms ($25), apartments ($30 to $65), and cabins with kitchen ($45).

To get there, go 10 miles north of Mt Shasta on I-5, passing Weed; take the Edgewood and Gazelle exit, turn west and follow the signs for four miles.

YREKA
• pop 7500 • elev 2295 feet

About 40 miles north of Mt Shasta on I-5, Yreka is inland California's northernmost city. A pleasant town with its roots in the Gold Rush days, Yreka is a fine place to stop with some good places to stay and eat.

Most places of interest are along Main and Miner Sts, including the chamber of commerce (☎ 842-1649) on W Miner St. The Klamath National Forest Headquarters (☎ 842-6131) is at 1312 Fairlane Rd.

Things to See & Do
Yreka is proud of its **Yreka Western Railroad,** fondly known as *The Blue Goose.* The 1915 Baldwin steam engine, pulling both covered and open-air cars, chugs at 10 mph through the Shasta Valley to the tiny town of **Montague,** 7.5 miles away, with views of Mt Shasta looming in the distance. The train depot is just east of I-5; take Miner St and go under the freeway, or take the freeway's Central Yreka offramp. The depot opens an hour before the train leaves, and features a 1000-foot working model railroad, historic railroad memorabilia, and a gift shop. Call ☎ 842-4146 for departure times and reservations; cost is $9 for adults, $4.50 for children three to 12.

The **Siskiyou County Museum** (☎ 842-3836), 910 S Main St, has an outdoor section with several historic buildings brought here from around the county. Behind the

museum, the **Yreka Creek Greenway** has a visitors center, pathways through the greenery, informative plaques along the Yreka Creek, and several good picnic areas. The **Siskiyou County Courthouse** at 311 4th St was built in 1857 and has a collection of gold nuggets in the foyer.

Places to Stay
Waiiaka Trailer Haven (☎ 842-4500), 240 Sharps Rd, has tent/RV sites at $10/20 per day; it's not the most attractive place, but it is in town. There's also camping at *Humbug Creek,* about 12 miles west of Yreka, and in Klamath National Forest; the forest headquarters has information.

Several comfortable motels are found up and down Main St, including the *Ben Ber Motel* (☎ 842-2791), 1210 S Main St; *Klamath Motor Lodge* (☎ 842-2751), 1111 S Main St, with a swimming pool and a shady lawn; and *Heritage Inn* (☎ 842-6835), 306 N Main St, with rooms set back from the street. All charge around $30/40 in the summer and offer winter discounts. There are more on the south end of town, just off I-5 at the Fort Jones exit. For a bit more luxury, the *Best Western Miner's Inn* (☎ 842-4355), 122 E Miner St, at the Central Yreka exit, has two heated swimming pools and charges $46/51.

What's in a Name?
You may ask yourself, 'Why Yreka?' When, in 1851, Abraham Thompson discovered gold in nearby Black Gulch, there was no town to name. Only six weeks later, over 2000 prospectors were on hand, raising a 'tent city' with a few rough shanties and cabins thrown in. Originally known as Thompson's Dry Diggings, the settlement later moved to its present site, nearer the creek, and was re-named Shasta Butte City. In 1852, when Siskiyou County was formed, the town won the title of county seat by only one vote over Deadwood, in Scott Valley. Its name was then changed again, to Wyreka, later Yreka, the Shasta Indian name for Mt Shasta. ■

Places to Eat

The *Pleasantry Restaurant,* 322 W Miner St, is locally famous for its omelets and sourdough pancakes at breakfast, and avocado sandwiches at lunch. *Poor George's* on the south end of town at 108 Oberlin Rd, a couple of doors west of Main St, is another place locals rave about, with large portions, good prices, and a friendly hometown atmosphere. Don't be discouraged by the outside appearance, it's nicely done inside. *Grandma's House,* 123 E Center St, between Main St and I-5, is another popular place for its homestyle cooking and salad bar. *Nature's Kitchen,* 412 S Main St, serves healthy vegetarian and meat dishes, and espresso drinks.

For Chinese food at good prices and without the MSG try *Ming's,* 210 W Miner St, and the *Wah Lee Chinese Restaurant,* 520 S Main St. *Lalo's,* 219 W Miner St, serves good Mexican food. *Sue's Coffee & Cones,* 117 W Miner St, sharing space with the chamber of commerce, is a small-town soda fountain with hot fudge and other sundaes, thick malts, hot dogs, and so on.

Getting There & Away

Bus Buses running along I-5 stop at the Greyhound depot (☎ 842-3145) at the Mini Mart at 2301 Fairlane Rd, east of the freeway on the southern outskirts of town – you'll have to take a taxi to get there or away.

STAGE bus line has daily buses running throughout the region. The weekday Scott Valley route connects Montague, Yreka, Fort Jones, Greenview, and Etna. Twice a week buses go from Yreka down the Klamath River to Happy Camp and back. The STAGE office (☎ 842-8295, 800-247-8243) is at 411 4th St.

Car About 25 miles north of Yreka on I-5, Siskiyou Summit (elev 4310 feet) catches many storms in winter and closes often – even when the weather is just fine on either side of the mountain. Check the CHP's recorded information line (☎ 842-4438) for road conditions before you travel this way. The same number provides information on winter road conditions for all of Siskiyou County.

If you're going to or from the coast, the fastest and easiest route is via freeway, taking I-5 through Ashland, Medford, and Grants Pass, Oregon, then heading south on Hwy 199 to Crescent City (or vice versa); the trip this way takes about 5½ hours. Hwys 96, 3, and 299 will also get you to the coast; they are very scenic but are also slow and winding. If you do take one of these scenic routes, it's best to start early in the day.

SCOTT VALLEY

Southwest of Yreka, Hwy 3 passes through the beautiful Scott Valley, a pristine agricultural valley nestled among towering mountains. Here is where the Scott Bar Mine operated for 110 years. Traveling south from Yreka, Hwy 3 passes **Fort Jones,** with its small museum of Native American artifacts. Another 12 miles brings you to **Etna.** Known for its tiny *Etna Brewing Company* (☎ 467-5277), 131 Callahan St, you can drop in any Saturday from 1 to 5 pm for a tour and a taste (otherwise by arrangement). After a drink, try the *Sengthong* Thai restaurant (☎ 467-5668), 434 Main St; locals come all the way from Mt Shasta and Weaverville to eat here. Continuing south out of the valley, Hwy 3 passes over Scott Mtn Summit (5401 feet) and joins the Trinity Heritage National Scenic Byway, passing Trinity Lake, and finally arriving at Weaverville.

KLAMATH NATIONAL FOREST

With 1,700,000 acres, Klamath National Forest covers a huge area of California's extreme north. It's bordered on the west by the Six Rivers National Forest, on the south by the Trinity Alps Wilderness, on the north by the Oregon border, and it extends in a patchwork pattern east as far as Yreka, with one far-flung district extending east of Yreka all the way to Lava Beds National Monument.

The Klamath includes three major rivers – the Klamath, Salmon, and Scott Rivers – providing opportunities for everything from slow, lazy canoeing and inner tubing to challenging Class V whitewater rafting and kayaking. Rafts, canoes, and kayaks can be rented locally, and a number of tour companies offer organized river trips; the ranger stations can provide details.

Other attractions include five wilderness areas. The 223,500-acre **Marble Mountain Wilderness** has almost 100 lakes, part of the Pacific Crest Trail, and is relatively easy to access. The 500,000-acre **Trinity Alps Wilderness** features Alpine terrain, lakes and streams, and a 400-mile system of trails. The 12,000-acre **Russian Wilderness** includes high, craggy granite formations and over 20 lakes. The 153,000-acre **Siskiyou Wilderness** on the west side of the forest is rugged and seldom visited. A small portion of the **Red Buttes Wilderness** is also within the forest, though most of it is in the Rogue River National Forest across the Oregon border. Topographic maps and advice on current conditions on all of these wilderness areas are available at the ranger stations. The Klamath National Forest Supervisor's Office is at 1312 Fairlane Rd, Yreka (☎ 842-6131).

The Klamath Basin hosts the largest concentration of eagles in the lower 48 states.

Northeastern California

☎ 916

Where the high desert plateaus of Modoc and Lassen Counties in the north give way to the mountains of the northern Sierras, life seems to proceed at a slower-pace. Its people often appear genuinely happy to greet a visitor. So far removed is it from big-city living that many native Californians never see the places mentioned in this section, though they're some of the most beautiful parts of the state. It's worth taking the time to pass through and experience these little-known areas. There's a lot of snow here in winter, which may be a deter-

rent if you don't like winter sports, but the rest of the year it's quite easy to travel here – traffic, congestion, and smog are definitely not problems.

KLAMATH BASIN WILDLIFE REFUGES

Six national wildlife refuges collectively form the Klamath Basin Wildlife Refuges: the Tule Lake, Lower Klamath, Clear Lake, and Bear Valley refuges are wholly within California, Upper Klamath straddles the California-Oregon border, and the Klamath Marsh is in Oregon. Both Bear Valley and Clear Lake (not to be confused with the Clear Lake just east of Ukiah) are closed to the public to protect their delicate wildlife habitats, but the rest are open daily during daylight hours and charge no admission.

These refuges provide habitats for birds migrating along the Pacific Flyway; 75% to 80% of all the birds on the flyway stop at these refuges, some only temporarily, some to mate, make nests, and raise their young. There are always birds here, and during the spring and fall migrations, there can be hundreds of thousands.

The spring migration peaks in March, some years seeing over a million birds fill the skies; in April and May, songbirds, waterfowl, and shore birds arrive, some to stay and nest, others to rest and build up their energy before they continue north. In summer around 45,000 ducks, 2600 Canada geese, and many other water birds are raised here. The fall migration begins in early September, and within two months peak numbers of over a million birds are present. In winter, the Klamath Basin refuges host the largest concentration of bald eagles in the lower 48 states, with 500 to over 1000 in residence from December to late February. The Tule Lake and Lower Klamath refuges are the easiest places to see these eagles, and other raptors (including hawks and golden eagles) can also be seen at this time. The first northbound migrating birds begin to arrive in February.

The Tule Lake and Lower Klamath Refuges attract the largest numbers of birds, and auto trails have been set up through these refuges; a free pamphlet from the visitors center shows the routes. Self-guided canoe routes have been established in the Tule Lake, Upper Klamath, and Klamath Marsh Refuges – rent canoes at Klamath Marsh.

Information

The Klamath Basin Visitor Center (☎ 667-2231) is on Hill Rd, five miles west of Hwy 139 near the town of Tulelake, on the west side of the Tule Lake refuge. Follow the signs from Hwy 139 or from Lava Beds National Monument (see below). This information center services all six refuges. It has a good six-minute slide program about the birds and the refuges, and plenty of information on these and other wildlife refuges. It's open weekdays from 8 am to 4:30 pm, weekends and holidays until 4 pm.

Places to Stay

There's camping nearby at Lava Beds National Monument, and on Hwy 139 near the tiny town of Tulelake are a couple of motels. Try *Park Motel* (☎ 667-2913), half a mile south of town, and the *Ellis Motel* (☎ 667-5242), half a mile north of town. Both run around $30 with regular and kitchenette units available.

Wildlife Refuge Tour

California is on the Pacific Flyway, a migratory route for hundreds of species of birds heading south in the winter and north in the summer. Flyway regulars include everything from tiny hummingbirds, finches, swallows, and woodpeckers to eagles, swans, geese, ducks, cranes, and herons.

Wildlife refuges are established to protect habitats for many kinds of wildlife; the ones in northern California mostly safeguard wetlands used by migrating waterfowl. There are birds to see at any time of year, but the most spectacular times are during the spring and fall migrations, when hundreds of thousands of birds fill the sky.

Several refuges are within easy driving distance of one another, each with slightly different birds. The Klamath Basin National Wildlife Refuges are all within about an hour's drive of one another; about a 1½-hour drive east is the Modoc National Wildlife Refuge at Alturas. Another detour brings you to the Ash Creek Wildlife Area near the junction of Hwys 299 and 139, about an hour southwest of Alturas. Others are just over the border in Nevada and Oregon.

A ranger-suggested route for touring the refuges begins at the Ash Creek Wildlife Area southwest of Alturas on Hwy 299. After visiting the nearby Modoc National Wildlife Refuge, try the large Sheldon National Wildlife Refuge across the border in Nevada, about a 1½ hour drive from Alturas, and the Hart Mountain National Antelope Refuge in Oregon, about two hours from Alturas or Sheldon. From Hart Mountain it's about a 90-minute drive north to the Malheur National Wildlife Refuge in southeastern Oregon. Then heading southwest again, visit the Klamath Basin National Wildlife Refuges in southern Oregon and northern California.

Rangers have plenty of information about the wildlife in their own and nearby refuges. A free pamphlet called *National Wildlife Refuges* shows all the refuges in the USA and is available at any of the refuges. ■

CALIFORNIA

LAVA BEDS NATIONAL MONUMENT

Lava Beds National Monument, off Hwy 139 and immediately south of the Tule Lake National Wildlife Refuge, is a remarkable nine-by-eight-mile landscape of volcanic features, including lava flows, craters, cinder cones, spatter cones, shield volcanoes, and especially lava tubes.

Lava tubes are formed when hot, spreading lava cools and hardens on its surface and sides, where it's exposed to cold air. The inside lava is thus insulated, keeping it hot and flowing, which ultimately leaves an empty tube as the process continues. Nearly 200 such tubular caves have been found in the monument, and many more are likely yet to be discovered.

Near the visitors center on the south side of the park is a short loop drive providing access to many **lava tube caves** with names like Mushpot, Hercules Leg, and Blue Grotto. The visitors center provides free flashlights and helmets for explorations of the caves; it's essential you use a high power flashlight, good shoes (lava is sharp), and that you not go exploring in caves alone. Mushpot, the cave nearest to the visitors center, has been installed with lighting and informative signs to make for easy exploration of the cave.

Other notable features of the region include the tall black cone of **Schonchin Butte,** where there's a magnificent lookout over the area; **Mammoth Crater,** the source of most of the area's lava flows; and ancient **petroglyphs** at the base of a high cliff on the north end of the monument. A leaflet explaining the origin of the petroglyphs and their probable meaning is available in the visitors center. Don't miss the hundreds of bird nests in holes high up in the cliff face.

Another intriguing feature of the monument is **Captain Jack's Stronghold** on the north end of the monument, a labyrinth of lava formations where Modoc leader Kintpuash, known as Captain Jack, led a band of 160 Modoc Indians in fighting off a contingent of the US Army that eventually outnumbered them 10 to one. Skirmishes between early settlers and the native Modocs finally culminated in an 1873 conflict that came to be known as the Modoc War. The fighting dragged on for several months and became a great shame to the US Army – a sort of Vietnam War for its era, with the might of the US military rendered ineffective by a small group of relatively primitive but determined people fighting for their homeland. The booklet will guide you on a number-by-number tour through the Stronghold; allow plenty of time. This and other books about the Modoc War and related historical and geological topics are available at the visitors center.

Just opposite Captain Jack's Stronghold and the petroglyphs is the Tule Lake Wildlife Refuge, open during daylight hours.

Information

The Visitor Center (☎ 667-2282), in the south end of the monument, has free maps and plenty of information about the monument and its volcanic features and history, plus flashlights and helmets you can use for exploring the caves. From Easter to Christmas it's open every day from 8 am to 6 pm; call for hours during the rest of the year.

Places to Stay

There is a tree-shaded, 42-site campground beside the visitors center, where camping runs $10 a night in summer, $6 in winter when there's no running water in the campground. There's always water available at the visitors center. Otherwise there are several motels on Hwy 139 in nearby Tulelake – see the Klamath Basin National Wildlife Refuges section for details.

MODOC NATIONAL FOREST

Modoc National Forest covers almost two million acres of California's northeast corner. At **Medicine Lake Highlands,** 14 miles south of Lava Beds National Monument on the western edge of the forest, Medicine Lake is a beautiful crater lake surrounded by pine forest and interesting volcanic formations. Four campgrounds are spaced around the lake making it a great spot for camping, swimming, and other recreation. Notable geologic features of the area include the 570-acre **Medicine Lake Glass Flow,** the 8760-acre **Burnt Lava Flow** and the 4210-acre **Glass Mountain Glass Flow.** Roads are closed by snow from around mid-November to mid-June, but it's still popular for winter sports.

Devil's Garden, north of Alturas in the central part of the forest, is an open plateau full of western juniper and other plants.

The **Warner Mountains,** on the east side of the forest, are a spur of the Cascade Range. About 80 miles from north to south and 10 miles from east to west, the mountains are divided at Cedar Pass (elev 6305 feet), east of Alturas, into the North Warners and South Warners. There the **Cedar Pass Ski Hill** (☎ 233-3323) offers downhill and cross-country skiing. Close by are the *Cedar Pass* and *Stough Reservoir* USFS campgrounds. The **South Warner Wilderness Area** contains 77 miles of hiking and riding trails; the best time to use them is from July to mid-October. Weather on the Warners is extremely changeable and snowstorms have occurred there at all times of year, so always be prepared.

Also in the South Warners, the lovely 160-acre **Blue Lake** is a fine spot for camping and fishing, with a campground open from Memorial Day to mid-October. The 1.5-mile Blue Lake Trail, beginning at the campground, and the 5.5-mile High Grade Trail in the North Warners, are two of the forest's most popular trails.

Maps and information on the forest are available at the Modoc National Forest Supervisor's Headquarters in Alturas (see below).

ALTURAS
• *pop 3000* • *elev 4372 feet*

Small, pleasant, and friendly, Alturas is the seat of Modoc County and the principal service town for the state's northwestern cattle and alfalfa ranchers. 'Where the West Still Lives' – the Modoc county slogan – is a fitting description; major annual events include spring and fall cattle drives, the rodeo, and a county fair.

On the high, flat desert of the Modoc Plateau, with the Warner Mountains towering in the east and beyond them, Surprise Valley, Alturas is removed from the rest of California both by geography and attitude. But, considering that Alturas is only about a three-hour drive from Redding, Reno, or Mt Shasta, and 1½ hours from Susanville or Klamath Falls it really isn't that remote. If you do get to Alturas, you'll find an attractive little town with friendly people, good places to stay and eat, and plenty to see and do, including a beautiful wildlife refuge just three miles from town.

Alturas gets extremely cold in winter, hot in summer, and sees thousands of migrating birds fly to the wildlife refuge in the spring and fall.

Alturas is at the junction of Hwys 299 and 395. Most businesses are along Main St in the one mile section south of its T-intersection with 12th St on the north end of town. County Rd 56, which crosses Main St on the south end of town between the museum and the chamber of commerce (☎ 233-4434), at 522 S Main St, heads east to the wildlife refuge and Dorris Lake.

The Modoc National Forest Supervisor's Headquarters (☎ 233-5811), on 12th St (Hwy 299) a few blocks west of town, has information and permits for all types of recreation in the area; it's open Monday to Friday, 8 am to 5 pm.

Things to See & Do
When in town, go to the **Modoc County Museum** (☎ 233-6328), 600 S Main St, with hundreds of interesting historical items and a remarkable collection of books with stories about the Wild West history of Modoc County. It's open in the summer, Tuesday to Saturday from 10 am to 4 pm. The 1914 Beaux Arts-style **Modoc County Courthouse,** at the corner of Modoc and Court Sts, has a lovely stained-glass window and historical displays in the rotunda.

Murals around town portray elements of Modoc County life, such as the spring and autumn cattle drives, the rodeo, and the wildlife refuge.

The **Modoc National Wildlife Refuge,**

three miles southeast of Alturas, is definitely worth a visit. A signboard provides a map of the refuge and suggests an auto tour, with tips for birdwatchers, and lots of information on the Pacific Flyway and the 232 species of birds found here. For pamphlets and more information about the various birds, check with the rangers at the refuge headquarters (☎ 233-3572), open weekdays from 8 am to 4:30 pm. You'll see the most birds if you come in the early morning, with binoculars.

Birds are present throughout the year but peak numbers are seen during the spring and fall migrations (mid-March to late-May, September and October). From mid-December to mid-February fewer birds visit the frozen wetlands, though bald eagles can still be seen. The refuge is open every day, sunrise to sunset, and charges no admission.

A little further east on County Rd 56, **Dorris Reservoir** allows swimming, boating, and waterskiing from June to October, but from mid-October to January there's no public access at all, as the reservoir becomes a refuge for wildlife.

Places to Stay
Camping *Sully's Trailer Lodge* (☎ 233-2253) is one block east of the museum on County Rd 197 at the corner of County Rd 56; it's a quiet park with tent/trailer spaces for $11/14. A USFS campground, *Cedar Pass,* is on Hwy 299, about a 15-minute drive east of Alturas. It's a beautiful spot with large trees by a stream, and it's free, as is the *Stough Reservoir campground* a few miles further east on Hwy 299.

Hotel, Motels & B&B The *Niles Hotel* (☎ 233-4200), 304 S Main St, is a beautifully restored historic landmark full of interesting details, with attractive, comfortable rooms at $45 to $65.

On Hwy 299 about a mile east of Main St, the *Rim Rock Motel* (☎ 233-5455) is a pleasant motel in the countryside with a view of the Warner Mountains, as is the nearby *Drifters Inn Motel* (☎ 233-2428). Both have rooms at around $27/31. There

are plenty more places on N Main St also in the $30 range.

Dorris House (☎ 233-3786), a B&B on the shore of Dorris Reservoir on the outskirts of town near the Modoc Wildlife Refuge, has four rooms in a two-story 1912 ranch house for $45.

Places to Eat
The *Beacon Coffee Shop Restaurant,* 206 N Main St on the corner of 2nd St, is a home-style restaurant good for all meals, open every day from 6 am to 11 pm. Its specialties are roasted chicken and barbecue ribs, to eat there or take out. The *Act One Espresso Bar & Bakery,* 126 N Main St, is a restaurant, coffeehouse, and bakery with organic and vegetarian food, and a good variety of delicious baked goods; closed on Sunday.

Nipa's, 1001 N Main St, serves an imaginative selection of tasty Thai, French, and California cuisine every day from 11 am to 9 pm. For more international fare, the *Brass Rail Restaurant,* half a mile east of town on Hwy 299, serves Basque dinners family-style. A popular landmark of the town, it's open for lunch from noon to 2 pm, dinner 5:30 to 10 pm, closed Monday.

Also for dinner, Niles Hotel (see above) has the *High Grade Room* (☎ 233-4761), a lovely restaurant with fine atmosphere and good food; prime rib and steak are the house specialties. The historic saloon, a living page of Wild West history, is worth visiting whether you're thirsty or not.

SURPRISE VALLEY
• *pop 1500* • *elev 4460 feet*
Long and narrow, Surprise Valley is bordered on the west by the Warner Mountains and on the east by the high, flat, dry peaks of Nevada's Hays Canyon Range.

The biggest surprise is its alkaline lakes – eerie white lakes with nothing living in them, and often dry. Surprise Valley's 'big town' is tiny **Cedarville** (population 800), 24 miles east of Alturas, which looks and feels like an old Wild West town. The Modoc National Forest has a ranger station one block off Main St (☎ 279-6116) where you can ask about local natural wonders including the Warner Mountains, the South Warner Wilderness, and various area hot springs. At the north end of the valley, 26 miles above Cedarville, are **Fort Bidwell** – originally a fort but now a small town – and the **Fort Bidwell Indian Reservation**.

From May to October there's camping at the *Modoc County Fairgrounds* (☎ 279-2315), except during the mid-June rodeo and the county fair during the last three weeks of August. There's also the *Drew Hotel* (☎ 279-2423), with rooms at $30/40, the *Cressler-Hill House* (☎ 279-2650), with rooms at $55 including breakfast – both attractive historic places on Main St in the center of Cedarville – and the *Sunrise Motel* (☎ 279-2161), half a mile west of town on Hwy 299, with rooms at $35/40. For food, try the *Country Hearth Restaurant & Bakery* or *Desert Deli Pizza,* both on Main St.

SUSANVILLE
• *pop 12,700* • *elev 4255 feet*
Susanville is on a high desert plateau, which feels quite remote from the rest of the world though it doesn't really take all that long to get to other places. It's 38 miles east of Chester and Lake Almanor, 85 miles north of Reno, and 96 miles south of Alturas. Primarily a service town for the surrounding cattle and timber district, Susanville experienced a jump in economics and population when construction began on an expansion of the state prison on the west end of town.

If you happen to be traveling through this part of California, Susanville has basic services. The Lassen National Forest Supervisor's Office (☎ 257-2191), 55 S Sacramento St at Main St, has maps and information about the forest. The town's oldest building, named after the town's founder, **Roop's Fort,** 75 N Weatherlow St, houses a museum open weekdays in the summer.

Places to Stay & Eat
Sixteen miles northwest of Susanville,

Eagle Lake is a large lake where swimming, fishing, boating, waterskiing, and camping attract visitors from late spring until fall. Five campgrounds, administered through the Lassen National Forest, are on the south shore of the lake. A bit more peaceful, *Antelope Lake* is about 15 miles south and has three campgrounds administered by the Plumas National Forest.

Motels along Main St, none of them very exceptional, range from $30/35 to $42/50. They include the *Sierra Vista Motel* (☎ 257-6721), the *River Inn Motel* (☎ 257-6051), *Susanville Inn* (☎ 257-4522), and the *Super Budget Motel* (☎ 257-2782), 2975 Johnstonville Rd at Main St. The *Roseberry House B&B* (☎ 257-5675), 609 N St, two blocks north of Main St, has four rooms from $55 to $85.

Ask the chamber of commerce where you can get a good meal and they'll tell you to go to Reno! Nevertheless there are a few cafes on Main St that have been surviving in Susanville for quite awhile. A plaque outside the *Pioneer Cafe,* 724 Main St – a combination bar, saloon, card room, billiards room and cafe – declares that a saloon has been on this site since 1862, and that this is the oldest established business in northeastern California. The cafe's hours depend on demand. Other historic cafes on Main St include the *Grand Cafe*, 730 Main St, established in 1909, and the *St Francis Cafe* at the Old St Francis Hotel on the corner of Main St and South Union St.

Getting There & Away
A bus between Red Bluff and Susanville, stopping on the way at Mineral (for Lassen Volcanic National Park), Chester (for Lake Almanor), and Westwood, operates every day except Sunday; see Red Bluff in the Sacramento Valley chapter for specifics.

LAKE ALMANOR
Lake Almanor and the surrounding area provide relaxing, nature-oriented recreation year round. With a 52-mile shoreline, it takes about an hour to drive around the lake. **Chester** is the main town on the lake; the chamber of commerce and ranger

station there have details on every type of lodging, and recreation in, on, and around the lake, in the surrounding national forest, and in nearby Lassen Volcanic National Park. The chamber of commerce (☎ 258-2426) is at 529 Main St (Hwy 36) and is open weekdays from 10 am to 4 pm in the summer; until 2:45 pm the rest of the year. The Almanor Ranger Station of the Lassen National Forest (☎ 258-2141), also on Main St about a mile west of town, is open weekdays from 8 am to 5 pm.

In **Westwood,** a tiny town a few miles east of Chester, is a historical museum telling the story of Paul Bunyan and Babe the blue ox and other local legends; phone for hours (☎ 256-3709). Also in Westwood is the start of the **Bizz Johnson Trail,** a 25-mile historical trail between Westwood and Susanville, once a part of the old Southern Pacific railway line, now converted to a trail that can be traveled by foot, mountain bike, horseback, or cross-country skis (no motorized vehicles). It's easiest to do the trail in the Westwood-to-Susanville direction, as it's mostly downhill that way; pamphlets are available in Chester and Susanville.

Bodfish Bicycles (☎ 258-2338), 152 Main St in Chester, rents bicycles. You can rent boats and other water sports equipment at many places around the lake.

Places to Stay
Camping You'll find plenty of camping around the lake and in the surrounding Lassen and Plumas National Forests, both of which have sites on the lake's south shore. Nearest to Chester, the *North Shore Campground* (☎ 258-3376), two miles east of town on Hwy 36, has tent/RV sites ($13/16) right on the lakeshore.

Motels The *Seneca Motel* (☎ 258-2815), 545 Decar and Martin Way, is quieter than the places right on the highway. It's a pleasant, old-fashioned place with a picnic and barbecue area; rooms go for $31/37, $5 more for family/kitchen units. The *Antlers Motel* (☎ 258-2722), 268 Main St, has

rooms at $30/35, plus larger family units and weekly rates. The *Timber House Lodge* (☎ 258-2729) and the *Black Forest Lodge* (☎ 258-2941) also have motel rooms (see Places to Eat).

B&Bs The *Bidwell House* (☎ 258-3338), 1 Main St, is the relocated summer home built by John and Annie Bidwell (see the Chico section). Rooms are $50 to $98, with a separate cottage at $135 per night. The *Cinnamon Teal B&B* (☎ 258-3993), 227 Feather River Drive, has three rooms from $65 to $85 and a suite at $95.

Places to Eat
Chester is your best bet for getting something to eat around the lake. The *Kopper Kettle Cafe,* 243 Main St, is great for breakfast and lunch, with homestyle food and giant portions; half-orders are available. It has great hospitality and small-town atmosphere – lots of locals eat here. The *Knotbumper Restaurant,* 274 Main St, is an attractive, cozy little place for lunch or dinner.

The *Timber House Restaurant* (reservations ☎ 258-2989), at the corner of Main and 1st Sts, is a bar and restaurant known for steak, prime rib, and seafood. The food is a little expensive, but the 'early-supper specials' from 4:30 to 6:30 pm are about half price. The *Chester Saloon & Restaurant,* 159 Main St, is also popular with locals, with an eclectic menu and outdoor dining in summer. The *Corner Pocket* (☎ 258-2800), 118 Watson Rd at Main St, is a cheerful delicatessen and pizza house with billiards, games, and free delivery in town. Further west on Main St, about 10 miles from town, the *Black Forest Lodge* (☎ 258-2941) is recommended for its German and American cuisine, and trout fresh from the ponds. It's open Friday through Sunday from 8 am to 8 pm, with longer hours in summer.

Getting There & Away
A bus between Red Bluff and Susanville stops at Chester, Mineral, and Westwood every day except Sunday; see Red Bluff in

NANCY KELLER

Shasta Dam, Lake Shasta, Northern Mountains

NANCY KELLER

The Sacramento River

NANCY KELLER

McCloud Reservoir

Black Butte, near Mt Shasta

Paul Bunyan & Babe the Blue Ox, Klamath

Castle Crags, Mt Shasta area

On the road again, Northern Mountains

Totem pole in Weed

the Sacramento Valley chapter for specifics.

LASSEN NATIONAL FOREST

Lassen National Forest covers 1.2 million acres in an area called the 'crossroads,' where the granite Sierras, the volcanic Cascades, the Modoc Plateau, and the Central Valley meet. The forest completely surrounds Lassen Volcanic National Park. It contains six recreation areas – Eagle Lake, Lake Almanor, Hat Creek, Silver Lake, High Lakes, and Deer Creek – all with campgrounds; the forest has 47 altogether. Recreational opportunities in the forest are practically unlimited.

Special points of interest include a one-third-mile walk through the Subway Cave lava tube, the 1½-mile volcanic Spatter Cone Trail, 7700-foot Antelope Peak, the 900-foot, 14-mile Hat Creek Rim escarpment, Willow Lake, Crater Lake, and the 32-mile Journey Through Time self-guided auto tour with 17 informative stops. If you're feeling ambitious you can also do a 170-mile loop drive, the Scenic Byway, passing many points of interest. It takes about five hours to do the whole thing, or you can do only part of it.

The forest contains 460 miles of hiking trails. About 120 miles of the Pacific Crest Trail pass through the forest, plus the 17 miles that pass through the national park. Other major trails include the 25-mile Bizz Johnson Trail, the 18-mile Hole-in-the-Ground to Black Rock Trail, the six-mile Spencer Meadows National Recreation Trail, and the 3½-mile Heart Lake National Recreation Trail.

The forest also contains three wilderness areas. The **Caribou Wilderness** and **Thousand Lakes Wilderness** are best visited from mid-June to mid-October; the **Ishi Wilderness,** at a much lower elevation in the Central Valley foothills east of Red Bluff, is more comfortable to visit in the spring and fall, as it's often extremely hot (over 100°F) in summer.

Information

The Lassen National Forest Supervisor's Office is at 55 S Sacramento St, Susanville (☎ 257-2191). District Ranger offices include Almanor Ranger District (☎ 258-2141), Eagle Lake Ranger District (☎ 825-3176), and Hat Creek Ranger District (☎ 336-5521).

LASSEN VOLCANIC NATIONAL PARK

Lassen Volcanic National Park is like a living lesson in volcanic landscapes. In addition to the spectacular Lassen Peak, the world's largest plug-dome volcano, rising 2000 feet over the surrounding landscape to a height of 10,457 feet above sea level, the park also contains boiling hot springs and mud pots, steaming sulfur vents, fumaroles, lava flows, tube caves, cinder cones, craters, crater lakes, and more. The road through the park wraps around Lassen Peak on three sides and provides access to the geothermal areas, lakes, and hiking trails. The park contains 150 miles of hiking trails, including a 17-mile section of the Pacific Crest Trail, and seven campgrounds.

Lassen Peak is classified as an active volcano. Its most recent eruption took place in 1915, when the volcano blew a giant cloud of smoke, steam, ash, and volcanic matter seven miles into the atmosphere. The national park was created the following year, to protect the volcanic landscape. Some of the areas destroyed by the blast, such as the appropriately named Devastated Area, are slowly recovering.

It's possible to drive through the park only in summer, usually from around June to October, though a few times in recent years the road has been closed by snow well into July – when we went in June one year, the road through the park was still under 40 feet of snow.

Information

When you enter the park you'll be given a pamphlet with a map and general information. Topographic maps and more specialized publications about the park's history, natural features, and other topics are also available.

The park headquarters (☎ 595-4444) is

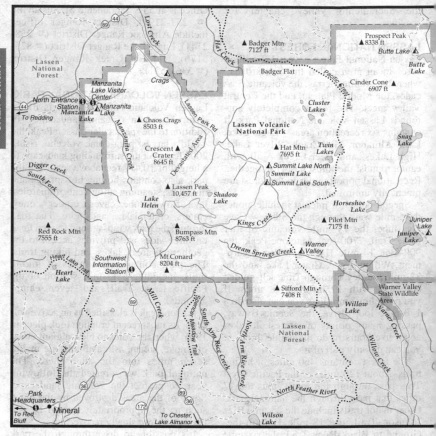

on Hwy 36 about a mile west of the tiny town of Mineral; it's open Monday to Friday from 8 am to 4:30 pm most of the year, daily in summer. The Southwest Information Station is at the park's southern entrance; at the northern entrance is the Manzanita Lake Visitor Center (☎ 335-7575) and the Loomis Museum, open daily from 9 am to 5 pm, but only in summer.

Places to Stay
Seven campgrounds are within the park, with many more in the surrounding Lassen National Forest. Various lodges, cabins, small resorts, and so on are nearby outside

the park; a list of them is published in the park newspaper. Otherwise, Chester, Red Bluff, and Redding all make convenient bases for visits to the park.

Getting There & Away
The park has two entrances. The north entrance, at Manzanita Lake, is reached via Hwy 44, coming 47 miles east from Redding. The south entrance is reached up a five-mile road taking off from Hwy 89, at a turnoff five miles east of Mineral, where the park headquarters is found. From this turnoff on Hwy 89 it is 48 miles west to Red Bluff, 25 miles east to Chester, 60

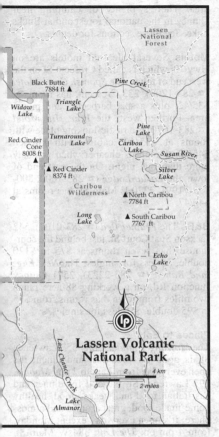

Lassen
National
Forest

Black Butte
7884 ft ▲

Pine Creek

Widow
Lake

Triangle
Lake

Red Cinder
Cone
8008 ft
▲

Turnaround
Lake

Pine
Lake

Caribou
Lake

Susan River

▲ Red Cinder
8374 ft

Silver
Lake

Caribou
Wilderness

▲ North Caribou
7784 ft

Long
Lake

▲ South Caribou
7767 ft

Echo
Lake

Last Chance Creek

Lassen Volcanic
National Park

0   2   4 km

0   1   2 miles

Lake
Almanor

County, which is characterized by mountains, high pine forests, lakes, the Plumas National Forest, and the Feather River. With its relatively dense population, tiny Quincy is the 'big city' of Plumas County. It's a pleasant place for a stop if you're driving through the mountains on Hwy 70, which passes right through the town, or if you're traveling between the mountains and the Central Valley via Hwy 70, through the magnificent Feather River Canyon.

The **Feather River** is the most noted attraction of the area; Plumas County is named for it *(plumas* is Spanish for 'feathers') and it's popular for swimming and fishing in summer. **Bucks Lake,** a 20-minute drive from Quincy, is popular in summer, too; in winter, snow renders the road to the lake impassable to cars, so snowmobilers get free rein. The Plumas National Forest provides unlimited opportunities for camping, hiking, fishing, and other activities near Quincy.

Orientation

Highway 70 is Quincy's main artery. Passing through town, it splits into two one-way streets, with traffic on Main St heading east, and traffic on Lawrence St heading west. Most everything you need is on, near, or between these two streets, which form the heart of Quincy's low-key commercial district. Jackson St, running parallel to, and one block back from Main St, is another important thoroughfare.

Information

The Plumas County Visitors Bureau (☎ 283-6345, 800-326-2247), 91 Church St between Main and Lawrence Sts, has a helpful staff with countywide information. It's open Monday to Friday from 8 am to 5 pm, with additional Saturday hours (also 8 am to 5 pm) in summer.

The Plumas National Forest Supervisor's Office (☎ 283-2050), 195 Lawrence St, has maps and information on the forest, and will send you free information if you phone to request it. The office is open Monday to Friday, 8:30 am to 5 pm. The Quincy Ranger District office (☎ 283-0555), 39696

miles east to Susanville, and 65 miles southeast to Quincy.

A bus between Red Bluff and Susanville, stopping on the way at Mineral, Chester, and Westwood, operates every day except Sunday (see Red Bluff in Sacramento Valley). Mineral is the stop closest to the park. There's no public transport within the park, though, or on the five miles between Hwy 36 and the park entrance.

QUINCY
• *pop 5000* • *elev 3423 feet*
Nestled in a pleasant valley in the northern High Sierra, Quincy is the seat of Plumas

Hwy 70, four miles north of Quincy, also has information; it's open Monday to Friday, 8 am to 4:30 pm.

The AAA office (☎ 283-1014), 20 Crescent St, is on the west end of town where Hwy 70 becomes Main St; it's open Monday to Friday from 8:30 am to 5 pm.

Things to See

The large **Plumas County Courthouse** on the west end of Main St, built in 1921, is said to be the county's most impressive structure, with huge interior marble posts and staircases and a 2000-pound bronze-and-plate glass chandelier hanging in the lobby.

In the block behind the courthouse, the **Plumas County Museum** (☎ 283-6320), 500 Jackson St at the corner of Coburn St, is worth a stop if you're passing through Quincy; it's full of exhibits on the history of Plumas County, with its pioneer days, early mining and timber, construction of the Western Pacific Railroad, and the Maidu Indians, with plenty of historical photos and relics. Hours are Monday to Friday from 8 am to 5 pm; 10 am to 4 pm on weekends and holidays from May to September; admission is $1.

The tourist office has a free pamphlet outlining a 30-minute **Heritage Walk,** which basically covers Main and Jackson Sts between Church and Buchanan Sts, with details on the historical homes and buildings.

Activities

Winter activities are popular in the area; cross-country ski gear and snowshoes can be rented at Sierra Mountain Sports (☎ 283-2323), 501 W Main St. Snowmobile tours are available at Bucks Lake Marina at Bucks Lake (☎ 283-4243) and in La Porte at O'Rourke's Outdoor Adventures (☎ 675-2729). Ask the tourist office for their *Winter Recreation* pamphlet.

Places to Stay

If you plan to stay in or around Quincy in summer, it's a good idea to make reservations, as it's a small town in a tourist-heavy area. There's plenty of camping near Quincy in the national forest and at Bucks Lake. See those sections for details.

Motels Several pleasant motels are on Hwy 70, which is called Crescent St on the west end of town. The *Spanish Creek Motel* (☎ 283-1200), 233 Crescent, has rooms at $35/42, plus a spa, barbecue, and picnic area. Further west, the *Pine Hill Motel* (☎ 283-1670) is a rustic-looking place with rooms at $35/40, cabins with kitchen $45/50, though its cheaper when you stay more than one night. On the east end of town, the *Lariat Lodge* (☎ 283-1000, 800-999-7199), 2370 E Main St, has rooms at $40/47.

B&Bs The *Feather Bed* (☎ 283-0102), 542 Jackson St at Court St, just behind the courthouse, has seven rooms at $75 to $120 double, $5 less for singles. The *New England Ranch* (☎ 283-2223), 2571 Quincy Junction Rd, on a working 88-acre ranch two miles from town, has rooms from $75 to $95 double, $10 less for singles.

Places to Eat

The *Morning Thunder Cafe,* 557 Lawrence St, is good for breakfast and lunch; it's open every day from 7 am to 2 pm. *Moon's,* 497 Lawrence St, is good for dinner and has Italian food and steaks, good, healthy home-made food, great aromas and atmosphere; it's open every day except Monday, from 4 pm on. *The Loft,* 384 W Main St, has 'delightful dining' for lunch and dinner, every day except Sunday. The *Feather River Co-Op Natural Food Market* is at 30 Harbison St, just off Main St, near The Loft.

BUCKS LAKE

About 17 miles southwest of Quincy and 32 miles northeast of Oroville, Bucks Lake is a beautiful, clear mountain lake surrounded by pine forest. It's popular in summer for camping, hiking, fishing, boating, waterskiing, and other recreation. Boats can be rented at Bucks Lake Marina and Bucks Lake Lodge (see Places to Stay).

Bucks Lake Pack Station & Stables (☎ 283-2532) offers horseback riding. The Pacific Crest Trail passes through the Bucks Lake wilderness, and there are other good hiking trails, too.

In winter, road access to the lake is closed by snow but it's still popular for cross-country skiing and snowmobiling. Bucks Lake Lodge, which stays open all year, rents winter sports gear, or it can be rented in Quincy.

The lake adjoins the 21,000-acre Bucks Lake Wilderness, a section of the Plumas National Forest; any of the forest ranger stations have information about hiking, fishing, camping, and other recreation on the lake and in the wilderness area.

Places to Stay & Eat

Several USFS campgrounds offer basic facilities for $3 to $12 per night; they include the *Grizzly Creek, Lower Bucks, Mill Creek, Sundew,* and *White Horse campgrounds* and the *Hutchins Group Camp.* Any Plumas National Forest Ranger station will have details, and reservations can be made through Destinet.

Commercial campgrounds include *Bucks Lakeshore Resort* (☎ 283-2333) and the *Haskins Valley PG&E Campsite* (☎ 800-743-5000). *Bucks Lake Marina* (☎ 283-4243) offers camping, housekeeping cabins, and boat rentals. Most of the campgrounds and services are open from around June to October.

Bucks Lake Lodge (☎ 283-2262) has a campground and various sizes of housekeeping cabins, for two to 10 people, for $49 to $79 per night, with cheaper weekly rates; it's open all year, with boat rentals and fishing tackle in summer, snowmobiling and cross-country skiing in winter. The restaurant at the lodge is known for good food; locals often drive out from Quincy for dinner.

PLUMAS-EUREKA STATE PARK

Within the Plumas-Eureka State Park is **Johnsville,** an Old West mining town where people still live today, and the mining camp where more than $8 million

worth of gold was processed, coming from 36 mines on and near Eureka Peak (elevation 7450 feet). The old stamp mill and other historical features are preserved, and the park visitors center doubles as a mining history museum (☎ 836-2380). Summer activities include hiking, with three main hiking trails ranging from easy to strenuous, fishing at Jamison Creek, Eureka Lake, and Madora Lake, and activities and interpretive programs put on by the park visitors center.

In winter, there's cross-country and downhill skiing in the park at the **Plumas-Eureka Ski Bowl** (☎ 836-2317, 836-2380). With two pomas, a rope tow, and a 650-foot vertical drop, it's a relaxed ski field good for beginning and intermediate skiers; it's open Friday through Sunday, usually from around mid December to April. Outside the ski bowl, there are plenty of other possibilities for cross-country skiing in the park, as well as other trails nearby in the Lakes Basin Recreation Area and starting from the Gray Eagle Lodge. Skis can be rented at Blairsden Mercantile (☎ 836-2589) in nearby Blairsden.

Places to Stay & Eat

There's camping in the park on a first-come, first-served basis from May 1 to October 15. Other camping is nearby in Plumas National Forest; ask at any of the ranger stations for details.

There are various lodges and restaurants in and near **Graeagle,** a small town one mile in from the highway, but they tend to be expensive. Cheaper accommodations are found in Portola, about 10 miles east on Hwy 70. There's one restaurant at Johnsville, in the park, and several more in nearby Graeagle.

Getting There & Away

The turnoff to the park is marked on Hwy 70, and the park itself is five miles off the highway.

PORTOLA

• *pop 2200* • *elev 4850 feet*

A small mountain town straddling the

Middle Fork of the Feather River, Portola's pride and joy is its **railroad museum** (☎ 832-4131), with over 30 locomotives and over 80 freight, caboose, and passenger cars. The museum is open daily from 10 am to 5 pm and admission is free. Train rides are given on summer weekends from 11 am to 4 pm in the summer or you can arrange to operate a locomotive yourself, with an instructor, for $75; call ☎ 832-4532 for details.

Seven miles north of Portola, in the Plumas National Forest, **Lake Davis** is good for trout and bass fishing all year round. **Frenchman Lake** is also popular, but it's farther away. Go southeast towards Reno for 20 miles to the turnoff at Chilcoot, then 12 miles north to the lake.

The Eastern Plumas County Chamber of Commerce (☎ 832-5444) is on Hwy 70, a short distance from town. It's open weekdays from 10 am to 2 pm, until 4 pm in summer.

Places to Stay

There's camping at Lake Davis in summer, or a bit further afield, at the Plumas-Eureka State Park, about 15 miles west of Portola, and at Frenchman Lake. Otherwise, there are several trailer camps along Hwy 70 west of Portola.

The *Sierra Motel* (☎ 832-4223), 380 E Sierra Ave (Hwy 70), has fine rooms at $35/40. *Pullman House B&B* (☎ 832-0107), 256 Commercial St, with rooms from $50 to $95, is conveniently situated in town, opposite the Good & Plenty Cafe. The *Silver Lady B&B* (☎ 832-1641), 100 Escondido Way, with rooms at $65, is in the Delleker district, about a mile west of town.

Places to Eat

The friendly little *Good & Plenty Cafe,* 241 Commercial St, is open 24 hours for ample portions of good food. The *Canyon Cafe,* 448 W Sierra Ave (Hwy 70), is open for breakfast and lunch. *The Willows,* 120 Pine St on the corner of Hwy 70, has a pleasant atmosphere with indoor or patio seating and good deli food.

For dinner, try the *Log Cabin,* 64 E Sierra Ave (Hwy 70), a local landmark specializing in German food, sometimes with live music.

PLUMAS NATIONAL FOREST

Covering 1,146,000 acres in the northern Sierra Nevada, Plumas National Forest extends roughly from Lake Oroville in the southwest, to Lake Almanor in the northwest, to Honey Lake in the northeast, and Frenchman Lake and Lake Davis in the southeast. The mountains are covered with evergreen forest, mostly ponderosa and sugar pine, Douglas, red, and white fir. The forest contains over 100 lakes and more than 1000 miles of rivers and streams, including the magnificent Feather River Canyon, which is traversed by Hwy 70.

The forest has over 50 campgrounds and dozens of hiking trails through the forest. Maps and information on the forest are available from the Supervisor's Office in Quincy (☎ 283-2050), 195 Lawrence St; the Quincy Ranger District office (☎ 283-0555), 39696 Hwy 70; or from the Oroville Ranger District office (☎ 534-6500), 875 Mitchell Ave, in Oroville.

Western Mountains

☎ 707

Between the Central Valley and the coast, the Coastal Mountain Range is occupied by national forests all the way from the Oregon border south to just above Clear Lake, at the north of the Wine Country. North of the Central Valley, the Coastal Range fans out into other mountain ranges: the Cascades, the Siskiyou Mountains, the Trinity Alps, the Salmon Mountains, the Marble Mountains, the Scott Bar Mountains, and others. At their higher elevations, the mountains are forested with evergreen conifers, including ponderosa pine, sugar pine, incense cedar, and red, white, and Douglas fir; at lower elevations are hardwoods, including oak, cottonwood, dogwood, and beech.

SIX RIVERS NATIONAL FOREST

Hugging the west side of the Klamath and Trinity National Forests and the Siskiyou and Trinity Alps Wilderness Areas, Six Rivers National Forest is a long, narrow swath of forest extending over 100 miles from north to south but only about five to 10 miles from east to west, starting at the Oregon border and going south all the way to the Yolla Bolly-Middle Eel Wilderness on the north end of Mendocino National Forest.

The six rivers for which the forest is named are the Eel, Klamath, Mad, Smith, Trinity, and Van Duzen Rivers. The forest has 15 campgrounds, but you can camp anywhere in the forest with a free campfire permit.

The Six Rivers National Forest Supervisor's Office (☎ 442-1721) is at 507 F St in Eureka.

MENDOCINO NATIONAL FOREST

Sixty-five miles long from north to south and 35 miles wide, the Mendocino National Forest includes over a million acres of forested mountains and canyons. Elevation ranges from 750 feet at Grindstone Creek Canyon in the Sacramento Valley foothills on the east side of the forest, up to the 8092-foot South Yolla Bolly Mtn in the north part of the forest.

Several recreation areas – Lake Pillsbury, Middle Creek-Elk Mountain, Letts Lake, Fouts, Eel River, and Plaskett Lake – all have campgrounds; altogether there are 42 within the forest, but you can camp anywhere for free with a free campfire permit. The forest has three national recreation trails: the Ides Cove Loop Trail in the Yolla Bolly Wilderness, the Travelers Home Trail at the Middle Fork of the Eel River, and the Sled Ridge Trail beginning at Middle Creek Campground. What it does *not* have is a single paved road.

Lake Pillsbury, probably the forest's most visited spot, attracts hikers, campers, boaters, and anglers, but being rather remote – 11 miles up a gravel road – it's still uncrowded. The *Lake Pillsbury Resort* (☎ 743-1581) has camping, cabins, fishing boat rentals, and a grocery store, and there's camping at four USFS campgrounds.

Two wilderness areas are within the forest: the 37,000-acre Snow Mountain Wilderness, with 52 miles of hiking trails, and part of the Yolla Bolly-Middle Eel Wilderness, with 40 miles of hiking trails.

Information

The Mendocino National Forest Supervisor's Office, 825 N Humboldt Ave, Willows can be reached at ☎ 916-934-3316, or try their 24-hour recorded information line (☎ 916-934-2350).

YOLLA BOLLY-MIDDLE EEL WILDERNESS

The 147,000-acre Yolla Bolly-Middle Eel Wilderness, between the North and South Yolla Bolly Mountains at the headwaters of the middle fork of the Eel River, includes territory from the Mendocino, Shasta-Trinity and Six Rivers National Forests. The name Yolla Bolly comes from the Wintu Indian language, *yo-la* meaning 'snow-covered' and *bo-li* meaning 'high peak.'

The best time to visit is in June and July, though it's possible to visit some areas from early May to mid-October. Precautions must be taken for erratic weather conditions at all times of year.

CLEAR LAKE

Just south of Mendocino National Forest, Clear Lake is a popular recreational lake with a shoreline over 100 miles long. Mt Konocti, towering over the lake at 4200 feet, is classified as an active volcano, and the lake itself is of volcanic origin. In late summer the thriving algae sometimes gives the lake a murky green appearance, while at other times of year it's clear blue. The algae in the lake makes it a great habitat for fish, especially bass, and it's also home to a variety of birds.

On the lake's southwest shore, **Clear Lake State Park** (☎ 279-4293) has hiking trails, fishing, boating, and camping. In Lower Lake, the **Anderson Marsh State**

Historic Park (☎ 279-4293) has a large marshy area, a 35-acre Pomo Indian archaeological site, a model Pomo Indian village, the restored historic John Still Anderson Ranch House, hiking trails, and bird watching. You'll often hear the terms 'upper lake' (the northwest portion) and 'lower lake' (the southeast portion), as the lake narrows in the middle to form two sections.

LAKEPORT
• *pop 4400* • *elev 1340 feet*

On the western shore of Clear Lake, Lakeport is the Lake County seat. The 1871 **Old County Courthouse** at 255 Main St is a state historic landmark; inside, the small but interesting **Lake County Historical Museum** (☎ 263-4555) has interesting Pomo Indian artifacts and other exhibits. **Library Park** on the lakeshore has picnic areas, a children's playground, and a gazebo where concerts are held.

Boats can be rented from a number of places including *On The Waterfront* (☎ 263-6789), 60 3rd St, and *Disney's Water Sports* (☎ 263-0969), 41 S Main St. Other boat rentals are available around the lake, including *Blue Fish Cove* (☎ 998-1769), 10573 E Hwy 20, in Clearlake Oaks. The visitor information center here in Lakeport has details on these and other attractions around the lake.

Information

The Lake County Visitor Information Center (☎ 263-9544, 800-525-3743), 875 Lakeport Blvd, has information on everything around the lake and the county. In summer it's open Monday to Friday from 8:30 am to 5:30 pm, Saturday 10 am to 6 pm; winter hours are Tuesday to Friday from 8:30 am to 5:30 pm, Saturday 10 am to 4 pm.

Places to Stay & Eat

Lakeport has many motels and restaurants. Lakeshore motels include the *Anchorage Inn* (☎ 263-5417), 950 N Main St, with rooms at $48 from mid-May to mid-October, $38 the rest of the year; the *Clear Lake Inn* (☎ 263-3551), 1010 N Main St, with rooms at $45/49; and the more expensive *Skylark Shores Resort Motel* (☎ 263-6151), at 1120 N Main St.

Park Place, 50 3rd St, is the town's most popular restaurant. It's open every day from 11 am to 9 pm and has a deck overlooking the lake. The more expensive *Anthony's* (☎ 263-4905), 2509 Lakeshore Blvd, is a popular Italian dinner house where reservations are suggested. Library Park is great for a picnic.

Getting There & Away

Greyhound has a daily San Francisco-Lakeport bus that makes 15 stops along the way and takes five hours. The bus leaves Lakeport in the morning and returns from San Francisco in the afternoon. There is no depot in Lakeport, but the bus makes a flag stop on Main St; call Greyhound for reservations, as departure times vary. Driving time between San Francisco and Clear Lake is about 2½ to three hours.

North Coast

From Bodega Bay and the beautiful Russian River resort area up to the Oregon border, California's rugged north coast holds some of the state's finest attractions including forests of 1000-year-old coast redwoods and a rocky, brooding coastline still being carved by crashing waves.

North of the Golden Gate Bridge, the Pacific Coast Hwy (Hwy 1) and the Redwood Hwy (Hwy 101) separate. Heading north, Hwy 1 snakes along the coast past magnificent scenery and tiny coastal towns, while Hwy 101 heads through a series of fertile inland valleys before entering the great redwood forests.

The north coast also has many other highlights, including lakes, rivers, bays and coastal lagoons, charming towns, a historic railroad (the 'Skunk Train'), and an individualistic culture very different from what you find in the big cities. All in all California's north coast is a very special part of the world.

Russian River

☎ 707

About a 1½- to 2-hour drive north of San Francisco, the lower Russian River is a beautiful area of magnificent scenery, with the river coursing through a hilly landscape of coast redwood forest, vineyards, and a few tiny towns. A popular resort area offering enjoyable activities and a laid-back attitude and pace of life, it attracts lots of visitors in summer; the rest of the year it's a lot quieter.

The Russian River begins in the mountains north of Ukiah and flows south, touching communities along the way including Ukiah, Hopland, Cloverdale, and Healdsburg, making a sharp turn west towards the ocean just south of Healdsburg. It's this area of the lower river, after it's made the turn, that is known as the Russian River resort area, or simply the Russian River for short. Little towns include Forestville, Rio Nido, Guerneville, Monte Rio, and Duncans Mills. Small towns away from the river, but still considered part of the Russian River area, include Cazadero in the mountains a few miles north of the river, and Occidental in the redwood forest a few miles south of Monte Rio.

North Coast map showing Oregon border region, including To Coos Bay, To Grants Pass, To Medford, Crescent City, Klamath National Forest, Yreka, Pacific Ocean, Redwood National Park, Shasta-Trinity National Forest, Weed, Mt Shasta, Hoopa Valley Indian Reservation, Trinity Lake, Arcata, Eureka, Shasta Lake, Redding, Eel River, To Sacramento, Leggett, Mendocino National Forest, Round Valley Indian Reservation, Black Butte 7448 ft, Fort Bragg, Mendocino, Willits, Ukiah, Point Arena, Clear Lake, Cloverdale, Santa Rosa, Bodega Bay, To San Francisco.

With a population of 7000, Guerneville is the river's biggest town; it has resorts, restaurants, and many other services, and the liveliest ambiance of any of the towns on the river. Four miles downriver, past the Northwood golf course, Monte Rio has a river beach, a bridge, a couple of places to stay and eat, and the turnoff to Occidental. Bohemian Grove, where bigwigs of politics and industry congregate for a camp-out each summer, is in the hills outside town. Further downriver, Duncans Mills, with a population of only 26 souls, is a tiny restored historic town. Occidental, a few miles south of Monte Rio via the Bohemian Highway, is an idyllic little historic town in the redwoods, and a good destination for a scenic drive; Cazadero, a few miles north of the river, has a remote, away-from-it-all feel.

Orientation & Information

River Rd, connecting Hwy 101 just north of Santa Rosa with Hwy 1 on the coast at Jenner, is the main artery of the lower Russian River region, hugging the river all the way from Forestville to the coast. Highway 116, coming northwest from Cotati through Sebastopol, is another important route.

The Russian River Chamber of Commerce (☎ 869-9000) is at 16200 1st St, Guerneville. The Russian River Region Visitor Information Center (☎ 869-9212) is at 14034 Armstrong Woods Rd.

River Activities

Many sandy beaches and swimming holes all along the river make pleasant spots for picnics, swimming, and relaxing. Canoes, paddle boats, inner tubes, and other craft are available in summer at Johnson's Beach (☎ 869-2045) at the river end of Church St in downtown Guerneville.

Burke's Canoe Trips (☎ 887-1222) at 8600 River Rd, Forestville, rents canoes from April to September for a variety of trips on the river. Overnight camping is available at their campground in a redwood grove beside the river.

There's fishing in the Russian River year round, with king and silver salmon from late August to November, steelhead from November to April, shad in late May and June, and bass and catfish in summer. King's Sport & Tackle (☎ 869-2156) at 16258 Main St, Guerneville, is the local center for fishing gear and information.

Mike's Bike Rental (☎ 869-1106) at 16442 Main St, Guerneville, rents mountain bikes, cruisers, and car racks, and can offer advice about routes.

Armstrong Redwoods State Reserve

The Armstrong Redwoods State Reserve (☎ 869-2015, 865-2391) at 17000 Armstrong Woods Rd, about two miles north of Guerneville, is an 805-acre park preserving a magnificent stand of old-growth redwood forest set aside by Colonel Armstrong, an early lumberman here. This is the only grove of virgin redwoods in this area. Armstrong Woods is open for day use, with hiking trails and interpretive nature trails, and an outdoor amphitheater. If you drive in there's a $5 day-use fee, but you can park at the entrance and walk or bicycle in for free – the amazing grove of giant trees is right there near the entrance.

The Armstrong Woods Pack Station (☎ 887-2939) operates year-round horse trail rides with everything from 1½-hour trail rides, and full-day lunch rides, up to three-day pack trips.

Wineries

The Korbel Champagne Cellars (☎ 887-2294) at 13250 River Rd, Guerneville, is a large, picturesque 1886 winery producing some of America's premium award-winning champagnes. Free winery tours and tastings are offered daily, year round.

Other wineries in the area include:

Mark West Estate Winery (☎ 544-4813), 7010 Trenton-Healdsburg Rd, Forestville; tasting, picnic area, tours by appointment.

Sea Ridge Winery (☎ 874-1707), 13404 Dupont Rd, Occidental; tasting, picnic area, tours by appointment.

Topolos at Russian River Vineyards (☎ 887-1575, 800-867-6567), 5700 Gravenstein Hwy N (Hwy 116), Forestville; tasting, dining, tours by appointment.

Special Events
The big events of the year in Guerneville include the Russian River Rodeo, Stumptown Parade & BBQ the third weekend in June; the Russian River Blues Festival at Johnson's Beach in June; the Russian River Jazz Festival in September and the Russian Heritage Christmas in December.

Places to Stay
The chamber of commerce and the Russian River Region Visitor Information Center have a complete list of the great number of accommodations available in every category.

Camping The Austin Creek State Recreation Area at Armstrong Redwoods State Reserve (☎ 869-2015, 865-2391), has drive-in sites at Bullfrog Pond for $10; cold water is available, but no showers. Primitive hike-in and equestrian backcountry trail campsites are $7, with pit toilets.

A great number of commercial campgrounds in Guerneville and along the river are also good for camping. They include the *Casini Family Campground* (☎ 865-2255, 800-451-8400), 22855 Moscow Rd, Duncans Mills, on the river; *Johnson's Beach Campground & Cabins* (☎ 869-2022), 16241 1st St, on the river in downtown Guerneville; and *Schoolhouse Canyon Campground* (☎ 869-2311), 12600 River Rd, Guerneville; near the river, with a private river beach.

Hotels, Resorts & Cottages The area has everything from simple family-style resorts with old wooden cabins where the same

families return summer after summer, to lively (or quieter) gay resorts. *Cazanoma Lodge* (☎ 632-5255), 1000 Kidd Creek Rd, Cazadero, on a large acreage with a waterfall and a fine restaurant; *Fife's* (☎ 869-0656), 16467 River Rd, an attractive, 'mostly gay' resort right on the river, on the west side of Guerneville; *Johnson's Beach Resort* (☎ 869-2022), 16241 1st St, right on the beach in downtown Guerneville; *Riverlane Resort* (☎ 869-2323), 16320 First St, with family-style cabins on the river in downtown Guerneville; and *Sweet Reunion Resort* (☎ 869-9769, 800-310-0804 (CA), 800-997-3312), 16124 Drake Rd, Guerneville; cottages, vintage silver trailers & RV hookups, on the river.

B&Bs In the area look for the *Huckleberry Springs Country Inn* (☎ 865-2683, 800-822-2683), 8105 Beedle Rd, Monte Rio, a 60-acre mountaintop retreat with sweeping views from the deck, pool, or spa; *Raford House* (☎ 887-9573), 10630 Wohler Rd, Healdsburg, a restored 1880 Victorian mansion on a five-acre parcel overlooking a vineyard; and *Ridenhour Ranch House Inn* (☎ 887-1033), 12850 River Rd, Guerneville, beside Korbel winery.

Places to Eat
Guerneville The *Last Great Hiding Place* (☎ 887-9506) at 15025 River Rd, is a local favorite with tables inside as well as outside on two river-view terraces overlooking Midway Beach. *Journey's End* (☎ 887-9647) at 6544 Front St is a pleasant coffeehouse serving food, baked goods, and great coffee.

Also along here, *Breeze Inn Bar-B-Q* (☎ 869-9208, 869-9209) at 15640 River Rd makes excellent barbecued meats as well as a few vegetarian dishes for the veggies in the crowd.

Jirk's Pizza Cafe (☎ 869-0651) at 16205 1st St serves pizza, pasta, burgers, and sandwiches inside or on the outdoor deck in the rear. *Fife's* (☎ 869-0656) at 16467 River Rd, on the west end at the resort of the same name, offers attractive gourmet dining both indoors and outside, with

CALIFORNIA

breakfast and brunch served on the deck overlooking the pool.

The *Applewood Restaurant* (☎ 869-9093) at 13555 Hwy 116, across the Guerneville Bridge at the beautiful Applewood Estate Inn, is an elegant restaurant winning rave reviews; it's open for dinner Tuesday to Saturday nights, reservations essential.

Mexican restaurants include *Lalita's Mexican Cantina* (☎ 869-3238) at 16255 Main St and *Mi Casita* (☎ 869-9626) at 16380 Mill St.

The *Coffee Bazaar* (☎ 869-9706) in the Cinnabar building at 14045 Armstrong Woods Rd, a block north of the main intersection of Main St and Armstrong Woods Rd, is a popular local hangout for coffee, baked goods, and ice cream. *Brew Moon* (☎ 869-0201) at 16248 Main St is a tiny coffeehouse with occasional poetry or music in the evening.

Around the River Every little town along the river also has places to eat. In Forestville, the *Forestville Inn Mexican Restaurant* (☎ 887-1242) at 6625 Front St (Hwy 116), right in the center of the tiny town, serves Mexican food inside or out in a lovely Spanish-style courtyard, especially pleasant in summer. Nearby, *Chez Marie* (☎ 887-7503) at 6675 Front St is a small country French restaurant.

North of the river, Cazadero also has good places to eat, especially the *Cazanoma Lodge* (☎ 632-5255) at 1000 Kidd Creek Rd with its fine German and American dinners and Sunday brunch, with an 80-foot waterfall and a trout farm providing fresh trout for the restaurant, open March through December

Entertainment
The Jungle (☎ 869-1400) at 16135 Main St, Guerneville, offers disco dancing on weekends in summer. *Molly's Country Club* (☎ 869-0511) at 14120 Old Cazadero Rd, just off River Rd, Guerneville, has country & western dancing every Friday and Saturday night year round, with lessons in line dancing and two-step on Sundays.

The *Rainbow Cattle Company* (☎ 869-0206) at 16220 Main St, Guerneville, is a popular gay bar; the bar at the Last Great Hiding Place (☎ 887-9506) at 15025 River Rd, Guerneville, is also popular.

Getting There & Away
Sonoma County Transit (☎ 575-7433, 800-345-7433) has a daily bus route (No 20) connecting Santa Rosa and the Russian River area, plus a weekday route (No 28) serving Guerneville, Monte Rio, Duncans Mills, and Rio Nido.

OCCIDENTAL
• *pop 500* ☎ *707*
Occidental is a lovely little town nestled in the redwood-covered hills a few miles south of the Russian River and west of Sebastopol. Founded as a logging town in the 19th century, it attracts visitors for its charming atmosphere, interesting little shops and its fine places to eat, especially the two Italian family restaurants which are the town's most prominent features. The scenic drive to get to Occidental, whichever way you come, is one of the highlights of western Sonoma County.

Places to Stay
The historic 1879 *Union Hotel* (☎ 874-3555, 823-1717) at 3703 Main St, offers lodging in 11 motel rooms out behind the old hotel, which is now a restaurant and saloon; rooms are $42 weekends, $30 the rest of the week. Across the street, the *Occidental Lodge* (☎ 874-3623) at 3610 Bohemian Hwy has a swimming pool and 24 rooms for $54 on weekends, $42/46 single/double the rest of the week. *The Inn at Occidental* (☎ 874-1047, 800-522-6324) at 3657 Church St is a Victorian B&B with eight rooms for $125 to $195 on Friday and Saturday nights, $95 to $165 the rest of the week.

Places to Eat
The *Union Hotel* dining room (☎ 874-3555, 823-1717) and *Negri's Italian Dinners* (☎ 823-5301), opposite one another on Main St right in the center of town, have been attracting visitors to Occidental for

ample family-style Italian meals since the 1930s.

The Union Hotel also has the *Union Cafe* for coffee and baked goods, open every day from 6 am. The *Union Hotel Saloon*, a popular gathering spot and watering hole for friendly locals, looks like it hasn't changed a thing since it was built in 1879; live music is often presented here on weekends.

Howard's Station Cafe (☎ 874-2838) at 75 Main St, in the center of town, is great for breakfast and lunch.

SEBASTOPOL
• *pop 7750 ☎ 707*

An attractive little town in a countryside of rolling hills and apple orchards 50 miles north of San Francisco and 12 miles west of Santa Rosa, Sebastopol is famous for the Gravenstein apples which are the area's major crop; it's also getting a reputation among antique buffs for its many antique shops. Historic Main St was spruced up several years ago and it now houses many interesting little shops. The big weekend flea market is another attraction.

Orientation & Information
The crossroads of Hwys 116 and 12 is Sebastopol's major intersection. Highway 116, called Main St in the center of town, is the main commercial street; in the heart of town, southbound highway traffic uses Main St, while northbound traffic uses Petaluma Ave, one block to the east. At the north end of Main St, the road makes a 90-degree turn at the Safeway store, after which it's called Healdsburg Ave; continuing north out of town towards Forestville and the Russian River, about eight miles away, it's called Gravenstein Hwy N. South of town, heading towards Cotati, Hwy 116 is called Gravenstein Hwy S; this is where most of the antique shops are, and the flea market.

The Sebastopol Chamber of Commerce (☎ 823-3032) is at 265 S Main St.

Things to See & Do
The many antique shops and collectives on the south end of town and along Graven-

stein Hwy S are an attraction for antique buffs as well as for ordinary browsers. The **Sebastopol Antique Mall** (☎ 823-1936) at 755 Petaluma Ave houses many varied shops; while you're there, pick up a copy of the free *Cochran's Art, Antiques & Collectibles* newspaper, published in Petaluma, which contains a map showing 16 antique shops along Gravenstein Hwy S and lots of other places around the area.

Midgley's Country Flea Market (☎ 823-7874) at 2200 Gravenstein Hwy S, is the region's largest flea market, held on weekends.

The free *Sonoma County Farm Trails* pamphlet, available at the chamber of commerce and many other places around Sebastopol and Sonoma County, is a fine publication with a map and information on dozens of nearby farms where you can buy everything from apples to wreaths, with a chart showing when each thing is harvested.

Special Events
Annual events in Sebastopol include the Apple Blossom Parade & Festival in April and the Gravenstein Apple Fair held under the oaks in Ragle Park in August.

Places to Stay
There are no places to stay within the Sebastopol city limits, but three B&Bs are in the countryside nearby. The *Gravenstein Inn* (☎ 829-0493) at 3160 Hicks Rd is a National Historic Landmark with a six-acre apple orchard, a wisteria arbor, and a heated swimming pool; rooms are $80 to $120. *Lamb Meadow B&B* (☎ 823-4794) at 1327 Cooper Rd has one room for $90 and a large suite for $120. *Raccoon Cottage* (☎ 545-5466) is a rustic country cottage amidst oaks, fruit trees, and English gardens, renting for around $70 to $95 a night, depending on the length of stay.

Places to Eat
The *East West Cafe & Bakery* (☎ 829-2822) at 128 N Main St, is a great place to eat, hang out, and enjoy the coffee, healthy food, and comfortable atmosphere.

Coffee Catz (☎ 829-6600) at 6761 Sebastopol Ave (Hwy 12 heading to Santa Rosa), a 'roastery & coffee club' in the Gravenstein Station with historic railway cars on display, is another very popular place for coffee, cafe fare, and live music.

Viva Mexico (☎ 823-5555) at 841 Gravenstein Hwy S, a simple little takeaway with tables under an awning out front, was voted the 'best Mexican take-out restaurant in Sonoma County' for 1995. There's a larger indoor branch, the *Viva Mexico Tropi-cal* (☎ 824-8482) at 7235 Healdsburg Ave. The *Thai Pot* (☎ 823-1324) at 6961 Bodega Ave offers Thai food to eat there or to go. *Mary's Pizza Shack* (☎ 829-5800) at 790 Gravenstein Hwy N serves up famous pizza in a family-style pizza parlor.

The town's favorite fancy restaurant is *Chez Peyo* (☎ 823-1223), two miles south of town at 2295 Gravenstein Hwy S, opposite the flea market, popular for its country French cuisine.

Entertainment
Jasper O'Farrell's (☎ 823-1389) at 6957 Bodega Ave, near the corner of Main St, is a traditional Irish-style pub with live music or other entertainment every night. The *Main Street Theatre* (☎ 823-0177) at 104 N Main St, at the main intersection with Bodega Ave, presents theater performances Thursday to Sunday throughout the year; phone for schedule and reservations. *Sebastopol Cinemas* (☎ 829-3456) at 6868 McKinley St, one block east of Main St and one block north of Hwy 12, has five movie theaters.

Getting There & Away
Sonoma County Transit (☎ 575-7433, 800-345-7433) operates several daily bus routes connecting Sebastopol with Santa Rosa, Cotati/Rohnert Park, Occidental, and the Russian River area.

The daily Mendocino Transit Authority (MTA) Coast Bus (☎ 884-3723) comes down the coast from Point Arena, turning inland south of Bodega Bay, with stops at Bodega and Sebastopol on the way to Santa Rosa, coming south down the coast every morning and returning from Santa Rosa by the same route in the afternoon.

Along Hwy 101

North of Santa Rosa, Hwy 101 heads north through a series of fertile valleys, joining the Pacific Coast Hwy (Hwy 1) at Leggett.

Some highlights of this area include the Sonoma and Mendocino County wine country regions, Lakes Sonoma and Mendocino, the picturesque Anderson Valley, and the two hot springs near Ukiah. The highway passes along the upper Russian River for much of its distance.

HEALDSBURG
• *pop 9750* ☎ *707*
Healdsburg is a small, pleasant town centered around a shady Spanish-style plaza. The Russian River, Lake Sonoma, and over 60 wineries all within a half-hour drive attract more than a million visitors to Healdsburg each year – a figure that seems hard to believe when you stroll around the unpresuming little plaza.

Orientation & Information
The heart of town is the Healdsburg Plaza, bordered by Healdsburg Ave, Center St, Matheson St, and Plaza St.

The Healdsburg Area Chamber of Commerce (☎ 433-6935, 800-648-9922 within California), 217 Healdsburg Ave, is south of the plaza. The post office is at 404 Center St.

Things to See & Do
The green, shady Healdsburg Plaza is, surrounded by shops and cafes; free concerts are held here on summer Sunday afternoons. The **Healdsburg Museum** (☎ 431-3325) at 221 Matheson St, has exhibits on northern Sonoma County history; it's open Tuesday to Sunday from 11 am to 4 pm, with free admission. A **walking tour** guidebook to Healdsburg's historic homes is available at the museum, at City Hall at

126 Matheson St, and at Toyon Books (☎ 433-9270) at 104 Matheson St.

Healdsburg Veterans Memorial Beach on the river, about a mile south of the plaza, is popular for swimming, fishing, canoeing, and picnics in summertime.

WC 'Bob' Trowbridge Canoe Trips (☎ 433-7247, 800-640-1386) at 20 Healdsburg Ave rents canoes and kayaks from April to October for a variety of trips on the Russian River. Their Alexander Valley campground is available to their customers for $5 per person, with a barbecue buffet dinner served there every Saturday night.

Special Events

Major annual events in Healdsburg include the Russian River Wine Road Barrel Tasting in March, the Russian River Wine Festival in May, and the Harvest Time in the Alexander Valley in October.

Places to Stay

Camping There's camping at Lake Sonoma (see the Around Healdsburg section) and at the *Cloverdale Wine Country KOA Camping Resort* (☎ 894-3337, 800-368-4558) at 26460 River Rd in Cloverdale, about 15 miles north of Healdsburg.

Motels On the north edge of town at the Dry Creek Rd exit from Hwy 101, the *Vineyard Valley Inn* (☎ 433-0101, 800-499-0103) at 178 Dry Creek Rd has 25 rooms for $65 and up on summer weekends, $45 Sunday to Thursday year round. The *Best Western Dry Creek Inn* (☎ 433-0300, 800-222-5784) at 198 Dry Creek Rd has 104 rooms for $89/69 in summer/winter.

Older motels on Healdsburg Ave a few blocks south of the plaza include the *Fairview Motel* (☎ 433-5548) at 74 Healdsburg Ave with rooms for $42/52 single/double in summer, $36/42 the rest of the year, and the *L&M Motel* (☎ 433-6528) next door at 70 Healdsburg Ave with regular rooms for $50/40 in summer/winter, or with kitchenette $58/40.

B&Bs In town, the *Healdsburg Inn on the Plaza* (☎ 433-6991) at 116 Matheson St has 10 rooms on an upper floor, with a roof garden and solarium, for $145 to $195. The *George Alexander House* (☎ 433-1358) at 423 Matheson St, in a 1905 Queen Anne Victorian three blocks east of the plaza, has four rooms for $80 to $130. The *Camellia Inn* (☎ 433-8182, 800-727-8182) at 21 North St has nine bedrooms in an elegant 1869 Italianate Victorian townhouse for $70 to $135. The *Haydon Street Inn* (☎ 433-5228) at 321 Haydon St, also in a Queen Anne Victorian, has six rooms and a separate cottage for $95 to $165.

In the countryside north of town, the *Belle de Jour Inn* (☎ 431-9777) at 16276 Healdsburg Ave has four cottages for $135 and $195. Half a mile west of town, the *Madrona Manor* (☎ 433-4231, 800-258-4003) at 1001 Westside Rd has 20 rooms in a luxurious country mansion with a swimming pool, carriage house, and garden suite for $140 to $240.

Places to Eat

On Healdsburg Ave south of the plaza, the *Singletree Inn* (☎ 433-8263) at 165 Healdsburg Ave is a pleasant, old-fashioned place for breakfast and lunch, open every day from 6 am to 3 pm. *Mangia Bene* (☎ 433-2340) at 241 Healdsburg Ave is a good yet inexpensive Italian restaurant with pleasant ambiance, open every day for lunch and dinner.

Several other good places to eat are situated around the plaza. On the north side, the *Plaza Street Market* (☎ 431-2800) at 113 Plaza St is an attractive European-style deli/cafe. *Bistro Ralph* (☎ 433-1380) at 109 Plaza St is a casual but elegant little restaurant with good food, serving lunch on weekdays and dinner every night.

A block north of the plaza, *Ravenous* (☎ 431-1770) at 117 North St, next door to the Raven Theatre, is very popular for its interesting food and enjoyable ambiance. The *China Restaurant* (☎ 433-4122) at 336 Healdsburg Ave is an attractive Chinese restaurant.

About five minutes' drive north of town,

the *Cafe at the Winery* (☎ 433-3141) at the Chateau Souverain winery, 400 Souverain Rd, Geyserville, is a favorite for its country French cuisine and its attractive ambiance, with a view overlooking the vineyards; it's open for dinner Friday, Saturday, and Sunday, reservations recommended.

Entertainment
Molly Malone's Irish Pub & Grille (☎ 431-1856) at 245 Healdsburg Ave has something going on every night, with live dance music Thursday, Friday, and Saturday nights; other nights feature a weekly schedule of karaoke, open mike, darts, and pool competitions.

Getting There & Around
Bus Greyhound (☎ 800-231-2222) serves Healdsburg with two northbound and two southbound buses daily, using a flag stop at the bench in front of the gas station on Dry Creek Rd at Hwy 101. Sonoma County Transit (☎ 576-7433, 800-345-7433) has a daily local bus route (No 60) to/from Santa Rosa and north to Cloverdale.

Bicycle Healdsburg Spoke Folk Cyclery (☎ 433-7171) at 249 Center St rents bicycles.

AROUND HEALDSBURG
☎ 707
Wineries
Smack in the middle of the northern Sonoma County wine country, Healdsburg is surrounded by wineries and vineyards. Those mentioned here are the more famous, but there are plenty of others, including tiny family wineries that can be the most charming of all; you can contact the chamber of commerce for a complete listing.

Chateau Souverain (☎ 433-3141), 400 Souverain Rd, Geyserville; tasting, cafe.
Clos du Bois (☎ 433-5576, 800-222-3189), 19410 Geyserville Ave, Geyserville; tasting, tours by appointment.
Dry Creek Vineyard (☎ 433-1000, 800-864-9463), 3770 Lambert Bridge Rd, Healdsburg; tasting, picnic area.

Ferrari-Carano Vineyards & Winery (☎ 433-6700), 8761 Dry Creek Rd, Healdsburg; tasting, tours by appointment.
Hop Kiln Winery (☎ 433-6491), 6050 Westside Rd, Healdsburg; historic tasting room, picturesque picnic area, and pond.
Simi Winery (☎ 433-6981), 16275 Healdsburg Ave, Healdsburg; tasting, picnic area and a 'dynamic tour program recognized as one of the wine industry's best.'

Lake Sonoma
Eleven miles northwest of Healdsburg, 2700-acre Lake Sonoma is popular for camping and water recreation. Formed by Warm Springs Dam in 1983, the lake has two major arms and many smaller coves.

The dam, 319 feet high and 3000 feet long, is on the south end of the lake. Nearby, the visitors center (☎ 433-9483) has historical exhibits, maps for the 40 miles of hiking trails, and other information.

About half a mile west of the dam, the Lake Sonoma Marina (☎ 433-2200) rents every type of water recreation you can think of. To get there from Hwy 101, take the Dry Creek Rd exit on the north end of Healdsburg and head northwest for 11 miles, through the beautiful Dry Creek Valley with its miles of vineyards, a very scenic drive.

Camping around the lake includes 113 sites at the Liberty Glen campground, a developed drive-in campground with hot showers on a ridge overlooking the south end of the lake; sites here are $12/6 in summer/winter, all first come, first served and rarely crowded. Fifteen other campgrounds are dotted around the lake, all primitive boat-in or hike-in sites; all of these are free, requiring only that you sign in at the visitors center.

HOPLAND
• *pop 800* ☎ 707
This little town just three blocks long on Hwy 101 is known as the gateway to the Mendocino County wine country. The town was named for its most prominent crop: hops were grown here starting in 1866 but Prohibition brought the industry to a halt.

The town languished until 1977, when Fetzer Vineyards renovated the old high school and opened it as a wine-tasting room. The event that put Hopland back on the map was the opening of the Mendocino Brewing Company in 1983, the first brew pub to open in California since Prohibition and the second in the nation. Now one of Northern California's best known, it attracts visitors from near and far, as do the Fetzer and Milano wineries, and the Jepson Vineyards north of town.

Places to Stay & Eat

The *Thatcher Inn* (☎ 744-1890, 800-266-1891) at 13401 Hwy 101 S is a charming, beautifully restored 1890 Victorian hotel with 20 double rooms from $100 to $155, breakfast included. Guests and non-guests alike are welcome for breakfast, lunch, and dinner served in the dining room and on the garden patio.

The *Mendocino Brewing Company* (☎ 744-1361, 744-1015) at 13351 Hwy 101 S, in the next block, is famous for its award-winning Red Tail Ale and other brews. The tavern hosts live music on Saturday nights and open mike night every other Friday; also here are a pleasant outdoor beer garden and the *Hopland Brewery Tavern Restaurant*.

Next door, *The Cheesecake Lady* (☎ 744-1441) at 13325 Hwy 101 S is famous for its wide variety of award-winning cheesecakes and other goodies; across the street, the *Bluebird Cafe* (☎ 744-1633) at 13340 Hwy 101 S is a pleasant cafe.

The *Fetzer Vineyards Tasting Room* (☎ 744-1737) at 13500 Hwy 101 S is also nearby, open every day from 10 am to 5 pm. The *Milano Winery* (☎ 744-1396) at 14594 Hwy 101 S and the *Jepson Vineyards* (☎ 468-8936) at 10400 Hwy 101 S are other Hopland wineries.

ANDERSON VALLEY
☎ 707

A beautiful agricultural valley with vineyards, apple orchards, sheep pastures, oak trees, and redwood groves, Anderson Valley is northwest of Hopland and south-west of Ukiah. Visitors primarily come here to visit the wineries and to make the 25-mile scenic drive along Hwy 128 from Yorkville to Navarro. Tiny **Boonville** and **Philo** are the valley's principal towns.

Boonville is linguistically famous for its unique language, 'Boontling,' developed here around the turn of the century, when Boonville was a pretty remote place; the language was developed so that the locals could communicate privately around outsiders, as well as for their own amusement. Try asking for a 'horn of zeese' (a cup of coffee) or some 'bahl gorms' (good food) while you're there.

Orientation & Information

Highway 128 travels 57 twisty miles between Hwy 101 at Cloverdale and Hwy 1 on the coast at Albion. Highway 253, heading west 19 miles from Hwy 101 just south of Ukiah to Boonville, is an alternative route and the easiest way to get here from Ukiah.

Information about Anderson Valley is available from the chamber of commerce in Ukiah or from the Anderson Valley Chamber of Commerce (☎ 895-2379) in Boonville.

Things to See & Do

The Anderson Valley Historical Museum (☎ 895-3207) on Hwy 128, one mile north of Boonville, has exhibits of Pomo Indian baskets and agricultural artifacts from the valley.

The valley has over a dozen wineries, see the listing under Around Ukiah.

Hiking, bicycling, fishing, canoeing, and kayaking are other popular activities here.

Special Events

The chambers of commerce in Boonville and Ukiah have information on these events, all held at the Mendocino County Fairgrounds in Boonville unless otherwise noted: the Spring Wildflower Show, held the last Sunday and Monday of April; the Spring Fair in May; the Woolgrower's Barbecue & Sheep Dog Trials the third weekend in July; the Wine Tasting Cham-

of Commerce publishes a free color pamphlet with a map and information on 33 wineries and vineyards around the area.

Almost all of the 33 wineries offer tasting, most during scheduled hours, some by appointment only; a few offer tours as well. Some of the area's better-known wineries include:

Parducci Wine Cellars (☎ 462-9463), 501 Parducci Rd, Ukiah; tasting, tours, gifts.

Weibel Vineyards (☎ 485-0321), 7051 N State St, Redwood Valley; tasting, picnic areas.

Fetzer Vineyards (☎ 744-1250), 13500 Hwy 101 S, Hopland; tasting, gifts, gardens, picnic areas.

Scharffenberger Cellars (☎ 895-2957), 8501 Hwy 128, Philo; tasting daily, tours by appointment.

Kendall-Jackson/Edmeades Estate (☎ 895-3009), 3500 Hwy 128, Philo.

Husch Vineyards (☎ 895-3216), 4400 Hwy 128, Philo; tasting.

Vichy Springs

Just a five-minute drive east of Ukiah, the Vichy Springs Resort (☎ 462-9515) at 2605 Vichy Springs Rd is a famous old hot springs with the distinction of being the only warm and naturally carbonated ('champagne') mineral baths in North America. Opened in 1854 and named after the world-famous Vichy Springs in France, this spring is the oldest continuously operating mineral springs spa in California; the two cottages here, built in 1854, are the two oldest structures standing in Mendocino County.

Around the turn of the century, Vichy Springs was a bustling place, popular for day trips from San Francisco; luminaries including Mark Twain, Jack London, and Robert Louis Stevenson have all come here for the restorative properties of the waters, which can be drunk as well as bathed in.

Facilities include a heated outdoor mineral hot tub, 10 indoor and outdoor tubs with natural 90°F waters, a grotto with a ladle for sipping the effervescent waters, and a massage room. The 700-acre grounds also feature hiking trails to the old Cinnabar mine shaft, up Grizzly Creek, and to a

40-foot waterfall, with 20 more miles of trails nearby.

Overnight accommodations include 12 rooms, built of redwood in the 1860s, for $89/130 single/double, a one-bedroom cottage with kitchen for $155 and a two-bedroom cottage with kitchen for $165, all with a fine buffet breakfast included. RV parking costs $15 per night, plus the all-day use fee of $25, $15 for two hours or less. Swimsuits are required.

To get to Vichy Springs from Hwy 101, take the Perkins St exit and go east for about a mile, until you run into the mountain, then turn left and follow the signs for another two miles to the springs.

Orr Hot Springs

The Orr Hot Springs Resort (☎ 462-6277) at 13201 Orr Springs Rd, about 13 miles northwest of Ukiah, is a famous old hot springs where clothing is optional. Facilities include a communal redwood hot tub, an outdoor tile-and-rock heated pool, four individual porcelain tubs, a cold swimming pool, sauna, massage room, gardens, camping areas, lodging, a library, lounge, and a communal kitchen (bring your own food). Day use of the springs, from 10 am to 10 pm, costs $15 per person.

Overnight lodging rates include full use of all facilities. Options include camping, with walk-in tent sites and a vehicle camping area, for $30 per person; a dorm room holding up to 12 people on futons for $30.50 per person; private rooms for $71/95 most of the week, discounted to $59/78 Monday through Wednesday nights; and private cottages with kitchen for $129 most of the week, $110 Monday through Wednesday.

To get there from Hwy 101, take the N State St exit , go north a quarter mile to Orr Springs Rd, turn west and keep going for 13 miles. Orr Springs Rd is a winding mountain road and it takes at least 45 minutes to drive those 13 miles.

Lake Mendocino

This is a 1822-acre lake formed in 1958 by the completion of Coyote Dam on the East

Fork of the Russian River, and is set in rolling hills just five miles northeast of Ukiah. It's a popular spot for camping and water recreation. In summer, boats are available to rent; the marina (☎ 485-8644) is on the north end of the lake. Coyote Dam, 3500 feet long and 160 feet high, is on the lake's southwest corner; the east part of the lake is a 689-acre protected wildlife habitat. A hiking trail goes all the way around the lake.

Traditionally this valley was the home of Pomo Indians. The Pomo Visitor Center (☎ 485-8285), on Marina Drive on the north side of the lake, is modeled after a Pomo roundhouse, with interesting exhibits on the Pomo, the valley, and the US Army Corps of Engineers who built the dam and manage the lake.

The lake has nearly 300 varied campsites in four campgrounds, most with hot showers. Sites are $12 to $14 in summer, $8 in winter, and are first come, first served year round.

The most convenient access to the lake is to turn east from Hwy 101 onto Hwy 20, a few miles north of Ukiah; before long you'll see the lake on your right; turn right from Hwy 20 onto Marina Drive and follow the signs to the marina, visitors center, campgrounds, etc.

WILLITS
• *pop 5000* ☎ *707*

Willits is a small nondescript but friendly little town on Hwy 101, 22 miles north of Ukiah. Its primary industry is wood products manufacturing, however Willits' greatest claim to fame for visitors is that it's the eastern terminus of the Skunk Train.

Orientation & Information
Highway 101 goes right through the center of town. On the south end of town is the intersection of Hwy 101 and Hwy 20, which heads 34 miles west out to the coast.

The Willits Chamber of Commerce (☎ 459-4113) is at 239 S Main St. The post office is at 315 S Main St.

Things to See & Do
The **Skunk Train**, operating the 34 miles between Willits and Fort Bragg, is Willits' primary tourist attraction; see the Fort Bragg section for details. The Skunk Train depot is on E Commercial St, three short blocks east of Hwy 101.

Two blocks further east, the **Mendocino County Museum** (☎ 459-2736) at 400 E Commercial St houses exhibits of historical artifacts of Mendocino County. Outside the museum, the Roots of Motive Power exhibit has demonstrations of steam logging and other historic machinery, and the Redwood Empire Railroad History Project offers demonstrations of a steam locomotive.

Special Events
Willits' Frontier Days & Rodeo, held every year in the week of the 4th of July, is a celebration of the town's frontier history; the rodeo, held every year since 1926, is California's oldest continuously-held rodeo and attracts many visitors.

Places to Stay
Camping The *Willits/Ukiah KOA* (☎ 459-6179), on Hwy 20 1½ miles west of Hwy 101, has a swimming pool, hiking trails, hot showers, and other amenities; it has tent/RV sites for $18/23, and one-room 'kamping kabins' for $30. *Hidden Valley Campground* (☎ 459-2521, 800-458-8368) at 29801 Hwy 101 N, 6½ miles north of town, has tent/RV sites for $15/17.

Motels Several motels are found along Hwy 101, some offering Skunk Train packages. The *Skunk Train Motel* (☎ 459-2302) at 500 S Main St has regular rooms for $32, rooms with kitchen for $40 to $50. Next door, the *Pepperwood Motel* (☎ 459-2231) at 452 S Main St has regular rooms for $65/55 in summer/winter, $10 extra with kitchen.

The *Old West Inn* (☎ 459-4201) at 1221 S Main St is a Western theme motel with rooms for $59/45 in summer/winter. The *Pine Cone Motel* (☎ 459-5044) at 1350 S Main St has rooms for $45 and up in summer, $29/34 single/double off season, higher for a two-bedroom unit with kitchen. The *Lark Motel* (☎ 459-2421) at 1411 S Main St, with free Skunk Train pick-up and delivery, has rooms for $40/30 in summer/winter. The *Holiday Lodge Motel* (☎ 459-5361, 800-835-3972) at 1540 S Main St has a swimming pool, free Skunk Train pick-up and delivery, and rooms for $45/48 single/double in summer, $35/38 off season, with continental breakfast included.

The *Baechtel Creek Inn* (☎ 459-9063, 800-459-9911) at 101 Gregory Lane is a more upmarket motel with swimming pool, spa, etc; rooms are about $100 in summer, $69/79 single/double off season, but cheaper with a Skunk Train package, available only in summer.

Places to Eat

The *South Main Restaurant* (☎ 459-9335), 708 S Main St, is a basic restaurant serving all meals. The *Cactus Garden Cafe* (☎ 459-1932), popular for lunch Monday to Saturday, and *Marisa's* (☎ 459-2146), with authentic Mexican food, are in the Willits Country Mall at 212 S Main St. The *Loose Caboose Cafe* (☎ 459-1434) at 10 Wood St, just off Main St, is a deli with train decor popular at lunch time.

The *Tsunami Restaurant* (☎ 459-4750) at 50 S Main St serves 'non-traditional Japanese and Mendonesian cuisine.' *Gribaldo's Cafe* (☎ 459-2256) at 1551 S Main St is popular with local old-timers. *Laruso's* (☎ 459-9022) at 251 E Commercial St, two blocks east of Main St towards the Skunk Train depot, is a fancier place for steak, seafood, pasta, and cocktails.

Getting There & Away

The Greyhound bus station (☎ 459-2210, 800-231-2222) at 99 N Main St is served by two northbound and two southbound buses daily. The daily Mendocino Transit Authority North Coast Inter City Rider ('CC Rider') bus (☎ 800-696-4682) stops at Fort Bragg, Willits, Ukiah, Hopland, and Santa Rosa.

Lower North Coast

Appropriately known as the Pacific Coast Hwy, Hwy 1 twists and snakes along the rugged coastline from Bodega Bay until it turns inland to meet the Redwood Hwy (Hwy 101) at Leggett, about 160 miles north.

The coast is usually cool and foggy in summer, cold and rainy in winter – the best times of year to visit are spring and autumn, especially around September and October, when the fog lifts, the ocean sparkles blue and the summer tourists have mostly gone home. In summer and on autumn weekends the many fine campgrounds along the coast tend to fill up, so reserving in advance is practically a necessity if you want to get a space.

Highlights of this part of the north coast include the picturesque town of Mendocino and its environs, the popular Skunk Train, the many fine state parks including the historic Fort Ross built by the Russians, and of course the rugged beauty of the coastline itself. Beaches range from wide swaths of windswept dunes to secluded rocky coves. Tidepools are a special treat at low tide, with their starfish, barnacles, mussels, sea urchins, sea anemones, hermit crabs, and other marine life.

Unlike the coasts of Southern California, here you're more likely to need a warm jacket or windbreaker than a bikini and suntan oil. Rather than sunbathing and swimming, walking on the sand, exploring tidepools, searching for unusual shells and driftwood, and gazing at the horizon are the main attractions of the beaches here; other activities include surfing, surf fishing, deep sea fishing, crabbing, river fishing for salmon and steelhead trout, and abalone diving in season.

Whale-watching is a popular attraction from December to April, when the California gray whales migrate along the coast; you can spot the whales from almost any point or headland jutting into the sea, or on whale-watching boat trips from Bodega

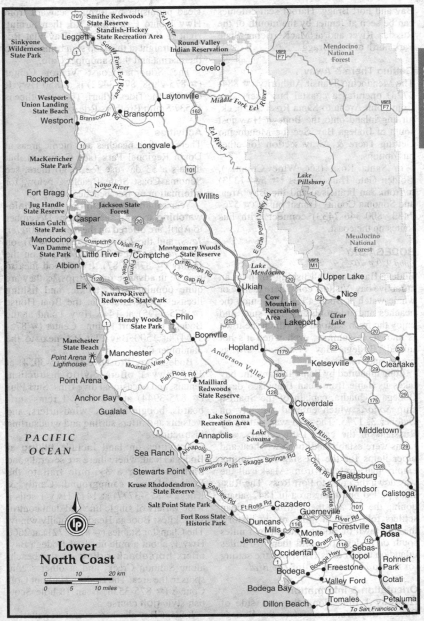

Lower North Coast

0   10   20 km

0   5   10 miles

PACIFIC OCEAN

Sinkyone Wilderness State Park

Leggett

Smithe Redwoods State Reserve

Standish-Hickey State Recreation Area

Eel River

Round Valley Indian Reservation

Covelo

Mendocino National Forest

USFS F7

Rockport

South Fork Eel River

Laytonville

Middle Fork Eel River

USFS F7

Westport-Union Landing State Beach

Westport

Branscomb Rd

Branscomb

Eel River

Longvale

USFS M1

MacKerricher State Park

Novo River

Willits

Lake Pillsbury

Fort Bragg

Jug Handle State Reserve

Jackson State Forest

Russian Gulch State Park

Caspar

Mendocino

Van Damme State Park

Little River

Comptche

Comptche

Ukiah Rd

Montgomery Woods State Reserve

Orr Springs Rd

Low Gap Rd

E State Potter Valley Rd

Lake Mendocino

Mendocino National Forest

Albion

Flynn Creek Rd

128

Ukiah

Upper Lake

Elk

Navarro River Redwoods State Park

Philo

253

Cow Mountain Recreation Area

Lakeport

Clear Lake

Nice

29

Hendy Woods State Park

Boonville

Manchester State Beach

Manchester

Point Arena Lighthouse

Hopland

Anderson Valley

175

Kelseyville

29

281

Clearlake

Point Arena

Mountain View Rd

Fish Rock Rd

Mailliard Redwoods State Reserve

101

128

53

29

Anchor Bay

Gualala

Lake Sonoma Recreation Area

Cloverdale

Russian River

175

Middletown

29

PACIFIC OCEAN

1

Annapolis

Lake Sonoma

Sea Ranch

Annapolis Rd

Stewarts Point

Stewarts Point - Skaggs Springs Rd

Dry Creek Rd

Westside Rd

128

Healdsburg

Kruse Rhododendron State Reserve

Seaview Rd

Salt Point State Park

Ft Ross Rd

Cazadero

Windsor

Calistoga

101

Fort Ross State Historic Park

Duncans Mills

Seaview Rd

River Rd

Guerneville

Forestville

River Rd

Santa Rosa

12

Jenner

Monte Rio

116

Graton Rd

Sebastopol

Rohnert Park

Occidental

116

Freestone

Cotati

Bodega

Bodega Hwy

Valley Ford

Petaluma

Bodega Bay

Tomales

Dillon Beach

To San Francisco

Bay and Fort Bragg. Harbor seal colonies can be seen at Jenner by the mouth of the Russian River and at MacKerricher State Park north of Fort Bragg.

Getting There & Away
The Mendocino Transit Authority (☎ 884-3723) operates a coastal bus every day from Point Arena to Santa Rosa and back, turning inland onto the Bodega Hwy just south of Bodega Bay. See the Mendocino Getting There & Away section for other bus options.

In Santa Rosa (see Wine Country), Golden Gate Transit buses (☎ 544-1323) to/from San Francisco and the Bay Area, and Sonoma County Transit buses (☎ 576-7433, 800-346-7433) connect with bus routes up the coast.

BODEGA BAY
• *pop 950* ☎ *707*
Bodega Bay is a small fishing town on an attractive bay. Visitors come here to hike or whale-watch at Bodega Head, to enjoy the beaches and tidepools, to fish, surf, and enjoy the fresh seafood for which the town is known. In summer, even when it's hot inland, Bodega Bay is almost always breezy and fresh.

Long inhabited by Pomo Indians, the bay takes its name from Juan Francisco de la Bodega y Quadra, captain of the Spanish ship *Sonora* which entered the bay on October 3, 1775. The area was settled by Russians in the early-19th century, and farms were established to grow wheat and other items for the Russian fur-trapping empire that stretched from Alaska all the way down the coast to Fort Ross. The Russians pulled out of the area in 1842, abandoning the fort and their farms; American settlers followed. In more recent history, the tiny town of Bodega, about two miles south of Bodega Bay and then two miles inland on the Bodega Hwy, was the setting for Alfred Hitchcock's film *The Birds*.

Orientation & Information
Highway 1 runs along the east side of Bodega Bay. You can get to the Bodega

Head peninsula by turning seaward from Hwy 1 onto East Shore Rd, then turning right at the stop sign onto Bay Flat Rd; going straight at this stop sign brings you to the marina and the Sandpiper Cafe.

The Sonoma Coast Visitor Center (☎ 875-2868, 875-3422) is at 850 Hwy 1, opposite the Tides Wharf. The post office is at 537 Smith Brothers Rd.

Activities
There are fine beaches and picnic areas at Doran Regional Park (see Camping), but there's a $3 day-use fee to go there; see Sonoma Coast State Beaches, below, for information on free beaches.

Year-round **sportfishing**, and **whale-watching** trips in season from December to April, are offered on the *New Sea Angler, Jaws,* and the *Predator* (☎ 875-3495), on the *Challenger* (☎ 875-2474), and on the *Dandy* (☎ 875-2787). It's a good idea to reserve in advance for all trips, as they are quite popular. Bait, tackle, and fishing licenses are available at the Boat House (☎ 875-3495) at 1445 Hwy 1 and at the Bodega Bay Sport Fishing Center (☎ 875-3344) at 1500 Bay Flat Rd, next to the Sandpiper Cafe.

Bodega Bay Pro Dive (☎ 875-3054) at 1275 Hwy 1 offers **diving** instruction, rentals, and occasional dive trips. Surf Plus (☎ 875-3944) at 193 Hwy 1 rents surfboards, boogie boards, windsurfers, and wetsuits and offers surfing and windsurfing instruction.

Activities on land include **hiking** at Bodega Head, where there are several good trails including a 3½-mile trail to the Bodega Dunes campground. Candy & Kites (☎ 875-3777) at 1415 Hwy 1 sells a wide variety of single line and dual control sport kites; Bodega Head is usually windy. The Chanslor Stables (☎ 875-2721) at 2660 Hwy 1, about a mile north of Bodega Bay, offers **horseback riding** on the beach, along Salmon Creek, and at other scenic spots in the area. The Bodega Harbour Golf Course (☎ 875-3538) is an 18-hole Scottish-style **golf** course.

Bodega Bay also has several art galleries.

Special Events

The Bodega Bay Fishermen's Festival held in April is the big event of the year, attracting thousands of visitors; activities include the blessing of the fishing fleet, a flamboyant parade of decorated boats and vessels of all kinds, an arts & crafts fair, outdoor food stalls, dances, races, a kite flying contest, and more.

Places to Stay

Vacation home rentals are an option, but they tend to be expensive, upwards of $100 a night. Try Vacation Rentals International (☎ 875-4000, 800-548-7631), Bodega Bay & Beyond (☎ 875-3942, 800-888-3565), Coastal Vistas (☎ 875-3000, 800-788-4782), or the Bodega Harbor Inn (☎ 875-3594).

Camping Campgrounds here are popular and often full in summer and on balmy autumn weekends. Sonoma County Regional Parks (☎ 527-2041) operates two: *Doran Park* (☎ 875-3540) and *Westside Campground* (☎ 875-2640), right beside the bay; both have beaches, hot showers, fishing, and boat ramps. Doran Park has four exposed and rather windswept camping areas on the narrow spit of land between the bay and the ocean; to get there, turn seaward from Hwy 1 onto Doran Park Rd or Doran Beach Rd. Westside Campground, on the bay side of Bodega Head, is also quite open and exposed.

Hotels, Motels & B&Bs The *Bodega Harbor Inn* (☎ 875-3594) at 1345 Bodega Ave, a block from Hwy 1, is the most economical lodging in town, with cottage-style rooms starting at $48. The *Holiday Inn* (☎ 875-2217, 800-346-6999), 521 Hwy 1, with a fine view of the bay, has rooms starting at $79 in winter, $105 in summer. The *Studio Room With A View* (☎ 875-3018) at 1140 Hwy 1, with a deck and view, rents for $95/105 on weekdays/weekends in summer, $75/95 in winter. The *Inn at the Tides* (☎ 875-2751, 800-541-7788), 800 Hwy 1, has rooms at $120/145 on weekdays/weekends in summer, $109/129 in

winter. The attractive 78-room *Bodega Bay Lodge* (☎ 875-3525, 800-368-2468) at 103 Hwy 1 is more expensive, with rooms starting at $150.

The *Chanslor Guest Ranch & Horse Stables* (☎ 875-2721) at 2660 Hwy 1, about a mile north of Bodega Bay, has horse riding and a variety of B&B rooms starting at $70.

Places to Eat

The *Tides Wharf Restaurant* (☎ 875-2777) at 835 Hwy 1, and the *Lucas Wharf Restaurant & Bar* (☎ 875-3522) nearby at 595 Hwy 1, are the two largest and best-known restaurants. Specializing in seafood, they both sit right on the waterfront, with big picture windows affording a view of the fishermen unloading their catch from the docks just outside the windows. Lucas Wharf has a fish market and deli where you can get less expensive deli fare and smoked fish to eat at the tables inside or out; The Tides has a fish market and a snack bar with tables inside and out.

Smaller, cheaper, and more popular with locals, the *Sandpiper Dockside Cafe & Restaurant* (☎ 875-2278) at 1410 Bay Flat Rd, is a casual, cheerful place offering fresh seafood and other fare and a fine view of the pier, the marina, and the bay. To get there, turn seaward from Hwy 1 onto East Shore Rd and go straight ahead at the stop sign, to the marina.

Getting There & Away

Mendocino Transit Authority coast buses (☎ 884-3723) operate every day from Point Arena to Santa Rosa and back, via Bodega Bay.

SONOMA COAST STATE BEACHES

The 12-mile stretch of rugged, rocky coast heading north from Bodega Bay to Jenner contains 14 state beaches, collectively named the Sonoma Coast State Beaches (☎ 707-875-3483): south to north they are the Bodega Dunes, Salmon Creek, Miwok, Coleman, Arched Rock, Marshall Gulch, Carmet, Schoolhouse, Portuguese, Gleasons, Rock Point, Duncan's Landing, Wright's, and Goat Rock State Beaches. Some are tiny beaches tucked away in little coves; others are wide expanses of tawny sand.

Two of the state beaches have campgrounds. One mile north of Bodega Bay, *Bodega Dunes Campground* has campsites nestled into high sand dunes; sites are $14 (hike/bike sites $3 per person), with hot showers available. Six miles north of Bodega Bay, *Wright's Beach* has beachside sites without much privacy, and bathrooms but no showers; sites are $19. Reservations are made through Destinet year round.

JENNER
☎ *707*

The tiny, picturesque town of Jenner is perched on the hills at the mouth of the Russian River. Stop at the Hwy 1 turnouts just north of the town for a view of the harbor seal colony at the river mouth.

Bridgehaven (☎ 865-2473) at the south end of the Russian River Bridge has tent and RV sites for $20 on weekends, $15 on weekdays. On Willow Creek Rd, on the east side of Hwy 1 just south of the Russian River Bridge, the *Willow Creek* and *Pomo Canyon* hike-in environmental state campgrounds are first come, first served, with sites at $9 per night. Willow Creek has no water; Pomo Canyon has cold water faucets. Sonoma Coast State Beaches (☎ 875-3483) has details.

The *Jenner Inn* (☎ 865-2377) at 10040 Hwy 1 is the most prominent building in town; it has B&B rooms at $75 to $175 per night, more expensive vacation rental homes, and a restaurant open for lunch and dinner from Friday to Tuesday. *River's End* (☎ 865-2484, 869-3252) at 11048 Hwy 1, a little to the north and overlooking the river, has hotel rooms and cabins at $98 per night, plus a restaurant. The *Seagull Deli*, at Seagull Gifts & Deli opposite the gas station, offers deli fare, espresso, and outdoor tables with a fine view of the river.

FORT ROSS
STATE HISTORIC PARK
☎ *707*

Eleven miles north of Jenner on Hwy 1, Fort Ross was the southernmost American outpost of the 19th-century Russian fur trade. In March 1812, a group of 25 Russians and 80 Alaskans arrived and began to build the wooden fort at Fort Ross, near the site of Meteni, a Kashaya Pomo Indian village. The fort was established as a base for sea otter hunting operations, to grow wheat and other crops to supply Russian settlements in Alaska, and as a base for trade with Spanish Alta California. The Russians dedicated the fort on August 13, 1812 and occupied it until 1842, abandoning it because the sea otter population was decimated and the agricultural production was never as great as hoped for.

Fort Ross today is an accurate historical reconstruction of the Russian fort; only one building is original. Most of the original construction was dismantled and carried away to Sutter's Fort in California's Central Valley.

The fort is open every day from 10 am to 4:30 pm; admission is $5 per vehicle. The visitors center (☎ 847-3286) has good displays about the history of the fort and an excellent library of California history, nature, and other topics. On Living History Day, held the last Saturday in July, costumed volunteers bring the fort's history back to life.

Places to Stay

Within the park, about three quarters of a mile south of the fort, the *Reef Campground* has 21 cold-water campsites (no showers) nestled into a sheltered seaside gully. The campground is open from April to November; the sites cost $10 per night and are first come, first served.

At **Timber Cove**, about 2½ miles north of Fort Ross on Hwy 1, there's camping at *Sea Coast Hideaways* (☎ 847-3278), on a bluff overlooking the sea and a private, secluded beach in a little cove; sites are

$17, or $19 with hookups, and amenities include hot showers, an outdoor hot tub, boat rentals, scuba gear rentals, fishing bait and tackle, and more. They also rent private homes and cabins in the area, starting at $195 for two nights. Also on Hwy 1 at Timber Cove, the luxurious *Timber Cove Inn* (☎ 847-3231) has rooms starting at $78 on weekdays, $110 on weekends. The lodge has a restaurant serving all meals.

Two miles north of Timber Cove on Hwy 1, **Stillwater Cove Regional Park** (☎ 847-3245, 527-2041) has 23 campsites under Monterey pines; hot showers are available and the sites, all first come, first served, are $14 per vehicle, or $3 per person for hike/bike sites. About half a mile north of this, the *Stillwater Cove Ranch* (☎ 847-3227) at 22555 Hwy 1 has six guest rooms at $40 to $70 on weekdays, $10 more on weekends. A mile further north, the *Salt Point Lodge* (☎ 847-3234) at 23255 Hwy 1 has 16 rooms, some with ocean view and all with hot tub accessible, for $50 to $137, and a restaurant serving all meals.

SALT POINT STATE PARK

Salt Point State Park (☎ 707-847-3221) is a 6000-acre coastal park with hiking trails, picnic areas, tidepools, a pygmy forest, the 317-acre **Kruse Rhododendron State Reserve**, two campgrounds, and an underwater reserve at Gerstle Cove that is one of California's first underwater parks, good for swimming, snorkeling, and diving.

The Kruse Rhododendron State Reserve is a short distance inland; to get there, turn east from Hwy 1 onto Kruse Ranch Rd and follow the signs. Growing abundantly in the filtered light of the redwood forest, the rhododendrons reach heights of 30 feet or more, with a magnificent display of pink blossoms in springtime, especially around April and May.

The two campgrounds, *Woodside* and *Gerstle Cove*, both signposted from Hwy 1, offer sites under Monterey pines; they have cold running water but no showers. Sites are $14 per vehicle, hike/bike sites $3 per person; make reservations through Destinet from March through October.

GUALALA
☎ 707
The tiny coastal town of Gualala was founded in 1858 as a lumber mill town. The **Gualala Point Regional Park** (☎ 785-2377), one mile south of town, has an attractive campground in a redwood grove beside the Gualala River, on the east side of Hwy 1; hot showers are available and sites are $14 per vehicle, or $3 per person for hike/bike sites, all first come, first served year round. Hiking trails lead along the river, to the beach and coastal bluffs, and to Whale Watch Point. The *Gualala River Park* (☎ 884-3533), another campground in a redwood grove beside the Gualala River, is open in summer; to get there, turn east from Hwy 1 onto Old State Rd on the south end of town and follow the signs.

The historic 1903 *Gualala Hotel* (☎ 884-3441), on Hwy 1 at the center of town, has a saloon, a restaurant, and 19 comfortable guest rooms for $44 with shared bath, $55 to $65 with private bath. Other places to stay, all on Hwy 1 and more expensive, include the *Gualala Country Inn* (☎ 884-4343), the *Surf Motel* (☎ 884-3571), both right in town, and the *Whale Watch Inn B&B* (☎ 884-3667), overlooking the sea five miles north of town.

POINT ARENA
• *pop 440* ☎ 707
Point Arena is a small fishing town on a windswept point where a lighthouse has stood for over a century. The **Point Arena Lighthouse & Museum** (☎ 882-2777), 115 feet high, is open every day from 11 am to 2:30 pm, with guided tours; admission is $2.50. Today's lighthouse is the second to stand on this spot; the original, built in 1870, was toppled by the 1906 earthquake.

At the lighthouse, several former US Coast Guard homes are available as vacation rentals; phone the Point Arena Lighthouse Keepers (☎ 882-2777) for details.

On Hwy 1 in town, the *Sea Shell Inn* (☎ 882-2000) at 135 Main St has 32 rooms from $45 to $66, and the *Point Arena B&B* (☎ 882-3455) at 300 Main St has three rooms sharing two bathrooms at $55 with breakfast, $50 without. A mile west of town at Arena Cove, overlooking Point Arena's small cove and pier, the *Coast Guard House Inn* (☎ 882-2442) has seven rooms from $75 to $175, while the more expensive historic *Wharfmaster's Inn* (☎ 882-3171), a restored Victorian built in 1862 as the wharfmaster's home, has 22 rooms in four buildings starting at $110 on weekdays, $135 on weekends.

Good places to eat on Main St include the *Bookends* cafe and bookstore, *Pangaea*, and *Pepper's*. At Arena Cove, the *Galley Restaurant & Bar* has a view over the cove and pier; *Simply Delicious Pizza* is downstairs.

MANCHESTER STATE BEACH

Seven miles north of Point Arena, half a mile north of the tiny town of Manchester, a turnoff from Hwy 1 leads to Manchester State Beach, a long, wide beach with two campgrounds. The *Mendocino Coast-Manchester Beach KOA* (☎ 707-882-2375), the fancier of the two, has attractively landscaped grounds with campsites spread amongst Monterey pines, a heated swimming pool, hot tub spa, cooking pavilion, hot showers, laundry, children's playgrounds, hiking trails, and more. Cost is $26 for tent or RV sites, $38 for cabins.

Further along on the same road, **Manchester State Park** (☎ 707-937-5804) has a campground in the coastal scrub near the beach with cold running water (no showers); sites are $9 in summer, $7 in winter, or $2 per person for hike/bike sites, all first come, first served.

ELK
☎ 707

Elk is a very tiny coastal town; its most notable feature is the **Greenwood State Beach**, with picnic areas but no camping.

Several B&Bs take advantage of the quiet beauty of the coast here. They include the *Griffin House at Greenwood Cove* (☎ 877-3422) at 5910 S Hwy 1 with garden/oceanfront cottages starting at $80/125; the *Elk Cove Inn* (☎ 877-3321) at 6300 S Hwy 1 with rooms and cottages starting at $98; and the *Sandpiper House* (☎ 877-3587) at 5520 S Hwy 1 with lodgings starting at $110.

NAVARRO RIVER REDWOODS STATE PARK

The Navarro River, with Hwy 128 snaking along beside it, meets the sea about five miles north of Elk and 10 miles south of Mendocino. The Navarro River Redwoods State Park (☎ 707-937-5804), beginning at the river mouth and extending upriver along Hwy 128 for 12½ miles, has two primitive campgrounds with pit toilets but no water: the *Navarro Beach* campground at the intersection of Hwys 1 and 128, and the *Paul M Dimmick* campground on Hwy 128, eight miles east of Hwy 1.

HENDY WOODS STATE PARK

Inland about 20 miles along Hwy 128, Hendy Woods State Park (☎ 707-937-5804) offers picnic areas, hiking trails, and a campground with hot showers and campsites at $14 from May to mid-October, when they can be reserved through Destinet; the rest of the year they are $12 and first come, first served.

VAN DAMME STATE PARK

Three miles south of Mendocino, Van Damme State Park is best known for its unusual **pygmy forest**, where a combination of acidic soil and an impenetrable layer of hardpan just below the surface create a natural bonsai forest with trees decades old growing only a few feet high. A raised wheelchair-accessible boardwalk provides easy access to the pygmy forest; to get there, turn east from Hwy 1 onto Little River Airport Rd, half a mile south of the Van Damme State Park entrance, and go 3½ miles. Or you can hike up from the camping area on the 3½-mile Fern Canyon Scenic Trail, crossing back and forth over Little River.

Other features of the park include a visitors center (☎ 707-937-4016) with a museum, videos, and summer programs, a 30-minute marsh loop trail departing from near the visitors center, a sandy beach, and camping areas. Lost Coast Adventures (☎ 707-961-1143, 800-961-1143) out of Fort Bragg offers two-hour sea cave kayak tours.

Camping includes 74 hookup sites with hot showers in two areas, one just off Hwy 1 in the Little River canyon and one in a highland meadow. There are also nine walk-in environmental sites, a 1¾-mile hike up Fern Canyon.

Maps and information are available at the visitors center or at the Mendocino State Parks headquarters (☎ 707-937-5804) on the east side of Hwy 1 at Russian Gulch State Park, two miles north of Mendocino.

MENDOCINO
• *pop 1100* ☎ *707*

The charming, picturesque little town of Mendocino, perched on a bluff overlooking the rugged Pacific Coast, is noted for its Cape Cod style of architecture and its active artistic community. Built as a lumber mill town in the 1850s by transplanted New Englanders, Mendocino thrived in the late-19th century, with ships transporting the redwood lumber from Mendocino Bay to San Francisco. Activity declined after the mills shut down in the 1930s, until in the 1950s the town was rediscovered by artists and became a bohemian haven. Tourists followed the artists to Mendocino, and have been following them ever since. The entire town, with its historic buildings lovingly restored, is on the National Register of Historic Places.

Attractions for visitors include art galleries and shops, charming Victorian B&Bs and other quality places to stay and eat, a couple of historic house museums, and the natural beauty of the nearby coastal areas. Mendocino is a very popular tourist destination in summer, when it gets overrun; the rest of the year the ambiance is more relaxed.

Information
The Ford House Visitor Center & Museum (☎ 937-5397) at 735 Main St has maps and information about the town and the nearby state parks, plus exhibits, books, videos, audio cassette tours of Mendocino; there's a $1 donation to tour the museum.

The Mendocino State Parks Headquarters (☎ 937-5804) on the east side of Hwy 1 at Russian Gulch State Park, two miles north of Mendocino, has information on all the state parks in the area. The post office is at 10500 Ford St.

Books & Publications
If you want to get out and explore the surroundings, *The Hiker's Hip Pocket Guide to the Mendocino Coast* and *The Hiker's Hip Pocket Guide to the Mendocino Highlands*, both by Bob Lorentzen (Bored Feet Publications, 1992) are fine resources.

Things to See & Do
The **Mendocino Art Center** (☎ 936-5818, 800-653-3328) at 45200 Little Lake St is the artistic heart of Mendocino, with two art galleries, live theater productions, arts & crafts fairs, and a nationally recognized program of over 200 arts classes; write or phone to request a schedule of classes. Many other art galleries are also found

---

Mendocino, Star of the Silver Screen
Mendocino is only a tiny town but over 50 films for the big screen and television have been filmed here – starting with *The Promise*, a silent film made here in 1916. Some of the more well-known motion pictures filmed here have included *East of Eden* starring James Dean (1954); *The Island of the Blue Dolphins* (1964), filmed on the south Mendocino coast; *The Summer of '42* (1970); *Same Time, Next Year* (1978); and the well-known *Murder, She Wrote* TV series starring Angela Lansbury (1984-1988). ∎

CALIFORNIA

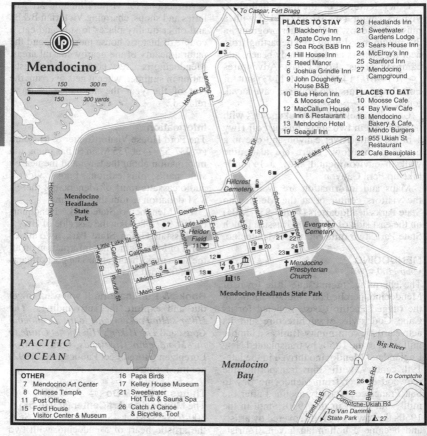

Mendocino

To Caspar, Fort Bragg

PLACES TO STAY
1 Blackberry Inn
2 Agate Cove Inn
3 Sea Rock B&B Inn
4 Hill House Inn
5 Reed Manor
6 Joshua Grindle Inn
9 John Dougherty
   House B&B
10 Blue Heron Inn
   & Moosse Cafe
12 MacCallum House
   Inn & Restaurant
13 Mendocino Hotel
19 Seagull Inn

20 Headlands Inn
21 Sweetwater
   Gardens Lodge
23 Sears House Inn
24 McElroy's Inn
25 Stanford Inn
27 Mendocino
   Campground

PLACES TO EAT
10 Moosse Cafe
14 Bay View Cafe
18 Mendocino
   Bakery & Cafe,
   Mendo Burgers
21 955 Ukiah St
   Restaurant
22 Cafe Beaujolais

Hesser Dr

Lansing St

Palette Dr

Mendocino
Headlands
State
Park

Hillcrest
Cemetery

Little Lake Rd

School St

Hesser Drive

Little Lake St

Covelo St

Howard St

Lansing St

Evergreen St

Evergreen
Cemetery

William St

Woodward St

Little Lake St

Kasten St

Ford St

Heider
Field

Calpella St

Kelly St

Carlson St

Ukiah St

Albion St

Main St

Mendocino
Presbyterian
Church

Mendocino Headlands State Park

Bundle St

**PACIFIC
OCEAN**

*Mendocino
Bay*

Big River

Big River Rd

To Comptche

Front Rd

Comptche-Ukiah Rd

To Van Damme
State Park

OTHER
7 Mendocino Art Center
8 Chinese Temple
11 Post Office
15 Ford House
   Visitor Center & Museum

16 Papa Birds
17 Kelley House Museum
21 Sweetwater
   Hot Tub & Sauna Spa
26 Catch A Canoe
   & Bicycles, Too!

around Mendocino; the tourist offices have a complete list.

The **Kelley House Museum** (☎ 937-5791) at 45007 Albion St is a historical museum in an 1861 home with relics, a library for research about early California and the local area, and interesting scrapbooks. It's open every day from 1 to 4 pm from June to August; September to May it's only open Friday to Monday; admission is $1. **Ford House** (see Information) is another historic home museum. Another historic building, the **Chinese Temple** on Albion St between Kasten and Woodward Sts, was built in 1852; you can look in the windows to see the old Chinese altar and other artifacts.

At 955 Ukiah St, **Sweetwater Gardens Lodge, Hot Tub & Sauna Spa** (☎ 937-4140, 800-300-4140), offers private hot tubs, private or group hot tubs and saunas, and massage and bodywork, all at affordable prices.

Mendocino also has some fine natural attractions. The **Mendocino Headlands State Park** is crisscrossed by trails, with pleasant walks overlooking the bluffs and rocky coves.

On weekends, free guided walks are a pleasant pastime. The 1½-hour **Mendo-**

cino **Bird Walk** along the Mendocino Headlands trails departs from Papa Birds (☎ 937-2730, 800-845-0522) on Albion St every Saturday morning at 10 am; bring binoculars and warm clothing. A free **History Walk** departs from the Ford House every Sunday at 2 pm.

At **Big River**, a quarter mile south of Mendocino on Hwy 1, Catch A Canoe & Bicycles, Too! (☎ 937-0273, 800-320-2453) rents mountain bikes, canoes, outrigger canoes, and single and double kayaks for self-guided trips up the eight-mile-long Big River tidal estuary, the longest undeveloped estuary in Northern California. There are no highways or buildings, only beaches, salt marshes, stream beds, historic logging sites including century-old train trestles, wooden pilings and log dams, forest, and abundant wildlife. A logging road up the river provides unofficial access for bicycles and hikers on Sundays in summer, every day in winter. Catch A Canoe is just inland from Hwy 1 on the Comptche-Ukiah Rd.

Special Events
The chamber of commerce office in Fort Bragg has information on these and other events in the area: in March there's the Mendocino Whale Festival, with wine and clam chowder tasting; in May, Mendocino Heritage Days, a 10-day celebration of the town's history, with a parade, games, pancake breakfast, and outdoor food, arts & crafts, and a film festival; in July the Mendocino Music Festival, a one- to two-week summer concert series on the Mendocino Headlands; and in December, the Mendocino Coast Christmas Festival, with tree lighting, music, inn tours, and other events in Mendocino, Fort Bragg, and Little River.

Places to Stay
Camping The *Mendocino Campground* (☎ 937-3130) on the Comptche-Ukiah Rd just east of Hwy 1, a quarter mile south of Mendocino, is an attractive campground with hot showers, plenty of trees, a nature trail, and campsites for $15/17 on weekdays/weekends.

About five miles north of Mendocino, the *Caspar Beach Campground* (☎ 964-3306) at 14441 Point Cabrillo Drive, in a sheltered gully next to Caspar Beach, has tent/RV sites at $15/20.

Hotels, Inns & B&Bs Accommodations in Mendocino, most in restored Victorian homes, virtually all have charm, character, comfort, high style and high price tags. If you want something cheaper, try the less expensive motels in Fort Bragg, just 10 miles to the north.

Mendocino Coast Reservations (☎ 937-1913, 937-5033) at 1000 Main St makes reservations and provides information for over 70 vacation homes and 50 B&Bs in the area.

The *Mendocino Hotel* (☎ 937-0511, 800-548-0513) at 45080 Main St, built in 1878 overlooking the sea, has an elegant Victorian dining room, a more casual garden bar and cafe, and rooms from $65 to $225. The *MacCallum House Inn* (☎ 937-0289) at 45020 Albion St, built in 1882, also has a fine restaurant, and rooms from $75 to $210.

Other places right in town include the *Seagull Inn* (☎ 937-5204) at 44594 Albion St, with rooms from $65 to $125; the *Headlands Inn* (☎ 937-4431) at the corner of Albion and Howard Sts, with rooms from $105 to $189; the *Blue Heron Inn* (☎ 937-4323) at 390 Kasten St at the corner of Albion St, with a good restaurant and three rooms from $80 to $90. Right on Main St are the *Sears House Inn* (☎ 937-4076) at No 44840 with eight rooms from $50 to $100 and *McElroy's Inn* (☎ 937-1734) at No 998 with four rooms from $50 to $75.

On Little Lake Rd are the *Joshua Grindle Inn* (☎ 937-4143) at No 44800 with rooms from $90 to $155; and the most expensive place in town, *Reed Manor* (☎ 937-5446), which faces Little Lake Rd but has its entrance through the block on Palette Drive, with rooms starting at $175. Nearby, on the corner of Lansing St, the

Hill House Inn (☎ 937-0554) at 10701 Palette Drive has rooms from $110 to $175. Further out on Lansing St overlooking the ocean, are the *Agate Cove Inn* (☎ 937-0551) at No 11201 with ocean view rooms from $99 to $199, and the *Sea Rock B&B Inn* (☎ 937-5517) at No 11101 with cottages from $85 to $165. The *Blackberry Inn* (☎ 937-5281, 800-950-7806), north of town at 44951 Larkin Rd, has various accommodations from $85 to $135, with a $20 to $30 discount on weekdays from November through March.

Another alternative right in town is the *Sweetwater Gardens Lodge Hot Tub & Sauna Spa* (☎ 937-4140, 800-300-4140) at 955 Ukiah St, where the room rates of $55 to $110 give you free access to all spa facilities – a special treat after hours, when everything is quiet and you have the hot tubs and spa facilities all to yourself.

Places to Eat
For a fine view over the bay, you can't beat the aptly named *Bay View Cafe* at 45040 Main St opposite the Ford House, with an upstairs dining room and outdoor deck.

The *Mendocino Bakery & Cafe* at 10485 Lansing St is a great place for casual, inexpensive dining and general hanging out; in addition to their baked goods they have a variety of salads, soups, hot meals, and 'gourmet quality at family prices,' with live acoustic music and a pleasant outdoor patio alongside the indoor cafe. In the rear, *Mendo Burgers* serves up popular beef, turkey, and vegetarian burgers.

Moving up the economic spectrum, *Cafe Beaujolais* (☎ 937-5614) at 961 Ukiah St is probably Mendocino's most famous restaurant; reservations are definitely a good idea. From May to September it's open on weekends from 9 am to 2:30 pm in addition to the daily dinner hours. Next door at 955 Ukiah St, is the *955 Ukiah St Restaurant*.

You can dine on European cuisine in Victorian elegance at the fancy dining room of the *Mendocino Hotel* (☎ 937-0511) at 45080 Main St; breakfast and lunch are served every day in the hotel's *Garden Bar & Cafe* to one side. Another fine old Victo-

rian inn, the *MacCallum House Inn* (☎ 937-5763) at 45020 Albion St, also has an elegant restaurant, open for dinner Friday to Tuesday. Or there's the smaller *Moosse Cafe* (☎ 937-4323) at the Blue Heron Inn on the corner of Kasten and Albion Sts, open for lunch, dinner, and Sunday brunch.

Entertainment
The Mendocino Art Center and the many galleries around town always have something going on. Mendocino Theatre Company performances are presented at the Mendocino Art Center's *Helen Schoeni Theatre* (☎ 937-4477). The Mendocino Bakery & Cafe (see Places to Eat) features live acoustic music.

Getting There & Away
The Mendocino Stage (☎ 964-0167) and the Mendocino Transit Authority (MTA) (☎ 800-696-4682) operate buses on daily runs along the coast from Fort Bragg south to the Navarro River Junction (Hwy 128) and back, with stops at Caspar, Caspar Beach, Russian Gulch State Park, Mendocino, Little River, and Albion.

Another MTA bus operates daily from Fort Bragg to Santa Rosa via Willits, Ukiah, and Hopland; at Santa Rosa you can connect with Golden Gate Transit (☎ 544-1323) and Sonoma County Transit (☎ 576-7433, 800-346-7433).

JUG HANDLE CREEK FARM
Five miles north of Mendocino, the Jug Handle Creek Farm (☎ 707-964-4630) offers accommodations in a 180-year-old farmhouse up on a hill on the east side of Hwy 1. The farmhouse has a nature center and library, a fully equipped kitchen where you can cook, and seven bedrooms for $18 per person from April to September, $15 per person the rest of the year, $20 per person on holidays; there are also two cabins at $22 per person, with use of the house facilities. Guests are expected to do one hour of chores per day. Bring your own sleeping bag or bedding; towels are provided. This is a popular place, especially with university students (who get a dis-

NANCY KELLER

Fort Ross State Historic Park, North Coast

NANCY KELLER

Sittin' on the dock of Humboldt Bay, Eureka

NANCY KELLER

The Russian River is a favorite of local anglers.

NANCY KELLER

The wind-swept beaches of the Sonoma coast

NANCY KELLER

Old lighthouse, Trinidad

NANCY KELLER

Pastels on the plaza, Arcata

NANCY KELLER

Coastal bluffs, North Coast

NANCY KELLER

Carson Mansion, Eureka

counted rate of $12/10 per person in summer/winter), so it's a good idea to make reservations in advance, especially for weekends.

RUSSIAN GULCH STATE PARK

Two miles north of Mendocino on Hwy 1, Russian Gulch State Park has scenic trails, a small waterfall, rocky headlands, a small sandy beach, many trees and rhododendrons, picnic areas, and attractive campsites with hot showers and plenty of vegetation. Camping is available only from April through October, with reservations through Destinet; the 30 sites are $14, or $3 per person for hike/bike sites, and day-use parking is $5. The Mendocino State Parks headquarters (☎ 707-937-5804) is on the east side of Hwy 1, opposite the campground entrance.

JUG HANDLE STATE RESERVE

Midway between Mendocino and Fort Bragg, the Jug Handle State Reserve has an 'ecological staircase' – five wave-cut terraces ascending in steps from the seashore, each about 100 feet and 100,000 years removed from the one before it. Each terrace has its own distinct geology and vegetation; on one level is a pygmy forest similar to the better-known one at Van Damme State Park. A pamphlet for a five-mile self-guided ecological staircase nature trail is available at the parking area just off Hwy 1, or from the Mendocino State Parks headquarters (☎ 707-937-5804) at Russian Gulch State Park. Other features of the reserve include a half-mile Headlands loop trail and a sandy beach in a lovely little cove just north of the parking area.

JACKSON STATE FOREST

Heading east over the mountains for 34 miles from Fort Bragg to Willits, Hwy 20 passes through the 816-sq mile Jackson Demonstration State Forest. Demonstration trails, with trail guides to explain the ecology, history, and management of the redwood forest, include the Forest History Trail, the Tree ID Trail, and the Chamberlain Creek Demonstration Trail. Free maps

and information are available at the California Department of Forestry office in Fort Bragg.

The forest contains two main camping areas, Camp One and Camp 20, each with a number of separate campgrounds, some open seasonally, some year round. The campgrounds are primitive – bring your own water. Camping is free, but you need a free campfire permit, available at the Department of Forestry office in Fort Bragg or from the resident camp hosts.

FORT BRAGG
• pop 6100 ☎ 707

About 10 miles north of Mendocino on Hwy 1, Fort Bragg is less conspicuously 'touristy' than Mendocino; food and lodging are generally cheaper here, making it a good alternative base for visiting the area.

The town takes its name from the fort established here in 1857, named for Colonel Braxton Bragg, a veteran of the Mexican-American War. The fort was abandoned in 1867; in 1885 a lumber company was established on the old fort site, and in the same year, the California Western Railroad, later nicknamed the Skunk Train, was established to get the big redwood trees out of the forest and down to the coast. Today the Skunk Train is a popular tourist attraction.

Orientation

Fort Bragg is basically a 'Main St town,' Main St being Hwy 1. Most everything you need is on or just off Main St; the post office and a few restaurants are on Franklin St, which runs parallel to Main St, one block to the east. Fort Bragg's commercial district lies in the two miles between Pudding Creek on the north end of town and the Noyo River and Noyo Harbor at the south end, with its boat docks and several good restaurants.

Information

The Fort Bragg-Mendocino Coast Chamber of Commerce (☎ 961-6300, 800-726-2780) at 332 N Main St has abundant

CALIFORNIA

information about Fort Bragg, Mendocino, and the surrounding area. The Department of Forestry office (☎ 964-5674) at 802 N Main St, has maps and information about the Jackson State Forest. The post office is at 203 N Franklin St .

Things to See & Do

Fort Bragg's pride and joy is the **Skunk Train** (☎ 964-6371), with a variety of historic engines and cars making daily runs between Fort Bragg and Willits, about 40 miles over beautiful redwood-forested mountains. The train got its nickname in 1925 when passenger service was established using stinky gas-powered steam engines. Today the historic steam and diesel locomotives have no odor, and it's a delightful trip through the mountains, the redwood forest, and along Pudding Creek and the Noyo River, crossing 30 bridges and two deep mountain tunnels.

The Skunk Train operates daily except Thanksgiving, Christmas, and New Year's Day. Departures are from both ends of the line; you can take the train one way or roundtrip in either direction or just to Northspur, the halfway point. Phone to check the schedule. Cost is $26 for a full-day roundtrip, or $21 for half-day round-trips to Northspur, and one-way trips between Fort Bragg and Willits, children ride for half price. The depot in Fort Bragg is at the foot of Laurel St, one block west of Main St, in the center of town. In Willits the depot is on E Commercial St, three blocks east of Hwy 101.

A free pamphlet from the chamber of commerce details a self-guided **walking tour** of historic Fort Bragg. The **Guest House Museum** (☎ 961-2823) at 343 N Main St, built in 1892, holds historical photos and relics of Fort Bragg's logging history; it's open Tuesday to Sunday from 10 am to 2 pm, admission is $1.

The **Mendocino Coast Botanical Gardens** (☎ 964-4352) at 18220 N Hwy 1 two miles south of town, cover 47-acres from the highway out to the coastal bluffs; the admission price of $5 includes a trail map. The gardens are open every day from 9 am

to 5 pm March to October, 9 am to 4 pm from November to February.

On the north end of town, **Glass Beach** is named for the sea-polished glass found there; it's reached by a short trail leading towards the sea from Elm St, off Main St on the north end of town. Other coastal trails lead around both sides of **Noyo Bay** on the south end of town.

Activities

A number of small boats at Noyo Harbor offer deep-sea fishing, coastal cruises, and whale-watching cruises in season (they say you see the most whales in February and March). Signs for many of the boats are posted around Noyo Harbor, and at the chamber of commerce; they include Anchor Charters (☎ 964-4550, 964-3854), the *Misty II* (☎ 964-7161), the *Noyo Belle* (☎ 964-3104, 964-5355), the *Patty C* (☎ 964-0669), and the *Tally Ho II* (☎ 964-2079).

Lost Coast Adventures (☎ 961-1143, 800-961-1143) at 19275 S Harbor Drive offers kayak, skin diving, and scuba diving rentals, guided two-hour kayak tours from April 1 to October 31 operating from Van Damme State Park (three miles south of Mendocino), and bicycle rentals at Pudding Creek and MacKerricher State Park, just north of Fort Bragg.

Sub-Surface Progression (☎ 964-3793) at 18600 N Hwy 1, a mile south of town, offers snorkeling and scuba diving tours, guided kayak trips, abalone diving tours, deep-sea fishing, and whale-watching, and all necessary gear. Abalone season is from April 1 to June 30 and from August 1 to November 30.

The Ricochet Ridge Ranch (☎ 964-7669) at 24201 N Hwy 1, opposite Mackerricher State Park just north of town, offers horse rides on the beach and into the redwoods.

Special Events

The chamber of commerce has information on events in Fort Bragg, Mendocino, and the surrounding region. Events include: the Fort Bragg Whale Festival the third weekend in March, featuring microbrewed beer and clam chowder tasting; the Rhododendron Show the last weekend in April; the World's Largest Salmon BBQ – at Noyo Harbor on the Saturday closest to the 4th of July; Paul Bunyan Days on Labor Day weekend, celebrating California's logging history with a logging show, fiddlers' contest, parade, and children's games; and the various Christmas celebrations including a Lighted Truck Parade of decorated trucks, tree lighting, music, and more.

Places to Stay
Camping The *Pomo RV Park & Campground* (☎ 964-3373) at 17999 Tregoning Lane, 2½ miles south of town, has tent/RV sites at $16/22. Or there's the *Woodside RV Park & Camp Grounds* (☎ 964-3684, 800-207-8772) at 17900 N Hwy 1, about a mile south of town, with plenty of trees and tent/RV sites at $13.50/19.

Motels Starting from the south end of town, the *Coast Motel* (☎ 964-2852, 800-280-2852) at 18661 Hwy 1, a quarter-mile south of Hwy 20, has 28 rooms, some with kitchen, starting at $36. The *Surf Motel* (☎ 964-5361) at 1220 S Main St has 54 rooms starting at $45. The *Tradewinds Lodge* (☎ 964-4761, 800-524-2244) at 400 S Main St is one of the largest motels in town, with 92 rooms starting at $69 in summer, $59 the rest of the year. The *Ebb Tide Lodge* (☎ 964-5321, 800-974-6730) at 250 S Main St is an attractive motel with 31 rooms starting at $49 in summer, $40 in winter. The *Fort Bragg Motel* (☎ 964-4787, 800-253-9972) at 763 N Main St has a variety of rooms at $38 and up.

B&Bs Fort Bragg has several good B&Bs to choose from. As in Mendocino, most are in large, beautifully restored Victorian-era homes. The *Rendezvous Inn* (☎ 964-8142, 800-491-8142) at 647 N Main St has rooms from $75 to $110, and a fine restaurant serving dinner Wednesday to Sunday. The *Country Inn B&B* (☎ 964-3737) at 632 N Main St has rooms from $89 to $139. The *Grey Whale Inn* (☎ 964-0640, 800-382-7244) at 615 N Main St has rooms from $88 to $165.

Four blocks east of Main St, the *Colonial Inn* (☎ 964-9979) at 533 E Fir St has eight rooms from $56 to $90. On a bluff overlooking the Noyo River at the south end of town, the *Lodge at Noyo River* (☎ 964-8045, 800-628-1126) at 500 Casa del Noyo Rd has rooms from $90 to $140.

Places to Eat
For breakfast you can't beat *Eggheads* at 326 N Main St, a popular little restaurant serving over 40 kinds of omelets and other breakfast specialties, half-pound burgers, and other treats at lunch time. A few doors down, the *Fort Bragg Grille* at 356 N Main St is also popular for breakfast and lunch, or there's the *Home Style Cafe* at 790 S Main St, with hearty food.

For fine dining, try the *Rendezvous Inn* (☎ 964-8142) at 647 N Main St, serving dinner Wednesday to Sunday, reservations recommended. The *North Coast Brewing Company Taproom & Grill* at 444 N Main St is a popular restaurant and pub, closed Monday.

Viraporn's Thai Cafe on Chestnut St half a block east of Main St, is a casual, inexpensive little restaurant; it's open for lunch weekdays, dinner nightly. Nearby, *D'Aurelio & Sons* (☎ 964-4227) at 438 S Franklin St is popular for pizza and pasta, with an inexpensive menu and casual family atmosphere; it's open evenings only.

Noyo Harbor has several good seafood restaurants. Probably the most attractive is the *Wharf Restaurant & Lounge* with a beautiful view of the harbor. Nearby, *Cap'n Flint's*, is a more casual restaurant with that same great harbor view. Also at the harbor, *El Mexicano* is an inexpensive Mexican family restaurant serving homestyle Mexican food; closed Sunday.

Entertainment
The *Headlands Coffeehouse* (☎ 964-1987) at 120 E Laurel St, half a block east of Main St, is a great place to enjoy many varieties of coffee, light meals, and baked goods; live acoustic music or poetry readings take place every evening. It's open weekdays from 7 am to 10 pm, weekends

9 am to midnight, closed Tuesday. The *North Coast Brewing Company* (☎ 964-2739) at 455 N Main St is a popular restaurant and pub.

The *Fort Bragg Footlighters Little Theater* (☎ 964-3806) at the corner of Laurel and McPherson Sts, features gay '90s-style musicals, comedy, and melodrama on Wednesdays and Saturdays at 8 pm in summer. The *Gloriana Opera Company* (☎ 964-7469) gives performances year round at various locations. In Caspar, about five miles south of Fort Bragg, the *Caspar Inn* (☎ 964-5565) features rock, rhythm 'n blues, world beat, and other music Thursday, Friday, and Saturday nights, and an acoustic open mike every Sunday at 8 pm.

Getting There & Around
See the Mendocino section for bus information.

Fort Bragg Cyclery (☎ 964-3509), 579 S Franklin St one block east of Main St, rents bicycles at $10 for two hours, $20 per day, or $50 per week.

MACKERRICHER STATE PARK
On the coast about three miles north of Fort Bragg, MacKerricher State Park (☎ 707-937-5804) covers eight miles of rugged coastline from Pudding Creek in the south to Ten Mile River in the north, with beaches, sand dunes, coastal bluffs, tidepools, and an eight-mile coastal hiking trail. Other attractions include Lake Cleone, a freshwater lake good for fishing, boating, and hiking, and Laguna Point, a good spot for watching harbor seals year round and whales in season. Horseback rides on the beach are offered by the Ricochet Ridge Ranch (☎ 707-964-7669) on Hwy 1 opposite the park.

The attractive campgrounds here offer hot showers and 142 drive-in sites nestled into coastal trees, plus 10 more attractive and secluded walk-in sites just 50 yards from the parking area. The walk-in sites are first come, first served year round; other sites can be reserved through Destinet from April through mid-October, a wise idea if you want to get a space, as this is a very popular park. Sites are $14 in summer, $12 in winter, or $3 per person for hike/bike sites; there is no day-use fee to visit the park.

WESTPORT
• *pop 100* ☎ *707*
Clinging to a coastal bluff 14 miles north of Fort Bragg on Hwy 1, Westport is only a tiny village today; in the late 1800s and early 1900s it was a much more important place, a shipping port with a population of 3000 and the longest logging chutes in California.

There's camping a couple of miles north of town at the *Westport-Union Landing State Beach* (☎ 964-2964), with primitive sites on a coastal bluff for $7 per vehicle or $3 per person for hike/bike sites. Half a mile north of town, the *Wages Creek Beach Camp* (☎ 964-2964), 37700 N Hwy 1, has hot showers and campsites near the beach for $17 in summer, $10 in winter.

Other accommodations in Westport include the *Pelican Lodge & Inn* (☎ 964-5588) with a restaurant, the *Westport Inn* (☎ 964-5135), the *Seagate Guest House* (☎ 964-5595), the *De Haven Valley Farm* (☎ 961-1660), and the *Howard Creek Ranch* (☎ 964-6725).

Upper North Coast

Highway 1 (the Pacific Coast Hwy) and Hwy 101 (the Redwood Hwy) join at Leggett, a small settlement 45 miles north of Fort Bragg. From Leggett, Hwy 101 heads north by an inland route for about 80 miles until it meets the sea at Eureka on Humboldt Bay, California's largest bay north of San Francisco. Along the way it passes through some awe-inspiring groves of giant coast redwoods in several state parks, notably the Humboldt Redwoods State Park with its famous Avenue of the Giants. Even if you're only driving north or south on Hwy 101 on your way to somewhere else, it's definitely worth it to get off the highway and drive on the beautiful Avenue of the Giants instead.

Eureka, a fishing and former lumbering town hugging the shore of Humboldt Bay, is the largest town on California's far north coast; it's known for its many fine old Victorian buildings and its delicious fresh seafood. A little further north on Humboldt Bay, Arcata is a pleasant university town with a youthful ambiance reminiscent of the 1960s. Humboldt Bay is good for bird watching, with several wildlife refuges around the bay.

From Arcata northwards, the highway hugs the coast most of the way to the Oregon border, about another 100 miles, passing magnificent scenery for its entire distance; the spectacular virgin groves of giant redwood trees in the Redwood National and State Parks are an unforgettable experience.

Hwys Heading Inland

Highways crossing the Coast Range, connecting the coast with the interior, are slow, winding, and scenic, mostly snaking through the mountains in river canyons.

Highway 36, between Fortuna and Red Bluff, is extremely winding and a particular ordeal to traverse. Highway 299 between Arcata and Redding, dubbed the Trinity Scenic Byway, is also a long haul with about 3½ hours of mountainous curves, but it's a beautiful drive and it's the primary connection between the coast and the interior. From Hwy 299, Hwy 96 branches northwards and goes up the Trinity and Klamath Rivers, through Happy Camp, to join I-5 just north of Yreka, not far from the Oregon border.

Heading northward from Crescent City into Oregon you can keep on hugging the coast on Hwy 101, which continues as the coast highway in Oregon, or you can head inland on Hwy 199, called the Smith River National Scenic Byway, through the Smith River National Recreation Area.

LEGGETT
• *pop 200* • *elev 952 feet* ☎ *707*

If you're traveling north, Leggett is where

CALIFORNIA

you'll catch your first glimpse of the giant coast redwood forests. Beside the South Fork of the Eel River, Leggett is a very small settlement; you can easily drive right through it and never know you've been there. But it does have some fine places to stay and to linger if you're so inclined.

The **Chandelier Drive-Thru Tree Park** (☎ 925-6363) on Drive-Thru Tree Rd (Hwy 271) has 200 acres of virgin redwood forest with picnic areas, nature walks, and the Chandelier Tree, which has a square hole allowing cars to drive through. The park is open every day from 8 am to dusk; admission is $3 per vehicle.

The 1012-acre **Standish-Hickey State Recreation Area** (☎ 925-6482) on Hwy 101 has virgin and second-growth redwoods, swimming holes and fishing in the Eel River, picnic areas, and hiking trails ranging from easy to strenuous. There are three campgrounds with hot showers in a wooded area beside the river, two of them open all year. A couple of miles further north on Hwy 101, the **Smithe Redwoods State Reserve** is another redwood grove, but without developed trails or other facilities.

Nine miles north of Leggett on Hwy 101, **Confusion Hill** (☎ 925-6456) has a gravity house, water running uphill and other oddities, a children's petting zoo, a snack bar, and a small train making a 1¼-mile scenic loop through the forest. It's open daily from 9 am to 7 pm in summer, 11 am to 4 or 5 pm in winter; admission is $3.

Places to Stay

There's camping at the *Standish-Hickey State Recreation Area* and at the *Redwoods River Resort* (☎ 925-6249) at 75000 Hwy 101, in a redwood grove beside the Eel River, opposite Confusion Hill. The resort is a fun family place, with plenty of recreational activities. Camping is $14 per site (more with RV hookups); other accommodations include camping cabins (no kitchen) for $30, fully-equipped cabins with beds, linen, kitchen, etc for $60, and lodge rooms with kitchen access for $55/70 for two/four people.

The HI *Eel River Redwoods Hostel* at the *Bell Glen Resort* (☎ 925-6425) at 70400 Hwy 101, 2½ miles north of the Hwy 101/Hwy 1 junction, is a well-equipped hostel offering 'bunk & breakfast' in dorm rooms ($12, $14 for non-members) and bungalows, with a large common area and kitchen open every day, year round. Six deluxe B&B cottages, open from mid-April to late November, are $95 to $130. A sauna and outdoor hot tub are available, and there's a swimming hole in the river. A restaurant and a rathskeller pub serving food are open on weekends and as needed.

The *Leggett Motel* (☎ 925-6266) at 67672 Drive-Thru Tree Rd (Hwy 271) has nine old fashioned cottages for $35/40 with one/two beds.

Places to Eat

Ne-Bob's, also sometimes called *Andrea's*, is a pleasant restaurant-cafe with good food at good prices, and tables both inside and on the lattice-covered patio out front. To get there from Hwy 101, turn onto Hwy 1, then immediately turn left onto Hwy 271 (Drive-Thru Tree Rd), and you'll see it on your right.

The Price's Peg House (☎ 925-6444), 69501 Hwy 101, opposite the Standish-Hickey State Recreation Area, is a deli and country store with tables inside and outside. The restaurant and pub at the *Bell Glen Resort* (see Places to Stay) are open on weekends, and sometimes more often.

Getting There & Away

Greyhound buses going north and south on Hwy 101 stop at The Price's Peg House (see Places to Eat). Buses will also stop at the Bell Glen Resort by request.

RICHARDSON GROVE STATE PARK

Richardson Grove State Park (☎ 707-247-3318) is a popular 1500-acre park in a lovely virgin redwood grove where many of the trees are over 1000 years old and over 300 feet tall. The South Fork of the Eel River runs through the park, and there are ranger-led campfire programs and interpretive nature walks in summer.

The park has three campgrounds, one open all year, with hot showers. Also in the park, the Richardson Grove Lodge (☎ 707-247-3415) operates seven rustic cabins, each with one bedroom, a fully-equipped kitchenette, private bath, barbecue, picnic tables, and propane heating. They're $65 in summer, $52 the rest of the year, and are closed during January and February.

BENBOW LAKE

The 1200-acre **Benbow Lake State Recreation Area** (☎ 707-247-3318) is on the banks of the South Fork of the Eel River, where a summer dam forms the 26-acre Benbow Lake every year from May to September.

Campsites with hot showers are open year round. The campsites, in a grove of oak trees, tend to be loud because they're near the highway.

Beside the lake, the elegant *Benbow Inn* (☎ 707-923-2124, 800-355-3301), 445 Lake Benbow Drive, is a large Tudor-style country inn opened in 1926 and now a National Historic Landmark. Rooms are priced from $110 to $295, with off-season discounts, and the restaurant here is world-class (reservations recommended). Various special events are held throughout the year, especially at Thanksgiving, and all through December until New Years Day. Summer events on Benbow Lake include Jazz on the Lake, the Summer Arts Fair, and Shakespeare on the Lake.

GARBERVILLE

• *pop 1350* • *elev 479 feet* ☎ *707*

Garberville, with its tiny sister town of **Redway** two miles away, became famous on the underground grapevine in the 1970s for the *sinsemilla* grown in the surrounding hills; you still see many lefties and back-to-the-landers around, though the heyday of the '70s is long gone. Today Garberville and Redway are quiet little towns with a few good places to eat and basic services; though it's tiny, this is 'town' for the surrounding rural areas.

Information

The Garberville-Redway Chamber of Commerce (☎ 923-2613, 800-923-2613) at Suite E in the Jacob Garber Square, 773 Redwood Drive at the corner of Church St, has plenty of brochures and information on the region. For local news, unusual music, and other interesting broadcasting, check out KMUD radio at 91.1 FM. The post office is on Sprowel Creek Rd.

Special Events

Reggae on the River is the major event of the year, drawing over 8000 fans to 'the best reggae fest in the US' held the first weekend in August at French's Camp, beside the Eel River, eight miles south of Garberville. Tickets, sold for both days only (no one-day tickets available), go on sale on April 1 at the Mateel Community Center in Redway (☎ 923-3368); tickets sell out very quickly. For a free brochure, send a SASE to the Mateel Community Center, PO Box 1910, Redway, CA 95560.

Other events include the Avenue of the Giants Marathon in May; the Redwood Run, a Harley-Davidson run through the redwoods usually on the 1st weekend in June, and the Garberville Rodeo also in June; the Hemp Festival in November; and the Winter Arts Fair in mid-December, with magnificent arts & crafts.

Places to Stay

The closest camping to town is the Benbow Lake State Recreation Area.

Several motels are on Redwood Drive. The *Lone Pine Motel* (☎ 923-3520) at 912 Redwood Drive has a swimming pool, hot tub, and other amenities; rooms are $38 to $54 from May to October, $30 to $42 from November to April. The *Humboldt Redwoods Inn* (☎ 923-2451) at 987 Redwood Drive is another fine motel, with rooms at $45 to $50 in summer, $38 to $42 in winter. Fancier motels include the *Motel Garberville* (☎ 923-2422) at 948 Redwood Drive with rooms from $54 to $58 in summer, $42 to $48 in winter, and the *Best Western Humboldt House Inn* (☎ 923-2771, 800-528-1234) at 701 Redwood Drive with rooms starting at $81 in summer, $52 in winter.

Places to Eat

One of Garberville's best-loved restaurants, the small *Woodrose Cafe* (☎ 923-3191) at 911 Redwood Drive has been serving delicious organic food since 1977, with both meat and vegetarian selections. Across the street, the *Waterwheel Restaurant* (☎ 923-2031) at 924 Redwood Drive is a basic family restaurant with reasonable prices; at dinner there's a choice of Italian dinners or American steak and seafood. The small *Cafe Gerberville* (☎ 923-3551) at 770 Redwood Drive is another good place, popular with locals; it's closed Sunday.

Sicilito's (☎ 923-2814) at 445 Conger St, one block east of Redwood Drive, is a fun restaurant with American, Mexican, and Italian food, pizza, steak, seafood, and hamburgers. A big screen TV provides entertainment, as does the decor with hundreds of historic items. Another international option in Garberville is Chinese food at the *Cadillac Wok* (☎ 923-2343) at 373 Sprowel Creek Rd, just west of Redwood Drive.

The *Mateel Cafe* (☎ 923-2030) at 3342 and 3344 Redwood Drive in Redway, about two miles northwest of Gerberville, is one of the area's most famous and popular restaurants. French chef Pierre Gaudé prepares excellent salads, sandwiches, burgers, pizza, pasta, steak, seafood, Italian and Thai selections, espresso drinks, and magnificent desserts, all at reasonable prices. Also in Redway, the *One World Fountain* (☎ 923-3276) at 55 Briceland Rd serves organic foods.

Getting There & Away

Greyhound buses traveling on Hwy 101 stop at the Singing Salmon (☎ 923-3388) at 432 Church St, half a block east of Redwood Drive.

HUMBOLDT REDWOODS STATE PARK
☎ 707

The 80-sq mile Humboldt Redwoods State Park holds some of the world's most magnificent old-growth redwood forest. Some of the most famous features of the park include the awe-inspiring Founders Grove, Rockefeller Grove, and the Avenue of the Giants. The Park Visitor Center (☎ 946-2263) on the Avenue of the Giants just south of Weott has information about the park, the redwoods, history, and natural history, with useful books and maps.

The **Avenue of the Giants** is a 32-mile stretch of scenic highway winding through numerous groves of old growth redwoods, running parallel to Hwy 101 and the Eel River. A free *Avenue of the Giants Auto Tour* map/brochure is available at either end of the Avenue and at the park visitors center. The southern entrance to the avenue is six miles north of Garberville, the northern entrance is a few miles south of Fortuna, and there are several other access points.

The park has a number of spectacular named trees, including the Giant Tree, the world champion coast redwood, in the Rockefeller Forest. That honor was held by the Dyerville Giant in Founders Grove until it fell in March 1991 when hit by another falling tree; a walk along the length of the 362-foot Dyerville Giant, with the width of its trunk towering high overhead, helps to appreciate how huge these big old trees are. The Founders Tree in Founders Grove is another spectacular tree, as are the Tall Tree (also called the Rockefeller Tree) and the huge Flatiron Tree in the Rockefeller Forest, which fell in January 1995.

The park has over 100 miles of trails for hiking, biking, and horseback riding, ranging in difficulty from easy to strenuous. Easy hiking trails through Founders Grove, the Rockefeller Forest, the Drury-Chaney Loop Trail and the High Rock Trail are all very popular, and there are plenty of others; a booklet with maps and directions for 22 spectacular walks is available at the visitors center.

Happy Horse Hill (☎ 943-3008) at 1989 Elk Creek Rd, Myers Flat, offers one-hour horseback trail rides through the forest for $15 per person, children welcome.

Places to Stay

Camping The park has three developed campgrounds, two environmental campgrounds, five trail camps, a hike-bike camp, two group camps and an equestrian camp. The developed campgrounds, all with solar-heated showers, include *Burlington*, open year round beside the park visitors center; *Hidden Springs* and *Albee Creek*, open from late May to mid-October.

Motels Several of the tiny towns along the Avenue of the Giants have attractive motels. Starting from south to north, the *Madrona Motel & Resort* (☎ 943-1708) at 2907 Avenue of the Giants in Phillipsville (population 250) is simple, quaint and old fashioned but attractive, with single/double rooms at $38/43, a kitchen unit for $57 and a two-bedroom house for $75 per night.

The *Miranda Gardens Resort* (☎ 943-3011) at 6766 Avenue of the Giants in Miranda, right beside the Eel River, is a lovely place with a heated swimming pool, a children's playground, and rooms starting at $65 in summer, $55 in winter; deluxe cottages, some with kitchen, whirlpool, and fireplace, are $110 to $175.

In Myers Flat (population 200), the *Log Chapel Inn* (☎ 943-3315) at 12840 Avenue of the Giants is a simple place with single/double rooms for $30/35. Across the road, the *Historic Myers Inn* (☎ 943-3259) at 12913 Avenue of the Giants is a B&B with rooms for $75.

Further north in Redcrest (population 320), the *Redcrest Motor Inn Resort* (☎ 722-4208) at 26455 Avenue of the Giants has cabins starting at $40 ($9 more with kitchen), Indian teepees for $20, campsites at $14/19 for tents/RVs, and bicycle sites for $10.

SCOTIA
• *pop 1000* • *elev 164 feet* ☎ *707*

Scotia is a rarity in the modern world: it's one of the last 'company towns' left in California, entirely owned and operated by the Pacific Lumber Company (PALCO), the largest redwood lumber mill in the world, which built the town beside the giant lumber mill in 1887 for its employees and their families. Today Scotia is a manicured, organized, and wholesome little town with housing and services for some 270 families.

The two interesting things to do in Scotia – besides just strolling around and seeing what it feels like to be in a 'company town' – are to take a tour of the giant redwood lumber mill and to visit the museum. The **Scotia Museum & Visitors Center** (☎ 764-2222, ext 247), on Main St at the corner of Bridge St, is only open in summer.

Free self-guided tours of the lumber mill are offered weekdays from 7:30 to 10:30 am and 11:30 am to 2 pm. In summer when the museum is open, you must stop by there to pick up your free permit for the tour; the rest of the year, permits are given out at the guard shack at the front of the mill. The tour of the redwood mill takes about 1 to 1½ hours and allows you to see everything from the de-barking of the giant trees to their conversion to board lumber.

Places to Stay & Eat

The *Scotia Inn* (☎ 764-5683) on Main St is an attractive historic inn with rooms from $55 to $150; the dining room is open for dinner Wednesday to Sunday nights from 5 to 9 pm. Groceries, sandwiches, salads, coffee, and the like are available at *Hoby's Market* opposite the inn. Otherwise there are several motels and little restaurants in Rio Dell, across the river from Scotia.

Getting There & Away

Redwood Transit System operates bus routes heading north and south from Scotia; see the Eureka Getting Around section for details.

GRIZZLY CREEK REDWOODS STATE PARK

Grizzly Creek Redwoods State Park (☎ 707-777-3683), on the banks of the Van Duzen River 18 miles east of Hwy 101 on Hwy 36, has redwood groves, campgrounds, activities, and a museum inside a restored old stage coach stop. Campgrounds with hot showers are open year round.

FERNDALE
• pop 1450 • elev 30 feet ☎ 707

Ferndale is an idyllic little dairy farming community founded in 1852 that feels as if time has somehow passed it by. Situated about 20 miles south of Eureka, the town still has the old Victorian buildings and homes built over a century ago, still in use, well-preserved, and lovingly tended. Shops with arts and antiques and pleasant restaurants along Main St provide for visitors, and the town has two museums and various places to stay, but Ferndale is not just a tourist trap – it's an authentic, charming 19th-century farming village in an otherwise busy world. It's no surprise that the entire town is a state historic landmark, listed on the National Register of Historic Places.

Orientation & Information
'Downtown' Ferndale is a five-block section of Main St lined with Victorian-era buildings and shops. The *Victorian Village of Ferndale* map, with a visitors' guide and walking tour, is available free from a rack at the Kinetic Sculpture Museum, where you'll also find many other brochures, and from a number of Main St merchants. The Ferndale Chamber of Commerce (☎ 786-4477) has a telephone recording with information on current events, and they will send out information about Ferndale by request.

The post office is at 536 Main St.

Things to See & Do
Top on the list of things to do in Ferndale is to take a historic walk around town, seeing the fine old Victorians and the interesting shops on Main St. As the original settlers began to grow wealthy from the successful dairy farms they operated, some built large, ornate Victorian mansions known as 'butterfat palaces.' The **Gingerbread Mansion** at 400 Berding St, now a B&B (see Places to Stay), is the most famous, but there are plenty of other interesting old homes and buildings in town.

The **Ferndale Museum** (☎ 786-4466), one block west of Main St at the corner of Shaw and 3rd Sts, has hundreds of artifacts and exhibits on the area's history. It's open Wednesday to Saturday from 11 am to 4 pm and Sunday from 1 to 4 pm.

Kinetic sculptures that have run in the annual Arcata-to-Ferndale Kinetic Sculpture Race are on display at the **Kinetic Sculpture Museum** at 580 Main St, open every day from 10 am to 5 pm; admission is free but you can make a donation. The race was born in 1969 when Ferndale artist Hobart Brown decided to spruce up his son's tricycle to make it more interesting, creating a wobbly, five-wheeled red 'pentacycle.' Initially, five odd contraptions raced down Main St on Mother's Day, at the end of the Ferndale Arts Festival. The race was expanded in the early '70s to two days coming from Fields Landing, on Humboldt Bay south of Eureka; by now it has grown to a three-day, 38-mile amphibious event coming all the way from Arcata, attracting thousands of spectators and usually around 40 to 60 entrants (but one year there were 99). The race is held every year on Memorial Day weekend.

Special Events
The chamber of commerce has information on many events held throughout the year, including the Bicycle Tour of the Unknown Coast on Mother's Day weekend (☎ 839-8296, 800-995-8356); the Kinetic Sculpture Race on Memorial Day weekend (see above); the Scandinavian Festival and Parade (☎ 786-9853) in June; the Humboldt County Fair & Horse Races for 10 days in mid-August (☎ 786-9511, 725-1306); *Oktoberfest*, a full weekend of ethnic foods, music, and dancing (☎ 786-4477); and the *Christmas Celebrations* including a Lighted Tractor Parade, tree lighting ceremony, arts & crafts sales, horse and carriage rides, concerts, and theater productions.

Places to Stay
Camping The *Humboldt County Fair-*

grounds (☎ 786-9511) at the corner of Van Ness and 5th Sts offers camping on the lawn out in front of the fairgrounds, with tent/RV sites for $5/10. To get there from Main St, turn west onto Van Ness, on the north side of town, and go a few blocks down.

Hotels & Motels The *Francis Creek Inn* (☎ 786-9611) at 577 Main St, has four comfortable, homey rooms at $45/55 a single/double, including Danish and coffee in the morning. The *Ferndale Laundromat & Motel* (☎ 786-9471), nearby at 632 Main St, has two units, each with two bedrooms, kitchen and private bath, for around $35 to $40 for singles, $40 to $45 for doubles. The *Victorian Inn* (☎ 786-4949), 400 Ocean St at Main St, is a Victorian-era hotel with a restaurant, bar, and 12 rooms from $75 to $95. The *Fern Motel* (☎ 786-4050) at 342 Ocean St has rooms and suites for $60 and $75.

B&Bs Ferndale's elegant Victorians naturals for B&Bs, and there are several excellent ones to choose from. The *Gingerbread Mansion* (☎ 786-4000) at 400 Berding St, a fancy 1899 Queen Anne-Eastlake Victorian mansion at the corner of Berding and Brown Sts, one block east of Main St, is the most photographed Victorian in Ferndale. Now converted to a four-star B&B, it offers the utmost in service and elegance, with nine large rooms from $140 to $350.

Grandmother's House (☎ 786-9704) at 861 Howard St is a turn-of-the-century Queen Anne Victorian with three guest rooms for $65 and $75.

The *Shaw House* (☎ 786-9958) at 703 Main St was the first permanent structure to be built in Ferndale; the town's founder, Seth Shaw, started building the gabled Carpenter Gothic Victorian home in 1854, though it was not completed until after his death in 1872. The house, called 'Fern Dale' for the six-foot-tall ferns that grew here, housed the new settlement's first post office, of which Shaw was the postmaster – and that's how the town of Ferndale got its name. Today it's a B&B with five rooms from $75 to $135.

Places to Eat
There are plenty of good places to eat along the few blocks of Main St, including a bakery and coffeehouse, several lunch time places, a candy-making shop, and a Mexican-American restaurant, *Roman's*, which on Sundays has a special champagne brunch and dinner buffet. Stroll along and see what captures your fancy.

Entertainment
The *Ferndale Repertory Theatre* (☎ 725-2378) at 447 Main St, a top quality live theater company, offers productions year round. If a production is on while you're in the area, don't miss it – this is Ferndale's pride and joy.

THE LOST COAST
☎ 707
California's 'Lost Coast,' with its southern border where Hwy 1 turns inland north of Rockport, and its northern border around Ferndale, became 'lost' when the state's highway system was put in place earlier this century. The steep, rugged King Range, rising to around 4000 feet less than three miles from the coast, with near-vertical cliffs plunging into the sea and the high rainfall (averaging 100 inches annually) exacerbating the unstable soil and rock conditions, all conspired to make it next to impossible to build a highway here. So the Pacific Coast Hwy was routed inland and in time, legislation was passed to protect the region from development. Today the Lost Coast is one of California's most pristine coastal areas.

The south part of the Lost Coast is composed of the King Range National Conservation Area and the Sinkyone Wilderness State Park. The area north of the King Range is more accessible, but the scenery is not as dramatic. Shelter Cove, the only sizable community on the Lost Coast, is an isolated settlement on a remote cove 25 miles west of Garberville.

The best time to visit the Lost Coast is

probably in spring and autumn when there's the best chance of clear weather. If you'll be doing any hiking along the coast, late spring (around late April and early May) is an especially good time as not only might the weather cooperate, but you can view the California gray whales migrating.

North of the King Range
The northern section of the Lost Coast is accessible year round by Mattole Rd, which is paved. It takes about three hours to drive on this road the 68 miles from Ferndale in the north, out to the coast at Cape Mendocino, and then cut inland again to reach Humboldt Redwoods State Park and Hwy 101. Don't expect wild redwood forests, as are found on Hwy 101 – the vegetation here is mostly grassland and pasture with scattered cattle ranches. You'll pass through three tiny farming villages: **Capetown, Petrolia,** and **Honeydew**. The only gas station is at the Honeydew Post Office/Market/Hangout, but it's open sporadically and can't be counted on; be sure to fill your gas tank before you start the drive. Allow plenty of time, as the road is slow going. Though the drive is pleasant enough, the wild, spectacular scenery of the Lost Coast is not here, but further south in the less accessible regions.

There's camping at the AW Way County Park (☎ 445-7651) on Mattole Rd six miles southeast of Petrolia, between Petrolia and Honeydew.

King Range National Conservation Area
The 94-sq-mile King Range National Conservation Area, operated by the BLM, covers 35 miles of virgin wilderness coastline, with ridge after ridge of steep mountains plunging almost vertically into the surf, and the rugged King Range, with King's Peak the highest point at 4087 feet. The BLM office in Arcata administers the conservation area, so it's best place to ask current information. Maps are available from the BLM offices in Arcata and Ukiah. For camping outside developed campgrounds you'll need a free campfire permit,

available from the California Department of Forestry or the BLM offices in Arcata and Ukiah.

Hiking One of the area's most attractive and alluring features is the **Lost Coast Trail**, following 24 miles of coast from the Mattole Campground on the north end to Black Sands Beach at Shelter Cove on the south end. The prevailing northerly winds make it best to hike the trail from north to south. Highlights of the trail include an abandoned lighthouse at Punta Gorda, remnants of old shipwrecks, tidepools, and a great abundance of marine and coastal wildlife including sea lions, seals, and over 300 species of birds. The trail is mostly level, passing along beaches and over rocky outcrops; consult tide tables, as some rocky outcroppings are passable only at low tide. The hike takes three to four days from end to end.

A good shorter day hike along part of the Lost Coast Trail can be made by starting at the Mattole Campground trailhead and hiking three miles south along the coast to the abandoned lighthouse at Punta Gorda, and back again, with beautiful tidepools along the way. The Mattole Campground is easy to reach; it's at the ocean end of Lighthouse Rd, a four-mile road which intersects with Mattole Rd just southeast of Petrolia.

Other notable trails in the King Range are the **King Crest Trail** and the **Chemise Mountain Trail,** both designated as National Recreation Trails, and there are several other trails besides. The 16-mile King Crest Trail is a fairly easy trek along the main coastal ridge north of Shelter Cove. From the end of the Lost Coast Trail at Black Sands Beach in Shelter Cove, you can hike up the hill through the Shelter Cove community (about five miles on a paved road) to the Wailaki and Nadelos recreation sites, which are trailheads for the Chemise Mountain Trail, a ridge trail which connects with the Lost Coast Trail in the Sinkyone Wilderness State Park.

Shelter Cove
A seaside resort and retirement community

with beautiful homes on a windswept cove just above Point Delgada, Shelter Cove is surrounded by the King Range National Conservation Area. It's a very remote and isolated place, with just one road for access – a 23-mile paved road winding over the mountains from Garberville and Redway that takes a good hour to drive.

Places to Stay & Eat The *Shelter Cove Campground & Deli* (☎ 986-7474) at 492 Machi Rd, right in town, has hot showers and 100 campsites at $12/18 for tents/RVs. The deli has tables both inside and out on an ocean-view deck; fish & chips is their specialty. Or there's free camping in undeveloped campsites at Black Sands Beach,

Marijuana

Just as Napa, Sonoma, and Mendocino Counties are known for their wines, and the far north coast for its redwoods, Northern California as a whole is known for its marijuana, especially the *sinsemilla* (Spanish for 'without seeds') grown here, which connoisseurs say is some of the highest-quality pot in the world.

In the 1970s, Sonoma, Mendocino, and Humboldt counties were a virtual 'green triangle,' with the illegal marijuana crop being the biggest money-maker in their economies. The hills and remote areas of all of these counties (and other places in Northern California as well) were full of

hippies and 'back-to-the-land' types growing marijuana out in the boonies.

There was an amazing amount of pot around and prices were low; an ounce of good-quality pot might cost $10 in the '60s, $20 in the '70s, but if you knew anyone who grew it, you might get a whole shopping bag full for that price, or for free.

All that changed in the 1980s when the government Campaign Against Marijuana Planting (CAMP) program started. CAMP sent helicopters buzzing over the hills and remote areas with special infrared scopes that could detect marijuana plants. Some growers moved their operations indoors under grow-lights, and got nabbed when the local electric company reported houses that were suddenly using much more electricity than before.

CAMP fueled a vicious circle of problems. One thing it did was create a paranoid and suspicious atmosphere. It also drove prices sky high, as the supply-and-demand ratio shifted with less of it around. When the prices skyrocketed, the big money interests involved caused still further problems, with rip-offs and violence, people arming themselves to defend their crops, worrying about police informers, etc.

CAMP is still going on. And marijuana is still grown. Northern California sinsemilla is still some of the finest pot in the world. But it's all on a much smaller scale than it was in the '70s, and prices are high. It's well known that it's not a good idea to go straying onto other people's property; if you should happen upon someone's crop you could be in big trouble.

Cultivation, sale, and/or transportation of any amount of marijuana, and possession of over one ounce, are all felonies punishable by prison time. People caught cultivating can not only be sent to prison, but their land can be confiscated by the government, since it was being used in a criminal activity. Possession of less than one ounce, for strictly personal use, is treated more leniently; this is an infraction, with a penalty of a simple fine. ■

or the nearby Wailaki and Nadelos Recreation Sites.

Other places to stay at Shelter Cove include the *Shelter Cove Beachcomber Inn* (☎ 986-7733) at 7272 Shelter Cove Rd; the *Shelter Cove Motor Inn* (☎ 986-7521) at 205 Wave Drive; the *Marina Motel* (☎ 986-7595) at 461 Machi Rd; and a luxury suite at *The Lighthouse* (☎ 923-4143). *Pelican's Landing* (☎ 986-7793) on Wave Drive offers dining with steak, seafood, and cocktails.

Sinkyone Wilderness State Park

The 7367-acre Sinkyone Wilderness State Park, named for the Sinkyone Indians who once lived here, is another pristine stretch of coastline. The Lost Coast Trail continues here for another 22 miles, from Whale Gulch on the north end to the Usal Campground at the south end, six miles north of Hwy 1, and takes about three days to hike.

Near the north end of the park, the Needle Rock Ranch House (☎ 986-7711) serves as a visitors center where you can check in, register for a campsite, and get maps and trail guides. Upstairs in the ranch house are two unfurnished bedrooms available for 'indoor camping;' reservations can be made up to nine weeks in advance.

To get to the Needle Rock Ranch House, drive west from Garberville and Redway on Briceland Rd for 21 miles to Four Corners, where you turn left (south) and continue about another four miles down a very rugged road to the ranch house; it takes about 1½ hours. There's also road access to the Usal Campground at the south end of the park; from Hwy 1, about three miles north of Rockport, the unpaved County Rd 431 takes off from the highway at milepost 90.88 and goes six miles up the coast to the campground.

EUREKA

• *pop 25,000* ☎ 707

The largest town on California's far north coast, Eureka hugs the shore of Humboldt Bay, a long, narrow bay that is the state's largest bay and seaport north of San Francisco, with a significant fishing fleet. At first glance when you drive into town on Hwy 101, which goes right through the town, Eureka doesn't look too impressive – the highway is a thunder of traffic, motels, fast-food joints, gas stations, and so on, giving a bad impression. Getting away from the highway, however, especially if you go into Old Town just a couple of blocks off the highway, you find beautiful historic Victorian homes, an attractively refurbished commercial district, many good restaurants, and other attractions.

History

Humboldt Bay is said to have been formed about 10,000 years ago, at the end of the last ice age, when the sea rose and flooded the inland valley. About 14 miles long, the bay was home to the Wiyot Indians before Europeans arrived. Although various early European explorers had plied the coast of California, the bay's narrow entrance kept it from being discovered until 1806 when Captain Jonathan Winship of the US vessel *O'Cain*, which was chartered to the Russian-American Fur Company searching for sea otter, sailed into the bay.

The bay was not settled at that time, however, and it seems to have been forgotten. Legend or history – it's hard to tell which, as accounts differ – relate that the bay was rediscovered and the town of Eureka founded when whaler James T Ryan sailed into the bay in spring of 1850, shouting 'Eureka!': Greek for 'I have found it!' This was a popular expression at the time, and this was not the only place to be named Eureka; nevertheless, the name stuck here, the town was founded, and later on, when the first state congress met, 'Eureka' was adopted as the California motto, and was put on the new state seal. The bay was named after German naturalist Baron Alexander von Humboldt.

During the 1840s and '50s when miners were active on the Trinity and Klamath Rivers further inland, Eureka and Arcata served as important supply bases and trading posts for the mining camps. It wasn't long before lumbering became as important as mining, and then surpassed it. By 1854 there were seven lumber mills in Eureka, and more in Arcata, with schooners taking the lumber to San Francisco and other burgeoning settlements along the coast. At one point over 75 lumber mills were in operation around Humboldt Bay. Railroad systems were laid down to get the big trees from the forests to the mills; it required a strong engine and many flatbed cars to get each giant redwood tree out of the forest. The first overland connection between Humboldt Bay and the outside world came in 1914 with the establishment of the Northern Pacific Railroad coming north from San Francisco.

Today, most of the lumber mills have closed, with only one mill, the Louisiana Pacific pulp mill on the Samoa Peninsula opposite Eureka, left in operation on the bay. Fishing is still an important industry, and there's plenty of good seafood to be found.

Orientation
Highway 101 passes right through Eureka. On the south end of town it's called Broadway. Where it passes through downtown it becomes 4th and 5th Sts; 4th is one way eastbound, 5th westbound. East-west-running streets are numbered, starting at the waterfront on the north end of town and working their way inland; north-south streets are lettered, starting on the west end of town and working their way eastward. Heading north on R St takes you over the Samoa Bridge (Hwy 255), first to Woodley Island and then to the Samoa Peninsula, just four minutes across Humboldt Bay from Eureka.

Information
The Eureka-Humboldt County Convention and Visitors Bureau (☎ 443-5097, 800-346-3482), 1034 2nd St at the corner of L St, has maps and information about Eureka, Arcata, and all of Humboldt County. The Eureka Chamber of Commerce (☎ 442-3738, 800-356-6381) at 2112 Broadway also has visitor information.

The Six Rivers National Forest Headquarters (☎ 442-1721) at 1330 Bayshore Way, off Broadway on the south end of town near Henderson St, has maps and information about the forest.

The Going Places shop (☎ 443-4145) at 328 2nd St has a good selection of travel guidebooks and maps. The AAA office (☎ 443-5087) is at 707 L St. The post offices are at the corner of 5th and H Sts, and 337 W Clark St, east of Broadway St.

Things to See & Do
In Town Old Town, along 2nd and 3rd Sts from C St to M St, is a pleasant place to stroll around; formerly Eureka's skid row area, Old Town has been refurbished into a district of trendy boutiques, shops, art galleries, cafes, and restaurants.

Eureka has many fine old Victorian homes. The *Eureka Visitors Map* available free at the tourist offices shows routes for scenic and architectural drives and walks. The most famous Victorian of all is the ornate **Carson Mansion** at the east end of 2nd St at M St. Home of lumber baron William Carson in the 1880s, it's said that it took 100 men a full year (1884-85) to

Carson Mansion

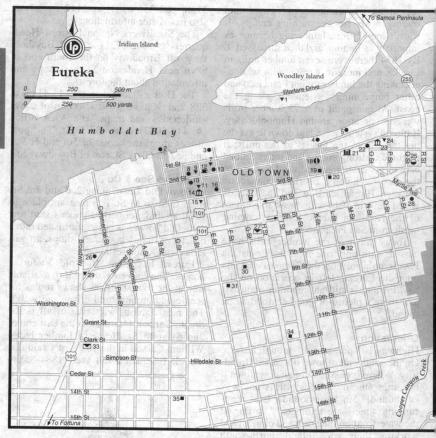

build the mansion. Today the mansion is occupied by a private men's club, Ingomar, and is not open to the public. The pink house at 202 M St, opposite Carson Mansion, is an 1884 Queen Anne Victorian designed by the same architects and built as a wedding gift for Carson's eldest son.

The **Clarke Memorial Museum** (☎ 443-1947), 240 E St at the corner of 3rd St, in the former Bank of Eureka building, has an especially impressive American Indian collection and thousands of other interesting items. The museum's largest historical artifact is the structure itself. Built 1911-12 of marble, granite, and tile, the building was

the leading bank in Eureka until the 1950s, and today it is on the National Register of Historic Places. The museum is open Tuesday to Saturday from noon to 4 pm; admission is free. Another museum, the small **Humboldt Bay Maritime Museum** (☎ 444-9440) is at 1410 2nd St, one block east of Carson Mansion; it's open every day from 11 am to 4 pm, admission is free.

A relic of Eureka's more recent past is the **Romano Gabriel Wooden Sculpture Collection**, on display in a large glass case in a little triangular plaza just off the sidewalk on 2nd St between D and E Sts. The city moved the collection from Gabriel's

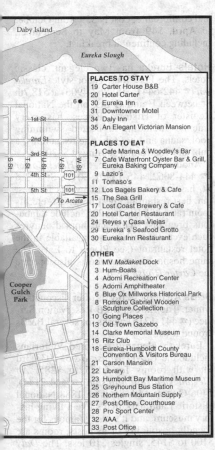

Daby Island

Eureka Slough

PLACES TO STAY
19 Carter House B&B
20 Hotel Carter
30 Eureka Inn
31 Downtowner Motel
34 Daly Inn
35 An Elegant Victorian Mansion

PLACES TO EAT
1 Cafe Marina & Woodley's Bar
7 Cafe Waterfront Oyster Bar & Grill,
   Eureka Baking Company
9 Lazio's
11 Tomaso's
12 Los Bagels Bakery & Cafe
15 The Sea Grill
17 Lost Coast Brewery & Cafe
20 Hotel Carter Restaurant
24 Reyes y Casa Viejas
29 Eureka's Seafood Grotto
30 Eureka Inn Restaurant

OTHER
2 MV *Madaket* Dock
3 Hum-Boats
4 Adorni Recreation Center
5 Adorni Amphitheater
6 Blue Ox Millworks Historical Park
8 Romano Gabriel Wooden
   Sculpture Collection
10 Going Places
13 Old Town Gazebo
14 Clarke Memorial Museum
16 Ritz Club
18 Eureka-Humboldt County
   Convention & Visitors Bureau
21 Carson Mansion
22 Library
23 Humboldt Bay Maritime Museum
25 Greyhound Bus Station
26 Northern Mountain Supply
27 Post Office, Courthouse
28 Pro Sport Center
32 AAA
33 Post Office

1st St
2nd St
3rd St
4th St
5th St
To Arcata
101
Cooper Gulch Park

front yard to preserve it after he passed away in 1977, having created the sculptures that delighted the locals for 30 years.

The **Blue Ox Millworks Historical Park** (☎ 444-3437, 800-248-4259) at the ocean end of X St is another interesting historical place, where antique tools and mills are used in the production of gingerbread trim and other decoration for old Victorian buildings. A real working museum owned by Eric and Viviana Hollenbeck, this is one of very few places in the world that you can see this being done; a one-hour tour takes you through the entire mill and other historical buildings. The $5

admission is well worth it. It's open Monday to Saturday from 9 am to 5 pm, with possible Sunday hours in summer.

Yet another historical site in Eureka is the **Fort Humboldt State Historic Park** (☎ 443-7952), just off Broadway St on the south end of town; turn inland onto Highland Ave and you'll see the entrance gate. The fort was established in 1853 on a high bluff affording a view of Humboldt Bay and its entrance. General Ulysses S Grant was stationed here in 1853 before he went on to lead the northern army to victory in the Civil War and later become president of the USA. The fort has indoor and outdoor exhibits about logging, and several reconstructed fort buildings. The park is open daily from 9 am to 5 pm; admission free.

The **Sequoia Park & Zoo** is a beautiful redwood grove with bicycle and hiking trails, picnic areas, a children's playground, a duck pond and a tiny zoo. The park is always open; the zoo is open Tuesdays to Sundays from 10 am to 7 pm from May to September, closing at 5 pm, the rest of the year. Admission is free, but donations are suggested.

On Humboldt Bay One of Eureka's most delightful activities is the Humboldt Bay Harbor Cruise on the MV *Madaket* (☎ 445-1910). The oldest passenger vessel in continuous use in the USA, the *Madaket* was built and launched here on June 6, 1910, and has served in Humboldt Bay all her life, ferrying passengers and workers to the lumber mills and other places around the bay for many years before the Samoa Bridge was built in 1972. The cruise passes many places of interest around the bay, while a host tells stories about history and natural features, giving you an experience you could never get from land. The 1¼-hour cruises depart several times daily from May to October, from the dock at the foot of C St; phone for reservations and for the current schedule.

Hum-Boats (☎ 443-5157) at the bay end of F St offers kayak and sailboat rentals and instruction, kayak tours, and sailing rides. Northern Mountain Supply (☎ 445-1711),

125 W 5th St at the corner of Commercial St, rents canoes, inflatable kayaks, Kiwi kayaks, and camping gear.

Special Events
Many enjoyable events are held every year in Eureka and nearby in Arcata. Events in Eureka include: the Redwood Coast Dixieland Jazz Festival in March; the Rhododendron Festival in April; the Tour of the Unknown Coast Bicycle Race in May; a series of summer concerts in Sequoia Park from June to August; the Humboldt Arts Festival in July and August, featuring concerts, plays, and art exhibits; and the December Christmas Celebrations, including a Truckers' Christmas Convoy Parade, the Eureka Inn Christmas Celebration, and more.

Places to Stay
Camping Near town, the *Eureka KOA* (☎ 822-4243, 800-462-KAMP) at 4050 N Hwy 101, on the east side of the highway about four miles north of Eureka, has tent/RV sites for $18/24, cabins for $32. The *Fortuna KOA* (☎ 725-3359, 800-404-0600) at Hwy 101 at the Kenmar Rd exit, 18 miles south of Eureka, has tent/RV sites for $19/25, cabins for $32. There's also camping on the Samoa Peninsula, across the bay from Eureka.

Motels Dozens of motels line Hwy 101 where it goes through town, but they are exposed to the roar of highway traffic; you'll get a more peaceful sleep away from the highway noise. The *Bayview Motel* (☎ 442-1673) at 2844 Fairfield St, just off Henderson St near the corner of Broadway, is near the highway but it's perched on a high bluff overlooking the bay; it's quiet, clean and pleasant, with a comfortable, homey family atmosphere and rooms decorated not like motel units but like pleasant guest rooms at $42/46 single/double.

Also away from the highway, the *Downtowner Motel* (☎ 443-5061), 424 8th St at the corner of E St, has an outdoor heated swimming pool, indoor sauna and hot tub, and 72 spacious rooms that are clean, quiet,

and comfortable; cost is $39 from October to April, $49 from May to September, including continental breakfast.

Hotels Eureka has two elegant, classic hotels. The luxurious Tudor-style *Eureka Inn* (☎ 442-6441, 800-862-4906) at 518 7th St between F and G Sts, on the National Register of Historic Places, has every amenity including a heated swimming pool, sauna and hot tub, fine restaurants, a pub, and 100 rooms starting at $120.

Another elegant place, the *Hotel Carter* (☎ 444-8062, 445-1390), 301 L St at 3rd St, has earned numerous awards for best inn, best restaurant, best breakfast, etc; its room rates of $105 to $225 include a fabulous breakfast, wine and hors d'oeuvres each evening, with dinner available in the hotel restaurant (see Places to Eat). The same hospitable owner/hosts also operate the *Carter House B&B*.

B&Bs All of these B&Bs offer discounts in winter. The Eureka B&B Reservation Service (☎ 441-1215) works for several B&Bs around town.

Eureka's elegantly restored Victorians include the *Carter House B&B*, 1033 3rd St, with rooms for $125 to $285. *An Elegant Victorian Mansion* (☎ 444-3144), 1406 C St at 14th St, is an 1888 National Historic Landmark that's like a living history museum, and it's justly famous for the friendly hospitality of its hosts; rooms are $100 to $145, singles $10 less. The *Daly Inn* (☎ 445-3638, 800-321-9656), 1125 H St at 12th St, is a 1905 Colonial Revival mansion with generous grounds, a garden patio, and rooms from $80 to $135. *Shannon House* (☎ 443-8130) at 2154 Spring St, an 1891 Victorian in a quiet residential neighborhood, has rooms for $75 and $85.

Places to Eat
An outdoor Farmer's Market (☎ 441-9699) is held at the Old Town Gazebo on the corner of 2nd and F Sts from July to October on Tuesdays from 10 am to 1 pm.

Eureka's best-known eatery, the *Samoa Cookhouse* (☎ 442-1659) is the 'last surviving cookhouse in the West.' An old lumber camp cookhouse with a museum in one part of the building, the whole place is like a slice out of Eureka's past. Diners are seated all together at long tables covered with checkered cloths, then served 'all-you-can-eat' of course after course of hearty dishes. Dinner includes soup, salad, two types of meat, potatoes, vegetables, apple pie, and coffee, tea or iced tea; breakfast and lunch are similarly hearty meals. It's on the Samoa Peninsula, four minutes north of town over the Samoa Bridge; follow the signs. It's open every day from 6 am to 3 pm and from 5 to 9 pm, and Sunday straight through from 6 am to 9 pm. Seating is first come, first served.

Many other good places to eat are right in town, mostly in Old Town. The gourmet restaurant at the *Hotel Carter* (☎ 444-8062, 445-1390), 301 L St at 3rd St, has won many awards for excellence; it's famous both for its breakfasts, a four-course meal and lavish buffet served every morning from 7:30 to 10 am, and its gourmet dinners with a 30-page wine list served every night from 6 to 9 pm. Reservations are recommended for both meals. Eureka's other fine hotel, the Eureka Inn (☎ 442-6441, 800-862-4906) at 518 7th St between F and G Sts, offers elegant dining in its *Rib Room*, specializing in prime rib, and more casual dining at its *Bristol Rose Cafe*.

For simpler fare, *Los Bagels Bakery & Cafe*, 403 2nd St at the corner of E St, is a branch of the popular Arcata cafe-bakery-hangout; it's open from 7 am to 5 pm, closing earlier on weekends and altogether on Tuesdays. Around the corner, the *Eureka Baking Company* at 108 F St has a wide variety of baked goods, coffee, and a few tables.

Seafood is of course popular in this seaport town, and Eureka has many fine seafood restaurants. The *Cafe Waterfront Oyster Bar & Grill* (☎ 443-9190), 102 F St at the corner of 1st St with a view of Humboldt Bay, is a fun, pleasant place that's popular for seafood and not too expensive. *The Sea Grill* (☎ 443-7187) at 316 E St is also known for good seafood; it's open for lunch Tuesday to Friday, dinner Monday to Saturday. *Lazio's* (☎ 433-9717) at 327 2nd St is another pleasant and popular seafood restaurant, open every day for lunch and dinner, with brunch on weekends.

A more casual seafood restaurant, *Eureka's Seafood Grotto* (☎ 443-2075), at the corner of 6th St and Broadway, is a bustling family-style seafood eatery with large portions and reasonable prices. *Cafe Marina & Woodley's Bar* (☎ 443-2233), on Woodley Island with decks and a view overlooking the marina, is a pleasant seafood restaurant.

For excellent Italian food, visit *Tomaso's* (☎ 445-0100) at 216 E St – you'll know you're nearby when you smell the enticing aromas wafting out onto the sidewalk. Famous dishes here include the spinach pies, tomato pies, and chicken or seafood cannelloni.

Reyes y Casa Viejas (☎ 445-4960), 1436 2nd St at the corner of P St, near the Maritime Museum, is a favorite for Mexican food; it's open for lunch Tuesday to Friday, dinner Tuesday to Saturday.

The *Lost Coast Brewery & Cafe* (☎ 445-4480) at 617 4th St is a popular micro-brewery pub and cafe serving a variety of brews and pub foods; it's a fun place.

Entertainment

The Eureka Inn (see Places to Stay) has live music upstairs in the *Palm Lounge* from Thursday to Sunday nights; downstairs in the *Rathskeller Pub* there's karaoke on Wednesday and Thursday nights, live music Friday and Saturday nights, and a variety of other entertainment, especially around the Christmas season. The *Ritz Club* at the corner of 3rd and F Sts has DJ dance music Thursday, Friday, and Saturday nights. The *Lost Coast Brewery & Cafe* (☎ 445-4480), 617 4th St, is a popular pub.

Getting There & Around

Air The Arcata-Eureka Airport, about 20 miles north of Eureka (11 miles north of Arcata) on Hwy 101, is served by three airlines: Horizon Air (☎ 800-547-9308),

Sierra Expressway (☎ 800-963-5987), and United Express (☎ 800-241-6522).

Bus Greyhound (☎ 442-0370, 800-231-2222), with a bus station at 1603 4th St at the corner of Q St, has two northbound and two southbound buses every day.

The Redwood Transit System (☎ 443-0826) at 133 V St operates buses weekdays between Scotia in the south and Trinidad in the north, with stops at all the little towns along the way including Fortuna and Arcata; these buses make a number of stops along 4th and 5th Sts as they pass through Eureka. In Scotia the buses connect with another bus route, Garberville-Scotia, with stops at various places in the Humboldt Redwoods State Park. Another bus route goes between Eureka and Blue Lake, via Arcata. Local city buses with a number of routes around Eureka are operated by Eureka Transit Service (☎ 443-0826), with service every day except Sunday.

Car Car rental companies in and near Eureka include Avis (☎ 443-3155, airport 839-1576, 800-831-2847), Budget (☎ 839-4374, 800-527-0770), and Enterprise (☎ 443-3366).

Bicycle The *Pro Sport Center* (☎ 443-6328), 508 Myrtle St at the corner of 5th St, rents bicycles by the full or half day.

AROUND EUREKA
☎ 707
Samoa Peninsula
The 7-mile-long, half-mile-wide Samoa Peninsula is the north spit of Humboldt Bay; it's said the place got its name from its resemblance to Pago Pago Harbor. The peninsula's most famous attraction is the **Samoa Cookhouse** (see Places to Eat, Eureka), but it has other attractions too.

You can go to the beach on the sea side anywhere along the peninsula, walking through the dunes. At the south end of the peninsula is the **Samoa Dunes Recreation Area** with picnic areas and access to the bay, ocean, and fishing; it's operated by the BLM (☎ 822-7648). The recreation area is open from sunrise to sunset; admission is free.

There's camping at the *Samoa Boat Ramp County Park* (☎ 445-7651), on the bay side of the peninsula about four miles south of the Samoa Bridge, for $8 a night. There's not much to it – basically it's just some picnic tables and a toilet block beside a parking lot.

Humboldt Bay National Wildlife Refuge
On the south end of Humboldt Bay, the Humboldt Bay National Wildlife Refuge (☎ 733-5406) is an important refuge for over 200 species of birds migrating on the Pacific flyway each year. Peak season for most species of waterbirds and raptors is from September through March, and peak season for black brant geese and migratory shorebirds is from mid-March to late April, but many birds can be seen year round, including shorebirds, gulls, terns, cormorants, pelicans, egrets, and herons. The refuge also harbors seals. It has two interpretive trails, the 1½-mile Hookton Slough trail (three miles roundtrip) and the 1¾-mile Shorebird Loop trail. A free map brochure is available at the refuge entrance and at the tourist offices. To get to the refuge, turn seaward from Hwy 101 at the Hookton Rd exit, 11 miles south of Eureka, and follow the signs. The refuge is open daily from sunrise to sunset.

ARCATA
• pop 15,400 ☎ 707
Nine miles north of Eureka, Arcata is a pleasant university town overlooking Humboldt Bay with a youthful, laid-back ambiance reminiscent of the 1960s. Humboldt State University (HSU), the northernmost campus in the state university system, is strong on environmental studies and both the university and the town have a distinct tilt to the left.

Arcata was called Union Town when it was founded in 1850; the name was changed to Arcata in 1860. Originally a depot and base for the Trinity gold fields in the mountains to the east and for nearby lumber camps, Arcata grew and became a lumber town with a number of mills. In the late 1850s Bret Harte worked in Arcata as a journalist; the town became the setting for some of his stories.

Orientation

Arcata is an attractive town sloping down a hill towards Humboldt Bay. At the top of the hill are HSU and Hwy 101. G and H Sts, connecting with Hwy 101 at the top of the hill, are the main streets going from the freeway into town, with G St going one way up the hill and H St going one way coming downhill. The heart of the town is the Arcata Plaza, between G and H Sts, 8th and 9th Sts. Finding addresses is a snap in downtown Arcata; the streets are all laid out on a grid, with numbered streets crossing lettered streets. The Giuntoli Lane exit off Hwy 101, where several budget hotels are found, is a couple of miles north of town; Hwy 299, the Trinity Scenic Byway going east to Weaverville and Redding, intersects Hwy 101 about one mile north of town.

Information

Arcata Chamber of Commerce & Visitor Information (☎ 822-3619) at 1062 G St, is

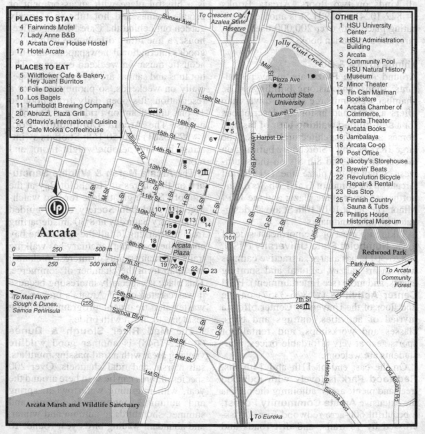

PLACES TO STAY
4 Fairwinds Motel
7 Lady Anne B&B
8 Arcata Crew House Hostel
17 Hotel Arcata

PLACES TO EAT
5 Wildflower Cafe & Bakery, Hey Juan! Burritos
6 Folie Douce
10 Los Bagels
11 Humboldt Brewing Company
20 Abruzzi, Plaza Grill
24 Ottavio's International Cuisine
25 Cafe Mokka Coffeehouse

OTHER
1 HSU University Center
2 HSU Administration Building
3 Arcata Community Pool
9 HSU Natural History Museum
12 Minor Theater
13 Tin Can Mailman Bookstore
14 Arcata Chamber of Commerce, Arcata Theater
15 Arcata Books
16 Jambalaya
18 Arcata Co-op
19 Post Office
20 Jacoby's Storehouse
21 Brewin' Beats
22 Revolution Bicycle Repair & Rental
23 Bus Stop
25 Finnish Country Sauna & Tubs
26 Phillips House Historical Museum

Arcata

0   250   500 m
0   250   500 yards

next to the Arcata Theater. Their free *Map Guide to Arcata* has plenty of useful information about the town and the region. The BLM office (☎ 825-2300) at 1695 Heindon Rd a couple of miles north of town (take the Giuntoli Lane exit from Hwy 101) has information on the Lost Coast and the King Range National Conservation Area.

The post office is at the corner of 8th and H Sts, on the southwest corner of the plaza.

Arcata has some excellent bookstores, with books you don't usually find. The Tin Can Mailman (☎ 822-1307), 1000 H St at the corner of 10th St, is a magnificent used bookstore with over 125,000 used books of all kinds on two floors. Arcata Books (☎ 822-1024) at 959 H St is another fascinating place with over 200,000 used, new, rare, and antiquarian books.

Things to See & Do
Around **Arcata Plaza** are many restaurants, shops, and historic buildings. The chamber of commerce's free town map offers a route and historical descriptions for a **self-guided walking tour** of historic homes and their architectural styles. The large 1857 Jacoby's Storehouse building on the corner of H and 8th Sts on the southwest corner of the plaza, the 1915 Hotel Arcata on the corner of G and 9th Sts on the northeast corner of the plaza; and the 1914 Minor Theater at 1013 10th St are all designated historic landmarks.

Taking up most of the northeast side of town, **Humboldt State University** (HSU, ☎ 826-3011) has a large, attractive campus with an art gallery, cultural and sporting events, and more (see Entertainment). **HSU Center Activities** (☎ 826-3357) on the 2nd floor of the University Center offers a myriad of activities, outings and trips, classes and workshops, and rentals of sports gear at very affordable prices; nonstudents are welcome.

On the east end of 11th and 14th Sts, **Redwood Park** is lovely with redwood trees and picnic areas; adjoining the park is the extensive **Arcata Community Forest**, a beautiful 600-acre redwood forest crisscrossed by 18 trails, and dirt roads and paved roads good for hikers and mountain bikers. A free Community Forest map is available from the chamber of commerce.

The **HSU Natural History Museum** (☎ 826-4479) at 1315 G St, between 13th and 14th Sts, is a small museum with many exhibits of fossils, open Tuesday to Saturday from 10 am to 4 pm, admission free. The **Phillips House Historical Museum** (☎ 822-4722) at the corner of 7th and Union Sts is a historic 1854 home museum open for guided tours on Sundays from noon to 4 pm, admission by donation.

The **Finnish Country Sauna & Tubs** (☎ 822-2228) at the corner of 5th and J Sts is a blissful place with an assortment of private saunas and hot tubs in a lovely garden out behind the Cafe Mokka coffeehouse, a fine little coffeehouse with baked goods, international newspapers, and live acoustic music on weekend evenings. The hot tubs and saunas are very popular, especially on weekends, so phone ahead for a reservation. It's open daily from noon to 11 pm, until 1 am on Friday and Saturday nights. The **Arcata Community Pool** (☎ 822-6801) at 1150 16th St offers swimming, hot tub, aerobic/weight room, and more.

The **Arcata Marsh & Wildlife Sanctuary** on the shores of Humboldt Bay at the foot of I St is a great place for bird watching; the Audubon Society offers guided walks every Saturday at 8:30 am, departing from the parking lot all the way at the bay end of the road. The sanctuary has walking trails and many points of interest; pick up a free map from the chamber of commerce. This place is especially interesting because it was created out of Arcata's progressive wastewater treatment program, enabling residents to 'flush with pride.'

The **Mad River Slough & Dunes** (☎ 822-7648) is another good wildlife viewing area, with a trail passing mudflats, salt marsh, and tidal channels. Over 200 species of birds can be seen here around the year, with migrating waterfowl in spring and autumn, songbirds in spring and summer, shorebirds in autumn and winter, and abundant wading birds year round. To get there from town, go west on Samoa Blvd for about three miles and then turn right at the Manila turnoff (Young St).

The **Azalea State Reserve** (☎ 445-6547) is on Hwy 200, one mile east of Hwy 101, about three miles north of town. It's lovely when the azaleas bloom from around late April to the end of May, but not so dramatic at other times.

Special Events
The most famous event of the year is the three-day **Kinetic Sculpture Race** (☎ 725-3851) held on Memorial Day weekend, the last weekend in May, see the entry under Ferndale.

Other events include the Arcata Bay Oyster Festival held the Saturday before Father's Day, in June; the July 4th Jubilee; the September Northcountry Fair; and Pastels on the Plaza, the first Saturday in October.

Places to Stay
Camping There's good camping at Patrick's Point State Park, 16 miles north of Arcata, and further north at Humboldt Lagoons State Park. Closer in, the Clam Beach County Park (☎ 445-7491) on Hwy 101 about eight miles north of town offers primitive camping in the dunes; facilities include pit toilets and a few cold water faucets.

Hostel The *Arcata Crew House Hostel* (☎ 822-9995), 1390 I St near the corner of 14th St, is a summer youth hostel open from June 1 to August 24, with beds at $10 a night; it's a popular place, so advance reservations are a good idea.

Hotels & Motels *Hotel Arcata* (☎ 826-0217, 800-344-1221), at 708 9th St on the corner of G St on the north side of the plaza, is a beautifully restored historic hotel built in 1915. The charming, comfortable rooms, all with private bath and clawfoot tubs, are $60/65 single/double.

In town, the *Fairwinds Motel* (☎ 822-4824), 1674 G St at 17th St, has rooms that are basically OK, but the noise from

Hwy 101 just a few feet behind the motel is very loud; singles/doubles are $40/45. Other motels are two miles north of town at Hwy 101's Giuntoli Lane exit. They include *Motel 6* (☎ 822-7061, 800-466-8356) at 4755 Valley West Blvd with rooms for $30/36; the *Comfort Inn* (☎ 826-2827) at 4701 Valley West Blvd with rooms from $40 to $75; the *North Coast Inn* (☎ 822-4861) at 4975 Valley West Blvd with rooms starting at $49; and the *Best Western Arcata Inn* (☎ 826-0313, 800-528-1234) at 4827 Valley West Blvd with rooms at $79/83 in summer, $52/56 in winter.

B&B The *Lady Anne B&B* (☎ 822-2797), 902 14th St at I St, has five rooms with private bath in a fancy Queen Anne Victorian mansion, for $75 to $95.

Places to Eat
The *Arcata Co-Op* at the corner of 8th and I Sts is a large natural foods supermarket open every day from 9 am to 9 pm (8 pm Sunday). From May to November, a *Farmers Market* meets on the Arcata Plaza on Saturdays from 9 am to 1 pm.

Los Bagels at 1061 I St is a great place for coffee, bagels, and other baked goods, and general hanging out; it's closed Tuesday. The *Cafe Mokka Coffeehouse* (☎ 822-2228) at the corner of 5th and J Sts is a pleasant coffeehouse with a Bohemian atmosphere, international newspapers, live acoustic music on weekend evenings, and the Finnish Country Sauna & Tubs in the yard out back. It's open Sunday to Thursday from noon to 11 pm, Friday and Saturday to 1 am.

Up the hill, the *Wildflower Cafe & Bakery*, 1604 G St at 16th St, is a fine place for baked goods and tasty, wholesome, inexpensive organic vegetarian meals of all kinds. *Hey Juan! Burritos* at 1642½ G St is a hip, cheap little Mexican cafe and takeaway with just five tables where you can get a basic but good, filling meal for around $4.

The *Humboldt Brewing Company* (☎ 826-2739) at 956 10th St between H and I Sts serves lunch, dinner, and pub food including famous buffalo wings, in addition to its good homemade brews; there's live music on weekends.

Arcata also has several more substantial restaurants, where reservations are a good idea. On the downstairs level of the historic Jacoby's Storehouse building on the corner of 8th and H Sts, *Abruzzi* (☎ 826-2345) is a good Italian dinner house; the entrance is easiest to find if you walk around the corner onto H St, to the rear of the building. Upstairs, the *Plaza Grill* (☎ 826-0860) is a steak-and-seafood restaurant with a fun, lively atmosphere, open for dinner every night from 5 pm until late.

Popular, quality gourmet restaurants with an international flair include *Folie Douce* (☎ 822-1042) at 1551 G St, a tiny restaurant with gourmet pizza as well as more exotic fare, and a 270-item wine list; it's open for dinner only, and closed Sunday and Monday. Or there's *Ottavio's International Cuisine* (☎ 822-4021) at 686 F St at 7th St, with an imaginative, eclectic menu of European and Asian cuisines; it's closed Mondays.

Entertainment

Jambalaya (☎ 822-4766) at 915 H St, near the plaza, offers live jazz, blues, and other music with weekly jam nights, poetry nights, and other entertainment; the schedule is posted at the door. On the south side of the plaza, *Brewin' Beats* (☎ 822-5053) at 773 8th St is a bar and dance hall with varied music. The *Humboldt Brewing Company* (☎ 826-2739) at 956 10th St between H and I Sts features live music on weekend nights, mostly rock 'n roll.

For mellower sounds, check out the *Cafe Mokka Coffeehouse* (☎ 822-2228) at the corner of 5th and J Sts, with live acoustic music on weekend evenings, usually European folk music.

The *Arcata Theater* (☎ 822-5171) at 1036 G St and the *Minor Theater* (same telephone) at 1013 H St have frequently changing movies and bargain matinees.

Humboldt State University Center Arts (☎ 826-4411, 826-3928) sponsors performances, concerts, international music, and cultural events.

Getting There & Around

Greyhound buses traveling on Hwy 101 stop at the bus stop on F St between 7th and 8th Sts. There's a catch if you're boarding the bus here, however: you must have a Greyhound ticket before the driver will let you on – the bus drivers don't sell tickets – and there's nowhere in Arcata to buy one. The nearest place to buy a ticket is at the Greyhound station in Eureka. Local buses will drop you right at the door of the Eureka Greyhound station.

The Redwood Transit System buses (see Eureka) stop in Arcata on their weekday Trinidad-Scotia and Eureka-Blue Lake routes.

Revolution Bicycle Repair & Rental (☎ 499-9877) at the corner of 7th and F Sts, rents mountain bikes, cruisers, bike racks, and bicycle gear.

TRINIDAD
• *pop 432* ☎ *707*

About 12 miles north of Arcata, this attractive, affluent little historic town on Trinidad Bay looks freshly painted and well cared for. Attractions here include hiking on Trinidad Head and the beautiful Trinidad State Beach, surfing on Luffenholtz Beach, visiting the museum and old lighthouse, and just strolling around.

The town and bay have a long history. Originally settled by Tsurai Indians, Trinidad Bay was discovered by Europeans several times, beginning in 1595. The Spanish sea captains Hezeta and Bodega anchored here on June 9, 1775 and named the bay 'La Santisima Trinidad' (the Holy Trinity), placing a monument to the Spanish king on Trinidad Head where the white granite cross is today. But it wasn't until the 1850s that Trinidad became the site of a booming settlement, after Josiah Gregg and seven companions tramped over the mountains from the Klamath and Trinity gold fields in 1849 searching for a convenient sea transport link to the mining regions and rediscovered the bay, going on to rediscover Humboldt Bay as well.

Like Eureka and Arcata, Trinidad became an important base and supply port for the inland gold fields, with schooners bringing supplies up from San Francisco and returning with redwood lumber from the north coast forests.

Orientation & Information
The town is very small and it's easy to get your bearings here. Taking the Trinidad exit from Hwy 101 brings you to the town's major intersection, the corner of Main St, Patrick's Point Drive, and Scenic Drive, where an information kiosk is stocked with free town maps and tourist brochures. The *Discover Trinidad* brochure has a good town map showing hiking trails on Trinidad Head and Trinidad State Beach.

From this corner, Patrick's Point Drive heads north along coastal bluffs past motels, campgrounds, and B&Bs to Patrick's Point State Park. Scenic Drive heads south to Luffenholtz Beach. Or, if you go about three blocks straight ahead on Main St, you come to the entrance to Trinidad State Park.

Things to See & Do
Several attractive hiking trails are at **Trinidad State Beach** and **Trinidad Head**; the free town map from the information kiosk shows where they are. The state beach, on an exceptionally beautiful cove, has picnic areas and is for day use only. The Trinidad Head trail, with a fine view of the coastline and excellent whale watching in season, starts from the parking lot at the base of the head.

The **Trinidad Memorial Lighthouse** is at the corner of Trinity and Edwards Sts, on a bluff overlooking Trinidad Bay. Two blocks further down Edwards St towards Trinidad Head, is the **Humboldt State University Marine Laboratory** (☎ 826-3671). Half a block inland from the lighthouse, the **Trinidad Museum** (☎ 677-0227) at 529-B Trinity St is open from May to October on weekends from 1 to 4 pm.

Scenic Drive, which is indeed on a very scenic drive along the coastal bluffs, passes several tiny coves with a view back towards Trinidad Bay for two miles before opening onto the long, broad expanse of **Luffenholtz Beach**, which further south is called Little River State Beach and then Clam Beach County Park. The long, regular waves at Luffenholtz Beach make it a popular surfing beach; surfers can also be seen in the waves at Trinidad State Beach. North of town, along Patrick's Point Drive, you can see and hear California sea lions barking on the rocks just offshore.

Trinidad is famous for its good fishing. Sport fishing trips can be arranged through Bob's Boat Basin & Gift Shop (☎ 677-3625), Salty's Sporting Goods (☎ 677-3874), Shenandoah Charters (☎ 677-3344), and Trinidad Bay Charters (☎ 839-4743, 800-839-4744). The harbor is at the bottom of Edwards St, at the foot of Trinidad Head.

Places to Stay
Camping & Cottages Five miles north of town, Patrick's Point State Park is excellent for camping. On Patrick's Point Drive, heading north from town along the coast, the *Deer Lodge Campground* (☎ 677-3554) at No 753 and the *Viewcrest Lodge Campground* (☎ 677-3393) at No 3415 have tent/RV sites for $12/16; Viewcrest Lodge also has nine cottages from $48.50 to $120 in summer, with discounts off-season. Closer in, the *Hidden Creek RV Park* (☎ 677-3775) at 199 N Westhaven Drive, just east of Hwy 101 at the Trinidad exit, has tent/RV sites for $12/19.

The *Bishop Pine Lodge* (☎ 677-3314) at 1481 Patrick's Point Drive is a peaceful, old fashioned place with 13 cottages for $60/50 in summer/winter, $8 more with kitchen; one two-bedroom cottage is $80 year round.

Motels The *Trinidad Inn* (☎ 677-3349) at 1170 Patrick's Point Drive has rooms from $40 to $55 year round, with kitchens available on request. The *Sea Cliff Motel* (☎ 677-3485) at 1895 Patrick's Point Drive has four rooms; with/without kitchen at $46/40 in summer, $4 less in winter. *Patrick's*

CALIFORNIA

Point Inn (☎ 677-3483) at 3602 Patrick's Point Drive has 10 rooms at $50 to $80 in summer, $40 to $60 in winter.

B&Bs Trinidad has three excellent B&Bs. Right in town, overlooking the harbor and Trinidad Head, the *Trinidad Bay B&B* (☎ 677-0840) at 560 Edwards St has four rooms in an attractive Cape Cod-style home from $105 to $155. The *Lost Whale Inn* (☎ 677-3425) at 3452 Patrick's Point Drive has eight rooms, five with ocean view, for $120 to $150 in summer, $100 to $130 in winter. Trinidad's newest B&B, the *Turtle Rocks Inn* (☎ 677-3707) at 3392 Patrick's Point Drive has spacious ocean view rooms with glassed-in decks for $90 to $155.

Places to Eat

The *Larrupin' Cafe* (☎ 677-0230), north of town at 1658 Patrick's Point Drive, is Trinidad's most famous restaurant; people drive from everywhere in the area to come and eat here. The ambiance is comfortable and the varied international menu features many mesquite-grilled specialties. It's open for dinner Thursday to Monday from 5 to 9 pm; reservations recommended. On Luffenholtz Beach, about two miles south of town, *Merryman's* (☎ 677-3111) at 100 Moonstone Beach Rd is a popular upscale dinner house right on the beach, with great sunset views.

At the harbor, the *Seascape Restaurant* (☎ 677-3862), specializing in seafood, is open every day from 7 am to 9 pm. In town, the *Trinidad Bay Eatery & Gallery* at the corner of Trinity and Parker Sts is pleasant for breakfast and lunch.

Getting There & Away

Trinidad is served by Redwood Transit System buses; see the Eureka section for details.

PATRICK'S POINT STATE PARK

Patrick's Point State Park (☎ 707-677-3570) at 4150 Patrick's Point Drive is a beautiful 640-acre park on a coastal bluff jutting out into the Pacific.

The park's many features include the long, broad Agate Beach where people collect sea-polished agates on the sand; the Rim Trail, a two-mile walk along the bluffs all around the edge of the point, with access to several rocky outcrops excellent for whale-watching in season; a nature trail and several other hiking trails, some on and around unusual rock formations including Ceremonial Rock and Lookout Rock; extensive tidepools at Palmer's Point, Abalone Point, and Agate Beach; a native plant garden, and colonies of seals and sea lions. Also very interesting is Sumeg, a replica of a traditional Yurok Indian village, with traditional-style Yurok buildings of hand-hewn redwood, where Native Americans come to hold traditional ceremonies; you are welcome to walk around the village and to enter the buildings.

The park has three campgrounds, all with hot showers and attractive, secluded sites. The Abalone and Penn Creek campgrounds are sheltered under trees, while the Agate campground, overlooking Agate Beach, has sites open to the sun. Day use is $5.

HUMBOLDT LAGOONS STATE PARK

Humboldt Lagoons State Park (☎ 707-488-2041, 677-3570) stretches for miles along the coast, with long sandy beaches and three large coastal lagoons – Big Lagoon, Stone Lagoon, and Freshwater Lagoon – all excellent for bird watching. There's drive-in camping in a cypress grove beside Big Lagoon; campsites with flush toilets and cold water, but no showers, are $10 a night. Further north at Stone Lagoon, a boat-in campground beside the lagoon has six primitive campsites for $7 per night.

ORICK

• *pop 6500* ☎ *707*

The tiny town of Orick is unremarkable in itself, but the Redwood National & State Parks Information Center here is highly recommended for a stop if you're heading north. Some of the parks' most attractive features, including Lady Bird Johnson Grove, Tall Trees Grove, and Fern Canyon, are not far from Orick.

The Redwood National & State Parks Information Center (☎ 488-3461), beside the beach on Hwy 101 a mile south of town, is a great source of maps and information about the parks; it's here you can pick up your free permit to visit Tall Trees Grove in Redwood National Park.

Two miles north of town, *Rolf's Park Cafe* (☎ 488-3841) on Hwy 101 at the corner of Davison Rd, the turnoff for Fern Canyon, is operated by a German chef, Rolf Rheinschmidt, and his sons Stefan and Gerry. People travel far out of their way to come and eat here; the food is magnificent, with a menu of many unusual dishes including elk, buffalo, and wild boar, plus a wide variety of German and seafood dishes, with generous portions and interesting selections for all meals. Their winter break is from December 1 to February 15. Rolf's also operates eight motel rooms, with singles/doubles for $28/38.

REDWOOD NATIONAL PARK

Special attractions of this 177-sq-mile park include the Lady Bird Johnson Grove and Tall Trees Grove.

The **Lady Bird Johnson Grove**, where this national park was dedicated, features an easy one-mile loop trail. To get to the grove, turn east off Hwy 101 onto Bald Hills Rd and go 2½ miles.

Further along on Bald Hills Rd, **Tall Trees Grove** is a remarkable redwood grove with several of the world's tallest trees. Only 35 vehicles are allowed in to visit the grove each day; pick up a free permit from the park information center at Orick. A shuttle bus service from the visitors center to the grove sometimes operates in summer.

Several longer hiking trails, including the beautiful 8.5-mile **Redwood Creek Trail**, also allow access to Tall Trees Grove. A free backcountry permit, available at the park visitors center, is required to hike this trail, and it can only be done from late May to late September, when summer footbridges are in place. Or you can come on horseback – Tall Trees Outfitters (☎ 707-488-5785), based three miles north of

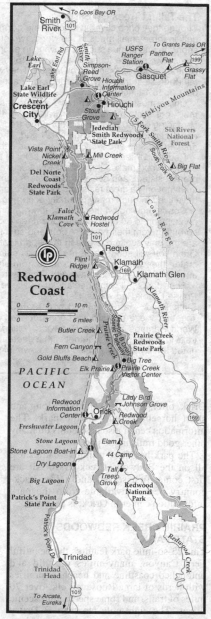

The Tallest Trees On Earth

Though they once covered much of the northern hemisphere, today redwood trees grow only in three small areas of the world, two of them in California and one in China, with a separate and unique species growing in each of these places. Coast redwoods *(Sequoia sempervirens)* are found in a narrow 450-mile-long strip along the Pacific Coast from central California to southern Oregon. They can live up to 2200 years, grow to 367.8 feet tall (the tallest tree ever recorded), and achieve a diameter of 22 feet at the base, with bark up to 12 inches thick.

Unlike most trees which have a deep taproot, coast redwoods have no taproot and their root system is shallow in relation to their height – only 10 to 13 feet deep and spreading out 60 to 80 feet around the tree. The structure of coast redwoods has been compared to a nail standing on its head. The trees sometimes fall due to wind, but they are very flexible and sway in the wind as if they're dancing.

Redwood trees are named for the color of their wood and bark. The high tannin content of their wood makes it resistant to insects and disease; the thick, spongy bark is even more resistant, and has a high moisture content. The bark insulates the trees and gives them not only a great resistance to insects and disease but also to fire; ancient redwoods have lived through many naturally-occurring forest fires during their long lifetimes.

Cones growing on the ends of the branches are about the size of an olive and each contains up to 50 or 60 seeds. Coast redwoods reproduce not only by seed, but also by sprouting from their parent's roots and stumps, using the established root systems; they are the only coniferous tree in the world that can reproduce by sprouts as well as seed. Often you will see a circle of redwoods standing in a forest, sometimes around a wide crater; these are trees that sprouted from one parent tree, which may have deteriorated into compost long ago, leaving the ring of trees standing to form the next generation.

Four parks, all with spectacular redwood forests – Redwood National Park and the Prairie Creek Redwoods, Del Norte Coast Redwoods, and Jedediah Smith Redwoods State Parks – are managed cooperatively as the Redwood National & State Parks. Together these parks have been declared an International Biosphere Reserve and a World Heritage Site. The *Redwood National Park Trail Guide* pamphlet shows hiking trails in all four parks, together with a general map and information about each trail. Each of the three state parks also has its own information center with more detailed maps. ∎

Orick, offers pack trips and other long and short horseback tours in the park. The information center also has details on many other good trails in the park.

The park has three primitive campsites, all on the Redwood Creek Trail. All are first come, first served and a free backcountry permit, available from the park information center in Orick, is required.

PRAIRIE CREEK REDWOODS STATE PARK

This 23-sq-mile park features the beautiful Fern Canyon, many miles of wild and untouched coastline and beaches, prairies with herds of large Roosevelt elk, over 70 miles of trails, and some spectacular scenic drives. The eight-mile **Newton B Drury**

Scenic Parkway, passing through amazingly beautiful virgin redwood forests, runs parallel to Hwy 101 and is well worth taking. Along the way are many turnouts, with hiking trails branching off for endless explorations through the forest. **Big Tree**, near the south end of the parkway, is just 100 yards down a paved path from the parking area beside the road. Other scenic drives in the park include the **Coastal Drive** heading past Gold Bluffs Beach to **Fern Canyon.**

Fern Canyon is an enchanting canyon with sheer 60-foot-high walls covered with several species of ferns. An easy half-mile loop trail takes you through the canyon and up into some fine redwoods. Fern Canyon is right beside the beach, about 1½ miles

Man vs Redwood

In the past 150 years, what nature hadn't already done to reduce the range of the coast redwood, man has helped do. California's Gold Rush of the 1850s is well known; lesser known is the fact that a similar 'timber rush' was going on at the same time on the north coast. The ancient redwood forests were decimated for lumber to build California's new settlements, including San Francisco.

Timber continues to be the primary industry on the north coast, though it's been drastically reduced in recent times. Most of the ancient forests are gone now; those that remain are largely found in state and national parks; only about 6000 acres of unprotected old-growth redwood forest remains. Conflict between environmentalists and loggers continues to rage on the north coast, as people see the forest in different ways. In 1918 the Save-the-Redwoods League began working to preserve the last remnants of the old growth redwood forests for future generations, buying old growth groves from the lumber companies and dedicating them as state and national parks and reserves. Today the league (☎ (415) 362-2352), 114 Sansome St, Room 605, San Francisco, CA 94104, is still working to protect the last remaining virgin redwood forests. Other groups also work to protect the great trees; the Save-the-Redwoods League will have information about them. ■

Coast redwoods (left) are taller and narrower than their inland counterpart, the Giant sequoia (right).

north of the Gold Bluffs Beach campground; there's a $5 day-use fee. To get to Fern Canyon, turn west from Hwy 101 onto Davison Rd, follow a gravel road for four miles until you reach the beach, then go another four miles north along the beach road.

This park has 28 hiking trails, ranging from very easy to strenuous. Several short, easy trails including the Five-Minute Trail, the Revelation Trail, the Nature Trail, and the Elk Prairie Trail begin at the Elk Prairie Visitor Center.

Other notable trails include the easy Fern Canyon loop trail, the easy Coastal Trail, the moderate Ossagon Trail, and the strenuous Zigzag Trail No 1. The South Fork-Rhododendron-Brown Creek Loop is especially wonderful in spring when the rhododendrons and other wildflowers are in bloom; do it in the Brown Creek-Rhododendron-South Fork direction.

The Prairie Creek Visitor Center (☎ 707-488-2171), on the south part of the Newton B Drury Scenic Parkway six miles north of Orick, is open daily in summer.

The park has two developed campgrounds, two backcountry campsites and one environmental campsite. *Elk Prairie*, an attractive, developed campground with hot showers, is in the redwoods beside Elk Prairie, where herds of Roosevelt elk can often be seen, just off the south end of the Newton B Drury Scenic Parkway.

Gold Bluffs Beach, the other developed campground with hot showers, is on the beach about 1½ miles south of Fern Canyon. The campsites are open and exposed, but windbreaks have been erected around many of the sites.

KLAMATH
• *pop 200* ☎ *707*

Besides the Klamath River, the town of Klamath's most noticeable landmark is the giant redwood carving of Paul Bunyan and Babe the Blue Ox towering over the parking area at the entrance to the **Trees of Mystery** (☎ 482-2251, 800-638-3389) on Hwy 101, five miles north of the Klamath River Bridge. The featured attraction here is a 30- to 45-minute walk along a trail passing a number of unusual trees, more redwood carvings and other oddities; cost for the walk is $6/3. It's free, though, and worth a stop even if you don't want to do the walk, the **End of the Trail Museum** is an outstanding museum of American Indian arts, crafts, and other artifacts.

Klamath River Jet Boat Tours (☎ 482-7775, 800-887-5387) offers jet boat tours of the Klamath River from May through October, with morning, afternoon, lunch, and dinner trips. The trip is fully narrated, with plenty of stops for photos of remarkable views and the abundant wildlife including bears, elk, deer, otters, mink, eagles, osprey, and hawks, and seals and sea lions at the river mouth.

Klamath has a drive-through tree, called the **Tour-Thru Tree**, 400 yards off the highway; access to the tree is during daylight hours and it costs $2 to drive through. This is one of several such trees at various places along Hwy 101.

Fishing is good in the Klamath River. The **Salmon Festival** in August, with a salmon barbecue and traditional Yurok Indian arts, crafts, and dances, is hosted by the Yuroks and is Klamath's major event of the year. The World Championship Jet Boat Races are held on the Klamath River, at Klamath

The Klamath Chamber of Commerce (☎ 800-200-2335) has information on attractions and events in Klamath.

Places to Stay & Eat
Camping & Cabins Redwood National Park has a few campgrounds in the Klamath area; the park map shows where they are. The *Mystic Forest RV Park* (☎ 482-4901) at 15875 Hwy 101, about three quarters of a mile south of the Trees of Mystery, has hot showers, a spa, swimming pool, and rec room, with tent/RV spaces for $12/15. The *Chinook RV Resort* (☎ 482-3511) at 17465 Hwy 101, 1½ miles north of the Klamath River Bridge, has tent/RV spaces for $16. *Camp Marigold* (☎ 482-3585, 800-621-8513) at 16101 Hwy 101, four miles north of the Klamath River bridge, is a charming, relaxed, old fashioned little resort with cabins-with-kitchen, a six-bedroom lodge, and camping. Cabins range from $35 to $55, cheaper off-season or by the week; the lodge is $135 a night; and tent/RV spaces are $10/12 in a separate camping area, with free hot showers and full hook-ups available.

The *Riverwoods Campground* (☎ 482-5591), on the south bank of the Klamath River at 1661 W Klamath Beach Rd, two miles west of Hwy 101, is bordered by Redwood National Park on three sides and by the Klamath River on the fourth side; tent/RV sites are $11/13.

Hostel The HI *Redwood Hostel* (☎ 482-8265) at 14480 Hwy 101, is in the large, historic DeMartin House on the coast overlooking the beautiful False Klamath Cove. It adjoins a couple of fine hiking trails including the Coast Trail and the Redwood Hostel Trail. Bunks in separate-sex dorm rooms are $10 a night; reservations are advised, as this is a very popular place. Check-in is from 4:30 to 11 pm; the hostel is closed each day from 9:30 am to 4:30 pm and there's an 11 pm curfew.

Motels On Hwy 101 opposite the Trees of Mystery, *Motel Trees* (☎ 482-3152) has a tennis court, restaurant, and 23 rooms for $40/44 single/double.

The *Requa Inn* (☎ 482-8205) at 451 Requa Rd, west of Hwy 101 on the north bank of the Klamath River, is a famous country inn that has operated here throughout an eventful history ever since 1885. Its 10 rooms are $70 to $95 including breakfast; the restaurant, a local favorite (reservations recommended), is open for dinner every night, except during January, when the inn is closed.

DEL NORTE COAST REDWOODS STATE PARK

This 7000-acre park contains beautiful redwood groves and eight miles of unspoiled coastline. Over 30 miles of hiking trails range from half a mile to 20 miles in length, and in difficulty from easy to strenuous. Several trails begin at the Mill Creek Campground; others at the beach and picnic area at False Klamath Cove, where the hostel is situated. **Endert's Beach** on the north end of the park, accessible from Enderts Beach Rd or the Last Chance/ Coastal Trail, has magnificent tidepools at low tide, as does **Hidden Beach**, about two miles south of False Klamath Cove, accessible by the Coastal Trail or the Hidden Beach Trail.

Maps and information about the park are available at the Redwood National & State Parks Headquarters in Crescent City and at the Redwood National & State Parks Information Center in Orick.

Mill Creek Campground (☎ 707-464-9533), a developed campground with hot showers and 145 campsites, is in a beautiful redwood grove 2½ miles east of Hwy 101; the turnoff is about seven miles south of Crescent City. The campground is open all year, but may be closed at times in winter due to snow and ice. The park also has a couple of primitive campgrounds.

CRESCENT CITY

• *pop 8800* ☎ *707*

On a crescent-shaped bay, Crescent City is the only sizable coastal town north of Arcata. Although Crescent City has been here since 1853, when it was founded as a port and supply center for inland gold mines, it has very few old buildings, as over half the town was destroyed by a tsunami (tidal wave) in 1964. It's all been rebuilt now and it's a pleasant enough place when the sun is shining. Like the rest of the north coast, however, Crescent City is often socked in by fog in the summer, and cold and wet in winter, with about 100 inches of rain falling annually. Fishing (including shrimp and crab) and the Pelican Bay maximum security state prison just outside town are the town's main economic bases.

Orientation & Information

It's virtually impossible to get lost in Crescent City's small 'downtown' area. Highway 101 passes along the east side of town, with southbound traffic on L St and northbound traffic on M St. The tiny commercial area is centered along 3rd St.

The Crescent City-Del Norte County Chamber of Commerce (☎ 464-3174, 800-343-8300) at 1001 Front St has free town maps and plenty of information on the surrounding areas.

The Redwood National & State Parks Headquarters (☎ 464-6101), 1111 2nd St at the corner of K St, has free maps and information about all of the four parks under its jurisdiction.

The post office is at the corner of 2nd and H Sts.

Things to See & Do

The **Battery Point Lighthouse** (☎ 464-3089) at the south end of A St, built in 1856, is still in operation on a tiny, picturesque little offshore island which you can easily walk to at low tide. From April through September the lighthouse is open as a museum, with tours for $2, Wednesday to Sunday from 10 am to 4 pm, tide permitting.

The **Del Norte Historical Society Museum** (☎ 464-3922) at 577 H St at 6th St has historical exhibits including a fine collection of local Tolowa and Yurok Indian artifacts, exhibits on Del Norte County's pioneer past, the '64 tsunami and many other aspects of the county's history. The museum is open May through September, closed Sundays; admission is $1.50.

About a quarter mile south of town, **Undersea World** (☎ 464-3522), 304 Hwy 101 S, is a small aquarium with nothing of the impressive magnitude of some of California's other coastal aquariums. But if you're not too jaded by visits to more lavish aquariums, a visit here is very enjoyable, with the friendly staff taking you on an informative 45-minute guided tour of the aquarium, explaining all about the local marine life. Admission is $6.

You can see cheese being made at the **Rumiano Cheese Company** (☎ 465-1535) at the corner of 9th and E Sts, with a cheese tasting room open weekdays in summer, with shortened hours in winter.

Special Events
Special events in and near Crescent City include the World Championship Crab Races, the third weekend in February; the Redwood Country Open Fiddle Contest at the Del Norte County Fairgrounds in April; the Crescent City Bay Blues Festival with invited microbreweries at Beachfront Park in early June; Easter in July, celebrating the lily bloom at Smith River, seven miles north of Crescent City; the *Del Norte County Fair* in August; and Seafest in September. The *Sea Cruise Classic Car Show* has over 50 classes of car-show competition, plus music, dance, food, and brews the first weekend in October.

Places to Stay
Camping There's plenty of good camping in the state parks near Crescent City. Otherwise, *Florence Keller Park* (☎ 464-7230) has camping and picnic areas in a beautiful

---

Crescent City's Great Tsunami
On March 28, 1964, most of downtown Crescent City was destroyed by a great tidal wave, more accurately, a tsunami. Here's how it happened.

At 3:36 am a giant earthquake – at 8.5 on the Richter scale the most severe earthquake ever recorded in North America – occurred in Alaska on the north shore of Prince William Sound. The first of the giant ocean swells created by the earthquake reached Crescent City a few hours later. Altogether there were four waves, each higher than the last. The swells were so huge that they did not stand up like ordinary waves on the shore; when each one came, it simply seemed as if the level of the entire ocean was rising.

The third wave came almost up into the town. By this time the residents were awake, had heard about the Alaska earthquake and were fearful of what might happen; when the third wave receded some of the residents rejoiced, thinking the danger was over. Then a very eerie thing happened: the water in the bay receded to such an extent that the entire bay was empty of water, leaving boats that had been anchored offshore sitting in the mud. This was caused by the suction in the trough of the fourth wave, as it approached the town.

When the fourth wave surged in, the frigid water moved powerfully, rising all the way up to 5th St. It knocked buildings off their foundations, carried away cars, trucks, and anything that wasn't bolted down, and even a lot of things that were. Many residents stayed in their houses as they floated off their foundations, adrift.

By the time the fourth wave receded, it had destroyed 29 blocks of the town, damaging or displacing over 300 buildings. Five bulk gasoline storage tanks exploded; 11 people were killed and three are still missing.

In the wake of the tsunami, the townspeople came together to help one another, and aid poured in. Many old-timers are still remembered for their heroic acts during and after the wave, helping to save their neighbors and to rebuild the town.

Today you can still see the effects of the tsunami that changed the town forever. In odd places you may come upon a giant piling weighing several tons, washed up onto land and left where it lay.

This is why, although Crescent City is an historic town, there are virtually no historic buildings to be seen here. The waterfront is now a broad, grassy expanse of park. And the modern little downtown shopping center, built to replace some of the town's old businesses, has an unusual but very appropriate name – Tsunami Landing. ■

redwood grove, with campsites for $10. To get there, take Hwy 101 north from town for three miles, take the Hwy 199 exit west (left), going over the freeway, and follow the signs.

Five miles north of town, the *Crescent City Redwoods KOA* (☎ 464-5744) at 4241 Hwy 101 N is a 21-acre campground with 10 acres of redwoods and many amenities including hot showers, laundry, recreation areas, nature trails, and more. Summer/ winter rates are $19/16 for tents, $23/20 for RVs, $35/29 for one-room 'kamping kabins' and $40/34 for two-room 'kamping kabins.' It's often closed in January and February.

Motels A great many motels line Hwy 101 around town. Beware of highway noise at these places.

Half a mile south of town, the *Curly Redwood Lodge* (☎ 464-2137) at 701 Hwy 101 S is a pleasant, comfortable older motel opposite the harbor with covered parking and large, attractive rooms for $60/37 in summer/winter. The entire motel was built from the lumber from just one curly redwood tree; a brochure at the desk tells the story. Next door, the *Super 8 Motel* (☎ 464-1111) at 685 Hwy 101 S has rooms for $60 in summer, $42.50/45 single/double in winter; it's not as attractive but some of the rooms face away from the highway.

The *Crescent Beach Motel* (☎ 464-5436) at 1455 Hwy 101 S, two miles south of town on a pleasant stretch of beach, has 27 rooms, most facing the beach with ocean views and patios, for $58/45 in summer/ winter. Also south of town, the *Bay View Inn* (☎ 465-2050, 800-446-0583) at 310 Hwy 101 S has pleasant rooms for $59/49.

In town, off the highway and hence quieter, the *El Patio Budget Motel* (☎ 464-5114) at 655 H St is a basic, inexpensive motel with 24 rooms, including some family rooms and some with kitchen; singles/doubles are $30/32 in summer, $25/27 in winter.

B&Bs The *Lighthouse Cove B&B* (☎ 465-6565) at 215 S A St, near the Battery Point

Lighthouse, has a suite for $150 with a glassed-in oceanfront sitting room, spacious outdoor deck and fine view overlooking the sea.

Places to Eat

Glen's Restaurant & Bakery at the corner of 3rd and G Sts is a bright and cheerful place for breakfast, lunch, or an early dinner. Old fashioned and friendly, this is one of the town's old favorites; it was situated at 1238 2nd St from October 1947 until the 1964 tidal wave moved it to its present location. It's open Tuesday to Saturday from 6:30 am to 6:30 pm.

Alias Jones Cafe & Bakery at 983 3rd St has espresso drinks and hot meals or baked goods for breakfast, hot and cold sandwiches, salads, and burgers for lunch; closed Sundays. *Cafe Clyde* at 260 I St, open for lunch and dinner, is a coffeehouse with live music Wednesday to Saturday nights, starting around 8:30 pm.

About a mile north of town at the corner of Hwy 101 and Northcrest Drive, the *Good Harvest Espresso Bar & Cafe* is known for its good, healthy food; it's open for breakfast and lunch. Also north of town is *Rowland's Coffee Shop & Restaurant* at 400 Hwy 101 N.

The *Da Lucciana Ristorante Italiano* (☎ 465-6566) at 105 N St, just off Hwy 101, is a favorite with locals for seafood, steaks, and Italian food; it's open for dinner every night from 5 pm, reservations recommended. Half a mile south of town and one block west of Hwy 101, the *Harbor View Grotto* (☎ 464-3815) at the corner of Citizens Dock Rd and Starfish Way (follow the signs from Hwy 101), with a view overlooking the harbor, is popular for seafood, steak, prime rib, and simpler fare.

The *Hunan Plaza Royal Restaurant* (☎ 465-3456) at 1193 2nd St, on the corner of 2nd and L Sts, is good for Chinese food.

Getting There & Away

Air North of town, the small Crescent City airport is served by United Express (☎ 800-241-6522).

CALIFORNIA

Bus The Greyhound bus station (☎ 464-2807) at 500 E Harding Ave, just east of Northcrest Drive about a mile north of the downtown area, has two northbound and two southbound buses daily.

Locally, Redwood Coast Transit (☎ 464-9314, 464-4314) operates a bus route between Crescent City, Klamath, and Redwood National Park, with many stops along the way. The bus makes two runs daily, Monday to Saturday.

Car Car rental companies in Crescent City include Enterprise (☎ 464-4228, 800-325-8007) and U-Save Auto Rental (☎ 464-7813, 800-272-8728).

JEDEDIAH SMITH REDWOODS STATE PARK

About five miles northeast of Crescent City, Jedediah Smith Redwoods is the northernmost of California's redwood state parks. A few miles inland, at the confluence of the Smith River and Mill Creek, it's often sunny here in summer, when Crescent City on the coast is socked in with fog.

A lovely picnic area on the bank of the Smith River is near the campground and a fine swimming hole; the easy half-mile **Stout Grove Trail**, departing from the other side of the campground and crossing the river over a summer footbridge, takes you to **Stout Grove**, the park's most famous redwood grove. Several other trails can also be started near the campground and picnic area; altogether the park has 19 hiking trails, ranging in length from half a mile to eight miles and in difficulty from easy to strenuous.

Park rangers lead guided inflatable kayak trips down the Smith River in summer; prices are economical and the trips are very popular. Lunker Fish Trips (☎ 707-458-4704, 800-248-4704) at 2095 Hwy 199 in Hiouchi rents innertubes, rafts, and inflatable kayaks in summer; they also rent mountain bikes and in fall, winter, and spring they offer guided wilderness and fishing trips for salmon, steelhead, and cutthroat trout on the Smith, Eel, Klamath, and Mattole Rivers (all 'big fish' rivers).

Maps and information about the park are available at the Hiouchi Information Center (☎ 707-458-3310, 464-9533) on Hwy 199 in Hiouchi, about five miles east of Hwy 101; Hwy 199 meets Hwy 101 three miles north of Crescent City. The center has exhibits including historic photos and a Tolowa Indian canoe; it's open May through October. You can tune your radio to 1610 AM in this area and get information about the park. Information and maps are also available at the Redwood National & State Parks Headquarters in Crescent City.

Places to Stay

The *Jedediah Smith Campground*, in a beautiful redwood grove beside the Smith River on Hwy 199 about five miles east of Hwy 101, is a developed campground with hot showers and 107 campsites.

The *Hiouchi Motel* (☎ 458-3041) at 2097 Hwy 199 in Hiouchi has 17 rooms for $27/45 single/double.

LAKE EARL STATE WILDLIFE AREA

Half a mile north of Crescent City, Lake Earl State Wildlife Area includes 5000 acres of wildlife habitat in a varied terrain with beaches, sand dunes, marshes and other wetlands, meadows, wooded hillsides, and two lakes: Lake Earl and the smaller Lake Talawa, connected to Lake Earl by a narrow waterway.

Wildlife here include over 250 species of birds, with resident as well as migrating birds; deer, coyote, raccoons, sea lions, seals, and migrating California gray whales can also be seen here. Cutthroat trout can be caught in the lakes. Wildflowers are a special attraction in spring and early summer. The park has about 20 miles of hiking and horseback trails, most of them level and sandy.

The Lake Earl State Park Headquarters (☎ 707-464-9533) at 1375 Elk Valley Rd has maps and information about the park, as does the Lake Earl Wildlife Area Headquarters (☎ 707-464-2523) at 2591 Old Mill Rd. A free park map is also available at the chamber of commerce in Crescent City.

The park has two primitive campgrounds: one a walk-in where you must provide your own water, the other a walk-in and equestrian site with non-potable water. Both are quiet and private; cost is $7 per site.

NORTH TO OREGON

From Crescent City there are two routes going north into Oregon. Highway 101, the coast highway, crosses into Oregon about 20 miles north of Crescent City and continues up the coast towards Brookings and Coos Bay.

Three miles north of Crescent City, Hwy 199 branches off from Hwy 101 and heads northeast into Oregon by an inland route towards Cave Junction and Grants Pass, where it meets I-5. On the way, Hwy 199 goes along the middle fork of the Smith River, passing first through **Jedediah Smith Redwoods State Park** and then continuing on through the **Smith River National Recreation Area** (see the Northern Mountains chapter). This route has been dubbed the **Smith River National Scenic Byway**, and it is indeed scenic; free brochures about the route and about the national recreation area, with its hiking trails, camping, etc are available from the park office on Hwy 199 at Gasquet, a few miles beyond Hiouchi.

Consult Lonely Planet's *Pacific Northwest USA – a travel survival kit* (1995) if you're heading up into Oregon.

Central Coast

California's central coast stretches from Monterey Bay to Ventura Harbor, 273 miles of unadulterated beauty perched at the continent's edge.

Monterey Peninsula

Spectacular coastal scenery, a colorful history as the old Spanish and Mexican capital of California, a superb aquarium, and lots of money all come together on the Monterey Peninsula, jutting into the Pacific just over 100 miles south of San Francisco. Historic Monterey and easy going Pacific Grove at the north of the peninsula are linked by the scenic 17-Mile Drive to the wealthy little enclave of Carmel to the south. Beyond Carmel the wild scenery of Point Lobos make a fine introduction to the awesome Big Sur coastline.

MONTEREY BAY

The Monterey Bay is one of the world's richest and most varied marine environments with a majestic coastline, a diverse range of marine life including its famous kelp forests, and the many marine mammals including sea otters, seals and sea lions, elephant seals, dolphins, and whales. The protected waters of the Monterey Bay National Marine Sanctuary extend 50 miles out to sea from San Simeon in the south all the way to San Francisco in the north, where they merge into the Gulf of the Farallon National Marine Sanctuary.

Monterey Bay itself is an extraordinarily rich body of water. Starting only a few hundred yards offshore from Moss Landing the Monterey Canyon plummets to a depth of over 10,000 feet. In summer the upwelling currents carry cold water from this deep submarine canyon, spilling a rich supply of nutrients up towards the surface level to feed the bay's diverse marine life. These frigid currents also account for the bay waters' generally low temperatures and for the fog that often blankets the peninsula during the summer months.

MONTEREY
• *pop 32,000* ☎ 408

California's Spanish and Mexican history is encountered elsewhere but nowhere is evidence of the state's Latin heritage richer than in Monterey. There are numerous

---

Sea Otters

Sea otters are one of the Monterey Bay Aquarium's major attractions but these charming creatures can be found all around the Monterey Bay and as far north as Santa Cruz. Not long ago the sea otter was on the brink of extinction, ruthlessly hunted down by 18th- and 19th-century fur traders because of its exceptionally dense fur. Sea otter fur can have over one million hairs per square inch, the thickest fur of any mammal. The sea otter population was finally reduced to a tiny group on the Big Sur coast but they are now totally protected although the once-plentiful animals only number about 2500 in California.

Sea otters are one of the few animals to use tools. They may be seen floating on their backs using a rock to break open shellfish which they place on their chests. Their playful nature and the relaxed looking way they loll around is what makes them so attractive. Friends of the Sea Otter has a Sea Otter Center (☎ 625-3290) at The Barnyard, just south of Carmel. They organize sea otter spotting trips on Saturdays from April to November. Sea otters can often be seen around the Monterey Bay Aquarium but other good places to see them include the marina wharfs and Fisherman's Wharf in Monterey, several of the rocky points along 17-Mile Drive at Pebble Beach and the Point Lobos Reserve. ■

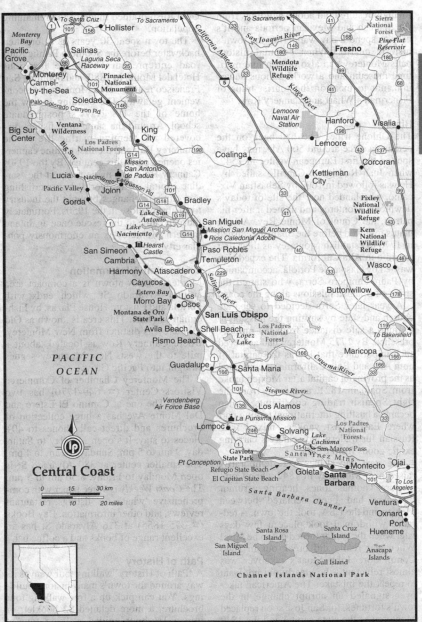

To Santa Cruz
To Sacramento
To Sacramento

Monterey Bay
Pacific Grove
Salinas
Laguna Seca Raceway
Monterey
Carmel-by-the-Sea
Palo-Colorado Canyon Rd
Soledad
Pinnacles National Monument
Hollister

Sierra National Forest
Pine Flat Reservoir
San Joaquin River
Mendota Wildlife Refuge
Fresno
Kings River
Hanford
Visalia
Lemoore
Lemoore Naval Air Station

Big Sur Center
Ventana Wilderness
Big Sur
Los Padres National Forest
King City
Coalinga
Kettleman City
Corcoran
Pixley National Wildlife Refuge

Lucia
Pacific Valley
Gorda
Jolon
Nacimiento-Fergusson Rd
Mission San Antonio de Padua
Bradley
Lake San Antonio
Lake Nacimiento
San Miguel
Mission San Miguel Archangel
Rios Caledonia Adobe
Kern National Wildlife Refuge
Wasco

San Simeon
Cambria
Harmony
Hearst Castle
Atascadero
Paso Robles
Templeton
Salinas River
Buttonwillow

Cayucos
Estero Bay
Morro Bay
Los Osos
Montana de Oro State Park
Avila Beach
Pismo Beach
San Luis Obispo
Shell Beach
Los Padres National Forest
Lopez Lake
To Bakersfield
Maricopa

PACIFIC OCEAN

Guadalupe
Santa Maria
Cuyama River

Vandenberg Air Force Base
Los Alamos
Sisquoc River
Los Padres National Forest

Central Coast

0   15   30 km
0   10   20 miles

Lompoc
La Purisima Mission
Solvang
Lake Cachuma
San Marcos Pass
Santa Ynez Mtns
Montecito
Ojai

Pt Conception
Gaviota State Park
Refugio State Beach
El Capitan State Beach
Goleta
Santa Barbara
To Los Angeles
Santa Barbara Channel
Ventura
Oxnard
Port Hueneme

San Miguel Island
Santa Rosa Island
Santa Cruz Island
Anacapa Islands
Gull Island
Channel Islands National Park

lovingly restored old adobe buildings from the Spanish and Mexican periods and it's easy to spend a day wandering the town's historic quarter. When colonial history palls Monterey can also offer a fine maritime museum and a world-famous aquarium, not to mention the tourist traps of Fisherman's Wharf and Cannery Row.

History

The Ohlone tribe, who had been on the peninsula since around 500 AD, may have spotted the first European visitor in 1542, when Juan Rodriguez Cabrillo sailed by. He was followed in 1602 by Sebastián Vizcaíno, who landed near the site of today's downtown Monterey and named it after his patron, the Count of Monte Rey. A long hiatus followed before the Spanish returned in 1770 to establish Monterey as their first presidio in Alta California. The expedition was led by Gaspar de Portolá, accompanied by Padre Junipero Serra, who started the string of Spanish missions along the coast.

A year later Serra decided to separate church and state by shifting the mission to Carmel, a safe distance from the military presence. By 1775 Monterey had achieved such importance that it was the capital of both Alta and Baja California. It continued as the provincial capital after Mexico broke from Spain in 1821, and freed from the tight Spanish trading constraints it also became a bustling international trading port where East Coast yankees mixed with Russian fur traders and seafarers carrying exotic goods from China.

The stars and stripes were temporarily raised over Monterey in 1842 when Commodore Thomas Jones, hearing a rumor that war had been declared between Mexico and the USA, took the town. A red-faced withdrawal took place a few days later when the rumor turned out to be false! When war really did break out in 1846 Commodore John Sloat's takeover was almost reluctant – he clearly did not want to repeat the mistake. The American takeover signaled an abrupt change in the town's fortunes, for San Jose soon replaced Monterey as the state capital and the 1849 Gold Rush drained much of the remaining population.

The town spent 30 years as a forgotten backwater before the Southern Pacific Railroad entrepreneurs built the luxurious Hotel del Monte in 1880, and booming San Francisco rediscovered Monterey as a convenient getaway. The building is now the home of the US Navy's postgraduate school. Around the same time fishers discovered the teeming marine life in the Monterey Bay and the first sardine canneries opened early this century. By the 1930s Cannery Row had made the port the 'sardine capital of the world' but overfishing and climatic changes brought the industry to an abrupt close in the 1950s. Fortunately tourism came to the rescue once again and modern Monterey is an enormously popular city.

Orientation & Information

Monterey's downtown is a compact area around Alvarado St, which ends with Portola and Custom House Plazas, by Fisherman's Wharf. This area is known as Old Monterey as distinct from New Monterey, where Cannery Row is located, about a mile to the west. New Monterey segues straight into Pacific Grove.

The Monterey Chamber of Commerce Visitors Center (☎ 649-1770) has two offices. The one at Camino El Estero and Del Monte Ave has a huge collection of brochures and direct call phones to 40+ places to stay. It's open Monday to Saturday, 9 am to 5 pm; Sunday, 10 am to 4 pm. The smaller center at 380 Alvarado St is open Monday to Friday, 8:30 am to 5 pm. The *Coast Weekly* is a free paper with comprehensive 'what's on' listings, restaurant reviews, and other information. Bay Books (☎ 375-1855) at 316 Alvarado St has an excellent range of books and a coffee bar.

Path of History

A 'Path of History' walking tour weaves its way around the town's many historic buildings. You can pick up a free walking tour brochure, a more detailed $2 booklet, or join a 1¼-hour guided walking tour at

CALIFORNIA

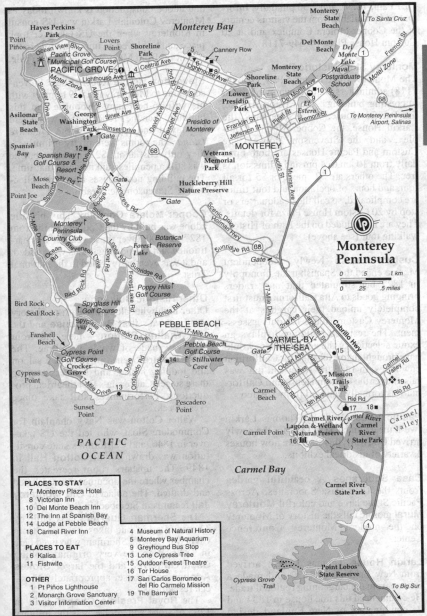

Monterey Bay

To Santa Cruz

Monterey State Beach

Point Piños

Hayes Perkins Park

Lovers Point

Ocean View Blvd
Pacific Grove
Municipal Golf Course

PACIFIC GROVE

Shoreline Park

Cannery Row

Del Monte Beach

Del Monte Lake

To Monterey Peninsula Airport, Salinas

Motel Zone

Fremont St

Lighthouse Ave
Central Ave

Motel Zone
Asilomar Ave
Alder St
Park Ave
Pine St
2nd St
Pine St

Monterey State Beach

Shoreline Park

Monterey State Naval Postgraduate School

El Estero

Sinex Ave
David Ave
Prescott Ave

Asilomar State Beach

George Washington Park

Sunset Drive

Gate

Presidio of Monterey

Lower Presidio Park

Franklin St
Jefferson St

MONTEREY

Del Monte Ave
Dela St
Pearl St
Fremont St

Spanish Bay

Spanish Bay Golf Course & Resort

Moss Beach

Point Joe

Bay Rd
Spanish Bay Dr
17-Mile Drive
Forest Lodge Rd
Congress Rd
Sloat Rd
Gate

Veterans Memorial Park

Huckleberry Hill Nature Preserve

Scenic Drive
Herman Hwy

Pacific St
Munras Ave

Gate

Monterey Peninsula Country Club

Stevenson Drive
Ocean Rd
Bird Rock Rd

Botanical Reserve

Forest Lake

Sunridge Rd
Sunridge Rd

Gate

Monterey Peninsula

Bird Rock
Seal Rock

Spyglass Hill Golf Course

Lopez Rd
Sloat Rd
Forest Lake Rd

Poppy Hills Golf Course

0   .5   1 km
0   .25   .5 miles

Fanshell Beach

Spyglass Hill Rd

Ronda Rd

PEBBLE BEACH

Stevenson Drive
17-Mile Drive

Cabrillo Hwy

2nd Ave
Carpenter St

Cypress Point Golf Course

Crocker Grove

Portola Drive
Ondulado Rd
Drive

Pebble Beach Golf Course
Stillwater Cove

Gate

CARMEL-BY-THE-SEA

Ocean Ave
Junipero Ave
Scenic Dr
8th Ave

15

Cypress Point

17-Mile Drive

13

Pescadero Point

Carmel Beach

Mission Trails Park

Carmel Valley Rd

Rio Rd

19
Rio Rd

Sunset Point

PACIFIC OCEAN

Carmel Point

13th Ave

Carmel River

17
18

Carmel River

Carmel Valley

Carmel River Lagoon & Wetland Natural Preserve

16

Carmel River State Park

Carmel Bay

Carmel River State Park

Point Lobos State Reserve

Cypress Grove Trail

To Big Sur

PLACES TO STAY
7   Monterey Plaza Hotel
8   Victorian Inn
10 Del Monte Beach Inn
12 The Inn at Spanish Bay
14 Lodge at Pebble Beach
18 Carmel River Inn

PLACES TO EAT
6   Kalisa
11 Fishwife

OTHER
1   Pt Piños Lighthouse
2   Monarch Grove Sanctuary
3   Visitor Information Center

4   Museum of Natural History
5   Monterey Bay Aquarium
9   Greyhound Bus Stop
13 Lone Cypress Tree
15 Outdoor Forest Theatre
16 Tor House
17 San Carlos Borromeo
    del Rio Carmelo Mission
19 The Barnyard

10:15 am, 12:30, and 2:30 pm daily. Information is available from the visitors centers at the Cooper-Molera Complex and at 20 Custom House Plaza (☎ 649-7118).

Monterey State Historic Park

The Monterey State Historic Park (☎ 649-7118) administers six of downtown's most interesting buildings: the Custom House, the Pacific House, Casa Soberanes, the Larkin House, the Cooper-Molera Complex, and the Stevenson House. The Custom and Pacific Houses are both open daily from 10 am to 4 pm and admission is free. The others are $2 apiece or $5 for all four, and hours of operation and tour times are complicated, so call the headquarters or stop by 20 Custom House Plaza for details. They are all included on the Path of History walking tour (see above).

Custom House Newly independent Mexico ended the Spanish trade monopoly in 1822 but stipulated that any traders bringing goods to Alta California must first completely unload their cargoes at the Monterey Custom House for duty assessment. The restored building displays an exotic selection of the goods traders would have brought in to exchange for Californian cow hides. In 1846 the American flag was raised over the Custom House and California was formally annexed from Mexico.

Pacific House Built by Thomas Larkin (we'll meet him later) in 1847 for the newly arrived US Army, this structure now houses a variety of historical exhibits.

Casa Soberanes A beautiful garden fronts the 1842 Casa Soberanes. Across Pacific St the large and colorful **Monterey Mural** mosaic tells the history of Monterey on the modern Monterey Conference Center.

Larkin House Thomas Larkin arrived from New England in 1832 and made a fortune from the burgeoning regional trade. He commenced this fine house in 1834 and its combination of New England design and adobe construction is known today as Monterey Colonial. Larkin was US consul in Monterey when the US takeover took place and he played an important role in the transition from Mexican to American rule.

Stevenson House Robert Louis Stevenson came to Monterey in 1879 to meet with his wife-to-be Fanny Osbourne and this building, then the French Hotel, was where he stayed and reputedly wrote *Treasure Island*. The rooms were pretty primitive – they only cost about $2 a month – but he was still a penniless unknown at that time. The building now houses a superb collection of Stevenson memorabilia.

Cooper-Molera Complex This historic adobe was built by the Cooper family from 1827 to 1900. Over those years it was partitioned and extended, gardens were added, and it was eventually willed to the National Trust.

Other Historic Buildings

Other highlights along the Path of History are the town's **first Brick House** and the old **Whaling Station** – note the front walkway made of whale vertebrae. The **First Theatre** opened in 1847 as a saloon and lodging house, and soldiers staying there staged California's first theatrical productions. Performances still take place every week.

Walter Colton was Navy chaplain for Commodore Sloat, who led the US takeover in 1846, and California's state constitution was drawn up in **Colton Hall** in 1849. The upstairs room recreates the chamber where the document was debated and drafted. The adjacent **Old Monterey Jail** features in Steinbeck's *Tortilla Flat*.

The **Sherman Quarters** was built by Thomas Larkin but takes its name from Civil War General Sherman, who lived here in 1847. Both the very original-looking **Casa Gutiérrez** and the larger **Stokes Adobes** now house, appropriately, Mexican restaurants.

The **Royal Presidio Chapel**, built in 1795 of stone and adobe, was the military headquarters of Spanish and Mexican Monterey and the original mission church was built on this site in 1770 but was shifted only a year later to its permanent site in Carmel. Until the 1820s the town was almost all contained within the presidio's fortified walls but as Monterey expanded it all gradually disappeared, leaving the chapel as a sole reminder.

Maritime Museum

The Maritime Museum of Monterey (☎ 373-2469) is in Customs House Plaza. Monterey has a plentiful supply of retired admirals, who regularly donate their naval miscellanea to the museum, so there's an excellent collection including the Fresnel lens of Point Sur Lighthouse, lots of maritime memorabilia, a great ship-in-a-bottle collection, and interesting displays on Monterey's history, particularly the rise, and rapid fall, of the sardine business. The museum is open Tuesday to Sunday, 10 am to 5 pm and entry is $5/3. In July and August it also opens Monday and hours are extended.

Fisherman's Wharf

Like its larger namesake in San Francisco the wharf is a tourist trap at heart, but good fun nevertheless. There's a plentiful supply of restaurants, regular visits by noisy seals, and it's the base for a variety of boat trips including whale watching expeditions.

Monterey Peninsula Museum of Art

The Museum of Art has two centers in Monterey. The branch at 559 Pacific St (☎ 372-5477) has a variety of exhibits with particular emphasis on Californian artists and a superb photographic collection. Housed in the early adobe villa La Mirada (☎ 372-3689), at 720 Via Mirada, the second site has exhibits that explore early Californian history and look at life on the peninsula in the 1920s.

Entry is $3 to each museum or $5 to both. The Pacific St museum is open Wednesday to Saturday 11 am to 5 pm and Sunday 1 to 4 pm. La Mirada has the same

hours but is closed Wednesday as well as Monday and Tuesday.

Cannery Row

John Steinbeck's novel *Cannery Row* immortalized the business that Monterey lived on for the first half of this century. The sardine-canning business really took off during WWI, when supplies of Atlantic sardines were inaccessible, but two-thirds of the catch actually ended up as fertilizer or sardine oil. Predictions that overfishing could decimate the business were ignored when the catch reached a peak of 250,000 tons in 1945 but just five years later the figure had crashed to 33,000 tons and by 1951 most of the sardine canneries had closed down, many of them mysteriously catching fire.

In its heyday Cannery Row was a hectic, noisy, and very smelly place. The cannery bells summoned the workers whenever the ships came in, day or night. Nowadays, Cannery Row is a non-stop enclave of restaurants, bars, and tourist shops. A statue of Steinbeck presides over the new incarnation of his old stamping ground – Laida Café still stands at 851 Cannery Row, but it's now known as Kalisa's.

Monterey Bay Aquarium

Cannery Row's one really worthwhile attraction justifies a trip to the Monterey area all on its own. Opened in 1984, the aquarium (☎ 648-4888) is on the site of Monterey's largest sardine cannery and, apart from temporary displays, its state of the art exhibits are devoted solely to the rich marine life of the Monterey Bay. The aquarium is open daily from 10 am to 6 pm; in summer and on holidays from 9:30 am. Entry is $11.75/5.75 but at peak times there can be long entry lines; there are nearly two million visitors a year. You can get around this problem by obtaining tickets in advance (☎ 800-756-3737 in California) or from many Monterey hotels.

Life-size models of whales and other marine mammals hang from the roof and the aquarium's star exhibits include the gigantic Kelp Forest where seven-inch-thick acrylic panels separates visitors from a third of a million gallons of water. Bay marine life swims between the towering fronds of kelp and feeding takes place at 11:30 am and 4 pm. Children love the tidal pools where they can pick up starfish and other shallow water creatures or the pool where bat rays can be gently stroked. Sea otter feeding time is a prime attraction at 10:30 am, 1:30, and 3:30 pm but these charming animals can often be seen basking in the open Tide Pool outside the aquarium, where they are quite free to come and go. Harbor seals also drop in here.

Opening in 1996 a major extension to the aquarium will include a jellyfish gallery, a plankton gallery with microscopes, and a pioneering deep sea exhibit displaying life from deep in the Monterey Canyon. The aquarium also has an excellent shop and a restaurant.

Activities
Surfing The Monterey Peninsula may have beautiful beaches but the water that laps them is icy cold. Swimming, even in the middle of summer, is strictly for the hardy but there are still plenty of water sports. The peninsula has some great surfing spots, but often not for beginners. Strong rip currents and unpredictable rogue waves lie in wait for the unwary, not to mention those famous sharks. Local surfers vote Asilomar Beach (just south of Pacific Grove) and Moss Landing (north of Monterey and Marina) as having the best and most consistent breaks. For surf gear and rentals head to one of the two On the Beach stores, in Carmel (☎ 624-7282) on Ocean Ave and Mission St, and in Monterey (☎ 646-9283) at 693 Lighthouse Ave.

Scuba Diving The Monterey Bay's famous kelp forest and its rich variety of marine life makes this a renowned scuba diving site. The Aquarius Dive Shop has two waterfront locations, at 32 Cannery Row (☎ 375-1933) and at 2040 Del Monte Ave (☎ 375-1933). Their dives go straight out from the shore and are rated as some of

the best shore dives in the country. Equipment rental costs $50 to $60 and in the bay's chilly waters includes a full wet suit, hood, and gloves. Dives, with a maximum of four people per guide, cost $50 for a single tank dive, $80 for a two-tank dive.

Kayaking Monterey Bay Kayaks (☎ 373-5357) rents open and closed kayaks for $25 a day, offers instruction courses every weekend, and operates a variety of natural history tours. Their 3½-hour Monterey Bay kayaking tours operate on Fridays, Saturdays, and Sundays all year and also on weekdays in the summer and cost $45.

Whale Watching The season is from December to March. Whale-watching boats leave from Fisherman's Wharf and two-hour trips cost around $15.

Bicycling On dry land, cycling is a very popular peninsula activity. The three-mile-long waterfront ride, from Monterey past Fisherman's Wharf and Cannery Row to Pacific Grove, is very popular. Baycycle Tours (☎ 649-1700) operate a variety of half- and full-day bicycle tours from $55 including winery tours, Pebble Beach tours, rides down to Big Sur, and other adventures.

Adventures by the Sea (☎ 372-1807) have outlets at 201 Alvarado St (the waterfront end), at 299 Cannery Row, and at Lovers Point in Pacific Grove. They rent out bicycles for $6 an hour, $18 a half day, or $24 all day and they also rent roller blades and kayaks. There's a bicycle recreation trail right along the waterfront through Monterey. Monterey Moped Adventures (☎ 373-2696) at 1250 Del Monte Ave rents bicycles and mopeds.

Special Events
The Monterey Peninsula is a festive place with a wide range of activities through the year. Popular events include the Monterey Wine Festival (☎ 656-9463) in March and the internationally famed Monterey Jazz Festival (☎ 373-3366) in September; reserve well in advance.

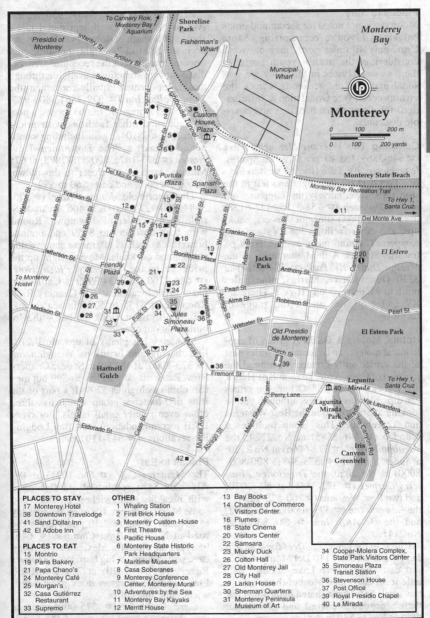

Monterey

Places to Stay

Monterey is not noted for accommodations bargains; if you're economizing, Santa Cruz, only 40 miles north, may be worth considering; the nearest youth hostel is there as well. Prices in Monterey are seasonal and rise on weekends. Check the visitors center (see Orientation & Information) for direct phone bookings and possible discounts.

Camping The *Veterans Memorial Park* (☎ 646-3865) has 40 'primitive' campsites, ie no electricity. Take Hwy 68 west to Skyline Forest Drive then right and left at the stop sign. Alternatively the *Laguna Seca Recreation Area* (☎ 758-3185, 422-6138) has a much bigger site with showers, hookups, and other facilities for RVs and tent campers. It's nine miles east on Hwy 68 towards Salinas. A third alternative is the *Marina Dunes RV Park* (☎ 384-6914) at 3330 Dunes Drive, Marina, nine miles north of Monterey along Hwy 1. There are RV and tent sites and a full range of facilities.

Hotels, Motels & B&Bs A group of economical motels can be found 2½ miles east of the center on N Fremont St around the junction of Casa Verde, just south of Hwy 1 and just east of Hwy 68. Off-season prices can dip as low as $30 here, although you're looking at $60 to $80 in the Best Westerns and Travelodge. This group includes a *Motel 6* (☎ 646-8585) at No 2124; the *Vagabond Motel* (☎ 372-6066) at No 2120; a *Super 8 Motel* (☎ 373-3081, 800-800-8000) at No 2050, the *Travelodge Monterey/Carmel* (☎ 373-3381) at No 2030; and two Best Westerns (☎ 800-528-1234) – the *Ramona Inn* (☎ 373-8000) at No 2332, and the *De Anza Inn* (☎ 646-8300) at No 2141.

Closer to the center the *Del Monte Beach Inn* (☎ 649-4410), 1110 Del Monte Ave, is just east of El Estero Lake, about a half mile from the center. Most of the rooms in this small hotel have shared bathrooms but there's a good breakfast and prices can drop as low as $40 in the low season.

El Adobe Inn (☎ 372-5409), 936 Munras Ave, is a neat and well-kept motel just a short stroll south of downtown. Rooms are normally $82 to $99 a night, including continental breakfast in the reception area, but discounts are sometimes available through the visitors center. Equally convenient the *Sand Dollar Inn* (☎ 372-7551, 800-982-1986), 755 Abrego St, has 63 rooms, a pool and spa, and other facilities with prices from $64 to $104, again including continental breakfast. The *Downtown Travelodge* (☎ 373-1876, 800-578-7878) at 675 Munras Ave is even closer to downtown, also has a pool, and costs $60 to $99.

The historic old *Monterey Hotel* (☎ 375-3184, 800-727-0960) is at 406 Alvarado St right in the center of downtown. Rooms with bath cost $89 to $159 and include breakfast as well as afternoon and evening snacks and cocktails. Moving right up the price scale the *Monterey Plaza Hotel* (☎ 646-1700, 800-334-3999 in California) has a great location at 400 Cannery Row. Rooms cost $155 to $235 in season and they don't just overlook the bay – they're built right out over it.

Monterey has plenty of upscale B&Bs, like the big and luxurious *Victorian Inn* (☎ 373-8000) at 487 Foam St near Cannery Row. Rates may dip as low as $99 but they can climb as high as $299. It's part of the Inns of Monterey group which has three other even pricier small hotels. For other B&B recommendations, call Bay Lodging Reservations at ☎ 647-1107.

Places to Eat

The *Monterey Café* (☎ 646-1021) at 489 Alvarado St is resolutely old fashioned with breakfast, sandwiches, omelets, and some Mexican dishes. It's open Wednesday to Monday, 7 am to 2:30 pm. Across the road at No 462, *Papa Chano's* (☎ 646-9587) is the place for Mexican-style cheap eats, particularly for big burritos. The *Paris Bakery* (☎ 646-1620) at 271 Bonifacio Place and Washington does great sandwiches and fine coffee.

Casa Gutiérrez (☎ 375-0095) serves straightforward and low-priced ($5 to $8)

Mexican dishes in a historic adobe building at the corner of Calle Principal and Madison St. Right across the road at 500 Hartnell St the Stokes Adobe also houses a Mexican restaurant: *Supremo* (☎ 373-3737) makes a noted margarita as well as good food.

There are lots of seafood restaurants along the wharf; you don't even need to pay to eat here as many places offer clam chowder samples out front at meal time.

They treat you right at *Spadaros Ristorante* (☎ 372-8881) at 652 Cannery Row (at Hawthorne St), which serves lunch and dinner every day. Among an Italian menu, the daily special usually includes the day's fresh catch. Very tasty pastas are around $9, other entrees are around $13. The *Sardine Factory* (☎ 373-3775) at 701 Wave St, Cannery Row, has mood rooms with a maritime flair and expensive seafood, which seemed to fill all patrons to happiness.

For expense account dining, or a special occasion, *Fresh Cream* (☎ 375-9798), in the Heritage Harbor complex across from Fisherman's Wharf, serves up delicious Continental dishes with a picture-window view of the wharf. When you walk in, you see about 25 national and local culinary awards lining the walls – and when you eat you understand why: try the lobster ravioli appetizer and the rack of lamb as an entree, while anything you choose from the wine list will be excellent. Entrees are around $30. Dinner is served daily or try lunch on Fridays; reservations are recommended.

You'll hear local folks talking about these places: though the food and decor aren't exactly the same, *Tarpy's Roadhouse* (☎ 647-14443) at 2999 Monterey/Salinas Hwy 1 (at Hwy 68 and Canyon Del Rey); Carmel's *Rio Grill* (☎ 625-5436) at 101 Crossroads Blvd in the mall; and downtown Monterey's *Montrio* (☎ 648-8880) at 414 Calle Principal are owned by the same people and have a similar ambiance. Montrio is definitely the showpiece bistro, and has recently garnered national accolades for it's combination of comfort and California cuisine. (I never knew a barstool could be so inviting!) Brunch at Rio Grill

included a great variation on eggs benedict: two poached on a bed of sauteed spinach greens and wild mushrooms covered in a red pepper cream sauce ($9). Entrees average $12, lunches $9, and are served daily, brunch on Sunday.

Entertainment

Coffeehouses *Morgan's* (☎ 373-5601) at 498 Washington St makes some of the best coffee in town. It's a nice relaxed place with live music. *Samsara* (☎ 373-5282) at 461 Alvarado and *Plumes* (☎ 373-5282) at Alvarado and Franklin Sts are other popular coffee dives.

Bars The *Mucky Duck* (☎ 655-3031) is a very English-looking pub at 479 Alvarado St in downtown Monterey but most of the activity at night is around Cannery Row. *O'Kane's Irish Pub* (☎ 375-7564) on the corner of Prescott Ave and Wave St, is a popular bar especially during the 5 to 7 pm happy hour. *Doc Ricketts' Lab* (☎ 649-4241) at 95 Prescott Ave has live music Thursday to Saturday nights with cover charges typically around $5. The original Doc Ricketts was a pioneering marine scientist, immortalized in Steinbeck's *Cannery Row*. Upstairs on the 3rd floor at 625 Cannery Row, *Planet Gemini* (☎ 373-1449) has live music or, on Thursday to Saturday nights, comedy with a cover charge of $5 or $6.

Theater & Cinema The *First Theatre* (☎ 375-4916) at Pacific and Scott Sts puts on Victorian melodramas in an appropriate venue, the state's first theater. Performances take place September through June on Friday and Saturday nights, July through Labor Day on Wednesday and Thursday as well. Tickets cost $8/5.

Local cinemas include the multi-screen *Galaxy 6* (☎ 655-4617) at 280 Del Monte Center; *Lighthouse Cinemas* (☎ 372-7300) at 525 Lighthouse Ave in Pacific Grove; the fine old *State Cinema* (☎ 372-4555) at 417 Alvarado St; and the *Dream Theater* (☎ 372-1494) at 301 Prescott Ave.

Getting There & Away

Air American Airlines, Delta, and United Airlines operate to Monterey Peninsula Airport and there are direct connections to Los Angeles and San Francisco. The airport is only about three miles from the town center.

Bus Greyhound buses operate twice a day between Los Angeles and San Francisco via Monterey. They stop at the Exxon gas station at 1024 Del Monte Ave, just east of El Estero Lake. Fares are San Francisco $19 one way, $36 roundtrip; Los Angeles $47 one way, $94 roundtrip; Santa Cruz $8.50. Bus services connect with the Amtrak station in Salinas. Stage Coach Express (☎ 657-1881) operates daily between Monterey and San Jose Airport while Monterey-Salinas Airbus (☎ 442-2877) operates to both the San Jose and San Francisco Airports.

Car Monterey is 120 miles south of San Francisco (scenically and slowly by Hwy 1, more quickly by Hwys 101 and 156). If you're heading down the Big Sur coast and you don't already have your own wheels it's worth thinking about renting some. The big rental operators are all represented on the peninsula or there's Rent-a-Wreck (☎ 373-3356) at 95 Central Ave, Pacific Grove. The coast doesn't lend itself to public transport; stopping and starting is what it's all about. Big Sur is just 26 miles south of Monterey

Getting Around

Bus Monterey-Salinas Transit (MST) operates buses around the peninsula, inland to Salinas, and south to Big Sur. The whole peninsula (which includes Monterey, Pacific Grove, and Carmel) counts as one zone and a single journey costs $1.25, or $3.75 for a day pass. From the peninsula south to Big Sur or inland to Salinas costs $2.50. An all-zones day pass is $7.50. The Monterey Transit Plaza at Simoneau Plaza at the south end of Alvarado St is the terminal for Monterey services. Useful routes include Nos 1, 2, or 14 to downtown Pacific Grove; No 1 goes via Cannery Row; No 19 to Pebble Beach; Nos 4, 5, 22, or 24 to Carmel; No 22 continues south to Point Lobos and Big Sur; Nos 20 and 21 go to Salinas. MST's the WAVE (Waterfront Area Visitors Express), which connects Cannery Row and Fisherman's Wharf, runs from Memorial Day to Labor Day and costs $1/50¢.

Car Monterey traffic can be horrendous on summer weekends and when you finally reach Cannery Row car parking can be a problem. Meters run to 10 pm, seven nights a week, and cost 75¢ an hour. Get quarters from the change machines on Wave St at Hoffman.

AROUND MONTEREY
Laguna Seca Raceway

Just off Hwy 68, about midway between Salinas and Monterey, the Laguna Seca Raceway (☎ 648-5100, 800-327-7322) attracts auto racing fans for an annual round of the Indy Car World Series, and motorcycle enthusiasts for a round of the World Superbike Championship. Back in the '50s races used to take place on a road circuit in the Del Monte Forest at Pebble Beach but the track was very unsafe and the Laguna Seca track replaced it.

PACIFIC GROVE
• *pop 17,000 ☎ 408*

There's little of interest in Pacific Grove but it does make an interesting alternative to staying in Monterey. It's a quiet, relaxed little resort, with architecture reflecting its Victorian origins and a great location right at the tip of the peninsula. Cannery Row is approximately equidistant between downtown Monterey to the east and Pacific Grove to the west.

Orientation & Information

Lighthouse Ave is the main shopping street of Pacific Grove. The Visitors Center (☎ 373-3304) at the chamber of commerce is a block north at the junction of Central and Forest Aves. It's open Tuesday to Friday, 9 am to 5 pm; Saturday, 11 am to 3 pm.

Monarch Butterflies

Butterflies come and go in a day don't they? Well nobody told that to the monarch butterflies that spend the whole winter in Pacific Grove.

Monarchs follow a remarkable migration pattern, starting in the spring along the central California coast and heading north and east. These migrating monarchs live for about four weeks during which time they fly north, mate, lay their eggs on milkweed leaves and die. In three to six days the eggs hatch, and the larva or caterpillars start out on a 15- to 20-day milkweed eating binge which will see its weight increase by a factor of over 2500. The caterpillar then suspends itself from a stem or leaf and enters the chrysalis or pupa stage from which a butterfly emerges about 10 days later. Once its wings have dried and hardened the new monarch starts off on another four week journey to the north.

Over the spring and summer four or five successive generations of monarchs travel further and further north, crossing the border into Canada and traveling as far as milkweed, their food source, extends. Finally, as the nights lengthen and temperatures drop, the northward migration ends by early October and the final generation turns south to fly 2000 miles back to their overwintering grounds. Covering as much as 100 miles a day and flying as high as 10,000 feet the monarchs start to turn up back in California during October.

The overwintering generation of monarchs live for six to nine months, clustering on trees at a number of favorite sites along the central California coast. In late winter rising temperatures and longer hours of daylight trigger their dormant sex drive; mating takes place and by March the monarchs are again heading north.

In Pacific Grove, butterfly trees are found in George Washington Park and in the Monarch Grove Sanctuary on Grove Acre Ave. Natural Bridges State Park in Santa Cruz and Pismo Beach near San Luis Obispo are other favorite monarch sites. Californian monarchs have developed a fondness for introduced Australian eucalyptus trees. ■

Museum of Natural History

Fronted by a gray whale model, the museum (☎ 648-3116) has some of that old-fashioned 'dead zoo' flavor that natural history museums were once notorious for. But there are also interesting exhibits about Big Sur, sea otters, and the monarch butterflies for which Pacific Grove is famous. It's at 165 Forest Ave on the corner with Central Ave and is open Tuesday to Sunday, 10 am to 5 pm. Admission is free, donations welcome.

Point Piños Lighthouse

Continue through Pacific Grove right to the northern tip of the Monterey Peninsula to find the oldest continuously operating lighthouse on the West Coast. It's been warning ships of this hazardous point with the same lenses and prisms and in the same lighthouse building since 1855. There are exhibits on its history and on local shipwrecks. The lighthouse (☎ 648-3116) is open Saturdays and Sundays, 1 to 4 pm. Entry is free but donations are welcome.

Special Events

The Butterfly Parade, marking the return of the monarchs to Pacific Grove, is in October.

Places to Stay

Quiet Pacific Grove can make a good alternative to the tourist buzz of Monterey or the smug affluence of Carmel. The cluster of motels at the northern end of Lighthouse Ave includes the *Pacific Grove Motel* (☎ 372-3218, 800-858-8997) at Lighthouse and Grove Acre Aves. It has a pool, a pleasantly quiet setting and singles at $54 to $84, doubles at $64 to $94. The *Butterfly Grove Inn* (☎ 373-4921, 800-337-9244) at 1073 Lighthouse Ave is very similarly priced.

The *Centrella Bed & Breakfast Inn* (☎ 372-3372) at 612 Central Ave is a pleasant B&B close to downtown and the sea. Built in 1904 the *Pacific Grove Inn* (☎ 375-2825) at 581 Pine Ave at Forest Ave looks properly authentic and rooms cost from

$88 to $118 in season. There are also three two-bedroom units.

Places to Eat

Peppers Mexicali Café (☎ 373-6892) at 170 Forest Ave, between Lighthouse Ave and Central Ave, blends Mexican and Latin American flavors with some distinctly Californian ingredients to produce dishes like salmon tacos and swordfish fajitas. It's closed Tuesdays.

Lighthouse Ave has a number of straightforward diners and *Bookworks* (☎ 372-2242) at No 667, which combines a bookshop with a very popular cafe. Lighthouse Ave also has an international bunch of restaurants like *El Cocodrilo* (☎ 655-3311) at No 701, which claims to produce 'the spirit and flavor of tropical America' with interesting salads, pastas, and Caribbean, Mexican, and Latin American entrees. It's closed Tuesdays. The flavors are Italian at *Pasta Mia* (☎ 375-7709) at No 481, one of the best Italian restaurants on the peninsula, or you can move to the Middle East at the stylish *Petra* (☎ 649-2530) at No 477.

Pasta and very reasonably priced seafood are the order of the day at the popular and much recommended *Fishwife* (☎ 375-7107). It's at 1996½ Sunset Drive, close to the intersection with 17-Mile Drive at Asilomar, and, like so much of Pacific Grove, it's closed on Tuesdays.

17-MILE DRIVE

Monterey, Pacific Grove, and Carmel are linked by the spectacularly scenic 17-Mile Drive which winds through Pebble Beach (☎ 800-654-9300), the private estate which most effectively symbolizes the peninsula's affluence. There are five entry gates to Pebble Beach and for non-residents entry costs $6.50 per car including a guide map. Bicycles enter free, but on weekends and holidays can only use the Pacific Grove gate.

Pebble Beach has fancy hotels (the *Lodge at Pebble Beach* and the *Inn at Spanish Bay*), golf courses (half a dozen of them) and the 5000-acre Del Monte Forest.

ADRIENNE COSTANZO

As you drive along 17-Mile Drive® you'll spot the Lone Cypress Tree® – both trademarks of Pebble Beach Land Company.

The 17-Mile Drive winds around the rugged coastline and up into the Del Monte Forest but it's the coastal stretch which is the most interesting and makes a fine, if somewhat circuitous, method of getting from Pacific Grove to Carmel.

From the Pacific Grove gate the drive winds by **Spanish Bay**, where Gaspar de Portolá dropped anchor in 1769. Rocky **Point Joe** has been the site of a number of ship wrecks, when mistaken for the entrance to Monterey Bay. Sea lions, harbor seals, and many birds can be seen around **Bird Rock** where there is a one-mile nature walk. A little further, **Seal Rock** and then **Fanshell Beach** also attract seals and other bay life. **Cypress Point Lookout** offers one of the finest views along the whole drive, somewhat spoilt by one of the ugliest wire fences. The road continues through **Crocker Grove** with its Monterey Cypress and reaches the **Lone Cypress**, inspiration for far too many local artists and photographers and also the symbol of the Pebble Beach Company.

CARMEL-BY-THE-SEA
• *pop 4500* ☎ *408*

Carmel began as a planned seaside resort in the 1880s and by the early 1900s had already established a reputation as a slightly bohemian retreat. The artistic flavor survives but these days 'wealthy' is just as descriptive an adjective; Carmel positively glows with self satisfaction. It's easy to see why this perfect vision of a Californian seaside village exerts such an attraction; leafy Carmel has a neat grid of picturesque homes, an impressive coastal frontage, an upscale shopping street and a beautiful Spanish mission.

Orientation & Information
Visitor information is available from the Carmel Business Association (☎ 624-2522) on San Carlos St, between 5th and 6th Aves above the Hog's Breath Inn. It's open Monday to Friday, 9 am to 5 pm; Saturday, 11 am to 5 pm.

The town's prettily picturesque appearance is ensured by local bylaws which forbid street lights, sidewalks, or even, in the central area, mailboxes. Residents have to pick up their mail from the post office. Since there's no mail delivery there are also no street numbers so addresses always have to specify which block you're looking for. Parking meters are also banned and even public phones and newspaper vending boxes are picturesquely rehoused with shingles!

The town's artistic temperament may still be strong but affluence has brought a distinctly right wing brand of bohemianism. In *Freedom of Speech*, a local free paper, a page devoted to what a good thing a gun can be probably tells it all.

There's a Brentano's bookshop on Mission St between Ocean and 7th, a Books Inc on Ocean Ave between Mission and

Carmel-by-the-Sea

PLACES TO STAY	6 Carmel Music
1 Carmel Wayfarer Inn	7 Post Office
2 Carmel Fireplace Inn	8 Carmel Business
32 The Homestead	Association,
	Visitors Center
PLACES TO EAT	12 Golf Arts & Imports
8 Hog's Breath Inn	13 Weston Gallery
9 Cactus Jacks	14 Galerie Blue Dog
10 Jack London's	15 Carmel Cutlery
11 General Store &	17 Mediterranean Market
Forge in the Forest	18 Augustina
16 Ristorante Piatti	19 Anderle
20 Caffé Napoli	22 Caffé Cardinale
21 Carmel Bakery	23 It's Cactus
25 Toots Lagoon	24 Vanguard
27 La Boheme	26 Conway of Asia
	28 Wings America
OTHER	29 Photography West
3 Bay Bike Rentals	Gallery
4 Red Lion Tavern	30 Tuck Box
5 Carmel Art Association	31 Carmel Village Theatre

San Carlos, or try Travels on the corner of Ocean Ave and Dolores St for travel books, but Carmel's best known book outlet is the Thunderbird Bookshop & Café (☎ 624-1803) in The Barnyard shopping center, just outside of town.

San Carlos Borromeo del Rio Carmelo Mission

The original Monterey mission was founded by Padre Junipero Serra in 1769 but poor soil and, probably more important, the military presence of the presidio, forced the move to the riverside site in Carmel in 1771. Although Serra founded many other missions in California this, the second mission, remained his base and he died here in 1784 and was buried in the mission beside his compatriot Padre Juan Crespi.

The mission church was originally built of wood, then replaced by an adobe construction and, in 1793, by the present stone church. In the 19th century the mission went into decline; it was secularized in 1834 and virtually abandoned in 1836 when the padre moved to Monterey. The ruin was roofed over in 1884, which at least slowed the decay, but not until 1931 was real restoration commenced. Today it is one of the most attractive and complete of the Californian missions with an interesting museum relating the story of Serra and the missions. Serra is buried in the church which was given the status of 'minor basilica' by the pope in 1960.

The mission (☎ 624-3600) is at 3080 Rio Rd, off Hwy 1 on the south side of Carmel. It's open Monday to Saturday, 9:30 am to 4:30 pm; Sunday 10:30 am to 4:30 pm. In summer it stays open until 7:30 pm. A $2/1 donation is suggested for entry to the museum and church.

Tor House

Poet Robinson Jeffers was one of the creators of the Carmel ethos and Tor House, his picturesquely rugged home at 26304 Ocean View Ave off Scenic Rd, a few blocks from Carmel Bay, has become a pilgrimage point. Tours operate Friday and Saturday, hourly from 10 am to 4 pm and the cost is $5/1.50 but numbers are limited to six per tour so it's wise to book by phoning ☎ 624-1813 Monday to Thursday, ☎ 624-1840 Friday and Saturday.

Places to Stay

The whole Monterey Peninsula has a reputation as an expensive place to stay and prices reach their apogee in Carmel's selection of sleek small hotels and cozy B&Bs. Many places impose a two-night minimum stay on weekends and rooms can be hard to find, particularly on summer weekends. Campers can go four miles up Carmel Valley Rd and turn right up Schulte Rd to *Saddlemountain* (☎ 624-1617) or *Riverside* (☎ 624-9329), both places take RVs and tents.

There's nothing 'cheap' in Carmel, Motel 6s are definitely not welcome, but the *Carmel River Inn* (☎ 624-1575) is at least below the stratosphere some of the time. This fairly straightforward place has spacious grounds and some two-bedroom units. It's on Hwy 1, south of town by the river, and has rooms from $65/75 up to as high as $130.

Right in the center, on the corner of Lincoln St and 8th Ave *The Homestead* (☎ 624-4119) has comfy rooms and cottages, all with attached bathroom, from $65 to $90. The *Carmel Wayfarer Inn* (☎ 624-2711) on the corner of Mission St and 4th Ave has singles at $68 to $88 and doubles at $78 to $98. Also centrally located the *Carmel Fireplace Inn* (☎ 624-4862, 800-634-1300) is on the corner of San Carlos St and 4th Ave. Rooms range from $65 to $140. Not quite so centrally located, the *Colonial Terrace Inn* (☎ 624-2741, 800-345-1818) is on San Antonio Ave between 12th and 13th, just one block back from the beach. The well equipped rooms range from $85 to $185 in season. It's one of Carmel's Inns by the Sea group, which can be booked by calling ☎ 800-433-4732. Carmel has many other places to stay, most of them small, most of them relatively exclusive.

Places to Eat

Carmel restaurants can be surprisingly down to earth and the prices are not always as outlandish as you might expect. The *Carmel Bakery* on Ocean Ave between Dolores and Lincoln is the place for baked goods. Head to the *Mediterranean Market* (☎ 624-2022) on Ocean Ave and Mission St for picnic goodies to take to the beach or to Point Lobos.

Toots Lagoon (☎ 625-1915), usually preceded with 'the fabulous,' on Dolores St between Ocean and 7th, has been turning out straightforward food of the steak, burgers, ribs, and pasta variety for a couple of decades. Prices are very reasonable for Carmel and the bar is a popular gathering spot. *La Boheme* (☎ 624-7500), on Dolores

Carmel's celebrity dining experience is the *Hog's Breath Inn*, owned by former Mayor Clint Eastwood.

St near 7th, lays on the European romantic look with a shovel but the set three-course meal for $20 is good value. *Caffé Napoli* (☎ 625-4033), on Ocean Ave near Lincoln, is a very popular small southern Italian restaurant with pizzas and pastas, mainly around $8 or $9, plus other dishes.

Jack London's (☎ 626-0909) is a small bar and restaurant in a lane off San Carlos St between 5th and 6th. Their burgers are around $6, pasta dishes around $9. On San Carlos *Cactus Jacks* (☎ 626-0909) is an equally popular Mexican restaurant with fajitas and other dishes at $9. The town's ex-mayor and most famous resident, Clint Eastwood's *Hog's Breath Inn* (☎ 625-1044), on San Carlos St between 5th and 6th, can't be ignored – where else could you start the day with a Magnum Force Omelette or lunch on a Dirty Harry Burger.

The *General Store & Forge in the Forest* (☎ 624-2233), at the corner of 5th and Junipero, offers simple American/Californian food, with an outside area under umbrellas around roaring fires. *Ristorante Piatti* (☎ 625-1766), on the corner of 6th and Junipero, is part of the California chain of stylish Italian restaurants.

Entertainment

For coffee try *Caffé Cardinale* (☎ 626-2095), Ocean Ave between San Carlos and Dolores. Lots of places have popular bars but the *Red Lion Tavern* (☎ 625-6765), in a lane off Dolores St between 5th and 6th, is a very British pub. The *Tuck Box* (☎ 624-6365), on Dolores St between Ocean and 7th, is equally British but here it's tea and cakes rather than beer. It's closed Monday and Tuesday.

On summer weekends outdoor performances take place at the *Outdoor Forest Theatre* (☎ 626-1681), just north of the center. The *Carmel Bach Festival* (☎ 624-1521, 800-513-2224) takes places in late-July and early August. The *Golden Bough Playhouse* (☎ 622-0100) on Monte Verde St between 8th and 9th is the local repertory theater. Movies are shown at the *Carmel Village Theatre* (☎ 625-1200) at Dolores St and 7th Ave.

Things to Buy

Carmelites were clearly born to shop and Carmel-by-the-Sea has plenty of outlets to satisfy the urge. Not chain shops, mind you. They're banned in central Carmel although 'chain' must be spelt differently in Italy and England, as you will find places like Benetton and Crabtree & Evelyn.

But other shops are here en masse and in particular a quite amazing number of art galleries, craft galleries, and shops selling all those things you don't need, but are nice to have anyway. Lots of them sell things only the very rich (plenty of them in Carmel) or tourists (plenty of them too) would buy. Carmel galleries are laden with happy dolphin sculptures, local scenery oil paintings (would you believe paintings of golf courses?), and pictures by artists who discovered impressionism a century too late. There are even Carmel galleries where the artists paint in the front window, so you'll know they *really* are Carmel artists. These 13 interesting places to shop are a totally personal and idiosyncratic selection:

- Anderle (☎ 624-4199), Lincoln St between Ocean and 7th – nice stuff from South-East Asia, particularly Indonesia
- Augustina (☎ 624-2403), Lincoln St between Ocean and 7th – rhinestone cowboy gear, fringed leather jackets, appliqued boots, and the like.
- Carmel Art Association (☎ 624-6176), Dolores St between 5th and 6th – works by many local artists
- Carmel Cutlery (☎ 624-6699), Dolores St between 6th and Ocean – 'collectible knives' is the subtitle: knives (lots of them), plus scissors, swords, and the odd battleaxe
- Carmel Music (☎ 624-8078), Dolores St between 5th and 6th – guitars
- Conway of Asia (☎ 624-3643), Dolores St between Ocean and 7th – oriental rugs and all

sorts of interesting artifacts from Tibet, the sub-continent and northern South-East Asia
- Galerie Blue Dog (☎ 626-4444), 6th Ave between Lincoln and Dolores – George Rodrigue has decided when you do something good you might as well stick to it. He paints pictures of his dog Tiffany, who died in 1980.
- Golf Arts & Imports (☎ 625-4488), Dolores St between 5th and 6th – not just paintings of the sand trap on hole seven but a host of arcane golfing bits and pieces that only a golfing nut could find interesting
- It's Cactus (☎ 626-4213), Mission St between Ocean and 7th – colorful Mexican crafts, not high art but not cheap junk either, an interesting and fun shop
- Photography West Gallery (☎ 625-1587), Dolores St between Ocean and 7th – interesting photography by a variety of established and up and coming photographers
- Vanguard (☎ 622-9034), Lincoln St between Ocean and 7th – Vargas nudes, those cheesecake pinups of the '50s have assumed the position of high art
- Weston Gallery (☎ 624-4453), 6th Ave between Dolores and Lincoln – Any commentary on Carmel galleries has to mention this one. Yes, Edward Weston was a Carmel native son, Ansel Adams helped to create a Carmel school of photography, and some of the work displayed here is terrific.
- Wings America (☎ 626-9464), Dolores St between Ocean and 7th – 'The difference between the men and the boys is the price of their toys' and this is a big boy's toy shop full of aviation memorabilia and superb (and commensurately expensive) wooden models of aircraft.

Getting There & Away

Carmel is only four miles south of Monterey by Hwy 1. See the Monterey Getting Around section for MST bus information.

Getting Around

Free unlimited car parking can be found on 3rd Ave just east of Junipero Ave. Carmel Yellow Cab (☎ 624-3885) is the only taxi service in Carmel. Bicycles can be rented from Bay Bike Rentals (☎ 625-2453) on Lincoln St between 5th and 6th.

AROUND CARMEL
Point Lobos State Reserve

Dubbed 'the greatest meeting of land and sea on earth,' Point Lobos (☎ 624-4909)

makes a wonderful finale to the peninsula and a fitting introduction to the spectacular scenery of Big Sur. The reserve, with its dramatically rocky and convoluted coastline, takes its name from the *Punta de los Lobos Marinos*, the 'point of the sea wolves,' named by the Spanish for the howls of the resident sea lions. It encompasses 554 land acres as well as 750 submerged acres that are good for scuba diving, though limited by ecologically motivated restrictions. There's a terrific selection of short walks, most of them less than a mile in length, which take in wild and inspiring scenery. Favorite destinations include Sea Lion Point and Devil's Cauldron, a blowhole and whirlpool that gets splashy at high tide. At the end of the main road, Bird Island is good for bird watching and for starting out on long hikes.

The reserve entrance is on the west side of Hwy 1, about four miles south of Carmel. It's open daily from 9 am to 4 pm. Admission is $7 per vehicle, $2 for walk-ins.

Carmel Highlands

The 12-mile stretch between Carmel and Big Sur is popular for scuba diving and bird watching. Cypress and redwood trees are plentiful, and sea lions like to hang out on the offshore rocks. South of Point Lobos is Carmel Highlands, an 11-mile stretch of private land where bizillion dollar homes cling to cliffs above the Pacific. When you pass the Rocky Point Restaurant (☎ 624-2933), a pricey seafood eatery with a stunning location and good bloody marys, you have, according to local reference, left Carmel Highlands and entered Big Sur.

Garrapata State Park

This small state park, where Soberantes Creek dumps into the sea, has a day-use area equipped with restrooms, picnic tables, barbecues, and a parking lot. The trail leading down to the beach is one of the few beach access points between Carmel and Big Sur. The $6 day-use fee is avoided by parking on Hwy 1.

Upper Central Coast

The austere Santa Lucia Range runs from Big Sur to San Simeon, separating the Pacific Ocean from the San Joaquin Valley. The range's west side plunges directly into the sea while the east side's rolling foothills support ranches and vineyards. Travel here is either along Hwy 1 (along the coast) or Hwy 101 (on the east side of the mountains). The two highways converge in San Luis Obispo and near Monterey, but once you get on Hwy 1 between those two cities you're committed, so be sure you have the time for this slower, scenic route. The Nacimiento-Fergusson Rd over the Santa Lucia mountains is the only connecting road between San Simeon and Carmel.

Highway 1 from Point Lobos to Morro Bay journeys along some of California's most dramatic coastline where wind and water are continually shaping the Santa Lucia Range into rugged cliffs and rocky promontories. Coastal redwoods grow

Driving Hwy 1

Completed in 1937 after 18 years of construction (by mostly convict labor), Hwy 1 was California's first Scenic Hwy, and certainly deserves the title. The curvy two-lane highway is not meant for quick travel: driving straight from Carmel to San Luis Obispo takes about five hours, but scenic breaks are integral to the trip. From December to March whales migrate north from Baja, a fantastic roadside attraction.

Summer brings fog and heavy traffic, and the highway is often closed during winter storms. Buy gas in Carmel or San Luis Obispo to avoid exorbitant gas prices, and bring your own food for picnicking. Beach access is limited since much of the land along Hwy 1 is private (trespassing laws are strictly enforced), and swimming is discouraged because of undertows and rip currents. Trails that do lead to the beach require tennis shoes or sturdy sandals. ■

along the Big and Little Sur Rivers, and the Ventana Wilderness supports the only Santa Lucia Fir trees in the world. Tourist 'sights' consist of coves, campgrounds, and state parks, until you reach Hearst Castle.

Highway 101 is more interesting than I-5 but not nearly as scenic as Hwy 1. Built along *El Camino Real*, the route connecting California's missions, the highway gives access to several historical sites and Pinnacles National Monument. Otherwise, the scenery is mostly rolling fields and pastures.

BIG SUR
• *pop 1200* ☎ *408*

Big Sur is an experience rather than one tangible place. Its raw beauty is awe-inspiring, its folksy residents endearing. There are no traffic lights, banks, or shopping centers, and when the sun goes down, the moon and stars are the only street lights.

History

The Esselen tribe, known to date back at least 3000 years in the area, occupied settlements along the coast, surviving primarily on acorns, rabbit, deer, bear, and sea mammals. They were wiped out by diseases brought by the Spanish before the first US settlers arrived.

Big Sur was named by Spanish settlers living in Carmel's mission, who referred to the unexplored wilderness as *el pais grande del sur* (the big country to the south). They named the two coastal rivers *el rio grande del sur* (the big river to the south) and *el rio chiquito del sur* (the little river to the south). The names were made official by the coming of Big Sur's post office in the 1900s.

In 1852, Juan Bautista Rogerio Cooper, harbormaster of Monterey, filed claim to Rancho El Sur, stretching from Cooper Point to the mouth of the Little Sur River. The headquarters for the rancho are now part of Andrew Molera State Park.

Homesteaders arrived in the early 1900s and supported the canning, and lumbering industries. At the turn of the century, Big

Big Sur

0   3   6 km
0   2   4 miles

1 Bixby Bridge
2 Little Sur River Bridge
3 Point Sur Light Station
4 River Inn Resort, Six Bells Pub
5 Big Sur Campground & Cabins
6 Riverside Campground & Cabins
7 Ripplewood Resort,
   Glen Oaks Motel
8 Big Sur Ranger Station,
   Pine Ridge Trailhead
9 Ventana Campground,
   Ventana Resort
10 Nepenthe, Cafe Kevah
11 Henry Miller Memorial Library
12 Deetjen's Big Sur Inn
13 Coast Gallery
14 Esalen Institute

Sur supported a larger population than it does today. Electricity arrived in the 1950s, and TV reception in the 1980s.

Orientation

Tourists often wander into businesses along Hwy 1 and ask 'How much further to Big Sur?' In fact, there is no town of Big Sur. Rocky Point marks Big Sur's northern end, and the Esalen Institute defines the southern end.

Information

If Big Sur has a hub, it is Big Sur Center (called 'the village'), 15 miles south of Rocky Point. Here lie the post office and the Big Sur Bazaar (☎ 667-2197), a combination market, deli, and all-purpose shop which stocks camping supplies, film, maps, and regional natural history books. This is the most affordable place to get food if you're on a budget, and they stock a variety of picnic supplies. It's open daily until 8 pm.

The *El Sur Grande*, a free newspaper published once a year, lists all of Big Sur's campgrounds, parks, and businesses. It is available at nearly every stop along Hwy 1, or by contacting El Sur Grande (☎ 667-2100), PO Box 87, Big Sur, CA 93920.

For information concerning Los Padres National Forest, the Ventana Wilderness, or any state parks, stop by the USFS Big Sur Ranger Station (☎ 667-2315), 2 miles south of Big Sur Center. The office is open daily from 8 am to 4:30 pm, and has maps posted. For road information call ☎ 757-2006.

Bixby Bridge

Bixby Bridge spans Bixby Creek in a graceful 320-foot arch, two miles south of Rocky Point. Completed in 1932 and originally called the 'Rainbow Bridge,' it is supported by 600,000 pounds of steel reinforcement and 825 truckloads worth of concrete. Before the bridge was built, travelers had to trek 14 miles inland on the Old Coast Rd which heads east from the bridge's north side and re-connects with Hwy 1 across from Andrew Molera State

Park. You can still make the adventure with a sturdy car.

Little Sur River Bridge

South of Bixby Bridge the highway rises to the lofty Hurricane Point headlands, then drops to the low-lying Little Sur River Bridge. Here the Little Sur River makes a gentle sweep – a favorite subject for local artists – before it meets the sea, turning the water bright blue with its heavy lime deposits. During the dry season the river forms a lagoon behind a sandbar. *Pico Blanco*, the white and green striped mountain to the east, stands 3709 feet tall and was revered by the Esselen Indians as the sacred birthplace of man and beast.

Point Sur State Historic Park

Point Sur is that imposing volcanic rock that looks like an island but is actually connected to land by a sand bar. The land between the highway and Point Sur is private, but on Wednesdays and weekends you can take a free three-hour tour of the 1899 Point Sur Light Station atop the rock. For tour information call ☎ 625-4419.

Andrew Molera State Park

Once part of Juan Bautista Cooper's 9000-acre Rancho El Sur, Andrew Molera State Park now has $3 walk-in campsites equipped with fire pits, vault toilets, and drinking water. Among eucalyptus trees just north of the meadow is the Cooper Cabin, the oldest structure in Big Sur. A gentle half-mile trail leads past the campground to a beautiful beach where the Big Sur River runs into the ocean. From here several trails head south, along the bluffs above the beach.

Molera Trail Rides (☎ 625-8664), in a barn near the entrance to Andrew Molera State Park, offers two-hour guided trail rides for $40. Beyond their barn is the **Molera Educational Sanctuary & Ornithology Center**, open to the public Monday to Friday from 9 am to 4 pm.

Pfeiffer Big Sur State Park

Pfeiffer Big Sur State Park is the largest

state park in Big Sur. Named after Big Sur's first European settlers – Michael and Barbara Pfeiffer, who arrived in 1869 – the park occupies 680 acres of the former Pfeiffer Ranch Resort and contains the original homestead cabin and the graveyard where the Pfeiffers are buried. The rustic administration buildings and Big Sur Lodge were built in the 1930s by the CCC. Campsites, which cost $22, are beside the Big Sur River in a flat-bottomed valley shaded by redwood groves. Hiking trails loop through the park and head into the adjacent Ventana Wilderness (see below). Summer crowds are the drawback to this otherwise idyllic scene.

Immediately south of the park, the USFS is headquartered at the Big Sur Ranger Station (☎ 667-2423), where you can buy maps for any of Big Sur's state parks and get backcountry permits and trail information. The office is open from 8:30 am to 4:30 pm daily. The Pine Ridge Trailhead, in the south end of the parking lot, is the major access point for the Ventana Wilderness. Overnight parking costs $4 per car, per day. For detailed hiking information, see below.

Sycamore Canyon Rd, the second road south of Point Sur Station on the west side of Hwy 1, winds two miles down to **Pfeiffer Beach**. The road is rugged and narrow but the beach is worth the trip.

Henry Miller Memorial Library

Housed amidst gardens and sculptures, the Henry Miller Memorial Library (☎ 667-2574), three miles south of Point Sur Station, is Big Sur's most cultural venue. The library has all of Miller's written and painted works, translations of his books, and a great collection of Big Sur and Beat Generation material. Grabbing a book and hanging out on the deck is encouraged. Hours vary, but in summer are generally daily from 11 am to 5 pm; October to May weekends only. Admission is $1.

Coast Gallery

The Coast Gallery & Cafe (☎ 667-2301), four miles south of the Henry Miller Library, is made of redwood water storage tanks that originally served the Oakland Naval Facility. The gallery was a show-place for bohemian artists' work in the 1950s, but now has a haphazard collection geared towards tourists.

Partington Cove

From the west side of Hwy 1, a well-marked fire road descends half a mile along Partington Creek, to Partington Cove, an alleged landing for bootleggers during Prohibition. You can still see a wooden foot-bridge and tunnel built in the 1870s as well as the old landing's fittings, which were revived during the construction of Hwy 1 in the 1920s.

Julia Pfeiffer Burns State Park

Julia Pfeiffer Burns State Park extends two miles south from Partington Cove along both sides of Hwy 1. At the park entrance (on the east side of Hwy 1) are forested picnic grounds along McWay Creek and an old cabin (on the creek's north side, just past the picnic area) that housed the Waters, the first homesteaders on the land that is now JP Burns State Park. The Waters built Saddle Rock Ranch here in the 1900s. The Ewoldsen Trail offers good views of the ocean and Santa Lucia mountains.

The park's highlight is California's only coastal waterfall – 50-foot **McWay Falls** drops straight into the sea (onto the sand at low tide). To reach the waterfall viewpoint, take the trail heading west from the park entrance and cross beneath Hwy 1. Nearby, two walk-in campsites sit on a semi-protected bluff. The price is $23 per night, and reservations must be made through Destinet.

Esalen Institute

Marked only by a lighted sign reading 'Esalen Institute, By Reservation Only,' Esalen is world-renowned for its seminars and natural hot springs. Workshops deal with anything that 'promotes human values and potentials' – from African Dance to Yoga to exploring the inner game of golf.

The Esalen baths are fed by a natural hot

spring and sit on a ledge above the ocean, below the center's main building. From 1:30 to 3:30 am, the baths are open to the public for a $10 fee. If you can stay up this late and are comfortable with nudity, the experience – sitting beneath the stars, hearing the waves crash below – is well worth it.

When space is available, you can stay at Esalen and use the baths without participating in a seminar. Accommodations are in standard rooms ($125 per night) with one or two other people, or in bunk rooms ($85) that sleep four to six people. The price includes three meals, and drops $10 if you stay two or more nights. For reservations and a free catalogue with seminar dates and details call ☎ 667-3000.

Ventana Wilderness

The Ventana Wilderness lies within the northern part of Los Padres National Forest, which straddles the Santa Lucia Mountains and runs parallel to the Big Sur coast for its whole length. Most of the wilderness is covered with oaks and chaparral, though canyons cut by the Big Sur and Little Sur Rivers support virgin stands of coastal redwoods. Scattered pockets of Santa Lucia Fir (found no other place in the world) grow in rocky outcroppings at the highest elevations (above 5000 feet).

The Ventana is especially popular with backpackers (day-hikers usually stick to coastal trails). One favorite destination is Sykes Hot Springs, natural mineral pools (ranging from 98° to 110° F) surrounded by redwoods, about 11 miles from the Wilderness boundary via the Pine Ridge Trailhead. Backcountry/fire permits are available from the Big Sur Ranger Station and Pacific Valley Station (listed below).

The main entry to the Wilderness is the Pine Ridge Trailhead at the Big Sur Ranger Station. The Pacific Valley Ranger Station (☎ 927-4211), south of Big Sur, gives access to the southern half of the wilderness. A good access point in this area is from the Kirk Creek Campground, listed below.

The Ventana has the country's largest

concentration of mountain lions (one cat per 10 square miles). See Dangers & Annoyances in Facts for the Visitor.

Places to Stay

Camping All three state parks in Big Sur offer camping. There are also some private campgrounds. *Big Sur Campground & Cabins* (☎ 667-2322) has trailer and tent sites on the Big Sur River for $22, and tent cabins for $40. Cabins with bathrooms and kitchens are $80 to $130. The camp store stocks the basics, and there are laundry facilities, hot showers, volleyball and basketball courts, and a playground. A half mile to the south, *Riverside Campground & Cabins* (☎ 667-2414) has similar prices and facilities.

Or try the *Ventana Campground* (☎ 667-2688), where woodsy, secluded campsites cost $20, and attract a relatively subdued crowd.

Inns & Resorts The *River Inn Resort* (☎ 667-2700, 800-548-3610) has a big lawn that slopes down to the Big Sur River, and there's live Dixieland jazz on Sunday afternoon. Food costs around $8 for lunch, $15 for dinner. Rooms that look out toward the Big Sur River and have access to a heated pool are $55/65. The gift shop – the Heartbeat – has a good selection of Native American art and handmade drums.

Cabins at the *Ripplewood Resort* (☎ 667-2242) cost $45 to $80 and have kitchens and private bathrooms. The cabins along the river are peaceful and surrounded by redwoods, but those on Hwy 1 can be quite noisy. Their coffee shop is good for breakfast and lunch, with $4 omelets and Big Sur's best burgers for $5. The adjacent market stocks fresh produce and picnic supplies. Next door, the *Glen Oaks Motel* (☎ 667-2242) has clean and simple rooms with phones for $45/55.

On high at the *Ventana Resort* (☎ 667-2331, 800-628-6500), rooms face the ocean or the mountains and are equipped with a spa, fireplace, and robes; prices start at $140. Below the ritzy resort is the Ventana Campground; see above.

Deetjen's Big Sur Inn (☎ 667-2377) is Big Sur's most pleasant accommodation – a rustic conglomeration of rooms, redwoods, and wisteria along Castro Creek. Rooms cost $70 to $140 (including coffee and homemade muffins) and get booked far in advance. Cancellations are frequent, but it's hard to make last minute reservations by phone, so stop by on the day you want to stay if you haven't booked ahead.

Places to Eat

The Six Bells Pub (☎ 667-2355), next to the River Inn Resort, is a good place for a beer and a game of darts, and is where locals congregate to watch major televised events (few people in Big Sur have their own TV). The cook makes wonderful soups, fish & chips, and veggie burgers, and most things cost under $5. Food is served until 10 pm, and the bar is open until around midnight.

Known for its elaborate gardens, cliffside location, and eccentric owners who have lived in Big Sur for the past 40 years, Nepenthe (☎ 667-2345) is a great place for a drink at sunset. The bar and dining room have redwood beams, huge glass windows (facing the sea), and open onto a patio that sprawls atop the cliffs. The menu involves local produce, fresh herbs, game, and seafood. Just below the main restaurant, Cafe Kevah has salads, soups, and sandwiches for under $10, and serves brunch on the patio starting at 9 am.

The Norwegian-style dining room at Deetjen's Big Sur Inn (☎ 667-2377) always has a fire blazing and classical music playing. Blueberry pancakes are great for breakfast (served 8 to 11:30 am) and the dinner menu is always interesting; reservations are advised.

SOUTH OF BIG SUR
☎ 408

South of the Esalen Institute, Hwy 1 straightens out considerably and there is a wider sweep of lowlands between mountain and sea. The landscape is barren and wild compared to Big Sur's river-fed valley, and services are few and far between.

Lopez Point, a prominent south-facing promontory, defines the northern end of Lucia Bay. The Lucia Lodge (☎ 667-2391) sits 500 feet above the bay with cabins for $85 to $165, and has a restaurant with a fabulous southwest view and overpriced lunch and dinner.

A half mile south of the lodge, a large white cross on the highway marks the entrance to the **New Camaldoli Immaculate Heart Hermitage**. This self-sufficient community of Benedictine monks devotes their lives to prayer and meditation. For information on retreats write to the Guestmaster, Immaculate Heart Hermitage, New Camaldoli, Big Sur, CA 93920, or call ☎ 667-2456.

About four miles south of Lucia, Kirk Creek Campground is rather unprotected but offers easy access to a sandy beach, and has flush toilets. On the Nacimiento-Fergusson Rd, which cuts over to Hwy 101, are the Nacimiento Campground and Ponderosa Campground. Both have tent sites with vault toilets for $6. Nearby, the Nacimiento Ridge gives views of the ocean and eastern foothills of the Santa Lucia Range.

One of the nicest spots between Big Sur and San Simeon, Plaskett Creek Campground, south of Pacific Valley on the east side of Hwy 1, has large, grassy sites shaded by Monterey cypress. Trails to the beach leave from the west side of the highway, directly across from the campground, and about a half mile to the north is a turn-out for the **Sand Dollar Beach** Picnic Area which has trails to the longest sandy beach in the area. South of Sand Dollar Beach is a series of coves known for their jade deposits. In 1971 three divers recovered a 9000-pound jade boulder that measured eight feet long and brought in $180,000. The best time to find jade – which is black or blue-green and looks dull until you dip it in water – is during low tide or after a big storm.

Named for an offshore outcropping that looks like a fat lady, **Gorda** (Spanish for 'fat') is best known for its annual Jade Festival, held the first weekend in October. The Gorda General Store & Deli (☎ 927-3918) has camping supplies, and the adjacent *Whale Watchers Cafe* serves food from 8:30 am to 8 pm. Gas prices are steep, but the station has clean restrooms and public showers. Four small houses with kitchens, fireplaces, and private decks cost $125 to $185 and sleep four to six; contact the General Store & Deli.

HEARST CASTLE
Perched high on a hill overlooking pastures and the Pacific, Hearst Castle is a monument to wealth and ambition. William Randolph Hearst – America's legendary newspaper magnate – based his 'enchanted hill' on a Mediterranean village, on 127 acres with 165 rooms, four guest houses surrounding a central plaza and 'cathedral,' which he used as private quarters and entertainment rooms. Hearst's art collection was so vast that an accurate calculation of it's size or value was never possible. Spanish cathedral ceilings are covered with flags from the Palio in Siena, Italy, which hover above a French refectory table set with paper napkins and Heinz ketchup. The display of wealth borders on grotesque and the amalgam of styles and periods is enough to make any architect or historian blanch. The visit is worthwhile, however, if only to see something uniquely American.

Construction on the Hearst Castle began in 1919. Upon Hearst's death, the 'ranch' was left to his heirs, but unable to afford the maintenance, they donated it to the University of California. They too denied it, and the state took it over as a museum.

Organized Tours
There are four tours of the estate, all of which leave by bus from the visitors center at the bottom of the hill and include the estates' two pools. Tours take about two hours – 30 minutes in transit, 30 minutes being told not to chew gum or touch priceless objects, and one hour shuffling through buildings and gardens with throngs of people.

Tour 1 This is the best for first timers. It includes entertainment rooms in the main house, the esplanade and gardens, and one of the guest cottages.

Tour 2 This tour shows the upper floors of the main house, including Hearst's private suite, study and library, and the pantry and kitchen.

Tour 3 Good for those interested in architecture, this tour shows the least altered building, suites built in Hearst's final years (totally different from anything else on the estate), and a video about Hearst Castle's construction.

Tour 4 This tour, available April to October, shows a 'hidden terrace and gardens,' which were part of the original plans but later covered up in construction. The tour also shows the esplanade, a guest cottage, the pool dressing rooms, and wine cellar.

Tickets cost $14 ($8 for children ages 6 to 12 years old) and are reserved through

William Randolph Hearst

Born in 1863 with a proverbial 'silver spoon' in his mouth, William Randolph Hearst was the only son of Senator George and Phoebe Apperson Hearst, self-made millionaires from near Rosebud, Missouri. Though spoiled as a child, William did not get the true object of his desire – his father's *Examiner* newspaper – until he was 21. With a $20 million fortune behind him, Hearst could afford to make enemies where other papers could not, namely in the business and political arenas. His papers uncovered stories that other papers were afraid to publish, becoming a voice and champion of blue collar workers and, though not openly, Democratic ethics.

With his father's money, Hearst acquired and built a tremendous publishing empire, encompassing over 50 newspapers across the USA. Out-selling his competition became an obsession. Hearst invented news if there wasn't any and created the 'banner headline' (announcing the news of the day in a few short words), becoming the king of 'yellow journalism' and 'muckraking.' Much of the sensationalism that soils today's media can be contributed to his ethics (the San Francisco *Examiner*, and *Good Housekeeping* and *Cosmopolitan* magazines are still run by the Hearst Corporation).

Hearst's obsession for power came to a climax with his construction of *La Cuesta Encantada*, the Enchanted Hill, known as Hearst Castle. When his mother died in 1919 and Hearst, at age 56, no longer had to ask his parents for money, he went all out to confirm his financial power. He chose the family ranch at San Simeon to build his private home. Though originally a reasonably sized project, the house grew to accommodate Hearst's expansive interest in art and in Hollywood actress Marion Davies. As Hearst purchased cathedral ceilings, refectory tables, Grecian urns, and roman columns, Marion Davies invited Hollywood's elite to spend weekends at 'the ranch,' playing tennis, swimming, watching movies in a full-scale theater, and driving through the zoo and gardens stocked with rare, exotic animals and plants. Architect Julia Morgan supervised construction on tireless weekend trips from her office in San Francisco.

As soon as one building or branch was 'complete,' Hearst would inform Morgan that he had bought a French tapestry or Egyptian statue that needed exhibition place. Money was not an issue to Hearst, but bills were known to go unpaid for several years. The project was unfinished when he died in 1951. According to the movie *Citizen Kane*, Orson Welles' rendition of Hearst's life, Hearst died an unhappy and tormented man. Photos and reports from his last years, however, show that Hollywood wanted to pay him tribute using his own sensational technique. ∎

Destinet. During the week from October to May, you can often get tickets without reservations, though tours and tour times might be limited. Call ☎ 800-444-4445 for reservations.

SAN SIMEON
☎ 805

The 'original' San Simeon is a small beachside settlement on the west side of Hwy 1, across from the entrance to Hearst Castle. The Hearst Corporation still owns most of the land here, and the Julia Morgan houses which once housed Hearst Castle staff are now home to cowboys who run the corporation's 80,000 acre cattle ranch. The Sebastiani Store, built in 1887 as a whaling station, is still going strong, with a good inventory of food, picnic supplies, and Hearst souvenirs. Their cafe has a nice deck and serves breakfast and lunch from May to September. Adjacent to the buildings, William Randolph Hearst State Beach has a nice sandy stretch with intermittent rock outcroppings and a rickety wooden pier ($5 day-use fee).

Three miles south of the original San Simeon (just off the Hearst Corporation's property), modern San Simeon is a mile-long strip of unexciting motels and restaurants. The San Simeon Chamber of Commerce (☎ 927-3500, 800-342-5613) is next door to Plaza del Cavalier. Along Hearst and Castillo Drives, which run parallel to Hwy 1, the *Sands Motel* (☎ 927-3243) has oceanside rooms for $30 and an indoor pool. The *Silver Surf Motel* (☎ 927-4661, 800-621-3999) has a pool and spa, and rooms surrounding a garden for $29.

San Simeon State Beach
Six miles south of the original San Simeon, San Simeon State Beach includes a long sandy beach and, on the east side of Hwy 1, *San Simeon Creek Campground* and *Washburn Campground*. They're side by side on the east side of Hwy 1, and together have over 200 sites. Sites at San Simeon Creek, which has hot showers and flush toilets, cost $22, while sites at Washburn are primitive and cost $7. For reservations call ☎ 927-2020.

CAMBRIA
• *pop 2480* ☎ 805

Cambria is a self-proclaimed artists' village surrounded by hills, about a half mile from the coast. The town's charm almost completely disappears under the feet of summer tourists, but from late October to late May, it's a good place to spend the afternoon amidst shops and art galleries. The Seekers Collection & Gallery (☎ 927-4352), 4090 Burton Drive, has two stories of glass art and tableware displayed like museum pieces. Cambria is also the nicest place to stay while visiting Hearst Castle.

Moonstone Beach (Cambria's coastal half) has low bluffs and an accessible white sand beach across from a strip of mid- and high-priced motels. The Village is the inland part of Cambria, east of where Moonstone Beach Drive crosses Hwy 1 and becomes Main St. At the beach's northern end, Leffingwell Landing State Park has a picnic area shaded by Monterey Cypress.

South of Cambria, off Hwy 1, **Harmony** (population 16, just like the T-shirt says) consists of an old creamery that houses artists' workshops and deserves a quick browse.

Places to Stay Cambria's lodgings are concentrated along Moonstone Beach Drive, though the most affordable places are in the Village. Prices fluctuate with the seasons. Plan to pay 20% to 30% more on weekends and from May to September. The *Cambria Palms* (☎ 927-4485), 2662 Main St, has worn-out rooms for $30/45. Next door, the *Creekside Inn* (☎ 927-4021, 800-269-5212), 2618 Main St, charges $7 more and has much newer facilities. For beachside accommodation, try the *Cambria Shores Inn* (☎ 927-8644, 800-433-9179), 6276 Moonstone Beach Drive, whose rooms cost $65/75 year round and include refrigerators and a continental breakfast.

Places to Eat *Soto's Market* (☎ 927-4411), 2244 Main St, has heaping sandwiches for around $3, plus fresh produce and bulk foods. *Linn's Restaurant & Bakery*, 2277 Main St, has a huge menu and is famous for its chicken pot pie ($6) and dessert items. Prices are $5 to $11 for lunch and dinner. The *Redwood Cafe* (☎ 927-4830), 2094 Main St, serves the best breakfast around.

The *Sea Chest* (☎ 927-4514), an updated fish house on Moonstone Beach Drive, has good Oysters Rockefeller ($7) and fresh fish or steak dinners for around $15.

ESTERO BAY
☎ 805

Estero Bay is a long, shallow, west-facing bay with Cayucos at its north end and Montana de Oro State park at its south end. Morro Bay, a deep inlet guarded by Morro Rock and separated from the ocean by a 12-mile long sand spit, sits about halfway between the two and has most of Estero Bay's services and tourist activity. Morro Rock is the bay's unmistakable landmark, used as a navigation marker since the Portola expedition in 1769.

Cayucos
• *pop 2995*

At the Bay's north end, small and slow-paced Cayucos (ki-YOU-kiss) offers a glimpse of local beach life without many tourists. The town developed around the mouth of Cayucos Creek and a wharf and warehouse built by Captain James Cass in 1867. Remnants of Cass' Landing – a rickety old pier and warehouse – are central to Cayucos' sandy beach. Ocean Ave (the main thoroughfare which runs parallel to Hwy 1) is lined with turn-of-the-century buildings, shops, and restaurants.

Cayucos' gentle waves are good for beginning surfers, and along the coast (north of the pier) is an old Chumash site that you can explore by kayak. Good Clean Fun (☎ 995-1993), south of the pier at 136 Ocean Front St, rents kayaks for $35 per day and surfboards for $5 an hour.

Places to Stay & Eat Cayucos' motels, on the south end of Ocean Ave, charge around $45/55 during winter, $50/65 in summer. Rooms at the *Sea Esta Motel* (☎ 995-3932), 100 S Ocean Ave, cost $28 year round and look as if they have not been touched since 1962. The *Cayucos Motel* (☎ 995-3670) charges $35/45 during winter, $65 in summer, and has a nice patio overlooking the ocean.

For good Italian food, try *Lou & Shenly's* (☎ 995-2626), 49 S Ocean Ave, whose owner came from Italy 30 years ago, but still knows how to make great *penne all'arrabiata*. Dinners are $6 to $10, and a large pizza costs $15.

Morro Bay
• *pop 11,000*

Apart from its kitschy Embarcadero, Morro Bay is an honest-to-goodness fishing town whose livelihood depends more on the day's catch than it does on tourism. Behind the facade of shell shops and fish & chips restaurants, the harbor bustles with maritime activity and in the evening small boats unload rock cod, salmon, and shellfish for inspection by local buyers.

The intriguing mass of **Morro Rock** is one in a chain of nine volcanic peaks between Morro Bay and San Luis Obispo, and is about 23 million years old. Herons and peregrine falcons nest among the high crevices, but rock climbing is prohibited for humans. North of the rock, **Morro Strand State Beach** offers a wide sandy shore and campsites in a parking-lot setting with flush-toilets and cold showers for $14. Make reservations directly through the park by calling ☎ 772-7434.

South of the rock is the Embarcadero and 'downtown' Morro Bay; Morro Bay Blvd and Pacific St (going east-west), and Morro Ave and Main St (going north-south) are the main thoroughfares. On Friday from 2 to 7 pm, the **Friday Night Market** takes over the north end of the Embarcadero with fresh fish and produce stands, arts & crafts booths, and food vendors. This is the main stage for the Morro Bay Harbor Festival

CALIFORNIA

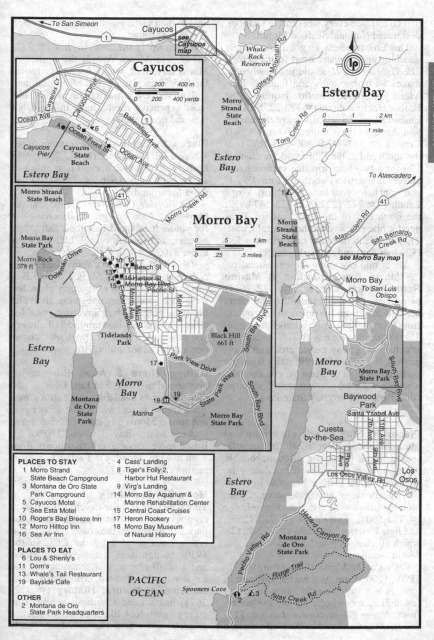

Cayucos

0   200   400 m
0   200   400 yards

Estero Bay

0   1   2 km
0   .5   1 mile

Morro Bay

0   .5   1 km
0   .25   .5 miles

PACIFIC OCEAN

PLACES TO STAY
1   Morro Strand
    State Beach Campground
3   Montana de Oro State
    Park Campground
5   Cayucos Motel
7   Sea Esta Motel
10 Roger's Bay Breeze Inn
12 Morro Hilltop Inn
16 Sea Air Inn

PLACES TO EAT
6   Lou & Shenly's
11 Dorn's
13 Whale's Tail Restaurant
19 Bayside Cafe

OTHER
2   Montana de Oro
    State Park Headquarters

4   Cass' Landing
8   Tiger's Folly 2,
    Harbor Hut Restaurant
9   Virg's Landing
14 Morro Bay Aquarium &
    Marine Rehabilitation Center
15 Central Coast Cruises
17 Heron Rookery
18 Morro Bay Museum
    of Natural History

that takes place every weekend in October, designated National Seafood Month.

The Embarcadero is good for people watching and is where **boat tours** depart. The *Tiger's Folly II*, an old paddlewheeler, makes $6 harbor tours and features Dixieland jazz; for information inquire at the Harbor Hut Restaurant (☎ 772-2255), 1205 Embarcadero. To actually leave the harbor you have to pay more. Central Coast Cruises (☎ 541-1435, 800-676-1677), at the south end of the Embarcadero, charges $20 for a two-hour trip that explores seal and sea lion territory north of Morro Bay. If you want to try your hand at **fishing**, Virg's Landing (☎ 772-1222, 800-932-3474), at the north end of the Embarcadero, is as good a place as any on the Central Coast. They run daily rock cod boat trips for $32 ($22 half day) and rent poles for $5.

About midway along the Embarcadero, the **Morro Bay Aquarium & Marine Rehabilitation Center** (☎ 772-7647) helps nurse sick seals, sea lions, and otters back to health and is open to the public from 9 am to 5 pm daily; admission is free. The Embarcadero ends at Tidelands Park, which has a grassy picnic area and playground. If you head up the stairs from the park and go right on Main St, you can take a scenic walk (about two miles) through Bluff Park to Morro Bay State Park.

Places to Stay Motels cluster around Main St and Harbor Blvd. In the off-season, room prices are often negotiable when you show up in person, but during the summer and the Harbor Festival, in October, reservations are imperative. Chain motels downtown are the *Econolodge* (☎ 772-5609), *Travelodge* (☎ 772-1259), and *Best Western El Rancho* (☎ 772-2212), which all charge around $55 in winter and $80 in summer.

Rooms at the *Morro Hilltop Inn* (☎ 772-1890), 1200 Morro Ave, are the cheapest in town at $35 in winter, $55 in summer. A few dollars more but right on the waterfront, *Roger's Bay Breeze Inn* (☎ 772-5607), at the north end of the Embarcadero

next to the PG&E plant, has rooms for $35 to $65 year round.

A step up is the *Sea Air Inn* (☎ 772-4437), 845 Morro Ave at the corner of Morro Bay Blvd, which has spiffy rooms for $35/55 in winter, $60/80 in summer, and serves a continental breakfast. The most expensive rooms have in-room hot tubs and ocean views.

Places to Eat Locals recommend the *Whale's Tail Restaurant* (☎ 772-7555), 945 Embarcadero, which doesn't have much of a view but has good fish for around $11 and pasta for around $9.

The *Bayside Cafe* (☎ 772-1465), at the Morro Bay State Park marina, is a hang-out for young locals and has good fish tacos, burgers, and oysters on the half shell for under $10.

Dorn's (☎ 772-4415), above the Embarcadero at 801 Market St, is a Morro Bay institution known for its clam chowder, fresh fish, and extensive wine list. The decor is elegant, but anything goes for attire. Full dinners cost around $18, though you can make a meal of appetizers, chowder, and bread for under $10.

Getting There & Away Bus service between Morro Bay, San Luis Obispo, and San Simeon is available on Central Coast Area Transit buses, which cost $3 per ride and stop at Morro Bay Park, on Shasta Ave between Morro Bay Blvd and Harbor St. Buses leave about every two hours from 7 am to 4 pm, Monday to Friday. For information call ☎ 541-2228.

Morro Bay State Park

This state park is quite developed and used regularly by area residents. Most of the park lies away from the coast, amidst eucalyptus trees planted by the CCC in the 1930s, though there is some beach access and a small marina that rents canoes and kayaks for $6 an hour. The **Morro Bay Museum of Natural History** (☎ 772-2694) has a good Chumash exhibit (the other exhibits look like high school science projects) and a nice view of Morro Rock.

Museum hours are 10 am to 5 pm daily, and admission is $2.

Just south of the park entrance is a eucalyptus grove where you can spot herons feeding their young from late February to May.

The *Morro Bay State Park Campground*, in the southern end of the park about two miles south of downtown Morro Bay, has beautiful sites surrounded by eucalyptus and cypress trees for $14. There is hot water and trails to the beach. Reservations are made through Destinet.

Montana de Oro State Park

South of Morro Bay and the joint communities of Los Osos and Baywood Park, Montana de Oro State Park covers 8000 acres of mountain and seaside terrain. Its coastal bluffs are a favorite spot for hiking, biking, and horseback riding. The northern half of the park includes a row of sand dunes (some 85 feet high) and the 12-mile-long sand spit that separates Morro Bay from the Pacific. The park's southern section consists of finger-like bluffs and an ancient marine terrace which (after seismic uplifting) is now a series of 1000-foot peaks. In the spring, the mountains are covered by bright wildflowers that give the park its name, which means 'mountain of gold' in Spanish.

South of the park entrance, **Spooner's Cove** is a popular beach and picnic area and home to the park headquarters (☎ 528-0513), which doubles as a natural history museum and sells maps and bottled water. Headquarters is open from 11 am to 3 pm October to March, noon to 4 pm March to September. The adjacent day-use facilities cost $5. You can park at any of the trailheads or turn-outs along Pecho Valley Rd for free.

Several hiking trails, including the Bluff Trail that skirts the cliffs and has beach access points, and the Alan Peak Trail that climbs to the park's highest point (1649 feet), start from the parking lot next to the headquarters. The best access to the sand dunes is along the Hazard Canyon Reef Trail, on Pecho Valley Rd about halfway

between the park entrance and headquarters. With a 4x4 vehicle, you can reach the sand spit via Sand Spit Rd (also called 'Army' and 'Dune Buggy Rd'), which intersects Pecho Valley Rd a half mile north of the park entrance.

Montana de Oro State Park Campground is Estero Bay's nicest campground. It winds along a narrow canyon with each site near the creek or against the hillside, and is near hiking trails and beaches. A 12-mile, 20-minute drive along a windy road is required to reach the campground, so it's not recommended as a quick place to crash. Sites cost $7 including picnic tables, fire pits, and pit toilets; there is drinking water, but no showers. Reservations can be made through Destinet.

ALONG HWY 101

Small agricultural towns along the inland route, Hwy 101, offer little in the way of accommodations, but good Mexican restaurants abound. The stretch between Carmel and San Luis Obispo (about 100 miles) is easily traveled in one day. If you want to stay overnight, there is camping at Pinnacles National Monument and plenty of motels in Paso Robles.

Salinas

• *pop 120,000* ☎ *408*

California's 'salad bowl' was also the birthplace of John Steinbeck. Only 17 miles from Monterey, this hard working farming town makes a strong contrast with the conspicuous affluence of nearby Monterey and Carmel. The historic center of the town is along Main St, just south of Hwy 101. The chamber of commerce (☎ 424-7611) at 119 E Alisal St, three blocks east of Main St, has some tourist information.

The **Boronda Adobe** (☎ 757-8085), at 333 Boronda Rd at the junction with W Laurel Drive, is the centerpiece for the local historical society. It's open daily from 10 am to 2 pm. Monterey makes much more mileage out of Steinbeck than Salinas but there is a **Steinbeck Center** (☎ 753-6411) at 371 Main St with displays and information. The **Steinbeck Public**

Library (☎ 758-7311) is at 350 Lincoln Ave, two blocks west. Also close to the Center is Steinbeck's birthplace and boyhood home (☎ 424-2735) at 132 Central Ave; it's now a restaurant open for lunch on weekdays only. There's a Steinbeck festival in August each year. Salinas also has a major rodeo in July and an international airshow in October.

Places to Stay & Eat There's no reason to stay overnight in Salinas but there are a number of motels along Main St at the Hwy 101 offramps. Restaurants can be found along Main St and a block over on Salinas St. *La Fogata* (☎ 757-5690) at 232 Main St is a straightforward Mexican restaurant with good-value lunch specials. On weekend nights *La Chapala* (☎ 757-4959) at 438 Salinas St puts on Latin and Tejano music.

Getting There & Away Monterey-Salinas Transit (MST) buses (☎ 424-7695) for the Monterey Peninsula (No 20 via Marina or No 21 via Hwy 68, $2.50) operate from the Transit Center at 110 Salinas St and also stop at the Amtrak station. Bus No 28 operates to Santa Cruz via Castroville, No 29 via Prunedale. Greyhound buses (☎ 424-4418, 800-231-2222) also stop on Salinas St at the junction with W Gabilan St. Salinas is on the Los Angeles-San Francisco Amtrak railway route (☎ 422-7458, 800-872-7245) and is the nearest stop to the Monterey Peninsula.

Pinnacles National Monument
Pinnacles National Monument, 12 miles northeast of Hwy 101, gets its name from the spires and crags which rise abruptly out of the oak and chaparral-covered hills of the Salinas Valley. The rocks are remains of an ancient volcano that formed along the San Andreas Rift Zone about 23 million years ago. Their arches, spires, crags, and lumps are the result of millions of years of erosion.

Hiking trails climb to the heart of the formations and wind past caves, natural springs, and the Bear Gulch Reservoir – a nice spot for picnicking and sunbathing. Although the Pinnacles' volcanic tufa is a bit crumbly, rock climbing is popular here and climbing access signs direct people to the best spots, most of which are on the east side.

Orientation & Information The rock formations divide the park into East Pinnacles, accessible from Hwy 25, and West Pinnacles, accessible from Hwy 101. While there is no road connecting the two sides, you can hike from one side to the other in about an hour. There are ranger stations with maps, books, and bottled water at both entrances, and a nice visitors center at the east entrance.

Campsites at the privately-owned *Pinnacles Campground Inc* (☎ 408-389-4462), at the East Pinnacles entrance, cost $14 and include hot showers. The Chaparral Ranger Station in West Pinnacles has primitive campsites for $12 per night, but is closed Friday to Sunday from March to May when the campground is converted to a day-use area.

Just off Hwy 101, the small town of **Soledad** has a bank, gas station, market, a few Mexican restaurants, and some budget motels.

Mission San Miguel Archangel
North of Paso Robles off Hwy 101, Mission San Miguel (☎ 408-467-3256) is the most accessible and one of the most authentic California missions. Established in 1797 as a stop-over between Mission San Antonio and Mission San Luis Obispo de Tolosa, Mission San Miguel was number 16 in the chain of 20 missions. There has not been much restoration work on the buildings as is evident from their rough and water-stained appearance, and murals painted by Chumash Indians using pigment from local rock are still visible in the main church.

A self-guided walking tour begins in the gift shop and goes through the mission's interior rooms and garden; allow half an hour. The enormous cactus in front of the mission was planted about the same time the mission was built. The mission is open daily, and masses are held Sundays and Holy Days.

Rios Caledonia Adobe

A quarter mile south of the mission is the Rios Caledonia Adobe (☎ 408-467-3357), which stands on mission property that Governor Pio Pico illegally sold to Petronillo Rios in 1846. Using Chumash labor, Rios built the two-story adobe as a ranch headquarters and hacienda for his family, and eventually turned it into an inn and stage stop on the route between Los Angeles and San Francisco. Original adobe bricks are visible where the whitewash has peeled off. The adobe is open daily and is free.

Mission San Antonio de Padua

This mission's remote location makes it a pain to reach, but it's well worth the trip. The lack of surrounding development is thanks to the US military, which owns the land, now Fort Hunter Ligget, an active army base. The mission was built in 1771 with a Salinian Indian labor force. The interior is quite elaborate, but the highlight is the mission grounds where you can see the remains of a grist mill, rip saw, corral, reservoir, and irrigation system. Plan on spending two hours at the mission and another hour driving to and from. Admission is free.

A quarter mile before the mission's entrance, on a small hill, is the Spanish-style Hacienda Inn, designed by Julia Morgan for William Randolph Hearst and originally called the **Milpitas Ranch House**. The inn is now owned by the military, but has a dining room and bar which are open to the public. Lunch and dinner are served Monday to Friday, and the bar is open nightly from 7 pm to midnight. The food is neither gourmet nor military grub, but you can get a big steak and all the trimmings for $8.

Getting There & Away From the north, take the Jolon exit (just before King City) and follow the Jolon Rd (G14) 20 miles south to Mission Rd. From the south, take the Hwy 101 exit marked San Antonio Mission/Lake San Antonio Recreation Area (north of Bradley) and head 22 miles northwest on G18. You'll pass a few markets and gas stations on the north shore of Lake San Antonio – good for swimming – and pass through a military check point. From here, Mission Rd goes another five miles to the mission.

You can also reach the mission from Hwy 1, via the Nacimiento-Fergusson Rd.

Lake Nacimiento

About 12 miles west of Hwy 101 on Lake Nacimiento Rd (clearly marked from the highway), Lake Nacimiento is best visited on the way to or from Mission San Antonio (listed above), unless you are a water skier, in which case it deserves priority status. With its sprawling inlets, the reservoir is considered one of the best water-ski spots in the USA. The lake is crowded with boats from April to October (especially on weekends and holidays) and has a real party atmosphere.

Most lakeshore property is privately owned. *Lake Nacimiento Resort* (☎ 408-238-3256, 800-323-3839), the only public access, charges a $10 day-use fee, which includes use of a swimming pool, hot tub, horseshoe pits, and basketball and volleyball courts. There is also a restaurant that serves good breakfast and lunch and marginal dinners. Campsites cost $20, and trailer and lodge accommodations start at $60; reservations are advised. Power boat rentals cost $30 to $50 an hour or $175 per day, and canoes, kayaks, and peddle boats rent for $5 to $10 an hour.

Paso Robles
• *pop 20,800* ☎ 805

Traditionally the hub of surrounding ranches, Paso Robles is a lively town with a decidedly western feel. Recently, ranchers have found wine grapes more lucrative than beef so vineyards are replacing cattle and Paso Robles is becoming increasingly chic. The city council recently restored the old town square into a lovely park. Across from the park at 1103 Spring St, the historic

Paso Robles Inn (☎ 238-2660) served as a stage stop in the early 1900s, and has been functioning as a hotel and restaurant ever since. Rooms are overpriced at $65 to $105, but the restaurant is good and has a folksy atmosphere.

For information and maps, stop by the chamber of commerce (☎ 238-0506), on Park St one block east of Spring St and half a block north of the town square, from 8 am to 5 pm Monday to Friday, 10 am to 4 pm on Saturday.

Places to Stay Paso Robles' accommodations are concentrated along Spring St, the town's main thoroughfare. The *Melody Ranch Motel* (☎ 238-3911), 939 Spring St, has adequate rooms for $34/40 and a small pool. Quite a bit nicer, the *Adelaide Motor Inn* (☎ 238-2770, 800-549-7276) is one block west of the Hwy 101/ 46 junction, next to the Black Oak Restaurant. Rooms cost $40/47 and the pool is heated. Also see the Paso Robles Inn, listed above.

Around Paso Robles
South of Paso Robles, **Templeton** activity revolves around its old granary, in continuous use since 1902, and a handful of specialty stores. *AJ Spurs* (☎ 434-2700), 508 Main St, is the area's most popular restaurant, filled with hunting trophies, cowboy gear, old photographs, and jovial people. Chicken, fish, or steak cost around $15, including vaquero soup, tequila beans, potatoes, and a root beer float. Off Main St, restored homes built during the 1900s railroad boom line shady streets.

The **wine country** surrounding Paso Robles has not yet attained the notoriety, throngs of people, or price level of Napa or Sonoma, and is worth a day's exploration. Most wineries are concentrated along Hwy 46 and west of Hwy 101 just north of Templeton. There are also several along Vineyard Drive, which intersects Hwy 101 south of Templeton. Most vineyards have tasting rooms and offer free tours. Try Meridian Vineyards (☎ 237-6000), on Hwy 46 seven miles east of Hwy 101, open daily except Tuesdays, and Jan Kris Vineyard

(☎ 434-0319), on Bethel Rd between Vineyard Drive and Hwy 46 west, open daily. Bonny Doon (☎ 239-5614), three miles west of Hwy 101 on Hwy 46 west, is known for dessert wines. They're open for tasting and 'knee-deep wading in the stream of consciousness' (from their brochure) from 11 am to 5:30 pm daily.

Lower Central Coast

The lower Central Coast is dominated by San Luis Obispo and Santa Barbara, both lively college towns with plenty of places to stay and eat and lots to see and do. South of San Luis Obispo, Southern California development begins in earnest and the highways become less interesting, used more as travel corridors than exploration routes. Highway 101 is the primary north-south thoroughfare, though Hwy 1 offers a glimpse of small towns populated by Mexican farm workers and surrounded by sugar beet and lettuce fields.

SAN LUIS OBISPO
• *pop 43,000* ☎ 805
San Luis Obispo (SLO) is a lively yet laid-back town, centered physically around Mission San Luis de Tolosa and culturally around California Polytechnic State University (Cal Poly). From September to May, music flows from pubs and cafes on Higuera St (the main drag) where you can hear everything from New Age electric grunge to Dixieland in one block. When school is not in session the town is quieter and the year-round population of ranchers and oil-refinery employees is more visible.

SLO's reasonably priced accommodations and proximity to beaches, state parks, and Hearst Castle (45 miles north), make it a good Central Coast hub.

History
Legend has it that Father Junipero Serra rang a bell on the bank of San Luis Creek to attract local Chumash Indians of the Tixlini community. When they came to find what

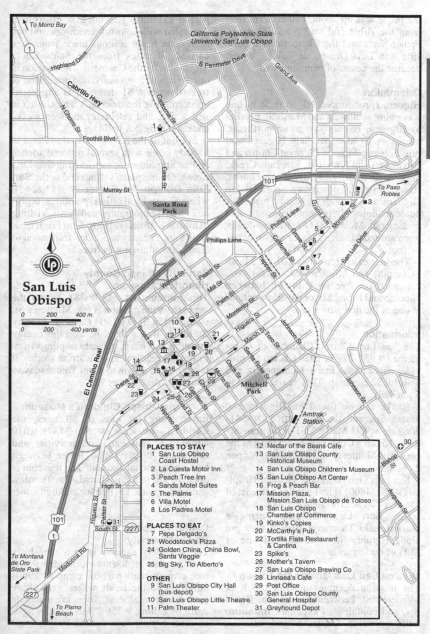

To Morro Bay

California Polytechnic State
University San Luis Obispo

S Perimeter Drive

Grand Ave

Highland Drive

Cabrillo Hwy

N Chorro St

Foothill Blvd

California St

Cass St

Murray St

**Santa Rosa
Park**

Phillips Lane

To Paso
Robles

Phillips Lane

Grove St

Pepper St

California St

Grand Ave

Monterey St

San Luis Drive

**San Luis
Obispo**

0   200   400 m
0   200   400 yards

Walnut St

Peach St

Mill St

Palm St

Monterey St

Higuera St

Marsh St

Toro St

Santa Rosa St

Johnson Ave

Broad St

El Camino Real

Dana St

Nipomo St

Broad St

Garden St

Chorro St

Morro St

Osos St

**Mitchell
Park**

Amtrak
Station

Johnson Ave

Bishop St

Augusta St

High St

Higuera St

Parker St

South St

To Montana
de Oro
State Park

Madonna Rd

To Pismo
Beach

PLACES TO STAY	
1	San Luis Obispo Coast Hostel
2	La Cuesta Motor Inn
3	Peach Tree Inn
4	Sands Motel Suites
5	The Palms
6	Villa Motel
8	Los Padres Motel

PLACES TO EAT	
7	Pepe Delgado's
21	Woodstock's Pizza
24	Golden China, China Bowl, Santa Veggie
25	Big Sky, Tio Alberto's

OTHER	
9	San Luis Obispo City Hall (bus depot)
10	San Luis Obispo Little Theatre
11	Palm Theater

12	Nectar of the Beans Cafe
13	San Luis Obispo County Historical Museum
14	San Luis Obispo Children's Museum
15	San Luis Obispo Art Center
16	Frog & Peach Bar
17	Mission Plaza, Mission San Luis Obispo de Toloso
18	San Luis Obispo Chamber of Commerce
19	Kinko's Copies
20	McCarthy's Pub
22	Tortilla Flats Restaurant & Cantina
23	Spike's
26	Mother's Tavern
27	San Luis Obispo Brewing Co
28	Linnaea's Cafe
29	Post Office
30	San Luis Obispo County General Hospital
31	Greyhound Depot

the jingle was all about, Father Serra read from the Bible and said mass. Together, Father Serra and the Chumash built Mission San Luis Obispo de Tolosa, which became the center of community life.

Orientation

Higuera (pronounced HI-gera) St is one way going southwest and Marsh St, parallel to Higuera, is one-way going northeast. Monterey St also parallels Higuera and runs between Mission Plaza (at Chorro and Broad Sts) and Hwy 101. San Luis Creek, once used to irrigate Mission orchards, flows through downtown parallel to Higuera and provides a shady place for outdoor dining, impromptu concerts, and making out. Most of SLO's sites are downtown around Mission Plaza, easily reached on foot.

The best exits from Hwy 101 are Marsh St (south) and Monterey St (north). You can park for free on Palm St, between Nipomo and Broad Sts, or pay 25¢ per hour at one of the downtown lots.

Information

The San Luis Obispo Chamber of Commerce (☎ 781-2777), 1039 Chorro St, provides a free phone line to local motels, and a useful $2 city map. They're open 9 am to 5 pm daily.

Banks can be found on Higuera and Marsh Sts, and the post office (☎ 541-3062) is at 893 Marsh St. For fax transactions, Kinko's Copies (☎ 543-3363), at the corner of Monterey and Morro Sts, is open 24 hours.

San Luis Obispo County General Hospital (☎ 781-4800) is half a mile southeast of Monterey St at 2180 Johnson Ave.

The **San Luis Obispo Farmer's Market**, held Thursdays from 6 to 9 pm along Higuera St, is considered one of SLO's best attractions.

Mission San Luis Obispo De Toloso

The mission occupies a solid block of Monterey St, between Chorro and Broad Sts, and contains an excellent **museum** with extensive Chumash and mission period exhibits. The mission **church** is decorated with colorful woodwork and has high open beam ceilings made from logs carried 40 miles from the Santa Lucia Mountains by the Chumash. The mission is open 9 am to 5 pm daily, and admission is free (though a $1 donation is suggested upon entering the museum). The church is still active, and celebrates mass on weekends and religious holidays.

In front of the mission, Mission Plaza is a shady space with several restored adobes and an amphitheater overlooking San Luis Creek. On the plaza's south end is the **San Luis Obispo Art Center** (☎ 543-8562), which shows local artists' paintings, sculpture, and photography and hosts visiting exhibits – usually from San Francisco. Hours are Tuesday to Sunday from noon to 5 pm, and admission is free.

San Luis Obispo County Historical Museum

This museum (☎ 543-0638), across the street from the mission at 696 Monterey St, is housed in SLO's 1904 Carnegie Library Building. Better than the average county museum, this has historical samplings from Chumash, nautical, and Victorian worlds. It is open from 10 am to 4 pm Wednesday to Sunday. Admission is $2.

San Luis Obispo Children's Museum

Entertaining for kids of all ages, the Children's Museum (☎ 544-5437), 1010 Nipomo St, has hands-on activities and interactive displays that teeter between being educational and fun. The museum is open 10 am to 5 pm Thursday to Tuesday, and admission is $3 (free for children under two years).

California Polytechnic State University

The Cal Poly campus is in a nice hilly setting north of downtown. Students lead free campus tours past the campus' 1960s buildings to the fields where agriculture projects are in process. Tours are available daily by calling ☎ 756-2792. Besides agriculture, architecture is Cal Poly's most important subject. The campus' unlikely highlight is the **Friends of Shakespeare Press Museum** (☎ 756-1108) which contains a Gold Rush-era collection of printing presses and type sets. The collection belonged to Charles Palmer, an antique collector and poet who earned the nickname 'little Shakespeare' in California's gold fields. To make an appointment to see the collection, call ☎ 756-1108 from 9 am to 5 pm Monday to Friday.

To reach the campus, take Grand Ave north from Hwy 101 or Monterey St and follow it to the campus entrance.

Activities
Hiking There are plenty of good hikes around SLO, many of which start from Poly Canyon Rd, on the Cal Poly campus. Hiking maps and parking information are available at the booth on the right as you enter the campus. Parking in designated lots costs around $2.50 per day.

Popular day hikes are to Bishop Peak and Cerro San Luis Obispo which offer panoramic views of San Luis Obispo Bay and surrounding ranch land. A hiking map and description sheet is available from the chamber of commerce.

Bicycling For bicycling, bike shops and the chamber of commerce sell the excellent *San Luis Obispo County Bike Map* for $1. You can rent a bike from the Alamo Bicycle Touring Company (☎ 781-3830) for $25 per day ($15 for three hours), which offers delivery and pick-up services since they don't have a shop.

Special Events
In February, Mardi Gras is celebrated with a boisterous New Orleans-style parade (though with a definite West Coast flavor) down Higuera St.

In April, SLO's streets are adorned with colorful renditions of everything from Keith Haring to Reubens paintings during the Italian Street Painting Festival. La Fiesta, in May, celebrates SLO's Spanish heritage with food, dancing, music, and craft booths. The Mozart Festival in July

and August features Mozart's works performed by musicians from all over the world. For information about any of these events, contact the chamber of commerce.

Places to Stay
Camping The nearest campgrounds are at Montana De Oro State Park, listed under Estero Bay, above.

Hostel The *SLO Coast Hostel* (☎ 544-4678) is next to Cal Poly at 1292 Foothill Blvd. Single-sex dorm accommodations with four or eight beds per room cost $13 per night, and there is a large common area and well-equipped kitchen facilities. The unexciting atmosphere is mostly due to the 11 pm curfew, though the distance from downtown is also a factor. The hostel is open from 5 to 10 pm for check-in, and closed from 9 am to 5 pm.

Hotels & Motels SLO's motels are concentrated on the north end of Monterey St. To avoid traffic noise, request a room facing away from Monterey. Charming but tiny yellow cottages at *The Palms* (☎ 543-0230) 1628 Monterey St, cost $25 and are the best deal in town.

Going north to south, *La Cuesta Motor Inn* (☎ 543-2777, 800-543-2777), 2074 Monterey St, has a pool and jacuzzi, continental breakfast, free local phone calls, and rooms for $64/74. The *Peach Tree Inn* (☎ 800-227-6396), 2001 Monterey St, has a continental breakfast and flowery lobby. The simple rooms are overpriced at $55/70, unless you can get one of the new rooms in the back that face San Luis Creek.

The *Sands Motel Suites* (☎ 544-0500, 800-441-4657), 1930 Monterey St, has rooms away from the street and a comfortable lobby. Their $54 rooms are a good value but sell out quickly, leaving only overpriced $89 rooms.

Owned by a friendly family, the *Villa Motel* (☎ 543-8071), 1670 Monterey St, has newly renovated units for $38/44, and *Los Padres Motel* (☎ 543-5017), 1575 Monterey St, has decorated rooms for $45.

The *Embassy Suites* (☎ 549-0800), 333

Madonna Rd (southwest of town off Hwy 101), offer SLO's most deluxe accommodations for $139 to $152, including breakfast and two hours of cocktails each evening.

Besides those listed above, there are three Best Westerns, a Travelodge, Super 8, Holiday Inn, Howard Johnson, and Vagabond Inn.

For something a little more unusual, try the *Madonna Inn* (☎ 543-3000), just west of Hwy 1/101 on Madonna Road, where the decor can be called 'interesting' at best. The Caveman Room is carved out of solid rock, and the lobby men's restroom has an automatic waterfall urinal. Each of the 109 rooms are unique, with prices from $65 to $210. The staff is very accommodating to people who just want to stop by and gaze.

Places to Eat

SLO has a good variety of ethnic food, and most restaurants have a vegetarian selection. *Woodstock's Pizza* (☎ 541-4420), 1000 Higuera St, is SLO's landmark pizza joint – fast, greasy, and always crowded. Pizzas come on white or whole wheat crust and cost around $15 for a large, $2 per slice. From 11 am to 3 pm, Monday to Friday, $4 will get you all the pizza you can eat and all the soda you can drink.

The *SLO Brewing Co* (☎ 543-1843), between Higuera and Marsh Sts at 1119 Garden St, has good burgers, veggie burgers, grilled meats and fish, and large salads for under $10. The atmosphere is loud and the homemade brews are worth sampling.

Also popular is *Big Sky* (☎ 545-5401), 1121 Broad St, whose 'modern food' tends to be hit or miss. The Big Sky Noodle Bowl, Blackened Chicken Salad, and Japanese Eggplant Sandwich are outstanding favorites; the Jambalaya should be avoided. Prices are $4 to $7; fresh fish around $10.

For good cheap Mexican food, line up with the locals at *Tio Alberto's* (☎ 546-9646), 1131 Broad St, where you grab paper napkins and plastic utensils and wait for your number to be called. Carnitas (pork) burritos, tortas, and tamales are house specialties – all under $6. *Pepe Delgado's* (☎ 544-6660), 1601 Monterey St, is good for sit-down Mexican meals and potent margaritas. Lunch is around $5, dinner around $10, and there is always a wait on Friday and Saturday nights.

There are three all-you-can-eat Chinese restaurants next door to each other in the 600 block of Higuera St. *Golden China* charges $5 for lunch, $7 for dinner and generally has the best quality. *China Bowl* and *Santa Veggie* charge $6 for lunch, $8 for dinner, and have more vegetarian items plus unlikely American dishes like brownies and Caesar salad. Lunch is served from 11:30 am to 2:30 pm, dinner from 5 to 9 pm.

Entertainment

Coffeehouses SLO's alternative scene revolves around *Nectar of the Beans Cafe* (☎ 545-0870), 940 Chorro St, which features experimental music and serves strong coffee until midnight. *Linnaea's Cafe* (☎ 541-5888), a tiny coffee house-cum-music venue just across from the Brewing Co at 1110 Garden St, hosts folk and acoustic guitarists and is open until 1 am.

Bars *Mother's Tavern* (☎ 541-8733), 729 Higuera St, is the college crowd's favorite for boozing and carousing. Across the street, the *Frog & Peach Bar* (☎ 595-3764), has a wide beer selection, subdued British atmosphere, and live jazz on Friday and Saturday nights.

Spike's (☎ 544-7157), 570 Higuera St, is a beer-lover's dream with around 70 different beers available (45 on tap). If somehow you manage to guzzle one of everything, you get a commemorative T-shirt to remember your liver by. *McCarthy's Pub* (☎ 544-0268), 1019 Court St, is a dark, no-nonsense bar popular with alternative types from the college.

Popular for billiards and beer, the *SLO Brewing Co* (see Places to Eat, above) attracts a thirty-something crowd. Live bands (usually reggae) play Thursday to Saturday nights, starting at 9:30 pm, and Irish folk bands play every second and last

Wednesday of the month during Irish Happy Hour, when pints cost $1 from 5:30 to 7 pm.

Tortilla Flats Restaurant & Cantina (☎ 544-7575), 1051 Nipomo St, is SLO's cure for Saturday Night Fever.

Theater & Cinema The *Palm Theatre* (☎ 541-5161), 817 Palm St, is an old-style movie house that shows foreign and classic films nightly. Tickets are $5 ($3 on Monday).

Live productions are performed at the *San Luis Obispo Little Theatre* (☎ 543-3737), 888 Morro St, Thursday to Saturday nights and on Sunday afternoons.

Getting There & Away
Air American Eagle Airline (☎ 800-433-7300) has daily flights to Los Angeles and San Francisco from the small San Luis Obispo County Airport (☎ 541-1038), south of downtown between Hwy 1/101 and Broad St.

Bus Greyhound Bus Lines runs six daily buses to Los Angeles for $30, five to Santa Barbara for $17, and six to San Francisco for $35; no discounts are offered on roundtrip tickets. The Greyhound station (☎ 543-2121) is south of downtown, one block east of Higuera St at 150 South St.

Central Coast Area Transit (CCAT) (☎ 781-4472) has buses that go to Morro Bay, where you can catch a bus to Cayucos, Cambria, and San Simeon. Buses leave hourly from 6 am to 6 pm Monday to Friday, from the San Luis Obispo City Hall on Osos St. Tickets cost $3 with one transfer. Schedules are available at the chamber of commerce.

Green Tortoise buses stop at the Denny's restaurant (☎ 543-7220), off the Los Osos exit just south of downtown, en route to Los Angeles and San Francisco.

Train North- and south-bound trains leave once daily from SLO's Amtrak station (☎ 541-0505), at the southern end of Santa Rosa St. Tickets to Los Angeles cost around $55, to Santa Barbara $45, and to

San Francisco $68 to $116, depending on availability.

Getting Around
Trolley The free SLO Trolley makes a continuos loop along Marsh, Higuera, Nipomo, Monterey, and Palm Sts, daily from noon to 5 pm (Thursdays until 9:30 pm to coincide with the Farmer's Market). Catch the trolley from well-signed stops on the right side of the street.

Bus The CCAT buses listed under Getting There & Away (above) make regular 10-minute trips between City Hall and the Cal Poly Campus. Buses run Monday to Friday, 7 am to 5 pm and cost $3.

Car Thrifty Car Rental (☎ 544-3777) charges around $35 per day and will deliver a vehicle to the train or bus station, or your motel. For taxi service, call Yellow Cab Co at ☎ 543-1234.

SAN LUIS OBISPO BAY

About eight miles southwest of San Luis Obispo, the small communities of Avila Beach, Shell Beach, Pismo Beach, Grover Beach, and Oceano border San Luis Obispo Bay, the bay Cabrillo called *Todos Santos* (all saints) because of its beauty. When Mission San Luis de Tolosa was built in 1772, the bay was its main port, connected to San Luis Obispo by narrow gauge railroad. After San Francisco's big fire in 1906, this was the official port of entry to the USA.

Today the bay is bordered by oil refineries and beach towns that survive on tourism. If you hear a steady siren for three to five minutes, tune your radio to 920 AM, 1400 AM, or 98.1 FM – Diablo Nuclear Power plant, just east of the bay, might be doing something weird.

Avila Beach
• *pop 384* ☎ *805*
Furthest north on San Luis Bay, where San Luis Creek meets the sea, sunny Avila Beach has an old wooden fishing pier which divides the beach in two: north of the

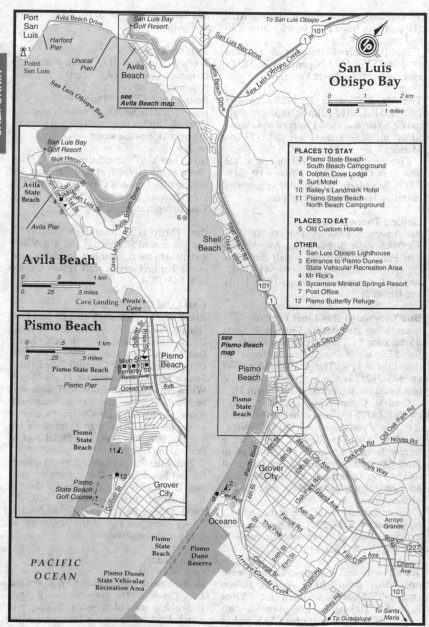

Port San Luis
Avila Beach Drive
Harford Pier
San Luis Bay Golf Resort
To San Luis Obviso
San Luis Bay Drive
101
1
Point San Luis
Unocal Pier
Avila Beach
San Luis Obispo Creek

San Luis Obispo Bay

0   1   2 km
0   .5   1 miles

see Avila Beach map

Avila Beach Drive

San Luis Bay Golf Resort
Blue Heron Drive
Avila State Beach
Front St
San Miguel St
San Luis St
Cave Landing Rd
Avila Beach Drive
4
5
Avila Pier
6

Shell Beach
Shell Beach Rd
Ocean Blvd

Avila Beach

0   .5   1 km
0   .25   .5 miles

Cave Landing　Pirate's Cove

101
1

PLACES TO STAY
2　Pismo State Beach
　South Beach Campground
8　Dolphin Cove Lodge
9　Surf Motel
10　Bailey's Landmark Hotel
11　Pismo State Beach
　North Beach Campground

PLACES TO EAT
5　Old Custom House

OTHER
1　San Luis Obispo Lighthouse
3　Entrance to Pismo Dunes
　State Vehicular Recreation Area
4　Mr Rick's
6　Sycamore Mineral Springs Resort
7　Post Office
12　Pismo Butterfly Refuge

Pismo Beach

0   .5   1 km
0   .25   .5 miles

Dolliver St
Price St
Main St
Pomeroy St
Hinds Ave
Ocean View Ave

Pismo Beach

Pismo State Beach
Pismo Pier

8
10

Pismo State Beach
11

Price Canyon Rd

see Pismo Beach map

Pismo Beach
Pismo State Beach

Pismo State Beach Golf Course
12
Grover City
Dolliver St

4th St
Atlantic City Ave
1st St
Oak Park Rd
Oak Park Blvd
Grand Ave
Ash St
Farroll Rd
Old Oak Park Rd
Noyes Rd
James Way

Grover City

Oceano
Pier Ave
2
3
4th St
13th St
The Pike
24th St
Elm St
Clienega St
Halcyon Rd
Pacific Blvd
Arroyo Grande Creek

Arroyo Grande
Branch
227
Fair Oaks Ave
Cherry Ave

PACIFIC OCEAN

Pismo State Beach
Pismo Dune Reserve

Pismo Dunes State Vehicular Recreation Area

Valley Rd
101
To Santa Maria
To Guadalupe

pier families spend their weekend outings, while the south side is populated by beer-drinking, frisbee-throwing college students. Front St, referred to as 'the board-walk' faces the water and is lined with bikini shops, board rental stands, and bars. *Mr Rick's* is a good place for a drink, and the lush patio of the *Old Customs House* (☎ 595-7555), 324 Front St, is popular for bloody marys, breakfast, and lunch.

A mile north of the fishing pier is **Harford Pier**, central to the working harbor of Port San Luis. The *Olde Porte Inn* at the end of the pier has fresh seafood for $6 to $11, and a popular bar where Jimmy Buffet tunes rule. For $1 you can buy a bag of smelt from the fishmonger next door and feed the sea lions.

Just south of Avila Beach, **Cave Landing** is a 150-foot promontory used as dock for large ships in the early 1900s. A rocky trail from the parking lot's south end leads down to the cave and to **Pirate's Cove**, a beautiful sandy beach where clothing is optional. A sign reads 'Respect people's privacy – don't be a gawker!' but locals recommend that women not go alone unless there are plenty of people around. High tides, responsible for the cove's interesting rock formations, will sweep your stuff out to sea if you don't put it near the cliffs.

At **Sycamore Mineral Springs Resort** (☎ 595-7302), rooms start at $170 and meals cost around $20, but you can have a soak in a natural mineral spring, a swim, and a shower for $10 – towels, robes, and soap included. Reservations are recommended if you want to visit after 7 pm; 'happy hour' is from 4 to 6 pm when you get a $2 discount. The springs are open 24 hours.

Shell Beach

Shell Beach is a neighborhoodish alternative to its touristy surroundings. Businesses are along Shell Beach Rd which parallels Hwy 101 for about one mile. Ocean Blvd, lined with a grass parkway and picnic tables, gives access to the beach and some nifty tidepools.

Shell Beach has cheaper accommodations than Pismo Beach, mostly on Shell Beach Rd near Hwy 101. The *Ocean View Motel* (☎ 805-773-2113), 1001 Shell Beach Rd, has exceptionally friendly owners and rooms for $28 in winter, $38 in summer.

Pismo Beach
• *pop 7850* ☎ *805*

Pismo Beach is a tacky tourist town known for clams and sand dunes. Today the beach is pretty much clammed out, though you still see people with clam rods (cylindrical tubes with pulleys running through their center) trying their luck from a half hour before to a half hour after sunset, as clamming laws require. Clamming doesn't require any instruments though – just twist your foot into the wet sand to about ankle level and feel with your toes for something hard. If you do find one, you can keep it if it is 4½ inches in diameter and you have a California fishing license (available at sport shops and liquor stores). The biggest clam shell in town is in front of the Pismo Beach Chamber of Commerce (☎ 773-4382) at 581 Dolliver St.

In mid-October, the **Pismo Beach Clam Festival** celebrates the beloved clam with an arts & crafts fair, music, and food booths, drawing people by the thousands. From late-November to March, thousands of migrating monarch butterflies land on Monterey Cypress and eucalyptus trees in the **Pismo Butterfly Refuge**, just south of the Pismo Pier.

Central Pismo Beach, a conglomeration of tourist shops and restaurants around the Pismo Pier, borders a wide sandy beach which extends south for about 10 miles. **Pismo Dunes Vehicular Recreation Area** dominates the middle and south part of this stretch, where the beach turns to sand dunes. Here you can drive along the beach and access a primitive campground where sites cost $6; reserve through Destinet.

Places to Stay *North Beach Campground* is about one mile south of the Pismo Pier. It has grassy sites shaded by eucalyptus trees, easy beach access trails, and new bathrooms. *South Beach Campground* is about four miles south, near the entrance to Pismo Dunes in the small community of Oceano. Dune warriors fill this campground and don't mind the parking lot atmosphere. Sites cost $16 at both places, and can be reserved through Destinet.

Most motels are near the beach on Cypress and Dolliver Sts, and on the short streets between Cypress and Hwy 101. Pismo Beach has dozens of motels, but rooms fill up quickly and prices are high from May to September, and during the Clam Festival in October. Housed in a refurbished 1920s hotel, *Bailey's Landmark Hotel* (☎ 773-5566, 800-262-7557), 701 Price St, is out of the tourist hubbub but walking distance to the Pismo Pier. Rooms cost $40 to $70 (depending on the view) from Sunday to Thursday, $50 to $90 on Friday and Saturday.

Closer to the beach, the *Surf Motel* (☎ 773-2070), 250 Main St, has rooms for $40/55 in winter, $65/85 in summer, including donuts and coffee and use of a heated pool. Steps from the beach, the *Dolphin Cove Lodge* (☎ 773-4706), 170 Main St, has rooms for $45 to $85 year round and offers discounts if you stay for three or more days.

Places to Eat There are several good chowder houses directly up from the pier on Pomeroy St, including *Splash Cafe* (☎ 773-4653) where you can get excellent clam chowder ($2.50), fish sandwiches ($4), and crab cocktail ($3) without even putting your shoes on. Across the street, the *Black Pearl Coffeehouse* (☎ 773-6631) has strong coffee, healthy muffins ($2), and a young local scene. Ironically, the best place in town has nothing to do with fish: *Giuseppe's* (☎ 773-2870), two blocks north of the end of Pomeroy at 891 Price St, specializes in Southern Italian food.

PISMO BEACH TO SANTA BARBARA
Along Hwy 1
Between Pismo Beach and Santa Barbara, Hwy 1 is forced inland by Vandenberg Air Force Base and its Missile Test Center which occupies the coast. If you take the train along this part of California, as Jack Kerouac was fond of doing, you'll see a part of the coast hidden from motorists. Land not owned by the government is planted with sugar beets and lettuce, harvested by Mexican laborers. Guadalupe and Betteravia are about 85% Mexican and have some truly authentic Mexican restaurants. **Lompoc**, the largest town along the highway, is a quiet military town with wide shady streets and a county museum. In the spring wildflowers turn the surrounding hills into a brilliant mosaic.

La Purisima Mission Just east of Hwy 1, on Hwy 246 about two miles from Lompoc, La Purisima Mission is one of two missions run by the State Park Service instead of the Church. Totally restored in the 1930s by the CCC, the mission's buildings are fully intact and decorated as they were during the mission period – right down to blankets on the cots and grinding stones in the courtyard. The mission fields still support livestock and the gardens are planted with medicinal plants and trees used by the Chumash. Within the garden, you can see fountains and ground-level troughs where women did the wash – one for the Indians and one for the mission women. The original mission was actually three miles south but rebuilt here after a major earthquake in 1812.

Surrounding the mission are 15 miles of hiking and horse trails, maintained by the Park Service. At the park entrance is a museum and bookstore (☎ 805-733-3713), open 11 am to 4 pm, which has a good selection of local history books and a free trail map. The park is open from 9 am to 5 pm daily; mission buildings close at 4 pm. Admission is $5.

Solvang
• *pop 4500* ☎ *805*
In 1911, three Danish farmers established the Atterdag College folk school in the Santa Ynez Valley to pass on their Danish traditions to future generations. The small

farming community of Solvang, whose name means 'sunny field,' grew up around the school. Today the quasi-Danish berg is a tacky conglomeration of 'authentic' Danish bakeries and gift shops full of wooden shoes and dinnerware.

The one redeeming piece of culture is the **Elverhoy Museum** (☎ 686-1211), housed in a replica 18th-century Jutland farmhouse, two blocks south of the main shopping district at the corner of Second St and Elverhoy Way. Its collection of *papierklip* (paper cut-out) art, period clothes and furniture, farm tools, and old photographs is worth a look. Hours are 1 to 4 pm Wednesday to Sunday, and admission is free.

Amidst the faux-front stores and European flags downtown is the **Hans Christian Andersen Museum** (☎ 688-2052), in the Bookloft Building at 1680 Mission Drive. It has a small collection of old books, manuscripts, and paper cut-outs inspired by Andersen's bed-time favorites.

Solvang's cultural loner is the **Mission Santa Inez** (☎ 688-4814), 1760 Mission Drive, hemmed in by civilization and a parking lot which used to be a vegetable garden. Founded at the height of missionary prosperity in 1804, the mission is an active parish and school. If you are planning to visit other missions, don't bother with this one. Hours are from 9 am to 4:30 pm daily, and admission is $2.

Places to Eat Among the many 'authentic' Danish bakeries, locals recommend *Birkholms Jr* (☎ 688-3872), 1555 Mission Drive, for shortbread cookies and pastries. They have indoor and outdoor tables where you can have a coffee with your sweets.

The *Solvang Restaurant* (☎ 688-4645), 1672 Copenhagen Drive, serves *aebleskivers* (ball-like pancakes dusted with powdered sugar) as well as 'normal' American breakfasts and lunches for under $5. For dinner try the huge all-you-can-eat smorgasbord ($9) at the *Danish Inn Restaurant* (☎ 688-4813), 1547 Mission Drive, or the reliable split pea soup at *Pea Soup Andersen's*, in Buellton at the Hwy 246/101 junction.

Santa Ynez Valley
From Hwy 101, six miles north of Solvang, you can head southeast through Solvang on Hwy 154 which cuts through the lovely Santa Ynez Valley and San Marco Pass to Santa Barbara. This route takes twice as long as going directly down Hwy 101, but is much more scenic and offers hiking, swimming, and camping opportunities (see Los Padres National Forest, below).

Refugio & El Capitan State Beaches
West of Santa Barbara on Hwy 1/101, Refugio (pronounced re-FOO-hee-o) and El Capitan State Beaches have grassy picnic areas, lifeguard stations, and beautiful campgrounds. Refugio is a popular surf spot and hangout for students. The small campground is right next to the beach. The El Capitan campground, perched on low bluffs above the beach, is more popular with families. A 2½-mile trail runs along the bluffs connecting the two. First come, first served campsites cost $14 and have flush toilets, picnic tables, and barbecues.

SANTA BARBARA
• *pop 85,500 ☎ 805*

Sandwiched between the Pacific Ocean and Santa Ynez Mountains, Santa Barbara is often called the California Riviera because of its affluent population, Mediterranean architecture, and seaside location. Five colleges in the area, including the University of California at Santa Barbara (UCSB), give the town a youthful vivacity and balance Santa Barbara's yacht clubs and retirement communities. Though definitely a beach city, much of Santa Barbara's charm lies inland. The downtown has outstanding architectural integrity, a masterpiece of a courthouse, and noteworthy art and natural history museums. Rising abruptly and majestically to the north, the Santa Ynez foothills offer great hiking and camping opportunities.

History
Until about 200 years ago, Chumash Indians thrived in the Santa Barbara area, living in villages along the coast and in the Santa

Ynez Mountains. In 1542, Juan Cabrillo entered the channel, put up a Spanish flag, and went on his way. Sebastian Vizcaino, a cartographer for the Duke of Monterey, landed in the harbor on December 4, 1602 (the feast day of St Barbara) and literally put Santa Barbara on the map. But being claimed and named by Spain didn't affect Santa Barbara's Chumash until the mission and presidio were built in the mid-1700s.

The padres converted the Chumash and taught them to wear clothes and change their traditional diet of acorn mush, roots, and fish to meat. The Chumash contracted European diseases that eventually decimated the tribe.

Easterners started arriving in force with the 1849 Gold Rush, and by the late 1890s Santa Barbara was an established vacation spot for the rich and famous. The American Film Company, founded at the corner of Mission and State Sts in 1910, was the largest in the world for about three of its 10 years in existence, but since then Hollywood has used Santa Barbara mostly as a get-away.

Orientation

Santa Barbara is on a south-facing promontory, with the Santa Ynez Mountains (part of Los Padres National Forest) rising abruptly to the north.

Downtown Santa Barbara is laid out in a square grid with State St as the main thoroughfare which divides streets into East and West (though State actually runs northwest – southeast). 'Lower' State St (south of Ortega St) has Santa Barbara's concentration of bars and shady characters, while 'upper' State St (north of Ortega St) is where the nice shops and museums are. Cabrillo Blvd hugs the coastline and turns into Coast Village Rd as it enters Montecito; Stearn's Wharf is at the south end of State St, and the Santa Barbara Yacht Harbor is a half mile west, off Cabrillo Blvd.

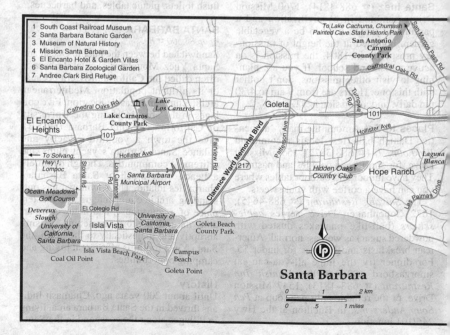

1 South Coast Railroad Museum
2 Santa Barbara Botanic Garden
3 Museum of Natural History
4 Mission Santa Barbara
5 El Encanto Hotel & Garden Villas
6 Santa Barbara Zoological Garden
7 Andree Clark Bird Refuge

To Lake Cachuma, Chumash Painted Cave State Historic Park

San Antonio Canyon County Park

San Marcos Pass Rd

Cathedral Oaks Rd

Lake Los Carneros

Goleta

Turnpike Rd

101

El Encanto Heights

Cathedral Oaks Rd

Lake Carneros County Park

101

Hollister Ave

Patterson Ave

To Solvang, Hwy 1, Lompoc

Hollister Ave

Storke Rd

Los Carneros Rd

Fairview Rd

Clarence Ward Memorial Blvd

217

Hidden Oaks Country Club

Laguna Blanca

Hope Ranch

Santa Barbara Municipal Airport

Las Palmas Drive

Ocean Meadows Golf Course

El Colegio Rd

Devereux Slough

University of California, Santa Barbara

Isla Vista

University of California, Santa Barbara

Goleta Beach County Park

Coal Oil Point

Isla Vista Beach Park

Campus Beach

Goleta Point

Santa Barbara

0   1   2 km
0   .5   1 miles

Santa Barbara is surrounded by small affluent communities: Mesa and Hope Ranch to the west, Montecito and Summerland to the east. UCSB is just west of Hope Ranch in Isla Vista, and most of Santa Barbara's college crowd lives around the campus or in neighboring Goleta.

Information

Tourist Offices The Downtown Organization Visitors Information Center (☎ 965-3023), 504 State St, has the best selection of maps and brochures, but is often so busy that the staff can't answer questions. Hours are 9 am to 5 pm Monday to Friday. Their smaller office is near Stearn's Wharf at the corner of Cabrillo Blvd and Santa Barbara St and is open weekends too.

The Hot Spots Visitors Center (☎ 564-1637), housed in a 24-hour cafe at 36 State St, has a hotel reservation board hooked up to a free telephone, plus maps and brochures, and an ATM. There is a staff person on hand from 9 am to 9 pm Monday to Saturday, noon to 5 pm on Sunday.

Telecommunications The main post office (☎ 546-2266) is housed in an Art Deco/Spanish Colonial Revival building at 836 Anacapa St.

All of the visitors centers listed above sell international phone cards and have facilities where you can use them. For fax transmissions and computer services, try Kinko's (☎ 966-1114), just off State St at 26 E Victoria (behind Copeland's Sports).

Money Numerous banks and ATMs are on State St; general banking hours are 9 am to 5 pm Monday to Thursday, 9 am to 6 pm Friday, and Saturday 9 am to 2 pm.

Paul Brombals (☎ 687-3641), four miles north of downtown at 3601 State St, gives the best foreign currency exchange rate. It is open 10 am to 5 pm Monday to Friday, Saturday 10 am to 2 pm.

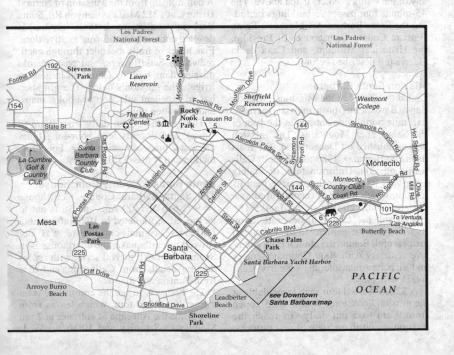

Bookstores Pacific Travelers Supply (☎ 963-4438), 529 State St, has a good selection of local guides and natural history books, and a large map inventory. They're open from 10 am to 6 pm Monday to Saturday, 11 am to 6 pm Sunday. For a more general selection, Earthling's Bookstore (☎ 965-0926), 1137 State St, has three floors worth of books and a cafe that is open until 11 pm.

Laundry Bubbles & Beans (☎ 898-9999), at the corner of Mission and De la Vina Sts, is open from 6:30 am to 9:30 pm daily, and sells espresso along with soap.

Medical Services The Med Center (☎ 682-7411), three miles north of downtown at 2954 State St, has a 24 hour emergency room.

The Red Tile Walking Tour
Pick up a free *Red Tile Walking Tour* map at any of the visitors centers listed above. The 45-minute tour passes 23 buildings including the Santa Barbara Art Museum, Santa Barbara County Courthouse, El Presidio, the Historical Museum, and Casa de la Guerra (all described below).

Mission Santa Barbara
Called the Queen of the Missions, Mission Santa Barbara sits on a majestic perch a half mile north of downtown at the foot of the Santa Ynez Mountains. The mission was established on December 4 (the feast day of St Barbara), 1786 as the tenth California mission. Unfortunately, its stately exterior is much more impressive than its interior, which has been reconfigured as a museum with glassed-in artifacts. The church still has Chumash decorations on its walls, and the gardens in the courtyard are peaceful. Behind the church is an extensive cemetery with 4000 Chumash graves and elaborate mausoleums of early California settlers.

A $2 self-guided tour map is available at the mission bookstore (☎ 682-4713), open from 9 am to 5 pm daily. To reach the mission, go north on State St and turn east

on Los Olivos. Walking takes about 20 minutes from downtown and is enjoyable because of all the nice homes in the area (especially along Santa Barbara St). Bus No 22 heads downtown from the east side of the mission at 15 minutes past the hour from 9:15 am to 6:15 pm, Monday to Saturday.

Museum of Natural History
Visit Santa Barbara's Museum of Natural History (☎ 682-4711), a half mile north of the mission at 2559 Puesta del Sol Rd, just to see its beautiful architecture and landscaping. Highlights of the museum include an extensive Chumash exhibit and the entire skeleton of a blue whale, though other exhibits are quite mediocre.

Hours are 9 am to 5 pm Monday to Saturday, 10 am to 5 pm Sunday and holidays. Admission is $4.

Santa Barbara Botanic Garden
A half mile up from the Museum of Natural History, at 1212 Mission Canyon Rd, Santa Barbara's extensive botanic garden is devoted entirely to California's native flora. Five miles of trails meander through cacti, redwoods, wildflowers, and past the old mission dam, built by Chumash Indians to irrigate the mission's fields. The gift shop has an excellent selection of books, maps, and recreation guides.

The garden is open daily from 9 am to sunset, and docents lead hour-long tours daily at 2 pm. Admission is $3. For information call ☎ 563-2521.

Santa Barbara County Courthouse
The Santa Barbara County Courthouse (☎ 962-6464), 1100 Anacapa St, is not to be missed. Completed in 1929, after Santa Barbara's original courthouse was destroyed by earthquake, the courthouse is in Spanish-Moorish revival style, with reproduction details from California, and tiles from Tunisia and Spain.

The best way to see the courthouse is on a free docent-led tour, which leaves from just inside the Anacapa St entrance at 2 pm Monday to Saturday and 10:30 am Wednesday and Friday. Be sure to see the mural room and go up the 80 foot clocktower for a view of the city. The courthouse is open Monday to Saturday 8 am to 5 pm, Sunday 9 am to 5 pm.

Santa Barbara Museum of Art
The Santa Barbara Museum of Art (☎ 963-4364), 1130 State St, has a varied collection with works by Monet, Matisse, and Chagall, Hopper and O'Keefe, but Asian art and classical sculpture dominate the permanent collection on the ground floor. Traveling exhibits are displayed on the second floor.

Museum hours are 11 am to 5 pm Tuesday to Saturday, noon to 5 pm Sunday. Admission is $3, free on Thursdays (when the gallery stays open until 9 pm), and the first Sunday of the month. Free docent-led tours are offered at 1 pm.

Contemporary Arts Forum
Above the California Pizza Kitchen in the Paseo Nuevo center (roughly the corner of Chapala and De La Guerra Sts), the Contemporary Arts Forum (☎ 966-5373) is where Santa Barbara's contemporary artists show their works. Hours are 10 am to 5 pm Tuesday to Saturday, and admission is free.

Santa Barbara Historical Museum
This museum (☎ 966-1601), 136 E De La Guerra St, has a great collection of Santa Barbara memorabilia including antique furniture, an intricately carved coffer that belonged to Padre Junipero Serra, and exhibits on Santa Barbara's involvement in toppling the last Chinese monarchy.

The museum is open 10 am to 5 pm Tuesday to Saturday, noon to 5 pm Sunday, and is free. Free guided tours are offered Wednesday, Saturday, and Sunday at 1 pm. The museum bookshop has a good selection of Santa Barbara and California history books.

El Presidio de Santa Barbara State Historic Park
Although most of the grounds are under excavation and restoration, the Presidio (☎ 966-9719), 123 E Canon Perdido St, is one of the few original Spanish Colonial buildings in California. Founded in 1782 to protect the missions between Monterey and San Diego from Indians, the Presidio was the last Spanish outpost in California. It acted as a social and political hub, and as a stopping point for Spanish military traveling along the coast.

The best preserved building (most have been turned into attorneys' offices) is the Presidio Chapel which contains restored 18th-Century decorations. A 15-minute slide show gives a history of the buildings and tells about reconstruction plans. The Presidio is open daily from 10:30 am to 4:30 pm, and admission is free.

Stearn's Wharf
Stearn's Wharf, a rough wooden pier that extends into the harbor from the south end of State St, is a favorite place to eat seafood and watch sea lions. Built in 1872 by John Peck Stearn, it is the oldest continuously operating wharf on the West Coast – during the 1940s it was owned by James Cagney and his two brothers.

The **Sea Center** (☎ 963-1067), run by the Museum of Natural History, features touch tanks filled with starfish and sea anemones. The center is open from 10 am to 5 pm daily (closed Wednesday); the tanks are open from noon to 4 pm. Admission is $2.

Santa Barbara Yacht Harbor
A half mile west from Stearn's Wharf, the harbor is a great place for strolling and eating seafood. A walk along the breakwater affords a nice view of the city with the mountains in the background. This harbor is also the departure point of most fishing boats and sightseeing cruises.

Santa Barbara Zoological Garden
The Santa Barbara Zoological Garden (☎ 962-5339), off Cabrillo Blvd near East Beach at 500 Ninos Drive, has gorgeous gardens as well as monkeys, elephants, and giraffes. The 100-year-old vegetation was once part of a palatial estate.

The zoological gardens are open 9 am to 6 pm daily from May to September, 10 am to 5 pm October to April. Admission is $5, and on the grounds are a restaurant, picnic grounds, and a nice playground.

Just west of the zoo, near the intersection of Cabrillo Blvd and Hwy 101, the **Andree Clark Bird Refuge** consists of a lagoon, gardens, and a path from which to observe nesting freshwater birds. A kiosk in the parking area (on the north side of the refuge, off Cabrillo Blvd) provides interpretive maps.

Chumash Painted Cave State Historic Park

About 12 miles northwest of downtown, Painted Cave Rd heads north from Hwy 154 and leads to Chumash Painted Cave State Historic Park. Marked only by a brown and yellow Park Service sign the park is easy to miss, so look for cars parked on both sides of the road. A dirt path leads from the road back to the cave where Chumash Indians painted bright pictographs around 200 years ago. The cave is protected by a metal screen, so a flashlight is helpful for getting a good view.

South Coast Railroad Museum

Located in Goleta, eight miles northwest of downtown Santa Barbara, the South Coast Railroad Museum (☎ 964-3540), 300 N Los Carneros Rd (a quarter mile from the Los Carneros exit off Hwy 101), occupies a 1901 Southern Pacific Railroad depot, moved to its present location in 1985. It holds a sizable collection of railroad artifacts, old photographs, and a 300-sq-foot model railroad.

The museum is open from 1 to 4 pm Wednesday to Sunday. The best time to visit is Wednesday and Friday from 2 to 3:30 pm, and Saturday from 1 to 4 pm, when you can ride the miniature train. Admission (and the train ride) is free.

Santa Barbara Farmer's Market

Local growers and artisans sell fruit, vegetables, flowers, honey, nuts, and arts & crafts at the colorful Santa Barbara Farmer's Market, held Tuesday evenings on the 500 block of State St and Saturday mornings on the corner of Santa Barbara and Cota Sts. St musicians and food vendors usually show up at the evening market, especially in the summer. For information call ☎ 962-5354.

Beaches

The long sandy stretch between Stearn's Wharf and Montecito, **East Beach** is Santa Barbara's largest and most popular beach. At its east end, across from the Biltmore Hotel, Armani swimsuits and Gucci sunglasses abound at **Butterfly Beach**.

Between Stearn's Wharf and the harbor, **West Beach** has calm water and is popular with families and tourists staying in nearby motels. On the other side of the harbor, **Leadbetter Beach** is a good spot for surfing and windsurfing, and has stair access to a grassy picnic area atop the cliffs.

West of Santa Barbara at the junction of Las Palmas and Las Positas Rds, **Arroyo Burro Beach** (also called Hendry's) is small and isolated. There is a parking lot, picnic area, and cafe that serves food until 7 pm.

Off Hwy 101 18 miles southeast of Santa Barbara in Carpenteria, **Rincon Beach** is a world-famous surf spot.

Parks

Alice Keck Park & Memorial Garden and Alameda Park flow together in a profusion of trees, lawns, ponds, and botanic gardens. Further north, between the mission and Museum of Natural History on Mission Canyon Rd, Rocky Nook Park has nice picnic and barbecue sites beneath old oak trees.

Activities

Hiking The Santa Ynez foothills (part of Los Padres National Forest) are 20 minutes by car from downtown. The hills are laced with hiking trails, most of which cut through rugged chaparral and steep canyons, and offer incredible coastal views. The trailheads closest to downtown are off

CALIFORNIA

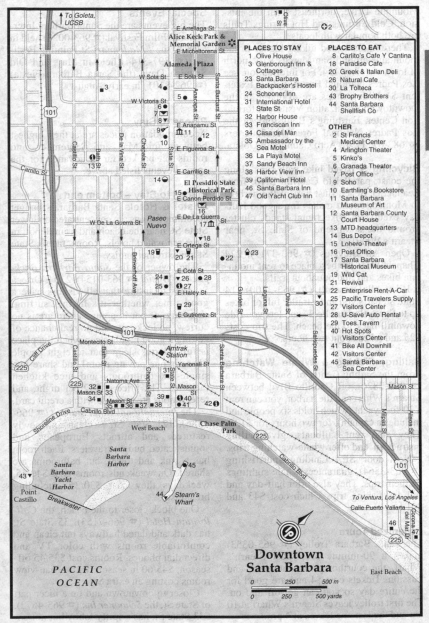

PLACES TO STAY

1 Olive House
3 Glenborough Inn &
   Cottages
23 Santa Barbara
   Backpacker's Hostel
24 Schooner Inn
31 International Hotel
   State St
32 Harbor House
33 Franciscan Inn
34 Casa del Mar
35 Ambassador by the
   Sea Motel
36 La Playa Motel
37 Sandy Beach Inn
38 Harbor View Inn
39 Californian Hotel
46 Santa Barbara Inn
47 Old Yacht Club Inn

PLACES TO EAT

8 Carlito's Cafe Y Cantina
18 Paradise Cafe
20 Greek & Italian Deli
26 Natural Cafe
30 La Tolteca
43 Brophy Brothers
44 Santa Barbara
   Shellfish Co

OTHER

2 St Francis
   Medical Center
4 Arlington Theater
5 Kinko's
6 Granada Theater
7 Post Office
9 Soho
10 Earthling's Bookstore
11 Santa Barbara
   Museum of Art
12 Santa Barbara County
   Court House
13 MTD headquarters
14 Bus Depot
15 Lobero Theater
16 Post Office
17 Santa Barbara
   Historical Museum
19 Wild Cat
21 Revival
22 Enterprise Rent-A-Car
25 Pacific Travelers Supply
27 Visitors Center
28 U-Save Auto Rental
29 Toes Tavern
40 Hot Spots
   Visitors Center
41 Bike All Downhill
42 Visitors Center
45 Santa Barbara
   Sea Center

**Downtown
Santa Barbara**

0   250   500 m
0   250   500 yards

Mountain Drive, northeast from the mission. Cold Springs and Hot Springs Trails are both popular with locals.

There is also good hiking higher in the mountains around San Marcos Pass, north of town via Hwy 154. For information, see Los Padres National Forest, below. Excellent $1 hiking maps are available at the Downtown Organization Visitors Information Center, Earthling's Bookstore, or the Los Padres National Forest Headquarters (☎ 683-6711), 42 Aero Camino, in Goleta.

Bicycling A paved bike path runs along the coast, parallel to Cabrillo Blvd, from Leadbetter Beach (just east of the harbor) to Montecito, and makes for a good half-day excursion. Bike rental stands cluster around the south end of State St, near Stearn's Wharf.

Open Air Bicycles (☎ 963-3717), 224 Chapala St, is the best place to rent mountain bikes and find out about trails.

Bike All Downhill (☎ 963-3700), 14 State St, carts you and a trailer full of bikes up to Santa Barbara Peak, and lets you ride downhill back to the beach. The trip costs $25 and takes about two hours.

Sailing, Fishing & Whale Watching
From the Sailing Center of Santa Barbara (☎ 962-2826), off Cabrillo Blvd between Stearn's Wharf and the harbor, you can rent a 30-foot yacht (which holds six people and includes a captain), for two hours for $135. They also rent sailboats, give sailing instruction, and offer whale-watching trips.

Next door, SEA Landing Sportfishing (☎ 963-3564), guarantees whale sightings on their trips. They also offer half-day and full-day fishing trips which cost $43 and $91.

Organized Tours
The Santa Barbara Trolley (☎ 965-0353) makes a 90-minute loop past Stearn's Wharf, the courthouse, art museum, and mission. Tickets cost $4 and are good for the entire day so you can get off and on. The first trolley leaves Stearn's Wharf at 10 am and the last one leaves at 4 pm.

Special Events
The big events are the Santa Barbara International Film Festival (☎ 963-0023) held in March, the *I Madonnari* St Painting Festival (☎ 897-3144) held in May, and Old Spanish Days (the Santa Barbara Fiesta) (☎ 962-8101) in early August.

Places to Stay
Accommodation prices are at their highest between mid-May and September, and rooms get booked far in advance for the special events listed above.

Places to Stay – bottom end
Hostel & Hotels Santa Barbara's budget accommodations are concentrated on lower State St, near the beach and train depot, in large renovated hotels. Rooms facing State St are extremely noisy.

The owner of the *Santa Barbara Backpackers Hostel* (☎ 963-0154), 210 E Ortega St, tries to insure that all visitors have a good time, whether it's hiking, surfing, shopping, or bar-hopping. There is no curfew, no lock-out, and no real chance of getting a good nights sleep when the place is full. Dorms sleep four to eight people (there is one private room) and share two single-sex bathrooms and nice kitchen facilities. The price is $12 per night, and reservations are possible with a credit card.

The *International Hotel State St* (☎ 966-6586), 121 State St, is clean and newly restored, and attracts Europeans and sophisticated budget travelers. Each room has a sink and towel, but bathrooms are shared. On weekends rooms cost $40/45, weekdays they cost $30/35, including breakfast.

One block closer to the beach, the *Californian Hotel* (☎ 966-7153), 35 State St, has dark and dated hallways but clean and comfortable rooms with color TV and direct dial phones. Rooms cost $35/45 off-season, $45/60 in season, with ocean-view rooms costing an extra $10.

Closer to downtown and on a nicer part of State St, the *Schooner Inn* (☎ 965-4572), 533 State St, has a spiffy lobby but not-so-nice rooms which, at $50/60 year round, are overpriced half the year.

Places to Stay – middle

Most of Santa Barbara's mid-range motels are along Cabrillo Blvd, west of State St, within a block of the beach. Quality and price don't vary much: rooms with two beds, a TV, air conditioning, and a continental breakfast cost $65 to $90 in winter, $80 to $115 in summer. Rates are often negotiable if you stay more than four nights. Rooms without a view cost about $20 less than those which look towards the ocean, and are actually less noisy if they sit back from Cabrillo.

The *Harbor View Inn* (☎ 963-0780, 800-755-0222), 36 W Cabrillo Blvd, has a pool, spa, gardens, and rooms starting at $85 in winter, $120 in summer. The *Sandy Beach Inn* (☎ 963-0405), 122 W Cabrillo Blvd, has a flowery lobby, wine and cheese in the afternoon, and rooms for $45 in winter, $55 in summer. One block west, the *La Playa Motel* (☎ 962-6436), 212 W Cabrillo Blvd, has similar facilities and identical rates.

Rooms at the *Ambassador by the Sea Motel* (☎ 965-4577), 202 W Cabrillo Blvd, face a lovely garden, pool and sundeck, and start at $60 in the winter, $85 in the summer.

There are also a few places just off Cabrillo on Bath St. *Casa del Mar* (☎ 963-4418, 800-433-3097), 18 Bath St, has rooms with kitchens and fireplaces for around $60 in summer, $75 in winter. Small and simple, the *Harbor House* (☎ 962-9745), 104 Bath St, has individually decorated rooms for $50 in winter, $65 in summer. Across the street, the *Franciscan Inn* (☎ 963-8845), 109 Bath St, has a pool, spa, and guest laundry. Rooms cost $55/65 in winter, $65 to $110 in summer.

Places to Stay – top end

Most top-end accommodations are north of downtown in the hills and east in Montecito. B&Bs are plentiful and mostly found in residential neighborhoods near upper State St.

Hotels Considered *the* hotel in Santa Barbara for many years, *El Encanto Hotel & Garden Villas* (☎ 687-5000), 1900 Lausen Rd, sits on a hill above the mission with a great view of downtown and the ocean. Nestled among 10 acres of lush gardens, its secluded cottages with private patios start at $120.

More popular among today's rich and famous is the *Four Seasons Biltmore* (☎ 969-2261), 1260 Channel Drive, in Montecito. Situated on 20 acres, this place caters to the golf and tennis crowd. Rooms here start at $300.

The *Santa Barbara Inn* (☎ 963-0744), just east of State St at 901 E Cabrillo Blvd, is a full-service convention facility right across from the beach. Winter rates are around $100, while summer prices start at $150.

B&Bs Rooms at the small and charming *Old Yacht Club Inn* (☎ 962-1277), one block off Cabrillo (east of State St) at 431 Corona Del Mar, cost $90 to $150 and are a good value but are often booked months in advance.

In a residential neighborhood three blocks west of downtown, the *Glenborough Inn & Cottages* (☎ 966-0589, 800-962-0589), 1327 Bath St between Victoria and Sola Sts, has 11 rooms that cost $75 to $175 year round.

Also in a residential neighborhood, near the mission, the *Olive House* (☎ 962-4902, 800-786-6422), 1604 Olive St, is a 1904 Craftsman-style house with a terraced garden, large sundeck, and grand piano. Rooms cost $70 in winter, $105 to $175 in summer.

Places to Eat

Eating in Santa Barbara can be quick and cheap or truly gourmet. The concentration of restaurants is in the 500 and 600 blocks of State St, Santa Barbara's 'restaurant row.' Since most restaurants post their menus, surprises are limited. The Paseo Nuevo shopping area on State St has a number of upscale cafes where you can get Chinese food, salads, pasta, and pizzas for under $10 – *Rudy's* makes good burritos for around $5. If you want a really good meal for around $5, head to Isla Vista and eat ethnic with UCSB students.

A local institution, the *Greek & Italian Deli* (☎ 962-6815) at the corner of State and Ortega Sts, has great sandwiches, gyros, Greek salad, and hot lunch specials for around $5. Three blocks south, the *Natural Cafe* (☎ 962-9494), 508 State St, is a totally California experience, serving cha-cha-cha chicken burritos, veggie-rice combos, Zen burgers, Buddha burritos, and Yogananda lasagna. Prices are $4 to $7.

The *Santa Barbara Shellfish Co* (☎ 963-4415), on Stearn's Wharf, is a fish counter where you get fresh crab, chowder, and fish for $4 to $10, and sit at picnic tables on the pier. Beware of aggressive seagulls and pelicans – they're experts at dive-bomb dining.

Down at the Santa Barbara Yacht Harbor, *Brophy Brothers* (☎ 966-4418) is a lively restaurant and oyster bar where locals go to get seafood and bloody marys. A full meal costs $8 to $11; oysters, clam chowder, and terrific sourdough bread is under $10.

The *Paradise Cafe* (☎ 962-4416), 702 Anacapa St, has a simple menu of meat, fish, pasta, and salads, and a breezy 'beach club' atmosphere. Most lunch items are around $8 and dinners cost $8 to $15; hearty appetizers are $3 to $6.

Three miles east of downtown in Montecito, *Palazzio* (☎ 969-8565), 1151 Coast Village Rd, serves heaping bowls of pasta, Caesar salad, and buttery garlic rolls to a trendy young crowd. Portions are enormous! Be prepared to wait at least 20 minutes for a table on Friday and Saturday night.

Authentic Mexican food is found at *La Tolteca* (☎ 963-0847), 616 E Haley St, a 'mexicatessen' famous for its enchiladas and tamales, which you can eat there or take out. Prices are $3 to $8. For Southwest style Mexican food, good margaritas, and a colorful atmosphere, try *Carlito's Cafe Y Cantina* (☎ 962-7117), north of downtown at 1324 State St.

Entertainment

The Independent arrives at newsstands on Thursday and has thorough events listings and reviews in its 'This Week' section. Also good is the *Santa Barbara News-Press* which has a daily events calendar and special Friday issue called *Scene* that details the weeks events.

Coffeehouses New coffeehouses and cafes spring up in Santa Barbara almost weekly, so your best bet is to cruise State St (between Cota and Anapamu Sts) for an appealing scene. Two local favorites are: *Espresso Roma* (☎ 962-4721), 728 State St, with high ceilings, pieces by local artists on the walls, and strong espresso drinks, and *Cafe Siena* (☎ 963-7344), 1101 State St, which is a little cleaner and gets a more hip crowd.

Bars & Clubs Santa Barbara's raging after-dark scene revolves around lower State and Ortega Sts. *Toes Tavern* (☎ 965-4655), 416 State St, is a classic surf bar with pool tables, a variety of beer, and surf videos in constant play. Live bands, usually reggae or wannabe Ventures, perform on weekends and demand a $3 cover charge.

Looking like a cross between a warehouse and a love den, the *Wild Cat* (☎ 962-7970), 15 W Ortega St, is the ultimate '70s revival bar. The crowd is diverse and the place offers a good mix of music (no cover charge). On the other side of State St, *Revival* (☎ 730-7383), 18 E Ortega St, is Santa Barbara's hottest (in all senses of the word) dance club. The action starts around – but never before – 10 pm. The cover charge is from nothing to $7.

Soho (☎ 962-776), above McDonald's at 1221 State St, has live jazz nightly and only charges admission for weekend and big-name shows. Shows start at 8 pm Monday and Tuesday, 8:30 pm Wednesday and Thursday, and 9:30 pm Friday and Saturday.

Theater To find out current theater happenings, call the Santa Barbara Theatre Alliance 24-hour hotline at ☎ 962-4636, ext 5545.

The *Lobero Theater* (☎ 963-0761), 33 E Canon Perdido St, California's oldest continuously operating theater, is home to the State Theatre of California and Santa Barbara Chamber Orchestra, and presents musicals, comedies, children's theater, and films.

Built in 1930, the *Granada Theatre* (☎ 963-9503), 1216 State St, hosts the Santa Barbara Civic Light Opera, which performs an annual series of musicals and operettas. The *Arlington Theater* (☎ 963-4408), 1317 State St, is home to the Arlington Center for the Performing Arts and Santa Barbara Symphony.

The *Center Stage Theater* (☎ 963-0408), on the upper level of the Paseo Nuevo Center, hosts small productions and is home to the Santa Barbara Shakespeare Company.

UCSB also has occasional events in Campbell Hall, the large performing arts center on campus, and in the Halten and Studio Theaters, also on the UCSB campus. For information call ☎ 893-3535.

Things to Buy
Shops along State St feature summery clothes year round. Santa Barbara's shopping malls are mostly indoor/outdoor affairs filled with flowers and plants – most shops are open until 6 pm, and a few in the Paseo Nuevo (listed below) are open until 9 pm.

Paseo Nuevo, on State St, has Nordstrom, the Broadway, and most upscale retail chains.

Along Brinkerhoff Avenue, a small lane bordered by State, W Cota, W Haley, and De La Vina Sts, some of Santa Barbara's only remaining Victorian-style houses have been converted to antique shops.

The best place to purchase nautical goods – from maps to deck shoes – is at The Chandlery (☎ 965-4538) in the Santa Barbara Yacht Harbor.

Getting There & Away
Air The small Santa Barbara Airport (☎ 683-4011), eight miles east of downtown off Hwy 101, at 500 Fowler Rd, has commercial service to Los Angeles and San Francisco on commuter planes. The major airline carriers serving the airport are American Eagle (☎ 800-433-7300), Skywest (☎ 800-453-9417), United Express (☎ 800-241-6522), and US Air Express (☎ 800-428-4322).

Bus Greyhound has nine buses per day to Los Angeles for $12, and six per day to San Francisco for $35; roundtrip fares save a few dollars each way. The Greyhound bus station, a magnet for transient types, is downtown at 33 W Carrillo St.

Train Three southbound trains and one northbound train leave daily from Santa Barbara's train depot (☎ 963-1015), downtown at 209 State St. The general fare to Los Angeles is $20 and to San Francisco (via Oakland) is $67.

Getting Around
Bus The Downtown-Waterfront Shuttle runs every 10 to 15 minutes from 10 am to 6 pm, and goes from Stearn's Wharf to the north end of State St, and along Cabrillo Blvd from the Yacht Harbor to the Zoo. The fare is 25¢ per ride.

Santa Barbara Metropolitan Transit District (MTD) buses cost 75¢ per ride and run from 6 am to 11:15 pm Monday to Saturday. The buses cover downtown and also go west to Goleta and east to Carpenteria (via Montecito and Summerland). For information, stop by the MTD headquarters (☎ 683-3702), downtown at 1020 Chapala St, open from 6 am to 7 pm Monday to Friday.

Car Avis, Budget, and Hertz have kiosks in the main airport terminal, as well as downtown. The most affordable rent-a-car service is U-Save Auto Rental (☎ 963-3499), 510 Anacapa St, which charges $30 per day for a mid-size car with 150 free miles. Enterprise Rent-A-Car (☎ 569-3636), 624 Santa Barbara St, charges $38 per day and will pick you up and drop you off anywhere in the Santa Barbara area.

CALIFORNIA

Taxi For taxi service, Yellow Cab Company (☎ 965-5111) or Mann's Cab (☎ 684-0234) both operate 24 hours.

LOS PADRES NATIONAL FOREST

The Los Padres National Forest starts in the Santa Ynez foothills just east of Santa Barbara and extends north and west over one million acres. The best access from Santa Barbara is by way of Hwy 154 northwest.

Paradise Rd, which crosses Hwy 154 north of San Marco Pass, offers the best access to developed facilities. At the Paradise Rd/Hwy 154 junction, the *Cold Springs Tavern* (☎ 967-0066) is *the* congregating point for hikers and campers – a fun place to have a beer. They also serve a good burgers and fries for around $5.

About five miles up the road is a USFS Los Padres National Forest ranger station, open 8 am to 5 pm Monday to Saturday, with posted maps and information. There are three campgrounds before the ranger station and one just past it, all of which are near the Santa Ynez River and cost $8 per night for up to eight people.

At **Red Rocks** (clearly marked from the ranger station), the Santa Ynez River pools among rocks and waterfalls making a great swimming and sunning spot. There are many hiking trails from here.

At the bottom of San Marcos Pass, surrounded by oaks, **Lake Cachuma Recreation Area** has a large campground with $13 sites, picnic tables, barbecues, and flush toilets. Sites are first come, first served and fill quickly with weekend warriors from Los Angeles.

SANTA BARBARA TO LOS ANGELES
☎ 805

Once upon a time, the land south of Santa Barbara was nothing but sugar beet, lima bean, and citrus orchards, harvested mostly by Japanese laborers. Despite their industrious reputation and active roles in the community, most Japanese were sent to the Gila River Relocation Camp in Arizona during WWII.

Oxnard still grows an abundance of strawberries, celery, and lettuce (nowadays Mexicans supply the work force), but modern economic livelihood is concentrated underground in oil. Most drilling moved offshore in the 1930s, but the area still reaps tax benefits and houses much of the labor force. Increasingly, the area's monotone housing developments supply mid-range houses for Los Angeles commuters. Oil and engineering enthusiasts might stop at the **Santa Paula Union Oil Museum** (☎ 933-0076), two blocks north of the Hwy 101 10th St exit in Santa Paula. The museum has a permanent hands-on, multi-media exhibit about petroleum and Union Oil's history. Hours are 10 am to 4 pm Thursday to Sunday, and admission is free.

Ventura

Ventura's Main St, north of Hwy 101 via Seaward Ave, has an odd assortment of antique and thrift shops that could entertain a bargain hunter for an afternoon, and a concentration of museums that center around the **Mission San Buenaventura** (☎ 643-4318), 211 E Main St, built in 1809. A fraction of its former self but still beautifully decorated, the church is the only one in California that has not missed a Sunday service in over 100 years. Visiting hours are 10 am to 4 pm daily.

The mission was actually completed, but because of bad planning had to be leveled and rebuilt. You can see the original foundation and related artifacts in the **Albinger Archaeological Museum** (☎ 643-5823), next door to the mission, open from 10 am to 4 pm Wednesday to Sunday.

Across the street in Figueroa Plaza, the **Ventura County Historical Museum** (☎ 653-0323) has two rooms dedicated to Chumash history. Museum hours are 10 am to 5 pm Tuesday to Sunday, and admission is $3.

Ventura Harbor, southwest of Hwy 101 via Harbor Blvd, is where boats depart for the Channel Islands. Even if you don't embark on an island adventure, **Channel Islands National Park Headquarters** (☎ 644-8262), 1901 Spinnaker Drive, has an interesting natural history display, a three-story look out from where you can see the islands (on a clear day). Next door is Island Packers, the main outfitter for island excursions (see Channel Islands, below).

Ojai

North of Ventura via Hwy 33, Ojai is a resort community that flourished about 20 years ago but now looks quite aged. The exception is the *Ojai Valley Inn* (☎ 646-5511, 800-642-6524), on the west end of town and well signed from the highway. The Inn has a bustling golf course and restaurants.

The **Arcade**, a Mission Revival-style building on Ojai Ave (the main thoroughfare), houses shops and art galleries. Just south of Ojai Ave, on Montgomery St, the **Ojai Valley Museum** (☎ 646-2290) is interesting mostly because it is housed in a Depression-era firehouse built by WPA workers.

Bart's Books (☎ 646-3755), two blocks north of Ojai Ave at 1302 W Marlijta St, demands at least a half-hour browse, while the Krotona Library (☎ 646-2653), west of downtown at 2 Krotona Hill (well-marked from Ojai Ave), caters to 'seekers of the truth.'

CHANNEL ISLANDS NATIONAL PARK
☎ *805*

The five northern Channel Islands (an eight-island chain lying off the coast from Newport Beach to Santa Barbara) and their surrounding ocean comprise Channel Islands National Park. Isolated from the mainland and located in a transition zone between warm water from the tropics and cold water from Arctic seas, the islands have unique flora and fauna, and extensive tidepools and kelp forests.

Originally inhabited by the Chumash and Gabrielino Indians (who were taken to the mainland missions in the early 1800s), the islands were owned by sheep ranchers and the US Navy until the mid 1970s when conservation efforts began. San Miguel, Santa Rosa, Anacapa, and Santa Barbara Islands are now owned by the National Park Service, while Santa Cruz is 90% owned by the Nature Conservancy and 10% by the Gherini family who once operated the island as one big ranch.

Anacapa, which is actually three separate islets, is the closest to the mainland and thus gets the most visitors. A visitors center and picnic area sits atop the island's narrow plateau (reached by 153 steps) and snorkeling and swimming are possible in Frenchy's Cove. San Miguel Island is known for its abundance of seals, sea lions, and sea otters.

Channel Islands National Park Headquarters (☎ 644-8262), on the mainland in Ventura Harbor at 1901 Spinnaker Drive, is the starting point for most island trips. It has a good film about the islands, plus exhibits, maps, and information.

Places to Stay

Camping is permitted on Anacapa year round, on Santa Barbara from late-May to September, and on San Miguel from July to September. All campgrounds are primitive, and you must pack everything in, including water. The campground on Santa Barbara is large, grassy, and surrounded by hiking trails, while the one on Anacapa is high, rocky, and isolated. Camping on San Miguel, with its unceasing wind and volatile weather, is only for the hearty. Camping permits are required (no charge) and can be obtained from park headquarters in Ventura.

The only established accommodations are on the private east end of Santa Cruz Island. Operated by the same people, two ranches offer rustic accommodations and attract quasi-adventurous off-the-beaten track types with money. *Scorpion Ranch* is the more popular one, known for nearby sea caves and good kayaking. Here, full-service accommodations with meals cost $90 per person, and 'BYOG' (bring your own gear) trips where you bring your own food and sleeping bags and stay in the ranch house cost $60 per person per day. At *Smuggler's Ranch*, you can stay in the 1889 adobe ranch house or a beach cabin for a minimum of three days (two nights) for $60 per person per night; kitchen facilities but no meals are available. For information and reservations, call Horizon West/Guided Travel Adventure at ☎ 800-430-2544.

Getting There & Away
Island Packers, the park's concessionaire, is located in Ventura Harbor, next to the Channel Islands National Park Headquarters. As the name suggests, their main purpose is to pack people to the islands and leave them for a few days; round-trip service is about $480 per person.

They also offer one-day excursions ($52) with optional ranger-led hikes, snorkeling, and tidepool explorations, narrated half-day cruises with no landing ($21), and whale-watching trips ($21). Channel crossings take one to four hours, and landing is never guaranteed because of changeable weather and tides.

Reservations are suggested for weekend, holiday, and summer trips, and require advance payment. If they cancel a trip because of bad weather, you receive a full refund if you don't want to reschedule. For recorded information call ☎ 642-7688; for reservations call ☎ 642-1393, or write Island Packers, 1867 Spinnaker Drive, Ventura, CA 93001.

San Joaquin Valley

The San Joaquin Valley extends roughly 300 miles from Stockton to Bakersfield, between the Sierra Nevada and the Coastal Range. The San Joaquin River's major tributaries – the Kings, San Joaquin, Merced, Tuolumne, Stanislaus, and Caliveras Rivers – flow west from the Sierra Nevada and join the San Joaquin proper, which flows north to the delta where it meets the Sacramento River and flows to the Pacific. Together the Sacramento and San Joaquin Valleys constitute the Central Valley or Great Valley.

Though not too exciting for travelers, the San Joaquin Valley is very important to California's economy. Often called the most productive valley in the world, much of the United States' walnuts, almonds, grapes, peaches, apricots, plums, oranges, olives, tomatoes, and cotton are produced in the valley and it holds five of the top 10 agricultural counties in the US. Crops are cultivated on an enormous scale, with most land in the hands of big corporations that own at least 5000 acres and use pesticides, massive irrigation systems, and Mexican laborers. Human and environmental rights activists point angry fingers at these farming practices for over-taxing the land and exploiting workers. John Steinbeck painted a classic literary portrait of farming life during the Depression in the Great Valley in *The Grapes of Wrath*.

For travelers, the San Joaquin Valley is a corridor to be passed through quickly – especially from June to September when temperatures reach 100°F by 11 am. Interstate 5 offers a streamlined route (popular with truckers) between San Francisco and Los Angeles, which takes about six hours to drive; the only roadside attractions are gas stations and fast-food stops. Highway 99 follows an old wagon route, parallel to the railroad, between Bakersfield and Sacramento, connecting the valley's important towns. Listening to the radio reveals true valley culture: a mix of Christian rock, country & western, and Mexican folk.

THE SACRAMENTO DELTA

The Sacramento Delta, where the Sacramento and San Joaquin Rivers meet and flow towards San Francisco Bay, contains 1000 miles of waterways. Once upon a time, most of this water flowed into the Pacific through San Francisco Bay, but today it is siphoned and redirected to supply 40% of California's drinking water and 45% of its irrigation; about half of the original flow actually makes it out to sea.

A major part of California's political and environmental arena, the delta is also a favorite place for boating, water skiing, and hunting. Highways 4 and 12 head east from I-80 and connect to Hwy 160 which runs atop the Sacramento River levee.

Towns along Hwy 160 survive on boat traffic and agriculture. **Rio Vista** has a

---

Tule Fog

Radiation or Tule (TOO-lee) fog causes an average of 24 deaths per year on San Joaquin Valley roads, including Hwy 99 and I-5. As thick as proverbial pea soup, the fog limits visibility to about 10 feet – making driving conditions almost impossible. The fog is worst from November to February, when cold mountain air settles on the warm valley floor and condenses into fog as the ground cools at night. The fog often lifts for a few hours during the afternoon, just long enough for the ground to warm back up and thus perpetuate the cycle.

Call the California Highway Information Network (☎ 800-427-7623) to check road conditions before traveling through the valley. If you end up on a tule-covered road, drive with your low-beams on, keep a good distance from the car in front of you, stay at a constant speed, avoid sudden stops, and never try to pass other cars. ■

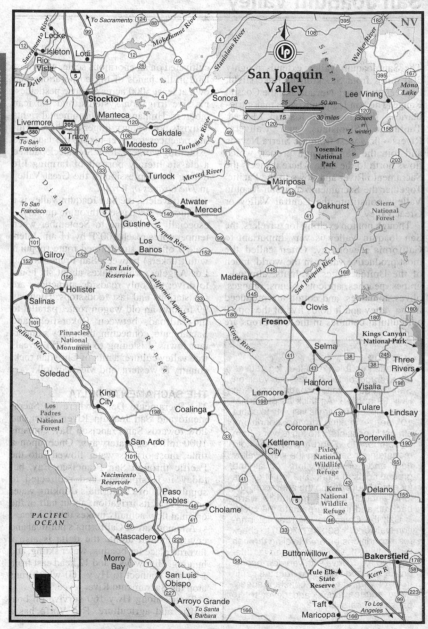

public beach and boat launch facility, and is home to *Foster's Bighorn* (☎ 707-374-9993), 143 Main St, a funky bar with over 300 wild game trophies – including a 13-foot elephant head – on its walls. Northeast, **Iselton** has an interesting main street lined with corrugated tin buildings with faded Chinese characters above many of the doors. Isleton's Crawdad Festival, at the end of June, draws people from all over the state.

Built by Chinese farmers after a fire wiped out the Chinatown of Walnut Grove in 1912, the one street in **Locke** sits below the highway and levee. Dilapidated buildings lean towards each other over the street, giving the place a broken feeling and its shops and galleries an undue air of authenticity. Locke's unlikely centerpiece is *Al the Wops*, a grungy bar with crumpled dollar bills on the ceiling and faded pictures on the wall. People come here to drink heavily and eat huge steaks ($11) served with pasta, bread, fries, and salad – served family style on red checked tablecloths.

More in touch with the town's heritage is the **Dai Loy Museum**, an old gambling hall filled with photos and relics from some of Locke's original families. The museum is open weekends from 10 am to 5 pm and costs $1.

STOCKTON
• *pop 409,000 ☎ 209*

Stockton has an impressive city hall and civic center, elaborate churches, and stately homes. Its port connects to San Francisco via a deep-water channel, making it an important loading/unloading point for San Joaquin Valley agriculture. During the Gold Rush, Stockton was the main disembarkation point for men and goods headed to the Southern Mines. The garish **Hotel Stockton**, downtown at the corner of Weber and El Dorado Sts, is in a sad state of disrepair. Looking like a California Mission in drag, the hotel was built in 1910 for $500,000 and hosted Stockton's most important guests during its heyday. Revitalization plans are in the future.

Today, Stockton is a conglomeration of boarded-up buildings, dilapidated houses, and potentially dangerous neighborhoods. The population is about 25% Hispanic, which makes Stockton a festive place to be on May 5th (Cinco de Mayo) and a good place to eat Mexican food. The University of the Pacific (UOP) has been important throughout Stockton's history, but doesn't support any college neighborhoods. Apart from the excellent Haggin Museum and the historic Magnolia District (of interest to architecture buffs), Stockton is one of California's most avoidable cities. Stockton's Asparagus Festival in mid-May, one of California's largest agricultural fairs, puts a green-golden hue of joviality over the city with asparagus cook-offs and tastings, carnival rides, and arts and crafts booths.

Orientation & Information
The main thoroughfares are Pacific Ave (which becomes Center St south of Harding Way) and El Dorado St going north-south, and Park St, Weber St, and Harding Way going east-west. Most visitors get off I-5 at Pershing Ave and head two blocks north to the Haggin Museum.

Maps and information are available at the Stockton San Joaquin Convention & Visitor's Bureau (☎ 943-1987, 800-350-1987), downtown off Center St at 46 W Fremont St. The bureau is open weekdays from 9 am to 5 pm.

Haggin Museum
The Haggin Museum (☎ 462-4116), 1201 North Pershing Ave, is also the San Joaquin Historical Pioneer Museum and has an excellent collection of American landscape paintings including works by Albert Bierstadt, famous for his portraits of Yosemite Valley. The museum also has a good collection of Stockton relics and, in the basement, some colorful horse-drawn fire engines and Native American (mostly Yokut and Pomo) trading and ceremonial baskets. Museum hours are Tuesday to Sunday from 1:30 to 5 pm. Admission is free, though a large coffer suggesting a $2 donation guards the door.

Surrounding the museum, **Victory Park**

is a shady picnic or barbecue spot with large trees and a duck pond. In the evening people run laps around the park (clockwise, always clockwise).

Magnolia District
About one mile east of the Haggin Museum via Acacia St (on Victory Park's south side), the historic Magnolia District stands as testimony to Stockton's more prosperous days. Eden Park, on Acacia between El Dorado and Hunter Sts, is a good place to park your car. From here, walk one block north on Hunter to Magnolia St, where most of the beautiful homes – Queen Anne, Arts & Crafts, and California Bungalow styles – are located. The visitors center has a detailed pamphlet on the history and architecture.

Places to Stay & Eat
There is a well-located *Days Inn* (☎ 948-6151, 800-325-2525), at the corner of Weber and Center Sts near downtown and the port. Rooms cost $42/50 and various discounts are available. In a more suburban location, north of downtown at 4540 N El Dorado St, the *Acorn Inn* (☎ 478-2944) has a pool and rooms for $30.

There are authentic Mexican restaurants downtown if you care to brave the stares of the local crowd. Also authentic but more user-friendly is *Miguel's* (☎ 951-1931) at 7565 Pacific Ave. Truly *the* place to go in Stockton is *Ye Olde Hoosier Inn* (☎ 463-0271), off the east end of Harding Way at 1537 North Wilson Way, which serves homemade mashed potatoes and gravy, chicken fried steak, and hoosier burgers. The 'recession menu,' served until 5:30 pm, includes soup, salad, an entree, dessert and rolls for around $5. An assortment of antiques hang about the walls – including a lantern that belonged to Mark Twain.

LODI
☎ 209
Creedence Clearwater Revival says it all with the song 'Oh Lord, Stuck in Lodi Again.' It's the hub of the Lodi-Woodbridge wine region, which specializes in Zinfandel grapes, and a gas stop for people en route to the delta. For information on where to go wine tasting, contact the Lodi Chamber of Commerce (☎ 367-7840) at 35 S School St downtown.

MODESTO
•*pop 175,000* ☎ 209
Despite its agricultural roots, Modesto's most famous product is George Lucas who immortalized Modesto in his movie *American Graffiti* and gave it the reputation as 'cruising capital of the world.' Until 1992, each July brought thousands of car enthusiasts and nostalgia buffs to Modesto to cruise McHenry Ave, listen to Buddy Holly tunes, and wear their high school letterman's jacket and poodle skirts. Unfortunately the tradition came to an end when the cruise-fest turned into a near riot and gangs threatened general safety. Now weekend cruising is prohibited (though people still rev their engines on weekend nights) and the festival has been canceled indefinitely.

Otherwise Modesto is much the same as other valley towns, with an old downtown surrounded by sprawling strip-mall lined boulevards. The area's biggest employers are the Ernest & Julio Gallo wineries, and the Tri-Valley Grower's cannery – the largest fruit cannery in the world. The Modesto Arch, at the corner of 9th and I Sts delineates the good and bad parts of town – avoid the area west of 9th St after dark.

Things to See
Housed in the 1912 city library, the **McHenry Museum** (☎ 577-5366), 1402 I St, has a mishmash of medical, dental, mining, and farm equipment. The museum is open from noon to 4 pm Tuesday to Sunday. In the museum basement, the **Central California Art League Gallery** (☎ 529-3369), has regional arts and crafts displays. At 906 15th St, 1½ blocks away, is the **McHenry Mansion** (☎ 577-5344), a grand showcase for replica rugs and wallpapers and original Victorian furniture. One-hour tours are given Tuesday, Wednesday, Thursday, and Sunday from 1 to

4 pm, and Friday and Saturday from noon to 3 pm. In the blocks east of the museum and mansion, especially along 14th St and Sycamore Ave, are numerous homes built in the early 20th century.

Places to Stay

Modesto's accommodations are concentrated north of downtown along Orangeburg Ave, which runs parallel to Hwy 99. The best values are along McHenry Ave which runs north from Needham St, downtown, to become Hwy 108. The *Capri Inn* (☎ 524-7374), 602 McHenry, has no-frills rooms for $34. A few blocks north, the *Sundial Lodge* (☎ 523-5642), 808 McHenry, has a small outdoor swimming pool and rooms for $48/52. Downtown, the *Red Lion Hotel* (☎ 526-6000, 800-547-8010), 1150 9th St, is Modesto's convention center and nicest accommodations with a swimming pool, restaurant, and rooms for $105/120; special rates are available mid-week and for various club members.

Places to Eat

St Stan's Brewery (☎ 524-4782), 821 L St at the corner of 9th St, combines brewery, pub, and restaurant. Tours are given on Saturdays at 2:30 pm (reservations are required). The pub lets you sample different brews ($3) and the restaurant serves mediocre salads, pasta, burgers, and chicken for $6 to $11; appetizers are a better value.

India Oven (☎ 572-1805), 1022 11th St, serves tasty Indian food, and has an all-you-can-eat lunch buffet for $4.50. A semi-yuppie local crowd hangs out at *DeVa* (☎ 572-3382), at the corner of 12th and J Sts, a coffeehouse and bistro that serves huge salads, fancy sandwiches, and hot items like polenta and vegetable lasagna for around $7.

OAKDALE
☎ 209

On the way to Yosemite, 13 miles east of Modesto on Hwy 108, Oakdale is home to the western division of **Hershey Choco-**

late USA (☎ 848-8126), just off the highway at 120 S Sierra Ave. A mosaic of sweets, the visitors center sells every Hershey product available. Free factory tours leave the visitors center weekdays every half hour from 8:30 am to 3 pm.

MERCED
•*pop 60,000* ☎ 209

Merced is an attractive place to spend the night and meet Yosemite-bound travelers. The 10th University of California campus will be built near Merced in the coming years.

Orientation & Information

Merced is at the junction of Hwy 99, and highways 59 and 140. The downtown is just east of Hwy 99 along Main St, between J and R Sts; numbered streets run parallel to Hwy 99. Fast-food restaurants, gas stations, and the Merced Mall are east of downtown along Olive St. The Merced Chamber of Commerce/Convention & Visitor's Bureau (☎ 384-3333, 800-446-5353), 690 W 16th St at the end of N St (adjacent to the bus depot), has information about Merced and Yosemite, and is open weekdays from 9 am to 5 pm.

Things to See & Do

The stately **Merced County Courthouse**, built in 1874, houses a local history museum (☎ 723-2401) open Wednesday to Sunday from 1 to 4 pm.

Widely publicized but poorly run, the **Yosemite Wildlife Museum** (☎ 383-1052), 2040 Yosemite Parkway one mile east of Hwy 99, is a taxidermy display cum gun shop that is best avoided unless you're in the market for a new rifle. About six miles north of Merced, off the Atwater exit from Hwy 99, the **Castle Air Museum** (☎ 723-2178) has a worthwhile display of restored military aircraft, uniforms, and WWII propaganda. Hours are daily from 1 to 4 pm, and admission is free.

The Merced Farmers Market is held Saturday morning at the corner of 19th and N Sts. If you stay long enough to explore, there is a nice path along both sides of Bear

Creek and a beautiful city park on the north side of the creek between M and R Sts.

Places to Stay

Hostel The *Merced Home Hostel* is in the European tradition, offering two rooms/four beds with available kitchen facilities, and meals are served with the family and other travelers. It gets full quickly on weekends from May to September. The hostel will pick up/drop off people traveling from bus and train stations, closes during the day, and has an 11 pm curfew. Call ☎ 725-0407, between 5 and 10 pm for information, reservations, and directions. For HI/AYH members, a bed is $10 or $13 for non-members.

Motels If hosteling isn't your thing, try the *Happy Inn* (☎ 722-6291), just east of Hwy 99 on Hwy 140 next to Carrows Restaurant, which has clean rooms for $27/30 and an outdoor pool. Two blocks east on Hwy 140, the *Cozy Inn* (☎ 722-6224), is worn but pleasant and has rooms for $35/45.

Places to Eat

For good, greasy, and ultra-authentic Mexican food, head to *Mario's Taco Shop* (☎ (209) 723-0194), one block off Main St at 51 W 16th St. Large combinations with rice and beans cost $4, and five rolled supreme tacos cost $2. Just as good but a few dollars more is *La Nita's* (☎ (209) 723-2291), north of downtown on 18th St between S and T Sts, which has table service and serves beer.

Getting There & Away

Bus One of the few routes to Yosemite National Park open year round, Hwy 140 heads east from Merced, through Mariposa, to Yosemite Lodge. Buses depart daily at 6:10 am, 10 am, and 3 pm from Merced's bus station (☎ 385-6849), 690 W 16th St at the west end of N St, and stop to meet north and southbound Amtrak trains. Fare is $17; people with Amtrak rail passes ride for free.

Train The Amtrak station (☎ 722-6862) is at the corner of 24th and K Sts, near the Merced County Courthouse, and is open daily from 7:15 am to 8:15 pm. There are four northbound trains per day, connecting Merced to San Francisco ($30), and three southbound trains which go to Los Angeles ($48) via a bus connection in Bakersfield. Buses to Yosemite meet the early train from San Francisco and the afternoon train from Los Angeles.

Car Enterprise Rent-A-Car (☎ 722-1600), at the corner of 16th and V Sts, charges $72 for a three-day weekend rental which includes 450 free miles; Weekdays the cost is $37 with 100 free miles per day. If you call ahead, an agent will meet you at the train or bus station.

FRESNO
•*pop 406,000* ☎ 209

Historically the most important city in the San Joaquin Valley, Fresno was once home to millionaires who made fortunes in citrus and raisin crops. Still one of the United States' most productive counties, Fresno's leading crops are grapes, plums, cotton, and nectarines; half of the nation's nectarines are grown in Fresno County. California State University, Fresno (student population 19,000) is considered one of the best agricultural schools in the US. Bus service from Fresno to Sequoia National Park makes it yet another 'gateway' to the Sierra Nevada.

Fresno is also the country's largest test-ground for fast food chains. Among the endless sprawl of strip malls, you will find nearly every fast food restaurant in existence. In Fresno, sampling the latest fast food products not only gives you a 'coming attractions' glimpse of the market, but turns your lunch into a marketing statistic. Though Fresno's landscape generally matches its fast food flavor, its cultural scene far surpasses that of any other city in the valley. Its museums are worth a visit, and the Tower District – Fresno's artsy alternative 'hood' – has some excellent restaurants and theaters.

MARISA GIERLICH

Mission San Miguel, Central Coast

MARISA GIERLICH

Having a snack with the locals

PAUL BURGIN

PAUL BURGIN

The Roman Pool (left), and the Neptune Pool (right) at Hearst Castle

Fruit stand, Central Coast

McWay Falls, Julia Pfeiffer Burns State Park, Big Sur

Orientation & Information

There are two distinct parts to Fresno: the old downtown which revolves around lettered streets (H to M) and streets named after local counties (Tulare, Merced, Inyo); and, extending north and east of downtown, the newer part of Fresno with the main thoroughfares of Shaw and Olive Aves (going east-west) and Palm and Blackstone Aves (going north-south).

The Fresno City & County Convention & Visitor's Bureau (☎ 233-0836, 800-788-0836), downtown at 808 M St, is open weekdays from 8 am to 5 pm. Two blocks southeast, the Holiday Inn Centre Plaza (☎ 268-1000) has maps and brochures in its lobby which is open 24 hours. Services including banks and pharmacies are on most major thoroughfares north of downtown.

Forestiere Underground Gardens

If you only see one thing in Fresno, make it the underground gardens of Baldasare Forestiere (☎ 271-8734), marked by a large yellow sign on Shaw Ave, one block east of Hwy 99. After migrating from Sicily in the 1890s, Forestiere bought 70 acres of land with hopes of planting citrus groves. He found, however, that beneath his land was

PLACES TO STAY
16 Fresno Downtown Motel
18 Holiday Inn Centre Plaza

PLACES TO EAT
2 Cafe Intermezzo
3 Butterfield's Brewing Company
4 Daily Planet

7 Veni Vidi Vici
15 Santa Fe Basque Bar & Restaurant

OTHER
1 Fresno Art Museum
5 Roger Rocka's Music Hall
6 Tower Theater
8 Laundomat Performance Space

9 Storyland
10 Playland
11 Fresno Zoo
12 Fresno Metropolitan Museum
13 Community Hospital
14 Moux Home
17 Fresno City & County
   Convention & Visitors Bureau

solid hardpan, impossible for planting anything. To escape the intense summer heat, he dug a basement out of the hardpan beneath his house and found that, with proper illumination from skylights, he could grow trees in pots beneath the ground. Eventually Forestiere cleared out some 70 subterranean acres for crops and his own living quarters. By altering the skylights he engineered a year-round growing season and was able to sustain himself and sell his produce – over 20 different crops – at local market. He even had a fish pond which he stocked with trout and cod.

After Forestiere died in 1946, his family preserved the gardens and registered them as a historic landmark. Weekend tours leave hourly from noon to 3 pm, and cost $4.

Fresno Art Museum

The Fresno Art Museum (☎ 485-4810), 2233 N 1st St in Radio Park, is Fresno's pride and joy. One of its more interesting twists is an exhibition of art related to social change featuring about 30 artists per year. The permanent collection has bits and pieces from France and South America, including some post-impressionist graphics. The museum is open Tuesday to Friday from 10 am to 5 pm, and on weekends noon to 5 pm. Admission is $2 and free on Tuesdays.

Fresno Metropolitan Museum

Of special interest to anyone with children, this museum of art, history, and science (☎ 441-1444), downtown at 1515 Van Ness Ave, has three stories of hands-on science exhibits, plus a small laser show. There is also a thorough William Saroyan exhibit, dedicated to Fresno's most beloved son. The museum's floor plan is a bit confusing so it's hard to understand how big the place really is; it takes a good two hours to cover the entire thing. Museum hours are daily from 11 am to 5 pm. Admission is $4.

Meux Home

Built in 1888 by Dr TR Meux, a Confederate surgeon, the Meux Home (☎ 233-

8007), at the corner of Tulare and R Sts, is a good example of Victorian architecture. The well-trained docents give an educational spiel on the Victorian Era: 'When people loved to think about death and pretend sex didn't exist.' Though the only original parts of the house are its windows, light fixtures, and hardware, period furniture and clothing is displayed throughout. The house is open Friday to Sunday from noon to 3:30 pm, and tours are given on demand; closed in January. Admission is $3.

Kearney Mansion

More interesting but less central, the Kearney Mansion (☎ 441-0862), six miles west of downtown on Kearney Blvd, belonged to M Theo Kearney, one of Fresno's first raisin barons. The house was built in 1903, and is beautifully restored with about half of its original furnishings and exquisite Art Nouveau wallpapers. Tours are given hourly Friday to Sunday from 1 to 3 pm. Entry is $3.

Tower District

At the east end of Olive Ave, around Wishon, Fern, and Fulton Sts, Fresno's Tower District centers around the restored Tower Theater (☎ 485-9050), built in 1939, which is now a center for the performing arts. Surrounding the theater are used-clothing stores, record shops, and cafes which cater to a diverse and hip crowd. The best time to experience the Tower District is on weekend nights when restaurants fill-up around 9 pm and people hang out in the streets to see and be seen. Pick up a copy of *Talk of the Tower*, available at most stores and cafes, which lists the current events and exhibits around the neighborhood.

Roeding Park

On Olive Ave just west of Hwy 99, Roeding Park is a shady spot to picnic and escape the summer heat. There is a $1 per vehicle entrance fee. It's also home to the **Chaffee Zoological Gardens** (☎ 498-2671), also called the Fresno Zoo. The small but well-tended zoo has a good collection of average zoo animals – monkeys, lions, tigers, elephants – plus a great tropical rain forest. The zoo is open March to October daily from 9 am to 5 pm, November to February 10 am to 4 pm. Admission is $4.50. For an extra $2, you can purchase a plastic key at the gift shop which activates recorded information at exhibits throughout the zoo – fun for people under 10.

Adjacent to the zoo are **Playland** and **Storyland** – kiddie havens. There is no admission fee to enter Playland, but its mini roller coasters, rides, and games cost 50¢ a pop. Storyland has oversized fairytale figures, castles, and cottages which 'come to life' when you insert the magic key you purchase at the entrance for $2 (just like at the zoo). They have performances of childhood favorites on weekends. Playland is open year round. Storyland is open May to September on weekdays from 10 am to 3 pm, weekends 10 am to 5 pm (October to April, weekends only). Admission is $3 for people over 12, $1.50 for children. For information call ☎ 264-2235.

Special Events
During the third weekend in April, nearby Clovis hosts the biggest two-day rodeo in California, complete with rodeo events, a carnival, and a street dance on Saturday night. A completely different crowd attends the Tower District's music, dance, and arts festival at the end of May; call ☎ 237-9734 for information. On August 14th, the eve of the Feast of the Immaculate Conception, is the Blessing of the Grapes, an Armenian tradition celebrating the first fruit of the season. The Fresno Fair, the largest in California, takes place the first two weeks in October and ends with a huge Ragtime Festival where costumed people play music and dance in the streets.

Places to Stay
Fresno's accommodations are the valley's most expensive. The best deals are found in chain motels along Motel Drive, north of downtown off Hwy 99. Next to Roeding Park, just east of Hwy 99 at the Olive Ave

exit, the *Best Western Parkside Inn* (☎ 237-2086) has rooms for $48/52. The *Travelers Inn* (☎ 800-633-8300) has motels on Blackstone, Jensen, and Shaw Aves, with rooms for $40/45. Near the convention center, the *Fresno Downtown Motel* (☎ 268-0621), 2127 Inyo St between L and Van Ness, charges $35/45 for old but clean rooms.

Amidst the strip malls and food chains along Shaw Ave, the *Picadilly Inn* (☎ 226-3850, 800-468-3522), 2305 W Shaw Ave, is a semi-upscale motel with an outdoor pool and hot tub and a good restaurant. Rooms cost $94/104. Near the train station and across from the convention center, the *Holiday Inn Centre Plaza* (☎ 286-1000), 2233 Ventura St, has a nice atrium, pool, hot tub, and fitness center; rooms cost $83/93.

On Hwy 180 (Kings Canyon Rd), 14 miles east of Fresno, the *Little House on Kings Canyon Road* (☎ 266-2519) rents a two-bedroom guest house with a fully-equipped kitchen, in the middle of a 20-acre vineyard. The price is $60 for one person, plus $10 for each additional person.

Places to Eat
For an introduction to the local scene and a good cup of coffee, head to *Cafe Intermezzo* (☎ 497-1456), 747 E Olive. They also serve good salads, huge pizzas and calzones Sunday to Thursday until 10 pm and Thursday to Saturday until around midnight. A few doors down, *Butterfield's Brewing Company* (☎ 264-5521), serves burgers, sandwiches, and pasta for $5 to $11, and makes their own beer. If you care to venture off the fast food track, Fresno has quite a few worthwhile restaurants. The *Santa Fe Basque Bar & Restaurant* (☎ 226-2170), across from the train station at 935 Santa Fe Ave, looks more like a seedy bar than a place to eat. The bar is a hangout for Fresno's few remaining Basque old-timers, but the dining room in back serves family-style meals with soup, salad, meat, vegetables, bread, and desert for $7 ($4 without the meat). The food isn't always great, but

portions are generous and the atmosphere is lively.

For excellent Vietnamese food, try *Kim's Restaurant* (☎ 225-0406), 5048 N Maroa Ave; be sure to get the Vietnamese coffee.

The Tower District is a popular spot for dinner, especially for late-night weekend meals. The fun and funky *Veni Vidi Vici* (☎ 266-5510), 1116 N Fulton St one block south of Olive Ave, has an outdoor patio with live music on weekends and serves food until midnight. The menu includes smoked salmon fettucini, roast duck pizza, and polenta with Thai black bean sauce. Prices are $6 to $10 for lunch, $8 to $16 for dinner. A bit more sophisticated is *Daily Planet* (☎ 266-4259), next to the Tower Theater at 1211 N Wishon Ave, which has a huge wine list and great desserts. The four-course fixed-price menu is a good value for $35; otherwise come for drinks and appetizers or coffee and dessert and watch the crowd.

Entertainment

Fresno's after dark scene happens in the Tower District. Cafe Intermezzo (see Places to Eat) shows movies on Tuesday and Wednesday nights, and many of the restaurants have live music on weekends. The *Laundromat Performance Space* (☎ 222-3341), 1114 N Fulton St, has eclectic theater, music, dance, and performance art; shows are usually free, and quality seems to vary according to lunar phases.

More reliable is *Roger Rocka's Music Hall* (☎ 266-0211), 1226 N Wishon, known for its Broadway dinner theater. The entertainment is good for the $12 price; dinner costs $10 extra but is better spent at a bona fide restaurant. The *Tower Theater for the Performing Arts* (☎ 485-9050), 815 E Olive St, gets headliners like Brian Wilson, Merle Haggard, and Patty LaBelle.

Getting There & Away

Air The Fresno Air Terminal, east of Hwy 41 at the east end of Shields Ave, is the airline hub for the San Joaquin Valley. It is serviced by American Eagle, Delta, Westair/United Express, Skywest, and USAir. Most flights to/from Fresno stop in Los Angeles, San Francisco, or Phoenix. The No 26 bus runs from the airport's main entrance to downtown (near the courthouse at Van Ness and Tulare Sts) from 6:40 am to 6:30 pm daily and costs 75¢. For information call Fresno Transit (☎ 488-1122).

Bus Highway 41 goes north to Yosemite, and Hwy 180 (Kings Canyon Rd) goes east to Kings Canyon and Sequoia National Parks. Greyhound connects Fresno to Los Angeles 16 times daily for $19, and San Francisco eight times daily for $29. The bus depot (☎ 268-9416) is downtown at 1033 H St.

Train Fresno is on the main Amtrak route between San Francisco ($39) and Bakersfield ($38), and gets four northbound and four southbound trains daily. The train station (☎ 486-7651) is downtown at the corner of Tulare and Q Sts.

BLOSSOM TRAIL

To make an attraction of the profuse blossoms on the fruit orchards each spring, the Fresno County Visitor's & Convention Bureau has mapped out a 67-mile route designated the 'Blossom Trail' through peach, plum, nectarine, almond, and citrus groves. The red, white, and pink flowers usually blossom from late February to late March, depending on the weather.

The trail starts on Ashlan Ave, off Hwy 99 and Hwy 41, and proceeds as follows: head east on Ashlan Ave, turn south on Riverbend, turn east on Belmonst, south on Oliver, east on Hwy 180, south on Hwy 63 (Hills Valley Rd), west on Manning Ave, north on Frankwood, west on Annadale, north on Academy, and west on Jensen St, which leads back to Hwy 99, south of Ashlan Ave. Average driving time is 2½ hours. The route is lined with crop-identification signs for those who can't tell a peach blossom from a plum blossom, and directional signs for those who confuse north and south.

Placed at the route's end – on Jensen St just east of Hwy 99 – **Simonian Farms**

(☎ 209-237-2294) is actually a good place to start the tour. It has maps and information, and is the main place to buy fruit and nuts along the route.

At the beginning of the route, along Ashlan Ave, **Clovis** has a restored downtown which, over the past 10 years, has become increasingly popular with antique hounds. As a result, even old tin cans fetch a tidy sum. Along Manning Ave, the route passes through **Reedley**, a cute little Mennonite tourist town whose main attraction is the **Mennonite Quilting Center** (☎ 209-638-3560), 1012 G St between 10th and 11th Sts, open weekdays from 9:30 am to 4 pm and on Saturday 10 am to 2 pm. On Monday mornings the Mennonite Women's Quilting Guild is there, stitching away.

HANFORD
•*pop 54,000* ☎ *209*

Hanford is one of the nicest towns in the San Joaquin Valley, with a restored downtown and lively business climate. Centered around the Kings County Courthouse, built in 1896, Hanford's downtown is noteworthy for its old architecture.

Things to See & Do
As told by the history displays in the **Hanford Carnegie Museum** (☎ 582-3454), 109 E 8th Sts, most of Hanford's brick buildings along Court and 7th Sts were built by railroad agencies in the early 1900s. Hanford's **Taoist Temple**, built in 1893, is at the center of China Alley – in what used to be a bustling Chinatown. To reach China Alley from downtown, take 7th St (away from the railroad tracks) to Green St, turn left and China Alley is clearly visible on the right.

Places to Stay & Eat
Downtown Motel (☎ 582-9036), 101 N Redington St, between 6th and 7th Sts, is the area's most affordable place to stay. Rooms cost $30/37.

The one lasting business in China Alley is the landmark *Imperial Dynasty Restaurant* (☎ 582-0196), owned by the same

family since 1894. Oddly enough, the restaurant serves pricey continental cuisine and is known for its Cordon Bleu and escargots.

Housed in the old jail on the courthouse's ground floor, *Bastille* (☎ 583-9544) serves good margaritas and tap beer and has live music starting at 8 pm, Monday to Saturday. Across the street, the 1924 Art-Deco style Fox Theater (☎ 584-7423), gets a fair share of big-name country & western singers including Merle Haggard and George Jones.

Getting There & Away
Amtrak trains connect Hanford to San Francisco ($46) and Los Angeles ($31) four times daily. The train station (☎ 582-5236) is off 7th St at 200 Santa Fe Ave.

VISALIA
•*pop 92,000* ☎ *209*

Visalia is the oldest town between Stockton and Los Angeles, and has undergone more thorough revitalization than other valley towns. Its downtown, centered at the intersection of Court and Main Sts, three blocks north of Hwy 98, has a number of good coffeehouses and Italian restaurants, and the restored Fox Theater, at the corner of Main and Encina Sts, which plays current movies nightly.

Things to See & Do
South of downtown on Hwy 63 (Mooney Blvd), **Mooney Grove Park** (☎ 733-6612), is a wonderful sprawl of shaded grass where people picnic, run, and fly kites. Within the park is the **Tulare County Museum** (☎ 733-6616) open Thursday to Monday 10 am to 4 pm, which has a typical collection of photographs, clothing, and farm equipment. Visalia's **Chinese Cultural Center** (☎ 625-4545), between Hwy 99 and downtown one block south of Hwy 198 on Akers Rd, is built in the traditional Chinese style – without nails. The building is primarily used for private parties, though anyone can go in and have a look at the collection of Chinese games, vases, serving vessels, and books on display.

Places to Eat

Visalia's *Little Italy* (☎ 734-2906), 303 W Main St, serves some of the best Italian food east of San Francisco. The spicy penne Siciliana is recommended, and all pizzas are cooked in a wood-fired oven. The lunch menu, served weekdays 11 am to 2 pm, is limited but everything on it is under $10. Dinner, served nightly from 5 to 9:30 pm, costs $8 to $15. For authentic border-style Mexican food, seafood dishes, and handmade tortillas, go to *Colima* (☎ 733-7078), 111 E Main, open daily from 8 am to 9 pm.

Getting There & Away

Visalia is serviced by Greyhound-Trailways which has seven daily buses to Los Angeles ($28) and five daily to San Francisco ($34). Visalia's bus station is a half mile east of downtown on Mineral King Ave. Amtrak shuttle buses stop here to make the train connection in Hanford (see above); for information call Amtrak.

BAKERSFIELD

•*pop 360,000* ☎ *805*

Bakersfield is most often associated with oil (the Kern River field was discovered here in 1899 and is still California's richest), country music (it is the birthplace of Merle Haggard), and race cars. These associations and an occasional oil-scent make Bakersfield what some like to call the 'armpit of California.'

If you don't visit in mid-summer (when temperatures rarely drop below 100°F) it's not that bad of a place. The downtown is a pleasant mix of restored buildings and new county offices, and the streets bustle with suit-clad business people at lunchtime. At night, cafes host live music and performance art, and rough-'em-up cowboy bars swing to country & western bands. Students at California State University, Bakersfield (known for its petroleum engineering department) add a youthful air during the week, but commute home to valley towns on weekends. Bakersfield also has the best Basque restaurants in Califor-

nia, run by families whose not-so-distant ancestors tended sheep on Colonel Thomas Baker's 136-sq-mile field.

Orientation & Information

The Kern River flows north of downtown separating the business district from unsightly oil fields. Truxton and Chester Aves are the main downtown thoroughfares; numbered streets run parallel to Truxton, lettered streets run parallel to Chester Ave. Many businesses are in the malls along Stockdale Hwy and Ming Ave, south of downtown off Hwy 99.

The Greater Bakersfield Chamber of Commerce (☎ 327-8751) and Convention & Visitors Bureau (☎ 325-5051), are in the same building, next to the Convention Center at 1033 Truxton Ave. There's another outpost at the corner of F and 19th Sts. All are open weekdays from 8 am to 5 pm.

Kern County Museum

A visit to the Pioneer Village at the Kern County Museum (☎ 861-2132, 323-8368), 3801 Chester Ave, could easily occupy an hour, or whole afternoon if you're traveling with kids. The village is composed of old houses, offices, and cabins, brought from their original locations, restored, and furnished as they were in their original state. You can enter quite a few of them, including an old oil warehouse with an exhibit on the history of oil. The main museum has a typical county history collection with a Bakersfield twist – Merle Haggard's cowboy boots. The museum is open weekdays from 9 am to 5 pm, Saturday 10 am to 5 pm, and Sunday noon to 5 pm. Tickets cost $5; ticket sales stop at 3:30 pm, and the Pioneer Village starts to shut down around 4 pm.

Bakersfield Museum of Art

The art museum (☎ 323-7219), 1930 R St, has changing exhibits of regional and California art that are generally of good quality. The gardens surrounding the building are lovely. Hours are Monday to Saturday 10 am to 4 pm, and admission is $2.

California Living Museum

Northwest of Bakersfield on Alfred Harrel Hwy, the California Living Museum (CALM, ☎ 872-2256), is a zoological and botanical garden whose unspectacular displays concentrate on California animal and plant life. It's in a nice rural spot beside the Kern River. Hours are 9 am to 4 pm Wednesday to Sunday, and admission is $3.

Raceways

Bakersfield's raceways, in full swing from March to October, are its biggest tourist draw. A night at these races gives you a chance to drink Budweiser, chew tobacco, and curse loudly as souped-up cars go screaming by. Weekend events, some with high-profile sponsors and large cash prizes, draw people from all over the state. Smaller races get a local crowd. Ticket prices vary from $7 to $18. Except for really big events, tickets are available at the gate only.

The **Bakersfield Raceway** (☎ 399-2210), is a quarter-mile drag strip famous for its Budweiser-sponsored race in January. On friday night Test-N-Tune 'grudge races' you can drive-up in any kind of vehicle (provided you have a valid drivers license and the car has seat belts) and race around the track. It costs $10 to run your car and $5 to watch. To reach the raceway, take the Hwy 46 exit off Hwy 99, turn right onto Famoso Rd and go east four miles; from downtown, take Hwy 65 north and go west on Famoso.

Home to NASCAR events, the **Mesa Marin Raceway** (☎ 366-5711) is a half-mile oval where cars do 25 to 100 laps at speeds way over 100 miles an hour. Races are held Friday and Saturday nights, usually around 7 pm.

Special Events

The Bakersfield Jazz Festival, held downtown in mid-May, is gaining more popularity each year for big name artists like BB King, Dianne Schurr, and Natalie Cole.

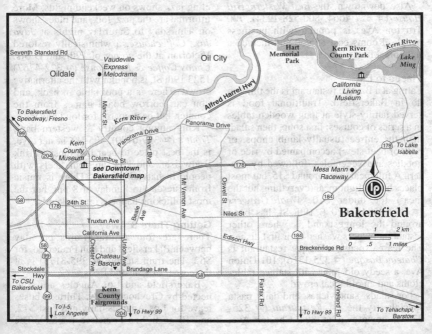

Arts and crafts, antiques, livestock, carnival rides, and rodeo events come together at the Kern County Fair, held during September at the Kern County Fairgrounds, near downtown at 1142 South P St.

Places to Stay

Chain motels are easily visible from Hwy 99, and there are a bunch of budget motels on Union Ave, south of downtown (east of Hwy 99 via E Brundage Lane/Hwy 58). Camping is available at Lake Ming, 10 miles east of downtown off Alfred Harrel Hwy, for $18 per night.

Downtown, the *Padre Hotel* (☎ 322-1419), at the corner of 18th and H Sts, was *the* place to stay in Bakersfield in the 1940s, when most people traveled by train or bus. Condemned as a fire hazard in the 1970s, the owner fought to keep the first floor open and now rents rooms for about $28 per night. The rooms are actually quite nice, and the lobby and coffeeshop are definitely cause for nostalgia.

Also downtown, the *Best Western Hill House* (☎ 327-4064, 800-528-1234), 700 Truxton Ave, is popular with business people. Rooms cost $55/60 and include a light breakfast.

Places to Eat

Eating at a Basque restaurant is the thing to do in Bakersfield. Traditional food is served family-style at long wooden tables in a series of courses: first soup, then salad, then the entree (usually lamb chops, or pork or beef stew) accompanied by rice or noodles and vegetables, followed by dessert. A full meal costs around $15, but most places have a light meal (everything but the meat) for under $10. *Wool Growers* (☎ 327-9584), 620 E 19th St, has been around the longest and is where other restaurant owners washed their first dishes. The least expensive Basque restaurant is *Chateau Basque* (☎ 325-1316), 101 Union Ave, a seedy old joint with stained tablecloths and an old local crowd.

For salads, sandwiches, and daily pasta specials, try the *Ivy Restaurant* (☎ 325-9725), downtown at 804 Chester Ave,

which has an upscale coffee shop setting and prices under $10; their adjacent pantry, open from 8 am to 3 pm, serves lunch and is popular for coffee and scones. *Goose Loonies* (☎ 631-1242), 1623 19th St, is a sports bar – quite loud on weekend nights – which serves heaping burgers, sandwiches, and pasta dishes for around $6. They also have gyros, moussaka, and souvlaki, inspired by the Greek owner.

Entertainment

For a corny but entertaining evening, check out the *Vaudeville Express Melodrama* (☎ 393-7886), a dinner theater where you cheer the hero, hiss the villain, and question your own integrity. Tickets cost $13, and occasionally sell out on weekends.

The best part about Bakersfield's music scene is that shows only cost the price of a beer or a cup of coffee. *City Lights* (☎ 633-2283), at the corner of Chester and 18th Sts, combines San Francisco and LA ambiance in its restaurant and bar, and gets traveling jazz shows on weekend nights. More informal are the jazz, folk, and blues shows on Thursday to Saturday nights at *Java Jazz Coffeehouse*, a whimsically restored Victorian at the corner of 19th and D Sts. *Chaos Coffee & Fun House* (☎ 322-4267) 1523 19th St, is popular with the alternative crowd. There is a pool table in back, and you can borrow board games from the counter, but be prepared for loud music.

King among country & western bars, *Trout's* (☎ 399-6700), 805 N Chester Ave, is the best place to hear live music, drink Budweiser, and kick up your heels with people in hats and boots. There is music from Tuesday to Sunday at 8 pm, but the most rollicking happens on weekends.

Getting There & Away

There are four Amtrak trains per day between Bakersfield and San Francisco, for $62. The train station (☎ 395-3175) is at the corner of 15th and F Sts.

Bakersfield and Los Angeles are connected by Greyhound only. Thirteen buses leave for Los Angeles daily and cost $12, and 10 go to San Francisco for $30. The

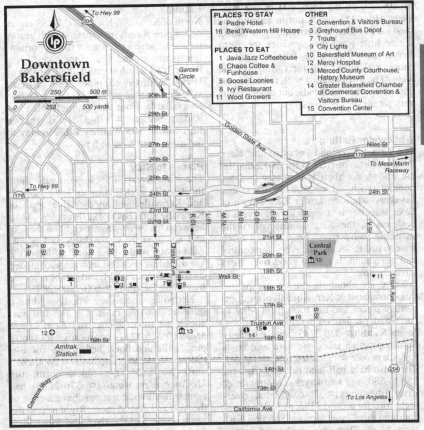

Downtown Bakersfield

To Hwy 99
204

0   250   500 m
0   250   500 yards

Garces Circle

To Hwy 99
178

30th St
29th St
28th St
27th St
26th St
25th St
24th St
23rd St
22nd St
21st St
20th St
19th St
18th St
17th St

Golden State Ave

Niles St

178

To Mesa Marin Raceway

24th St

Central Park
🏛 10

▼ 11

Wall St

Truxtun Ave
■ 16

🏛 13

15
14

16th St

12 ✚
16th St

Amtrak Station

14th St
13th St

To Los Angeles ↓

California Ave

204

Campus Way

A St. B St. C St. D St. E St. F St. G St. H St. Eye St. Chester Ave. K St. L St. M St. N St. O St. P St. R St. S St. S St. Union Ave. V St.

PLACES TO STAY	OTHER
4 Padre Hotel	2 Convention & Visitors Bureau
16 Best Western Hill House	3 Greyhound Bus Depot
	7 Trouts
PLACES TO EAT	9 City Lights
1 Java Jazz Coffeehouse	10 Bakersfield Museum of Art
6 Chaos Coffee & Funhouse	12 Mercy Hospital
5 Goose Loonies	13 Merced County Courthouse; History Museum
8 Ivy Restaurant	14 Greater Bakersfield Chamber of Commerce; Convention & Visitors Bureau
11 Wool Growers	15 Convention Center

Greyhound depot (☎ 327-5617) is downtown at 1820 18th St.

KERN RIVER
☎ 619

Designated a Wild and Scenic River, the Kern starts near Mt Whitney and journeys 170 miles to its final destination in the valley. It is dammed in two places to create **Lake Isabella**, which supplies irrigation water to the southern San Joaquin Valley. About 70 miles east of Bakersfield, this is California's largest freshwater lake; it's a fingery body of water with coves and rock

promontories, surrounded by stark, chaparral-covered mountains. The lake actually lies in the southern Sierra, but most people access it through Bakersfield. Highway 178 follows the Kern River's edge between Bakersfield and Lake Isabella, through the Sequoia National Forest and past USFS campgrounds and picnic areas. Summer temperatures hover around 105°F, and there is little protection from the sun. People naturally spend most of their time on or in the water.

The town of Lake Isabella (pop 2500) is a strip of markets, banks, gas stations, and restaurants, on the south end of the lake. Here, Hwy 155 heads north, around the west side of lake, to **Kernville** (pop 3000), a cute little town that straddles the Kern River about two miles from the lake's shore, and is the hub for rafting on the Kern. The town swarms with recreationalists on summer weekends, but otherwise is very serene.

Whitewater Rafting

The Upper Kern and Forks of the Kern (both sections of river north of Kernville) are known for their whitewater and are popular with adventurous rafters and kayakers, while the Lower Kern (south of Lake Isabella) is a good family river. In both cases, the Kern is known as the 'working man's river,' because you often have to paddle – continuously – for control and navigation. It's not a good river for a leisurely float.

There are about six rafting companies that operate out of Kernville; all offer competitive prices and run trips from May to August, depending on the river conditions. Sierra South (☎ 376-3745), has a Lickety Split trip which takes one hour and costs $18, for people with limited time or money. They also have half- and full-day trips for $50 to $80, and rent kayaks. Mountain & River Adventures (☎ 376-6553), does overnight trips for around $175, as well as one-hour and three-hour trips for $16 and $30, respectively. They rent kayaks and mountain bikes for $7 per hour, $28 per day.

Hiking

North of Kernville, Hwy 122/Mtn 99 enters dense pine forests interspersed with grassy meadows where there are a few opportunities to hike around. One of the nicest is the **River Trail** which starts on the east side of Hwy 122/Mtn 99, 20 miles north of Kernville (at the three-lane bridge). Information is available from the Cannell Meadow Ranger Station (☎ 376-3781), downtown Kernville at 105 Whitney Rd, Monday to Saturday from 8 am to 5 pm.

Places to Stay

There are five USFS campgrounds along the 10-mile stretch between Lake Isabella and Kernville, and another five north of Kernville on Hwy 122/Mtn 99. Most between the two towns are right on the lake and are used by water-skiers and people with boats, while those north of Kernville are a bit less crowded and are surrounded by trees. Sites cost $14, and can be reserved by calling Destinet (☎ 800-280-2267).

Kernville's motels are woodsy and have quite reasonable rates. On the hill just above the town square, the *Kern Lodge Motel* (☎ 376-2224), has rooms with knotty pine walls and floral bedspreads for $40 ($60 on weekends), and has several kitchen units for $65. One block north, the *McCambridge Motel* (☎ 376-2288) has similar facilities, but rooms have a view of the river and cost $5 more. Right next to the town square and the river, the *River View Lodge* (☎ 376-6019) has rooms for $45 to $75 ($50 to $85 on weekends).

Sierra Nevada

Over 400 miles long and from 60 to 80 miles wide, the Sierra Nevada creates a massive barrier along most of eastern California, separating the Central and Owens Valleys. This impressive range (the longest in the continental US) is one big block of granite, tilted westward along a series of faults, with a steep eastern side and gently rolling western foothills. The highest peaks, including Mt Whitney, are along the Sierra Nevada Crest in the east, while Yosemite, Kings Canyon, and Sequoia National Parks sit high in the west with the Gold Country at their feet. Between the crest and foothills lies a granite world woven with canyons, rivers, lake basins, and meadows – some of California's most majestic and pristine scenery. Most development is around Lake Tahoe, Yosemite, and Mammoth Lakes, where ski and tourist industries simultaneously choke and enhance the Sierra's recreational appeal.

Geology

About 140 million years ago, the Pacific Plate dove beneath the westward moving North American Plate, its surface melting into magma with the intense heat and friction. Some of the magma rose to the surface through volcanoes (like those around Mammoth Lakes) while most of it cooled to form the granite block which would become the Sierra Nevada. Over the next 50 to 80 million years this granite block uplifted along faults on its eastern side, tilting west to form an asymmetrical range. As the mountains rose, the streams draining them became fast-flowing rivers and started carving V-shaped valleys (trending east-northwest) into the western slope. Glaciers, which covered the higher parts of the range about three million years ago, scraped the V-shaped valleys into U-shaped valleys and left behind the Sierra's most remarkable topography – erratic boulders, scoured peaks, and valleys such as Yosemite and Kings Canyon.

The Sierra's lower western slope, around 2000 feet, is covered with California black oak, chaparral, manzanita, and high grasses characteristic of its mild climate. Above 2000 feet, this foliage gives way to dense conifer forests of pine and fir, meadows, and large rock outcroppings. In what is called the High Sierra, above 9000 feet, soil was taken away by glacial activity, leaving a polished granite landscape of peaks, basins, and ridges where foxtail and white-bark pine are about all that grow. The Sierra tops out on its eastern side along the Sierra Crest, where peaks rise to about 9000 feet near Lake Tahoe and get gradually higher in the south where they reach above 14,000 feet.

Lake Tahoe

Brilliantly blue and totally surrounded by mountains, Lake Tahoe sits like a jewel in California's eastern crook. The California-Nevada state line cuts lengthwise through the lake; the western shore is in California and the eastern shore is in Nevada. Along the highway, the obvious signs that you've crossed from California to Nevada are boxy casinos and slot machines in every grocery store.

Lake Tahoe Stats

Lake Tahoe is the third-deepest lake in North America, with its greatest depth measured at 1645 feet and its average depth 1000 feet. The bottom of the lake, about 4500 feet in elevation, is lower than the Carson Valley floor, at the bottom of the Carson Range in Nevada. The lake is 22 miles long, 12 miles wide, and has about 72 miles of shoreline. ∎

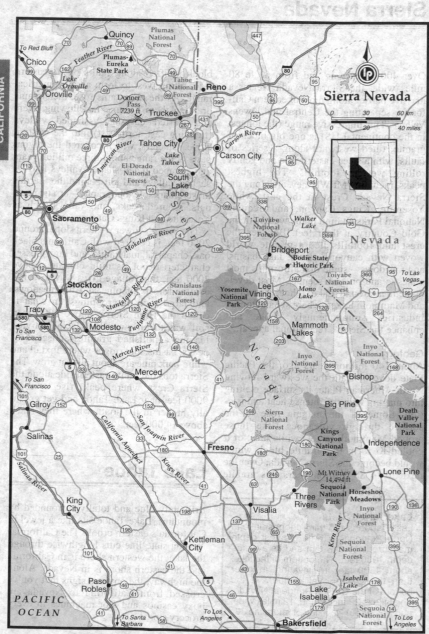

Wanting to drive around the lake is probably instinctual, but it's not necessarily the best way to see the lake. First of all, it's a long drive – about three hours without stopping – with the lake only visible about 60% of the time. During much of the winter a round-the-lake trip isn't an option since Hwy 89 (Emerald Bay Rd), which runs along the west shore connecting South Lake Tahoe and Tahoe City, closes when there is too much snow.

Really the best way to experience what Tahoe has to offer is to get out of the car. The north shore (accessible via I-80) has destination resorts and cute towns with good shopping, while the south shore (via Hwy 50) has casinos, cheap accommodations, and good hiking nearby. The low-key west and east shores are good day trips from either end. Emerald Bay and DL Bliss State Park, on the west shore, should not be missed if Hwy 89 is open. Skiers have choices on both shores: Squaw Valley and Alpine Meadows on the north, Heavenly Valley and Kirkwood (you need your own transportation to get here) on the south. Backpackers should start at Emerald Lake and head southwest into Desolation Wilderness.

Geology

The Tahoe Basin formed between the Carson Range (east) and the Sierra Nevada (west) when the Sierra Nevada block uplifted 50 to 80 million years ago. Lava flowing from Mt Pluto, on the north shore, formed a dam across the basin's outlet and created a lake several hundred feet higher than the present lake. Eventually a new outlet, the Truckee River, was eroded from the lava dam and is the lake's one present outlet, flowing from its northwest shore.

Getting Around

Tahoe Area Rapid Transit (TART, ☎ 916-581-6365, 800-736-6365) buses connect Tahoe City (the hub), Truckee, Squaw Valley, Alpine Meadows, Tahoe Vista, Incline Village, Kings Beach, Homewood, and Tahoma. In summer they extend service down the west shore to Meeks Bay Resort where you can transfer to a South Lake Tahoe bus. Buses run from about 6 am to 6 pm and cost $1.

TRUCKEE & DONNER SUMMIT
• pop 3484 • elev 5820 feet ☎ 916

Named after a Northern Paiute chief who led Frémont from Montana to Los Angeles

---

Outdoor Dangers & Annoyances

Bears are hooked on people food and know that campgrounds are a good place to find it. Never leave food unattended in picnic areas or campsites, and always use the food storage containers provided. Bears have good eyesight, and know what grocery bags, backpacks, and ice chests look like, even when covered with a blanket in the back of a car. When camping in the backcountry, hang your food and smelly things (deodorant, toothpaste, etc) at least 25 feet from the ground. Bear-resistant food canisters ($12) are available at sporting goods shops and in national parks.

Mountain lion sightings have increased in the lower western Sierra, especially in areas with lots of deer. Rangers recommend to stay calm if you meet a lion, hold your ground, try to appear large by raising your arms or grabbing a stick, and if the lion gets aggressive or attacks, fight back, shout, and throw objects at it.

Ticks may carry Lyme disease or borelliosis (relapsing fever), both transmitted by bite. Check your clothes, hair, and skin after hiking, and sleeping bag if it's been out under the trees. Early symptoms of both diseases are similar to the flu: chills, high fever, headache, digestive problems, and general aching. Advanced Lyme disease may result in arthritis, meningitis, neurological, or cardiac problems.

Giardiasis is a water-borne intestinal disease that results in chronic diarrhea, abdominal cramps, bloating, fatigue, and weight loss (not a fun way to slim down). Don't drink stream, lake, or snow water without boiling it for five minutes or treating it with a Giardia-rated water filter or iodine-based purifier.■

The Donner Party

In the 1800s, more than 40,000 immigrants and emigrants traveled west along the California Overland Trail in search of a better life in the 'Land of Sunshine.' High drama was common on this arduous journey, but the story of the ill-fated Donner Party takes the prize for morbid intensity. The Donner Party left Springfield, Illinois, in April 1846. George Donner had a family of seven, Jacob Donner a family of five, and James Reed had family of seven plus two hired hands and a cook. Intending to make the trip as comfortable as possible, the families had two wagons apiece (one of the Reed's wagon's was two-stories) and a large herd of livestock. Though supposedly one of the best outfitted parties to embark on the journey west, this over abundance of supplies led to their demise.

They had a smooth trip to Independence, Missouri, where a large group of emigrants joined them to make the party about 87 people. From here on it was slow going, and by the time they reached Fort Bridger in July they were running behind schedule. When Lansford Hastings told them of a 'short cut' around the south end of the Great Salt Lake which would save several hundred miles, it sounded pretty good. What Hastings didn't mention was that this route had never been used by wagons (he also said that the Great Salt Desert was only 40 miles wide when in fact it was more than 80). Though some in the party decided to go the traditional Fort Hall route, the majority followed the Donners via this 'Hastings cut-off.'

Things started to get grim. At one point it took them three weeks to travel 36 miles. James Reed fought with another member of the party and killed him, and was thus banished in the middle of the desert. Oxen and livestock began to die of heat exhaustion and dehydration, and wagons had to be abandoned. By the time the party reached the eastern foot of the Sierra Nevada, many people were walking and provisions were already running short.

A few months earlier, several men were sent ahead to bring back supplies and they returned to the party just before they reached the Truckee Pass in November. Thus when they encountered a fierce snowstorm which made the pass impassable, they were not too concerned: they had food to last a month and certainly the weather would clear by then. But the weather didn't clear. The snow fell for weeks on end until it reached a depth of over 20 feet – the most snow recorded in the past 100 years.

By winter the party was split in three: about half were camped at Truckee (now Donner) Lake; most of the others (including George Donner who had slashed his hand trying to carve a new wagon axle) were at Alder Creek, about six miles from the lake; and the Breen family, an Irish-Catholic family of 10, was in a cabin built two years before by another emigrant party.

James Reed, the fellow banished in the desert, made it to Sutter's Fort, California, by mid-October. Fearing that his family was trapped by winter storms, he put together the first rescue party which arrived at the camps in mid-February. With most livestock and oxen buried in snow, people were surviving on boiled ox hides. Most were too weak to travel, so the rescue party could only evacuate six people. By the time the second rescue party came in March, people had resorted to cannibalism. Journals and reports tell of 'half-crazed people living in absolute filth, with naked, half-eaten bodies strewn about the cabins.' Again, only a few of the strongest survivors could be rescued. By mid-April, when a final rescue party arrived, the only person remaining at the lake camp was Lewis Keseberg. At the Alder Creek Camp, the rescuers found George Donner's body cleansed and wrapped in a sheet, but no sign of Tasmen Donner, George's wife who refused to leave her husband even though she was strong enough to go with earlier rescue parties. Keseberg admitted to surviving on the flesh of those who had died, but denied the accusations that he had killed Tasmen Donner for fresh meat. He spent the rest of his life trying to clear his name.

Altogether 40 people survived, including the entire Breen family and five people they cared for in what became known as Starved Camp, and 47 people perished. The most definitive histories written about the tragedy are George R Stewart's *Ordeal By Hunger*, and Joseph A King's *Winter of Entrapment: A New Look at the Donner Party.* ∎

in 1846, Truckee is a charming old mining and railroad town that survives on tourism. It has a good amount of restaurants, interesting shops, and a restored hotel which makes it a good base for exploring Tahoe's north shore.

West of Truckee via I-80, Donner Lake is surrounded by small, woodsy resorts and private cabins – a low-key alternative to Tahoe action. This is also where the unfortunate Donner Party lodged during their fateful (and famous) winter.

History
Built in 1863 as Coburn's Station, Truckee was a rendezvous for miners and lumberjacks, with its fair share of saloons, gambling halls, and bordellos. In 1868, during a race to finish the first transcontinental railroad, workers built east and west from Truckee making it a railroad center. A few years later it was site of the West's first big train robbery – the Verdi Robbery – when seven bandits made off with $41,000 in gold. The **Old Truckee Jail Museum** (☎ 582-0893), at the corner of Jiboom and Spring Sts, has some interesting relics from these old days. It's open weekends from 11 am to 4 pm (free).

Orientation & Information
Truckee's businesses lie along Commercial Row which intersects I-80 and becomes Donner Pass Rd (to Donner Lake and the state park) at the west end of town. West River St runs along the Truckee River, parallel to Commercial Row. Bridge St makes the town's east border, connecting I-80 and Hwy 267 which goes southeast to Incline Village.

The Truckee Donner Visitors Center (☎ 800-548-8388), housed in the train depot at the west end of Commercial Row, gives out a 'visitor bag' full of maps, brochures, and local bus schedules. They also have a car rental service ($35 per day) and public restroom.

The Sierra Mountaineer (☎ 587-2025), at the corner of Bridge and Jiboom, has a good selection of maps, guides, and camping/climbing equipment; their staff is helpful with trail recommendations. The Bookloft (☎ 582-8302), at Bridge St and W River Drive, has a good local and natural history selection and is open until 9 pm. The USFS Truckee Ranger Station (☎ 587-3558) is a mile northeast of town on Hwy 89.

A big shopping center with banks, gas stations, and a market is west of town at the I-80/Hwy 89-South junction.

Donner Memorial State Park
At the Murphy Cabin site on the east end of Donner Lake, this park is on one of three sites where the Donner party spent the winter of 1846 waiting to continue over Donner Pass to Sutter's Fort, the end of their eight month journey from Illinois. A highway-side memorial shows how high the snow got that year; most of the party froze or starved to death while some survived on cannibalism (see the sidebar on previous page).

The **Emigrant Trail Museum** (☎ 587-3841) does a great job chronicling the Donner party's journey and has a worthwhile film. Admission is $2 and can be used towards the park's $5 day-use fee. From the museum, the Emigrant Trail winds through the forest past other cabin sites and a memorial erected in 1918. Though its history is gruesome, the park is lovely and has a nice campground (see Places to Stay), sandy beach, and cross-country ski trails.

Donner Lake
Because of its small size, Donner is much warmer than Tahoe making swimming and water-skiing quite comfortable. Most campers and boaters go to the beach and marina on the east end of the lake at the state park ($5 day-use fee), which is nice but small. Families favor West End Beach ($2.50), at the west end of Donner Pass Rd, for its volleyball, basketball, snack stand, and roped-off swimming area. Docks along the lake's north shore (visible from Donner Pass Rd) are public and free (unless fenced off) and quieter than the beaches.

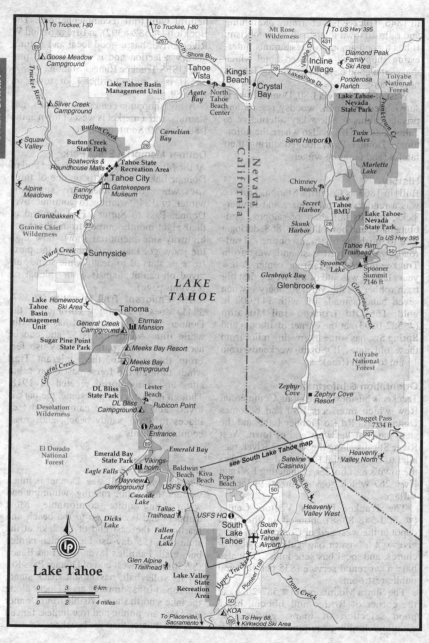

To Truckee, I-80
To Truckee, I-80
89
267
North Shore Blvd
Mt Rose Wilderness
431   To US Hwy 395

Goose Meadow Campground
Tahoe Vista
Kings Beach
Village Dr
Incline Village
28
Lakeshore Dr
Diamond Peak Family Ski Area

Silver Creek Campground
Agate Bay
North Tahoe Beach Center
Crystal Bay
Ponderosa Ranch
Toiyabe National Forest

Truckee River

Squaw Valley
Burton Creek
Carnelian Bay
Lake Tahoe-Nevada State Park

Lake Tahoe Basin Management Unit

Burton Creek State Park
28
Sand Harbor
Twin Lakes
Marlette Lake
Franktown Cr

Boatworks & Roundhouse Malls
Tahoe State Recreation Area
Tahoe City
Alpine Meadows
Fanny Bridge
Gatekeepers Museum
Chimney Beach
Secret Harbor
Lake Tahoe BMU

Granlibakken
89
Skunk Harbor
28
Lake Tahoe-Nevada State Park
To US Hwy 395
50

Granite Chief Wilderness
Ward Creek
Sunnyside
LAKE TAHOE
Spooner Lake
Tahoe Rim Trailhead
Spooner Summit 7146 ft

CALIFORNIA
NEVADA

Lake Tahoe Basin Management Unit
Homewood Ski Area
Tahoma
Glenbrook Bay
Glenbrook
Glenbrook Creek

General Creek Campground
Ehrman Mansion
Toiyabe National Forest

Sugar Pine Point State Park
Meeks Bay Resort

General Creek
Meeks Bay Campground

DL Bliss State Park
Lester Beach
DL Bliss Campground
Rubicon Point
Zephyr Cove
Zephyr Cove Resort

Desolation Wilderness
Park Entrance
Dagget Pass 7334 ft
207

El Dorado National Forest
89
Emerald Bay
see South Lake Tahoe map
Stateline (Casinos)
Heavenly Valley North

Emerald Bay State Park
Vikingsholm
Baldwin Beach
Kiva Beach
Ski Run Blvd

Eagle Falls
Bayview Campground
Cascade Lake
USFS
Pope Beach
50
Heavenly Valley West

Dicks Lake
Tallac Trailhead
USFS HQ
South Lake Tahoe
South Lake Tahoe Airport

Fallen Leaf Lake

LP

Lake Tahoe

Glen Alpine Trailhead
Lake Valley State Recreation Area
Upper Truckee R
Pioneer Trail

0   3   6 km
0   2   4 miles
50
KOA
To Placerville, Sacramento
89
To Hwy 88, Kirkwood Ski Area
Trout Creek

Activities

There are several equipment rental shops that cater to all seasons. Porter's Ski & Sport (☎ 587-1500), in the Lucky-Longs Center at the I-80/Hwy 89 junction, has just about everything. For guided back-country tours and skills seminars, Alpine Skills International (☎ 426-9108) is highly respected. Their base camp is at Donner Pass where they offer a 'bunk & breakfast' for $23, but you must register in advance for their courses. Call for a catalog, or write PO Box 8, Norden, CA 95724.

Alpine Skiing Ski areas around here are smaller and less flashy than Squaw Valley and Alpine, but are still good. Most are west of town, off I-80 or Donner Pass Rd, and all have full service lodges with rentals, ski school, equipment shops, and a restaurant/cafeteria. **Northstar-at-Tahoe** (☎ 562-1010), off Hwy 267 southeast, is the closest big-time resort – a favorite with families and intermediate skiers. They have 10 lifts, a gondola, 2200 vertical feet, and loads of other activities; lift tickets are $42. Locals recommend **Sugar Bowl** (☎ 426-3651), south of Donner Pass Rd, for steep terrain and good atmosphere (the lodge area resembles a Tyrolean village). They have eight lifts, 1500 vertical feet, and $37 tickets.

Smaller, cheaper areas include **Boreal Ski Area** (☎ 426-3666) with 10 lifts, 600 vertical feet, and $33 tickets; **Donner Ski Ranch** (☎ 426-3635), off Donner Pass Rd, with six lifts and 750 vertical feet, and $20 ($10 midweek) tickets; **Tahoe Donner** (☎ 587-9444), with 600 vertical feet, and a $34 Beginners Special including ticket, rentals, and lessons (lift tickets are $13); and **Soda Springs** (☎ 426-3666), whose two lifts and 650 vertical feet are open weekends only (tickets are $20).

Cross-Country Skiing South of I-80 off Soda Springs Rd, the **Royal Gorge Cross Country Ski Resort** (☎ 426-3871) is the largest cross-country ski resort in the USA, with 321 km of trails and four surface lifts. Hard-core skiers consider this *the* spot to ski. With so much terrain, however, there is plenty of variety and it never feels crowded. Trail passes cost $19 ($16 midweek).

With 70 km of groomed trails, **Tahoe Donner** has $15 passes, and night skiing Wednesday to Saturday from 5 to 8 pm. In addition, **Northstar-at-Tahoe** has 65 km ($15).

Places to Stay

Camping The Donner Memorial State Park campground is divided in three, with restrooms and hot showers at each: the *Creek Campground* is nicely shaded and near Donner Creek, but sites are close together; *Ridge Campground* is the smallest with the best access to the campfire center; and the *Splitrock Campground* is the most removed from day-use activities and has the most sites. Sites cost $14 and can be reserved through Destinet.

There are also nice USFS campgrounds on Hwy 89 south of Truckee, next to the Truckee River: *Granite Flat* is the largest, with flush toilets and pull-through sites; *Goose Meadow* is smaller and better protected from highway noise; and *Silver Creek* gets the most crowded because it's closest to Tahoe City. All sites cost $14 and are reservable (☎ 800-280-2267).

Hotels A stage stop in the 1860s, home to railroad laborers in the 1870s, then a lumbermen's boarding house for many years, the *Truckee Hotel* (☎ 587-4444, 800-659-6921), just off Commercial at 10007 Bridge St, is the most historical place to stay. Its recent restoration, homey atmosphere, and nice decor also make it the nicest. European rooms (with a sink but no bathroom) cost $70 to $110, standard rooms are $90 to $110, including breakfast.

Southeast of town on Hwy 267, the *Truckee Tahoe Inn* (☎ 587-4525) has a nice views, a cozy lobby, and modern rooms for $65 to $90.

Donner Lake Village (☎ 800-621-6664), on Donner Lake Rd, has decent condos and suites for $70 to $125 ($10 more for a view), a private beach, marina, and pool.

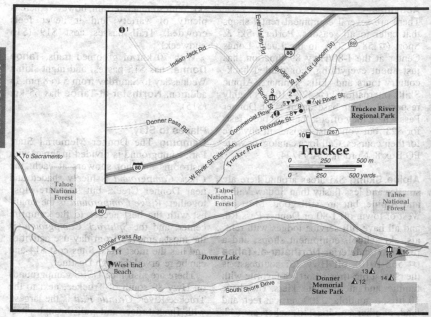

Built in the 1920s, the *Rainbow Lodge* (☎ 800-500-3871) at Royal Gorge Cross Country Ski Resort, off I-80, has classic mountain lodge charm, with a huge fireplace and cozy rooms for $99 ($69 without private bath). Ski trails are right out the door.

Places to Eat

Earthly Delights Bakery (☎ 587-7793), on W River St, is a good spot for coffee, pastries, and bread.

Among the restaurants on Commercial Row, *OB's Pub* (☎ 587-4164) has been there the longest and has basic lunch and dinner items for under $10. Next door, *Theresa's* (☎ 587-2626), has nicer atmosphere and good burgers ($6).

The Passage (☎ 587-7619), in the Truckee Hotel, is the local hang-out and has the best food in town. The atmosphere is casual – lots of wood, brass and big,

colorful paintings – and they often have live music on weekends.

On a hill overlooking the town and river, off Hwy 267, the *Cottonwood* (☎ 587-5711) is more for partying than eating. It has a lively happy hour from 4 to 6 pm, live jazz on Saturday nights, and a great patio.

Getting There & Around

Reno-Cannon International Airport (☎ 702-328-6499) is the closest commercial airport to north Lake Tahoe and services most flights to the area. Truckee-Tahoe Airport is primarily for charter flights; the next-closest commercial airport is in South Lake Tahoe.

There are four buses to Reno ($8) and five to Sacramento/San Francisco ($18/32) daily. The Greyhound ticket counter opens one hour before buses depart.

Amtrak trains and Greyhound buses both stop at the Truckee train depot in the same

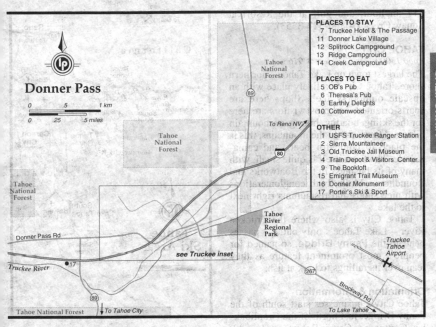

Donner Pass

PLACES TO STAY
7 Truckee Hotel & The Passage
11 Donner Lake Village
12 Splitrock Campground
13 Ridge Campground
14 Creek Campground

PLACES TO EAT
5 OB's Pub
6 Theresa's Pub
8 Earthly Delights
10 Cottonwood

OTHER
1 USFS Truckee Ranger Station
2 Sierra Mountaineer
3 Old Truckee Jail Museum
4 Train Depot & Visitors Center
9 The Bookloft
15 Emigrant Trail Museum
16 Donner Monument
17 Porter's Ski & Sport

CALIFORNIA

building as the visitors bureau, at the west end of Commercial Row. Eastbound trains to Reno ($12) leave at 5 and 9:27 am, and westbound trains to San Francisco ($49) leave at 5:18 pm daily. Tickets are bought on board.

The Truckee Trolley (☎ 546-1222) leaves from the train depot at the west end of Commercial Row hourly from 7:30 am to 6:30 pm, with one route to Donner Memorial State Park and West End beach, and another to the Northstar Resort and Truckee-Tahoe Airport. One-way fare is $1, and an all-day pass is $2.

SQUAW VALLEY USA
☎ 916
In 1955, Alexander Cushing developed Squaw Valley USA (☎ 800-545-4350) into a resort equipped to host the 1960 Olympic Winter Games. Recently the mountainside facilities were overhauled and updated, and a deluxe golf and conference center – the Resort at Squaw Creek – was added. Now Squaw is a year-round village with restaurants, plenty of lodging, and enough activities to make the lazy person wince.

Summer and winter activities are based from the main lodge, at the bottom of the tram/gondola, where there are equipment rental shops, restaurants, visitor information, and lift ticket sales. Squaw has 40 chair lifts, 2830 vertical feet, and some of the best skiing in California; lift tickets are $43.

In summer, High Camp, at the top of the gondola, serves as a scenic spot for bungee jumping, ice skating, and outdoor swimming, while the bottom of the mountain is a mountain bike park ($35 all day). A round-trip ride on the gondola is $13 ($3 after 5 pm); with ice skating and swimming it's $20.

Other activities include horseback riding at Squaw Valley Stables (☎ 583-7433) for

$17 an hour, and golf at the Resort at Squaw Creek (☎ 800-327-3353).

TAHOE CITY
• *pop 1300* • *elev 6240 feet* ☎ *916*

The largest town on Lake Tahoe's northern shore, Tahoe City is a lively place with an upscale outdoorsy feel. Shops here are sports-oriented, and most visitors are here for the skiing, boating, hiking, or mountain biking. After a day in the mountains, this is the place to come for beers and camaraderie. The town itself is quite small, with many of its business in the Boatworks and Roundhouse Malls, both conglomerations with nice shops and restaurants right next to the lake.

Tahoe City is also where the Truckee River – Lake Tahoe's only outlet – passes beneath the **Fanny Bridge**, so named for people's most prominent feature as they lean over its railings to look at fish.

Orientation & Information
Tahoe City's businesses start south of the Fanny Bridge, just north of the Granlibakken Conference Center Resort, on Hwy 89. Highway 28 heads northeast from Hwy 89 as N Lake Blvd, Tahoe City's main drag. From this junction, Hwy 89 goes north (as River Rd) to Squaw Valley and Truckee, and south, along the lake's west side, to South Lake Tahoe. Hwy 28 continues around the lake's north and east shore.

At the junction, the North Lake Tahoe Chamber of Commerce (☎ 581-6240) has lodging, dining, shopping, and activities information. They're open weekdays from 9 am to 5 pm. The Book Shelf (☎ 581-1900), in the Boatworks Mall, has good maps, Lake Tahoe books and guides, and is open until 9 pm (8 pm Sunday).

Gatekeeper's Museum
Near the south end of Fanny Bridge on Hwy 89, this museum (☎ 583-1762) has a large Native American basket collection and old Tahoe memorabilia including ski equipment and photos. The surrounding park is nice for picnicking. The museum is

open Wednesday to Sunday from 11 am to 5 pm (free).

Activities
Porter's Ski & Sport (☎ 583-2314), 501 N Lake Blvd, is a good source of trail maps and equipment. They rent mountain bikes and in-line skates ($4 an hour/$18 all day), water skis ($13 a day), alpine and cross-country skis ($16/8); ski rentals cost $3 less on weekdays.

There is a nice paved path along the Truckee River, north of town, popular for running, walking, skating, and leisurely biking. The same path extends south of town, but is more exposed to Hwy 89 traffic.

Hiking & Biking There are some great day-hikes in the Granite Chief Wilderness, east of Tahoe City. The Five Lakes and Whiskey Creek Trails, from the Alpine Meadows parking lot, give steep but immediate access to beautiful alpine lakes and the Pacific Crest Trail; from here you can access backcountry trails, good for overnight trips – no wilderness permits required.

A trailhead for the Tahoe Rim Trail is just off Hwy 89 (north of Fanny Bridge) on Fairway Drive, across from the Fairway Community Center. No bikes are allowed for the first eight miles of this stretch, but you can access the bikeable part via dirt roads in Burton Creek State Park; maps are available at Porter's. Watson Lake, 12 miles from the trailhead, is a good overnight destination for hikers. The lake is stocked with trout and surrounded by wildflowers in the spring.

Skiing Between Tahoe City and the turnoff for Squaw Valley USA (listed above) is the road to **Alpine Meadows** (☎ 583-4232), a top notch resort that gets its 'second-best' status only because Squaw is so huge. Locals like Alpine for its friendly atmosphere and steep backside bowls. Alpine has 12 lifts, 1800 vertical feet, and $43 lift tickets.

Northeast of town off Hwy 28 via Fabian and Village Rds, **Lakeview Cross-Country Ski Center** (☎ 583-9353), has 65 km of groomed trails which wander through Burton Creek State Park. They have a well-respected ski school ($18 for a half-day lesson, including rentals; $11 rentals only), and nice lodge. Passes are $14. Serious cross-country skiers should check-out Royal Gorge (under Truckee).

Rafting The Truckee River is gentle and wide as it flows from the lake – perfect for novice rafters who like to drag a six-pack behind the boat. Raft companies set up along Hwy 89 in town and charge $22 to $55 per boat. They provide transportation back from the River Ranch Lodge (☎ 583-4264) at the end of the run. The lodge is famous for its strawberry margaritas and big patio overlooking the roughest part of the ride.

Places to Stay
Accommodations get booked far in advance for 4th of July and Labor Day weekends, December 26 to January 1, and the weeks before and after Easter Sunday (depending on when it falls and how much snow there is). Squaw Valley Central Reservations (☎ 800-545-4350) books motel rooms, condos, and houses in the Squaw Valley area, though sometimes they have places available at other locations on the north shore. This is an affordable way to go for long stays and large groups. Tahoe Vista (listed below) has a bunch of affordable motels and cabins and is serviced by bus year round.

Camping Just outside of town on Hwy 28, the *Tahoe State Recreation Area* (☎ 583-3974) has flush toilets, showers, and 31 sites close to the lake for $14; reservable through Destinet. There are three USFS campgrounds north of town on Hwy 89, listed under Truckee.

Motels Downtown, the *Tahoe City Inn* (☎ 800-800-8246) 790 N Lake Blvd, is the most affordable in town with $45 rooms ($60 to $95 on summer weekends). The *Rodeway Inn* (☎ 583-3711, 800-624-8590), 645 N Lake Blvd, is a good value with basic rooms for $66 to $76. For a splurge, the *Tahoe Marina Lodge* (☎ 800-748-5650) is a good choice. They have lakeside rooms for $92, condos starting at $120, and a private beach.

Places to Eat
The all-around favorite restaurant, bar, and hangout is *Rosie's Cafe* (☎ 583-8504), at 640 N Lake Blvd. Their menu is straightforward, with a few Mexican items (mostly under $10).

Grazie! (☎ 583-0233), in the Roundhouse Mall, is a casual spot with a lakeside deck and good Italian food for around $8. For interesting beer, hearty appetizers, and large salads, try the *Bluewater Brewing Company* (☎ 581-2583), next to Safeway in the Lighthouse Shopping Center at the east end of town.

Jakes (☎ 583-0188), in the Boathouse Mall, has a great view and a pleasant deck.

Specialties include shrimp scampi ($12), seafood linguine ($14), and charbroiled steaks. For a deluxe dinner that might break the bank (prices start at $18), everyone and their mother recommends *Wolfdale's Cuisine Unique* (☎ 583-5700), 790 N Lake Blvd, which serves gourmet food from a small, seasonal menu and has an extensive wine list.

Getting Around

In summer, the Tahoe City Trolley zips people around town for free, stopping at the malls, Gatekeeper's Museum, and requested destinations.

THE NORTH & EAST SHORES

Between Tahoe City and Glenbrook, Nevada, are a handful of lakeside communities that buzz with tourist activity from June to September and, not as loudly, from December to whenever the snow melts. While the towns are not very exciting – usually just motels and shopping centers strung along Hwy 28 – they have good Lake Tahoe beach access and affordable accommodations. The lake's northern California-Nevada state line crosses Hwy 28 at Crystal Bay (where a sad conglomeration of casinos tries to look like South Lake Tahoe), so that all of the east shore is in Nevada. The parks on this side of the lake are epic in summer.

Tahoe Vista
• *elev 6232 feet* ☎ *916*

This strip of motels along Hwy 28 (N Lake Blvd) is quite woodsy (almost charming) and much less glitzy than Kings Beach, its larger neighbor immediately east. North Tahoe Regional Park is north of the highway, at the end of National St, with hiking, biking, and cross-country ski trails, and nice picnic facilities. On the lake, the North Tahoe Beach Center (☎ 546-2566) has health spa facilities ($5 a day), a sandy beach, and canoe/kayak rentals ($7 an hour).

Places to Stay & Eat *Beesley's Cottages* (☎ 546-2448), 6674 N Lake Blvd, are cute and whimsical and surrounded by a grassy lawn that slopes down to the lake. Rooms in the small, basic motel are $70, one bedroom cottages start at $100. Across the road, the *Cedar Glen Lodge* (☎ 546-4281, 800-341-8000) has friendly owners and new rooms for $40 to $90. Straddling the highway, the *Vista Shores Resort* (☎ 800-535-9671), 6731 N Lake Blvd, has mountainside rooms for $55 to $85, and lakeside cottages starting at $110, plus a private beach and swimming pool. The *Franciscan Lakeside Lodge* (☎ 546-6300), 6944 N Lake Blvd, has the same set up and similar prices.

Restaurant pickin's along here are slim but good. The *Seedling Cafe* (☎ 546-3936) at 7801 N Lake Blvd, serves excellent vegetarian food for under $10 (open until 9 pm), and *The Boulevard* (☎ 546-7213), 6731 N Lake Blvd, has some of the best Italian food on the lake. The menu is very authentic, with items like insalata Caprese (tomatoes, fresh mozzarella, basil, and olive oil), fettucini carbonara, penne puntanesca, and tiramisu; dinner for two is around $40.

Incline Village (Nevada)
• *pop 4500* • *elev 6269 feet* ☎ *702*

Incline's Lakeshore Drive, which skirts the lake while Hwy 28 (Tahoe Blvd) swings northeast, is lined with million-dollar homes and private beach clubs – one of the most prominent displays of wealth on the lake. A paved bike path runs along Lakeshore Drive with good views of water and wealth. Businesses here are along Village Blvd, between Hwy 28 and Lakeshore Drive, and at the Village Blvd/Hwy 28 junction. The Village Ski (☎ 831-3537) is a good place for bike and ski rentals, and the Incline Village/Crystal Bay Visitors Bureau (☎ 800-468-2436), on Hwy 28 at the east end of town, has local maps and lodging information.

Golfers should check out **Incline Championship Golf Course** (☎ 832-1144), north of Hwy 28 via Country Club and

Fairway Drives, one of the lake's most popular courses open for public play. Northeast of town, off Hwy 28 and Country Club Drive, **Diamond Peak Family Ski Area** (☎ 831-3249) has downhill skiing with seven chair lifts and mostly intermediate runs ($35 lift tickets), and 35 km of groomed cross-country ski trails ($12 passes).

Mt Rose (Nevada)
• *elev 8900 feet* ☎ *702*
North of Incline Village, off Hwy 431 (Mt Rose Hwy) which connects with Hwy 395 to Reno, Mt Rose has the profile of a woman lying on her back with clasped hands resting on her stomach. An early miner, looking at her from Reno, named the mountain Rose after his sweetie.

The Mt Rose Wilderness lies northwest of the highway, with good access from the Mt Rose Summit and Tahoe Meadows Trailhead, a half-mile west of the summit. Wilderness permits are self-register at the trailheads where there are posted maps, restrooms, and free parking. The wilderness is interspersed with private land, so get a good map before doing any overnight trips (day hikes are generally OK).

On the other side of the highway, **Mt Rose Ski Area** (☎ 800-754-7673) is low-key, uncrowded, and popular with locals. It has five lifts, 1440 vertical feet, and interesting views of both wilderness and Reno, and $38 lift tickets.

Ponderosa Ranch (Nevada)
For a worn-out piece of Western Americana, visit the Ponderosa Ranch (☎ 702-831-0691), off Hwy 28 just south of Incline Village, where the Western TV classic *Bonanza* was filmed. Tours of the Cartwright Ranch include old film clips and a barn full of props and antiques used on the set, plus a staged gunfight on 'Main Street.' There is also a petting zoo, shooting gallery, and old buildings which function as stores and restaurants. The ranch opens April to October from 9:30 am to 5 pm; admission is $10.50.

Sand Harbor (Nevada)
If it weren't for the swarms of summer tourists, this place would be ideal. The harbor sits on the northeast shore where two sand spits have formed a beautiful shallow bay with brilliant turquoise water and white sand beaches. **Diver's Cove**, a popular scuba spot, is at the north end, where the bottom drops off a bit and underwater rock formations attract fish.

The area is managed by the Nevada State Park Service which charges $5 per vehicle and maintains a small visitors center (☎ 702-831-0494) with good maps and hiking information. The beach has lifeguards, restrooms, a snack stand, and boat rentals. In July and August, the harbor hosts a reputable Shakespeare Festival (☎ 800-486-2463) with outdoor performances beside the lake – fantastic! Tickets are $12 and sell out quickly.

Lake Tahoe Nevada State Park
This excellent state park spans most of the ridge along the lake's east shore, encompassing beaches, lakes, and miles of trails. There are beach access points all along Hwy 28. Most of them are undeveloped, word-of-mouth spots where you'll see cars parked along the highway but no developed parking lot or trailhead; it's a steep half-mile hike down to the lake. There are two official parking lots (across from each other on the highway) for Chimney Beach, often full by 10 am.

At the park's south end, **Spooner Lake**, at the Hwy 50/Hwy 28 junction, has the most facilities and the best park information. The lake is stocked with trout and has restrooms, nice picnic facilities ($4 per vehicle), and a cross-country ski area (☎ 702-749-5349) with 91 km of groomed trails ($12 trail pass). The Marlette Flume Trail follows the path of an old flume that carried logs by water to lumber mills and mines at Virginia City. The trail goes north from Spooner Lake with the Tahoe Rim Trail, then goes around the west side of Marlette Lake (the Rim Trail goes around the east side). The trail's west side drops straight down to the lake, making it quite treacherous for mountain bikes but great for hiking and cross-country skiing. There is a scenic primitive campsite on the east side of Marlette Lake and at Twin Lakes, about two miles north.

WEST SHORE
☎ *916*

The west shore of Lake Tahoe, between Emerald Bay and Tahoe City, has some of the lake's nicest state parks and swimming beaches. The 'towns' along Hwy 89 – Meeks Bay, Tahoma, Homewood, and Sunnyside – are little more than gatherings of cabins and resorts (Tahoma has a general store and post office) – a good destination if you're looking to sit by the lake and not be entertained. **Ski Homewood** (☎ 525-2992) is the area's only ski hill, a small, friendly affair with nine lifts, $32 lift tickets, and challenging back runs.

Sunnyside
The deck of *Sunnyside Lodge* (☎ 583-7200) is *the* place to be in the summer. They serve lunch, dinner, and loads of cocktails around sunset when people are just coming off the trails. They also have pricey lakeside accommodations and a full-service marina with boat rentals and a water-ski school ($75 per hour for three people).

Just north, across the highway, Cycle-paths (☎ 581-1171) rents bikes ($8 per hr) and in-line skates ($5 per hour), and is a good source of hiking, biking, and skiing information.

Tahoma
Tahoma has the west side's concentration of places to stay and eat, as well as the area's general rendezvous, *Obexer's Market* (☎ 525-7962), a well-stocked deli and market open daily until 9 pm. Just north of the market, the *Tahoma Meadows B&B* (☎ 525-1553, 800-355-1596) has a beautiful garden and darling cabins for $65. Next door, the microscopic *Stony Ridge Cafe* (☎ 525-0905) serves excellent breakfasts, and lunch until 3 pm.

The *Norfolk Woods Inn* (☎ 525-5000) has a variety of plush rooms and rustic cabins for $75 to $110, including breakfast. Across the highway, *Tahoe Cedars Lodge* (☎ 525-7515) has small, rustic cabins for $47 and its own beach.

Sugar Pine Point State Park
Between Meeks Bay and Tahoma, Sugar Pine Point is a well-developed park with a swimming pier, tennis courts, and a nature center. The **Ehrman Mansion** (☎ 525-7982), a beautiful estate built in the 1920s, is the park's major attraction. It is open daily from 10 am to 5 pm (free).

On the west side of Hwy 89 is the park's well-forested *General Creek Campground* with 175 year-round sites, and hiking and cross-country ski trails. Sites ($14) are reservable through Destinet.

Meeks Bay
This long, shallow bay with its wide sweep of shoreline stays light longer than other spots because it has a meadow on its west side which lets in the afternoon sun. It also has warm water by Tahoe standards.

Meeks Bay Resort (☎ 525-7274) has had the same owners for 40 years. They rent small cabins for $75 per night, large ones for $1000 per week, and tent sites for $15. Adjacent is the USFS *Meeks Bay Campground* with $14 sites (reservable by calling ☎ 800-280-2267) and much nicer surroundings but no hot water.

DL Bliss State Park
If you only have one day on the lake, this is a good place to spend it. Some of the prettiest sections of the lake, Rubicon Point and the DL Bliss beach harbor boast clear turquoise water, white sand, and big boulders which people jump off into the lake – beware of low water and protruding rocks should you decide to take the plunge. From the beach's south end you can connect with the Rubicon Trail (the official trailhead is just past the park entrance), a four-mile hiking trail which skirts the water's edge, south to Emerald Point. Beach and trailhead parking costs $5 and is extremely

limited – the lots usually fill up by 10 am, in which case you must walk the steep 1½-miles from the park entrance to the beach.

The large *DL Bliss Campground* (☎ 525-7277) has flush toilets, potable water, tables, and fire pits. Sites ($19) are reservable through Destinet, with sites 140 to 160 having the best lake access.

SOUTH LAKE TAHOE
• *pop 23,586* • *elev 6260 feet* ☎ *916*

Here at the southeastern extent of the lake, the state line cuts through the trees dividing Stateline (Nevada) and South Lake Tahoe (California) – the 'glitziest' and ugliest developments on the lake. Boxy casinos loom above the lake and swaths of ski runs loom above the casinos, while Hwy 50 lines the lake with mini malls, motels and, on the Nevada side, 'chapels' where you can get married in 15 minutes for $45 – rings and flowers included.

There is only a small gap in the development where the lake is visible from Hwy 50; the best views are from the Heavenly Valley ski area and the top floors of casinos, and the best beach access is west of town off Hwy 89. The south shore's concentration of million-dollar homes and boats are in the Tahoe Keys, a network of docks and waterways northwest of Hwy 50 via Keys Blvd.

Orientation & Information
Highway 50 (Lake Tahoe Blvd) wraps around the south shore of the lake between Spooner Summit and the 'Y' where it joins Hwy 89 (Emerald Bay Rd). Highway 89 is often closed west of Tallac Historic Site when there is heavy snow.

Traffic along Hwy 50 is a real problem: it gets totally jammed around noon and 5 pm, and on weekends, while in winter Sunday evenings (when skiers head back down the mountain) are the worst. A good alternate route is Pioneer Trail which branches east off of Hwy 89/Hwy 50 (south of the Y) and re-connects with Hwy 50 at Stateline. The speed limit is strictly enforced along Pioneer Trail.

The South Lake Tahoe Chamber of Commerce (☎ 541-5255), 3066 Lake Tahoe Blvd, has brochures, maps, and a friendly staff. A smaller branch at the junction of Hwy 89 and Hwy 50 is primarily a bathroom stop and orientation point for people coming down the hill.

For topo maps, head to the USFS ranger station (☎ 573-2600) just past the Y on Emerald Bay Rd, or the USFS visitors center at the Tallac Historic Site, open summer weekends. The Sierra Bookshop (☎ 541-6464) in the shopping center at the Y has a great selection of local history books and guides.

Stateline (Nevada)
For about a half mile, Hwy 50 resembles the Las Vegas Strip on a much smaller scale. Caesar's Tahoe, Harrah's, and Harvey's are the 'big three' casinos, with lavish entertainment, tons of slot machines and gaming tables, multiple restaurants, and resort-like accommodations. Harrah's has a terrific Family Fun Center for kids, open until midnight. The Horizon and Bill's are smaller and less flashy; Bill's is especially friendly for people who don't have gambling experience. About a mile north of the others, the Lakeside Inn has a local atmosphere and nice view of the lake. Gaming guides, which explain casino game rules, are available at all casinos (free).

All of the casinos are open 24 hours a day, 365 days a year. As in Reno and Las Vegas, there are no windows or clocks on the walls, climate control is in full effect, and waitresses bring free cocktails as long as you are playing – all devices to make you forget what time it is and how much money you are spending.

Lake Tahoe Historical Society Museum
Next door to the chamber of commerce, this museum (☎ 541-5458) has a rustic collection of 'stuff' from early settlers, and some nice Native American (mostly Washoe) baskets, jewelry, and ceremonial garb. It's open on weekends from noon to 4 pm and from June to September daily; admission is $1.

CALIFORNIA

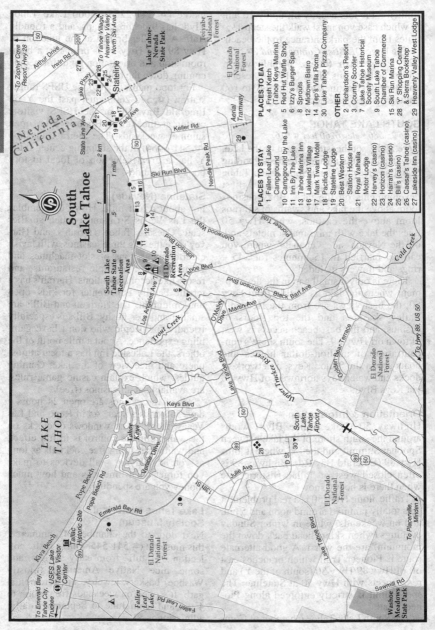

South Lake Tahoe

PLACES TO STAY

1   Fallen Leaf Lake
    Campground
10 Campground by the Lake
11 Inn By The Lake
13 Tahoe Marina Inn
16 Lakeland Village
17 Mark Twain Motel
18 Pacifica Lodge
19 Stateline Lodge
20 Best Western
    Station House Inn
21 Royal Valhalla
    Motor Lodge
22 Harvey's (casino)
23 Horizon (casino)
24 Harrah's (casino)
25 Bill's (casino)
26 Caesar's Tahoe (casino)
27 Lakeside Inn (casino)

PLACES TO EAT

4   Fresh Ketch
    (Tahoe Keys Marina)
5   Red Hut Waffle Shop
6   Izzy's Burger Spa
8   Sprouts
12 Midtown Bistro
14 Tep's Villa Roma
30 Lake Tahoe Pizza Company

OTHER

2   Richardson's Resort
3   Country Scooter
7   Lake Tahoe Historical
    Society Museum
9   South Lake Tahoe
    Chamber of Commerce
15 Ski Run Marina
28 'Y' Shopping Center
    & Sierra Bookshop
29 Heavenly Valley West Lodge

CALIFORNIA

Tallac Historic Site

About three miles northwest of the junction of Hwys 50 and 89 on Emerald Bay Rd, the Tallac site encompasses 150 acres and three luxurious estates from the early 1900s. Elias 'Lucky' Baldwin bought Tallac Point in 1880 and built a luxurious resort including a hotel, casino, promenade, and tennis courts – one of the few and most opulent on the lake at that time. Eventually the estate was parceled and sold. The Pope Estate was built in 1894 and the Heller estate **Valhalla** was built in 1924. The Pope Estate acts as interpretive center and has art exhibits, living history demonstrations, and offers guided tours on summer weekends. Valhalla is the site of various activities, including the Summer Arts & Music Festival from June to August.

Surrounded by pines and connected by paved hiking/biking paths, the entire area now serves as a big park with beach access and beautiful picnic grounds. The **Baldwin Museum** (☎ 541-5227), in the Baldwin house, is worth a visit for its Washoe exhibit and old photos of Lake Tahoe. It opens in summer Thursday to Monday from 10 am to 4 pm, weekends only the rest of the year.

Near the parking lot at the west end of the site, the USFS Lake Tahoe Visitor Center has good natural history exhibits, short interpretive trails, and a Stream Profile Chamber where you can see trout and salmon through an underwater window. The forest service puts an annual Kokanee Salmon Festival here, during the October/November salmon run.

Emerald Bay

This long, narrow bay off the southwest corner of the lake is one of Lake Tahoe's major attractions. It contains the lake's only island and has waters that truly justify its name. Highway 89 wraps around the bay's southern rim, affording great views from pull-outs and designated scenic points. The Eagle Falls parking lot, on Hwy 89 just as it turns north, the main stopping point, has a short trail to Eagle Falls and restrooms.

Trails from the west side of Hwy 89 lead to Desolation Wilderness.

Below Hwy 89 at the lake's edge, **Vikingsholm Castle** (☎ 525-7277) is reached by boat or a steep one-mile descent from the Vikingsholm parking lot (just past the Eagle Falls lot) on Hwy 89. This storybook mansion, built by Laura Knight in 1928, incorporates pre-industrial craftsmanship and Scandinavian design with carved wooden ceilings and furniture in Viking motif. The $2 tour, given June to September daily from 10 am to 4 pm (weekends only the rest of the year) is worthwhile. The stone ruins atop Fannette Island were once Laura Knight's tea house.

Skiing

Heavenly Valley Ski Resort This ski area (☎ 586-7000) is Lake Tahoe's biggest (in terms of acreage), with 3500 vertical feet (wow!), 23 lifts and a gondola operating year round. Heavenly has two parts: Heavenly North (the Nevada side) accessible from Kingsbury Grade, north of Stateline off Hwy 50; and Heavenly West, at the end of Ski Run Blvd which intersects Hwy 50 south of the casinos. Heavenly West is the base for the gondola and has the main lodge. Most runs are long and narrow, below tree line, with great views of the lake, and about half the terrain is intermediate. Heavenly North has fewer crowds, and also has a full-service lodge (cafeteria, rental shop, ski school) and ticket sales. Lift tickets cost $42 ($18 half-day); discount tickets are available at most Safeway stores. The gondola runs in summer from 10 am to 6 pm; tickets are $11 ($8 after 6 pm). Shuttles from the casinos go to Heavenly West.

Kirkwood Ski Area About 40 miles southwest on Hwy 88 (via Hwy 89), Kirkwood (☎ 800-967-7500) is an extreme-skier's playground. The drive through Hope Valley to get there is beautiful and, for advanced skiers, the skiing is worth the drive. Because Kirkwood's base is 1000 feet higher than Heavenly's, it gets better snow and holds it longer. It has 11 lifts, 2000 vertical feet, cliffs, cornices, and epic open bowls. Lift tickets cost $39. Kirkwood also has a full cross-country trail system with 80 km of groomed track. The cross-country lodge is on Hwy 88 just before the main Kirkwood entrance. Trail passes are $12.

Hiking

The chamber of commerce and USFS visitors center at Tallac has free hiking information and a good recreation map of Lake Tahoe for $7. A favorite hike is up Mt Tallac (five miles), the glacier-gouged peak above the lake's southwest corner. The Tallac Trailhead, south of Hwy 89 via a rough road, just past Tallac Historic Site (across from Baldwin Beach), also gives access to Desolation Wilderness which is outlined below.

There is also good hiking from the Glen Alpine Trailhead at Fallen Leaf Lake, south of Hwy 89 via Fallen Leaf Lake Rd, and the Eagle Lake Trailhead, on Hwy 89 at Emerald Bay.

A scenic hike is along the Tahoe Vista Trail from the top of the Heavenly Valley gondola (see Skiing above).

Biking

The USFS visitors center at Tallac sells good mountain biking maps for $2.50. There is a paved bike path from the foot of Rufus Allen Blvd (at the stop light on Lake Tahoe Blvd, just past the chamber of commerce) to the Baldwin Beach turn-off on Emerald Bay Rd. The path skirts the lake at times, goes through the Tahoe Keys, and passes the Tallac Historic Site. Country Scooter (☎ 544-3500), near the path at 800 Emerald Bay Rd, rents bikes, skates, and scooters. Numerous well-marked rental shops with similar wares and prices are along Lake Tahoe Blvd.

Boating & Swimming

There is a free public beach and picnic area across from the chamber of commerce at the small South Lake Tahoe State Recreation Area. On Emerald Bay Rd are some really nice beaches – Baldwin, Pope, and Kiva – with good swimming and picnic tables and barbecues (day-use fee of $5 per car).

Ski Run Marina (☎ 544-0200), on Hwy 50 at the foot of Ski Run Blvd, has the best boat rental rates: $59 per hour for a jet ski, $70 per hour for a power boat.

Reminiscent of summer camp, Richardson's Resort (☎ 800-544-1801), is on Emerald Bay Rd, with a nice beach, kayak and canoe rentals ($12 per hour), and a general store. On the other side of Stateline, four miles north, Zephyr Cove Resort (☎ 702-588-3508) is a woodsy resort with a swimming area, boat rentals, volleyball courts, and an outdoor bar and restaurant. Both swarm with kids in summer and charge a day-use fee (around $3).

Organized Tours

Touring the lake by boat is worthwhile. The *Tahoe Queen* (☎ 541-3364), leaves from the Ski Run Marina, off Hwy 50 at the foot of Ski Run Blvd, for two-hour cruises to Emerald Bay ($14) and back. They also have sunset dinner cruises with live music ($18), and in winter a fun ski package ($18) which includes a boat trip to the north shore, bus ride to Squaw Valley or Alpine Meadows, and boat trip home with cocktails and live music.

The *MS Dixie II* (☎ 702-588-3508) leaves from Zephyr Cove Resort, four miles north of Stateline on Hwy 50. Their prices and itinerary are identical to the *Tahoe Queen*; they also have a champagne brunch cruise ($18) which skirts the lake's east shore.

Places to Stay

The South Lake Tahoe Visitor's Authority (☎ 800-288-2463) makes free room reservations which often include meals, casino shows, and ski lift tickets. Most casino hotels offer good deals from September to mid-November and March to May. Harrah's and Caesar's offer packages including a double room, breakfast, lift tickets, transportation to/from the lifts (usually Heavenly Valley), and a few gaming tokens for about $115 per person, per night (two night minimum).

Camping & Hostel Camping in South Lake Tahoe ain't cheap, and it's only possible when the snow melts. Information is available at the USFS visitors center on Emerald Bay Rd.

On the west side of Emerald Bay, the *Bayview Campground* is right off Hwy 89 and the *Eagle Point Campground* is on the tip of picturesque Eagle Point, overlooking the lake. Both have $14 sites, reservable through Destinet. The *Fallen Leaf Lake Campground* (☎ 800-280-2267), south of Emerald Bay Rd on Fallen Leaf Lake (take Fallen Leaf Lake Rd), is really nice and quiet.

Right in the thick of things, the *Campground by the Lake* (☎ 542-6096), behind the chamber of commerce on Hwy 50, has hot showers, flush toilets, and $20 sites. There is good beach access, but lots of noise from the highway. The *South Lake Tahoe KOA* (☎ 577-3693) is south of town at the Hwy 50/Hwy 89 junction.

In South Lake Tahoe, there is *Doug's Mellow Mountain Retreat* (☎ 544-8065), four blocks off Hwy 50 at 3787 Forest in South Lake Tahoe, an independent hostel run by a hard-core ski bum. Beds in Doug's house cost $13 and carry no curfew.

Motels There are hundreds of small motels in South Lake Tahoe, mostly along Hwy 50 and on the small streets off Ski Run Blvd. Rooms go for $50 to $65 at the low-end places, $80 to $130 at the high-end places, with lower rates on weekdays and in fall and spring. Behind the Liquor Barn on Hwy 50 the *Tahoe Marina Inn* (☎ 541-2180), has nice rooms for $65 to $90 with lake views, an outdoor pool, and a quiet sandy beach. On the other side of Hwy 50 at No 3300, the *Inn By the Lake* (☎ 542-0330, 800-877-1466) is an upscale convention motel with elegant rooms (some with water views) starting at $85. There are restaurants, boat rentals, and a shuttle stop for Heavenly Valley and casino buses within walking distance of these places.

In Stateline, there is an especially good concentration of motels on the lake side of Hwy 50 across from the casinos, between Stateline Blvd and Park Ave. The *Mark Twain Motel* (☎ 544-5733, 800-232-6363), 947 Park Ave, has friendly owners and clean rooms for $30 on weekdays, $65 on weekends. The *Pacifica Lodge* (☎ 544-4131, 800-735-3887), 931 Park Ave, has plain rooms for $55 on weekdays, $70 weekends, plus a pool and hot tub. Next on Park Ave, *Stateline Lodge* (☎ 544-3340, 800-826-8885) is old fashioned through and through – from the sign to the owners. Rooms are $45 midweek, $75 on weekends.

The nicest place in this pocket is the *Best Western Station House Inn* (☎ 542-1101, 800-822-5888), 901 Park Ave. Rooms cost $98 midweek, $108 on weekends, with a full breakfast. Across from the lake, the *Royal Valhalla Motor Lodge* (☎ 544-2233, 800-999-4101), 4104 Lakeshore Blvd, has a nice pool, private beach, and rooms for $57 to $77 during midweek and $80 to $98 on weekends.

Casinos These multi-level coin boxes in Stateline tend to be overpriced, but offer all kinds of amenities including health spas, 24-hour room service, and transportation to and from ski areas. Rooms ($85 to $130) are typically clean and boring unless you get a suite which might have a lake view or in-room Jacuzzi, and cost an extra $100. *Harrah's* (☎ 800-648-3773) and *Harvey's* (☎ 800-648-3361) have the nicest decor, with Harvey's having a new gym and spa. Rooms at *Caesar's Tahoe* (☎ 800-648-3353) are a bit worn, but guests have free access to their indoor pool surrounded by plants and waterfalls. The *Horizon* (☎ 800-648-3322) has the most basic rooms for $10 to $20 less than its neighbors.

Resorts In South Lake Tahoe, next door to the Tahoe Marina Inn at 3535 Hwy 50, *Lakeland Village* (☎ 544-1685, 800-822-5969) is a good spot for families. They have a private beach with an outdoor grill, a lakeside clubhouse, and cabins for up to 10 people with kitchens, lofts, and fireplaces; prices are start at $115.

In Hope Valley, southeast of Lake Tahoe

on Hwy 88, *Sorensen's* (☎ 694-2203, 800-423-9949) is a magical year-round resort with woodsy cabins, a cozy dining room, and access to cross-country ski and hiking trails and good fishing. B&B rooms cost $70 to $90, and cabins cost $90 to $115 for two to four people, $130 for six.

Places to Eat

For breakfast, locals go to the *Red Hut Waffle Shop* (☎ 541-9024) 2723 Hwy 50, which always has a line out front, or the *Midtown Bistro* (☎ 541-6768), above Baskin Robbins at 3330 Hwy 50, with a rooftop deck that's great in summer.

A fun place to go for breakfast or lunch is *Zephyr Cove Lodge* (☎ 588-6644) at the Zephyr Cove Resort, four miles north of Stateline on Hwy 50. The restaurant has a big rock fireplace and pine ceilings, and serves tasty pancakes ($4), steak and eggs ($6), and their famous mushroom sour cream burger ($6.50). Dinner prices are $8 to $14.

Bright lights and loud clinking aside, casinos offer the best values in town. *Harrah's*, *Harvey's*, and the *Horizon* offer all-you-can-eat buffets for around $10 (locals recommend the Horizon), and every casino

has a 24-hour coffee shop. *Llewellyns*, on the top floor of Harvey's, is one of the south shore's most elegant restaurants and has an unbeatable view. Entrees start at $18.

For good burgers, join the locals at *Izzy's Burger Spa* (☎ 544-5030), 2591 Hwy 50. *Sprouts* (☎ 541-6969), across from the chamber of commerce on Hwy 50, is a natural food cafe with big sandwiches, black bean burritos, and fresh smoothies for under $5.

Dark and cavernous *Tep's Villa Roma* (☎ 541-8227), 3450 Hwy 50, has classic Italian dishes ($8 to $15) and a great soup and salad bar serving homemade garlic rolls. For good pizza and atmosphere, try the *Lake Tahoe Pizza Company* (☎ 544-1919), just south of the Hwy 50/Hwy 89 junction. The seafood pizza ($15) and spinach special ($12) are recommended.

At the Tahoe Keys Marina, west of Hwy 50 via Keys Blvd, the *Fresh Ketch* (☎ 541-5683) has consistently good seafood and steaks for $9 to $18, great oysters Rockefeller ($6), and a nice view.

Getting There & Away

The South Lake Tahoe Airport (☎ 544-5810), just south of town on Hwy 50/Hwy

WAYNE BERNHARDSON
Found in Desolation Wilderness, and just about every national park, marmots are one of the most accessible 'wild' animals around.

89, is serviced by Reno Air (☎ 800-736-6247), with daily flights to San Francisco, Los Angeles, and San Diego.

Greyhound buses leave from Harrah's five times daily to Sacramento ($18) and San Francisco ($10). Amtrak buses leave for Sacramento ($17) three times daily from in front of the shopping center at the junction of Hwy 50/Hwy 89. Tickets can be bought at a travel agency or on board.

The *Tahoe Casino Express* connects South Lake Tahoe and Stateline to the Reno airport with 14 shuttles daily ($15) that stop at Harrah's, Harvey's, Horizon, and Caesar's.

Getting Around
The South Lake Tahoe Stage (☎ 542-6877) buses run 24 hours a day and make 50 stops along Hwy 50 between the Lakeside Inn (north of Stateline) and the Hwy 50/Hwy 89 junction. The fare is $1.25.

Most casinos have free shuttles that run until 2 am and will stop at any motel. In winter, the Heavenly Valley shuttle ($1) runs from the Main Lodge at Heavenly West to all the casinos, the intersection of Hwy 50 and Ski Run Blvd, and several motel areas.

DESOLATION WILDERNESS
☎ *916*

This wilderness area, the most heavily used per acre in the US, spreads south and west from Lake Tahoe, encompassing 100 sq miles of forests, lakes, and peaks. Contrary to what its name suggests, the wilderness is vibrantly beautiful and alive with trees, birds, fox, deer, bears, and marmots. Retreating glaciers formed Desolation Valley, sweeping away its soil and leaving huge, polished rock faces in its upper elevations. Trees don't grow in this area, but conifer-like shrubs grow as big as trees and wildflowers sprout between the rocks. Camping on these smooth, flat granite surfaces is great, and hiking and climbing is fast and easy.

A wilderness permit quota system limits overnight camping from June 15 to the first weekend in September. Reservations can be made by calling the USFS (☎ 644-6048, 573-2674), but overnight permits must be obtained in person at the USFS Lake Tahoe Visitors Center in South Lake Tahoe, or the Camino Ranger Station on Hwy 50; maps and information are available at both. Day-hikers can self-register at the trailheads.

From Hwy 50, the best access is from Wrights Lake, at the north end of Wrights Lake Rd, where there is plenty of parking, posted maps, and a nice campground with $14 sites (reservable through Destinet). Trailheads from South Lake Tahoe are south of Hwy 89 (Emerald Bay Rd), across from the Tallac Historic Site, and at Emerald Bay.

Yosemite National Park

☎ *209*

With over three million visitors per year, Yosemite is one of the most visited places in the US – and for good reason. Seeing photographs of the valley's glacier-swept profile, with Half Dome on one side and El Capitan on the other, is no substitute for experiencing it in person. Waterfalls thunder from granite walls that stretch 3000 feet above the valley floor which is covered with meadows and groves and swept by the Merced River. East of the valley, lone granite peaks rise to over 13,000 feet above flowery meadows and gem-like lakes. Even with the crowds, traffic, and congestion, Yosemite is awesome and stunning. And with tourist activity concentrated in 6% of the park (mostly in Yosemite Valley), outdoors enthusiasts need only hit the trails to find solitude and wilderness.

The western part of the park is densely forested with a mild climate, resembling the foothills to the west, while the east side along the Sierra Nevada crest is a sub-alpine environment. Yosemite Valley, on the southwest side of the park, is the park's foremost destination, home to most visitor facilities and campgrounds. Tuolumne

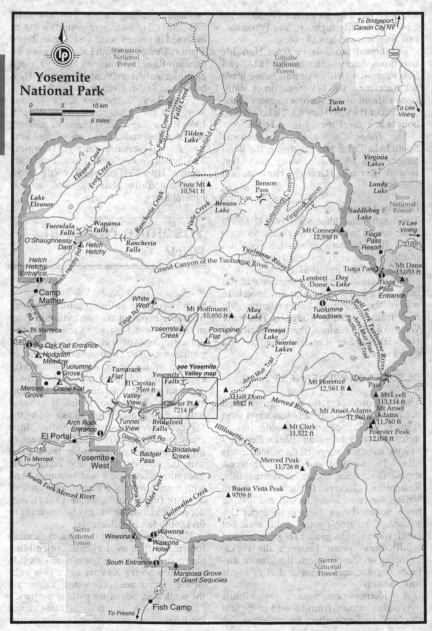

Yosemite National Park

To Bridgeport,
Carson City NV

Stanislaus
National
Forest

Toiyabe
National
Forest

Twin
Lakes

To Lee
Vining

Virginia
Lakes

Lundy
Lake

Inyo
National
Forest

Saddlebag
Lake

To Lee
Vining

Tioga
Pass
Resort

Mt Dana
13,053 ft

Tioga
Pass
Entrance

Eleanor Creek

Frog Creek

Falls Creek

Tilden
Lake

Saddlebag Canyon

Pacific Crest Trail

Piute Mt
10,541 ft

Benson
Pass

Benson
Lake

Matterhorn Canyon

Virginia Canyon

Mt Conness
12,590 ft

Tioga Pass

Lake
Eleanor

Rancheria Creek

Piute Creek

Tuolumne River

Tueeulala
Falls

Wapama
Falls

O'Shaughnessy
Dam

Hetch
Hetchy

Rancheria
Falls

Hetch Hetchy Rd

Grand Canyon of the Tuolumne River

Lembert
Dome

Dog
Lake

Lyell Fork Tuolumne River

John Muir Trail

Pacific Crest Trail

Hetch
Hetchy
Entrance

Camp
Mather

Evergreen Rd

To Manteca

Big Oak Flat Entrance

Hodgdon
Meadow

Tuolumne
Grove

Crane Flat

Merced
Grove

White
Wolf

Tioga Rd

Yosemite
Creek

Mt Hoffmann
10,850 ft

May
Lake

Porcupine
Flat

Tenaya
Lake

Sunrise
Lakes

Tuolumne
Meadows

Tamarack
Flat

Yosemite
Falls

El Capitan
7569 ft

Valley
View

see Yosemite
Valley map

Glacier Pt
7214 ft

Half Dome
8842 ft

Mt Florence
12,561 ft

Merced River

John Muir Trail

Donahue
Pass

Mt Lyell
13,114 ft

Mt Ansel
Adams
11,760 ft

Mt Ansel Adams
11,760 ft

Foerster Peak
12,058 ft

Arch Rock
Entrance

El Portal

Tunnel
View

Bridalveil
Falls

Glacier Point Rd

Badger
Pass

Bridalveil
Creek

Illilouette Creek

Mt Clark
11,522 ft

Yosemite
West

Wawona Rd

Alder Creek

Merced Peak
11,726 ft

South Fork Merced River

Chilnualna Creek

Buena Vista Peak
9709 ft

Sierra
National
Forest

Wawona

Wawona
Hotel

South Entrance

Sierra
National
Forest

Mariposa Grove
of Giant Sequoias

To Merced

To Fresno

Fish Camp

0   5   10 km
0   3   6 miles

MARISA GIERLICH

Lake Mary, near Mammoth

MARISA GIERLICH

Tioga Pass Resort

MARISA GIERLICH

Tioga Pass, near Yosemite

MARISA GIERLICH

Eerie volcanic landscape at the Mono Craters

MARISA GIERLICH

Mt Whitney, highest point in the continental US

MARISA GIERLICH

Twin Lakes, near Bridgeport, has great fishing

DAVE SKIBINSKI

Tufa formations, Mono Lake

NANCY KELLER

Majestic Yosemite Falls

MARISA GIERLICH

Bridalveil Fall, Yosemite

TOM DOWNS

El Capitan, rock climber's dream

Meadows, off the Tioga Rd (closed in winter), is the high country hub. Other interesting areas within the Park are Hetch Hetchy and Wawona.

History

The Ahwahneechee, a group of Central Valley Miwok and Eastern Sierra Paiutes, lived in the Yosemite area for 4000 years before whites set foot in Yosemite Valley. Their main staples were black oak acorns and fish from the Merced River, though occasionally they trapped deer and rabbits. During the fall and winter they lived in the valley, then in spring headed to the eastern high country where they traded with Paiutes from the Mono Lake area.

In 1833, a group of explorers looking for a trans-Sierra route saw Yosemite Valley from its eastern rim, but did not descend its steep walls. In the 1850s, as miners settled the Sierra's western foothills, the Mariposa Battalion was formed to find 'threatening' Native Americans living in the mountains. On one of these missions, the battalion followed a group of Ahwahneechee into the valley – the first non-Native Americans to enter. Four years later, James Mason Hutchings, a San Francisco newspaperman, organized the first tourist party to the valley which included artist Thomas Ayers. Ayers's sketches of the trip were the first printed publicity advertising Yosemite's scenic wonders.

As visitors increased, conservationists such as Hutchings and Fredrick Law Olmstead recognized the importance of protecting the valley and the grove of giant sequoia trees south of the valley. In 1864 Abraham Lincoln signed a bill preserving and protecting these two areas under the Yosemite Grant to California. This was the first state park in the world, and the foundation of what is now the National Park System. With major campaigning by John Muir, the area around the valley and grove were established as Yosemite National Park in 1890, and in 1906 the valley and grove were seceded by the state of California to be included in the national park.

From 1890 to 1914, the US army managed and administered the park. During the Spanish-American War, the first civilian rangers were employed and in 1914 the first 'park rangers' were authorized by the Department of the Interior. Today the park is run according to a General Management Plan created in 1980 which emphasizes education through interpretation and environment-first (as opposed to people-first) ethics. Yosemite Concession Services (YCS) manages all concessions in the park, from tent cabins to ice cream stands.

Geology

As the Sierra block uplifted and tilted west the slow-moving Merced River increased in flow and cut a 3000-foot canyon into the rock – the V-shaped Yosemite Valley.

The Ice Age covered the valley with glaciers for about 2½ million years. As the glaciers retreated (about 14,000 years ago) they scoured Yosemite's V into a 'U,' breaking off enormous granite slabs along vertical 'joints' formed by stress and strain when the granite was forming beneath the earth's surface. Yosemite has six types of granite – a high concentration for such a small area- and each has its own rate of erosion. So while some walls withstood the glacial action, others crumbled, giving Yosemite Valley it's unique profile. El Capitan, a granite monolith which stands 3593 feet from base to summit, is flanked by rock slides (mostly covered with trees) of weaker granite.

Over the past 6000 years about 10,000 feet of sediment has collected in the bottom of Yosemite's U, creating a flat valley floor. Tenaya Canyon, from the valley's northeast corner, is a good example of a U-shaped valley that hasn't been filled in. The several glaciers that still exist today in

'In the face of Yosemite scenery cautious remonstrance is vain; under its spell one's body seems to go where it likes with a will over which we seem to have scarce any control.'

John Muir, *The Yosemite*, 1911 ■

Yosemite, from a mini Ice Age about 600 years ago, are retreating.

Flora & Fauna

Yosemite's wide range of elevations nurture diverse species of trees, plants, birds, and animals. At lower elevations, the most common trees are small leaf maple, black oak, ponderosa pine, dogwood (which bloom with big white flowers in spring), and incense cedar (the cedar's shaggy red bark makes it look like a Giant Sequoia or Redwood, but its wood is much harder). Higher elevations have mostly ponderosa and Jeffrey pines, and Douglas fir trees – all of them shorter than low elevation trees because of the harsher climate.

Giant sequoias grow in three isolated groves in the park: the Mariposa Grove, off Hwy 41; the Tuolumne Grove, off the Tioga Rd; and the Merced Grove, which is off Big Oak Flat Rd near the Big Oak Flat Entrance.

Wildflowers bloom in April and May in the valley, late May and June at higher elevations. The best place to see wildflowers – lupine, iris, shooting star, Indian paintbrush, monkey flower, mule ear, Mariposa lily – is around Tuolumne Meadows.

Wildlife, except Western gray squirrels and mule deer, is most abundant outside Yosemite Valley. In 1986, California bighorn sheep, native to the area, were reintroduced after being wiped out by hunting and disease. The herd lives in the high country on the park's eastern edge, sometimes seen from Hwy 120. American black bears, which can be golden to dark brown to black, live in all parts of the park. Though not generally aggressive, they do attack when startled and mother bears may charge to protect their cubs.

Steller's jays are numerous in the valley and known for swiping food off campground tables. More rare and interesting are Peregrine falcons which raise their young on rock ledges above the valley floor.

There are numerous endangered, threatened, and sensitive species in the park, including the golden eagle, Yosemite toad, Sierra Nevada red fox, and California wolverine. The Yosemite Wilderness Center (☎ 372-0740) in Yosemite Village is a good place to get information.

Orientation & Park Entry

There are three primary approaches to Yosemite: Hwy 41 from Fresno, which enters at South Entrance and goes on to pass Wawona and Glacier Point Rd; Hwy 140 from Merced, which passes El Portal and enters at Arch Rock Entrance; and Hwy 120 from the San Francisco Bay Area and Manteca, which enters at Big Oak Flat Entrance, traverses the park as the Tioga Rd (closed in winter), and heads east to Lee Vining and Mono Lake via Tioga Pass. Directions are well-signed, and all roads access Yosemite Valley.

Gas prices are about 30% higher in the park. There are gas stations at Wawona, El Portal, the Tioga Rd/Big Oak Flat Rd junction (closed in winter), Tuolumne Meadows, and in the valley near Yosemite Lodge.

Yosemite's entrance fee is $5 per vehicle, $3 for people on foot, bicycle, or horseback. There are ranger stations with maps, information, and posted campground availability at all park entrances, though Yosemite Valley is the headquarters. Upon entering the park, you'll receive a NPS map and the *Yosemite Guide*, a bi-monthly newspaper with current ranger programs, park activities, and a shuttle bus map and schedule. The *Yosemite Magazine* is available (free) at most shops and visitors centers and gives a bit more detail about park history, personalities, and more.

Books

A really good general guidebook is *The Complete Guidebook to Yosemite* (Yosemite Association, 1994) by Steven P Medley, available for $10 at the valley and Tuolumne Meadows visitors centers, and most gift shops. Jeffrey P Schafer's *Yosemite National Park: A Natural History Guide to Yosemite and Its Trails* (Wilderness Press, 1992) is a great hiking companion and includes a detailed map of the park. *My*

First Summer in the Sierra (1911) and *The Yosemite* (1912) are John Muir at his eloquent, tree-loving best.

Photography

Aspiring Ansel Adams' should check out sunrise at Mirror Lake or Yosemite Falls, and sunset from Valley View, Tunnel View, or Glacier Point (all outside the valley). Sentinel Bridge, near Housekeeping Camp (in the valley), offers an epic shot of Half Dome. Slide and print film is widely available and reasonably priced.

Camera walks led by professional photographers leave the Ahwahnee Hotel or Valley Visitors Center daily at 8:30 am (free); check the *Yosemite Guide* for current information.

Hiking

Yosemite has over 800 miles of trails that go far beyond the beaten tourist path. The best way to enjoy the park's natural splendor is to take to the backcountry, even if it is only two miles in and only for one night. Wilderness permits (free) are required year-round for all overnight trips. A quota system limits the number of people leaving from each trailhead each day: half of the quota is available first-come, first served

Legendary Half Dome

According to Native American legend, one of Yosemite Valley's early inhabitants went down from the mountains to Mono Lake where he wed a Paiute named Tesaiyac. The journey back to the valley was difficult, and by the time they reached what was to become Mirror Lake, Tesaiyac decided that she wanted to go back down to live with her people at Mono Lake. Her husband refused to live on such barren, arid land with no oak trees from which to get acorns. With a heart full of despair, Tesaiyac began to run towards Mono Lake and her husband followed her. When the powerful spirits heard quarreling in Yosemite, they became angry and turned the two into stone: he became North Dome and she became Half Dome. The tears she cried made marks as they ran down her face and formed Mirror Lake.

True or not, Half Dome is Yosemite's most distinctive monument. It is 87 million years old and has a 93% vertical grade – the sheerest cliff in North America. Climbers come from around the world to grapple with its legendary 'north face,' but good hikers can reach its summit via an 8½-mile trail from Yosemite Valley. The trail gains 4900 feet in elevation and has cable handrails for the last 200 yards. It *can* be done in one day, but is more enjoyable if you break it up by camping (Little Yosemite Valley is the most popular spot) one night along the way. ■

NANCY KELLER

no earlier than 24 hours before you want to begin; the other half may be reserved (☎ 372-0740) in advance no earlier than 24 weeks and no later than two days before your trip for a $3 fee.

Before you get your permit, know how many people are in your party, entry and exit dates, starting and ending trailheads, and your principle destination. Permits can be obtained from the Yosemite Valley Wilderness Center, Wawona Ranger Station, Tuolumne Valley Permit Kiosk (off the Tioga Rd near Tuolumne Meadows Lodge), Big Oak Flat Information Station, and Hetch Hetchy Entrance Station. More detailed hiking information is given in specific area listings below. The best place for camping/backpacking supplies is at the Curry Village Mountain Sport Shop (☎ 372-8396) in Yosemite Valley. The Tuolumne Meadows Store (☎ 372-1328) has sleeping bags and pads, stoves, foul weather gear, and a good selection of freeze-dried food (open May to October).

Hiking Note Be aware of Yosemite's altitude range, especially in the valley where steep trails gain altitude quickly, and in the Tuolumne Meadows area where trails start at around 9000 feet. Take it slow and allow your body to adjust.

Rock Climbing

With 3000-foot granite monoliths and a mild climate, Yosemite is a climber's mecca. When you see a person hanging from the mass of Half Dome or a single light shining from El Capitan in the middle of the night, the meaning of 'Go Climb A Rock' (a well-known Yosemite slogan) becomes clear. Most climbers stay at Sunnyside walk-in campground in the valley. People looking for climbing partners or equipment post notices on the bulletin board here, and resident climbers are helpful in suggesting routes. The best place to go for equipment and printed information is the Curry Village Mountain Sport Shop (☎ 372-8396) in Yosemite Valley. They have climbing books to loan, maps, and a knowledgeable staff. Climbers rec-

ommend the *Climber's Guide to the High Sierra* (Sierra Club Books, 1972) by Steve Roper.

The Yosemite Mountaineering School (☎ 372-1244 September to May, 372-1335

John Muir

Born in Scotland in 1838, John Muir came to America with his father in 1849 and settled near the Fox River in Wisconsin. After studying botany and geology at the University of Wisconsin, he set out on what would be a never-ending journey through the wilds. He accompanied research expeditions to the Arctic and the Yukon, and discovered Glacier Bay in Alaska. But more than anywhere else, Muir is synonymous with the Sierra Nevada. He spent most of his life studying the range's geology and plant life, and scouting the area between Yosemite Valley and Mt Whitney, where the 200-mile John Muir Trail now pays him tribute.

Though he discovered 75 glaciers and mapped much of the Sierra for the first time, Muir is best known for his eloquent writings.

His love for the outdoors was so extreme that he spent most of his time in solitude, among trees, cliffs, rocks, and waterfalls, using his pen to commune with the environment.

Yosemite was his special love. In *My First Summer in the Sierra* (1911), he wrote about his first view of Yosemite Valley:

> Never before had I seen so glorious a landscape, so boundless an affluence of sublime mountain beauty. The most extravagant description I might give of this view to any one who has not seen similar landscapes with his own eyes would not so much hint its grandeur and the spiritual glow that covered it.

His articles and lobbying efforts were the foundation of the campaign that established Yosemite as a national park in 1890. He died in 1914, one year after the losing the battle against Hetch Hetchy Reservoir to the city of San Francisco. ∎

June to August) has beginner and intermediate rock climbing classes ($65) held at 8:30 am daily in Tuolumne Meadows (June to August) or the valley. Equipment is provided, and climbing shoes are available to rent ($6); rentals are only available with a lesson.

The meadow across from El Capitan, and the northeast end of Tenaya Lake (off the Tioga Rd) are good for watching climbers dangle from granite (binoculars are needed for a really good view). Look for the haul bags first – they're bigger, more colorful, and move around more than the climbers, thus are easier to spot.

Horseback Riding
Yosemite Concession Services manages all stables within the park. Rates are $31 for two hours, $44 for four hours, and $65 all day (about nine hours). No experience is needed, but reservations are advised, especially at the valley stables.

Winter Activities
According to locals, Yosemite is at its best when the snow falls. Accommodations are cheaper, the park is less crowded, and the weather in the valley stays mild. Roads in the valley are plowed, and Hwys 41, 120, and 140 are kept open (the Tioga Rd closes with the first snow fall). Be sure to buy snow chains before approaching the park, as prices double once you hit the foothills.

There is a big ice skating rink at Curry Village, a snow play area at Crane Flat Campground, and a free shuttle from the valley to **Badger Pass Ski Area** (☎ 372-1244), California's oldest operating ski area. It is primarily a beginner and intermediate hill, with 10 chair lifts, 900 vertical feet, $25 lift tickets, a good ski school, and full-service lodge.

For cross-country skiing, there are 45 km of groomed trails (free) from Badger Pass (including a scenic 10-mile trail to Glacier Point) and marked backcountry trails to the valley's south rim. The **Yosemite Cross Country Ski School** (☎ 372-8444) offers learn-to-ski packages ($40), guided tours ($35), and equipment rentals ($15). There

are marked, ungroomed trails from the Crane Flat Campground on the park's north side (no facilities).

Two backcountry ski huts with beds, cooking facilities, bathrooms, wood stoves, and water, are available for overnight stay: the Yosemite Association (☎ 372-2317) operates the Ostrander Ski Hut, in a gorgeous spot on the bank of Ostrander Lake; and YCS (☎ 372-1244) operates the Glacier Point Hut. Reservations are required for both.

Accommodations
For individual listings see Places to Stay in the following sections.

Campground Reservations Reservations are mandatory for Yosemite Valley campgrounds (except walk-in sites) year round, and for Hogdon Meadow, Crane Flat, and half of Tuolumne Meadows from May to October. Make reservations up to but no earlier than eight weeks in advance by calling Destinet. From mid-May to mid-September, campgrounds are usually reserved by the first day of the eight-week period, so try to call exactly eight weeks before you want to arrive. Have an idea of which campground and which space you want (suggestions are given under each campground listing under Yosemite Valley, Tulumne Meadows & Tioga Rd, Hetch Hetchy, and Wawona, below), and have a Visa or MasterCard ready for payment. Prices are $11 to $17 per night.

Don't fret if reservations are full. Except during Labor Day, 4th of July, and Veteran's Day weekends, there are usually spots at first-come, first-served campgrounds if you arrive by check-out time (10 am in the valley, noon everywhere else). These include: Wawona, Bridalveil Creek, Tamarack Flat (no water), White Wolf, Yosemite Creek, and Porcupine Flat.

High Sierra Camps The six High Sierra Camps (HSC) are set about nine miles apart in the park's high country near Tuolumne Meadows. Each one has canvas tents for four to six people, a communal dining room, and bathroom with running water and hot showers. Beds have sheets and down comforters, and meals (breakfast and dinner) are very hearty. This is a great way to experience the backcountry without having to carry much food or equipment. The cost is $42 per person, including two meals. If there happens to be a cancellation, hikers not staying at the camp can get a meal for around $10.

The camps are (clockwise) at Tuolumne Lodge, Vogelsang, Merced Lake, Sunrise Lake, May Lake, and Glen Aulin. Tuolumne Lodge, just off the Tioga Rd, gets non-hikers and is a popular start/end point for the loop. May Lake is a mile off the road, thus popular for one-night trips. A short season (late-June to September) and high demand requires a lottery for reservations. Applications are accepted from October 15 to November 30, and the lottery is in December. For an application write to the High Sierra Desk, Yosemite Reservations, 5410 E Home Ave, Fresno, CA 93727.

Other Accommodations Yosemite Concession Services manages all non-camp accommodations in the park, including cabins and tent cabins. Their 'Accommodation, Rates and Packages' brochure, with seasonal rates and a send-in reservation form, is available at visitors centers or from Yosemite Reservations (☎ 252-4848), 5410 E Home Ave, Fresno, CA 93727. Places get booked well in advance for summer months. Detailed information is given below under specific parts of the park.

Yosemite West Condominiums (☎ 454-2033), and Yosemite West Cottages (☎ 642-2211) offer vacation rentals in a private development within the park, 15 miles west of the valley on Hwy 41 (the Wawona Rd). Further from park activities, the Redwoods Guest Cottages (☎ 375-6666), one mile east of Wawona on Chilnualna Falls Rd, has one- to five-bedroom units with kitchen and fireplace. These are good alternatives when YCS places are full. Accommodations near the park, in the small towns along major access routes, tend to be overpriced, especially in summer.

Getting There & Away
Daily Greyhound buses go to/from Merced ($17) year round and connect with north and southbound Amtrak trains at the Merced train depot (☎ 722-6862). Buses to Yosemite leave at 6:10 am, 10 am, and 3 pm; those from Yosemite leave from Yosemite Lodge around 3:45 pm (call for current schedules). VIA Bus Lines (☎ 384-7441) connects Yosemite to the Fresno Air Terminal, via Wawona, Fish Camp, and Oakhurst ($22, 3½ hours). Buses leave Curry Village at 8:30 am, Fresno at 2 pm.

YOSEMITE VALLEY
☎ 209

With sheer granite monoliths towering 3000 feet above a lush forest floor, the effect of Yosemite Valley is what gothic architects must have in mind when they construct foreboding towers and elaborate cornices. Though crowds are often so thick that staying in the valley is unpleasant, or at least unsatisfying, a visit to the valley is mandatory for all first-timers in the park. This is where you really *know* you're in Yosemite. It's also where you'll find the best visitor facilities, park information, educational programs, and some classic Yosemite views.

Orientation
The valley is on the park's southwest side, 35 miles from South Entrance (Hwy 41), 13 miles from Arch Rock Entrance (Hwy 140), 29 miles from Big Oak Flat Entrance (Hwy 120 west), and 58 miles from Tioga Pass Entrance (Hwy 120 east). A one-way road makes an 8½ mile loop around the valley floor, giving access to campgrounds and visitor facilities. Yosemite Village is the hub, with nearly as much activity (from June to September) at Curry Village and Yosemite Lodge. Each has a free day-use parking lot. To avoid traffic and angst, park in one of these lots and get around by shuttle bus (free), bicycle (available for rent in Yosemite Village and Camp Curry; $18

per day), or on foot. Most facilities are within a mile of each other.

Information

Tourist Offices Yosemite Village is information central for the whole park. At the Valley Visitor Center (☎ 372-0299), you'll find a kiosk out front for simple questions and lodging information, a park concessions courtesy phone, a message board, and museum-quality exhibits about the park. The bookstore has a good selection of maps and guides with hours daily from 9 am to 6 pm. There are smaller information stations at Curry Village and Yosemite Lodge.

The Yosemite Wilderness Center (☎ 372-0740), near the visitors center, issues wilderness permits and has topo maps and trip planning guides.

Money There is a Bank of America office (open daily 8 am to 4 pm) and a 24-hour ATM in Yosemite Village (next to the Village Store). The bank cashes personal checks with a drivers license, state ID, or passport. The Village Store (open until 10 pm), Tuolumne Meadows Store, and Wawona Grocery Store will cash a check for $20 over your purchase. Shops and restaurants accept travelers checks in US dollars only, and American Express cards are not accepted anywhere in the park.

Post & Telecommunications The post office in Yosemite Village accepts general delivery and has a fax machine; the zip code is 95389.

Laundry & Showers There is a coin-op laundry at Housekeeping Camp open in summer from 8 am to 11 pm, and at Curry Village, open year round from 8 am to 6 pm. Showers are available at Housekeeping Camp and Curry Village for $2 (free for camp guests). Those at Curry Village are much nicer, but close from noon to 4 pm and 10 pm to midnight.

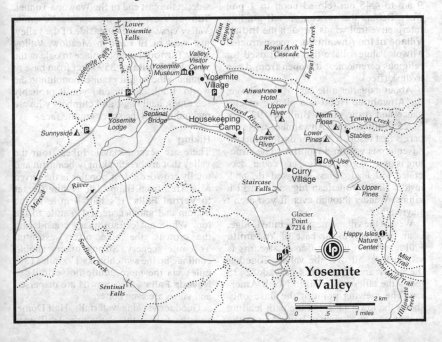

Yosemite Valley

Recycling There are recycling centers at the Village Store and Curry Village (summer only) which accept glass, aluminum, plastic, and newspaper, and give 5¢ refunds for beer and soda cans. There are also glass and aluminum receptacles at campgrounds and picnic areas.

Medical Services For emergencies call ☎ 911. A medical clinic (☎ 372-4637) and dental clinic (☎ 372-4200) are in Yosemite Valley, on the Ahwahnee Hotel road near Yosemite Village. Hours vary, but doctors can be reached by phone 24 hours a day.

Things to See

Yosemite Village is a good starting point from which to see the valley's star attractions. Next to the Valley Visitor Center, a museum complex houses the **Yosemite Museum Gallery** which has changing exhibits, and the **Indian Cultural Exhibit** with a large Miwok and Paiute basket collection and nice gift shop. Hours are daily 9 am to 4:45 pm (closed noon to 1 pm; free). Behind the museum, a self-guiding interpretive trail winds through the **Indian Village of the Ahwahnee**, a reconstructed Miwok-Paiute village that is still used for religious ceremonies; it's open from dawn to dusk (free).

About a quarter mile east of the village, the **Ahwahnee Hotel** is a picture of elegance and rustic grace. Built in 1927 for $1.25 million, the Ahwahnee was the park's first resort, a popular destination for adventurous well-to-do tourists. The structure is of local granite, pine, and cedar, decorated with leaded glass, sculpted tile, and, inside, Native American rugs and Turkish kilims. Wander through even if you aren't staying there.

West of the village, near Yosemite Lodge, is an easy path to the base of **Yosemite Falls,** whose double-tiered stream is visible from all over the valley. Together the upper and lower falls cascade 2425 feet – the tallest waterfall in North America. The viewing point at the base only shows the lower falls, but the path leading to it gives a good view of both. Across the

valley, a short jaunt from the Bridalveil Fall parking lot leads to the base of 620-foot **Bridalveil Fall**. The Ahwahneechee call the fall *Pohono*, Spirit of the Puffing Wind, as gusts often blow the falls from side to side. This fall is especially nice around sunset.

At the valley's southeast end, where the Merced River rushes around two small islands, **Happy Isles** is the starting point for several popular hikes, and home to the Happy Isles Family Nature Center (open May to October; free). The center has hands-on nature exhibits and free 'Explorer Packs' full of games, books, and educational toys that kids can use for the day.

One of the best views in the park is from **Glacier Point**, 3214 feet above the valley floor on the south rim. You can reach the point via Glacier Point Rd (off Hwy 41) by car, tour bus (from the valley; $18), cross-country skis, or by foot via the Panorama or Four Mile Trail. Take the bus one way ($9) and hike up or down. On the valley's south side, at the east end of the Wawona Tunnel, **Tunnel View** gives the classic Yosemite Valley view. On the other side of the valley, just west of El Capitan Meadow, **Valley View Turnout** is a good place to ogle at the size of **El Capitan** – 3593 feet from base to summit – the largest granite monolith in the world. Look closely and you'll probably see ropes, haul bags, and climbers who are reckoning with the sheer granite face.

Hiking

There are several classic hikes from the valley that are breathtakingly beautiful and totally crowded. Most popular is the paved Mist Trail from Happy Isle Nature Center to **Vernal Falls**. It's half a mile to the bottom and another steep 1½ mile to the top. While not extraordinary considering the crowds, the hike offers essential Yosemite scenery. Strong hikers should continue up the switchbacks 1½ miles (3½ miles via the more gentle horse trail) to **Nevada Falls** where crowds are dispersed and views are even better.

Good for viewing waterfalls, Half Dome, and the valley, the Panorama Trail goes from Happy Isles Nature Center to **Glacier Point**. It's a tough 8½ miles going up, but coming down is a cinch. For $10 you can ride the bus one way to/from Glacier Point; check bus schedules in the *Yosemite Guide* or at Yosemite Village, Curry Village, Yosemite Lodge, or the Ahwahnee Hotel.

At the valley's east end, a paved half-mile trail goes from Mirror Lake Junction to **Mirror Lake**. You can also access the trail by heading east on the bike path from Yosemite Village, the Ahwahnee Hotel, or Upper River Campground. Ansel Adams took many a photo here, as early morning and evening light catches the reflection of Half Dome in the lake. From here, a three-mile trail makes a loop along Tenaya Creek with nice views of its U-shaped canyon.

Arduous, but worthwhile for waterfall enthusiasts, the hike to the top of Yosemite Falls gains 2700 feet of elevation in 3½ miles – now that's steep. The trail leaves from behind Sunnyside walk-in campground, passes Columbia point, the top of Lower Yosemite Falls (a good turn around point for some), and continues to the top of the upper falls.

Rafting

Floating the Merced River, from Stoneman Bridge to Sentinel Beach, is a leisurely way to soak up Yosemite views. Raft rentals are available at Curry Village for $12.50, including equipment and shuttle service back to the village (two person minimum). Paddles, life jackets, and the shuttle ride cost $2 each with your own raft or inner tube. Rafting above Yosemite Stables or below Cathedral Beach Picnic Area is forbidden.

Ranger Programs

Daily ranger-led walks, slide shows, and educational programs give insight to the valley on a very general level. Good ones include 'Explore Yosemite,' 'Legacies,' and 'The Ever-changing Landscape.' Most are held at the Valley Visitor Center, Curry Village, or Yosemite Lodge; look in the *Yosemite Guide* for a current schedule. There are often evening programs at the

Ahwahnee Hotel (a great setting) that aren't publicized, but open to anyone; check the marquee in the lobby for the night's program.

The park's most noteworthy entertainer is actor Lee Stetson who does a one-man show about the life of John Muir. One of three different performances ('The Spirit of John Muir' is recommended) is given nightly (except Sunday) at the Valley Visitor Center auditorium, behind the center's main building. Tickets are $5.

Organized Tours

While tours are good for covering a lot of ground with someone else in the driver's seat, four of the five tours offered are in big tour buses and make few stops. Your best bet is the two-hour Valley Floor Tour ($15) in an open-air tram, which stops at points of interest including Yosemite Falls, Bridalveil Falls, and El Capitan; the moonlight version of this (summer only) is spectacular. Other tours are listed in detail in *Yosemite Magazine* and at departure points: Yosemite Lodge, Curry Village (summer only), the Ahwahnee Hotel, and Village Store (mid-May to mid-October) in Yosemite Village.

Places to Stay

Camping All campgrounds, except Sunnyside Walk-In, require reservations made through Destinet. They have flush toilets, picnic tables, fire rings, and food storage boxes, and cost $14 per site. Check in/out time is 10 am. From June to September, camping in the valley is like living in an apartment building with very thin walls.

Largest and furthest from Yosemite Village, *Upper Pines* has the most trees and nicest sites (especially sites 188 to 240). *Lower Pines* is similar, with sites 150 to 166 being the best. Across the river, *North Pines* is near the stables and has nice group and backpacker sites. Closest to Yosemite Village, *Upper River* and *Lower River* cater mostly to tent campers, but are quite noisy.

Cabins & Motels All room reservations/cancellations are made through Yosemite

Reservations (☎ 252-4848), 5410 E Home Ave, Fresno, CA 93727.

Housekeeping Camp has tent cabins, a small visitors center, grocery store, laundry, and pay showers. The tent cabins are basically a concrete slab with a bunk bed, double bed, mirror, and electrical outlet, plastic sides and roof ($42). Each one has its own picnic table and fire grate. Sites 204 to 219 and 228 to 250 are on the river.

At *Curry Village*, the tent cabins ($40) have four beds on a wooden platform, and are very close together. Wooden cabins without bath ($53) are a bit nicer but still crowded together, while those with bath ($72) are spacious and cozy. There are also modern rooms here, right in the thick of Curry Village activity, for $82.

Yosemite Lodge gets large tour groups and has the park's most popular restaurant and bar. Standard rooms cost $82 ($61 without bath), and modern 'lodge' rooms with TV and phone cost $98. There are also cabins for $72 ($53 without bath).

The park's deluxe accommodations are at the elegant *Ahwahnee Hotel*, where rooms and cottages cost $210, and are usually booked a year in advance.

There are also some nice but pricey B&Bs just outside the valley (but in the park) in Yosemite West, a private development. *Yosemite West High Sierra B&B* (☎ 372-4808), has a large living room and deck for guest use and friendly owners who really know the park. Rooms are $75 to $125.

Places to Eat

The best spots for self-catering are *Dengan's Deli* and the *Village Store* (open until 10 pm), both in Yosemite Village.

Prices around the valley are reasonable and most menus have vegetarian items. Popular with climbers, the *Terrace Lounge* at Curry Village has good pizza ($12 large), pitchers of beer and margaritas, and a nice deck. Next to it, the *Dining Pavilion* is a self-service cafeteria with mediocre breakfast, lunch, and dinner for around $5. In Yosemite Village, the *Pasta Place* serves (what else?) large portions of pasta with a choice of sauce and Caesar salad for $6.

Locals like the *Mountain Broiler Room* at Yosemite Lodge for its patio and casual atmosphere, but the food is overpriced, with OK prime rib, steak, and seafood dinners starting at $16. A worthwhile dining splurge is the *Ahwahnee Hotel Dining Room*, where the room itself is a feast for the eyes and the food is truly gourmet. Go for a scone and coffee ($3.50) just for the experience. Breakfast and lunch are under $10, dinner is around $20. Reservations (☎ 372-1489) and a coat and tie (for men) are required at dinner.

Getting Around

To enjoy the valley, you must get out of the car. A free shuttle bus runs September to October from 7 am to 10 pm, October to mid-November 9 am to 10 pm. They operate at 20-minute intervals; stops include all day-use parking lots and campgrounds, Yosemite Village, Curry Village, Yosemite Lodge, the Ahwahnee Hotel, and popular trailheads.

Bike rentals are available at Curry Village for $5 an hour, $16 per day. A two-way bike path (clearly marked on the NPS map) makes a six-mile loop around the valley, giving access to all campgrounds, picnic areas, and visitor facilities; spur trails go to the Happy Isles Nature Center and towards Mirror Lake.

TUOLUMNE MEADOWS & TIOGA RD
☎ 209

At 8500 feet, Tuolumne Meadows is the largest sub-alpine meadow in the Sierra. Its wide open fields and clear blue lakes are a dazzling contrast to Yosemite's densely forested valley, and the surrounding granite peaks – part of the Sierra Nevada crest – appear small and close, though most are between 10,000 and 13,000 feet. This area is more typically 'High Sierra' than it is 'Yosemite:' in summer it blooms with wildflowers and services hikers on the John Muir Trail, and in winter it sits under a blanket of snow, crossed by backcountry skiers and snowshoers.

Tioga Rd (Hwy 120), built as a mining road in 1882, is the only road to traverse the park from east to west. Tioga Pass, at its east end (outside park boundaries) is the highest pass in the Sierra, at 9945 feet. Besides great scenery, the road offers relatively uncrowded campgrounds, excellent day hikes, and the chance to see climbers at close range. At the road's west end, just after its junction with Big Oak Flat Rd, are two giant sequoia groves: the Merced Grove, the most serene in the park since it requires a two mile hike to reach (the trailhead is on the south side of the road, near a post marked B-10), and the Tuolumne Grove, the park's smallest, cut through by a six-mile loop road.

Orientation & Information
It is 46 miles from the Tioga Pass Entrance to the Big Oak Flat Entrance, about a two-hour drive. Tuolumne Meadows, which stretches for about two miles, 16 miles west of the Tioga Pass Entrance, is the only hub. At the meadow's west end, the Tuolumne Meadows Visitor Center (☎ 372-0263), has hiking maps of the area and general guide books. A half-mile east, the Tuolumne Meadows Store (☎ 372-1328) is well-stocked with topo maps and camping supplies. A ranger kiosk, just off the road near Tuolumne Meadows Lodge, issues wilderness permits. You can get a shower for $2 at the Tuolumne Meadows Lodge. A free shuttle bus connects these places from mid-May to September, and two buses daily make the 2½-hour trip between the lodge and Yosemite Valley ($13 one way).

Hiking
There are loads of small glacial lakes in this area, good day hike destinations. Just west of the Tioga Pass Entrance, the trail to Gaylor Lakes advances immediately to a high-altitude environment: it's one mile to Middle Gaylor Lake, another two to the upper lakes. The altitude and steep terrain make this one quite difficult.

The John Muir Trail parallels the Lyell Fork of the Tuolumne River at Tuolumne Meadows, connecting the visitors center, campground, and lodge. This is an easy two-mile section with nice swimming holes, meadows, and dome views.

A steep 1½-mile trail from the Dog Lake parking lot (near Tuolumne Meadows Lodge) heads around the east side of Lembert Dome to Dog Lake, whose grassy shore is good for picnicking and swimming. From here you can continue five miles to Young Lakes, or go back around the west side of the dome to end up at the Tuolumne Meadows stables.

West along Tioga Rd, trailheads are well marked for the Cathedral Lakes, Sunrise Lakes, and May Lake trails, all highly recommended. From May Lake you can climb two steep miles (unmarked) to the top of Mt Hoffmann, the geographical center of the park, for a panoramic view.

Places to Stay & Eat
At Tioga Pass, two miles east of park boundaries, are four nice USFS campgrounds with flush toilets, picnic tables, and fire grates. The rustic *Tioga Pass Resort* (☎ 372-4471) has housekeeping cabins and motel rooms for $300 to $450 a week, and serves excellent pie and pancakes.

In Tuolumne Meadows, the *Tuolumne Meadows Lodge* (☎ 252-4848) has canvas tent cabins with four beds, a wood stove, and candles (no electricity) for $41. Breakfast or dinner in the campy dining room is fun, but you pay for its remote location. Near the visitors center, the large *Tuolumne Meadows Campground* is half first-come, first-served, with nice spots along a creek; sites A77 to 87, C43 to 49 and 86 to 95, and G1 to 16 are good. The Tuolumne Meadows Store has good picnic items, and the grill next door has food for under $5.

The campgrounds between Tuolumne Meadows and Big Oak Flat are the most likely to have a spot when the rest of the park is full. There is a beautiful walk-in campground on the west end of Tenaya Lake ($3), not far from the road. *Porcupine Flat* is really woodsy, with a bumpy road and pit toilets. In a recent burn area, *Yosemite Creek* is quite ugly but usually has empty sites. *Tamarack Flat* is set back from the road with sites along Tamarack Creek.

A mile north of the road, *White Wolf* is in a charming world of its own. The lodge has a great porch and rustic dining room, tent cabins ($42), wood cabins with bath ($62), and a lovely campground.

HETCH HETCHY
☎ 209

After an environmental debate that knocked the wind out of John Muir, the 1913 Raker Bill allowed the City of San Francisco to construct O'Shaughnessey Dam in the Hetch Hetchy Valley, blocking the Tuolumne River to create Hetch Hetchy Reservoir. The eight-mile-long reservoir now submerges an area said to be as beautiful as Yosemite Valley while it supplies the majority of San Francisco's water and hydroelectric power.

The area around Hetch Hetchy reservoir gets the park's least amount of traffic. Its low elevation and arid landscape make it less scenic than other parts of Yosemite, but it is a good place to start long trips into the park's quiet northern reaches. There is a nice backpacker's camp at the reservoir's west end (near the dam), popular with people who know the park well. A gentle hiking trail crosses the dam, goes through a tunnel, and heads along the north shore past Tueeulala, Wapama, and Rancheria Falls (six miles). This is a good afternoon trip in spring or fall, but should be completed before 3 pm in summer when temperatures soar. At Rancheria Falls, the trail splits to go northeast through the Tiltill Valley and east (and eventually north) through Pleasant Valley to the Sierra's high country.

WAWONA
☎ 209

Sixteen miles south of the valley, Wawona is Yosemite's historical center, home to the park's first headquarters and site of its first tourist facilities. The Wawona Grocery Store (☎ 375-6574) acts as 'downtown'

Wawona, with a post office, deli, and bus stop. The **Pioneer History Center** has an outdoor collection of stage coaches and some of the first buildings in the park (moved here from various points), including remnants of Clark's Station, built by the park's first guardian in 1857. Nearby, the *Wawona Hotel*, built in 1875, is a picture of vintage elegance, with manicured grounds, a covered porch, and wooden deck chairs for anyone to use. Rooms here start at $70 ($90 with bath). Meals in the bright Victorian dining room (☎ 375-6556) are casual at breakfast and lunch, formal and expensive for dinner when reservations are required.

Mariposa Grove

A trip to this giant sequoia grove, once John Muir's favorite, is about as unnatural as a nature experience gets. A free bus (or your car) takes you six miles from Wawona (two from the park's South Entrance) to the grove parking lot where a diesel powered open-air tram ($7) makes the two-mile drive through the trees to the Mariposa Grove Museum. You can walk the trail which is somewhat better, but still crowded and exposed to tram noise, or the longer outer loop trail that gets relatively little traffic; there's a good interpretive map (50¢) at the trailhead on the east end of the parking lot.

Despite the tourist racket, the trees themselves are impressive – several are over 3000 years old and 300 feet high. The Wawona Tunnel Tree, which toppled over in 1969, was the famous drive-through tree that first gave the grove its notoriety.

YOSEMITE GATEWAYS
☎ 209

The small towns on Yosemite's western fringe are mostly old mining towns that now thrive on the park's overflow. These are good places to stay if you arrive without a tent or room reservation. From the east, the nearest town is Lee Vining (nine miles east of Tioga Pass; closed in winter), listed in the Eastern Sierra section.

Oakhurst & Around

Situated at the junction of Hwys 41 and 49, Oakhurst is the last place with normal gas prices, supermarkets, banks, and automotive stores before entering the park from the south. While most traffic is Yosemite bound, a fair amount of people pass through Oakhurst en route to Bass Lake, a popular fishing and boating spot. The City Park and Fresno Flats Historical Park, both southeast of Hwy 41 near the historic town center, offer shady spots to stretch your legs.

Chain motels are your best bet here, though they're relatively expensive. The *Shilo Inn* (☎ 683-3555), *Best Western Yosemite Gateway* (☎ 683-2378), and *Holiday Inn Express* (☎ 642-2525) are all on Hwy 41. Each has a pool and rooms for around $60 ($85 from June to September). North of these, the small *Snowline Lodge* (☎ 683-5854) is also good, with rooms starting at $40 year round.

Fifteen miles north, **Fish Camp** is smaller and less commercial. Its *Marriott Tenaya Lodge* (☎ 683-6555) is a wonderful but expensive place to stay, with two pools, a fitness center, woodsy grounds, and cozy log rooms starting at $150. The deli, with nice atmosphere and huge sandwiches ($5), is a good lunch stop.

Mariposa & Around

About halfway between Merced and Yosemite Valley at the Hwy 140/49 junction, Mariposa is the largest and most interesting town near the park. Born as a mining and railroad town during the Gold Rush, it has a stately courthouse built in 1854 (the oldest in continuous use west of the Mississippi), and a History Center (☎ 966-2924), at the east end of town next to the Bank of America, with mediocre mining and railroad exhibits. The **California State Mining & Mineral Museum** (☎ 742-7625), a mile south of town off Hwy 49 at the fairgrounds, is worth a stop ($2).

The *Mother Load Lodge* (☎ 966-2521), *Mariposa Lodge* (☎ 966-3607), and *Best Western Yosemite Station* (☎ 966-7545), all on Hwy 140, are good places to stay with rooms for around $50.

El Portal Just outside the park entrance, El Portal sprawls for about seven miles along Hwy 140. *Savage's Trading Post* (☎ 379-2301), at its west end where the South and Main Forks of the Merced River meet, is the town's well-known tourist trap – a gift shop and restaurant erected on the site of a trading post used by miners and Miwok in the 1850s. The lodge has decent rooms for $62. Further east, the *Cedar Lodge Resort* (☎ 379-2612), *Yosemite View Lodge* (☎ 379-2681), and *Dell Hart Lodge* (☎ 379-2308), each have a pool, restaurant, and $45 to $95 rooms.

Hwy 120 West

Visitor facilities are sparse along this route, but there are two good spots to swim: Don Pedro Reservoir, 11 miles west of Groveland, and at Rainbow Bridge on the Tuolumne River, three miles east of Buck Meadows Lodge. **Groveland** has the most choices of restaurants and lodging, and has an adorable town center (along the highway) with restored Gold Rush-era buildings. Along the highway, the *Hotel Charlotte* (☎ 962-6455) has vintage rooms with shared bath for $65, and an upscale restaurant, while the *Groveland Motel* (☎ 902-7865) has modern rooms for $55. *PJ's Cafe* is a good spot for pizza, burgers, and sandwiches. Further east, the *Buck Meadows Lodge* (☎ 962-5281) has standard rooms for $55 to $70, and a country-style coffee shop. Railroad enthusiasts should make a point to stop in **Jamestown**, listed in the Gold Country chapter.

Kings Canyon & Sequoia National Parks

☎ 209

South of Yosemite, on the Sierra's western slope, the adjacent Kings Canyon and Sequoia National Parks encompass some of the world's most incredible pieces of

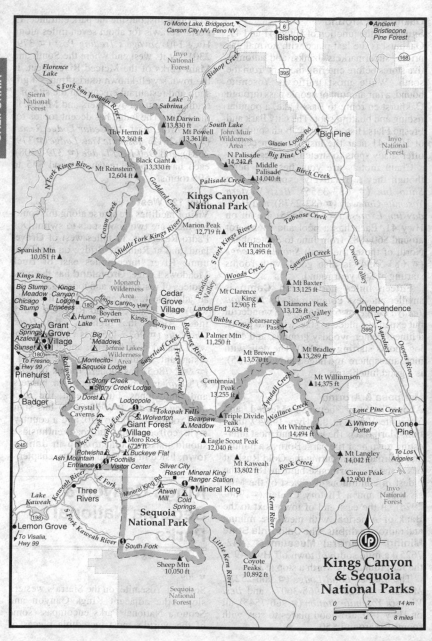

To Mono Lake, Bridgeport,
Carson City NV, Reno NV

Ancient
Bristlecone
Pine Forest

Bishop

Florence
Lake

Inyo
National
Forest

Sierra
National
Forest

S Fork San Joaquin River

Lake
Sabrina

Bishop Creek

Mt Darwin
13,830 ft

Mt Powell
13,361 ft

South Lake
John Muir
Wilderness
Area

Big Pine

The Hermit
12,360 ft

Glacier Lodge Rd

Inyo
National
Forest

N Palisade
14,242 ft

Big Pine Creek

Birch Creek

Black Giant
13,330 ft

Mt Reinstein
12,604 ft

Goddard Creek

Palisade Creek

Middle
Palisade
14,040 ft

N Fork Kings River

Kings Canyon
National Park

Taboose Creek

Crown Creek

Middle Fork Kings River

Marion Peak
12,719 ft

S Fork Kings River

Mt Pinchot
13,495 ft

Spanish Mtn
10,051 ft

Sawmill Creek

Woods Creek

Owens Valley

Kings River

Monarch
Wilderness
Area

Mt Clarence
King
12,905 ft

Mt Baxter
13,125 ft

Big Stump
Meadow
Chicago
Stump

Kings
Canyon
Lodge
Princess

Cedar
Grove
Village

Kings Canyon HWY

Lands End

Paradise
Valley

Diamond Peak
13,126 ft

Onion Valley

Independence

Hume
Lake

Boyden
Cavern

Kings Canyon

Bubbs Creek

Kearsarge
Pass

LA Aqueduct

Grant
Grove
Village

Crystal
Springs
Azalea
Sunset

Big
Meadows

Jennie Lakes
Wilderness
Area

Palmer Mtn
11,250 ft

Mt Bradley
13,289 ft

Mt Williamson
14,375 ft

Owens River

To Fresno,
Hwy 99

Pinehurst

Montecito-
Sequoia Lodge

Sugarloaf Creek

Ferguson Creek

Roaring River

Mt Brewer
13,570 ft

Tyndall Creek

Stony Creek
Stony Creek Lodge

Centennial
Peak
13,255 ft

Badger

Dorst

Crystal
Caverns

Lodgepole

Wolverton

Tokopah Falls

Bearpaw
Meadow

Triple Divide
Peak
12,634 ft

Wallace Creek

Mt Whitney
14,494 ft

Lone Pine Creek

Whitney
Portal

Lone
Pine

Giant Forest
Village

Moro Rock
6725 ft

Eagle Scout Peak
12,040 ft

Mt Langley
14,042 ft

To Los
Angeles

Marble Fork

Yucca Creek

Potwisha
Buckeye Flat

Ash Mountain
Entrance

Foothills
Visitor Center

Silver City
Resort

Mineral King
Ranger Station

Mt Kaweah
13,802 ft

Rock Creek

Mineral King

Cirque Peak
12,900 ft

E Fork

Mineral King Rd

Redwood Cr

Three
Rivers

Atwell
Mill

Cold
Springs

Inyo
National
Forest

Lake
Kaweah

Kaweah River

S Fork Kaweah River

Sequoia
National Park

Kern River

Lemon Grove

To Visalia,
Hwy 99

South Fork

Little Kern River

Sheep Mtn
10,050 ft

Coyote
Peaks
10,892 ft

Sequoia
National
Forest

Kings Canyon
& Sequoia
National Parks

0   7   14 km

0   4   8 miles

nature. Giant sequoias stand as the most massive living things on earth and the awesome canyon of the South Fork of the King's River rivals any in the Sierra. Despite this superlative world, crowds are sparse thanks to its relative inaccessiblity and the usual amusement park atmosphere is absent. Designed primarily as hiking and backpacking parks, there are few drive-by sites but loads of trails for all abilities. Each park has its own history and defining characteristics, but they are run and managed as one unit.

History

The Kaweah and Potwisha Indians, sub-tribes of Central Valley Yokuts, lived as hunter-gatherers in the western foothills along the Marble Fork of the Kaweah River. In 1858 they led Hale Tharp, a cat-tleman from Three Rivers, into the Giant Forest along the west side of Moro Rock. Tharp spent summers here for the next 30 years and entertained John Muir who wrote of the area in magazines and periodicals.

The Gold Rush brought logging and grazing to the Grant Grove area, and mining to Mineral King, causing alarm in early conservationists. Visalia journalist George Stewart, called the 'Father of Sequoia National Park,' started a stir in the San Joaquin Valley with newspaper articles about the effects of logging the Big Trees. Valley farmers sent their message to Washington, DC, via representatives, and in 1890 Sequoia became the second national park in the US, with the four sq miles around Grant Grove becoming Grant Grove National Park a few months later. Kings Canyon was designated a national park in

Giant Sequoias

In the same family as the California coast redwood and Dawn sequoia (recently discovered in China), the giant sequoia *(Sequoiadendron giganteum)* grows only on the Sierra's western slope, between 5000 and 7000 feet. Giant sequoias are the largest living things on earth in terms of volume. They can grow to 300 feet tall, 40 feet in diameter, and live up to 3000 years – the eldest is estimated to be 3500 years old. The main cause of death for the trees is their own size – they topple under their own weight, not supported by their fragile roots.

Sequoia groves might be more abundant if the trees weren't so finicky. They require plenty of ground water for their wide, shallow root system, a heavy snow pack to trim limbs and dead branches so they won't blow over in a storm, and frequent fires (their thick, soft bark is full of air – very fire resistant) to pop-open their tight cones and free the seeds inside. Aside from Yosemite, look for sequoia groves around Kings Canyon & Sequoia National Parks and the similarly gigantic California coast redwood tree along the Pacific coast.■

GENERAL SHERMAN

MARISA GIERLICH

CALIFORNIA

1940, encompassing Grant Grove and nearby Redwood Mountain.

Flora & Fauna

The parks' low foothills (to 5000 feet) are covered with manzanita, California black oak, and the tall yucca whose fragrant flowers bloom in early spring. The foothills is the only area in which you have to watch for rattlesnakes while hiking.

From 5000 to 9000 feet, forests include sugar, ponderosa, Jeffrey, and lodgepole pine, fir, and incense cedar. A 200-mile stretch north of the Kings River encompasses eight giant sequoia groves, while the remaining 67 are concentrated along a 60-mile belt south of the river. For more on the unusual sequoia, see the sidebar in the Yosemite National Park section. Deer and Douglas squirrels are predominant, though coyotes and bobcats are also at these elevations.

In the high country, above 9000 feet, forests give way to stark granite landscapes dotted with lakes and foxtail and white-bark pine.

Information

The entrance fee is $5 per car, $3 for people on foot or bike. Upon entering the parks you'll receive a good NPS map and copy of *Sequoia Bark*, a quarterly newspaper with phone numbers, hours, and descriptions for all visitor facilities, including those in the nearby national forests. All main visitor facilities are on the Generals Hwy (see below).

There are no banks or check cashing facilities in the parks, though most places will accept personal and travelers checks. Camping supplies are limited and of marginal quality, and gas is about 50% more expensive than in the San Joaquin Valley. The nearest banks and sporting goods stores are in Reedley, 45 miles west off Hwy 180, and Three Rivers, eight miles southwest on Hwy 198.

Hiking & Backpacking

With trail mileage 10 times greater than road mileage, these parks are a back-packer's dream. Kings Canyon and Mineral King offer the best backcountry access, while the Jenny Lakes Wilderness Area (accessible from Big Meadows Trailhead near Big Meadows Campground) has pristine meadows and lakes at lower elevations. Wilderness permits, required for all overnight trips, are available at visitors centers and ranger stations (free), as are topo maps and hiking guides. Trails are usually open by mid-May and quotas go into effect when necessary (usually July and August). For current trail conditions and backcountry information, call ☎ 565-3708. The Bearpaw Meadow Camp (see Places to Stay) offers an overnight destination for those without proper camping gear.

Winter Activities

Grant Grove and Giant Forest offer great snow shoeing and cross-country skiing on marked, groomed trails. Since the Generals Hwy is not plowed between the two, you're best to choose one or the other as a destination.

Trails from Grant Grove connect with those in the Sequoia National Forest and some maintained by Montecito-Sequoia Lodge (☎ 565-3388), a private cross-country ski resort on the Generals Hwy. Grant Grove Village (including the market and restaurant) is in full-swing, with ski and snowshoe rentals, nightly programs at the visitors center, cabin and campground accommodations, and naturalist-guided snowshoe walks on weekends only. Giant Forest is a little more subdued, with only the Lodgepole Visitor Center, campground, and laundry open. Ski activity here is at the Sequoia Ski Touring Center (☎ 565-3435), 2½ miles south of Lodgepole in Wolverton, an excellent day-use facility with rentals, lessons, and a retail shop.

Accommodations

Accommodations in the parks are managed by Guest Services International (GSI), a private concessionaire. Reservations are made through the Reservations Department (☎ 561-3314), PO Box 789, Three Rivers, CA 93271. Grant Grove is the only lodge open year round (others close from early October to May). Campgrounds are first-come, first-served, with $10 sites, flush toilets, bear boxes, tables, and fire pits; *Lodgepole*, the biggest and busiest, is the one exception where sites must be reserved through a reservation system (☎ 800-365-2267). GSI also operates the *Bearpaw Meadow Camp*, 11½ miles from Giant Forest on the High Sierra Trail, where hikers can stay for about $42 per night including showers, two meals, bedding, and towels. The necessary reservations are made through the Reservations Department starting January 2.

For details on specific campgrounds, see Places to Stay in the following sections.

Getting There & Away
The parks spread from the western Sierra Nevada foothills east to the Sierra Nevada crest, though roads only penetrate the very western portion. Highway 180 makes a gentle climb from Fresno to the Big Stump Entrance Station, four miles west of Grant Grove; from here you can go north into Kings Canyon or south along Generals Hwy. In the south, Hwy 198 runs from Visalia through Three Rivers past Mineral King Rd to the Ash Mountain Entrance Station, at the south end of the Generals Hwy. In winter, Generals Hwy is closed between Grant Grove and Giant Forest, with Rte 245 (west of the park) as the only connection between the two.

GENERALS HWY
☎ 209
Built between 1921 and 1934, this road connects Grant Grove (in Kings Canyon National Park) to Giant Forest and the rest of Sequoia, giving access to the main visitor facilities, campgrounds, and, most importantly, the trees everyone comes to see. Along its 48 miles between Grant Grove (in the north) and the Ash Mountain Entrance Station, the highway winds from about 6500 feet, where the Big Trees are, to chaparral covered foothills at around 2000 feet. You can drive the full distance in

about two hours, and totally defeat the purpose of being here. You should allow for time out of the car – the only way to experience the trees. You could easily spend a day at each site listed below.

Information
Grant Grove and Lodgepole are the two visitor hubs along the highway, each with a visitors center (see below), gas station, market, showers ($2), post office, and laundry. Grant Grove facilities are open year round, while those at Lodgepole (except the visitors center and laundry) close from mid-October to late May. At the south end of the highway, the Foothills Visitor Center is one mile north of the Ash Mountain Entrance, the first you'll encounter when entering from the south on Hwy 198. All visitors centers have day-hike and topo maps, books, and information for both parks, and are open daily 8 am to 5 pm (from October to May until 4 pm).

Grant Grove
When the bill to create Sequoia National Park was before Congress in 1890, DK Zumwalt, a resident of Visalia, persuaded the bill's sponsor to establish General Grant National Park around the small Sequoia grove standing among clear-cut forests. The thumb-like four sq miles, surrounded by Sequoia National Forest, stood as one of the smallest national parks for 50 years until it became part of Kings Canyon National Park in 1940.

Near the Hwy 180/Generals Hwy/Kings Canyon Hwy junction, Grant Grove Village is a focal point of the parks. The Grant Grove Visitor Center (☎ 335-2856) has a good history exhibit and the true to scale 'Sequoia room.' From behind the visitors center a road goes northeast two miles to **Panoramic Point**, a good spot to view Kings Canyon and start scenic hikes. A mile northwest from the village, the **General Grant Grove** encompasses the General Grant Tree, estimated to be over 3500 years old, and the Fallen Monarch, a massive tree which housed early pioneers, shepherders, and US Cavalry horses.

Redwood Mountain Grove

About six miles south of Grant Grove, this is the most extensive concentration of Sequoias and one of the most pristine since it is not accessible by car. A seven-mile trail loops through the grove along Redwood Creek (flanked by azalea blossoms in May and June) where the trees are dense though not as huge as in other groves. The trail is on the south side of the highway across from the Quail Flat turn-off, about half a mile east of the Redwood Mountain Overlook (no facilities).

Giant Forest & Lodgepole

The Giant Forest area is Sequoia's core, a good destination for first-time visitors to the park. 'Discovered' in 1958 by Hale Tharp and named by John Muir in 1875, these three sq miles contain the parks' most massive trees, including General Sherman – the largest living thing on earth. At the north edge of the forest, **Lodgepole** has an excellent visitors center (☎ 565-3782) with natural history exhibits and a slide show. Five miles south, **Giant Forest Lodge & Village**, Sequoia's first guest facilities, sit among the noble giants – right on top of their fragile root system. With some of the trees poised to topple, all services will be out of the village by 1998.

The centerpiece of Giant Forest, half way between Lodgepole and Giant Forest Village, is the **General Sherman Tree and Congress Trail**. A parking lot gives access to the short trail around the big tree and the two-mile, paved Congress Trail passes impressive tree groupings such as the 'House' and 'Senate.' To get away from the crowds, continue to the five-mile Trail of the Sequoias which puts you in the heart of the forest.

There are also nice meadows in Giant Forest where you can see the trees in their entirety – top to bottom. At the south edge of Giant Forest Village, **Crescent Meadow Rd** leads to a lovely picnic area surrounded by meadows and several easy hikes, including one to Tharp's Log where Hale Tharp spent summers in a fallen tree. Before reaching the picnic area, the road passes **Moro Rock**, a solid granite monolith often compared to Yosemite's Half Dome. The best part about this rock is the quarter-mile carved granite staircase that leads to its very top, where the view is unbeatable.

Crystal Cave

Discovered in 1918 by two fishermen, this cave extends around 3 miles into the earth and has formations estimated to be 10,000 years old. It was formed by an underground river that cut soft limestone into large chambers and passageways which filled as the water table rose. Cascade Creek eventually eroded a mouth to the cave, draining the water and exposing the rock to air. Secondary formations – stalagmites and stalactites – grew on floors and ceilings in the form of curtains, domes, columns, 'cave bacon,' and 'cave popcorn,' all of milky white marble. The 50-minute cave tour covers a half mile of chambers and includes detailed interpretation. Tickets ($4) are available at the Lodgepole and Ash Mountain visitors centers (not at the cave) and sell out quickly; May to mid-September tours are every hour from 8 am to 4 pm. The cave itself is northwest of Generals Hwy, up a steep and narrow road, about an hour from both visitors centers; the half-mile trail from the parking lot to the cave is mostly stairs.

The Foothills

At about 2000 feet, the foothills surrounding the south end of Generals Hwy have a hot, dry environment compared to the rest of the park. Potwisha Indians lived here until the early 1900s, surviving mostly on acorn meal. A vivid pictograph and remains of a village site can be seen at Hospital Rock picnic area, below the sheer face of the rock which dominates the valley. Swimming holes abound along the Marble Fork of the Kaweah River, especially near Potwisha Campground (see Places to Stay).

Hiking

The day-hike map for Giant Forest, available at visitors centers ($1.50), is useful for making sense of the 40 miles of foot-trails concentrated in its three sq miles. Trails here are quite gentle, with most of them along meadows and the forest floor. The five-mile Trail of the Sequoias passes the most 'famous' named trees along the Congress Trail then makes its way past Ponderosa pine, rock outcroppings, and fern grottoes. With Moro Rock accessible by car, the Moro Rock Trail from Giant Forest Village stays uncrowded and offers views of the San Joaquin Valley. The High Sierra Trail, from the Crescent Meadow parking lot, is good for views east.

The Lodgepole area offers glacial scenery and some long hikes into high lake basins; trailheads are behind the visitors center at the back of the campground. The short and easy Tokopah Falls Trail skirts the Marble Fork of the Kaweah River and ends at a multi-level cascade. The Twin Lakes Trail climbs hard for the first mile, mellows out at Cahoon Meadow, then climbs along Clover Creek to the lakes at the foot of Siliman Crest – a good day's adventure.

Places to Stay

Camping The concentration of NPS campgrounds is in the Grant Grove area. Across from the visitors center, *Sunset* has hillside sites with some that overlook the western foothills and San Joaquin Valley, while sites at *Azalea* are well-dispersed with some bordering a meadow. *Crystal Springs* is the least attractive, with neither ground cover nor privacy. Campgrounds are first-come, first-served, with $10 sites.

South of Grant Grove on Sierra National Forest land, *Big Meadow Campground*, six miles northeast of the highway on a well-marked road, has two units with pit toilets and $7 sites. Just off the highway, *Stony Creek Campground* is one of the nicest around, with $8 creekside sites which get the afternoon sun, and flush toilets. Half of the 49 sites are reservable (☎ 800-280-2267). A bit further south, the NPS *Dorst Campground* is near the small Muir Grove of Sequoias and quite secluded.

Behind the Lodgepole Visitor Center and

market, *Lodgepole* is the only reservation campground in the park (☎ 800-365-2267) and the only one open year-round. Sites are spread along the Marble Fork of the Kaweah River with good fishing and hiking; sites 58 to 62, 38 to 45, 202 to 218, and 189 to 199 are especially nice.

In the foothills, *Buckeye Flat* and *Potwisha* both have riverside sites near swimming holes. These are good in spring and fall, when the higher elevations get cold, but hot and buggy in summer.

Motels & Lodges *Grant Grove Lodge* (☎ 335-2314) has rustic cabins with kerosene lamps and wood-burning stoves for $35, and housekeeping cabins with private bath and electricity for $62 to $78. Privately owned *Montecito Sequoia Lodge* (☎ 565-3388), nine miles south of Grant Grove, is open to nightly visitors from September to May. It maintains its own cross-country ski trails, and has a pool and hot tub. Spring and fall rates are $60 per person including breakfast and dinner; winter rates are $20 more, including lunch and a trail pass.

About half-way between Grant Grove and Giant Forest, *Stony Creek Lodge* (☎ 561-3314) has a big river-rock fireplace in its main room, and old but nice motel rooms with private bath for $78 (closed September to May). Until 1998, *Giant Forest Lodge* (☎ 561-3314) has rustic cabins ($35), housekeeping cabins ($62 to $78), and motel rooms ($94) that would be $50 cheaper anywhere else.

Places to Eat

The Lodgepole Market is the largest in the parks, though the Grant Grove Market (open year round) is your best bet after September.

The *Grant Grove Restaurant*, open year-round from 7 am to 8 pm, has a comfortably average coffeeshop atmosphere with food to match (under $10). From May to October, the *Lodgepole Deli* serves fresh salads, sandwiches, and pizza until 8 pm, and has a nice patio. The *Giant Forest Lodge Dining Room*, open until 9 pm, is the parks' fanciest eatery, but neither the food nor atmosphere justify the prices. Better to eat at the *Giant Forest Cafeteria*, where mediocre cafeteria-style food is spruced up by a friendly atmosphere and big log fireplace.

KINGS CANYON
☎ 209

About four miles north of Grant Grove, the Kings Canyon Hwy enters Sequoia National Forest for its 2000-foot descent to Cedar Grove along the South Fork of the Kings River. Views from the road – massive granite ridges, peaks, and domes in the distance with logging roads and clear-cut as foreground – show a major difference between national park and national forest land-use policies. They also give a glimpse of the stunning backcountry that makes the canyon a favorite place among serious climbers and hikers.

The canyon itself is the deepest in the lower 48 states at 8200 feet. At its west end is a world of rust, chartreuse, and golden rock sloping down to the river in big chunks and blade-like ridges. Towards its east end, near Cedar Grove Village, walls are sheer and further apart, and the valley gains a floor to become U-shaped. The road into the valley and trails leading from it are the main attractions.

Orientation & Information
Cedar Grove Village is 31 miles from Grant Village, about an hour's drive. Here is a visitors center (☎ 565-3793) with maps and information, a market/deli/lodge, and gas station with $2 showers and a laundry. Village services open from 8 am to 7 pm late-May to mid-October, though the visitors center closes in early September. Six miles past the village, Roads End is just that, with trailheads, overnight parking, and a ranger kiosk (the Backpackers Information Station, see Backpacking below) that issues wilderness permits.

Hume Lake
Created in 1900 as a dam for logging operations, Hume Lake is now surrounded by a thick forest of second-growth pine, cedar, and fir. The three-mile road from Kings Canyon Hwy (about 7½ miles from Grant Grove) to the lake is well-marked and maintained, but rarely used outside of hunting season (mid-September to November). The lake itself is stocked with trout and warm enough for swimming. A primitive USFS campground on the lake's south end has undeveloped sites ($3) near the water.

Big Stump Meadow
About 3½ miles north of Grant Grove, two marked forest service roads (about a mile apart) head west from the highway through what John Muir, in *The Mountains of California* (1894), called 'the northernmost assemblage of Big Trees that may fairly be called a forest.' About five years after Muir's visit, lumbermen turned the forest into a Sequoia cemetery. The first road goes to Converse Basin Grove, where the Chicago Stump stands. This is the remains of a tree that was supposedly bigger than the General Sherman until it was cut down and sent to Chicago for the 1892 Colombian Exposition, where disbelieving Easterners called it a 'California hoax.' The second road goes two miles to Big Stump Meadow, where a concentration of stumps and fallen logs make good picnic platforms and photo subjects (especially with black & white film). A half mile past the meadow, a marked trail from the road goes to the Boole Tree, third-largest of the big trees and the only old one surviving in the area.

Boyden Cavern
This limestone cave has whimsically shaped formations – stalagmites, stalactites, domes – near its entrance. While interesting to visit, it can be skipped if you're planning to see Crystal Cave which is larger and more impressive (but requires more walking to see). The entrance/ticket booth (☎ 736-2708), 11 miles west of Cedar Grove on the highway, sells $6 tickets for the 45-minute tour from 10 am to 5 pm daily as long as the road is open. Half a mile past the cave on the left (north),

a road cut reveals an incredible black and white marble vein, indicative of what lies within most of the canyon walls.

Hiking

You needn't bring a tent to enjoy the canyon's trails. There are numerous gentle paths along the valley floor which offer views of the enticing peaks on all sides. The Cedar Grove day-hike map ($1.50) available at the visitors center and market, is useful for these hikes. The Zumwalt Meadow Loop is really nice but often crowded, while the one-mile connecting trail from Roads End to the meadow is less traveled: together they make a good trip. From Roads End, the Bubbs Creek trail offers a good view but climbs a set of nasty switchbacks before putting you next to the creek, while the Paradise Valley trail follows the river the entire way. (Mist Falls makes a good destination on this trail.)

Backpacking

Topo maps are available from the Cedar Grove Visitor Center from May to September, and from the Grant Grove Visitor Center (see Generals Hwy) year round. The Backpackers Information Station at Roads End has a posted map that shows mileage and the location of bear-proof food storage boxes (which may determine where you camp) and a very up-to-date information and message board. Wilderness permits are necessary for any overnight trip. During peak season, permits to certain areas (usually Paradise Valley and the Rae Lakes Loop) are limited. At this time, rangers issue permits at the station from 7:15 am to 2:45 pm, with permits for the following day not issued until 1 pm. The rest of the year permits are self-register.

The Paradise Valley (Woods Creek) and Bubbs Creek Trail both connect with the John Muir/Pacific Crest Trail, which together form the 43-mile Rae Lakes Loop – a very popular trip. The Copper Creek Trail heads north through somewhat lower terrain.

Places to Stay & Eat

Facilities in the canyon start to close in mid-September.

In the national forest before the road descends, the *Princess Campground* has $11 sites next to a huge meadow. Down at Cedar Grove there are four NPS campgrounds, all near the village. *Sentinel* and *Sheep Creek* have riverside sites (arrive by noon to snag one) and thick cedar and pine groves nearby, while *Moraine* and *Canyon View* (tenters only) are above the river on a steep embankment with sparse ground cover.

Motel rooms at the *Cedar Grove Lodge* (☎ 561-3314) have a private bath and two big beds, but hardly justify the $76 price. Though a bit isolated, the *Kings Canyon Lodge* (☎ 335-2405), 13 miles west of Cedar Grove, is a better value. Rooms with private bath cost $62, and cabins cost $70 to $150 (with up to six people). Their cafe has good breakfast and lunch daily, dinner on weekends, and a cozy atmosphere. The Cedar Grove Snack Bar serves fast food for under $5.

MINERAL KING AREA
☎ 209

At the south end of Sequoia, Mineral King is at the end of a curvy, steep, narrow 25-mile road which manages to weed out all but those with a mission. This is the park's backpacking mecca and a good place to find solitude year round. The valley sits at 7500 feet, surrounded by serrated peaks, lake basins, and mountain passes that reach upwards of 11,000 feet. Rock here is softer than in other parts of the Sierra, so the valley's walls are sloped instead of sheer, and crimson and purple in color. These odd characteristics led early explorers to think the area was loaded with precious metals. From the 1860s to 1890s, the valley (called Beulah) witnessed heavy silver mining and lumber activity. There are still old shafts and stamp mills around, though it takes some exploring to find them. In 1965, the Walt Disney Corporation proposed a massive ski area in the valley but, after serious debate, did not succeed.

Orientation & Information

The Mineral King Rd heads southeast from Hwy 198, between Three Rivers and the Ash Mountain Entrance (outside park boundaries). The ranger station (☎ 565-3768), about 24 miles down the road, has maps and a good mining exhibit and issues wilderness permits (necessary for overnight trips). May to September it opens on weekends from 7 am to 3:30 pm; permits are self-register the rest of the year. Three miles west of the ranger station, the *Silver City Resort* has showers, a small market, and, usually, gas. It is open until mid-September.

Hiking

When the ranger station is closed, get topo maps at the Foothills Visitor Center (☎ 565-3141), one mile east of the Ash Mountain Entrance. Most trails start steep and mellow out after three or four miles. Be aware of the high elevation, even on short hikes. Nice day hikes go to Mosquito, Eagle, and White Chief Lakes (all stocked with trout). For long trips, locals recommend the Little Five Lakes Basin and, further on along the High Sierra Trail, Kaweah Gap, surrounded by the sawtooth Black Kaweah, Mt Stewart, and Eagle Scout Peak – all above 12,000 feet.

Places to Stay & Eat

There are two campgrounds on Mineral King Rd: *Atwell Mill*, about five miles west of the ranger station, with no running water; and *Cold Springs*, across from the ranger station, which has two loops along the river and some secluded spots off the road.

The *Silver City Resort* (☎ 561-3223), three miles west of the ranger station, has rustic cabins for around $75 and a charming little cafe with excellent pie (pie only on Tuesday and Thursday). It's open from late May to early September. Buy groceries and supplies at the *Village Market*, open daily from 9 am to 6 pm (5 pm Sunday).

THREE RIVERS

• *elev 6000 feet* ☎ 209

Eight miles outside the Ash Mountain Entrance Station, this little river town is an access hub for the parks and weekend getaway for San Joaquin Valley residents. Sierra Drive, the main drag, is lined with woodsy motels, stores, and artists' studios and galleries. Midway through town, Three Rivers Village has a post office, good pizza parlor, and the best market (open from 8 am to 6 pm; Sunday until 5 pm) for buying supplies en route to the parks.

The Naturedome (☎ 561-6560), 42249 Sierra Drive, is a geodesic dome (built in harmonious convergence with nature spirits) with a large deck overlooking the Kaweah River. It features local artists' work, live music, and workshops on everything from meditation to finger-painting. The River Envy Iris Farm (☎ 561-3630), 43429 Sierra Drive, produces a variety of irises, including some genetically engineered to smell like grape juice and orange popsicles! The farm is open to the public from April 1 to June 4 (prime blooming season), during which the display grounds bloom with a rainbow of colors, and staff are on hand to answer questions. During the Three Rivers Redbud Festival, held the first weekend in May, artisans set up booths along Sierra Drive and hundreds of people converge for general merrymaking.

The Eastern Sierra

The Sierra Nevada's eastern slope rises abruptly from the Owens Valley Floor to jagged 14,000-foot peaks marking the Sierra Nevada crest. For many, this is the best side of the Sierra because it offers immediate access to alpine scenery, high mountain lakes, and large meadows. Creeks and rivers that tumble from the mountains into the Owens River carve canyons which serve as infiltration points to the otherwise daunting barrier. Most of these drainages are designated national recreation areas, with developed campgrounds, small resorts, and well-marked trailheads. Roads are usually paved and partially plowed in winter, giving access to backcountry ski trails. Most trails cross the Sierra Nevada crest, accessing wilderness areas and national parks in the west.

The arid Owens Valley lies at the base of the mountains, with the ancient White Mountains, nearly as high but much older than the Sierra, to the east. Once as prosperous as the Central Valley in agriculture, Owens Valley is now a desert-like wasteland, drained by the California Aqueduct to water Los Angeles.

For those who don't enjoy the outdoors, the Eastern Sierra holds little in the way of diversions and Hwy 395 is a long haul (brutally hot in summer) to be made quickly. Highway towns, which sprang up as stage stops and supply stations during the 1850s, are extremely 'redneck' for California – filled with gun shops, bars, and pick-up trucks.

Orientation

The Eastern Sierra extends from Bridgeport in the north to Hwy 178 in the south. The mountains are lowest and easiest to access north of Bishop, where Mammoth Lakes provides a good destination for hikers, bikers, and skiers, and Bridgeport is popular with anglers. From Bishop south, where the Sierra's peaks are highest and the Owens Valley slopes gently downwards, getting into the mountains often requires at least a 25-mile drive up curvy, narrow roads. The easiest access to high, dramatic scenery is from Rock Creek (near Mammoth Lakes), Bishop Creek (near Bishop), and Whitney Portal (near Lone Pine). South of Lone Pine, the Owens Valley tilts south while the Sierra Nevada tops out along peaks over 14,000 feet, including 14,494 foot Mt Whitney – highest in the contiguous US.

Two-lane Hwy 395, in a constant state of repair and expansion, runs the length of the range. Well-marked roads head west into the mountains. Little towns along the highway offer accommodations, food, camping supplies, and reasonably priced gas.

Pack Trips

Trails to the Eastern Sierra's high country are short, steep, and often rocky – better navigated by horse or mule than a hiker with a heavy pack. On 'spot trips,' an outfitter carries your gear (and you, if desired) to a chosen destination and leaves you to hike out or picks you up days or weeks later. Most nearby outfitters also offer full-service trips, where they provide everything from meals to tents to naturalist guides. Spot trips cost about $125 per person, while full-service trips usually cost that much per day. Some reputable outfitters (also called 'pack stations') include: Virginia Lakes Pack Outfit (☎ 702-867-2591), HC Rte 1, Box 1070 A, Bridgeport, CA 93517; Bishop Pack Outfitters (☎ 619-873-4785), 247 Cataract Rd, Aspendell, CA 93514; and Rock Creek Pack Station (☎ 619-935-4493 summer, 619-872-8331 winter), PO Box 248, Bishop, CA 93514.

Getting Around

Greyhound buses travel Hwy 395 between Los Angeles and Carson City (Nevada), stopping in Lone Pine, Independence, Big Pine, Bishop, Mammoth Lakes, Lee Vining, and Bridgeport. The southbound bus leaves Carson City at 8:20 am, the northbound leaves LA at 4:35 am, for the 12½-hour trip ($59).

Each summer several hiker/backpacker shuttles are operated by sporting goods stores and/or climbing schools. Your best bet is to ask at a store in Bridgeport, Mammoth Lakes, Bishop, or Lone Pine. Backpacker Shuttle Service (☎ 619-872-2721) has a good reputation. They'll transport you to/from trailheads in the Lone Pine area for about $15 per person. Also, resorts and lodges will often provide rides to/from their location to the nearest town for a negotiable fee.

BRIDGEPORT
• *pop 500* • *elev 6500 feet* ☎ 619
Bridgeport is the first town of any importance between Carson City and Mammoth Lakes, and unlike most places along Hwy 395, it is downright cute. Its main street is

as American as apple pie, with classic old storefronts and an impressive 1880 courthouse trimmed in red and surrounded by a gracious lawn. A few blocks away in the old Bridgeport schoolhouse, the Mono County Museum (☎ 932-5281), open daily from 10 am to 5 pm (free), has one of the better historical collections in the Eastern Sierra. But Bridgeport truly lives for things out-of-doors and outside the city limits: Twin Lakes is a popular fishing destination, Bodie State Historic Park is one of California's best-preserved ghost towns, and hot springs await travelers who don't shirk nudity or wash-board roads. Bridgeport Lake, two miles north on Hwy 182 is nothing spectacular, but has plenty of fish and warm water for swimming and waterskiing.

Orientation & Information

Highway 395 jogs east through Bridgeport as Main St, with the turn-off to Twin Lakes at the west end of town and turn-off to Bridgeport Lake at the east end. Highway 270, to Bodie, heads east from Hwy 395 south of the city limits. The Bridgeport Ranger Station (☎ 932-7070), just south of town on the highway, has posted maps and issues permits (required from July 1 to August 15) for the Hoover Wilderness, accessible by trail from Twin Lakes. The best place for fishing information is Ken's Sporting Goods on Main St, open till 8 pm (9 pm Friday and Saturday). They have a variety of maps, fishing, hunting, and camping gear, and an ice box full of locally caught fish on display in front of the store. The town's laundry is one block off Main St on Sinclair, open daily from 7 am to 9 pm.

Places to Stay & Eat

All businesses are on Main St. Built as a stage stop on the road to Bodie, the *Bridgeport Inn* (☎ 932-7380) has been in operation since 1877. Supposedly there are nostalgic 'spirits' cruising the halls, though the rooms are said to be 'ghost free.' Hotel rooms cost $49 with no TV or private bathroom, and must be paid for with a credit card. Out back, modern motel rooms which look pale and sterile compared to the hotel's garish decor, cost $61. The bar has loads of charm and is a good spot for a drink, while the dining room is good for breakfast, lunch (under $10), and a fancy dinner; fresh local trout is usually available ($14).

The *Silver Maple Inn* (☎ 932-7383) has friendly owners, well-kept grounds, and nice rooms for $50 to $80. From late October to May, the *Walker River Lodge* (☎ 932-7021) is often the only place open. They have a heated pool, hot tub, and rooms for $80 to $120 in summer, $50 to $65 in winter.

About eight miles from town, off the road to Twin Lakes on Robinson Creek, *Doc and Al's Robinson Creek Resort* (☎ 932-7051) has new cabins with showers and kitchens which sleep 4 to 10 people ($63 to $93) and rustic cabins with a communal shower and toilet ($38 to $60). Campsites cost $12 ($15 with a full hookup) with use of all facilities.

Locals drink, play pool, and eat pizza at *Rhino's Bar & Grille*, but recommend the *Virginia Creek Settlement* (☎ 932-7780), 14 miles south on Hwy 395, for good steaks and Italian food (under $10).

TWIN LAKES
☎ 619

With most places open for fishing season from June to November, this is primarily a summer destination revered for its population of trout, Kamloop and Kokanee salmon, and trails to the Hoover Wilderness and eastern, lake-riddled reaches of Yosemite National Park.

The road to Twin Lakes intersects Hwy 395 at Bridgeport and heads 12 miles through pastures and foothills, past several nice campgrounds on Robinson Creek, before reaching the lower lake. Here, a dirt road goes south to *Lower Twin Lake Campground* and *Sawmill Campground*, both USFS with pit toilets, water, and $11 sites on the lake's quiet eastern shore. Past the campground turn off, *Twin Lakes Resort* (☎ 932-7751) has seven housekeeping cabins for $82 to $125, and a small store with fishing gear and information. At the west end of the upper lake, the road ends at *Mono Village* (☎ 932-7071), a huge affair that offers cheap but crowded accommodations, boat rental and launch facilities, and a greasy spoon restaurant (open daily from 6 am to 10 pm). The campground, big enough to require street signs, has $18 sites; motel rooms cost $45; and cabins without bath are $65 to $90. Trailheads begin behind Mono Village, and at the terminus of the Lower Twin Lake/Sawmill Campground Rd which has a day-use parking lot.

BUCKEYE HOT SPRINGS

These are the area's best hot springs and the hardest to find. The springs surface atop a steep embankment above Eagle Creek and trickle down into pools that have been outlined with rocks. The largest pool, right next to the creek, is cold when the creek is high. A smaller one, next to a solo tree at the top of the embankment, commands a great view of the surrounding forest. Buckeye Hot Springs Rd runs between Hwy 395 (north of Bridgeport) and Twin Lakes Rd which originates in Bridgeport and goes west; the springs are about 11 miles from both, at a half-circle turn-out on the south side of the road. West of the springs, at a bridge spanning Eagle Creek, a road goes two miles to the USFS *Buckeye Campground* with tables, fire grates, potable water, pit toilets, and $7 sites. You can camp for free in undeveloped spots along Eagle Creek on both sides of the bridge.

BODIE STATE HISTORIC PARK
☎ 619

The combination of its remote location and unrestored buildings makes Bodie one of California's most authentic ghost towns. Gold was discovered along Bodie Creek in 1859, and within 20 years the place transformed from a rough mining camp to an even rougher mining town with a population of 10,000 and a reputation for lawlessness. Hotels, saloons, gambling halls, and

GREG HERRIMAN
Find the ghosts of the gold mining past in Bodie.

brothels were centers of activity and received much of the $100 million worth of ore that came from the surrounding hills. When the gold supply petered out, people moved elsewhere (mostly to the Comstock Lode in Nevada) and left Bodie's buildings to the elements. Five percent still remain, maintained by the State Park Service but untainted by restoration work.

An excellent museum and visitors center (☎ 647-6445), open May to September, has historical maps, exhibits, and daily guided tours (free). The park is open late May to September from 9 am to 7 pm, the rest of the year from 9 am to 4 pm; there is a $5 fee per vehicle, $3 for walk-ins. Hwy 270, which connects Bodie and Hwy 395 (13 miles), is unpaved for the last three miles, and often closed in winter. There aren't any developed campgrounds around, but the park is surrounded by BLM land where dispersed camping is allowed with a campfire permit, available from the Bridgeport Ranger Station (☎ 932-7070).

Mono Lake

In 1941 the City of Los Angeles Department of Water and Power (DWP) bought most of the Mono Basin and diverted four of the five streams feeding Mono Lake to the California Aqueduct to provide water to Los Angeles. Over time, the lake level dropped 40 feet and doubled in salinity. In 1976, David Gaines began to study the environmental concerns surrounding the lake's depletion and found that it would totally dry up within about 20 years. As the major breeding ground for California gulls and habitat of eared grebes and red-necked phalaropes, this was a major threat to California's bird population. Gaines formed the Mono Lake Committee in 1979 and through numerous campaigns and court battles has managed to win water from the City of LA.

A fluke of nature aided current courtroom progress. In 1989 a heavy-snow season caused dams to overflow into previously dry spillways, re-watering streams which had not seen water for 10 years. When fish were found in the streams, the courts ruled that although the DWP technically 'owned' water rights, they could not allow the fish to die and thus were obliged to maintain the streams at a level in which fish can survive. In 1994, a landmark ruling required the lake level to rise to 6377 feet above sea level (which will take an estimated 15 years) before the DWP can take water from the lake or its tributaries. Bumper stickers and T-shirts with the 'Save Mono Lake' slogan now read 'Restore Mono Lake.' ■

VIRGINIA LAKES & LUNDY LAKE
☎ *619*

South of Bridgeport, Hwy 395 parallels Virginia Creek until it reaches Conway Summit (8138 feet) and drops down into the Mono Basin. The view south from the summit shows the area's topography, with Mono Lake, backed by the Mono Craters, backed by June and Mammoth Mountains – all products of volcanic activity.

Just north of Conway Summit, the Virginia Lakes Rd heads west along Virginia Creek to a cluster of lakes flanked by Dunberg Peak and Black Mountain. A trailhead at the end of the road gives access to the Hoover Wilderness and the Pacific

Crest Trail which continues down Cold Canyon to Yosemite National Park. There is a pocket of lakes at around 9000 feet elevation (2½ to 5 miles from the trailhead) that are said to have some of the Eastern Sierra's best fishing. In high snow seasons, the small cascades that fall from lake to lake turn into crashing waterfalls. *Virginia Lakes Resort* (☎ 937-0326) at the road's end, has a cafe and general store that sells fishing tackle and licenses.

Between Conway Summit and Mono Lake, Hwy 167 heads east to Hawthorne, Nevada, and the Lundy Lake Rd goes about five miles west to Lundy Lake. This is a gorgeous spot, often overlooked and thus uncrowded. The lake is long and narrow, with steep canyons – good for fishing and great for hiking – feeding its west end. A mining town sat above the lake's northwest end from 1879 to 1884, evident from the old mining equipment and tailings scattered about. The *Lundy Lake Resort* has tent and RV spaces ($18), showers, laundry, boat rentals, and a store. A few miles past the resort on a good dirt road is trailhead parking for the Hoover Wilderness with self-register wilderness permits. From here you can head over Lundy Pass to Saddlebag Lake, two miles north of Tioga Pass and just outside Yosemite National Park.

MONO LAKE
☎ 619

This glistening expanse of alkaline water that spreads lazily across the white-hot desert landscape is North America's second-oldest lake. Though the basin and lake are Ice Age remnants, formed more than 700,000 years ago, the area's most interesting features come from volcanic related activity. Appearing like drip sand castles on and near the lake shore, Mono's tufa (pronounced TOOfah) towers form when calcium-bearing freshwater springs bubble up through alkaline water.

Whether exploring the lake or not, the Mono Basin Scenic Area Visitor's Center (☎ 647-3044), just north of Lee Vining on Hwy 395, has a beautiful view of the lake, good interpretive displays and information.

Also a worthwhile stop, the Mono Lake Committee Visitor Center (☎ 647-6595) in Lee Vining on the west side of Hwy 395, has maps, a great selection of books and shirts, and a 20-minute free slide show about the lake's natural and political history. They also offer interpretive talks and hikes, photo excursions, and canoe tours.

There are examples of tufa towers all around the lake, but the best concentration is at the **South Tufa Reserve** on the lake's southern rim. Here a mile-long interpretive trail explains, in detail, the towers' formation. This is also a good place for swimming, although Navy Beach (just east of the Tufa Reserve) is a bit better.

Away from the lake shore, between the South Tufa Reserve and Hwy 120, is the **Panum Crater**, the youngest (about 640 years old) and smallest of the Mono Craters which string south to Mammoth Mountain. There is a nice trail around the crater rim, and a short but steep 'plug trail' that puts you at the crater's center among rock formations, shiny black obsidian, and pumice stones that resemble popcorn.

On the lake's north shore are the **Black Point Fissures**, narrow crags that opened when Black Point's lava mass cooled and contracted about 13,000 years ago. Reaching the fissures requires a substantial – but worthwhile – hike (east of the County Park off Hwy 395 or south of Hwy 167), that is usually hot and very dry. Check at one of the visitors centers before heading out.

Lee Vining
This is Mono Lake's utilitarian addition where you can eat, sleep, gas up, and buy post cards. It is also where Hwy 120 heads west over Tioga Pass to Yosemite National Park (closed in winter). There are six creekside campgrounds just west of town off Hwy 120 with pit toilets, running water, and $7 sites. Just before the turn off, the Lee Vining Ranger Station (☎ 647-3000) issues wilderness permits and has sparse information about Yosemite.

In town, the *El Mono Motel* (☎ 647-6310) has been operating since 1927 but

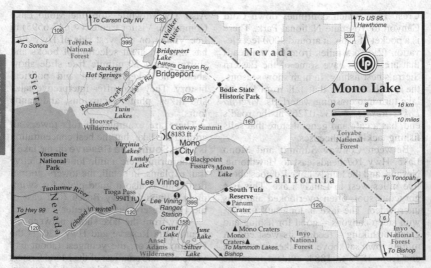

has been renovated a few times (no phones); rooms are $50 October to May, $65 to $75 in summer. A few blocks south, the *Best Western Lakeview Lodge* (☎ 647-6543) is considerably nicer, with rooms starting at $65 ($72 in summer). *Bodie Mike's Pizza* (☎ 647-6432) is a good night spot with pizza, salads, and beer for under $10. For big breakfasts, old fashioned food, and local color, go to *Nicely's Restaurant* (☎ 647-6477).

JUNE LAKE LOOP
☎ 619

Between Mono Lake and Mammoth Lakes, Hwy 158 makes a 14 mile loop west of Hwy 395. This scenic route passes Grant, Silver, Gull, and June Lakes, flanked by massive Carson Peak to the west and Reversed Peak to the east. The area could detain outdoorsy types for a good week, though it is just as easily a nice half-hour detour off Hwy 395. All of the lakes are good for trout fishing (Grant Lake has a few Kokanee salmon) and Grant and Silver Lakes both have free public boat launches. June Lake Village, a cute gathering of small businesses, is at the south end of the route. The mountains immediately west are

part of the Ansel Adams Wilderness which runs into Yosemite National Park, easily reached by trail.

Activities

At Silver Lake, the Frontier Pack Station (☎ 872-1301) has one-hour rides for $20 and week-long trips to Yosemite for about $500. Silver Lake Resort (☎ 648-7355) rents boats and fishing tackle for $6 an hour and sells fishing licenses. Between the resort and pack station, the Rush Creek Trailhead is a departure point for wilderness trips with a day-use parking lot, posted maps, and self-registration permits. From June to October a wilderness permit quota is in effect and a guardian at the trailhead issues permits on a first come, first served basis from 8 am to 4 pm. Gem and Agnew Lakes make spectacular day hikes, while Thousand Island and Emerald Lake (both on the Pacific Crest/John Muir Trail) are good overnight destinations.

On the south end of the loop near June Lake, **June Mountain Ski Area** (☎ 648-7733) is friendly, uncrowded, and fun with quite challenging slopes, long runs, and 2590 vertical feet. It was recently bought by the proprietors of Mammoth Mountain (who plan to connect the two resorts by 1996) and overhauled with new lifts and lodge facilities. There are 11 lifts and tickets cost $36.

Places to Stay & Eat
The *Silver Lake Campground* has grassy $7 sites next to Rush Creek and is near the Silver Lake Resort (below). There are two reservation campgrounds (☎ 800-280-2267) on June Lake, each with running water and $14 sites: the *June Lake Campground* is small and shady, but crowded by June Lake Village and Marina; the *Oh Ridge Campground*, on an arid ridge above the lake's south end, has nice views and beach access but not much shade. Across from Oh Ridge is a family-style private campground with a store, hot showers ($3), and $12 sites.

The *Silver Lake Resort* (☎ 648-7525) is a hub of activity, with a store, showers ($2.50), and woodsy cabins for around $60. Their cafe serves excellent pancakes, large omelets, and lunch from 6 am to 2 pm. Between Silver and Gull Lakes, the *Fern Creek Lodge* (☎ 800-621-9146) isn't lakeside, but has nice cabins for $45 ($180 for up to eight people) with kitchen and fireplace. They have a well-stocked store, and restaurant, and laundry across the street, all open from daily 7 am to 9 pm.

In June Lake Village, the *Heidelberg Inn* (☎ 648-7781, 800-483-6493) has an old Bavarian exterior with modern American rooms and cabins starting at $70. Across the road, next to its namesake, the *Big Rock Resort* (☎ 648-7717) has nice cabins for $68 to $115, and the *Boulder Lodge* (☎ 648-7533) has a pool, tennis courts, and worn in rooms and cabins starting at $49. *Schat's Dutch Bakery* (☎ 648-7613) is a good breakfast and lunch stop, while the *Tiger Bar* (☎ 648-7551) is the place to be in the evening (especially during ski season) for burgers, fish, and beer.

MAMMOTH LAKES
☎ 619

Mammoth Lakes is mostly just called 'Mammoth,' an indication of how much attention the lakes themselves get. While the pocket of alpine lakes west of town are as beautiful as any in the Sierra, Mammoth Mountain, with its world-class skiing and summertime mountain bike park, attracts more visitors. The town is basically a conglomeration of shopping centers and condominiums, with no particular center, spread over a few sq miles. Its lack of charm is made up for by its friendly, laidback atmosphere, good restaurants, not-too-pricey accomodations, and the stellar surroundings.

Orientation & Information
At the Mammoth Lakes turn-off from Hwy 395, Rte 203 heads west for three miles to central Mammoth. At the first major intersection, Rte 203 becomes Main St and Old Mammoth Rd heads south to Old Mammoth, the original town site, and Mammoth Basin. At the second intersection, on the east end of town, Main St makes a sharp turn north and becomes Minaret Rd which dead-ends at Mammoth Mountain Ski Area Main Lodge. Straight ahead from the second intersection, Lake Mary Rd goes to Mammoth Basin. Most businesses are on Main St between the intersections, and south on Old Mammoth Rd where it crosses Meridian Blvd.

The Mammoth Lakes Ranger Station (☎ 924-5500) and Mammoth Lakes Visitors Bureau (☎ 800-367-6572) share a new building on the north side of Rte 203, just before Old Mammoth Rd. This one-stop information center issues wilderness permits and has accommodations and campground listings, road and trail condition updates, and information on local attractions. At the Old Mammoth Rd/Meridian Blvd junction, Minaret Village Shopping Center has a bank, supermarket, movie theater (☎ 934-3240), and bookstore.

Historic Mammoth
Believe it or not, Mammoth did not spring to life with the invention of the chair lift. It was originally a mining and lumber town with stamp mills, sawmills, flumes, waterwheels, and a rough-and-tumble main

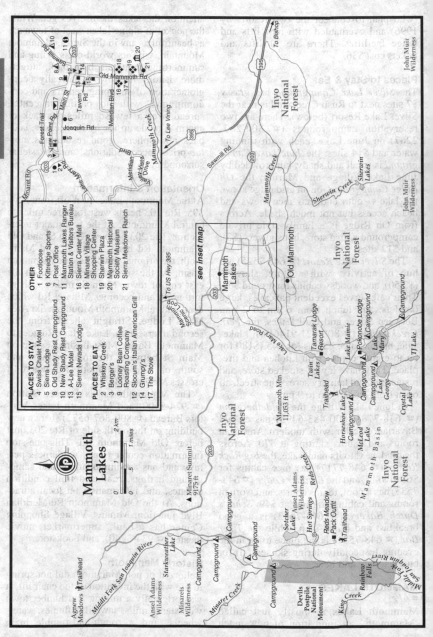

street of tent cabins and saloons. Most of the town, on the west end of Old Mammoth Rd, was burned to cinders, but a 14-foot fly wheel and some other old structures remain. The Mammoth Historical Society Museum (☎ 934-6918), just east of where Old Mammoth Rd turns abruptly west, has the most evidence of the old town in photographs and gives out tour maps for the old town. It's open June to October daily from 9:30 am to 4:30 pm (free).

Devils Postpile National Monument
This monument's 60-foot, multi-sided columns of blue-gray basalt are the most conspicuous and interesting product of the area's volcanic activity. The columns formed when lava, which flowed through Mammoth Pass, cooled and fractured vertically. A glacier came through later to give them their cracked, shiny surface. Surrounding the monument, **Reds Meadow** has terrific camping and fishing, and a well-used 1½-mile trail to Rainbow Falls, a 101-foot sheet cascade. Reds Meadow Pack Station (☎ 934-2345) has a reputable horseback-riding school and pack trips into the Minarets Wilderness.

You must visit the area by shuttle, since Minaret Rd (the only access) is closed to cars from 7:30 am to 5:30 pm, unless you have 11 or more people, a camping permit for one of the area's campgrounds, or overnight reservations at Reds Meadow Pack Station (see Places to Stay). Shuttles leave about every half hour from the Mammoth Mountain Inn, across from the ski area's Main Lodge ($7 roundtrip), and stop at campgrounds, view points, the Devils Postpile Visitors Center (☎ 934-2289), where the half-mile trail to the columns begins, and Reds Meadow Pack Station; you can get on and off as much as you like.

Mammoth Mountain Ski Area
This is a true recreationalist's resort, where playing hard and having fun are more important than whose name is on your ski parka. The mountain (☎ 934-2571), an inactive volcanic peak, has 27 chair lifts,

two gondolas, and enough terrain to keep anyone – beginner to expert – busy for a week. The combination of tree-line and open bowl skiing is great and the 3100 vertical feet give some long cruising runs, as well as vertically steep slopes at the top. There are three hubs at the base of the mountain – **Main Lodge, Warming Hut 2,** and **Chair 2 Outpost** – each with parking and ticket sales. The Main Lodge and Hut 2 have rental shops and ski schools.

In summer, the Main Lodge area has a rock-climbing wall, orienteering courses, and outdoor concerts (at the Yodeler Pavilion, across the main parking lot), while the ski runs are used as a mountain bike park ($20 lift ticket, $35 bike rentals). This is the site of the Kamikaze Downhill, held the last weekend in June, the fastest mountain bike race on the circuit. A free shuttle (☎ 934-0686) connects the mountain to motels and shopping centers of downtown Mammoth during ski season, July and August, and a new monorail (known as 'the toaster') connects Main Lodge and Chair 2.

Other Activities
Downhill skiing and mountain biking are best on Mammoth Mountain. There are numerous rental shops around town, with competitive prices and good equipment; these are the best places to get trail suggestions and information about guided trips. Footloose (☎ 934-2400), on Minaret Rd north of Main St, is good for ski rentals and equipment, while Mammoth Sporting Goods (☎ 934-3239), in the Sierra Center Mall at the Old Mammoth Rd/Meridian Blvd junction, has a good general selection. Kittredge Sports (☎ 934-7566), on Main St west of Old Mammoth Rd, is good for backpacking gear.

Hiking There are three main trailheads, all with parking lots, good day-hikes, and longer trails over the Sierra crest: Horseshoe Lake, in Mammoth Basin, is at a high elevation so you needn't hike far to reach alpine scenery and has a good trail down into Red's Meadow; also in Mammoth

Basin, Lake Mary gives easy access to small alpine lakes backed by the impressive Mammoth Crest; trails from Agnew Meadows (on the Devils Postpile/Reds Meadow Rd, accessible by shuttle bus) go north along the Pacific Crest/John Muir Trail into the Minaret Wilderness, surrounded by some of the Sierra's most stunning sawtooth peaks and cirque lakes.

Cross-Country Skiing In winter, the above-mentioned trails (especially to Reds Meadow) are popular with backcountry skiers. Right in town, behind New Shady Rest Campground (near the visitors bureau), Blue Diamond Trails has 30 km of groomed trails maintained by the USFS. South of town on Old Mammoth Rd (where it turns west), Sierra Meadows Ranch (☎ 934-6161) has groomed trails in a wide open meadow (good for beginners) with views of Mammoth Mountain and Mammoth Rock. The Tamarack Cross Country Ski Center, in Mammoth Basin, has groomed track and skating lanes, marked backcountry trails, and a rustic lodge (see Places to Stay) with rentals and lessons; $15 day pass, $15 rentals.

Places to Stay
Mammoth Properties Reservations (☎ 800-227-7669) has an armada of condominiums and cabins available for rent – a practical and affordable option for large groups.

Camping The USFS 'Campground Schedule,' available at the ranger station, lists all campgrounds' fees, number of sites, and elevations. The nicest campgrounds around are in Mammoth Basin, on the shores of Twin Lakes, Lake Mary, and Lake George.

They're first-come, first-served, with flush toilets and lovely $14 sites. There are seven USFS campgrounds off Minaret Rd, out towards Devils Postpile, on the Middle Fork of the San Joaquin River. All of these offer great fishing and hiking, and have reservable sites ($10, ☎ 800-280-2267) that fill up quickly. Campground reservations allow you to drive into this area, otherwise restricted to the Devils Postpile/Reds Monument shuttle bus. Less scenic but handy to town are *New Shady Rest* and *Old Shady Rest Campgrounds*, behind the visitors bureau on Rte 203. These have $14 first-come, first-served sites, flush toilets, ranger programs, and lots of kids.

Motels The *A-Lee Motel* (☎ 934-6709) 1548 Tavern Rd, is the cheapest place in town, with no frill rooms starting at $38. Almost identical, the *Swiss Chalet Motel* (☎ 934-2403), is at 3776 View Point Rd which swings north of Main St just east of the Minaret intersection. A bit nicer, the *Sierra Nevada Lodge* (☎ 934-2515), 164 Old Mammoth Rd, has been here forever. It has a cozy lobby, hot tub, and $48 to $56 rooms, more in winter. The *Sierra Lodge* (☎ 934-8881, 800-356-5711), on Main St halfway between Old Mammoth Rd and Minaret, is a good choice with new rooms for $75, more on weekends and winter. A good value for its location and amenities, the elegant *Mammoth Mountain Inn* (☎ 934-2581, 800-228-4947), across from the Main Lodge, has standard rooms ($85), four-person suites ($115), and lofts for up to 13 people ($175); prices are $25 higher on winter weekends.

Lodges On the shore of Lower Twin Lake, *Tamarack Lodge Resort* (☎ 934-2442, 800-237-6879) is charming, rustic, and run by friendly people. The cozy lodge has a fireplace, bar and reading area where guests congregate, and excellent restaurant. In winter it's a popular cross-country ski spot, so rates are at their highest: rooms are $80 ($60 with shared bath) and cabins start at $120; prices are more on weekends. Less expensive, *Pokonobe Lodge & Marina*

(☎ 934-2437) has simple old cabins on the north end of Lake Mary for $65 to $85 (summer only). The Reds Meadow Pack Station (☎ 873-3928) in Reds Meadow occasionally rents cabins to non-clients – a good deal at $45 (shared bath).

Places to Eat

The place to be in the morning is *Looney Bean Coffee Roasting Company* (☎ 934-1345), on Main St just west of Old Mammoth Rd, with strong brew fueling many a hike and ski; they have a few breakfast items (good homemade granola) and sandwiches. For bigger breakfasts, *The Stove* (☎ 934-2821), on Old Mammoth Rd south of Meridian, is the all-time favorite, with three-egg omelets, blueberry pancakes, and juice served in Mason jars. Across the street in Sherwin Plaza, *Anything Goes* (☎ 934-2424) steams their eggs with an espresso machine! They have excellent soups and salads for lunch (under $10), and a seasonal dinner menu (starts at $11) with good vegetarian options. The best burgers in town are at *Berger's* (☎ 934-6622), on Minaret Rd north of the Main St intersection, open for lunch and dinner.

Dining and drinking are integral to Mammoth's nightlife, especially in winter. *Whiskey Creek* (☎ 934-2555), at the Main St/Minaret Rd intersection, is an old standby with unexciting but reliable food ($10 to $15), a good bar scene, and live music. *Slocum's Italian American Grill* (☎ 934-7647) on Main St east of Old Mammoth Rd, is a good splurge, with excellent grilled meat and fish, creative pasta specials, and nice ambiance. The sand volleyball court at *Grumpy's* (☎ 934-8587), on Old Mammoth Rd just south of Main St, is a popular summer hangout and the saloon is full year round; the straightforward menu features chili and hot sandwiches.

Getting There & Away

Mammoth Airport, southeast of town off Hwy 395, is mostly for private planes, though TW Express (☎ 800-221-2000) has one daily flight to San Francisco, and two to Los Angeles.

Greyhound buses stop at McDonald's parking lot, across from the visitors bureau on Rte 203. The southbound bus comes through at 12:30 pm, the northbound at 1:30 am; buy tickets onboard.

AROUND MAMMOTH LAKES
☎ 619

Convict Lake

Five miles south of Mammoth and two miles west of Hwy 395, this is one of the prettiest lakes in the area, with lucid emerald water and two massive peaks – Mt Morrison and Laurel Mountain – as a backdrop. The lake is named for a group of unfortunate convicts that only made it this far after a jail break. A gentle trail goes around the lake, through aspen and cottonwood trees, and a trailhead on the southeast shore goes to Genevieve, Edith, Dorothy, and Mildred Lakes in the John Muir Wilderness.

Below the lake on an arid ridge, the USFS *Convict Lake Campground* has terraced sites ($10), flush toilets, and a view of the Owens Valley. Nearby, the *Restaurant at Convict Lake* (☎ 943-3803) is popular with Mammoth locals. It has a nice bar, burgers for lunch ($5), and pasta, leg of lamb, and grilled venison for dinner ($10 to $15).

Rock Creek

The road up Rock Creek Canyon climbs past big boulders and wide meadows to end at the Mosquito Flat parking lot – the highest point reached by car in the Eastern Sierra at 10,300 feet. From here there are easy trails to Little Lakes Valley, where you expect Heidi to come yodeling through the hills at any moment. The scenery here is about as good as it gets on a day hike. Longer trails go over Mono Pass to the John Muir Wilderness. Some people come just for the homemade pie (often gone by 2 pm) at the *Rock Creek Resort*, on Rock Creek Lake, which also has showers ($3), camping supplies, and fishing licenses.

There are 10 USFS campgrounds along the nine-mile stretch between Hwy 395 and Mosquito Flat, all first-come, first-served, with $11 sites and flush toilets. Favorites are *Pine Grove*, *Upper Pine Grove*, both small, shady, and near a meadow where wild iris blooms, and *Big Meadow*; *East Fork* is the largest. The campground at *Rock Creek Lake*, just before Mosquito Flat, has $3 walk-in sites, and group sites at water's edge. A ranger kiosk at the canyon entrance posts current campground availability and issues wilderness permits.

In winter, the place turns into a Nordic ski paradise, and *Rock Creek Lodge* (☎ 935-4170) has the run of the place. Cabins are cozy and rustic, and for $70 per person you get a ride to the lodge from where the road closes, excellent breakfast and dinner, and plenty of good conversation.

BISHOP
•*pop 3680* ☎ 619
The largest town south of Mammoth Lakes, Bishop is a major pit stop for Southern Californians on a weekend recreation mission. The old part of town has classic Western Americana character, with covered sidewalks, classic 1950s neon signs, and hunting and fishing stores aplenty. If you like country music, chewing tobacco, and mounted antlers, this is a good place to have a drink (any bar will do). The new parts of town, along the highway north and south, are just utilitarian sprawl with fast food restaurants, chain motels, and gas stations. During 'Mule Days,' the last weekend in May, the town hosts horse and mule events (some serious but most silly) and everyone becomes a cowhand.

Orientation & Information
Bishop has Hwy 395's sharpest curve, where it meets Hwy 6 (to Benton, Nevada) at a right angle. The town extends south of this junction for about three miles along Hwy 395 (Main St), with the old part surrounding the intersection of Hwy 395 and Hwy 168 (Line St) which goes west into the mountains and separates north and south Main St. The White Mountain Visitor Center & Ranger Station (☎ 873-2500), 798 N Main St, issues wilderness permits and has trail and campground information

for the White Mountains, Big Pine, Rock, and Bishop Creek Recreation Areas. A few doors south, the visitors center and chamber of commerce (☎ 873-8405), in front of the City Park on the highway, has information on Death Valley and Mammoth Lakes.

Laws Railroad Museum
Off Hwy 6, four miles northeast of Bishop, this extensive collection (☎ 873-5950) of old buildings is worth at least an hour's stop. The central exhibit is the 1883 Laws railroad depot, a train and passenger depot which serviced the narrow-gauge line used to transport people and agriculture from near Carson City to just south of Lone Pine through the then-fertile Owens Valley. Other historic buildings, including Bishop's first church, have been moved here and hold antiques and exhibits of all kinds. Hours are daily 10 am to 4 pm; admission is $2.

Paiute Shoshone Indian Cultural Center
Just west of central Bishop, the land is part of the Bishop Indian Reservation, the northernmost of four in the Owens Valley. A few miles out Hwy 168, the center acts as administrative headquarters, a gathering place for tribal members, and an educational facility for the general public. Displays show the basketry, tools, clothing, and dwellings of Paiute and Shoshone tribes, and give thorough explanations of Indian life and culture – historic and modern. It opens weekdays from 9 am to 5 pm, weekends 10 am to 4 pm.

Activities
The Owens River Gorge, nine miles north of town on the east side of Hwy 395, has excellent rock climbing and the Buttermilk Hills, west of town on both sides of Hwy 168, are good for bouldering. Most staff at Wilson's Eastside Sports (☎ 873-7520), 206 N Main St, are experienced climbers with good route suggestions; the shop rents equipment and sells maps and guide books.

Nine miles west of town, Hwy 168 heads into the Sierra along both forks of Bishop

Creek. The south fork ends at South Lake, surrounded by jagged peaks, and the north fork ends at Sabrina Basin, with Lake Sabrina and North Lake as its dual centerpiece. Fishing is good in all of the lakes (North Lake is least crowded), and hiking trails from them lead through the John Muir Wilderness to Sequoia National Park. Rainbow Packers (☎ 873-4177) within Parcher's Resort near South Lake, have one-hour horseback rides for $20. At North Lake, Bishop Pack Outfitters (formerly Schober's, ☎ 873-4785) is recommended for long pack trips.

Places to Stay

Camping On the south edge of town, family-style *Brown's Campgrounds* (☎ 872-8533) has grassy sites for $10 ($13 with hookups), showers, a laundry, nightly movies, and a game room.

Eleven USFS campgrounds along Bishop Creek, nine miles west of town via Hwy 168, are surrounded by trees and are close to fishing and hiking (see Activities). A ranger kiosk on the highway (just before the road splits), has maps and information. *Willow Campground* on the south fork, and *Sabrina Campground* on the north, are recommended.

Motels Most places in Bishop are along Hwy 395, with unexciting rooms for $40 to $60. Rooms at the *Village Motel* (☎ 873-3546), one block east of Hwy 395 on Elm St (north end of town), are old but clean and cost $37. The *Outdoorsman Motor Lodge* (☎ 873-6381) has a nice guest lobby, coffee, and donuts, and rooms for $36/42 per single/double. A bit newer, the *Bishop Inn* (☎ 873-4284, 800-576-4080), 805 N Main St, has a pool, spa, and rooms for $52/63. Bishop's deluxe accommodations are the *Creekside Inn* (☎ 872-3044, 800-273-3550), 725 N Main St, with two pools, a hot tub, continental breakfast, and $90 rooms.

Places to Eat

A mandatory stop for anyone passing through, *Erick Schat's Bakkery* (☎ 873-

7156), 763 N Main, started making shepherd bread in 1938 and has been going strong ever since. Now they have a soup-salad-sandwich bar, and espresso drinks. *Amigos Mexican Restaurant* (☎ 872-2189), 285 N Main, serves coastal Mexican food (good fish tacos and ceviche), and *Jack's Waffle Shop* (☎ 872-7971), 437 N Main, has straightforward coffeeshop food. *Whiskey Creek* (☎ 873-7174), 524 N Main, has a nice bar and patio, good food, and the town's freshest atmosphere.

BISHOP TO LONE PINE
☎ 619

Big Pine & Big Pine Creek

While Big Pine is nothing in itself, it offers a place to stay while exploring the Ancient Bristlecone Pine Forest (below). The *Bristlecone Motel* (☎ 938-2067) has large, old rooms with phone and TV ($35), and showers for non-guests ($3). The *Big Pine Motel* (☎ 938-2282) and *Starlight Motel* (☎ 938-2011) are the other two options, with similar rooms and rates.

West of Big Pine via Glacier Lodge Rd (the only stop light in town), Big Pine Creek Canyon has good camping, fishing, and hiking. Campsites are $9 with pit toilets, and about half are reservable (☎ 800-280-2267); an information kiosk at the canyon entrance has information and wilderness permits. The scenery here is not spectacular compared to canyons further north, but trails lead to the Palisade Glacier – the southernmost in the US and largest in the Sierra. Glacial run-off turns the lakes below a milky turquoise color which looks great on film. It's a three-mile hike to the first waterfalls, another 1½-miles before you reach a lake, then another two to see the glacier; experienced mountaineers climb its icy face with crampons and ice picks – fun to watch.

Ancient Bristlecone Pine Forest

The Great Basin bristlecone pines found here are the oldest living things on earth, some over 4000 years old. The oldest trees are squatty and gnarled, with exposed roots and wide-reaching limbs. Soil depletion takes place at a rate of six inches per 1000 years here, telling the age of those trees whose roots are a few feet above ground. Visiting the forest is an all day affair but worth the time and effort, if only for the astonishing view of the Sierra Nevada and Owens Valley from atop the White Mountains. Dry and stark, this range was once higher than the Sierra but is much older and thus heavily eroded.

To reach the forest, head northeast from Hwy 395 on Hwy 168 (just north of Big Pine) and follow the signs up, up, up the curvy road to where it ends at a visitors center and parking lot. From here, there are self-guiding trails ($1 brochures at the trailhead) through different groves. The longest one, 4½ miles, offers views of the Sierra and Deep Springs Valley (east) and passes the Methuselah 'Forest of the Ancients' where the very oldest trees are. A dirt road (popular with mountain bikers) continues on past the Patriarch Grove Picnic Area, a little-used facility among a stand of bristlecones, to the Mt Bancroft Research Station, run by the University of California, Berkeley.

The only place to stay up here is at *Grandview Campground*, before the visitors center, which has an awesome view and $7 sites; bring your own water.

Independence
This sleepy highway town, named for a Civil War fort founded here on Independence Day (1862), has a few unlikely attractions. One block west of Hwy 395 on Market St, is Mary Austin's (an early American author) childhood home with a nostalgia-ridden plaque on the gate. Further west on Market St, the **Eastern California Museum** (☎ 878-2010) has an excellent Paiute basket display, an old California guidebook library, and thorough exhibit about Manzanar (below) and its residents. It opens from 10 am to 4 pm (closed Tuesday); free. Across from the stately courthouse on the highway, the 1927 *Winnedumah Hotel B&B* (☎ 878-2040) has a rustic lobby with games, a fireplace, and piano that once entertained Gary Cooper,

Bing Crosby, and Gabby Hayes; cute historic rooms cost $45.

West of town via Onion Valley Rd (Market St in town), Onion Valley offers two nice campgrounds and a trailhead for the Kearsarge Pass Trail, an old Paiute trade route. This offers the shortest backside access to Kings Canyon National Park. Golden Trout Lakes, northwest from the trailhead, is a good day-hike destination. There is a ranger station at the end of the road with posted maps, trail information, and wilderness permits. A herd of California Bighorn Sheep live south of Onion Valley around Shepherd Pass, in the upper reaches of the John Muir Wilderness.

Manzanar National Historic Site
Two months after the Japanese bombed Pearl Harbor, President Roosevelt signed an order for all Japanese on the West Coast to be placed in relocation camps. Manzanar was the first permanent camp, built in 1942 among pear and apple orchards five miles south of Independence. At full operation, Manzanar held 10,000 people in its one sq mile and was one of the biggest 'towns' (the only one surrounded by sentry posts and barbed wire) in Owens Valley. Not much remains of the parks, rock gardens, or buildings, though the large wooden auditorium still stands. Roads through the camp are very sandy, so your best bet is to park at the entrance (on Hwy 395, marked by two stone, pagoda-like police posts) and explore by foot. The best educational material and artifacts regarding the site are in the Eastern California Museum in Independence. There aren't any facilities or interpretive displays at the site.

LONE PINE
• *pop 2800* • *elev 8371 feet* ☎ 619

Lone Pine is famous for three things: the Alabama Hills, Mt Whitney, and the turnoff for Death Valley. Founded in the 1800s as a supply post for Owens Valley ranchers and farmers, Lone Pine experienced a boom during 1850s mining activity and then 100 years later when movie stars such as Cary Grant, Gary Cooper, and Hopalong

CALIFORNIA

Cassidy made movies in the Alabama Hills, just west of town. Nowadays, recreationalists are more numerous than movie stars and Lone Pine has turned into somewhat of a tourists' crossroads, 90 miles from Death Valley and 14 miles from Whitney Portal, the departure point for ambitious hikers. The locals, however, look more like they belong in an old Western than in a modern sports video.

South of Lone Pine, Hwy 395 passes what *was* Owens Lake, now drained to water lawns in Los Angeles, and continues through the desert-like southern part of the Owens Valley. From here you can see where the Sierra Nevada tapers to an unexciting end, arid and stark compared to its northern reaches.

Orientation & Information

Highway 395 runs through Lone Pine as Main St, lined with motels, gas stations, restaurants, and a bank. Whitney Portal Rd heads west from Hwy 395 at the town's one stop light, and Hwy 136 to Death Valley heads southeast from Hwy 395 two miles south of town.

The Interagency Visitor Center (☎ 876-6222), two miles south of town at the Hwy 395/136 junction, has exhibits, books, maps, trail, and campground information for Death Valley and all of the Sierra Nevada, plus clean restrooms and potable water; it's open daily from 7 am to 6 pm. The Mt Whitney Ranger Station (☎ 876-6200), on Main St in Lone Pine, issues wilderness permits and has local trail and road conditions posted. The *Lone Pine Visitor Guide*, a newspaper published by the chamber of commerce (☎ 876-4444) is available at most shops and restaurants, and has local maps and some well-planned daytrip itineraries. There's a coin-op laundry just off the highway on Post St, open daily 8 am to 7 pm.

Alabama Hills

These hills, remnants of a mountain range much older than the Sierra Nevada, consist of big red boulders and outcroppings surrounded by sage and scrub. If the scene looks familiar, it's because numerous old films including *How the West Was Won* and *Gunga Din* were made here. Movie Rd, west of town via Whitney Portal Rd, makes a loop around the hills and passes near most of the film locations (the Interagency Visitor Center has a history sheet and map for locating the exact spots). The films take center stage at the Lone Pine Film Festival, held the first weekend in October. When Hollywood's elite were in town, they stayed at the Dow Villa Motel (still in operation) and carved their names (still visible) in the walls at the trading post on Main St. There are no developed trails among the hills, but the sparse brush makes for easy wandering – just keep an eye out for rattlesnakes.

Places to Stay & Eat

The one star attraction among Lone Pine's typical highway motels is the *Dow Villa Hotel* (☎ 800-824-9317), 310 S Main St, which lodged movie stars like John Wayne when they came to make movies in the Alabama Hills. Built in 1923, the place has been updated but still retains much charm. There is a comfortable lobby, TV room and library, and an outdoor pool. Rooms in the hotel ($23 to $40) share a bath, while those in the modern motel section ($56 to $62) have their own. Other good lodging options include the *Mt Whitney Motel* (☎ 876-4207), 305 N Main St, with a pool and quiet, modern rooms for $36 to $55, and the *Best Western Frontier* (☎ 876-5571), south of town on Hwy 395, with standard rooms for $50 and deluxe rooms for four people for $79, including a light breakfast.

Locals recommend *PJ's Cafe*, 446 S Main St, which is open 24 hours. The *Totem Cafe*, 131 S Main St, serves big breakfasts and fresh salads and sandwiches until 5 pm. *Sierra Cantina*, 123 N Main St, has a nice all-you-can-eat buffet with vegetarian options.

Twenty miles south of Lone Pine in **Olancha**, the *Ranch House* (☎ 764-2363) is the area's best place to eat. In a dilapidated ranch house with high ceilings, big wooden booths, and red-checked table-cloths, this unlikely destination serves down-home American food like corn bread, biscuits and gravy, sheepherder's potatoes, soupy ranch-style beans (a good vegetarian dish), and homemade pie. Breakfast and lunch are under $10, dinner is $8 to $14; it's open daily 6 am to 10 pm.

AROUND LONE PINE
☎ 619

Whitney Portal

You needn't be a mountain climber to enjoy this pine oasis, tucked away below the Sierra's highest peaks, 13 miles west of Lone Pine via Whitney Portal Rd. Though most traffic is headed to the highest point of the continental US – 14,494-foot Mt Whitney – there are trails, campgrounds, and waterfalls right at the portal, a nice side trip for anyone. The campground here has

> ### Climbing Mt Whitney
> At 14,494 feet, Mt Whitney is the highest point in the contiguous 48 states, climbed by over 2000 people a year. Though the trail to the summit is well-marked and maintained, it challenges the average body with its elevation gain: about 6000 feet over 11 miles (an unmarked 'mountaineers route' makes the same climb in four miles). Most people in good physical condition can make the climb, especially if they take a few days to do it. Often the biggest problem is getting a wilderness permit. Inquire at the Lone Pine Ranger Station because with a permit, you can stay at one of two basecamps along the route, adjust to the altitude, and make the summit without carrying too much weight. Without a permit you have to make the hike in one day which often leads to altitude sickness and fatigue. If you go for it, bring a flashlight in case you don't make it all the way down by sunset. A recommended guide is *Mt Whitney Guide for Hikers & Climbers* by Paul Hellweg & Scott McDonald (1994). ∎

lovely terraced sites ($10) next to a creek, pit toilets, and potable water. The drawback is availability: most sites are reservable (☎ 800-280-2267) and the others fill up quickly. There's a better chance at the first-come, first-served walk-in campgrounds, adjacent to the main campground, with the same facilities and $3 sites. The tiny Whitney Portal Store sells maps, outdoors gear, and a few groceries, and makes good burgers ($4) and 12-inch pancakes that cost 'a buck' each – eat three and they're free. This is also the place to get trail information from people coming off the mountain (the store owner has made the summit over 50 times).

The Whitney Trail is nice for hiking even if you don't hit the top, and the Meysan Lakes Trail, from the back of the campground, offers a low-key hike past beautiful meadows and lakes. Before the CCC paved Whitney Portal Rd, climbers started the Whitney ascent in Lone Pine. Four miles of this early trail were recently restored to make a scenic low-elevation hike between the Portal and Lone Pine Campground, well-signed off Whitney Portal Rd. The campground is hot and dry, but a good alternative if the Portal campground is full; sites are $10 with running water and pit toilets.

Horseshoe Meadows

Six miles from Lone Pine off Whitney Portal Rd, Horseshoe Meadows Rd heads south and climbs a series of steep switchbacks to reach Horseshoe Meadows Recreation Area at 10,000 feet. The elevation makes for an desolate landscape with short trees scattered sparsely over a sand and rock ground cover. Most people come here to fish and hike the trails which head into the Golden Trout Wilderness over Cottonwood and Trail Passes. Cottonwood Lakes, a native home to golden trout, is a popular day hike destination with good fishing. Longer hikes, over the Sierra Crest, lead to Sequoia National Park in the west. The trailheads are well-marked from a day-use parking lot at the end of the approach road, where there is also a picnic area and campground with large, open sites ($11) and flush toilets. The Cottonwood Pack Station (☎ 878-2015), the only business up here, does spot trips into High Sierra camps for about $300 per person.

Los Angeles

LA is a survivor. It seems to be always at the mercy of nature's whims (from devastating earthquakes and drought to almost-annual mudslides and brush fires) and society's vagaries (from race riots to crimes of passion that make soap operas look maudlin). Yet it continues to grow and flourish, attracting a United Nations of immigrants from Latin America, the Pacific Rim, and countries around the globe. Despite its natural disasters, crime and violence, jammed freeways, poor air quality, and so-called plastic personality, LA is a place that no traveler should omit from a 'must see' list.

The big houses, fast cars, fancy clothes, elegant restaurants, and designer drugs, of which LA has more than its share, may be the aggrandizement of 'the American dream.' They are a statement of LA mentality: what you see may be gone tomorrow, so live as fully as possible today.

In Southern California, where cinema is the ultimate art form, and 'The Industry' (as motion picture production is known) willingly shields its public from the 'real world,' it's sometimes hard to separate fact from fiction. You can't avoid The Industry if you try: round one corner, police have cordoned off a major building while filming takes place inside; and every third person you speak to is a budding actress serving cocktails (as she waits for her agent to call back) or a struggling screenwriter parking cars.

The City of Los Angeles is relatively small compared to the metropolis with which its name is synonymous. Hollywood, for instance, is a part of LA, while West Hollywood and Beverly Hills are separate cities. A network of freeways at once makes sense and nonsense of this urban sprawl, connecting all corners but creating a metropolis with no real nucleus. Consequently, Angelenos have an almost total dependence on the automobile... and in recent years the cellular telephone.

HISTORY

The earliest residents of the LA area were the Gabrieleño Indians and the Chumash Indians, who arrived between 5000 and 6000 BC. The Gabrielenos were hunters and gatherers who lived inland (their staple food was the acorn, finely ground and made into bread or porridge), while the Chumash lived on the coast as masterful sea trawlers whose middens of discarded shells reached 30 feet high. Rain was too scarce and inconsistent for sustained agriculture.

The first European known to have laid eyes upon the Los Angeles basin was Juan Rodriguez Cabrillo, who sailed the coast in 1542. He observed a brown haze over the landscape – from campfires at the Gabrieleño village of Yangna, located near the modern LA city center – and called Santa Monica Bay, from which he looked, *Bahia de los Fumos,* or 'Bay of Smokes.' LA's fabled smog has been around longer than most folks might have imagined.

The Mission Era

There were two in greater LA: the Mission San Gabriel Archangel, built in 1771, and the Mission San Fernando Rey de España, founded in 1797. (Restorations can still be visited.) The Gabrieleños who gathered at these missions and built their communities around them had no previous concept of heaven or hell, but they traded hard labor for salvation, meanwhile exposing themselves to a variety of diseases, from measles to syphilis, that effectively wiped out their people.

In 1781, the missions embarked on a plan to create separate agricultural communities to produce food and support their expansion. Forty-four *pobladores,* or settlers, were assigned from San Gabriel to establish a new town near the village of Yangna, on the banks of a cottonwood-lined stream about nine miles southwest of the mission. The town they established, El

CALIFORNIA

Pueblo de Nuestro Señora la Reina de los Angeles del Río Porciúncula ('The Town of Our Lady the Queen of the Angels of the Porciuncula River'), was named for a saint whose feast day had just been celebrated.

Los Angeles, as the pueblo became known, grew into a thriving farming community. Taking full advantage of long sunny days and limited water, the settlers developed orange and olive groves, vineyards and wheat fields, and herds of cattle, sheep, and horses.

Ranchos

Upon Mexican independence in 1821, many of that new nation's citizens looked to California to satisfy their thirst for private land. By the mid-1830s, the missions had been secularized, with a series of governors doling out hundreds of free land grants. This gave birth to the rancho system. The *rancheros*, as the new landowners were called, prospered and quickly became the social, cultural, and political fulcrums of California.

Joseph Chapman, a blond Boston millwright-cum-pirate, became the first Yankee, or *Yanqui*, Angeleno in 1818; he was known as *El Inglés*, 'The Englishman.' Others followed slowly; by the mid-1830s there were still only 29 US citizens residing in Los Angeles. But these few would buy entire shiploads of imported goods from seafarers and in exchange deliver full cargoes of 40,000 hides. In setting up a system of credit for rancheros, they established California's first banking system.

Jedediah Smith, who established the first overland route to the states, arrived at the San Gabriel mission from across the Sierra Nevada in 1826. Kit Carson, a legend of the American West, helped pave the Santa Fe Trail to Los Angeles in 1832. But most Easterners didn't know much about Los Angeles until 1840, when Richard Henry Dana's *Two Years Before the Mast*, gave an account of his mid-1830s experience in the coastal hide-and-tallow trade. 'In the hands of an enterprising people, what a country this might be,' Dana wrote of Los Angeles, then with a population of just over 1200.

From Small Town to Big City

With California statehood, Los Angeles was incorporated (on April 4, 1850) and made the seat of broad Los Angeles County. It was an unruly city of dirt streets and adobe homes, of saloons, brothels, and gambling houses that thrived on the fast buck. But by 1854, Northern California's Gold Rush had peaked and the state was thrust into a depression. As unemployed miners swarmed to LA and other cities, banks and businesses that had harnessed their futures to miners' fortunes closed their doors.

But a bit of wheeling and dealing brought a railroad spur line to LA in 1876, via the San Joaquin Valley. In 1885, the Atchison, Topeka & Santa Fe Railroad directly linked LA across the Arizona desert to the East Coast, and the competition dropped coast-to-coast rail rates to a mere $1 per person.

Coincidental with the arrival of the railroad was the establishment of an orange-growing industry in Southern California. Around 1874, three Brazilian navel (seedless) orange trees were shipped from the federal Department of Agriculture to Eliza and Luther Tibbetts, botanists in Riverside, a town east of LA.

As California oranges found their way onto New York grocery shelves, coupled with a hard-sell chamber of commerce advertising campaign, Easterners heeded the advice of crusading magazine and newspaper editor Horace Greeley to 'Go West, young man.' LA's population jumped from 2300 in 1860, to 11,000 in 1880, to more than 50,000 in 1890. It reached 100,000 in 1900.

Never mind that there was no natural harbor, or that the supply of fresh water was inadequate to support even a small town. A sharp mind and a willing spirit could overcome these obstacles.

The first of these needs was addressed by the construction of a harbor at San Pedro, 23 miles south of City Hall. Work began in 1899; the first wharf opened in 1914, the year the Panama Canal was completed. Suddenly 8000 miles closer to the Atlantic seaboard, San Pedro became the busiest harbor on the West Coast.

But bringing drinkable water to the growing city would require a much more complex solution. The sporadic flow of the Los Angeles River (as the Río Porciúncula became known) may have been adequate for the original pueblo, but even supplemented by scattered artesian wells, the local water supply wasn't nearly sufficient.

In 1904, city water-bureau superintendent William Mulholland visited the Owens Valley, on the southeastern slopes of the Sierra Nevada 233 miles northeast of LA, and returned with a startling plan. Voters gave him the $24.5 million he needed to build an aqueduct to carry melted snow from the mountains to the city, and by November 1913, Owens River water was spilling into the San Fernando Valley. Its flow has been increased from 26 million gallons daily when it opened to 525 million gallons daily now. The system remains controversial, especially to Owens Valley ranchers and to environmentalists, but it supplies more than 75% of the city's water. Most of the rest, as well as Southern California's electricity, comes from dams on the Colorado River, 200 miles east.

To the Present

LA's population soared to one million by 1920, and two million by 1930, largely having to do with the discovery of oil. In 1892, when Edward Doheny dug a well near downtown Los Angeles, a sophisticated and highly profitable oil industry took off in the region. The demand for exporting much of that oil also caused a boom in shipping and related harbor industries.

During WWI, the Lockheed brothers and Donald Douglas established aircraft manufacturing plants in the area. Two decades later, with another world war brewing, the aviation industry employed enough people to help lift LA out of the Depression. By the end of WWII billions of federal dollars were poured into Southern California military contracts, and thousands of families had moved to the region to work at the plants. Through the Cold War years, increased dependence on federal spending led some critics to call LA a 'Federal City.'

Capitalizing on the influx of aviation employees, a new real estate boom brought about whole new suburbs south of LA. Lakewood, just north of Long Beach, is the classic example: the entire city was developed almost overnight to house employees of McDonnell-Douglas.

During the war, and the years immediately following, the railroads drew thousands of Black maintenance workers from Texas and Louisiana to LA. Still more Blacks came when it became apparent that a vibrant community was developing in South Central LA. What had been just a small colony before the war grew by 1950 into one of the nation's great Black cultural centers.

More than 14 million people live within a 60-mile radius of the city center. The City of LA proper boasts 3.5 million. Of that, whites represent about 48%, Latinos 28%, blacks 17%, Asians and Pacific Islanders 7%. The percentages are similar countywide.

Today, if metropolitan LA were a nation of its own, its gross national product would rank 14th in the world. Tourism ($5.5 billion a year) and entertainment (movies, television, radio, and recording produce $4 billion annually) rank high on the list of income earners, as does aviation. Less 'sexy' but equally important manufacturing industries include petroleum and refining, electronics, pharmaceuticals, and processed food.

Race Relations Policy-makers had turned a blind eye to growing ethnic friction for decades, including a spell of urban warfare between Anglos and Latinos in 1943. In the 1960s, South Central LA was faced with increasing tension which came to a boil in August 1965 in the Watts riots. Thirty-four people died and more than a thousand were wounded in six days of burning and looting.

South Central Los Angeles, populated mainly by blacks and Latinos, saw subsequent riots in 1979 and 1992. The latter, a direct result of the notorious Rodney King beatings and trial, cost 51 lives and $1 billion in property damage. Oddly, much of the violence in 1992 was directed at Korean shopkeepers in fringe neighborhoods and in Koreatown, perhaps reflecting resentment over the apparent ease with which these newcomers had established successful businesses.

A strand of hope lies in the city's unified response to natural disasters. Major earthquakes in the San Fernando Valley in 1971 and 1994 brought out the best in Angelenos: looting was at a minimum, goodwill at a maximum.

The Industry It is the film industry (known simply as 'The Industry'), that symbolizes 20th-century LA. Independent producers were attracted here beginning in 1908 for LA's sunny climate which allowed indoor scenes to be shot outdoors – essential with the unsophisticated photo technology of the day. Any location, from ocean to desert to alpine forest, could be depicted nearby. What's more, the proximity of the Mexican border enabled film makers to rush their equipment to safety if they were challenged by collection agents for patent holders like Thomas Edison.

Studios were constructed in Culver City and Universal City, but the capital of filmdom was the LA suburb of Hollywood. Soon moviegoers were succumbing to the romance of Southern California as portrayed in silent films. Organ music accompanied one-reel comedies and Westerns that made stars of Charlie Chaplin and Tom Mix. And directors like DW Griffith and Cecil B DeMille became luminaries in their own right. 'Talkies' soon eclipsed the silent films, and color cinematography later made the movies seem more real than ever. Fads followed popular movies, shaping styles around the world.

GEOGRAPHY & CLIMATE
The most notable aspect of LA's geography is that it straddles one of the world's major fault zones. Not only does the great San Andreas Fault run from northwest to southeast at a distance of 33 miles from downtown LA at its nearest point; more than three dozen lesser faults also crisscross the metropolitan area like cracks on an eggshell.

Despite its desert climate, most of LA is protected from temperature extremes and humidity by the mountain ranges to its north and east. Average temperatures are around 70°F (21°C), with summer highs usually in the mid 80s to low 90s and winter lows typically in the mid 50s to low 60s. The desert reaches of Los Angeles County commonly get heat in excess of 100°F in summer, while the mountains support ski resorts without artificial snowmaking equipment. Downtown LA gets an average 186 days of sunshine a year.

ORIENTATION
Greater LA occupies a broad coastal plain, framed on its west and south by the Pacific Ocean, on its north by the San Gabriel Mountains, and on its east by smaller ranges that run to the Mojave Desert. The Santa Monica Mountains separate Hollywood and Beverly Hills from the workaday San Fernando Valley to the north; adjacent Orange County, home of Disneyland and Newport Beach, extends along the coast to the southeast.

The city's meandering boundaries, which extend 50 miles from San Fernando to San Pedro, 25 miles from Pacific Palisades to Highland Park, comprise only a fraction of LA County which encompasses more than 80 incorporated cities (many of them surrounded by the City of LA itself). LA is connected to the San Francisco Bay Area by I-5, which also runs south to San Diego and continues to the Mexican border. The alternative to I-5 from San Francisco is US 101, which enters LA as the Ventura Fwy, becoming the Hollywood Fwy and ending where it joins I-5 in the city center.

From San Diego and the south, I-5 is the obvious choice of route. At Irvine, the 405 (San Diego) Fwy branches off I-5 and takes a westerly route to Long Beach and Santa Monica, avoiding downtown LA entirely

CALIFORNIA

and rejoining I-5 near San Fernando. It can be a time-saver if you're headed to the West Side.

If you're coming into LA from Las Vegas or the Grand Canyon, you'll want to take I-15 which continues south to San Diego and is crossed by I-10 (westbound from Palm Springs) near Ontario; this route continues through downtown LA to Santa Monica.

Getting around in LA need not be hard if you have an automobile and a basic understanding of its famous network of restricted-access freeways. Some communities of visitor interest (namely Beverly Hills and West Hollywood) aren't on the freeway system and must be reached via city streets.

Maps

Handout maps may be insufficient if you plan on spending any length of time exploring the nooks and crannies of greater LA. The driver's bible is the annual edition of *The Thomas Guide* to Los Angeles County ($15.95), or *The Thomas Guide* to LA and Orange Counties ($25.95).

Less pricey but sufficiently detailed maps are available from the Automobile Association of Southern California (☎ 213-741-3111), in a Spanish Colonial mansion downtown at 2601 S Figueroa St. The California Map Center, 3211 Pico Blvd, Santa Monica, has an excellent selection.

INFORMATION
Tourist Offices

Maps, brochures, lodging information, and discounted tickets to theme parks and other attractions are available from the Los Angeles Convention and Visitors Bureau (☎ 213-624-7300). Its main office, downtown at 633 W 5th St (on the 60th floor), is open weekdays 9 am to 5 pm. More user-friendly are the Downtown Visitor Information Center (213-689-8822), 695 S Figueroa St, and the Hollywood Visitor Information Center (☎ 213-461-4213) in the turn-of-the-century Janes House, 6541 Hollywood Blvd, open daily except Sunday 9 am to 5 pm.

Foreign Consulates

The addresses and telephone numbers of consulates not listed can be found in the Pacific Bell yellow pages under Consulates & Other Foreign Government Representatives.

The largest in LA include:

Australia
  611 N Larchmont Blvd, in Hancock Park (☎ 213-469-4300)
Canada
  300 S Grand Ave, Suite 1000, downtown (☎ 213-346-2700)
Israel
  6380 Wilshire Blvd, in the Fairfax District (☎ 213-651-5700)

Major Freeways

LA's major freeways include:

I-5 Golden State Fwy From downtown northwest to Bakersfield.
I-5 Santa Ana Fwy From downtown southeast to Irvine.
I-10 San Bernardino Fwy From downtown east to San Bernardino.
I-10 Santa Monica Fwy From downtown west to Santa Monica.
I-60 Pomona Fwy From I-5 downtown east to 10 at Beaumont.
I-101 Hollywood Fwy From I-5 and I-10 downtown northwest to Hwy 170 in North Hollywood.
I-101 Ventura Fwy From Hwy 134 in North Hollywood west to Ventura.
I-110 Harbor Fwy From I-101 downtown south to San Pedro.
I-110 Pasadena Fwy From I-101 downtown north to Pasadena.
I-210 Foothill Fwy From I-5 in Sylmar east to I-10 in Pomona.
I-405 San Diego Fwy From I-5 in San Fernando southeast to I-5 at Irvine.
I-605 San Gabriel River Fwy From I-210 in Duarte south to I-405 in Long Beach.
I-710 Long Beach Fwy From I-10 in Alhambra south to Long Beach.
I-118 Ronald Reagan Fwy From north San Fernando Valley to Simi Valley ■

Coping With Traffic

It should come as no surprise that, in terms of volume, Los Angeles has the worst traffic in the US. If you're entering Los Angeles by car, you may want to time your arrival away from heaviest commuter hours (roughly 7 to 10 am, 3 to 7 pm). Unfortunately, there's really no guarantee that you'll avoid tie-ups, which can occur at any time of day and add more than an hour to your travel time. If you have two or more people riding in a car, you may be entitled to drive in the speedier car pool (High Occupancy Vehicle – HOV) lane. City streets are usually a poor alternative to freeways, unless you are going a short distance. ■

Japan
　　350 S Grand Ave (☎ 213-617-6700)
Mexico
　　2401 W 6th St, next to MacArthur Park (☎ 213-351-6800)
New Zealand
　　12400 Wilshire Blvd, Suite 1150, in West Los Angeles (310-207-1605)
South Africa
　　50 N La Cienega Blvd, Beverly Hills (☎ 310-657-9200)
UK
　　11766 Wilshire Blvd, Suite 400, in West Los Angeles (☎ 310-477-3322)

Money

Most major currencies and leading brands of travelers checks are easily exchanged in LA. The best rates are usually obtained at banks. For new arrivals, LA International Airport has currency exchange offices in the Tom Bradley International Terminal.

Among foreign exchange brokers, one of the most dependable is Thomas Cook (☎ 800-287-7362) with locations downtown at 735 Figueroa St, in Beverly Hills at 452 N Bedford St, and in West Hollywood at 901 Santa Monica Blvd.

American Express (☎ 213-659-1682) has its main office downtown at 8493 W 3rd St, open weekdays 9 am to 7 pm and Saturday 10 am to 6 pm. There are other AmEx offices downtown at 901 W 7th St (☎ 213-627-4800); at 327 N Beverly Drive, Beverly

Hills (☎ 213-274-8277); and at 251 S Lake Ave, Pasadena (☎ 818-449-2281).

Taxes A combined total tax of 8.5% applies to all hotel and restaurant bills as well as most shopping. It does *not* apply to grocery shopping, except for certain items like alcoholic beverages. You can expect an additional tourist tax of 5 to 10% on hotel rooms; the amount varies from city to city, even within the Los Angeles area.

Post & Telecommunications

Post offices are open weekdays from 9 am to 5 pm and Saturday from 9 am to noon.

The main post office (☎ 213-617-4543) is next to the railroad station, north of downtown and east of El Pueblo de Los Angeles, at 900 N Alameda St. Collect your general delivery mail weekdays between 8 am and 3 pm. There's also a philatelic office here for stamp collectors.

Other handy post offices are at 325 N Maple Drive, Beverly Hills (☎ 310-247-3400); 1248 5th St, Santa Monica (☎ 310-576-2626); and 1601 Main St, Venice (☎ 310-396-3191).

You'll find Mail Boxes Etc and Kinko's Copies franchises throughout the LA area for fax services. For telegrams, contact Western Union, has several locations including 1454 4th St, Santa Monica (☎ 310-394-7211).

CALIFORNIA

There are several area code districts in the greater LA area:

Downtown LA	☎ 213
Hollywood	☎ 213
Beverly Hills	☎ 310
West LA	☎ 310
Santa Monica	☎ 310
Pasadena	☎ 818
San Fernando Valley	☎ 818

Travel Agencies

Council Travel (☎ 800-223-7402) has a LA branch (☎ 310-208-3551) at 10904 Lindbrook Drive, in Westwood. STA (☎ 310-394-5126), 120 Broadway, Suite 108, in Santa Monica, is also good for discount fares. Both companies have several offices in the metropolitan area.

Bookstores

For travel books, visit Traveler's Bookcase (☎ 213-655-0575), 8375 W 3rd St, near the Beverly Center; or Distant Lands (☎ 818-449-3220), 62 S Raymond Ave, Pasadena. California Map Center (☎ 310-829-6277), 3211 Pico Blvd, offers an excellent selection of maps and travel guides. Nations (☎ 310-318-9915) at 502 Pier Ave in Hermosa Beach is another excellent choice to stock up on maps, guides, and travel gear. A Different Light Bookstore (☎ 310-854-6601), 8853 Santa Monica Blvd, is the area's number one gay bookstore. Sisterhood Bookstore (☎ 310-477-7300) at 1351 Westwood Blvd, has material geared towards women travelers.

Book Soup, 8818 Sunset Blvd, West Hollywood, is a favorite place for everyone from students to celebrities to find newspapers and magazines from all over the world. Another celebrity bookstore is The Bodhi Tree, 8585 Melrose Ave, West Hollywood, a New Age-specialty shop made famous in Shirley MacLaine's books. Far more bizarre, however, is Amok, 1764 N Vermont Ave, Los Feliz, a bookstore where the extreme and the unlikely are the norm. Also try Dutton's Brentwood (☎ 310-476-6263) at 11975 San Vicente Blvd.

On Santa Monica's 3rd St Promenade, The Midnight Special Bookstore, has a wide selection of titles including a fair amount of radical political literature, while Hennessy & Ingalls is the city's best forum for books on every possible art form.

Newspapers & Magazines

The *Los Angeles Times*, first published in 1881, is LA's (and one of California's) largest newspaper. The *LA Weekly*, issued on Thursdays and available free from bookstores, video stores, restaurants, and convenience stores, is worth reading for its entertainment listings and personal ads.

The monthly *LA Magazine* is a high-

Email & Internet Access

A multimedia megalopolis, Los Angeles offers scant hindrance to anyone wishing to make use of that fine new friend of travelers, the Internet. If carrying your own laptop and modem is an option, one of the easiest ways to log on is to be sure when making hotel reservations that your room is equipped with a free phone line. Some, like the Hyatt Regency (☎ 800-233-1234) and the New Otani Hotel and Garden (☎ 800-421-8795), cater primarily to business travelers, so this won't be a problem. When traveling without such hardware, another simple way to connect is to swing by any public library branch, all of which are equipped to allow Web browsing and access to chat groups, though not to send or receive email.

For complete online access, a new wave of business has begun to take up the slack. CafeNet (☎ 213-467-3552) has begun placing coin-operated (25¢ per three minutes) computer stations in cafes throughout the area. Among the best-suited of these sites is the funky Highland Grounds (☎ 213-466-1507) at 742 N Highland Ave. Electronic Cafe International (☎ 310-828-8732), 1649 18th St, Santa Monica, offers a more complete setup than the single sites in the above cafes, as well as hosting periodic cybernaut events and classes. Cyber Java (☎ 310-581-1300), 1029 Abbott Kinney Blvd, also has several complete workstations as well as videophone facilities. ∎

RICK GERHARTER
No one ever said LA needed another media outlet.

brow glossy whose restaurant listings and reviews are digested with gusto by locals, while *Buzz,* also monthly, offers spirited critiques of Industry goings-on and local media. If you really want to keep up with the show-biz scene, keep an eye out for 'the trades': *Variety* and the *Hollywood Reporter.*

Medical Services

Major hospitals include the USC Medical Center (☎ 213-226-2622), 1200 N State St; the Hollywood Presbyterian Medical Center (☎ 213-660-5350), 1300 N Vermont Ave, near Barnsdall Park; the Cedar-Sinai Medical Center (☎ 213-855-5000), 8700 Beverly Blvd, near Beverly Hills and West Hollywood; and the UCLA Medical Center (☎ 310-825-3901), 10833 LeConte Ave, in Westwood.

Planned Parenthood (☎ 213-223-4462) has 10 clinics in the LA area.

Emergency

In case of emergency, phone ☎ 911 and request assistance from police, fire department, ambulance, or paramedics.

Some other crisis contacts include:

AIDS Hot Line
　☎ 800-342-2437
Alcohol & Drug Referral Hotline
　☎ 800-252-6465
Crisis Response Unit
　☎ 800-833-3376
Poison Information Center
　☎ 800-777-6476
Rape & Battering Hotline
　☎ 310-392-8381
Rape Crisis Center
　☎ 310-392-8381
Suicide Prevention Hotline
　☎ 800-333-4444

Dangers & Annoyances

Crime Much has been written about crime in LA. If you take ordinary precautions, chances are you won't be victimized. If you have something stolen report it to the police.

Perhaps it is too obvious to state that you should avoid 'bad' neighborhoods, especially after dark. Much of South Central LA and East LA are plagued with interracial gang activity, so be informed of the dangers before wandering into those areas.

Depending as much as LA does upon the automobile, it should come as little surprise that car thefts and car jackings are rife there. Rental cars are particular targets: do not leave valuables behind when you park, and keep your windows rolled up and your doors locked if anyone approaches your vehicle.

Smog The very word 'smog' – smoke and fog – was coined in LA, where air pollution has been a severe problem for more than 50

What to Do in an Earthquake

In the extremely unlikely event that you're in LA during a major earthquake – such as the January 1994 Northridge temblor – here's what to do:

If you are indoors, stay indoors. Immediately take cover under a desk or table, or failing that, a doorjamb. Stay clear of windows, mirrors, or anything with a danger of falling, like bookshelves or file cabinets. If you are outdoors, get into an open area away from buildings, trees, and power lines. If you are driving, pull over to the side of the road away from bridges, overpasses, and power lines.

Afterward, check first for personal injuries, then for fire hazards (such as gas leaks or electrical-line damage) and spilled chemicals or medicines. As the city water supply may be polluted, you should boil it before you drink until notified otherwise.

Most Californians are prepared with an emergency kit for major earthquakes. It includes a first-aid kit, portable radio, flashlights and extra batteries, blankets, essential medications, three days' worth of food, three gallons of water per person, and various other items.

Look in the inside front cover of any telephone directory for more details, or call the *Earthquake Preparedness Hotline* (☎ 818-908-2671). ∎

---

years. In the desert skies, the noxious fumes rising from the city's freeways and factories are trapped beneath a warm inversion layer. The problem is worst during the peak summer heat, mainly in the San Fernando and San Gabriel Valleys. Offshore breezes keep the beach communities the cleanest. Thanks to strict environmental measures in recent years, the problem has more-or-less stabilized: it may not be getting any better, but at least it isn't getting much worse.

CENTRAL LOS ANGELES

It's only fitting that LA's downtown area is framed by freeways rather than any particular geographic boundary. You'll find the Hollywood (101) Fwy to the north, the Harbor (110) Fwy to the west, the Santa Monica (10) Fwy to the south, and a bird's nest of other freeways across the aqueduct-like Los Angeles River to the east.

Orient yourself at the Civic Center, America's second largest complex of government buildings (next to Washington, DC), at the northwest corner of this parallelogram. Northeast of here, across the 101 Fwy, are El Pueblo de Los Angeles, Chinatown, and, beyond them to the north, Dodger Stadium. Southeast is Little Tokyo; west, across the 110 Fwy, is the Pacific Stock Exchange. Southwest is the main business district; further south are the Gar-

ment District, the convention center, and, past the 10 Fwy, Exposition Park.

Parking is costly in downtown LA; a combination of walking and inexpensive DASH mini-buses is a much more practical way of getting around than by car.

Civic Center

Extending eight blocks east to west from San Pedro to Figueroa Sts, the Civic Center contains the most important of LA's city, county, state, and federal office buildings. The US Federal Courthouse Building, where the infamous OJ Simpson murder trial took place in 1995, is at 312 N Spring St; and the Parker Center, 150 N Los Angeles St, is where law-enforcement officers coordinated anti-riot activities in 1992. The most recognizable building is certainly the 28-story, 1928 **Los Angeles City Hall** (☎ 213-485-2891), 200 N Spring St, which served as the 'Daily Planet' building in *Superman* and the police station in *Dragnet*. You can get a free 45-minute guided tour (by reservation, two weeks in advance) or excellent view from the observation deck (at the foot of the pyramid which caps its 28 stories: take an express elevator to the 22nd floor, then change to a second lift to the tower).

Catty-corner from City Hall at 202 W 1st St, is the *Los Angeles Times building* (☎ 213-237-5757), whose lobby contains a giant globe and a worthwhile historical exhibit. Free 45-minute tours are offered weekdays at 11:15 am and 3 pm.

The complex of three theaters – Dorothy Chandler Pavilion, Ahmanson Theater, and Mark Taper Forum – known collectively as **The Music Center of LA County** (☎ 213-972-7211), 135 N Grand Ave, dominates the west end of the Civic Center mall between 1st and Temple Sts. Free one-hour guided tours (☎ 213-972-7483) of all facilities are offered year round from the Chandler Pavilion, though they are of most interest when going to see a performance.

North across Temple St from City Hall is the **LA Children's Museum** (☎ 213-687-8800), 310 N Main St, where kids can enjoy hands-on learning experiences. It's open summer weekdays from 11:30 am to 5 pm and weekends from 10 am to 5 pm; weekends only the rest of the year. Admission is $5.

El Pueblo de Los Angeles
This 44-acre state historic park commemorates the site where the city was founded in 1781 and preserves many of its earliest buildings. Its central attraction for most visitors is **Olvera St,** a narrow, block-long passageway between Main and Alameda Sts and Cesar E Chavez Blvd (a stretch of Sunset Blvd renamed for the agrarian labor leader). Restored as an open-air Mexican marketplace in 1930, Olvera St is lined with shops, restaurants, and stalls of vendors selling hand-woven clothing, leather belts and bags, handmade candles, and piñatas. A visitors center in the 1887 **Sepulveda House** (☎ 213-628-1274), 622 N Main St, whose back entrance extends to Olvera St, houses an LA history exhibit; it's open Monday through Saturday 10 am to 3 pm.

At its south end, Olvera St opens into the **Old Plaza** around which the original pueblo was built. Facing the plaza on the west is the **Church of Nuestra Señora la Reina de los Angeles** (☎ 213-629-3101), 535 N Main St, originally built of adobe by Franciscan monks and native laborers between 1818 and 1822.

Directly across Alameda St from El Pueblo is **Union Station** (☎ 213-683-6875), 800 N Alameda St, one of LA's oft-overlooked architectural treasures. This classic beauty, built in 1939 in Spanish Mission style with Moorish and Moderne details, is worth a stop even if you aren't hopping aboard a train.

Chinatown
Fewer than 5% of LA's 200,000 Chinese make their home in the 16 sq blocks of Chinaown, but the district that surrounds Broadway and Hill St north of El Pueblo is clearly their social and cultural center. Dozens of restaurants, and shops whose inventories vary from cheap kitsch to exquisite silk clothing, inlaid furniture, antique porcelain, and intricate religious art line the streets. In passages like **Bamboo Lane** and **Gin Ling Way,** the 'Street of the Golden Palace,' you'll find traditional acupuncturists and herbalists.

Little Tokyo
Immediately southeast of the Civic Center is Little Tokyo, roughly bounded by 1st and 4th Sts on the north and south, Alameda St on the east, and Los Angeles St on the west. First settled by early Japanese immigrants in the 1880s and thriving by the 1920s, the neighborhood was effectively decimated by the anti-Japanese hysteria of the WWII years. Thanks in part to an injection of investment from the 'old country,' today Little Tokyo is again the social, economic, and cultural center for the Southland's Japanese population of nearly a quarter-million. Along the streets and outdoor shopping centers you'll find sushi bars, bento houses, and traditional Japanese gardens.

Housed in a historic Buddhist temple that underwent a $30-million renovation, the **Japanese American National Museum** (☎ 213-625-0414), 369 E 1st St, exhibits objects of work and worship, photographs, and art that relate the history of Japanese emigration to, and life in, the USA. It's open Tuesday to Sunday 10 am to 5 pm, Thursdays to 8 pm. Admission is $4.

Old Chinatown

Chinese first settled in LA just southeast of the old Plaza on an adobe-lined alleyway known as Calle de los Negros – a name that should have served as an ominous warning for making issue of the dark skin of the street's previous residents, who were mestizos and mulattos. Chinese – primarily men – were drawn to LA as the Sierra gold strikes dwindled, the transcontinental railroads were completed, and racism made life in other towns less tolerable. Life in Los Angeles wouldn't offer much of an improvement for many years.

In October 1871, 19 local Chinese men were killed in an anti-Chinese race riot known as the Chinese Massacre. As in other towns, hard times had turned hard-working Chinese into scapegoats. Still, the Chinese persisted, and they carved niches for themselves within the larger LA community. Chinese were most successful running small farms and distributing produce throughout LA. Eventually, women arrived from China and the men had wives and started families. Old Chinatown spread eastward, across Alameda St.

In the 1930s, however, a large portion of Old Chinatown was demolished to make room for Union Station. Less than two decades later, the rest of the old neighborhood had been torn down for freeway construction. The touristy plaza of New Chinatown, which opened several blocks to the north in 1938, has been the cultural center for this vibrant community ever since. ■

The Museum of Contemporary Art at the **Temporary Contemporary** (MOCA at the TC, ☎ 213-626-6222), 152 N Central Ave, houses temporary exhibits, in an enormous, redesigned warehouse loft. Exhibits here tend to be even more avant-garde than those at MOCA, with the raw warehouse design as an ideal viewing space.

DOWNTOWN
Bunker Hill
Three blocks south of the Music Center, where Grand Ave crests the hill, Bunker Hill was once LA's most fashionable residential neighborhood a century ago. By the 1940s it was a slum. Today, it is again a vital district, with skyscraper condominiums, multi-level courtyards, and city-commissioned sculpture. Its crowning commercial complexes are California Plaza, 300 S Grand Ave, and the Wells Fargo Center, 333 S Grand Ave, which has a free Gold Rush history museum on its ground floor.

At the north end of California Plaza at 250 S Grand Ave, the **Museum of Contemporary Art** (MOCA, ☎ 213-626-6222), designed by Japanese architect Arata Isozaki, houses a collection of paintings, sculptures, and photographs from the 1940s to the present that is considered one of the world's most important representations of the period. It's open Tuesday to Sunday 11 am to 5 pm; entry is $6, except Thursday nights, when admission is free from 5 to 8 pm.

Financial District
One of the features that characterizes downtown LA's urban-renewal projects of the 1980s and early '90s is a network of elevated walkways – a 'pedestrian skyway,' as it were – interconnecting many of its major hotels and office buildings. From the Hotel Inter-Continental at California Plaza, 251 S Olive St, you can walk with relative impunity past the city's impressive new Ketchum Downtown YMCA, 401 S Hope St, and the 444 Building (best known as home to the attorneys of *LA Law*), 444 S Flower St, to **The Westin Bonaventure**, 404 S Figueroa St, whose quintet of cylindrical glass towers are instantly recognizable to any regular moviegoer. The view from its 34th-floor revolving cocktail lounge is extensive.

South down Figueroa and Flower Sts rise numerous other skyscrapers and hotels, but none has the classic character of the 1923 **Biltmore Hotel**, 506 S Grand Ave, whose

CALIFORNIA

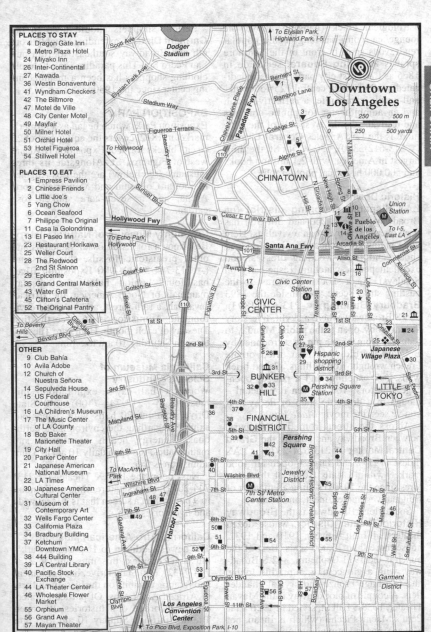

PLACES TO STAY
- 4 Dragon Gate Inn
- 8 Metro Plaza Hotel
- 24 Miyako Inn
- 26 Inter-Continental
- 27 Kawada
- 36 Westin Bonaventure
- 41 Wyndham Checkers
- 42 The Biltmore
- 47 Motel de Ville
- 48 City Center Motel
- 49 Mayfair
- 50 Milner Hotel
- 51 Orchid Hotel
- 53 Hotel Figueroa
- 54 Stillwell Hotel

PLACES TO EAT
- 1 Empress Pavilion
- 2 Chinese Friends
- 3 Little Joe's
- 5 Yang Chow
- 6 Ocean Seafood
- 7 Philippe The Original
- 11 Casa la Golondrina
- 13 El Paseo Inn
- 23 Restaurant Horikawa
- 25 Weller Court
- 28 The Redwood
   2nd St Saloon
- 29 Epicentre
- 35 Grand Central Market
- 43 Water Grill
- 45 Clifton's Cafeteria
- 52 The Original Pantry

OTHER
- 9 Club Bahía
- 10 Avila Adobe
- 12 Church of
   Nuestra Señora
- 14 Sepulveda House
- 15 US Federal
   Courthouse
- 16 LA Children's Museum
- 17 The Music Center
   of LA County
- 18 Bob Baker
   Marionette Theater
- 19 City Hall
- 20 Parker Center
- 21 Japanese American
   National Museum
- 22 LA Times
- 30 Japanese American
   Cultural Center
- 31 Museum of
   Contemporary Art
- 32 Wells Fargo Center
- 33 California Plaza
- 34 Bradbury Building
- 37 Ketchum
   Downtown YMCA
- 38 444 Building
- 39 LA Central Library
- 40 Pacific Stock
   Exchange
- 44 LA Theater Center
- 46 Wholesale Flower
   Market
- 55 Orpheum
- 56 Grand Ave
- 57 Mayan Theater

Downtown
Los Angeles

To Elysian Park,
Highland Park, I-5

Dodger
Stadium

Scott Ave

Elysian Park Ave

Stadium Way

Figueroa Terrace

Beaudry Ave

To Hollywood

Chavez-Ravine Place

Pasadena Fwy

Bernard St

Bamboo Lane

College St

Alpine St

CHINATOWN

N Main St

N Broadway

N Spring St

N Hill St

New High St

El Pueblo
de los
Angeles

Union
Station

To I-5,
East LA

Sunset Blvd

Cesar E Chavez Blvd

Hollywood Fwy

To Echo Park,
Hollywood

Santa Ana Fwy

Arcadia St

Aliso St

Commercial St

Alameda St

Temple St

Court St

Colton St

**CIVIC
CENTER**

Civic Center
Station

Broadway

Spring St

Main St

Los Angeles St

Figueroa St

Hope St

Bixel St

To Beverly
Hills

Beverly Blvd

1st St

2nd St

1st St

2nd St

Ohio St

Japanese
Village Plaza

Grand Ave

Olive St

Hill St

**BUNKER
HILL**

3rd St

Hispanic
shopping
district

3rd St

**LITTLE
TOKYO**

Pershing Square
Station

**FINANCIAL
DISTRICT**

4th St

5th St

**Pershing
Square**

5th St

Maryland St

Beaudry Ave

Boylston St

6th St

To MacArthur
Park

Wilshire Blvd

Ingraham St

Wilshire Blvd

Broadway Historic Theater District

6th St

Jewelry
District

Harbor Fwy

7th St

7th St/ Metro
Center Station

Maple Ave

Spring St

Main St

Los Angeles St

Garland Ave

8th St

8th St

9th St

Wall St

San Julian St

9th St

9th St

Olympic Blvd

Blaine St

Flower St

Figueroa St

110

**Los Angeles
Convention
Center**

Olympic
Blvd

Olympic Blvd

Grand Ave

Hill St

Olive St

Broadway

**Garment
District**

11th St

To Pico Blvd, Exposition Park, I-10

0   250   500 m
0   250   500 yards

astrological clock (hanging above the lounge/tea room) has long been a popular rendezvous spot. In front of the Biltmore sprawls **Pershing Square,** set aside in 1866 as LA's first city park. It was rededicated in 1995 with a central 125-foot pink-and-purple campanile, a reflective pool, and an amphitheater for public concerts and festivals. On the west side of the Biltmore is the Los Angeles **Central Library** (☎ 213-612-3320), 630 W 5th St, the third largest in America, with 2.1 million books and 500,000 historical photographs.

Historic Downtown

LA's **Hispanic shopping district** (on Broadway between 2nd and 5th Sts) has been overlooked by urban revivalists. Here you can find good, cheap Mexican food, $5 shoes, and frilly wedding dresses, and excellent people-watching (especially on Sundays). For a shocking contrast to the bustling street scene, step inside the 1893 **Bradbury Building** (☎ 213-626-1893), 304 S Broadway, where a skylit, five-story atrium lobby, open to the public Monday to Saturday from 9 am 5 pm, is surrounded by Belgian marble, Mexican tile, ornate French wrought-iron railings, glazed brick walls, oak paneling, and a pair of open-cage elevators. You've seen it in detail – though in a dramatic state of decay – if you've seen the movie *Blade Runner.*

Across the street from the Bradbury, between Broadway and Hill St, the **Grand Central Market** (☎ 213-624-2378) is LA's oldest (1917) and largest open-air food market, with 48 stalls (some of them fixtures since the 1930s) selling all manner of fruit and vegetables, meat, and seafood.

South along Broadway is the **Broadway Historic Theater District**, whose dozen theaters, all built between 1910 and 1932, house more than 15,000 seats. Best of the bunch is the 1911 Orpheum, 842 S Broadway, with a gilt ceiling, a marble lobby, and two huge bronze-and-crystal chandeliers. A couple of blocks away is the Mayan Theater, 1038 S Hill St, styled in 1926 after Peru's Machu Picchu (which is Incan, not Mayan), now a Latin nightclub.

Serious shoppers should head to the **Garment District**, extending roughly from 6th and Broadway southeast to 16th and San Pedro Sts. This paradise for wholesale clothing shoppers has been a manufacturing center since the 1930s.

EXPOSITION PARK

Exposition Park, which began as a farmer's market in 1872, covers the equivalent of 25 sq city blocks south of Exposition Blvd and west of Figueroa St. Alongside its three museums (see below) are the Los Angeles Memorial Coliseum and Memorial Sports Arena, and a seven-acre sunken rose garden.

LA County Museum of Natural History

Best known for its dinosaur skeletons and other prehistoric fossils, this museum (☎ 213-744-3466), 900 Exposition Blvd, has four 'habitat halls' that display mammals of North America, the African savannah, a rain forest, and an arctic environment. Admission is $6, free the first Tuesday of each month. Hours are Tuesday through Saturday 10 am to 5 pm.

California Museum of Science & Industry

Worth a half-day's exploration, this museum (☎ 213-744-7400), 700 State Drive, contains 20 halls with 'hands-on' exhibits regarding the environment, earthquakes, energy, health, economics, and mathematics. It's open daily 10 am to 5 pm; admission is free.

Next door, the IMAX Theater (☎ 213-744-2019), shows nature films (daily noon to 9 pm; $6) on a screen that is 70 feet wide and five stories high.

California Afro-American Museum

The newest addition to Exposition Park's museum complex, this museum (☎ 213-744-7432), 600 State Drive, has permanent and rotating exhibits on the history and arts of African Americans. Of particular interest are recorded oral histories. It's open Tuesday through Sunday 10 am to 5 pm; free.

University of Southern California

Across from Exposition Park at Hoover St and Exposition Blvd, USC, founded in 1880, is one of the oldest major private universities on the West Coast. Free one-hour walking tours (☎ 213-740-2311) of the campus are offered weekdays 10 am to 2 pm.

On campus is the Fisher Gallery (☎ 213-740-4561), 823 Exposition Blvd, that shows important temporary exhibitions; there are other museums on campus of limited interest. Call the university for opening hours and details.

At the northeast corner of campus, the 1926 Moorish-style **Shrine Auditorium** (☎ 213-749-5123), 665 W Jefferson Blvd, is home to the Grammy Awards, the American Music Awards, and (every other year) the Academy Awards.

MID-WILSHIRE

Once a path followed by the Yangna Indians between their village in the Elysian Hills and the tar pits of Hancock Park, Wilshire Blvd was extended 16 miles from the city to the sea in the late 19th century. It passes through an eclectic variety of neighborhoods, including Koreatown; ultra-elite Hancock Park; the now-faded Miracle Mile (an important shopping district in the 1930s); and the Fairfax District, LA's primary Jewish neighborhood. Further west Wilshire continues through Beverly Hills, Westwood, and finally Santa Monica to where it meets the Pacific Ocean.

Just over a mile from LA's downtown core at Wilshire Blvd at Alvarado St, MacArthur Park is one of LA's coolest spots for a picnic (though best avoided at night), and a likely location to begin a westbound exploration of Wilshire Blvd.

Koreatown

Beginning at 8th St, two blocks south of Wilshire, this square mile (roughly extending south to Pico Blvd between Vermont and Western Aves) is home to fully one-third of LA's 160,000 Koreans, making it the largest 'Koreatown' this side of Pusan. The main thoroughfare, Olympic Blvd, is lined with shops and restaurants. The area suffered heavy damage during the 1992 LA riots and is still undergoing reconstruction.

Fine Architecture

As Wilshire crosses through Lafayette Park a half-mile past MacArthur Park, it enters an area of particular architectural interest.

The First Baptist Church, 760 S Westmoreland Ave, south of Wilshire between Virgil and Vermont Aves. This church's rose windows are like those of the cathedral at Chartres, France, and its gold-embossed ceiling resembles that of an Italian palace.

I Magnin Wilshire, 3050 Wilshire Blvd at Vermont Ave. This grand Art Deco tower closed for business in 1993 and is awaiting a prescription for reuse.

The Ambassador Hotel, 3400 Wilshire Blvd at Catalina St. Built in the 1920s and home of the infamous Coconut Grove nightclub, it was at this hotel that Senator Robert Kennedy was assassinated after winning the 1968 California primary election. Closed for over six years, it is now owned by Donald Trump and rented out only to set-hungry film companies.

The Wilshire Boulevard Temple stands further west, at Wilshire and Hobart Blvds. Visit weekdays from 10 am to 4 pm to see its 135-foot, mosaic-inlaid dome, the Old Testament murals on its inside walls, and its gallery on the history and customs of important Jewish holidays.

The Wiltern Center, 3790 Wilshire Blvd at Western Ave – hence the name 'Wil-tern' – is a 12-story Art Deco masterpiece built in 1931. It contains the Wiltern Theater, a restored movie palace that must be seen from the inside to be appreciated, which now serves as one of LA's finest concert venues. ■

La Brea Tar Pits

One of the world's most important paleontological sites, these pits supplied tar (*brea* in Spanish) used by Native Americans and early settlers to waterproof roofs and boats. In 1906 scientists learned the bubbling black pools had been a unique trap for all manner of animal and plant life since the Pleistocene Era, beginning 40,000 years ago. The fossilized skeletons of such long-extinct mammals as saber-tooth cats, ground sloths, mammoths, and mastodons were among the treasures yielded in excavations of the pits, along with 200 more species of birds, reptiles, insects, and plant life. An observation pit (☎ 213-857-6311) at Wilshire Blvd and Curson Ave lets you see how a specimen appears in the seeping tar; it's open weekends 11 am to 2 pm, with free guided tours of the grounds Wednesday through Sunday at 1 pm.

Tar pit discoveries are exhibited at the adjacent **George C Page Museum of La Brea Discoveries** (☎ 213-936-2230), 5801 Wilshire Blvd, open Wednesday to Sunday 10 am to 5 pm. Admission is $5, free the first Tuesday of each month.

LA County Museum of Art

Just west of the tar pits in Hancock Park is LACMA (☎ 213-857-6111), 5901 Wilshire Blvd, considered one of the best art museums in the US (and, indeed, the world) for its size, variety, and the importance of its works. Composed of several buildings surrounding a central courtyard, collections include Western paintings (especially German expressionism), sculpture, textiles, and decorative arts; Japanese Art including rare Shin'enkan temple paintings; contemporary paintings; and temporary exhibits that run the gamut from Jain religious art (from India) to Annie Leibowitz photographs. It's open Tuesday to Thursday 10 am to 5 pm, Friday 10 am to 9 pm, weekends 11 am to 6 pm. Admission is $6, free the second Wednesday of each month.

Other Museums Other collections along this stretch of Wilshire Blvd include the

RICK GERHARTER
La Brea tar pits

Craft & Folk Art Museum (☎ 213-937-5544), 5800 Wilshire Blvd, the **Museum of Miniature Art** (☎ 213-937-6464), 5900 Wilshire Blvd, and the **Petersen Automotive Museum** (☎ 213-930-2277), 6060 Wilshire Blvd, which depicts the history of the car as it relates to Southern California.

Fairfax District

Though many liberal Jews have scattered to the four winds within the metropolis, Orthodox and Hassidic Jews remain strong in this area which centers around Fairfax Ave between Santa Monica and Wilshire Blvds. For visitors, the main point of interest is the **Farmer's Market** (☎ 213-933-9211), 6333 W 3rd St at Fairfax Ave (see Things to Buy). It's as good a place as any to grab a bite and spend time people-watching.

The **Silent Movie Theater** (☎ 213-653-2389), 611 N Fairfax Ave at Melrose Ave, is popular for its vintage organ music and silent films.

SOUTH CENTRAL

Most visitors – and many residents – tend to avoid South Central LA, an impoverished district that ranges south on either side of the Harbor (110) Fwy from Exposition Park and Martin Luther King Jr Blvd. Many of its neighborhoods and commercial strips were hard hit by the 1992 riots, as they were by the Watts riots of 1965. While not a traditional tourist destination, South Central has a culture and history entirely its own; especially for those interested in LA's black heritage, it should not be overlooked.

Watts Towers

The area's best known attraction is the Towers of Sabato (Simon) Rodia (☎ 213-847-4646), a state historic park at 1765 E 107th St, about eight miles south of downtown off Graham Ave and Santa Ana Blvd. In 1921, Italian immigrant Rodia, an unschooled tilesetter, began assembling a free-form sculpture from discarded pipes, steel rods, bed frames, and cement, embellishing them with shards of glass, tile, porcelain, and seashells. The eight towers (the two tallest are 99 and 97 feet) are considered among the world's greatest works of folk art. Tours ($1) are offered Saturdays and Sundays 10 am to 4 pm. The adjacent **Watts Towers Art Center** (☎ 213-569-8181), 1727 E 107th St, sponsors art exhibits, classes, and special programs.

Black Cultural Centers

After visiting the Watts Towers, you can drive west on 108th St to Central Ave, then north past LA's colossal Main Post Office (☎ 213-586-1705), 7001 S Central Ave, to the Dunbar Hotel **Black Historical Cultural Museum** (☎ 213-234-7882), 4225 S Central Ave, just a few blocks south of

Martin Luther King Jr Blvd. Almost every prominent African American who visited LA in the 1930s and '40s stayed in this hotel.

About five miles due west in the Crenshaw district, the **Museum in Black** (☎ 213-292-9528), just south of Martin Luther King Jr Blvd at 4331 Degnan Blvd, displays more than 1000 masks, figurines, beads, and other artifacts from Africa, and a myriad of works by African Americans. It's open Tuesday to Saturday from noon to 6 pm; free. There are also some great entertainment venues around here, see Entertainment for more information.

HOLLYWOOD

Though its name remains synonymous with The Industry and many of the great early movie palaces still stand, modern Hollywood is fighting a tough battle against deterioration, street crime, and the wrecking ball. An urban renewal project launched by the City of LA in 1991 is projected to bear fruit 20 years into the 21st century; in the meantime, Hollywood is a place of nostalgia spread beneath its most recognizable landmark, the 'HOLLYWOOD' sign on the crest of the Hollywood Hills above Beachwood Canyon. You can reach the 50-foot-tall letters by hiking up a trail from the end of Beachwood Drive.

The **Janes House** (☎ 213-461-9520), 6541 Hollywood Blvd, a rare remnant of the mansions that lined this street, houses a visitors center with a historic exhibit and area maps.

The Cinema District

Running from La Brea Ave across Highland Ave, this area is still lively with movie lovers. Mann's – formerly known as

RICK GERHARTER

Hollywood Walk of Fame

RICK GERHARTER

Grauman's – **Chinese Theater** (☎ 213-464-8111), 6925 Hollywood Blvd, near its west end, may be Hollywood's most famous individual site. The broad courtyard before its front entrance is renowned for the memories left in concrete by more than 150 screen legends, from prints of Betty Grable's legs to Jimmy Durante's nose.

The Chinese Theater is located near the west end of the **Hollywood Walk of Fame,** which stretches east from Sycamore to Gower Sts and down Vine three blocks from Yucca St to Sunset Blvd. More than 2000 marble-and-bronze stars inlaid in the sidewalk exalt stars of movies, television, radio, theater, and the recording industry.

In the summer of 1996, the new **Hollywood Entertainment Museum** opened in the Galaxy Theater at 7021 Hollywood Blvd. The 33,000-sq-foot facility will offer exhibits that trace the history of the entertainment industry here. Meanwhile, the mezzanine of the **Hollywood Roosevelt Hotel,** 7000 Hollywood Blvd, location of the first Academy Awards ceremony, has an excellent, museum-type display.

Nearby, the 1926 **El Capitan Theater** (☎ 213-467-7674), 6838 Hollywood Blvd, had the honor of premiering *Citizen Kane,* and now shows world premieres of Disney movies. A block away is Hollywood's first movie palace, built in 1922: the 1100-seat **Egyptian Theater,** 6712 Hollywood Blvd, originally had live caged monkeys at its doors and usherettes clad in Cleopatra-style garb.

Opposite at 6522 Hollywood Blvd is a gallery known as LACE, for **Los Angeles Contemporary Exhibitions** (☎ 213-957-1777), which provides cutting edge artists with a space to show their painting, sculpture, video and still photography, music, and performance art. Just uphill is the landmark **Capitol Records Tower,** 1750 N Vine St, designed as a stack of records topped by a stylus.

Hollywood Hills
Two to three generations ago, such stars as Ethel Barrymore and Gloria Swanson made their homes along the rugged ridges that rise above Hollywood, and in canyons like Laurel, Nichols, Runyon, and Beachwood.

Today, the Hollywood Hills are getting a new infusion of life from young actors like Lou Diamond Phillips and Rebecca de Mornay.

Nestled at the foot of the hills, the open-air **Hollywood Bowl** (☎ 213-850-2000), on Highland Ave, is the summer home of the Los Angeles Philharmonic Orchestra and concerts by big-name entertainers. Adjacent is movie director Cecil B DeMille's original 1913 horse barn, now the **Hollywood Studio Museum** (☎ 213-874-2276), 2100 N Highland Ave, with exhibits on early film making, including costumes and a replica of DeMille's office.

Hollyhock House

Between Sunset and Hollywood Blvds at Vermont Ave, surrounded by Barnsdall Park, the Hollyhock House (☎ 213-485-2116), 4800 Hollywood Blvd, was Frank Lloyd Wright's first LA house and is still considered one of his finest works. Built in 1918–20 on commission for oil heiress Aileen Barnsdall, the house's abstract geometrical motif reflects that of a hollyhock plant. Tours of the building and its original furnishings are offered daily except Monday, every hour from noon to 3 pm; entry is $1.50.

The house is part of a complex that also

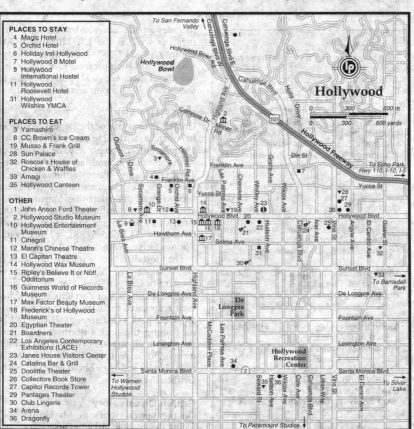

PLACES TO STAY
4 Magic Hotel
5 Orchid Hotel
6 Holiday Inn Hollywood
7 Hollywood 8 Motel
9 Hollywood International Hostel
11 Hollywood Roosevelt Hotel
31 Hollywood Wilshire YMCA

PLACES TO EAT
3 Yamashiro
8 CC Brown's Ice Cream
19 Musso & Frank Grill
28 Sun Palace
32 Roscoe's House of Chicken & Waffles
33 Amagi
35 Hollywood Canteen

OTHER
1 John Anson Ford Theater
2 Hollywood Studio Museum
10 Hollywood Entertainment Museum
12 Mann's Chinese Theatre
13 El Capitan Theatre
14 Hollywood Wax Museum
15 Ripley's Believe It or Not! Odditorium
16 Guinness World of Records Museum
17 Max Factor Beauty Museum
18 Frederick's of Hollywood Museum
20 Egyptian Theater
21 Boardners
22 Los Angeles Contemporary Exhibitions (LACE)
23 Janes House Visitors Center
24 Catalina Bar & Grill
25 Doolittle Theater
26 Collectors Book Store
27 Capitol Records Tower
29 Pantages Theater
30 Club Lingerie
34 Arena
36 Dragonfly

Kings of Kitsch

Near the corner of Hollywood Blvd and Highland Ave are several unusual museums – of sorts. If you're interested in perhaps learning something about Hollywood's unreal view of the world you might step into one or all of these cultural centers:

For starters, there's **Ripley's Believe It or Not! Odditorium** (☎ 213-466-6355), its rooftop tyrannosaurus beckoning passers-by to examine its 300 exhibits of the weird and wild. Next door is the **Guinness World of Records Museum** (☎ 213-463-6433), which isn't a whole lot different from Ripley's except that its achievements – depicted with animated displays – somehow seem more plausible. The **Hollywood Wax Museum** (☎ 213-462-5991) features 220 celebrities including film stars from The Industry's early years to the present (ooh! Tom Cruise!), plus other entertainers, sports greats, and political leaders.

If celebrities in wax don't do it for you, maybe famous brassieres will. **Frederick's of Hollywood Lingerie Museum** (☎ 213-466-8506) combines an interesting 'evolution of lingerie' section with a Celebrity Lingerie Hall of Fame. Turn the corner on Highland Ave for the **Max Factor Beauty Museum** (☎ 213-463-6668), and celebrate of the role of cosmetics in creating many a star image. ■

Frank's Wild Years

He once called it 'the great American commonplace.' Later, 'a busted flush.' 'Los Angeles is much worse than the average American city, there is more of it to be ugly,' he tells us. To hear the city so soundly trounced might come as little surprise today, but to know that the speaker did his grousing more than 70 years ago is to wonder what there was to badmouth. Worse still if the speaker happens to be the premier American architect.

That Frank Lloyd Wright bore little love for LA is no secret; fortunately, his distaste is not his only legacy. To see the six homes Wright built locally, begin your tour in Pasadena and continue east into Hollywood. Remember, though, all but Hollyhock House are private residences!

Millard House (1923), 645 Prospect Crescent, Pasadena.
Hollyhock House (1920), Barnsdall Park, Vermont Ave at Hollywood Blvd, Hollywood.
Storer House (1923), 8161 Hollywood Blvd, Hollywood.
Ennis-Brown House (1924), 2655 Glendower Rd, Los Feliz.
Freeman House (1924), Glencoe Way, Hollywood.
Sturges House (1939), Kenter Canyon, off Skyewiay Drive, Brentwood. ■

includes art education and workshop buildings, as well as the **LA Municipal Art Gallery** (☎ 213-485-4581), 4804 Hollywood Blvd, which presents changing exhibitions of fine art; it's open Tuesday to Sunday 12:30 to 5 pm; admission is $1.

GRIFFITH PARK

Griffith Park is one of the largest city parks in America, with 4213 acres including two 18-hole golf courses, a wide variety of sports and playground facilities, the Greek Theater, (a big-name outdoor concert venue, see Entertainment), and wilderness seen more by mule deer than human intruders. For hiking information stop by the Griffith Park Ranger Station & Visitors Center (☎ 213-665-5188), 4730 Crystal Springs Drive, from 6 am to 10 pm.

The most direct route into Griffith Park is via Vermont Ave. You can also enter via Western or Canyon Aves. Get directly onto either Griffith Park or Zoo Drives by taking their respective exits from I-5, which runs along the park's eastern edge. Highway 134 runs along the park's northern edge and gets you in via the Victory Blvd exit (which meets Zoo Drive just inside the park). MTA buses No 96 and No 97 both have service to Griffith Park.

Griffith Observatory

On the upper slopes of Mt Hollywood, facing the city, the Griffith Observatory and

Planetarium (☎ 213-664-1191), 2800 E Observatory Rd, has been a local landmark since 1935. (You may recognize it from scenes in *Rebel Without a Cause*.) The facility comprises a twin refracting telescope available for public viewing, a Hall of Science with astronomy exhibits, a 600-seat planetarium theater, and a laserium that screens psychedelic images with rock-music accompaniment. Take your turn at the telescope any clear night except Monday from 7 to 9:45 pm, or beginning at dusk in summer. The Hall of Science is open daily in summer 12:30 to 10 pm; Tuesday to Sunday 2 to 10 pm the rest of the year. There's no charge for the observatory; adults pay $4 for the planetarium and $6.50 for the laserium. Showtimes vary, so call ahead for information.

Kid Stuff

Many of the park's children's attractions are in its southeast corner, where Los Feliz Blvd crosses the Golden State (5) Fwy. There's a one-third scale model of an 1880s steam engine that runs a 1½-mile loop, a miniature stagecoach, a track for pony rides, tennis courts, and a swimming pool. An antique 1926 carousel operates nearby (daily in summer, weekends the rest of the year). To get to it, follow Crystal Springs Drive up the park's eastern flank.

Gene Autry Museum

Gene Autry, born in Texas in 1907, became a millionaire several times over by recording nine gold records – including 'Rudolph, the Red-Nosed Reindeer' and 'Back in the Saddle Again' – from the 1930s through the '60s. Known as 'The Singing Cowboy,' he parlayed his earnings into three music publishing companies, four radio stations, a Palm Springs resort, and a Major League Baseball team, the California Angels.

In 1988, Autry opened his Gene Autry Western Heritage Museum (☎ 213-667-2000), 4700 Zoo Drive, and it is already recognized as one of the world's most comprehensive collections on the history and evolution of the American West. The $54 million, two-story museum's 10 galleries skillfully combine scholarship and showmanship. There are exhibits on natural history, native and Hispanic roots, and the much-romanticized westward migration of the mid-19th century, and other displays on the cowboy lifestyle, firearms, art and sculpture (including works by Charles Russell and Frederic Remington), and the making of the Hollywood Western. There's also a children's gallery, a cafe, and a gift shop. It's open daily except Monday from 10 am to 5 pm; admission is $7 for adults, $5 for seniors and students, $3 for children 12 and under. ∎

Cemetery Crawl

Scattered throughout the LA basin, no place better demonstrates the lively art of death glorified than the Forest Lawn Cemeteries.

The 'flagship' of the Forest Lawn empire is **Forest Lawn Memorial Park-Hollywood Hills** (☎ 818-241-4151), which bounds Griffith Park to the northwest. Many legends of filmdom are resting there, among marble buildings and bronze statues honoring the American War of Independence. Highlights include replicas of Philadelphia's Liberty Bell and Boston's Old North Church; a 60-foot Washington Memorial; and a 30-by-165-foot mosaic, 'The Birth of Liberty.' There's also a Museum of Mexican History.

You may find **Forest Lawn Memorial Park-Glendale** (☎ 213-254-3131) even more impressive. It features the world's largest religious painting, Jan Stykam's 45-by-195-foot 'The Crucifixion;' a stained-glass interpretation of da Vinci's 'The Last Supper;' and a 20-by-30–foot mosaic version of 'The Signing of the Declaration of Independence.'

If famous tombstones are what you're looking for, immediately north of the Paramount Lot is **Hollywood Memorial Cemetery** (☎ 213-469-1181), a 65-acre sanctuary which may contain more stars' graves than any other such refuge. Here lie Douglas Fairbanks, Rudolph Valentino, Cecil B DeMille, Tyrone Power, Peter Lorre, Jayne Mansfield, Richie Valens, and many other greats and not-so-greats. ∎

Los Angeles Zoo

Located at 5333 Zoo Drive (☎ 213-666-4090), near the junction of the Golden State (5) and Ventura (134) Fwys, this zoo doesn't compete for superlatives with the world-famous San Diego Zoo to the south. Nevertheless, it's worth a visit for animal lovers. There are separate continental areas for North and South America, Eurasia, Africa, and Australia, plus the Adventure Island children's zoo with creatures native to the American Southwest. It's open daily 10 am to 5 pm, except Christmas; entry is $8.25 for adults, $5.25 for seniors, $3.25 for children 2 to 12.

Travel Town

On the north side of Griffith Park just off the Ventura (134) Fwy, Travel Town (☎ 213-662-5874), 5200 N Zoo Drive, is an outdoor transportation museum that specializes in pre-WWII railroad antiques such as steam locomotives, cabooses, trolley cars, and a huge model-train network that runs Sundays from 11 am to 2:30 pm. It's open weekdays from 10 am to 5 pm, weekends and holidays until 6 pm; free.

WEST HOLLYWOOD

Wedged between Hollywood and Beverly Hills, embracing the Sunset Strip, part of Melrose Ave, and a long stretch of Santa Monica Blvd, this incorporated city is known far and wide for its enormously popular restaurants, nightclubs, theaters, art galleries, and boutiques. Its Pacific Design Center has helped establish the city's fame as an interior-design capital, while the Beverly Center is one of LA's shopping hubs.

Sunset Strip

Eclectic as ever, the famed Sunset Strip – Sunset Blvd between Laurel Canyon Blvd and Doheny Drive, where the westbound street curves south to follow the contours of the landscape – is all that it's cracked up to be, attracting every variety of LA character to its stores (Virgin & Tower Records), clubs of all types, and chic hotels and snazzy restaurants.

Sunset has hauntingly famous spots such as the 1927 **Château Marmont Hotel** (☎ 213-656-1010), 8221 Sunset Blvd, where the comedian John Belushi died of a drug overdose, and the **Viper Room**, 8852 Sunset Blvd, where young actor River Phoenix died of drug-related complications in 1993; and celebrity-owned joints including Dennis Hopper and Peter Fonda's **Thunder Roadhouse**, 8371 Sunset Blvd, where Patrick Swayze and Mickey Rourke bought their Harley Davidsons, and Dan Aykroyd's **House of Blues**, 8430 Sunset Blvd, which hosts great music and celebrity watching. Go to launching pads such as the **Comedy Store**, 8433 Sunset Blvd, where David Letterman, Robin Williams, and Roseanne got their starts.

A few blocks of Sunset read like a where's where of LA rock history: the **Whisky A Go Go** at No 8901, the **Roxy** at No 9009, the **Rainbow Bar & Grill** at No 9015, and **Gazzarri's** at No 9039, were regular gigs for the Doors, Jimi Hendrix, Bob Marley, Bruce Springsteen, and Van Halen, to name a few.

The Sunset Shuttle (☎ 310-858-8000), run by the City of West Hollywood, offers shuttle-bus service up and down the Strip.

The Design District

At the heart of a triangle framed by Santa Monica, Beverly, and La Cienega Blvds is the Pacific Design Center (☎ 310-657-0800), 8687 Melrose Ave, known to locals as the 'Blue Whale,' which contains more than 200 showrooms in its 1.2 million sq feet of floor space. This is the cornerstone for the so-called Avenues of Design – mainly Melrose Ave and Robertson and Beverly Blvds – which contain some 300 additional design shops and showrooms. There are another three dozen art galleries in the vicinity, including the **Margo Leavin Gallery** (☎ 310-273-0603), 812 N Robertson Blvd, unmistakable for Claes Oldenburg's 'Knife Slicing Through Wall' sculpture.

Melrose Ave

Imagine the Sunset Strip on Venice Beach,

and you have some idea of what Melrose Ave is all about. Expect to see skinhead motorcyclists, magenta- and lime-haired grunge rockers, and pierced-nosed head-bangers searching for the latest in fashion alongside Armani-clad businessmen. Wild shop windows and ostentatiously colorful facades reflect the diversity of humankind. A stark contrast to the trendy frenzy that is Melrose, most residents on the surrounding side streets are Orthodox Jews.

Architecture addicts will want to detour two blocks north from Melrose at Kings Road to see the **Schindler House** (☎ 213-651-1510), 835 N Kings Rd, designed by Viennese immigrant architect Rudolph Schindler who lived here until he died in 1953. Tours are offered weekend after-noons by appointment.

Another 1½ miles east of La Brea, **Paramount Studios** (☎ 213-956-5575), 5555 Melrose Ave, is open to those who call ahead for a two-hour guided walking tour.

BEVERLY HILLS

Throughout the world, mere mention of the name 'Beverly Hills' conjures an image of fame and wealth. The reality of this stylish and sophisticated city-within-a-city is not so different from the myth portrayed by filmdom. Among the winding, tree-lined streets that climb the Santa Monica Mountain foothills are the lavish estates – sprawling Spanish haciendas, stately Tudor mansions, French Provencial farmhouses – for which the city is famous. **Rodeo Drive** is lined with a veritable 'Who's Who' of fashion designers' shops, beginning at the front doors of the sumptuous Regent Beverly Wilshire Hotel (☎ 310-275-5200) at 9500 Wilshire Blvd.

You can get directions to the stars' homes from street-corner vendors wherever you see a scribbled 'Star Home Maps' sign. One of the more intriguing is **Greystone Park**, 905 Loma Vista Drive, used in many movies, including *The Bodyguard* and *Indecent Proposal*. Another landmark is the 1912 **Beverly Hills Hotel & Bungalows** (☎ 310-276-2251), 9641 Sunset Blvd,

nicknamed 'The Pink Palace,' whose Polo Lounge is a famous refuge for Industry 'power lunches.'

Century City

Adjoining Beverly Hills at its southwest corner, once was the enormous backlot of 20th Century Fox studios. Now it's an important business and entertainment center whose main street is Avenue of the Stars, which runs in a southerly direction from Santa Monica Blvd to Pico Blvd, marked by the Century City Shopping Center and Marketplace on its north end, and a huge business-and-theater complex, built in 1975 by Minoru Yamasaki, who also was the architect of New York's World Trade Center.

Museum of Tolerance

Just south of Beverly Hills and just east of Century City, the new Museum of Tolerance (☎ 310-553-8403), 9786 W Pico Blvd, presents a gut-wrenching look some of the more appalling examples of human behavior. The oppression of blacks in America and the 20th-century Holocaust in Europe are primary focuses. Hours are Monday to Thursday 10 am to 5 pm, Friday 10 am to 3 pm, Sunday 11 am to 5 pm. Admission is $7.50.

WEST SIDE

The quiet, affluent neighborhoods of Bel Air and Brentwood and the beautifully landscaped Westwood campus of the University of California, Los Angeles (UCLA), dominate that part of LA flanking the San Diego (405) Fwy between Beverly Hills and Santa Monica. Westwood Village is today LA's single biggest center of first-run movie houses. The 1931 Spanish tower of Mann's Village Theater, 961 Broxton Ave, and the 1937 Art Deco design of Mann's Bruin Theater, 948 Broxton Ave, dominate the village, which is a favorite of students not only for its proximity to UCLA, but also for its inexpensive cafes and youth-oriented stores.

CALIFORNIA

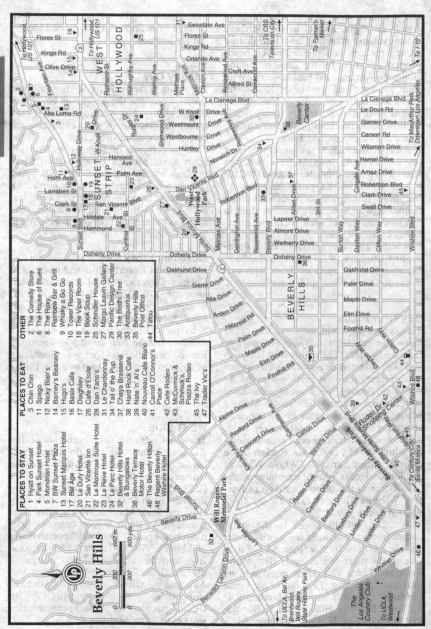

Armand Hammer Museum of Art & Cultural Center

At the foot of the village at the corner of Wilshire Blvd and Westwood Blvd, this museum (☎ 310-443-7000) displays the late industrialist's personal collection worth $450 million of Impressionist and post-Impressionist paintings. Hours are Tuesday to Saturday 11 am to 7 pm, Sunday until 6 pm; admission is $4.50 for adults.

University of California, Los Angeles

Established in 1919, UCLA encompasses 90 buildings on a 419-acre campus and has an enrollment of about 35,000 students. Guided campus tours (☎ 310-825-4321) are offered weekdays at 10:30 am and 1:30 pm (by reservation) from the visitors center in the Ueberroth Building, 10945 Le Conte Ave. On campus, the Fowler Museum of Cultural History (☎ 310 825-4361), Circle Drive N, exhibits a world-class collection of art and artifacts from Latin America, Africa, Asia, and the Pacific, while the Wight Art Gallery (☎ 310-825-9345), Circle Drive N at Circle Drive E, has more than 70 works including masterpieces by Matisse, Miró, Rodin, and Henry Moore. Schoenberg Hall (☎ 310-825-2101), Circle Drive E, houses a collection of rare stringed instruments and sponsors thrice-weekly noon concerts from October through May.

SANTA MONICA

The seaside city of Santa Monica is one of the most agreeable in the greater LA area. With its early-20th-century pleasure pier, its hotels and restaurants on a bluff over-looking the Pacific Ocean, its pedestrian-friendly downtown, and its colorful Main St district, this is a great place to pass an afternoon and evening.

The north end of Santa Monica is notable for the fashionable shopping street of **Montana Ave.** The street extends three miles from Ocean Ave to 26th St, then into Brentwood; the best stretch for shoppers and diners is between 7th and 17th Sts. Look for boutiques, salons, and fine continental- and California-cuisine restaurants.

The heart of Santa Monica is the **3rd St Promenade,** a pedestrian mall that extends for three long blocks from Wilshire Blvd south to Broadway. Here you'll find street entertainment (especially on weekends), restaurants, bars, and movie theaters. The south end of the Promenade is anchored by **Santa Monica Place**, Broadway between 2nd and 4th Sts, a three-story, 150-store, sky-lit galleria whose Atelier showcases current work from the USC School of Fine Arts.

Two blocks west of the Promenade, Ocean Ave follows **Palisades Park** atop a bluff overlooking ocean beaches. The sunsets from here are unparalleled in the LA area. At the south end of Palisades Park, Colorado Ave leaps over the Pacific Coast Hwy and ends on the **Santa Monica Pier.** The West Coast's oldest surviving pleasure pier, it has a 'fun zone' with arcades and rides (including the 1920s carousel featured in *The Sting*), seafood restaurants, and gift shops.

Also there's **Main St**, running south for two miles from Pico until it enters the community of Venice at Rose Ave, where it verges on the ultra-trendy, especially around its intersection with Ocean Park Blvd. Main St has taken off since 1989, when contemporary architect Frank O Gehry was commissioned to re-engineer a turn-of-the-century egg-processing plant into the urban village. A principal tenant is the **Santa Monica Museum of Art** (☎ 310-399-0433), 2437 Main St, which exhibits contemporary Californian and European artists and performers. Nearby are the **Gallery of Contemporary Photography** (☎ 310-399-4282), 2431 Main St, and the **Gallery of Functional Art** (☎ 310-450-2827), 2427 Main St, the latter a center for wry social commentary through sculpture.

Take Ocean Park Blvd three miles east, turn right on 28th St, and you'll find yourself at the Santa Monica Municipal Airport, where pioneer aviator Donald Douglas, Sr, built his first aircraft. Some of those planes,

CALIFORNIA

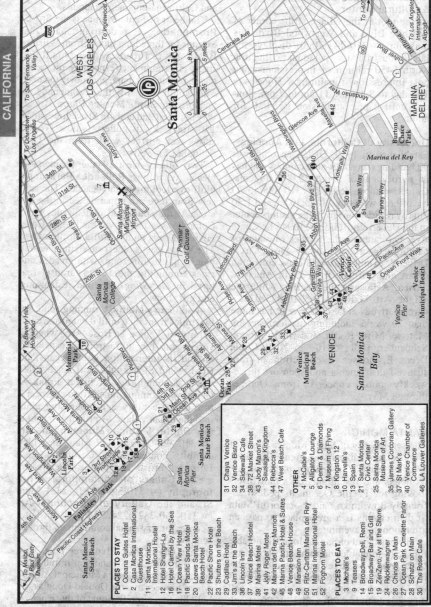

PLACES TO STAY
1   Oceana Suites Hotel
2   Casa Monica International
    Guesthouse
11 Santa Monica
    International Hostel
12 Hotel Shangri-La
16 Hotel Carmel by the Sea
17 Ocean View Hotel
18 Pacific Sands Motel
20 Loews Santa Monica
    Beach Hotel
22 Pacific Shore Hotel
23 Shutters on the Beach
29 Cadillac Hotel
33 Jim's at the Beach
36 Lincoln Inn
37 Venice Beach Hostel
39 Marina Motel
41 Jolly Roger Motel
42 Marina del Rey Marriott
45 Marina Pacific Hotel & Suites
48 Venice Beach House
49 Mansion Inn
50 Ritz-Carlton Marina del Rey
51 Marina International Hotel
52 Foghorn Motel

PLACES TO EAT
3   Michael's
9   Teasers
14 Broadway Deli, Remi
15 Broadway Bar and Grill
19 ZenZero, Ivy at the Shore
24 Röckenwagner
26 Chinois on Main
27 Ocean Park Omelette Parlor
28 Schatzi on Main
30 The Rose Cafe

31 Chaya Venice
32 Venice Bistro
34 Sidewalk Cafe
38 72 Market Street
43 Jody Maroni's
    Sausage Kingdom
44 Rebecca's
47 West Beach Cafe

OTHER
4   McCabe's
5   Alligator Lounge
6   Denim & Diamonds
7   Museum of Flying
8   Kingston 12
10 Harvelle's
13 Spain
21 Santa Monica
    Civic Center
25 Santa Monica
    Museum of Art
35 James Corcoran Gallery
37 St Mark's
40 Venice Chamber of
    Commerce
46 LA Louver Galleries

RICK GERHARTER

'You are here,' Melrose-style

RICK GERHARTER

RICK GERHARTER

Temples of the Industry, LA movie palaces

RICK GERHARTER

Frederick's of Hollywood

RICK GERHARTER

Celebrity worship

RICK GERHARTER

The Griffith Observatory, site of the knife fight in *Rebel without a Cause*

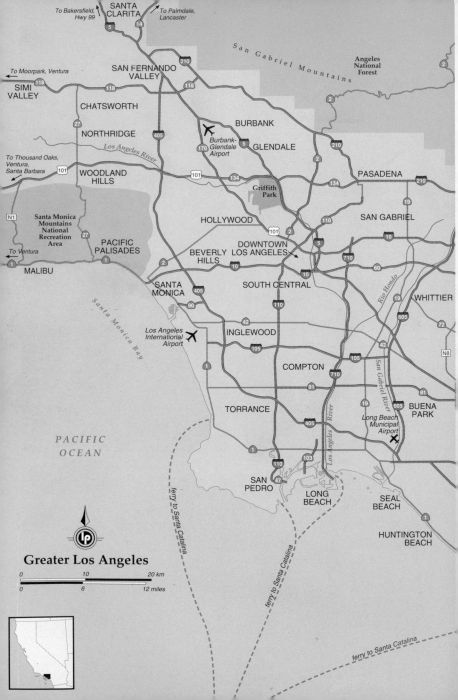

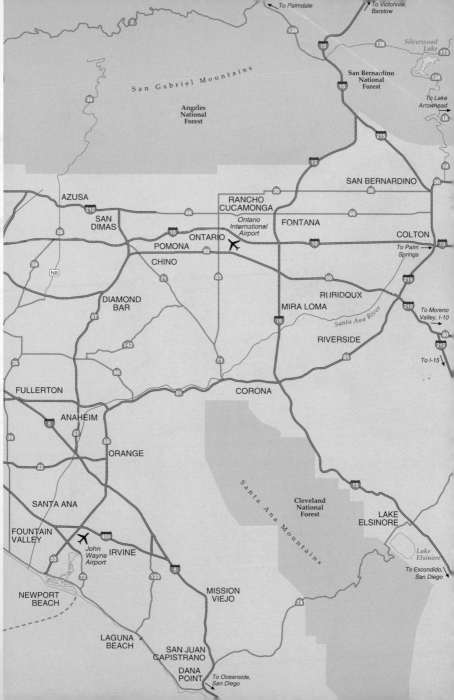

Inside the Bradbury Building

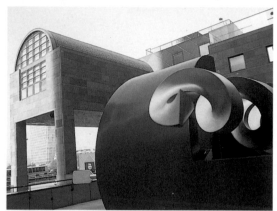

LA Museum of Contemporary Art

Chiat-Day, Inc

Downtown Los Angeles skyscrapers, the domino effect

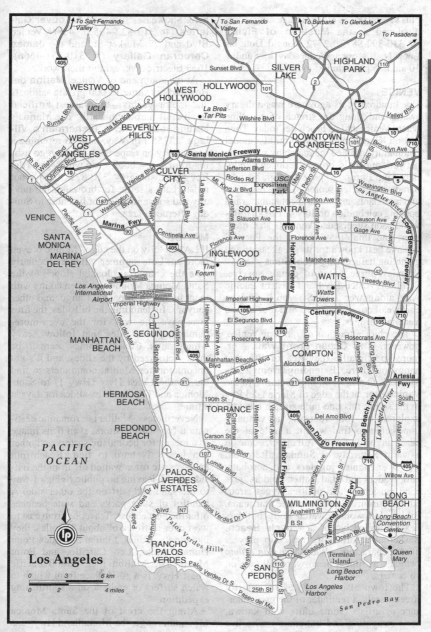

Los Angeles

0   3   6 km

0   2   4 miles

plus several dozen other vintage aircraft are displayed at the **Museum of Flying** (☎ 310-392-8822), 2772 Donald Douglas Loop N. It's open Wednesday to Sunday 10 am to 5 pm; admission is $7.

VENICE

One hundred years ago there was a dreary swampland along the stretch of coastline where Venice and its beach lies today. Then Abbott Kinney, on a quest to build a model community, drained the marsh by a 16-mile network of canals, brought a dozen gondoliers from Europe to pole through his new paradise, attracted scores of new residents and merchants, and had a spectacular grand opening celebration on July 4, 1905. Hollywood soon superseded Venice's star, however, and this 'Playland of the Pacific' became best known for its speakeasies and gambling halls during Prohibition.

Today, three miles of canals survive. South of Venice Blvd and east of Pacific Ave, along wee Dell St, you'll find an enclave of cozy bungalows and four arched Venetian bridges.

The chief attraction of modern Venice, however, is its **Ocean Front Walk** – or, more specifically, the slice of life that hangs out here. Extending from Santa Monica's Ocean Park, on the north, to the **Venice Pier**, at the edge of Marina del Rey to the south, this one-mile stretch must be explored by foot (parking is virtually impossible to find within a mile of the beach anyway). For the full effect, come on a warm Saturday or Sunday afternoon. You'll encounter jugglers and acrobats, tarot readers and Mad Hatter vendors, jugband musicians, and political types circulating petitions to decriminalize marijuana. Bikini-clad women watch body builders flex well-oiled biceps at **Muscle Beach.** Basketball courts attract pickup players like the characters in *White Men Can't Jump* (which was filmed here) who will take on all comers.

The town also has scores of colorful street murals, a reminder of the preponderance of artists (some quite well known, most struggling and bohemian) who live here. Showcases like the **LA Louver Galleries** (☎ 310-822-4955), 45 N Venice Blvd and 77 Market St, and the **James Corcoran Gallery** (☎ 310-451-4666), 1633 Electric Ave, exhibit their work.

At the south end of Venice, **Marina del Rey** harbors some 10,000 private sailboats and motor yachts – the largest artificial small-craft harbor on Earth. The Marina's leading tourist site is **Fishermen's Village**, 13755 Fiji Way, built to resemble a community on Cape Cod. You *can* go fishing from here – book a trip with Marina del Rey Sportfishing (☎ 310-822-3625) – but most visitors settle for browsing the novelty and souvenir shops or listening to Sunday afternoon jazz.

MALIBU

If LA is a 'city on the edge,' Malibu is even more so. Late summer wildfires regularly raze the chaparral-cloaked slopes of the Santa Monica Mountains, often taking with them homes in Topanga, Latigo, and other canyons. In denuding the hillsides, the fires also pave the way for the even-more-damaging mudslides that follow heavy winter rains. Coastal homes seem to be most victimized by the slides, and it's not uncommon for Malibu commuters to find the Pacific Coast Hwy (Hwy 1) to Santa Monica and LA closed by slides for days at a time.

Nevertheless, Malibu is a romantic destination for many visitors, even if its image as a mecca for hedonistic surfers and other sun lovers is hard to find. Beachfront enclaves are often walled off from the outside world, leaving no public rights-of-way to the sand and surf on the other side. A handful of state parks and state beaches offer the best access. Traveling from east to west over a stretch of about 25 miles, they include Las Tunas, Malibu Surfrider, Point Dume, Zuma, Leo Carrillo, and Point Mugu. The Malibu Pier, 23000 Pacific Coast Hwy, is a good place from which to watch surfers or embark on a sportfishing expedition.

Along the crest of the Santa Monica Mountain range, the Mulholland Hwy runs

50 miles from Leo Carrillo Beach to the Hollywood (101) Fwy; the panoramic views from the road are simply astounding.

J Paul Getty Museum

By far the best reason to go to Malibu is this museum (☎ 310-458-2003), 17985 Pacific Coast Hwy, near Santa Monica just west of Sunset Blvd. A replica of a 79 AD Pompeiian villa, it houses one of the world's most valuable art collections: Getty endowed it with a trust that is now worth $3 billion. Displayed among its magnificent indoor and outdoor gardens are a fantastic array of Greek and Roman antiquities; its additional treasures of European decorative arts and painting (including van Gogh's 'Irises') are scheduled to be moved upon completion of the new Getty Center in Bel Air, in 1997. The gift shop and tea room at this museum are worth a visit in themselves. It's open Tuesday to Sunday 10 am to 5 pm; admission is free, but parking res-

ervations are required, preferably a week in advance. Under no circumstances should you miss this incredible museum.

PASADENA

Resting in the shadow of the lofty San Gabriel Mountains, Pasadena was established in 1873 by Midwestern settlers who gave it a Chippewa name meaning 'crown of the valley.' The town incorporated in 1886, and before long five commuter trains a day linked it with downtown LA. After Southern California's first freeway, the Arroyo Seco Pkwy (since designated I-110, the Pasadena Fwy), connected LA and Pasadena in 1940, more commuters settled in Pasadena. About 135,000 people now call the city home, as do the famed Tournament of Roses (see Special Events), Rose Bowl, and the acclaimed think-tank of the California Institute of Technology.

Old Town

This 14-block historic district of late-19th and early-20th century buildings whose main intersection is at Colorado Blvd and Fair Oaks Ave, is the heart of Pasadena. Streets and hidden alleyways of the newly gentrified area are lined with restaurants and coffeehouses, upscale boutiques and bookstores, antique stores and novelty shops, nightclubs and cinema complexes.

Norton Simon Museum

A short walk west from Old Town takes you to the Norton Simon Museum (☎ 818-449-6840), 411 W Colorado Blvd, with its outstanding collection of works by Boticelli, Cézanne, Degas, Goya, Matisse, Monet, Picasso, Raphael, Rembrandt, Renoir, Rubens, Toulouse-Lautrec, and van Gogh. There are also notable exhibits of Hindu and Buddhist sculpture from India and Southeast Asia. It's open Thursday to Sunday noon to 6 pm; admission is $4.

Millionaire's Row

Pasadena's Millionaire's Row, which extends on either side of Orange Grove Blvd from the Norton Simon Museum, is home to many of the city's lavish early-

---

Public Art

Nothing bridges gaps in common experience like the visual arts. LA-area artists – surrounded by speakers of over 80 languages, many living in poverty that keeps museum visits, performances, and movies out of reach – are taking steps to ensure their messages are heard by those residents who need it most. The Social & Public Art Resource Center (SPARC, ☎ 310-822-9560) is one such group dedicating itself to the production, exhibition, and preservation of multi-ethnic art projects, notably the city's nearly 1000 murals. SPARC and the Mural Conservancy of Los Angeles (MCLA, ☎ 310-470-8864) provide docent-led tours of LA's 'street gallery,' showcasing the works of particular muralists or neighborhoods, about a dozen times per year. Cost of tours are $25 for adults, $20 for students and seniors. Some of the areas most often visited are East LA, downtown, South Central, Hollywood, and Venice, with most tours introducing at least one of the featured artists. Call in advance for a schedule of upcoming tours. ■

LA Botany

Known for its traffic and freeways, LA nevertheless has much to offer in the way of peaceful and exotic garden settings. The following list includes gardens around Greater Los Angeles worth making a special effort to visit:

Los Angeles State & County Arboretum (☎ 818-821-3222), 301 N Baldwin Ave, Arcadia.
The arboretum recreates many of the world's major landscapes, arranged by continent around a spring-fed lake. That's one reason this 127-acre garden is so popular with movie makers – including John Huston, who filmed much of *The African Queen* here.

Huntington Library, Museum & Gardens (☎ 818-405-2141), 1151 Oxford Rd, San Marino.
The Botanical Gardens span 150 acres and contain more than 14,000 different species of trees, shrubs, and flowering plants in 15 separate gardens. A highlight is the Desert Garden, featuring the widest array of mature cacti and other succulents in the USA. Other visitor favorites are the Japanese Garden and the Shakespearean Garden. An English tea room (☎ 818-683-8131) serves light afternoon meals.

Descanso Gardens (☎ 818-952-4400), 1418 Descanso Drive, La Cañada Flintridge.
A year-round delight for flower lovers, some 100,000 camellias are in bloom from October through March; lilacs and orchids are at their best in April; roses and other annuals blossom beginning in May. Flower shows feature other varieties throughout the year. Bird lovers have identified 150 species in the gardens.

Japanese Garden at the Tillman Water Reclamation Plant (☎ 818-756-8166), 6100 Woodley Ave, Van Nuys.
The traditional garden, which includes bridged ponds, stone lanterns, bonsai sculpture, and a tea house, is built atop a water-treatment facility at the northern edge of the Sepulveda Basin Recreation Area. Book ahead to join a free guided tour of the garden.

Virginia Robinson Gardens (☎ 310-276-5367) 1008 Elden Way, Beverly Hills.
With a week's notice, you can visit this 1920s estate. The six-acre gardens include many rare palms and flowering trees.

Hannah Carter Japanese Garden (☎ 310-825-4574), 10619 Bellagio Rd, Bel Air.
By reservation, you can wander this garden on the edge of the UCLA campus. Built in 1961, it features a teahouse and imported vegetation.

Rancho Santa Ana Botanic Garden (☎ 909-625-8767), 1500 N College Ave, Claremont.
The 85-acre garden displays the world's largest array of native California plants. Trails writhe through species from deserts, mountain woodlands, and the coast.

Orcutt Ranch Horticulture Center (☎ 818-883-6641), 23600 Roscoe Blvd, Canoga Park.
Huge live-oak trees, some perhaps as old as six centuries, shade a Spanish-style ranch house built in 1920. The City of Los Angeles conducts gardening classes on the grounds. ■

20th century buildings, many of them designed by architects Charles and Henry Greene between 1903 and 1910. Of note are the **Tournament House and Wrigley Gardens** (☎ 818-449-4100), 391 S Orange Grove Blvd, the former estate of William Wrigley, Jr; the imposing **Vista del Arroyo Hotel**, a couple of blocks from Wrigley's estate at 125 S Grand Ave, now home to the Ninth Circuit US Court of Appeals; and Pasadena's most infamous landmark: the **Colorado St Bridge** (1913). 'Suicide Bridge,' as it came to be known, was the area's favorite jumping

spot for those hard hit by the 1929 stock market crash.

Pasadena Historical Museum

Housed in the 18-room neo-Classical Fenyes Estate at 470 W Walnut St, where Orange Grove Blvd crosses over the Ventura (134) Fwy, this museum (☎ 818-577-1660) has original antique furnishings and paintings on the main floor, archival photos in the basement, and a display of Finnish folk art in the outlying sauna house. Guided tours are offered Thursday to Sunday from

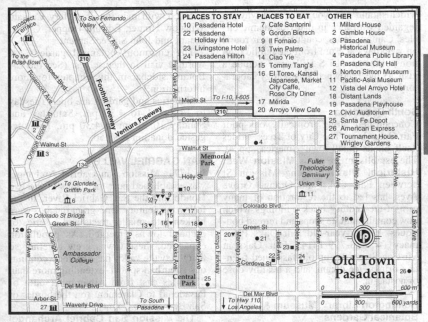

PLACES TO STAY
10 Pasadena Hotel
22 Pasadena Holiday Inn
23 Livingstone Hotel
24 Pasadena Hilton

PLACES TO EAT
7 Cafe Santorini
8 Gordon Biersch
9 Il Fornaio
13 Twin Palms
14 Ciao Yie
15 Tommy Tang's
16 El Toreo, Kansai Japanese, Market City Caffe, Rose City Diner
17 Mérida
20 Arroyo View Cafe

OTHER
1 Millard House
2 Gamble House
3 Pasadena Historical Museum
4 Pasadena Public Library
5 Pasadena City Hall
6 Norton Simon Museum
11 Pacific-Asia Museum
12 Vista del Arroyo Hotel
18 Distant Lands
19 Pasadena Playhouse
21 Civic Auditorium
25 Santa Fe Depot
26 American Express
27 Tournament House, Wrigley Gardens

1 to 4 pm (closed in August). Admission is $4.

The Gamble House

At 4 Westmoreland Place, a block north from the Historical Museum, the Gamble House (☎ 818-793-3334) is considered the world's best example of Craftsman-style bungalow architecture. A 1908 Greene-and-Greene design, it was commissioned by Cincinnati's Gamble family (of Proctor & Gamble renown), and is now a study center maintained by the School of Architecture at the University of Southern California. Original furnishings share attention with the polished teak woodwork and Tiffany glass. This was the home of mad scientist Doc Brown (Christopher Lloyd) in the three *Back to the Future* movies. Guided tours are offered Thursday through Sunday noon to 3 pm; admission is $4.

Nearby, the **Millard House**, also known as La Miniatura, at 645 Prospect Crescent, was designed in new Aztec style by Frank Lloyd Wright in 1923.

Pasadena Civic Center

Italian Renaissance and Spanish Colonial architectural styles meet Beaux Arts in this complex a few blocks east of Old Town, just north of Colorado Blvd. The magnificent Pasadena City Hall (☎ 818-405-4222), 100 N Garfield Ave, built in 1927 around a courtyard garden and fountain, is flanked by the 1927 Pasadena Public Library (☎ 818-405-4066), 285 E Walnut St and the 1933 Civic Auditorium (☎ 818-449-7360), 300 E Green St, annual home to television's Emmy Awards ceremony.

The imperial Chinese facade of the nearby **Pacific-Asia Museum** (☎ 818-449-2742), 46 N Los Robles Ave, houses galleries of ancient and contemporary works from Asia and the Pacific Islands. It's open Wednesday to Sunday from 10 am to 5 pm; admission is $3, free the third Saturday of the month.

California Institute of Technology

Twenty-two Nobel laureates have taught at Caltech (☎ 818-395-6327), 551 S Hill Ave, which should give you some idea why it's regarded with awe in many academic circles. Campus tours, conducted year round on weekdays at 2 pm from the public relations office at 315 S Hill Ave, include a visit to the renowned seismology laboratory.

South Pasadena

Concentrated along ironically oak-poor Fair Oaks Ave, 'The City of Trees' prides itself on its small-town America appeal. The establishment of its **Mission West Historical District,** along Mission St between Fair Oaks and Orange Grove Aves, has led to the restoration of many turn-of-the-century brick buildings which now contain antique shops and retread boutiques. Eighty-year-old Fair Oaks Pharmacy (☎ 818-799-1414), Fair Oaks at Mission St, serves up old-fashioned fountain drinks, ice cream, and a healthy dose of nostalgia.

Huntington Library, Museum & Botanical Gardens

Southeast of Pasadena in San Marino (named after the world's oldest republic), Henry E Huntington's 1910 manor and grounds (☎ 818-405-2141), 1151 Oxford Rd, are one of Southern California's not-to-be-missed attractions.

The library's collection of rare English-language books, maps, and manuscripts rivals that of the British Museum: among those on permanent display are a Gutenberg Bible, the Ellesmere manuscript of Chaucer's *Canterbury Tales,* Benjamin Franklin's handwritten autobiography, and a double folio edition of Audubon's *Birds of America.*

The original home is now the **Huntington Art Gallery,** whose collection of 18th-century British and French paintings – among them Thomas Gainsborough's 'Blue Boy' and portraits by Sir Thomas Lawrence, Sir Joshua Reynolds, and George Romney – ranks with the world's great art museums. The **Virginia Steele Scott Gallery of American Art** exhibits works from the 1730s to the 1930s: its walls are

adorned with paintings by Mary Cassatt, Winslow Homer, Edward Hopper, Gilbert Stuart, and John Singer Sargent.

The enormous botanical gardens are worth a visit in themselves. (See the LA Botany sidebar in this chapter for more information.)

Galleries and gardens are open Tuesday to Friday 1 to 4:30 pm, Saturday and Sunday 10:30 am to 4:30 pm. The suggested donation is $7.50.

SAN GABRIEL VALLEY

In 1771, Mission San Gabriel Archangel was established near the banks of the Rio Hondo and the San Gabriel River. In the following century, land-grant ranchos were broken into smaller tracts and a series of orchard towns emerged. As population expanded, these towns grew together so that today the valley has become a continuous suburban sprawl, extending more than 25 miles east from Alhambra (south of Pasadena) to Claremont (on the border of San Bernardino County).

The **Mission San Gabriel Archangel** (☎ 818-457-3035), 537 W Mission Drive, is a 19th-century restoration built upon the ruins of the original church, constructed by Gabrieleño workers between 1791 and 1805 and based upon the cathedral in Cordova, Spain. Artifacts, including remnants of California's first winery, are on display in the mission museum, open daily 9:30 am to 4 pm. Donations are requested.

GLENDALE & BURBANK

These twin communities lie at the far eastern end of the San Fernando Valley, between Griffith Park (the easternmost extent of the Santa Monica Mountains) and the Verdugo Hills (a sub-range of the San Gabriel Mountains). The towns boomed in the 1920s, and today have populations diverse in their ethnicity and religion.

Brand Park, in northwest Glendale, is home to the **Brand Library & Art Galleries** (☎ 818-548-2051), 1601 W Mountain St. Built as a private mansion in 1904, with white domes and arches, it houses an art and music library, a gallery of modern

Getting into a Studio

If you want to be sure to see a particular TV star, your best bet is to watch them taping their show. Doing so is easy, and tickets are free – but plan ahead.

For tickets, contact Audiences Unlimited (☎ 818-506-0067), which handles arrangements for many of the studios in town including Warner Bros, Universal Studios, Disney, and CBS. They also book audiences for the smaller Sunset-Gower and Renmar studios.

Here's how to contact some of the major studios directly:

CBS Television City Shows include *Wheel of Fortune, The Price Is Right,* and *Family Feud.* 7800 Beverly Blvd (☎ 213-852-2624)

Fox Television Center This is where *Coach,* and *Married . . . With Children* are taped. 5746 Sunset Blvd, Hollywood (☎ 213-856-1520)

NBC Television Jay Leno's *Tonight Show* is the biggest draw, or call ☎ 818-340-3551 for tours (weekdays 9 pm to 3 pm, hourly). 3000 W Alameda Ave, Burbank (☎ 818-840-3537)

Paramount Studios Its most popular studio-audience shows include *Frasier, Wings,* and *Leeza.* Two-hour guided walking tours of the historic studios are available by reservation (☎ 213-956-5575). 5555 Melrose Ave, Hollywood (☎ 213-956-5000)

Warner Bros Studios Popular TV programs produced here include *Murphy Brown, Full House,* and *Step by Step.* The studio's 12-person VIP tours (weekdays 10 am to 2 pm, by reservation) give behind-the-scenes tours of many of the studio operations. Hollywood Way and Olive Ave, Burbank (☎ 818-954-1744) ■

art, an arts & crafts studio, and a performance hall. It's open Tuesday and Thursday 1 to 9 pm, Wednesday until 6 pm, Friday and Saturday until 5 pm.

Walt Disney Productions, Warner Bros Studios, the National Broadcasting Company (NBC), and Columbia Pictures' Television Division all make their homes in Burbank, and NBC and Warner Bros both welcome visitors.

SAN FERNANDO VALLEY

Fully one third of the population of LA lives in the Valley, a broad, flat region of 220 sq miles that is as well known for its earthquakes (the devastating Sylmar quake of 1971 and the Northridge tremor of 1994) as for its seemingly endless commercial strips and tract homes.

Four freeways provide a framework for the Valley. The Ventura (101) Fwy, on the south, parallels Ventura Blvd, which begins at Universal City and runs west 17 miles through Studio City, Sherman Oaks, Encino, Tarzana, and Woodland Hills. The Hollywood (170) Fwy runs northwest through Universal City and North Hollywood, joining the Golden State (5) Fwy at Sun Valley and continuing through San Fernando. The Simi Valley-San Fernando (now called the Ronald Reagan 118) Fwy crosses I-5 at Mission Hills and proceeds west through Granada Hills and Chatsworth. Finally, the San Diego (405) Fwy bisects the Valley, crossing I-101 at Sherman Oaks and joining I-5 at San Fernando.

Universal Studios

Universal Studios Hollywood (☎ 818-508-9600), 100 Universal City Plaza, has the world's largest movie and television studio and an interesting theme park worth a day's exploration. The hillside studios sprawl across 420 acres, the upper and lower sections connected by a quarter-mile-long escalator. Trams leave from the bottom of the escalator to explore locations used in hundreds of classic movies (like *Animal House, Home Alone,* and *The Sting*) and TV shows (such as *Leave It to Beaver, McHale's Navy,* and *Murder, She Wrote*). There are special effects exhibits, musical-comedy revues, and an Animal Actors Stage with performances by several dozen animals, including Beethoven, the canine movie star. Actors are frequently seen not only on sound stages but also in restaurants (there are at least eight within the park) and wandering the grounds.

Universal Studios is open 7:30 am to 11 pm in summer, 9 am to 7 pm the rest of the year. Admission is $31 for ages 12 and

CALIFORNIA

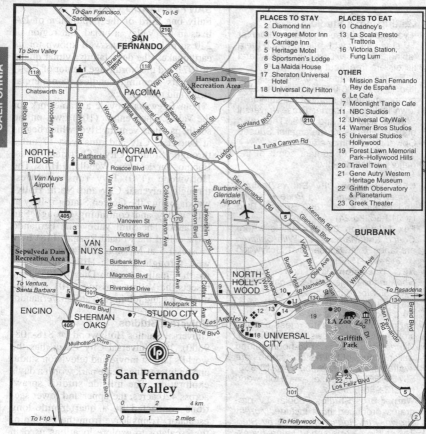

PLACES TO STAY
2 Diamond Inn
3 Voyager Motor Inn
4 Carriage Inn
7 Heritage Motel
8 Sportsmen's Lodge
9 La Maida House
17 Sheraton Universal Hotel
18 Universal City Hilton

PLACES TO EAT
10 Chadney's
13 La Scala Presto Trattoria
16 Victoria Station, Fung Lum

OTHER
1 Mission San Fernando Rey de España
6 Le Café
7 Moonlight Tango Cafe
11 NBC Studios
12 Universal CityWalk
14 Warner Bros Studios
15 Universal Studios Hollywood
19 Forest Lawn Memorial Park–Hollywood Hills
20 Travel Town
21 Gene Autry Western Heritage Museum
22 Griffith Observatory & Planetarium
23 Greek Theater

older; $24.95 for seniors (60 and older) or children (3 to 11).

Beside Universal Studios is **Universal CityWalk** (☎ 818-622-4455), 1000 Universal Center Drive, an innovative shopping, dining, and entertainment promenade featuring whimsical facades, from a '57 Chevy bursting through a freeway sign to a 27-foot gorilla guarding a music store entrance.

Mission San Fernando Rey de España
Founded in 1797, this mission (☎ 818-361-

0186), 15151 San Fernando Mission Rd, was the second Spanish mission built in the LA area (after San Gabriel; see below). The highlight of a visit is the mission's 1822 Convento, built with four-foot-thick adobe walls and 21 Roman arches. Also open for viewing are the 19th-century workshops of weavers, potters, carpenters, saddle makers, and blacksmiths; the house where the *mayordomo,* or ranch foreman, lived; a cemetery; a historical museum and archival center; and beautiful grounds sprinkled with statues and a 35-bell carillon. It's open daily 9 am to 5 pm; donations are requested.

ACTIVITIES
Hiking
Urban hiking is your best bet, but if you need to get space and a bit of greenery, LA's surrounding mountains are good day-hike destinations. The rugged mountains rise abruptly behind Malibu are encompassed by the Santa Monica Mountains National Recreation Area (☎ 818-597-1036), more than 234 sq miles of erratically vegetated hills under NPS administration. Topanga State Park (☎ 310-455-2465), climbs the mountain ridge to the east of Griffith Park, with a network of trails extending through its 9000 acres all the way to adjacent Will Rogers State Historic Park.

Biking
Although most of LA is not particularly inviting to cyclists, the county has more than 200 miles of bike trails. Best of the bunch is the South Bay Bicycle Trail, a flat, 22-mile paved path that follows the beach south from Santa Monica to Torrance Beach, with a jog around the yacht harbor at Marina del Rey. There are other more adventurous paths from Azusa to Long Beach (the 37-mile San Gabriel River Trail), from Commerce to Long Beach (the 20-mile Los Angeles River Path, which is probably the fastest way to get to a beach from anywhere near downtown LA), from Long Beach to Newport Beach (the 21-mile Oceanside Bike Path), and through

---

Adobe Buildings
Built with mud and clay bricks dried under the sun, adobe buildings are a signature of the Southwestern US. Greater LA has numerous examples of Spanish-era adobe architecture, which began with the area's two missions, at San Gabriel and San Fernando.

Avila Adobe is LA's oldest house. Built in 1818 by rancher Don Francisco Avila, it was damaged in the 1971 Sylmar earthquake but later restored. 10 E Olvera St (☎ 213-680-2525)

Andres Pico Adobe suffered heavy damage in the 1994 Northridge quake and is under reconstruction. Built in 1834, this second-oldest house in Los Angeles will eventually reopen for public tours. 10940 Sepulveda Blvd, Mission Hills (☎ 818-365-7810)

Centinela Adobe was also built in 1834 and is often overlooked, though it is one of LA's oldest existing structures. 7634 Midfield Ave, Westchester (☎ 310-649-6272)

Leonis Adobe dates from 1844. The two-story, Monterey-style ranch house has been restored to its appearance during its mid-19th-century heyday. 23537 Calabasas Rd, Calabasas (☎ 818-222-6511)

Rancho de los Encinos State Historical Park preserves a mid-19th-century stagecoach stop, including a nine-room adobe built in 1849 (it was huge for the time) and a two-story limestone cottage from 1870. 16756 Moorpark St, Encino (☎ 818-784-4849)

Pio Pico State Historic Park dates from 1850. The two-story adobe hacienda of Don Pio Pico, last Mexican governor of California, is now the centerpiece of this 9000-acre state park. 6003 Pioneer Blvd, Whittier (☎ 310-695-1217)

Casa Adobe de San Rafael remains from Rancho San Rafael in Glendale. Built in the early 19th century, and restored in 1932, the one-story hacienda nestles in a eucalyptus grove. 1330 Dorothy Drive

Catalina Verdugo Adobe also remains from the Rancho San Raphael, and was built in 1875. It's a private residence and can be viewed only from the street. 2211 Bonita Drive

Shadow Ranch Park includes an adobe-and-redwood home built in 1872, surrounded by a stand of eucalyptus said to be the first brought to Southern California from Australia. 22633 Vanowen St, Canoga Park (☎ 818-883-3637) ■

Griffith Park (an eight-mile trail that passes the LA Zoo and the Gene Autry Museum).

The best place to rent a bike is near the beach. Try Citycycle (☎ 310-450-4567), 1901 Main St, Santa Monica; the Venice Pier Bike Shop (☎ 310-301-4011), 21 Washington Blvd, Venice; or Spokes N Stuff (☎ 310-306-3332), 175 Admiralty Way, Marina del Rey.

Horseracing
Santa Anita Park (☎ 818-574-7223), 285 W Huntington Drive, is considered to be one of the best tracks in America. During the thoroughbred season, which runs from Christmas through April, visitors can watch morning workouts from 7:30 to 9:30 am weekdays and get a continental breakfast at Clocker's Corner; tram tours of the grounds are offered weekends at 8 am.

ORGANIZED TOURS
Most LA-area tour companies operate year round, with stepped-up schedules during the peak visitor periods of summer and the Christmas holidays. Gray Line's Starline Tours (☎ 213-856-5900, 800-279-5800), 6451 Hollywood Blvd, specializes in Hollywood tours, including theaters and movie stars' homes. For specialized tours of the glamour and scandal of Hollywood, sometimes in mini-vans, contact Casablanca Tours (☎ 213-461-0156) at the Roosevelt Hotel, 7000 Hollywood Blvd, or Hollywood Dream Tours (☎ 213-957-9280), 6919 Hollywood Blvd.

Grave Line Tours (☎ 213-469-3127) in Hollywood explores the final resting places of big-screen notables, and the venues of various other deaths, murders, and scandals – all in a refurbished hearse.

The LA Conservancy (☎ 213-623-2489),

BEACHES OF LA COUNTY

Northern Beaches
If skimpy bikinis and fast food picnics aren't to your taste, the northern end of the Santa Monica Bay is a welcome sanctuary. Beaches abound that will delight nature-lovers with miles of hiking, tide-pool gazing, swimming, surfing, diving, fishing, and sunbathing (clothing optional). For more information on the LA County coastline, call the chamber of commerce in the area you plan to visit, or the visitor's bureau information center (☎ 213-628-3101).

Point Dume Area The northernmost tip of the Santa Monica Bay, Point Dume begins where Kanan-Dume Rd meets PCH (Hwy 1). On its south side, **Paradise Cove** is a breathtaking private beach (admission fee charged) with a fishing pier and restaurant; no surfing or surf fishing is allowed. Further south, near Malibu Cove Colony Drive, an unmarked stairway leads to **Escondido Beach,** perhaps the best diving spot in the bay. Point Dume itself has a rocky, 215-foot north face that attracts technical climbers, while **Westward Beach** below boasts nature trails that join Zuma Beach to the north. A stairway at Westward Beach Rd (next to Monroe's restaurant) leads to a platform for whale-watching.

Zuma Beach County Park Two miles further up PCH, Zuma is LA's largest and sandiest county-owned beach, with all the 'dudes' and 'Bettys' to prove it. Rough surf and oily hardbodies may convince you to drive on, but if *Baywatch* brought you to LA, stop here to worship.

Point Mugu Beaches On the northern end of a magnificent 25-sq mile state park you reach Point Mugu. **Sycamore Cove** and **Thornhill Broome Beach** are popular for surf fishing and sunbathing; steep drop-offs and crashing surf make them less than ideal for swimmers. Primitive camping sites are available at Thornhill Broome or just across PCH at Sycamore Canyon. **Mugu Lagoon,** 1½ miles north of Point Mugu Rock, is the largest coastal estuary lagoon between San Diego and Morro Bay. Unfortunately, the land is part of the Navy's

727 7th St, offers an extensive program of walking tours – most of them on Saturday mornings – that includes classic architecture, the Broadway movie palaces, and historic homes. Air LA Tours (☎ 310-641-1114), 3000 N Claybourn Ave, Burbank, offers helicopter flights over Hollywood and Beverly Hills by day or night.

For boat tour information, see Santa Catalina Island in the Around Los Angeles chapter.

SPECIAL EVENTS

Special events in LA county run the gamut; here are some highlights:

January & February
The Tournament of Roses Parade – a cavalcade of enormous flower-coated floats proceeds along Pasadena's Colorado Blvd every New Year's Day (☎ 818-795-4171)
The Rose Bowl – the football game takes place later the same day (☎ 818-449-7673)
Oshogatsu – the Japanese New Year celebration, takes place in Little Tokyo with traditional foods, music, and dance (☎ 213-628-2725)
Chinese New Year – festivities take place in late January or early February and feature traditional revels in the heart of Chinatown; (☎ 213-617-0396)
African American History Month – February when African American history is celebrated with films, lectures, exhibits, and performances (☎ 213-295-0521).

March
The Academy Awards – bringing actors and film makers out in their designer finery
LA Marathon – the 26-mile race that begins at the Memorial Coliseum and proceeds through Chinatown, Hollywood, and Echo Park. Phone ☎ 310-444-5544 for information or to register to run.

April
Nondenominational Easter – services held at

Pacific Missile Test Center and is usually off-limits; weekend tours are given by the PMTC public affairs office (reservations required, ☎ 805-989-8094), but not for fewer than 15 adults. Ask about joining in on a pre-planned tour.

South Bay Beaches
Manhattan Beach Manhattan is the northernmost of a series of beachfront communities that run south from the airport area to the Palos Verdes Peninsula. It is also, perhaps, the nearest thing you'll find to the 'California Dream.' Between the beach, jam-packed on summer days with surfers and volleyball players, and the American-as-apple-pie residential districts inland, is an upscale downtown district lined with neat boutiques and restaurants, indicating a high degree of attention to modern city planning.

Hermosa Beach From the end of the Hermosa Beach Fishing Pier (rental equipment and bait available), you gaze north and south at superanimated surfers, east down Pier Ave at several blocks of funky bars and shops, and across a sweep of beach town at perhaps the least expensive housing along this entire shore. That doesn't mean it's cheap (this *is* LA), but prices are low enough to attract a high concentration of, well, laid-back dudes.

It's a mile and a half from the Manhattan pier to the Hermosa pier. Shortly after the turn of the 20th century, an electric trolley ran along this strand on its way from Marina del Rey to Redondo. Today, the 22-mile South Bay Trail, an urban bikeway, traces the same route. One of Hermosa's landmarks is the *Lighthouse Cafe* (☎ 310-372-6911), 30 Pier Ave, a nightclub decades old that now features live rock & roll most nights.

Redondo Beach Redondo is perhaps the most intriguing of the beach communities. At its north end is King Harbor, a small-boat marina and fishermen's haven. In the heart of town, at the end of Torrance Blvd, are Monstad Pier and Fisherman's Wharf, the biggest surfside pleasure complex south of Santa Monica. Joined at their seaward end, the pier and the wharf are chockablock with restaurants, bars, souvenir shops, and a fishing dock with a cafe that will cook what you catch. ■

sunrise in the famed Hollywood Bowl (☎ 213-850-2000)

May

Cinco de Mayo – festivities abound near Olvera St and other Chicano centers (☎ 213-625-5045)

June

Gay Pride Week – includes a flamboyant parade down Santa Monica Blvd in West Hollywood and a myriad smaller festivities

July

Summer Pops Festival – at the Hollywood Bowl beginning with a 4th of July concert with fireworks – and continuing through September (☎ 213-850-2000)

Festival of the Arts & the Pageant of the Masters – California's largest art fair at Laguna Beach in Orange County in July and August

August

The International Surf Festival – brings world class surfers to the waves at Manhattan, Hermosa, and Redondo beaches

September

The Los Angeles County Fair – the world's largest in Pomona (☎ 909-623-3111)

October

AFI-LA International Film Festival – from late October to early November – is one of the largest in the country, with more than 75 features from around the world. Call ☎ 213-856-7707 for a schedule of screenings.

November & December

Pasadena's Doo Dah Parade – a whacked-out parody of the traditional Rose Parade, with such staple marchers as a precision briefcase drill team. (Beware artificial seagulls 'anointing' unsuspecting onlookers!)

Hollywood Christmas Parade – movie and television stars join Santa Claus, ringing in the season from flashy floats riding down Hollywood Blvd

Christmas Boat Parades – ostentatiously herald the season with twinkling yachts cruising beach-town harbors, notably in Long Beach, Newport, and Marina del Rey

Las Posadas – candle-lit processions – including one on Olvera St – that relive Mary and Joseph's journey to Bethlehem and honor the Christ child in colorful, Latin fashion.

PLACES TO STAY

Greater LA has a wide variety of accommodations in all price categories, although finding a cheap bed between Memorial Day (late May) and Labor Day (early September) or over the Christmas holidays can be as difficult as finding a smog-free day in Pasadena.

Your best bet for bottom-end lodging in the LA area, in the $15 to $20 per night range, is at a hostel or in university housing. The information bureau at UCLA (☎ 310-825-4321) has a listing of dorm rooms. You might also snag a summer room at a sorority or fraternity house: call UCLA's Inter Fraternity Council (☎ 310-825-8409) or Pan-Hellenic Sorority Council (☎ 310-206-1285). In summer, USC (☎ 213-740-0031), near downtown, and Loyola Marymount University (☎ 310-388-2975), near LAX, often have rooms.

Hostels are generally well-maintained and well-located, with a concentration in the Venice/Santa Monica area near the beach. Bottom-end motels run about $35 to $60 per night, double occupancy. You'll find large numbers of these off the beaten tourist track, which behooves you to have a car. There are plenty of cheap lodgings in Hollywood, some of which rent by the hour (with an extra charge for waterbeds); but you wouldn't want to get under the sheets in many of them.

The closer you are to the coast or to upscale neighborhoods like Beverly Hills, the more likely your accommodations will cross the line into middle range, about $65 to $95 per night for two. The more removed from attractions your lodging is, the better buy you'll get for the price.

You'll find top end properties, sometimes including a rare B&B, in the $100+ range. Greater LA has a variety of luxury five-star and 'boutique' hotels that cost from $150 per night to more than $400, and suites to $2000. These are clustered in downtown, Beverly Hills, West Hollywood, and Santa Monica.

Prices fluctuate with vacation trends: on the beaches and in heavily touristed areas, rates may be increased by 10 to 30% in summer and over the Christmas to New Year holidays. Hotels that cater to business travelers have high rates during the week, while in Malibu it's weekend rates that are jacked up.

'Transient occupancy' tax on all hotel and motel rooms in LA is 14% of the bill, including city, county, and state taxes. Tax percentages may vary somewhat in other cities, including Santa Monica and Long Beach.

Free hotel reservation services include the Hotel Reservations Network (☎ 800-964-6835) and the Central Reservation Service (☎ 800-548-3311).

Hostels

In the Hollywood Hills, just off the Hollywood (101) Fwy at 2775 N Cahuenga Blvd, is *Banana Bungalow Hollywood,* (☎ 213-851-1129), that looks like a cut-rate resort village. Formerly a rambling old motel on 7 acres, it has 200 dormitory beds (in rooms of four or six, each with its own cable TV and bathroom facilities) and another 35 private rooms. Facilities include a cafe, small store, kitchen, swimming pool, weight room, laundry, and library. Shuttle service to area attractions is free. Rates (including breakfast) are $15 for dorm beds, $45 per double room.

Two other hostels are not as much fun but cheaper and more centrally located. The *Hollywood Wilshire YMCA* (☎ 213-467-4161), 1553 N Hudson Ave, charges $12 for each of its 30 dorm beds, including breakfast; rooms have TVs and safes, and the Y offers a fitness center, two swimming pools, a laundry room, and a full kitchen. The *Hollywood International Hostel* (☎ 213-850-6287), 7038 Hollywood Blvd, has basic hostel facilities for $11 per bed; a few double rooms are available for $30.

Local headquarters for the Hosteling International system, the *Santa Monica International Hostel* (☎ 310-392-0325 or 393-9913), 1436 2nd St, Santa Monica, has 238 dorm beds in a huge ivy-covered brick building that once served as city hall. A block from the 3rd St Promenade and a short walk from the beach, it has a huge kitchen, laundry, travel store, 2 am curfew, and $15 beds. Reserve ahead in summer.

A few blocks south is the 50-room *Casa Monica International Guesthouse* (☎ 310-576-6292), 1032 7th St, Santa Monica, where you'll pay $15 for a bunk bed in a small dorm, $20 including dinner, or $30 for two for a private room (with a private bath!). All rates include breakfast. There's a kitchen as well as laundry, music rooms, and TV rooms. Reservations are advised in summer.

Another trio of hostels are in Venice, just south of Santa Monica. The *Airport (Interclub) Hostel* (☎ 310-305-0250), 2221 Lincoln Blvd, handles 74 people in dorms of four, six, and (ouch!) 22 beds for $15 a night, $95 a week. Breakfast is another $3 per day, but shuttle buses to LAX are free. You must present a passport to stay here (US is OK), and foreign visitors have preference when it's crowded. Drinking and smoking are permitted.

The *Venice Beach Hostel* (☎ 310-392-6277, 396-0824), 1515 Pacific Ave, is dark and rundown, but will do in a pinch. A block from the famed Ocean Front Walk, there's no curfew and no limit on how long you can stay. Beds are $11 a night plus a $15 deposit for keys and bedding. Very few women wind up here; they feel more comfortable in the dormitory rooms at *Jim's at the Beach* (☎ 310-399-4018), 17 Brooks Ave. Passports are required to stay at this beachside hostel for $15 a night or $90 a week.

Perhaps the prettiest location for a LA-area hostel is that of HI's *Los Angeles International Hostel* (☎ 310-831-8109), 3601 S Gaffey St, Building 613, San Pedro. Housed in old army barracks at Fort MacArthur, the hostel faces Angel's Gate Park on a hilltop looking due south toward Santa Catalina Island. The only negative is that you've got to clear out between 9:30 am and 4 pm. There are separate men's and women's dorms, kitchen facilities, and a store; HI members pay $10, non-members $15. A few private rooms are available at $30 a night.

Hotels – Central Los Angeles

Bottom End With no hostels in the downtown area, pickings are slim for budget travelers. Outside of the undesirable mission district, the best places to look for low-priced rooms are on the south side of the city center, between the Garment District and the Convention Center; west of the city center, around Wilshire Blvd; and in Chinatown.

The *Stillwell Hotel* (☎ 213-627-1151), 838 S Grand Ave, has an Indian restaurant and Asian art in the lobby, and rooms for $39 (single with shared bath) to $69 (double with private bath). Side-by-side two blocks west are the *Orchid Hotel* (☎ 213-624-5855), 819 S Flower St, with spartan but adequate rooms priced $30 to $42; and the *Milner Hotel* (☎ 213-627-6981), 813 S Flower St, with $50 to $65 rooms, including breakfast.

A few blocks further west, the *Motel de Ville* (☎ 213-624-8474), 1123 W 7th St, has rooms for $35 to $45, a restaurant and an outdoor swimming pool – albeit not an especially well maintained one. Next door, the *City Center Motel* (☎ 213-628-7141), 1135 W 7th St, has a pool and rooms for $45 to $55.

In the heart of Chinatown, Best Western's *Dragon Gate Inn* (☎ 213-617-3077), 818 N Hill St, has $49 to $62 rooms (each with a refrigerator), laundry facilities, a nice little restaurant, and a Chinese herbalist's shop.

Middle Easily the favorite in this price range, the *Hotel Figueroa* (☎ 213-627-8971), 939 S Figueroa St, has a tiled lobby, beautiful outdoor swimming pool and spa surrounded by a lush garden, two restaurants, a bar, spacious rooms, and a price tag of $68 to $78 single, $74 to $84 double.

The *Kawada Hotel* (☎ 213-621-4455), 200 S Hill St, is another good choice, with TVs and VCRs in each of the $62 to $95 rooms.

On the edge of Chinatown near Olvera St and Union Station, the four-story *Metro Plaza Hotel* (☎ 213-680-0200), 711 N Main St, has rooms with refrigerators, microwave ovens, and in-house movies for $59 single, $69 to $75 double.

Best Western's *The Mayfair* (☎ 213-484-9789), 1256 W 7th St, has rooms for $50 to $75 single, $60 to $85 double, with the lower rates applicable weekends and off-season (November through March). A luxury hotel when built in 1928, The Mayfair still has a touch of faded elegance in its skylit lobby, plus a restaurant and lounge, fitness center, and rooftop sundeck.

There aren't many B&Bs in LA, so *The Inn at 657* (☎ 213-741-2200), 657 W 23rd St, near USC, is a rarity. Five nonsmoking rooms are priced $65 to $95 single, including breakfast, snacks, and drinks.

Still further south, the *Salisbury House* (☎ 213-737-7817), 2273 W 20th St, has five rooms in a beautiful early-20th century Craftsman-style bungalow with original stained glass. Rooms are $70 to $95.

Top End Featured in many movies, the five glass cylinders of *The Westin Bonaventure* (☎ 213-624-1000), 404 S Figueroa St, contain 1368 guest rooms plus 94 suites, 20 restaurants, five bars, 40 retail stores, a pool and fitness deck the size of a football field, and staff from 85 different countries. Rates start at $89, but expect to pay more.

Little Tokyo's *Miyako Inn* (☎ 213-617-2000), 328 E 1st St has Japanese-style rooms, with tatami floors, shoji screens, and low beds, for $89 to $102 single, $99 to $112 double.

Downtown LA's finest hotel is *The Biltmore* (☎ 213-624-1011), 506 S Grand Ave, built in 1923 and recently restored for $41-million. Palatial rooms start at $185/215 single/double, with many rooms in the $250 range.

Across the street is the *Wyndham Checkers Hotel* (☎ 213-624-0000), 535 S Grand Ave, which has marble bathrooms and a rooftop spa. Rooms are $169/$205 single/double weekdays, $99/$115 weekends.

Hotels – Mid-Wilshire
Bottom End On Wilshire Blvd itself, you get adequate rooms at the *Dunes Wilshire Motor Hotel* (☎ 213-938-3616), 4300 Wilshire Blvd, $53/62 single/double, with a swimming pool, laundry, and kitchenettes on request. Other likely prospects in the vicinity are the *Executive Motor Inn-Mid Wilshire* (☎ 213-385-4444), 603 S New

Hampshire Ave, $40 to $60; the *Good-Nite Inn* (☎ 213-385-7141), 1903 W Olympic Blvd in Koreatown, $50 to $70; the *Westlake Plaza Inn* (☎ 213 483-6363), 611 S Westlake Ave near MacArthur Park, $45 to $65; and the *Wilshire Comfort Inn* (☎ 213-385-0061), 3400 W 3rd St, $40 to $54.

Middle The *Park Plaza* (☎ 213-384-5281), 607 S Park View St, facing MacArthur Park, is a great old Art Deco building from the 1920s with a vaulted lobby, ceiling frescoes, and crystal chandeliers, a restaurant, bar, indoor pool, and fitness center. Rooms are $50 to $70, with suites up to $90.

Also in this category are the *Chancellor Hotel* (☎ 213-383-1183), 3191 W 7th St, a historic and well-maintained residence hotel with meals included in the $60 to $80 rate; and the *Wilshire Royale Hotel* (☎ 213-387-5311), 2619 Wilshire Blvd, another restored Art Deco palace with rooms in the $80 to $100 range.

Top End Slightly off the beaten track, six blocks south of Wilshire in Koreatown, the *Oxford Palace Hotel* (☎ 213-389-8000), 745 S Oxford Ave, is a handsome 'boutique' hotel with rooms for $79 to $149, including breakfast, refrigerators, VCRs, and in-room movies. Also in this vicinity is the *Sheraton Town House* (☎ 213-382-7171), 2961 Wilshire Blvd, whose spacious rooms overlook a park-like courtyard with a pool and tennis courts. Rates start around $100.

Hotels – Hollywood

Bottom End In the heart of Hollywood, a short canter from the Walk of Fame, is the *Orchid Suites Hotel* (☎ 213-874-9678), 1753 N Orchid Ave, with kitchenette rooms for $50 to $75. The spacious rooms in the nearby *Magic Hotel* (☎ 213-851-0800), next door to the Magic Castle at 7025 Franklin Ave, have full kitchens as well as a swimming pool; rates run $45 to $85.

A pleasant property at the east end of Hollywood, not far from Griffith Park, is the *Hollywood Downtowner Motel* (☎ 213-464-7191), 5601 Hollywood Blvd, with

well-kept rooms and a swimming pool. Rates are $38 to $48. The *Hollywood 8 Motel* (☎ 213-467-2252), 1822 N Cahuenga Blvd, has rooms for $30 to $45.

Middle The *Hollywood Metropolitan Hotel* (☎ 213-962-5800), 5825 Sunset Blvd, is a modern high-rise with a flamboyant Art Deco lobby, restaurant, bar, and free parking. Its 90 rooms run $69 to $98, including breakfast.

Top End Relive bygone days of glory at the *Radisson Hollywood Roosevelt Hotel* (☎ 213-466-7000), 7000 Hollywood Blvd, opposite Mann's Chinese Theatre. Rooms are small but furnished with antiques, and priced $99/109 single/double. Facilities include restaurants, bars, a swimming pool, and a fitness center.

You'll get more modern treatment at the 470-room *Holiday Inn Hollywood* (☎ 213-462-7181), 1755 N Highland Ave, where rooms cost $89 to $129 single, $104 to $139 double, $30 higher in June and July.

Hotels – West Hollywood

Bottom End Your best bets in the low end are not actually in West Hollywood, but in the adjacent Fairfax District. Try the *Bevonshire Lodge Motel* (☎ 213-936-6154), 7575 Beverly Blvd, with rooms priced $39 to $45; or the *Farmer's Daughter Motel* (☎ 213-937-3930), 115 S Fairfax Ave, near the Farmer's Market, with rooms at $58 to $65. Both have swimming pools, and rooms in the Farmer's Daughter also have small refrigerators.

Middle Popular with gays, the *San Vicente Inn* (☎ 310-854-6915), 837 N San Vicente Blvd, is a B&B with nine private cottages built around a garden courtyard and pool. Rates are $79/89 single/double. On the Sunset Strip, the *Park Sunset Hotel* (☎ 213-654-6470), 8462 Sunset Blvd, has rooms at $69/74 single/double. Nearby, Best Western's *Sunset Plaza Hotel* (☎ 213-654-0750), 8400 Sunset Blvd, has rooms for $69 to $92 single, $75 to $92 double.

Top End When you close in on the top end in West Hollywood, the city's proclivity for French style becomes clear. The *Le Reve Hotel de Ville* (☎ 310-854-1114), 8822 Cynthia St, has suites ($109 to $160) with living rooms and fireplaces, and *Le Parc Hotel de Luxe* (☎ 310-855-8888), 733 W Knoll Drive, has suites ($124 to $154) and a rooftop tennis court.

Also in the European mode is the *Beverly Plaza Hotel* (☎ 213-658-6600), 8384 W 3rd St at La Cienega Blvd, a six-story boutique hotel with $110/120. More urbane is the *Hyatt on Sunset* (☎ 213-656-1234), 8401 Sunset Blvd, with $119 to $135 single, $144 to $160 double rooms.

The *Château Marmont* (☎ 213-626-1010), 8221 Sunset Blvd, is a Norman-style castle with whimsical charms that drew Greta Garbo and Howard Hughes to live in isolation. Room rates start at $150, with suites at $195 to $650.

The *Mondrian Hotel de Grande Classe* (☎ 213-650-8999), 8440 Sunset Blvd, features a 60-foot homage to Dutch painter Piet Mondrian on its facade; rooms start at $160, and go up to $365. The *Bel Âge Hotel de Grande Classe* (☎ 310-854-1111), 1020 N San Vicente Blvd, just off the Sunset Strip, has suites priced $195 to $500, with one-bedrooms occasionally discounted to $125. Away from the hustle and bustle, in quiet residential neighborhoods, are *Le Dufy Hotel de Luxe* (☎ 310-657-7400), 1000 Westmount Drive, with $149 to $199 suites, and *Le Montrose Suite Hotel de Gran Luxe* (☎ 310-855-1115), 900 Hammond St, whose suites cost $145 to $195.

If you have money for this sort of indulgence, however, go for the *Sunset Marquis Hotel & Villas* (☎ 310-657-1333), 1200 N Alta Loma Rd, also favored by numerous visiting actors, rock musicians, and other celebrities. With three acres of gardens, its own recording studios, and 12 private villas, it's an oasis amid the madness. The smallest rooms (junior suites) are priced at $215; rates climb to $1200 for a two-bedroom villa.

Hotels – Beverly Hills

Middle There are a couple of moderately priced options in LA's stronghold of opulence and wealth. The *Beverly Terrace Motor Hotel* (☎ 310-274-8141), 469 N Doheny Drive, and the *Crescent Hotel Beverly Hills* (☎ 310-247-0505), 403 N Crescent Drive, both offer rooms and swimming pools in the $60 to $85 range.

Top End The *Carlyle Inn* (☎ 310-275-4445), 1119 S Robertson Blvd, on the edge of West Hollywood, has rooms for $105/115 single/double, including a breakfast buffet and afternoon tea and cocktails. The *Beverly Hills Ritz Hotel* (☎ 310-275-5575), 10300 Wilshire Blvd, has rooms ($95/115) overlooking a luxurious garden and pool.

Beverly Hills' most luxurious hotels are among the world's finest. The *Regent Beverly Wilshire* (☎ 310-275-5200), 9500 Wilshire Blvd, perhaps LA's single best place for star-gazing, recently underwent a $100-million renovation. Built in 1928 in Italian Renaissance style with French neoclassical touches, its rooms are priced from $255/275; if you want the Presidential Suite, that'll run you $4000 a night.

The *Peninsula Beverly Hills* (☎ 310-551-2888), 9882 Little Santa Monica Blvd, has French Renaissance architecture approached by a circular driveway through a carefully tended garden. Most rooms are $265 to $315, villas are $390 to $2500.

The *Beverly Hills Hotel and Bungalows* (☎ 310-276-2251), 9641 Sunset Blvd, reopened in June 1995 after a two-year renovation closure. In doing so, it stepped into the 21st century with early 20th century flair. Rooms and bungalows are $205 to $320.

The *Beverly Prescott Hotel* (☎ 310-277-2800), 1224 S Beverwil Drive, is a lovely boutique hotel with rooms for $185, and an imaginatively designed Jerry Garcia Suite for $300.

Hotels – West Side

Middle Short of student accommodations, one of the least expensive choices for UCLA visitors is the *Royal Palace Westwood* (☎ 310-208-6677), 1052 Tiverton Ave, Westwood, one block north of Wilshire Blvd. It has various-sized rooms priced $60 to $82 single, $66 to $96 double. A few blocks away, the *Hilgard House Hotel* (☎ 310-208-3945), 927 Hilgard Ave, Westwood, has rooms with spas in a three-story brick building for $99.

Top End The *Hotel del Capri* (☎ 310-474-3511), 10587 Wilshire Blvd, Westwood, is a charmer with $95 to $110 rooms on four stories surrounding a terrace and swimming pool; continental breakfast is delivered to your door. Just down the road, the *Westwood Plaza Hotel* (☎ 310-475-8711), 10740 Wilshire Blvd, Westwood, has rooms for $120 to $140.

On a tree-lined residential block just a few steps from the UCLA campus, the *Westwood Marquis Hotel and Gardens* (☎ 310-208-8765), 930 Hilgard Ave, Westwood, has personalized service, arty restaurants and a bar, and a full fitness room. All rooms are suites, priced at $200 to $250.

If I had to spend the rest of my life in just one LA hotel, I would choose the resort-like *Hotel Bel Air* (☎ 310-472-1211), 701 Stone Canyon Rd. Nestled in 11 acres of subtropical forest in the Santa Monica Mountain foothills above Beverly Hills, this two-story, pink, 1920s Mission-style hotel and its various outbuildings are a great getaway. There's a restaurant and bar, swimming pool and fitness center, wonderful garden with a swan pond and waterfalls, and a continual parade of celebrities. Rooms cost $245 to $395 single, $275 to $435 double, and suites are $550 to $2000.

Hotels – Santa Monica Area

Bottom End There's not a lot to choose from here, especially during the summer season. You might try the *Pacific Sands Motel* (☎ 310-395-6133), 1515 Ocean Ave, Santa Monica, with 50 rooms in the $50 to $60 range; don't expect quiet solitude,

however. Another possibility is the *Hotel Carmel by the Sea* (☎ 310-451-2469), 201 Broadway, Santa Monica, in a similar price range. In costly Malibu, the *Malibu Riviera Motel* (☎ 310-457-9503), 28920 Pacific Coast Hwy, has managed to keep prices down somewhat.

The classic in this category is Venice's *Cadillac Hotel* (☎ 310-399-8876, 399-1930), on Ocean Front Walk at 8 Dudley Ave. A 1930s Art Deco hotel, it has nine four-person dorm rooms for $20 per person, 30 private rooms priced $54/64, and one $99 suite with a view from Malibu to Catalina Island. Leave your passport at the desk and you'll also have access to a gym, sauna, laundry, and sundeck.

Other low-cost motels include the *Marina Motel* (☎ 310-821-5086), 3130 Washington Blvd, Venice, with $45/50 rooms, and the *Jolly Roger Motel* (☎ 310-822-2904), 2904 Washington Blvd, Marina del Rey, with $50 to $75 rooms and a pool.

Middle In Santa Monica, you'll be guaranteed a comfortable bed in the $65 to $95 range at any of several chain hotels. (See the information on hotel chains in the Facts for the Visitor chapter for phone numbers of chain hotels.)

Another option is the *Pacific Shore Hotel* (☎ 310-451-8711), 1819 Ocean Ave, Santa Monica. Rooms are $89.

A few miles north, the *Topanga Ranch Motel* (☎ 310-456-5486), 18711 Pacific Coast Hwy, Malibu, has trim white cottages across the highway from the beach for about $60 to $80.

A particularly lovely B&B is *The Venice Beach House* (☎ 310-823-1966), 15 30th Ave, a 1911 California Craftsman bungalow with nine antique-filled rooms just a few steps from the boardwalk. Rooms with a shared bath cost $80 to $90, those with private baths run $130 to $150.

Also in Venice is the *Mansion Inn* (☎ 310-821-2557), 327 Washington Blvd, with charming rooms just four blocks from the beach. Rates are $63 to $71; rooms with lofts cost $95 to $125. Mid-range alternatives in Venice, clean and well-kept but without as much character, include the *Lincoln Inn* (☎ 310-822-0686), 2447 Lincoln Blvd, $68 to $78 single, $73 to $86 double, and the *Marina Pacific Hotel & Suites* (☎ 310-452-1111), 1697 Pacific Ave, $80 to $90 single, $90 to $100 double.

In Marina del Rey, the *Foghorn Motel* (☎ 310-823-4626), 4140 Via Marina, has rooms with refrigerators priced $59 to $79 October through March, $80 to $100 during the summer season.

Top End Santa Monica's *Hotel Shangri-La* (☎ 310-394-2791), 1301 Ocean Ave, designed to resemble a ship's prow, is a 1939 Art Deco artists' and writers' retreat overlooking the beach from atop the Palisades near downtown. Continental breakfast and afternoon tea are both included in the tab, which starts at $110 but climbs quickly to $205 (for a kitchen) or $260 (for a studio suite).

The romantic *Channel Road Inn* (☎ 310-459-1920), 219 W Channel Rd, Santa Monica, is set in a hillside garden with rooms facing the Pacific Ocean. There are free bicycles, a library, spa, and laundry. Rooms with shared baths are $95; more elaborate lodging is $165 to $200.

Loews Santa Monica Beach Hotel (☎ 310-458-6700), 1700 Ocean Ave, was LA's first luxury hotel directly on a beach when it opened in 1989. Rooms go for $205 to $415 single, $20 more for a double, with suites to $2500.

Just down the coast, the plantation-style *Shutters on the Beach* (☎ 310-458-0030), 1 Pico Blvd, Santa Monica, offers panoramic views – not to mention great people-watching – from its restaurants, lounges, and pool deck. Rooms are $225 to $350.

Numerous larger Santa Monica hotels in the $100-plus range include the *Radisson Huntley Hotel* (☎ 310-394-5454), 1111 2nd St, with comfortable rooms ($95 to $145 single, $105 to $155 double) and a rooftop bar and restaurant with magnificent views; the *Ocean View Hotel* (☎ 310-458-4888), 1447 Ocean Ave, with $95 to $145 rooms; and the *Oceana Suites Hotel* (☎ 310-393-0466), 849 Ocean Ave, at $99 to $109

single, $119 to $149 double, whose rooms all have kitchens.

South of Santa Monica, the *Marina del Rey Marriott* (☎ 310-822-8555), 13480 Maxella Ave, has rooms for $129, with occasional weekend discounts to $89. The *Marina International Hotel* (☎ 310-301-2000), 4200 Admiralty Way, Marina del Rey, has elegant rooms at $119 to $129, plus 25 courtyard bungalows for $185 to $250. Both offer free parking and LAX shuttle service.

The *Ritz-Carlton Marina del Rey* (☎ 310-823-1700), 4375 Admiralty Way, has its own marina with charter yachts, as well as lighted tennis courts, a pool, and a spa. The palatial rooms of the 12-story hotel start at $179, with deluxe units up to $395 and suites to $1200.

In Malibu, seven miles north of the town center via Pacific Coast Hwy, the *Malibu Country Inn* (☎ 310-457-9622), 6506 Westward Beach Rd, offers a quiet retreat with 15 rooms ($85 to $95 single, $115 to $165 double, with the higher rates in summer), a restaurant and a small pool. By the Malibu Pier, the *Malibu Beach Inn* (☎ 310-456-6444), 22878 Pacific Coast Hwy, has rooms with fireplaces and balconies overlooking the surf. Rates are $115 to $180 Sunday to Thursday, $150 to $195 Fridays and Saturdays.

Hotels – LAX Area

Bottom End Apart from the inexpensive chain hotels, all of which seem to have airport-area lodgings, there are numerous other budget spots. Most offer free shuttle service to and from LAX.

There's almost always vacancy at the 770-room *Airport Marina Resort Hotel* (☎ 310-670-8111), 8601 Lincoln Blvd, Westchester, with rates at $49 standard and $79 deluxe. Other good options along the ma-and-pa lines: *Dai-Ichi Hotel* (☎ 310-673-2400), 4330 W Century Blvd, Inglewood, with rooms at $28 to $45; the *Vista Motel* (☎ 310-397-9194), 4900 Sepulveda Blvd, Culver City, with rooms at $30 to $40; the *Sunburst Motel* (☎ 310-398-7523),

3900 Sepulveda Blvd, Culver City, with rooms at $55 to $65.

Middle Check out the chain hotels, or try one of these: *Continental Plaza LA Airport Hotel* (☎ 310-645-4600), 9750 Airport Blvd, with basic rooms at $75; the *Crown Sterling Suites LA Airport* (☎ 310-640-3600), 1440 E Imperial Ave, El Segundo, with two-room suites at $89; or the pleasant *Wyndham Garden Hotel* (☎ 310-641-7740), 5990 Green Valley Circle, Culver City, walking distance from the Fox Hills shopping mall with rooms for $59 to $79 single, $69 to $89 double.

Top End There's plenty to choose from along LAX's 'hotel row,' Century Blvd. Biggest of the big are the 1164-room *Los Angeles Airport Hilton & Towers* (☎ 310-410-4000), 5711 W Century Blvd, with singles from $99 and doubles from $119; and the *Los Angeles Airport Marriott* (☎ 310-641-5700), 5855 W Century Blvd, with rooms from $79 weekdays, $109 weekends.

Other massive properties include: the *Sheraton LA Airport Hotel* (☎ 310-642-1111), 6101 W Century Blvd, with 801 rooms; the *Doubletree Hotel-LA Airport* (☎ 310-216-5858), 5400 W Century Blvd, with rooms at $79 to $109 single, $10 more for a double, $10 more on weekends; the *Hyatt at LA Airport* (☎ 310-337-1234), 6225 W Century Blvd, with rooms at $89 to $99, to $139 weekends; and the *LA Renaissance Hotel-International Airport* (☎ 310-337-2800), 9620 Airport Blvd, with rooms at $110 to $175.

Removed from the rush but a short shuttle ride away is the nice *Red Lion Hotel-LA Airport* (☎ 310-649-1776), 6161 Centinela Ave, Culver City, with rooms at $95 to $120 single, $10 more double.

Hotels – Pasadena
Bottom End Pasadena's 'motel row' is E Colorado Blvd, paralleling the Foothill (210) Fwy from Lake Ave all the way to Rosemead Blvd. There are literally dozens of budget-priced motels along this strip,

some in better repair than others, including such chain properties as Best Western, Comfort Inn, Econo Lodge, Holiday Inn, Ramada, and Travelodge.

Some of the better non-chain motels include the *Siesta Inn* (☎ 818-795-2017), 2855 E Colorado Blvd, with air-con rooms for $35 to $40; the *Regal Inn Motel* (☎ 818-449-4743), 3800 E Colorado Blvd, a well-kept place with a swimming pool and rooms at $35 to $42; and the *Westway Inn* (☎ 818-304-9678), 1599 E Colorado Blvd, with a pool, sauna, spa, guest laundry, and rooms at $44 to $49 single, $48 to $56 double.

Closer to central Pasadena is the *Livingstone Hotel and Apartments* (☎ 818-795-3311), 139 S Los Robles Ave, a well-worn residential hotel that keeps seven one-bedroom units with private baths, double beds, and telephones, open for short-term travelers. There's a TV in the lobby and a Japanese restaurant in the hotel basement. Rates are $40 to $43 single, $45 to $48 double. Ask for a room with a sun porch.

Middle A charming B&B in the heart of Old Town, the *Pasadena Hotel* (☎ 818-658-8172), 76 N Fair Oaks Ave, has 12 rooms in a restored turn-of-the-century building furnished with Edwardian antiques. Rates are $65 to $85 single (shared bath) or $95 to $100 (private); doubles pay $80 to $150. Parking is $5 per day.

The *Saga Motor Hotel* (☎ 818-796-3121), 1633 E Colorado Blvd, is above average for being on the 'strip,' with free continental breakfasts and a swimming pool and spa. Rooms are $62/65.

Top End The *Pasadena Holiday Inn* (☎ 818-449-4000), 303 E Cordova St, is centrally located and has a swimming pool, two tennis courts, and rooms at $88 to $128. Decorated with marble and skylights, the *Pasadena Hilton* (☎ 818-577-1000), 150 S Los Robles Ave, has rooms for $119 to $150 single, $134 to $175 double.

B&B enthusiasts will find two lovely homes in South Pasadena. Each of the four rooms at *The Artists' Inn* (☎ 818-799-

596 Los Angeles – Places to Stay

5668), 1038 Magnolia St, is decorated with attention to art history, and all have private baths. They cost $80 to $90 single, $90 to $100 double. The *Bissell House* (☎ 818-441-3535), 201 Orange Grove Ave, is a restored 1887 Victorian house with stained-glass windows; three rooms run $100 to $150.

The *Ritz-Carlton Huntington Hotel* (☎ 818-568-3900), 1401 S Oak Knoll Ave, Pasadena, is a sumptuous Mission-style hostelry surrounded by a magnificent 23-acre garden. Rooms start at $165 and climb to $500.

Hotels – San Fernando Valley

Bottom End Busy Ventura Blvd, running west from Universal City to Calabasas, is a commercial strip with dozens of motels. Recommended are the *Heritage Motel* (☎ 818-981-0500), 15485 Ventura Blvd, Sherman Oaks; the *St George Motor Inn* (☎ 818-345-6911), 19454 Ventura Blvd, Tarzana; and the *Vagabond Inn* (☎ 818-347-8080), 20157 Ventura Blvd, Woodland Hills; each with pools and singles/doubles in the $45 to $60 range.

Traveling north from Ventura Blvd on Sepulveda Blvd, try the *Carriage Inn* (☎ 818-787-2300), 5525 Sepulveda Blvd, Sherman Oaks, with a pool, restaurant and bar, and $59 to $69 rooms; the *Voyager Motor Inn,* 6500 Sepulveda Blvd, Van Nuys, with rooms for $39 single, $44 to $65 double; and the *Diamond Inn* (☎ 818-891-5172), 8609 Sepulveda Blvd, North Hills, with rooms for $36 single, $40 to $50 double.

Middle A handsome garden with waterfalls and a swan pond are the centerpiece of the *Sportsmen's Lodge* (☎ 818-769-4700), 12825 Ventura Blvd, Studio City, which has a restaurant, an English pub, a huge pool, and a spa. All rooms have private patios, and cost $85 to $95.

Top End A 1920s villa and bungalows surrounded by expansive gardens, *La Maida House* (☎ 818-769-3857), 1159 La Maida St, North Hollywood, has 11 rooms ($100 to $125) with private baths, a solarium, pool, and gym, and serves gourmet meals.

A short walk or a shorter shuttle ride from Universal Studios Hollywood is the 21-story *Sheraton Universal Hotel* (☎ 818-980-1212), 333 Universal Terrace Pkwy, with rooms for $135 to $150 single, $155 to $170 double. The Sheraton's 24-story, steel-and-glass neighbor, the *Universal City Hilton & Towers* (☎ 818-506-2500), 555 Universal Terrace Pkwy, has rooms at $129 to $180 weekdays, $105 to $145 weekends.

PLACES TO EAT

Folks in San Francisco may disagree, but the fact remains: LA represents the cutting edge of cuisine in the Western Hemisphere. As a cosmopolitan crossroads, LA attracts people from every corner of the Earth – and with them comes their food. Creative chefs (many of them now celebrities, like the celebrated Wolfgang Puck) take bits and pieces from different traditions and combine them in a variety of fashions. Here, more than in any other city on the West Coast, you'll find French Thai, Chinese Italian, and Pacific Rim food. Vanguards include Santa Monica's ZenZero, whose menu offers the likes of blackened (Cajun) sea bass (Chilean) and air-dried duck (Chinese) with cranberry-apple (Oregonian) chutney (Indian), with other spots in upscale districts such as West Hollywood, Beverly Hills, Santa Monica, Pasadena, and downtown LA.

Ethnic districts are the best places to find cheap, good Mexican, Chinese, and Japanese food prepared in the vernacular. There are also plenty of hamburger joints and hole-in-the-wall diners.

Consider any restaurant where you can dine for less than $10 to be 'budget;' $10 to $20 as 'moderate;' and over $20 as 'top end.' Although dining is a casual affair in LA, you still should dress according to price. A jacket is appropriate for men at better restaurants. Most moderate and top end restaurants take reservations; at the more popular, in fact, you should call days or even weeks ahead. If you're a serious foodie, keep your eyes open for LA restaurant guides written by Merrill Shindler or Paul Wallach, two noted food critics.

Central Los Angeles
Civic Center A classic old-time cafe and bar, *The Redwood 2nd St Saloon* (☎ 213-617-2867), 2nd St between Hill and Broadway, serves great burgers and good lunches at budget prices. *Epicentre* (☎ 213-625-0000), Kawada Hotel, 200 S Hill St, is a moderately expensive California-cuisine bistro.

El Pueblo de Los Angeles You'll find good eats on Olvera St. *El Paseo Inn* (☎ 213-626-1361), at No 11, has Sonorastyle Mexican peasant fare and mariachi entertainers; dinner costs $6 to $14. *Casa la Golondrina* (☎ 213-628-4349), at No 17, has authentic Mexican food for slightly less. There are lots of cheap food stalls, too.

Almost opposite Union Station stands *Philippe The Original* (☎ 213-628-3781), 1001 N Alameda St. Established in the 1920s, it claims to have invented the French dip sandwich. Meals start at about $4 (open 6 am to 10 pm).

Chinatown For seafood, try *Ocean Seafood* (☎ 213-687-3088), 750 N Hill St (dinner $6 to $15), a large, upstairs, Hong-Kong-style place; it's also a dim sum parlor from 8 am to 3 pm.

One block east are *Yang Chow* (☎ 213-625-0811), 819 N Broadway, great for Mandarin (dinner about $19), and the *Chinese Friends Restaurant* (☎ 213-626-1837), 984 N Broadway, for Hunanese (dinner $4 to $10). Between them is *Little Joe's* (☎ 213-489-4900), 900 N Broadway, a classic Italian-American restaurant where lunch will run you $6 to $10, and dinner costs $7 to $18.

Another block west, the *Empress Pavilion* (☎ 213-617-9898) on the 3rd floor of Bamboo Plaza, 988 N Hill St, is the single best place in LA for dim sum (full midday meals are under $12).

Above Chinatown, right by Dodger Stadium, the *Los Angeles Police Academy Revolver and Athletic Club* (☎ 213-222-9136), 1880 Academy Rd, Elysian Park, gives you the opportunity to dine among the cops on hearty breakfasts and lunches from 6 am to 2 pm. Meals run $3 to $8.

Little Tokyo The best place for traditional Japanese cuisine, if you're looking for something in the middle range, is the *Restaurant Horikawa* (☎ 213-680-9355), 111 S San Pedro St, with teppan, sushi, kaiseki, and other specialties (lunch $8 to $12, dinner $14 to $35).

Weller Court, 123 S Ellison Onizuka St, has three floors of restaurants of many kinds, priced from budget to top end. Here's where you'll get Japanese favorites such as okonomiyaki and curries.

Financial District In the budget category, don't miss Mayor Richard Riordan's own *The Original Pantry* (☎ 213-972-9279), 877 S Figueroa St. It's open 24 hours, seven days a week, with home-cooked American meals for $5 to $10 served by aging tuxedoed waiters.

Grand Ave between 5th and 6th Sts has an overload of great restaurants. The *Water Grill* (☎ 213-891-0900), 544 S Grand Ave, may be LA's best seafood eatery (lunch $12 to $18, dinner $19 to $25).

Downtown's least pricey restaurants are in the *Grand Central Market* (☎ 213-624-2378), 317 S Broadway, with all manner of takeaway and counter dining. Nearby are two huge cafeterias (no booze, cash only) that have been an integral part of downtown for decades: *Clifton's Cafeteria* (☎ 213-627-1673), 648 S Broadway, and *Vickman's* (☎ 213-622-3852), 1228 E 8th St.

Mid-Wilshire
Westlake Catty-corner from MacArthur Park is *Langer's Delicatessen* (☎ 213-483-8050), 704 S Alvarado St, famous for pastrami sandwiches. Lunch costs $5 to $10, dinner $10 to $14.

Koreatown Best of many Korean restaurants in this district is *Korean Gardens*

(☎ 213-388-3042), 950 S Vermont Ave (meals $9 to $15). But not all is Korean: *El Cholo* (☎ 213-734-2773), 1121 S Western Ave, is one of LA's earliest and best Mexican spots (it's now pricey with lunch $16 to $24, dinner $22 to $35); for budget Nicaraguan meals there's *La Plancha* (☎ 213-383-1449), 2818 W 9th St.

South Central
Janet's Jerk Chicken Pit (☎ 213-296-4621), 1541 W Martin Luther King Jr Blvd, owned by a former Air Jamaica flight attendant, serves Jamaican food ($6 to $15) from noon to 9 pm daily. *Murray's Cafe* (☎ 213-778-2224), 5974 S Broadway, has Southern/soul food that many pro athletes claim is 'the best.' Meals run $6 to $11.

Hollywood
The old standby – a haunt of entertainment industry types since it opened in 1919 – is *Musso & Frank Grill* (☎ 213-467-7788), 6667 Hollywood Blvd. You'll still get gruff service and basic American food for $7 to $25. Another famous Hollywood restaurant is *Yamashiro* (☎ 213-466-5125), 1999 N Sycamore Ave, on a hillside overlooking Mann's Chinese Theater. An exact replica of a Japanese palace amid 12 acres of gardens, it offers great views along with Japanese and continental food. Dinners run $25 to $35.

Almost opposite Mann's is the restaurant that claims to have invented the hot-fudge sundae. Whether Clarence Clifton Brown did so or not, *CC Brown's Ice Cream*, 7007 Hollywood Blvd, is still a great place to try one.

Around the east end of the Walk of Fame are *Roscoe's House of Chicken & Waffles* (☎ 213-466-7453), 1514 N Gower St, with great soul food and huge breakfasts, and the *Sun Palace* (☎ 213-465-7181), 1718 N Vine St, an old-time Chinese place with low to moderate prices.

Sunset Blvd Traveling west on Sunset from downtown LA you'll find numerous restaurants of interest. The building that houses *El Cid* (☎ 213-668-0318), 4212 W Sunset Blvd was an original DW Griffith movie studio; now it's a Spanish restaurant (dinners about $25) with nightly flamenco dancing. Also on Sunset, you might try one of these budget-priced spots: *Fifty Fifty Sunset* (☎ 213-913-1656), at the obvious address, for Thai food; *Paru's* (☎ 213-661-7600), at No 5140, for South Indian vegetarian; and *Amagi* (☎ 213-464-7497), at No 6114, for Japanese.

On a side street off Sunset between Highland and Cahuenga is *The Hollywood Canteen* (☎ 213-465-0961), 1006 N Seward St. Located in a district of sound stages and film-processing plants, it attracts show-biz types for solid American home cooking at low to moderate cost.

West Hollywood
Sunset Strip The Sunset Plaza area at the corner of Horn Ave has an overflow of celebrity-populated restaurants. Here is chef Wolfgang Puck's famous *Spago* (☎ 310-652-4025), 1114 Horn Ave, with California cuisine for around $18 to $26; *Chin Chin* (☎ 310-652-1818), 8618 Sunset, California-style Chinese meals for around $15; *Le Dôme* (☎ 310-659-6919), 8720 Sunset, a top end French restaurant that singer Elton John helped establish; and *Nicky Blair's* (☎ 310-659-0929), 8730 Sunset, a northern Italian spot (dinner around $35) with the ultimate Industry bar scene.

For elegant meals on the strip, many prefer *Diaghilev* (☎ 310-854-1111), 1020 N San Vicente Blvd, a superior Franco-Russian restaurant (dinners around $25) in the Bel Âge Hotel.

Santa Monica Blvd West Hollywood embraces Santa Monica Blvd from its 7100 block (at La Brea Ave) to its 9100 block where it enters Beverly Hills. Traveling west, the *Basix Cafe* (☎ 213-848-2460), at No 8333, has budget-priced pasta and pizza. The stars come out in the morning for power breakfasts at *Hugo's* (☎ 213-654-3993), at No 8401. *Barney's Beanery* (☎ 213-654-2287), at No 8447, is such a 'dive,' it's 'in:' Choose from 40 omelets, 40 burgers, and 80 beers.

Upscale spots along this boulevard include *Café d'Étoile* (☎ 310-278-1011), at No 8941, with continental cuisine at moderate cost; *Dan Tana's* (☎ 310-275-9444), at No 9071, a northern Italian celebrity hangout with moderate to top end prices; and *La Masia* (☎ 310-273-7066), at 9077, a Spanish classic famous for its paella (around $25).

Melrose Ave Many Angelenos consider *Patina* (☎ 213-467-1108), a French restaurant at No 5955, to be the city's single best dining experience. Lunch runs $18 to $22, dinner $35 to $40. Vegetarian plates are available. *Citrus* (☎ 213-857-0034), at No 6703, is another restaurant that ranks high among LA foodies; chic California-French dinners run about $40.

Along the most frenetic section of Melrose – between La Brea and Fairfax – look for *Georgia* (☎ 213-857-0034), at No 7250, a gourmet soul food restaurant whose many partners include Denzel Washington, Eddie Murphy, and Debbie Allen; or *Tommy Tang's* (☎ 213-937-5733), at No 7313, for non-traditional Thai cuisine. Dinner at either of these runs in the $15 to $20 range, as it will at *Caffé Luna* (☎ 213-655-8647), at No 7463, a charming open-air trattoria. Up the price scale (dinners $27 to $37) is the *Chianti Ristorante e Cucina* (☎ 213-653-8333), 7383 Melrose Ave, serving Italian cuisine since 1938.

South along La Brea Ave, from Melrose to Wilshire, is yet another restaurant row. *Pink's Famous Chili Dogs* (☎ 213-931-4223), at No 711 N, has been around since 1939, and the prices are still under $5.

Fairfax District You can't go wrong at *Canter's Delicatessen* (☎ 213-651-2030), a 24-hour landmark at No 419 N, with meals around $6 to $10; *Tom Bergin's* (☎ 213-936-7151), at No 840 S, with Irish pub fare around $6 to $11; or the *LA Farmers Market* (☎ 213-933-9211), 6333 W 3rd St at the corner of Fairfax, with all manner of takeout dining within the open-air market.

Beverly Center This shopping center, which has identified a district, is framed by Beverly Blvd and 3rd St, La Cienega and San Vicente Blvds.

You'll get basic meals in the $10 to $15 range at the *Hard Rock Cafe* (☎ 310-276-7605), 8600 Beverly Blvd. Or grab a hot dog at *Tail o' the Pup*, 329 N San Vicente Blvd. It's been around for 50 years. Nearby at 1415 S La Cienega Blvd, *Versailles* (☎ 310-289-0392), has some of the city's best Cuban food. Meals ($8 to $12) include wonderfully spiced black beans & rice, and fried plantains.

Beverly Hills
This is primarily where the rich and famous dine, though there are a few affordable hang-outs that have been around for years. Perhaps the all-time classic is *Nate 'n' Al's* (☎ 310-274-0101), 414 N Beverly Drive, a New York-style deli with meals for $5 to $15.

In the Via Rodeo complex at 2 Rodeo Drive opposite the Regent Beverly Wilshire Hotel, *McCormick and Schmick's* (☎ 310-859-0434) is a moderately priced hangout for excellent seafood, popular with producers and screenwriters. The adjacent *Piazza Rodeo* (☎ 310-275-2428) has light Italian fare for $12 to $15. North up Rodeo Drive, the *Cafe Rodeo* (☎ 310-273-0300), 360 Rodeo Drive, serves continental dinners in the $20 to $35 price range.

Carroll O'Connor's Place (☎ 310-273-7585), 369 N Bedford Drive, another block west, has American and continental meals in the low to moderate price range. The actor sometimes visits to sing along at the piano bar. On Little Santa Monica Blvd, *Nouveau Café Blanc* (☎ 310-888-0108), at No 9777, has moderately priced French-Japanese cuisine.

Meals at the original *Trader Vic's* (☎ 310-274-7777), 9876 Wilshire in the Beverly Hilton, run in the $30 range. First opened in 1934, Vic's serves continental cuisine with a Polynesian flair.

Along Robertson Blvd in east Beverly Hills, you'll find *The Ivy* (☎ 310-274-8303), 113 Robertson Blvd, where the

Industry dines on California cuisine for a hefty $50 at lunch, $75 at dinner.

In the nearby Century City Shopping Cener, *DIVE!* (☎ 310-788-3483), 10250 Santa Monica Blvd, is a great place for fantasy-seekers: just enter the yellow submarine. One of a new national chain whose partners include Steven Spielberg and Jeffrey Katzenberg, it effectively submerges you into an aquatic world. The menu, priced budget to moderate, is highlighted by – what else? – gourmet submarine sandwiches and made-to-order potato chips with exotic dipping sauces; it's also a good place just to have a drink.

West Side

Westwood Heading south from the UCLA campus along Westwood Blvd, you'll find a couple of classic student hangouts: *Old World* (☎ 310-208-4033), with burgers, pizzas, and simple meals, at No 1019; and *Alice's Restaurant* (☎ 310-208-3171), at No 1043, with omelets, sandwiches, salads, and anything else you want. Both have dinners in the low-moderate price range. *Asuka* (☎ 310-474-7412), 1266 Westwood Blvd, claims to have the largest sushi bar in LA (dinners $10 to $15).

On the west side of Westwood Village, *Stratton's Grill* (☎ 310-208-0488), 1037 Broxton Ave, is a popular bar and grill with American dinners priced $4 to $11. *Mongolian BBQ* (☎ 310-824-3377), 1064 Gayley Ave, has all-you-can-eat noodle meals at budget prices.

West LA Where Westwood and Pico Blvds intersect, the *Westside Pavilion* is at the southeast corner. This large shopping mall has a low-cost food court within. On the north side of Pico, opposite the mall, is one of LA's best-loved restaurants: *The Apple Pan* (☎ 310-475-3585), 10801 W Pico Blvd, serving great burgers, good pie, and coffee since 1950. Don't expect to pay more than $7.

Along Wilshire Blvd are two of the city's best Chinese restaurants. The *Gourmet West Inn* (☎ 310-478-8928), 11701 Wilshire, has moderately priced Mandarin and

Sichuan specialties. The *Fragrant Vegetable Restaurant* (☎ 310-312-1442), 11859 Wilshire, is a Buddhist vegetarian cafe with a 60-entree menu; lunch is only about $6, dinner $15.

In nearby Brentwood, *Mezzaluna* (☎ 310-447-8667), 11750 San Vicente Blvd, has gained its greatest fame as the restaurant where Ronald Goldman worked, and Nicole Brown Simpson dined, on the night they were murdered. The modern Italian restaurant has dinners for about $24.

Santa Monica

Either side of the 3rd St Promenade, walking north from the Santa Monica Place Mall, is lined with small restaurants and cafes, most offering moderately priced meals. Among them are the *Broadway Bar and Grill* (☎ 310-393-4211), 1460 3rd St, with burgers and more exotic grills; the *Broadway Deli* (☎ 310-451-0616), 1457 3rd St, a 200-seat deli-bar-bakery serving three meals daily; *Remi* (☎ 310-393-6545), 1451 3rd St, a creative Italian spot with prices that approach top end; and *Teasers* (☎ 310-394-8728), 1351 3rd St, with nouvelle cuisine dinners at $6 to $13. Just past the mall is elegant *Michael's* (☎ 310-451-0843), 1147 3rd St, a continental restaurant with lunches around $20, dinners $35.

Along Ocean Ave, atop the bluffs facing Palisades Park and the Santa Monica beach, are some of the city's finest restaurants, including *ZenZero* (☎ 310-451-4455), 1535 Ocean Ave, with some of LA's finest Pacific Rim dinners priced $15 to $26; and *Ivy at the Shore* (☎ 310-393-3113), 1541 Ocean Ave, a celebrity favorite with American and continental cuisine at bust-the-wallet prices: lunch runs from $30 to $40, dinner $60 to $70.

Near Santa Monica's east end, *Hamburger Henry's* (☎ 310-828-3000), 3001 Wilshire, serving burgers (at $6 to $8) that have won eight gold medals at the California State Fair.

Ocean Park Traveling south down Main St through the hip Ocean Park area, from Pico Blvd to the edge of Venice, you'll encounter an eclectic mix of restaurants. *Röckenwagner* (☎ 310-399-6504), 2435 Main St, offers gourmet fixed price lunches ($13) and nouvelle French dinners (around $35) in a serene but funky setting; try the grilled Portobello mushroom sandwich and save room for dessert. Wolfgang Puck's *Chinois on Main* (☎ 310-392-9025), 2709 Main St, is a whimsical California-French-Chinese restaurant that will hit you up for $25 at lunch, $45 to $50 at dinner. The *Ocean Park Omelette Parlor* (☎ 310-399-7892), 2732 Main St, specializes in $3 to $5 omelets. *Schatzi on Main* (☎ 310-399-4800), 3110 Main St, an Austrian-American restaurant owned by Arnold Schwarzenegger and Maria Shriver, has lunches under $10, dinners around $15.

Venice

For budget diners, the *Venice Bistro* (☎ 310-392-3997), 323 Ocean Front Walk, and the *Sidewalk Cafe* (☎ 310-399-4457), 1401 Ocean Front Walk, both offer meals for under $10. There are no better sausages – anywhere – than those sold at *Jody Maroni's Sausage Kingdom* (☎ 310-306-1995), a boardwalk stand at 2011 Ocean Front Walk. Or you can get excellent

salads, casseroles, and ice cream at *The Rose Cafe* (☎ 310-399-0711), 220 Rose Ave, two blocks off the beach, for a similar price.

Most of Venice's by-the-water eateries are of the top end variety, however. Favorites include *Chaya Venice* (☎ 310-396-1179), 110 Navy St, a French-Japanese spot that attracts many celebrities; *72 Market Street* (☎ 310-392-8720), 72 Market St, a continental restaurant (among whose partners is Dudley Moore) noted for its seafood; *Rebecca's* (☎ 310-306-6266), 2025 Pacific Ave, a too-trendy gourmet Mexican restaurant; and the *West Beach Cafe* (☎ 310-823-5396), 60 N Venice Blvd, which serves continental cuisine.

Away from the beach, *Casablanca* (☎ 310-392-5751), 220 Lincoln Blvd, is noted for its Mexican seafood and handmade tortillas, served hot off the griddle.

Malibu

Malibu's restaurants are all fairly pricey, except for sandwich shops in strip malls. For a nice dinner out, try *Moonshadows* (☎ 310-456-3010), 20356 Pacific Coast Hwy, for steak and seafood; *Alice's Restaurant-Malibu* (☎ 310-456-6646), 23000 Pacific Coast Hwy, for gourmet seafood with distinctly California touches (like a cactus ratatouille and a walnut pesto); *Granita* (☎ 310-456-0488), 23725 W Malibu Rd, Wolfgang Puck's Mediterranean-style restaurant in the Malibu Colony; and *Geoffrey's* (☎ 310-457-1519), 27400 Pacific Coast Hwy, with Pacific Rim and continental dishes.

In the canyons and hills above Malibu are a couple of classic restaurants. The *Inn of the Seventh Ray* (☎ 310-455-1311), 128 Old Topango Rd, Topanga, offers natural foods – vegetarian, fish, and poultry – in continental preparations at $5 to $14 for lunch, $15 to $28 for dinner. The romantic, rustic, and highly-recommended *Saddle Peak Lodge* (☎ 818-222-3888), 419 Cold Canyon Rd, Calabasas, is in its fifth decade of serving American and continental cuisine specializing in game; dinners are $20 and up.

Arnold Schwarzenegger uses unique methods for frying up his schnitzel at Schatzi on Main.

Pasadena

A person could spend months in Old Town Pasadena and still not have sampled every restaurant. Walking west on the south side of Colorado Blvd from the intersection of Fair Oaks Ave, you'll pass *Tommy Tang's* (☎ 818-792-9700), 24 W Colorado, with non-traditional Thai food in the $15 range; and *Ciao Yie* (☎ 818-578-7501), 54 W Colorado Blvd, with Chinese-Italian dishes (like mu shu calzone) at $7 to $16.

A left turn down DeLacey Ave will direct you to *Twin Palms* (☎ 818-577-2567), 101 W Green St, the Kevin Costner-backed country Provincial restaurant with indoor and outdoor seating around a huge courtyard (with two palms, of course). Dinners run $15 to $20.

There are more moderately priced choices in the One Colorado complex, including *Gordon Biersch* (☎ 818-449-0052), 41 Hugus Alley, a brewpub serving California cuisine; *Il Fornaio* (☎ 818-683-9797), 24 W Union St, an Italian cucina; and *Cafe Santorini* (☎ 818-564-4200), serving Mediterranean dishes on a rooftop.

South from Colorado on Fair Oaks, both sides of the street are lined with restaurants. There's *El Toreo*, 21 S Fair Oaks, for budget Mexican; the *Market City Caffe* (☎ 818-568-0203), at No 33, for mid-priced Italian (great antipasti); *Kansai Japanese*, for budget noodles, at No 36; and the *Rose City Diner* (☎ 818-793-8282), a '50s-style American coffeeshop, at No 45.

On E Colorado Blvd from Fair Oaks, *Mérida* (☎ 818-792-7371), at No 20, may be LA's best Yucatecan-Mexican restaurant with $3 to $7 meals.

One of Pasadena's best dining deals is the *Arroyo View Cafe* (☎ 818-666-2833) on the ground floor of the Bank of America Building at Green and Marengo. You can eat full meals, daily, for no more than $4.25.

South of Old Town, one of Pasadena's best restaurants is the *Parkway Grill* (☎ 818-795-1001), 510 S Arroyo Pkwy, which grows its own herbs for grilled meats and fish. Dinners run $13 to $22.

South Pasadena Area

South Pasadena's best restaurant is *Shiro* (☎ 818-799-4774), 1505 Mission St. Dinners in the French-Japanese Pacific Rim tradition (if that *is* a tradition) run $30 to $35. The ginger-encrusted catfish is incredible.

In the Huntington Gardens, 1151 Oxford Rd, San Marino, the *Rose Garden Tea Room* (☎ 818-683-3131) offers a buffet of sweets and finger sandwiches with afternoon tea for $11 per person.

Glendale & Burbank

Though it doesn't offer much in the way of tourist attractions, Glendale has more than its share of good restaurants. In the downtown area, at 219 N Central Ave, there's *Clancy's Crab Broiler* (☎ 818-242-2722), with fresh seafood at $10 to $14. On Brand Blvd, there's *Jax* (☎ 818-500-1604), 339 N Brand, for steak, seafood, and superb live jazz nightly.

Across the street from the NBC Studios in Burbank, and a hangout for many employees, is *Chadney's* (☎ 818-843-5333), 3000 W Olive Ave, a steak-and-seafood house with moderately priced meals. Close to Warner Bros Studios, *La Scala Presto Trattoria* (☎ 818-846-6800), 3821 Riverside Drive, has good Northern Italian dinners for only about $10.

Universal City

Among the generous handful of restaurants in Universal CityWalk, all of them moderately priced, are *Gladstone's* (seafood), *BB King's Blues Club* (barbecue), *Camacho's Cantina* (Mexican), *Morisawa Sushi* (Japanese), and *Lighthouse Beach* (burgers and such). Nearby is *Victoria Station* (☎ 818-777-8180), 100 Universal Terrace Pkwy, a touristy steak-and-seafood restaurant with dinner in the $20 range.

Fung Lum (☎ 818-763-7888), 222 Universal Terrace Pkwy, has 200 staff to handle 1000 diners. Chinese dinners run $15 to $20.

ENTERTAINMENT

Your best sources of information about LA's entertainment are the Calendar section of daily *Los Angeles Times* and the free *LA Weekly*, published Fridays (but usually available Thursday nights).

Music

For highbrow music lovers, there's no finer place to go in Los Angeles than the *Music Center of Los Angeles County* (☎ 213-972-0700), 135 N Grand Ave, at the Civic Center in downtown LA. Currently undergoing a major expansion, it nevertheless is home to four performing companies, Broadway stage productions, the Academy Awards ceremonies, and more.

The Music Center's Ahmanson Theater presents major long-run musicals like *Phantom of the Opera* and *Miss Saigon*. The Mark Taper Forum is strictly for stage plays. The Dorothy Chandler Pavilion is home to the Los Angeles Philharmonic Orchestra (conducted by Esa-Pekka Salonen), the Los Angeles Opera, the Los Angeles Master Chorale & Sinfonia Orchestra, and the American Youth Symphony. Depending upon the event and seating preference, ticket prices range from $19 to $95.

Perhaps even better known is the *Hollywood Bowl* (☎ 213-850-2000), 2301 N Highland Ave, Hollywood, whose summer series offers everything from popular vocalists to pops orchestras, including the LA Philharmonic and the Glendale Symphony Orchestra (conducted by Lalo Schifrin). Very near the Bowl is the *John Anson Ford Amphitheatre* (☎ 213-466-1767), 2580 Cahuenga Blvd, Hollywood, whose own summer series includes dance, opera, and theater.

Notable classical groups include the Los Angeles Chamber Orchestra (☎ 213-622-7001), 315 W 9th St, downtown, and the Los Angeles Mozart Orchestra (☎ 213-851-7100), which performs 18th-century music at the *Wilshire-Ebell Theater*, 4401 W 8th St, in the Mid-Wilshire district. The Pasadena Symphony Association (☎ 818-793-7172) has a huge following for its concerts at the *Pasadena Civic Auditorium*, 300 E Green St, Pasadena. Musical stage productions are also mounted here.

The leading venues in greater LA for major rock concerts are the *Universal Amphitheater* (☎ 818-980-9421), Universal CityWalk, Universal City, and the *Greek Theater* (☎ 213-665-1927), 2700 N Vermont Ave, Griffith Park. In southern LA County, near Long Beach, the *Cerritos Center for the Performing Arts* (☎ 800-300-4345), 12700 Center Court Drive,

---

What's This Thing Called Swing?

In most other cities, the Swing Era ended in 1945, but in cutting edge LA things are just getting started. You got me right, Daddy-O, this town swings!

We're not talking about the surviving members of the Glen Miller Orchestra, we're talking about serious swingers who can really shake a leg – and they play music that'll make you do the same. This isn't a straight retro-scene, either. In typical LA fashion, anything goes in the swing revival. So what you get is a cross between jazz, blues, rockabilly, and country & western. Cab Calloway, Louis Jordan, Elvis Presley, and Bob Wills all exert a certain amount of influence.

For big band blues of the jump variety, see Laura Burgo fronting the Big Town 7. For swing with a rockabilly twist, check in and see the Royal Crown Revue or Jimmy and the Gigolos. For swing of the Western variety, seek out Big Sandy and his Fly-Rite Boys or the Dave and Deke Combo.

You can find new swing at the Brown Derby (213-663-8979) and the Atlas Bar & Grill (213-380-8400) any night of the week. In Long Beach, the Foothill Club (710-495-5196) swings hard most nights as well.

Stepping into one of these clubs, you may well wonder: Where'd all these kids learn to dance like this? And where'd they get those zoot suits? But don't sweat it if you can't swing with the best of 'em right off. There are others in blue jeans and T-shirts who can't do a one-step, not to mention two, out there with you. ∎

Cerritos, also hosts major concerts. The more intimate *Wiltern Theater* (☎ 213-388-1400), 3790 Wilshire Blvd, has jazz and other concerts that draw smaller crowds.

Tickets for events at all of these locations can be purchased directly from TicketMaster (☎ 213-480-3232).

The Club Scene

As LA is the entertainment capital of the world, it would be folly to try to list every venue for live music and dancing. This is a mere sampling. Unless otherwise specified, you must be 21 to enter nightclubs. Expect to pay a cover charge of anywhere from $5 to $15, especially on Friday and Saturday nights. Popular clubs (which change according to a 'who's hot who's not' trend) often have crowds lined up out the door waiting to get in. And getting in is not always guaranteed: the best looking, best dressed people tend to be 'chosen' first. Dress codes, often enforced but usually unofficial, usually prohibit torn jeans, shorts, and bare feet.

Central Los Angeles There's live rock at *Al's Bar* (☎ 213-625-9703), 305 S Hewitt St, and the *Impala Cafe* (☎ 213-621-2170), 418 E 1st St, in Little Tokyo – the latter a vegetarian coffeehouse that welcomes teens.

Latin music holds forth at the *Mayan Theater* (☎ 213-746-4287), 1038 S Hill St; *Grand Ave* (☎ 213-747-0999), 1024 S Grand Ave; and at *Club Bahía* (☎ 213-250-4313), 1130 W Sunset Blvd.

The Silver Lake area, whose population is largely gay, boasts *Spaceland* (☎ 213-412-4442), 1717 Silver Lake Blvd, with extreme alternative music; *Rudolpho's* (☎ 213-969-2596), 2500 Riverside Drive, whose eclectic offerings include a 'gay salsa' night once a month. Nearby is *El Cid* (☎ 213-668-0318), 4212 W Sunset Blvd, with outstanding flamenco performances direct from Spain.

Catch One (☎ 213-734-8849), 4067 W Pico Blvd, a very outré club with strip shows for all persuasions, male and female; and *The Mint Lounge* (☎ 213-937-9630),

6010 W Pico Blvd, perhaps the city's best blues club.

South Central *Babe and Ricky's Inn* (☎ 213-235-4866), 5259 S Central Ave, is a long-established neighborhood blues club. A product of members of the Watts Writers Workshop and jazz drummer Billy Higgins, the *World Stage* (☎ 213-293-2451), 4344 Degnan Blvd in the Crenshaw district, plays mainly reggae and world beat. Just around the corner at 3347½ W 43rd Place, *Fifth Street Dick's Jazz Coffee House* (☎ 213-296-3970) attracts a thirsty crowd of hipsters and features live music nightly.

Hollywood Traveling east from La Brea Ave, near Mann's Chinese Theater, you'll encounter some great jazz clubs on Hollywood Blvd, including the *The Cinegrill* (☎ 213-466-7000), 7000 Hollywood Blvd in the Roosevelt Hotel; *Boardners* (☎ 213-462-9621), 1652 Cherokee Ave; and the *Catalina Bar & Grill* (☎ 213-466-2210), 1640 N Cahuenga Blvd.

Two blocks south of Hollywood Blvd on Sunset Blvd, *Club Lingerie* (☎ 213-466-8557) at No 6507, features alternative rockers on the way up. On Santa Monica Blvd in Hollywood, look for *Dragonfly* (☎ 213-466-6111), a leading alternative rock club at No 6510, and *Arena* (☎ 213-462-1742), a huge gay-oriented disco at No 6655.

West Hollywood Along the Sunset Strip, west from Fairfax Ave, are some of the most established rock clubs in LA, including *Coconut Teaszer* (☎ 213-654-4773), 8117 Sunset, with raw rock for the 18+ crowd, and the tri-level *Roxbury* (☎ 213-656-1750), 8225 Sunset, whose cellar attracts top-name national acts and celebrity drop-ins. Line up early or plan on dining at *The House of Blues* (☎ 213-650-1451), 8430 Sunset, to get in the door.

Further down Sunset, *Club Brasserie* (☎ 310-854-1111) in the Bel Âge Hotel, 1020 N San Vicente Blvd, is an old-style jazz venue; the *Viper Room* (☎ 310-358-1880), 8852 Sunset, is actor Johnny Depp's

---

Smoke of Choice

Fast on the heels of recent restrictions on public smoking in California has come an anti-nonsmoking backlash of sorts. Of particular interest to cigar smokers is a new crop of 'cigar lounges,' where men *and* women congregate to smoke stogies, drink beer or wine, and share industry gossip in voices turning raspy to gravelly.

Three dollars will buy you a mild Arturo Fuente, but you can certainly spend more than that. If you relish the thought of puffing leisurely on a Habana Gold or a Padrón Diplomatico – with no scowls from pesky nonsmokers – check out one of these tobacco havens:

Hamilton's is a throwback to the days of British sportsmen's clubs. It's owned by actor George Hamilton (love at first light?), who often shows up for a smoke, and features a painted portrait of him sitting on a horse. Jacket required. 97135 S Santa Monica Blvd, Beverly Hills (☎ 310-278-0347)

Phillip Dane's Cigar Lounge is a cigar aficionado's 'retreat,' where the female shop-keepers are true cigar aficionadas; they will help you choose from an enormous selection of stogies in their walk-in humidor. 9669 S Santa Monica Blvd, Beverly Hills (☎ 310-285-9945)

The Big Easy calls itself a 'cigar sanctuary' and delivers with a generous selection of choice cigars. Step into their walk-in humidor, make your selection, then find a comfortable chair and puff away. 12604 Ventura Blvd, Studio City (☎ 818-762-3279) ∎

---

notorious nightclub (where River Phoenix died) that attracts acts from Carol Channing to Johnny Cash to Porno for Pyros; the *Whisky a Go Go* (☎ 310-535-0579), 8901 Sunset, still presents the kind of rock that once spawned the Doors; and *The Roxy* (☎ 310-276-2222), 9009 Sunset, presents rock, rhythm & blues, country, and more in its intimate and historic setting. Neither the Whisky nor The Roxy has an age requirement.

Santa Monica Blvd is the location of many of West Hollywood's wildest gay clubs, including *Checca* (☎ 213-850-7471), at No 7323, with occasional floor shows; *7969* (☎ 213-654-0280), at No 7969, tending very outrageous erotic entertainment; *The Palms* (☎ 310-652-6188), at No 8572, a long-established lesbian bar; and *Rage* (☎ 310-652-7055), at No 8911, a trendy men's dance club. At the Beverly Hills end of this strip are *La Masia* (☎ 310-273-7066), 9077 Santa Monica Blvd, which has two dance floors for live salsa and merengue music, and *Doug Weston's Troubador* (☎ 310-276-6168), 9081 Santa Monica Blvd, which has evolved over three decades from a leading folk club to a rock venue. There's no age requirement.

Luna Park (☎ 310-652-0611), 665 N Robertson Blvd near Melrose Ave, has two stages presenting music that ranges from the the bizarre to the sublime. Over at 575 S Fairfax Ave, *Molly Malone's Irish Pub* (☎ 213-935-1577), specializes in Irish folk, rock, and rhythm & blues.

Beverly Hills The hottest club off Rodeo Drive is *Tatou* (☎ 310-274-9955), 233 N Beverly Drive, with live cabaret downstairs and a celebrity-conscious disco upstairs. *Orsini's* (☎ 310-277-6229), 9575 W Pico Blvd, is an elegant disco that attracts well-dressed young professionals, while the *Century Club* (☎ 310-553-6000), 10131 Constellation Blvd, Century City, is a dance club.

West LA Popular clubs in West LA include *Lunaria* (☎ 310-282-8870), 10351 Santa Monica Blvd, for jazz; *Zabumba* (☎ 310-841-6525), 10717 Venice Blvd, for Brazilian rock; and the *Music Machine* (☎ 213-350-4142), 12220 W Pico Blvd, for reggae and world-beat music. *Club Mambo* (☎ 310-837-3775), 11620 Wilshire Blvd, Brentwood, presents live salsa for dancing several nights a week.

Santa Monica Area A block north of the 3rd St Promenade, *Harvelle's* (☎ 310-395-1676), 1432 4th St, has long been a leading live blues club. *Spain* (☎ 310-477-6500), 115 Santa Monica Blvd, presents classical Spanish guitar and flamenco shows. Up Wilshire Blvd from the Promenade, *Kingston 12* (☎ 310-451-4423), 814 Broadway, is a full-time Jamaican reggae club.

Not far from the Santa Monica Airport, *Denim & Diamonds* (☎ 310-452-3446), 3200 Ocean Park Blvd, is a large and very popular country & western club. Nearby are two all-ages clubs: the *Alligator Lounge* (☎ 310-449-1844), 3321 Pico Blvd, whose nightly musical offerings range from alternative to zydeco, and *McCabe's* (☎ 310-828-4403), 3101 Pico Blvd, which presents international folk, blues, country, and solo rock performers in a no-alcohol atmosphere.

At Venice, *St Mark's* (☎ 310-452-2222), 23 Windward Ave, presents jazz, blues, and salsa in an old church. The *Sidewalk Cafe* (☎ 310-399-5547), 1401 Ocean Front Walk, stages acoustic musicians in a boardwalk coffeehouse.

San Fernando Valley On the second floor of Universal CityWalk is *BB King's Blues Club* (☎ 818-622-5464), 1000 Universal Center Drive, Universal City. With a seating capacity of 350, this club serves up Southern cuisine and hospitality and a nightly roster of top touring blues performers.

Sherman Oaks' *Moonlight Tango Cafe* (☎ 818-788-2000), 13730 Ventura Blvd, features big bands and swing dancing, complete with conga lines. *Le Café* (☎ 818-986-2662), 14633 Ventura Blvd, has an intimate attic where top-name jazz musicians play nightly.

In North Hollywood, *The Palomino* (☎ 818-764-4010), 6907 Lankershim Blvd, is a classic country music theater.

Theater
Theater in LA is a natural partner to the film industry. Many stage actors go on to successful movie careers; conversely, film

stars may return to the stage to hone their acting skills. There are more than 100 stage groups and facilities in the metropolis; call ☎ 213-688-2787 for information on all shows, performance times, and locations. You can also get tickets and information by calling Theatix (☎ 213-466-1767).

Major Theaters The *Mark Taper Forum* at the Music Center (☎ 213-972-0700), 135 N Grand Ave, emphasizes the development of new plays and presents US and world premieres. The *Ahmanson Theater* in the same complex is a venue for major Broadway plays. You will also see leading musical productions (like *Sunset Blvd* and *Beauty and the Beast*) at the *Shubert Theater* (☎ 800-447-7400), 2020 Ave of the Stars, Century City, and at the *Pantages Theater* (☎ 213-468-1770), 6233 Hollywood Blvd, considered one of America's finest examples of Art Deco-Renaissance architecture. The *UCLA James A Doolittle Theater* (☎ 213-462-6666), 1615 N Vine St, is probably the top stage in LA for touring theater.

The outdoor *John Anson Ford Theater* (☎ 213-466-1767), 2580 Cahuenga Blvd, hosts LA's annual Shakespeare Festival each July. Built in the 1930s, the Ford has a hillside backdrop of palms and cypresses that gives it a particularly intimate feeling.

Neighborhood Stages The *Los Angeles Theater Center* (☎ 213-485-1681), 514 S Spring St, is the leading theater downtown. Nearby, the *Bob Baker Marionette Theatre* (☎ 213-250-9995), 1345 W 1st St, is the only ongoing puppet theater in the US, and its shows are geared for adults as well as children.

The greatest concentration of small theaters are along a stretch of Santa Monica Blvd. There's the *Actors Gang Theater* at No 6201, *The Complex* at No 6476, *Second Stage* at No 6500, the *Hudson Theater* at No 6539, the *Attic Theater* at No 6562, and the *Celebration Theater* at No 7051.

Two theaters noted for their daring original presentations are *Stages Theatre Center* (☎ 213-465-1010), 1540 N McCadden Place, and the *Ivar Theatre* (☎ 213-464-1364), 1605 N Ivar St at the Inner City Cultural Center.

In Beverly Hills, *Theatre 40* (☎ 310-277-4221), 241 Moreno Drive, is one of LA's oldest professional companies. Its annual season includes eight classic and modern plays.

Santa Monica boasts the *Santa Monica Playhouse* (☎ 310-394-9779), 1211 4th St, where three to five different productions – comedies, musicals, dramas, even fairy tales – are performed weekly, often by noted actors. Above Malibu, the *Will Geer Theatricum Botanicum* (☎ 310-455-3723), 1419 N Topanga Canyon Blvd, Topanga, has an outdoor amphitheater where a resident professional acting company performs Shakespeare and works by other playwrights every summer.

The 1927 *Pasadena Playhouse* (☎ 818-356-7529), 39 S El Molino Ave, has been designated the official State Theater of California. Refurbished and reopened in 1985, it now offers an annual program of at least a half-dozen different plays, from classics to world premieres.

In North Hollywood, theater center for the San Fernando Valley, the *Actors Alley Repertory Theater* (☎ 818-508-4200), 5269 Lankershim Blvd, has a subscription series in the historical El Portal Theatre featuring musicals, comedy, drama, and new works.

Ethnic Theater The *Bilingual Foundation of the Arts* (☎ 213-225-4044), 421 North Ave 19, Highland Park, claims to be 'the only theatre on the West Coast presenting Hispanic world drama in English and Spanish.' *Plaza de la Raza* (☎ 213-223-2475), 3540 N Mission Rd, Lincoln Park, doesn't try English; instead, this Latino cultural center encourages Spanish-language arts through theater, dance, and music.

The *East West Players* (☎ 213-660-0366), 4424 Santa Monica Blvd, Silver Lake, are the leading Asian American theater company in the US.

At the Japanese American Cultural & Community Center in Little Tokyo, the *Japan America Theater* (☎ 213-628-2725), 244 S San Pedro St, has an annual season of theater and concerts featuring Japanese and other Asian American artists.

The *Unity Arts Center* (☎ 213-993-7245), 412 S Park View, offers a stage for works by people of many nationalities, including Korean and Hispanic.

Comedy

One of the best values for entertainment in LA is comedy. On any given night, comedy stars – some of them very famous – may be loosening their chops in one of LA's many comedy clubs. At the very least, you will likely be treated to a hilarious evening with one of next year's comic sensations: LA is where the funny people come to make it big.

In West Hollywood comedy clubs abound. Perhaps most notable is the *Groundling Theater* (☎ 213-934-9700), 7307 Melrose Ave, a repertory company whose alumni include Peewee Herman, Phil Hartman, and Julia Sweeney. Topname stand-ups still appear regularly at *The Improvisation* (The Improv, ☎ 213-651-2583), 8162 Melrose Ave. Nearby are the *Acme Comedy Theater* (☎ 213-525-0202), 135 N La Brea Ave, and the MICE improv troupe at the *West Hollywood Playhouse* (☎ 818-762-7547), 666 N Robertson Ave.

Santa Monica has a few venues, including a good improv troupe *Upfront Comedy* (☎ 310-319-3477), 123 Broadway Ave. In Pasadena there's the *Ice House* (☎ 818-577-1894), 24 N Mentor Ave, LA's first comedy club and still one of its best. Bigname comedians like Dennis Miller and Gabe Kaplan appear there regularly. If you're spending your time in South Central, a comedy club catering primarily to Black audiences is the *Comedy Act Theater* (☎ 310-677-4101), 3339 W 43rd St, Crenshaw.

Dance

Dance productions aren't as widely publicized as music and theater, but there remains a great deal of ballet, modern, tap, jazz, ethnic, traditional, and performance-art dancing in LA. Performers like Martha

Nomomania

The Dodgers may be nearly as ethnically diverse as Los Angeles itself but in 1995 the team's number-one attraction was Hideo Nomo, the only Japanese player in Major League Baseball. So many Japanese fans have made a pilgrimage to Dodger Stadium that Japanese travel agents have started to include a Dodgers game in their itineraries and the stadium has opened a Japanese restaurant.

But Nomo's popularity doesn't stop with his countrymen – American fans have also taken a real interest in him. His appeal is largely due to an extremely unorthodox pitching style. In winding up for each pitch, Nomo twists on his knee, his foot still pointing towards home plate, until the rest of his body is facing the opposite direction. Then he rears his upper body back, for that little something extra, and thrusts all his weight and leg power into his throwing motion. Nearly every pitch is launched at speeds exceeding 90 mph.

The ultimate accolade came in July '95, when Nomo was selected starting pitcher for the National League in the 'mid-summer classic,' the annual All Star Game. One hundred and fifty Japanese journalists turned up to cover the event. Back in Japan, over 15 million fans watched the game on TV at home and nearly a quarter of a million more watched on giant TV screens set up in major cities. Some, believe it or not, even turned up late for work. Nomo is undoubtedly not the only Japanese player capable of cutting it in American baseball (he began in Japan playing for the Kintetsu Buffaloes) but the Japanese sense of responsibility to an employer makes it very difficult for even the most talented players to move to the bigger pool. Luckily for the Dodgers, Nomo is a nonconformist. ■

Graham, Alvin Ailey, and Bella Lewitzky got their start here.

The best source for information on performances is the Dance Resource Center of Greater Los Angeles (☎ 213-227-9162).

Two venues have regular dance performances scheduled: *LA Contemporary Exhibitions* (LACE, ☎ 213-957-1777), 6922 Hollywood Blvd, Hollywood, and *Highways Performance Space* (☎ 310-453-1755), 1651 18th St, Santa Monica.

Cinema

Many of LA's multiplex theaters have six screens or more; the largest is the *Universal City 18 Cinemas* at Universal CityWalk (☎ 818-905-3767). Among the most popular theaters for studio previews is the *Westwood Theater* (☎ 310-208-7664), 1050 Gayley Ave, Westwood. See geographical entries for classic theaters, and check the newspapers for current ads and listings.

Many theaters throughout the metropolis cater to foreign-language audiences. Examples are the *Orpheum* (☎ 213-239-0937), 842 S Broadway, and the *State* (☎ 818-792-6227), 703 S Broadway, downtown, for Spanish speakers; *Kuo-Hwa Cinemas*

(☎ 818-282-5899), 250 W Valley Blvd, San Gabriel, for Chinese speakers; and the *Rani Theater* (☎ 818-773-3848), 5269 Lankershim Blvd, North Hollywood, for speakers of Urdu-Hindi and other languages of India and Pakistan.

Spectator Sports

Baseball The National League's Los Angeles Dodgers (☎ 213-224-1400) play 81 games from April to October at Dodger Stadium, 1000 Elysian Park Ave, just north of downtown LA. Orange County's California Angels play in the American League at Anaheim Stadium.

Football Both of LA's professional football teams – the Rams and the Raiders – picked up and moved in early 1995. The city hopes to attract a new pro team in 1996. In the meantime, USC (☎ 213-740-2311) and UCLA (☎ 310-825-2106), compete in the Pac-10 Conference for the right to play in Pasadena's Rose Bowl game on January 1.

Basketball The city has two professional teams in the National Basketball Association: the Los Angeles Lakers, who play at the Great Western Forum (☎ 310-419-3100), Manchester Blvd and Prairie Ave in Inglewood, and the Los Angeles Clippers, who play at the LA Sports Arena (☎ 213-748-6136), 3939 S Figueroa St, Exposition Park.

UCLA's basketball team, the Bruins, is one of the best college teams in the USA; in 1995, the Westwood team won the national collegiate championship. Call ☎ 310-825-2106 for tickets.

Ice Hockey The Los Angeles Kings of the National Hockey League play at the Forum (☎ 310-419-3100) in Inglewood. The Anaheim Mighty Ducks, given that name by their Disney owners, are an Orange County franchise.

THINGS TO BUY

Most LA residents do their serious shopping in multi-story malls, some of them with upwards of 200 stores in a single building. But when they want to take a more whimsical approach to shopping, they head for a handful of streets where the people-watching is as much fun as the window browsing.

The most unique boutique is in the LA County Hall of Administration, near the Civic Center at Temple and Hill Sts, where the county Coroner Department's bizarre Skeletons in the Closet gift shop sells items such as beach towels with chalk outlines to benefit the city's Youthful Drunk Driving Program.

Shopping Districts

In addition to those listed below, one of greater LA's newest shopping streets is **Universal CityWalk,** which opened in 1993 adjacent to Universal Studios. The fanciful promenade has 40 shops, restaurants, and entertainment venues. Don't go expecting to find bargains; go for the amusement value. Two other popular shopping districts are the UCLA student-oriented **Westwood Village,** just north of Wilshire Blvd along Westwood Blvd, and the gentrified **Pasadena Old Town** area,

surrounding the intersection of Colorado Blvd and Fair Oaks Ave.

Visitors intent on ethnic souvenirs should head for Mexican **Olvera St,** in El Pueblo de Los Angeles; **Chinatown,** especially along Broadway and Hill Sts; and **Japanese Village Plaza,** between 1st and 2nd Sts east of San Pedro St, in Little Tokyo.

Melrose Ave Extending from north La Brea Ave near Hollywood to La Cienega Blvd in West Hollywood, this is the place to come for 21st century funk. The greatest concentration of hip shops and boutiques runs roughly from Alta Vista Blvd west nine blocks to Spaulding Ave. Everyone's got their own favorite shops; mine include Spike's Joint West, 7263 Melrose, for logo apparel from the popular director; Vinyl Fetish, 7305 Melrose, for imported British records and music paraphernalia; the Wound & Wound Toy Co, 7374 Melrose, for wind-up toys and music boxes; La Luz de Jesus, 7400 Melrose, for Mexican folk art; Zulu and Wacko, 7416 Melrose, for novelty items; Leathers & Treasures, 7511 Melrose, for biker jackets, cowboy boots, and trashier stuff; and Aardvark's, 7579 Melrose, for second-hand clothing.

Ocean Front Walk Vendors of all types display their wares along Venice Beach, just south of Santa Monica. Among the wacky street life, you'll find items from silk Italian ties to bronze dancing Shiva icons from India to bronze cowbells from Switzerland to spiked leather bikinis to backpacks made entirely from hemp. Permanent shops sell sunglasses, famous prints and posters, socks (five pair for $2!), and a variety of clothes.

3rd St Promenade This mid-city pedestrian mall extending from the Santa Monica Place shopping mall on Broadway three blocks north to Wilshire Blvd, is the heart of Santa Monica. Street musicians and other buskers, not to mention Hollywood entertainment scouts, keep this strip busy day and night. The best shops are those that

---

Flea Markets

Flea markets or swap meets: call them what you will, the LA area has plenty. Nourished by a remarkably diverse population with some equally eclectic tastes, these massive gatherings can make for the best bargain shopping around. Whether you're hunting a Stickley settle or a Hopalong Cassidy pocket knife, you'll seldom find it for a better price (or have half the fun in bargaining). The first four below, held on successive Sundays every month, are the best of the bunch. Arrive early and wear those walking shoes.

Pasadena City College Flea Market, first Sunday of the month from 6 am to 3 pm. Admission is free and it's the best for music. 1570 E Colorado Blvd, Pasadena (☎ 818-585-7906)

Rose Bowl Flea Market, second Sunday of the month from 6 am to 4:30 pm. It's the largest in the land, with over 1500 vendors descending upon Pasadena's scenic Arroyo Seco. Admission is $10 before 9 am, when all the best goodies are gotten, $5 after. 1001 Rose Bowl Drive, Pasadena (☎ 213-588-4411)

Long Beach Outdoor Antique & Collectible Market, third Sunday of the month from 8 am to 3 pm. Veteran's Memorial Stadium, Conant St between Lakewood Blvd and Clark Ave, Long Beach (☎ 213-655-5703)

Santa Monica Outdoor Antique & Collectible Market, fourth Sunday of the month from 6 am to 3 pm. Possibly the poshest of the lot, with Victorian to post-Modern wares and tasty food besides! Airport Ave off Bundy Ave, Santa Monica (☎ 213-933-2511)

Melrose Weekend Market, Sundays 9 am to 5 pm. Fairfax High School parking lot, Melrose and Fairfax Aves, Hollywood (☎ 213-465-7665)

Burbank Monthly Antique Market, fourth Sunday of the month from 8 am to 3 pm. Admission is $3. Main St. and Riverside Drive, Burbank (☎ 310-455-2886)

The Roadium, runs daily from 7 am to 3 pm. Admission is 50¢, except Wednesday when the week's treasures arrive and the price jumps to $1.25 adults, 75¢ seniors. 2500 Redondo Beach Blvd, Torrance (☎ 213-321-3709) ■

---

appeal to readers (see Books, below), artists, and import lovers.

Rodeo Drive Known the world over for its up-up-upscale designer boutiques and jewelry stores, art galleries, antique shops, and high-priced salons, Rodeo provides a tangible definition of Beverly Hills. Start at the cobblestoned Two Rodeo Drive complex on Wilshire Blvd opposite the Regent Beverly Wilshire Hotel; from there, follow Rodeo north three blocks, across Dayton Way and Brighton Way, to Little Santa Monica Blvd. Names along here include Giorgio Armani, Cartier, Christian Dior, and Gucci to name a few.

Design District Perhaps the single best area for the art lover to explore is the triangle in West Hollywood bounded by Santa Monica, La Cienega, and Beverly Blvds. The heart of the district is the Pacific Design Center, 8687 Melrose Ave at San Vicente Blvd, which has more than 1.2 million sq feet of floor space and 200 showrooms exhibiting state-of-the-art furniture and home accessories. It's mainly intended as a wholesale outlet for retailers, but the public is invited to browse. Among three dozen art galleries in the area are the Margo Leavin Gallery, 812 N Robertson Blvd, specializing in contemporary international art; the Herbert Palmer Gallery, 802 N La Cienega Blvd, displaying 20th-century American and European masters; and the Gideo Gallery, 8748 Melrose Ave, featuring 16th- to 19th-century etchings and lithographs.

Garment District You can't do better in terms of price and variety than to shop in this downtown LA district, which extends roughly from 6th St and Broadway southeast to 16th and San Pedro Sts. A manufacturing center since the 1930s, you'll find wholesale prices on all manner of garb. At its heart is The Cooper Building, 860 S Los Angeles St, with more than 50 factory-outlets selling designer brands.

Nearby, on S Hill St between 6th and 7th Sts, is LA's old **Jewelry District** where prices for watches, gold, silver, or gems are 40 to 70% less than elsewhere in the city. Try the St Vincent Jewelry Center, 650 S Hill St, or the Fox Jewelry Plaza, 608 S Hill St, each with dozens of outlets.

Shopping Malls

The typical Southern California shopping mall seems to grow in proportion to the number of major department stores by which it is anchored. Top-end stores that you'll find throughout the metropolis include the locally owned Bullock's and Robinson's-May. Also look for Neiman-Marcus and Saks Fifth Avenue, both top-of-the-line department stores, and Nordstrom a department store known for its shoe selection.

The largest shopping mall in the LA area is the Glendale Galleria, a two-story, 270-store center at Central Ave and Colorado St. Others with 150 shops or more include Beverly Center, 8500 Beverly Blvd, West Hollywood; Century City Shopping Center and Marketplace, 10250 Santa Monica Blvd; Westside Pavilion, 10800 Pico Blvd, West LA; Santa Monica Place, Colorado Ave at the 3rd St Promenade; and the Sherman Oaks Galleria, 15301 Ventura Blvd.

Open-Air Markets

The city's best-known is the **Farmer's Market**, 6333 W 3rd St in the Fairfax District. There are some 150 shops and stalls here, many vending fresh produce or an international selection of hot and cold foods, but many more selling unique craft and gift items, from T-shirts to oil paintings. A downtown LA institution since 1917, the **Grand Central Market**, 317 S Broadway, has four dozen vendors that hawk fresh fruits and vegetables, meat and seafood, hand-tossed tortillas, and homemade Chinese noodles. Also downtown is one of the most colorful destinations in the

city: the **Wholesale Flower Market** (☎ 213-622-1966), at 754 S Wall St, where you'll get the best selection of fresh flowers before the sun comes up.

Antiques

Perhaps the best place to look for deals is the monthly **Rose Bowl Flea Market**, held the second Sunday of every month from 9 am to 3 pm in the vast parking lot of Pasadena's famous sports stadium.

Major antique markets in the LA area include the **Santa Monica Antique Market**, 1607 Lincoln Blvd, with more than 150 dealers and 20,000 sq feet of display space; **The Antique Guild**, 8800 Venice Blvd, Culver City, covering two acres; and **Antiquarius**, near Hollywood's Pacific Design Center at 8840 Beverly Blvd, an art and antique mall with more than 40 shops.

Souvenir Stores

For film aficionados, Collectors Book Store, 1708 N Vine St, Hollywood, is an essential stop for its inventory of film memorabilia, including old scripts, movie posters, and publicity stills. Another outstanding shop fairly bursting with nostalgia is the Larry Edmunds Book Shop, 6644 Hollywood Blvd.

On Melrose Ave, Chic-a-Boom, 6817 Melrose, carries vintage movie memorabilia; Fantasies Come True, 8012 Melrose, sells animation stills; and Name That Toon, 8483 Melrose, not only has a current animation gallery, it also boasts the world's only Gumby museum.

GETTING THERE & AWAY
Air

In Westchester, 17 miles southwest of downtown LA, Los Angeles International Airport (LAX, ☎ 310-646-5252) is the third-busiest airport in the world, and the hub of travel throughout the Pacific Rim region. Good-value roundtrip fares to the East Coast typically run around $400; to Chicago around $300; slightly less to Denver or Dallas; and less than $100 (sometimes as little as $19) to San Francisco.

LAX has nine terminals, all but one of which (including the five-tier Tom Bradley International Terminal) focus around a two-level, central traffic loop that encloses the control tower and heliport, parking garages, and an observation-deck restaurant. The airport postal center and first aid office are located in the Tom Bradley International Terminal (TBIT).

Free shuttle buses circle the terminal area on a continuing schedule; look for these blue-and-green vehicles in front of the baggage claim areas, located on each terminal's lower (arrival) level along with car-rental agents and other ground transportation services. Ticketing and check-in are on each terminal's upper (departure) level. A free mini-bus equipped with a wheelchair lift for the handicapped can be reached at ☎ 310-646-6402.

Bus

Greyhound Lines serves LA from cities all over North America. The main LA terminal (☎ 213-629-8400) is in a seedy district east of downtown, south of Little Tokyo, at 1716 E 7th St at Alameda St. The area is a bit rough, but the station itself is safe enough inside. There are other LA-area Greyhound stations at 1409 N Vine St, Hollywood (☎ 213-466-6382); 1433 5th St, Santa Monica (☎ 310-394-5433); and 1711 S Manchester Blvd, Anaheim (☎ 714-999-1256).

Green Tortoise (☎ 415-285-2441, 800-227-4766) buses offer weekly service up and down the West Coast; summer trips to Alaska and the East Coast, winter tours to Mexico and Baja California, and a Mardi Gras extravaganza between LA and New Orleans. Fares are around $69 from Seattle to LA via San Francisco. Be sure to reserve. Greyhound's fare is identical, but it's nowhere near as much fun.

Train

Amtrak arrives and departs from Union Station (☎ 213-624-0171), downtown at 800 N Alameda St. The one-way fare between San Francisco and LA is $75. There is also regular east-west service from LA to Phoenix, New Orleans, and points beyond, as well as several trains daily to and from San Diego.

Car

Try Auto Driveaway (☎ 310-421-0313), 2735 E Carson St, in Lakewood. There's a $300 deposit (cash or travelers check) which will be held in the event of an accident or if you travel beyond the limited time or mileage for the trip. You must be 21 or older, have a valid driver license, and be able to provide references in the original city and your destination.

GETTING AROUND

LA is an enormous metropolis with many forms of public transportation. The Metropolitan Transportation Authority (MTA) oversees an extensive system that includes buses, heavy rail street cars, and a new subway. Still, by far the area's most popular mode of transportation remains the automobile. Before rushing headlong into the bumper-to-bumper mélange, though, you ought to consider all of your transportation options.

The Paratransit Referral Service Info Line (☎ 800-431-7882) can refer mobility-impaired people to door-to-door transportation services in LA County.

To/From the Airport

Bus A free MTA connector bus stops outside each terminal every 10 to 20 minutes around the clock and drops you at Lot C of the LAX Transit Center, on the corner of 96th St and Vicksburg Ave. Here you can connect to public buses that will take you anywhere in greater LA. For more information, see Bus, below.

Train To catch the Metro Green Line, take the free shuttle (on the lower level, under the LAX shuttle signs) to the Metro Green Line Aviation Station. Trains run south to Redondo Beach and east to Norwalk. On an eastbound train, you can transfer at the Wilmington Station to the Metro Blue

Line, which will take you north to downtown LA or south to Long Beach. Fare is $1.35.

Shuttles Private shuttle buses are a compromise in time and expense between taxis, which are quite costly, and exhaustingly slow public transportation. Your choice of shuttle service will depend upon your destination: inquire at the ground-transportation desk near each baggage claim (open daily from 8 am to midnight). Most shuttles operate 24 hours and provide door-to-door service. Fares are usually $10 to $15. All American Shuttle (☎ 310-641-4090, 800-585-2529), Prime Time (☎ 800-262-7433), and Super Shuttle (☎ 310-450-2377, 800-258-3826) all have minibuses that serve the greater LA and Orange County areas.

If you're staying near the airport, Airport Coach (☎ 800-772-5299) provides service to hotels.

If you're headed out to the San Fernando Valley, FlyAway (☎ 818-994-5554) runs direct service from LAX to the Van Nuys Airport Bus Terminal.

Taxi These are plentiful and cost about $20 to Santa Monica, $30 to downtown or Hollywood, up to $70 to Disneyland.

Bus

A network of 208 separate bus routes spans the metropolis. The fare is $1.10, plus another 25¢ for each transfer you require; express buses (which use the freeways) cost 35¢ more. A monthly pass, if you're going to be in town that long, is $42.

For full information on MTA bus routes, including maps, timetables, and passes, visit the MTA ticket counter on Level C of the ARCO Plaza, 515 S Flower St, downtown, open weekdays from 7:30 am to 3:30 pm, or call MTA (☎ 213-626-4455) from 5:30 am to 11:30 pm. There are other customer centers downtown at 419 S Main St and down the street at 1016 S Main St, in Hollywood at 6249 Hollywood Blvd in the mid-Wilshire area at 5301 Wilshire Blvd, and in the San Fernando Valley at 14435 Sherman Way, Van Nuys.

MTA Bus Routes
Here are a few of the more commonly used MTA routes from downtown LA. Most services run from 5 am to 2 am at intervals of every 15 minutes or so.

No 1, Hollywood Blvd
No 2, Sunset Blvd
No 4, Santa Monica Blvd (24 hours)
No 10, Melrose Ave
No 20, Wilshire Blvd (24 hours)
No 22, to Santa Monica via Wilshire Blvd
No 27, to Beverly Hills (nonstop)
No 33, to Venice Beach
No 60, to Long Beach
No 79, to Huntington Library & Gardens
No 96, to Burbank Studios
No 436, to Venice Beach (express)
No 439, to LAX and South Bay (express)
No 446, to San Pedro (express)
No 456, to Long Beach (express)
No 460, to Disneyland (express) ■

The Santa Monica Municipal Bus Lines (☎ 310-451-5444), popularly known as 'The Big Blue Bus,' serves much of West Los Angeles, including Westwood, Pacific Palisades, and LAX, as well as Santa Monica and Venice. The fare is only 50¢. Also, the No 10 express runs to downtown on the Santa Monica Fwy for $1.25. Transfers are available to MTA and Culver City buses. Buses run Monday to Saturday from 5:30 am to midnight and Sundays from 6:30 am to midnight.

Downtown LA is also served by a minibus system – the Downtown Area Short Hop (DASH, ☎ 800-252-7433) – that runs a pair of circuits weekdays from 6:30 am to 6:30 pm and Saturdays from 10 am to 5 pm. Buses stop every 6 to 15 minutes (more during rush hours) and cost just 25¢ (exact change). Four separate routes, three of them meeting at City Hall, extend from Chinatown south to Exposition Park.

Metro Rail

Run by the MTA (☎ 213-626-4455), Metro Rail's 22-mile Blue Line, which opened in 1990, operates between downtown LA and

Long Beach every 15 minutes daily from 5 am to 10 pm; full fare is $1.35. The Red Line, which opened in 1993, runs underground from Union Station through the central business district to MacArthur Park and Western Ave; fare is 25¢. It will soon extend to Hollywood and the San Fernando Valley. The 20-mile Green Line runs west from Norwalk, crosses the Blue Line at the Imperial Highway in Wilmington, and extends to LAX and Redondo Beach. The Red and Blue lines join at the downtown Metro Center, 7th and Flower Sts. Tickets are dispensed by coin-operated machines.

Metrolink (☎ 800-371-5465) extends

Big Red Cars

Long before the freeways were built – even before William Mullholland brought water to the Los Angeles Basin – the many corners of this far-reaching, seemingly unplanned metropolis were connected by a complex network of electric railways which, by 1911, were consolidated under Henry E Huntington's Pacific Electric Railway. Known as 'The Big Red Cars,' LA's old streetcars are romanticized today by train buffs and oldtimers.

At their peak, the Red Cars covered over 1100 miles of track stretching as far east as San Bernardino, west to the coast, north to San Fernando, and south to Huntington Beach. Pacific Electric even built a subway line in 1925, which ran from downtown to Hollywood. Subsidiary lines connected more communities in between, creating smaller commercial centers and lessening reliance on the urban core.

Ultimately, Angelinos' preference for the automobile spelled the doom of fixed-rail transit in LA. Not only did autos intrude on the trains' rights-of-way, public funds shifted towards the building of more roads, while trains fell into a state of neglect. Beginning in the late 1930s, Red Car lines were discontinued at a steady rate. When the last Red Car had its final run, from downtown to Long Beach in April of 1961, all of the trains had been either junked or sold to the Argentine capital of Buenos Aires. ■

from Union Station south through Orange County to Oceanside, east to Riverside and San Bernardino, north and west to Santa Clarita and Ventura County.

Car

By far the best way to get around is by car. Despite the sheer volume of traffic, the city is not hard to get around, especially if you stick as much as possible to the major arterials like Santa Monica and Wilshire Blvds. Street signs are large, easy to read, and usually posted far enough ahead of major intersections. It's wise to map out your route before you start driving, and as much as possible avoid rush hours: roughly speaking, 6:30 to 9:30 am and 3:30 to 6:30 pm.

Parking is one of the biggest bugaboos for LA drivers. Metered parking will probably cost you 25¢ per 15 minutes, and may be limited to one hour. See Car in the Getting Around chapter for more on this.

If you're going to rent a car, the best place to do so may be near the airport upon your arrival. Agencies are located throughout the LA area, but bargaining power goes furthest at LAX. Costs are highest in summer and over the Christmas holidays, lowest on weekends any other time of the year. Expect to pay $25 to $45 per day, $120 to $200 per week.

Some agencies which may have lower rates are:

Avon
    1100 S Beverly Drive (☎ 213-850-0826)
Penny
    12425 Victory Blvd (☎ 818-786-1733)
Rent-A-Wreck
    12333 W Pico Blvd (☎ 310-478-0677, 800-535-1391)
Ugly Duckling
    10620 Venice Blvd (☎ 310-478-4208)

If money is no object, you can rent everything from a Rolls-Royce to a Jaguar at the likes of Elegant Rent-A-Car (☎ 310-247-0277, 800-577-4528), 9797 Wilshire Blvd, Beverly Hills; and Luxury Line (☎ 310-823-6000), 4100 Admiralty Way, Marina del Rey.

CALIFORNIA

Rail Transit Redux

Visitors who haven't been to Los Angeles for many years may be surprised to see fixed-rail transit operating once again in the city. Ever since the old Pacific Electric system faded out in 1961, gridlock, smog, and social unrest have pointed to the need for the return of trains. A long time passed before anything was done about it, though.

For 15 years, beginning in the mid-'60s, ballot initiatives for the development of a new system failed. When a ballot initiative passed in 1980, calling for a half-cent sales tax to fund a new rail transit system, it still took another nine years before the first stretch of track was laid.

Ironically, when the Metro Rail Blue Line began service in 1989, it ran along exactly the same course as the old Long Beach Line. Similarly, the new Red Line subway, which began service in 1993, reproduces the Pacific Electric subway discontinued in 1955. Whether the return of fixed-rail transit effectively addresses LA transportation problems remains to be seen. Success depends largely on public response, which thus far has been luke-warm.

By the time the MTA rail transit system is completed in 2010, it will span 400 miles countywide and cost an estimated $6.5 billion. Talk about a heavy roundtrip fare! ∎

Taxi

You can't just thrust your arm out and expect to hail a taxi in LA. Except for those lined up outside airports, train stations, bus stations, and major hotels, cabbies only respond to phone calls. Fares are metered; you pay $2 at flagfall, $1.80 per mile. There are additional charges for luggage (50¢ per piece) and passengers over three (75¢ per person).

Checker
    (☎ 213-258-3131, 800-300-5007)
Independent
    (☎ 213-385-8294, 800-521-8294)
United Independent
    (☎ 213-653-5050, 800-822-8294)
Yellow Cab
    (☎ 213-934-6700, 310-278-2500)

Limousines

Chauffeur-driven limousines cost about $50 an hour, usually with a minimum use of three hours. The yellow pages has several pages of limo companies.

Bicycle

Cyclists are entitled to their share of any city street in LA. Freeways, on the other hand, are reserved for automobiles. Be aware that the presence of cyclists on LA's streets is relatively small and riding aggressively is likely to antagonize already uncharitable motorists.

Get a detailed map of LA's bike paths from the city Department of Transportation (☎ 213-485-2265), 200 N Spring St, 12th Floor. The best place to rent bicycles is from one of the many concessions along the beachfront bike paths.

Of LA's city buses only Bus No 130 to Artesia has a bike rack. MTA's MetroRail allows cyclists with a permit ($6) to ride during restricted hours on weekdays (unrestricted on weekends). Call MTA's Passenger Service (☎ 213-922-6235) to get more information. MetroLink also allows bikes, as long as you have a bicycle permit (☎ 213-808-5465) and the conductor determines that there is enough space on the train for you.

Around Los Angeles

LONG BEACH
• pop 430,000 ☎ 310

The second-largest city in the greater Los Angeles area (after LA itself), Long Beach is also one of the metropolis' most diverse and exciting communities. If driving from downtown LA, to get there take the 110 Fwy south to the 405 Fwy south to the 710 Fwy west. If you want to try out the modern Metro Rail system, catch a Blue

Line train in downtown LA and ride it all the way down to the Long Beach Plaza.

Queen Mary & The Waterfront

To casual visitors, Long Beach is best known for its **Queen Mary Seaport** (☎ 435-3511), 1126 Queens Hwy. At the south end of the Long Beach (710) Fwy, the *Queen Mary* has been a major attraction since it was permanently moored here in 1971. The 50,000-ton Art Deco luxury passenger liner was launched in 1934 and made 1001 crossings of the Atlantic (including service as a WWII troop ship) before it was retired in 1964. Recently it was purchased from the City of Long Beach by the Disney Corporation.

Don't miss taking a guided tour; they're offered daily from 10 am to 6 pm, 9 am to 9 pm in July and August. Admission is $7 for adults, $6 for those over 55 and $4 for kids 4 to 11. In addition, 365 staterooms are maintained as hotel accommodations, supplemented by elegant restaurants and lounges, a wedding chapel, and numerous gift shops.

The ship's entrance path weaves through the Queen's Marketplace, a kitschy takeoff on 19th-century British architecture. You'll also find the tallest free-standing bungee tower in North America: MegaBungee (☎ 435-1880) is 210 feet tall, with a 75% rebound. Leap before you look for $85.

The huge dome-like shell adjacent to the *Queen Mary* once housed billionaire aviator Howard Hughes' bizarre flying boat, the *Spruce Goose*. Today the dome is used as a Warner Bros movie set, most recently for the 1995 *Batman* movie that starred Val Kilmer and Nicole Kidman.

Directly across Queensway Bay is **Shoreline Village** (☎ 435-2668), a shopping-and-dining complex that surrounds a small marina beside Shoreline Aquatic Park. An antique carousel, built in 1906, is the village centerpiece.

Visitors can take thrilling two-seater parasailing flights (Skyrider Parasails, ☎ 493-4979) or book daily dinner cruises through the Port of Long Beach Harbor.

Deep-sea fishing launches depart for half-day and full-day excursions daily around 7 am from Long Beach Harbor. Try Belmont Pier Sportfishing (☎ 434-6781), Belmont Pier, or Long Beach Sportfishing (☎ 432-8993), 555 Pico Ave.

Downtown

The liveliest street in downtown Long Beach is **Pine Ave,** from the west side of Long Beach Plaza to Ocean Blvd at the convention center. This three-block stretch and its cross streets have numerous restaurants, nightspots, and interesting shops. The city's new restaurant row is Pine around Broadway. The *Blue Cafe* (☎ 983-7111), 210 Promenade, *System M* (☎ 435-2525), 213A Pine Ave, and the *Cohiba Club* (☎ 491-5220), 110 Broadway, keep night owls hopping.

Readers head to *Acres of Books* (☎ 437-6980), 240 Long Beach Blvd, an Art Deco warehouse of 'nearly one million' used books, whose aisles sci-fi author Ray Bradbury faithfully prowls. The *Bert Grimms Tattoo Studio* (☎ 432-9304), a few blocks away at 22 S Chestnut Place, claims (1) to be the nation's longest-operating tattoo parlor (since 1927) and (2) to have tattooed gangsters like Bonnie Parker and Pretty Boy Floyd.

Naples

Alamitos Bay surrounds the isle of Naples, built by Arthur Parson (a chronological and philosophical contemporary of Venice's Abbot Kinney) in the 1920s. Parson's success at community planning was more lasting than Kinney's – the **Rivo Alto Canal** still circles a network of curving lanes built up with garden-shrouded bungalows. See Naples by foot or, better yet, by water.

The authentic boats of *Gondola Getaway* (☎ 433-9595), 5437 E Ocean Blvd, will cruise you à la Venice – that's Venice, *Italy* – through the Rivo Alto as you relax. The cost is $55 per couple, by reservation only, engagement rings and champagne not included.

LOS ANGELES HARBOR
☎ 310

South of Central Los Angeles via the 110 freeway, LA's harbor is within the city limits for purely economic reasons: geographically it is closer to the South Bay and Long Beach, where most of its workers live. Since 1923 it has been the busiest port on the West Coast, ahead of San Francisco and Seattle.

Things to See & Do
The Harbor's tourist center is the **Villages at Ports o' Call** (☎ 831-0287), where you can take one-hour harbor tours (from Berth 77), browse atmospheric gift shops, and eat fresh seafood (drop in on the fresh fish market, point to a couple of live crabs, and they'll be steamed as you wait). Deep-sea fishing launches depart for half-day and full-day excursions around 7 am daily; Los Angeles Harbor Sportfishing (☎ 547-9916), has been recommended.

Near Ports o' Call is the **Maritime Museum** (☎ 548-7618), occupying a former ferry terminal on Berth 84 at 6th St. A wide-ranging exhibit on local nautical history includes the bridge of the US Navy cruiser *Los Angeles*, scale models of the *Titanic*, maritime artifacts, and numerous paintings with marine themes.

It's a short drive south to the **Cabrillo**

Shoestring Corridor
The City of LA *does* have boundaries, but if you were to trace the city's limits you'd end up with an indescribable shape. The patchwork look is the result of decades of expansion, during which LA absorbed smaller towns around it.

The most interesting aspect of the shape is the narrow strip known as the Shoestring Corridor, which was annexed in 1906. Twenty miles long, but just a quarter of a mile wide, this strip slices through the cities of Gardena, Carson, Torrence, and Lomita, and connects central LA to the city's harbor in San Pedro. On a clearly demarcated map, it appears that the City of Angels has the tail of a devil. ■

Marine Aquarium (☎ 548-7562), 3720 Stephen White Drive, San Pedro, a favorite of the school-age set. Among the 38 tanks displaying colorful fish and other marine life, is a 'touch tank' where visitors are encouraged to pick up starfish, sea urchins, sea cucumbers, and other tidepool denizens. Whale-watching tours (☎ 832-4444) can be booked here between Christmas and early April.

Landlubber whale watchers have a great observation post at **Point Fermin Park** (☎ 548-7756), Paseo del Mar at Gaffey St, San Pedro's southernmost cape. Occupying a cliff top due north of Santa Catalina Island, which is easily visible some 17 miles away. The park's Victorian lighthouse (now a private residence) dates from 1874. A short uphill walk from Point Fermin will take you to the **Fort McArthur Reservation and Angels Gate Park** (☎ 548-7705), 3601 S Gaffey St, part US Air Force facility, part park and museum, and part youth hostel (see LA's Places to Stay). The Fort McArthur Military Museum (☎ 548-2631), open weekends, displays the inner workings of the US armed forces' main West Coast defense battery from WWII.

SANTA CATALINA ISLAND
☎ 310

Santa Catalina is one of the largest of the Channel Islands, a chain of semi-submerged mountains that rise from the floor of the Pacific Ocean between Santa Barbara and San Diego. It was left relatively untouched until 1811, when the native seafaring Indians were, tragically, resettled on the mainland. Most of the island has since been in private ownership. It was purchased in 1919 by William Wrigley, Jr, heir to the chewing gum fortune; he built a mansion and a casino, and briefly made Catalina the spring training headquarters for his major-league baseball team, the Chicago Cubs. (Interestingly, it was reporting on the Cubs that first brought Ronald Reagan from Chicago to California.)

Even after the Mediterranean-flavored port town of Avalon began attracting

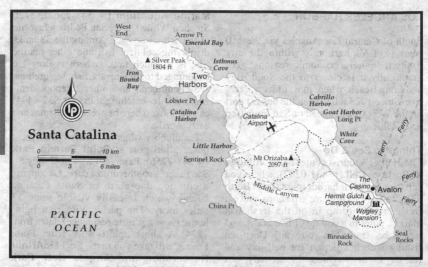

tourists in the 1930s, Catalina's interior and most of its coastline remained largely undeveloped. In conjunction with Los Angeles County, the nonprofit Santa Catalina Island Conservancy (☎ 510-1421) was able to buy 86% of the 8-by-21-mile island from the Wrigley Family in 1975, assuring its preservation. It has a unique ecosystem, with 400 species of endemic and indigenous plant life, more than 100 types of birds, and numerous animals, including deer, goats, boar, foxes, and several hundred wild American bison descended from those brought to Catalina in 1925 for the filming of Zane Grey's *The Vanishing American.*

Avalon

Most of Catalina's 3000 permanent residents (the population quadruples during the summer tourist season) live in Avalon, the island's only town, on the southeast shore. The Catalina Island Chamber of Commerce (☎ 510-1520) has a visitors center on the municipal Pleasure Pier, open daily; stop in for maps, brochures, and information on tours.

A sweep of small hotels and restaurants faces Avalon Bay, framed on the southeast

by Cabrillo Mole Pier and the northwest by the island's famed **Casino** (☎ 510-2500), 1 Casino Way. The white, circular, Spanish Moderne-style Casino, tall as a 12-story building, was designed for Wrigley in 1929. There was legal gambling here until the 1940s – today, there's a Catalina Island Museum (☎ 510-2414) of human and natural history (open daily 10:30 am to 4 pm; $1 admission), and a Casino Art Gallery (☎ 510-0808) featuring the work of island artists.

On a bluff overlooking the Casino is the **Chimes Tower,** given to the city by Mrs Ida Wrigley in 1925. Inlaid Catalina-made tiles are a distinction of the tower, which rings every 15 minutes throughout the day. Nearby are architect Rudolph Schindler's Modernist 1928 Wolfe House, 124 Chimes Tower Rd, its balconied floors stacked on a steep hillside, and the 1929 adobe *Zane Grey Hotel* (☎ 510-0966), 199 Chimes Tower Rd. Now a quiet 17-room inn, the Zane Grey was formerly the home of its namesake, the Western writer.

The **Wrigley Memorial and Botanical Garden** (☎ 510-2288), 1400 Avalon Canyon Rd, is about 1½ miles inland from Avalon Bay. A spiral staircase climbs the

130-foot tower of the memorial, built in 1934 of blue flagstone and decorative tile. Surrounding it is the 38-acre garden, which specializes in cacti, succulents, and other plants native to the island. It's open daily 8 am to 5 pm; adults pay $1, kids under 12 are free.

Two Harbors
Besides Avalon, the only development on Catalina is Two Harbors, which occupies an isthmus near the island's northwestern end. You can reach this pretty community by boat from Avalon or the mainland with Catalina Channel Express (☎ 510-1212), or by the 23-mile road from Avalon aboard an Island Safari bus (☎ 510-0683). There's a beachfront campground, a picnic ground, a dive shop, a general store, a restaurant and saloon, and the hilltop *Banning House Lodge* (☎ 510-0303), an 11-room B&B that dates from the early-20th century.

Organized Tours
The best way to see the island is on a tour. Most begin from the Avalon Pleasure Pier in the heart of town.

By sea, the Santa Catalina Island Company (☎ 510-2500) offers 40-minute tours of the island's undersea gardens in a 'semi-sub.' The 60-foot vessel carries 36 passengers. You can also see the seas from a glass-bottom boat operated by Catalina Adventure Tours (☎ 510-2888). Adult fares for both run about $8. There are also dining cruises and coastal trips to Two Harbors, with adult fares around $40; inquire at either pier for information.

A good way to explore the island by land is with the Santa Catalina Island Company's four-hour Inland Motor Tour (☎ 510-2500). Trips leave Avalon daily at 9 am and cost $23 for adults, $20 for seniors, $14 for children under 12. Jeep Eco-Tours (☎ 510-1421) offers off-road journeys on the island's back roads, accompanied by either a botanist or a wildlife naturalist (your choice). There are also $8 Avalon city tours (contact Catalina Adventure Tours, ☎ 510-2888) and $23 van trips out of Two Harbors with Island Safari (☎ 510-0683).

Places to Stay
Camping If you plan to camp on Catalina, visit the *Hermit Gulch Campground* (☎ 510-8368) just outside of Avalon, or call ☎ 510-2800 for information on Catalina's other four campgrounds. All camps can provide maps and free camping permits.

Hotels Catalina's hoteliers depend heavily upon summer business, and rates are staggered accordingly. Each lodging has different ideas about the beginning and end of the tourist season, however: inquire when you book your room.

In Avalon, the *Hotel Villa Portofino* (☎ 510-0555), 111 Crescent Ave, recreates an Italian Riviera scene with 34 rooms and a harborview sundeck. Rates are $55 to $225 low season, $90 to $300 high season. The *Hotel Vista del Mar* (☎ 510-1452), 417 Crescent Ave, has 15 rooms with fireplaces facing the harbor. Rates are $65 to $195 low season, $95 to $275 high season.

The old Wrigley Mansion was built on a hilltop on the east end of Avalon. Today it is the *Inn on Mount Ada* (☎ 510-2030), 398 Wrigley Rd, a luxurious six-room B&B. The 7000-sq-foot, Georgian colonial estate still has the Wrigleys' original antique furnishings.

The *Catalina Canyon Resort* (☎ 510-0325), 888 Country Club Drive, a half-mile inland from the harbor, is a 72-room Mediterranean-style complex amid palm and banana trees. Rates are $85/95 per single/double in the low season; $125/135 in the high season.

Places to Eat
Restaurants in Avalon are pricey. Good restaurants along waterfront Crescent Ave include *Ristorante Villa Portofino* (☎ 510-0508), at No 111 in the Hotel Villa Portofino, for top-end Italian; *The Channel House* (☎ 510-1617), at No 205, for continental; the *Harbor Grill* (☎ 510-0171), at No 313, for steaks and seafood; and *Pirrone's* (☎ 510-2034), at No 417, serving mainly seafood.

Getting There & Around

There are regular cruises to Avalon from Long Beach and San Pedro, as well as from Redondo Beach and Newport Beach. The main purveyors are Catalina Channel Express (☎ 519-1212), from Long Beach and San Pedro; Catalina Cruises (☎ 800-538-4554), from Long Beach, San Pedro, and Redondo; and Catalina Passenger Service (☎ 714-673-5245), from Newport. There's also a helicopter service, Island Express (☎ 510-2525), from the Queen Mary Seaport for those with money to burn.

Only 10-year Catalina residents are allowed to have cars on the island. Bicycles and golf carts can be rented for travel around Avalon; if you plan on cycling beyond the square-mile city limits, you'll need to buy a $50 permit (☎ 510-1421).

BIG BEAR
☎ 909

Surrounded by the San Bernardino National Forest, Big Bear is an outdoorsy destination favored by families for its various sports activities and after-dark entertainment. For the large populations of San Bernardino and LA, cabins built near the lake and Southern California's two largest ski areas offer getaway resort accommodations. Recently, area merchants re-vamped downtown Big Bear Lake (called Big Bear Village) with sidewalks and benches to make it nice for browsing.

Orientation

There are two distinct parts to Big Bear: the city of Big Bear Lake, along Hwy 18 on the south shore of Big Bear Lake; and Big Bear City which sits at the lake's east end at the Hwy 18/38 junction. The former, which centers around Big Bear Village, has motels, restaurants, and shops that service the ski areas, while the latter is mostly residential.

Highway 18 from San Bernardino and Lake Arrowhead hits the lake at its east end from where you can go south (right) to the city of Big Bear Lake or along the north shore to where the Big Bear Ranger Station and most hiking trails are. Hwy 38 (the 'back way') from Redlands reaches the lake at its southeast end near Big Bear City.

Information

Most sport shops and motels have information on outdoor activities, while realty

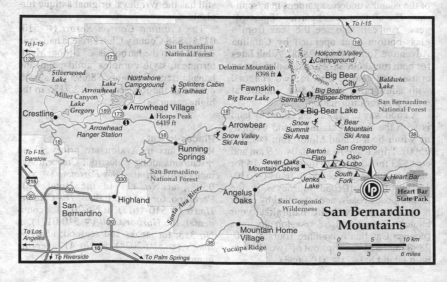

San Bernardino Mountains

offices supply area maps. In Big Bear Village, the Big Bear Lake Chamber of Commerce (☎ 866-4607), 630 Bartlett Road, has lodging information and will make reservations for free. The Big Bear Ranger Station (☎ 866-3437), on Hwy 38 on the north shore, has camping information, wilderness permits and topo maps. They're open from 8 am to 4:30 pm (closed Sunday).

Skiing

With an 8000-foot ridge rising above the lake's south side, Big Bear is known for its downhill skiing. Snow usually falls by mid-December and lasts until March or April, with cannon-like snow-making machines producing supplementary snow whenever temperatures fall below 28°F. The snow is usually good from about 9 am to noon, after which it becomes wet and heavy and then turns to ice. Groomed runs and moguls are good up here, but don't expect powder to be fun. The best part about Big Bear skiing is the weather – sunshine 90% of the time, and shorts and T-shirt temperatures in spring.

Big Bear has two main ski mountains, both near Big Bear Lake off Hwy 18: **Snow Summit** (☎ 866-5766), with 12 lifts (including two high-speed quads), 1200 vertical feet, and $42 lift tickets; and **Bear Mountain** (☎ 585-2519), with 11 lifts, 1665 vertical feet, and $40 tickets. While Snow Summit has more terrain, Bear Mountain is a favorite among locals for its steep upper runs. Smaller areas, good for beginners and low intermediates, are **Snow Forest** (☎ 866-8891) and, 11 miles west of Big Bear on Hwy 18, **Snow Valley** (☎ 867-2751).

You can rent equipment at many places along Hwy 18 in Big Bear Lake, and at the base lodge of all ski areas. Skis, boots, and poles rent for around $9.50 per day, with a discount offered for weekly rentals. The rental shops near Snow Valley on Hwy 18 are usually a few dollars cheaper.

Hiking

In summer, people trade their skis for hiking boots and mountain bikes. The best hiking and most accessible trailheads are on the lake's north shore, off Hwy 38. The Pacific Crest Trail (PCT) runs along a 2400-foot ridge two miles north of the highway, accessible via Van Duesen Canyon Road (3N09) which heads north from the highway at the west end of Big Bear City, and Poligue Canyon Road (2N09), one mile west of the Big Bear Ranger Station. An easy two mile hike up the Cougar Crest Trail, whose trailhead and parking lot are half a mile west of the ranger station, accesses the PCT and offers a view of Big Bear Lake and Holcomb Valley. For detailed hiking brochures and maps, stop by the ranger station..

Mountain Biking

As in most mountain towns, the latest craze in Big Bear is mountain biking. Snow Summit (☎ 866-5766) offers chair lift service to bikers for $7 ($18 for an all-day pass) and maintains 60 miles of roads and trails for all levels. They also host several downhill races each year, including the Grundig World Cup Downhill in mid July. Popular riding areas that don't require the chair lift are Holcomb Valley, Delamar Mountain, and Van Duesen Canyon, off Hwy 38 on the north shore. Team Big Bear Mountain Bikes (☎ 866-4565), at the base of Snow Summit ski area, rents bikes for $6.50 an hour ($32 all day) and publishes an annual *Mountain Biking Guide to Big Bear Lake* available in most sport shops (free). Less aggressive cyclists will enjoy the gentle bike path along the lake's north shore.

Places to Stay

There are hundreds of small motels along Hwy 18 (Big Bear Blvd) in Big Bear Lake, most offering standard accommodations for around $70 per night. Rates drop by $10 on weekdays in summer, ($20 in winter) and go up about $20 on holiday weekends and from December 26th to January 1st. Renting a cabin is often the most affordable option for big groups planning to stay at least two nights. Cabins usually have a full kitchen and bath, and can range from small and shabby to huge and elegant with prices that vary accordingly. The Big Bear Lake Resort Association (☎ 866-7000), above the Chamber of Commerce in Big Bear Village, has a thorough list of accommodations and makes cabin reservations for free.

Camping Campgrounds around the lake are operated by the USFS and have picnic tables, fire rings, and potable water. Sites (except at Holcomb Valley and Big Pine Flat, both of which are first come, first served) are reservable through Destinet. Popular with mountain bikers and close to town, *Pineknot Campground*, a quarter mile east of Snow Summit at the top of Summit Blvd, has 48 spaces, running water, and $11 sites. On the north shore near the ranger station, *Serrano* is the only campground with showers and RV hookups. It has 150 spaces, $12 tent sites and $20 RV sites.

The *Hanna Flat Campground*, two miles north of Hwy 38 via Rim of the World Drive (a maintained dirt road which veers off Hwy 38 in front of the fire station in Fawnskin), is remote but not too hard to reach – and is a popular spot for adventurous families. It has 88 spaces and $12 sites. More remote and less crowded are the $10 sites at *Big Pine Flat*, four miles past Hanna Flat, and the $7 sites at *Holcomb Valley Campground*, four miles north of Hwy 38 via Van Duesen Canyon Road (2N09).

Motels The best deal in town are the $45 rooms at *Jensen's Lakefront Lodge* (☎ 866-8271), half a mile west of Big Bear Village on Lakeview Drive. The rooms haven't been updated since they were built in 1976, but they are clean, spacious, quiet, and have a view of the lake.

A long time favorite with a recent facelift, the *Honey Bear Lodge* (☎ 800-628-8714), three blocks from Big Bear Village at 40994 Pennsylvania Ave, has spacious rooms with TV, microwave, and refrigerator for $50/70 a single/double. They also offer ski and mountain bike packages which include lodging and a lift ticket for $49 per person.

In the thick of Big Bear Lake action, the *Robinhood Inn* (☎ 866-4643, 800-990-9956), corner of Hwy 18 (Big Bear Blvd) and Pine Knot Ave, has friendly owners, a hot tub, and rooms for $50 to $90. Ask for an inside room to avoid traffic noise.

For a splurge try the new *Northwoods Resort* (☎ 800-866-3121), on the west edge of Big Bear Village, whose woodsy rooms ($89 to $150) have fireplaces and in-room Jacuzzis, or *Switzerland Haus Bed & Breakfast* (☎ 800-335-3729), at the base of Snow Summit, with $150 rooms and hearty breakfasts.

Places to Eat
Breakfast and dinner are the most important meals at Big Bear, since lunch is usually had on a mountain or trail. Self catering is a good way to save money when skiing: there is a large Vons supermarket with a deli and bakery at the east end of the lake on Hwy 38.

The *Teddy Bear Restaurant* (☎ 866-5415) is a local favorite for breakfast (try the buckwheat pancakes; $2) though the service can be very slow. West of the village on Hwy 18, *The Alpine* (☎ 866-2002) and *The Sugar Bear* are also good breakfast choices with most items under $5.

Popular for its upstairs bar and hearty German food, *Hansel's* (☎ 866-9497), in Big Bear Village, serves huge omelets ($6) for breakfast, sandwiches, and entrees like sauerbraten ($11) for lunch and dinner. *Che Faccia* (☎ 878-3222) has casual but elegant atmosphere and outstanding Italian food for $8 to $13. For a good steak and local color head to *Cowboy's Steak House* (☎ 866-1486), at the Hwy 18/Lakeview Drive intersection, where most items are around $10. On Saturdays the bar gets packed with people waiting to be seated for the huge $15 prime rib dinner.

Getting There & Away
Mountain Area Regional Transit Authority (MARTA, ☎ 584-1111) buses connect Big

Bear with San Bernardino's Greyhound Station four times daily ($4.50). The driver can tell you where to disembark to catch the Big Bear Trolley which runs between the ski mountains, Big Bear Lake, and Big Bear City.

If you have a large group, consider the door-to-door Big Bear Shuttle (☎ 585-5514) which charges $140 for one person, then $10 per extra person for up to 10 people. They will pick you up in any part of LA, with advanced reservations.

LAKE ARROWHEAD
☎ 909

This sophisticated mountain community was one of LA's first weekend getaway destinations. Today the lake has a large year-round population which owns rights to the lake, making it difficult (if not impossible) for the general public to get wet. Basically the only way to obtain lake access is by staying at the Arrowhead Resort (see below) or renting a cabin or condo with lake access. But people still flock to Arrowhead on weekends to hike the surrounding trails, shop, and ski at nearby Snow Valley.

About 10 years ago, developers with heaps of economic foresight but little concern for nostalgia razed Arrowhead's rustic old town center and built Arrowhead Village, a spiffy collection of shops and designer outlets on the lake's south shore. This is now Arrowhead's center of activity, home to most services and restaurants. Small communities such as Blue Jay, Crestline, and Rimforest provide inexpensive entertainment and places to stay while exploring the area.

Orientation & Information
Highway 18 from San Bernardino passes south of the lake as Rim of the World Drive (a National Scenic Byway) and connects with Hwy 330, from Redlands, before heading east to Big Bear. Most small communities lie along this road. To reach the lake and Lake Arrowhead Village, two miles north of Hwy 18, turn north on Hwy 189 or 173 (they converge just south of the village).

There are banks, a post office, and supermarket in Blue Jay, a mile south of Arrowhead Village. Most realty offices have decent area maps and can help find accommodations, though the best spot for area information is the Lake Arrowhead Communities Chamber of Commerce (☎ 337-3715) in Lake Arrowhead Village, open weekdays from 9 am to 5 pm. For campground and trail information, maps, and wilderness permits, stop by the Arrowhead Ranger Station (☎ 337-2444), on Hwy 18 a quarter mile east of the Hwy 173 turn-off.

Things to See & Do
An example of the worst kind of American tourism, **Lake Arrowhead Village** surrounds a large parking lot with chain stores meant to resemble Bavarian cottages and music piped in over outdoor speakers. There is a sidewalk that skirts the lake and a promontory covered with a small patch of grass that is popular for picnicking, and stands where you can buy 'duck food' ($1) to feed mallards and geese. McKenzie Waterski School (☎ 337-3814) operates from a dock in front of the village, offering a one-hour lesson or ride for $30. This is also where you can catch the *Arrowhead Queen,* a miniature paddlewheeler that makes a 1½-hour tour of the lake.

Lovers of the outdoors will probably want to skip the village entirely and head to the hills. **Deep Creek** offers good hiking and mountain biking, with access to the Pacific Crest Trail. To reach the area, take Hwy 173 around the south shore of the lake and turn east on Hook Creek Rd. Two miles past the small town of Cedar Glen, the pavement ends and road 2N26Y continues two miles to the Splinters Cabin site where there is a parking lot and marked trailheads. Two miles north along the creek is Devil's Hole, a favorite swimming hole where clothing is optional.

More tame and accessible is the **Heap's Peak Arboretum Trail**, two miles east of the ranger station on Hwy 18. This half-mile trail loops through a lovely garden with views of Lake Arrowhead. Another nice, moderate trail is the **North Shore**

Recreation Trail (3W12) which begins from the North Shore Campground (site No 10) just off Hwy 173 via Hospital Road on Lake Arrowhead's northeast side.

Blue Jay has a terrific indoor-outdoor **skating rink** called the Blue Jay Ice Castle, which has entertained three generations of visitors. The rink is open year round, and a two-hour session costs $7. **Snow Valley** (☎ 867-2751), east of Arrowhead on Hwy 18, offers mountain biking in summer and skiing and snowboarding in winter. Across from Snow Valley, **Rim Nordic** (☎ 867-2600) has cross-country skiing and **Snow Drift** (☎ 867-2640) in the small town of Arrowbear, has sled and inner-tube rentals.

Places to Stay
Camping Campgrounds around Arrowhead are run by the USFS, and sites can be reserved through Destinet. *Dogwood Campground*, off Hwy 18 near the Hwy 189 turn-off, is the largest and most popular in the area, with 93 sites ($12 tent; $16 RV). A quarter mile (via Hospital Road) from Hwy 173 on the northwest shore of Lake Arrowhead, *North Shore* has 27 sites ($10) surrounded by oak trees and access to hiking trails.

Motels Staying at the luxurious *Lake Arrowhead Resort* (☎ 336-1511), next to the village on Hwy 173, makes a trip to the lake worthwhile if you can afford the $120 (minimum) rooms. They have a beautiful lobby with a large fireplace, a pool, hot tub, fitness center, and private beach. Another good and more affordable option near the lake is the *Tree Top Lodge* (☎ 337-2311), a half mile from the lake on Hwy 173, which has a pool, access to a private dock, and $70/85 rooms in a woodsy setting. Ask for a room off the highway to avoid traffic noise.

There are also a few places to stay in Crestline, west of Arrowhead via Hwy 18 then Lake Gregory Drive, on the west shore of Lake Gregory. The *North Shore Inn* (☎ 338-5230, 800-300-5230), across from the lake at the corner of Lake Gregory and Lake Drive, has new rooms with microwaves and coffeemakers for around $55 on weekdays, $65 weekends. A few blocks west on Lake Drive, the *Sleepy Hollow Cabins Motel* (☎ 338-2718) has a small pool and play yard, and motel rooms for $60 and cabins for $65 to $85.

Places to Eat
The best view in town is from the patio of the *Arrowhead Deli* or *Belgian Waffle Works*, both in Arrowhead Village. Ask around for a good breakfast spot and 9 out of 10 people will tell you to go to the *Cottage Restaurant* (☎ 337-1212), in the tiny community of Rim Forest on Hwy 18. Portions are large enough to feed several people, or sustain one hungry person through the day, and everything is around $7. From the look of the place and the volume they do, it appears they're so busy they haven't had a chance to clean in a few years.

The *Borderline Family Restaurant* (☎ 336-4363), in Blue Jay, serves straightforward food for under $10 and has a kids menu. For a splurge, try the *Antlers Inn* (☎ 337-4020), on Hwy 189 half way between Arrowhead Village and Hwy 18. This rustic old lodge serves exquisite meals of grilled meats and fish for around $15 and has an extensive wine list.

Getting There & Away
Lake Arrowhead is directly north of San Bernardino via Hwy 18 (Rim of the World Drive), about 1½ hours from LA. The 40-mile stretch between San Bernardino and the lake is quite beautiful when there is no smog.

MARTA buses (see Big Bear, above) traveling between Big Bear and San Bernardino stop at Lake Arrowhead Village.

SAN GORGONIO WILDERNESS
South of Big Bear is the least developed part of the San Bernardino National Forest, including 92 sq miles of trees, lakes, and barren slopes designated as the San Gorgonio Wilderness. This area encompasses

Mt San Bernardino and San Gorgonio Peak (called Greyback), both over 10,000 feet high. A multitude of hiking and equestrian trails, including the Santa Ana River, Lost Creek, and South Fork Trails, traverse the area's steep and rugged terrain. At low elevations the area is very arid, hot in the summer and full of rattlesnakes. At higher elevations, oak and manzanita are joined by cedar, fir, sugar and lodgepole pines. Black bears, coyote, deer, and squirrel are common, and bald eagle sightings are frequent in the Hart Bar campground area. Backed by Mts San Gorgonio and San Bernardino, Jenks Lake, two miles south of Hwy 38 is a scenic spot for picnicking and easy hiking (take the turn-off across from Barton Flats Campground, instead of Jenks Lake Rd, to avoid a long drive).

Highway 38 runs along the wilderness' northern periphery, giving access to trailheads, campgrounds, and the few services in the area. A free wilderness permit, required for day hikes and camping, is available from the Mill Creek Ranger Station (☎ 909-794-1123), 10 miles east of Redlands on Hwy 38, open from May to September weekdays 8 am to 5 pm and on Saturday 6:30 am to 3:00 pm. They have a wilderness trail map for $3, and USGS quadrangles.

Places to Stay & Eat

The campgrounds along Hwy 38 are owned by the USFS, managed by L&L Enterprises, and are reservable through Destinct. Tent sites cost $7, RV sites are $14. *Hart Bar Campground* is the largest in the area, with 94 sites and flush toilets. Sites here are spacious and flat, surrounded by large ponderosa pines that offer beauty but not much privacy. A few miles further west, *South Fork Campground* is the most intimate in the area with secluded, shady sites, but is subject to highway noise. *Oso-Lobo*, *San Gorgonio*, and *Barton Flats* are all connected by one hiking trail and have similar surroundings of oak and pine. Oso-Lobo gets large groups and has the oldest facilities, while Barton Flats is the most popular and has hot showers.

Non-campers can stay at *Seven Oaks Mountain Cabins*, west of the campgrounds on Hwy 38, which has charming little no-frills log cabins ($70) beside the Santa Ana River, a volleyball and tennis court, and lodge with games and a big fireplace.

The best place to eat is *The Oaks Restaurant*, on Hwy 38 in Angelus Oaks, which serves usual American fare (including vegetarian items) from 6:30 am to 9 pm daily for under $10. The general store next door is a good place to buy supplies.

Orange County

While most people consider a trip to Disneyland an integral part of the California experience, few stop to consider what lies around it. Similarly, while most people don't leave the state without setting foot on the sand, they are usually content with the beaches near Los Angeles or San Diego. Thus Orange County is not a tourist destination in itself, and many people pass right through forgetting that the expanse of urbanity that seems to be the southern end of Los Angeles is actually its own governing body. Aside from Disneyland and Laguna Beach, Orange County should not be first priority on an itinerary. Once here, however, there are some interesting museums and nice beaches, all serviced by an excellent public transportation system.

Orange County identifies itself as a 'county' more than any other in Southern California, with strong county-wide publications such as the daily *Orange County Register,* which some say is better than the *Los Angeles Times,* and *Orange County Weekly,* which has useful entertainment reviews and in-depth articles. Inland towns have mostly Latino populations whose ancestors came here when orange crops were the main source of income. Both the demographics and the landscape changed quite a bit in the 1970s and '80s when several large corporations set up their headquarters here, starting a trend that has kept Orange County one of the fastest growing urban centers in the US. Until 1995, when the county was forced to declare bankruptcy, it was also one of the richest. The resident community, however, remains safely within California's highest per capita income brackets and is most often characterized by its political conservatism.

Information
The Anaheim/Orange County Convention and Visitor's Bureau (☎ 714-999-8999), across from Disneyland at 800 W Katella Ave, has county-wide lodging, dining, and transportation information which they'll send you for free. They're also helpful answering questions over the phone.

Getting There & Away
The Amtrak stations in Fullerton, Irvine, and San Juan Capistrano, all on the Los Angeles – San Diego route, get about eight northbound and 10 southbound trains per day. Orange County Transportation Authority (OCTA, ☎ 714-636-7433) buses stop at all the stations and destinations listed in this chapter; fare is $1 and transfers are free. If you're planning to travel by public transportation, it's worthwhile to get a copy of the OCTA bus system map (free), available at train stations, most chambers of commerce, and by calling OCTA.

Orange County is also home to John Wayne Airport (☎ 714-252-5200), just off I-405 in Irvine, which is quickly becoming a major airport. Currently, Alaska, American, America West, Continental, Delta, Northwest, Reno Air, Southwest, TWA, United, and US Air service the airport, though prices are not as competitive as those from San Diego or Los Angeles.

DISNEYLAND
☎ 714
Opened in 1955 by Walt Disney himself, Disneyland (☎ 999-4565) is 'imagineered' to be the 'happiest place on earth,' from the impeccably clean, pastel colored sidewalks to the personal hygiene of park employees, all of whom are referred to as 'cast members.' Buildings, rides, costumes, and characters are brightly colored and always in good spirits, for cast members know that if they treat one person rudely they're very likely to lose their jobs. While Disney's guidelines are exceptionally strict for those on the payroll (Walt is said to have been a tyrannical employer), the resulting order creates the perfect atmosphere for Mickey

Orange County

0   8   16 km
0   5   10 miles

Mouse, Donald Duck, Goofy, Pluto, and the host of other characters that have made Disney an integral part of an American childhood. This is *not* the real world and many people travel long distances for just that reason.

You can see the entire park in a day, but it requires two or three days to go on all the rides, especially in summer when lines are long. Disneyland is possibly the best place in the USA for people-watching, so non-riders needn't worry about being bored – strolling around the park, encountering life-sized Disney characters, and looking at fanciful architecture and decorations is

very entertaining. In fact, among the smiles you even forget the grotesque suburban sprawl outside the park.

Orientation & Highlights

The park is divided into four different 'lands' that center around Sleeping Beauty's Castle – the big pink palace in park advertisements. **Adventureland** has a jungle theme and is home to the park's latest attraction: Indiana Jones and the Forbidden Eye, which has three different tracks so you never get the same ride twice. **Frontier-land** has Western attractions like the Golden Horseshoe Revue (a stage show popular with the older crowd) and Big Thunder Mountain (a roller coaster through an Old West mining town). **Fantasyland** is where the character-inspired rides are, such as Peter Pan, Snow White, and Alice in Wonderland. **Tomorrowland** is home to Space Mountain (the park's hairiest roller coaster), Star Tours, and the 3-D film production of Captain EO, starring Michael Jackson (Mickey Mouse's long lost brother?). Main Street, USA – the entrance access lined with shops, an old-fashioned arcade, and the Candy Emporium – is where you're most likely to find life-sized characters hanging out. Mickey's Toontown is a recent addition whose wacky buildings make the rest of the park look 'normal.'

Besides the above mentioned attractions, a few stand-bys remain favorites among Disneyland aficionados: Pirates of the Caribbean, the Haunted Mansion, Bear Country Jamboree, and the Jungle Cruise. History buffs will want to look into the Walt Disney Gallery (above the entrance to Pirates of the Caribbean), which has old prints and unrealized plans for other Disney projects. Circle Vision, across from Star Tours, is another obscure but interesting attraction, with a 360° movie screen where they show stunning documentaries of the USA.

Ultra-efficient visitors will want to hit all of the attractions in one area before heading to the next, though the park's size and lay-out makes that quite unnecessary. Lines tend to be shortest first thing in the morning, late in the evening, and around meal times (noon to 1:30 and 5:30 to 7 pm). Crowds in Fantasyland, which has most of the kiddy rides, thin-out after dark. The nightly Main Street Electrical Parade (10 pm), with gigantic floats covered with thousands of tiny colored lights, also draws people away from the rides, though it's really worth seeing in itself.

Information
Hours are Monday to Friday from 10 am to 6 pm; weekends, holidays, and in summer from 9 am to midnight. Parking is $6, and a one-day pass including all rides and attractions costs $30 ($28 for those over 60 and 3 to 11); a small discount is available for multiple-day passes. There are $1 lockers, complimentary strollers and wheelchairs, and a lost & found just inside the entrance at the head of Main Street, USA. This is also a good meeting place if your party gets separated.

Upon entering you'll receive a map and brochure with listings of all the park's restaurants, shops, and attractions. In summer the tickets lines are staggering; you can avoid the crush by buying your ticket at the Disneyland Hotel and riding the monorail into the park (which lets you off in Tomorrowland). Hotel parking costs $15.

Places to Stay – hostels
The clean and friendly HI *Fullerton Hacienda Hostel* (☎ 738-3721), 1700 N Harbor Blvd, is the cheapest place around, with $17 beds. It has a nice porch, a ping-pong table, and kitchen facilities, though it's closed from 9:30 am to 5 pm and has a midnight curfew. OCTD bus No 43A to Disneyland stops out front.

Places to Stay – motels
There are literally hundreds of motels in the blocks surrounding Disneyland, most of which have $70 rooms and the basic amenities. This is a good place to opt for a chain motel – Best Western, Motel 6, Days Inn – since they are reliably clean and usually offer shuttle service to the park. From June to September, prices are $10 to $20 higher than those listed below.

Bottom End A few blocks east of Harbor Blvd at 425 W Katella, the *Samoa Motel* (☎ 776-2815) has island decor and East Indian owners. Rooms ($30 to $40) are ancient but spacious and the courtyard is filled with large palms and a small pool.

In the midst of big, fancy motels the *Village Inn Motel* (☎ 774-2460), 1750 S Harbor Blvd, makes you feel like you're at grandma's house, with brown shag carpet, blue plaid bedspreads, and knotty pine

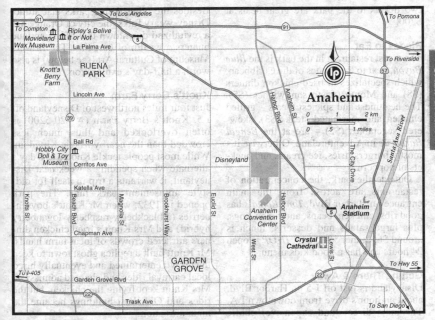

walls. Doors are painted different colors because the friendly owner from Mexico has an easier time with 'red, green, blue' than '136, 137,' etc. Rooms cost $38.

Middle Striving to be the best in an oversaturated market, the *Candy Cane Inn* (☎ 774-5284, 800-345-7057), 1747 S Harbor Blvd, has a free breakfast of cereal, bagels, muffins, juice, coffee, and tea served in a breakfast room decked with flowers, a private shuttle to the park, a pool and hot tub open until 11 pm, and impeccable modern rooms. Prices are $65 to $95, with discounts for more than two nights stay.

The *Tropicana Inn* (☎ 635-4082), 1540 S Harbor Blvd, is an excellent value with very nice rooms for $48, a large pool, shuttle service to the park and Amtrak and Greyhound stations, and an in-house car rental service. A few doors down and run by the same company, the brand new *Park Inn International* (☎ 635-7275) has similar

facilities, plus a complimentary breakfast and refrigerators in every room. Prices are about $10 more.

Good choices for chain motels are the *Best Western Anaheim Inn* (☎ 774-1050, 800-854-8175), 1630 S Harbor Blvd, which has a free shuttle and in-room VCRs, and the *Econo Lodge* (☎ 772-5721, 800-854-0199), 1570 S Harbor Blvd, whose rooms are set back from the boulevard, making them some of the quietest around.

Top End Almost rivaling the park in terms of activities and entertainment, the *Disneyland Hotel* (☎ 778-6600) is very worthwhile if you plan on staying more than one night. A monorail runs between the hotel and park, making it easy to go back and forth, and hotel guests get to enter the park an hour and a half before the general public. One-night stands are expensive at $175 to $240, but multiple-night packages, which include parking ($15), breakfast, and two tickets to the park are great deals at $200.

Places to Eat

The nicest restaurant in the park is the *Blue Bayou*, next to the Pirates of the Caribbean, which specializes in fried chicken dinners ($8) and Monte Cristo sandwiches ($5). The healthiest and spiciest meals – grilled chicken and marinated steak ($3), skewered vegetables ($2) – are at the *Bengal Barbecue* in Adventureland. Otherwise it's mostly burgers, fries, ice cream, and buckets of popcorn.

Outside the park, the concentration of restaurants are across from the main entrance on Harbor Blvd. *Tony Roma's* has good ribs, chicken, beans, and onion rings, plus large salads and desserts; lunch is around $6, dinner $8 to $13. *IHOP* is open 24 hours and has a good kids menu.

Getting There & Away

Disneyland is just off I-5 on Harbor Blvd, about an hour's drive from downtown LA. The most direct (and expensive) public transportation is the Airport Coach Bus (☎ 800-772-5299), which runs between LAX and the Disneyland Hotel every half hour; tickets are $20 ($32 roundtrip). Greyhound buses go to Anaheim's Greyhound station (☎ 999-1257), about three blocks from the park, eight times daily ($6).

All San Diego-bound Amtrak trains stop at Anaheim's Amtrak station (☎ 385-1448), on the grounds of Anaheim Stadium. Tickets between Anaheim and LA cost $8. From here you can catch the No 52 bus westbound (across Katella Ave in front of the station) every half hour for the 20-minute, $1 trip to the park.

AROUND DISNEYLAND

☎ 714

People generally avoid interior Orange County – Fullerton, Garden Grove, Santa Ana – which is plagued by smog, traffic, and seemingly ceaseless strips of fast food restaurants, car dealerships, and low-grade housing developments. There are, however, some diamonds in this urban rough.

Besides the other theme parks that attract Disney-weary folks, the city of Orange has a revitalized downtown that offers antique hunters a wealth of bargains. The Bowers Museum of Cultural Art (see below) is also worth a half-day's exploration.

Knott's Berry Farm

Just four miles northwest of Disneyland off I-5, Knott's Berry Farm (☎ 220-5200) is often overlooked and thus much less crowded than the nearby Magic Kingdom. While most people tackle Knott's as a day's alternate when spending a week near Disneyland, it warrants a trip in itself for old-style amusement park fans. The park opened in 1932, when Mr Knott's boysenberries (a blackberry-raspberry-loganberry hybrid) and Mrs Knott's fried chicken dinners attracted crowds of local farm hands. Mr Knott built a replica ghost town to keep the crowd entertained and eventually hired local carnival rides and charged admission. Mrs Knott kept frying the chicken, but the rides and Old West buildings became the main attraction.

The park continues its Old West theme with staged gun fights, gold panning demonstrations, and steam train rides. Rollercoaster highlights include Montezuma's Revenge, which makes an upside-down loop as high as a three story building then does it again backwards; the six loop Boomerang (which also goes backwards); and the Jaguar which sweeps around the park in a smooth, tame way. Big Foot Rapids sloshes down a faux whitewater river and leaves you absolutely soaked, while the Parachutes take you high above the park and leave your stomach there while dropping you to the ground at breakneck speed. Camp Snoopy (*Peanuts* characters – Snoopy, Charlie Brown, Lucy, Linus – are the park's equivalent of Disney's Mickey Mouse, et al) is a kiddy wonderland made only for people under four feet tall. Knott's can be a blow to the budget: carnival games where you can win stuffed toys cost $1 a pop, and places to pan gold, make candles, and dress-up in old-fashioned clothes cost around $3.

Shops sell Knott's jams and preserves (a worthwhile gift for non-Californians) and you can still get fried chicken dinners ($10) with mashed potatoes, hot biscuits and gravy, and boysenberry pie at the restaurant next to the park entrance (if the line for dinner seating is long, check the restaurant's back entrance – near the Snoopy Souvenir shop – which is usually less crowded).

On weekends in October Knott's is host to what is possibly California's best and scariest Halloween party, 'Knott's Scary Farm.' Professional performers in costume haunt the park, special rides and attractions are put up for the occasion, and lights around the park are dimmed or turned off.

Information Admission is $29, $26 for those over 60, and $23 for children 3 to 11; weekends after 5 pm it's $14. From late May to September hours are Sunday to Thursday 9 am to 11 pm, weekends and holidays 9 am to midnight; the rest of the year it's open Monday to Friday 10 am to 6 pm, Saturday 10 am to 10 pm, Sunday 10 am to 7 pm. It's closed Christmas Day.

Getting There & Away Knott's is on Beach Blvd, south of I-5 and Hwy 91 in the city of Buena Park. There is a bus stop a block north of the park on Beach Blvd. OCTD bus No 99 goes to Amtrak's Fullerton Station (☎ 992-0530), on the LA-San Diego route, and MTA bus No 460 goes to downtown LA.

Ripley's Believe It Or Not & Movieland Wax Museum

These two only-in-America museums are one block apart and across Beach Blvd from each other (a half mile north of Knott's Berry Farm), and are run as a joint operation. Don't fall for the 'buy both tickets for a bargain' gimmick though, since Ripley's (☎ 522-7054) is the only one worth seeing while Movieland (☎ 522-1154) is a waste of time and money. Robert L Ripley traveled the globe in the 1920s and '30s, collecting weird and exotic artifacts from Africa, Asia, and the Pacific

Islands. While the Disney-esque display is probably less impressive today than it was back then, the pieces of folklore and documentation of human oddities provide some twisted entertainment. Movieland on the other hand, is a dizzying maze of wax figures that don't hold a candle to the people they're made to portray. Maybe the attraction lies in seeing your favorite stars look really bad for once.

Ripley's is open from 10 am to 6 pm and costs $11, and Movieland is open from 9 am to 7 pm and costs $13; a joint ticket costs $19. Kids tickets (ages 4 to 11) are about half price.

Hobby City Doll & Toy Museum

About two miles south of Knott's Berry Farm on Beach Blvd, Hobby City (☎ 527-2323) is a group of 23 specialty art and craft shops that sell everything from cake decorating equipment to model race car kits. The Doll & Toy Museum here, housed in a half-scale model of the White House, is the best entertainment value around: admission is $1, and the collection of dolls is exceptional. Besides every type of Barbie doll made, the museum has Russian dolls from the 1800s, and replicas of TV, movie, and sports personalities, rock stars, and presidents that serve as an interesting example of the USA's pop culture over the last 60 years. Unfortunately, the display spaces are a bit shabby. Hobby City is open daily from 10 am to 6 pm.

Bowers Museum of Cultural Art

Housed in a gracious Mission-style complex built in 1932, this museum (☎ 567-3600) has a rich permanent collection of pre-Columbian, African, Oceanic, Asian, and Native American art, and features changing exhibitions of traditional indigenous art. It is truly astonishing that such a storehouse exists in Santa Ana (an otherwise non-descript Orange County city) and that it receives little notoriety among Southern California's general public. The building itself, restored in 1994, is an architectural gem surrounding a large courtyard where hands-on crafts demonstrations are held most weekends. The galleries are comfortable and insightful narration accompanies the various exhibits that include ritual objects, sculpture, jewelry, costumes, and weapons. One block south, the Bowers Kidsmuseum keeps kids entertained with hands-on exhibits relating to world cultures.

Hours are Tuesday to Sunday from 10 am to 4 pm and Thursday nights until 9 pm (closed Monday); the Kidsmuseum is open Tuesday to Friday from 2 to 5 pm, weekends 10 am to 4 pm. Admission (good for both museums) is $4.50, $3 seniors/students, and $1.50 ages 5 to 12.

Crystal Cathedral
You needn't agree with Robert Schuller's teachings or be an 'Hour of Power' fan to appreciate the architecture of the Crystal Cathedral (☎ 971-4000), which sits just west of I-5 (via Chapman Ave) in Garden Grove. Looking like a cross between a modern office complex and a *Superman* movie set, the cathedral has 10,661 windows, seating capacity for 3000 people, and an organ with 16,000 pipes (and its own million-dollar endowment fund) – all in the shape of a four-point star. The building, designed by Phillip Johnson, is surrounded by gardens, a reflecting pool, and fountains, and can be visited alone or on a free tour that leaves from the visitors center every half hour. Be sure to visit the free-standing modern Gothic prayer chapel on the cathedral's north side; its pillars are made of eight different types of Italian marble, and inside is a five-piece lead crystal cross that weighs 200 pounds.

Schuller's congregation, part of the Protestant Reform Church (descended from the Dutch Reform Church) formerly worshipped at the Orange County Drive-In movie theater, where Schuller preached from atop the snack stand. Now the congregation boasts 1600 members and Schuller's 'Hour of Power' is broadcast on TV networks around the world. Donations from the combined audience funded the building's construction, and when the cathedral was dedicated in 1980 it was 100% debt-free.

Orange
The city of Orange, about six miles southeast of Disneyland, has the only planned downtown and best collection of antique and consignment shops in Orange County. Originally part of Rancho Santiago de Santa Ana, the land was given to lawyers Alfred Chapman and Andrew Glassell as legal fees in 1869. They laid out a one-sq-mile town surrounding a plaza (at the intersection of Chapman and Glassell Sts) which still acts as the center of activity. In the blocks north and south of the plaza, you'll find serious antique shops such as Anthony's Fine Antiques, 114 N Glassell, which has a hand-carved wooden facade that came from the Spanish embassy in Buenos Aires, and not-so-serious stores with vintage Batman lunch boxes and colorful California pottery. At the north end of Glassell are several funky used clothing stores and cafes frequented by students from Chapman University (also on Glassell).

Besides the good browsing, people know Orange for *Felix's Cafe* (☎ 633-5842), whose pink tablecloths decorate the southwest corner of the plaza. Their excellent Cuban and Spanish food comes with black beans, rice, and fried plantains (*maduros*), and costs around $6 for lunch, $10 for dinner. Specialties include *Palomilla* (steak grilled with parsley and onions), *arroz con pollo* (chicken and saffron rice), and fish with a spicy tomato sauce and creamy spinach.

Getting There & Away From Disneyland, take OCTA bus No 46 or 50; from the coast, take No 53 or 74 to South Coast Plaza, then catch the No 59 northbound.

Orange County Beaches

The surfers, artists, and retirees that inhabit Orange County's beach towns give the coast its own vibe, distinct from the rest of the county. Besides Newport Beach, the small beach communities, strung roughly 10 miles apart along Pacific Coast Hwy (PCH), are very relaxed despite the area's fast-paced development. Oil rigs sit about a mile offshore all along the coast and are scattered among the houses and businesses inland, giving the landscape a surreal appearance.

Orange County Transit Authority (OCTA, ☎ 714-636-7433) bus No 1 runs north-south between Long Beach and San Clemente along Pacific Coast Hwy, stopping in Seal Beach, Sunset Beach, Huntington Beach, Newport Beach, Corona del Mar, Laguna Beach, Dana Point, San Juan Capistrano, and San Clemente every 20 minutes. The last northbound bus leaves San Clemente at 8:06 pm, and the last southbound bus leaves Long Beach at 8:29 pm. On Saturday, buses are hourly and stop running two hours earlier. Fare is $1 and transfers, good for up to two hours, are free.

SEAL BEACH
☎ 310
Unlike towns whose business district is spread out along Pacific Coast Hwy, Seal Beach has a very walkable downtown that lies along a few blocks of Main St, between Pacific Coast Hwy and Ocean Ave, which skirts the beach. At the end of Main St, the **Seal Beach Pier** extends 1885 feet over the ocean. The current pier, built in 1985, replaced the 1906 original that was swept to sea by the winter storms of 1981-82. Seal Beach Sportfishing (☎ 598-8677), at the end of the pier, offers half-day fishing trips for $20, and whale-watching trips from January to March for $12.

Main St has some interesting antique and consignment clothing stores, and the Courtyard Nursery, 225 Main St, which does a pretty good job at imitating the Garden of Eden. The Bay Theater (☎ 431-9988), 340 Main St, shows alternative films preceded by live music from the theater's Wurlitzer pipe organ that once entertained patrons at New York's Paramount theater.

Away from its charming downtown, Seal Beach has a huge naval weapons research station and is home to Leisure World, one of Southern California's first and most exclusive retirement communities.

Bolsa Chica State Beach & Ecological Preserve
The three-mile stretch of Pacific Coast Hwy between Seal Beach and Huntington Beach is flanked on one side by Bolsa Chica State Beach, and on the other side by an Ecological Preserve of the same name. Less attractive than neighboring beaches, Bolsa Chica has dark and dusty sand, and faces a monstrous oil rig half a mile off shore. It is, however, a popular spot for parties since bonfires are allowed in the concrete pits along the beach. Parking costs $5, and there are restrooms and snack stands about every quarter mile down the beach.

Across Pacific Coast Hwy, terns, mergansers, pelicans, pintails, grebes, and endangered Belding's Savannah sparrows congregate among pickleweed and cordgrass in a restored salt marsh designated as the Bolsa Chica State Ecological Preserve. Oil derricks and a housing development loom nearby, but with a set of binoculars focused on the birds this can be an interesting stop. A loop trail starts from the parking lot on Pacific Coast Hwy and makes a tour around the area's northern waters.

Places to Stay
Popular with an RV crowd that spends months at a time in one spot, the *Bolsa Chica State Park Campground* has 60 spaces ($15) that can be reserved through Destinet. Just south of Seal Beach, in the small community of Sunset Beach, are a few small motels on Pacific Coast Hwy.

CALIFORNIA

Most of these are walking distance to the beach and have rooms for under $50. The *Lighthouse Inn/Islander Motel* (☎ 592-1993), 16555 Pacific Coast Hwy, has new rooms for $50 ($60 for an ocean view) and older motel rooms for $30, plus a small pool and hot tub. A few blocks north, rooms at the *Sunset Bed & Breakfast* (☎ 592-1666) are very small but have plush decor and come with a continental breakfast; prices are $40 to $60.

Places to Eat

Affordable eats are everywhere here, as are pricey seafood dinners. Despite what's on the menu, dress is usually casual and thongs are generally accepted as real shoes. *Nick's,* on Main St in Seal Beach, is a hole-in-the-wall deli that makes great breakfast burritos ($3) of chorizo, potatoes, eggs, cheese, and bacon (a veggie version is available) and huge sandwiches for under $5. Half the crowd in here still has salt water in their hair. Two blocks west, at the corner of Main and Ocean, the *Kinda Lahaina Broiler* (☎ 569-3864) has a large patio, ocean-view tables, and good seafood and steaks. Lunch is around $7, dinner around $13, and there are $8 specials from 4 to 7 pm.

Favorite eating spots in Sunset Beach (both near the motels on Pacific Coast Hwy) are *Woody's,* a post-surf hang out with good omelets and burgers, and the *Sunset Beach Brewery*, which serves salads, pasta, pizza, and excellent home-made beer in a lively atmosphere.

HUNTINGTON BEACH

☎ *714*

Once the least polished and most low key of Orange County's beaches, Huntington has recently been bombarded with glitzy chain restaurants and horrendous architecture. Away from the center of tourist activity (the corner of Pacific Coast Hwy and Main St across from the Huntington Pier) Huntington's roots are still intact: surfers outnumber yuppies, 1940s beach cottages house most of the population, and oil derricks are a common lawn adornment.

Since George Freeth and Duke Kahana-moku gave surfing demonstrations in Huntington in 1914, Huntington has been one of Southern California's most popular surf destinations, earning the title 'Surf City, USA' from surf daddies Jan and Dean. The **Huntington Pier** is site of the Ocean Pacific (OP) Pro surf contest – a landmark event held annually in early September – and across from the pier (on Main St) is the Surfing Walk of Fame (like Hollywood's Avenue of the Stars with sand and salt).

International Surfing Museum

This museum (☎ 960-3483), on Olive St half a block off Main St, is one of the few of its kind in California, a mecca for surf-culture enthusiasts and an entertaining place to spend an hour or two. Exhibits chronicle the sport's history with photos, early surfboards and surfwear, and surf music records by the Beach Boys, Jan and Dean, and the Ventures. There is also a good display about women in surfing. Admission is $2.

Huntington Art Center

Away from the hustle and bustle of down-town, Huntington's newly remodeled Art Center (☎ 374-1650) sits at the east end of Main St across from the public library and city hall. The exhibit space is excellent, with high ceilings and concrete floors which go well with the mostly contemporary installations. Films are shown on the first and third Friday of each month ($3), and the gift shop has a unique selection of cards, clothes, and house decor. Hours are noon to 6 pm, until 9 pm Thursday and Friday, until 4 pm Sunday; admission is free.

Places to Stay

Huntington is home to the area's only hostel, and it's a real peach: the *Colonial Inn Youth Hostel* (☎ 536-3315), 421 8th St, has four-person dorms ($12), doubles ($14), a nice kitchen, a living room and backyard, free breakfast, no curfew, and is a three block walk to downtown and the beach.

Huntington has a few budget motels across from the beach on Pacific Coast Hwy, including the *Sun 'n' Sands Motel* (☎ 536-2543), with nice $70 rooms and a pool; and the somewhat crusty *Huntington Shores Motel* (☎ 536-8861, 800-554-6799), a favorite among truck drivers (don't ask what they're doing out west) for their complimentary breakfast and free donuts and coffee; rooms are $55 to $70.

The *Quality Inn* (☎ 536-7500, 800-228-5151), on Pacific Coast Hwy just north of the Huntington Pier, has dependably clean rooms with cable TV and ocean views for $75 to $90. The nicest accommodations in the area are at the *Waterfront Hilton Beach Resort* (☎ 960-7873, 800-822-7873), a quarter-mile south of the pier, with a spa, fitness center, fancy restaurant, and ocean view rooms starting at $110.

Places to Eat
The *Sugar Shack,* on Main St in Huntington Beach, is a breakfast and lunch institution, with local lore decorating the walls and a straightforward coffee shop that serves food for under $10 (under $5 for breakfast). Across the street, *Wahoo's Fish Tacos* serves tacos and burritos with black beans and rice for around $5 and conscientiously lists the caloric and fat content of menu items. Italophiles should make it a point to eat at *Ritmo Trattu,* next to Starbucks on Main St, a tiny trattoria operated by two brothers from Naples who do things just like mamma does in the homeland. The *bruscetta pomodoro* appetizer with tomatoes, basil, and garlic ($3) is a meal in itself, and all of the sandwiches (served on *ciabatta* bread) and pastas ($5 to $8) are recommended.

NEWPORT BEACH
☎ *714*
Newport is the largest and most sophisticated of Orange County's beach towns, with one of the biggest pleasure-craft harbors in the US and shopping that rivals Beverly Hills. There is plenty to do both on and off the beach here, but things are very spread out. Pacific Coast Hwy passes through the part of Newport that centers around harbor activity, with boat dealerships, yacht clubs, and large seafood restaurants clustered in buildings that once served as shipping warehouses for the Irvine Ranch. South of Pacific Coast Hwy via Balboa Blvd, the Balboa Peninsula makes a six-mile barrier between Newport Harbor and the ocean. This is where most tourist activity is, including beaches and the Balboa Fun Zone. North of Pacific Coast Hwy, inland Newport is a sprawl of upscale tract homes that house a good chunk of Orange County's corporate workforce. The University of California, Irvine (UCI), northeast of Newport, lends a great deal to the area's young population.

Orientation & Information
Highway 55 (Newport Blvd) is the main access road from I-405. It intersects Pacific Coast Hwy then becomes Balboa Blvd which goes to the very end of the Balboa Peninsula. Highway 73 (MacArthur Blvd), which joins Pacific Coast Hwy at Newport's south end, and Jamboree Rd also connect I-405 to Pacific Coast Hwy, passing UC Irvine and Fashion Island shopping center.

The Newport Beach Conference & Visitors Bureau (☎ 722-1611), at the northeast corner of Hwy 55 and Pacific Coast Hwy, has good lodging and dining guides and a detailed map. The *Daily Pilot* newspaper has local news and entertainment listings, while *The Log* – available from the visitors bureau and most nautical shops – has boating news for all of Southern California.

Balboa Peninsula
This strip of land, about six miles long and a quarter-mile wide, has a long white sand beach on its ocean side and stylish homes – including Rudolph Schindler's 1926 Lovell House (on 13th St) – facing the harbor. The **Newport Pier** is the center of fishing activity and the peninsula's most rowdy nightlife, while the **Balboa Fun Zone** and **Balboa Pier** (about half-way down the peninsula) support the most tourism. The Fun Zone was built on the site of the 1905 **Balboa Pavilion,** an entertainment

CALIFORNIA

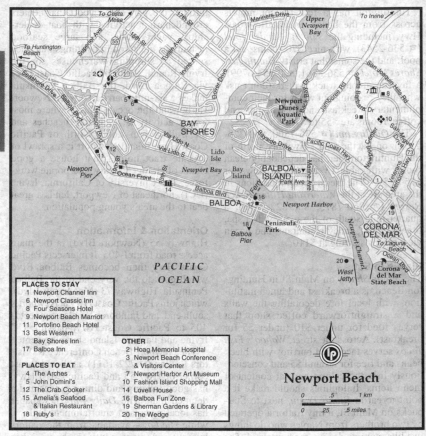

PLACES TO STAY
1   Newport Channel Inn
6   Newport Classic Inn
8   Four Seasons Hotel
9   Newport Beach Marriot
11 Portofino Beach Hotel
13 Best Western
    Bay Shores Inn
17 Balboa Inn

PLACES TO EAT
4   The Arches
5   John Domini's
12 The Crab Cooker
15 Amelia's Seafood
    & Italian Restaurant
18 Ruby's

OTHER
2   Hoag Memorial Hospital
3   Newport Beach Conference
    & Visitors Center
7   Newport Harbor Art Museum
10 Fashion Island Shopping Mall
14 Lovell House
16 Balboa Fun Zone
19 Sherman Gardens & Library
20 The Wedge

Newport Beach

0   .5   1 km
0   .25   .5 miles

destination that older generations from all over Southern California remember as *the* place to go on a Sunday afternoon. Now the place has a Ferris wheel, arcade games, touristy shops, and restaurants, but little of its old charm.

At the very tip of the peninsula, just west of the jetty, is **The Wedge**, a body surfing and knee-boarding spot famous for its perfectly hollowed waves that can get up to 30 feet high. The yellow flag with a black-ball in the middle (atop the lifeguard stand) means this location is illegal to surf, due to dangerous water conditions. The Wedge is

not a good place for learning how to handle the currents; new-comers should head north a few blocks for calmer water. Also at the peninsula's end is a small park with a nice view of the channel – great for boat-watching and picnicking.

Activities There are several boat excursions from here: Balboa Boat Rentals (☎ 673-7200) rents kayaks ($10 and hour), sailboats ($25), and motor boats ($45); Showboat Cruises (☎ 673-0240) offers 90 minute tours of Newport Harbor ($8); and Davey's Locker (☎ 673-1434) has half-day fishing trips ($30) and whale-watching excursions ($12). This is also where boats to Catalina Island depart.

Balboa & Lido Islands

Within Newport Harbor are these two densely populated islands, both with small shopping districts and upscale beach houses. Balboa Island connects to the mainland via Marine Ave, which crosses Pacific Coast Hwy as Jamboree Rd. There is also a car ferry from the Balboa Fun Zone that goes to Balboa every 10 minutes ($1 per car, 35¢ per person) from 6:30 am to midnight (until 2 am Friday and Saturday). The ferry lands at the east end of the island, 11 blocks from the businesses and restaurants on Marine. It's only about a mile and a half around the island, making it a good place to explore by foot or bike.

Lido Island is inland from Balboa and connected to the mainland by Via Lido, which crosses Balboa Blvd just south of Pacific Coast Hwy. Streets here are especially narrow and houses appear to be built one on top of the other. Via Lido wraps around the entire island (about a mile), past upscale beachwear shops and the restored Lido Theater, which shows classic and foreign films.

Fashion Island

This enormous shopping center is nearly as big as Newport's real islands (Balboa and Lido) and has twice as much parking. Considered one of *the* places to shop, eat, and see movies in Orange County, Fashion Island has major department stores – Bullock's, Robinson's May, Nieman Marcus – plus many small boutiques and chain stores, organized around an open-air mall decorated with fountains, trees, and benches. Even non-shoppers can enjoy a few hours here without feeling claustrophobic.

Newport Center Drive makes a circle around the complex, connecting to Pacific Coast Hwy, Hwy 73 via San Miguel Rd, and Jamboree Rd via Santa Barbara Dr. The Atrium Court, near Robinson's May, has a concierge desk and farmer's market with fresh produce and food stands. Stores are open Monday to Friday from 10 am to 9 pm, Saturday until 6 pm, and Sunday noon to 6 pm.

Newport Harbor Art Museum

In an obscure location between Jamboree Rd and Fashion Island, this museum (☎ 759-1122), 850 San Clemente Drive, is worth visiting if you're interested in contemporary art. Exhibits usually feature artists whose work has a common theme, from industrial technology to the children of Thailand. There is a nice sculpture garden near the back of the museum, and a gift shop with oversized art books and jewelry. Classic, foreign, and art-related films are shown most Thursday nights ($4) at 6 pm; check listings in the *OC Weekly* or call. Museum hours are Tuesday to Saturday 10 am to 5 pm, Sunday noon to 5 pm; admission is $4.

Corona del Mar

On the east side of the Newport Channel, about six miles south of I-405, Corona del Mar is a ritzy bedroom community with elegant stores and restaurants spread along Pacific Coast Hwy. The beach here – two blocks south of Pacific Coast Hwy via Marguerite Ave – is really nice, surrounded by rocky cliffs, with restrooms and volleyball courts maintained by the State Park system. Parking costs $5 per vehicle, but there is usually free parking atop the cliffs behind the beach, along Ocean Blvd.

Besides the beach, the community's prize attraction is the **Sherman Library & Gardens** (☎ 673-2261), which occupies an entire block of Pacific Coast Hwy. Begun in 1966, the gardens are extremely lush and well-maintained, with especially nice orchids and a pond of huge koi. The small research library holds a wealth of California historical documents and a few paintings by early California landscape artists. Hours are from 10:30 am to 4 pm (the library is closed weekends and holidays) and admission is $2.

Newport Harbor Christmas Boat Parade

The week before Christmas brings thousands of spectators to Newport Harbor to watch the nightly parade of decorated boats, a tradition begun here in 1919. The parade begins at 6:30 pm and lasts about two-and-a-half hours. There is usually grandstand seating provided by the Newport Harbor Jaycees (☎ 451-2178) for $7 per person, though the best way to see the parade is from the water. Balboa Boat Rentals (☎ 673-7200) rents boats for six to 12 people ($100 to $220 for four hours; reservations are recommended), and the Newport Harbor Area Chamber of Commerce (☎ 729-4400) has a list of private boat rentals that changes annually.

Places to Stay

A good choice for budget travelers is the *Newport Channel Inn* (☎ 642-3030), one mile north of Newport Blvd at 6030 W Coast Hwy, which charges $39/44 in winter, $59/65 in summer, and is right across from the beach. Closer to the harbor and peninsula, the *Newport Classic Inn* (☎ 722-2999), between Newport Blvd and the Balboa Bay Club at 2300 W Coast Hwy, has rooms for $65 in winter, $76 in summer.

In the heart of Balboa's action, between the Balboa Fun Zone and Balboa Pier, the *Balboa Inn* (☎ 675-3412) is a grand old hotel with newly renovated rooms for $90 ($125 with an ocean view). Also on the peninsula, three blocks from the Newport Pier at 1800 W Balboa Blvd, the *Best Western Bay Shores Inn* (☎ 675-3463) has standard rooms for $92 to $129 in winter, $109 to $139 in summer, including breakfast, free VCR and video rental, and use of beach mats, chairs, and boogie boards. For a romantic fling, try the classy *Portofino Beach Hotel* (☎ 673-7030), 2306 W Oceanfront, whose rooms have marble bath tubs and fireplaces ($100 to $150) and views of the Newport Pier. Their restaurant, *Renato*, is said to have some of the best Italian food in Orange County, with dinner for two costing as much as a room.

There are several large resort hotels near Fashion Island that cater to business travelers and conventions. The *Newport Beach Marriott* (☎ 640-4000), 900 Newport Center Drive, is the least expensive, with rooms for $89 to $134, while the *Four Seasons Hotel* (☎ 759-0808), 690 Newport Center Drive, has rooms starting at $200.

Places to Eat

Ask most Southern Californians about Newport Beach, and they'll inevitably mention *The Crab Cooker* (☎ 673-0100), 2200 Newport Blvd near the Newport Pier. Begun as a fish market in the 1940s, the place now relies on restaurant patrons willing to wait in hour-long lines to eat red clam chowder, grilled fish, and romano mashed potatoes served on paper plates with plastic forks. The menu and prices – which run from $7 to $23 – depend upon the daily catch.

Another Newport Beach institution is *The Arches* (☎ 645-7077), at the corner of Pacific Coast Hwy and Newport Blvd, which received its liquor license in 1922. Specialties include steak Diane, beef Wellington, and soft-shell crab, though John Wayne swore by the New York steak. Prices are discriminatory – most dishes are over $20 – but the dress code is not. Down the block, *John Dominis* (☎ 650-5112), 2901 W Coast Hwy at Riverside, is worth a stop if only to see the 2000-gallon indoor lagoon that meanders through the restaurant. Dinners run from $17 to $35, and don't worry, the fish in the lagoon are friends, not food.

Amelia's Seafood & Italian Restaurant (☎ 673-6580), 311 Marine Ave on Balboa Island, is a good place for seafood and

pasta (under $10) and is open for lunch and dinner. The *Ruby's* (☎ 675-7829) at the end of the Balboa Pier is the original of what is now a chain of '40s-style diners. Their burgers and sandwiches (around $5) are served in plastic baskets with mounds of fries, and their milkshakes ($2) are almost a meal in themselves.

Getting Around
OCTA (☎ 636-7433) bus No 53 stops at the corner of Pacific Coast Hwy and Newport Blvd and goes south to the end of the Balboa Peninsula, and north to South Coast Plaza and John Wayne Airport; the No 65 covers the Peninsula, Pacific Coast Hwy from Newport Blvd to MacArthur Blvd, Fashion Island, and UCI.

AROUND NEWPORT BEACH
University of California, Irvine
UCI is the up-and-coming University of California campus whose scientific research departments are increasingly well-funded, and whose basketball team – the Anteaters – surprised the collegiate world several years ago by beating top-seated University of Nevada Las Vegas (UNLV). Although the campus is not too exciting in terms of architecture (most of it was built in the 1970s and '80s), it occasionally hosts interesting lectures or sporting events. The student union (☎ 824-5011), where you'll find a student-staffed information center and a good bookstore, is well marked off Campus Drive, south of I-405 via MacArthur Blvd.

South Coast Plaza
This is Orange County's largest and snazziest mall, with classical music piped in over the speakers and stores such as Cartier, Giorgio Armani, and Burberry's. A colorful carousel in the main building (near Sears) entertains children, and the Laguna Beach Art Museum Annex (just behind the carousel) has changing exhibits and an interesting store.

There are three parts to the mall: South Coast Plaza main building, marked by Nordstrom, Sears, Bullock's, Saks Fifth

Avenue, and Robinson's May; Crystal Court, with the Broadway on one end and another Robinson's May on the other; and South Coast Plaza Village, which houses administrative offices, the beautiful new Orange County Center for the Performing Arts, and several good restaurants. Free shuttle buses stop outside the main stores every 20 minutes.

South Coast is well-marked off I-405 via Bristol St. A good place to park is on the northeast side of the main building (off Sunflower Blvd), near Nordstrom. A concierge in Nordstrom's men's department has a map and information for the entire mall. Across the street, *Planet Hollywood* is a good if not-too-wild place to have a salad, sandwich, or decadent dessert surrounded by authentic Hollywood memorabilia such as John Wayne's high school yearbook and Freddy Kreuger's glove.

LAGUNA BEACH
☎ 714
Secluded beaches, low cliffs, glassy waves, waterfront parks, eucalyptus-covered hillsides, and a host of art galleries and boutiques make Laguna Beach Orange County's (and one of Southern California's) most popular seaside destinations. An early gathering spot for California artists and home of the renowned Festival of the Arts and Pageant of the Masters, Laguna draws artists and art collectors from all over the world, especially during July and August. Thanks to stringent building codes which, according to a long time resident, 'took longer to draft than the US Constitution,' the town has great architectural integrity. Crowds of tourists are thick on summer weekends, but away from 'the village' (the central business district) and Main Beach (where the village meets the shore) there is plenty of uncrowded sand and water.

History
Laguna's earliest inhabitants, Ute-Aztecas and Shoshone tribes, called the area 'Lagonas' because of two freshwater lagoons in what is now Laguna Canyon. The name

'Lagona' held until 1904, when mail carriers kept delivering residents' mail to Long Beach. Never part of a rancho or land grant, Lagona began to attract homesteaders in 1872, when the Timber Cultures Act gave people 160 acres of land, provided they planted 10 of those acres with trees. Homesteaders in this area planted eucalyptus trees, imported from Australia, which eventually became a landmark for Laguna artists.

In 1903, San Francisco artist Norman St Claire moved to Laguna and painted watercolors of the surf, cliffs, and hills. His work and letters home about Laguna's climate attracted other artists to the area. By 1917, about 40 of the town's 300 inhabitants were artists, most of whom were influenced by Monet and Impressionism and were thus called the California 'plein-air' school (often called the Eucalyptus school because the trees appeared in so many of their works). In 1918, Edgar Paine opened a gallery and formed the Laguna Beach Art Association, which still functions as a major part of the community.

The 1920s and '30s brought the most lasting development to Laguna. In 1926 Pacific Coast Hwy was opened between Newport Beach and Dana Point, giving

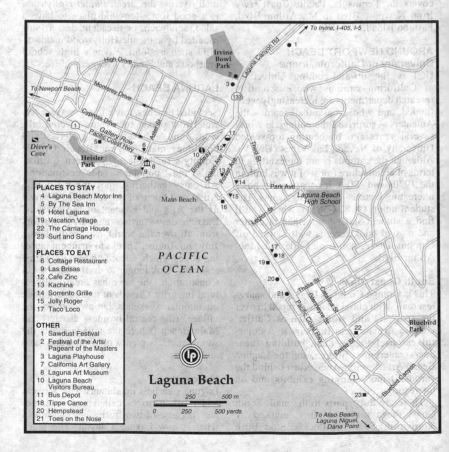

Laguna Beach

PLACES TO STAY
4 Laguna Beach Motor Inn
5 By The Sea Inn
16 Hotel Laguna
19 Vacation Village
22 The Carriage House
23 Surf and Sand

PLACES TO EAT
6 Cottage Restaurant
9 Las Brisas
12 Cafe Zinc
13 Kachina
14 Sorrento Grille
15 Jolly Roger
17 Taco Loco

OTHER
1 Sawdust Festival
2 Festival of the Arts/
  Pageant of the Masters
3 Laguna Playhouse
7 California Art Gallery
8 Laguna Art Museum
10 Laguna Beach
   Visitors Bureau
11 Bus Depot
18 Tippe Canoe
20 Hempstead
21 Toes on the Nose

Laguna three access routes. Mary Pickford, Douglas Fairbanks, Mickey Rooney, and Bette Davis vacationed here regularly and helped establish the Laguna Playhouse (still in operation) and the Festival of the Arts, still the town's biggest attraction, which began in 1932.

Orientation

Though the town stretches for about seven miles along Pacific Coast Hwy, attractions are concentrated in the village, along Broadway, Ocean, and Forest Sts and their intersections with Pacific Coast Hwy (all within a quarter-mile). Across Pacific Coast Hwy from the village, Main Beach and Heisler Park (atop the bluffs to the north) offer the most public beach access. Four miles south, Laguna Niguel is home to the fancy Ritz-Carlton Hotel and Salt Creek, a favorite of local surfers. To reach Laguna from I-405, take Laguna Canyon Rd (Hwy 133) west; this passes the Festival of the Arts site and hits the east end of the village, where it splits into Broadway, Ocean, and Forest.

Information

The Laguna Beach Visitors Bureau (☎ 376-0511), one block off Pacific Coast Hwy at 252 Broadway, has maps, local bus schedules, Festival of the Arts information, and will make lodging reservations for free. From June to September hours are Monday to Saturday 8 am to 5 pm, Sunday 10 am to 4 pm. The free weekly, *Coastline News,* available at stands and restaurants around town, lists local happenings from city council activities to poetry readings.

Parking lots in the village cost about $3 a day and fill up quickly in the summer. If possible, park at your motel and take public transportation (see Getting Around below), or at the high school on Park St, three blocks northeast of Forest Ave.

Laguna Art Museum

Showplace for the Laguna Art Association, founded in 1918, this museum (☎ 494-8971), at the corner of Pacific Coast Hwy and Cliff Drive, has three levels of exhibit space and an interesting gift shop. Changing exhibits feature California art, usually focusing on one or two artists. In the absence of important traveling exhibits, the museum shows pieces from its permanent collection, mostly early California landscapes and vintage photographs. Hours are 11 am to 5 pm (closed Monday), with free docent tours at 2 pm (except Thursday and Friday). Admission is $5.

Beaches

Main Beach fronts the village with volleyball and basketball courts, a wooden boardwalk, and colorful tile benches. This is the best place for swimming since the water is calm, rocks are absent, and lifeguards are on duty year round. At the north end of this beach, a path heads up the bluff (past Las Brisas Restaurant) to Heisler Park, a long skinny stretch of grass accented by hibiscus, roses, and bougainvillea. Several sets of stairs lead down to the sand, including those at the north end of the park that go to Diver's Cove, a deep protected cove popular with guess who.

In Laguna Niguel, eight miles south of the village, are Aliso Beach and Salt Creek – both less crowded than the beaches near town. Aliso has a pier and a sub-Pacific Coast Hwy tunnel that leads to a grassy park and hikeable Aliso Creek Canyon. The point break at Salt Creek is popular with surfers. Both have parking lots that run $1 per hour, and both are accessible by bus from the village.

Dana Point

Ten minutes down the road, Dana Point is one of California's best whale-watching locales. Excursion boats leave from the Dana Point Marina (☎ 496-6137) from January to March when giant gray whales move south towards the Sea of Cortez. Also of maritime interest is Dana Point Harbor, home to a full-scale replica of the *Pilgrim,* the ship Richard Henry Dana wrote about in his novel *Two Years Before the Mast,* and the Orange County Marine Institute (☎ 496-2274), which has a good aquatic and sea-life museum.

CALIFORNIA

Festival of the Arts

This is Laguna's landmark event, a seven-week, juried exhibit of 160 artists whose work varies from paintings to hand-crafted furniture to scrimshaw. Begun in 1933 by local artists who needed to drum up buyers for their work, the festival now attracts patrons and tourists from all over the world and offers added attractions such as the Junior Art Gallery featuring children's art, free daily workshops conducted by artists, and live entertainment.

A year after the Festival of the Arts began, artists who did not make the juried exhibition started their own festival to take advantage of the art-seekers passing through town. They set up directly across from the festival (on Laguna Canyon Rd, half a mile from the village) mocking its formal atmosphere by scattering sawdust on the ground. Local journalist Dick Nall coined the name Sawdust Festival which has remained ever since. Many people actually enjoy this festival more, since the arts and crafts are utilitarian and quite affordable. A $3 ticket allows you to enter both festivals which are open daily from 10 am to 11:30 pm.

Perhaps the most interesting aspect of the fair is the Pageant of the Masters, where human models stand perfectly still for three minutes to re-create famous paintings. This also was begun in 1933 as a 'sideshow' to the main festival. Tickets ($15 to $40) need to be ordered weeks in advance, though you can often pick up last-minute cancellation tickets at the gate. Nightly performances begin at 8:30 pm. For information call the Laguna Festival of the Arts (☎ 494-1145, 800-487-3378).

City shuttle busses (50¢) run continuously from 10 am to midnight from parking lots on Laguna Canyon Rd and the village to the festival.

Places to Stay

Accommodations get booked far in advance for summer months, during which time prices are generally $20 higher than those listed below. The visitors bureau has a limited lodging brochure and makes reservations for free.

Motels The best deals in town are the $48 rooms at the *Laguna Beach Motor Inn* (☎ 494-5294), 985 N Coast Hwy. They are old, but clean and spacious, with ocean views and only a short walk to the beach and village. Ask for a room away from the highway. A few blocks south, *By the Sea Inn* (☎ 800-297-0007), 475 N Coast Hwy, charges $80 to $110 for small rooms with new carpet, wallpaper, and beds. Rooms look out over the small pool and hot tub (the ocean is visible in the distance) and the lobby has free coffee and pastries. Formerly the stomping ground of Hollywood stars, the restored *Hotel Laguna* (☎ 494-1151, 800-524-2927), at Laguna Ave and Pacific Coast Hwy, offers slightly shabby rooms in a great location for $70 to $110.

Vacation Village (☎ 494-8566, 800-843-6895), south of the village on Pacific Coast Hwy, has a pool, a spa, and kitchen units; rooms that sleep four run $120, doubles around $75. The *Surf and Sand* (☎ 497-4477, 800-524-8621) is another moderately upscale choice, with a pool, sundeck, restaurant, private beach, and ocean-view rooms for $150.

B&Bs Laguna is a popular honeymoon destination, so clientele at these upscale accommodations is often surprisingly young. Housed in a Spanish-style old Laguna home, the *Casa Laguna Inn* (☎ 494-2996, 800-233-0449), 2510 S Coast Hwy, has cozy rooms and individual cottages starting at $70, including a hearty breakfast and afternoon tea. Rooms at the *Carriage House* (☎ 494-8945), 1322 Catalina St, surround a lovely courtyard and have their own sitting rooms and kitchens (and complimentary bottle of California wine); rates are $125, including breakfast. The beach is two blocks west and the village is about half a mile south.

Ritz-Carlton When the *Ritz-Carlton Laguna Niguel* (☎ 240-2000, 800-241-3333), west of Pacific Coast Hwy via Ritz-

Carlton Drive, was built in 1985, it had the eight miles of ocean, cliffs, and trees between it and the village to itself. Now the sprawl along Pacific Coast Hwy connects the hotel to the rest of town, and the view of central Laguna is shared by million-dollar homes in Ritz Cove and golfers on the Monarch Bay Golf Links. Still, the Ritz-Carlton offers lap-of-luxury accommodation in an opulent setting. There are two pools, a full spa, tennis courts, terraced paths to the beach (which happens to be a great surf spot), a library and smoking lounge, and several restaurants. Rooms start at $215 and go to 10 times that much for a deluxe suite. The most affordable experience here is a drink in the Lobby Lounge – a grand place to watch the sunset.

Places to Eat

A Laguna institution with one of the best views, *Las Brisas* (☎ 497-5434), next to Laguna Art Museum at 361 Cliff Drive, serves Mexican seafood dishes ($20) in the dining room and appetizers and soft tacos ($7) on the patio bar. If you stop at only one watering hole, make this it. For breakfast, the institutional equivalent is the *Cottage Restaurant* (☎ 494-3023) across Pacific Coast Hwy from the museum. They've got big wooden tables, copies of the *LA Times* and the *Orange County Register,* good coffee, and great cranberry orange pancakes ($3.50). At *Taco Loco,* a favorite among surfers and vegetarians, you can get blackened chicken, swordfish, or tofu and mushrooms in a taco, burrito, salad, quesadilla, or sandwich ($2 to $5).

Three blocks from the beach at 350 Ocean Ave, *Cafe Zinc* (☎ 494-6302) is where locals in-the-know go to get their cafe lattes, muffins, and fresh salads (under $8). Seating is mostly at outdoor tables, and the adjoining market has good picnic items. For straightforward coffeeshop food with an ocean view, head to the *Jolly Roger* at the corner of Laguna and Pacific Coast Hwy – any restaurant this old must be doing something right.

The *Sorrento Grille* (☎ 494-8686), 370 Glenneyre, and *Kachina* (☎ 497-5546), 222 Forest Ave, are considered two of the area's best restaurants, with dinner for $20 and lunch for under $10. The former has Mediterranean food, while the latter features Southwest ingredients (black beans, corn, squash, duck) prepared à la Laguna with a very artistic flair.

Things to Buy

Most Laguna galleries sell the work of a single artist, which make them more museum-like than hodge-podge tourist traps so often passed-off as art galleries. While the village has a good number of the former, it also has a fair share of the latter, where you can buy landscape watercolors for around $30 and prints for around $12. For a more serious art tour head to Gallery Row, a few blocks north of the village on the east side of Pacific Coast Hwy. This string of upscale galleries – Gallery McCollum, Peter Blake Gallery, Left Bank Gallery, Schaar Gallery – has modern, contemporary, abstract, and landscape paintings (a few sculptures), most by local artists. Across from the Laguna Art Museum, the **California Art Gallery** is a small but well-stocked place whose staff knows its way around California plein-air work.

About a quarter mile south of the village along Pacific Coast Hwy are funky and more affordable shops such as **Tippe Canoe**, a well-known consignment store, **Hempstead**, which sells products made from leafy green plants, and **Toes on the Nose**, a surf shop with a fine collection of Hawaiian relics and vintage surfboards.

Getting Around

Laguna Transit (☎ 497-0746) buses leave every 20 minutes from the outdoor bus depot at the east end of Broadway, going south to Laguna Niguel, and north for about four miles on Pacific Coast Hwy, stopping near most motels. This is also where OCTA buses stop between Long Beach and San Clemente.

MISSION SAN JUAN CAPISTRANO

This is one of California's most visited and most beautiful missions, with a lush garden and graceful arches. The charming Father Serra Chapel – whitewashed and decorated with colorful symbols – is the only building still standing where Father Junipero Serra said Mass. Father Serra founded this mission on November 1, 1776, and tended it personally for many years. With access to San Clemente harbor and as the only development between San Diego and Los Angeles, this was one of the most important missions in the chain. Like most, it acted as a gathering point for travelers and local land owners, and sustained its own activity with mills, granaries, livestock, crops, and other small industry.

Plan on spending at least an hour looking at the grounds and exhibits in the mission museum. The bookstore and gift shop both have mission and early California related materials. The mission is open daily from 8:30 am to 5 pm; admission is $4.

This mission is also where the legendary swallows return each year – on March 19, the feast of Saint Joseph – after wintering in South America, just like the song says.

Surrounding the mission are converted adobes that now house Mexican restaurants (Pedro's Tacos is recommended), art galleries and gift shops. Two blocks south, across Via Capistrano, is a historic district with several adobes dating back to the mission's founding when they housed business people who thrived from mission activity.

Getting There & Away

The San Juan Capistrano Amtrak station (☎ 240-2972), housed in a converted rail car one block from the mission at 26701 Verdugo St (behind L'Hirondelle restaurant), gets eight southbound and 10 northbound trains per day en route between Los Angeles and San Diego. OCTA buses No 91 and 398 stop in front of the station and go south to Pacific Coast Hwy where the No 1 heads north to Orange County beach cities.

SAN ONOFRE STATE BEACH

The longest undeveloped stretch between Los Angeles and San Diego is marked by San Onofre nuclear power plant and San Onofre State Beach. While there is no correlation between splitting atoms and catching waves, this is one of the best surf spots in Southern California. The rocky bottom gives the waves consistency, while the flat wide bay makes for gentle rollers that break about a quarter mile out – perfect for longboarding. North of San Onofre, Upper and Lower Trestles are point breaks whose big, hollow tubes are beautiful to watch and a challenge to surf.

Basilone Rd gives access to the beaches from I-405. The day-use parking lot costs $6 per vehicle and is next to the beach. Two miles south (well-marked off Basilone), *San Onofre State Park campground* (☎ 492-4872) has $16 sites, reservable through Destinet, with showers and ocean views. Nighttime activity is pretty friendly in this campground, with surfers and travelers willing to share beers and surf stories. Trails lead from the campground down to the beach (about half a mile).

San Diego Area

San Diego County comprises 4200 sq miles, extending about 60 miles between Orange and Riverside Counties to the north, to the Mexican border in the south, and about 70 miles from the Pacific seashore over the coastal mountain range to the deserts of Anza-Borrego. The area has a great variety of landscapes, superb coastline, near-perfect climate, and a population of over 2.5 million people and still growing.

People looking for a laid-back California lifestyle are often disappointed with the pace and pollution of LA, but find what they want in San Diego. Conservative, comfortable, affluent San Diego lacks the high profile and international recognition of San Francisco or Los Angeles, but it's a very pleasant place to visit, especially if you like beaches, water sports, or, surprisingly, theater.

The metropolitan part of the county includes the city of San Diego itself, and a number of suburban communities from swanky La Jolla and Coronado to the almost Mexican San Ysidro. For information about the attractions in the northern and eastern parts of the county, and the neighboring Mexican city of Tijuana, see the Around San Diego section. Anza-Borrego State Park is covered in the chapter on the California Deserts, though it is actually within San Diego County.

San Diego

• *pop 1,110,500* ☎ *619*

HISTORY
As a city, San Diego is very new. Though human occupation of the area goes back a long way, there are very few sites in the county which are genuinely older than a century. The long period of Native American habitation has left very few tangible remains, and despite an abundance of Spanish place names and Spanish-style architecture, only half a dozen structures in the county actually date from the periods of Spanish and Mexican rule.

The Kumayaay
Though originally a desert people, the Kumayaay adapted readily to the Southern California environment. They lived in small villages around the bay, making short trips to the Cuyamaca mountains to hunt and gather acorns, and hung out closer to the beach in summer, catching fish and birds and collecting shells. They didn't cultivate crops, but they used a large number of local plants for food, fiber, and medicine. The most distinctive artifacts of the Kumayaay are baskets and nets skillfully woven from sage, tulle, reeds, and grasses. Some good examples can be seen at the Museum of Man in Balboa Park. With the arrival of Europeans, the identity of the various native groups was obscured by the practice of naming them for the nearest mission – those near San Diego were called Diegueños, those near San Luis Rey were called Luiseños, and so on.

Mission Period
Juan Rodríguez Cabrillo's expedition made the first European contact with California in 1542. His ships sat out a storm in the San Diego Bay which he named San Miguel, and after six days they continued their northward journey. The next was Sebastián Vizcaíno, in 1602. He entered the bay on the feast day of San Diego de Alcalà, and could not resist renaming the place San Diego.

When the Spanish finally decided to occupy Alta California, 40 men under Father Junípero Serra founded the first of the California missions, on the hill now known as the Presidio. Disease struck the settlement from the beginning, and the

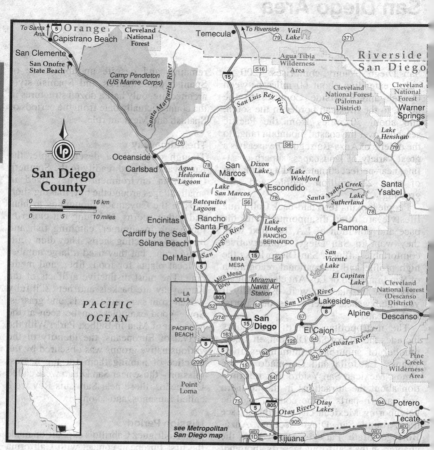

San Diego County

0   8   16 km
0   5   10 miles

PACIFIC OCEAN

see Metropolitan San Diego map

Kumayaay made a number of attacks – 19 of the original settlers died in the first six months, and the mission was almost abandoned. The mission eventually achieved some stability; at its height there were 1500 converted Kumayaay in the congregation.

Missionary activity continued further north, and other missions were established in the San Diego area, including San Luis Rey Francia in 1798, and the *asistencias* (satellite missions) of San Antonio de Pala (1815), and Santa Ysabel (1818).

The grants of land for *ranchos* and the breakup of the missions (1833) displaced Native Americans. Many of the Kumayaay fell into poverty and began raids on isolated ranchos and travelers. The small community of San Diego became a civilian *pueblo* in 1835, with an *alcade* (a combination mayor and magistrate) who had wide powers and dispensed harsh justice to rebellious Indians. Despite the prosperity of the ranchos, San Diego itself remained a ramshackle village at the base of the Presidio hill, with only a few hundred residents.

Early American Period
The 1849 Gold Rush bypassed San Diego, as did the first rail link to Southern Califor-

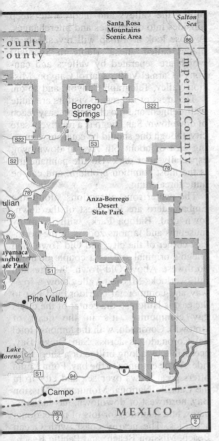

ahead, especially after 1872 when a fire devastated much of the original settlement.

The discovery of gold in the hills east of San Diego started a frenetic mining boom, but it was nearly all over by 1874 – the town of Julian is one of the few surviving gold mining settlements. The population fell from 4000 to 2000 in the years after the gold played out. Despite the efforts of the city's boosters, San Diego did not acquire an industrial base in the 19th century – the main economic activity was real estate speculation, and the city saw several cycles of boom and bust.

Panama-California Exposition
To celebrate the 1914 completion of the Panama Canal, San Francisco hosted the Panama-Pacific International Exposition, but San Diego was not to be ignored and held its own exposition, which ran for most of 1915 and 1916. In an effort to give the city a distinctive image, the exposition buildings were consciously designed with a romantic Spanish-Mexican style. Developers, architects, and the public took to this fashion with enthusiasm. San Diego's Mediterranean style, Mission architecture, and Spanish street names derive more from this deliberate image building than from its actual heritage as a small and remote colonial Spanish outpost.

Modern San Diego
Glenn H Curtiss developed ship-based aircraft on San Diego Bay, and the city soon became the home of US naval aviation. Ryan Airlines built the *Spirit of St Louis* for Lindbergh's trans-Atlantic flight in 1927, and Consolidated Aircraft opened its factory in 1931 – San Diego at last had an industry. A steady revenue from naval and military bases helped San Diego weather the Depression, along with WPA projects like the race track at Del Mar and San Diego State University, but there were nevertheless shanty towns of poor immigrants from the dustbowl and industrial areas. In 1935, as the Depression eased, San Diego staged another big event, the California-Pacific Exposition, with more

nia, and by 1855 the population was still only about 800. Some business people saw the city's potential as a port – in the 1850s William Heath Davis, a former sea captain and San Francisco property speculator, bought 160 acres of bayfront land, and erected prefabricated houses, a wharf, and warehouses. But the development, dubbed Davis' Folly, was ahead of its time, and failed to attract either commercial or government support. In 1867 Alonzo E Horton, another San Francisco speculator and businessman, acquired 960 acres of waterfront land and promoted it as 'New Town,' this time the new subdivision really went

Hispanic architecture appearing in Balboa Park.

Following the bombing of Pearl Harbor, the headquarters of the US Pacific Fleet was moved to San Diego. The boom in wartime activity transformed the city – vast tracts of instant housing appeared, public spaces were turned into training camps, storage depots, and hospitals, and the population doubled in a couple of years. The war, the marines, the navy, and naval aviators were the subjects of films in which San Diego was featured, albeit incidentally – from *Guadalcanal* to *Sands of Iwo Jima*. The wartime role, and the associated publicity, more than anything else put San Diego on the American map.

Post-war San Diego became a booming city in a booming state. The naval and military presence provided an expanding core of activity, employing up to a quarter of the workforce. The climate and the seafront location have also been major factors in the city's growth. Recreation facilities like Mission Bay helped attract visitors, who now contribute a big slice of the county's income. The downtown area has been revitalized. Education and research are now major activities too, while the San Diego Padres baseball team, and the San Diego Chargers football team, have both been successful representatives of the city.

ORIENTATION

San Diego is a pretty easy place to find your way around. The airport, train station, and Greyhound terminal are all in or near the downtown area, which is a compact grid east of San Diego Bay. The main north-south freeway is I-5, which parallels the coast from the Camp Pendleton Marine Corps Base in the north to the Mexican border at San Ysidro. Also going from north to south, I-805 is a detour from I-5, bypassing the downtown area to the east. Interstate 8 runs east from Ocean Beach, up the valley of the San Diego River (called Mission Valley), past suburbs like El Cajon and on to Imperial Valley and Arizona.

It's difficult to appreciate the topography as you cruise the freeways, which often follow the valleys and incorporate steep hillsides into overpasses and interchanges. A close look at a map will reveal lots of places called 'mesa' (table in Spanish) which are separated by valleys and canyons – Carmel Valley, Carrol Canyon, Mission Valley, Telegraph Canyon, and so on.

The areas of interest to visitors are quite well-defined, and mostly within easy reach of downtown. San Diego is a relatively safe city, though one should be cautious venturing east of about 6th Ave in downtown, especially after dark. Hostile panhandling is the most common problem, and can be quite threatening.

The waterfront attractions along the Embarcadero are just west of the downtown grid. Balboa Park, with its many museums and famous zoo, is in the northeast corner of the city, and Old Town, San Diego's original site, is a couple of miles northwest. Above Old Town, the Presidio hill overlooks Mission Valley, now a freeway and commercial corridor, and just to the east is Hillcrest, the center of the city's gay community (it's in the heart of Uptown). Coronado, with the famous Hotel del Coronado, is across San Diego Bay, accessible by a long bridge or a short ferry ride. At the entrance to the bay, Point Loma offers great views over sea and city from the Cabrillo National Monument. Mission Bay, northwest of downtown, has lagoons, parks, and facilities for lots of recreational activities. The nearby coast, with Ocean Beach, Mission Beach, and Pacific Beach, is the epitome of a Southern California beach scene, while La Jolla, a little further north, is a more upmarket seaside area.

INFORMATION
Tourist Offices

Downtown, the International Visitors Information Center (☎ 236-1212) is on 1st Ave at F St – it's on the side of the Horton Plaza complex, at 11 Horton Plaza. The center has lots of free printed information and a knowledgeable staff. It's open Monday to Saturday from 8:30 am to 5 pm, and in summer on Sunday from 11 am to 5 pm.

Another visitors center (☎ 276-8200) at

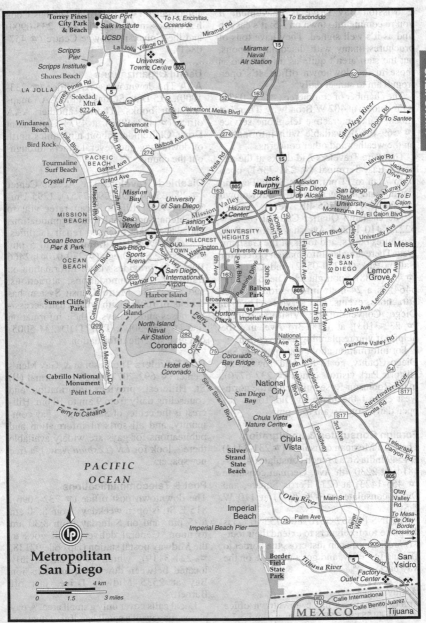

Metropolitan
San Diego

0   2   4 km
0   1.5   3 miles

E Mission Bay Drive is convenient if you're coming into town on I-5; it's easy to find as it's well signed. They have tons of brochures, many with discount coupons, but the staff aren't quite as informative as those in the downtown office. It's open from 9 am to sunset daily.

The chamber of commerce (☎ 234-0331) is downtown at 402 W Broadway. There's a 'Local Talk' interactive telephone service (☎ 569-1000) available with information on the weather and other concerns.

There are Travelers Aid desks at the airport's East Terminal (☎ 231-7361) open from 7 am to 11 pm; in the Santa Fe train station; and in the main office downtown (☎ 232-7991) at 1765 4th Ave.

The Gaslamp Quarter Council (☎ 233-5227), 410 Island Ave, has information, brochures books, and tours of the Gaslamp area. There are also information offices for Balboa Park (☎ 239-0512) and Coronado (☎ 437-8788). Spotlight San Diego (☎ 551-6464) is a 24-hour information line for attractions, events, and services. The San Diego Convention & Visitors Bureau (☎ 232-3103), at 1200 3rd Ave, may be helpful if you're planning a convention.

For information about state parks in San Diego County, go to the Old Town State Historic Park visitors center (☎ 237-6770), in the Robinson-Rose building at the northwest end of the plaza in Old Town. It's open daily from 10 am to 5 pm.

Foreign Consulates & Immigration

There's a Mexican consulate (☎ 231-8414) at 1549 India St, a French consulate (☎ 239-4814) at 2230 4th Ave, German consulate (☎ 455-1423) at 6215 Ferris Square, and Dutch consulate (☎ 696-7941) at 110 W C St.

The INS (☎ 557-5570, 800-755-0777) is the place for foreigners to extend their tourist cards. Or you can just cross the border to Tijuana for a day, and get a new one on the way back.

Money

American Express has a downtown office (☎ 234-4455) at 258 Broadway, and a La Jolla branch (☎ 459-4161). Thomas Cook has offices in Horton Plaza (☎ 235-0900) and the University Towne Centre (☎ 457-0841).

Useful Organizations

AAA The downtown AAA office (☎ 233-1000), 815 Date St, has all the AAA maps and tour books. There's another AAA office (☎ 483-4960) at 4973 Clairemont Drive, Clairemont, about nine miles north of downtown, and several others throughout the county.

Disabled Travelers The Access Center (☎ 293-3500, TDD 293-7757), 1295 University Ave Hillcrest, can refer you to wheelchair-accessible accommodations and wheelchair sale and repair facilities. It's open weekdays from 9 am to 5 pm. Accessible San Diego (☎ 279-0704), 2466 Bartell St, provides visitor information on transport, accommodations, attractions, and tours. The Metro Transit System has dozens of routes with wheelchair accessible buses and trolleys – their information line (☎ 233-3004, TTY/TDD 234-5005) can give specific information.

Gay Travelers The Lesbian & Gay Men's Center (☎ 692-2077), at 3916 Normal (!!) St, Hillcrest, provides information and counseling daily from 9 am to 10 pm. Hillcrest is the center of San Diego's gay community, and all sorts of information and publications for gays are widely available there – look for *LN (Lesbian News)*, a free newspaper.

Post & Telecommunications

The downtown post office (☎ 232-5096), 815 E St, is open weekdays from 8:30 am to 5 pm, and on Saturday from 8:30 am to noon. General delivery mail goes to the Midway postal station (zip code 92138, ☎ 221-3119), which is inconveniently located between downtown and Mission Bay at 2535 Midway Drive, just off Barnett.

Local calls cover only a small area. A pay phone may want a small handful of quarters for a few minutes' call across town – have a credit card ready when you can.

Bookstores
Every shopping mall has at least one bookshop. The ones combined with a coffeeshop can be extremely pleasant. UCSD has an excellent bookstore on campus, and a branch downtown in the American Plaza opposite the train station. Wahrenbrooks Book House (☎ 232-0132), 726 Broadway, is one of the most established downtown outlets, as is William Burgett (☎ 238-7323), at 800 Broadway.

There are a number of shops specializing in travel books. Le Travel Store (☎ 544-0005), 745 4th Ave in the Gaslamp, has an excellent range of maps, travel guides, equipment, and a very helpful staff. Traveler's Depot (☎ 483-1421), 1655 Garnet Ave, Pacific Beach, also has a good stock.

Newspapers & Magazines
The daily *San Diego Union-Tribune* is not a bad rag, but it is pretty much a local paper. For information on what's happening in town, and particularly on the active music, art, and theater scene, pick up a free *San Diego Reader* from just about any convenience store. It comes out every Thursday, but they can be all gone by the weekend.

A number of free publications have useful information and discount coupons between the advertisements. *San Diego This Week* actually comes out twice per month with good listings of events and coupons, and is widely available. *Guide to Downtown* is a similar magazine which emphasizes downtown eating and entertainment. The *Guest Quick Guide* is big on shopping and eating, but doesn't have coupons.

Medical Services
Urgent medical attention is available 24 hours a day at the Mercy Hospital (☎ 294-8111), 4077 5th Ave; and Mission Bay Hospital (☎ 274-7721), 3030 Bunker Hill St.

DOWNTOWN
San Diego's downtown is adjacent to the waterfront in the area first acquired, subdivided, and promoted by Alonzo Horton in 1867. In the 1960s, downtown succumbed to a combination of uninteresting office developments and creeping inner-urban dereliction.

Redevelopment has saved central San Diego, with Horton Plaza and the Gaslamp Quarter attracting people for shopping, dining, and entertainment. The downtown area as a whole is not compellingly attractive, but there is enough interest in a couple of key precincts to make a trip downtown worthwhile.

The main drag is Broadway, which goes east from the waterfront right through the middle of town. It's a functional street, with the Santa Fe train station and the trolley depot at one end, a few cheap hotels, the bus station, and a couple of top-end hotels. The new, large, ultra-modern Horton Plaza shopping mall and downtown magnet occupies a seven-block area south of Broadway, while the renovated Gaslamp Quarter extends for about eight blocks between 4th and 6th Ave from Broadway south to Harbor Drive and the Embarcadero. East of the Gaslamp, particularly along and around Market St, are the soup kitchens, homeless shelters, and the Salvation Army.

Horton Plaza
This is the centerpiece of San Diego's downtown redevelopment. Conceived and promoted by mall developer Ernie Hahn, this huge project involved the leveling of seven city blocks and the construction of a five-level complex with a multi-screen cinema, two theaters, 2300 parking spaces, restaurants, cafes, and 140 shops lining a crescent-shaped open courtyard. It was designed by Jon Jerde, using the 'festival-marketplace' concept of urban renewal, and completed in 1985 at a cost of over $145 million.

OK, it's another shopping mall, but like it or not, the architecture is innovative. From the outside it's a little uninviting, but

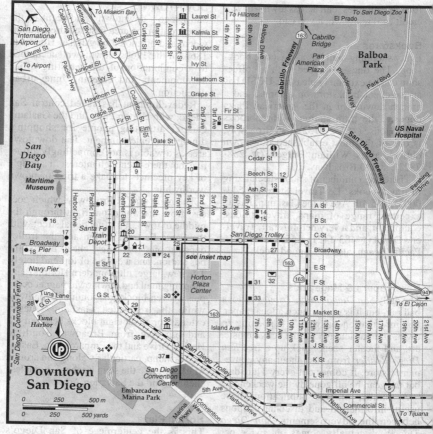

Downtown San Diego

inside, it has the toy-town arches and balconies typical of post-modernism. The 1907 Jessop Clock provides a touch of nostalgia, and the color scheme is anything but dull. The top-floor food court is not cheap but great for yuppie-watching and the city view. The curved spaces and changes in level can be disorienting, so you may see more and stay longer than you intended – in places it feels like you're walking through a MC Escher drawing.

The Horton Plaza Center (☎ 238-1596) is open weekdays from 10 am to 9 pm, Saturday 10 am to 6 pm, and Sunday 11 am to 6 pm though some shops and restaurants have extended hours. Parking is validated with purchase.

The Paladion

Another shopping center, The Paladion (☎ 232-1627) is not as big or as popular as nearby Horton Plaza, but is even newer and more upmarket. Inside it's super glossy, and has tenants like Tiffany, Gucci, Cartier, Nina Ricci, and Versace.

Gaslamp Quarter

When Horton first established New Town San Diego, 5th Ave was its main street and home to its main industries – saloons, gam-

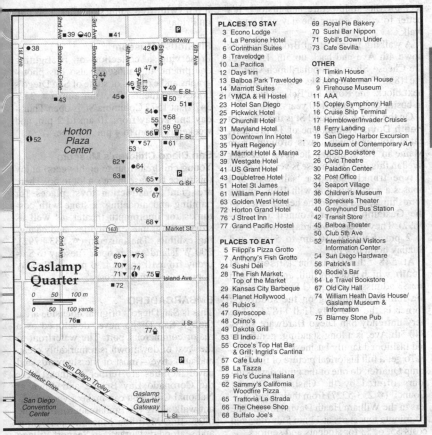

PLACES TO STAY
3 Econo Lodge
4 La Pensione Hotel
6 Corinthian Suites
8 Travelodge
10 La Pacifica
12 Days Inn
13 Balboa Park Travelodge
14 Marriott Suites
21 YMCA & HI Hostel
23 Hotel San Diego
25 Pickwick Hotel
27 Churchill Hotel
31 Maryland Hotel
33 Downtown Inn Hotel
35 Hyatt Regency
37 Marriot Hotel & Marina
39 Westgate Hotel
41 US Grant Hotel
43 Doubletree Hotel
51 Hotel St James
61 William Penn Hotel
63 Golden West Hotel
72 Horton Grand Hotel
76 J Street Inn
77 Grand Pacific Hostel

PLACES TO EAT
5 Filippi's Pizza Grotto
7 Anthony's Fish Grotto
24 Sushi Deli
28 The Fish Market;
     Top of the Market
29 Kansas City Barbeque
44 Planet Hollywood
46 Rubio's
47 Gyroscope
48 Chino's
49 Dakota Grill
53 El Indio
55 Croce's Top Hat Bar
     & Grill; Ingrid's Cantina
57 Cafe Lulu
58 La Tazza
59 Fio's Cucina Italiana
62 Sammy's California
     Woodfire Pizza
65 Trattoria La Strada
66 The Cheese Shop
68 Buffalo Joe's

69 Royal Pie Bakery
70 Sushi Bar Nippon
71 Sybil's Down Under
73 Cafe Sevilla

OTHER
1 Timkin House
2 Long-Waterman House
9 Firehouse Museum
11 AAA
15 Copley Symphony Hall
16 Cruise Ship Terminal
17 Hornblower/Invader Cruises
18 Ferry Landing
19 San Diego Harbor Excursion
20 Museum of Contemporary Art
22 UCSD Bookstore
26 Civic Theatre
30 Paladion Center
32 Post Office
34 Seaport Village
36 Children's Museum
38 Spreckels Theater
40 Greyhound Bus Station
42 Transit Store
45 Balboa Theater
50 Club 5th Ave
52 International Visitors
     Information Center
54 San Diego Hardware
55 Patrick's II
60 Bodie's Bar
64 Le Travel Bookstore
67 Old City Hall
74 William Heath Davis House/
     Gaslamp Museum &
     Information
75 Blarney Stone Pub

bling joints, bordellos, and opium dens. While more respectable businesses grew up along Broadway, the 5th Ave area became known as the Stingaree, a notorious red-light district. By the 1960s it had declined to a skid row of flop houses and bars, but its seedy atmosphere had made it so unattractive to investors that many of its older buildings survived by default. When developers started thinking about demolition and rebuilding, local protests and the Gaslamp Quarter Council saved the area.

Wrought iron streetlamps, in the style of 19th-century gaslamps, have been installed, along with trees and brick side-walks. Restored buildings dating from the 1870s to the 1920s now house restaurants, bars, galleries, and theaters. The 16-block area south of Broadway between 4th and 6th Aves is designated a National Historic District, and development is strictly controlled. There's still a bit of sleaze though, with a few porno shops and some very downmarket hotels, but they give some character to the area, which might otherwise be gentrified to the point of artificiality. The most enjoyable time to visit is on a warm evening when people throng the streets and crowd the outdoor tables (see Places to Eat and Entertainment). To get a feel for the architecture and history, it's better to come during the day and take a walk.

A walking tour starts at Broadway, goes down 4th Ave and back up 5th. Look for the Cheese Shop, a popular lunch spot, in the 1890 Carriage Works building; in the next block, the Royal Pie Bakery has been in business for about 110 years.

On the corner of Island St is the **William Heath Davis House**, one of 14 prefabricated houses which Davis brought from Maine in 1850, though he never actually lived in this one. The house is very plain, of a type frankly called a 'salt-box,' and houses a small museum with 19th-century furnishings, and is also the headquarters of the Gaslamp Quarter Council (☎ 233-4692). They're open weekdays from 10 am to 2 pm, Saturday 10 am to 5 pm, and Sunday noon to 4 pm.

At 548 5th Ave is the **Museum of Death**, which is deadly dull, and not worth the $3 admission. At the G St intersection, the Italianate building on the southwest corner is the Old City Hall (1874). The very untrendy San Diego Hardware store, 840 5th Ave, is a long-standing, genuinely old fashioned family business.

To get a full historical picture of the Gaslamp Quarter, do one of the guided walking tours offered by the Gaslamp Quarter Council (☎ 233-5227) from their headquarters in the William Heath Davis House. The 90-minute tour starts at 11 am Saturday and costs $5, or $3 for students and seniors.

Museum of Contemporary Art

Opposite the train station at 1001 Kettner Blvd, this MCA (☎ 234-1001) is the downtown branch of the La Jolla-based institution which has shown innovative artwork to San Diegans since the '60s. Indeed, it's the only branch of MCA until the rebuilding of the La Jolla complex is complete in early 1996. The ever-changing exhibits of painting and sculpture are publicized widely (see the *Reader*, or call the gallery). The museum is open Tuesday to Sunday from 10:30 am to 5:30 pm (admission $3; $2 for students and seniors), and it's open until

8 pm (with free admission after 5:30 pm) on Friday.

Firehouse Museum

Preserving a collection of firefighting equipment, this museum also has photographs and exhibits of some of San Diego's hottest moments. The museum (☎ 232-3473), at 1572 Columbia St, is open Thursday and Friday from 10 am to 2 pm, and weekends 10 am to 4 pm; it's free.

San Diego Children's Museum

Young children (four to eight years) enjoy this place because there's a lot to do. There are giant construction toys, places for painting and modeling, a stage with costumes for impromptu theater, as well as story telling, music, activities, and changing exhibits. The museum (☎ 233-8792), 200 W Island Ave, is open Tuesday to Saturday from 10 am to 4:30 pm, on Sunday noon to 4:30pm, and costs $4.

EMBARCADERO

This is San Diego's original dockside area, though San Diego never developed as a major commercial port. The waterfront to the west of downtown is remarkably clean and attractive – most of the shipyards and naval facilities are further southeast near the Coronado Bay Bridge and down at National City. You can make a very pleasant walk along the Embarcadero, from the interesting Maritime Museum, past ships and seafood restaurants, to Seaport Village and the San Diego Convention Center.

Maritime Museum

The Maritime Museum (☎ 234-9153) consists of three restored vessels moored at 1306 N Harbor Drive, just north of the Ash St corner. It's not hard to find the museum as the masts of the square-rigged *Star of India*, over 100 feet high, make a good landmark. Built on the Isle of Man and launched in 1863, it plied the England-India trade route, carried immigrants to New Zealand, became a trading ship based in Hawaii, then worked the Alaskan salmon fisheries. It's a handsome ship, but don't expect anything romantic or glamorous on board; this is an old workhorse, not the Love Boat. Also moored here are the *Berkeley* and the *Medea*.

The museum is open daily from 9 am to 8 pm, and the $6 ticket gives admission to all three vessels; it's $4 for seniors and older children, $2 for kids under 13, and a family ticket is $12.

Seaport Village

Neither a port nor a village, this collection of novelty shops, restaurants, and snack outlets has an unconvincing maritime theme with nostalgically re-created turn-of-the-century seafront architecture. It's touristy and twee, but not a bad place to look for souvenirs. Seaport Village (☎ 235-4014) opens daily from 10 am to 9 pm (to 10 pm in summer), and there are two hours free validated parking.

San Diego Convention Center

A very successful attempt to boost the city as a site for major conventions, this unusual-looking complex opened in 1989 and is booked solid until about 2007. The design, by Arthur Erickson, is said to be inspired by an oceanliner and features large cylindrical windows (ocean waves?) and a roof space sheltered by white Teflon 'sails.' The convention center (☎ 525-5000) sometimes offers tours.

Look around the masts in the nearby Marriott's marina for the **Embarcadero Marina Park**, where there's a public fishing pier and an open-air amphitheater which has free concerts on summer evenings.

BALBOA PARK

Maps of Alonzo Horton's 'additions' to San Diego, from 1868, show a 1400-acre 'City Park,' at the northeast corner of what was to become the downtown area. The decision to provide for such a large park is usually attributed to 'far-sighted civic leaders,' but it was probably also consistent with the short-term interests of the shrewd Mr Horton. By restricting the areas available for future development, the value of

the land in his subdivision would be enhanced. Though the expansive park looked good on the map, it was just empty, barren land. By 1890 the city had over 35,000 people, but the park was still bare hilltops, chaparral, and steep-sided *arroyos* (gullies).

By the turn of the century, the Balboa Park had became a well-loved part of San

---

The Legacy of Kate Sessions

Kate O Sessions graduated in botany from the University of California at Berkeley in 1881, a time when few women attended university, and even fewer studied the natural sciences. She came to San Diego as a school teacher, but soon began working as a horticulturist, establishing gardens for the fashionable homes of the city's emerging elite. In 1892, in need of space for a nursery, she proposed an unusual deal to the city officials – she would have the use of 30 acres of city-owned Balboa Park for her nursery in return for planting 100 trees a year, and donating 300 others for use throughout the city. The city agreed to the arrangement, and Kate Sessions more than fulfilled her side of the bargain – within 10 years Balboa Park had shady trees, lawns, paths, and flower beds. Over 35 years she planted some 10,000 trees and shrubs, and became known as 'The Mother of Balboa Park.'

In 1910 she moved her nursery to the newly developing suburb of Mission Hills, where she persuaded developers to leave some of the canyons in their natural state and to lay out some streets following the contours of the land rather than imposing an orderly, rectangular grid. She later moved to Pacific Beach, where she is commemorated by the Kate Sessions Park. She was an active horticulturist up to the 1930s, working on gardens from Coronado to La Jolla. Her work surrounds the houses of some of San Diego's best-known architects, and the trademarks of her style, like shady arbors hung with Bougainvillea and informal plantings softening steep hillsides, define much of what is lovely in San Diego landscaping. ■

Diego, and a contest was held to find a suitable name. The winning entry honored Vasco Nuñez de Balboa, a Spanish conquistador and the first European to sight the Pacific Ocean.

The 1915-16 Panama-California Exposition developed the Spanish Colonial theme even further. Irving Gill's modern, minimalist architecture was rejected in favor of the Beaux Art style and Baroque decoration of New Yorkers Bertram Goodhue and Carlton Winslow. The exposition buildings were meant to be temporary, and constructed largely of wood, chicken-wire, and plaster, but they were so popular that many were retained. As the originals deteriorated, they were replaced with durable concrete structures. These buildings now house the museums along El Prado.

The Pacific-California Exposition was staged in Balboa Park in 1935, with new buildings erected southwest of El Prado around the Pan-American Plaza. Architecturally, the Spanish Colonial theme was extended to cover the whole New World, from indigenous styles (some of the buildings had pueblo Indian, and even Mayan influences) through to the 20th century. Most of these have been preserved too, and also house museums, theaters, and other exhibits.

The San Diego Zoo occupies 200 acres in the north of the park, and the eastern third is occupied by the sports facilities of Morley Field, with tennis courts, a swimming pool, velodrome, 9- and 18-hole golf courses, and even a Frisbee golf course. About a quarter of the original 1400 acres has been given over to the Cabrillo freeway, the US Naval Hospital, and other non-park uses, but Balboa Park retains extensive and beautiful green areas, and a large assortment of things to see and do.

Orientation & Information

If you just want to enjoy the gardens and the atmosphere, you can visit Balboa Park any time and just stroll around, but be a little cautious after dark.

To visit all the museums and attractions would take days, so it's a good idea to plan your visit. Start at the Balboa Park Information Center (☎ 239-0512), open daily from 9:30 am to 4 pm in the House of Hospitality on El Prado. They have a very helpful staff, lots of information, and a park map, and they sell the Balboa Passport, which costs $18 and is good for a single entry into nine of the park's museums for one week. If you only want to see a couple of the museums, and especially if you can visit on a Tuesday when one or more of the museums offer free entry, the passport is not such a good deal. Call the information center to find out which is the freebie museum of the week. Most of the museums are open from about 10 am to 4:30 pm, but many are closed on Monday and/or Tuesday.

Balboa Park is easily reached from downtown on a No 7, 7A, or 7B bus along Park Blvd. By car, Park Blvd provides easy access to parking areas (free) near most of the exhibits, but the most attractive approach is from the west, over the Cabrillo Bridge. Coming from the west, El Prado is the extension of Laurel St, and crosses Cabrillo Bridge with the Cabrillo Freeway 120 feet below. Make a point of driving this stretch of freeway (State Hwy 163) – the steep roadsides are hanging with greenery like a rainforest gorge.

The free Balboa Park Tram stops at various points on a continuous loop through the main areas of the park. (It's actually a bus rather than a tram, and is not to be confused with the Old Town Trolley tour bus.) Mostly, however, it's more enjoyable to walk between the attractions.

The description below starts with the attractions on El Prado, then those down the Pan-American Plaza, followed by some more scattered features, then the San Diego Zoo, which is worth a special trip.

California Building & Museum of Man

El Prado passes under an archway and into a quadrangle with the Museum of Man on its north side. Figures on either side of the arch represent the Atlantic and Pacific Oceans, while the decoration of the arch itself symbolizes the Panama Canal linking the two. This was the main entrance for the 1915 exposition, and the building was one of Goodhue's most ornate neo-Spanish Colonial creations, said to be inspired by the Churrigueresque church of Tepotzotlán, near Mexico City. Its single **Tower of California**, richly decorated with blue and yellow tiles, is an architectural landmark of San Diego.

Originally, the building displayed over 5000 ethnographic artifacts, including some which were specially made for the exposition – the cast concrete reproductions of Mayan carvings are still on display. The museum now specializes in Indian artifacts from the American Southwest, and has an excellent display of baskets and pottery from the San Diego area. Ask about temporary exhibits. The museum store sells good handicrafts from Central America and elsewhere. The Museum of Man (☎ 239-2001) is open Tuesday to Sunday from 10 am to 4:30 pm, and costs $4 for adults, $2 for children. It's free on the third Tuesday of each month.

Simon Edison Centre for the Performing Arts

This complex includes three theaters. Best known is **The Old Globe**, where visitors to the 1935-36 exposition enjoyed condensed, 40-minute renditions of Shakespeare's greatest hits. Saved from demolition in 1937, the theater became home to a popular summer series of Shakespeare plays, performed in full. In 1978 the whole complex was destroyed by an arsonist, but was rebuilt in the style of the Old Globe in England. It reopened in 1982, winning a Tony award in 1984 for its ongoing contribution to theater arts. The Old Globe, plus the **Cassius Carter Stage** and the outdoor **Lowell Davies Festival Theater**, are at the heart of San Diego's thriving live-theater scene. There are performances most evenings and matinees on weekends (☎ 239-2255 for details and bookings). Guided tours run on some weekends (☎ 231-1941 for tour information).

Plaza de Panama

This space, in the middle of El Prado, was the focus of the Panama-California Exposition. The equestrian statue on the south side is of **El Cid**, who led the Spanish revolt against the Moors in the 11th century. On the plaza's southwest corner, the **House of Charm** was the Indian Arts building for the exposition, but got its present name as a souvenir market for the 1935 effort. It is being rebuilt to its original form, and will house the Mingei Museum of Folk Art. (The Mingei is currently in the University Towne Centre, in La Jolla.)

San Diego Museum of Art

This 1924 building was designed by William Templeton Johnson in the Spanish *plateresque* style, so named because the heavy ornamentation resembles decorated silverwork. The facade is particularly ornate, with sculptures of Spanish artists (most of whom are represented inside the museum). The collection has a number of fine European paintings, though it has no really famous works. Some of the American landscape paintings are worth seeing, and there are some very interesting pieces in the Asian galleries. The **Sculpture Garden** is behind the cafe to the west of the main museum building. The museum (☎ 232-7931) is closed on Mondays, but free on the third Tuesday of each month. Admission is $5/2.

Timkin Museum of Art

Distinctive for *not* being in imitation Spanish style, this 1965 building houses the Putnam collection. The small but impressive collection includes works by Rembrandt, Rubens, El Greco, Cézanne, and Pisarro. There's also a wonderful selection of Russian icons, which will appeal even to those who are not fans of this art-form. Don't miss the Timkin (☎ 239-5548), which is free, but closed on Mondays and during September.

Botanical Building

This building looks just lovely from El Prado, reflected in the expansive lily pond.

Its central dome and two wings are covered with redwood lathes which let filtered sunlight into the collection of tropical plants, and ferns. Unfortunately, the interior planting can be pretty uninspired, but it's free and they change it every season, so have a look in anyway. It's open Tuesday to Sunday.

Casa del Prado
This is one of the handsomest buildings along El Prado, but there is little to draw the visitor inside. It was built as a temporary structure for the 1915 exposition and an earthquake in 1968 caused so much damage that the building was condemned. It was rebuilt with the support of community arts groups who now use it for theater and dance.

Casa de Balboa
The House of Commerce & Industry for the 1915 exposition was designed by Goodhue in the imitation Spanish Colonial style, and later used for a variety of purposes, until it burned down in 1978. The original building was faithfully reconstructed, including concrete decorations cast from pieces of the original. It now houses four museums, each with its own museum shop, and a small cafe. Admission to each museum is $3.

The **Museum of San Diego History** (☎ 232-6203) covers mainly the American period, from about 1848. It's open Wednesday to Sunday.

The **San Diego Hall of Champions Sports Museum** (☎ 234-2544) has numbing exhibits on San Diego sports people (baseballer Ted Wiliams and Olympic diver Greg Louganis are the best known). It's open daily.

The **San Diego Model Railroad Museum** has working models of actual railroads in Southern California. It's open Wednesday to Friday from 11 am to 4 pm, and on Saturday 11 am to 5 pm. It's free for children under 15.

The **Museum of Photographic Arts** (MoPA ☎ 239-5262) is not mere photography, so the works of art here may not appeal to everyone. Nevertheless, some of the exhibitions are very good, so it's worth finding out what's on. MoPA is open until 5 pm daily, and until 9 pm on Thursday.

Reuben H Fleet Space Theater & Science Center
One of Balboa Park's most publicized venues, this one features a hands-on science museum, and a huge-screen Omnimax theater. The hemispherical, wrap-around screen, and 152-speaker sound system create an interesting sensation, at least for a few minutes. The shows run for nearly an hour. The hands-on science display was also very innovative when this center opened in 1973, but it has been done often and better since. The theater (☎ 232-6866) has shows daily from 9:30 am to 9:30 pm, and entry costs $6/3. The Science Center (☎ 238-1233) can be included in the theater price for $7.50, or can be visited by itself for $2.50, or free on the first Tuesday of the month.

Natural History Museum
This 1933 William Templeton Johnson building houses lots of rocks, fossils, and stuffed animals, with an impressive dinosaur skeleton. It's at the east end of El Prado, and open every day. Admission is $6/2, and free on the first Tuesday of the month. The museum (☎ 232-3821) also arranges field trips and nature hikes in Balboa Park and further afield.

Spanish Village Area
Behind the Natural History Museum is a grassy square with a magnificent Moreton Bay Fig tree (sorry, no climbing). Opposite is a group of small tiled cottages, said to be 'an authentic reproduction of an ancient village in Spain,' which are rented out as artists' studios. You can watch potters, jewelers, painters, and sculptors churn out pricey decorative kitsch, and maybe a few pieces of taste and value. Most are open daily from 11 am to 4 pm. North of the Spanish Village is a 1924 **Carousel** and a **Miniature Railroad**; both operate on

weekends and holidays from 11 am to 5 pm, and charge $1 per ride.

Spreckels Organ Pavilion

Going south from Plaza de Panama, you can't miss the circle of seating and the curved colonnade in front of this organ, said to be the largest outdoor musical instrument in the world. Free concerts are held every Sunday at 2 pm, and during July and August on Mondays at 8 pm.

Pan-American Plaza

This plaza is now just a large parking lot southwest of the Spreckels Organ. As you approach it, the **United Nations Building**, is on your right. Nearby, the **House of Pacific Relations** (☎ 234-0739) is actually 15 cottages from the 1915 exposition; inside they feature furnishings and displays from many countries. They're open free of charge on Sunday afternoons.

Also of interest are the Palisades Building with the **Marie Hitchcock Puppet Theater** (☎ 466-7128); the **San Diego Automotive Museum** (☎ 231-2886), which has a varied collection of over 60 cars and motorbikes, perfectly restored and well displayed, with helpful and highlights like the 1933 Duesenberg Roadster, or the 1956 Gull Wing Mercedes; the **Aerospace Museum** (☎ 234-8291), with a very extensive display of aircraft – originals, replicas, and models (Don't miss the planes out front, or the courtyard, where a Phantom jet pursues an Russian MiG-17 between Art Deco standard lamps.) and the **Starlight Bowl**, where the Starlight Opera (☎ 544-7800) presents a summer season of musicals and light opera.

Centro Cultural de la Raza

This center for exhibitions of Mexican and Native American art is way out on the fringe of the main museum precinct (easiest access is from Park Blvd). The round, steel building is actually a converted water tank. Inside, the temporary exhibits of contemporary indigenous artwork can be very powerful. The Centro Cultural de la Raza

(☎ 235-6135) is open Wednesday to Sunday from noon to 5 pm, and it's free.

Marston House

In the far northwest corner of Balboa Park is the former home of George Marston, philanthropist and founder of the San Diego Historical Society. The house was designed in 1904 by noted San Diego architects William Hebbard and Irving Gill, and is a fine example of the American Arts & Crafts style. The society is currently restoring the interior as a showplace for Arts & Crafts furnishings and decorative objects. The Marston House (☎ 232-6203) is at 3525 7th Ave. The Historical Society conducts tours of the house ($3) and the gardens ($1 extra) on weekends from noon to 4 pm.

Gardens of Balboa Park

Balboa Park includes a number of quite distinct garden areas, reflecting different horticultural styles and different environments. One way to learn more about the gardens is to take one of the free, weekly Offshoot Tours, conducted by park horticulturists from mid-January to Thanksgiving. The Park & Recreation Department (☎ 235-1114) has more information, but reservations are not required – just be at the front of the Botanical Building by 10 am.

If you're exploring on your own, visit the **Alcazar Garden**, a formal, Spanish-style garden; **Palm Canyon**, which has over 50 species of palm; the **Japanese Friendship Garden** open on Friday, Saturday, and Sunday for $2, and on Tuesday, for free; the **Australian Garden**; the **Rose Garden & Desert Garden**, which is best in spring; **Florida Canyon** which gives an idea of the San Diego landscape before European settlement. The Natural History Museum (☎ 232-3821) conducts guided walks in the canyon.

San Diego Zoo

The zoo is one of San Diego's biggest attractions, and anyone remotely interested in the natural world should allow a full day to see it. Over 3000 animals, representing more than 800 species, are exhibited in a beautifully landscaped setting, typically in enclosures which reproduce their natural environment.

History The origins of the San Diego Zoo go back to the 1915 California-Panama Exposition, and the enthusiasm of one local man, Dr Harry Wegeforth. The exposition featured an assortment of animals in cages along Park Blvd. It's now San Diego folklore that Wegeforth, hearing the roar of one of the caged lions, exclaimed 'Wouldn't it be wonderful to have a zoo in San Diego – I believe I'll build one.' He started his campaign in 1916 in the newspaper, and soon formed the Zoological Society of San Diego. Dr Wegeforth then ensured that quarantine requirements made it almost impossible to remove exotic animals from the county, so the society was able to acquire much of the menagerie left over from the exposition.

As a private organization, the Zoological Society could not be given a site on public land, but in 1921 a nice compromise was reached. The society donated all the animals and facilities to the city, and the city provided 200 acres of Balboa Park to use as a zoo, which would be then be administered by the society. Though the site was bisected by canyons and largely barren, these problems were turned to advantage: canyons provided a means of separating different groups of animals to prevent the spread of disease, and they were individually landscaped to simulate appropriate natural settings.

Wegeforth also had a talent for extracting money from wealthy benefactors – John Spreckels, the millionaire sugar king, warned that the surgeon would 'cut you off at the pockets.' One of the first big donations was from Ellen Browning Scripps, who paid for a perimeter fence, which was to enforce the payment of admission fees as much as to keep the animals in.

Local support for the zoo resulted in unorthodox means of adding to its collection. Local people brought in various finds, like seals and snakes, which were never refused – rattlesnakes caught in Balboa Park were often traded profitably for animals from other zoos. In another exchange deal, the zoo provided fleas for a New York flea circus. The US Navy unofficially contributed an assortment of animals which had been adopted as mascots but could no longer be kept on ships. US Marines landing in Nicaragua were offered prizes if they captured beasties for Dr Wegeforth. During the 1930s Wegeforth himself traveled the world, collecting jaguars from Venezuela, orangutan from Borneo, and marsupials from Australia. On a trip to India, Wegeforth contracted pneumonia and malaria, and he died in 1941 – his final contributions to the zoo were three elephants which arrived two months after his death.

By the end of WWII, the San Diego Zoo had world-wide reputation, and it helped to rebuild the collections of European zoos which had been devastated by the war. The Zoological Society continued at the forefront of zoo management with the introduction of 'bioclimatic' habitats, allowing a number of different types of animals to share a simulated natural environment. In the 1960s the society started work on the 1800-acre Wild Animal Park, 32 miles north of the city (see Escondido), which provides free-range areas for many larger animals.

Information The zoo (☎ 234-3153) is in the northern part of Balboa Park and has a large free parking lot off Park Blvd. Bus No 7 will get you there from downtown. From late June to early September, entrance gates are open Monday to Wednesday from 9 am to 5 pm; Thursday to Sunday from 9 am to 9 pm. For the rest of the year, the gates are open from 9 am to 4 pm. The information booth is just to the left of the entrance as you come in – if you want to leave the zoo and return, they'll stamp your hand.

The regular daily admission price is $13/6. The 'deluxe admission package' costs $15/6.50, and includes a 40-minute guided bus tour ($3/2.50). On summer evenings, when the museum's open late, an evening admission, after 5 pm, costs

$6.75/2.75. Discount coupons for the zoo are widely available. A combined ticket to visit both the zoo and the Wild Animal Park, within a five-day period, costs $24/12.95.

It's wise to arrive early as many of the animals are most active in the morning. You might start with a tour in a double-decker bus, which gives a good overview of the zoo, and includes an informative commentary. Animal shows are held in the two amphitheaters (no extra charge), and they're usually entertaining, especially for kids who might need a rest anyway. The Skyfari cable car goes right across the park, and can save you some walking time, though you might have to wait in line to get on it.

Facilities are provided for disabled visitors – call the zoo (☎ 231-1515 ext 4526) for specific information.

Highlights The zoo and the Wild Animal Park share an active program of breeding endangered species in captivity, for re-introduction into their natural habitats. It has done this with species including Arabian oryx, Bali starling, and California condor. The zoo has also been recognized for its gardens. Some plants are now used for the specialized food requirements of particular animals. More recently, the zoo has developed its entertainment and educational role, with the opening of the children's zoo exhibit and outdoor theaters for animal shows. Most visitors will have their own favorites, but the koalas are so popular

The world's largest living lizard, the Komodo dragon is a favorite at the zoo.

that Australians may be surprised to find them a sort of unofficial symbol of San Diego. The Komodo dragon not only looks fearsome, but strides around the reptile house in a very menacing manner. In the same area is the children's zoo, where kids can pet small animals. The nearby animal nursery lets you look at the zoo's newest arrivals.

Tiger River is one of the newer bioclimatic exhibits, with a realistic, recreated Asian rainforest environment. Gorilla Tropics is an African rainforest. A third bioclimatic environment is the Sun Bear Forest, where these Asian bears are famously playful.

The large Scripps Aviary and Rainforest Aviary are both impressive structures where carefully placed feeders allow some very close-up viewing. Finally, don't miss the African Rock Kopje (outcrop), where klipspringers display their rock climbing abilities.

PRESIDIO HILL

In 1769 the first Spanish settlement in California was established on the Presidio hill, overlooking the valley of the San Diego River. Nothing remains of the original Presidio structures, but there are archaeological digs under way to unearth the past. A large cross, constructed with tiles from the original mission, commemorates Padre Serra.

American forces occupied the hill in 1846, during the Mexican-American War, and named it Fort Stockton. A flagpole, cannon, some plaques, and earth walls now comprise the **Fort Stockton Memorial**. The nearby **El Charro Statue** depicts a Mexican cowboy on horseback, and was a bicentennial gift to the city from Mexico.

It would be easy to believe that the **Junípero Serra Museum** is a well preserved Spanish Colonial structure, but in fact it was designed by William Templeton Johnson in 1929. The museum has a small but interesting collection of artifacts and pictures from the Mission and rancho periods, and gives a good feel for the earliest days of European settlement. The museum

(☎ 297-3258) is open Tuesday to Saturday from 10 am to 4:30 pm, and on Sunday noon to 4:30 pm. It costs $3 for adults, and is free for children under 12.

MISSION VALLEY
Though intermittent, the San Diego River was the most reliable source of fresh water for the crops and the livestock of the early missions. The river valley, now called Mission Valley, was frequently flooded until dams were completed upstream. In the 1950s and '60s there was disagreement over its development, but I-8 now runs the

---

Conversion, Lust & Revenge
The first missionaries visited the nearby Indian settlements with gifts and promises, and their first converts, whom they called *neophytes*, were encouraged to move into the mission compound where they lived and worked and contracted European diseases. The Spanish soldiers in the Presidio garrison abused the mission neophytes, and also raided Indian villages. According to Padre Serra's reports, soldiers would chase them on horseback, and 'catch an Indian woman with their lassos, to become prey for their unbridled lusts.' So, in 1774 the priests left the Presidio and started their new mission near a large Kumayaay village, well away from the bad influence of the military.

Unfortunately, they were also away from the protection of the military, and in November 1775 the increasingly resentful Kumayaay made a concerted attack on the mission and burned it to the ground. One of the priests, Luis Jayme, appealed to the attackers with arms outstretched crying 'Love God my children!' He was dragged away and beaten to death, becoming California's first martyr. The survivors retreated to the Presidio, and the Spanish authorities captured, flogged, and executed the leaders of the attack. After a few months, the missionaries returned to their site in the valley, and built a second mission, with a tiled roof to resist the flaming arrows of Indian attack – this became a standard feature of mission architecture. ■

---

length of the valley, interspersed with hotels and shopping centers. Some green open space remains, but much of it is golf courses and country clubs. The restored mission is definitely worth a visit for its historic value, but Mission Valley's most spectacular feature now is the multi-level interchange where I-8 crosses I-805.

Mission San Diego de Alcalá
Though the first California mission was established on the Presidio hill, Padre Junípero Serra decided in 1773 to move it a few miles upriver. The new site offered a better water supply and more arable land, but that was not the main reason for the move.

In 1784 they built a solid adobe and timber church which was destroyed by an earthquake in 1803. The church was promptly rebuilt, and at least some of it still stands on the slope overlooking Mission Valley. With the abolition of the mission system, the buildings were turned over to the Mexican government and fell into disrepair. By some accounts, they were reduced to a facade and a few crumbling walls by the 1920s.

Extensive restoration began in 1931, with financial support from local citizens and the Hearst Foundation. The pretty white church and the buildings you see now are probably about 95% restoration.

The visitors center (☎ 281-8449) has friendly and informative staff, some quite good books, and some very tacky souvenirs. The mission is open daily from 9 am to 5 pm, and costs $1 for adults. It's south of Friars Rd, just east of I-15.

OLD TOWN
The land beneath the Presidio hill was first cultivated by soldiers from the garrison, and was the place of the first civilian Spanish settlement in California. A plaza was laid out in the 1820s, and within 10 years it was surrounded by about 40 dark huts and a few larger, white-washed houses which comprised the Mexican Pueblo de San Diego. These half-dozen blocks were also the center of American San Diego until

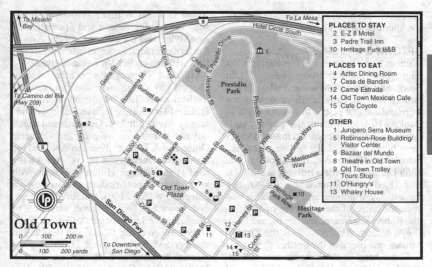

PLACES TO STAY
2 E-Z 8 Motel
3 Padre Trail Inn
10 Heritage Park B&B

PLACES TO EAT
4 Aztec Dining Room
7 Casa de Bandini
12 Carne Estrada
14 Old Town Mexican Cafe
15 Cafe Coyote

OTHER
1 Junipero Serra Museum
5 Robinson-Rose Building/ Visitor Center
6 Bazaar del Mundo
8 Theatre in Old Town
9 Old Town Trolley Tours Stop
11 O'Hungry's
13 Whaley House

Old Town

0   100   200 m
0   100   200 yards

after the fire of 1872, when the city's focus moved to the new Horton subdivision.

In 1968, Old Town became a State Historic Park, archaeological work was done, and the few surviving original buildings were restored. Other structures were rebuilt, and the area is now a touristy pedestrian precinct (there are parking lots around the edges). With the shady trees and the open plaza it's a pleasant place to spend an afternoon or an evening, but don't take it too seriously as a historical site. Bus Nos 3 or 5 from downtown will get you there, as will one of the Old Town Trolley tours.

The Old Town State Historic Park visitors center (☎ 237-6770) is in the Robinson-Rose building at the northwest end of the plaza, and is open daily from 10 am to 5 pm. They have some interesting information and books for sale, and the staff is very informative. If you're particularly interested in the historical background, pick up a copy of the *Old Town San Diego State Historic Park Tour Guide & Brief History*, or take one of the guided tours which leave the visitors center daily at 2 pm. The shops and especially the restaurants stay open late.

Along San Diego Ave, on the south side of the plaza, is a row of small, old-looking buildings, some of which house souvenir and gift shops. At 2482 San Diego Ave, two blocks from the Old Town precinct, the **Whaley House** has pretty plain architecture, but it is the original 1856 home of Thomas Whaley who moved to San Diego in 1851 and prospered as a merchant. There is an excellent collection of period furniture and clothing on display. The house is supposed to be haunted. The home (☎ 298-2482) opens Wednesday to Sunday from 10 am to 4:30 pm, and entry costs $3.

Just north of Old Town, the **Casa de Carrillo** dates from about 1820 and is the oldest house in San Diego. It is now the pro shop for the public Presidio Hills Golf Course (☎ 295-9476).

One of the worst examples of ersatz historical re-creation is **Heritage Park**, a clutch of Victorian houses, reconstructed on the northeast edge of Old Town. The houses, from various suburbs, were slated for demolition in the city's postwar development boom, but instead were transported to this site. Heavily restored, the buildings now house the likes of Ye Olde Doll Shoppe, a B&B, and a bridal boutique. Some information is available from the office (☎ 565-3600) on the ground floor of the Sherman-Gilbert house.

UPTOWN & HILLCREST

Without being too precise, Uptown is a triangle north of downtown, east of Old Town, and south of Mission Valley. In the late 1800s, the hills north of downtown were fashionable places to live – known as Bankers Hill, for some of the wealthy residents, or Pill Hill, because many doctors lived here. A few of the ornate, Victorian mansions still survive, most notably the 1889 **Long-Waterman house,** at 2408 1st Ave. Easily recognized by its towers, gables, bay windows, and veranda, it was once the home of the governor of California, Robert Waterman, and the focus of San Diego society. Also notable is the **Timkin house,** one block to the north.

At the heart of the Uptown area is **Hillcrest,** which was the first suburban real estate development in San Diego, linked to downtown by a trolley line up Bankers Hill, and close to the growing greenery of Balboa Park. Driving around, you'll see the work of many of San Diego's best known architects from the early 1900s, including

Irving Gill and William Templeton Johnson. The Mediterranean and Spanish Mission styles, and the influence of the Arts & Crafts movement, make an interesting contrast with the earlier Victorian houses.

Hillcrest is now the center of San Diego's gay community, and is one of its liveliest areas. To look around, start at the Hillcrest Gateway, which arches over University Ave at 5th Ave. Go north and check out the retro '50s style of the Corvette Diner, Bar & Grill, at 3946 5th Ave, and the fashionable menswear shops. Across the road is the Village Hillcrest Center, with very colorful postmodern architecture, a cineplex (☎ 299-2100), restaurants, shops, and News Etc (with a great selection of magazines and newspapers). Going east on University Ave, the 1928 Kahn Building at number 535 is an original Hillcrest commercial building with decorations bordering on kitsch. Going south on 5th Ave, there's a variety of bookstores with a good selection of non-mainstream publications, the Guild theater (☎ 295-2000), which shows alternative movies and old classics, and Off-the-Record, with an eclectic mix of music.

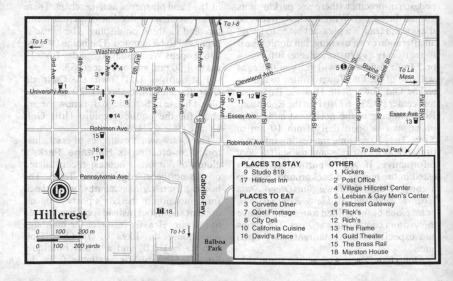

PLACES TO STAY
9 Studio 819
17 Hillcrest Inn

PLACES TO EAT
3 Corvette Diner
7 Quel Fromage
8 City Deli
10 California Cuisine
16 David's Place

OTHER
1 Kickers
2 Post Office
4 Village Hillcrest Center
5 Lesbian & Gay Men's Center
6 Hillcrest Gateway
11 Flick's
12 Rich's
13 The Flame
14 Guild Theater
15 The Brass Rail
18 Marston House

POINT LOMA

Point Loma is the peninsula which seems to hang down across the entrance to San Diego Bay, protecting it from the Pacific Ocean. At Cabrillo National Monument, on the southern tip, there are stunning panoramas over San Diego Bay and out to sea, and excellent exhibits on Point Loma's history and natural environment. It's one of the best places to visit in San Diego.

San Diego's first fishing boats were based on Point Loma, and the 19th-century whalers dragged carcasses onto its shores to extract the whale oil.

Given the strategic location, it's not surprising that the US military occupies much of Point Loma's land, though the biggest site is actually Fort Rosecrans National Cemetery, established in 1899. The Marine Corps Recruit Depot Command Museum (☎ 524-4426) covers marines engagements from Mexico to the Gulf War. It's off Pacific Hwy at Barnett Ave – look for the signs, and enter at Gate 4.

The wider, central part of Point Loma is a residential area, with some very swanky houses overlooking the best views.

The tidal flats of Loma Portal, where Point Loma joins the mainland, were used as an airstrip in 1927 by Charles Lindbergh, for flight testing the *Spirit of St Louis*. The following year a functioning airport was established – it was named Lindbergh Field and, with considerable expansion, it is now San Diego International Airport.

Cabrillo National Monument

This monument commemorates Portuguese explorer Juan Rodríguez Cabrillo, who led the first Spanish exploration of the West Coast. It is reached via Catalina Blvd, and there's an entrance fee payable at the gate – $4 per car; $2 if you're on a bike or a bus (No 6A from downtown). The monument is open from 9 am to 5:15 pm daily. The visitors center (☎ 557-5450) has an excellent presentation on Cabrillo's exploration, and very good exhibits on the native inhabitants and natural history of the area. The nearby lookout area has an imposing statue of Cabrillo, and a great view over Coronado Island, the bay and the city. For whale watching see Activities.

A short and scenic walk brings you to the 1854 **Old Point Loma Lighthouse**, on the top of the point. It closed in 1891, and in 1913 it was declared a national monument.

On the other side of the point, you can drive or walk down to the **Tidepools**, which are most interesting at low ebb tide. Look in the pools for anemones, starfish, crabs, limpets, and dead man's fingers, but don't damage or remove anything – it's all protected by law.

Ocean Beach

A seaside community which once had a somewhat sleazy reputation, OB (as it's commonly called) has moved upscale, but it's still a long way from pretentious and is one of the most enjoyable beach areas in San Diego. The half-mile-long Ocean Beach Pier is popular for fishing and a breath of fresh air. Just north of the pier, near the end of Newport Ave, is the beach scene headquarters, with volleyball courts and sunset barbecues. It can get crowded all the way up to near Voltaire St. North of there is Dog Beach, where dogs are unleashed and owners are supposed to clean up after them. A few blocks south of the pier is Sunset Cliffs Park, where watching the sunset is the big attraction. Falling from the cliffs is the big danger, as they can crumble easily.

There are good surf breaks to the south, off Point Loma, and to the north, around the seawalls at the entrance to Mission Bay – the hot surfers slalom the pilings of the pier. Others should beware of the rips and currents, which can be deadly.

Away from the sea, Newport Ave is well stocked with shops selling beachwear, surfing stuff, and recycled clothing. There are lots of antique shops in the 4800 and 4900 blocks of Newport Ave. Bars and cheap eateries abound.

Harbor Island & Shelter Island

Harbor dredgings were used to build Shelter Island (1950) and Harbor Island (1969), which are not really islands, but T-shaped peninsulas joined to the mainland by causeways. They now provide moorings for a huge flotilla of pleasure boats, and are covered with hotels, restaurants, boatyards, and parking lots. There's a classic view of San Diego from here, across the bay through a forest of masts. The pointy building on Shelter Island, which resembles the tower of the Hotel del Coronado, is the clubhouse of the San Diego Yacht Club, which held the America's Cup yachting trophy from 1987 to 1995.

CORONADO

The oh-so-respectable community of Coronado, with a population of 27,000, is right across the bay from downtown San Diego, and is a combination of middle-class suburbia, retirement village, and upscale seaside resort. Administratively, it is a separate city from San Diego, known for closely guarding its ambiance and environmental quality.

Coronado is joined to the mainland by a spectacular two-mile bridge which arches over the bay, and a long narrow sand spit, the Silver Strand, which runs south to Imperial Beach. Nevertheless, it's often referred to as Coronado Island, though the locals like to call it 'The Village.' The large North Island Naval Air Station occupies a big chunk of land which was once an island.

In 1888 Elisha Babcock and Hampton Story opened the Hotel del Coronado, the grandiose centerpiece of their resort, and by 1900 they were broke. John D Spreckels, the millionaire who bankrolled the first rail line to San Diego, took over Coronado, and turned the whole island into one of the most fashionable getaways on the West Coast.

Information

The Coronado Visitors Information Center (☎ 437-8788), upstairs at 1111 Orange Ave, opens weekdays 9 am to 5 pm, weekends 10 am to 4 pm. For an insight into Coronado history, try a Historical Walking Tour (☎ 435-4993), starting from the Glori-

etta Bay Inn Tuesday, Thursday, and Saturday at 11 am. The 90-minute guided tours take in many of Coronado's most interesting sites, and cost $5.

There's a $1 toll for cars coming over the bridge to Coronado, but it's free for vehicles with passengers. Bus Nos 901, 902, and 903 from downtown run the length of Orange Ave, to the Hotel del Coronado. Alternatively, come across on the ferry from Broadway Pier ($2), and use the Coronado Electric Shuttle to get around. The beach can have good surf in summer with a south swell and a north wind.

Hotel del Coronado

Commonly known as the Hotel Del (☎ 435-611), this place is a much-loved San Diego institution. Architecturally, it's pretty quirky, with a facade replete with conical towers, cupolas, turrets, balconies, and dormer windows. It's an all-timber building, and the cavernous public spaces reflect the architects' experience designing railway depots, though the acres of polished wood give the interior a warm, old-fashioned feeling.

The Del was where Edward (then Prince of Wales) first met Mrs Simpson (then Mrs Spenser) in 1920, though the two did not become an item until some years later. Other hotel guests have included many US presidents and other dignitaries – pictures and mementos are displayed in the hotel's History Gallery. Hotel Del achieved its widest exposure in the 1959 movie *Some Like it Hot*, and earned a lasting association with Marilyn Monroe. Take a cassette-guided tour ($3) from the Lobby Shop, or one of the personally guided tours ($10), which start at 10 am and 11 am on Thursday, Friday, and Saturday. There's an interesting resident ghost story too.

See Places to Stay and Places to Eat for more details.

Bicycling

The best way to spend a day here is to come across by the ferry, and cruise around Coronado by bike. You can rent them at the Ferry Landing Marketplace for about $5 an hour, or bring one on the ferry for 55¢. The main drag across Coronado is Orange Ave, which passes through the well clipped Spreckels Park, then swings south towards the Hotel del Coronado. There are some designated bicycle routes (get a map when you rent the bike) which avoid Orange Ave, because it can be busy.

MISSION BAY

The mouth of the San Diego River formed a shallow bay when the river flowed, and a marshy swamp when it didn't – the Spanish called it False Bay. After WWII, a fine combination of civic vision and coastal engineering turned the swamp into a 7-sq-mile playground, with 27 miles of shoreline, and 90 acres of public park. With finance from public bonds, and expertise from the Army Corps of Engineers, the river was channeled to the sea, the bay was dredged and millions of tons of sludge were used to build islands, coves, and peninsulas. A quarter of the land created has been leased to hotels, boatyards, and other commercial uses, repaying the bonds and providing an ongoing revenue for the city.

The attractions of Mission Bay run the gamut from luxurious resort hotels to free outdoor activities. Kite flying is popular in Mission Bay Park and there's delightful cycling on the miles of smooth bike paths – you can rent a bike just off East Mission Bay Drive, opposite the Hilton. Beach volleyball is big on Fiesta Island, as is the local fun game, Over-the-Line.

The waters around Fiesta Island are used by jet-skis, power boats, and water-skiers, and the Hilton Beach Resort (☎ 276-4010) rents out the necessary equipment. Overpowered 'Thunderboats' race on the bay during the third weekend of September. Sailing and windsurfing predominate in northwest Mission Bay – boats and boards can be rented from CP Sailing Sports (☎ 581-5939), on Vacation Island, and Mission Bay Sportcenter (☎ 488-1004), on Santa Clara Point.

The *Bahia Belle* (☎ 488-0551) is a floating bar disguised as a stern-wheeler paddle boat. It cruises between two resort hotels, the Catamaran and the Bahia, Tuesday to Saturday from 7:30 pm to 12:30 am in summer; Friday and Saturday only for the rest of the year. It's a beautiful way to see the bay, and costs $5, plus drinks.

Sea World

Undoubtedly one of San Diego's best known and most popular attractions, Sea World (☎ 226-3901) started here in 1964 and Shamu, its killer whale, has become an unofficial symbol of the city. Sea World is very commercial, but nonetheless entertaining, and even slightly educational. Its popularity can be a drawback, with long waits for some shows and exhibits at peak seasons.

At $27.95 for adults, and $19.95 for kids, it's a pretty expensive day. Discount coupons are available, but the extras really add up – parking costs $5, the food is expensive, and not many people escape without spending something on the ubiquitous Sea World souvenirs. Other options to get the best value for your ticket include a re-entry stamp, which lets you go out for a break and return later (good during summer when it opens till late), and deals which let you come again at greatly reduced prices.

It's easy to find by car – take Sea World Drive from I-5. By bus, take No 9 from downtown. The gates open in summer daily at 9 am, and for the rest of the year daily at 10 am. Tickets sales finish 1½ hours before closing time, which is around sunset most of the year, but as late as 11 pm in summer.

MISSION BEACH & PACIFIC BEACH

From the southern tip of Mission Beach to the north end of Pacific Beach ('the beaches') is three miles of solid So-Cal beach scene. Ocean Front Walk, the beachfront boardwalk, can get crowded with in-line skaters and bicyclists any time of the year. On a warm summer weekend, the main north-south road, Mission Blvd, is so crowded that the police just close it to further traffic. Parking becomes impossible, and suntanned bodies cover the beach from end to end. A bike is probably the best

CALIFORNIA

way to get around, or in-line skates – both can be rented from places like Beach Rentals, near the beach at Grand Ave, Pacific Beach; Hamel's (☎ 488-5050) at 704 Ventura Place, near the roller coaster in Mission Beach; or Mike's (☎ 488-1444) at 756 Ventura Place. Prices are around $5 per hour, $20 per day.

Down at the Mission Beach end, many small houses and apartments are rented for the summer season, and the hedonism is concentrated in a narrow strip between the ocean and Mission Bay. Up in Pacific Beach (or PB) the activity spreads inland, especially along Garnet Ave, which is well supplied with bars and restaurants. At the ocean end of Garnet, Crystal Pier is a popular place to fish or watch the surfers.

The surf on Mission Beach is a beach break, good for beginners. It's more demanding around Crystal Pier, where medium swells can give good left and right breaks over the sandbars. Tourmaline Park, at the far north end of the beach, is particularly popular with windsurfers.

Belmont Park

This family-style amusement park in the middle of the Mission Beach has been here since 1925. When it was threatened with demolition, concerted community action saved the classic wooden roller coaster and the large indoor pool known as The Plunge. More modern attractions include the Pirates Cove children's play zone, and Venturer II, with virtual amusement machines. There are also beachwear boutiques, a bar, and some places to eat. It's free to enter Belmont Park, you just pay for the attractions – the roller coaster is $2.50 and opens daily at 11 am.

LA JOLLA

La Jolla is the next suburb north of Pacific Beach, but a huge leap up in socioeconomic status – and people care about status in La Jolla. The name is often translated as 'the jewel,' and it's always pronounced in the Spanish way – la HOY-ya. The area was subdivided in the 1880s, but when Ellen Browning Scripps moved in,

Mission Bay & Beaches

CALIFORNIA

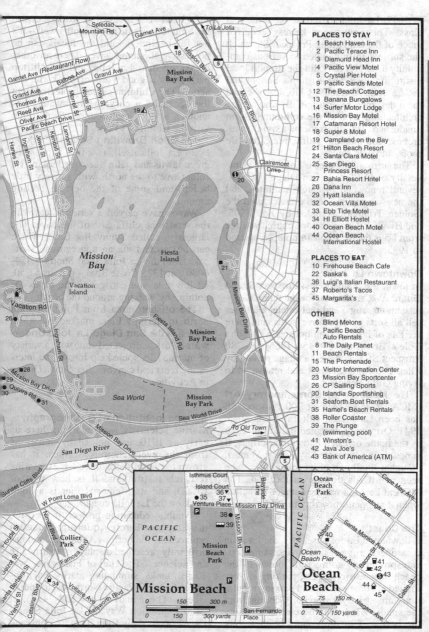

PLACES TO STAY
1 Beach Haven Inn
2 Pacific Terace Inn
3 Diamond Head Inn
4 Pacific View Motel
5 Crystal Pier Hotel
9 Pacific Sands Motel
12 The Beach Cottages
13 Banana Bungalows
14 Surfer Motor Lodge
16 Mission Bay Motel
17 Catamaran Resort Hotel
18 Super 8 Motel
19 Campland on the Bay
21 Hilton Beach Resort
24 Santa Clara Motel
25 San Diego
   Princess Resort
27 Bahia Resort Hotel
28 Dana Inn
29 Hyatt Islandia
32 Ocean Villa Motel
33 Ebb Tide Motel
34 HI Elliott Hostel
40 Ocean Beach Motel
44 Ocean Beach
   International Hostel

PLACES TO EAT
10 Firehouse Beach Cafe
22 Saska's
36 Luigi's Italian Restaurant
37 Roberto's Tacos
45 Margarita's

OTHER
6 Blind Melons
7 Pacific Beach
  Auto Rentals
8 The Daily Planet
11 Beach Rentals
15 The Promenade
20 Visitor Information Center
23 Mission Bay Sportcenter
26 CP Sailing Sports
30 Islandia Sportfishing
31 Seaforth Boat Rentals
35 Hamel's Beach Rentals
38 Roller Coaster
39 The Plunge
   (swimming pool)
41 Winston's
42 Java Joe's
43 Bank of America (ATM)

in 1897, La Jolla started to get some real class. The newspaper heiress acquired much of the land along Prospect St, which she subsequently donated to various community uses. Not only did she support local institutions like The Bishop's School and the La Jolla Woman's Club, but she had them designed by Irving Gill, who set the architectural tone of the community – an unadorned Mediterranean style with arches, colonnades, palm trees, red-tile roofs, and pale stucco.

The surrounding area is home to the University of California, San Diego (UCSD), several renowned research institutes, and the new-money residential area called the Golden Triangle, bounded by I-5, I-805, and Hwy 52. The space-age church you see from I-5 is the Mormon Temple, completed in 1993.

Downtown La Jolla

In town, the main streets, Prospect St and Girard Ave, are known for the three 'R's' – restaurants, rugs, and real estate. Galleries sell all sorts of decorative items, and there are lots of fashion boutiques as well. John Cole's Bookshop (☎ 454-4766), at 780 Prospect St, was once a cottage owned by Ellen Browning Scripps and renovated to Irving Gill's design.

The **Museum of Contemporary Art** (MCA, ☎ 454-3541), at 700 Prospect St, has been La Jolla's cultural focus since 1941. Originally designed by Gill in 1916 as the home of Ellen Browning Scripps, it is now being renovated by Robert Venturi, though a small part of its collection can be seen at MCA's downtown location. The MCA at La Jolla will be a major attraction when it re-opens, possibly in 1996.

The Coast

If downtown La Jolla is stuffy, the La Jolla coastline is rugged and invigorating. Private properties going right down to the beach can restrict access, parking is very limited at some points, and parking regulations are strictly enforced. Coming from the south, Windansea beach has arguably the best surf in the county, with a long

right-hand reef break that works best on medium to low tide and a south swell – it's not for beginners, and the locals can be possessive about the waves. There are other breaks up near La Jolla, and the clifftop park gives a good view of the surfers in action. The Children's Pool, protected from the ocean by a curving breakwater, was another Scripps contribution. Seals often visit the Children's Pool.

The **Ellen Browning Scripps Park** on Point La Jolla itself, is a tidy expanse of green lawns and palm trees overlooking La Jolla Cove to the north, with a lovely little beach, and some of the best snorkeling around.

Waves have carved a series of caves in the sandstone cliffs east of the cove. The largest is called Sunny Jim Cave, which can be reached via an underground staircase from the La Jolla Shell Shop (☎ 454-6080), at 1325 Coast Blvd – it costs $1.50. At low tide you can get to the caves for nothing by walking around the beach.

The offshore area from Point La Jolla north to Scripps Pier, marked by white buoys, is the **San Diego-La Jolla Underwater Park**, a protected zone with a variety of marine life, some kelp forest, and interesting reefs and canyons. See Scuba Diving in Activities.

Scripps Institution of Oceanography

Marine scientists were working here as early as 1910 and, helped by donations from the ever-generous Scripps, it has grown to one of the world's largest marine research institutions. It is now part of UCSD, and its Memorial Pier is a landmark on the La Jolla coast.

A public education project of the SIO, the **Stephen Birch Aquarium-Museum** replaces the old Scripps Aquarium, and has brilliantly presented displays of marine life and sciences. The Hall of Fishes has over 30 fish tanks, simulating marine environments from the Pacific Northwest to Indian Ocean. The aquarium (☎ 534-3474), at 2300 Exhibition Way off La Jolla Shores Drive, opens daily from 9 am to 5 pm, and

CALIFORNIA

PACIFIC OCEAN

Point La Jolla

Ellen Browning Scripps Park

La Jolla Cove

Alligator Head

La Jolla Bay

Boomer Beach

Coast Blvd S

La Jolla Caves

To Scripps, UCSD

Children's Pool

Shell Beach

Seal Rock

Coast Boulevard Park

Coast Walk

Torrey Pines Rd

La Jolla

Wipeout Beach

Whispering Sands Beach

To Pacific Beach

La Jolla Country Club

PLACES TO STAY	PLACES TO EAT	OTHER
2 La Valencia	8 José's	5 La Jolla Shell Shop
3 Prospect Park Inn	11 John's Waffle Shop	9 Post Office
10 Colonial Inn	12 Johnny Rocket's	15 John Cole's Bookshop
18 Bed & Breakfast Inn at La Jolla	13 Hard Rock Cafe	16 Museum of Contemporary Art
	14 Avanti Restaurant	17 La Jolla Woman's Club
	21 Harry's	19 La Jolla Brewing Company
PLACES TO EAT	23 The Pannikin	20 The Bishop's School
1 Top o' the Cove	24 Sammy's California Woodfired Pizza	22 The Comedy Store
4 Alfonso's	25 The French Gourmet	
6 La Terraza	26 Royal Thai Cuisine	
7 Star of India		

costs $8.50 for adults, $4.50 for students, and $3.50 for children.

Salk Institute

This institution for biological and biomedical research was founded by Jonas Salk, the polio prevention pioneer, in 1960. San Diego County donated 27 acres of land, the March of Dimes provided financial support, and Louis Kahn designed the building. Completed in 1965, it is regarded as a modern masterpiece, with its classically proportioned travertine marble plaza, and cubist, mirror-image laboratory blocks framing a perfect view of the Pacific. The Salk Institute attracts the best scientists to work in a research-only environment. The facilities are currently being expanded, with new laboratories designed by Jack McAllister, a follower of Kahn's work. The Salk Institute (☎ 453-4100) is at 10010 N Torrey Pines Rd, and you can make an appointment to tour the building with a volunteer guide on a weekday morning. Bus Nos 41 and 301 go along N Torrey Pines Rd, and you could take a beautiful walk from there to the institute then down to the beach.

Torrey Pines City Park

Some of the best beaches in the county are in this park, which covers the coastline from the Salk Institute up to the Torrey Pines State Reserve. The **Torrey Pines Glider Port**, at the end of Torrey Pines Scenic Drive, is the place for hang-gliders and paragliders to launch themselves into the sea breezes which rise over the cliffs. It's a beautiful sight – tandem flights are available if you can't resist trying it. Down below is **Blacks Beach**, where bathing suits are technically required but practically absent. Lots of gay guys hang out here.

Torrey Pines State Reserve

This reserve preserves the last mainland stands of the Torrey pine *(Pinus torreyana)*, a species adapted to the sparse rainfall and sandy, stony soils. Steep sandstone gullies are eroded into wonderfully textured sur-

JAMES LYON
Salk Institute, La Jolla

faces, and the views over the ocean and north to Del Mar are superb, especially at sunset. The visitors center, by the parking lot at the top of the access road, has good displays on the flora and fauna of the reserve. The building itself, a simple adobe, was built as a lodge in 1922 by (you guessed it) Ellen Browning Scripps, and donated to the newly established reserve. Several walking trails wind through the reserve and down to the beach. The reserve (☎ 755-2063) is open from 9 am till sunset daily. Entry and parking is $4 per car (free if you walk in) – if the ticket office is closed, get a permit from the yellow machine in the lower parking lot.

University of California, San Diego

A campus of the University of California, UCSD was established in 1960 and now has over 18,000 students and an excellent academic reputation. It's attractive enough, in its park-like setting of eucalyptus trees, but not exactly a vibrant place to visit. The most distinctive structure is the Central Library, an upside-down pyramid of glass and concrete. The UCSD bookstore (☎ 534-7323) has an excellent stock and helpful staff.

Spread around the campus is the **Stuart Collection** of outdoor sculptures, including Niki de Saint Phalle's *Sun God*, a large and colorful chicken, and Bruce Nauman's *Vices & Virtues*, which spells out seven of each in huge neon letters every evening. Details are available from the Visual Arts Building. In the Mandell Weiss Center for the Performing Arts is the **La Jolla Playhouse** (☎ 550-1010), known for its high-quality productions.

University Towne Centre

Ignoring the pretentious spelling, UTC (☎ 546-8858) is the best shopping mall in the classy northern suburbs. It has 160 stores with numerous specialty outlets. There's also a food court, an Olympic-size ice skating rink, six-screen movie theater, video arcade, and child-care center.

A particular attraction is the **Mingei International Museum of Folk Art**

Horton Plaza, San Diego

Botanical Building, Balboa Park

Hotel Del Coronado

Truth in advertising – predator & prey

Belmont Park Roller Coaster

The center of San Diego's gay community

La Jolla shores

San Diego Marriott Hotel at the Marina

San Diego surf pad

The aptly named Death Valley

CALIFORNIA

JAMES LYON

Offering books to the gods, UCSD's Central Library is about the most interesting thing on campus.

(☎ 453-5300), which has an excellent permanent collection of costumes, toys, jewelry, utensils, and other handmade objects from traditional cultures around the world. It's open Tuesday to Saturday from 11 am to 5 pm, and Sunday 2 to 5 pm, and costs $3 for adults, $1 for children. The Mingei is expected to move to Balboa Park in 1996.

Soledad Mountain

For a worthwhile 360° view of the northern suburbs, take Soledad Rd up to the park on this hill east of La Jolla. The large cross on top was the subject of a court case – residents objected to the sectarian religious symbol on publicly owned land.

SOUTH BAY & CHULA VISTA

Between downtown and the Mexican border, the South Bay area is the least affluent part of San Diego, and has relatively few attractions for visitors. It is interesting to see that San Diego does have a gritty side, where there are factories, warehouses, and neighborhoods of Mexican workers. If

you take the San Diego trolley to the San Ysidro border crossing, you'll see a reasonable cross-section.

A city of 60,000 within San Diego County, **National City** is a compact square just south of downtown. It was first developed in the 1870s, and retains several Victorian homes. In WWII, the city gave to the US Navy all the land fronting San Diego Bay, and it remains the home the US Pacific Fleet, a major source of employment and industry.

The city of **Chula Vista** extends from the bay to the hills, and despite sprawling suburbia it still has some of the citrus orchards for which it was once renowned.

The Sweetwater Marsh National Wildlife Refuge occupies much of Chula Vista's waterfront, and is one of the few areas of salt marsh left on the Pacific Coast. Some 210 bird species inhabit the refuge, several of them rare or endangered. The **Chula Vista Nature Center** (☎ 422-2473) has some very good exhibits. To get there, take the E St exit from I-5, and go west to the parking lot from which a shuttle runs to the nature center every 20 minutes or so. The shuttle also picks up from the E St trolley station. It's open daily from 10 am to 5 pm in summer, but closes on Mondays and public holidays for the rest of the year. Admission costs $3.50 for adults.

By far the least pretentious of San Diego's beachside communities, **Imperial Beach** was once a popular holiday spot for visitors from Imperial Valley. Its long stretch of sandy beach is the site of the US Open Sandcastle contest every July. The water is sometimes unsafe for swimming because of pollution from the Tijuana River – the new Border Environment Cooperation Commission is attempting to deal with the problem. The **Border Field State Park,** a coastal reserve, accessed from I-5, goes right to the Mexican border. It's open daily from 9:30 am to sunset; entry is $4 per vehicle.

One of the busiest international border crossings in the world, **San Ysidro,** 'Gateway to Mexico,' is largely populated by Mexican Americans and well supplied with Mexican restaurants, money changers, and sellers of Mexican auto insurance, particularly along San Ysidro Blvd.

ACTIVITIES
Surfing
Surfing is popular along the San Diego coast, and the surf can get crowded. Fall offers the best chance to find strong swells and offshore Santa Ana winds. In summer, swells come from the south and southwest, and in winter, from the west and northwest. Spring brings more frequent onshore winds, but can still be good. For the latest beach, weather, and surf reports call ☎ 221-8884.

The best surf breaks, going from south to north, are at Imperial Beach (especially in winter), Coronado (especially in summer with north wind and south swell), Point Loma (reef breaks which are less accessible, but therefore less crowded; best in winter), Ocean Beach, Pacific Beach, Bird Rock (good in summer at low tide), Windansea (hot reef break, best in summer, but crowded), La Jolla Cove (works with a big

swell – over 10 feet), La Jolla Shores (best in winter with a south wind). Further up, in North San Diego County, there are breaks at Cardiff State Beach, San Elijo State Beach, Swami's, Carlsbad State Beach, and Oceanside.

Scuba Diving
There are dive sites all along the coast of San Diego County, with some of the best diving in the San Diego-La Jolla Underwater Park. Watch for the spectacular, bright orange Garibaldi fish, which is now a protected species. Beginning divers train off Kellog Park and La Jolla Cove. Other dive sites, including the 100 foot deep La Jolla Canyon, are for more experienced divers. It's forbidden to remove or damage any marine life or natural features in the park. Further out are forests of the giant Californian kelp, one of the world's fastest growing plants, which can increase its length by up to three feet per day. Islands off the Baja California coast also offer some of the best diving.

Quite a few operators conduct scuba courses, sell or rent equipment, fill tanks, and arrange trips. Check the Yellow Pages, or try: Buhrow Into Surf & Dive (☎ 477-5946), 1536 Sweetwater Rd, National City; Explorer Dive & Travel (☎ 226-3843), 4967 Newport Ave, Ocean Beach; OE Express (☎ 454-6195), 2158 Avenida de la Playa, La Jolla; Del Mar Oceansports (☎ 792-1903), 1227 Camino del Mar, Del Mar, or any of the Sport Chalet stores (☎ 224-6777). Charter operations which take diving trips include Islandia Sportfishing (☎ 222-1164), and Altair Classic Yacht Charters (☎ 297-8824).

Fishing
A state fishing license is required by people over 16 years (see the Outdoor Activities chapter). Over a dozen lakes have bass, crappie, bluegill, trout, and catfish. Most charge a fee of around $4 per day. A recorded service (☎ 465-3474) provides fishing information.

The most popular public fishing piers are Imperial Beach Municipal Pier, Embarcadero Fishing Pier, Shelter Island Fishing Pier, Ocean Beach Pier, and Crystal Pier at Pacific Beach. The best time of year for pier fishing is from about April to October.

Offshore catches include barracuda, bass, and yellowtail. In summer, albacore is a special attraction. Many firms run full-day and half-day charter fishing trips, including Fisherman's Landing (☎ 222-0391), Fish n' Cruise Charter Association (☎ 224-2464), H&M Landing (☎ 222-1144), and Point Loma Sport Fishing (☎ 223-1627). Most are based at Shelter Island Marina, Quivira Basin in Mission Bay, and at Oceanside Harbor in North San Diego County.

Boating

Power and sail boats, row boats, and canoes can be rented on Mission Bay – try Mission Bay Sportcenter (☎ 488-1004) at 1010 Santa Clara Place; CP Watersports at the Hilton (☎ 275-8943) and Dana Inn (☎ 226-8611); or Seaforth Boat Rentals (☎ 223-1681), 1641 Quivira Rd.

Experienced sailors can charter yachts for trips on San Diego Bay and out into the Pacific. Quite a few charterers are based around Shelter Island, including Set Sail (☎ 224-3791), 2131 Shelter Island Drive; Shelter Cove Marina (☎ 224-2471), 2240 Shelter Island Drive; San Diego Yacht Charters (☎ 297-4555), 1880 Harbor Island Drive; and Harbor Sailboats (☎ 291-9568), 2040 Harbor Island Drive.

Whale Watching

The Cabrillo National Monument **Whale Overlook** has a shelter and information about gray whales. If you're lucky, you'll spot their water spouts off Point Loma. Park rangers present special programs during the migration season – the whales pass on the way south from mid-December to late February, and on the return trip during March.

Many whale-watching cruises operate daily during the winter whale migration. The cost is around $15 for adults and $8 for children for a three-hour trip – some of them will guarantee a sighting. Contact H&M Landing (☎ 222-1144), Hornblower/Invader Cruises (☎ 234-8687), or San Diego Harbor Excursions (☎ 234-4111).

Hang-Gliding & Para-Gliding

Glider riders hang at Torrey Pines Gliderpark (☎ 452-3202), 2800 Torrey Pines Scenic Drive, La Jolla, which is famous as a gliding location. Tandem flights in a hang glider are $150 for 30 minutes; tandem para glider flights are $100 for 15 to 20 minutes.

Experienced pilots can join in if they have a USHGA Hang 4 rating, and take an associate membership of the Torrey Pines Hang Glider Association. Training programs for para glider and hang glider pilots are offered by UP International at La Jolla (☎ 452-7230), but training flights are at less demanding sites.

Hot-Air Ballooning

Brightly colored hot-air balloons are a trademark of the skies above Del Mar, on the northern fringe of the metropolitan area. For pleasure flights, contact Skysurfer Balloon Company (☎ 481-6800), 1221 Camino del Mar; Del Mar Balloon (☎ 259-3115), 13443 Barbados Way; or Sunset Balloon Flights (☎ 481-8891), 3443 Tripp St, San Diego. Flights are usually at sunrise or sunset, and cost around $120.

ORGANIZED TOURS

Several companies run narrated tours of the city and surrounding attractions. Grayline (☎ 491-0011) has four-hour city tours twice daily for $24/10 for adults/children, and trips to Tijuana, Wild Animal Park, La Jolla, Coronado etc. San Diego Scenic Tours (☎ 273-8687) covers the city, harbor, and Tijuana for similar prices.

Old Town Trolley

Not to be confused with the Metropolitan Transit System's trolleys, which run on rails, the Old Town Trolley is a bus done up to resemble an old-fashioned street car. Old Town Trolley Tours (☎ 298-8687) do a loop around the main attractions near downtown, and you can get on or off at any number of them, staying as long as you wish to look around. It's a quite good introduction to the city, and the commentary is entertaining. It costs $16/7.

The Old Trolley also gives tours of some of the military bases, call ☎ 800-628-9868 for information.

Naval & Military Bases
Old Town Trolley Tours also tours the San Diego Naval Station, North Island Naval Air Station, ships in port, and other military facilities ($20 for adults, $7 for children). On weekends, the navy itself often conducts free tours of ships in port – call ☎ 437-2735 to find out if any are open.

Harbor Cruises
Two companies depart from Broadway Pier: Hornblower/Invader Cruises (☎ 234-8687) has one- and two-hour cruises for $10 and $15 (kids half price); and Harbor Excursion (☎ 234-4111).

SPECIAL EVENTS
The calendar is full of community, cultural, and sporting events. Some of the most interesting and unusual are listed below. A recorded service (☎ 239-9696) gives information about current happenings.

January
    Penguin Day Ski Fest – people do things without wetsuits, on water-skis and blocks of ice (☎ 276-0830)
February
    Chinese New Year – Chinese food, culture, and martial arts at Del Mar Fairgrounds (☎ 234-4447)
March
    Ocean Beach Kite Festival – kite making, decorating, flying, and competitions at Ocean Beach (☎ 531-1527)
    Saint Patrick's Day Parade – 6th Ave (☎ 299-7812)
April
    San Diego Crew Classic – national college rowing regatta, Crown Point Shores (☎ 226-4590)
    San Diego Earth Fair – an Earth Day parade and environmental displays in Balboa Park (☎ 496-6666)

May
    Cinco de Mayo – the Mexican national day is celebrated with gusto in Old Town and elsewhere in the county (☎ 296-3161)
    American Indian Cultural Days – Native American dancing, music, and arts displays in Balboa Park (☎ 281-8964)
    Pacific Beach Block Party – lots of music and fun on Garnet Ave (☎ 483-6666)
June
    Indian Fair- native American cultural exhibition at the Museum of Man in Balboa Park (☎ 293-2011)
    Ocean Beach Street Fair & Chili Cook-Off – popular two-day street party (☎ 224-4906)
    Del Mar Fair – from June 15 to July 4, a huge county fair with headline acts and hundreds of carnival rides and shows, at the Del Mar Fairgrounds (☎ 755-1161)
July
    4th of July – one of the most popular parades is in Coronado (☎ 437-8068)
    Sand Castle Days – amazing sand castle-building competition at Imperial Beach (☎ 424-6663)
    Old Globe Festival – renowned Shakespearean festival, at the Old Globe Theatre in Balboa Park (☎ 239-2255)
    Over-the-Line Tournament – lots of over-the-top teams compete in this very local variant of beach softball, on Fiesta Island (☎ 688-0817)
August
    Hillcrest City Fest – street fair in one of San Diego's liveliest districts (☎ 299-3330)
    Miramar Air Show – Blue Angels and Top Guns show the right stuff at Miramar Naval Air Station (☎ 537-4084)
    Summerfest Chamber Music Festival – a two-week series with international performers (☎ 459-3728)
September
    San Diego Street Scene – street festival with music on outdoor stages in the Gaslamp Quarter (☎ 557-8487)
    Thunderboat Races – unlimited hydroplane championship on Mission Bay (☎ 268-1250)
October
    Halloween – features an underwater pumpkin carving contest for scuba divers at La Jolla (☎ 565-6054)
November
    Thanksgiving Dixieland Jazz Festival – Dixieland bands converge on the Town & Country Hotel (☎ 297-5277)
December
    Christmas on El Prado – crafts, carols,

and candlelight parade in Balboa Park
(☎ 239-0512)

Harbor Parade of Lights – dozens of decorated, illuminated boats float through the harbor (☎ 297-5917)

Old Town Posadas – a traditional Latin Christmas celebration that takes place in Old Town (☎ 237-6771)

PLACES TO STAY

Tourism is a major industry here, and there are over 45,000 hotel rooms in the county. In the summer season (roughly Memorial Day to Labor Day) accommodations, particularly near the beaches, are heavily booked and prices are higher. Taxes in San Diego County add 10.5% to the bill.

Apart from what's listed below, there is a wealth of summer rental accommodation in the beach areas. If you have a group of friends or family, and you want to stay for more than a few days, renting a place can be an excellent idea. Try calling agents like *Mission Bay Vacations* (☎ 539-7220, 800-882-8626), or *Penny Realty* (☎ 539-3900, 800-748-6704), but call early.

Places to Stay – bottom end

Camping There are several campgrounds around San Diego, but only two allow tent camping. *Campland on the Bay* (☎ 274-4212, 800-422-9386), 2211 Pacific Beach Drive, has over 40 acres fronting Mission Bay. There's a restaurant, pool, boating facilities, and full RV hookups. Sites cost $19 to $37 in winter, $26 to $52 in summer, depending on proximity to the water. The location is great, but the tent area is not very attractive and can be crowded. Bookings are a good idea in the warmer months. The *KOA* (☎ 800-762-2267), 111 N 2nd Ave in Chula Vista, is about five miles southeast of downtown and charges $26 for tent sites, $32 for RV sites, and has cabins from $34 to $42.

Hostels The HI *San Diego Hostel* (☎ 525-1531) is centrally located at 500 W Broadway, handy to the Amtrak and Greyhound stations and the trolley to Tijuana. It's in the same building as the YMCA, and offers basic dorm rooms for $12 per night, or $15

for non-members. It's open from 8 am to 11 pm. HI's *Elliott Hostel* (☎ 223-4778), at 3790 Udall St in Loma Portal, is tricky to find if you're driving, and not convenient without a car. It's closer to the beaches and has a good atmosphere, and also charges $12. The *Inn at the YMCA* (☎ 234-5252), 500 W Broadway, has single/double rooms with shared bathroom for $20/30, which are quite OK as a budget option.

Several private hostels offer basic budget backpacker accommodations for international travelers. Downtown, the *Grand Pacific Hostel* (☎ 232-3100, 800-438-8622), 437 J St, is a Victorian-era hotel refitted with six-bed dorms ($12 to $14 per bed) and some double rooms ($30). The price includes breakfast cereal and coffee, and they do a $3 dinner most nights. It has good lounge and kitchen areas, and offers day tours, in-house parties, and free information. It's right in the Gaslamp Quarter, so can be a bit noisy, but the young crowd here doesn't mind. Another downtown hostel is *Jim's San Diego*, (☎ 235-0234) at 1425 C St, which is handy for Balboa Park, but not in a good area. It charges $13 per night for a dorm bed. It's OK, but not as well run as it could be.

Only a couple of blocks from the ocean, *Ocean Beach International Hostel* (OBI or O-Bee for short; ☎ 223-7873, 800-339-7263), 4961 Newport Ave, charges $12.50 to $15 for a bed in a dorm with three others, and it's a friendly, fun place with helpful staff – popular with European travelers. Bus No 35 from downtown passes Newport Ave a block east of the hostel. Right on Mission Beach, *Banana Bungalows* (☎ 237-1440), 707 Reed Ave, has a top location, a beach-party atmosphere, and is reasonably clean, but it's pretty basic and can get crowded. They have dorm beds for $11 in the big, badly ventilated room in the back, and for $15 in more pleasant six-bed rooms. The communal area is a patio which fronts right onto the boardwalk, and is a great place for breakfast or a beer.

Downtown Note that some of the cheapest downtown hotels provide what is sometimes called SRO (single room occupancy); they rent basic rooms, by the day week or month, to people who might otherwise be homeless. Low-budget travelers often stay in these places and find them quite OK, though some regular guests can be, well, colorful characters. Many developers would like to get rid of SROs, especially in 'improving' areas like the Gaslamp Quarter, but they serve a useful social function, and are a relief from total gentrification. Rates are cheaper by the week, but they typically charge a key deposit. In the cheapest rooms, you share a hall bathroom.

In the same building as the Greyhound station, the *Pickwick Hotel* (☎ 234-9200), at 132 W Broadway, is a little worn with zero charm and smallish rooms, but it's adequate, and costs only $25/35 plus tax and key deposit. Also with a central location, the *Hotel San Diego* (☎ 234-0221), 339 W Broadway, is old but quite comfortable, for $35 a double.

For something different, try the *Churchill Hotel* (☎ 234-5186), at 827 C St. It's done out like a medieval castle, and has bizarre theme rooms (Wild West, Jungle Safari, Chrome-a-Rama) from $42, but ordinary rooms, some with shared bath, cost around $30.

In the Gaslamp Quarter, the *Golden West Hotel* (☎ 233-7596), 720 4th Ave, has a big lobby but is definitely bottom-end, with single/double rooms from $15/26. Another cheapie is the *Maryland Hotel* (☎ 239-9243), 630 F St, with very basic rooms from $17/25, or $25/32 with a private bathroom. *J Street Inn* (☎ 696-6922), at 222 J St, has single-person units with kitchenettes from $25. The *Downtown Inn Hotel* (☎ 238-4100), 660 G St at 7th Ave, is also a good value, units from $24/34 to $39/49.

La Pacifica Hotel (☎ 236-9292, fax 236-9988), 1546 2nd Ave, is a new budget hotel, very clean and well-designed, and only five blocks from the center of town. The rooms have basic cooking facilities, and there's a laundry, market, and deli on the premises. Singles/doubles cost from $40/45 to $50/60. A little further out, *La Pensione Hotel* (☎ 236-8000, 800-232-

4683), at 1700 India St, has the same ownership, the same high quality rooms, and the same low prices.

There's a bunch of budget motels near the east end of Ash St, the cheapest of which are *Days Inn* (☎ 239-9113, 800-325-2525), 1449 9th Ave, with rooms from $39/40, and *Balboa Park Travelodge* (☎ 234-8277), at 840 Ash St.

Near Downtown The *E-Z 8 Motel* chain has eight establishments around San Diego, and they all have budget-priced rooms that are clean and comfortable. The most central are in Mission Valley (☎ 291-8252), at 2484 Hotel Circle Place; near Old Town (☎ 294-2512), at 4747 Pacific Hwy; and near the Sports Arena (☎ 223-9500), at 3333 Channel Way. Prices vary depending on the location and the season – around $32 to $44.

Corinthian Suites (☎ 236-1600), 1840 4th Ave, between downtown and Hillcrest, has rooms with kitchenettes from only $39 to $55. *Padre Trail Inn* (☎ 297-3291), at 4200 Taylor St right by Old Town, is pretty cheap and conveniently located. There's a pool, bar, and restaurant, and air-con rooms with one/two beds cost $49/59 in summer, or $39/41 at other times. *Old Town Inn*, (☎ 260-8024, 800-643-3025), 4444 Pacific Hwy, has singles/doubles starting at $34/36, but some rooms are double this price.

Hillcrest The *Hillcrest Eagle Inn* (☎ 298-9898), 3942 8th Ave, just north of University Ave, has cheap, small rooms with shared bathrooms from $15 to $20, and is tolerable if you can't afford anything else. *Studio 819* (☎ 542-0819), 819 University Ave, is much better, with nice, new, modern, little rooms with a bathroom, kitchenette, and phone, starting at $29/32 – bigger rooms cost up to $39/42, but they're all cheaper by the week.

East San Diego Coming into town from the east, there are standard budget motels along El Cajon Blvd near San Diego State University, though the area hasn't got much else going for it. Look for the *Campus Hitching Post Motel* (☎ 583-1456), at 6235 El Cajon Blvd, with rooms around $40; the *Imperial Motel* (☎ 463-9245), at 6624 El Cajon Blvd, which is only slightly more expensive. Others include *Aztec Budget Inn* (☎ 582-1414, 800-225-9610), at 6050 El Cajon Blvd; and *Lamplighter Inn* (☎ 582-3088, 800-545-0778) at 6474 El Cajon Blvd.

Point Loma There are budget motels on Rosecrans St, the main commercial road going to Point Loma. The cheapest places include *Arena Inn* (☎ 224-8266, 800-742-4627), at 3330 Rosecrans, and *Loma Lodge* (☎ 222-0511, 800-266-0511), at 3202 Rosecrans, both with pools and rooms from less than $40 per night.

Pacific Beach Motels near the beach can be a pretty good value at the off-season prices quoted here, but in summer (mid-June to mid-September) prices increase by 30% or more, and rooms can be scarce. *Pacific View Motel* (☎ 483-6117), at 610 Emerald St, is classic '60s in appearance and close to the beach, and only $36 for singles or doubles outside summer. *Pacific Sands Motel* (☎ 483-7555), 4449 Ocean Blvd, is also well-positioned and well-worn, with rooms from $40 to $60. Rooms at *Mission Bay Motel* (☎ 483-6440), 4221 Mission Blvd, overlook a parking lot and a busy street, but they cost only $40/45 for singles/doubles in the off season; $20 more in summer.

Mission Bay The *Mission Bay Super 8 Motel* (☎ 274-7888), 4540 Mission Bay Drive, is not on the beach, but it's handy to most attractions, and a good value at around $46. Other cheapies along this stretch of Mission Bay Drive include *Western Shore Motel* (☎ 273-1121), 4345 Mission Bay Drive, and *Sleepy Time Motel* (☎ 483-4222), 4545 Mission Bay Drive, with rooms from $30/35.

Places to Stay – middle
Downtown In the Gaslamp Quarter, the *William Penn Suites Hotel* (☎ 531-0833), 511 F St, has units with kitchen facilities from $79 to $109, but in the quiet seasons they are much cheaper – from $40. *Hotel St James* (☎ 234-0155), 830 6th Ave, was built in 1913 but has been thoroughly modernized. It's comfortable, with a bit more character than your average motel, and quite a good value for $59 a double.

There's another group of budget motels like *Days Inn* and *Econo Lodge* along Pacific Hwy, as you approach the downtown area from the north.

Hotel Circle Near Old Town, Hotel Circle N and Hotel Circle S, on either side of I-8, have a dozen or so mid-range motels. The cheapest are *Vagabond Inn* (☎ 297-1691, 800-522-1555), 625 Hotel Circle S, from $45/50; and *Fabulous Inn* (☎ 291-7700, 800-647-1903), 2485 Hotel Circle Place, from $46/56, more in summer. More expensive places, with recreational facilities, include *Handlery Hotel & Country Club* (☎ 298-0511, 800-223-0888), 950 Hotel Circle N.

Hillcrest In the heart of the area, *Hillcrest Inn* (☎ 293-7078), at 3754 5th Ave, welcomes straight and gay guests (no children), has a friendly atmosphere, and is quite a good value at $49 to $55. *Travelodge at the Zoo* (☎ 296-2101, 800-843-9988), at 2223 El Cajon Blvd, has a large pool and a bit more character than most chain motels, from $39 to $59. *Embassy Hotel* (☎ 296-3141), 3645 Park Blvd, is in a quiet location and well-priced at around $30/50.

Point Loma, Harbor Island, Shelter Island Hotels here tend to cater to conventioneers and yachties, and tend to be expensive, but the area is close to the airport, and has good views across the bay to the city. Some of the more economical places are *Vagabond Inn* (☎ 224-3371), 1325 Scott St, Point Loma, from $47/52 for singles/doubles; *Shelter Island Mariana Inn* (☎ 222-0561), 2051 Shelter Island Drive, right on the waterside, where the smaller rooms start at $70 and suites with kitchens cost much more.

Ocean Beach At 5080 Newport Ave, right by the beach, the *Ocean Beach Motel* (☎ 223-7191), has rooms with ocean views starting at $55 per night. Further north, also close to the sea, the *Ocean Villa Motel* (☎ 224-3481), at 5142 W Point Loma Blvd, is a family place ('no pets, no parties'), clean and well-run, with a pool and a variety of rooms from $45 in summer, or from $50 with kitchenette. The slightly worn *Ebb Tide Motel* (☎ 224-9339), at 5082 W Point Loma Blvd, has rooms with kitchens for $50.

Mission Beach An ordinary motel with a great location, within a couple of blocks of both ocean and bay beaches, the *Santa Clara Motel* (☎ 488-1193), at 839 Santa Clara Place, is not especially cheap, from around $60 in summer, but they may give you a good deal out of season.

Pacific Beach One of the most interesting places to stay in all San Diego is the *Crystal Pier Hotel* (☎ 483-6983, 800-748-5894) – the address is 4500 Ocean Blvd, but the rooms are actually cottages on the pier itself, right above the beach and the ocean. Dating from 1927, the distinctive arched entrance to the pier is a landmark at the end of Garnet Ave. Winter prices range from $85 per day for the original cottages (one to four people), up to $180 per day for newer and larger cottages (some sleep up to eight people), with a two-night minimum stay. Summer rates start at $140, with a three-night minimum.

Just north of the pier, *Diamond Head Inn* (☎ 273-1900), at 605 Diamond St, has rooms with kitchens from around $70 to $110 ($95 to $145 in summer), and the best rooms face the sea. *Beach Haven Inn* (☎ 272-3812, 800-831-6323), 4740 Mission Blvd, is a block back from the beach, with quite good rooms from about $50. A bigger place is *Surfer Motor Lodge* (☎ 483-7070), 711 Pacific Beach Drive, right on the beach with a pool and restaurant. They

have a variety of rooms, all with fridge, phone, and TV, from $66 to $73 and $87 for family units; summer prices are $77 to $92 and $118.

The Beach Cottages (☎ 483-7440), 4255 Ocean Blvd, has motel rooms, apartments, and beachfront cottages, priced from $55, $90, and $95 in winter; $90, $145, and $150 in summer. It's a well-run place, and you have to book early to get a cottage in summer.

La Jolla In the town itself, it's hard to find a room for under $100 – try the *Prospect Park Inn* (☎ 454-0133, 800-433-1609), 1110 Prospect St, where prices start at $80/90. For other reasonably priced choices, look north or south of town. *Andrea Villa Inn* (☎ 459-3311, 800-367-6467), 2402 Torrey Pines Rd, is a comfortable place, not too far from La Jolla Shores Beach, with all the amenities and rooms from $70/80. Nearby is the high-rise *Summer House Inn* (☎ 459-0261, 800-666-0261), 7955 La Jolla Shores Drive, from $79/89. Heading south, try *The Inn at La Jolla* (☎ 454-6121, 800-367-6467), at 5440 La Jolla Blvd, in the Bird Rock area, from $75/95.

Places to Stay – top end
B&Bs The Bed & Breakfast Directory for San Diego lists 30 B&Bs in the county. You can order a copy ($3.95) from the publisher (☎ 297-3130, 800-619-7266).

Close to downtown and Balboa Park, *Britt House* (☎ 234-2926), at 406 Maple St, is an 1887 Queen Anne-style mansion with a separate cottage and 10 guest rooms, mostly with shared bathrooms, from $95 a double.

Over the big bridge, *Coronado Victorian House* (☎ 435-2200), at 1000 8th St, Coronado, was built in 1894 and was recently restored. It has eight units, all with private bathrooms, and also offers dancing and fitness classes, local tours, murder-mystery theme nights, and gourmet food. Prices run from $175 to $375.

Further north, *The Bed & Breakfast Inn at La Jolla* (☎ 456-2066), at 7753 Draper

Ave, is a 1913 Irving Gill house with Kate Sessions garden – surely a San Diego classic. Sixteen rooms range in price from $85 to $225, but they all include trimmings like fresh flowers.

Downtown The classiest and most historic downtown hotel is the *US Grant Hotel* (☎ 232-3121, fax 232-3626), at 326 E Broadway. It's not very old (1910), but it was built by Ulysses S Grant, Jr, and named for his father, and it has housed a host of famous guests, including Charles Lindbergh, Albert Einstein, and Harry S Truman. It was handsomely renovated in the 1980s, and is beautifully appointed with antique-style furnishings. Year-round rates are from $135/155 to $155/175; suites from $295. Special packages can be substantially cheaper, so it's worth calling.

The *Horton Grand Hotel* (☎ 544-1886, 800-542-1886), 311 Island Ave, reconstructed on this site from two 19th-century hotels, is more nostalgic than historic, but lots of people are happy to pay from around $100/140 for a room with lace curtains and a gas-fueled fireplace – ask about special rates before you book.

In the Horton Plaza precinct, try the upscale chains like the *Doubletree Hotel* (☎ 239-2200, 800-222-8733), 910 Broadway Circle, with distinctive architecture, tennis courts, pool, and all the luxuries you could expect, from $99 to $179 per night.

Other big name hotels downtown include the *Hyatt Regency* (☎ 232-1234); *Marriott Hotel & Marina* (☎ 234-1500), next to the Convention Center; *Marriott Suites* (☎ 696-9800), 701 A St, above the Symphony Hall; and the *Westgate Hotel* (☎ 238-1818), at 1055 2nd Ave, opposite Horton Plaza.

Coronado Obviously *the* top-end place to stay is the *Hotel del Coronado* (☎ 522-8000, 800-468-3533), 1500 Orange Ave (see entry in this chapter). Apart from the historical ambiance there are tennis courts, a pool, shops, spa, restaurants, and the Pacific Ocean out back. Remember that nearly half the accommodations are in the adjacent seven-story block, a modern building with no historical feel at all, and the rooms in the original building are pretty ordinary. Prices run from $145 to $335 per night.

Harbor Island & Shelter Island If you like yachts and harbor views then you might want to stay on one of these landscaped breakwaters. The *Sheraton Harbor Island* (☎ 291-2900), 1380 Harbor Island Drive, offers the complete four-star experience for around $150. On Shelter Island, the *Bay Club Hotel & Marina* (☎ 224-8888), 2131 Shelter Island Drive, and the *Kona Kai Plaza Las Glorias* (☎ 222-1191), 1551 Shelter Island Drive, are less fancy and around $50 cheaper.

Mission Bay The best places on Mission Bay are like tropical resorts, with lush gardens and private beaches. One of the first and finest of these developments is the *San Diego Princess Resort* (☎ 274-4630), 1404 W Vacation Rd. High season rates start at about $150. Other resort hotels include the *Bahia Resort Hotel* (☎ 488-0551), 998 W Mission Bay Drive; *Catamaran Resort Hotel* (☎ 488-1081), 3999 Mission Blvd; and *Hyatt Islandia* (☎ 224-1234), 1441 Quivira Rd.

Pacific Beach For comfort in an area with character, consider the *Pacific Terrace Inn* (☎ 581-3500, 800-344-3370), right on the beach at 610 Diamond St. It's new and well-fitted, and rates range from $130 to $170 for rooms with ocean views; $210 to $450 for suites with 'spectacular ocean views' ($30 more in summer).

La Jolla There's a range of top-end choices here, many with an old-fashioned charm. Most famous is *La Valencia* (☎ 454-0771), 1132 Prospect St, with great views, pink walls, palm trees, and Mediterranean style, and rooms from $150 to $325 year round. Designed by William Templeton Johnson, it has attracted movie stars and millionaires since it opened in the 1920s.

Older and smaller, the *Colonial Inn* (☎ 454-2181), 910 Prospect St, dates from

Hang out and watch the waves crash in La Jolla.

JAMES LYON

1913 and maintains a refined atmosphere, with rooms from $150 to $250, but less in winter. For luxury and style right on the beach, check the *Sea Lodge* (☎ 459-8271), 8110 Camino del Oro, where most rooms have a seafront balcony or patio, and cost from $105/120 in winter up to $215/305 for the best rooms in summer. The *Sheraton Grande Torrey Pines* (☎ 558-1500) is a modern luxury hotel, further north at 10950 N Torrey Pines Road, which boasts a butler on every floor and rooms at $175/250.

PLACES TO EAT
Downtown
Grand Central Café (☎ 234-2233) at 500 W Broadway (in the YMCA building), offers plain, inexpensive food Monday to Saturday – $4 breakfasts, $5 to $6 lunches, and $7 dinners. The *Sushi Deli*, 339 W Broadway, has good-value Japanese food – a sushi platter with soup and salad runs

from $4 to $8. The *New Peking* (☎ 235-6900), 638 Broadway, does an all-you-can-eat lunch and dinner for $5. *China King*, at Broadway and 4th, open from 11 am to 9 pm, does it even cheaper with a buffet lunch or dinner for $4. In the US Grant Hotel, the *Grant Grill* (☎ 232-3121) is excellent but expensive.

Horton Plaza has a variety of eateries, scattered through the complex. *Planet Hollywood*, facing the Horton Plaza park, is a fun place with a movie memorabilia theme. The *Farmers Market*, on the ground floor, has a good selection of sandwiches and deli items. There's *La Salsa* (☎ 234-6906) for Mexican food, and on the top floor a Food Court with lots of choices, and the upscale *California Cafe Bar & Grill* (☎ 238-5440), with indoor and outdoor dining, a brilliant view from the top level, and famously fresh dishes for lunch, dinner, and Sunday brunch.

In the northwest corner of downtown at 1747 India St, *Filippi's Pizza Grotto* (☎ 232-5094) is about the oldest pizza place in town, and still one of the best, with inexpensive pizzas to eat in or take out. In the southwest corner of downtown, *Kansas City Barbeque*, at the corner of Columbia and Market, is a popular place for ribs, onion rings, and fried chicken, and slightly famous as the locale for the 'sleazy bar scene' in *Top Gun*.

Gaslamp Quarter

Over 65 places here offer everything from a quick breakfast to a gourmet dinner, with a range of prices to match. Some are mainly daytime operations, while others offer entertainment well into the night (see Entertainment). Many change their character and clientele as the day progresses, serving lunch to business people, light dinner to the theater set, and strong coffee to a late-night crowd. It's a great area to walk around and choose a place you like – many have a menu posted out the front. The ones listed below will give an idea of what's available.

Rubio's (☎ 231-7731), at 901 4th Ave, is one of a chain of Baja-style Mexican restaurants, with delicious fish tacos, and lots of other low-priced dishes. Around the corner in the E St Alley, *Chino's* (☎ 231-9200), is more upscale and offers the eclectic mix of 'original American cuisine with Southwest and Far-East flair.' At 926 5th Ave, *Gyroscope* (☎ 235-4635) has a good selection of Greek dishes at around $10.

El Indio (☎ 239-8151), 409 F St on the corner of 4th Ave, is one of the original Mexican restaurants, with good food and substantial servings from around $4. *Johnny M's* (☎ 233-1131), at 801 4th Ave and F St, is a restaurant come nightclub, which serves large main courses from $13 to $18. On the other side of F St, *Cafe LuLu* (☎ 238-0144) serves coffee and light meals till 4 am. Next door, the *Star of India* (☎ 544-9891), at 423 F St, is a 1st-class restaurant with north Indian food.

Further down 4th Ave, at No 770, *Sammy's California Woodfired Pizza*

(☎ 230-8888), offers its enormously popular pizza, with toppings including cilantro, sun-dried tomato, and low-fat cheese, from $8. On the corner of 4th Ave and G St, *The Cheese Shop* (☎ 232-2303) is a daytime deli much loved by locals for its great sandwiches and coffee.

The *Sushi Bar Nippon* (☎ 544-9779), 532 4th Ave, serves traditional sushi items from around $3 to $5, but the tab can add up if you're hungry. *Café Sevilla* (☎ 233-5979), 555 4th Ave, is Spanish, but similar in that the tapas, at $4 to $6, can add up to a hefty total, especially if you stay around to enjoy the atmosphere and the music – the place stays open till 2 am. *Sybil's Down Under* (☎ 239-9117), 500 4th Ave on the corner of Island, is downplaying its Aussie image these days, but it's still a friendly place with a varied menu and nighttime entertainment. Another fun place for eating and drinking is the *Blarney Stone Pub, Bar, Grill & Restaurant*, at 5th Ave and Island St, where salads and sandwiches cost $5 to $6.

On 5th Ave just north of G St is a group of quality Italian restaurants, including *Trattoria La Strada* (☎ 239-3400), 702 5th Ave, which specializes in Northern Italian food and has dishes at a wide range of prices. A block north, three places run by the Croce family, side by side on 5th Ave, offer both music and good food, but they're not. *Croce's Restaurant & Jazz Bar* (☎ 233-4355), 802 5th Ave, and *Croce's Top Hat Bar & Grill* (☎ 232-4338), next door, serve good salads, pastas, and American fare, while *Ingrid's Cantina*, next door again, features Southwestern dishes at around $10; breakfast is a good value. *La Tazza*, 825 5th Ave, is popular for its lunch specials ($6), and its late-night coffee; it opens 10 am to midnight most days, but until 2 am on Friday and Saturday nights.

One of the most fashionable places in town is *Fio's Cucina Italiana* (☎ 234-3467), at 801 5th Ave, a modern Italian place. It's pricey, but not outrageous, the food is very good and the wine list is extensive – reservations are a good idea. One block north is another place to see and be seen, the *Dakota Grill* (☎ 234-5554), 901 5th Ave on the corner of E St. It serves 1st-class California/Western cuisine. Starters are $5 to $6, salads $3 to $5, and main courses $13 to $18. They have their own microbrewed beers, and a big wine list. In true California style, there's an open kitchen where you watch the chef in action, and an atmosphere described as 'casual but elegant.'

The south end of the Gaslamp is more downmarket. *Buffalo Joe's Barbecue Grill & Saloon* (☎ 236-1616), 600 5th Ave, does great steak, ribs, and alligator (from $10 to $18), $5 lunch specials, and has live music, though not always with a Wild West feel. *Ruby's* (☎ 595-7829), at 322 5th Ave, is a retro 1940s-style diner with music to match. *The Old Spaghetti Factory* (☎ 233-4323), 275 5th Ave, caters to families with and Olde-Worlde-theme decor and large servings.

Embarcadero

The waterfront area is the place to eat seafood, and the various Anthony's outlets have been serving it up for decades. Their classiest, and costliest, place is *Anthony's Star of the Sea* (☎ 232-7408), built over the water at the end of Ash St. You can eat virtually the same seafood in simpler surroundings and for less money at *Anthony's Fish Grotto* (☎ 232-5103), right next door – entrees cost from $6 to $19. Cheapest of all is *Anthony's Fishette*, on a veranda south of the Grotto, where excellent fish & chips with coleslaw cost around $5, and you can still enjoy the same view over the harbor.

A little further south, the building at the tuna harbor has two seafood places. Downstairs is *The Fish Market* (☎ 232-3474), an oyster and sushi bar where a meal will cost about $9 to $13. Upstairs, the *Top of the Market* (☎ 234-4867) is more elegant and quite expensive.

To eat right on the harbor, take a brunch or dinner cruise with *Hornblower/Invader* (☎ 234-8687), departing from 1066 N Harbor Drive. A dinner cruise costs $40 for adults, $20 for children, plus drinks, tax,

and tips. On weekends, a buffet brunch costs $30, and they throw in the champagne.

Old Town

Mexican and Southwestern flavors predominate in the Old Town eateries. They go for contrived Mexican atmosphere (lots of margaritas, and mariachi bands cruising the tables), but the food can be good, outdoor tables are popular, and it makes for a pleasant evening. *Casa de Bandini* (☎ 297-8211), 2660 Calhoun St, is one of the most established places, serving good, reasonably priced meals like pollo asado ($9) or enchiladas ($7).

Bazaar del Mundo, on the northern corner of the Old Town Plaza has three restaurants, and can get crowded. Also there, *La Panaderia* is a Mexican bakery where you can grab a quick churro for dessert.

One of the least expensive places is the *Aztec Dining Room* (☎ 295-2963), at 2811 San Diego Ave, at the west end of Old Town. Other Mexican possibilities along San Diego Ave include *Carne Estrada*, for takeout tacos at the corner with Harney St; *Old Town Mexican Cafe* (☎ 297-4330), at No 2489, with food which is perhaps more authentic; and *Cafe Coyote* (☎ 291-4695), at 2461, for a Southwest influence.

Balboa Park

Cafe Del Rey Moro (☎ 234-8511), 1549 El Prado in the House of Hospitality, is the best, and dearest, place in the park, but it has quite reasonable lunch specials. Beside the Museum of Art, the *Sculpture Garden Café* is convenient for a pricey snack. There are usually some hamburger and hot dog stands on El Prado if you need a quick bite.

Albert's (☎ 231-1515), the new upscale restaurant in the zoo, has a varied menu and a great location in the Gorilla Tropics – it's well regarded but expensive. Other places at the zoo serve standard lunch items, but are not particularly a good value.

CALIFORNIA

Hillcrest

There are over 80 places to eat here, many are well out of the ordinary, and most are competitively priced. It's a great place to look around – you may have to look around because parking is often difficult (infractions cost $60).

A classic is *The Corvette Diner* (☎ 542-1001), at 3946 5th Ave, with a riot of '50s theme decor and an all-American menu with burgers, salads, sandwiches, and daily specials for around $6. More contemporary, and more expensive, is *California Cuisine* (☎ 543-0790), at 1027 University Ave, with pastas, seafood, and game, a good wine list, and an excellent reputation. Dinner entrees start at $14, but lunch specials are as low as $7.

Numerous ethnic restaurants serve everything from Sicilian to Sichuan. Vegetarians should try *Monsoon* (☎ 298-3155), in the Village Hillcrest Center, or *Kung Food* (☎ 298-7302) at 2949 5th Ave, a long-standing place with substantial main courses for around $8. For the cafe society experience, hang at the delightfully named *Quel Fromage* (☎ 295-1600), at 523 University Ave, or *David's Place* (☎ 294-8908), 3766 5th Ave, where proceeds are donated to AIDS charities. If you're around for breakfast, you could do worse than *City Deli* (☎ 295-2747) at 535 University Ave.

Coronado

Definitive Coronado dining is in the Hotel del Coronado (☎ 522-8496), where the Sunday brunch in the *Crown Room* is an institution for $24, often crowded and maybe overrated. The upscale restaurant in the famous *Prince of Wales* room is being renovated, but you can try the *Ocean Terrace Lounge*, where main courses cost from $10 to $15. Two restaurants in *Le Meridien Hotel* (☎ 435-3000) serve well-regarded and very expensive French cuisine.

The Beaches

Many places along the beach offer American fare from hot dogs to steak dinners. Garnet Ave has a wider variety of cuisine, and the numerous bars will also feed you between drinks. At the beach end of Garnet, across from Crystal Pier, *Kono's Surf Club Cafe* (☎ 483-1669), is a breakfast and lunch place for hungry surfers with few bucks. Get inexpensive Greek food until late at night at *Santorini* (☎ 490-0150), 1050 Garnet Ave. *Pacific Beach Weinie* (☎ 272-8577), 1313 Garnet Ave, is an old-style family-run eatery, serving until 3 am. A good breakfast place is the *Broken Yolk* (☎ 270-0045), at 1851 Garnet Ave, which has over 24 types of omelet.

Grand Ave, two blocks south of Garnet, has added possibilities, like the *Firehouse Beach Cafe* (☎ 272-1999), overlooking the beach at 722 Grand Ave, open for breakfast (from $4 to $5), lunch, and seafood dinners. A couple blocks to the east is a branch of *Rubio's* (☎ 270-4800), 910 Grand Ave, where you can get the original and famous fish tacos from $2.

At the *World Famous* (☎ 272-3100), at the beach end of Pacific Beach Drive, you can have breakfast, lunch, or dinner inside or out with a view of the ocean.

Further down in Mission Beach, *Saska's* (☎ 488-7311), 3768 Mission Blvd, serves steak and seafood from $9 to $19. *Luigi's* (☎ 488-2818), 3210 Mission Blvd, is an economical pizza and pasta place, with entrees around $6. *Roberto's Tacos*, on the corner of Mission Blvd and Ventura Place, opposite the roller coaster, has really tasty tacos, enchiladas, and burritos for under $2, to eat in or take out.

In Ocean Beach, there's a good selection of eating options on Newport Ave. *The Little Chef* (☎ 222-3255), No 4902, is good for breakfast, and has a multi-cultural selection dishes, burgers, and sandwiches, all around $5. *Margarita's* (☎ 224-7454), No 4955, is an inexpensive Mexican place with tasty dishes, many under $5.

La Jolla

There are many top restaurants here, most of them charging top dollar. Two good alternatives are *José's* (☎ 454-7655), 1037 Prospect St, which serves good-sized Mexican dishes from about $4, and *The Spot* (☎ 459-0800), 1005 Prospect St, with

Chicago-style pizzas, steaks, and seafood. Both have bars and are open late.

For breakfast or lunch, try *John's Waffle Shop* (☎ 454-7371), 7906 Girard Ave, where $5 will fill you with waffles or sandwiches. *Harry's* (☎ 454-7381), 7545 Girard Ave, and *The Pannikin* (☎ 454-5453), 7467 Girard Ave, are both La Jolla breakfast favorites, but the Pannikin stays open in the evening, while Harry's closes after lunch.

Johnny Rocket's (☎ 456-4001), 7863 Girard Ave, is one of those retro-'50s diners serving pretty good burgers and fries. *Sammy's California Woodfired Pizza* (☎ 456-5222), 702 Pearl St, serves very tasty pizza and salads.

More expensive places, with quality international cuisine include *Alfonso's* (☎ 454-2232), 1251 Prospect St, for Mexican and margaritas; *La Terraza* (☎ 459-9750), 8008 Girard, which has some excellent Italian dishes for under $10; the *Star of India* (☎ 459-3355), 1025 Prospect St, with lunch specials; the *French Gourmet* (☎ 454-6736), 711 Pearl St; and *Royal Thai Cuisine* (☎ 456-2063), 737 Pearl St. The *Hard Rock Cafe* (☎ 454-5101) on Prospect St is also reputed to serve good food.

If money is no object, make a reservation, dress up, and go to *Avanti* (☎ 454-4288), 875 Prospect St, for excellent gourmet Italian dishes; *The Sky Room*, (☎ 454-0771), on top of the Valencia Hotel at 1132 Prospect St, for the magnificent view as much as the classic continental cuisine; or the *Top o' the Cove* (☎ 454-7779), 1216 Prospect St, for those who really appreciate fine wine and high prices.

ENTERTAINMENT

There's an enormous amount going on in San Diego, and you'll need some local information. The free weekly *San Diego Reader* has pretty comprehensive listings and reviews of movies, theater, galleries, and gigs. The *Performing Arts Guide*, available from International Visitors Center, covers all the theater, music, and dance offerings over a two-month period.

Call Ticketmaster for event information (☎ 268-8526) and to book tickets (☎ 220-8497). Ticketron also has information (☎ 565-9949) and takes reservations (☎ 268-9686). Times Arts Tix (☎ 238-3810), in the little Horton Plaza park on Broadway, sells half-price theater tickets on the day of a performance, as well as full-price tickets to most major events in the area.

Bars & Clubs

Gaslamp Quarter The distinction between eating and entertainment venues can be fuzzy in this lively area, epitomized by the places run by the family of the late bluesman, Jim Croce. The bar at *Croce's Restaurant & Jazz Bar* (☎ 233-4355), 802 5th

---

The Shame of the Gaslamp

You can't ignore *Dick's Last Resort* (☎ 231-9100), at 345 4th Ave, a venue which thrives on its own negative publicity. The self-proclaimed 'Party From Hell Place' is a beer barn that advertises 'no ferns, no fine art, no elite atmosphere, and no class, ever.' Instead of happy hour, they have a weekday 'decompression deal' for the 'working stiff,' which features a 2½-hour 'supervisor slam-o-rama,' $1 draft beer, and $2 margaritas. Their 'worthless eats' are served not on plates but in plastic buckets. After 8 pm, they have live rock and jazz bands which get a rowdy reception. I also heard they had some particularly tacky decor, and deliberately rude staff, so I went to check it out.

The waitress was very friendly, and politely offered to take a drink order. I asked her if it were true that the staff at Dick's were rude. She replied, somewhat apologetically, that they usually were but that she just didn't feel like it that evening. I walked past the bar, which was festooned with women's underwear, and suddenly I heard someone yelling. It was the barman – 'Hey, you! What are you looking at? You look like a fucking tourist! Sit down, have a drink, and for Chrissake get yourself an *attitude!*' ∎

Ave, is regularly packed with jazz fans, while *Croce's Top Hat Bar & Grill* (☎ 232-4338), next door, is more of a blues/R&B venue.

Patrick's II (☎ 233-3077), at 428 5th Ave, is a popular R&B bar. *Bodie's Bar* (☎ 236-8988), at 528 F St, has heavy rock music most nights, while *Johnny M's 801 Club* (☎ 233-1131), 801 4th Ave, has a variety of bands.

Much fancier is *Club 5th Avenue* (☎ 238-7191), at 835 5th Ave, which attracts a well-dressed Latino crowd on weekend nights. Around the corner, the E St Alley, on the north side of E St, has *Club F* (☎ 231-9200), a 'high energy dance club,' and *The Blue Room*, a classy-looking coffee lounge, bar, and billiard parlor. Another billiard place is *Fats* (☎ 230-1868), at 379 4th Ave on the corner of J St, which has 36 tables, two bars, and a good atmosphere. Downstairs at 802 6th Ave, *Club Chubasco's* (☎ 234-8944) has a DJ and is very much for dancing.

Other interesting downtown venues include *Cafe Sevilla* (☎ 233-5979), 555 4th Ave, which has live Latin American music and dancing most nights; *La Gran Tapa* (☎ 234-8272), 611 B St, with flamenco guitar music and dancing; and *Olé Madrid* (☎ 557-0146), 751 5th Ave, which often features reggae bands.

Old Town Despite the name, *O'Hungry's* (☎ 298-0133), 2547 San Diego Ave, is more for drinking than eating. They serve beer by the yard, and sometimes have live music – it can be a fun place.

Hillcrest Nearly all the bars cater to a mainly gay clientele. Some of the most popular are *Kickers* (☎ 491-0400), 308 University Ave; *The Brass Rail* (☎ 298-2233), 3796 5th Ave; *Flick's* (☎ 297-2056), 1017 University Ave; and *Rich's* (☎ 295-0750), 1051 University Ave. A few blocks east of Hillcrest, *Pecs* (☎ 296-0889), 2046 University Ave, is a heavy leather scene, while to the west over I-5, *West Coast Production Company* (WCPC, ☎ 295-3724), 2028 Hancock St, has loud disco music and

a reputation as a meat market. *The Flame* (☎ 295-4163), 3780 Park Blvd, and *Club Bombay* (☎ 296-6789), 3175 India, are both lesbian clubs.

The Beaches In Pacific Beach, there's a bunch of bars and clubs on and around Garnet Ave, and near the beach – none of them overly sophisticated. *Blind Melons* (☎ 483-7844), 710 Garnet Ave, has mainly blues performers and some rock. A dance club popular with a young crowd, *Club Tremors*, 860 Garnet, has a low cover and cheap snacks. *Emerald City* (☎ 685-7550), 945 Garnet Ave, plays alternative, punk, industrial, or gothic, depending on the night. The *Daily Planet* (☎ 272-6066), 1200 Garnet, is a colorful bar for sports buffs and beer drinkers. The *Society Pool Hall* (☎ 272-7665), 1051 Garnet Ave, is billed as San Diego's plushest, and it offers 15 full-size tables, snacks, and a bar, from 11 am to 2 am daily.

In Ocean Beach, *Winston's* (☎ 222-6822), 1921 Bacon St, features live reggae most nights.

Microbreweries
A popular local brew is Karl Strauss, available at many bars but made at the *Old Columbia Brewery & Grill* (☎ 234-2739), 1157 Columbia St. Microbreweries typically offer at least a dozen types of beer, serve quite good value meals, and often have live entertainment. In the Gaslamp, *Brewski's* (☎ 231-7700), 310 5th Ave, has 16 types of beer, along with good food and sports on TV. In La Jolla, try *La Jolla Brewing Company* (☎ 456-2739), 7536 Fay Ave.

Coffeehouses
Though coffee hasn't reached cult status in San Diego, coffeehouses are popular nighttime venues, particularly with those below the legal drinking age. They often have live music. Some to try include *La Tazza*, in the Gaslamp Quarter; *Java Joe's* (☎ 523-0556), 4994 Newport Ave, Ocean Beach; *Zanzibar*, Garnet Ave, Pacific Beach.

Theater

Theater thrives in San Diego, and is one of the city's greatest attractions. Book tickets from the theater, or with one of the agencies listed above. Venues include:

Civic Theatre
in the Community Concourse, 202 3rd Ave at B St (☎ 236-6510)
Hahn Cosmopolitan Theatre
444 4th Ave (☎ 234-9583)
La Jolla Playhouse
at UCSD (☎ 550-1010)
Old Globe Theater
one of three theaters in the Simon Edison Complex in Balboa Park (☎ 239-2255)
San Diego Junior Theatre
Casa del Prado, Balboa Park (☎ 239-8355)
San Diego Repertory Theatre
79 Horton Plaza (☎ 231-3586)
Spreckels Theater
121 Broadway (☎ 235-9500)
Theatre in Old Town
4040 Twiggs St (☎ 688-2494)

Comedy Clubs

Two of the most established comedy venues are *The Improv* (☎ 483-4522), 832 Garnet Ave, Pacific Beach, and *The Comedy Store* (☎ 454-9176), 916 Pearl St, La Jolla. They both open nightly, serving meals, drinks, and laughs.

Cinema

The main downtown movie venue is the UA complex at Horton Plaza (☎ 234-4661), with seven theaters showing current release movies. The Village Hillcrest (☎ 299-2100) with five theaters, shows some European and classic movies, as well as current releases. The Guild Theater in Hillcrest (☎ 295-2000) also manages some adventurous showings.

Opera

The San Diego Opera season runs from January to May, with performances at the Civic Theatre (☎ 236-6510). Tickets cost from $20 to $90, but discount tickets may be available from Arts Tix, or from the theater just before a performance.

Symphony

The Fox Theatre, a heavily decorated Spanish-Rococo structure, originally opened as a cinema in 1929. In the 1980s the whole block, bounded by A and B Sts, and 7th and 8th Aves, was redeveloped, but fortunately the theater was retained. Sold to the San Diego Symphony and renamed Copley Symphony Hall, it was renovated and now hosts a 24-week winter season of orchestral concerts. For concert details, call ☎ 699-4205.

Spectator Sports

The big sports venue is San Diego-Jack Murphy Stadium (☎ 525-8282), 9449 Friars Rd, in Mission Valley. The San Diego Chargers football team (☎ 280-2111), and the San Diego Padres baseball team (☎ 283-4494), are both well-supported, so book in advance for big games.

The Sports Arena (☎ 224-4176), 3500 Sports Arena Blvd, is where the San Diego Sockers play soccer and the San Diego Gulls play ice hockey. It's also the venue for any big rock concerts visiting town. There are some strip joints and sleazy bars in the area – single women may find Midway Drive a bit threatening after dark.

THINGS TO BUY

The most expensive shops are downtown, in Horton Plaza and the Paladion Center, and in downtown La Jolla, and the University Towne Centre mall. There are numerous other shopping malls in the suburbs, and particularly in Mission Valley.

The Factory Outlet Center (☎ 690-2999), just west of I-5 in San Ysidro, has discount outlets for Nike, Levi's, and other big names. There's also the North County Factory Outlet Center (☎ 595-5222), 1050 Los Vallecitos Blvd, San Marcos. For really cheap stuff, try Kobey's Swap Meet (☎ 226-0650), a massive flea market in the parking lot of the Sports Arena, Thursday to Sunday from 7 am to 3 pm. Shopping in Tijuana is not particularly cheap, and it's hard to find good quality, even in Mexican handicrafts.

The Indian Arts Center, 2425 San Diego

Ave in Old Town, sells Navajo jewelry, rugs, and crafts. There's not much to buy that's uniquely San Diegan, but some of the nautical novelties at Seaport Village might come close. Every museum and visitor attraction has a gift shop, so souvenir hunters might find a stuffed Shamu at Sea World, a realistic rubber snake at the zoo, or an old photo at the Museum of San Diego History.

GETTING THERE & AWAY
Air
There are some direct international flights to San Diego, but it's not a major gateway. If you're flying in from abroad, you will most likely come via Los Angeles, and it's hardly worth getting a connecting flight to San Diego (the standard one-way fare is about $75). The flight from LA takes only about 35 minutes, but it's almost as quick to drive down, and it's just as cheap to rent a car in LA as in San Diego. For flights to/from other US cities, it's worth shopping around for cheap fares, and allowing about three weeks for advance purchase. Airlines serving San Diego include: Aeromexico, America West (worth checking for cheap fares), American, Continental, Delta, MarkAir, Northwest, Southwest, and USAir.

Bus
The Greyhound station (☎ 239-8082), at 120 W Broadway, has luggage lockers ($2 for 6 hours), phones, and is generally user friendly. Services include:

Los Angeles (2½ hours) – 13 direct buses per day; $10
Oceanside (1 hour) – 7 buses per day; $3.50
El Centro (2½ hours) – buses at 6.45 am, 3:15, and 10 pm; $11 (three of these continue to Phoenix, Tucson, and El Paso.)
San Ysidro/Mexican border (half hour) – 19 buses per day; $4

Train
The Santa Fe depot is one of the Spanish Colonial-style structures built at the time of the 1915 exposition. Colonnaded, clean,

and spacious, but not overdone, it is almost definitive San Diego architecture. It's easy to find, at 1050 Kettner Blvd, at the west end of C St.

Amtrak's only services to/from San Diego are along the coast. From the Santa Fe depot, the *San Diegan* goes to Los Angeles nine times daily, with stops at six stations in between. Three of these trains continue to Santa Barbara. The first train leaves at 5 am, and the last at 8:45 pm, and it takes about three hours to reach LA. Southbound services are similar, with trains arriving in San Diego between 7:50 am and 11:59 pm. There's some nice coastal scenery along the way. Call Amtrak for reservations and information.

GETTING AROUND
Most people get around San Diego by car, but you can reach most places on public transport. Metropolitan buses and the trolley lines are run by Metropolitan Transit Service (MTS), and several other bus companies serve surrounding areas. All sorts of local public transport tickets, maps, and information are available from the Transit Store (☎ 234-1060), 449 E Broadway, open weekdays from 8:30 am to 5:30 pm. They sell the Day Tripper Transit Pass for unlimited travel on local buses, the trolley, and bay ferry at $5 for one day, and $15 for four consecutive days.

To/From the Airport
Lindbergh Field is quite close to downtown, and easily reached with Bus No 2 or No 2A. Various shuttle bus services go to and from the airport, including Cloud Nine (☎ 800-974-8885), Super Shuttle (☎ 278-8877), and Sure Ride (☎ 800-870-4787). Between the airport and downtown costs about $4.

Bus
MTS covers most of the metropolitan area, and is most convenient if you're going to or from downtown, and not staying out late at

night. Get details from the Transit Store (see above), or from the telephone information service (☎ 233-3004). Fares are $1.75 for most trips, good for at least an hour (and including an interchange if you ask for a transfer), but on express routes it's $2: exact fare only.

Trolley

Two trolley lines run to/from the downtown terminal near Santa Fe train depot. One line goes south to the Mexican border at San Ysidro, the other goes east to El Cajon. They run every 15 minutes during the day (from 5 am), and every 30 minutes in the evening (the last trolley leaves the city about 12:15 am). Fares vary with distance, up to $2. A third line, going north to Old Town, is under construction.

Train

A new commuter rail service, the *Coaster*, operates up the coast to North San Diego County. In the metropolitan area, it stops at Sorrento Valley station, Old Town, and Santa Fe depot. It only runs in the morning, and the evening until about 6:30 pm – but daytime and evening services may be added at some stage.

Car

The big-name rental companies have desks at the airport, but the lesser known ones can be cheaper. It's definitely worth shopping around and haggling – prices vary widely, even from day to day with the same company. The west terminal at the airport has free direct phones to a bunch of car-rental companies – you can call several and then get a courtesy bus to the company of your choice. Also, car rentals are as cheap or cheaper in LA, so it might be preferable to get one there.

Pacific Beach Auto Rentals (☎ 581-6500), 861 Garnet Ave, Pacific Beach, charge from $16.95 per day, and maybe less by the week or month – that includes 100 free miles, and they let you take the car to Mexico. It's a good value for traveling around the county, but not if you plan a long trip. Thrifty (☎ 239-2281) rents compact cars from $100 per week with unlimited miles. West Coast (☎ 544-0606) has cars from $18.95 per day. Others to try include Admiral (☎ 696-9907), Getaway (☎ 233-3777), National (☎ 231-7100), Avis (☎ 231-7171), Dollar (☎ 234-3388), and Tropical (☎ 239-9017).

Taxi

Established companies include American Cab (☎ 292-1111), Orange Cab (☎ 291-3333), Silver Cab (☎ 280-5555), and Yellow Cab (☎ 234-6161). Fares are $1 to start and $1.40 per mile.

Bicycle

Some areas around San Diego are great for cycling, particularly Pacific Beach, Mission Beach, Mission Bay, and Coronado. MTS buses on some routes have a bike rack, and bikes can be transported without extra charge. These routes include No 9 between Downtown and Pacific Beach via Mission Bay, No 81 between Pacific Beach and La Mesa via San Diego State University, and No 41 between Fashion Valley Center and UCSD. The bike-rack routes are indicated by a bicycle symbol on the bus-stop signs. For more information call ☎ 233-3004. You'll need a permit to take a bike on the San Diego Trolley, obtainable from the Transit Store.

Bike rentals are available at Coronado, Mission Bay, and the beaches. Rent-a-Bike (☎ 232-4700), at 1st Ave and Harbor Drive, has a variety of mountain bikes, road bikes, kids bikes, and cruisers, and will deliver one to you, seven days a week.

Boat

A regular ferry goes between Broadway Pier and Coronado. The Harbor Hopper ferry (☎ 925-4677) does a route around Mission Bay, stopping at Sea World and the big hotels. Water Taxi (☎ 235-8294) makes a regular connection ($5) between Seaport Village and Coronado, where it stops at the Ferry Landing Marketplace and Glorietta Bay, and makes on-call trips to Shelter Island, Harbor Island, Chula Vista, and South Bay.

Around San Diego

NORTH COUNTY COAST

The North County extends up the coast from the pretty seaside town of Del Mar to the Camp Pendleton Marine Base. There are lots of beaches, and an almost continuous string of suburban communities.

From the south, N Torrey Pines Rd is the most scenic approach to Del Mar, and you can continue along the coast on S-21. A quicker route is I-5 which continues to Los Angeles. Bus No 301 departs from University Towne Centre and follows the coast road to Oceanside, while No 800 is a peak hour express service; for information call the North County Transit District (☎ 722-6283). Greyhound buses stop at Del Mar, Solana Beach, Encinitas, and Oceanside. The new *Coaster* commuter train service stops at Solana Beach, Encinitas, Carlsbad, and Oceanside.

Del Mar

• *pop 4860* ☎ *619*

This very pleasant seaside suburb has largely unspoiled ocean beaches, and a horse racing track which is also the site of the annual county fair. Downtown Del Mar (sometimes called 'the village,' like other swanky San Diego communities) has friendly outdoor cafes along Camino del Mar, and the neighborly Seagrove Park, overlooking the ocean. **Del Mar Plaza** (☎ 792-1555), on the corner of Del Mar Heights Rd and 15th St, is a very tasteful complex of upscale boutiques, galleries, and restaurants, designed by Jon Jerde of Horton Plaza fame.

Hot-air balloons are a common and colorful sight over Del Mar, especially at sunset. See the Activities section (above) for details.

Del Mar Racetrack & Fairgrounds The Del Mar Racetrack (☎ 755-1141) was started in 1937 by a group including Bing Crosby and Jimmy Durante, and its lush gardens and pink Mediterranean-style architecture are delightful. The thoroughbred racing season runs from mid-July to mid-September, and track admission costs $3.

From June 15 to July 4 the **Del Mar Fair** (☎ 755-1161) is a major event, with livestock exhibits, carnival shows, rides, and big-name performers every night.

Places to Stay & Eat Staying near the beach in Del Mar would be nice, and there are plenty of hotels, but it's not cheap. The *Del Mar Motel* (☎ 755-1534, 800-223-8449), 1702 Coast Blvd, is right on the beach and costs from $60/85 in winter to $95/120 in summer.

There are lots of nice-looking places to eat along Camino Del Mar south of 15th St, many with outdoor tables. Quintessential Del Mar village dining is at *Carlos & Annie's* (☎ 755-4601), at Camino Del Mar and 15th St – it's a good place for breakfast (from $5) and burgers (around $7).

Solana Beach

• *pop 12,962* ☎ *619*

Solana Beach is the next town north, not quite so posh, but with good beaches. There are some budget-priced motels along State Hwy 21, which follows the coast.

Mexican farm workers lived around here from the 1940s, and two long-standing Mexican restaurants are worth looking up – *Fidel's* (☎ 755-5292), 607 Valley Ave, and *Tony's Jacal* (☎ 755-2274), 621 Valley Ave (Valley Ave goes north of Via de la Valle, just west of I-5).

Off Lomas Santa Fe, just east of the coast road, the *Belly Up Tavern* (☎ 481-9022), 143 S Cedros Ave, is a very popular music venue which regularly hosts great bands – cover charge is $4 to $7, or even $10 for top attractions.

Cardiff-by-the-Sea

At Cardiff State Beach, the surf break on the reef is mostly popular with longboarders, but it gets very good at low tide with a big north swell. A little further north, San

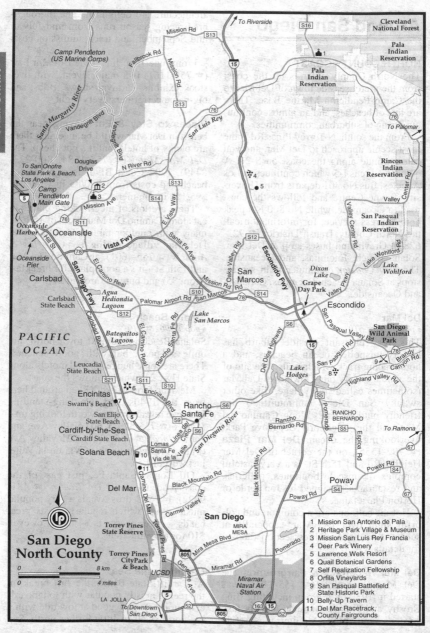

San Diego North County

0   4   8 km
0   2   4 miles

1 Mission San Antonio de Pala
2 Heritage Park Village & Museum
3 Mission San Luis Rey Francia
4 Deer Park Winery
5 Lawrence Welk Resort
6 Quail Botanical Gardens
7 Self Realization Fellowship
8 Orfila Vineyards
9 San Pasqual Battlefield
   State Historic Park
10 Belly-Up Tavern
11 Del Mar Racetrack,
   County Fairgrounds

Elijo State Beach has good winter waves. The campground at San Elijo State Beach (☎ 753-5091) overlooks the surf at the end of Birmingham Drive, and has tent and RV sites from $14 to $21 – book with Destinet.

Encinitas
• pop 55,386 ☎ 619

Conspicuous on the coastal bluff are the gold lotus domes of the Self Realization Fellowship, 216 K St, founded by Yogi Paramahansa Yoganada in 1937 – its **Meditation Garden** is open to the public Tuesday to Sunday from 9 am to 5 pm. They also conduct live-in retreats for those in need of spiritual renewal – call ☎ 753-1811 for details.

The beach below is called **Swami's**, and has one of the best breaks for experienced surfers. Big north swells produce a classic right, and attract so many surfers that the break is also known as Swarmy's.

The hills inland from here are used for commercial flower farms. In spring they produce bands of brilliant color which look spectacular from the highway.

The 30-acre **Quail Botanical Gardens** have a large collection of California native plants and sections for flora of various regions, including Australia and Central America. The gardens (☎ 436-3036) are open daily from 9 am to 5 pm and cost $2 for adults, $1 for children. Take the Encinitas Blvd exit from I-5.

In the 1920s **Rancho Santa Fe**; inland from Encinitas, was subdivided as a residential community that attracted Hollywood types like Bing Crosby, Douglas Fairbanks, and Mary Pickford. Architect Lilian Rice planned the community and designed many of the original homes in the elegant Spanish Mission style.

Places to Stay The *Royal Motor Inn* (☎ 436-4534), 1488 N Hwy 101, is small, quiet, and cheap, from $25/40. *Moonlight Beach Motel* (☎ 753-0623, 800-323-1259), 233 2nd St, is bigger and better positioned, and costs from $50.

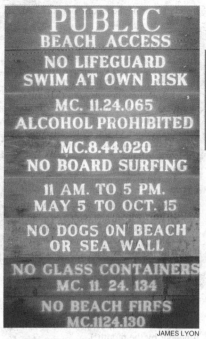

JAMES LYON

California's public beaches:
NO FUN ALLOWED

Carlsbad
• pop 63,126 ☎ 619

When the railroad came through here in the 1880s, it was found that water from the local wells had a high mineral content, supposedly identical to that from a spa in Karlsbad, Bohemia. To learn more of the town's history as a health resort, drop in at **Alt Karlsbad Haus** (☎ 729-3170), 2802-A Carlsbad Blvd. It has a small museum and gift shop. Other 19th-century buildings include the Victorian house (c 1890) at 2978 Carlsbad Blvd, which is now *Neiman's Restaurant*, and the original 1887 train station, which now houses the Carlsbad Visitors Bureau (☎ 434-6093), at 400 Carlsbad Village Drive. The Village Faire Shopping Centre, 300 Carlsbad Village Drive, has a small Children's Museum (☎ 720-0737), and sometimes has live outdoor music in the evenings. There are state beaches north and south of Carlsbad, as well as two lagoons.

Places to Stay & Eat One place you can't miss seeing is *Best Western Andersen's Inn* (☎ 438-7880), 850 Palomar Airport Rd, in the conspicuous Danish-style windmill near I-5. Rooms cost $65/85 ($10 more in summer), and the restaurant features the highly publicized pea soup, as well as mid-priced versions of the standard American fare. There are plenty of other eateries in Carlsbad Village.

You can camp at *Carlsbad State Park* (☎ 438-3143), where sites cost from $16 to $21 and can be booked through Destinet. There are plenty of other accommodations (the visitors bureau can refer you), but they tend to be expensive, especially in summer. Best value is probably the *Motel 6* (☎ 434-7135), at 1006 Carlsbad Village Drive, for $29/35, or one of its siblings in the area. The top-end option is *La Costa Resort & Spa* (☎ 438-9111), on Costa Del Mar Rd two miles east of I-5, with acres of grounds, all sorts of recreational facilities, and rooms from $215 to $400 per night (cheaper by the month!).

Oceanside
• *pop 128,398* ☎ *619*

A large proportion of Oceanside's population works on, or for, the big Camp Pendleton Marine Base, but most of the visitor interest is along the coast. The main thing to look at is the **Oceanside Municipal Pier,** extending over 1900 feet out to sea. It's so long that there's a little golf buggy to transport people to the end (25¢). There are bait and tackle shops, with poles to rent, and lights for night fishing, as well as snack bars and the mid-price *Oceanside Pier Restaurant.*

Oceanside dates from the 1880s, when the new Santa Fe coastal railway was completed. Very few buildings remain from this period, but there are some examples of work by Irving Gill and Julia Morgan. The Oceanside Visitor Information Center (☎ 721-1101), at 928 N Hill St, has a pamphlet with a self-guided history walk. A

number of 19th-century buildings have been reconstructed at **Heritage Park Village & Museum** (☎ 433-8297), a few miles east of town on Douglas Drive. The park is open daily, but you can only see inside the buildings on Sunday afternoons during summer.

Surfing Oceanside hosts major surfing competitions, notably the West Coast Pro-Am and the PSSA, both in June. The best surf is around the pier (good for spectators), and at the north end of the beach. You can rent a board from Beach & Bike (☎ 722-7101), 310 W Mission Ave, from $20 per day. The **California Surf Museum** (☎ 721-6876), 308 N Pacific St, has lots of photos and old boards – to appreciate it you'll need an interest in surfing *and* history. It's free, and open weekdays from noon to 4 pm, weekends 11 am to 5 pm (shorter hours in winter).

Oceanside Harbor At the northern end of Oceanside's waterfront, the extensive Oceanside Harbor (☎ 722-2133) provides slips for hundreds of boats. Helgren's (☎ 722-2133), 315 Harbor Drive S, offers a variety of charter trips for sportfishing and whale watching, around $22 to $32. At the south end of the harbor, Cape Cod Village has seafood restaurants and shops of a nautical flavor.

Mission San Luis Rey Francia Founded in 1798, this was the largest California mission and the most successful in recruiting Indian converts – it was known as 'the king of the missions,' and at one time some 3000 neophytes lived and worked here. After the Mexican government secularized the missions, San Luis fell into ruin – the adobe walls of the church, from 1811, are the only truly original parts remaining. Inside there are displays on work and life in the mission with some original religious art and artifacts. The mission (☎ 757-3651) is four miles inland, at 4050 Mission Ave (Hwy 76), and is open Monday to Saturday from 10 am to 4 pm, Sunday noon to 4 pm. Entry costs $3.

Places to Stay Budget motels are not hard to find, but may fill up on weekends and in summer. Close to I-5, there's a *Motel 6* (☎ 721-6662) at 1403 Mission Ave, and the *Sandman Motel* (☎ 722-7661), near the Oceanside Harbor Drive exit. In town, the *Dolphin Hotel* (☎ 722-7200), 133 Hill St, is an older place, with OK rooms at $25/31. Look for more upmarket chain motels.

Getting There & Away The Oceanside Transit Center, 205 Tremont St, is the station for Transit System buses, Greyhound (☎ 722-1587), and Amtrak (☎ 722-4622).

Camp Pendleton
Driving through on I-5, you can often see marines making amphibious attacks on the beaches. For a closer look, you can do a free self-drive tour of Camp Pendleton (☎ 725-5566), but there's not much to see except a **Landing Vehicle Museum**. The main gate is off I-5 just north of Oceanside, and you need to show your drivers license and vehicle registration.

San Onofre State Beach
A long and largely undeveloped beach area north of Oceanside, San Onofre gets good surf, and is reputed to have warm water because of the San Onofre nuclear power plant. Campsites cost $16 per night in summer – reservations can be made with Destinet.

NORTH COUNTY INLAND
Interstate 15 heads north from San Diego, through Rancho Bernardo (a residential community with miles of Mission-style houses) and Escondido to the Riverside County line. The number-one attraction is the Wild Animal Park near Escondido, but there are also some interesting historical sites, and the area provides access to the scenic backcountry around Palomar (see the Backcountry section). You can get out to Escondido by bus – call the North County Transit District (☎ 743-6283) for info. You really need a car to explore further.

Escondido
• *pop 108,635* ☎ *619*
Many people retire to this unexciting satellite city. Heritage Walk (☎ 743-8207), in Grape Day Park, is a collection of retired Victorian buildings which have also been moved here. A self-guided tour brochure is available at the old library, Thursday to Saturday from 1 to 4 pm. The chamber of commerce (☎ 745-2125), 720 N Broadway, has information about all of North San Diego County – their 'hotline' (☎ 800-848-3336) is available 24 hours.

There are plenty of places to stay; the chain motels are near I-15.

Wineries Spanish missionaries planted some of California's first grapevines around Escondido. Orfila Vineyards (formerly Thomas Jaeger Winery), (☎ 738-6500), at 13455 San Pasqual Rd, is open daily from 10 am to 6 pm. Deer Park Winery (☎ 749-1666), 29013 Champagne Blvd, open from 10 am to 5 pm, is touted as the world's only winery and car museum – it has over 100 American convertibles. Both wineries offer tastings, and sell wines by the bottle or the case, but they are almost invariably cheaper at supermarkets or big liquor stores.

Getting There & Away North County Transit (☎ 743-6283) bus No 810 is a peak-hour commuter service between downtown San Diego and the Escondido Transit Center at 700 W Valley Parkway. Greyhound (☎ 745-6522) buses use the same stop.

Wild Animal Park Since the early 1960s, the San Diego Zoological Society has been developing this 1800-acre, free-range animal park. The main attractions are the herds of giraffe, zebra, rhino, and other animals as they roam the open valley floor. Visitors take a 50-minute ride around the animal preserves on the Wgasa Bush monorail (actually an electric tram), which gives great views of the animals and includes an interesting commentary. The animals look wonderful

Lawrence Welk Resort
The Lawrence Welk Resort (☎ 749-3000, 800-932-9355), 8860 Lawrence Welk Drive, is about seven miles north of town. It incorporates the Lawrence Welk Dinner Theater (☎ 749-3448), which runs a summer season of light musicals, and the Lawrence Welk Museum, open daily from 10 am, which has memorabilia of Lawrence Welk's life and work. Lawrence Welk, aka 'Mr Bubbles,' was the man responsible for 'champagne music,' and he hosted the 'wunnerful, wunnerful' Lawrence Welk Show in the 1940s and '50s – it was the longest running music program in TV history. There's a museum on the premises also. The Lawrence Welk westauwant has a $10 buffet lunch which is a good value if you're hungry. ∎

in the wide open spaces, though often you can't get as close to them as you can in a regular zoo.

At the Petting Kraal you can often touch some of the youngest animals in the park. Animal shows are held in a number of areas, starting between 11 am and 4:30 pm. Get the map and schedule as you enter.

There's a full range of services, souvenir shops, and places to eat. San Diego Wild Animal Park (☎ 619-234-3153) is just north of Hwy 78, five miles east of I-15. Bus No 307 will get you there from Escon-

dido. The gates open daily from 9 am to 6 pm in summer, 9 am to 4 pm for the rest of the year. It costs $18.95 for adults, $11.95 for children 3 to 11 years, and $15.70 for seniors, including the monorail ride and all animal shows. Discount coupons are widely available. A combined ticket to visit both the San Diego Zoo and the Wild Animal Park within a five-day period costs $24/12.95. Parking is $3 extra. For a real safari experience, Photo Caravan tours go right in amongst the animals, but they're quite expensive, and reservations are required – call guest relations. Facilities are available for disabled visitors; call ☎ 619-738-5022 for information.

San Pasqual Battlefield State Historic Park
The USA won the Mexican-American War, but here at San Pasqual, in December 1846, they lost a battle with Californio lancers loyal to the Mexican government. Twenty Americans and 11 Mexicans were killed.

Today the battlefield is a peaceful park, a few miles east of Escondido. The visitors center (☎ 619-238-3380) has exhibits on the battle, and California's early history. It's open daily, free of charge.

Mission San Antonio de Pala
Built in 1810 as an asistencia to Mission San Luis del Rey, this was to have been one of a chain of inland missions, but the plan was abandoned, as was the whole mission system a few years later. This mission is largely reconstructed, and has a small museum (☎ 619-742-3317), open from 10 am to 3 pm daily except Tuesday, for $1.50. It's on an Indian reservation in a quiet, rural area, and it makes a pleasant stop along Hwy 76.

THE BACKCOUNTRY
Going inland from San Diego, you quickly get into sparsely populated rural areas a world away from the highly developed coast. Much of San Diego County's backcountry is occupied by the Cleveland National Forest, which offers hiking and mountain biking opportunities. Highway

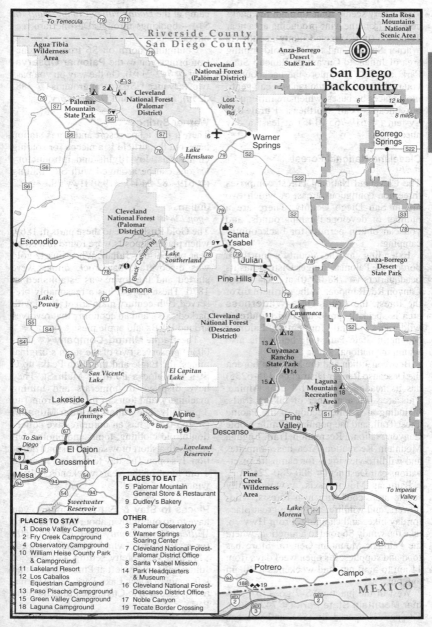

San Diego Backcountry

PLACES TO STAY
1 Doane Valley Campground
2 Fry Creek Campground
4 Observatory Campground
10 William Heise County Park
   & Campground
11 Lakeland Resort
12 Los Caballos
   Equestrian Campground
13 Paso Pisacho Campground
15 Green Valley Campground
18 Laguna Campground

PLACES TO EAT
5 Palomar Mountain
   General Store & Restaurant
9 Dudley's Bakery

OTHER
3 Palomar Observatory
6 Warner Springs
   Soaring Center
7 Cleveland National Forest-
   Palomar District Office
8 Santa Ysabel Mission
14 Park Headquarters
   & Museum
16 Cleveland National Forest-
   Descanso District Office
17 Noble Canyon
19 Tecate Border Crossing

79 is a very scenic route through the back-country, from the wine producing area near Temecula (in Riverside County), south via Warner Springs and the old gold mining area of Julian, to Cuyamaca Rancho State Park, and I-8. To explore the backcountry you really need a car, though you can get to most places by buses, which are infrequent but cheap – call Northeast Rural Bus System (☎ 619-765-0145) at least a day ahead.

Cleveland National Forest
☎ 619

The Cleveland National Forest comprises three non-contiguous areas, of which two are in San Diego County. There are a number of developed campgrounds, and you can obtain permits for backcountry camping.

Extending to the county's northern border, the Palomar Ranger District has its headquarters (☎ 788-0250) at 1634 Black Canyon Rd, Ramona. At the northern tip of the forest, the **Agua Tibia Wilderness** area is specially protected and requires a wilderness permit for entry. Palomar Mountain State Park (see below) is also within the national forest.

Between Julian and the Mexican border, the Descanso Ranger District (☎ 445-6235) has its headquarters off I-8 near Alpine. This area has a number of hiking trails, including a 37-mile section of the Pacific Crest Trail, and the popular 10-mile Noble Canyon National Recreation Trail. Laguna Mountain Recreation Area has campsites and wildlife viewing – for campsite reservations call Destinet (☎ 800-280-2267).

Palomar Mountain is a wonderfully scenic area, cool with lush forests, wild-flowers, and wildlife, and it's a great place for day hikes and camping. From Hwy 76, take the windy S6 road to a junction, where the Palomar Mountain General Store has food and supplies. It's open weekdays from 11 am to 5:30 pm, and weekends 8:30 am to 6 pm.

West of the junction, S-7 goes to **Palomar Mountain State Park** (☎ 742-3462). The park is open daily ($5), and you can

camp at the *Doane Valley Campground* for $14 – bookings through Destinet are recommended.

Continuing north on S6 from the junction brings you to the **Palomar Observatory** (☎ 742-2119). On the way up you pass two very nice USFS campgrounds (☎ 788-0250), *Fry Creek* and *Observatory*.

Warner Springs
There's just a spa resort and a gas station here, but the airfield is a mecca for soaring enthusiasts. Joy flights and introductory lessons can be arranged with Sky Sailing (☎ 619-782-0404), 31930 Hwy 79.

Julian
• *pop 1284* ☎ 619
The Gold Rush came to these parts in 1869, when placer deposits were found in a creek near present-day Julian. When quartz gold was discovered, hard-rock mines were started and the town was established in 1870. These days it has a reasonably preserved 19th-century main street (lined with parked cars), and an economy that revolves around B&Bs and apple pies.

The **Eagle Mining Company** (☎ 765-0036) preserves two of the town's original mines, the Eagle and the High Peak, up C St a few blocks north of Main St. They have displays of minerals and mining machinery, and tours of the mine from 1 to 3 pm daily. The **Julian Pioneer Museum** (☎ 765-0227) has an unimpressive collection of old clothing, tools, and photos, but it's worth a short browse, and a small donation. It's open Tuesday to Sunday 10 am to 4 pm most of the year; weekends only in winter.

Places to Stay & Eat For camping, you have to go out of town about three miles, to *William Heise County Park* (☎ 565-3600 for reservations), which has tent sites for $11, in a very pretty setting. Go west of Julian on Hwy 78, left at Pine Hills Rd and left again at Deer Lake Park Rd. Alternatively, go down to Cuyamaca Rancho State Park.

Accommodations in Julian are mostly

pricey B&Bs. Places fill up on weekends and holidays, and many have a two-night minimum stay. The chamber of commerce (☎ 765-1857), 2129 Main St, has information about many of them, but keeps irregular hours. About the most appealing is the *Julian Hotel* (☎ 765-0201), 12032 Main St, which dates from 1897. Most of the rooms don't have bathrooms, and it's not a great value at $38/64 for singles/doubles.

Lots of restaurants and cafes on Main St sell lunches and apple pies.

Near the town of Santa Ysabel on Hwy 78, *Dudley's Bakery* (☎ 765-0488) is enormously popular with San Diegans for homemade bread, cakes, and pastries.

Cuyamaca Rancho State Park

Delightful for the variety of its landscapes, Cuyamaca Rancho is a lush, cool contrast to the coastal areas and deserts. Though less spectacular than other California parks, its 33 sq miles embrace meadows with spring wildflowers, and forests of oak, willow, sycamore, and pine. Wild animals includes deer, raccoon, bobcat, and squirrel, and there's rich bird life.

The centrally located park headquarters (☎ 619-765-0755) opens on weekdays. During summer they have nature walks and campfire talks. Coming in from the south, there's a shop, pay phone, and a place to eat (closed Tuesday) at Descanso. There's also a shop, bar, and restaurant at Lake Cuyamaca, on the north side of the park. There's a $5 day-use fee, which you pay when you park.

The small museum next to the park headquarters has a good display on local Native Americans. It's open daily, free of charge.

The park is a nice area for hiking, with miles of well-defined trails – a popular 3½-mile climb goes to Cuyamaca Peak (6512 feet), offering a panoramic view. Many of the trails are open to mountain bikes. Most trails are also open to horses, and the *Los Caballos* campground is equipped with corrals. Holidays on Horseback (☎ 619-445-3997), 24928 Viejas Blvd, Descanso, arranges guided trail rides and overnight trips in the park.

There are two drive-in campgrounds in the park, *Green Valley*, and *Paso Pisacho*, charging $12 per site ($14 in summer). Call Destinet for reservations. There are also two undeveloped, walk-in campsites. *Lakeland Resort*, opposite the lake just outside the park's northern boundary, has cabins from $40 to $45.

Highway 79 goes right through the park, which can be approached from the north, via Julian, or the south, off I-8.

Tijuana, Mexico

• *pop 700,000 ☎ 52 (Mexico) + 66 (Tijuana)*

Visiting Tijuana is a real experience, not least because of the shocking contrast between the two sides of the border. Almost immediately you notice the pot holes in the sidewalk, the poverty of the street peddlers, and the almost chaotic atmosphere, especially compared with orderly, affluent San Diego. As a Mexican city, Tijuana is neither typical nor attractive, but as border towns go, it is almost an archetype, with gaudy souvenir shops, noisy bars, and sleazy backstreets. Though more respectable than it once was, it has never completely overcome the 'sin city' image it acquired during US Prohibition. It still attracts young Americans, who can get legally drunk from age 18, but these days old ladies and young families can feel

JAMES LYON
Immigrant crossing sign on the way to LA

comfortable in the main shopping streets, at least until sunset.

Tijuana (pronounced tee-HWAH-na and sometimes called 'TJ'), has a population unofficially estimated at 1.4 million. Just across the US border from San Diego's southern suburbs, it's a significant city in its own right, though in some ways the two cities are so interdependent that they can almost be regarded as a single urban area.

Speaking Spanish

It's easy to get around Tijuana without speaking much Spanish, but knowing just a bit will definitely help you, and is also respected by the locals. Here are some of the basics:

yes	*sí*	here	*aquí*
no	*no*	there	*allí*
thank you	*gracias*	coffee	*café*
you're welcome	*de nada*	tea	*té*
hello	*hola*	beer	*cerveza*
good morning	*buenos días*		

good afternoon	*buenas tardes*
good evening/night	*buenas noches*
goodbye	*adiós*
I don't speak Spanish.	*No hablo español.*
I understand.	*Entiendo.*
Where?	*¿Dónde?*
Where is . . . ?	*¿Dónde está . . . ?*
Where are . . . ?	*¿Dónde están . . . ?*
How much?	*¿Cuanto?*
How many?	*¿Cuantos?*
How much does it cost?	*¿Cuanto cuesta?*
It's very expensive	*es muy caro*
When?	*¿Cuando?*
How?	*¿Cómo?*
Why?	*¿Porque?*
Is there . . . ? Are there . . . ?	*¿Hay?*
I want	*Quiero*
I have	*Tengo*
I like . . .	*Me gusta . . .*
Do you have?	*¿Tienes?*

To make a verb negative, add *no* before the verb; I don't have is *No tengo*, I don't like is *No me gusta*.

and	*y*
to/at	*a*
for	*por, para*
of/from	*de, desde*
in	*en*
with	*con*
without	*sin*
before	*antes*
after	*después*
soon	*pronto*
now	*ahora*

Numbers

1	*uno*
2	*dos*
3	*tres*
4	*cuatro*
5	*cinco*
6	*seis*
7	*siete*
8	*ocho*
9	*nueve*
10	*diez*
20	*veinte*
30	*treinta*

Time

What time is it?	*¿Que hora es?*
At what time do you open/close?	*¿A qué hora abre/cierra?*

Telling time is fairly straightforward. Eight o'clock is *las ocho*, while 8:30 is *las ocho y treinta* or *las ocho y media* (eight and a half). However, 7:45 is *las ocho menos quince* (eight minus fifteen) or *las ocho menos cuarto* (eight minus one quarter). Times are modified by morning (*de la mañana*) or afternoon (*de la tarde*) instead of am or pm.

Days of the Week

Monday	*lunes*
Tuesday	*martes*
Wednesday	*miércoles*
Thursday	*jueves*
Friday	*viernes*
Saturday	*sábado*
Sunday	*domingo* ■

About 70% of Tijuana's economy is based on 'frontier transactions' like tourism, and another 15% is from *maquiladoras* (factories assembling products for the US market). Meanwhile, San Diego promotes Tijuana as one of its own tourist attractions, and depends on Tijuana for a supply of cheap workers. But beyond the shopping and entertainment precincts, Tijuana does have its own life, with office buildings, factories, and housing developments, as well as two universities and a rapidly growing population – it is one of the wealthiest cities in Mexico.

Orientation
Tijuana's central grid consists of north-south avenidas and east-west calles. Most of the calles have names as well as numbers, but are usually known by the number. South of Calle 1A, Avenida Revolución is the main commercial center. The Frontón Palacio Jai Alai, the big white building for Jai Alai games, is a landmark on the avenue. To the east, the 'new' commercial center straddles the Río Tijuana. Mesa de Otay, to the northeast, contains the airport, maquiladoras, residential neighborhoods, and shopping areas.

Information
For those venturing further down the Baja California peninsula, the book *Baja California – a travel survival kit*, published by Lonely Planet, is highly recommended.

Tourist Offices The Tijuana city tourist office, CANACO (☎ 85-84-72), on Calle 1A at the corner of Revolución, is open from 9 am to 7 pm daily. The Baja state tourist office, SECTUR (☎ 81-94-92), has an information booth on Revolución, diagonally across from CANACO, which keeps identical hours.

Foreign Consulates The US consulate (☎ 81-74-00) is at Tapachula 96, just behind the Club Campestre Tijuana (Tijuana Country Club). There are also consulates for Canada (☎ 84-04-61), France (☎ 86-55-54), and Germany (☎ 34-13-32).

Visas & Immigration If you're not going past the border zone (beyond Ensenada), or staying more than 72 hours, you don't need a visa or even a passport to enter Tijuana, but you should have some form of identification, with a photo. Returning to the USA, non-Americans can be subject to the full immigration bit, so must have a passport with a US visa. If your immigration card still has plenty of time on it, you will probably be able to re-enter with the same one; but if it has nearly expired, you will have to apply for a new one, and they may want to see your onward air ticket, sufficient funds, and so on.

Money Everyone accepts (even prefers) US dollars, and tourist prices are usually quoted in dollars. There are lots of *casas de cambio* which will change money and travelers checks at almost any hour. Bring small notes and coins, or you may have to accept change in pesos at very low rates. At most souvenir stalls and shops, prices are not marked, and haggling is expected.

Post & Telecommunications Tijuana's central post office, at Avenida Negrete and Calle 11A, is open weekdays from 8 am to 4 pm.

Tijuana has many public telephones and long-distance offices. The Central Camionera has several cabinas with an operator and a public fax. To call Tijuana from the USA, dial 011 (for international calls) + 52 (for Mexico) + 66 (for Tijuana) + the number. To call the USA from a pay phone, get a Ladatel phone card, and dial 95 + the area code (eg 619 for San Diego), then the number. For collect or person-to-person calls to the USA, dial 96, then the area code and number. Private telephone offices in Tijuana offer special deals, which are often cheaper.

Medical Services The Cruz Roja (☎ 132) is at Calle 10A and Avenida Pío Pico. The Hospital General (☎ 84-09-22) is north of the river on Avenida Padre Kino, west of Rodríguez, but many clinics cater to US visitors.

JAMES LYON

Tijuana is geared toward cheap entertainment for tourists.

Dangers & Annoyances

Coyotes and polleros – human smugglers – and their clients congregate along the river, west of the San Ysidro crossing. After dark, avoid this area and Colonia Libertad, east of the crossing. The **Zona Norte**, a very seedy red-light area, north of Calle 1A and west of Constitución, can also be dangerous, especially at night. Theft and pickpocketing has become more common in Tijuana in the last couple of years. The state government has a tourist protection service (☎ 88-05-55). For police, call ☎ 134.

Avenida Revolución

South of Calle 1A, Avenida Revolución ('La Revo') is Tijuana's tourist heart. Every visitor braves at least a brief stroll up this raucous avenue of seedy bars, restaurants, brash taxi drivers, tacky souvenir shops, zappy dance clubs, and street photographers with zebra-striped burros.

Frontón Palacio Jai Alai

Fast-moving jai alai matches at the Frontón (☎ 86-39-58), on Revolución between Calles 7A and 8A, resemble a hybrid between tennis and handball. Frontón staff explain details to neophyte betters, and the bilingual narration is also helpful. Matches on Mondays and Tuesdays start at 1 pm, and at 8 pm Thursday to Sunday. General admission is $2.

Centro Cultural Tijuana

This modern cultural center (CECUT, ☎ 84-11-11), at Paseo de Los Héroes and Avenida Independencia, is conspicuous for its spherical **Cine Planetario** (locally known as La Bola – 'The Ball'), which shows Imax films on a 180° screen ($4.50). The building behind has the **Museo de Las Identidades Mexicanas**, with rotating and permanent exhibitions on Mexican culture, which can be excellent; entry is $1. There's also an art gallery (free), theater and book shop. Hours are weekdays 11 am to 8 pm, to 9 pm weekends.

Plaza Fiesta Mall

Also at the junction of Paseo de Los Héroes and Independencia, across the traffic circle from CECUT, this shopping center imitates a Mexican village and somehow avoids being totally kitsch.

Bullfights

On Sundays, from April to October, *corridas de toros* take place at two bullrings: the famous Plaza Monumental near the beach, and the less spectacular El Toreo de Tijuana, Blvd Agua Caliente 100. Phone ☎ 85-22-10 for reservations (☎ 232-5049 in San Diego). Tickets cost from $4 to $16.

Places to Stay

Most visitors just come for the day, but if you stay too late there are plenty of accommodations available. Many places are much cheaper and rougher than anything in San Diego, but mid-range hotels are quite OK, and less expensive than equivalent lodgings on the other side of the line. The really cheap places in the Zona Norte should definitely be avoided.

Try the *Hotel Nelson* (☎ 85-43-03), Revolución 503, a longtime favorite for its central location and tidy rooms. Windowless singles or doubles with telephone and spotless toilets cost $24; a room with a view, TV, and street noise costs from $27. *Hotel Villa de Zaragoza* (☎ (66) 85-18-32), on Avenida Madero east of the Frontón, has clean, well-equipped rooms with aircon for $27.

Places to Eat

The venerable *Bol Corona*, across from Hotel Nelson, features a street-level bar and coffee shop, but the steakhouse upstairs is overpriced, and near a thunderous disco. Down an arcade off Revolución near Calle 3A, *Café La Especial* has decent Mexican food at reasonable prices, and is far quieter than the average La Revo eatery.

Tía Juana Tilly's, is a moderately expensive gringo hang-out, next to the Frontón

Palacio Jai Alai, while *Tilly's Fifth Avenue*, at Revolución and Calle 5A, is more of a nightspot. At Revolución and Calle 8A, *Sanborns* (☎ 88-14-62) has both a bar and a restaurant. For generous portions of reasonably priced pizza and pasta, try *Vittorio's* at Revolución 1269, on the corner of Calle 9A. *La Torta*, on Constitución between Calles 5A and 6A, is a clean, modern place serving quality tortas at moderate prices.

Several restaurants at the Plaza Fiesta mall, at Los Héroes and Independencia, are worth a try – *Saverio's* (☎ 84-73-72) has exceptional pizza, pasta, and seafood (prices are much higher than Vittorio's). Try also the Argentine-run *Buenos Aires* (closed Sunday) for beef or *Taberna Española* (☎ 84-75-62) for Spanish tapas.

Entertainment

The rowdy Avenida Revolución is the place for ear-splitting live and recorded music at places like the *Bol Corona*, *People's Bar*, *Hard Rock Café*, and many others.

Fancier discos and dance clubs are in the Zona Río, such as the kitschy *Baby Rock* at Diego Rivera 1482 near Los Heroes. Patrons dress well and start late.

Things to Buy

Jewelry, wrought-iron furniture, baskets, silver, blown glass, blankets, pottery, leather goods, and Mexicana of every description are available on Revolución and Constitución, at the municipal market on Niños Héroes between Calles 1A and 2A, and at the sprawling Mercado de Artesanías at Calle 1A and Ocampo. Auto body and upholstery shops along Ocampo offer real bargains.

Getting There & Away

Air Flights to Mexican cities can be substantially cheaper from Tijuana than from San Diego, LA, or other US cities, but this depends on the exchange rate. To US cities, it would be better to fly from San Diego.

Bus Only ABC local buses and the US-based Greyhound use the handy but dilapi-

CALIFORNIA

dilapidated downtown terminal, at Avenida Madero and Calle 1A. From the Plaza Viva Tijuana, near the border, ABC and Autotransportes Aragón go to Ensenada.

Both ABC and Greyhound (☎ 26-17-01) also use the Central Camionera, about five km southeast of downtown. From Calle 2A, east of Constitución, take any 'Buena Vista,' 'Centro', or 'Central Camionera' bus. The gold-and-white cabs (Mesa de Otay), from Avenida Madero between Calles 2A and 3A, are quicker and more convenient, and still cheap.

Buses from San Diego's Greyhound station (US$4) depart almost hourly between about 5:30 am and 12:30 am. Greyhound buses to San Diego from the Central Camionera also have connections to Los Angeles (US$18). Mexicoach (☎ 232-5049 in San Diego, 85-69-13 in Tijuana) has seven daily buses between San Diego's Amtrak station and the Frontón Palacio Jai Alai.

Trolley The trolley runs from downtown San Diego to San Ysidro, every 15 minutes from about 5 am to midnight. From the San Ysidro stop take the pedestrian bridge over the road, and go through the turnstile into Mexico. You don't need a taxi to get to the middle of town – just follow the footpath to the right and walk through the largely

deserted tourist trap of Plaza Viva Tijuana, take another pedestrian bridge across the Río Tijuana, and walk another couple of blocks to the north end of Avenida Revolución.

Car If you're just going to Tijuana for a day, don't drive your car – the traffic is frenetic, parking is a pain, and there may be a long wait to cross back into the US. It's better to drive to San Ysidro, leave your car in a day parking lot (about $5), and walk across the border. If you want to go further down into Baja, a car is useful. You'll need Mexican auto insurance, which is widely available for about $6 per day. It's much cheaper to rent a car in San Diego than in Tijuana, but make sure the rental company will let you take it across the border.

Border Crossings The San Ysidro crossing is open 24 hours. Mesa de Otay, about 6 miles east of town, is open from 6 am to 10 pm and is much less congested.

Getting Around
Local buses go everywhere for 2.50 pesos (about 40¢), but slightly more expensive 'route taxis' are much quicker. Tijuana taxis lack meters – most rides cost about 10 to 25 pesos (around $1.60 to $4), but beware of overcharging.

Artist's Palette, Death Valley

JAMES LYON

Trona Pinnacles, Upper Mojave Desert

Treasure Island, Las Vegas

The neon heavens of
Las Vegas

Next gas, 41 miles – Great Basin, Nevada

Valley of Fire, Nevada

Opera house, Pioche, Great Basin

California Deserts

Forget about green. After a while the starkness of the desert landscape, the clarity of the light, and the feeling of wide open spaces will become beautiful in their own way. The desert climate is easy to appreciate – sometimes intensely hot, but rarely oppressive, it has long been regarded as healthy, especially by those from colder, wetter, and greener places.

Outside the Resort Cities around Palm Springs, and the irrigated agricultural area of the Imperial Valley, California's deserts are sparsely populated. The most spectacular areas, especially Death Valley and Joshua Tree National Parks and Anza-Borrego State Park, attract many visitors at certain times, but for most of the year they are not crowded. At lesser known or less accessible places, like the Trona Pinnacles or the Algodones Dunes, and the long stretches of road between them, solitude is likely to be a real attraction. The harshness and the isolation of the desert can also present real dangers and visitors should be well prepared and take proper precautions.

History

Since pre-historic times, people have lived in those corners of the desert where springs, streams, or lakes can sustain them, and the signs of this ancient occupation can be found at several desert sites. For the early European explorers, like Juan Bautista de Anza and Jedediah Smith, the desert was a barrier between the habitable west coast and the settled areas to the south and east. The trails they pioneered, like the De Anza Trail and the Spanish Trail, can still be traced. Miners also came and went, establishing towns that died as the minerals played out and leaving their scattered, spooky skeletons in the desert.

Permanent European settlements came only with dependable water supplies, first with agricultural communities in the Imperial and Coachella Valleys, and then the

health and holiday resorts of Palm Springs. The military took over huge areas for training in WWII, and still has three million acres of weapons test sites, desert training centers, gunnery ranges, live bombing areas, and the large Edwards Air Force Base, used for aircraft testing and space shuttle landings.

Desert Protection & Conservation

In October 1994, the California Desert Protection Act was passed by Congress, giving additional environmental protection to millions of acres of California deserts. Death Valley and Joshua Tree were both upgraded from national monuments to national parks, and 1.3 million acres were added to the protected area of Death Valley. The act also created the East Mojave National Preserve, which transferred the management of the former East Mojave National Scenic Area from the Bureau of Land Management (BLM) to the National Parks Service (NPS).

Though generally welcomed by conservationists, these changes have some controversial features. Existing mining activities will be allowed to continue in the extended areas of Death Valley National Park, and this is seen as an erosion of the level of protection offered by national park status. Hunting is permitted in the East Mojave National Preserve, though it is not exactly a preservation activity. Then there is the question of funding the land management – the Republican Congress allocated the NPS an additional $1 per year to manage the 1.4-million-acre East Mojave National Preserve.

Most of California's deserts are recognized as being of international environmental significance. They now form part of the UN-designated Mojave & Colorado Deserts Biosphere Preserve. ∎

Hot Enough For You?

Temperatures vary with the seasons and the altitude. The hottest temperature ever recorded in the US was 134°F (57°C) in Death Valley on July 10, 1913. Summer temperatures commonly exceed 120°F (around 50°C) in the lower elevations of the California deserts. The *average* daily maximum temperature in July is 116°F in Death Valley, and 107°F in Palm Springs. It's usually around 10° to 15°F cooler at higher levels – the July average in Barstow (at 2100 feet) is 101°F. A rule of thumb is that temperatures fall by about 1°F for every 300 feet of elevation gain.

These figures are not the whole story, however. The reported and commonly quoted figure is the air temperature measured in the shade – a thermometer in the sun can rise rapidly to well over 150°F, and may literally burst. Sun blazing through the windows will turn a car into a little hothouse, and the temperature inside can reach 160°F within minutes – this can be fatal for children or pets. When it's this hot, adhesives soften, boxes disintegrate, pages fall out of books, plastics melt, and photographic film can change color. Exposed surfaces reach truly blistering temperatures after a few hours in the sun – the temperature on the desert floor can exceed 200°F. You can literally fry an egg on the ground. ■

Geography

About one quarter of California is desert. The area roughly south and east of Palm Springs is the 'low desert,' called the Colorado Desert (around the valley of the Colorado River), which is actually part of the great Sonora Desert, most of which lies in Arizona and Mexico. The area roughly north of Palm Springs, south of the Sierra Nevada mountains, and east of Bakersfield is the 'high desert,' named the Mojave, which extends into northwest Arizona, southern Nevada, and the southeast corner of Utah. The low desert is mostly less than 600 feet above sea level, while the high desert averages about 2000 feet, though there are peaks of over 1000 feet in the low

desert area, and Death Valley, which drops below sea level, is in the middle of the high desert.

The distinction is really one of ecology. The low desert is characterized by cacti, particularly the cholla, ocotillo, and prickly pear. A few of the large saguaro cacti exist in the southeast corner of the state, but are more common in Arizona and Mexico. The most distinctive high desert plant is the Joshua tree, seen throughout the Mojave. Joshua Tree National Park straddles the transition zone between the high and low deserts, and is a good place to observe the differences.

Flora

The desert plants can look drab from a passing car, but they are easy to appreciate with a short walk and a close look. Adaptations to the arid climate include thin, spiny 'leaves,' which resist moisture loss and deter grazing animals. Many plants have the ability to produce flowers and seed during brief periods of moisture, then become almost inert for the rest of the year. The best times to see the flowers blooming are in February and March in the low desert, extending into April and May at the higher elevations.

Small streams run down from the mountains in valleys and gorges that support tiny, oasis ecosystems, shaded by palm trees. Though palm trees are almost emblematic of Southern California, only one variety is native – the Washingtonia palm *(Washingtonia filifera,)* which grows in desert oases. It's a handsome tree, and produces stalks of small black berries that are quite tasty. The soils of the low desert are actually very fertile, and with irrigation they grow a variety of hot weather crops such as dates, grapes, cotton, and citrus trees.

Visitors centers at the various desert parks and reserves have excellent displays and information on desert plants and environment, and usually sell good-quality reference books. Some desert plants are described in the Flora section of the Facts about California chapter.

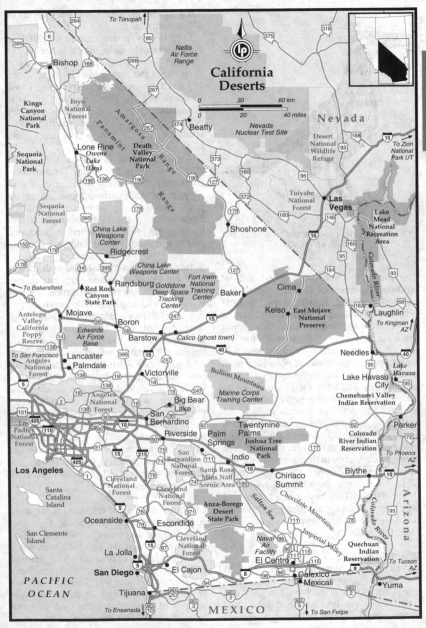

Roadrunners are cuckoos that race up to 15 miles an hour.

Fauna

The desert also supports a good deal of wildlife, but much of it is nocturnal, and not easily spotted. Roadrunners, the little gray birds with long straight tails, can often be seen running beside roads, though not often pursued by coyotes, who are usually too wily to show themselves. Desert tortoises are not so fast, but not often seen either: often road kill victims, they are now endangered. The cute kit fox will sometimes approach a camp at night, but bobcats are very shy. Smaller animals include the jackrabbit and the kangaroo rat, and a variety of lizards, snakes, spiders, and insects adapted to desert life. If you look in sandy patches early in the morning you will often see tracks of critters that passed in the night, but that may be all you'll see of the desert fauna. The best places for bird watching are oases – anywhere with water; the Salton Sea has several varieties of migratory birds.

Desert Travel

Extremely high temperatures and lack of water are the most obvious hazards of desert travel. Extremely cold nights and flash floods are less obvious risks. You should also be aware of some poisonous wildlife, vicious plants, and the dangers of old mineshafts.

Surprisingly, a temperature of 120°F in the desert can be quite tolerable because of the very low humidity – so long as you keep out of the sun, drink plenty of water, and don't try anything too strenuous. Those who live and work in the desert get little consolation from the cliché that 'it's a dry heat,' especially when repeated by visitors spending a few days by the swimming pool of an air-conditioned resort.

Another surprise is how cold the desert gets in winter and at night. Temperatures commonly drop below freezing on a January night and snow-capped mountain peaks surround some of the hottest valleys. Snow is less common at lower elevations, but the sight of snow-covered Joshua trees, palms, and cacti is not unknown.

Water It's absolutely essential to drink lots of water. Perspiration and evaporation keep the body cool, but the rate of moisture loss is high. Take regular drinks even if you don't feel thirsty – don't try to ration your water consumption. Beverages with alcohol, caffeine, or sweeteners will actually reduce the amount of water available to cool your body – drink extra water to compensate for their dehydrating effects, or better still, avoid them altogether, at least during the day. Allow one gallon of water per person per day, and twice that if you're walking, climbing, cycling, or doing any other outdoor activity. Carry an extra gallon of water per person in case you get stuck, as well as a few gallons of radiator water for your car. Always carry water in non-breakable containers.

Clothing Wear a hat that shades the head and neck. It's best to wear loose, light colored clothing that covers most of the body. Short shorts, sandals, and tank tops leave too much skin exposed to the heating effects of the sun. Thick-soled shoes are necessary to protect your feet from the hot ground. Carry warmer clothing for night wear – at least a sweater and a windbreaker – plus extra layers in winter.

Sunburn (caused by UV radiation) is a separate problem, distinct from the heating effects of the sun (which is infra red radiation). To protect against sunburn, use a high SPF sunscreen, lip balm, and good quality sunglasses.

Desert Survival The biggest danger is being stranded in the desert without adequate supplies of water. An interesting back-road drive can become a disaster if a car breaks down or gets stuck in sand. Even a short walk can turn into a fatal ordeal if you get lost or injured.

To avoid getting stuck, take a map and compass and know where you're going. Ensure your vehicle is in good condition and don't push it beyond its limits. Never venture alone into remote areas. Always tell someone where you're going and when you'll be back.

If you do get stuck, stay with your vehicle and wait for rescue. A car is easier to spot from a distance than a lone walker. If you become hopelessly lost while walking, seek the closest shady spot and stay put. People walking around in the desert can become exhausted and/or dehydrated very quickly. A few basic emergency supplies can greatly prolong desert survival. Have at least a gallon of water per person in reserve. Take a mirror, matches, and maybe some flares so you can signal for help. A tent or groundsheet can provide vital sun protection, and increase your visibility. A flashlight, pocketknife, first aid kit, and extra food may also be useful.

Flash Floods Flooding can occur after heavy rains, even if the downpour is many miles away. It is unwise to camp or park in streambeds or washes if there is even the slightest chance of rain in any upstream area.

Poisonous Animals Black widow spiders, scorpions, rattlesnakes, and centipedes are all venomous, but are unlikely to attack. See the Facts for the Visitor chapter for more information.

Pointy Plants Obviously, cacti have spikes. Less obvious are the tiny barbs, which make the spikes so difficult to pull out of your skin. Bring strong tweezers or pliers to extract them.

Mines There are hundreds, perhaps thousands, of abandoned mineral mines in the California deserts. Watch out for holes or shafts, which can be hard to see and easy to fall into. Old shafts are very dangerous as the supporting timbers have usually deteriorated, and the air may contain poisonous gases. Never enter old mines.

Explosives Much of the desert has been used for military training and testing. Though this is mostly in defined areas, unexploded bombs and shells have turned up in many places and should never be touched. It would be unwise to enter any area marked as a live bombing range.

Getting Around

The main towns of the desert can all be reached by bus, and some by rail as well, but to get out into the desert itself you really need your own transport. You can rent cars in the desert towns, but rentals are usually cheaper in the coastal cities, so you might as well drive yourself the whole way. Don't even think about hitching – you could die waiting for a lift out there.

Desert Driving Much of California's desert is accessible on paved roads and requires no more than a normal car, driven with normal care. Many car rental contracts do not allow the vehicle to be driven off normally trafficked roads.

As you travel into more remote areas, it's increasingly important to make sure the car is in good condition, and you have spare gasoline, oil, and coolant. You might also carry a tire pump, a shovel to dig your wheels out, and a board or traction mats, in case you get stuck in loose sand. For really rough roads a 4WD is best, but regular cars can travel most unpaved roads if the clearance between the underside of the car and the ground is adequate. Off-road driving is prohibited on all public land, except in areas designated for ORV use.

Get some cardboard or plastic sun-shields, or use towels to cover the steering wheel, dashboard, and seats. Even a few minutes parked in the sun can leave the interior too hot to touch.

Check tires before you start a day's hot-weather driving and make sure they are at full pressure – an under-inflated tire can overheat very quickly. Never deflate a tire which has become hot after driving.

Watch the temperature gauge of your car. If it starts to heat up, turn off the air conditioning. If it continues to get hotter, pull over, face the front of the car into the wind, keep the engine running, and dribble water over the front of the radiator (*not* over the engine or fan). Turning the car heater on to the max can also help.

Tours An alternative to driving may be a tour from the nearest city. For tours to Joshua Tree National Park, look for an operator in Palm Springs; for Anza Borrego, check operators in San Diego; for Death Valley, try in Las Vegas.

Palm Springs & Coachella Valley

☎ *619*

The so-called Resort Cities extend the length of the Coachella Valley, forming an almost continuous sprawl of suburbs and golf courses. Palm Springs is the original, best known, and most visited area, famous as a winter retreat for Hollywood stars, but increasingly a well-scrubbed retirement home for the moderately rich. Going south-east down the valley, Cathedral City, Rancho Mirage, and Palm Desert may be slightly less prestigious, but they all have swanky resorts and retirement communi-ties, and they all seem to survive without visible industries or downtown areas. At the far end of the valley, Indio originally serviced the railroad and the surrounding

agricultural areas, and still resembles a rural town.

To get things in perspective – the valley has about 250,000 people, 10,000 swim-ming pools, 85 golf courses, and more plas-tic surgeons per head than anywhere else in the US.

Most visitors (about 3.5 million per year) come in the cooler months, to play golf or just enjoy the desert climate. There's a growing gay scene in Palm Springs and Cathedral City, and college kids in the thousands descend on the town for spring break. But once you've seen Palm Canyon Drive and the few attractions in town, there's not much to do except hang around a pool or play golf. The real interest is in visiting the nearby canyons, mountains, and desert areas.

History

Cahuilla people occupied the canyons on the southwest side of the Coachella Valley, where permanent streams flowed from the San Jacinto mountains. They also used the hot springs where the city of Palm Springs now stands, so the early Spanish visitors gave them the name 'Agua Caliente,' mean-ing 'hot water.' In 1851, the Cahuilla staged a revolt against American authorities and, though it was put down, their land rights were recognized in the 1852 Treaty of Temecula. However, the treaty was not rat-ified by Congress, and was superseded by a new arrangement in 1876.

In order to promote the construction of a railroad from Los Angeles to Yuma, Ari-zona, the valley was divided into a checker-board of square-mile sections, and the odd-numbered sections were granted to the Southern Pacific Railroad. The even-numbered sections were given to the Agua Caliente as their reservation. The railroad was built, the company sold most of its land, and the whole valley was progres-sively developed as farm land, and later with health spas, hotels, and resorts.

It was not until the 1940s that surveys established the exact boundaries of the sec-tions, and by then much of the Indian land had been built on. Though they couldn't sell the land, the Indians were able to charge rent, and as the valley has grown more affluent, the several hundred Indians who can establish tribal membership have become very wealthy.

At the southern end of the valley, Indio was a construction camp for the railway in the 1870s, and its artesian water was tapped to irrigate the first crops. Date palms from Algeria were introduced in 1890, and have become the major fruit crop of the valley, along with citrus fruits and table grapes. Later, water was brought all the way from the Colorado River.

In Palm Springs, the first hotels were for those who sought the health benefits of the natural hot springs, and a desert climate. From the late 1920s it became popular as a resort area, and as a winter getaway for Hollywood stars. One of the city's first councilwomen, Ruth Hardy, was responsible for many of the restrictive ordinances that saved Palm Springs from the excesses of uncontrolled development, including bans on two-story houses and large outdoor advertisements.

Orientation

The Resort Cities extend over 25 miles from Palm Springs to Indio, with most of the communities along Hwy 111, south of I-10. Going up and down the valley, it's often quicker to take the interstate than to follow Hwy 111 through miles of suburbs and dozens of traffic lights.

Palm Springs has a reasonably compact downtown area, centered on about four blocks of Palm Canyon Drive, with shops, banks, restaurants, and some things to see. In this area, traffic goes south on Palm Canyon Drive and north on Indian Canyon Drive. Tahquitz Canyon Way divides these streets into north and south. The ritziest residential area is Little Tuscany, on the slopes to the west of N Palm Canyon Drive. Go to the top of Chino Canyon Rd for a view over town.

Restaurants and chain motels are spread out along E Palm Canyon Drive and Hwy 111 to Cathedral City. Some of the main attractions are just outside of Palm Springs,

particularly the Aerial Tramway that ascends the San Jacinto mountains to the west, and the Indian Canyons in the Agua Caliente reservation, south of town.

Information

The Palm Springs Visitor Center (☎ 778-8418), 2781 N Palm Canyon Drive near the turn-off to the aerial tram, has a helpful staff with information about local hotels and attractions. Hotel referrals and bookings (☎ 800-347-7746) are available weekdays from 9 am to 5 pm, weekends until 6 pm. For other information, call ☎ 800-417-3529.

Free publications with visitor information include *Desert Key* magazine and *Desert Guide. Lifestyle Magazine* (☎ 321-2685) has information for the gay community.

The Palm Springs post office (☎ 325-9631) is at 333 Amado Rd. Desert Hospital

---

Palm Springs Celebs

A long list of Hollywood stars have lived or stayed in Palm Springs, including Jean Harlow, Al Jolson, Nat King Cole, Liberace, Dean Martin, Jack Warner, Liz Taylor, Spencer Tracy, Bing Crosby, Lawrence Olivier, Goldie Hawn, and Kirk Douglas – name dropping comes easy in a place with streets like Dinah Shore Drive and Gene Autry Trail. Former President Gerald Ford makes frequent golfing forays to the valley, and also has a Drive named after him.

The town is also associated with some well-known scandals, romances, and marriages – Clark Gable and Carol Lombard; Frank Sinatra and Ava Gardner; Elvis and Priscilla (who honeymooned here); Bob and Dolores Hope (Dolores is much more popular in Palm Springs than Bob); the evangelical Jim and Tammie Bakker; and Zsa Zsa Gabor (plus six or eight of her husbands).

Sonny Bono, late of Sonny and Cher, owns a fashionable restaurant here and was once mayor of Palm Springs. He now represents the area in Congress. ■

(☎ 323-6511), 1150 N Indian Canyon Drive, provides 24-hour emergency care.

Palm Springs Desert Museum

Some of the most interesting exhibits in the museum are the large dioramas and displays of desert plants and wildlife – they're informative and very well done. There are also some excellent Cahuilla baskets, temporary and permanent exhibitions of Western American art, and a fine sculpture collection. Be sure to pick up a museum guide when you enter, as all the wings and galleries are identified only by the names of museum benefactors, which must be gratifying for the donors but is not very helpful for visitors.

The Desert Museum (☎ 325-7186) is at 101 Museum Drive, west of Palm Canyon Drive behind Desert Fashion Plaza. Entry is $5, but it's free on the first Tuesday of the month. It opens from 10 am to 4 pm (to 5 pm on weekends); closed on Mondays, holidays, and during the summer.

Village Green Heritage Center

This grassy little square at 221 S Palm Canyon Drive has some 'heritage' attractions, the best of which is Ruddy's General Store (☎ 327-2156), a reproduction of a 1930s general store, with authentic period fittings and goods in their original packages (open October to June from Thursday to Sunday, weekends only in other months).

The Agua Caliente Cultural Museum (☎ 323-0151) has pictures and artifacts on the tribe's history (closed Monday and Tuesday). The 1884 McCallum Adobe, said to be the home of Palm Springs' first white settler, has been reconstructed on this site and has a collection of old pictures and artifacts. The Little House, next door, is another relocated pioneer house, made of old railroad ties. Tours of the houses (☎ 323-8297) are given from October to May – call for times.

Hot Springs

The original hot springs are now part of the Spa Hotel & Casino (☎ 325-1461), at 100 N Indian Canyon Dr, which is still owned by the Indian community. Day visitors can use the spa for $15.

Oasis Water Park

With 12 water-slides and a large wave pool, Oasis Water Park (☎ 327-0499), 1500 Gene Autry Trail, is a lot of fun in the hotter months, but closed from November to April. They charge by height – $17 if you're over 60 inches, free if you're under 40 inches, and $11.50 if you're somewhere in between. Discounts and coupons are available. Hours are 11 am to 6 pm.

Moorten Botanic Gardens

If you're really interested in desert plants you might find this place worth a visit, though it's not very attractively laid out and there's little in the way of informative signs or pamphlets. The gardens (☎ 327-6555), 1701 S Palm Canyon Drive, are open daily and charge $3 admission.

Aerial Tramway

A real highlight of a visit to Palm Springs is a trip in this cable car, which climbs nearly 6000 vertical feet, from the desert floor up to the San Jacinto mountains, in about 14 minutes. You ascend through visibly different vegetation zones from the Valley Station (2643 feet) to the Mountain Station (8516 feet). It's 30° to 40° cooler as you step out into pine forest at the top, so bring some warm clothing – the trip up is said be the equivalent of driving from Mexico to Canada.

The Mountain Station has a bar, cafeteria, observation area, and a theater showing a short film on the tramway. The views over the valley are brilliant, and it's worth allowing some time at the top to enjoy the San Jacinto Wilderness State Park, where there are hiking trails (some paved and suitable for wheelchairs) and primitive campgrounds. A **cross-country ski center** (☎ 327-6002) operates from December to April if there is enough snow.

The standard tramway hours are daily from 10 am to 8 pm, on weekends and holidays from 8 am. In daylight savings time, the last car goes up at 9 pm, and the last car comes down at 10:45 pm. A roundtrip costs $16/10 for adults/children, and various discounts are available. A Ride 'n' Dine combination, which includes a buffet dinner at the top, is available after 4 pm for $20/13. It's not a bad dinner for $4, but the deal may not allow enough time for a leisurely look around at the top.

Indian Canyons

Streams flowing from the San Jacinto Mountains sustain a rich variety of plants in the canyons around Palm Springs. The canyons were home to Indian communities for hundreds of years, and are now part of the Agua Caliente Reservation. A walk up these canyon oases, shaded by fan palms and surrounded by towering cliffs, is a real delight. From downtown, go south on Palm Canyon Drive for about two miles to the reservation entrance, where you pay a $5 admission; hours are 8 am to 5 pm in fall and winter, until 6 pm in spring and summer.

Closest to town is **Andreas Canyon,** where there's a pleasant picnic area. Nearby are imposing rock formations where you can find Indian mortar holes, used for grinding seeds, and some rock art (see California's Indians in Facts about California). The trail up the canyon is an easy walk.

About a 20-minute walk south from Andreas Canyon is **Murray Canyon,** which can't be reached by road and is therefore less visited. It's a good place for bird watching, and bighorn sheep might be seen on the slopes above the canyon.

Following the winding access road to the end brings you to **Palm Canyon,** which is the most extensive of the canyons, some 15 miles long, with good trails and a store selling snacks and souvenirs. In the morning, look for animal tracks in the sandy patches.

Another canyon just west of town, **Tahquitz Canyon,** is currently closed to visitors, though you may be able to see it with one of the hiking groups listed below (under Tours). It is noted for its waterfalls

and swimming holes, and once supported a large Indian population.

The Living Desert

This outdoor museum and botanic garden presents a wide variety of desert plants and animals, including some exotic species, and has exhibits on desert geology and Indian culture. The Living Desert (☎ 346-5694), 47-900 Portola Ave, Palm Desert, is open September to mid-June, daily from 9 am to 4:30 pm, and costs $7/3.50. Between Thanksgiving and New Year, from 6 to 9 pm, the museum also presents its WildLights show for an additional $4. Discounts are available.

Miscellaneous Museums

There are quite a few other attractions in and around the valley, which may be worth a visit if you have the time and a particular interest. One of the weirdest is **Cabot's Old Indian Pueblo Museum** (☎ 329-7610), 67616 E Desert View Ave, Desert Hot Springs, which is a ramshackle, junk-filled, old house built by an eccentric, desert-loving recluse. It costs $2.50 and opens weekends and most other days.

The **Museum of the Heart** (☎ 324-3278), at the Eisenhower Medical Center, 39-600 Bob Hope Drive, Rancho Mirage, explains all about heart attacks and how to avoid them, while giving you a chance to step inside a giant aorta. The suggested donation is $2.50, but if you're about to pay for a coronary bypass they may overlook it.

Another very specialized attraction is the **Jude E Poynter Golf Museum** (☎ 341-0994), on Fred Waring Drive east of Monterey Ave, in Palm Desert. It features a set of clubs owned by Gerald Ford, lots of photos of lots of golfers, and a fine display of clubs from the late gutta-percha period (1885-1900).

Way down in Indio, the **Coachella Valley Museum & Cultural Center** (☎ 342-6651), 82-616 Miles Ave, actually has some quite interesting displays on the early days of date farming and how people lived here before air conditioning, as well as the usual old kitchen utensils, farm equipment, and school desks. It opens daily except Monday, and costs $1.

West of town, near Banning, the **Malki Museum** (☎ 849-7289), on the Morongo Indian reservation, has a small, disorganized collection that includes some old and very interesting Cahuilla artifacts. They publish some fine pamphlets on Indian history and culture. The museum is open Wednesday to Sunday from 10 am to 4 pm.

Golf

Golf is huge here, with over 80 public, semi-private, private, and resort courses, with a total of 1463 holes. There are several big tournaments annually, and the College of the Desert even has a School of Golf Management. Green fees run from $26 to $215, depending on the course, the season, and the day of the week. Most hotels can make arrangements for their guests to play on at least one local course. You can receive substantial savings through Stand-by Golf (☎ 321-2665), which can provide guaranteed tee-times, at a discount, for same-day or next-day play at 20 courses. They are open daily from 7 am to 9 pm.

Hiking

There are lots of enthusiastic local hikers, and it's a great way to see the desert. Most of the hiking is in the canyons, and in the San Jacinto and Santa Rosa Mountains. Trail Discovery Outdoor Guide Service (☎ 325-4453) does guided hiking and running trips, locally and in Joshua Tree National Park. A two-hour hike is $25 per person, a half-day trip is $45, and a full-day trip $75 (less for groups of five or more). The Palm Springs Desert Museum (☎ 325-7186) conducts short hikes on Fridays and Saturdays, and visitors may be able to join in – call for information. Visitors may also be able to join trips run by the Coachella Valley Hiking Club; call their information number (☎ 345-6234) during business hours.

Hiking and rock climbing equipment and information is available at The Great Outdoors (☎ 773-4880), 73-360 Hwy 111,

Palm Desert. The owners of this shop have a good knowledge of the area.

Bicycling

There are several bike paths in Palm Springs and the valley. Local groups sometimes arrange group rides – try calling the Desert Cyclery (☎ 321-2453), 70053 Hwy 111, Rancho Mirage.

Horseback Riding

Smoketree Stables (☎ 327-1372), 2500 Toledo Ave, Palm Springs, arranges trail rides, from a one-hour outing to an all-day trek. The cost is about $22 per hour and they take novice or experienced riders.

Hot-Air Ballooning

Several operators do hot-air balloon flights, including Sunrise Balloons (☎ 800-345-3272), in Indio, and American Balloon Charters (☎ 800-359-6837), in Palm Springs. Flights are usually around sunrise or sunset.

Organized Tours

Celebrity Tours About the best way to pick up on the gossip and glamour of Palm Springs is to take a trip with Celebrity Tours (☎ 770-2700), based at Rimrock Shopping Center, 4751 E Palm Canyon Drive. You can do it yourself with a map of the stars' homes from the visitors center ($5!), but you'll miss out on the amusing commentary and all the juicy gossip. Gray Line Tours (☎ 325-0974) also does tours that show off celebrity homes.

Desert Adventures This very professional operation runs guided jeep tours to the Indian Canyons, Santa Rosa Mountains, around the Bighorn Sheep Preserve, and to other areas that can be hard to get to, even with your own 4WD. The driver/guides are full of information about the natural environment and Indian lore. Tours cost about $25 per hour; $70 for half a day. Make a booking by calling ☎ 864-6530.

Covered Wagon Tours A leisurely two-hour tour of the Coachella Valley Preserve in a mule-drawn covered wagon follows the San Andreas fault, while guides describe many of the plants and how they were used by the Agua Caliente people. At the end of the trip there's an optional cowboy cook-out from the chuck wagon, and a country music singalong. It's $40 for the tour, $55 with dinner, and half price for kids. Reservations (☎ 347-2161) are required.

Special Events
Dinah Shore Weekend This event marks the biggest lesbian happening in the USA, when 25,000 women descend upon Palm Springs for the Dinah Shore Golf Tournament in March. While some women actually watch golf, most go just for the pool parties and events. The weekend used to be a Southern California affair, but in recent years has developed an international flavor with lesbians arriving from all over the globe. Book your room early, as accommodations are likely to fill. For a complete listing of the weekend's events, pick up the *Lesbian News* or *Female FYI*. Call ☎ 324-4546 for information and tickets.

Villagefest Every Thursday, from 6 to 10 pm, the downtown blocks of N Palm Canyon Drive are closed to traffic, and dozens of street stalls sell snacks, handicrafts, souvenirs, and produce. There is often live music as well. The desert evenings are balmy, and there's a good fun atmosphere.

Places to Stay
Many of the accommodations in Palm Springs are in expensive resort-style hotels, but there are some budget places around, and they all have swimming pools and aircon. Palm Springs has a problem with the word 'motel,' so there are lots of inns and lodges. Peak season is January and February, when prices really go up and rooms can be hard to find. Taxes add another 10% to 11% to these prices.

Camping There are several RV parks, but the only place for tent camping is way down in La Quinta, at the Lake Cahuilla County Park, at the west end of 58th Ave. There are 150 tent and RV sites, from $9 to $14. Reservations (☎ 800-464-6316) are recommended in the winter holiday season.

Bottom End About the cheapest night's stay is the *Pepper Tree Inn* (☎ 325-9505), 645 N Indian Canyon Drive; you won't be overwhelmed by the service but you'll pay only about $25/30 in summer and not much more in winter. *Budget Host Inn* (☎ 325-3904, 800-283-4678), 1277 S Palm Canyon Drive, is a better place, from $39 (up to $85 in peak season). Other cheapish places are on N Palm Canyon Drive, including *Desert Rose Inn* (☎ 327-2743), at No 1404, from $35 in low season to $55 in high season, and *Super 8 Lodge* (☎ 322-3757), at No 1900, from $45 to $55. *Travelodge* (☎ 327-1211), 333 E Palm Canyon Drive, has spacious rooms from $45 ($55/59 in winter). *Quality Inn* (☎ 323-2775, 800-472-4339), 1269 E Palm Canyon Drive, has similar prices.

If you're not looking for charm, there's a *Motel 6* (☎ 327-4200) at 660 S Palm Canyon Drive, and another (☎ 325-6129) at 595 E Palm Canyon Drive, which are bargains for Palm Springs at around $28/33 for singles/doubles, or $31/35 in winter and on weekends. However, they're often full. Other Motel 6 places are in Desert Hot Springs (☎ 251-1425), just north of I-10; Rancho Mirage (☎ 324-8475), at 69570 Hwy 111; and Indio (☎ 342-6311), at 82195 E Valley Pkwy.

Middle Mid-range accommodations offer a choice of the better quality chain motels, or somewhat more expensive places with a bit of character. *Howard Johnson Lodge* (☎ 320-2700, 800-854-4345), 701 E Palm Canyon Drive, has clean, modern, and reasonably priced double rooms for $44, $62 in winter. *Days Inn Suites* (☎ 323-3493), 411 E Palm Canyon Drive, costs from $51 in summer, but jumps to at least $92 in winter.

The *Spa Hotel & Casino* (☎ 325-1461), 100 N Indian Canyon Drive, is on the site of the original Agua Caliente Indians' mineral springs, and the hotel is still owned by the Indian community. Rooms cost from $54/74 in the off season, and around $150 in December.

One of the original Palm Springs hotels, *Casa Cody* (☎ 320-9346), at 175 S Cahuilla Rd, retains a quiet charm, with Santa Fe-style suites and villas set in shady, landscaped grounds. Prices start at $60 per night. *Ingleside Inn* (☎ 325-0046), 200 W Ramon Rd, is another venerable, classy Palm Springs institution, with rooms from $76 to $310 in summer, $95 to $375 in winter.

The *Happy Tanner Inn* (☎ 320-5984), 1466 N Palm Canyon Drive, is a 'clothing optional' place, at $68/89 year round. Some places cater expressly to gay clientele, many of them in the area around Warm Sands Drive and Parocela, like the *Inntimate* (☎ 778-8334) at 556 Warm Sands Rd, with rooms from $80 in winter, $69 in summer, and the similarly-priced *Inntrigue* (☎ 323-7505, 800-798-8781), 526 Warm Sands Drive. The *Inn Exile Hotel* (☎ 327-6413, 800-962-0186), at 960 Camino Parocela, has rooms from $81 to $113 all year round. *El Mirasol Villas* (☎ 327-5913), 525 Warm Sands Rd, is another gay-lesbian hotel; $70 in winter, $55 in summer.

Top End There's no shortage of luxury in Palm Springs. *La Mancha Private Villas* (☎ 323-1773 or 800-647-7482, 800-64-PRIVACY), 444 Avenida Caballeros, prides itself on absolute discretion. Double rooms, units, and villas cost between $95 and $675, and they won't breathe a word to anyone.

Other top-end resorts are in Rancho Mirage and Palm Desert. Most expensive is *Marriott's Desert Springs Resort & Spa* (☎ 341-2211), 74855 Country Club Drive, Desert Springs, where launches take you across an artificial lake to the restaurant. Rooms and suites cost from $235 to $2100 in winter, but less than half that in summer. The luxurious *Ritz-Carlton* (☎ 321-8282), 68-900 Frank Sinatra Drive, Rancho

Mirage, has rooms from $260 in winter, but in summer they go for as low as $89.

Places to Eat
Many of the restaurants in and around Palm Springs are pretentious and overpriced. Most of the Palm Springs places are on North, South, or East Palm Canyon Drive. The usual fast food franchises are less in evidence – the size and placement of their familiar signs is severely restricted – but you'll find some of them along Palm Canyon Drive north or south of the center. Outdoor eating areas are sometimes sprayed with a fine mist of water to keep them cool, which is a nice touch.

An old local favorite is the original *Las Casuelas* (☎ 325-3213), 368 N Palm Canyon Drive, with fine Mexican main courses from $7 to $12. Its offshoot, *Las Casuelas Terraza* (☎ 325-2794), 222 S Palm Canyon Drive, is in a great-looking Mexican-style building and has a menu and prices similar to the original. Also good is *Blue Coyote Grill* (☎ 327-1196), 445 N Palm Canyon Drive, which does Mexican and Southwestern food, with main courses from $7 to $13. *Cafe St James* (☎ 320-8041), 254 N Palm Canyon Drive, is an upscale restaurant with an international menu including some good vegetarian dishes.

Several places offer English cooking. Among them, *Churchill's Fish & Chips*, 665 S Palm Canyon Drive, has a British pub atmosphere and serves jolly good fish and chips for $7.50. They also have shrimp, scallops, and clams, as well as Guinness on tap for $2.75. Distinctly American is *Louise's Pantry*, a diner at 124 S Palm Canyon Drive, which has good breakfasts and lunch specials. Mid-range ethnic eateries in the same area are *Milano's Pasta & Pizza* and the *Flower Drum* Chinese restaurant.

Bono's (☎ 32-6200), 1700 N Indian Canyon Drive, is an Italian-American restaurant with a celebrity owner, an interesting menu, and a nice setting. It's quite expensive though, with pastas like linguini and clam sauce for around $13, and entrees like shrimp scampi for $19. Other top-end restaurants have excellent food, elegant surroundings, and also offer the hope of seeing a celebrity. Two of the best prospects, in the right season, are *Melvyn's* (☎ 325-2323), at the Ingleside Inn, 200 W Ramon Rd, which was 'featured on *Lifestyles of the Rich & Famous';* and *Le Vallauris* (☎ 325-5059), 385 W Tahquitz Canyon Way, 'Where the Stars entertain their friends.' A star might expect to pay around $25 for a friend's entree. Non-stars should make a reservation and dress up.

Entertainment
Palm Springs Follies This Zeigfeld Follies-style review includes music, dancing, showgirls, and comedy, in the historic 1936 *Plaza Theater* (☎ 327-0225), 128 S Palm Canyon Drive. The twist is that many of the performers are as old as the theater – they are all over 50, some up to 80. But this is not the amateur hour; Palm Springs can pull some big names out of its celebrity closet, and the show has been known to feature such stars as Bing Crosby, Doris Day, and Jack Benny. At $25 to $38, it's not cheap, but the cast from the past can turn in a great performance. They do evening shows and matinees, from November to May, and reservations are recommended.

Theater The *Annenberg Theater* (☎ 325-4490), in the Desert Museum, has regular music performances, theater, and dance.

Casinos Legal gambling is possible on Indian reservations, and a new casino is now operating in the *Spa Hotel* (☎ 800-258-2946) – the casino entrance is at 140 N Indian Canyon Drive. Near Indio, the *Fantasy Springs Casino* (☎ 800-827-2946), north of I-10 at Auto Center Drive, has entertainers and 24-hour gambling.

Clubs *Zelda's Nightclub & Beachclub* (☎ 325-2375), 169 N Indian Canyon Drive, is a longstanding and still popular place, attracting a mixed crowd for drinking and dancing ($6 cover). *Chiller's* (☎ 325-3215), 262 S Palm Canyon Drive, specializes in frozen cocktails and has a mix of dance music, live bands, and the occasional comedy act.

As the name implies *The Saloon*, 225 S Indian Canyon Drive, is a basic beer-drinkers bar with no pretensions. At the other extreme, *Touché* (☎ 773-1111), Bob Hope Drive and Hwy 111 in Rancho Mirage, is an upmarket restaurant and nightclub for people who want to dress up.

Gay Bars In Palm Springs, check the *Toolshed* (☎ 320-3299), 600 E Sunny Dunes Rd. There are lots more in Cathedral City, including *C.C. Construction Company* (☎ 324-4241), 68-449 Perez Rd, and *Choices* (☎ 321-1145), 68-352 Perez Rd.

Coffeehouses *LaLaJava* (☎ 322-6398), 245A S Palm Canyon Drive, makes a good cup. *Peabody's* (☎ 322-1877), 134 S Palm Canyon Drive, has live jazz on weekends.

Things to Buy
There are quite a few art galleries and antique stores, but unless you have a mega-budget you'll be looking more than buying. Coffman's Fine Art (☎ 325-0676), 457 N Palm Canyon Drive, has a good selection of American Indian and Western arts and crafts. Adagio Galleries (☎ 320-2230), 193 S Palm Canyon Drive, exhibit and sell contemporary paintings and sculpture, while B Lewin Galleries (☎ 325-7611), 210 S Palm Canyon Drive, has an extensive collection of paintings by the best Mexican artists.

The Desert Fashion Plaza (☎ 320-8282), 123 N Palm Canyon Drive, has a number of upmarket fashion outlets. Lots of stores in downtown Palm Springs sell 'resort wear,' which would be a typical Palm Springs purchase. Another local specialty is dates – the Coachella Valley produces 90% of the US supply. Edward's Date Shoppe (☎ 324-0223), in the Rimrock Plaza on Hwy 111 at Gene Autry Trail, has gift boxes, date cakes, and date milkshakes.

Getting There & Away
Air Palm Springs Regional Airport (☎ 323-8161) is served by Alaska Airlines, Ameri-

can Airlines, America West, Delta/Sky-west, United Airlines, and USAir Express.

Bus The Greyhound bus station (☎ 325-2053) is at 311 N Indian Canyon Drive. There are nine buses a day, between 6 am and 9 pm, to and from Los Angeles ($27). Amtrak buses go to Bakersfield, Fresno, Stockton, and Oakland, leaving the Indio train station daily at 8:35 am.

Train The Amtrak Sunset Limited train (Los Angeles-Miami) stops at Indio at three inconvenient times a week – westbound at 2:39 am Monday, Wednesday and Friday; eastbound at 1:09 am Monday, Wednesday, and Saturday. Buy tickets from an agent or on the train.

Car The I-10 from Los Angeles (about a two-hour drive) is the main route into and through the Coachella Valley, but Hwy 74, the Palms to Pines Hwy, is the more scenic route, and worth a detour.

Car rental companies include Thrifty (☎ 323-2212), Dollar (☎ 325-7333), Budget (☎ 778-1960), and Avis (☎ 778-6303).

Getting Around
To/From the Airport Buses on Line 21 run hourly between the airport and downtown Palm Springs.

Bus & Taxi The local bus service, Sunline, covers the whole valley from about 6 am to 10 pm. The air-con buses are clean, comfortable, and run every 20 to 30 minutes along the main routes, but they're not a fast way to get around. Line 111 follows Hwy 111 between Palm Springs and Indio (about 1½ hours). You can transfer to other lines that loop through the various communities. The standard fare is 75¢ (exact change required), plus 25¢ for a transfer. All the buses have wheelchair lifts and a rack for two bicycles. For more information call their customer service line at ☎ 343-3451.

Checker Cab (☎ 325-2868) and Valley Cabousine (☎ 340-5845) provide the area's 24-hour taxi service.

Joshua Tree National Park

☎ 619

Joshua Tree National Park is known for the distinctive Joshua trees, as well as for wonderfully shaped rock outcrops, popular with climbers. The park straddles a transition zone between the high and low deserts, and has a variety of plant life.

Information
The park headquarters is at the Oasis Visitor Center (☎ 367-7511), National Monument Drive in Twentynine Palms, just outside the park's northern boundary. It's open daily from 8 am to 4:30 pm and has useful information, books, and maps. The smaller Cottonwood Visitor Center is a few miles inside the park's southern entrance. Vehicle entry, good for seven days, costs $5; walkers, cyclists, and bus passengers are charged $3. For emergency assistance, call ☎ 909-383-5651.

Hiking
You really need to get away from your car to appreciate Joshua Tree's eerie landscapes and intriguing details. The visitors centers will give you maps and advice

The Joshua tree is a treelike species of the yucca.

about the following short, marked trails that focus on different features of the park – Fortynine Palms Oasis, Hidden Valley, Lost Horse Mine, Keys View & Inspiration Point, Ryan Mountain, Cholla Cactus Garden, and Lost Palm Oasis.

Overnight Hikes Longer hikes are possible, but are a real challenge because of the need to carry water – at least two gallons per person per day. Anyone going overnight into the backcountry must fill out a registration card (to aid in census-taking and rescue efforts) and deposit the stub in the box at the parking lot where they leave their car. Cars left overnight that are not identified on a registration card may be cited or towed away.

Rock Climbing
The many granite outcrops are smooth and steep-sided, but have interesting cracks and splits. The longest climbs are not much more than a 100 feet or so, but there are many challenging technical routes, and most can be easily top-roped for training. Some of the most popular climbs are in the Hidden Valley area. Keen climbers should get a specialized guide, like *Joshua Tree Rock Climbing Guide,* by Randy Vogel (Chockstone Press).

Bicycling
Joshua Tree is a popular place for cycling, though bikes must stay on established roads and trails. The *Bicycle Club* (☎ 365-3101), at 55379 Twentynine Palms Hwy, Yucca Valley, rents bikes for $15-25 per day, and down the road at No 56778, *Bike Business* (☎ 365-1078) repairs bikes.

Camping
There are nine campgrounds in the park, available on a first-come-first-served basis only. At busy times, during spring and fall, find a site early (before noon) and stake your claim. Water is available at *Black Rock Canyon* and *Cottonwood* campgrounds, which cost $8 per night, and close to *Indian Cove,* which costs $10. The other campgrounds are free, and have toilets, tables, and fire places, but you have to bring in your own water.

Backcountry camping is permitted, but not less than a mile from the nearest road, or 500 feet from the nearest trail, and not in any wash or day use area. No fires are permitted.

AROUND JOSHUA TREE NATIONAL PARK
Twentynine Palms
• *pop 11,821* ☎ *619*

Right by the north entrance to the national park, Twentynine Palms is a service town for the park, and the nearby Marine Corps base. The Oasis of Mara, behind the park visitors center, had the original 29 palm trees for which the town is named. The San Andreas Fault runs through the oasis, which is believed to be charged with psychic energy and attracts New-Age types.

Places to Stay This is the best place to find accommodations near the national park. *Motel 6* (☎ 367-2833), 72562 Twentynine Palms Hwy, is nice and clean, at $30/34 for singles/doubles. *Hill View Motel,* a little further out on the same road, is not as nice, but is cheaper at $20/25. There are plenty of other cheap places, though some are a little seedy, so check the room before you check in. *Best Western Gardens Motel* (☎ 367-9141), 71487 Twentynine Palms Hwy, is a good mid-range choice at $54/56.

The most interesting place to stay is *Twentynine Palms Inn* (☎ 367-3505), at 73950 Inn Ave, built on and around the oasis. They have a variety of old adobe and wood cabins, at a variety of prices – the cheapest ones from about $40/50 midweek during low season to $65/75 on weekends in high season.

Places to Eat For a fast-food fix go to the east side of the town center. In the same area, *Rocky's New York Style Pizza* has big servings and is popular with locals, and *El Ranchito* (☎ 367-2424) is recommended for Mexican meals, from $6 to $8.

CALIFORNIA

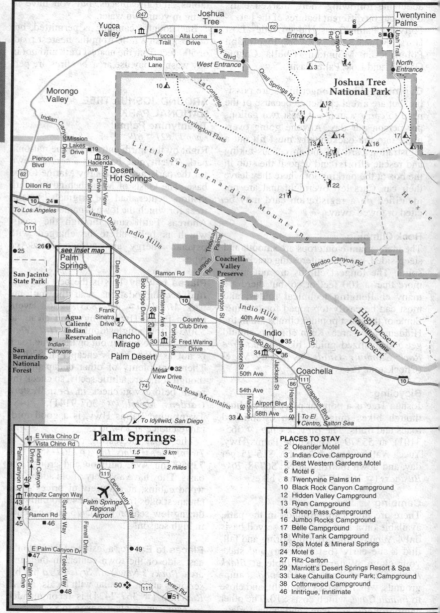

Yucca Valley

Joshua Tree

Twentynine Palms

247

62

Yucca Trail

Alta Loma Drive

Entrance

Canyon Rd

Utah Trail

North Entrance

Joshua Lane

West Entrance

Park Blvd

Quail Springs Rd

La Contenta

Covington Flats

Joshua Tree National Park

Morongo Valley

Little San Bernardino Mountains

Indian Canyon Drive

Mission Lakes Drive

Pierson Blvd

Hacienda Ave

Desert Hot Springs

Mountain View Drive

Palm Drive

Dillon Rd

Varner Drive

Hexie

To Los Angeles

111

Indio Hills

Thousand Palms

Coachella Valley Preserve

Ramon Rd

Berdoo Canyon Rd

San Jacinto State Park

see inset map

Palm Springs

Date Palm Drive

Canyon Rd

Washington St

Indio Hills

High Desert Transition Zone Low Desert

Agua Caliente Indian Reservation

Frank Sinatra Drive

Bob Hope Drive

Monterey Ave

Country Club Drive

Portola Ave

40th Ave

Indio

Dillon Rd

San Bernardino National Forest

Indian Canyons

Rancho Mirage

Palm Desert

Fred Waring Drive

Jefferson St

Indio Blvd

Jackson St

Coachella

Mesa View Drive

Santa Rosa Mountains

50th Ave

54th Ave

86

74

Airport Blvd

Madison St

Harrison St

Grapefruit Blvd

111

10

To Idyllwild, San Diego

58th Ave

To El Centro, Salton Sea

Palm Springs

E Vista Chino Dr

Vista Chino Rd

Indian Canyon Drive

Palm Canyon Dr

Tahquitz Canyon Way

Ramon Rd

Gene Autry Trail

Palm Springs Regional Airport

Sunrise Way

Farrell Drive

E Palm Canyon Dr

Toledo Way

Palm Canyon Drive

Perez Rd

111

0   1.5   3 km

0   1   2 miles

PLACES TO STAY

2 Oleander Motel
3 Indian Cove Campground
5 Best Western Gardens Motel
6 Motel 6
8 Twentynine Palms Inn
10 Black Rock Canyon Campground
11 Hidden Valley Campground
13 Ryan Campground
14 Sheep Pass Campground
16 Jumbo Rocks Campground
17 Belle Campground
18 White Tank Campground
19 Spa Motel & Mineral Springs
24 Motel 6
27 Ritz-Carlton
29 Marriott's Desert Springs Resort & Spa
33 Lake Cahuilla County Park; Campground
38 Cottonwood Campground
46 Inntrigue, Inntimate

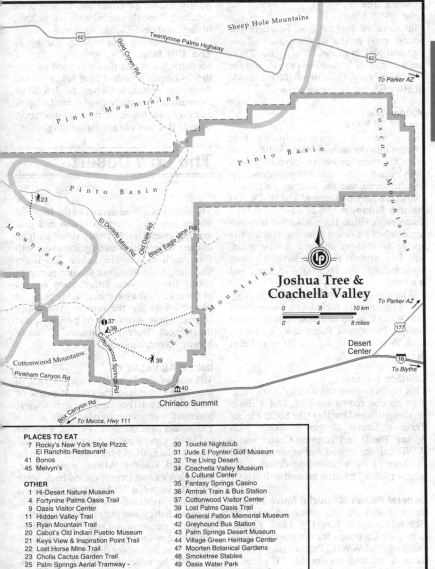

Joshua Tree & Coachella Valley

0   5   10 km
0   4   8 miles

Desert Center

To Parker AZ

To Blythe

Chiriaco Summit

To Mecca, Hwy 111

Joshua Tree
• *pop 3898* ☎ *619*

The town of Joshua Tree is where the access road to the west entrance of the national park branches off Hwy 62. There are a couple of basic places to eat, and the *Oleander Motel*, ($22/30) on the south side of Hwy 62, just east of the center.

Yucca Valley
• *pop 13,701* ☎ *619*

Going west, the town of Joshua Tree merges into the town of Yucca Valley, with Hwy 62 (here called Twentynine Palms Hwy) lined with unattractive commercial developments and the Institute of Mental Physics, a 'spiritual center.' The **Hi-Desert Nature Museum** (☎ 228-5452), 57117 Twentynine Palms Hwy, has a few interesting exhibits on desert flora and fauna – the spring wildflower displays can be good, and the scorpions are impressive. It's open Wednesday to Sunday from 1 to 5 pm, and it's free.

Along or near Twentynine Palms Hwy you'll find motels, including a *Super 8* and the *Desert View,* as well as several fast-food outlets. Twentynine Palms Hwy continues west then south to meet I-10 near Palm Springs.

Chiriaco Summit
This highway stop has a motel with standard air-con rooms for $28, and a diner serving grills and burgers (the $5.25 Desert Training Center Burger is made with Spam). The Desert Training Center was a WWII training ground that covered 18,000 sq miles of the surrounding desert – the largest military training ground in history.

General Patton Memorial Museum
The Desert Training Center was established by General George S 'Blood 'n' Guts' Patton, to prepare US troops for the North African campaign in WWII. Patton said of the harsh desert environment that, 'If you can work in this country, it will be no difficulty at all to kill the assorted sons of bitches you will meet in any other country.' The museum (☎ 227-3483) has a large but poorly explained collection of war junk recalling Patton's career, with an archive, library, and publications on sale.

An interesting non-military exhibit is **The Big Map**, a 5½-ton relief map of southern California that was used to plan the 242-mile aqueduct that brings water from the Colorado River to LA. The museum is open daily from 9 am to 5 pm, and costs $4, but there are some old tanks outside that you can see for nothing.

The Low Desert

☎ *619*

The rich agricultural district of the Imperial Valley is a monument to vision and pioneering enterprise, but only those with an interest in irrigation and agribusiness will find much to see. The Salton Sea looks intriguing on a map, but is uninspiring in reality, though it does attract many species of water bird. The most interesting parts for desert lovers are the remote Algodones Dunes, where thousands of people spend the whole winter in colonies of motor homes – a bizarre sight.

IMPERIAL VALLEY
The soil of the Imperial Valley is rich in alluvial deposits from the ancient course of the Colorado River, and its agricultural potential was recognized as early as the 1850s. Because the area is actually below sea level, water flowing down the Colorado River to the Gulf of Mexico was able to be channeled via the Alamo watercourse, through Mexican territory, then back north into the Imperial Valley. This ambitious plan was realized by CR Rockwood, George Chaffey, and their California Development Company, and was bankrolled by the sale of water rights to local water companies. The first water flowed in 1901, and by 1905 the valley had 67,000 acres irrigated and a population of 12,000. An agreement with the Mexican government in 1904 provided for half the diverted water to be supplied to Mexico where much of it

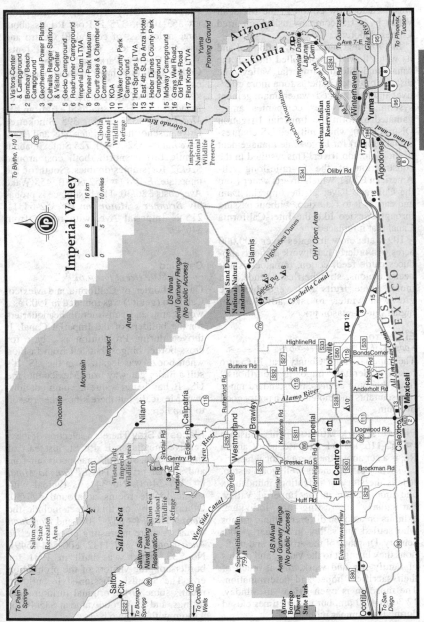

Imperial Valley

1 Visitors Center & Campground
2 Bombay Beach Campground
3 Geothermal Power Plants
4 Cahuilla Ranger Station & Visitor Center
5 Gecko Campground
6 Roadrunner Campground
7 Imperial Dam LTVA
8 Pioneer Park Museum
9 Courthouse & Chamber of Commerce
10 KOA
11 Walker County Park Campground
12 Hot Springs LTVA
13 East 4th St. De Anza Hotel
14 Heber Dunes County Park Campground
15 Midway Campground
16 Grays Well Road, Old Plank Road
17 Pilot Knob LTVA

was used to grow cotton in the Mexicali valley by a US company using imported Chinese laborers.

In 1905 the Colorado River flooded and its water flowed uncontrolled through the canals and into the Imperial Valley. The disaster provided impetus for a more effective and centralized water management system. Local water companies amalgamated to form the Imperial Irrigation District (IID), which initiated US congressional support for large-scale management of the Colorado River. This resulted in the construction of the 80-mile-long All-American Canal, which diverts water from the Colorado River at the Imperial Dam and carries it to Calexico, without passing through Mexico like the Inter-California Canal that it replaced.

IID water now irrigates over 500,000 acres. An orderly patchwork of fields produces cattle feed, cotton, tomatoes, sugar beets, melons, strawberries, lettuce, and more. Some fruits and vegetables are grown in winter, to take advantage of higher out-of-season prices.

El Centro
• *pop 31,384* • *elev -42 feet* ☎ *619*

The Imperial Valley County seat, El Centro has a moderately imposing courthouse, three shopping centers, the standard range of restaurants and motels, and a pretty good museum.

Pioneers Park Museum This museum (☎ 352-1165), 373 E Aten Rd, near Cannon Rd, is a cut above the average local historical society effort, and is well worth a stop. It tells the story of irrigation, inundation, and immigration in the Imperial Valley. Particularly interesting are individual exhibits on a dozen different ethnic groups who settled the valley in the early 20th century. Displays of the artifacts and traditions they brought to the valley, and photos of family life and work, reveal much of their sacrifice, hope, and determination. The museum is open Friday to Sunday, 12:30 to 4:30 pm, but is sometimes closed during the summer months.

Places to Stay The *El Centro KOA* (☎ 353-1051), 375 E Ross Rd, is about three miles east of central El Centro and has sites for RVs ($18.50) and tents. Walker County Park and Heber Dunes County Park both have free campgrounds; call ☎ 352-3308.

A number of inexpensive motels can be found near the Hwy 86/4th St exit from I-8. *Motel 6* (☎ 353-6766), 395 Smoketree Drive, just north of the interstate, and *Executive Inn* (☎ 352-8500), 725 State St, about a mile further north, both cost around $26/32 for singles/doubles. South of the interstate, *E-Z 8* (☎ 352-6620), 455 Wake Ave, costs $26/30. The best place is probably *Brunner's Motor Inn* (☎ 352-6431), 215 N Imperial Ave, with rooms from $46/49.

Calexico
• *pop 23,800* • *elev -1 foot* ☎ *619*

On the border of California and Mexico, Calexico (get it?) was founded in 1900 as a work camp and construction headquarters for the builders of the Imperial Canal. It thrived during Prohibition as a base for cross-border binges, but fell from fashion when booze was legalized in the US. It's still a major gateway from Mexico into the US. It has better value accommodations than Mexicali, but there's no other reason to stop here.

Places to Stay There's a selection of inexpensive motels on E 4th St, just east of Imperial Ave, all with small pools, air-con, and similar prices. The *El Rancho Motel* (☎ 357-2468), No 341, is typical with single/double rooms at around $27/30. Others nearby on this street include the *Border Hotel* (☎ 357-2707) and *Don Juan Motel*. A more interesting place is the *De Anza Hotel* (☎ 357-1112, 800-544-4549), No 233, which was built in 1931 for border-hopping visitors of the prohibition era. The Spanish Mission-style building retains some of the original furniture and fittings, and it's a good value at $35/44 for a room with one/two beds.

Places to Eat The De Anza Hotel serves a pretty good breakfast, lunch, and dinner. Otherwise, there are the usual fast-food places along Imperial Ave.

Getting There & Away Greyhound (☎ 357-1895) at 121 E 1st St, near the border crossing, has five buses daily to/from Los Angeles for $18.

Mexicali (Mexico)
• *pop 900,000* • *elev sea level* ☎ *619*
Much larger than its counterpart across the line, Mexicali is the capital of the Mexican state of Baja California, an educational center, and the terminus of Mexico's main northern railroad. It's a modern city with some grandiose monuments, but not much to see. Most tourists head straight through to mainland Mexico, Baja California, or the beaches of San Felipe.

The blocks near the border have lots of souvenir shops and touristy restaurants. Further south is La Chinesca, Mexicali's Chinatown, around the intersection of Avenida Juárez and Calle Altamirano. The Centro Cívico-Comercial (Civic & Commercial Center), about two miles southeast of the border post, is a modern complex with government offices, a medical school, bullring, cinemas, bus station, hospitals, and restaurants. Just south of there is the Zona Rosa, an area of fancy hotels and restaurants.

Visas & Immigration The border is open 24 hours. You don't need a visa or a passport to cross into Mexicali, but you should have some form of photo identification. Returning to the USA, non-Americans need to show a passport with a US visa. If you're going east into Sonora or south past San Felipe, or are staying more than 72 hours, you'll need a Mexican tourist card.

Places to Stay The family-oriented *Hotel México* (☎ 65-54-06-09), Lerdo de Tejada 476, between Altamirano and Morelos, has singles from $10, but rooms with air-con,

TV, a private bath, and parking cost extra. The respectable *Hotel Plaza* (☎ 65-52-97-57), Madero 366, charges around $20 a double. If you can afford more than $25, you'll get better accommodations on the US side.

Places to Eat It's worth coming over to Mexicali for Mexican food, and a big selection of Chinese restaurants. Quite a few restaurants are along Avenida Reforma, parallel to the border and two blocks south. An above average place, in price and quality, is *La Villa del Seri* (☎ 53-55-03), at Reforma and Calle D, which specializes in Sonoran beef, but also has excellent seafood and *antojitos*. Only three blocks southeast of the border crossing, the inexpensive *Alley 19,* at Juárez 8 near Azueta, is Mexicali's oldest Chinese restaurant, opened in 1928.

SALTON SEA
The largest lake in California, the Salton Sea is surprisingly unattractive. Filled with water in the 1905 flood, it was stocked with fish and soon attracted colonies of migratory birds. The Salton Sea State Recreation Area, on the eastern shore, has a visitors center (☎ 393-3052) with information about local fishing and bird watching. It's open daily from October to May. There are some failed lakeside resorts on the western shore, of which Salton City is the biggest and most depressing.

The Salton Sea National Wildlife Refuge (☎ 348-5278) provides a habitat for migrating and endangered birds, including snow geese, mallard, brown pelicans, bald eagles, and peregrine falcons. The Wister Unit of the Imperial Wildlife Area (☎ 359-0577) not only provides a habitat for waterfowl, but also permits hunting them in season.

Fishing has been adversely affected by increasing salinity, but it's still popular. The best fishing is for croaker, sargo, tilapia, and especially orangemouth corvina. Eating the fish is not recommended because of the high concentration of selenium. There are three boat launching ramps, and small boats may be launched anywhere round the shoreline.

Swimming is not pleasant because the water is murky with plankton and the salt stings the eyes. Swimming is not recommended at the south end of the sea because of pollution.

Camping

The Salton Sea State Recreation Area has several campgrounds, with tent and RV spaces ranging from $7 to $12.

Now You Sea it, Now You Don't

Fifteen million years ago, the area that is now the Imperial Valley and the Salton Sea was under the Pacific Ocean. Uplifts in the earth's crust created the mountains that now form Southern California's coastal range and the spine of Baja California. The ancient seabed was raised, lifting marine fossil beds hundreds of feet above sea level. Then, starting 12 million years ago, tectonic movements separated Baja California from the mainland, creating the elongated trough we call the Gulf of California. The gulf extended much further north than it does now – all the way to the San Gorgonio pass, beyond Palm Springs. The area of the Imperial Valley and the Salton Sea was under the sea again.

The Colorado River, flowing somewhat west of its present course, carried huge quantities of sediment into the northern end of this gulf – all the material eroded from the Grand Canyon ended up here. The sediment progressively built up, until it formed a gigantic levee that separated the Imperial Valley from the Gulf of California. The course of the Colorado shifted eastward, flowing directly into the gulf, and the water in the Imperial Valley began to evaporate, leaving a dry, empty basin.

Sometime later the river shifted again, perhaps in a large flood, filling the valley with fresh water to a height some 30 feet above sea level. This water line is clearly visible on the mountainside at Travertine Point, south of Indio, and it corresponds to the height at which the water would overflow the valley and run south to the gulf. This cycle was probably repeated many times, with the Colorado changing its course, filling the lake, clogging itself with silt, and then swinging back to the gulf, allowing the lake to become dry again.

Shells and mineral deposits indicate that there was a fresh-water lake here around 3000 years ago, and there are many sites which show that people lived on its shores, trapping fish and making extensive use of lakeside plants. Around five or six hundred years ago, the Colorado River changed its course again, the lake started to dry up, and these lakeside dwellers moved away. When Europeans first arrived, the whole Imperial Valley was dry, and its deepest part was a salty depression that was dubbed the Salton Sink. A US Army survey in 1852 found traces of the old lake, which they called Lake Cahuilla after the Cahuilla Indians who lived in the area at that time. (In fact, the Indians living along the shores of the ancient lake were probably not ancestors of the Cahuilla. More likely they were Yumans, whose descendants lived in the San Diego area and on the banks of the Colorado River when Europeans arrived.)

In 1905, the Colorado River again flooded and overflowed into irrigation channels, nearly inundating the entire valley once more. It took 18 months, 1500 workers, $12 million, and half a million tons of rock to put the Colorado River back on its course to the Gulf of Mexico. The previously dry Salton Sink had again become a lake, 45 miles long and 17 miles wide. It had no natural outlet and, as evaporation reduced its size, the natural salt levels became more concentrated. The Salton became an inland sea, with its surface actually 228 feet below the level of the sea in the Gulf of California.

Colorado River water continued to flow into the Imperial Valley via irrigation canals and pipelines, but years of irrigation has caused salt to percolate to the surface of farmland. This problem is being relieved by periodically flooding the land and flushing off the excess salt. Each year, this adds another 4½ million tons of salt to the Salton Sea, which now has 1½ times the salinity of sea water. Fewer types of fish can survive in the Salton Sea now, the number of water birds is thought to be declining, and the salt concentration continues to rise. Unless this problem is solved, the Salton Sea will become a Dead Sea. ∎

THE ALGODONES DUNES

Up to 300 feet high, these sand dunes along the eastern edge of the Imperial Valley were once beaches round Lake Cahuilla. The shifting sands were an obstacle for early European explorers and the builders of canals and roads.

When the dunes buried the first trails between the Imperial Valley and Yuma, a wooden road was tried. Sections of heavy timber planks, bound together with steel straps, formed the road's surface. When sand covered a section, it could be dragged to a new position by a mule team. The 'plank road,' continually being moved with the dunes, provided the only link across this strip of desert from 1916 to 1926, when a surfaced highway was built. Remnants of the plank road may be seen from Grays Well Rd, south of I-8, and there's a section in the Pioneer Park Museum near El Centro.

Much of the dunes area is open to ORVs (off-road vehicles), or OHVs (off-highway vehicles). If you want to get into it, contact Sandman Dune Tours (☎ 339-6644), which rents ORVs and does guided tours of two hours or longer. If you want to see some undisturbed dune country, try the Imperial Sand Dunes National Natural Landmark, north of Hwy 78 and west of Glamis. It's a preserve for desert plants and animals, closed to vehicles, but open for walkers.

Information

The public land in the dunes is under the control of the BLM. For information about ORV use, camping, or the general area, contact the El Centro Resource Area Office (☎ 337-4400), 1661 S 4th St, El Centro.

The Cahuilla Ranger Station & Visitor Center (☎ 344-3919), Gecko Rd south of Hwy 78, has some information about the dunes, but keeps limited hours. It opens on weekends and holidays between mid-October and Memorial Day.

Phones, food, and gas are available at Glamis, on Hwy 78. Elsewhere, there are virtually no facilities at all between the Imperial Valley and the Colorado River.

Places to Stay

The BLM operates free camping grounds at Midway, Gecko, and Roadrunner. They have toilets, but no water or other facilities. You can camp anywhere on undeveloped public land for up to 14 days. Long-term visitor areas (LTVAs) have been established for those who spend the whole winter in motor homes in undeveloped desert areas.

Anza-Borrego Desert

☎ 619

Don't be put off by the unappealing town of Borrego Springs – the Anza-Borrego Desert State Park has some of the most spectacular and accessible desert scenery you'll find anywhere. The human history goes back 10,000 years, recorded in ancient Native American pictographs. Spanish explorer Juan Bautista de Anza passed through in 1774, pioneering an immigrant trail from Mexico. The Mormon Battalion came this way to fight the Californios, and the Southern Emigrant Trail and the Butterfield Stageline followed a route along the Vallecito Valley, in the southern part of the park.

BORREGO SPRINGS

• pop 2244 • elev 590 feet ☎ 619

This little town is completely surrounded by the Anza-Borrego Desert State Park, and provides shops, restaurants, and gas to park visitors, as well catering to a seasonal population of hundreds of 'snowbirds' escaping northern winters. There are several golf courses, a couple of expensive resorts, and no fewer than seven mobile home and RV parks.

Peg Leg Smith Monument & Liars Contest

Northeast of town, where S22 takes a 90° turn to the east, there's a pile of rocks just north of the road. This is a monument to Thomas Long 'Peg Leg' Smith – mountain man, fur trapper, Indian fighter, horse thief,

CALIFORNIA

CALIFORNIA

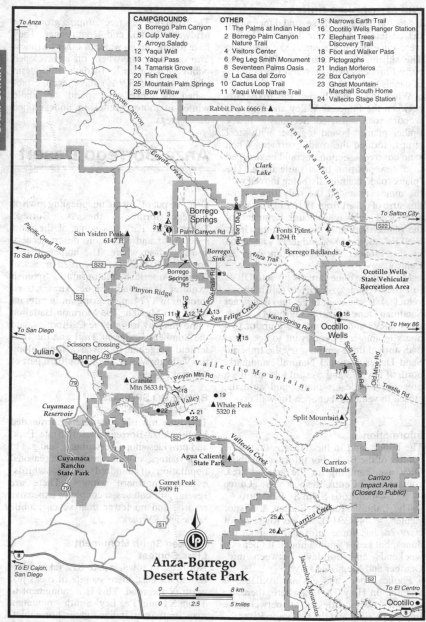

CAMPGROUNDS	OTHER	15	Narrows Earth Trail

CAMPGROUNDS
3 Borrego Palm Canyon
5 Culp Valley
7 Arroyo Salado
12 Yaqui Well
13 Yaqui Pass
14 Tamarisk Grove
20 Fish Creek
25 Mountain Palm Springs
26 Bow Willow

OTHER
1 The Palms at Indian Head
2 Borrego Palm Canyon
  Nature Trail
4 Visitors Center
6 Peg Leg Smith Monument
8 Seventeen Palms Oasis
9 La Casa del Zorro
10 Cactus Loop Trail
11 Yaqui Well Nature Trail

15 Narrows Earth Trail
16 Ocotillo Wells Ranger Station
17 Elephant Trees
   Discovery Trail
18 Foot and Walker Pass
19 Pictographs
21 Indian Morteros
22 Box Canyon
23 Ghost Mountain-
   Marshall South Home
24 Vallecito Stage Station

To Anza

Coyote Canyon

Coyote Creek

Rabbit Peak 6666 ft ▲

Clark Lake

Santa Rosa Mountains

6

Borrego Springs

Peg Leg Rd

Palm Canyon Rd

To Salton City
S22

San Ysidro Peak ▲
6147 ft

Pacific Crest Trail

2 1 3
4

5

S22

Borrego Sink

Fonts Point
▲ 1294 ft

Anza Trail

7 ▲

Borrego Badlands

8 ●

To San Diego

S2

Borrego Springs Rd

Pinyon Ridge

9

Ocotillo Wells
State Vehicular
Recreation Area

10

Yaqui Pass Rd

To San Diego

S3

11 12 14 13
San Felipe Creek

Kane Spring Rd

78

16

Ocotillo Wells

To Hwy 86

Julian ●

Scissors Crossing

Banner ● 78

15

V a l l e c i t o   M o u n t a i n s

Split Mountain Rd

Old Mine Rd

17

79

▲ Granite
Mtn 5633 ft

Pinyon Mtn Rd

18

Blair Valley

19

▲ Whale Peak
5320 ft

Trestle Rd

20

Split Mountain ▲

Cuyamaca
Reservoir

22

21
23

79

Cuyamaca
Rancho
State Park

S2

24

Vallecito Creek

Agua Caliente
State Park

Carrizo
Badlands

Garnet Peak
▲ 5909 ft

Carrizo
Impact Area
(Closed to Public)

25

26

Carrizo Creek

S1

8

To El Cajon,
San Diego

LP

**Anza-Borrego
Desert State Park**

0   4   8 km

0   2.5   5 miles

Jacumba Mountains

S2

To El Centro

Ocotillo ●

8

liar, and Wild West legend. Around 1829, Peg Leg passed through Borrego Springs on his way to Los Angeles, and supposedly picked up some rocks that were later found to be pure gold. Strangely, he didn't return to the area until the 1850s, when he was unable to find the lode. Nevertheless, he told lots of people about it (often in exchange for a few drinks), and many came to search for the gold, and add to the myths.

On the first Saturday of April, the Peg Leg Liars Contest is a hilarious event in which amateur liars compete in the western tradition of telling tall tales. Anyone can enter, so long as the story is about gold and mining in the southwest, is less than five minutes long, and is anything but the truth.

Places to Stay
Oasis Motel (☎ 767-5409), 366 Palm Canyon Drive, is OK and about the cheapest place in town, from around $40 in summer, $55 in winter. *Hacienda del Sol* (☎ 767-542), 610 Palm Canyon Drive, is similar, but both places are small enough that it's a good idea to call ahead. *The Palms at Indian Head* (☎ 767-7788), 2220 Hoberg Rd (turn north off Palm Canyon Drive), is an older resort hotel, now operated as a B&B, from $60 per night. It's near to the park visitors center, and has great desert views.

Resort hotels include *Palm Canyon Resort* (☎ 767-5341), 221 Palm Canyon Drive, which has new Old West-style buildings, an attached RV park, and rooms from $85 (or $55 in summer). The classiest place is *La Casa del Zorro* (☎ 767-5323), southeast of town at 3945 Yaqui Pass Rd, with attractive grounds, Southwestern architecture, and spacious rooms from $98 in winter, $80 at other times.

Places to Eat
Several undistinguished restaurants congregate along Palm Canyon Drive, with a few in The Mall, a small shopping center on the south side of the road. Most of them close around 8 pm, so don't time your dinner too late. *George's & Family Little Italy* (☎ 767-3938), in The Center at 590 W

Palm Canyon Drive, is probably a good choice. *Borrego's Kitchen* (☎ 767-5173), a tiny place on Palm Canyon Drive just east of Borrego Springs Rd, serves big portions of authentic Mexican food from only $6. The fanciest would be the restaurant at La Casa del Zorro (see Places to Stay).

ANZA-BORREGO DESERT STATE PARK
The park is large, some 600,000 acres, and you really need a car to get around it and access the many points of interest. Several main roads run through it, and numerous dirt side roads offer more possibilities – some of these require 4WD, so ask at the visitors center about current conditions. It is a good place for mountain biking, but it's forbidden to take any vehicle, including a bike, off the established roads.

Information
The park visitors center (☎ 767-5311), two miles west of Borrego Springs township, is built partly underground, and from the parking lot it just looks like a low scrubby hill. The walls are faced with local stone, and blend beautifully with the mountain backdrop. Around the center is a selection of plants that you'll encounter in the park, all clearly labeled. Inside, a small theater shows a short slide show on the natural history of the park, and there are exhibits on desert flora and fauna, and a good selection of publications. The staff are helpful and well-informed, and the center is open October through May, daily from 9 am to 5 pm; the rest of the year, on weekends only.

Summers here are extremely hot. The average daily maximum temperature in July is 107°, but it can reach 125°. It's slightly cooler at higher elevations, so stick to these areas.

Flora
The spring wildflowers in Anza-Borrego can be absolutely brilliant, depending somewhat on the amount of winter rain that has fallen. Verbena, dune primrose, desert sunflower, brittlebush, and desert lily are

just some of the varieties to be seen. The flowers start blooming in late February at the lower elevations and reach their best over the next few months at successively higher levels. Contact the park to find out exactly when and where the flowers are at their peak bloom.

Pupfish Sanctuaries

The desert pupfish (Cyprinodon macularius) is an Ice Age remnant species, now very rare and on the endangered list. Adapted to life in desert water holes and intermittent streams, the pupfish can live in fresh or salt water from near freezing point to over 100° F. Two ponds, one near the visitors center and one at the start of the Borrego Palm Canyon Nature Trail, are sanctuaries for this unique creature.

Borrego Palm Canyon Nature Trail

A popular self-guiding trail goes northeast from the Borrego Palm Canyon Campground, climbing 350 feet in 1½ miles to a palm grove and waterfall which make a delightful oasis in the dry rocky countryside.

Short Walks

A variety of other short trails have been laid out, many of them with informative little signs or self-guiding brochures – different trails highlight particular features. The one-mile Cactus Loop Nature Trail is a good place to see a variety of cacti. Nearby, the two-mile Yaqui Well Nature Trail has many labeled desert plants, and passes a natural waterhole that attracts a rich variety of birdlife, as well as the occasional bighorn sheep in winter. The Narrows Earth Trail, two miles east of Tamarisk Grove, is a short trail that highlights the local geology, but also has some unusual chuparosa shrubs, which attract hummingbirds.

A dirt road, which may require 4WD, goes three miles off S22 to within a few hundred yards of Seventeen Palms Oasis, which is a permanent water source and a great place to spot wildlife.

Going south from Ocotillo Wells is a road that leads to Split Mountain, where

you can walk along the gorge between 600 foot high walls. On the way you pass the Elephant Trees Discovery Trail, one of the few places to see a herd of the unusual elephant trees.

Font's Point

A four-mile dirt road goes south of S22 to Font's Point, which offers a spectacular panorama over the Borrego Valley to the west, and the Borrego Badlands to the south.

Blair Valley

This area, near S2 five miles southeast of Scissors Crossing, has pleasant campsites and some attractive walks, but is also of particular archaeological interest. Short trails lead to sites with Indian pictographs, and morteros (hollows in rocks used for grinding seeds).

A monument at Foot and Walker Pass marks a difficult spot on the Butterfield Overland Stage route, and in Box Canyon you can still see the marks of wagons on the Emigrant Trail. A steep, one-mile climb leads to Ghost Mountain, the remains of a house occupied by the family of desert recluse Marshall South.

Vallecito Stage Station

Going west, both the Southern Emigrant Trail and the Butterfield Stage crossed the fiercely hot and dry Imperial Valley then followed the Vallecito Creek up into the mountains for the final part of the journey to the coast. The Vallecito station was built in 1852 as a major stop on the route, though the present building is a 1934 reconstruction.

Camping

Borrego Palm Canyon Campground, two miles west of Borrego Springs, has tent sites with all the amenities for $14, but don't expect a shady haven. Tamarisk Grove Campground, on S3, 12 miles south of Borrego Springs near Hwy 78, is smaller and has more shelter, and has similar facilities for the same price. Book both through Destinet. Bow Willow Campground, off S2 in the southern part of the park, has only 14 sites, with water, toilets, tables, and fireplaces, for $9. There are several other campsites in the park (see map), which are free but have no water and minimal facilities. Camping is permitted just about everywhere, though not within 200 yards of any water source, and you can't drive off the roads or light a fire on the ground.

OCOTILLO WELLS STATE VEHICULAR RECREATION AREA

The town of Ocotillo Wells is on Hwy 78, just outside the eastern edge of the state park. On the north side of the highway is the Ocotillo Wells State Vehicular Recreation Area (☎ 767-5391), where 40,000 acres of dunes and dry washes have been sacrificed to meet the needs of OHVs. Dune buggies and dirt bikes race round in a storm of dust and engine noise, but though it looks like anarchy on wheels, there is actually a long list of regulations and restrictions. Camping is permitted anywhere in the area, but there are no established campgrounds and no water is available. Gas, food, and phones are available in Ocotillo Wells.

The Mojave

The Mojave Desert covers a vast area, from urban areas on the northern edge of LA County to the remote, almost unpopulated country of the Mojave National Preserve. Most people just pass through on their way to the Eastern Sierra, Death Valley, or Las Vegas, but those with the time will find a lot worth stopping for. It's not really feasible to explore the Mojave without your own vehicle.

ANTELOPE VALLEY
Palmdale & Lancaster
• *pop 68,842 & 97,291* ☎ 805
This area is dead flat, and it's difficult to see a valley, much less an antelope. The two main towns have a combined population of about 160,000, and dormitory

suburbs that seem to go on forever. A few things worth seeing are miles away from the urban area. If you need to stay here, you'll find motels off Hwy 14 at Palmdale Blvd, and Avenue K in Lancaster.

Antelope Valley California Poppy Preserve From mid-March to mid-May, the hills here are covered with wildflowers, particularly California's state flower, the golden poppy. An interpretive center (☎ 765-3533) has more information, and there are easy hiking trails. To get there, take the W Avenue I exit from Hwy 14, and continue west for about 13 miles. It's open daily in the blooming season, and entry costs $5 per car.

Antelope Valley Indian Museum Incongruously housed in a Swiss chalet, this museum (☎ 942-0662) has a very good collection of Indian artifacts from California and the Southwest. Official hours are 11 am to 3 pm on weekends from October to June, but call first to be sure. From Hwy 14 take the E Avenue I exit, go east about 8 miles, south to Avenue J, then east another 9 miles to 150th St, south to Avenue M, then east until you see the chalet up among the boulders on your left. It's free, but worth a donation.

Saddleback Butte State Park Rising 1000 feet above the desert floor, this granite butte has a great view if you make it to the top (and the air is clear). The park (☎ 942-0662) also has a good selection of desert plants and wildlife, and a *campground* with sites for $10 a night. From Hwy 14 take the E Avenue I exit, go east about 8 miles, south to Avenue J, then east another 10 miles. The park is on the right after 170th St.

VICTOR VALLEY
☎ 619
Victor Valley includes the residential communities of Victorville, Hesperia, and Apple Valley, with a total population of 250,000. Many of them are retirees, and two of them are legendary.

Roy Rogers – Dale Evans Museum

Roy Rogers ('King of the Cowboys') made more than 80 movies for the Republic studio between 1938 and 1952, as well as over 100 half-hour TV shows and a comeback movie in 1976. Many also featured his wife, Dale Evans ('Queen of the West'), and his horse Trigger ('The Smartest Horse in the Movies').

This museum, in a building resembling a fort from the Old West, has a mindboggling collection of souvenirs, awards, testimonials, photographs, and mementos. There are Roy's favorite cars and boats, autographed baseballs, dozens of guns, ornate saddles, the stuffed heads of animals killed on hunting trips to Africa, Asia, and Alaska, and a framed invitation to Ronald Reagan's inauguration. Trigger himself is here, saddled and stuffed. The museum was established by Roy and Dale themselves, and taken as a whole (including its visitors), it is well worth visiting as an authentic and unselfconscious piece of mid-20th-century Americana.

To get there, exit I-15 at Roy Rogers Drive in Victorville, and go west. Then take the first left, and look for the giant statue of Trigger out the front. The museum (☎ 243-4547) opens from 9 am to 5 pm daily and entry costs $4 for adults, with discounts for seniors, children, and AAA members.

UPPER MOJAVE

About 70 miles north of LA, you cross the LA county line, and you feel you are really out of the city. The Upper Mojave is harsh, inhospitable country, with sporadic mining settlements and vast areas set aside for weapons and aerospace testing.

Mojave

• *pop 3763* • *elev 2787 feet* ☎ *805*

The town of Mojave has Hwy 14, the Sierra Hwy, as its main street, with the railroad on its west side and a commercial strip of motels, shops, and eateries on the east side. Tourist information is available, sometimes, in the old, red, railroad caboose in the lot next to Mike's Family Restaurant. Driving through, you might think this town

has a huge international airport, but all those airliners are actually in storage here, where deterioration is minimal in the dry desert air.

Places to Stay The *Friendship Inn* (☎ 824-4523), 15620 Sierra Hwy, is a pretty comfortable place to stay, with a pool, cable TV, and single/double rooms for $27/32. *White's Motel* (☎ 800-782-4596) is also OK but marginally more expensive, and a big, red neon arrow makes it easy to find.

Around Mojave

Edwards Air Force Base Southeast of town, this 300,000 acre base (formerly called Muroc) is a flight test facility for the USAF, NASA, and civilian aircraft, and a training school for test pilots with 'the right stuff.' It was here that Chuck Yeager flew the Bell X-1 on the world's first supersonic flight, and shuttles glide in here after their space missions. Free tours of the air force base are available on Fridays by appointment (☎ 805-277-3517). Tours of the **NASA-Dryden Flight Research Facility** are available on weekdays, also by appointment (☎ 805-258-3446). Crowds gather at the East Shore Viewing Site when the space shuttles land; call ☎ 805-258-3520 for flight details.

Boron Thirty miles east of Mojave, Boron is the site of a huge open-cut borax mine. North of Boron, visible from Hwy 395, is a vast array of solar collectors, part of the LUZ corporation's electricity generating system.

Red Rock Canyon State Park This small park (☎ 805-942-0662) straddles Hwy 14, about 20 miles north of Mojave. Its very striking sandstone cliffs have eroded into weird formations that present a spectacular range of colors at sunrise and sunset; you may recognize it from the opening scenes of *Jurassic Park*. There are some marked hiking trails on which you can see Indian grinding holes and a variety of desert plants. The campground has 50 tent sites,

Alternative Energy

California is a massive consumer of fossil fuels, but it has also established some full-scale projects to exploit alternative sources of energy. The desert regions offer not just an abundant source of strong sunshine, but also excellent sites for wind generators and areas where geothermal energy can be tapped.

One of the first large solar energy power plants is near Daggett, east of Barstow. A field of pivoting mirrors tracks the sun and reflects its light onto a cylindrical collector at the top of a 60-foot tower, where a boiler produces water to drive a steam-powered generator. Nearby is a newer type of plant, where curved mirrors focus the sun onto horizontal pipes in which water is heated to power the generators. The mirrors rotate on a horizontal axis to follow the sun from east to west. The concept is simple, but the scale can be impressive; at the site near Boron these mirrors cover hundreds of acres of the desert floor.

More spectacular are the wind generators, with blades the size of airplane wings rotating on top of 80-foot towers that turn to face the prevailing wind. Thousands of these towers stand in lines at locations like the San Gorgonio Pass near Palm Springs and the Tehachapi Pass, west of Mojave, where geographical conditions reliably produce strong winds. As air in the desert heats and rises during the day, cooler air is drawn in from the coastal areas, accelerating as it goes through the narrow passes (the average wind speed in the San Gorgonio Pass is 15 to 20 mph). The older generators (many imported from Denmark), have a capacity of around 40 to 50 kW, but with technology rapidly developing, the newer turbines are much larger and have a capacity of around 500 kW. For more information, call the Desert Wind Energy Association at ☎ 329-1799.

The potential for geothermal energy also results from geographical circumstances. The Salton Trough, extending from the Gulf of California through the Imperial and Coachella valleys, was created by massive sections of the earth's crust moving apart. This movement creates fractures and stresses points, which not only cause earthquakes, but also allow molten magma to work its way close to the earth's surface, heating the ground water. In some places this creates natural hot springs; this heat can also be tapped to provide steam to power generators. Geothermal power plants operate at a number of sites near the Salton Sea, which is the deepest part of the trough, and the thinnest part of the earth's crust. ■

---

toilets, but no other facilities. Camping is $7 per night, and there is a day-use fee of $5. The visitors center is open on weekends (closed all summer).

Rand Mining District

Gold and silver ores discovered here in the 1890s were thought to resemble those in the Rand district of South Africa, hence the town names of Randsburg and Johannesburg. In 1900, thousands of people were working in mines here. Today it's almost deserted, and quite picturesque. There's a lot of old mining junk around – in the hills, on private property, and in the Desert Museum, on Butte Ave in Randsburg, which is open most weekends. The area hasn't been prettied-up or touristified yet, but there are a couple of places to stay.

In Randsburg, the *Whitehouse Saloon &*

Floozy House (☎ 619-374-2464) was originally the mine owner's house, later a brothel, and will now put you up for $45 a night, or provide you with a beer or a burger. The *Randsburg General Store* (☎ 619-374-2418) also has a couple of rooms, from $50 mid-week. Three miles away, on Hwy 395, the *Old Owl Inn* (☎ 619-374-2235) in Red Mountain is another ex-bar-and-brothel that is now an antique shop and B&B, with accommodations from $50 per night.

Ridgecrest
• *pop 27,725* • *elev 2289 feet* ☎ 619

This is the last sizable town before Death Valley, and not a bad place to stock up on water, gas, and supplies, or spend a night in reasonably priced accommodation. The town is here because of the China Lake

Naval Weapons Center on its eastern edge; you can see what this facility does by looking at the **China Lake Exhibit Center** (☎ 939-8645), from 7:30 am to 4:30 pm on weekdays.

It's also worth looking at the **Maturango Museum** (☎ 375-6900), which has good exhibits on Native American art and archaeology. It's on the corner of China Lake Blvd and Las Flores Ave, and is open Tuesday to Sunday from 10 am to 5 pm, for $1.

Places to Stay & Eat There are several budget motels south of town along S China Lake Blvd, including *El Rancho Motel* (☎ 375-9731) at $35/39, and a *Motel 6* (☎ 375-8784) at $25/29. China Lake Blvd has an almost complete set of the most popular fast-food franchises.

Around Ridgecrest
Little Petroglyph Canyon The rock walls here have a huge number of ancient petroglyphs, but the canyon is on the Naval Weapons Center Reserve and not open to the public. You may be able to see them on one of the tours conducted by the Maturango Museum on weekends during spring and autumn.

Pinnacles National Natural Landmark This strange group of rock pinnacles, up to 150 feet tall, are in stark and lonely desert country about 20 miles east of Ridgecrest. The pinnacles were formed when calcium-laden springs bubbled into the carbon-rich waters of an ancient lake, forming tufa spires of calcium-carbonate. This is the same process that created the spires in Mono Lake, 175 miles to the northwest, but here the lake has long since dried up, leaving the spires standing like a ruined city. The area is completely undeveloped, but camping is permitted. The Pinnacles are three miles down a dirt road, south of Hwy 178.

Trona An industrial complex here processes chemicals extracted from the dry bed of Searles Lake, which contains quan-

tities of just about every useful mineral known to science. A strong, sulfurous smell hangs in the air for miles around.

Ballarat A few ruins on the edge of a shining salt flat are all that remain of the mining camp of Ballarat, hopefully named after a city in the Australian goldfields. It's probably the only place in America with an Australian Aboriginal name.

BARSTOW
• *pop 21,472* • *elev 2106 feet* ☎ *619*
At the junction of I-40 and I-15, Barstow is about halfway between Los Angeles and Las Vegas, and lots of travelers break their journey here. They're not looking for charm, and they don't find any.

This area has been a crossroad for desert travelers for centuries. The Spanish priest Francisco Garces came through in 1776, and the 'Old Spanish Trail' passed nearby. By the 1860s, settlers on the Mojave River were selling supplies, mostly liquor, to California immigrants. Mines were established in the surrounding hills, but Barstow really got going after 1886, as a railroad junction. It still has a big rail freight business and serves a couple of military bases, as well as being the unofficial capital of the Mojave.

Orientation & Information
The Barstow Rd exit, heading north from I-15, takes you right past the California Desert Information Center (☎ 256-8313), which has some pretty good exhibits on desert environment and history, and lots of tourist information about Barstow and the Mojave. It's open daily from 9 am to 5 pm. Continue north on Barstow Rd and turn right on Main St, where you'll find a mile or so of motels and places to eat.

Mojave River Valley Museum
On Barstow Rd, two blocks north of I-15, this small museum (☎ 256-5452) concentrates on local history, and has some artifacts (or rocks?) from the Calico Early Man Site (see below). It's open from 11 am to 4 pm daily, and it's free.

Places to Stay

Budget motels on E Main St include *Stardust Inn* (☎ 256-7116), at No 901, with rooms from $24/29 a single/double; *Desert Inn* (☎ 256-2146), at No 1100, from $24/38; and *Barstow Inn* (☎ 256-7581), at No 1261, from $22/27.

For a slightly more expensive midrange place, try the *Quality Inn* (☎ 256-6891), 1520 E Main St, for $49/58; or the *Holiday Inn* (☎ 256-5673), at No 1511. The most comfortable accommodations are probably at the *Best Western Desert Villa* (☎ 256-1781, 800-528-1234), No 1984, where rooms start at $55/59, including breakfast.

Places to Eat

Apart from the standard, big-name places like *Carrows* and *IHOP*, both on E Main St, there are some local places of good value. The *Golden Dragon,* 1231 E Main St, serves substantial Chinese or Thai dishes for $6 to $8, and has good dinner specials. For Mexican food, go a mile or so from the main strip to *Rosita's* at 540 W Main St. On the way you'll pass a few of Barstow's bars. The *McDonalds* on E Main St is said to be their busiest US outlet. It's in an old railway carriage, along with a couple of other food shops and the tackiest selection of souvenirs you'll see anywhere.

Things to Buy

Factory Merchants (☎ 253-7342), at the Lenwood Rd exit off of I-15, just south of town, is a factory outlet center with over 50 stores selling fashions, footwear, and household goods. It's open daily from 9 am to 8 pm.

Getting There & Away

Buses and trains both arrive and depart from the historic railroad station, the Casa del Desierto, north of Main St. You'll really need a car to get around Barstow and the surrounding area.

Bus Greyhound (☎ 256-8757) has 10 buses per day to Los Angeles (2½ hours; $21.50) and San Diego (four hours; $31.50). Two buses per day go east to Las Vegas (2½

hours; $33.50) and on to Denver. Two Amtrak buses per day go to Mojave, Bakersfield, and Oakland.

Train Amtrak has two trains stopping at Barstow, the Desert Wind, going on to Las Vegas, and the Southwest Chief, from LA to Chicago.

Car Enterprise Rent-a-Car (☎ 256-0761), 620 W Main St, rents compact cars from about $30 per day, plus tax, with unlimited mileage.

AROUND BARSTOW
Rainbow Basin National Natural Landmark

Amazingly colorful layers of sedimentary rock can be seen here, folded and distorted into interesting formations. There's a scenic drive, and several short hiking trails. Many mammal fossils, from 12 to 16 million years ago, have been found at the site. The nearby *Owl Canyon Campground* is OK at $4 a night. To get there, take Fort Irwin Rd north of Barstow for six miles, then take Fossil Bed Rd west for two miles.

Calico Ghost Town

The mines around here produced millions of dollars worth of silver and borax, but as the ore played out and the price of silver fell, the town died, and was virtually abandoned by 1907. There was little left but foundations in 1951, when Walter Knott (of Knott's Berry Farm fame) began to rebuild it. Now it's a tourist attraction only marginally more authentic than Frontierland, and just as commercial. Entry is $5/2, and you pay extra to go gold panning, tour the Maggie Mine, ride a little steam railway, see the 'mystery shack,' or catch a show at the Calikage playhouse; these attractions are about $2.25 each. Calico Ghost Town (☎ 254-2122) is off I-15 about 10 miles north of Barstow, and is open daily from 7 am to dusk.

The Calico *campground* is a red earth parking lot, which costs $19 with a hookup, or $15 without. The *KOA* (☎ 254-2311), near the interstate, is better. The *Calico*

Motel (☎ 254-2419), on the south side of I-15, looks like it hasn't changed since the 1950s, but it's kind of cute and costs only $24/33.

Calico Early Man Archaeological Site

Artifacts found at the 'Calico Dig' have been dated to 200,000 years, which doesn't fit with the theory that the first Americans came from Asia less than 20,000 years ago. But are these stones really human tools? Some of them just look like rocks with chips in them, and no human bones have yet been found at the site. See for yourself on one of the site tours, Wednesday to Sunday from 8:30 am to 4:30 pm; call ☎ 256-3591 for tour times. The site is north of I-15, 15 miles east of Barstow.

EASTERN MOJAVE

Interstate 15 and Interstate 40 traverse the eastern Mojave, and most travelers never get off them. Smaller roads crisscross the desert between the interstates, giving access to a number of interesting, and uncrowded desert features. Some of these roads are unpaved, but most can be traveled by passenger cars. Those who really want to explore the area will find useful information in *Walking the Eastern Mojave,* by John McKinney & Cheri Race.

Afton Canyon

A permanent watercourse flows through this canyon, making it a mecca for wildlife. The campground has developed sites for $4. Afton Canyon Natural Area (☎ 256-3591) is south of I-15, 38 miles east of Barstow.

Mojave National Preserve

As a national scenic area, this large preserve (1.3 million acres) is jointly managed by the NPS and the BLM; the latter published a series of 22 *Desert Access Guides* with detailed information about many places of interest in the Mojave. For more information, call the Hole-in-the-Wall Visitor Center at ☎ 619-928-2572.

Kelso The old Kelso railroad depot is a handsome Spanish-style building. Two miles from town, the isolated Kelso Dunes, also called the Devils Playground, are delicately colored and beautifully shaped. They frequently produce a booming or singing noise as sand shifts down the 'slip-face' of the dunes.

Cima Dome Visible from Cima Rd, this perfectly formed, 1500 foot batholith is covered with a unique type of Joshua tree.

Hole-in-the-Wall Hiking trails lead through diverse plant communities, and past interesting rock formations. There are pleasant campgrounds here (at 4200 feet), and nearby at Mid Hills (5600 feet).

Providence Mountains State Recreation Area This is a state park (☎ 619-389-2281), accessed from Essex Rd. There are six primitive campsites ($12), but be well prepared – at 4300 feet it's hot in summer, cold in winter, wet in spring and fall, and can be windy at any time. There's a native botanic garden, and the 1¼ mile, self-guiding, Mary Beale Nature Trail. Within the recreation area, the **Mitchell Caverns Natural Preserve** (☎ 805-942-0662) is a limestone cave that you can only see on a $4 guided tour.

Old Route 66

Nostalgia buffs like to explore this old highway, sometimes called The Mother Road. Old 66 went from Chicago to LA – in California it crossed the Mojave from Needles to Barstow. The old route swings south of I-40 through Amboy, where there's an impressive volcanic crater, and Bagdad, where there used to be a café.

Death Valley

☎ 619

The name itself evokes all that is harsh, hot, and hellish in the deserts of the imagination – a punishing, barren, and lifeless place of Old Testament severity. Historically, the valley has not been as deadly as other parts of California, and naturalists are keen to point out that many plants and animals thrive here. Still, the average visitor expecting blazing sunlight, stark scenery, and inhuman scale will not be disappointed.

DEATH VALLEY NATIONAL PARK
The actual valley is about 100 miles from north to south, and from 5 to 15 miles wide, with the Panamint Range on its west side and the Amargosa Range on its east side. The Death Valley National Park covers a much larger area, which includes several other ranges and valleys to the north.

History
Native Americans The Timbisha Shoshone lived in the Panamint Range for centuries, visiting the valley from winter to early summer every year to hunt and gather food, particularly mesquite beans. They also hunted waterfowl, caught pupfish in marshes, and cultivated small areas of corn, squash, and beans. Encroachments made by mining and tourism interests saw the Shoshone become more sedentary, with many taking on paid work, some making baskets for the tourist market. In 1933, the tribe was allocated a village site near Furnace Creek, which they still occupy.

Mining The fractured geology of Death Valley left many accessible minerals. The earliest miners here, in the 1860s, sought gold, silver, copper, and lead, and a dozen mines were started in the surrounding mountains, each closing as the ore played out. The most sustained mining operation was the Harmony Borax Works, which extracted borate, an alkaline mineral used to make detergents, and other products. The stuff was shipped out in wagons pulled by 20-mule teams, and hauled 160 miles to a railhead at Mojave. By the late 1920s, most of the mining had ceased, though there was a brief resurgence during WWII, when minerals like manganese, tungsten, and lead were needed for wartime production.

Tourism Tents at Stovepipe Wells in the 1920s were the first tourist accommodations, followed by converted workers' quarters at Furnace Creek. In 1933, the area was designated a national monument, and for the next 11 years units of the Civilian Conservation Corps constructed roads, ranger stations, campgrounds, and entrance gates. The area under protection was increased in 1994, when Death Valley became the largest national park in the continental US.

Geology
The rock formations you see today were created by geological events that occurred as long as 500 million years ago. Extensive faulting and fracturing allows some of the oldest rocks to be visible on the earth's surface, when normally they would be hidden deep underground.

Limestone and sandstone from the earliest period, seen in the Panamint and Funeral Mountains, were formed on an ancient seabed and slowly lifted by movement in the earth's crust. From 250 to 70 million years ago, the rock strata were bent, folded, and cracked as converging tectonic plates pushed up mountain ranges. These stresses weakened the earth's crust, leading to a period of volcanic activity, distributing ash and cinders that provided much of the rich coloring seen in the valley.

About three million years ago, the tectonic plates began to move apart, causing major faults. One of these faults formed on the eastern side of what is now Death Valley, and another formed on the west of the Panamint Range. The valley floor and the mountain range together form a single geological structure, which is slowly rotating – the valley floor is subsiding while the range is being lifted. At the same time, erosion is carrying material down the mountains and depositing it in the valley. Much of this erosion occurred between 2000 and 10,000 years ago, when the climate was much wetter than at present, so the valley was filling with sediment even as its floor subsided. At Badwater, the lowest part of

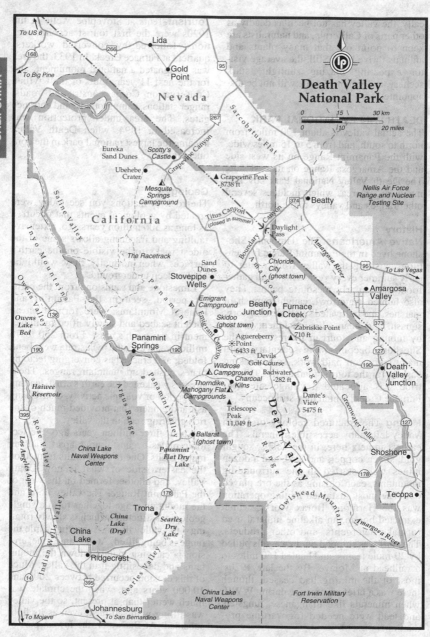

Death Valley National Park

0   15   30 km

0   10   20 miles

To US 6

Lida

266

Gold Point

95

Nevada

168

To Big Pine

267

Sarcobatus Flat

Grapevine Canyon

Eureka Sand Dunes

Scotty's Castle

Grapevine Peak 8738 ft

Ubehebe Crater

374

Beatty

Mesquite Springs Campground

Titus Canyon (closed in summer)

Nellis Air Force Range and Nuclear Testing Site

Saline Valley

California

Boundary Canyon

Daylight Pass

The Racetrack

Sand Dunes

Chloride City (ghost town)

95

To Las Vegas

Inyo Mountains

Stovepipe Wells

Amargosa Valley

Owens Valley

136

Emigrant Campground

Beatty Junction

Furnace Creek

373

Owens Lake Bed

Skidoo (ghost town)

Zabriskie Point 710 ft

190

Panamint Springs

190

AgUereberry Point 6433 ft

Devils Golf Course

Death Valley Junction

127

Haiwee Reservoir

Wildrose Campground

Charcoal Kilns

Badwater -282 ft

Dante's View 5475 ft

190

395

Argus Range

Thorndike, Mahogany Flat Campgrounds

Telescope Peak 11,049 ft

Death Valley

Greenwater Valley

Shoshone

Los Angeles Aqueduct

Rose Valley

China Lake Naval Weapons Center

Panamint Valley

Ballarat (ghost town)

Panamint Flat Dry Lake

Range

127

178

Tecopa

Trona

China Lake (Dry)

Searles Dry Lake

178

Owlshead Mountain

Amargosa River

China Lake

14

Ridgecrest

395

Indian Wells Valley

Searles Valley

China Lake Naval Weapons Center

Fort Irwin Military Reservation

Johannesburg

To Mojave

To San Bernardino

Amargosa River

the valley, the sediment layer is some 9000 feet deep.

Orientation & Information
It's not hard to find your way around the valley by car; there are only a few main roads and they're all well marked. Furnace Creek, toward the southern end of the valley, has most of the facilities for visitors, including a well-stocked general store (open 7 am to 10 pm), a post office, gas station, campground, restaurants, and accommodations. There's also a smaller store, accommodations, and a campground at Stovepipe Wells. Supplies and gas are expensive in the valley. Food and water are available, and gas is cheaper, in the north end of the valley at Scotty's Castle.

Entrance Fees The entrance fee of $5 per vehicle is valid for multiple entries over 10 days, and includes a good map of the park. Not all entrances have a fee collection station open at all times, but you are still expected to pay at one of the ranger stations. Make a point of doing so – the rangers have better things to do than chase fee evaders and the Parks Service needs the funding.

Furnace Creek Visitor Center This really excellent visitors center (☎ 786-2331) has a small museum on the natural

and human history of the valley, a good selection of books, maps, and information, and a moderately interesting slide show every half hour. The center is open daily from 8 am to 5 pm, sometimes later in the winter season.

Emergencies For 24-hour ranger assistance, call ☎ 786-2330. For other emergencies, dial ☎ 911.

When to Visit Winter is the peak season, when accommodations can be booked solid, campgrounds filled before 11 am, and people wait for hours to see Scotty's Castle. Autumn is less crowded, while spring is the best time for wildflowers. Death Valley used to be practically empty in summer, but it has become more popular in recent years, especially with European visitors who are keen to experience 120° temperatures. With an air-conditioned car, a summer trip is quite feasible, especially if you do your sightseeing in the early morning and late evening, spending the hottest part of the day by a pool, or at the higher elevations which are significantly cooler.

Driving Tour
This tour goes from south to north and back. Even starting outside the valley, you could do it all in a single day if you got going very early, which is always a good

Death in the Valley
A small party of forty-niners wandered into the valley when they separated from a larger emigrant group crossing western Nevada. Taking what they hoped would be a shortcut to the California goldfields, they entered the valley from the east in December, 1849. They crossed the valley floor, but could not get their wagons over the Panamint Range. Most of the party sheltered near a waterhole, while two young men, Lewis Manly and John Rogers, were sent to scout for a route west over the mountains. The captain of the group explored to the south, but after some days walking down the valley he turned back, dying before he reached the waterhole again.

The remainder of the party split up, with one group eventually making their way out over Towne Pass. The others, members of the Bennett and Arcan families, including women and children, waited for the two scouts. Manly and Rogers eventually returned, after 26 days and 600 miles in the wilderness, and guided the survivors out of the valley along the route now called Emigrant Canyon. As they left the valley, Mrs Bennett reputedly looked back and uttered the words 'Goodbye, death valley.' It's not surprising the name stuck; more remarkable is the fact that 24 of the 25 emigrants actually survived the ordeal in Death Valley. ■

thing to do in the desert. If you have more time, take one of the side trips listed later.

Start by driving up to **Dante's View**, which offers one of the best overall views of the valley at any time, but is absolutely brilliant if you can make it for sunrise. Heading down toward the central valley, take a short walk out to **Zabriskie Point**, which is also a great place to see the sunrise (and to wonder what that Antonioni film was all about). You can then backtrack about three miles to go through **Twenty Mule Team Canyon**, a windy one-way loop through an ancient lake bed – it makes you feel like an ant in a quarry.

Continue north to Furnace Creek, where you can get some breakfast, have a break, and sit in some shade. The **Borax Museum** in Furnace Creek Ranch will tell you all about the stuff, and there's a big collection of old coaches and wagons out the back. The National Park Visitor Center is just up the road, and you should see its exhibits on Death Valley. Further north again is a not-so-interesting interpretive trail through the ruins of the Harmony Borax Works.

From Furnace Creek you can drive 50 miles straight through to the north end of the valley, or stop for sightseeing on the way. If it's getting hot, go straight through and see the sights on the way back. When you get to the Grapevine ranger station, you'll have to pay the entry fee if you haven't done so yet (keep your ticket). A few hundred yards after the gate, turn right to Scotty's Castle, which is nearly 3000 feet above sea level and noticeably cooler. Even if you don't take a tour (see below), it's worth looking around the outside. You can get food here, and gas is cheaper than in the valley.

Going west after the Grapevine ranger station brings you to **Ubehebe Crater**, a half-mile-wide hole caused by the explosive meeting of superheated volcanic lava with cool groundwater. You can take a one-mile walk through this lunar landscape to the younger and smaller **Little Hebe Crater**.

Head back down the valley, and by the time you get to the scenic loop to the **Mesquite Flat Sand Dunes**, the temperature should be more bearable, and the sun will be lower in the sky, making the dunes more photogenic. Near the road, an old pump marks the site of the original **Stovepipe Wells**, which were tapped by pounding old stovepipes into the sand at a dried-up waterhole. Opposite the end of the loop, look for the field of arrowweed clumps called the **Devil's Cornfield**. Nearby is Stovepipe Wells Village, with a ranger station, store, and a pool you can use for $2.

Return to Hwy 190, drive back south through Furnace Creek, and branch right at the next junction. Two miles south is **Golden Canyon**, which really glows in the late afternoon. Six miles further is the turn-off for the **Artists Drive** scenic loop, which is also at its best around sunset – the spot called **Artists Palette** is particularly colorful. Across to the west, the valley floor is filled with lumps of crystallized salt in what is called the **Devil's Golf Course** – in the middle of this salt pan is the deepest part of the valley, 282 feet below sea level. The lowest point accessible by road is **Badwater** (-279.8 feet), a little further south. It's a pool of salty, mineralized water that is the only habitat of the soft-bodied Death Valley snail.

Scotty's Castle

This Spanish-Moorish pile was built in the 1920s for Chicago insurance magnate Albert Johnson. Walter E Scott, alias 'Death Valley Scotty,' had for years persuaded Johnson to bankroll his seldom-successful gold prospecting; eventually, after Johnson's doctor recommended he move to a warm, dry climate, Scotty convinced him to fund this elaborate vacation home. Scotty seems to have been something of a liar and a freeloader, and after supervising the construction of the house, and being a frequent long-term guest and caretaker, he began claiming it was his own.

When Johnson died in 1948, the house was willed to a charity, but Scotty was allowed to stay on until he died in 1954. The gardens were never finished, but part of the grand swimming pool can be seen outside. Inside are furnishings imported from Europe, handmade tiles, carved timber, and elaborate wrought-iron made especially for the house.

You can get the full story on one of the guided tours, which leave on the hour between 9 am and 4 pm. Tours cost $8, and there can be a long wait – call ahead to find out (☎ 786-2392). Don't be distraught if you miss it though – Scotty's Castle is an entertaining folly, but has no great architectural or historical significance.

Side Trips
There are many possible side trips to points of interest along the edges of the valley and in the surrounding ranges. Detailed information is available from the Furnace Creek Visitor Center, and it's wise to check with them first for information, maps, and an update on road conditions.

Emigrant Canyon Rd A scenic road climbs steeply up this canyon to Emigrant Pass (5318 feet). On the way, dirt roads turn off to Skidoo ghost town, and Aguereberry Point, which has superb views over Death Valley. These higher parts of the park are good to explore when it's really hot down below. Continue up Emigrant Canyon Rd and turn left up Wildrose Canyon to reach the Charcoal Kilns, a line of large, stone, beehive-shaped structures used to make charcoal for smelting silver ore.

The landscape here is sub-alpine, with forests of piñon pine and juniper, and can be covered with snow in winter. You may need a 4WD to reach the end of the road at Mahogany Flat (8133 feet). A trail goes from there to Telescope Peak (see below under Hiking).

The Racetrack Large rocks appear to have been moving across this mud flat, making long, faint tracks in the sun-baked surface. One theory is that winds push the rocks along when the valley is wet or icy. The Racetrack is 20 miles south of Ubehebe Crater, via a dirt road that sometimes requires 4WD.

Daylight Pass The Daylight Pass Rd (Hwy 374 to Beatty, Nevada) goes east of the valley, past a rough road to Chloride City ghost town. Off the Daylight Pass Cutoff, another rough road leads to the ruins of the Keane Wonder Mine.

Titus Canyon A 25-mile, one-way scenic road goes from the Daylight Pass Rd through this dramatic canyon to the floor of Death Valley. It's usually closed in summer, and may only be passable for 4WD vehicles.

Eureka Sand Dunes Rising up to 680 feet from a dry lakebed, these are perhaps the tallest dunes in the country. From the north end of the valley, near Ubehebe Crater, 44 miles of dirt road leads to the dunes. Unless there has been wet weather, the road can be traveled by a regular car.

Hiking
The visitors center has good maps and hiking information, and will encourage you to fill out a backcountry registration form. Rangers regularly conduct guided hikes, but not during summer. In the valley, the most popular hikes are to explore the numerous side canyons, like Mosaic Canyon, Golden Canyon, Natural Bridge Canyon, and Titus Canyon Narrows. At higher (and cooler) elevations, hiking trails skirt some of the old mining areas, like the Keane Wonder Mine and Chloride City. The hike to Wildrose Peak (9064 feet) from the charcoal kilns is an 8½-mile roundtrip, with a climb of nearly 3000 feet.

The most demanding hiking trail climbs seven miles and 3000 feet from Mahogany Flat to the summit of **Telescope Peak** (11,049 feet). From here it's possible to see both the highest and the lowest points in the continental US, Mt Whitney, and Badwater. Allow six to nine hours for the roundtrip, and don't attempt it in winter unless you're equipped for snow and ice climbing. The last two miles to the trailhead might be too rough for a regular passenger car, so you may have to start walking from the charcoal kilns – this will add about four miles, and 2000 feet, to the trip.

Bicycling

Bikes are only allowed on roads open to vehicle traffic – not on hiking trails. The visitors center has a list of suggested bike routes.

Horseback Riding

Furnace Creek Ranch (☎ 786-2345) arranges one- and two-hour trail and carriage rides, except during summer, for around $15 per hour.

Organized Tours

From October to May, Furnace Creek Ranch offers $20 to $30 bus tours to various parts of the valley. Call them (☎ 786-2345, ext 222) at least a day ahead for information and bookings.

Places to Stay

Apart from the campgrounds, all accommodations in the valley are operated by the Fred Harvey Consortium, and are overpriced with minimal standards of service. If you want a roof over your head, you get much better value in one of the towns around Death Valley; Beatty, Nevada, is the most convenient.

Camping As well as saving money, camping is a great way to experience the Death Valley environment. The campgrounds are not particularly appealing (some are like gravel parking lots with a toilet block), but the attraction is just being out there for the sunset, the stars, the sunrise, and the silence. In summer, camping at the lower levels is not really feasible – it's just too hot. Nearly all the campgrounds are run by the NPS, but bookings are only possible at Furnace Creek, through Destinet. The Fred Harvey Consortium has RV parks near its other facilities.

Furnace Creek Campground, with its entrance just north of the visitors center,

has 136 sites, for $10, close to the facilities of Furnace Creek. It's open all year, but it fills up early at busy times and it's very hot in summer; very few sites have any shade. Nearby, *Texas Springs* has a little more shade and costs only $6, but it's only open from October to April. The large *Sunset Campground,* also closed in the hotter months, is mainly for RVs ($6). *Furnace Creek Ranch* operates a trailer park that costs $20.

The *Stovepipe Wells Campground,* open October to April, has very little shade and lots of RVs ($6). There's also a 14-site RV park next to the general store, run by *Stovepipe Wells Village.*

The small *Emigrant Campground,* nine miles south of Stovepipe Wells, is free and open from April to October. At 2100 feet, it should be a little cooler, though it doesn't have any shade at all. Toward the north end of the valley, *Mesquite Springs,* at 1800 feet, is one of the more attractive campgrounds, open all year for $6.

In the Panamint Mountains, approaching Telegraph Peak, are three free campgrounds that have mild weather in summer. *Wildrose,* at 4100 feet, is open all year (unless it's snowed in), and water should be available in summer. *Thorndike* (7500 feet) and *Mahogany Flat* (8200 feet) are small sites, open March to November, and you may need a 4WD to reach them.

Backcountry Camping You can camp for nothing in most parts of the national park, so long as you're at least one mile from the nearest road and a quarter mile from any water source. The old mining areas are for day-use only; they don't want people in them after dark. It's a good idea to check with the visitor center first, and fill out a backcountry registration form.

Hotels The *Furnace Creek Ranch* (☎ 786-2345) has pretty ordinary cabins at $70 for one or two people ($50 in summer) and motel rooms at $98. Extra adults cost $14. Facilities include a large swimming pool, tennis courts, and a golf course. The top-end *Furnace Creek Inn Resort* (☎ 786-

2361) has elegant, Spanish-style, stone buildings, dating from 1927, an attractive swimming pool, tennis courts, and palm-shaded grounds. It's open from mid-October to mid-May and prices start at $225/275.

There are a couple of trees and a pool in Stovepipe Wells, but generally it's a pretty unattractive place. Accommodations at *Stovepipe Wells Village* (☎ 786-2387) include standard rooms at $53 for singles/doubles, and 'deluxe' rooms at $76. They also have 'patio rooms' at $38, but they won't tell you about these unless you ask, and even then they are reluctant to rent them. They're small, a bit worn, and the air-con is noisy, but they're OK, and definitely the cheapest rooms in the valley.

Places to Eat

Restaurants at the Furnace Creek Ranch include *Coyote's,* which has quite good Mexican meals from $10 to $14; *Tino's Italian Ristorante,* which has $7 sandwiches at lunchtime, pasta dishes at around $10, and entrees around $18; and the *Wrangler Steak House,* where steak and/or seafood dishes cost from $13 to $21. The *Corkscrew Saloon* is the only night life, and it's not a bad place for a drink. The *Furnace Creek Inn* has two pricey restaurants, one of which boasts a dress code.

The dining room at Stovepipe Wells Village serves fixed-price buffet meals that are not a particularly good value at $13.95 for soup and a main course, $16.95 with salad as well.

Getting There & Away

Bus There is no regular, scheduled service to Death Valley, though some charter buses and tours operate from Las Vegas.

Car & Motorbike Good roads come into Death Valley from every direction, and all of them offer some spectacular views. Given the cost of rooms inside the National Park, you may want to plan your route so you can spend a night nearby (see Around Death Valley, below). Gas is expensive in the park too, so fill up before you enter.

AROUND DEATH VALLEY

Beatty
• *pop 1623* ☎ *702*

This little Nevada town is the best bet for cheap accommodations near Death Valley, only 40 miles from Furnace Creek. *El Portal Motel* (☎ 553-2912) is a well run little place on the road to the national park, and good value at $35. *Stagecoach Hotel & Casino* (☎ 553-2419, 800-424-4946), on Main St north of town, looks like a tawdry gambling joint, but the rooms are quite good for $37/42. Other options include the *Phoenix Inn* (☎ 553-2250, 800-845-7401), at $33/36, and the slightly upscale *Exchange Club Motel & Casino* (553-2333), from $38/41.

On the way to Death Valley, a short detour goes to the not-very-interesting Ryolite ghost town.

Death Valley Junction
• *pop 8* ☎ *619*

The junction of Hwys 127 and 190, 12 miles east of the park boundary, is famous for the **Amargosa Hotel & Opera House** (☎ 852-4441, 800-952-4441), a creation of the multi-talented Marta Becket. Marta does a season of solo dance and mime performances in which she presents a varied and entertaining cast of characters. Shows are at 8 pm on Friday, Saturday, and Monday nights during November and from January to April; on Saturdays only in October and December. Tickets are $8/5; call first to book and confirm showtimes. The theater space has been fancifully decorated with an audience of renaissance figures painted by Marta herself. The few hotel rooms are priced at $35/45.

Pahrump
• *pop 7424* ☎ *702*

This Nevada town, 60 miles from Furnace Creek, has three motels on Hwy 160, including *Charlotta Inn Motel* (☎ 727-5445), and a *Days Inn* (☎ 727-5100). For more on Pahrump, see the Las Vegas & Canyon Country chapter.

CALIFORNIA

Panamint Springs
☎ 619

The *Panamint Springs Resort* (☎ 764-2010), right on the western edge of the park, has rooms from around $40 (which aren't a particularly good value), as well as campsites, RV hookups, and gas. There's a bigger selection further out on Hwy 395 at Lone Pine and Olancha (see the Sierra Nevada chapter).

Shoshone
• *pop 70* ☎ 619

The small town of Shoshone gives good access to Death Valley by a choice of two scenic routes. By the shorter, northern route it's 57 miles from Furnace Creek. The *Shoshone Inn* (☎ 852-4335) is the only place to stay, and not bad at $36/44.

You'll have a few more choices at Baker, but it's 58 miles further from Death Valley.

Lake Havasu & Colorado River

HAVASU NATIONAL WILDLIFE REFUGE
This is one of a string of protected areas along the lower Colorado River. Habitats include marshes, dunes, desert, and the river itself. Wintering geese, ducks, and cranes are found in profusion and, after their departure, herons and egrets nest here in large numbers. Bald eagles and ospreys are often sighted in winter, bighorn sheep are sometimes seen, and the elusive bobcat is also present, along with common desert mammals like coyotes, rabbits, and pack rats.

Orientation & Information
The section of the reserve north of I-40 is the Topock Marsh. South of I-40, the Colorado flows through Topock Gorge. The southern boundary of the reserve abuts the northern boundary of Lake Havasu State

Park, about three miles north of the famous (and still-standing) London Bridge.

The refuge headquarters (☎ 619-326-3853), 1406 Bailey Ave, Needles, is open Monday to Friday from 8 am to 4 pm, for maps, bird lists, and other information.

Boating
A day of canoeing or floating through Topock Gorge usually begins at either Golden Shores Marina (☎ 520-768-2325), or Park Moabi Campground (☎ 619-326 4777) in Needles. Both are just north of where I-40 crosses the Colorado River. Allow about seven hours for the float through the gorge.

The Jerkwater Canoe Company (☎ 520-768-7753) in Topock offers canoe rentals and guided day trips through the gorge, as well as a variety of overnight excursions along the river. Jet boat tours from Lake Havasu City are operated by Bluewater Charters.

Camping
There is no camping allowed in Topock Gorge. Camping is permitted on the Arizona side of the river, south of the gorge, everywhere except Mesquite Bay. Tent and RV camping ($7 and $14.50) is available at *Five Mile Landing* (☎ 520-768-2350) on the Arizona side of Topock Marsh, about six miles north of I-40 on Hwy 95.

LAKE HAVASU CITY
• *pop 24,363* ☎ 520

The Parker Dam, finished in 1938, created 46-mile-long Lake Havasu. Until 1963, there was no town along the lake. Developer Robert McCullouch planned Lake Havasu City, Arizona, as a center for water sports and light industry/business. Both he and the area received a huge amount of publicity when McCullouch bought London Bridge for $2,460,000, disassembled it into 10,276 granite slabs, and reassembled it at Lake Havasu City. The bridge, originally opened in London, England, in 1831, was rededicated in 1971 and has become the focus of the city's English

Village – a complex of restaurants, hotels, and shops built in English style.

The move was a huge success, and today Lake Havasu City is host to millions of visitors coming not just to see the strange sight of London Bridge in the desert, but to enjoy water sports, boat tours, shopping, golf, and tennis.

Orientation & Information

Hwy 95, the main drag through town, runs north-south. McCullouch Blvd is the main east-to-west street, and goes over London Bridge. Note that you can't turn from Hwy 95 onto McCullouch Blvd – you have to turn a block before or after and reach McCullouch via Lake Havasu Ave.

The chamber of commerce (☎ 855-4115, 800-242-8278), 1930 Mesquite Ave, is open Monday to Friday from 9 am to 5 pm. A visitors center at the English Village is open daily, 10 am to 4 pm. The post office (☎ 855-2361) is at 1750 McCullouch Blvd. The Havasu Samaritan Regional Hospital (☎ 855-8185) is at 101 Civic Center Lane.

Boating

There are many companies offering **boat tours** of the lake region. Narrated day and sunset tours cost about $12 with Dixie Belle (☎ 855-0888) or Miss Havasupai (☎ 855-7979). Bluewater Charters (☎ 855-7171) has jet boat tours at 9 am daily; they cover 60 miles in three hours. Fares are $20/11, free for kids under six. A cheap, quick cruise can be taken on the Colorado River Express ferry operated by the Chemehuevi Indian Tribe. They leave from English Village at 9 am, noon, and 5:30 pm daily, heading for the Havasu Landing Resort operated by the tribe on their California reservation. Fares are $2/1.

Fishing, water-skiing, or sightseeing boat **rentals** are available from Lake Havasu Marina (☎ 855-2159), 1100 McCullouch Blvd; Resort Boat Rentals (☎ 453-9613), in the English Village; or the Havasu Landing Resort (☎ 619-858-4593). Boat rentals vary from about $40 a day for a four-person fishing boat to as much as $300 a day for a ski boat. Jet skis and para-sailing are available from the Water Sports Center at the Nautical Inn (☎ 855-2141, ext 429).

Other Activities Fishing licenses, gear, and information for fishing are available from boat rental places and Bob Lee's Tackle Shop (☎ 855-6744) at 40 Capri Blvd.

Outback Off-Road Adventures (☎ 680-6151), 2169 Swanson Ave, offers 4WD desert tours for $65 half day, $130 full day with lunch. Groups of four or more and children get discounts.

Rent bicycles at Havasu Wheels (☎ 855-3119), 1665 Mesquite Ave.

Places to Stay

The winter season sees the lowest hotel prices; costs rise in summer, which in Lake Havasu City stretches from March to November. Reservations are a good idea for summer weekends and holidays.

Camping Lake Havasu State Park has two campgrounds. The *Windsor Beach Campground* (☎ 855-2784), two miles north on London Bridge Rd, and *Cattail Cove* (☎ 855-1223), 15 miles south on Hwy 95; both offer showers, a boat launch, and tent camping for $9 per day. Cattail Cove also has 40 RV sites with hookups. There are other camping areas near Parker Dam and also on the CA side of the lake.

Bottom End The cheapest places, with doubles around $25 midweek in winter, but rising to over $40 during summer/holiday weekends, cluster along Acoma Rd and London Bridge Rd. These include the *E-Z 8 Motel* (☎ 855-4023), 41 Acoma Blvd, and the *Windsor Inn* (☎ 855-4135), 451 London Bridge Rd, with a pool and spa. Both have kitchenettes. The cheapest of all (starting at $20/25) is the basic *Highlander Motel* (☎ 764-3013), 3350 London Bridge Rd, north of town.

Middle The *Havasu Travelodge* (☎ 680-9202), 480 London Bridge Rd, has a spa and exercise room and charges about

$45/50 for single/doubles midweek or $50/60 on weekends. Continental breakfast is included. The similarly priced *Pioneer Hotel* (☎ 855-1111), 271 Lake Havasu Ave, has a pool, spa, laundry room, as well as a nightclub with dancing.

Top End The *Holiday Inn* (☎ 855-4071), 245 London Bridge Rd, has rooms starting at around $50, but they are better than most for this price. Many rooms come with a refrigerator and a balcony. The hotel offers a pool and spa, bar and restaurant, and entertainment (music with dancing) most nights. There is also a coin laundry. The *Nautical Inn* (☎ 855-2141, 800-892-2141), 1000 McCullough Blvd, was the first of Lake Havasu's resort hotels; fishing, boating, water skiing, jet skiing, and parasailing are available. The inn also has a pool, spa, and golf and tennis facilities. Large rooms start at about $90 ($120 on weekends).

Places to Eat
A good area for a variety of restaurants is on or near the half-mile of McCullouch Blvd between Smoketree Ave and Acoma Blvd.

Shugrues (☎ 453-1400), 1425 McCullouch Blvd, is considered by many to be the best restaurant in town. Other good restaurants are found in the better hotels – the *Captain's Table* (☎ 855-2141) at the Nautical Inn, the *King's Retreat* (☎ 855-0888) at

the London Bridge Resort, and the *Bridge-Room* (☎ 855-4071) at the Holiday Inn all serve breakfast, lunch, and dinner at somewhat more economical prices. For Mexican food, *Casa de Miguel* (☎ 453-1550), 1550 S Palo Verde Blvd, is a popular spot, especially with younger eaters. Breakfast, lunch, and dinner can be had at the *Cafe Mocha Tree* (☎ 453-6444), 2126 McCullouch Blvd, which features crepes, quiches, Belgian waffles, and sandwiches.

Entertainment
Several of the hotels and restaurants mentioned above have lively nightlife. *Hussongs*, adjoining Casa de Miguel, is one of the most popular dance spots for the college-age crowd. Slightly more sedate dancing is found in the *Reflections Lounge* at the Holiday Inn and the *Captain's Cove* at the Nautical Inn.

Catch a movie at *The Cinema* (☎ 855-3111) or the *London Bridge Theater* (☎ 453-5454). Dinner plays are performed by the *Drury Lane Repertory Players* (☎ 453-5605) at the London Bridge Resort. Call the chamber of commerce for other performing arts information.

Getting There & Away
KT Bus departures for Phoenix and Las Vegas leave from the EZ Stop Food Mart (☎ 453-6633), 54 N Lake Havasu Ave, at the Texaco gas station.

Facts about Nevada

HISTORY

Archaeological evidence of human habitation in Nevada goes back many thousands of years. Remains found at Nevada sites include stone tools, arrow and spear points, and bones, as old as any in the Americas. The ancient Lake Lahonton, which covered much of western Nevada until about 7000 years ago, was home to communities who fished and hunted on its shores. Among the more interesting artifacts found in the region are fish hooks, baskets, and duck decoys made from tule reeds (the Nevada State Museum has good exhibits on these ancient societies). After the lake dried up, the region became inhabited by northern Paiute people, who were adapted to life in the desert and lived by hunting small animals and gathering food from the wild. The Paiute may be descended from the Lahontans – there are some similarities in the way they made woven baskets – but it's possible that they came to the area some time after the Lahontans had left.

Other ancient cultures waxed and waned in what is now the southeast part of the state. From around 4000 years ago, small nomadic groups lived by hunting bighorn sheep using a spear and *atlatl* – a notched stick used to throw a spear with greater power. This is clearly depicted in petroglyphs in the Valley of Fire State Park. At some point, the bow and arrow came into use and replaced the atlatl as the weapon of choice for nomadic hunters. Around 2500 years ago, a new group of people arrived, the Anasazi, who also inhabited areas to the east and south. They brought skills in basket making (they're sometimes referred to as the Basketmakers) and also a knowledge of agriculture. Living in extended nuclear families, they cultivated corn, squash, and beans, hunted small game, and lived in pit dwellings. Later they learned to make earthenware pots and constructed groups of adobe buildings similar to the pueblos built by their cousins in Utah, Arizona, and New Mexico.

Around 900 years ago, the Anasazi left southern Nevada for reasons which are not clear; one theory is that a prolonged drought at the time forced them to migrate to more productive agricultural lands. Southern Paiute hunter-gatherers, with whom the Anasazi had coexisted for many years, then had the area to themselves, at least for a few centuries. The Lost City Museum, at Overton, displays adobe and pit dwellings, and artifacts from several cultures dating back 10,000 years.

At the time the first Europeans arrived, there were four main Indian groups in Nevada. Northern Paiute occupied much of the northwest, but the Lake Tahoe area and the eastern foothills of the Sierra Nevada were Washoe country. Southern Paiute occupied most of the Mojave region, from around Las Vegas on into southern Utah, while Shoshone tribes lived in eastern Nevada and western Utah. Most of these Native Americans lived in bands of a few dozen people, and made seasonal migrations between mountains and valley areas. Each band required a substantial area of land, and consequently the total Native American population was quite low, probably under 100,000.

European Exploration

By the early 1800s, Europeans had been through most of the West, but had scarcely touched the area of modern Nevada. Spanish outposts were established in California and New Mexico, Spanish explorers had ventured into Utah, and Lewis and Clark had crossed the continent to the north of Nevada. As Mexico struggled for independence from Spain, it agreed with the US that the 42nd parallel (now Nevada's northern border) would be the northern limit of Mexican territory. After independence, the Mexican government was not as strict

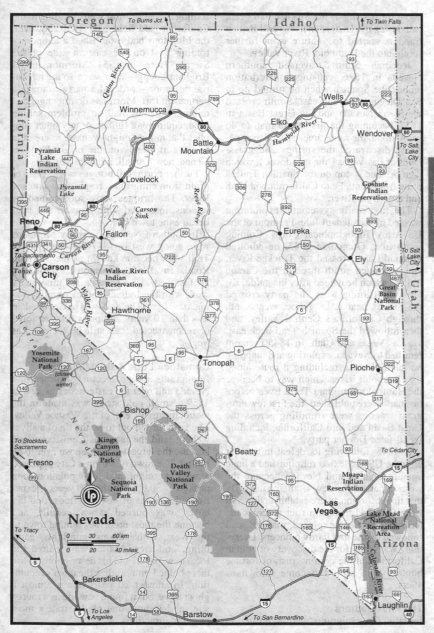

NEVADA

about trespassing as the Spanish had been, and during the 1820s American and British trappers started to venture even further south into the Humboldt River valley.

Jedediah Smith traversed southern Nevada in 1826, causing consternation among the Spanish when he turned up in San Diego. Returning east, Smith crossed the Sierra Nevada and the Great Basin in 1827, becoming the first white man to do so. At about the same time, a Spanish expedition discovered the springs and grasslands of Las Vegas ('the meadows'), which then became a stop on the Spanish Trail, a route from Santa Fe to California, via Utah and the Virgin River.

The first really systematic exploration was led by Lieutenant John Frémont of the US Army Topographical Corps. Coming south from Oregon in 1843, he admired Pyramid Lake, crossed the Truckee River, and continued south through the Carson Valley (which he named after his guide, Kit Carson). Turning west, the party crossed the Sierras near Lake Tahoe, went south through California's Central Valley, and then followed the Spanish Trail back east, via Las Vegas and Utah. In 1845 Frémont returned to Nevada, exploring and mapping northern Nevada, including a route along the Humboldt River which was to become the Humboldt Emigrant Trail. Even before his maps were published, the first few emigrant wagons were trundling across the Great Basin and into California, including the ill-fated Donner party.

In 1848, following its defeat in the war with the USA, Mexico relinquished a huge amount of land and Nevada became the western part of the new Utah Territory. By that time Mormons were established in Salt Lake City and the main routes across the territory had been explored, mapped, and followed by the first hardy pioneers. Everything was ready for the discovery of gold in California and the coming rush of fortune hunters who would become known as 49ers.

The First Settlers

Initially, few emigrants were interested in settling Nevada – most were heading to the California gold fields. By 1850, however, the Mormons had established a temporary trading post on the eastern side of the Sierras. Here, in 1851, Mormon leader Brigham Young – who was also the territorial governor – ordered a party to make a permanent fort. Mormons do not engage in mining, but they had no problem selling food, equipment, timber, or any other supplies that miners might want. A re-creation of the fort stands on the original site in Genoa, now a small, pleasant village.

Further north, toll bridges were set up to profit from emigrants crossing the Truckee River. The bridges were soon joined by saloons, inns, and supply posts, and later became the town of Reno.

In southern Nevada, so many Mormons were going west in 1847 that the Spanish Trail soon became known as the Mormon Road. In 1855, Mormons established another fort at Las Vegas, for missionary work with the Indians and to supply passing travelers. The fort was abandoned in less than 10 years, but parts of it, restored or reconstructed, can still be seen in Las Vegas.

Comstock Lode & the Mining Era

Immigrants and prospectors swarmed into Nevada and over the eastern Sierras, and in 1859 a small gold strike was made in the mountains to the east of the Washoe Valley. The gold turned out to be the tip of a silver iceberg, and the fabulous Comstock Lode became the largest silver deposit ever to be mined. The town of Virginia City appeared almost overnight, and its population soon peaked at 30,000. Within 20 years it experienced two major boom periods, two big busts, was burned down, rebuilt, and became the most notorious mining town in the West, with saloons, gunfights, gambling, and vice. Mark Twain edited the local newspaper, and his descriptions of life there helped immortalize the town's reputation. In another 20 years it was almost a ghost town, but it found new life as a tourist site, and is now one of the state's most popular attractions.

Its wealth helped Nevada progress to statehood. It was incorporated as part of the Utah Territory in 1861, when the US government needed all the resources it could find to fight the Civil War. In 1864, President Lincoln admitted Nevada to the Union as the 36th state, and gained the one extra vote needed to ratify the 13th Amendment abolishing slavery. The state slogan, 'battle born,' thus refers to the financing and politics of the Civil War, not to any battles fought on Nevada soil.

The frenetic mining of the Comstock stimulated activity elsewhere – from agriculture in the Washoe Valley and lumbering in the Sierras, to stock speculation and scandal in San Francisco. While California's quick-money mentality balked at bankrolling a transcontinental railroad, prospects for a rail link across the Sierras to the Comstock country offered sufficient profit potential to finance the most difficult part of the whole project.

The Indian populations were in trouble even before mining and railways made a major impact. The first few immigrants brought enough cattle to damage the grasses the Indians depended on, and their guns took a disproportionate share of the wildlife. If the Indians resisted, they were subject to brutal attacks and reprisals, and there were several battles in the 1860s. The mining industry devastated the natural resources on which the Indians depended, especially the piñon pine, which was clearcut along with most of the other trees in and around the mining areas, for fuel, construction, and to shore up the mines. By 1890, most of the Indians were on poorly run reservations which provided little chance of economic survival, forcing them into dependency.

By 1880, the Comstock Lode had played out, along with other, smaller finds throughout the state. Nevada's population declined steeply, from 62,000 in 1880 to 47,000 in 1890, and took 20 years to recover to the boom-time levels. The cattle industry had done well with the arrival of railroads in northern Nevada, but suffered in the severe winters in the 1880s. In the early-1900s new mineral discoveries revived the state's fortunes, with silver at Tonopah, copper near Ely, and gold at Goldfield.

Economic Diversification

This second mining period saw some diversification. Railroads built branch lines, which stimulated a revival of the cattle industry, and WWI saw a strong demand for beef. Irrigation projects turned the Carson and Washoe Valleys into productive agricultural areas, while motor vehicles and new roads made more of the state accessible. The Great Depression hit hard in Nevada, bringing a collapse in mineral and crop prices, and the failure of most of the state's banks. In 1931 the state government officially legalized gambling and created agencies to tax it, turning an illegal underground industry into a major tourist attraction and revenue source. At the same time they reduced the period of residency required to get a divorce under Nevada's liberal divorce laws, creating one of the most bizarre tourist attractions ever; thousands came to take the 'six-week cure,' and Reno made front pages and gossip columns nationwide during dozens of celebrity divorces.

Construction of the Hoover Dam was a Depression-era project, started in 1931 and finished in 1935, two years ahead of schedule. Not only did it provide much needed work and income for southern Nevada, but it provided an additional water and electricity supply which enabled Las Vegas to grow into a major city. WWII brought a number of military bases to Nevada, and new industries, like the extraction and processing of magnesium to meet the needs of the aircraft industry, which made Henderson (near Las Vegas) the first industrial area in southern Nevada.

Reno was the first city to make an industry out of gambling, but Las Vegas caught up and surpassed it in the 1940s and '50s, with gangsters like Benjamin 'Bugsy' Siegel providing plenty of investment funds, and the innovation of using big-name entertainers to draw people to the

NEVADA

casinos. The rest of the country, including the FBI, were less than impressed with Nevada's criminal connections and sleaze industries, but the state continued with its unconventional sources of revenue, and actually managed to impose some measure of control over the gaming industry. Billionaire Howard Hughes brought legitimate money to invest in Las Vegas, displacing some of the underworld casino owners, and bringing a semblance of respectability to the industry – not too much respectability though, as Hughes himself was decidedly weird and a little wickedness remains part of the Las Vegas attraction.

One attraction that has lost its appeal is nuclear testing. Nevada at first welcomed the nuclear test facility, northwest of Las Vegas, and locals held all-night parties which climaxed with a rooftop view of the big blast at dawn. The testing went underground in the 1960s, and has now stopped, but the site is proposed as a long-term nuclear waste dump. Nevada is not exactly jumping at the chance to acquire this new unconventional industry – it's not the sort of gamble they want the rest of the country to make on their land.

Another unfashionable industry is prostitution, which is neither officially legal nor actually banned by the state government. The regulation of prostitution has long been left up to the county administrations. It is illegal in the two largest counties (Clark County, which includes Las Vegas, and Washoe County, which includes Reno), but tolerated in many of the small counties that see no reason to become self-righteous about an activity that has gone unfettered since the mining days, and which brings in much-needed local taxes. There is some suggestion that the industry is declining because of concerns about AIDS, but don't expect it to disappear anytime soon.

A more likely future for Nevada is as a corporate and financial center, with the attractions of lower state taxes and less onerous government regulations. Already the state has done well with a Freeport Law, which makes warehousing free of tax – storage, distribution, and light manufacturing operations have boomed in Sparks ever since. Because gambling taxes provide so much of the state's revenue, there's no state income tax and no state tax on corporate profits. There is a minimum of red tape, and no requirement for a corporation's primary business or officials to be resident in the state. Despite rapid postwar growth, the state is still sparsely populated, and there is enormous potential for more development in outdoor adventure activities and ecotourism.

GEOGRAPHY

Roughly three quarters of Nevada is in the Great Basin – that high desert region of rugged ranges and broad valleys, which also extends into Utah, California, and Oregon. It's called a 'basin' because its rivers drain to inland lakes and sinks, and do not flow to the sea, but it's more descriptively known as the Basin & Range country – dozens of jagged north-south mountain ranges cross the state, dividing up the bottom of the so-called 'basin.'

Nevada's southern corner, around Las Vegas and the Colorado River, is part of the Mojave Desert, another high desert which extends from California. The western corner of the state, around Lake Tahoe, is geographically on the fringe of the Sierra Nevada mountain range, while a small area in the north is on the edge of the Columbia Plateau.

CLIMATE

Nevada is generally quite dry; most moisture from the Pacific's prevailing winds is lost as precipitation over California's mountains. Nevada's high elevations and inland location make for wide variations in temperature, over the course of the day and the year.

The Great Basin areas get about eight inches of precipitation per year, much of it falling as winter snow; *nevada* means snowy in Spanish. Summer days are hot, averaging around 90°F, while winter days range from cool to cold – around 35°F in the valleys, and colder in the mountains.

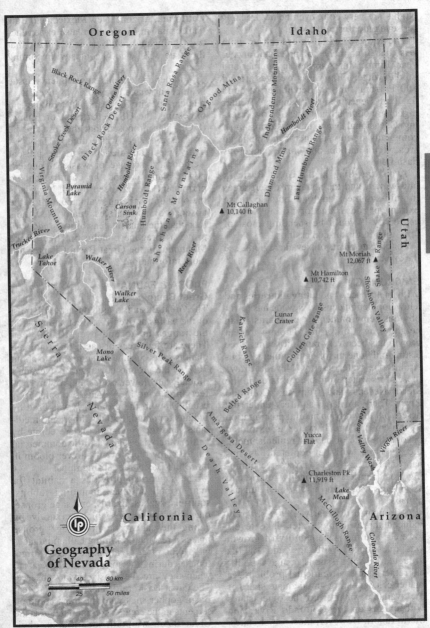

NEVADA

Geography
of Nevada

0   40   80 km
0   25   50 miles

Nights are very cold, even below freezing for seven months of the year.

The Mojave region is even drier, with less than four inches of precipitation per year. Temperatures are hot in summer and mild in winter – Las Vegas averages around 100°F from June to September, around 55°F in December and January. Winter nights are cool, but not often below freezing. Occasional heavy thunderstorms, most commonly during summer, can deluge an area within an hour and create dangerous flash floods.

Avoid traveling in the Great Basin in mid-winter, and the southern desert areas in mid-summer; anytime outside those extreme periods is fine for visiting Nevada, especially if you'll be spending most of your time in the air-con casinos.

For climate charts of Nevada regions, see the appendix.

ENVIRONMENT

With an absence of polluting industries and a low population density, Nevada has fewer obvious environmental problems than neighboring California. Though recent growth has been very rapid, it seems to be testing only one major environmental constraint: the water supply. Nevada draws most of its water from precipitation in the Sierra Nevada, and from the Colorado River. There are large aquifers under the desert, but they rely on natural precipitation to replenish them. If water is extracted beyond the rate of natural replenishment, the resource will be depleted, as has happened at Las Vegas. Excessive pumping from aquifers is critically referred to as 'mining water,' and is obviously unsustainable.

A drought in the early 1990s severely reduced the available water, lake levels lowered, and the sustainability of growth was questioned. With the end of the drought, the water issue is seen as a political rather than environmental problem – a matter of negotiating an adequate share of the available water from the other states with claims on the Colorado River and Sierra runoff. However, those other states,

California, Arizona, New Mexico, and Baja California (in Mexico) are also experiencing significant growth rates; it's likely that the issue will be hotly contested in coming years.

Another contentious environmental issue is nuclear waste. Nevada was used as a nuclear test site for years, but with the end of testing, the US Department of Energy (DOE) has proposed that the test site be used as a nuclear waste dump. The USA badly needs an alternative to the present 'temporary' storage of waste at nuclear power plants around the country, but no permanent site has been found. Nevada is the only option being evaluated, and in the absence of alternatives, many Nevadans fear that the current feasibility study will prove a foregone conclusion. See Yucca Mountain, in the Great Basin Chapter, for more information.

FLORA & FAUNA
Great Basin

The Great Basin is a high desert, with most of the basins at over 4000 feet and most of the ranges up to and over 10,000 feet. There are few trees or cacti; the dominant plant is sagebrush, which amounts to about 70% of the ground cover and is Nevada's official state flower. Sage can grow over 10 feet high, but in Nevada's basins it is usually low to the ground. It was used by Indians for smudge sticks, fiber, and medicines, and the young shoots are edible by cattle; otherwise sage has little commercial value. Many types of wildflower bloom in the Great Basin after spring rains.

The sagebrush provides a habitat for many small animals, including rabbits, squirrels, snakes, lizards, and sage grouse, one of the few species which can survive by eating the sage. The male sage grouse makes a resonant booming call and dances in specific places (called the lek) to attract females during the spring breeding season, when they are the most easy to observe. The Great Basin rattlesnake and the Great Basin gopher snake are the most common serpents in the area. A common lizard is the Great Basin whiptail, identifiable, obvi-

Altitude & Life Zones

An interesting feature of the Great Basin is the change in plant and animal habitats as you climb into the mountain ranges, which have been described as 'islands in a sea of sage brush.' A very rough rule of thumb is that a 1000-foot elevation gain is equivalent to a several-hundred-mile distance to the north, so the vegetation of the highest mountains is comparable to that of Canada. Biologists divide the elevations of the mountains into a series of 'life zones' which are useful in categorizing the changes you see, though the actual altitudes are somewhat generalized:

4500 to 6500 feet – Desert vegetation of cacti, agaves, yuccas, creosote, and sagebrush gives way to evergreen trees, first small junipers, and then piñon pine. (Juniper was a source of berries, fiber, and building material for Native Americans, while pine nuts were a dietary staple.)

6500 to 8000 feet – Stands of ponderosa pine are here, as well as oak, cottonwood, and aspen. Squirrels and chipmunks are common, as well as mule deer and the occasional mountain lion.

8000 to 9500 feet – The predominant trees are sugar pine, Douglas fir, and aspen, with a few shrubs in the shaded understory.

9500 to 11,500 feet – Spruce and fir trees dominate, with bristlecone pines growing right up to the tree line.

above 11,500 feet – The tree line is around this level, above which there are mosses, lichens, and small tundra-variety plants. ∎

ously, by its long thin tail. Larger animals include coyote, pronghorn antelope, and mountain lion, as well as thousands of feral horses and burros.

Bristlecone pines are Nevada's most interesting trees, capable of surviving in the highest, coldest, harshest environments, and are the oldest living things on earth – the oldest documented specimen was 4900

years old. The harsher the environment, the longer they live. The best place to see bristlecone pines, and to appreciate the life-zone transitions, is Great Basin National Park.

Birds include the small and elusive sage sparrow and sage thrasher, and larger raptors, like eagles, hawks, and falcons. Nevada's Great Basin is on the migratory flyway, and thousands of birds fly over in spring and fall from the Pacific Northwest, Canada, and Alaska, to summer sites in Texas, Mexico, and even further south. The Ruby Lake National Wildlife Refuge and the Stillwater Wildlife Management Area (near Fallon) are two of the best places for bird watching. Pelican colonies can be seen at Pyramid Lake.

Mojave Desert

The Mojave Desert covers parts of southern Nevada, southeastern California, north-western Arizona, and the extreme southeast of Utah – it's the smallest, driest, and hottest of the country's deserts. The Mojave is something of a transition zone between the Colorado-Sonora Desert and the Great Basin, with altitudes as low as 282 feet below sea level in Death Valley, but typically from 1000 to 2000 feet. The lowest areas are usually the hottest and driest, characterized by widely spread, shrubby vegetation, or empty sand dunes and dry lake beds.

At the higher elevations, the eerie Joshua trees grow up to 40 feet high, and are believed to live as long as 1000 years. Other members of the same family include the Utah yucca and the Mojave yucca, also called Spanish bayonet.

If there are sufficient winter rains, spring can carpet the desert with around 250 species of flower, of which, 80% are endemic to the Mojave. The indigo bush, desert primrose, paper flower, desert holly, and the catclaw will produce flowers in the right conditions. Creosote bushes are the most common of Mojave plants – and the most aromatic – often growing together with bursage, the favorite forage plant of

NEVADA

The fruits and flowers of yucca plants were a source of food for Native Americans.

burros. Small cacti, like the cholla and beavertail, are also common.

Large numbers of lizards and desert birds are present. The most interesting lizard is the colorfully patterned, venomous, but elusive Gila monster; the most common is the chuckwalla, a large lizard, frequently more than a foot long. The desert tortoise (Nevada's state reptile), is an endangered species, with preservation programs under way near Las Vegas and in California. There are several types of rattlesnakes, of which the Western diamondback and the Mojave rattler are the largest and most distinctive, not to mention the country's deadliest. Desert mammals include the coyote and the kit fox.

The bighorn sheep, Nevada's state animal, is a handsome beast that has long been hunted in the Mojave; it is clearly recognizable in ancient petroglyphs in the Valley of Fire State Park. Well-adapted to desert life, the bighorn eats more varieties of plant than any other hoofed animal. The Desert National Wildlife Refuge is a protected habitat for bighorn sheep, just north of Las Vegas.

For more information about the desert environment and desert travel, see the California Deserts chapter.

NATIONAL & STATE PARKS

Nevada has one national park, the highly recommended Great Basin National Park, and also the Lake Mead National Recreation Area. See the Las Vegas and Great Basin chapters for details. In addition there are two national forests, which between them include a dozen separate forest areas and 22 state parks.

The Humboldt National Forest, with its headquarters in Elko (☎ 738-5171) has two units in the northern reaches of the state. Areas in the forest of particular interest to visitors, at least those with an outdoor bent, are the Santa Rosa Mountains, north of Winnemucca; the Jarbridge Wilderness, north of Elko; and the Ruby Mountains, south of Elko. See the Great Basin chapter for more information.

The Toiyabe National Forest, with headquarters in Sparks (☎ 331-6444), has four units in the central and western parts of the state, some of them straddling the California border. The most interesting features are the Toiyabe Crest National Recreation Trail and the Arc Dome Wilderness, both south of Austin in the Great Basin, and the Mt Charleston area, near Las Vegas.

Of the state parks, the following are of particular interest and are described in more detail in the text:

Valley of Fire State Park Stunning desert scenery, rock formations, and ancient rock art, about 50 miles northeast of Las Vegas.

Spring Mountain Ranch State Park Delightfully green and picturesque old ranch, just west of Las Vegas.

Berlin-Ichthyosaur State Park An old ghost town and an ancient fossil site, about 60 miles south of Austin.

Fort Churchill State Park Evocative ruins of an 1860s army outpost, about 45 miles east of Carson City.

Cathedral Gorge State Park Spectacularly eroded canyon in the east of the state, 110 miles south of Ely.

Lake Tahoe Nevada State Park A great place for hiking, mountain biking, water sports, and cross-country skiing. See the Sierra Nevada chapter for details.

GOVERNMENT
Nevada has a bicameral legislature, with a 20-member Senate elected to four-year terms and a 40-member Assembly elected to two-year terms. The state judicial arm comprises a Supreme Court, plus a number of district courts. There are 16 counties, some with populations of only a few thousand. The Nevada Gaming Commission, one of the most important state bureaucracies, regulates the industry and collects the 'amusement tax,' a principle source of state revenue.

ECONOMY
Tourism and gaming together are the state's biggest industries, employing a third of the workforce and generating more income than all other industries combined. Within this total, about 40% is gambling revenues and 60% is revenue from accommodations, food, drink, entertainment, transportation, and all other tourist services. (This means that the average visitor who spends, $100 for accommodations and food on a trip to Nevada, will also lose an average of about $67 gambling.)

Mining is the second-biggest income earner, though mining revenues fluctuate with mineral prices, the opening of new mines, and the closure of old ones. Nevada is the major US producer of gold, silver, and other precious metals. Other mineral products include mercury, barite, sand, gravel, gypsum, manganese, and copper. The big Carlin County mine, opened in 1965, was the first new US gold mine in 30 years, and it now produces over one quarter of Nevada's gold. Modern mines are capital intensive though; for all its earnings, the industry employs less than 3% of Nevada's workforce.

Agricultural output is significant, with livestock its most important component; cattle are grazed on the vast acreage of the Great Basin, and often sent elsewhere for fattening and sale. The main crops are alfalfa, grains, potatoes, fruit, cotton, figs, and grapes, grown mostly in the western and southern corners of the state, and are dependent on irrigation.

POPULATION & PEOPLE
Nevada's population is only around 1.4 million, but it is among the fastest growing states in the country, with an increase of 39% during the 1980s. This growth is the result of immigration, not fecundity – only a quarter of the current residents were born in Nevada. The vast majority of people, nearly 90%, live in urban areas. Las Vegas, by far the biggest city, has nearly a million people, about 75% of the state's population. With such a big land area, and the small population mostly in a few towns and cities, it's no wonder that much of the state seems so empty.

Ethnically, the population is 95% American born, though there is a greater diversity in Las Vegas. There are several Native American communities, but they form only a tiny percentage of the population. Around 20,000 people, mainly in the north of the state, are of Basque ancestry, descended from 19th-century immigrant sheepherders.

CULTURE & SOCIETY
No one expects a big cultural scene in Nevada, with its short history and small population, but the state has established a Council on the Arts, and there are art galleries, public libraries, orchestras, and live theater in both Las Vegas and Reno.

If there is a local cultural tradition, it's

the culture of the cowboy and the American West. It's most diligently cultivated in Elko, where the Western Folklife Center organizes a Cowboy Poetry Gathering in January and a Cowboy Music Gathering in June. Away from the tourist haunts and casinos it's easy to find a bar with country & western music and, quite likely, some country dancing. Rodeo is a popular spectator sport, though the average cowboy these days does his riding in a pick-up truck. For men in rural areas, cowboy boots, checkered shirts, Stetson hats, and big belt buckles are the rule rather than the exception.

Driving across Nevada's lonely highways, you'll pick up lots of country & western music on the radio. Listen for immortal lyrics like 'I've sure got a weakness for cowboys;' 'That ain't my truck in your driveway;' or for some local interest, 'Hey baby let's go to Vegas, we can bet on love and let it ride.'

GAMBLING

Except for poker, all gambling pits the player against the house, and the house nearly always has a statistical edge. In order to enter the gambling pit, you must be 18 years old. The standard advice to gamblers is:

- Understand the game you are playing.
- Don't bet more than you can afford to lose.
- Quit while you're ahead.

There are several basic gambling options: machines, table games, keno, and the sports books. In terms of player numbers, machines are by far the most popular choice, because they require minimal levels of skill, and can be played with little money. Many casinos, especially in smaller towns, will offer not much more than a few blackjack tables, dozens of slot machines, and flat-top video poker games.

The Machines

Slot Machines The 'slots' are mind-numbingly simple – you put in a coin, and pull the handle (or push a button on some

electronic machines). Most machines take quarters, some take nickels, and a few take tokens of $1, $5, and even more. There are several variants on the number of spinning wheels and what combinations pay out, but there are no choices to make once you've put in the money. The probability of a win, and the size of the payout, are programmed into the machine.

The only important decisions a gambler must make are which machine to play, and when to stop. Some machines pay back a higher proportion of the money deposited than others. Those that return a lot to the player, as much as 97%, are called 'loose' – hence the signs advertising 'the loosest slots in town.' Loose slots are more likely to be found in the main gaming areas of big casinos. Slots with a lower return, down to 84% or even less, are more common in impulse gambling locations, like waiting rooms, bars, and bathrooms. But most players are gambling with a limited sum of money, and keep playing until it's all gone. If they play a loose machine, it just takes them a little longer to lose their stake.

'Progressive slots' offer a jackpot which accumulates, and many slots are now linked in networks to generate bigger jackpots. Often these pay off in the form of a new car, which is prominently displayed in the casino. The jackpots are factored in to the payout percentage, so there's no extra statistical advantage to the player, except that a payout of a few thousand dollars may induce someone to quit while they're ahead, instead of putting all the winnings back into the slot.

Video Poker Increasingly popular video poker games are often built into a drinks bar. For a quarter, they deal you five electronic cards, let you hold or draw, and pay off if you get a pair of jacks or better. They don't pay well though – a royal flush will pay 250 times the amount bet, but the odds against getting a royal flush are just over one in a million.

Table Games

The table games can involve complicated

betting options, and even more complicated payout levels, so it can be hard to figure out the house's statistical edge. All table games are played with chips, which can be bought from the dealer. If you have any left when you finish playing, go to the cashier to 'cash in your chips.'

Blackjack Basically the same as pontoon or 21, blackjack is the most popular table game in Nevada. Players bet against the dealer, with the object to draw cards which total as close to 21 as possible, without going over. Jacks, queens, and kings count as 10, an ace is worth either 11 or 1, and other cards are counted at face value. The player places a bet and is dealt two cards. The dealer then gets two cards, one facing up and the other concealed. The player can 'stand' on the cards dealt, or 'hit' (ie take more cards from the dealer, one at a time). Variants are to 'double down,' which means doubling your bet and taking one more card; or to 'split' a hand, if it has two cards of the same value, by matching the original bet and playing the cards as two separate hands.

Players draw cards until they stand on their total, or 'bust' (go over 21 and lose). The dealer then draws cards, and by house rules must hit on any total of 16 or less, or stand on any total of 17 or more. The player must score higher than the dealer to win. Most wins are paid at even money, except if a player is dealt blackjack (an ace plus a 10-value card), which pays 3 to 2, ie $3 for every $2 bet.

The skill is in knowing when to stand, draw, double down, or split, to maximize your chances of beating the dealer. Some gambling books publish charts which show the best move to make for every dealt hand and every up card the dealer may have. If you follow these exactly, your chances of a winning an even money payout are slightly less than 50%. Professional gamblers count the cards as they are dealt (even though more than one deck is used), and by knowing the probabilities of drawing given cards they can sometimes beat the odds, but card counting is regarded as cheating in Nevada,

and you won't be allowed to do it in any visible way.

Craps If you throw 2 dice, the up faces will add up to a number from 2 to 12. Craps has some very complicated ways of betting on this outcome. The possible bets are marked on the green felt of the playing table, but they're far from self-explanatory. A 'pass line' bet is that on the first roll (the 'come out' roll) the dice will total 7 or 11. If the dice total 2, 3, or 12, (called 'craps') the player loses. Any other number is a 'point,' and the dice are rolled again until either a 7 or the point number comes up – if a 7 comes up first, the player loses; if the point comes up, the player wins. A 'don't pass' bet is basically the reverse – if the come-out roll totals 7 or 11, the player loses; if it's 2 or 3 the player wins, while the 12 is a tie. If a point is established, the don't-pass better wins on a 7 and loses if the point is rolled again. All these bets pay even money, and the player has a statistical chance of winning which is just under 50%.

'Come' bets are placed after a point is established; 7 and 11 win, while 2, 3, or 12 lose. If it's none of these, the dice are thrown again until the point is thrown, and the player wins, or an even is thrown and the player loses. The don't-come bet is the reverse, except that 12 is a draw, not a win for the player. Come and don't-come bets pay even money, and again the odds of winning are just under 50%.

If you've already made a pass or come bet, and a point has been established, you can bet that the point will come up before a 7 is thrown. These bets pay off at a rate which is equal to the statistical chance of a win, so the house has no edge – this is called a 'free-odds' bet (or just an 'odds' bet), and it is the best chance you'll get in a casino. You don't have an advantage against the house, but at least the odds aren't against you, except that you have to place one of the less-favorable bets first.

Other options include a 'place bet' (that either a 4, 5, 6, 8, 9, or 10 will be rolled before a 7) or a 'field bet' (that the next roll will be either a 2, 3, 4, 9, 10, 11, or 12). The house has an edge of between 1.5% and 6.7% on these bets. 'One-roll' bets offer a chance to bet on various outcomes for a single roll, and the house edge is between 9% and 17% – pretty bad for the better.

In short, some craps bets are much better than others, but even on the best of them, with an optimum playing strategy, the odds are still against the player. The game is fast and complicated, so if you want to maximize you chances, take a lesson, watch some games, and don't expect to win in the long run.

Roulette This is the easiest game to understand, and the one that most clearly demonstrates the house edge. The roulette wheel has 38 numbers – from 1 to 36, plus 0 and 00. About half the numbers are colored red, the other half are black, while the two zeros are green. The table is marked with the numbers, and the various combinations which can be bet.

You can bet that a result will be odd or even, red or black, high (19 to 36) or low (1 to 18). All of these bets pay off at even money, but the chances of a win are less than 50% because the 0 and 00 don't count as odds or evens, red or black, high or low. Your chances are 18 in 38 (47.37%), not 18 in 36.

You can bet on a single number (including the 0 and 00), which will pay at 35 to 1, though there 38 possible outcomes. You can also bet on pairs of numbers, or groups of 4, 5, 6, or 12 numbers, and they all pay off at a level which gives the house a 5.26% advantage, except for the 5-number bet which is slightly worse.

Baccarat This game is offered in some Las Vegas casinos, but it's not very popular. Bets are placed, and the player and the banker are dealt 2 cards on which a point value is calculated; sometimes a third card is drawn, and the hand which is closer to 9

points wins. The rules are quite fixed, and the house edge is low, but there are no decisions for the player to make except the size of the initial bet.

Poker This is unusual for casino games because players bet directly against each other. The house provides the table, the cards, and the dealer, who sells the chips and deals the hands, and collects a 'rake' from each pot. If you're not already a good poker player, don't even think about getting involved in a casino game in Nevada. In any case, not many casinos offer public poker games, though the big places usually run semi-private games in back rooms for high rollers.

Wheel of Fortune
You sometimes see these near the slot machine area of a casino. You place your bet, spin the wheel, and in most cases lose your money. They don't offer good odds.

Keno
This game is like lotto; there are 80 numbered squares on a card, a player picks from 1 to 15 numbers, and bets 70¢ or $1 per number. At the draw, the casino randomly selects 20 of the numbers, and winners are paid off according to how many of the winning numbers they chose, as shown on a 'payoff chart.' The amount they pay off is distinctly less than the probability of selecting the numbers by chance, so the odds favor the house by over 20%.

Sports Betting
Some of the bigger casinos have a 'sports book' room, where sporting events from around the country are displayed on video screens which cover a whole wall. Players can bet on just about any ball game, boxing match, horse race, or hockey game in the country, except for events taking place in Nevada.

Las Vegas & Canyon Country

The triangle of southern Nevada is part of the Mojave Desert, which extends into California, northwest Arizona, and southern Utah. The main city is, of course, Las Vegas, a huge, internationally known destination, which everyone should see at least once.

Las Vegas is also a good base from which to explore other attractions of the region. Beautiful Red Rock Canyon is just out of town, while the forests and snow fields of Charleston Peak are less than an hour away. Also close are the imposing Hoover Dam, Lake Mead, and the gambling gulch of Laughlin. The brilliant Valley of Fire can be reached in a few hours, as can Death Valley in California. A day's drive brings you to the Grand Canyon and the massive Navajo Reservation in Arizona, or to Zion National Park and Bryce Canyon National Park in Utah. Still another option for a quick overview is an air tour.

Las Vegas

• *pop 881,000* • *elev 2174 feet* ☎ *702*

This is the original 'love it or hate it' town. Most people are dazzled by their first sight of the bright lights in Glitter Gulch and the Strip, and staggered by the scale and extravagance of it all, but many are overwhelmed almost instantly by its downright tackiness. If you've come for the gambling and the glitter, you'll love it – at least for a few days, until your money disappears. Kids love it – there are so many things here just for fun. Budget backpackers love it – they can get great meals for a few bucks, and great entertainment for free. But to anyone with cultural pretensions, it's tasteless, gaudy, vulgar, commercial, and crass. Las Vegas is a place people love to hate.

As a piece of modern America, Las Vegas is truly remarkable. In 90 years it has grown from nothing to nearly a million people. It's the fastest growing city in the nation, with greater recognition than many cities twice its size, and it's the biggest single attraction in the country, receiving nearly 30 million visitors a year. Amazingly, this has been achieved in an isolated location in the middle of a desert, almost entirely devoid of natural advantages. Las Vegas has made an industry of providing the whole country with something it wants: budget-priced glamour for mass consumption and the tantalizing hope of instant wealth. It manages to reach out for a family market, while still pretending to be a little bit naughty; titillation is the stock in trade.

History

The only natural feature to account for the location of Las Vegas is a spring north of downtown. It was used by Paiute Indians on seasonal visits to the area. In 1829 the spring was discovered by Rafael Rivera, a scout for a Mexican trading expedition, and the area became known to overland travelers as *las vegas,* 'the meadows,' a place with reliable water and feed for horses. Explorer John Frémont put the place on the map in 1844 when he drew the first map of the region. Las Vegas became a regular stop on the southern emigrant route to California, the so-called Spanish Trail. Mormons built the first structure in the 1850s, a small mission and fort which was abandoned by 1858. The fort became a ranch house, but there was little development until 1902, when much of the land was sold to a railroad company. The area which is now downtown was subdivided when the track came through, with 1200 lots sold in a single day, May 15, 1905. The date is now celebrated as the city's birthday.

As a railroad town, Las Vegas had machine shops, an ice works, and a good number of hotels, saloons, and gambling houses. In 1920 the population was 2300. The railroad laid off hundreds in the mid 1920s, but one Depression-era development gave the city a new life. The huge Hoover Dam (then known as Boulder Dam) project, commenced in 1931, provided jobs and growth in the short term, and the water and power for the city's long-term growth.

Also in 1931, Nevada legalized gambling and simplified its divorce laws, but unlike Reno, conservative Mormon politics in Las Vegas did not encourage business to capitalize on these changes. The first big casino on the Strip, El Rancho, was built by Los Angeles developers and opened in 1941.

The next wave of investors, also from out of town, were mobsters like 'Bugsy' Siegel, who built the Fabulous Flamingo in 1946. This set the tone for the new casinos – big and flashy, with lavish entertainment laid on to attract the high rollers. The underworld connections, if anything, added to the excitement of a Las Vegas as a tourist destination.

The glitter which brought in the high rollers also attracted smaller spenders, but in larger numbers. Southern California provided a growing market for Las Vegas entertainment, and improvements in transport made it accessible to the rest of the

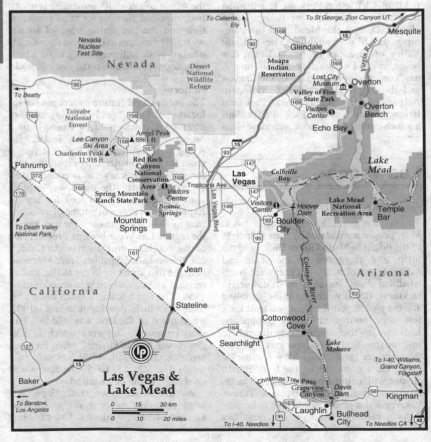

Las Vegas & Lake Mead

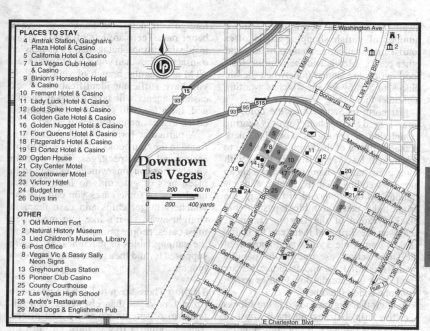

PLACES TO STAY
4 Amtrak Station, Gaughan's Plaza Hotel & Casino
5 California Hotel & Casino
7 Las Vegas Club Hotel & Casino
9 Binion's Horseshoe Hotel & Casino
10 Fremont Hotel & Casino
11 Lady Luck Hotel & Casino
12 Gold Spike Hotel & Casino
14 Golden Gate Hotel & Casino
16 Golden Nugget Hotel & Casino
17 Four Queens Hotel & Casino
18 Fitzgerald's Hotel & Casino
19 El Cortez Hotel & Casino
20 Ogden House
21 City Center Motel
22 Downtowner Motel
23 Victory Hotel
24 Budget Inn
26 Days Inn

OTHER
1 Old Mormon Fort
2 Natural History Museum
3 Lied Children's Museum, Library
6 Post Office
8 Vegas Vic & Sassy Sally Neon Signs
13 Greyhound Bus Station
15 Pioneer Club Casino
25 County Courthouse
27 Las Vegas High School
28 Andre's Restaurant
29 Mad Dogs & Englishmen Pub

Downtown Las Vegas

NEVADA

country. Vegas became a mass tourism destination. Most of Las Vegas' phenomenal development has occurred in the postwar period; as with other sun-belt cities, air conditioning and reliable water supplies made life in the desert not just bearable, but desirable.

Orientation

Two main highways come into Las Vegas, I-15 and Hwy 95, but there are no exits marked either 'Downtown,' or 'the Strip.' For downtown, exit Hwy 95 at Las Vegas Blvd (exit 75) or I-15 at Charleston (exit 41). Interstate 15 parallels the Strip, so work out which cross street will bring you closest to your destination. If it's your first time in Vegas, and you're not in a hurry, get off I-15 at Blue Diamond Rd (exit 33), and cruise the length of the Strip from south to north, right up to downtown.

Downtown Las Vegas is a reasonably compact grid, southeast of the Hwy 95/I-15 intersection. It is the original town center,

but it's not like downtown in any other city – the principal street, Fremont St, is lined with casinos and hotels, while public buildings, like the post office and city hall, are pushed out on the edge, a few blocks north. There's virtually no shopping, except for souvenirs, and even the train station is buried in the middle of Gaughan's Plaza Hotel & Casino. The blocks around the intersection of Main St and Fremont St are known as Glitter Gulch, and feature the smiling neon cowpersons Vegas Vic and Sassy Sally, who are long-time Las Vegas icons. A new downtown redevelopment project is making five blocks of Fremont St into a pedestrian precinct, shaded by a massive awning – it's a great idea.

Las Vegas Blvd goes through downtown and continues for about 10 miles to the south end of town. Most of the really big hotel/casinos, with their galaxies of colored lights, are located along a three-mile stretch of the boulevard known as the Strip. It isn't non-stop neon, though; huge vacant lots await the next new development, and a number of garish shopping malls offer tourist information, souvenirs, liquor, and other basics. Motels and the familiar fast-food outlets are slotted in between the big places, or occupy any site which is awaiting a grander fate.

Just north of Sahara Ave, the colossal, three-legged Stratosphere Tower is nearing completion, and promises to be a landmark at the north end of the Strip. From there to downtown, Las Vegas Blvd is lined with some pretty tatty looking buildings – cheap motels, wedding chapels, shops, and gas stations. At the south end of the Strip, the bright lights peter out a block past the big black pyramid of the Luxor. Traffic is heavy on the Strip and there can be traffic jams at 2 am. Unless you want to be part of the street action, use one of the parallel roads (Industrial Rd and Paradise Rd are good bets) or take the local buses to get from one end to the other.

A few other big casinos dot the blocks near the Strip, but beyond them, most of Las Vegas is ordinary, residential suburbs. North Las Vegas is a pretty tough area, while the city's western fringe has some of the biggest, fanciest houses. Southeast of Vegas, Henderson is a satellite suburb with some 'real' industries, like chemicals and metal processing.

Information

Tourist Offices The Las Vegas Visitor Center (☎ 892-7575) is in the Convention Center at 3150 Paradise Rd. They have racks of brochures and free books of information, and are open daily from 8 am to 5 pm. Quite a few businesses advertise themselves as 'tourist offices,' and they usually have maps, brochures, and discount books, but they are basically agents selling tours and hotel packages.

The California State Automobile Association (☎ 870-9171) is at 3312 W Charleston Blvd, open from 8:30 am to 5 pm weekdays.

Money Casino cashiers, open 24 hours, will change travelers checks and major

foreign currencies, but banks will give a better rate. There are lots of ATMs, many inside the casinos, but there may be heavier transaction fees than you'd be charged at an ATM at a regular branch of your bank. If you have sufficient identification, check cashing agents will take personal checks and, for a fee, will give you a guaranteed check that casino cashiers will accept.

A particular form of local currency is found in the 'fun books,' offered with many casino and hotel packages. They contain vouchers or coupons which can be used to place bets or get coins to insert in slot machines. In some cases you can use the vouchers to get chips and cash them in straight away, so it's like free money. In most cases, people promptly spend them at the gaming tables or machines, as they're supposed to, and then start losing their own money.

Tipping There seem to be more people to tip in Las Vegas than elsewhere, and this tends to offset the generally low prices. Valet parking is free at most casinos; tip around $2 and it's still a good value. Drinks are complimentary while you're playing the tables, but tip the waitress $1 or so for a round. Dealers only expect to be tipped (or 'toked') by winning players, maybe 10% of a good win, or with a side bet that the dealer collects if it wins. Buffet meals are self-serve, but it's nice to tip the person who brings you a drink or cleans your table.

Post The main office (☎ 385-8944) is downtown at 301 E Stewart St, and it's open weekdays from 9 am to 5 pm and Saturday mornings. General delivery mail sent to Las Vegas comes here, and can be collected, with photo ID, between 9 am and 3 pm.

Media The local newspaper is the *Las Vegas Review Journal*. For tourist information, free papers like *Today in Las Vegas* and *What's On in Las Vegas* are available in most hotels. Gig guides, local gossip, and alternatives to the casino scene are covered in two free local papers, *New Times* (weekly) and *Scope* (monthly).

Bookstores There's a Waldenbooks in Fashion Show Mall. The Gamblers Book Club (☎ 382-7555), downtown at 630 S 11th St, has books on every aspect of gambling, and some on Las Vegas history.

Gay & Lesbian Travelers The Gay & Lesbian Community Center (☎ 733-9800) is at 912 E Sahara Ave. Like most of Nevada, Las Vegas is not particularly gay friendly, and it's unwise for gay couples to show affection in public.

Medical Services Southern Nevada Memorial Hospital (☎ 383-2000), 1800 W Charleston Blvd, has 24-hour emergency service.

Gambling Problems Gamanon (Gamblers Anonymous, ☎ 731-0905) is at 900 Karen Ave. One of the best places for the treatment of problem gambling is the counseling center at the Charter Hospital (☎ 876-4357), 7000 Spring Mountain Rd. There is also the Nevada Council on Compulsive Gambling (☎ 364-0623).

Dangers & Annoyances Most of the tourist areas are well-lit and have people around all the time, so they're pretty safe. North Las Vegas is reputed to be an unsafe area, but there's not much reason to go there. The stretch of Las Vegas Blvd between downtown and the Strip can feel a bit threatening.

You'll notice smoke-free and Las Vegas are never in the same sentence: Vegas has ashtrays at every telephone, elevator, pool, shower, in the toilets, in taxis, and at the movies. A Surgeon General's warning should be posted at the airport.

Casinos & Gambling

Casinos make money if they can get the punters through the doors, and in Las Vegas the competition is so intense that casinos go to extraordinary lengths to get them in. At first it was cheap booze, food, and entertainment, but the newest casinos are trying to get the whole family, and they have theme-park-style amusements to keep the youngsters busy while the old folks feed the slot machines. With minor variations, most casinos offer the same range of gambling options – see Gambling in the Facts about Nevada chapter – if that's what you're here for. If you're serious about learning the games, consider taking the free lessons offered by the big casinos – see *Today in Las Vegas* for a current list of times. For information about the famous Las Vegas shows, see Entertainment; there's also information in Places to Stay and Places to Eat.

On the inside, casinos are gaudy, noisy, and deliberately disorienting. Long rows of slot machines are surrounded by mirrors, lights, and more slot machines, all beeping and ringing like demented computer games, and rattling the occasional win into a metal trough with as much noise as possible. You have to pass hundreds of these things to get to the bar, bathroom, restaurant, or registration desk of most big casinos. The tables for blackjack, craps, and roulette are less raucous and slightly more classy, but by the time you've found them you won't be able to see the exit.

Black globes with hidden cameras survey the scene constantly, while the cruising cocktail waitresses can be anything from gorgeous to grotesque, wearing fishnet stockings, togas, cowboy boots, grass skirts, or whatever else has been contrived to match the casino theme. Most of the customers are dressed somewhere between casual and slobby, and look slightly dazed if they're detached from a slot machine. There are special rooms for the real high rollers, where the stakes are higher, the waitresses prettier, and the people show how rich they are by losing hundreds or thousands without flinching.

The front entrance of a casino will tend to draw you in, though there's nowhere to park a car out front; leave it with a parking valet, or go around back, where there is usually a free parking lot or multi-story garage. The big casinos on the Strip are set

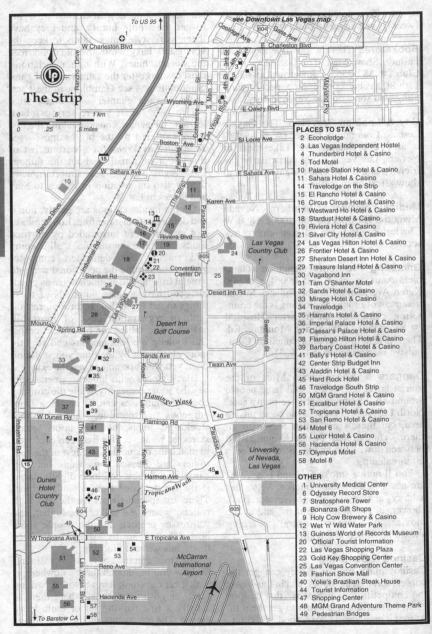

NEVADA

The Strip

see Downtown Las Vegas map

To US 95

W Charleston Blvd
Coolidge Ave
E Charleston Blvd
Gass Ave

0   .5   1 km
0   .25   .5 miles

Wyoming Ave
Boston Ave
St Louis Ave
E Oakey Blvd
W Sahara Ave
E Sahara Ave
Karen Ave
Riviera Blvd
Circus Circus Dr
Convention Center Dr
Stardust Rd
Desert Inn Rd
Mountain Spring Rd
Sands Ave
Twain Ave
W Dunes Rd
Flamingo Wash
Flamingo Rd
Harmon Ave
Tropicana Wash
W Tropicana Ave
E Tropicana Ave
Reno Ave
Hacienda Ave
To Barstow CA

Rancho Drive
Industrial Rd
Rancho Rd
Las Vegas Ave
S Main St
Commerce St
Fairfield Ave
S Las Vegas Blvd
3rd St
4th St
5th St
Maryland Pkwy
The Strip
Paradise Rd
Swenson St
Koval Lane
Audrie St
Monorail
Las Vegas Blvd
(The Strip)
Industrial Rd

Las Vegas Country Club
Desert Inn Golf Course
University of Nevada, Las Vegas
McCarran International Airport
Dunes Hotel Country Club

604
605

PLACES TO STAY

2   Econolodge
3   Las Vegas Independent Hostel
4   Thunderbird Hotel & Casino
5   Tod Motel
10 Palace Station Hotel & Casino
11 Sahara Hotel & Casino
14 Travelodge on the Strip
15 El Rancho Hotel & Casino
16 Circus Circus Hotel & Casino
17 Westward Ho Hotel & Casino
18 Stardust Hotel & Casino
19 Riviera Hotel & Casino
21 Silver City Hotel & Casino
24 Las Vegas Hilton Hotel & Casino
26 Frontier Hotel & Casino
27 Sheraton Desert Inn Hotel & Casino
29 Treasure Island Hotel & Casino
30 Vagabond Inn
31 Tam O'Shanter Motel
32 Sands Hotel & Casino
33 Mirage Hotel & Casino
34 Travelodge
35 Harrah's Hotel & Casino
36 Imperial Palace Hotel & Casino
37 Caesar's Palace Hotel & Casino
38 Flamingo Hilton Hotel & Casino
39 Barbary Coast Hotel & Casino
41 Bally's Hotel & Casino
42 Center Strip Budget Inn
43 Aladdin Hotel & Casino
45 Hard Rock Hotel
46 Travelodge South Strip
50 MGM Grand Hotel & Casino
51 Excalibur Hotel & Casino
52 Tropicana Hotel & Casino
53 San Remo Hotel & Casino
54 Motel 6
55 Luxor Hotel & Casino
56 Hacienda Hotel & Casino
57 Olympus Motel
58 Motel 8

OTHER

1   University Medical Center
6   Odyssey Record Store
7   Stratosphere Tower
8   Bonanza Gift Shops
9   Holy Cow Brewery & Casino
12 Wet 'n' Wild Water Park
13 Guiness World of Records Museum
20 'Official' Tourist Information
22 Las Vegas Shopping Plaza
23 Gold Key Shopping Center
25 Las Vegas Convention Center
28 Fashion Show Mall
40 Yolie's Brazilian Steak House
44 Tourist Information
47 Shopping Center
48 MGM Grand Adventure Theme Park
49 Pedestrian Bridges

way back from the street. There may be an escalator or a moving footpath to get you in, but when you want to leave, you'll be walking all the way.

Downtown casinos are less gimmicky, and concentrate on gambling. The casinos listed below, all on the Strip and listed from north to south, are worth visiting as attractions in themselves. It's free to get into the casinos, and many of the attractions are free too, though you may have to pay for rides or special exhibits, and you have to run the gauntlet of gambling temptations to get in or out.

Stratosphere Tower Opened on the Strip in 1996, this casino/hotel (☎ 800-998-6937) has a landmark 1149-foot tower. Not content with building the tallest observation tower in the country, they are putting a roller coaster on top of it, as well as a revolving restaurant and four wedding chapels. Only in Las Vegas.

Circus Circus One of the original casino-cum-theme-park places, Circus Circus has been enormously successful sucking in the crowds, and its owners have developed several of the other new and spectacular casinos on the Strip. This one features a variety of free circus acts in the tent-like interior, a 'midway' with carnival attractions, and a room of video games. Grand Slam Canyon (☎ 794-3912) is a mini amusement park, in a giant dome behind the casino, with a roller coaster, flume rides, dinosaurs, and a super slide. It's open daily from 10 am to 6 pm, until midnight on weekends. A one-day ticket with unlimited rides is $14/10, or get in for $3 and pay separately for rides.

Treasure Island From the street you'll notice the pirate ship and man o' war parked in the lagoon out front. Every 90 minutes from 4:30 pm to midnight, they stage a sea battle with lots of noise, smoke, and drama. Kids love it.

Mirage A fake volcano erupts in front of the Mirage every half hour, with lots of

smoke, noise, and flames coming from the water. Inside is a re-created tropical rain forest, and the white tigers used in the Siegfried & Roy stage show. A 2½-million-gallon tank holds five dolphins which you can see, from above and below the water, for $3.

Caesar's Palace You are drawn into this place past classic columns and 'ancient' statues, along a moving footpath which takes you into the gaming rooms, or to the Forum Shops. The Forum is an indoor imitation of a Roman street, with a painted sky which changes from dawn to dusk every three hours, and a fountain where marble statues come to life and deliver an homage to self-indulgence. The Omnimax theater (☎ 731-7900) shows special features.

MGM Grand With over 5000 rooms, this is the world's largest hotel; a massive, green-striped structure on Las Vegas Blvd at Tropicana. A large and silly-looking lion squats on the corner, looking across at the medieval turrets of Excalibur, and the Easter Island statues outside the Tropicana Ave. Enter between the lion's paws, and in the front lobby is the Emerald City special effects show, which exploits a Wizard of Oz theme. MGM Grand Adventure (☎ 891-7979) is a 33-acre theme park behind the main casino complex, with water rides, roller coasters, restaurants, and shops. It's open daily from 10 am to 6 pm (until 10 pm in summer), and costs $17/14 with unlimited rides and shows.

Excalibur Here is another huge hotel (4000 rooms), this time done out to look like a medieval castle with a heavily overworked Arthurian theme. A big attraction is the jousting knights, which are part of the dinner show. One of the few features that doesn't try to mimic olde England is the collection of Magic Motion Machines ($3) which create the illusion that you're doing something exciting.

Tropicana A tropical theme dominates in this casino, inelegantly known as 'the

Trop.' Polynesian statues stand out front, and there's a giant water park behind. There are poolside blackjack tables, so you can sit in the water and gamble – but where do you put the chips?

Luxor This remarkable pyramid structure is a sight in itself, with a sphinx and an imitation of Cleopatra's needle out the front. The beam of light pointing up from the pyramid's apex can be seen for miles. Inside is a huge atrium with more than the usual number of options for eating, drinking, and gambling. Attractions have an ancient Egyptian theme, like a 'Nile River Cruise' (a boat ride round the lobby), some special effects shows, and an unconvincing replica of King Tut's tomb. The attractions cost $4 to $5 each, or $15 for the lot, and don't seem to be a very good value.

Wet 'n' Wild
You can't miss this water park (☎ 734-0088), at 2601 Las Vegas Blvd S, and it looks mighty tempting on a hot day. There are some great water slides, like the 'High Roller' and the 'Bomb Bay,' a wave pool, and a river ride. It's open April through September, daily from 10 am to 6 pm, with extended hours in the hottest months. All-day entry costs $19 for anyone over nine years old; $15 for younger kids, but discounts are available, and may be cheaper for evenings in the summer.

Imperial Palace Auto Museum
A highlight for car buffs, this excellent collection includes a dozen Duesenbergs and lots of vehicles once owned by the rich and famous. There's a 1914 Rolls Royce owned by Czar Nicholas II; a 1935 Packard limo sent to Japan's Emperor Hirohito (the last US car exported to Japan?); a 1939 Mercedes used by Adolf Hitler (look for the marks where he tested the bullet-proofing); Krushchev's 1962 Chaika (a really gross car); and Howard Hughes' 1954 Chrysler (the air purifier cost more than the car). The collection of US presidents' cars alone is an automotive history. As well as these permanent displays, about 200 vehicles

(from a selection of over 800) are displayed on a rotating basis, changing monthly. The museum (☎ 331-3311) is in the Imperial Palace casino, 3535 Las Vegas Blvd S, and is open daily from 9:30 am to 11:30 pm. Entry is $7, but discounts, coupons, and freebies are available.

Guinness World of Records Museum
If you enjoy the detail, diversity, and authenticity of the Guinness Book of Records, you'll be disappointed in this museum. It has exhibits like an unrealistic mannequin of the world's tallest man, a grainy video clip of someone riding the world's smallest bicycle, and computers which display sporting records almost as quickly as you could look them up in the book. It's in a small mall at 2780 Las Vegas Blvd S, is open daily, and costs $5/3.

Liberace Museum
For the lowdown on high camp, come and see the costumes, cars, and candelabra of the pianist Liberace (1919-1987). In the library, photos and mementos from his early life, and a quiet acknowledgment of his long-term gay relationship, are of particular interest. The museum (☎ 798-5595, 800-626-2625), at 1775 E Tropicana, is open Sundays from 1 to 5 pm, other days from 10 am to 5 pm. It costs $6.50 for adults and $4.50 for seniors, but discounts are available, and the proceeds go to the Liberace Foundation which sponsors the musical education of talented young people.

Lied Discovery Children's Museum
This 'hands-on' science museum (☎ 382-3445) has exhibits which allow kids to make giant bubbles, be a radio disk jockey, or pilot a space shuttle simulator. It's in the same building as the Las Vegas Library (an interesting piece of architecture), at 833 Las Vegas Blvd N, about half a mile north of Hwy 95. Admission is $5, $4 for ages 12 to 17, and $3 for ages 3 to 11, who must be with an adult. It's open until 5 pm most days, Wednesdays until 7 pm, and is closed Mondays.

Las Vegas Natural History Museum

The most interesting exhibits here are the full-size dinosaur models and the diorama showing plants and animals of Nevada's deserts. The museum (☎ 384-3466) is in a factory-like building at 900 Las Vegas Blvd N. It is open daily from 9 am to 4 pm and costs $5/4/2.50 for adults/students/kids under 12.

Nevada State Museum

This is probably the best place to learn about southern Nevada's natural and social history, and has some interesting old photos and Indian artifacts. The museum (☎ 486-5205), 700 Twin Lakes Drive, in Lorenzi Park, is open daily from 9 am to 5 pm, and costs $2.

Old Las Vegas Mormon Fort State Historic Park

The remains of the Las Vegas Mormon fort (☎ 486-3511), 908 Las Vegas Blvd N, are pretty unspectacular compared with the modern metropolis, but this is where it all started in the 1850s. Here, an adobe quadrangle provided a refuge for travelers along the Mormon Trail, between Salt Lake City and San Bernadino. Some of the original walls still stand and a three-room display shows artifacts and photos from the early days. Outside are sample fields of the first crops grown here and an archaeological dig. Volunteer groups worked hard to preserve this site, and there are plans for more research, restoration, and reconstruction. The fort is a mile north of downtown, next to the Cashman Field sports center, and is surrounded by a wire fence. It is open most days, and you may have to ring the bell for the attendant.

Historic Buildings

Unsurprisingly, there aren't many. Not only is this a new city, but many of the original buildings have been demolished or rebuilt during its spectacular growth. Even on the Strip, 1960s landmarks like the Dunes Hotel and Vegas World have been razed to make way for newer and better attractions. There are a few survivors downtown, like the Victory Hotel, 307 S Main St. It's the oldest hotel in town, built in 1910 with an arcade in front to provide shade from the fierce sun; such arcade-fronts used to line most of Fremont St. The 600 block of 3rd St still has some of the railroad company houses from the same period. The 1931 Las Vegas High School, 315 S 7th St, has Art Deco detailing, while nearby, some substantial residences of the same era are built in Spanish mission style.

Organized Tours

Gray Line (☎ 384-1234) does tours of the city, but many more tours leave Las Vegas for Lake Mead National Recreation Area and national parks further afield. See the introduction to Canyon Country for company listings.

Special Events

Las Vegas hosts a huge number of conventions, trade shows, and major sporting events. The big ones fill hotel rooms and raise prices all over town. Many casinos have 'gaming tournaments,' which try to turn slot machine playing, keno, or blackjack into a competitive event, and these promotions occur all the time. For a list of upcoming events, call Las Vegas Events (☎ 731-2115), or the Convention & Visitors Bureau. Some of the big annual happenings include the Consumer Electronics Show at the Convention Center in January; the St Patrick's Day parade in March; Helldorado Days Rodeo & Western Festival in May; the Jaycees State Fair and the Cashman Field PGA Invitational Golf Tournament, both in October; and the National Finals Rodeo, at the Thomas & Mack Center in December.

Places to Stay

The best deals are midweek specials at the big casino hotels, where you can sometimes get a really great room for $20 to $25. On a busy Friday or Saturday, the same room might be as much as $100. It's a very competitive market, deals come and go by the hour, and bargains disappear if there's a big convention in town. Call

NEVADA

around the hotels before you arrive, and try some of the hotel booking services as well. Two worth trying are the Las Vegas Tourist Bureau (☎ 739-1482, 800-522-9555), and City-Wide Reservations (☎ 794-4481, 800-733-6644). Motel prices are less variable, but they still tend to be higher on Friday and Saturday nights, and they may have a two-night minimum.

Places to Stay – bottom end

Camping Some of the hotel/casinos on the Strip have RV parks for around $12, including Circus Circus, the Hacienda, and Stardust. They're about as attractive as a parking lot, and not suitable for tent camping, but you do have the use of the hotel facilities. The *KOA* (☎ 451-5527), a few miles south of town at 4315 Boulder Hwy, has tent and RV sites, a swimming pool, and slot machines on site, and charges $22 per double. The other options for tent campers are out of town, at Lake Mead or Mt Charleston.

Hostel The *Las Vegas Independent Hostel* (☎ 385-9955), 1208 Las Vegas Blvd, is popular with international backpackers, with four-bed dorms at $9, and a few double rooms for $20. There's a small kitchen, lounge, and laundry, and tea and coffee is included. It's pretty clean and well run, but it can get crowded, so check in early if you can (they don't take bookings). They also run cheap tours to Grand Canyon, Bryce Canyon, and Zion National Parks.

Motels – Downtown The ultra-cheap *Ogden House* (☎ 385-5200), 651 Ogden Ave, is managed by the El Cortez (see below) and charges only $18. The *Victory Hotel* (☎ 387-9257), 307 S Main St, is only a block from the bus station and costs $20 for a room with a double bed and shared bath, or $22 with private bath. It's very basic, but it has the distinction of being the oldest hotel in Las Vegas. The *Crest Budget Inn* (☎ 382-5642), 207 N 6th St, runs about $25. Near Ogden House, the *Downtowner Motel* (☎ 384-1441, 800-777-2566), 129 N

8th St, is also OK at $25/30 a single/double, or $35/40 on weekends. The *City Center Motel* (☎ 382-4766), 700 Fremont St, is close enough to the action, nothing special, but quite OK for $30/35, or $43/51 on weekends.

Motels – The Strip There are plenty of cheap motels around, which aren't as good a value as a casino special, but may be

---

Conservation, Vegas-style

Las Vegas is a byword for extravagance and consumption, where elaborate fountains and lakes evaporate into the desert air, acres of colored neon blaze all night long, and a typical hotel uses as much electricity as a town of 6000 people. It was therefore surprising to find, in the bathroom of a large casino-hotel, a card with the headline 'A Commitment to the Environment.'

The card said that the place is run by an 'environmentally aware company with a sincere commitment to recycling and energy conservation programs,' and went on to request that guests turn off the lights when they leave their room, turn off the air-con and heating when it isn't needed, and advised that 'in the interests of energy conservation' bed linen would be changed every other day. This was in a 20-story building, completely covered with colored lights burning from dusk to dawn, visible from 10 miles away.

It's hard not to be skeptical about this, but it does raise a serious question of how to reconcile conservation with self-indulgence. Certainly, some newer hotels are being built with systems to recycle waste water, and changing bed linen every other day may well be a major saving in power and water which doesn't compromise the glamour of the visitor's experience. It's also true that the casinos use only a small proportion of the water and energy consumed in Las Vegas. But if it were simply a question of turning off the lights when they weren't needed, a hard-core conservationist could well suggest pulling the plug on the whole city. ■

cheaper than a casino on weekends. The north end of the strip is not exactly charming, but it has a few motels. The *Tod Motel* (☎ 477-0022), 1508 Las Vegas Blvd S, is cheap enough at around $25, but has a somewhat sleazy reputation.

At the bottom end of the Strip, adjacent to the airport, are some bottom-end motels, like the *Olympus* (☎ 795-2897), 3941 Las Vegas Blvd S, which is one of the cheapest at under $25. Even further south, the *Glass Pool Inn* (☎ 739-6636, 800-527-7118), 4613 Las Vegas Blvd S, is famous for its swimming pool with big, round windows. Double rooms with kitchenettes begin at $34.

Places to Stay – middle & top end

Motels At the top of the Strip, *Econo Lodge* (☎ 382-6001), 1150 Las Vegas Blvd S, is a good, standard motel, at $40 midweek and $50 weekends, though it's no bargain by Las Vegas standards. In the center of the Strip, many other chain motels provide standardized mid-range accommodations. Three places are typical of the bunch: *Travelodge on the Strip* (☎ 735-4222), 2830 Las Vegas Blvd S; *Travelodge* (☎ 734-6801), 3419 Las Vegas Blvd S; and *Travelodge South Strip* (☎ 736-3443), 3735 Las Vegas Blvd S. *Center Strip Budget Inn* (☎ 739-6066, 800-777-7737), 3688 Las Vegas Blvd S, is a good value midweek at $30/40, but climbs to $50/60 on weekends.

Casinos – Downtown In terms of quality, most of the accommodations in casino-hotels are middle to top-end, but price-wise they are mostly low to mid-range. If you want to pay top-end prices, come on a busy weekend, and/or ask for a suite. While casinos can be an amazingly good value, the prices are amazingly volatile. Generally, the cheapest places are downtown.

The *El Cortez Hotel & Casino* (☎ 385-5200, 800-634-6703), 600 E Fremont St, has singles/doubles from only $23/28. *Gaughan's Plaza Hotel & Casino* (☎ 386-2110, 800-634-6575), 1 Main St, is right on top of the bus and train stations, with rooms from $30, rising to $50 during busy times.

California Hotel & Casino (☎ 385-1222, 800-634-6505), 12 Ogden Ave, is an inexpensive place with an inoffensive tropical decor and rooms from around $40 to $50. *Golden Nugget* (☎ 385-7111, 800-634-3454), 129 E Fremont St, is the best of the downtown hotels; its least expensive rooms are under $60, which is a great value for a place like this.

Casinos – The Strip Though some of the most expensive places are on the Strip, you can get special deals and bargains. These are listed in order of their official prices, which should correspond roughly to the relative price of special deals.

Circus Circus (☎ 734-0410, 800-634-3450), 2880 Las Vegas Blvd S, is a big, inexpensive place which appeals to families; rates begin at $21, but expect to pay $65 for a family of four. *Sahara* (☎ 737-2111, 800-634-6411), 2535 Las Vegas Blvd S, is an older hotel with no special gimmick or theme; it's very comfortable and has great specials, starting at $25. The *Stardust* (☎ 732-611, 800-634-6033), 3000 Las Vegas Blvd S, is a 1950s hotel, renovated in the '90s. Rates start at around $30, though that may put you in the barrack-like motel blocks out back. *Luxor* (☎ 262-4000, 800-288-1000), 3900 Las Vegas Blvd S, is a glass pyramid with an overworked ancient-Egyptian theme; rooms start at $49. The *MGM Grand* (☎ 891-7777, 800-929-1111), 3799 Las Vegas Blvd S, is a huge new place, with child-care and a theme park, with rooms from $69. *Caesar's Palace* (☎ 731-7110, 800-634-6661), Las Vegas Blvd S, is probably the best place on the Strip, with large, luxurious rooms starting at $100/115.

Places to Eat

All the casinos have restaurants, and the bigger ones can have four or more, serving different styles of food at different prices, with a variety of buffets and special meal deals. They tend to monopolize the eating options in the tourist areas, though there is a selection of the usual fast food franchises on the Strip. Most visitors will find the casinos offer more than enough variety and value for the duration of their stay, but the locals do have a life, and an appetite, away from the Strip – there are some good restaurants out there.

Casino Buffets & Specials The all-you-can-eat buffet is a Las Vegas dining institution, and one that can get pretty gross, as greedy diners pile their plates with mountains of schlock – as if eating $30 of food at a $5 buffet will recoup the $25 they've just lost in the slots. The cost depends on the time of day, and how badly the casino wants to suck you in.

Cheapest is the *Circus Circus* buffet, at $3 for breakfast (6 to 11:30 am), $4 for lunch (noon to 4 pm), and $5 for dinner (4:30 to 11:30 pm); it's a truly low-brow dining experience. The *Excalibur's* Round Table Buffet is just huge, and tests the limits of all-you-can-eat for breakfast, lunch, or dinner ($4, $5, or $6). The best buffet in town is a subject of local debate, but those commonly mentioned include the *Golden Nugget* for a $7.50 dinner, *Bally's Big Kitchen* for $12, and the Palatium Buffet at *Caesar's Palace* for $14.25.

As well as the buffets, most casinos advertise special, bargain-priced meals; a good one is the 12-ounce prime rib special ($4) at the *Frontier Hotel* between 11 am and 11 pm.

Casino Restaurants If you're not after buffets or bargains, the best approach is to get a copy of *Today in Las Vegas,* which lists dozens of casino restaurants according to the kind of cuisine on offer, and gives an indication of price.

There must be hundreds of restaurants in the casinos. For example, one of the big places, the Luxor (☎ 262-4000), has the following eating options: *Papyrus Restaurant,* offering 'Pacific Rim' cuisine with a variety of Asian and Southwestern entrees from $12 to $20; the *Millennium,* a 'high energy cafe' with standard American fare at slightly cheaper prices; a *Swensen's* ice cream parlor; the *Manhattan Buffet,* for $7.50 all-you-can-eat dinners; the *Pyramid*

Cafe, for 24-hour casual dining; the *Nile Deli,* for New York-style sandwiches; the upscale *Isis,* serving continental dishes at around $35; the *Sacred Sea Room,* serving expensive seafood; and, for poolside dining, the *Oasis Terrace.*

The *California Hotel* (☎ 385-1222), downtown, has a good reputation for its food in general. A fun place is *Planet Hollywood* (☎ 791-7827), at Caesar's Palace (though it doesn't fit the ancient Roman image). It has moderately expensive pastas, pizzas, grills, salads and vegetarian dishes, served amid a collection of Hollywood props. The most expensive place is probably the excellent *Charlie Trotters* (☎ 891-7337), in the MGM Grand, where the fixed-price dinner is $125, plus wine.

Other Restaurants Away from the casinos there are some interesting places where locals like to eat. A favorite is *Poppa Gars,* at 1624 W Oakey, with American standards, plus Cajun, Mexican, and game dishes, and lots of animal heads looking over your shoulder. The *Mad Dogs & Englishmen Pub* (☎ 382-5075), 515 Las Vegas Blvd, just south of downtown, serves English-style main courses and great fish and chips for around $8, and the quiet, dark interior is a relief from casino clatter – until the evening entertainment starts.

Two good international restaurants are *Yolie's* (☎ 794-0700), in Citybank Park Plaza at 3900 Paradise Rd, a Brazilian steakhouse serving a set meal for about $20; and *Chin's* (☎ 733-8899), in the Fashion Show Mall, where Chinese entrees are from $15. The best restaurant in town is quite possibly *Andre's* (☎ 385-5016), 401 S 6th St, a classic French restaurant, with a fine wine list, a refined but friendly atmosphere, and predictably high prices.

Entertainment
Casinos The major casinos offer several types of entertainment. The 'big room' shows can be either concerts by famous artists, Broadway musicals, or Vegas-style production shows (see the sidebar). These typically cost $25 to $35 – more for a really

big-name act – and sometimes include dinner or drinks. Lounge acts are smaller shows in smaller venues for smaller prices ($8 to $20), and can be both very entertaining and an excellent value. If two shows are scheduled nightly, there will be more smut in the later one.

Often seats cannot be reserved and are allocated on a first-come, first-served (or tip-the-usher) basis. For dinnertime performances, arrive two hours before showtime. There is an incredible amount on offer every night; for a listing, get a copy of *What's On in Las Vegas*. The most popular shows often sell out, so if your visit is on a weekend, attempt to reserve seats before you arrive. Below is a sample of the entertainment offered in some of the best-known venues.

- Aladdin (☎ 736-0420) specializes in country music, despite its Arabian Nights image, with two shows per night for $18.
- Bally's (☎ 739-4567) books big-name acts in its celebrity room ($28 to $39); its long-running *Jubilee!* musical ($42) features the Titanic sinking on stage.
- Caesar's Palace (☎ 731-7333) has big-name acts appearing at *Circus Maximus* ($50 to $60), though as yet, no gladiators.
- Excalibur (☎ 597-7600) has *King Arthur's Tournament* featuring jousting, jesters, and Merlin's magic, while spectators eat a medieval banquet ($30). An equestrian show with Royal Lipizzaren stallions takes place every afternoon ($7); various lounge acts also appear.

- Flamingo Hilton (☎ 733-3333) has *The Great Radio City Spectacular,* featuring the Rockettes; the dinner show is at 7:45 pm ($40) and the cocktail show is at 10:30 pm ($30); in *Bugsy's Celebrity Theater*, look for smaller shows.
- Harrah's big production is Spellbound for $25 (☎ 369-5222); comedy acts appear at The Improv (☎ 369-5000) for $14.
- Las Vegas Hilton has Andrew Lloyd Webber's *Starlight Express* (☎ 732-5755) for $40 to $45.
- Mirage (☎ 792-7777) is host to the very popular and long-running *Siegfried & Roy* magic show, complete with white tigers, which must make heaps at $78 a ticket.
- Riviera (☎ 794-9433) runs several shows including the latest version of the long-running *Splash* at $38 to $48 (☎ 477-5274); *Crazy Girls*, a topless revue, costs $15; *La Cage*, with female impersonators, is $17; and dinner shows with various comedy acts are $14.
- Treasure Island (☎ 894-7111) presents *Mystère,* featuring Cirque du Soleil, for $57.
- Tropicana has been running their classic production *Folies Bergère* (☎ 739-2411) for years, with a dinner show ($29) and a cocktail show ($23). The *Comedy Stop at the Trop* (☎ 739-2358) is a great value at $13.

Music & Bars There's a lot of night life in Vegas, even outside the casinos; *New Times* has the best listings. A popular dance spot among visitors and locals is the *Shark Club* (☎ 795-7525), 3765 E Harmon, which plays techno-pop, hip-hop, alternative, and top-40 music. Cover is $5 midweek, $10 on weekends. *Fremont St Reggae & Blues*

NEVADA

It's Showtime

The Las Vegas production show is a local institution, typically featuring a large cast, in elaborate costumes, performing in a music and dance spectacular, full of sound and color, signifying not very much. These are sometimes called 'continental' production shows, or 'European-style' revues, though this style of entertainment is extinct in Europe.

Maybe 50 years ago the sight of a semi-naked female was so risque that the whole performance had to be lavishly dressed up so that no one could call it sleazy. To judge by the promotional pictures, which usually feature the fabled Las Vegas showgirls, titillation is still their main attraction, along with images of glamour and extravagance.

They might seem like a dated art form, but some productions, like *Folies Bergère* at the Tropicana, and *Splash* at the Riviera, have been going for years. Lots of visitors see these shows, perhaps because it's part of their package, or perhaps they are enticed by a $2 discount coupon. Many seem pretty bemused after watching for an hour or so, and walk out wondering what it was all about. ■

(☎ 594-4640), 400 E Fremont St, has live bands on two stages. The bar at the *Hard Rock Hotel* (☎ 693-5000), 4455 Paradise Rd, is a mainstream venue with dancing, from the makers of the Hard Rock Cafe.

On the corner of Sahara Ave and the Strip, the *Holy Cow Brewery & Casino* has some fine beers and a fun atmosphere. You'll notice it by the large plastic cow outside.

Spectator Sports Big-time boxing bouts are the best known spectator sport in Las Vegas. The professional rodeo circuit has major events at the Thomas Mack Center, and there are also PGA golf tournaments, but no major league baseball or football.

Things to Buy
Downtown is remarkably devoid of shops. Fashion Show Mall (☎ 369-8382), on the Strip, has the most upscale stores, like Neiman-Marcus, Saks, Macy's, and so on. Two of the largest suburban shopping centers are the Boulevard Mall (☎ 735-8268), at 3528 Maryland Blvd, east of the Strip; and Meadows Mall (☎ 878-4849), 4300 Meadows Lane, off Hwy 95 west of downtown.

For more distinctly Las Vegas-style shopping, go to the Forum Shops (☎ 893-4300), in Caesar's Palace, with retailers they wouldn't have had in ancient Rome, including a Disney outlet, Versace, and Magnet Maximus (which specializes in fridge magnets). Other hotel/casinos have shopping plazas, which often sell stuff related to their design theme – the Luxor has shops with Egyptian arts & crafts, Treasure Island has a Moroccan shop, and the Flamingo has a shop in which everything sold bears a Flamingo logo.

The Bonanza Gift Shops, on the Strip at Sahara Ave, have an overwhelmingly large and tacky selection of souvenirs. Odyssey Records (☎ 384-4040), 1600 Las Vegas Blvd S, has a really great collection of CDs at competitive prices. At the Gamblers General Store (☎ 382-9903), 800 S Main St, you can buy your own slot machine

(they'll ship it), personalized poker chips, and anything else you need to start a casino.

Opportunists might find some real bargains in Las Vegas pawn shops, where less fortunate gamblers hock their jewelry, cameras, and musical instruments. You have to know what you're buying though – you can't expect a pawn shop to guarantee that a camera will work.

Getting There & Away
Air McGarran International Airport (☎ 261-5743) has direct flights from most US cities, and a few from Canada and Europe. You may get a better deal on airfares as part of a Las Vegas package than you would directly from the airlines. Airlines flying to Las Vegas include America West, American, Continental, Delta, Hawaiian, Northwest, Southwest, United, and USAir.

Bus The Greyhound bus station (☎ 382-2640), downtown on Main St, has 12 buses per day to/from Los Angeles ($37), three per day to San Diego ($32 – via San Bernardino), and other connections to San Francisco, Reno, and Lake Havasu (Arizona). Package tours to Las Vegas often include bus transportation for little more than the usual cost of accommodations.

Train The Amtrak station (☎ 386-6896) is downtown, inside Gaughan's Plaza Hotel & Casino. The *Desert Wind* runs daily between Los Angeles and Las Vegas, via Barstow and San Bernadino. The trip takes seven hours and costs $68 one way, but roundtrip specials may be as little as $70.

Car There are many car rental companies, and you can get quite good deals, though prices vary a lot with demand, and it pays to shop around. Some agencies to call include Alamo (☎ 737-3111), Dollar (☎ 739-8408), Thrifty (☎ 736-4706), and US Rent-A-Car (☎ 798-6100). Las Vegas Auto Driveaway (☎ 658-8500) may also be able to put you in a car leaving town.

Getting Around

To/From the Airport The airport is close to the south end of the Strip. Bell Trans (☎ 739-7990) and Gray Line (☎ 384-1234) offer a shuttle service to the airport for $5.

Bus Local bus service is provided by Citizens Area Transport (CAT, ☎ 228-7433). The most useful service for visitors is the regular shuttle up and down the Strip and connecting to downtown. It runs 24 hours a day. The standard fare is $1.25, regardless of distance, and you need the correct change.

The Strip Trolley (☎ 382-1404) does a circuit around the Sahara, the Hacienda, and the Las Vegas Hilton every 30 minutes ($1). The Downtown Trolley (☎ 229-6024) will start on a new route when the Fremont St work is finished. In fact neither of these are real trolleys, just small buses done up to look like trolleys.

Monorail A short, free monorail runs between Bally's and the MGM Grand, but you could almost walk it in the time you spend finding the monorail station, waiting for a train, and trundling along the track.

Taxi Standard fares are around $2.20 for the first mile, then $1.50 per mile. Try Whittlesea Cab (☎ 384-6111), Star Cab (☎ 873-2000), or Yellow Cab (☎ 873-2227).

Around Las Vegas

WEST OF LAS VEGAS
Red Rock Canyon

It's amazing to find this brilliantly scenic natural area just outside of Las Vegas. The canyon is actually more like a valley, with the steep, rugged Red Rock escarpment rising 3000 feet on its western edge. It was created around 65 million years ago, when tectonic plates collided along the Keystone Thrust fault line, pushing a plate of gray limestone up and over another plate of younger red sandstone.

Orientation & Information To get to the northern end of the canyon from Las Vegas, just go west on Charleston Blvd which turns into Hwy 159. Highway 159 runs the length of the valley, and has a 13-mile one-way scenic loop allowing you to drive past some of the most striking features.

The canyon is designated a national conservation area, and it's managed by the BLM, which has a good visitors center (☎ 363-1921) near Hwy 159, at the start of the one-way scenic loop. It's open daily from 9 am to 4 pm, and in summer 8 am to 5 pm. The scenic loop is open from 7 am to dusk. The visitors center will provide maps and information about a number of short hikes in the area. There is no overnight camping.

Spring Mountain Ranch State Park

South of the scenic loop drive, a side road goes off to the west, to Spring Mountain Ranch, underneath the steep Wilson Cliffs. The ranch was established in the 1860s, was owned by the Wilson family for over 70 years, then had various owners, including Howard Hughes, before the state bought it in 1974. It's amazingly green and lush, with white fences and an old red ranch house, like something from back east. The park is open for visits and picnics from 8 am to dusk daily, for a $3 day-use fee, and you can tour the ranch house on Fridays and weekends. Concerts and other entertainment are provided on summer evenings; call the visitors center (☎ 875-4141) for information.

Old Nevada & Bonnie Springs

At the southern end of Red Rock Canyon, Old Nevada (☎ 875-4191) is a tourist-trap reproduction of an 1880s mining town, complete with wooden sidewalks, staged gunfights, hangings, and a Boot Hill cemetery. There's also a restaurant, ice cream parlor, saloon, and motel. The adjacent Bonnie Springs Ranch (☎ 875-4191) has various types of farm animals, a petting zoo, and offers guided horseback riding trips. It's open daily from 10:30 am to 6 pm and costs $6.50/4.

NEVADA

Toiyabe National Forest

The Spring Mountains form the western boundary of the Las Vegas valley, with the highest point, Charleston Peak, 11,918 feet above sea level. It's an area of pine forests, higher rainfall, and lower temperatures, and is very popular with locals on weekends. As an isolated mountain range surrounded by desert, Toiyabe has evolved some distinct types of plant which are unique to the area.

Highways 156 and 157 turn southwest off of Hwy 95 north of Las Vegas, climb into the forest, and are later connected by scenic, 12-mile Hwy 158; driving the loop is possible unless the roads are closed by snow.

Sixteen miles north of Las Vegas, Hwy 157 follows Kyle Canyon up to the village of **Mt Charleston**, where there's a for the USFS district office (☎ 386-6899). At the end of the road is the trailhead for several hikes, including the demanding nine-mile trail that goes up to Charleston Peak. There are several campgrounds, open from about May to October, for $7 per night. The *Mt Charleston Hotel* (☎ 872-5500, 800-794-3456), is a comfortable place with a mountain lodge atmosphere, charging about $50 most nights, around $80 on weekends.

About 30 miles north of Las Vegas, Hwy 156 turns southwest from Hwy 95 and goes to **Lee Canyon Ski Area** (☎ 646-0793). It's a small, mostly intermediate ski area (1000-foot vertical drop) enjoyed by locals on weekends, with good scenery and a season from late-November to March. Lift tickets are $25. Call them to find out if the bus service is running from Las Vegas. There are a couple of campgrounds nearby that are open in the warmer months.

Pahrump

It might not look like it, but the real estate tracts spread out along this valley, between the Spring Mountains and the California state line, are home to 10,000 people and constitute one of the fastest growing areas in Nevada. Nevada's only winery, the big, white Pahrump Valley Winery (☎ 727-6900), produces white and rosé wines, and offers tours, tastings, and lunch and dinner in its own restaurant.

There are two casinos, Saddle West and Mountain View, which draw business from the California side, but it's fair to say that a high proportion of short-term visitors are here for something else. Pahrump is in Nye County, and has the closest legal brothels to Las Vegas, 70 miles away. These establishments are well-publicized in Vegas, and provide limos, and even light planes, to bring their customers in.

Jean & State Line

For those who just can't wait to start gambling, casinos have sprung up along I-15, on the 45 miles between the California state line and Las Vegas. Right on the border, two casinos, Primadonna and Whiskey Pete's, face each other across the freeway, each with big and bizarre theme-park gimmicks. The place is now commonly called State Line, and it is marked as such on some maps (don't confuse it with the Stateline near South Lake Tahoe). The roller coaster here is advertised as the highest and the fastest in the world.

About 15 miles from the border, exit 12 will leave you in Jean, where the big and garish Gold Strike Hotel & Casino looms on one side of the road and the big and garish Nevada Landing sits on the other. The Jean Visitor Information Center (☎ 874-1360) will give you lots of information about Las Vegas.

BOULDER CITY

• *pop 12,600* • *elev 2500 feet* ☎ *702*

This pretty town is unique in Nevada because it does not allow gambling. It was built in the 1920s and '30s to house workers near the dam site, and was a properly planned community. With its grassy parks, trees, and quiet streets, it's a lovely piece of old fashioned, small town America and a complete contrast with Las Vegas, only 23 miles away. A few of the original buildings survive around Hotel Plaza, including the Boulder Dam Hotel. The Hoover Dam Museum (☎ 294-1988), 444 Hotel Plaza, preserves some artifacts and records from the early days of the dam and the town.

There are a few places to stay, but they're not great value compared to Las Vegas. The historic *Boulder Dam Hotel* (☎ 293-1808), 1305 Arizona St, is the most interesting, while the *Sands Motel* (☎ 293-2589), 809 Nevada Hwy, is about the cheapest, from $32/37. The *Happy Days Diner* (☎ 294-2653), 512 Nevada Hwy, is a nifty '50s place with good, inexpensive American food.

LAKE MEAD NATIONAL RECREATION AREA
☎ 702

It is an hour's drive down Hwy 93 from Las Vegas to Lake Mead and Hoover Dam, the most-visited sites within the 2337-sq-mile Lake Mead National Recreation Area. The area encompasses both 110-mile-long Lake Mead and 67-mile-long Lake Mohave, and many miles of desert around the lakes. The Colorado River and the two lakes form the border between Arizona to the east and Nevada to the west. There are sparse motels, campgrounds, restaurants, marinas, grocery stores, and gas stations available.

The Boulder Dam (at the time the world's largest, and later renamed the Hoover Dam) was built between 1931 and '36, backing up the Colorado River to form Lake Mead. In 1953, the smaller Davis Dam was completed, forming Lake Mohave. The purposes of the dams were to provide flood control, irrigation, and hydroelectric power; and to supply water to the burgeoning population of the Southwest and Southern California.

Highway 93, which connects Kingman, Arizona, with Las Vegas, crosses the Hoover Dam and passes the main visitors center and park headquarters. Another important road is Hwy 68, which runs between Kingman and Laughlin, at the southern tip of the recreation area.

Hoover Dam
At 726 feet high, the concrete Hoover Dam is one of the tallest in the world. It has a striking beauty, with its strong, graceful

Hoover Dam, holding back the Colorado River in Art-Deco grandeur.

curve filling a dramatic red rock canyon, backed by the brilliant blue waters of Lake Mead. Its simple form and Art Deco design sit beautifully with the stark landscape. Its construction in the 1930s provided much-needed employment as the country struggled through the Great Depression.

The Alan Bible Visitor Center (☎ 293-8906), five miles west of the dam, has an interesting film on its history and construction. It's open daily from 8:30 am to 5 pm (4:30 pm in winter), and offers a 35-minute guided tour down to the power plant at the bottom of the dam wall. The power plant is not so interesting, but the view of the dam and the canyon from below is worth seeing. Tours run daily between 8 am and 6:45 pm in summer, 9 am to 4:15 pm for the rest of the year, and cost $5/2.50; there can be a long wait.

If you come by car, stop in the multi-floor parking lot before you reach the dam: shuttle buses to the dam depart from there.

NEVADA

Bus tours from Vegas are a good deal for about $20, and bypass the line for the underground tours. The *Snacketeria* at the Nevada spillway on the north side of the dam wall sells food, film, books, and souvenirs.

Lake Mead

Lake Mead is 110 miles long, with 500 miles of shoreline, and has a capacity equal to two years of the normal flow of the Colorado River. It's popular for fishing, boating, water-skiing, and even scuba diving, and there is some beautiful scenery in the surrounding country, most of which is undeveloped and protected as part of the recreation area. A stop at the Alan Bible Visitor Center, on Hwy 93 about 26 miles east of Las Vegas, will supply you with lots of information on the recreational possibilities, campgrounds, and natural history.

The usual scenic drive is along N Shore Road, from near the visitors center up to Valley of Fire State Park and Overton. Lake Mead Cruises (☎ 293-6180) does sightseeing trips ($14.50), breakfast cruises ($21), and dinner-dance cruises ($43), departing from the Lake Mead Resort Marina.

On the scenic drive, there are campgrounds at Boulder Beach, Las Vegas Wash, Callville Bay, Echo Bay, and Overton Beach. Accommodations, from around $60, are available at *Echo Bay Resort* (☎ 394-4000), which has a restaurant with $10 to $12 entrees, a bar, and store. There's also a store at Overton Beach, open 8 am to 6 pm.

Valley of Fire State Park

Near the north end of Lake Mead National Recreation Area, this park is a masterpiece of desert scenery – a fantasy of wonderful shapes carved in psychedelic sandstone. It's similar, in appearance and geology, to the desert landscapes of Utah, Arizona, and New Mexico, but easily accessible from Las Vegas, and not crowded with tourists.

The visitors center (☎ 397-2088) is just off Hwy 169, which runs through the park; it has excellent exhibits and information, and can suggest a number of short hikes. If

you stop in the park, there's a $3 day-use fee. Some of the most interesting formations are Elephant Rock, the Seven Sisters, and Rainbow Vista. The winding side road to White Domes is especially scenic, while Atlatl Rock has some very distinct and artistic petroglyphs.

The valley is at its most fiery at dawn and dusk, so staying in one of the two campgrounds ($7 for tent sites) is a good option. There are also accommodations at Overton, but Las Vegas is only 55 miles away.

Overton

Over 1000 years ago, a community of Anasazi Indians farmed here and built structures resembling the pueblos of the Southwest which are found nowhere else in Nevada. For some unknown reason, the Anasazi withdrew from the area, which was later occupied by Paiute people. Mormons settled the Muddy (or Moapa) River in 1864, but after seven years they also left, and it wasn't until 1880 that new settlers came, and stayed. Today it's a little agricultural town with a couple of motels, bars, and other businesses along the dusty main street.

The foundations of Pueblo Grande de Nevada were noted by Jedediah Smith in the 1820s. Outside what's called the **Lost City Museum** (☎ 397-2193), some adobe dwellings have been reconstructed on original foundations, which give an idea of the settlement's appearance. Inside is a collection of artifacts going back 10,000 years, information on the original inhabitants and early European settlers, and some interesting photos of archaeological excavations on the site. The museum is open daily from 8:30 am to 4:30 pm and costs $2.

Mesquite

Outside the recreation area, and just a dot on I-15 at the Nevada-Arizona border, Mesquite is a fast-growing place thanks to the large *Peppermill Oasis Resort Hotel & Casino* (☎ 800-621-0187). It has a great pool, health club, golf course, casino games, and four restaurants. There are a few other eateries in town, and some budget motels. It's 70 miles from Vegas, and a good base for those heading to Zion and Bryce Canyon National Parks in Utah, but the resort really seems to be banking on entertainment-starved visitors from Utah.

Lake Mohave & Laughlin
•*pop 3000* ☎ *702*

South of Hoover Dam, the Colorado River is impounded by the Davis Dam, near Laughlin, creating the long, narrow Lake Mohave. Access to the lake is from side roads off Hwy 95, one of which goes to Cottonwood Cove, where there's a campground and boats to rent. Further south, a rough road goes east over the Christmas Tree Pass, then south past Grapevine Canyon. A pleasant half-mile walk from the parking lot here will bring you to a small canyon with lots of Native American petroglyphs. The Katherine Landing Visitor Center (☎ 520-754-3272) is in Arizona, three miles north of Davis Dam, and is open daily from 8 am and 4 pm. Information is also available from ranger stations throughout the area. For advance information, call ☎ 293-8932.

Just south of Davis Dam is the booming gambling resort town of Laughlin. A dozen large casino-hotels line up along the west bank of the Colorado River, which is thick with power boats and jet skis. The casinos are almost as glittery as those in Las Vegas, but without quite as many gimmicks . . . yet. Entertainment tends towards country music and golden oldies. Comfortable casino accommodations are cheap here, and swimming in the lake is an option in summer, but there's no other reason to come here unless you want to gamble and you can't stand Las Vegas.

Places to Stay
There's a list of houseboating outfits, which offer a unique place to stay and way to tour the lake, under Accommodations in the Facts for the Visitor chapter. For the best accommodations deal, call the visitors bureau first (☎ 298-3321, 800-452-8445), or try calling the following casinos directly. *Don Laughlin's Riverside Resort Hotel &*

Casino (☎ 298-2535, 800-227-3849) is the original Laughlin casino, with lotsa-slots, restaurants, and an entertainment venue called 'The Losers' Bar.' The *Ramada Express Hotel & Casino* (☎ 298-4200, 800-272-6232) is done up with a railroad theme; their locomotive-shaped swimming pool and a train ride around the parking lot should amuse the kids. The *Colorado Belle Hotel & Casino* (☎ 298-4000, 800-458-9500) is a big place pretending to be a Mississippi riverboat, and the *Gold River Resort & Casino* (☎ 298-2242, 800-835-7904), another big place just south of the others, is a good bet for low room rates.

Canyon Country

Las Vegas is the antithesis of a naturalist's America. It is, however, surprisingly near some of the Southwest's most spectacular attractions. Lonely Planet's *Southwest USA – travel survival kit* extensively covers outdoor recreation in Arizona, Utah, and New Mexico, but for travelers with more interest than time to spare, the following section provides basic information for several easily accessible tours.

The information is organized as a loop itinerary, beginning from the Lake Mead National Recreation Area, east of Las Vegas, continuing east to the South Rim of the Grand Canyon in Arizona, northeast through Navajo country, and crossing the Colorado River and Lake Powell near the Utah border. From there travelers can continue northwest to Zion and Bryce National Parks in Utah or southwest to the North Rim of the Grand Canyon, again, in Arizona.

Summer travelers and those most interested in visiting national parks should consider skipping the South Rim of the Grand Canyon and head straight to St George, Utah, 120 miles northeast of Las Vegas, via I-15. From St George, Zion, Bryce, and the North Rim of the Grand Canyon are all within a few hours' drive. The entire loop can be done in three or four days, allowing

NEVADA

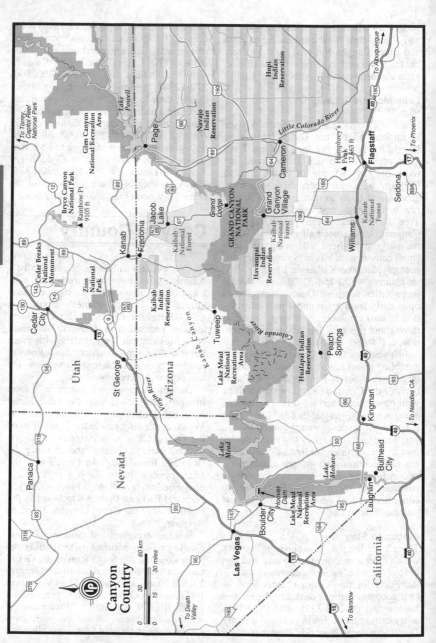

Canyon Country

just enough time to get a glimpse of each area, or you can take several weeks and fully explore each national park. Whichever your decision, the scenery is sure to be spectacular. So fill up the tank, find a good radio station, and wave goodbye to the Vegas Strip as it shrinks away in the rearview mirror. The best of the Southwest is just ahead!

Organized Tours

The vast majority of the many tours on offer out of Las Vegas go to Canyon Country areas. The most heavily promoted are air tours over the Grand Canyon. The main options are: a flight over Hoover Dam, Lake Mead, and the western portion of the Grand Canyon, for about $89; or an air and ground tour, which involves a similar flight, but also lands at Grand Canyon Airport and includes sightseeing at the South Rim, from about $150. Overnight trips, some with hiking or rafting options, cost around $200 to $300. You might save a few dollars by shopping around. Some operators to try include Air Nevada (☎ 702-736-8900), Adventure Airlines (☎ 702-736-7511), Vision Air (☎ 702-263-6263), and Scenic Airlines (☎ 702-739-1900).

One-day bus tours from Las Vegas are available to the Grand Canyon, Bryce Canyon, Zion, or Death Valley; they usually take about 10 hours and cost from about $110. Try Las Vegas Adventure Tours (☎ 702-564-5452), Ray & Ross Tours (☎ 702-646-4661), or Gray Line (☎ 702-384-1234).

LAKE MEAD TO THE GRAND CANYON

It is a 71-mile drive on Hwy 93 from Hoover Dam to **Kingman, Arizona,** where I-40 has surpassed historic Route 66 as the main traffic artery across northern Arizona. Highway 68 runs between Bullhead City, at the southern tip of Lake Mohave, and Kingman.

There are plenty of places to stay and eat in Kingman, especially on Route 66 which runs through the center of the town as Andy Devine Ave. While I-40 has none of the history and character of the highway it replaced, it's a beautifully constructed freeway and is great for getting across the state fast!

Williams
☎ 520

About 110 miles east of Kingman is the town of Williams. From here it's either a 60-mile drive north to Grand Canyon National Park on Hwys 64 and 180, or a 2¼-hour train ride aboard the restored steam engine-driven **Grand Canyon Railway.** Roundtrips depart Williams from March through October (and on winter weekends) daily at 9:30 am, and allow about 3½ hours at the canyon before returning at 5:30 pm. Coach-class fares are $49 roundtrip ($19 for kids 2 to 16), club-class (more room plus a bar) is $12 more, and 1st-class is $40 more, allowing access to the open-air back platform. Park admission is $4 extra. It's a short walk from the Grand Canyon train depot to the South Rim, but narrated bus tours of varying lengths are also offered, as are overnight packages with accommodations at either Williams or the Grand Canyon. Contact the railway (☎ 635-4000, 800-843-8724) for reservations.

Williams has numerous places to eat and stay, including most of the chains. Reservations are advised in summer unless you arrive by early afternoon; Reservations of the West (☎ 635-5351, 800-943-3310) provides free bookings for lodgings and excursions.

GRAND CANYON NATIONAL PARK

The Grand Canyon is Arizona's most famous sight – indeed, it is arguably the best known natural attraction in the entire country. At 277 miles long, roughly 10 miles wide, and a mile deep, the canyon is an incredible spectacle of differently colored rock strata. The many buttes and peaks within the canyon and its meandering rims all give access to fantastic views, but descending into the canyon for a day hike or a multi-day backpacking trip offers a better sense of the breathtaking variety in landscape, wildlife, and climate.

Although the rims are only 10 miles apart as the crow flies, it is a 215-mile, five-hour drive on narrow roads from the visitors center on the South Rim to the visitors center on the North Rim. Thus the park is essentially two separate areas and are treated individually in this chapter.

Geology

The oldest rocks, near the bottom of the inner canyon, are 1.7 billion years old – a good chunk of time even when compared to the age of the planet (4.6 billion years). However, the layers making up most of the canyon walls were laid during the Paleozoic Era, about 250 to 570 million years ago. These strata of the Grand Canyon were in place well before the Americas began drifting apart from the Old World, roughly 200 million years ago.

Some 60 to 70 million years ago – about the same time the Rocky Mountains were being formed – the massive Colorado Plateau emerged. For millions of years after this uplift, rivers flowed north from the north side of the plateau and south from the south side. The Grand Canyon began to form about 5.5 million years ago when a shifting of the San Andreas Fault created the Gulf of California. South-flowing rivers combined to form the lower Colorado River along the Arizona-California boundary and emptied into this new sea. Over time, the headwaters of the lower Colorado eroded through the Grand Wash Cliffs (northeast of Lake Mead) and connected with the upper Colorado system. This altered the river's course from its northward flow into Utah, to southward into the Gulf of California, and the combined rivers' erosion created the Grand Canyon.

Today's visitor can leave Flagstaff, skirting lava fields that are less than 1000 years old, and within a couple of hours be following a trail that leads to schist formations nearly two billion years old. The route is physically demanding, but even more challenging is the mental struggle to comprehend the awesome geological and temporal significance of the canyon.

GRAND CANYON – SOUTH RIM
☎ 520

The elevation of the South Rim ranges from 7000 to over 7400 feet, which is lower than the North Rim. More and better transportation facilities also make it more accessible; therefore, 90% of park visitors go to the South Rim. The foremost attraction is the rim itself, bordered by a 33-mile scenic drive with several parking areas, views, and trailheads. The second is Grand Canyon Village, with turn-of-the-century hotels and amenities of all kinds. If you'd rather get away from the topside traffic, hike down to the canyon bottom and stay at Phantom Ranch or one of the park's several campgrounds.

Orientation

At Grand Canyon Village, 60 miles from Williams, Hwy 64 turns east and becomes Rim Drive. As it exits the park, Hwy 64 continues east through the Kaibab National Forest and Navajo Indian Reservation to Cameron, a tiny community at the junction of Hwy 64 and Hwy 89. It's 53 miles from Grand Canyon Village to Cameron, and a further 51 miles south on Hwy 89 to Flagstaff.

Information

Tourist Offices The main visitors center is in Grand Canyon Village about six miles north of the South Entrance Station. If you can't find the information you need on the bulletin boards, rangers are available to assist you. Hours are 8 am to 6 pm year round, but may be extended in peak season.

A smaller visitors center is found at Desert View, near the east entrance of the park, about 25 miles east of Grand Canyon Village. Other centers include ranger stations near the Grand Canyon Railway depot, Indian Gardens below the South Rim, the River ranger station, Phantom Ranch at the canyon bottom, and Cottonwood campground below the North Rim.

Telephoning the park (☎ 638-7888) gets

you through to an automated system that directs your call to the appropriate office.

Fees & Permits Entrance to the park is $10 per private vehicle, $4 for bicycles and bus/train passengers. The entrance ticket is valid for seven days and can be used at any entrance point, including the North Rim. A $15 annual pass is available and Golden Access, Age, and Eagle Passes are honored.

For backcountry camping permits see Hiking & Backpacking in the North Rim section.

Climate & When to Go
Although the South Rim is open all year, the majority of visitors come in the months between Memorial Day and Labor Day. Avoid that time if possible, as it is very crowded indeed. Otherwise, the high season ranges from about April to November. June is the driest month, but summer thunderstorms make July and August the wettest. Weather is cooler and changeable in fall and you can expect snow and freezing overnight temperatures by November. Winter weather can be beautifully clear, but be prepared for occasional storms.

Grand Canyon Village
Visitors services include hotels, restaurants, campgrounds, coin-op laundry and showers, gift shops, pet kennels, churches, and transportation services. Car towing and mechanics (☎ 638-2631) are available, and a medical clinic (☎ 638-2551) is open weekdays 8 am to 5:30 pm, on Saturday 9 am to noon.

Organized Activities
Call the park's information service (☎ 638-7888) or ask at a visitors center about free, ranger-led activities. These occur year round, though with much greater frequency in summer. Programs include free-ranging Coffee on the Rim discussions in the mornings, half-hour talks throughout the day at Yavapai Observation Station, a variety of evening talks at the outdoor Mather Amphitheater or indoor Shrine of the Ages Auditorium, short hikes along the rim,

longer hikes into the canyon, and guided half-day hikes for those in good shape. During the summer there are Junior Ranger activities for 4- to 12-year-olds.

East & West Rim Drives
The West Rim is accessible by road for eight miles west of Grand Canyon Village, and by the unpaved Rim Trail which extends from Maricopa Point. At the end of the drive and trail is **Hermits Rest** where there is a snack bar and the trailhead for the Hermit Trial into the canyon; if you don't descend, you have to return the way you came.

Year round you can hike the western Rim Trail or cycle along the road. During the summer cars are not allowed along the drive to Hermits Rest, but free shuttle buses operate every 15 minutes.

The East Rim is longer and a little less-crowded than the West Rim, but offers equally spectacular views. There are no free shuttles or walking trails, but you can drive, bike, or take a narrated bus tour. The most accessible of the park's approximately 2000 Anasazi Indian ruins, **Tusayan,** is along this road. East Rim Drive ends at **Desert View**, the highest point on the South Rim, then leaves the park through the Navajo Indian Reservation to Cameron.

Rim Trail
The paved Rim Trail – which is accessible to wheelchairs – skirts the rim for about three miles from Yavapai Point to Maricopa Point. It extends unpaved further east to Mather Point and further west to Hermits Rest. The views are excellent and there are interpretive signs and brochures. Only foot and wheelchair traffic is allowed – no bicycles. Winter snow or ice may temporarily cover the trail.

Hiking & Backpacking
There are two important things to bear in mind when attempting any hike into the canyon. The first is that it is easy to stride on down the trail for a few hours, but an

NEVADA

uphill return during the heat of the day when you are tired can be very demanding. Allow two hours to return uphill for every hour of hiking downhill. The second is that temperatures inside the gorge are much hotter than at the rim and that water is scarcely available. Carry plenty of water and protection from the sun. In summer, temperatures can exceed 110°F in the inner gorge.

The two most popular below-the-rim trails are the Bright Angel Trail and the South Kaibab Trail. These are the only maintained trails and are also used by mule riders. Both are suitable for day hikes or, with a permit and advance reservations, overnight backpacking trips (see the North Rim section for details on permits). Both trails are steep and strenuous; nevertheless, they are considered the easiest rim-to-river trails in the canyon and even a short descent along part of these trails will completely alter your perspective.

Bright Angel Trail The trail leaves from the Rim Trail a few yards west of Bright Angel Lodge in Grand Canyon Village. From the trailhead (6900 feet), the trail drops to **Indian Gardens** 4.6 miles away (3800 feet), where there is a ranger station, campground, restrooms, and water. From Indian Gardens, an almost flat trail goes 1.5 miles to **Plateau Point,** with exceptional views into the inner gorge. The 12.2-mile roundtrip from the rim to Plateau Point is a strenuous all-day hike. There are resthouses after 1.5 miles (1130-foot elevation drop) and 3 miles (2110-foot elevation drop). The 1.5-mile resthouse has restrooms; both have water in summer.

Also from Indian Gardens, the Bright Angel Trail continues down to the Colorado River (2450 feet), which is crossed by a suspension bridge – the only bridge within the park. The Bright Angel campground is a short way north of the bridge and 9.5 miles from the South Rim. A few hundred yards beyond is Phantom Ranch, with water, food, accommodations, and a ranger station.

South Kaibab Trail This trail leaves the South Rim from near Yaki Point, about 4½ miles east of Grand Canyon Village. From the trailhead at 7260 feet, it's a 4800-foot descent to the river and the Bright Angel campground, 6.7 miles on foot. Clearly, South Kaibab is a much steeper trail than Bright Angel. It follows a ridge with glorious views. The first 1.5 miles drop 1300 feet to Cedar Ridge and this makes a good short half-day hike.

North Kaibab Trail From the Bright Angel campground on the north side of the river, the North Kaibab Trail climbs to the North Rim at 8200 feet in 14 miles. This allows a rim-to-rim crossing of the canyon. Extremely fit hikers can descend from the South Rim to the river and return or make a rim-to-rim crossing in one long day (the record for running rim-to-rim is now under four hours) but the NPS discourages such endeavors. Certainly during the summer the extreme temperatures make such attempts very dangerous for inexperienced hikers.

River Rafting
You can raft the Colorado River with a tour or arrange your own private trip. But before you throw a rubber raft into the back of a pickup and head up river, make sure you have serious river-running experience and a permit. Contact the NPS several months in advance.

Commercial trips aren't cheap – expect to pay up to $200 per person per day. Family discounts can be arranged, but small children are not allowed. Several companies are authorized to raft the Colorado through the national park; check the local telephone directory or contact the rangers for a listing. These trips fill up several months (even a year) in advance, so contact them early for information.

Organized Tours
Within the park, most tours are run by the Fred Harvey Company (☎ 638-2631). Reservations are advised in summer, but even then there are usually enough buses that

you can get on a tour the next day. A two-hour West Rim tour leaves in the morning, afternoon, and evening (for sunset) and costs $11. A four-hour East Rim tour leaves every morning and afternoon for $17. A ticket for both tours (which can be taken on the same or on separate days) costs $20. Six- to 15-year-olds are half-price.

Places to Stay

Reservations are essential in summer and a good idea in winter. Cancellations provide a lucky few with last-minute rooms, but don't count on it. If you can't find accommodations in the park, try Tusayan (four miles south of the South Entrance Station), Valle (31 miles south), Cameron (53 miles east), Williams (about 60 miles south), or Flagstaff (about 80 miles south).

Camping Campers should be prepared for freezing winter nights. Free backcountry camping is available by reservation only – see Hiking & Backpacking in the North Rim section. In Grand Canyon Village, *Mather Campground* has 320 sites (no hookups) for $10. Make reservations up to eight weeks in advance with Destinet. Otherwise it's first-come, first served.

The *Desert View Campground* near the east entrance has 50 campsites on a first-come, first-served basis from April to October. They are often full by lunchtime, so arrive early. There is water (but no showers or RV hookups) and fees are $10.

Lodges About 1000 rooms are available on the South Rim in a variety of lodges all run by the Fred Harvey Grand Canyon National Park Lodges (☎ 638-2401).

Phantom Ranch at the bottom of the canyon, has cabins sleeping 4 to 10 people and segregated dorms sleeping 10 people in bunk beds. Rates are $21 per person; bedding, soap, and towels are provided. Plentiful meals are available in the dining hall by advance reservation only. Snacks, limited supplies, beer, and wine are also sold.

Places to Eat

At the end of West Rim Drive, *Hermits Rest Snack Bar* is open from 9 am to 5 pm, in summer 8 am to 6:30 pm. *Desert View Cafeteria* near the east entrance is open from 9 am to 5 pm, in summer from 8 am to 6 pm.

Babbitt's Deli in the shopping center opposite the visitors center has a dining area or carry out from 8 am to 7 pm. Moderate prices and an American menu is available at the *Bright Angel Dining Room,* open from 6:30 am to 10 pm, in Grand Canyon Village. Next door, the *Arizona Steakhouse* serves steaks and seafood March through December from 5 to 10 pm.

By far the best place for quality food in an elegant setting is the *El Tovar* in Grand Canyon Village, where dinner reservations are recommended, especially in summer. Entrees are in the $15 to $25 range and smoking is not permitted.

Getting Around

Free shuttles operate along two routes during the summer only. One goes around Grand Canyon Village, stopping at lodges, campgrounds, the visitors center, Yavapai Observation Station, and other points. Buses leave every 15 minutes from 6 am to 10 pm and take 50 minutes for the entire loop. Stops are clearly marked.

The village loop bus connects with the West Rim shuttle at the Bright Angel trailhead (called the West Rim Interchange Stop). The West Rim shuttle operates every 15 minutes from 7:30 am to 7 pm, stops at eight scenic points along its route, and takes 90 minutes roundtrip. When the shuttle is running, private cars are not allowed along the West Rim Drive.

NAVAJO INDIAN RESERVATION
☎ 520

Leaving Grand Canyon Village along East Rim Drive/Hwy 64 offers many spectacular views. East Rim Drive ends at Desert View, then proceeds as Hwy 64 through the Navajo Indian Reservation to Cameron. Along the way is the Little Colorado River

Gorge Navajo Tribal Park with a scenic overlook – it's worth a stop.

From Cameron, heading north on Hwy 89 leads through the vast countryside of the Navajo reservation, which covers about 25,000 sq miles and the entire northeast corner of Arizona. As befits the nation's largest tribe – about one in seven Native Americans is Navajo – this is the largest reservation in the USA. About 75% is high desert and the remainder is high forest. Today, over half of the approximately 170,000 members of the Navajo nation live on this reservation.

Information
Tourist Office Information about the reservation is available from Navajoland Tourism Department (☎ 871-6436).

Photography Photography is permitted almost anywhere there's tourism. Taking photographs of people, however, is not appropriate unless you ask for and receive permission from the individual involved. A tip is expected.

Restrictions Alcohol and drugs are strictly prohibited throughout the reservation. The law of the land is as follows: it is a violation of federal, state, and tribal laws to disturb, destroy, injure, deface, or remove any natural feature or prehistoric object.

Things to Buy
There are numerous stands along Hwy 89 with Navajos offering their wares. These include hand-woven rugs with the distinctive Navajo patterns, traditional silverwork (often with turquoise and coral), jewelry, blankets, etc. There are also 'official' stores, however there is no guarantee that the quality of items in the stores will be any better than those at the roadside stalls. When you buy direct, you may find that you pay less and the sellers may still make more than if they had sold their wares to the official merchants.

GRAND CANYON – NORTH RIM
☎ 520

The differences between the North and South Rims of the Grand Canyon are in elevation and accessibility. The North Rim is over 8000 feet above sea level. Winters are colder, the climate is wetter, and the spruce-fir forest above the rim is much thicker than the forests of the South Rim. There is only one road in, so visitors must backtrack over 60 miles after their visit. Since it's such a long drive from any major city or airport, only 10% of Grand Canyon visitors come to the North Rim – though for visitors coming from Las Vegas it is the more accessible area. The views here are just as spectacular and North Rim visitors are drawn more by the lack of huge crowds and the desire for a more peaceful, if more spartan, experience of the canyon's majesty.

Orientation
Highway 89 splits a few miles before crossing the Colorado River, with Hwy 89 heading north to Page and the Glen Canyon/Lake Powell region, while Alt Hwy 89 heads northwest and crosses the Colorado by the Navajo Bridge at Marble Canyon. Fifty-five miles west, a USFS visitors center (☎ 643 7289) in Jacob Lake, on Alt 89 near the Hwy 67 intersection, has information, displays, and interpretive programs on the Kaibab National Forest.

It is 44 miles south on Hwy 67 from Alt Hwy 89 to the Grand Lodge. Almost 30 miles of paved roads lead to various other overlooks to the east.

Information
The visitors center (☎ 638 7864) is in the Grand Lodge (the North Rim's only hotel) and is open from 8 am to 6 pm from around mid-May through October. The usual NPS activities and information are available in summer.

In winter, the North Rim is considered open for backcountry day use only – those wishing to stay overnight will be backcountry camping which requires a permit. However, you may still enter the park even when services are closed. Depending on conditions, the road may be open in spring and fall, and you can cross-country ski in if the road is closed.

The park headquarters are at the South Rim. See that chapter for general information and entrance fees. The park's automated telephone system (☎ 638-7888) has both South and North Rim information.

Climate & When to Go

On the North Rim, overnight temperatures drop below freezing as late as May and as early as October. The hottest month, July, sees average highs in the upper 70°s F and lows in the mid 40°s F. The North Rim is wetter than the South; summer thunderstorms occur from July into early September. Winter snowfall is heaviest from late December to early March, when overnight temperatures normally fall into the teens and sometimes below 10°F. However, since visitor services are closed from October to mid-May (although intrepid travelers may still ski in), most visitors won't have to contend with such chilliness.

North Rim Drives

The drive on Hwy 67 through the Kaibab Plateau to the Grand Lodge takes you through thick forest. There are excellent views from the lodge, but to reach other overlooks you need to drive north from the lodge almost three miles and take the signed turn to the east to **Point Imperial** and **Cape Royal**. It is nine miles to Point Imperial, which, at a lofty 8803 feet, is the highest overlook in the entire park and has stunning views.

One of the most spectacular of the remote overlooks is the **Toroweap Overlook** at **Tuweep,** far to the west of the main park facilities. An unpaved road, usually passable to cars, leaves Hwy 389 nine miles west of Fredonia and heads 55 miles to the Tuweep Ranger Station. It is five more miles from Tuweep to the overlook where there is primitive camping but no water or other facilities.

North Rim Nordic Center

In winter, the Kaibab Lodge, on Hwy 67 about 25 miles south of Jacob Lake, becomes a cross-country skiing center run by Canyoneers, Inc (☎ 526-0924, 800-525-0924). A specially equipped 'snow van' transports skiers from Jacob Lake to the lodge from late December through mid-March (depending on snow). The center maintains about 25 miles of groomed ski trails, plus plenty of ungroomed trails, and you can rent skis if necessary. Accommodations, ski tours, and lessons are also available.

Hiking & Backpacking

In summer, the forests of the North Rim offer more backpacking potential than the South Rim, but there are fewer inner canyon hikes. The most popular quick hike is the paved half-mile trail from the Grand Lodge south to **Bright Angel Point** which offers great views at sunset. The 1.5-mile **Transept Trail** goes north from the lodge through forest to the North Rim Campground.

Two trailheads are at a parking lot two miles north of the lodge. The **Ken Patrick Trail** travels through rolling forest country northeast to Point Imperial, about 10 miles away. This trail is often overgrown and requires orienteering skills. About a mile along this trail, a fork to the right (east) becomes the Uncle Jim Trail, a fairly rugged, five-mile loop offering fine views from the rim.

The **North Kaibab Trail** plunges from the parking lot trailhead down to Phantom Ranch at the Colorado River, 5750 feet below and 14 miles away. This is the only maintained rim-to-river trail from the North Rim and it connects with trails to the South Rim. The first 4.7 miles are the steepest, dropping well over 3000 feet to **Roaring Springs,** a popular all-day hike and mule-ride destination. Cottonwood campground is about two miles further and 4000 feet below the rim. Phantom Lodge and the Bright Angel campground are seven miles below Cottonwood (see South Rim).

Backcountry Permits In the winter, the trails of the North Rim are regarded as backcountry use areas, as snow can accumulate to five feet. The USFS campground (see Places to Stay & Eat) is still open for backcountry use, however there are only two ways to get to the campground: either hike from the South Rim up to the North Rim via the North Kaibab Trail (a trip for only the truly Nordic) or cross-country ski from the Kaibab Lodge, or from Jacob Lake (52 miles), a route which takes three days.

Permits for Cottonwood Campground and any other backcountry campground must be applied for as far in advance as possible (up to five months) with the Backcountry Reservation Office (BRO, ☎ 638-7875). You can get reservations by mail (PO Box 129, Grand Canyon, AZ 86023), but there are no phone reservations. The office is on the South Rim – you can pick up permits from 1 to 5 pm weekdays. If you are beginning your hike from the North Rim, you can pick up your permit from the ranger station about 1½ miles north of the Grand Lodge. This is also where to go to get on the waiting list if you don't have a permit – though your chances are slim in summer, at best. The ranger station can also advise you of other, more remote backcountry campgrounds, most of which require a long drive on dirt roads followed by a hike.

Organized Tours

TW Recreational Services (see Places to Stay & Eat) offers daily three-hour narrated tours to Point Imperial and Cape Royal for $20, $10 for 4- to 12-year-olds.

Trail Rides (☎ 638-2292 in season, 801-679-8665 otherwise) offers mule rides for $10 for an hour (minimum age six), $30 for half day (minimum age eight), and $70 for an all-day tour into the Grand Canyon including lunch (minimum age 12). Advance reservations are recommended.

Places to Stay & Eat

The *North Rim Campground*, 1½ miles north of the Grand Lodge, has 83 sites for

$10 each. There is water, a store, snack bar, and coin-op showers and laundry, but no hookups. Reservations (☎ 619-452-8787, 800-283-2267) can be made up to eight weeks in advance and are highly recommended. All other campgrounds are undeveloped and require a backcountry permit.

The *Grand Lodge* (☎ 638-2611 in season) is operated by TW Recreational Services (☎ 801-586-7686), PO Box 400, Cedar City, UT 84721, and is often fully booked; reservations should be made as far in advance as possible. There are about 200 units in both motel rooms and a variety of rustic cabins sleeping up to five people. All have private baths and a few cabins have canyon views. Rates vary from $55 to $85 for a double and $70 to $100 for five people.

KANAB CANYON TO TORREY

Marked on most maps as Kanab Creek, this is actually the largest canyon leading to the Colorado River's north side. In places, Kanab Canyon is 3500 feet deep, splitting the relatively developed eastern Arizona Strip from the remote western part. From Fredonia, Arizona, Kanab Canyon goes south for 60 miles to the Grand Canyon; adventurous canyoneers enjoy hiking this route, while drivers of high-clearance vehicles can drive through Kaibab National Forest to Hack and Jumpup Canyons, two popular entry points into the lower part of Kanab Canyon. USFS permits are required in some stretches.

North of Kenab, Utah, Hwy 89 intersects with Hwy 12 heading east through Bryce Canyon, past three state parks, and terminates at Torrey on Hwy 24, about four miles from Capitol Reef National Park. The 122-mile long Hwy 12 is one of the most scenic roads in Utah.

BRYCE CANYON NATIONAL PARK
☎ 801

The Grand Staircase – a series of step-like uplifted rock layers stretching north from the Grand Canyon – culminates in the Pink Cliffs formation at Bryce Canyon. These cliffs were deposited as a 2000-foot-deep sediment in a huge prehistoric lake some 50 to 60 million years ago, slowly lifted up to over 7000 and 9000 feet above sea level, and then eroded into wondrous ranks of pinnacles and points, steeples and spires, cliffs and crevices, and the strangely named formations called hoodoos. These odd hoodoos lined up one behind the other have been likened to military platoons – superficially made up of identical soldiers, yet each one unique upon closer inspection. The pink-red color of the rock is also incredibly variable, and a shaft of sunlight can suddenly transform the view from merely magnificent to almost otherworldly.

Orientation

Scenic Hwy 12 is the main paved road to the park and cuts across the northern portion. (There is no entrance fee for driving through this northern corner). From Hwy 12 (14 miles east of Hwy 89) Hwy 63 heads south to the official park entrance, about three miles away. From here, a 20-mile dead-end drive continues along the rim of the 'canyon.' This rim drive climbs slowly past turnoffs to the visitors center (at almost 8000 feet), the lodge, campgrounds, scenic view points, and trailheads, ending at Rainbow Point, 9105 feet above sea level. Trailers are allowed only as far as Sunset Campground, about three miles south of the entrance. Vehicles over 25 feet in length have some access restrictions in summer. Shuttle buses are available along this road.

Information

The visitors center (☎ 834 5322) is the first main building along Hwy 63 after you officially enter the park. It is open daily from 8 am to 4:30 pm (except Christmas), or until 8 pm from Memorial Day to Labor Day. Entrance to the park is $3 per person or $5 per private vehicle, and entrance is valid for seven days. There is a free map available to all who enter the park.

Climate & When to Go

The park is open year round, with the period of May to September receiving about 75% of the approximately 1.6 million annual visitors. Summer high temperatures at the 8000 to 9000 foot elevation of the rim may rise above 80°F – and even hotter below the rim – so carry water and sun protection. Summer nights have temperatures in the 40°s F. June is relatively dry, but July and August see torrential storms.

Snows blanket the ground from about November to April, but most of the park's roads remain open. Some do remain unplowed and are designated for cross-country skiing or snowshoeing. Rim Rd is occasionally closed after heavy snow, but only until the plows have done their job.

Rim Drives

Almost every visitor takes all or part of the Rim Rd drive, either in their car or on the **shuttle bus**. The bus runs daily from May to September and runs every 30 minutes from 9 am to 5 pm, with extended hours at peak times. It begins from opposite Ruby's Inn outside the park and stops at the visitors center, campgrounds, lodge, and major overlooks in the northern part of the park. The cost is $4 and includes entrance to the park and unlimited rides – you can get off anywhere and hop another bus later.

Near the visitors center, short side roads go to several popular viewpoints overlooking Bryce Amphitheater (these are visited by the bus). Further away from the center, Rim Rd passes half a dozen small parking areas and view points on its way to Rainbow Point – all are worth a look.

Hiking & Backpacking

The views from the rim are superb, yet a completely different perspective is gained by ditching the traffic and taking a hike, either along the rim or, better still, below it. Remember when hiking below the rim that an uphill return to over 8000 feet can be strenuous – leave time for it and carry extra water. Also bear in mind that most trails skirt steep drop-offs – if you suffer from fear of heights, these trails are not for you.

The easiest hike is along the **Rim Trail**,

which is 5.5 miles long (one way) and skirts the Bryce Amphitheater. The one-mile section between North Campground and Sunset Point is the most level, with some parts accessible to wheelchairs and strollers.

One of the most popular of the many trails descending below the rim is the mile from Sunrise Point (at 8000) feet down to **Queen's Garden**, 320 feet below. From here, you can either return the way you came or continue descending further, connecting with the **Navajo Trail** for a more strenuous hike. Another trail suitable even for those with a fear of heights is the mile-long **Whiteman Connecting Trail,** which leaves Rim Rd about nine miles south of the visitors center. This trail follows an old dirt road which connects with the **Under-the-Rim Trail**; the descent is about 500 feet and you return the way you came.

If you really want to get away from the crowds, shoulder a pack and get down below the rim for a night or two. Backpackers must register at either the visitors center or (in summer) at the Nature Center, where rangers will issue you a free permit, discuss your route, tell you where to find water, and where camping is permitted. Note that backcountry campgrounds have no facilities, all water must be purified, no fires are allowed, and you must carry out *all* of your trash.

Organized Tours
Canyon Trail Rides (☎ 679-8665) operates horse or mule tours into the backcountry, which last from two hours to all day.

Places to Stay & Eat
Inside the Park The park service operates *North Campground* near the visitors center and *Sunset Campground* two miles south. Both have $7 sites and toilets and drinking water. Between the two campgrounds is the *General Store* for basic food and camping supplies – and coin-op showers and laundry in summer.

The 1924 *Bryce Canyon Lodge* (☎ 834-5361) is open from April 15 to November 1 with 110 rooms, a restaurant and bar, coin-

op laundry, and occasional entertainment. Reservations (☎ 568-7686) are essential.

Outside the Park The *Best Western Ruby's Inn* (☎ 834-5341) is a popular and unrelentingly 'Western' complex on Hwy 63, just north of the park entrance. They have a campground, hotel, restaurant, store, pool, hot tub, laundry, and post office. Horse, bike, and ski rentals are also available. During the summer there's even a rodeo most evenings – Yiiii Haaaa!

ZION NATIONAL PARK
☎ 801
Northeast of Kenab, Hwy 89 intersects with Hwy 9 which heads west into Zion National Park, where the rocks are so huge, overpowering, and magnificent that they are at once a photographer's dream and despair. Few photos do justice to the magnificent scenery found in this, the first national park established in Utah.

The highlight is Zion Canyon, a half-mile-deep slash formed by the Virgin River cutting through sandstone. Everyone wants to drive the narrow paved road at the bottom, straining their necks at colorful vistas of looming cliffs, domes, and mountains.

Orientation
Highway 9 is the main east-west road running through the park. It has splendid views but is also exceptionally steep, twisting, and narrow. A tunnel on the east side of Zion Canyon is so narrow that escorts are required for vehicles over 7 feet, 10 inches wide or 11 feet, 4 inches tall (☎ 772-3256; a $10 fee is charged). The main visitors center and campgrounds are at the mouth of Zion Canyon; lodging is nearby, either in the canyon or Springdale.

For the middle of the park, paved Kolob Terrace Rd leaves Hwy 9 at the village of Virgin and climbs north into the Kolob Plateau for about nine miles, then becomes gravel for two miles to Lava Point, where there is a ranger station and primitive campground. The road (which is closed from about November to May and is impassable after rain) continues out of the park as a dirt road to I-15 and Cedar City.

At the north end, Kolob Canyons Rd leaves I-15 at exit 40 and extends five miles into the park. There is a visitors center at the beginning of the road, but no camping. The road is over 5000 feet above sea level, is open all year, and has several scenic lookouts over the finger-canyon formations.

Information

The main visitors center (☎ 772-3256) is on Hwy 9, less than a mile from the south entrance, and is open daily from 9 am to 5 pm, 8 am to 8 pm in summer. The smaller Kolob Canyons Visitor Center (☎ 586-9548), at the beginning of Kolob Canyons Rd, is open 8 am to 4:30 pm.

Entrance to the park is $2 per person, $5 per private vehicle. Tickets are valid for seven days, and Golden Age, Eagle, and Access passes are accepted. The south and east entrance stations (at either end of the Zion-Mt Carmel Hwy) and all visitors centers provide free maps and informative brochures.

Climate & When to Go

From as early as March to as late as November, the campgrounds may fill to capacity, and in the high season they are often full by late morning, so arrive early if camping. Almost half of the park's visitors arrive in the Memorial Day to Labor Day period.

Summer weather is hot (over 100°F is common) so be prepared with plenty of water and sun protection. It drops into the 60°s F at night, even in mid-summer. The summers are generally dry with the exception of about six weeks from late July to early September – when the so-called 'monsoons,' short but heavy rainstorms, occur and dry canyon walls become waterfalls.

There is snow in winter, but the main roads are plowed and daytime temperatures usually rise above freezing even on the coldest days. Hikers climbing up from the

roads will find conditions even more wintry.

Spring weather is variable and hard to predict – rainstorms and hot, sunny spells are both likely. May is the peak of the wildflower blooms. Spring and early summer is also the peak of the bug season, so bring repellent.

Fall is magnificent, with foliage colors peaking in September on the Kolob Plateau and October in the Zion Canyon. By then, daytime weather is pleasantly hot and nights are around 50°F.

Zion Canyon

From the visitors center, it's about a seven-mile drive to the north end of the canyon. The narrow road follows the Virgin River, with nine parking areas along the way – most are signed trailheads. In order of increasing difficulty, the best trails accessible from the Zion Canyon road are outlined below. Which have the best views? All of them! All distances below are one way.

You can stroll or roll along the 100-yard, paved **Court of the Patriarchs Viewpoint Trail** or take an easy walk near the canyon's end along the paved and very popular **Gateway to the Narrows Trail**, about a mile long and fairly flat. (You can continue further along into The Narrows – a wet hike crossing the river as it flows through a narrow canyon – see Backpacking below.) The quarter-mile-long **Weeping Rock Trail** climbs 100 feet to a lovely area of moist hanging gardens. **Emerald Pools** can be reached by a mile-long paved trail or a shorter unpaved one climbing 200 feet to the lower pool; a shorter trail scrambles another 200 feet up to the upper pool. **Sandbench Trail** climbs almost 500 feet in two miles – there are great views but horses use this one too. **Hidden Canyon Trail** has a few long drop-offs and climbs 750 feet in just over a mile to a very narrow and shady canyon. **Angels Landing Trail** is 2.5 miles with a 1500-foot elevation gain. There are steep and exposed drop-offs, so don't go if you're afraid of heights, but the views looking back down are super. **Observation Point Trail** is almost four miles long with a 2150 feet elevation gain; it's less exposed than Angels Landing and has great views too.

Zion-Mt Carmel Hwy

The road east of Zion Canyon, Hwy 9, is somewhat of an engineering feat, with many switchbacks and a mile-long tunnel. East of the tunnel, the geology changes into slickrock, with many carved and etched formations of which the mountainous Checkerboard Mesa is a memorable example. It's just over 10 miles from the Zion Canyon turnoff to the east exit of the park, and there are several parking areas along the road. Only one, just east of the tunnel, has a marked trail (though other short walks are possible). This is the half-mile-long **Canyon Overlook Trail** which climbs over 100 feet and gives fine views into Zion Canyon, 1000 feet lower.

Backpacking

You can backpack and wilderness camp along the over 100 miles of trails in Zion. The most famous backpacking trip is through **The Narrows** – a 16-mile trip through canyons along the North Fork of the Virgin River – where in places the canyon walls are only 20 feet apart and tower hundreds of feet above you. The hike requires wading (sometimes swimming) the river many times. It is usually done from Chamberlain's Ranch (outside the park) to the Gateway of the Narrows Trail at the north end of Zion Canyon, to allow hikers to move with the river current. The trip takes about 12 hours and camping for a night is recommended. This hike is limited to June to October, and may be closed from late July to early September because of flash flood danger.

All backpackers need to get a free permit from either visitors center. These are issued the day before or the morning of a trip, and there is rarely any problem with selecting a route (with the exception of The Narrows, for which you may need to wait). Camping is allowed except for in a few restricted areas; ask a park ranger. Day hikers require

no permit, except for those attempting The Narrows in one day. Zion's springs and rivers flow year round but their water must be treated. Maximum group size is 12 people and animals are not allowed.

Neither are campfires allowed (except in The Narrows to allow wet hikers to dry out), so carry a camping stove or bring food which doesn't need to be cooked. Sun protection is essential, and insect repellent is priceless in spring and early summer.

Many backpacking trips require either retracing your footsteps or leaving a vehicle at either end of the trip. If you don't have two vehicles, ask at the visitors center, where a 'Ride Board' can connect you with other backpackers. Also, Zion Lodge (☎ 772-3213) has a shuttle desk and will arrange a ride for you for a fee.

Places to Stay & Eat

Between the south entrance and the main visitors center are two NPS campgrounds, *Watchman* and *South*. Both offer water and toilets – no showers – and cost $7 per site. Watchman is open year round, South from March to October, both on a first-come, first-served basis. *Lava Point* has a free, six-site campground just outside the east entrance, and free camping is permitted near the Mt Carmel Restaurant. For campers craving a hot shower, *Zion Canyon Campground* in Springdale lets anyone use theirs for a small fee.

Zion Lodge (☎ 586-7686) has motel rooms ($70) and cabins ($75 to $85), most with excellent view and private porches.

ZION TO LAS VEGAS

Twenty-eight miles after leaving the west entrance, Hwy 9 intersects I-15. Heading south on I-15 leads to St George and, eight miles further, to the Arizona state line. Here, through an area known as the Arizona Strip, I-15 winds through some breathtaking manmade canyons chiseled deep into red-rock slopes. On the other side, less than two hours' drive brings you back to Las Vegas, its neon-lit casinos, and the endless clamor of the slots.

NEVADA

Western Nevada

The western corner of the state is the birthplace of modern Nevada. It was the site of the first trading post and the first farms, and of the fabulous Comstock Lode, which spawned towns, financed the Union side in the Civil War, and earned Nevada its statehood. This chapter covers the main towns of the area, each with its own place in the state's development. Reno, and its neighbor Sparks, started as way stations for emigrants and grew to become centers of rail transport, entertainment, services, and education. Virginia City was the scene of the big mining bonanza. Carson City, the state capital, emerged from the orderly farming communities of the Carson Valley.

This part of Nevada is more densely settled than most of the state, and these days it seems more settled in character. Reno has largely rejected the boomtown mentality of Las Vegas, Virginia City stopped booming a long time ago, and the other communities have none of the Wild West rawness that still lingers in the towns of the Great Basin.

RENO
• pop 135,000 • elev 6018 feet ☎ *702*

It's hard not to think of Reno as a little Las Vegas, but Reno has a certain small-town charm, which is something no one will find in Las Vegas. You can see people fishing in the river that flows past the middle of downtown Reno, and the university campus is positively serene. Reno repeatedly reminds you that it's 'The Biggest Little City in the World;' what they really mean is it's a large country town with some big city excrescences. Virginia St has bright lights and biggish casinos, but it looks just a little too homely – more like a Glowing Gully than a Glitter Gulch. The irony is that in 1910, when the 'Biggest Little City' slogan was coined, Las Vegas was an insignificant, conservative, railroad junction with Mormon morality, while Reno was already regarded as a city of sin and was in the

process of promoting a prize fight which attracted 10,000 people.

If you want to gamble, the games inside the casinos are exactly the same as the ones in Las Vegas and you're just as likely to lose your money. Also, like Las Vegas, Reno is a good starting point for trips into the scenic surrounding areas. There's a little of the Las Vegas entertainment scene

Marriage & Divorce

While other states require residency periods, blood tests, and other time-consuming formalities, you can get married fast in Nevada. First off, you'll need a marriage license from the county court house (which in Reno is open from 7 am to midnight, seven days a week). You'll also need to be over 18 years old, have proof of identity and date of birth, and $35 cash. If either party has been previously married, the divorce must be final in the state where it was granted, and you'll need to give the date and the location of the decree.

Those from ages 16 to 18 can be married with the written consent of a parent or legal guardian. With special consent of the Nevada District Court, it is even possible to marry under the age of 16. With license in hand, you can find a wedding chapel, complete with a minister to tie the knot, for as little as $30.

Divorce is not quite so easy. It requires the parties to reside in Nevada for at least six weeks, after which they can go to a lawyer and file for divorce. Assuming the divorce is uncontested, the decree will take another one to four weeks, depending on how quickly the lawyer can obtain necessary documents from other states. The cost can be as low as $250, but can climb upwards of $500 if there are complications.

It's difficult now to imagine the 1930s perception of the divorce business as scandalous. Nevada has always had liberal divorce laws, but until 1931 they only applied to Nevada residents. (The period of stay required for residency began at one year, was changed to six months, then to three months to finally six weeks.) In most states, adultery was the most straightforward grounds for divorce, so even an uncontested Nevada divorce had a whiff of scandal about it. For whatever reasons, the liberal and simplified divorce laws in Nevada met a definite demand of residents from other states; over 5000 divorces were granted during the first year of the new, eased requirements. It seemed as if the state was not just permitting the dissolution of marriage, but actually encouraging it.

Much of the negative image was created by highly publicized celebrity break-ups, and some probably lived up to it. But it was the six-week residency period which provided grist for the rumor mills. It was common for the unhappily married couple to arrange a six-week holiday in Nevada, filling hotels with would-be divorcees, often with their new partners staying in the same place. Some hotels and resorts specialized in the divorce trade, like the Floyd Lamb Ranch near Las Vegas, and the Riverside Hotel in Reno. They provided comfortable accommodations and plenty of diversions, and were so discrete that they left everything to the imaginations of the gossip columnists. ■

here, but for over-the-top tackiness, Reno hasn't quite made it, though it seems to be trying.

History

In the 1850s, travelers on the Humboldt Trail to California crossed the Truckee River at Truckee Meadows (where Reno now stands), followed the river up into the mountains north of Lake Tahoe, and crossed the Sierra at Donner Pass – basically the route of today's I-80. Several people established river crossings and charged tolls; the most enterprising of them, Myron Lake, also built a hotel, saloon, and several miles of road to steer people to his bridge. When the mining boom started in Virginia City, Lake's crossing became a busy thoroughfare, and Lake became rich, acquiring most of the surrounding land.

When the Central Pacific railroad came through, Lake offered to donate land for a townsite if the company would establish a passenger and freight depot. A deal was done and, in May of 1868, lots were auctioned in a new town named after Jesse Reno, a Union general killed in the Civil War. In 1870, Reno became the seat of Washoe County, and in 1872 the Virginia & Truckee railroad linked it to the boomtowns of the Comstock Lode. By 1900 it was a rough railroad town of 4500 people, though it had acquired a university, thanks to some generous mining magnates.

As the mining boom played out and most of Nevada stagnated, Reno made an economic virtue of social vices. Gambling and prostitution were frontier traditions that became attractions in Reno as they were suppressed in increasingly respectable California. During Prohibition, Reno not only tolerated the speakeasies, but became a place for mobsters to launder their money. Reno was Nevada's 'Sin City.' Irrigation in the Carson Valley, agriculture, light industry, and warehousing have since helped to diversify the economy, along with tourism based on the attractions of Lake Tahoe and the region's history.

Reno was already a city of vices with gambling, boxing, and prostitution when Las Vegas was still sunk in virtue.

NEVADA

Orientation

The main highway to/from Reno is I-80, which heads west to Truckee (32 miles) and San Francisco and east to Salt Lake City and eventually New York. Highway 395 heads south through Carson City (30 miles) and Bishop to Southern California. Carry snow chains during winter, especially if you're thinking of driving through the Sierras. For road information call the Nevada Department of Transportation (☎ 793-1313).

Reno's downtown area, with most of the casinos, is along N Virginia St, north of the Truckee River. The Reno arch crosses Virginia St at Commercial Row, with the railroad tracks cutting through the town behind it. The sight of a giant freight train lumbering across the glittery stretch of casinos is one of Reno's wonderful incongruities. Interstate 80 cuts across the north side of the downtown area, heading east to the suburb of Sparks. The pleasant campus of the University of Nevada is just north of I-80. Highway 395 bypasses the city center on the east, and heads south towards Carson City.

South Virginia St, which is also the business route of Hwy 395 (Bus 395), runs several miles south of the river, with motels, commercial buildings, malls, several casinos, and the Reno-Sparks Convention Center.

The downtown area is in the process of redevelopment, so expect some major construction sites. One pleasant new feature is Riverwalk, a pedestrian path which follows the Truckee River the whole width of downtown, from the National Automobile Museum in the east, to beyond Wingfield Park in the west. Most visitors will stay in or near downtown, but McGarran Blvd makes a complete circle of the Reno-Sparks area if you want to have a look at the suburbs. The classiest area is Newland Heights, just southeast of downtown.

Information

Tourist Office The downtown visitors center (☎ 800-367-7366, 800-FOR-RENO) is a desk in the lobby of the National Bowling Stadium, 300 N Center St. They are open daily with enthusiastic volunteer staff and lots of brochures.

Media The daily *Reno Gazette-Journal* costs 35¢, and reports some international news, but it's not likely to win any Pulitzer Prizes. *Reno News & Review* is a free weekly with good entertainment listings. NPR is heard locally on KUNR-FM, 88.7.

Medical Services Emergency clinics are at St Mary's Regional Medical Center (☎ 323-2041), at 235 W 6th St, or at Washoe Medical Center (☎ 328-4100), 77

NEVADA

Pringle Way at Mill St, southeast of downtown.

Gambling Problems National Council on Problem Gambling has a 24-hour help line at ☎ 800-522-4700.

Casinos

Most of the casinos are downtown, along and around N Virginia St. The traditional Reno casino offers gambling and occasional entertainment (see Entertainment below). The Las Vegas-style theme-park casino concept is just starting to catch on here, especially at newer places. Circus Circus, 500 N Virginia St, has free circus acts every half hour or so, like its Las Vegas cousin. It's linked by a bridge over 5th St to the new, very Vegas-like Silver Legacy Resort, with a gigantic white ball looming behind a turn-of-the-century streetscape. Inside the ball is a 120-foot-high imitation mining rig with a sound-and-light show. The venerable Harrah's is still one of the biggest and fanciest casinos, so if you want to see a lot of people losing a lot of money, have a look in here.

Away from downtown, a few big casino-hotels stand like islands in the suburbs. The Peppermill, at 2707 S Virginia St, attracts

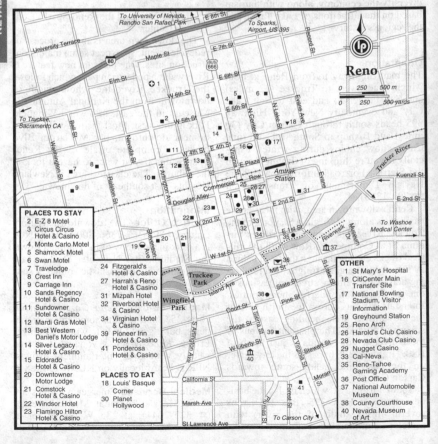

PLACES TO STAY
2 E-Z 8 Motel
3 Circus Circus Hotel & Casino
4 Monte Carlo Motel
5 Shamrock Motel
6 Swan Motel
7 Travelodge
8 Crest Inn
9 Carriage Inn
10 Sands Regency Hotel & Casino
11 Sundowner Hotel & Casino
12 Mardi Gras Motel
13 Best Western Daniel's Motor Lodge
14 Silver Legacy Hotel & Casino
15 Eldorado Hotel & Casino
20 Downtowner Motor Lodge
21 Comstock Hotel & Casino
22 Windsor Hotel
23 Flamingo Hilton Hotel & Casino
24 Fitzgerald's Hotel & Casino
27 Harrah's Reno Hotel & Casino
31 Mizpah Hotel
32 Riverboat Hotel & Casino
34 Virginian Hotel & Casino
39 Pioneer Inn Hotel & Casino
41 Ponderosa Hotel & Casino

PLACES TO EAT
18 Louis' Basque Corner
30 Planet Hollywood

OTHER
1 St Mary's Hospital
16 CitiCenter Main Transfer Site
17 National Bowling Stadium, Visitor Information
19 Greyhound Station
25 Reno Arch
26 Harold's Club Casino
28 Nevada Club Casino
29 Nugget Casino
33 Cal-Neva
35 Reno-Tahoe Gaming Academy
36 Post Office
37 National Automobile Museum
38 County Courthouse
40 Nevada Museum of Art

customers with titillating advertising, and dazzles them with psychedelic decor. The Reno Hilton, east of town near Hwy 395, is another really big place, pressing for family business with Fun Quest, a super video arcade that has a host of high-tech toys like Q-Zar laser tag ($6).

For an inside view at the gambling business with an introduction to the main casino games, take a tour with the Reno-Tahoe Gaming Academy (☎ 329-5665), 300 E 1st St. It costs $6, and includes a look from the other side of the surveillance cameras in one of the big casinos.

National Automobile Museum

For anyone even slightly into cars, or social history, this museum is a must. There are a great number and variety of perfectly restored vehicles on show, informatively labeled and displayed in settings which convey something of their era and social context. The collection includes some one-of-a-kind, custom-built, and experimental vehicles, like Bucky Fuller's 1934 Dymaxion, the 1938 Phantom Corsair that looks like a Batmobile prototype, and Ed Roth's 1961 Beatnik Bandit. Old advertisements, fashions, touring maps, and other automotive memorabilia help fill out the picture. There's even a chance to dress yourself up in 1930s gear and be photographed behind the wheel of an old classic.

The museum (☎ 333-9300) is at 10 Lake St, on the south bank of the Truckee River, an easy walk from downtown. It's open daily from 9:30 am to 5:30 pm and costs $7.50/2.50, but you can usually find a discount coupon that will save you a dollar.

National Bowling Stadium

One of Reno's most recent downtown developments, at 300 N Center St, is a venue for tournament-level 10-pin bowling (☎ 334-2695). It's not available for public play, but it will soon have spectator facilities, and the large geodesic dome out front is to be an IMAX theater with a wraparound screen. The Reno Visitor Information Center is in the lobby.

Nevada Museum of Art

There are some pretty interesting contemporary works here, as well as Native American baskets, and temporary exhibitions which can be excellent. The museum (☎ 329-3333), 160 Liberty St, is open Tuesday to Saturday from 10 am to 4 pm; Sunday noon to 4 pm. Admission is $3, but it's free on Friday.

Fleischmann Planetarium

Simulations of the night sky and assorted astronomical phenomena are projected onto a dome-like screen in this unusual building (which was *not* designed by Frank Lloyd Wright, though it is sometimes erroneously attributed to him). It also shows gee-whiz movies filmed especially for the wraparound screen. Some people like it. Shows last 90 minutes; call ☎ 784-4811 for times. The planetarium is on the University of Nevada campus, off N Virginia St.

Nevada Historical Society Museum

If you're interested in Nevada's history, you could spend a lot of time here. It's organized chronologically, and has a good account of the region's prehistory, and indigenous cultures, as well as the usual pioneer relics. It also covers 20th-century growth and politics. There's even a research library if you're really serious. The museum (☎ 688-1190) is on the University of Nevada campus, off N Virginia St, just north of the planetarium.

Wilbur May Center

Wilbur May (1898-1982) was a wealthy traveler, adventurer, pilot, rancher, and philanthropist who spent the latter half of his life in Reno. This center, run by the Wilbur May Foundation, has a mix of attractions. The **Wilbur B May Museum** has exhibits on May's life and displays of the many antiques, artifacts, trophies, and souvenirs which he collected, or shot, in his travels around the world. It's great if you have a taste for the eclectic and aren't turned off by taxidermy. Nearby, the **Arboretum** has outdoor gardens, with a collection of Great Basin desert plants, and

NEVADA

an indoor tropical garden. The **Great Basin Adventure** is a children's fun park with log rides and a petting zoo. The Wilbur May Center (☎ 785-5961) is in Rancho San Rafael Park, north of the university, and is open Tuesday to Sunday (Wednesday to Sunday in winter) from 10 am to 5 pm; admission costs $4/3.

Activities

There's a wealth of outdoor activities around Lake Tahoe: hiking, skiing, boating, fishing, and others (see the Sierra Nevada chapter). You can fish for trout in the Truckee River, right in the middle of Reno, but get a license from a sporting goods store first. Pyramid Lake, 32 miles north of town, is noted for the Lahontan cutthroat trout.

Reno is a minor center for sky sports, with big airplane and balloon races every September. A number of commercial operators arrange joy flights in balloons or sailplanes, most of them based at Minden, about 50 miles south. For soaring, try Soar Minden (☎ 782-7627) or Soar Truckee (☎ 587-6702). For hot-air balloons, call Alpine Adventures Aloft (☎ 782-7239) or Zephyr Balloons (☎ 329-1700).

Organized Tours

If you don't have a car or a lot of time, it's worth taking a tour to see Lake Tahoe, Virginia City, Carson City, and the less obvious parts of Reno and Sparks. Gray Line (☎ 331-1147) has various tours taking in most of the sights; a combination with Tahoe and Virginia City is $49. Cheaper, and perhaps more fun, is Hardy & Associates Scenic Tours (☎ 329-3114, 800-627-8222), which offers adults-only trips to all the major sights for $34.

Special Events

Like any place pressing for the tourist/convention trade, Reno has a full calendar of annual events. Some of the most interesting are also the most likely to fill the hotels, so plan your visit accordingly.

The Reno Rodeo (☎ 329-3877), one of the largest in the country, fills the Live-

stock Events Center each year with bucking broncos and bruised cowpokes from June 17 to 25. Hot August Nights (☎ 827-1955) is the summer's next big happening, with parades and concerts celebrating the cars and music of the 1950s and '60s. The Livestock Events Center (☎ 688-5767) again heats up from August 23 to 27 as the Nevada State Fair brings back that good old fair fun, with rides, games, and livestock events. Lastly, from September 14 to 17, the National Championship Air Races – the world's longest running airshow – rounds out Reno's events season with aerobatic exhibitions and aircraft displays at the Reno/Stead airport (☎ 972-6333), northwest of downtown.

Dates may vary, so call the visitors center (☎ 800-367-7366) to check.

Places to Stay

Bargains in quality casino accommodations aren't quite what they are in Vegas, but you can still find some good deals, though not on weekends and not when there's any big event on. Book ahead if you can; the visitors center gives referrals and advice. At the Greyhound station there's a notice board where motels advertise cheaper prices than they offer at the front desk. There's a free phone connection and they might even come and get you.

Hotels & Motels The *Mizpah Hotel* (☎ 323-5194), 214 Lake St, is one of those big, solid old railway-era hotels – probably the Motel 6 of 1922. Rooms are small but clean, there's no parking lot, and you pay extra for phone and TV. Prices also vary with the season, the day, and the number of people, but it's cheap. Rates are $15/18 midweek, low season, and $26/29 on a summer Saturday with phone and TV. The *Windsor Hotel* (☎ 323-6171), 214 West St, is another cheapie, but not really the best value at $22 for a single with shared bath.

Opposite the Greyhound station, the *Downtowner Motor Lodge* (☎ 322-1188), 150 Stevenson St, is your standard budget motel, at $35 midweek, $45 on weekends. *Crest Inn* (☎ 329-0808), 525 W 4th St is

OK, from $24 midweek. *Carriage Inn* (☎ 329-8848, 800-554-4822), 690 W 4th St, and *Mardi Gras* (☎ 329-7470), 200 W 4th St, are slightly more expensive. There are a few areas with cheap motels – as well as W 4th St, try around E 5th St. If you're arriving on a weekend, it would be wise to book a room.

There are plenty of chain motels too, including five *Motel 6* branches, an *EZ-8* (☎ 322-4588), 255 W 5th St, and a *Days Inn* (☎ 786-4070, 800-448-4555), 701 E 7th St, near the Wells Ave exit off I-80. The *Best Western Daniel's Motor Lodge* (☎ 329-1351, 800-528-1234), 375 N Sierra St, is a comfortable mid-range option at $35/54.

Casinos The cost of accommodations at the big casino-hotels varies with demand. To shop around, call the visitors center or try some establishments directly. The following are listed roughly in order from cheapest to the most expensive. If you want real top-end luxury, most of them have suites.

Circus Circus, 500 N Virginia St (☎ 329-0711, 800-648-5010)

Pioneer Inn, 21 S Virginia St (☎ 324-7777, 800-879-8879)

Ponderosa Hotel, 515 S Virginia St (☎ 786-6820, 800-228-6820)

Clarion, 3800 S Virginia St (☎ 825-4700, 800-723-6500)

Sands Regency, 345 N Arlington Ave (☎ 348-2200, 800-648-3553)

Fitzgerald's, 255 N Virginia St (☎ 785-3300, 800-648-5022)

The Peppermill, 2707 S Virginia St (☎ 826-2121, 800-648-6992)

Fantasy Motels Maybe it's an extension of the wedding and divorce industries, but there are a few places here specializing in exotic theme rooms for erotic couples. You can rent a Roman room, bordello room, Oriental suite, or a luxury cave. If you've ever fancied it on a zebra skin rug, circular bed, heart-shaped spa, or a 1958 Chevrolet, this might be your chance. Try the *Romance Inn* (☎ 826-1515, 800-662-8812),

2905 S Virginia St, where rooms cost $69 to $140 on weekdays, $110 to $180 on weekends. Further south is the *Adventure Inn* (☎ 828-2436, 800-937-1436, 800-YES-I-DO), 3575 S Virginia St, where prices run from $69 weekdays for the jungle room to $235 for a Saturday night in the Super Ocean Suite, waterfall included.

Places to Eat
In a short visit, you'll find the casinos offer more than enough value and variety. The all-you-can-eat buffets can be like feeding time at the zoo, but they're worth it if you're hungry. *Circus Circus* is the least expensive; *Fitzgerald's* is cheapish, and quite good; *Eldorado* is excellent, and only slightly more expensive.

The *Cal-Neva* is always a good bet, from the 99¢ breakfast, to the all-night food court, with lots of steak specials in between. *Kilroy's*, upstairs in the Nevada Club, is a classic diner which does all-American burgers, apple pies, and shakes, for very reasonable prices. *Le Moulin* (☎ 826-2121), at The Peppermill casino, is regarded as one of the best restaurants in town, with a long wine list and a menu of fine continental dishes which are quite reasonably priced; most entrees are under $20.

For a good Mexican meal in nice surroundings, try *Hacienda del Sol* (☎ 825-7144), 2935 S Virginia, where antojitos cost $4 to $5 and main courses around $9. They also have live entertainment. The *Blue Heron* (☎ 786-4110), 1091 S Virginia, is a vegetarian and health food restaurant, reasonably priced with substantial servings. Try a taste of Nevada's Basque culture at *Louis' Basque Corner* (☎ 323-7203), 301 E 4th St, where $15 will get you a filling meal with everything included.

Entertainment
It's a long way short of Las Vegas, but there is more than enough happening in Reno to keep you entertained for a few nights. Free papers like *Reno/Tahoe Showtime* and *Best Bets* have listings of all the casino shows. Some of the popular, long-running productions include *Splash,* at the Reno Hilton

NEVADA

(☎ 789-2285), and *American Superstars,* at the Flamingo Hilton (☎ 322-1111).

Nightclubbers could check *American Bandstand* (☎ 786-2222), at Harold's Club, for dance music; *Easy Street* (☎ 323-8369), 505 Keystone Ave, which plays both rock and country; or maybe the *Clarion Casino* (☎ 825-4700), for a slightly classier dance scene. *Hacienda del Sol* (☎ 825-7144), 2935 S Virginia, has good live music, as does the *Great Basin Brewing Company* (☎ 355-7711), 846 Victorian Ave, in Sparks.

Reno also has seasons of ballet, orchestral music, opera, jazz, and theater. Call the Sierra Arts Foundation (☎ 329-1324) to find out what's on.

Spectator Sports The best live sports to watch in Reno would be rodeo, at the Livestock Events Center (☎ 329-3877), or bowling, at the National Bowling Stadium (☎ 334-2695), 300 N Center St.

Getting There & Away
Air Reno-Cannon International Airport (☎ 328-6499) is a few miles southeast of downtown. Direct flights go mostly to the West Coast, but also to Dallas, Denver, and Chicago. The cheapest airlines serving Reno-Cannon are Reno Air and Southwest, but don't overlook the package deals which will include accommodations.

Other airlines flying into/out of Reno are America West, American, Delta, MarkAir, Northwest, Skywest, and United.

Bus The Greyhound station (☎ 322-2970) is at 155 Stevenson St. There are lots of buses to Sacramento ($19) and San Francisco ($34). A direct bus leaves for Los Angeles ($42) at 7:30 am, via Bishop; others go via Sacramento. Buses also go to/from Las Vegas and Salt Lake City. Package tours from California may include cheap bus fare as part of the deal.

Train The Amtrak station (☎ 329-8638) is at 135 E Commercial Row. A train arrives every afternoon from Sacramento ($52) and San Francisco ($58; both about six hours), and one departs in the other direction every morning. Roundtrip fares are not much more than one-way.

Getting Around
To/From the Airport RTC bus No 24 runs between the airport and downtown.

Bus The RTC Citifare bus system covers most of the metropolitan area. The routes generally go to and from downtown, where the focus is the CitiCenter Main Transfer Site, between E 4th St and E Plaza St, one block from Virginia St. There's a Customer Information Center there, or you can call for information (☎ 384-7433). All rides are $1 (exact change required) and transfers are free. Some routes operate Monday to Saturday from 7 am to 7 pm, but others have more restricted hours. Useful routes include Nos 7 and 8 (for the university), No 21 (for the Greyhound Station), and No 24 (for the airport).

Car All the main rental agencies are here, including Alamo, Budget, Dollar, Enterprise, and Thrifty. They're mostly based at the airport.

AROUND RENO
Sparks
• *pop 55,000* • *elev 4407 feet* ☎ *702*

Though Reno and Sparks are now virtually a continuous urban area, Sparks is actually a separate city. It was established in 1901 as a railroad maintenance depot and switching yard, and resisted Reno-style casinos and vice . . . at least until the 1950s when the railroad pulled out. Sparks grew strongly in the 1960s and '70s as a warehousing and light industrial center, with gambling as a minor attraction.

Serious efforts to attract visitors are quite recent, with the development of **Victorian Square.** This eight-block strip in the center of Sparks, next to I-80, has been remodeled in a pseudo-Victorian style. It has several casinos, restaurants, shops, and lots of parking spaces. It's interesting at night, with colored lights everywhere, but during the day it feels like a shopping mall parking lot. The **Sparks Museum** (☎ 355-

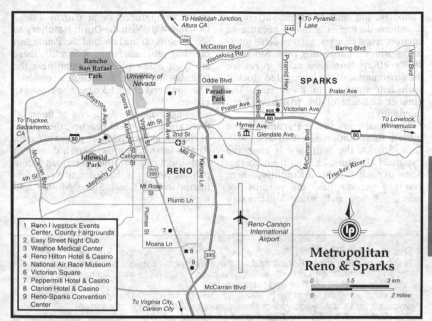

Metropolitan
Reno & Sparks

1 Reno Livestock Events
  Center, County Fairgrounds
2 Easy Street Night Club
3 Washoe Medical Center
4 Reno Hilton Hotel & Casino
5 National Air Race Museum
6 Victorian Square
7 Peppermill Hotel & Casino
8 Clarion Hotel & Casino
9 Reno-Sparks Convention
  Center

NEVADA

1144), 820 Victorian Ave, has exhibits from the early-20th century, like a replica barber shop and a collection of police shoulder patches.

Sparks' biggest attraction, in summer anyway, is the **Wild Island** waterpark (☎ 331-9453), north on Sparks Blvd off I-80, east of town. It's open daily from 11 am to 7 pm and costs $15/11. Airplane buffs might enjoy the **National Air Race Museum** (☎ 358-0505), 1570 Hymer St, with some full size planes and lots of models.

Pyramid Lake

A beautiful blue expanse in the red desert, Pyramid Lake is a popular place for recreation and fishing. The lakeshore was inhabited as long as 11,000 years ago, and the semi-nomadic Paiute visited the lake annually to pow-wow, and to harvest the fish which congregated for their spawning run up the Truckee River. Explorer John Frémont encountered the lake in 1843, and

named it for the small island which he thought resembled the Pyramid of Cheops. A Paiute village gave his party a meal which included the 'best tasting fish [he] had ever eaten.'

The great Paiute chief Winnemucca negotiated treaties with the European settlers as early as 1855, but two bloody conflicts occurred in 1860. In 1874, Pyramid Lake and the surrounding lands were declared an Indian reservation, though settlers and the railroad companies still managed to acquire portions of the best land; Truckee River water, which had always replenished the lake, was also siphoned off for irrigation, lowering the water level by over 100 feet.

For modern anglers, as it was for Paiute spearfishers, the most prized catch is the Lahontan cutthroat trout (in fact a type of salmon) which can grow up to 40 pounds and has the honor of being Nevada's official state fish. Along with the endemic cuicui, another remnant from ancient Lake

Lahontan, the cutthroat trout suffered a disastrous decline in numbers because of environmental changes, such as dams interfering with their spawning runs. Since the 1970s, efforts have been made to restore the environment of the lake and to stock it with fish spawned in hatcheries. The number and size of the fish have been improving.

The usual entry to the **Pyramid Lake Indian Reservation** is off of Hwy 445 from Sparks; the boundary is near the Pyramid Lake Store, 23 miles from Sparks. Some five miles further is **Sutcliffe,** where you can get supplies, and permits for camping, fishing, and boating. You can stay at the campground or at *Crosby Lodge* (☎ 476-0400). Visit the **Dunn Hatchery** to see exhibits on the lake and the Paiute fish breeding program. North of Sutcliffe there are quite a few places to camp near the lake, but they have no facilities or shade. The north end of the lake may be closed to visitors.

Going round the south end of the lake, there are a few sandy beaches, the village of **Nixon,** and several more places to camp. **Anaho Island,** near the eastern shore, is a bird sanctuary for the American white pelican. Nearby is the distinctive rock formation called Great Stone Mother and Basket.

The Mustang Ranch

This has become one of Reno's best-known attractions, despite a lack of official promotion and the fact that it's actually in the next county, nine miles away. Its background is a long story of Nevada politics and pragmatism.

Prostitution was a fact of life in Nevada's mining and railroad camps from the earliest days and was officially ignored in Reno throughout the notoriously corrupt 1920s and '30s. During WWII, the War Department compelled the Washoe County authorities to close down the 'cribs' in Reno's Lake St and Riverside red-light districts, mainly to counter the risk of venereal disease. For the first time prostitution was made officially illegal in the county, but not in response to any local moral outrage, nor out of concern for the exploitation of women.

In the mid-1950s, a man named Joe Conforte started a mobile brothel near Wadsworth, where the corners of Washoe, Lyon, and Storey Counties meet. He shifted the establishment between the three counties, and stayed ahead of the authorities (some of whom were persuaded to be less-than-enthusiastic in pursuit) until 1960, when he was jailed by the Washoe County district attorney.

On his release, Conforte opened a new brothel, the Mustang Ranch, just inside the Storey County line. Here he paid his local taxes, paid off the authorities, and campaigned for changes in the law. By 1971 the Mustang Ranch was the biggest taxpayer in Storey County, and the county commissioners voted in an ordinance which made brothels (or at least Conforte's brothel) legal. It was the first such ordinance in the USA.

After several years of legal and lucrative operation, Conforte acquired a new enemy. The IRS pursued him for over a decade on charges of income tax evasion. In 1990, with Conforte owing over $10 million in back taxes, the brothel was declared bankrupt and the IRS put the whole place up for auction: a 300-acre ranch, with offices, living quarters, catering facilities, a fancy lobby, large bar, and 100 bedrooms, each with bathroom, bidet, and interesting decor. It was sold for the bargain price of $2.5 million to a consortium which included Conforte's lawyer and which promptly appointed Conforte himself as manager.

The Mustang Ranch (☎ 342-0176) is back in business on a big scale, 24 hours a day, with dozens of working women. It's estimated that over 200,000 men per year visit the place, which will also provide services for couples, possibly for interested women, definitely not for gay men. To get there, take I-80 east from Reno to exit 23 and follow the well-worn road. They don't discuss prices over the phone. ∎

CARSON CITY

• *pop 40,500* • *elev 4660 feet* ☎ *702*

It's easy to be underwhelmed by Nevada's state capital, but it's a pleasant place with tree-lined streets, handsome old buildings, and a couple of good museums. It's accessible from Reno, Virginia City, or Lake Tahoe, and makes a good day trip.

History

The city was created almost solely by the initiative of New York businessman Abe Curry, who envisioned the site as a state capital before Nevada was even a state. With a mixture of vision, business acumen, and civic generosity, he acquired the land in 1858, had the town site platted, and set aside four blocks for a capitol building. The city was named after frontiersman Kit Carson, or perhaps for the Carson Valley (which, in any case, was named after Kit Carson, the scout for John Frémont's 1844 expedition).

With the discovery of gold and silver in the nearby hills, Carson City became a busy way station on the route to the mines, growing to more than 500 people within two years. In 1861, it was selected as the capital of Nevada Territory, and Curry provided, free of charge, a building in which the Territorial Assembly could meet. Its first sitting was, quite literally, on chairs provided by Abe Curry. By 1864, Nevada was a state, and Carson City was its capital. The short railway line to mining boomtown Virginia City, was completed in 1869 and soon extended to Reno, giving Carson City a small industrial base and a rail link to the rest of the country.

The rail link enabled Carson City to benefit from the mining booms at Tonopah and Goldfield, and the work of government provided an ongoing economic base. Nevertheless, Carson City stagnated with the rest of the state as the mining booms played out. Its population fell as low as 2000 in the Great Depression, but it benefited from the liberalization of gambling and divorce laws, and grew again in the 1930s and '40s. It has recovered strongly in the postwar period, with burgeoning government services and growth in the Carson Valley and Lake Tahoe regions.

Orientation

Carson City straddles Hwy 395, the main road to/from Reno, in the north. This is the main street, called Carson St as it goes through town. Highway 50 from Virginia City comes into town as Williams St. The street layout is a straightforward grid with most of the motels, restaurants, casinos, and public buildings along Carson St, south of Williams.

Information

The Carson City Chamber of Commerce (☎ 882-1565), 1900 S Carson St, is open weekdays from 8 am to 5 pm, from 10 am to 3 pm on weekends. They have a good map of town that plots a 2½-mile walking tour around most of the old historic buildings. The Talking Houses program has many of the old buildings broadcasting information about their past; get a brochure from the chamber of commerce, switch your radio to the AM band, and tune in to the frequencies they indicate.

Capitol Building & Museum

The Nevada State Capitol was built in 1857, complete with a silver-covered dome symbolizing its 'Silver State' status. New legislative chambers were completed in 1913, and the original Senate chamber now houses a museum of Nevada's state souvenirs. The old Assembly chamber has an exhibit on the USS *Nevada*. The Capitol Building & Museum (☎ 687-4810), at 101 N Carson St, is open weekdays from 8 am to 5 pm.

Nevada State Museum

Built in 1869 as a branch of the US Mint, this building of local sandstone looks suitably solid. It closed as a mint in 1893, and re-opened as a museum in 1941. Its various galleries have fine exhibits on many aspects of the state, as well as the coin press from the original mint, and an example of every coin it ever produced. The Ghost Town Gallery, reproducing a mining town streetscape, with recorded commentary by 'old timers,' is actually pretty interesting and not overwhelmingly contrived. Other galleries have stuffed versions of Nevada's animals and birds, with informative labels, a weapons collection, and a geological display. A large ichthyosaur fossil hangs over the stairs.

The museum basement has been converted into a re-creation of an underground mine, fitted out with genuine tools, timbers, ores, and artifacts from real mines around the state. It's a great exhibit, but leave it until last as you'll re-surface outside the museum. Another highlight is the ethnology and archaeology galleries, with dioramas showing Indian life in the Great Basin and around the lakes, and examples of Washoe baskets made by master basket-maker Dat-So-La-Lee.

The museum bookstore has an excellent collection of books on every aspect of Nevada, from Paiute culture to nuclear politics. The museum (☎ 687-4810), 600 N Carson St, is open daily from 8:30 am to 4:30 pm and costs $3 for adults, free for children under 18.

Nevada State Railroad Museum

The Virginia & Truckee Railroad endures here, with three perfectly restored steam locomotives, antique passenger carriages, and interesting exhibits on this historic short railroad. Built in a single year, the railroad climbed 1600 feet from the Carson Valley to Virginia City. From 1869 to 1948 it hauled massive quantities of timber, supplies, and everything else up to the mines, and carried back huge loads of ore. The trains are also featured in Hollywood Westerns from the 1930s to '50s. Short train rides, hauled by one of the old steam locomotives, cost $2/1; buy tickets at the Wabuska Station at the north end of the parking lot.

Stewart Indian Museum

In the 1880s, Senator William Stewart convinced the federal government to fund a school for Indian children, with the aim of teaching them trade skills, so they could

integrate into European society. It was quite a few years before the school, and the society, accepted that Native American culture was not extinct, and began to incorporate elements of the traditional heritage into the school program. The school was closed down in 1980, but the campus is still used by the Native American community. It's very pretty, with big trees and rustic stone buildings from the 1930s.

The museum (☎ 882-1808) has some good baskets and pottery, and old pictures of the school and its students, but it doesn't tell you much about the history or culture of Nevada's native people. The excellent photogravures by Edward E Curtis are worth seeing. It's at 5366 Snyder Ave, which branches off Hwy 395 about three miles south of town, and is open daily. Donations are appreciated, and there's a gift shop, too.

Casinos

If you're not casino-ed out after Stateline, Reno, or wherever else you've played, you'll find a few unspectacular examples here. Ormsby House (☎ 882-1890), 600 S Carson St, is the oldest and largest. The Best Western Carson Station Hotel & Casino (☎ 883-0900, 800-528-1234), 900 S Carson St, is popular and is the most likely spot for entertainment.

Organized Tours

A nice way to see the old areas of Carson City, at least in the warmer months, is from one of the horse-drawn wagons of Hoofbeats Historical Tours (☎ 884-3450).

Places to Stay

There are plenty of motels on Carson St at the north and south end of town, but they can fill up on a Friday or Saturday night and they aren't a very good value, anyway. One of the cheapest is the *Forty-niner Motel* (☎ 882-1123), 2450 N Carson St, at $32 per night. The *Frontier Motel* (☎ 882-1377), 1718 N Carson St, is only slightly more expensive at $32, but may go down to $27 midweek. Also try the *Downtowner*

Motor Inn (☎ 882-1333) at 801 N Carson St.

The chain motels here might be a better value; try *Motel 6* (☎ 885-7710), 2749 S Carson, or the mid-range *Days Inn* (☎ 883-3343), at 3103 N Carson St, from $40 mid-week to $45 at peak times. The *St Charles Hotel* (☎ 882-1887), 310 S Carson St, is an old place, renovated but with a bit of character. It's pricey at $39 for a shared bath, or $69 for a room with private bathroom, though this does include breakfast.

Places to Eat

Most of the restaurants, over 20 of them, are on Carson St. Two popular places serving American food are *Scotty's,* at 1480 N Carson St, with big, inexpensive lunches and dinners; and *Sierra's,* at 400 S Carson, for lunch only. International restaurants include *Szechuan Express,* 3697 S Carson St, with good, mid-priced specials, and *El Charro Avitia,* 4389 S Carson St, for excellent and inexpensive Mexican. The casinos also serve meals, which can be a good value. The best, and most expensive restaurant is *Adele's* (☎ 882-3353), with a first-class continental menu and an elegant atmosphere.

Getting There & Away

Greyhound buses (☎ 782-4544) stop at 111 E Telegraph Ave and at the Frontier Motel. There are connections to Reno at 4:55 am and 5 pm ($5.75), Las Vegas at 8:10 am ($56), and Los Angeles at 8:20 am ($56).

AROUND CARSON CITY
Genoa

This pretty village, at the edge of Carson Valley, nestled beneath the Sierras, was the first European settlement in Nevada, at that time the western edge of Utah Territory. After temporary camps in 1849 and 1850, a group of Mormons established a trading post here in 1851 and ran a good business provisioning emigrant groups for the final leg of the trip to California. Later, Genoa provided food for the miners of Virginia City and timber for their mines; big trees were cleared from the mountains and trans-ported to the valley in timber flumes down Jacks Valley and Clear Creek.

Mormon Station State Historic Park The wooden stockade here is sometimes said to be a restoration of the original Mormon Trading Post fort, but it doesn't look very credible. Maybe it's more of a reproduction – perhaps a rendition – of the original, but it is a good place for a picnic. There's a small museum and a ranger in the log cabin, which has a few pioneer pieces. It's open between May and October daily from 9 am to 5 pm.

Genoa Courthouse Museum The old Douglas County courthouse, a well-proportioned red brick building from 1863, has good exhibits on local history, with a couple of surprises. There's something on George Ferris, a local engineer who was inspired by the giant water wheels in Carson Valley and came up with a new type of attraction for the Chicago World's Fair: the Ferris Wheel. Another remarkable tale concerns 'Snowshoe' Thompson, a Norwegian who carried mail between Genoa and Placerville, CA, from 1856 to 1876. All through winter, twice per month, with 60 to 80 pound loads, he traveled the route on skis, taking two days to reach Placerville, and three days to return. The museum (☎ 782-2590) opens from 10 am to 4:30 pm daily in summer.

Walley's Hot Springs Off Hwy 208, a mile south of Genoa, these luxuriously developed hot springs are open to the public for $12 per day. Small cottages rent from about $80 per night, and the rusticated restaurant (☎ 782-8155) serves upper-middle-priced American food.

Places to Stay & Eat The *Genoa House Inn B&B* (☎ 782-7075) on Nixon St is an 1872 house with nice rooms, for which they charge around $65 and up. There's also the *Wild Rose B&B* (☎ 782-5697) on Main St. On the corner of Main and Nixon Sts, the *Genoa Country Store* has snacks and drinks, while a little further up Main

St, the *Pink House Restaurant* (☎ 782-3939), is quite expensive, with scallops or steak at around $18. Across the road, the *Genoa Saloon* claims to be the oldest bar in the state, and it looks it. Very atmospheric, it's a good place for a drink.

VIRGINIA CITY
• *pop 1500* • *elev 6220 feet* ☎ 702

If you're interested in history and can ignore commercialization, you'll enjoy a day in Virginia City, the greatest mining boomtown of the late-19th century and site of the fabulous **Comstock Lode**, now a National Historic Landmark. It's a touristy town, with a main street of old buildings housing souvenir shops, saloons, restaurants, and some pretty hokey 'museums,' but it's more authentic than many of the over-restored and reconstructed 'historic' towns you see around.

History
Locating the lode started with discoveries of placer gold in Six Mile Canyon, downstream near Dayton. Two Irish prospectors followed the canyon up and, in 1859, found gold in surface quartz at the head of the canyon, near the north end of what is now C St. Another prospector, Henry Comstock, fraudulently claimed that the dig was on his land, and conned the Irishmen into giving him a piece of their paydirt. It is appropriate that the Comstock Lode was named after a con-man, for though it yielded perhaps $400 million in precious metals (the estimates vary from under $300 million to over $700 million), several times this amount was traded in mining stocks and bonds by investors and speculators in San Francisco and elsewhere.

The initial digging for surface gold was impeded by a heavy, gray mud, which was soon found to contain as much as $3000 of silver per ton, as well as the gold. The ore body dipped steeply into the mountainside, so when the first finds were exhausted, deep mining operations were required. This meant major capital investments, share floats, stock certificates, and wild speculation. With rich deposits deep underground and claims on the surface inaccurately recorded, the Comstock became patchwork of overlapping lots on top of a labyrinth of shafts, contested by crooked lawyers in interminable cases which clogged the corrupt courts. The total area claimed was three or four times the actual acreage above the lode.

Nevertheless, the first five years of frenetic activity saw the development of new mines deep in the unstable ground, dozens of stamp mills to process the ore, and the completion of a toll road from the Carson Valley. The new town gained gas lines, a sewer system, and a population of 15,000.

It could take up to 20 mules to push the ore around the mining sites, as seen in this historic photo of Harmony.

It also gained a newspaper on which Samuel Clemens (before adopting his penname, Mark Twain) worked from 1862 to 1864. Nevada was admitted to the Union in 1864 and federal judges were able to sort out the mess of conflicting claims. Then the main mines hit the bottom of the lode, stock prices crashed, and the population slumped to 4000.

The crash allowed big investors like William Ralston and his associates to consolidate control of the mines, the stamp mills, and the new railway to Carson City. The town grew again as new mines went down to deeper parts of the lode, then declined again in 1870. In 1873, John Mackay, a rival of Ralston, struck it really rich when his Consolidated Virginia mine hit the Big Bonanza ore body, 1200 feet down in the Comstock Lode. Virginia City boomed again, with 30,000 people in the district by 1874. The following year a fire destroyed most of the town, but such was the new wealth that it was nearly all rebuilt within a year. Most of the structures in Virginia City today date from this reconstruction.

By 1878, even the Big Bonanza was played out, and the town barely survived, though there was an unspectacular industry of reprocessing the tailings with new cyanide mineral extraction techniques. By the 1930s Virginia City was down to 500 people and would have disappeared altogether if not for its tourism potential.

Orientation

Virginia City is built on a hillside, with interesting views of the old mines and the hills and valleys to the east. The main street is C St, with old buildings and verandas on either side, as well as most of the tourist attractions. B St, parallel to C St and one block up the hill, also has some old buildings. Go downhill to the railroad station, between D and F Sts, then see the Mackay Mansion, on D St, and further south, the Chollar mine. It's best to park your car and walk around the town; there's a parking lot on D St, at the north end of town, and another in the middle of C St.

Information

The chamber of commerce (☎ 847-0311) is in an old railroad car on C St, south of Washington. An informative little pamphlet, *Guide to Virginia City,* by Len Ettinger, is sold in town for $1. It has good maps and diagrams of the area.

The Way It Was Museum

There is a very diverse collection here, which gives a few angles on the Comstock's history. The models of the mine workings show how extensive the tunnels underneath you are – all 750 miles of them. The video on the Comstock provides a good background, as does the one about Mark Twain. The museum, at 66 North C St, is open daily from 10 am to 6 pm and costs $2; free for kids under 11.

The Castle

Mine engineer Robert Graves had this house built for his family in 1868. It's notable for its lavish interior and expensive furnishings, and for the fact that the house and contents survive largely intact. Bohemian crystal chandeliers, French wall paper, and Italian marble fireplaces were all shipped from Europe, around Cape Horn to San Francisco, and hauled over the Sierras by wagon. It's a great insight into the lives of the elite, in what was a very stratified society. The Castle is at 70 South B St, and can be seen by guided tour only; these are available from May to October, daily, for $3.

Mackay Mansion

It's not quite as lavish or as original as the Castle, but in this mansion you can see all the rooms, including the utility rooms, and it looks more lived in. But the main interest is the life of its one-time owner, John Mackay, an Irish miner who arrived at the Comstock with nothing in 1860. Through hard work, diligent study, and well-calculated risk, he became one of the 'Silver Kings,' and successfully challenged the big money bankers from San Francisco. He was also noted for his personal charm, civic leadership, and generous endowment

NEVADA

of the University of Nevada. The docent will tell you all about him, after he collects your $3 entry fee. It's at 129 South D St, and open from 10 am to 6 pm daily.

Chollar Mine

A 30-minute underground tour will show you how the other half lived on the Comstock. The most significant feature is the use of 'square-set' timbering, which was developed in the mines here. It enabled large ore bodies to be mined, at great depths, even in unstable ground. The system was invented by Phillip Deidesheimer in 1861; he did not patent it, but

actively encouraged its use in the Comstock because it was so much safer than earlier techniques. The mine (☎ 847-0717) is at the south end of F St, and tours ($4) are offered every afternoon between May and September.

Virginia & Truckee Railroad

This railroad was built in 1869, and ran to Carson Valley via Gold Hill and Silver City. For 70 years it hauled people, timber, supplies, and everything else up to the mines, and carried back huge loads of ore. Most of the track has been removed, but a narrated, 35-minute trip takes you through

---

Museum Madness

It will take the better part of a day to see Virginia City's staple attractions, but there are at least a dozen more. Some are of very limited interest, others are pretty good. The following are listed from north to south via C St.

Marshall Museum, North C St at Sutton St, displays gold, silver, precious stones, minerals, coins, etc, and you can pan for gold ($4).

Assay Office Museum, also at Sutton St, shows the workings of an assay office (donation).

Wild West Museum, 66 North C St, has tacky dioramas, a spook show, a crooked roulette wheel, and smutty old movieolas ($1, plus quarters to make the dioramas do their thing).

Red Light Museum, 5 South C St under the Julia C Bulette Saloon, is home to an unarousing collection of medical instruments, opium pipes, French postcards, letters, and so forth ($1).

Pipers Opera House, B St at Union, featured many stars of the 19th-century stage and has an interesting interior, with chandeliers, a sprung stage, and painted sets ($2).

Territorial Enterprise **Museum,** C St between Union and Taylor, houses presses and printing technology from Nevada's oldest newspaper ($2).

Mark Twain Museum, C St at Taylor, has more old printing technology and an overdone recorded commentary ($1).

Ponderosa Saloon Underground Mine Tours, South C St, raises the question: 'why shouldn't you have a mine shaft in the back of a saloon?' This one shows most of the mine features you'll see at the Cholla mine, and has a good commentary ($3.50/1.50).

Nevada Gambling Museum, 50 South C St, seems to interest most people with their collection of cheating devices ($1.50)..

Firemen's Museum, 51 South C St, has some beautifully restored fire fighting equipment (donation).

Territorial Prison Museum, South C St, is a really crummy collection of mannequin prisoners in fake, plywood cells (75¢).

Fourth Ward School Museum, South C St, is an impressive old building with displays on the history of the mining and Virginia City (donation). ■

the old mining areas to Gold Hill and back, behind a vintage steam locomotive. The train runs May through September and costs $4.50/2.25.

Places to Stay

It's feasible to commute from Reno, Carson City, or even Tahoe, but staying overnight lets you see the place with fewer tourists, less traffic, and more character. Accommodations are not of particularly good value, but check the *Comstock Lodge* (☎ 847-0233), 875 South C St, which has a bunch of new cottages with old-style furnishings, at $45/55, slightly more on weekends. The *Sugar Loaf Mountain Lodge* (☎ 847-0505), 430 C St, is similar, from $42/52 including a continental breakfast.

If you want to stay in an original 19th-century building, try the *Silver Queen Hotel* (☎ 847-0440), right in the middle of C St, where renovated rooms run from $45 to $90. A mile south of town, the *Gold Hill Hotel* (☎ 847-0111) claims to be Nevada's oldest (established 1859), and has rooms in the old part of the building from $35 to $50 low-season, $45 to $70 at busy times. Newer, more comfortable rooms go from $65 to $135.

The RV Park (☎ 847-0999), off Carson St, is pretty good, and takes tent campers from $4 per person, while RV sites with hookups cost $18 in high season.

Places to Eat

Most visitors are here for lunch, but it's nice to stay for dinner, when the streets aren't crowded with tourists and the commercial hype subsides. The *Brass Rail* has good value meals, including dinner, for under $10, and has some very nice tables with a beautiful view from a balcony out back. The *Delta Saloon* serves inexpensive American fare and also stays open for dinner. The *Julia C Bulette Saloon* does an OK lunch and snacks, but closes early in the evening. *Solid Muldoons* may be a better value, with burgers at $4 to $5, and pasta at $5.50. The fanciest place for dinner is *Comstock House Restaurant* (☎ 847-7319), which does a dinner-and-theater deal, with entrees around $17.

Saloons

Saloons must have been pretty common in old Virginia City, and a number of fine examples survive on C St, though some are packed with slot machines which do nothing for the historical ambiance. The *Old Washoe Club* has a great-looking bar, and the local millionaires' club used to meet upstairs. The *Silver Queen* is another great bar, with a big portrait of a woman made largely of silver coins. The *Delta Saloon* is the location of the much-touted 'suicide table' (go in and read the story), though its main business is slot machines. On the other side of the street, the *Bucket of Blood* has honky-tonk entertainment and a big window looking down the valley. The *Union Brewery & Saloon* makes its own beer and looks authentically rough and tough.

Nevada Great Basin

Geographically, nearly all of Nevada is in the Great Basin – a high desert of rugged ranges and broad valleys, which also extends into Utah, California, and Oregon. The southern corner, around Las Vegas, is in the Mojave; the western corner, around Lake Tahoe, is on the fringe of the Sierra Nevada; and a small area in the north is on the edge of the Columbia Plateau. But the rest of the state – vast, harsh, and sparsely populated – is Great Basin country. Most travelers pass through on one of several main highways across the state, so this chapter describes each of those routes, the places along the way, and some interesting detours.

The Great Basin is not a giant bowl, but rather a series of parallel, north-south mountain ranges and valleys. It is a basin in the sense that water does not drain out of

it – all the streams and rivers, such as they are, run into lakes, disappear underground, or just evaporate. The mountain ranges, some remote and almost totally unpopulated, are of great interest to outdoor enthusiasts, with wonderful opportunities for hiking in summer and skiing in winter. Most of the mountain ranges are part of the Toiyabe National Forest or the Humboldt National Forest, and USFS offices have excellent maps and information. Another good specialized source is *Hiking the Great Basin* by John Hart.

History

The Shoshone and Paiute lived here as hunter-gatherers for at least 700 years, gathering piñon pine nuts in the mountains in the warmer months, hunting rabbits, antelope, and fowl in the valleys during winter. Their culture, their way of life, and their very existence was almost totally overwhelmed by European settlement. This was not so much because of direct conflict, though there was plenty of that, but because cattle grazing, mining, and logging destroyed the natural resources on which the Indians depended.

Reservations were established early in the process of European settlement, often as a part of treaties in which Indians lost access to large areas of their traditional lands. Often, the reservations were poorly managed, and did little or nothing to preserve Indian culture or foster self-reliance. The main enterprises a visitor will see on reservations today are 'smoke shops,' in which tobacco products are sold free of local taxes. These have actually been quite successful in earning income for Indian communities.

Though the Great Basin was part of Mexico until 1848, Europeans began their exploration of the area much earlier. The first were American fur trappers who pioneered the trails along the Humboldt River.

Nevada Great Basin

The army soon sent Lieutenant John Frémont to explore and map the region, and he spent most of 1843 doing so, searching for the mythical San Buenaventura River which was supposed to flow west to the Pacific. When he was finally convinced that the river did not exist, it was Frémont who dubbed the area the 'Great Basin.'

In the years of the California Gold Rush, well-worn emigrant trails were established along the routes of trappers and explorers. This remote area was the last great barrier before crossing the Sierras to the promised land of California. Hundreds of thousands of emigrants passed through what was then the Utah Territory, though very few chose to settle in the Great Basin. The area's history is largely that of developing ways to bridge the distance: trails and roads, the Pony Express and the telegraph, the railroad and the highway. Then gold, silver, and other minerals were discovered and mining towns mushroomed right across the state; very few, however, continued to thrive after their lodes played out. Cattle ranching followed the railroad, and expanded to feed the miners. The Wild West period, with free-range grazing, lawless towns, and Indian skirmishes endured longer here than almost anywhere else in the country – the last stagecoach robbery in the US took place in Jarbridge in 1916.

Flora & Fauna

Many visitors wonder at the lack of trees in the national forests, as the lower slopes of the mountain ranges have nothing but desert vegetation, mainly sage, to cover them. Above 6000 feet, juniper trees begin to appear, and piñon pine trees a little higher, with an occasional patch of willow, aspen, or cottonwood. Around 8000 feet and up, higher rainfall and cooler temperatures favor the pine and fir trees, with the really tall spruces occurring up to 10,000 feet, and bristlecone pine at the upper limits of survival. These different plant communities support different types of animal, and it's a real delight to see changes in the various 'life zones' as you climb into the higher ranges. Because the ranges are sep-

Bristlecone pine, the oldest living thing on earth.

arated by broad, hot, dry valleys, many are like ecological islands, with species evolving in a particular area which are found nowhere else.

ALONG I-80

The fur trappers' route followed the Humboldt River from northeast Nevada to where it peters out in the Humboldt Sink, near Lovelock. By continuing southwest, it was possible to find the Truckee River and follow it up into the Sierras north of Lake Tahoe. This route was one of the earliest emigrant trails to Northern California, and was called the Humboldt Trail or the Emigrant Trail. Though not the most direct route across Nevada, it was chosen as the route of the Central Pacific Railroad because it avoided many of the Great Basin's steep north-south ranges. Building the transcontinental railroad from the west, the tracks reached Reno in May 1868, and had crossed the state within a year.

By the 1920s, a new automobile road, Hwy 40 – the Victory Highway – followed the same route. This was upgraded as part of the federal interstate highway program, and is now a section of the transcontinental I-80. It was one of the last sections to be completed – in 1983 the only traffic light on the road from New York to San Francisco was in the main street of Lovelock, Nevada.

Lovelock
• pop 2069 • elev 3975 feet ☎ 702

Founded in the 1860s, this small town is the capital of Pershing County, providing services to the surrounding farmlands and to travelers on the interstate. Two freeway exits, 105 and 107, lead to Cornell Ave, which has plenty of motels and places to eat. The visitor information office is at the chamber of commerce (☎ 273-7213), close to exit 105, while the nearby Marzen House (1876) has a folksy museum (closed Monday). The county courthouse, on Main St, is an interesting round building, with a pleasant, shady park and a public swimming pool nearby.

Seven miles west of town, **Giant Tufa Park** has a group of calcium carbonate spires which grew in the ancient Lake Lahontan.

Around Lovelock

Between 1860 and 1880 the Buena Vista Valley, east of I-80, was the scene of a small mining bonanza and a large speculative frenzy. It produced the foundation of a fortune for George Hearst (William Randolph's dad), and some good stories for Samuel Clemens.

For a slow but scenic detour, leave I-80 at Oreana (exit 119), take the rough road over the Humboldt Range, swing north through the pretty little village of Unionville, then follow Hwy 400 back to the interstate at Mill City (exit 149).

Winnemucca
• pop 6134 • elev 4324 feet ☎ 702

The biggest town on this stretch of I-80, Winnemucca has been a travelers' stop since the days of the Emigrant Trail, when many of the emigrants forded the Humboldt River here to take a cutoff trail to Northern California and Oregon. When the railroad came through in 1865, the town was named after the famous Paiute chief. In

the last decade, the town has grown rapidly because of large mining operations in the Osgood Mountains east of town.

From the interstate, exit 176 is at the west end of Winnemucca Blvd and exit 178 is at the east end. Most of the motels are along this street, with the town center around Melarkey and N Bridge Sts. The visitors bureau (☎ 623-5071), 50 Winnemucca Blvd, is open on weekdays from 8 am to 5 pm. The town also has a good library, at the corner of 5th St and Baud, several casinos, and a small red-light district.

The **Humboldt County Museum** (☎ 623-2912), on Jungo Rd north of the river, is in an old church (though it's closed on Sundays). It has an assortment of archaeological artifacts and Paiute baskets. The **Buckaroo Hall of Fame** (☎ 623-2225), 30 W Winnemucca Blvd, is dedicated to 'the old-time working cowboy' (also closed Sundays).

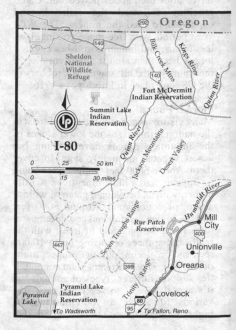

Places to Stay & Eat There are a dozen or more motels on Winnemucca Blvd, with prices that vary with the day and the season; summer prices are much higher. For example, *Motel 6* (☎ 623-1180), 1600 W Winnemucca Blvd, charges $36/42 per single/double in summer, but $28/34 for the rest of the year. The *Downtown Motel* (☎ 623-2398), 251 E Winnemucca Blvd, is one of the cheapest, with rooms from under $30. For more comfort, the *Thunderbird Motel* (☎ 623-3661), 511 W Winnemucca Blvd, charges $60/65 year round.

The *Winnemucca Hotel*, 95 Bridge St, is a nice old building with a restaurant that serves Basque food. Food is also available at the casinos, 24 hours a day.

Around Winnemucca

About 50 miles north of Winnemucca, the Santa Rosa Mountains in the Humboldt National Forest, are a remote and beautiful wilderness area. A good drive is to take Hwy 290 up Paradise Valley, take the dirt road which climbs over Hinkey Summit, then descend to *Lye Creek Campground*. From there you can continue west to meet Hwy 95.

There are lots of hiking possibilities. Snow will close the road from October to May, but it's great for snowmobilers and cross-country skiers. For information, contact the Santa Rosa Ranger District (☎ 623-5025) at 1200 E Winnemucca Blvd.

Battle Mountain
• *pop 3542* • *elev 4510 feet* ☎ 702

Pioneers battled with Shoshone near here in 1861, after which the area had a brief mining boom, then settled down to life as a railroad town. A new mining boom began in the 1980s, with huge operations extracting gold and silver from the surrounding hills. Two exits from the interstate (229 and 233) go to the two ends of Front St, which has motels, restaurants, and casinos on one

NEVADA

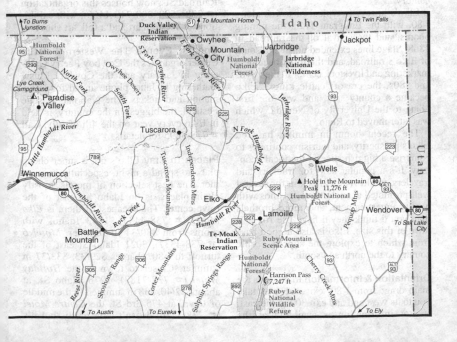

side, and the railway yards on the other. It's not a great place to stop because accommodations are often filled with mine workers and prices tend to be high.

South of Battle Mountain, Hwy 305 goes to Austin, 89 miles away. It's a good road which follows the Reese River between two mountain ranges, and it's very picturesque in a bleak, lonely, wide-open-spaces way.

Elko

• pop 15,000 • elev 5067 feet ☎ 702

This is cattle country, and Elko is a center of cowboy culture, with a calendar of Western-theme cultural events and a museum which is big on buckaroos, stagecoaches, and the Pony Express. The other cultural influence is Basque, and if this seems like a contrast, you won't be surprised that Basque sheepherders and Old West cattlemen had some violent conflicts over grazing rights around the turn of the century.

Elko's history is typical of towns along I-80, with the Emigrant Trail, the mining booms, and the arrival of the railroad in 1868. Stage lines extended north and south of Elko's railroad, and the town became a marketing and livestock center in the 1870s and '80s, the era of 'cattle kings.' Elko became a county seat, and was the first home to the University of Nevada, which was later moved to Reno.

The recent boom in mining has fed Elko's prosperity, and tourism continues to comprise a biggish slice of the local economy. It's a popular stop for truckers and travelers, while visitors flock in for several well-promoted annual events, casinos with quality entertainment, and more brothels than you'd think they'd have use for in a town of this size. Elko is also a good base from which to explore the superb, scenic country to the north and south.

Orientation & Information Idaho St is the main drag; from I-80, exit 301 will take you to its west end and exit 303 to the east. Visitor information is available at the chamber of commerce (☎ 738-7135), 1601 Idaho St, which is open weekdays from 9 am to 5 pm. For good maps, information, and advice about the backcountry, visit the USFS office (☎ 738-5171), 976 Mountain City Hwy, between exit 301 and downtown.

Northeastern Nevada Museum This modern museum has excellent displays on many aspects of the region, from pioneer life and Basque settlers, to wildlife and the latest techniques of gold mining and extraction. Exhibits include Indian artifacts, an original stage coach, photographs of the old mining towns, and an old Pony Express cabin. The museum (☎ 738-3418), 1515 Idaho Ave, is open daily from 9 am to 5 pm, Sunday 1 to 5 pm. It's free – but worth a donation – and there's a pleasant park out back.

Western Folklife Center The historic Pioneer Saloon, on the corner of 5th and Railroad Sts, now houses this organization (☎ 738-7508, 800-748-4466), with exhibitions of Western art and a folk art shop.

Special Events The Western Folklife Center organizes the Cowboy Poetry Gathering in January and the Cowboy Music Gathering in June; phone ahead for information and tickets. The National Basque Festival, the biggest in the country, is held in Elko every year on the 4th of July. Call ☎ 738-3295 for details.

Places to Stay Elko's not a super cheap place to spend a night, especially in summer. The best selection of motels, mostly chain places, is on Idaho St, east of the town center. The cheapest of them is *Elko Motel* (☎ 738-4433), 1243 Idaho, with rooms from $30/34 in summer. *Motel 6* (☎ 738-4337), 3021 Idaho St east of the turnoff to I-80, charges $29/33, $33/37 in summer. Closer to town is the *Holiday Motel* (☎ 738-7187), 1276 Idaho St, at about $32/40, $38 in summer. In the middle of town, at 475 3rd St, the *Centre Motel* (☎ 738-3226) doesn't look pretty, but it's

OK for $30/32. All these places have small heated pools that are open in summer.

Park View Inn (☎ 753-7747), 1785 Idaho St, is comfortable and charges $40/45 all year. The best place to stay is either the *Best Western Ameritel Inn* (☎ 738-8787), 1930 Idaho St, at $54/64, or the *Red Lion Inn & Casino* (☎ 738-2111, 800-545-0044), which charges from $50/55 in low season, and asks up to $79 in summer.

Places to Eat Apart from the complete set of fast food franchises on Idaho St, there are some interesting eating options, unless you're a vegetarian. The *Stockmen's Casino*, 340 Commercial St, has dinner entrees around $10, but this includes soup, salad, bread, and dessert. The *Red Lion Inn & Casino* does a buffet which might be a good value if you're really hungry. For Basque food, try the *Star Hotel*, 246 Silver St, or the *Nevada Dinner House* (☎ 738-8485), 351 Silver St; a full meal will run from $15 to $20.

Around Elko

Ruby Mountains This beautiful, rugged little range is like a jagged saw running south from Wells, though the best access is from Elko. Hwy 227 leads 20 miles to the picture-perfect village of **Lamoille**, where food and lodging (around $50) are available at *Pine Lodge* (☎ 753-6363). Just before the village, Lamoille Canyon Rd branches south, following the canyon for 12 miles past cliffs, waterfalls, and other glacial sculptures.

At the end of the road is a trailhead for the two-mile trail to Island Lake, and the 40-mile Ruby Crest Trail. The Ruby Mountains are now a declared wilderness area, with prominent peaks, glacial lakes, and alpine vegetation. It's brilliant terrain, but the hiking season is short – from about mid-June to mid-September. Other activities include horseback riding, for about $100 per day with Elko Guide Service (☎ 738-7539), and heli-skiing with Ruby Mountain Heli-Ski (☎ 753-6867). On the east side of the range, Ruby Lake National

Wildlife Refuge is a rest stop for migrating waterbirds and is also good for fishing.

In summer you can drive across the southern end of the range via the 7250 foot Harrison Pass, at the southern end of the Ruby Crest Trail. (John Frémont and Kit Carson crossed this pass in 1845.) Camping is possible at *Ruby Marsh Campground,* a BLM site near the lake, for $2; and *Thomas Canyon Campground,* halfway up Lamoille Canyon, for $6.

Tuscarora About 47 miles northwest of Elko – the last six miles via gravel road – you'll find this former mining town, which has come as close as a dozen people to ghost town status (ie deserted). Ceramicist Dennis Parks moved here in the 1960s, establishing a workshop, gallery, and ceramics school that put the place on the map, at least for potters.

Humboldt National Forest Highway 225 north of Elko is a paved road into the forest, going to Mountain City, through the Duck Valley Indian Reservation, and into Idaho. Mountain City has two cheapish motels, and a steakhouse/casino. There are quite a few campgrounds in the area, which is traversed by steep, rough, gravel roads.

One of the most remote towns in the state, **Jarbridge** is another old mining town, with a population of maybe 50 people. It has gas, food, accommodations, and campgrounds, and is the closest place to the Jarbridge Wilderness. If you want to explore this rugged, pristine, and nearly inaccessible area, first get information from the USFS in Elko, or from the Trading Post (☎ 488-2315) in Jarbridge.

Wells

• *pop 1256* • *elev 5630 feet* ☎ 702

At the junction of Hwy 93 and I-80, Wells has gas, food, and cheaper lodging than other towns along the interstate. Most of the motels are on 6th St. For trivia buffs, let it be known that Jack Dempsey started his boxing career here – as a bouncer in the local bars.

In the East Humboldt Range, about 12

miles southwest of town, *Angel Creek Campground* is beautifully located in a gully, while *Angel Lake Campground* is next to a cirque lake at 8300 feet. From Hwy 232, south of Wells, you can see the large natural window near the top of 11,300-foot Hole in the Mountain Peak.

Wendover
☎ 702

Wendover is a gambling boom town. Motels and casinos line up along Wendover Blvd, the main drag which continues into Utah. The state line is painted across the road, where the large cowboy statue of Wendover Will makes sure you don't miss it.

On the Nevada side, the Welcome Center (☎ 664-3414) has displays on Nevada, Wendover, and the WWII work at Wendover Air Force Base, which prepared the *Enola Gay* crew for dropping atomic bombs. On the Utah side, the Bonneville Speed Museum (☎ 801-665-7721) documents attempts to set land speed records on the nearby Bonneville Salt Flats.

Accommodations in Wendover tend to be expensive, especially on weekends. The *Super 8* (☎ 664-2888, 800-800-8000), 1325 Wendover Blvd, is about the cheapest, but you might find a better value on the Utah side.

ALONG HWY 50

This road is often described as 'the loneliest road in America,' a slogan usually attributed to a story in *Life* magazine. Local publicists figured that any superlative was good advertising, and used it as a tourism promotion theme – tourist offices will give you passports which you can get stamped along the way, and bumper stickers boasting 'I survived the loneliest road in America.'

In fact it's no great ordeal to cross Nevada on Hwy 50 – it's about two hours from Fallon to Austin (hardly exceeding the speed limit at all), a longish hour to the historic mining town of Eureka, and about 1½ hours more to Ely. From Ely, it's another hour to the Great Basin National

Park, which on its own is worth the whole trip, and is almost in Utah.

The route goes across the natural grain of the country – repeatedly you climb up the side of a range, go through a mountain pass, roll down the other side, cross a broad valley, and climb up the next range. This is 'range and basin' terrain. It must have been heart-breaking in a pioneer's covered wagon, but in a car, it's a lot more interesting than a long, straight, flat freeway. In several places you can make detours north or south of Hwy 50, typically driving along valleys between the ranges, and this is a quite different sensation.

West of Austin, Hwy 50 follows the route of the Overland stagecoach lines and the Pony Express (another promotional theme exploited by the Nevada Commission on Tourism). The first transcontinental telegraph line also took a central route across Nevada – via Ely, Eureka, Austin, and Fallon – putting the Pony Express out of business even as the railroad across the north made the stagecoach line obsolete.

As road traffic became more important, the Lincoln Highway (Hwy 50) was established almost exactly along the route of the telegraph line, but it was the northern route, the Victory Highway (Hwy 40), that attracted the federal funding and became I-80. The 'lonely' Lincoln was left to be a tourist attraction.

Silver Springs
☎ 702

There's not much at this crossroads of Hwy 50 and Alt Hwy 95, but eight miles south is the turnoff to **Fort Churchill State Historic Monument**. Built in 1860, the fort is an appropriate stop-off along Hwy 50, as it was established partly to protect the Pony Express and Overland stage lines. Its other functions were to deter Indian attacks on the mining settlements and, more importantly, to help ensure that both California and Nevada remained decidedly pro-Union in the Civil War.

The fort was abandoned in 1870, after just 10 years of service, and only a few adobe ruins remain. Even so, it's still worth

Lake Lahontan

There is a Lahontan Reservoir west of Fallon, but it's nothing compared to the original Lake Lahontan, which existed from around 50,000 years ago, and dried up between 3000 to 4000 years ago. In cooler, wetter times, the various arms of the 8500-sq-mile lake covered a large triangular area, between McDermitt (on the Oregon border) in the north, Susanville (California) to the west, and Mono Lake (California) to the south. The lakeshore was home to prehistoric peoples from around 10,000 to 7500 BC, when woolly mammoth, mastodon, bison, and caribou roamed the area. The Lovelock Cave archaeological site has yielded human remains, baskets, and tools – with fish hooks, nets, and duck decoys to indicate that it was a lakeshore community – dating back about 4000 years.

Around that time, Lake Lahontan was starting to dry up, and much of the population disappeared. Paiute people were inhabiting the area when Europeans arrived, having adapted to life in the desert. Petroglyphs indicate they'd been in the area a long time, but it's not certain whether they were descendants of the Lahontan people, if they displaced them, or if they came to the area some time after the Lahontans had left.

Mono Lake, Pyramid Lake, and Walker Lake are the scattered remnants of the once extensive Lake Lahontan, and other geological signs are widespread in western Nevada, from the salt pan at Eightmile Flats, to the tufa spires near Lovelock. Another Lahontan remnant is the cui ui fish, a species which existed as long as 50,000 years ago in the ancient lake. They thrived in Pyramid Lake until recent times, and were an important source of food for the Paiute. Now they are an endangered species, partly because the dam at the mouth of the Truckee River has blocked the natural access to their spawning areas, and efforts are being made to spawn them in hatcheries. ■

seeing. The fort's main quadrangle is quite discernible, and there are excellent interpretive signs, so it's easy to imagine the place filled with parading soldiers and cavalry horses. Incidentally, the fort was named – probably by a sycophant – after Sylvester Churchill, Inspector General of the US Army.

The visitors center (☎ 577-2345) has very good exhibits on life in the fort and is open daily from 8:30 am to 3:30 pm. Nearby, *Buckland Campground* has beautiful shaded sites for $6 per vehicle.

Fallon

• *pop 6500* • *elev 3963 feet* ☎ *702*

The seat of Churchill County and the self-proclaimed 'oasis of Nevada,' Fallon is the heart of an irrigated agricultural area whose main product is alfalfa. It's also home to the Fallon Naval Air Station, where crews rehearse carrier-based operations without the inconvenience of going to sea.

There's a good museum here, and three small casinos, but no real reason to spend the night. If you must, the cheapest place is probably *Fallon Lodge* (☎ 423-4648), 25 N Taylor St on the corner of W Williams Ave (Hwy 50 as it goes through town), which charges $28/35. More motels are found along W Williams Ave/Hwy 50 on the western edge of town. *La Cocina Mexican Restaurant* (☎ 423-2411), in the Depot Casino at 875 W Williams Ave, will fill you with good Mexican food for under $8.

Churchill County Museum It's worth stopping at Fallon to see this museum, which has good displays of Paiute artifacts, including a traditional dome-shaped shelter made from tule reeds. The tule duck decoys are particularly whimsical and well done. Some of the artifacts are from the important archaeological find at Hidden Cave, and the museum arranges tours of the site, which is generally closed to the public. Meet at the museum at 9:30 am on the second and fourth Saturday of the month. There are better-than-usual displays of early clothing, furniture, and household goods, including some very fine hand-stitched quilts. The museum (☎ 423-3677) is open daily from 10 am to 5 pm, though in winter it closes on Thursday and has shorter hours. It's at 1050 S Maine St (which is the main street, though it was named after the state of Maine).

Around Fallon

Grimes Point Archaeological Area

On the northeast side of the highway, about eight miles from Fallon, you'll see signs pointing to this area, where a marked trail leads past scores of boulders covered in ancient petroglyphs. These are thought to have been created between 400 and 7000 years ago, though the dating is uncertain. The pictures are believed to have been made by shamans, as part of rituals to ensure a successful hunt, but in fact their significance is not known for certain.

In the same area is the **Hidden Cave**, which has yielded many significant archaeological finds. To see the cave, take a two-hour guided tour with the Churchill County Museum (see above). The cave itself was created around 20,000 years ago, by the action of waves on the ancient Lake Lahontan.

Sand Mountain About 25 miles from Fallon, Sand Mountain is a 600 foot-high sweep of sand dunes which occasionally produces a low-pitched hum, caused by vibration of wind-blown sand crystals. The best time to hear the sound is a hot, dry evening, at a time when the dune is not covered with screeching ORVs. Nearby, the ruins of an old Pony Express station have been excavated from the sand.

Middlegate At the junction of Hwy 50 and Hwy 361, the Old Middlegate Station sells gas, burgers, beer, and hot dogs. Highway 361 goes south to Gabbs, where you turn off to reach the Berlin-Ichthyosaurus State Park (see below).

Cold Springs Around 52 miles east of Fallon (47 miles west of Austin) there's a historical marker and self-guided trail around the ruins of the Cold Springs Pony Express Station. It's a good place to get out of the car and put your head in the Great Basin.

Austin

• pop 370 • elev 6577 feet ☎ 702

It might look interesting after an hour or so of uninterrupted basin and range, but there's not much to see in Austin, just a few

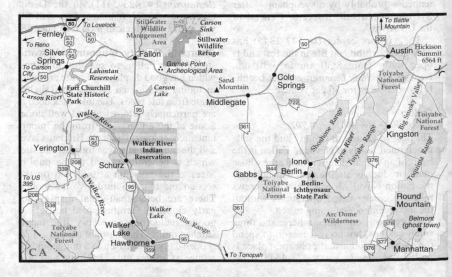

pleasantly old, almost decrepit buildings along the short main street. In the 1860s it had a population of 10,000, produced $50 million in silver, and generated a few Nevada legends. One was the Reese River Navigation Company, which sold stock on the basis of a scheme to run paddle steamers on a large trickle west of town.

A gravel side road goes south of the highway, to **Stokes Castle**, a box-like, three-story, stone structure surrounded by a chain link fence. It has a great view over the Reese Valley, and that's the best reason to go up here. The place was a folly built for mine magnate Anson P Stokes.

Information The USFS Austin Ranger District (☎ 964-2671) is north of the highway, a mile or so west of town, and is a good source for maps and information about hiking and other activities in the Toiyabe National Forest. They're open on weekdays from 7:45 am to 4:30 pm.

Places to Stay & Eat Three undistinguished motels are on the south side of the main street. The *Pony Canyon Motel* (☎ 964-2605) looks to be the best of them, for $32/36. The *International Hotel* is now

a restaurant, with OK food at basic prices. It was moved here in pieces from Virginia City in 1863, and is one of the oldest buildings in the state.

Around Austin

Toiyabe National Forest This national forest covers five separate mountain ranges in central Nevada, the most impressive of which is Toiyabe Range, extending south from Austin. A highlight is the demanding 73-mile Toiyabe Crest National Recreation Trail, which would require around five days to hike, but intermediate trailheads give access to shorter sections. The **Arc Dome Wilderness,** in the southern part of the range, is the largest in the state. There are four designated campgrounds with toilet facilities, and a fee of $2 is charged during the warmer months. *Big Creek Campground* is very pretty, and the most accessible, 13 miles southwest of Austin.

The USFS recommends two driving loops going south of Hwy 50. The shorter one (60 miles) goes from Austin, through Big Creek and Kingston, then back up the Big Smoky Valley. The longer one (100 miles) leaves Hwy 50 13 miles east of

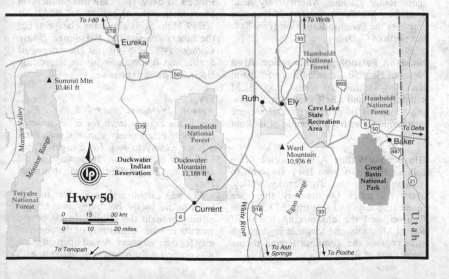

Austin, crosses the Toquima Range to Monitor Valley, then crosses the range again and returns by the Big Smoky Valley.

Berlin-Ichthyosaur State Park The two features of interest here are the ghost town of Berlin (born 1895, died 1911) and the fossil remains of half a dozen ichthyosaurs. You can walk round the town site any time (there are interpretive signs) or take a guided tour ($1) at 11 am on summer weekends.

The ichthyosaurs were carnivorous marine reptiles who lived here 225 million years ago, when this area was the western edge of the North American continent. Remains of over 40 icthyosaurs have been discovered, but the main find was of six specimens apparently trapped together in a muddy pool. This site was excavated in 1954 and is now protected by an A-frame shelter. Tours ($4) are given daily at 10 am, 2 pm, and 4 pm, during the summer, with shorter hours for the other seasons. Call ☎ 964-2440 to confirm times.

There's a nice campground nearby, costing $5. To get to the park, follow the picturesque Reese Valley on a dirt road southwest from Austin, and cross the Shoshone Range via Ione. Alternatively, head south from Middlegate on Hwy 361, and go east over the Paradise Range on Hwy 844, just north of Gabbs.

Hickison Petroglyph Recreation Area North of Hwy 50, 22 miles east of Austin, Hickison Summit has a rest stop, BLM campground, and a self-guided trail passing a number of petroglyphs. There are panoramic views from a couple of lookout points.

Big Smoky Valley A very scenic drive follows Hwy 376 from Hwy 50 south to Tonopah along the Big Smoky Valley, about 100 miles. On the way, there are interesting stops and side trips to Kingston Canyon, and the old mining towns of Round Mountain and Manhattan. A rough road crosses the Toquima Range to the ghost town of Belmont.

Eureka
• *pop 650* • *elev 6837 feet* ☎ *702*
Don't call this a ghost town; it may have sunk some from its peak population of 11,000, but it is still the seat of Eureka County. Between 1875 and 1890, $40 million worth of silver was extracted from a lead-rich ore in this area. During this time, hills were stripped of trees to make charcoal, while smelters belched lead-laden smoke, poisoning both plants and people for miles around.

Most of the sights can be seen on a short walk around town. The handsome brick County Courthouse, at Main and Bateman Sts, was finished in 1880 and, though it's still in use, is usually open to visitors. The **Eureka Sentinal Museum** (☎ 237-5484) displays late-19th-century newspaper technology and colorful examples of period reportage. It's open most days from 10 am to 4 pm, Sundays 10 am to 3 pm. The chamber of commerce (☎ 237-5484), in the same building, has additional information about the town. Stroll past other old buildings along Main St, to the 1880 **Eureka Opera House & Theater**, and catch the video on Eureka's history.

Places to Stay There are three motels on Main St; *Eureka Motel* (☎ 237-5247), at 10289 Main St, is about the cheapest, but the others are similar. *Parsonage House Cottage* (☎ 237-5746), at the corner of Spring and Bateman Sts, is an interesting B&B, but more expensive.

Ely
• *pop 4830* • *elev 6421 feet* ☎ *702*
Ely is the biggest town for miles around, the White Pine County seat, and is as good a place as any to stop for a night. Three highways converge on the town, and it's convenient to the Great Basin National Park.

Ely was established as a silver mining town in the 1860s, but large-scale copper mining brought the railroad in 1906, and was the economic mainstay of the community for over 70 years. A vast open pit mine was opened at Ruth, just west of town, with railway tracks spiraling into the abyss, and snaking 12 miles north to a smelter at McGill. The tracks ran another 90 miles north to join the Southern Pacific line at Cobre, east of Wells.

The mine closed down in 1979, and the population declined from its 1950s level of 12,000. Some new mining ventures have started, and tourism and a new state prison are also providing employment, but it's not exactly a boomtown at the moment.

Orientation & Information Aultman St is the main drag, running east-west through town. The White Pine Chamber of Commerce (☎ 289-8877) is at 636 Aultman, providing plenty of visitor information on weekdays from 8 am to 5 pm. On the blocks west of there you'll find the Jailhouse Motel & Casino (only slot machines), and the solid, 1920s Hotel Nevada (which has blackjack as well as slots), the biggest commercial buildings in town.

Nevada Northern Railway Museum Railroad transport was essential for moving the huge quantities of material from the open pit mine. The railway carried passengers from 1906 to 1941, but the vast majority of its work was hauling ore and overburden. For each ton of copper, 100 tons of ore were hauled to the smelter, and 420 tons of waste were taken to the tailings dumps. Railyards, a depot, and a complete railway workshop were established to support this operation. After the mine closed down, the Kennecott Corporation donated the whole shebang – locomotives, buildings, yard, and 32 miles of track – to the White Pine Historical Railroad Foundation, which now offers railway excursions pulled by historic steam engines, and shows off the depot and workshops as a working museum.

The 'Ghost Train of Old Ely,' pulled by a 1910 Baldwin steam locomotive, does a 1½-hour roundtrip ($14), passing downtown Ely, two ghost town sites, going through a curved tunnel, and up a scenic canyon. The 'Hiline Route,' usually pulled

by a 1952 Alco diesel, does a 1½-hour roundtrip ($10) through the Steptoe Valley and into the hills near McGill, where the smelter used to be. You can do both trips for $18, $16 for those over 65 or under 18, and $8 for kids under 12.

Walking tours of the depot and sheds let you see and touch a variety of old steam locomotives, carriages, and freight cars. Special vehicles, like the rotary steam snow blower and the wrecking crane, are particularly interesting. Tours ($2.50) depart at 9:30 am, 11:30 am, 2 pm, and 4 pm; call the museum (☎ 289-2085) to confirm. The museum is next to the handsome old East Ely railway station, at the north end of 11th St.

White Pine Public Museum This museum (☎ 289-4710) has the usual displays of stuff from the late 19th century, some mining and Indian artifacts, and several hundred dolls. It's worth a look if you have some time to spare, open daily from about 9 am to 4 pm, at 2000 Aultman St.

Places to Stay There are six motels on Aultman St and a couple more on High St, one block to the north. The *Rustic Inn* (☎ 289-4404), 1555 Aultman St, is OK, with rooms from $25. *Hotel Nevada* (☎ 289-6665), 501 Aultman, has some old-fashioned appeal, if not charm, at around $37. The *Four Sevens Motel* (☎ 289-4747), 500 High St, is nice and new and charges $40/46, but gives good discounts if business is slow.

On 7th St, south of the center at Ave O, *Motel 6* (☎ 289-6671) is one of the few places with a pool, charging $27/33; the *Copper Queen Hotel & Casino* (☎ 289-4884, 800-851-9526), on 7th St at Ave I, is probably the best in town, from $44/48.

Steptoe Valley Inn (☎ 289-8687), 220 E 11th St, is a twee B&B, with heavily decorated rooms from $63 to $74. There's also a *KOA* (☎ 289-3413) on Hwy 93 east of town, and several RV parks in the vicinity.

Places to Eat Casino-subsidized food at the *Hotel Nevada* is a pretty good value.

Señorita's on Aultman St at 5th St, has tasty Mexican main courses from around $8. For Chinese, try the *Good Friends Restaurant* at 1455 Aultman, where a set dinner will cost around $6.

Around Ely

The huge open-pit mine at **Ruth**, a few miles west, may not be accessible but you can't miss the mountainous tailings dumps. South of town, off Hwy 93, are the well-preserved **charcoal kilns** at Ward, which date from 1876. **Cave Lake State Recreation Area**, with an artificial lake stocked with trout, and several campgrounds, is also popular.

Great Basin National Park

This park is an absolute gem, and worth a long detour and a visit of several days if you enjoy nature and the great outdoors. The wonder is that mountains of over 11,000 feet rise abruptly from the desert, creating a full range of life zones and landscapes within a very limited area. In a few miles you climb from the desert, to piñon pine, to forests of fir and aspen, and finally reach the treeline where the hardiest bristlecone pines have lived for thousands of years. The highest peaks are snow capped in winter and embroidered with wildflowers in spring and summer – there's even a small glacier. The whole range sits like a temperate island surrounded by a sea of sagebrush, and is home to a wonderful variety of birds and animals. The wonders continue underground, where the Lehman Caves, richly decorated with limestone formations, are the main attraction for many visitors.

History In prehistoric times, the area supported a lakeside culture on the shores of the ancient Lake Bonneville. Around 800 years ago, there were small villages on the eastern side of the Snake Range, growing corn, beans, and squash. From about 1300 AD, Shoshone and Paiute hunter-gatherers occupied the area, using piñon pine nuts as their staple food.

Explorers, miners, and homesteaders arrived in the mid-1800s, with Absalom Lehman establishing a ranch in the 1860s. He discovered the cave here around 1885, and soon started guiding tours through it. Much of the Snake Range became a national forest in 1909, and the caves were declared a national monument in 1922. But, due to opposing efforts from mining and ranching interests, the area did not achieve the status of national park until 1986.

Information Coming in from the little settlement of Baker, the access road leads straight to the visitors center (☎ 234-7331), near the Lehman Caves. There is an excellent selection of books and maps, and the helpful rangers can answer just about any question and book a cave tour for you. The center is open from 7:30 am to 6 pm, 8 am to 5 pm in winter. Outside the center is a short nature trail with labeled plants, a cafe, and a gift shop, open May to October. Park entry is free. Gas, food, and limited accommodations are available in Baker.

In winter, much of the park is covered in snow and, as the upper roads are not plowed, access will be limited unless you come prepared for backcountry skiing or snow-shoeing. In summer, especially on weekends, the park can get a lot of visitors, but many come just to see the caves and drive the Wheeler Peak Trail. It rarely has that human zoo feeling, which can detract from the enjoyment of better-known parks.

Lehman Caves The caves have all those calcium carbonate formations usually found in limestone caves: stalactites, stalagmites, columns, curtains, flowstones, etc. Guided 1½-hour tours take you through a half mile of illuminated chambers and passages; make a booking and buy your ticket at the visitor center as soon as you arrive, as there can be a wait for the next available tour. During summer, tours leave on the hour between 9 am and 5 pm, with a candlelight tour at 6 pm. The rest of the year, tours are at 9 am, 11 am, 2 pm, and 4 pm. Tours cost $4/3, and the temper-

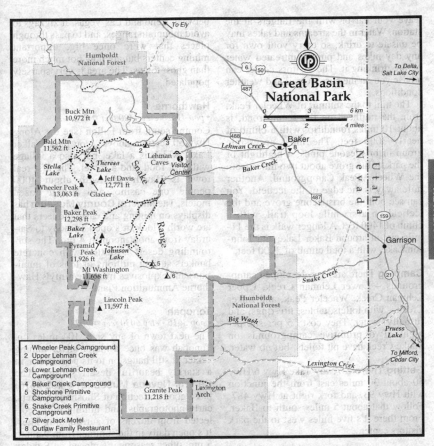

Great Basin National Park

1 Wheeler Peak Campground
2 Upper Lehman Creek Campground
3 Lower Lehman Creek Campground
4 Baker Creek Campground
5 Shoshone Primitive Campground
6 Snake Creek Primitive Campground
7 Silver Jack Motel
8 Outlaw Family Restaurant

ature inside is a constant 50° F, so bring a sweater.

Wheeler Peak This impressive peak, 13,063 feet high, is the second-highest point in the state, and has snow drifts even in the middle of summer. A paved road winds up its northern slopes to around 10,000 feet, offering great views of the Great Basin and a chance to experience the changes in temperature, landscape, and vegetation as you ascend. On the way, stop at some of the scenic lookouts and take one of the short walks. Try to allow two hours

at the top of the road, near Wheeler Peak Campground, to do the hiking circuit, through superb country, to Stella Lake and Teresa Lake. Ideally, take more time and do some longer hikes.

Hiking There are a number of excellent hikes which will take the best part of a day, but do not entail backcountry camping. Keep on established trails whenever possible, as the alpine ecosystem is more fragile than its rugged looks suggest. If you plan an overnight trip, there's a backcountry registration system; sign up where you leave your car or with the rangers at the station. Water in the streams and lakes may be unsafe to drink, so carry your own for any day hikes and purify untreated water before drinking it. The visitors center can advise you on the current trail and weather conditions.

The trail to the summit of Wheeler Peak, from the trailhead on the scenic road, is about 10 miles roundtrip, with a climb of nearly 3000 feet. The most accessible group of bristlecone pines, a highlight of the park, is the grove about two miles from the Wheeler Peak Campground. Another mile away is the edge of the icefield. You can see both the bristlecone grove and the icefield on a six-mile loop trail, with a climb of 1400 feet. A longer walk is the 11-mile circuit around Baker Lake and Johnson Lake, with a total climb of 3200 feet.

Camping There are four developed campgrounds – Lower Lehman Creek, Upper Lehman Creek, Wheeler Peak, and Baker Creek – with toilets, tables, fire rings, and (usually) water. They cost $5 per site per night. Two primitive campgrounds on Snake Creek have pit toilets, but no water.

Getting There & Away Take Hwy 6/Hwy 50 about 30 miles east from the junction with Hwy 93, and fork right at Hwy 487. Follow that about 5 miles south to Baker. From there it's five miles west to the park visitors center.

Baker

Don't expect too much, as the population here is only about 50, but you can stay at *Silver Jack Motel* (☎ 234-7323), a friendly little place charging $29/35. *Whispering Elms* (☎ 234-7343) has tent sites for $5, RV spaces for $15, and motel units for $35. For food, there's the *Outlaw Family Restaurant,* and for a drink, drop by the *Hitchin' Post.*

ALONG HWY 95

This is the main highway going vaguely north-south through the western part of the state, though it's hardly a direct route

between Reno and Las Vegas. It zigzags to avoid mountain ranges, and to pass through places that were once big, important mining centers but are now not much more than ghost towns. The area is very sparsely populated.

Hawthorne

• *pop 4162* • *elev 4320 feet* ☎ *702*

Coming south from Fallon (see the Along Hwy 50 section, above), you pass Walker Lake, which is a lake, but also a village with gas, food, and a motel. The first real town is Hawthorne, with about 4000 people, one casino, and a half dozen motels. The **Mineral County Museum** has displays on mining and early pioneers that are worth a look; it's open Tuesday to Saturday from about noon to 4 pm. The surrounding desert is dotted with concrete bunkers storing millions of tons of munitions and explosives from the army's Hawthorne Ammunition Plant.

Tonopah

• *pop 3616* • *elev 6030 feet* ☎ *702*

The next town of any size, 104 miles on, Tonopah was once a major silver mining center. It still hangs on to its population, in a starkly beautiful desert setting. The **Central Nevada Museum** (☎ 482-9676) has a good collection of Shoshone baskets, early photographs, and mining relics collected from dozens of surrounding sites. It's open daily in the summer from 9 am to 5 pm; other seasons it's closed on Sunday and Monday.

The restored *Mizpah Hotel* (☎ 482-6202, 800-646-4641), 100 Main St, dates from 1908 and is the most elegant place to stay, and it isn't too expensive; call and ask about their dinner, room, and breakfast package. The *Station House Hotel & Casino* (☎ 482-9777) has good, cheap food, 24 hours a day, and live entertainment most nights. The *S & D Tonopah Inn* (☎ 482-6266) is one of the cheapest places to stay, at around $25/30, and the *Best Western Hi-Desert Inn* (482-3511, 800-528-1234) is about the best, at $42/48. All of these places are on Main St.

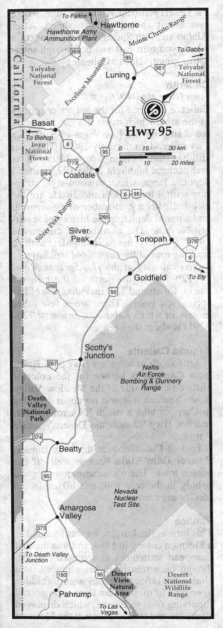

Hwy 95

0   15   30 km
0   10   20 miles

Goldfield

Another 25 miles south on Hwy 95 brings you to what was once the largest town in Nevada. It is now somewhat smaller, but it's still the seat of Esmeralda County (pop 1340).

Gold was discovered here in 1902, and the growth was spectacular – a tent city by 1903, it had a post office and railway station a year later, and over 10,000 people by 1907. Production and population peaked in 1910 with 20,000 people, then the decline was precipitous. The town flooded in 1913 (amazing to think of a flood in this place), the biggest mining company pulled out in 1919, and a fire in 1923 took out nearly all the buildings.

A few stone and brick structures survive, including the hotel, telephone exchange, high school, and the courthouse, which is still functioning. Another survivor is the *Santa Fe Saloon* (☎ 485-3431), an atmospheric place for a drink that has about the only accommodations in town.

Nevada Test Site

Continuing on Hwy 95 takes you past a boom area of another kind. To the east is the Nellis Air Force Bombing & Gunnery Range, and within it, the Nevada Test Site. In the 1950s, some 120 nuclear weapons were exploded in the atmosphere over the test site, and another 600 underground explosions were detonated over the next 30 years. The tests have now been discontinued following the Nuclear Test Ban Treaty, but a high incidence of cancer still shows up in the areas of southern Utah which were downwind of the atmospheric tests.

On the western edge of the test site is **Yucca Mountain**, a long, low ridge of volcanic rock, which the Department of Energy selected as the location for a high-level nuclear waste repository. Initially three sites were proposed, but Yucca Mountain is the only one now under consideration. The DOE has developed a specific proposal which is the subject of a feasibility study, due to be completed by 2001. Nevadans are divided on the proposal, a large project yielding jobs and revenue, that also has environmental risks that are difficult to assess, while no other part of the country seems willing to accept.

Highway 95 continues through Beatty, with side roads going west to Death Valley (see the California Deserts chapter). Along the way to Las Vegas, the mountains to the east have some of the most distinct and beautiful rainbow rock strata you'll see anywhere – maybe it's the radiation.

ALONG HWY 93

Highway 93 is a long road, extending from Canada down into Arizona, and is favored by snowbirds who pilot their RVs south every winter, and back north in the spring. It's the route you'd take from Las Vegas to the Great Basin National Park, passing great scenery, ghost towns, and few people.

From the south, Hwy 93 crosses the wall of the Hoover Dam, goes through Las Vegas, and joins I-15 for the next 22 miles. Diverging north, Hwy 93 goes alongside

the Desert National Wildlife Range, where you might spot a bighorn sheep. After Alamo and Ash Springs, there's a junction where you turn east and go through interesting countryside to Caliente.

Caliente

• *pop 1100* • *elev 4400 feet* ☎ *702*

Caliente is named for the hot water springs in the area, which made it a good location for a stop on the Las Vegas-to-Salt Lake City railroad, in the early 1900s. The town still has stone buildings from 1905, but its architectural highlight is the 1923 railroad depot, a large, white, mission-style structure with a long colonnade. Inside are the city hall, library, chamber of commerce, and a mural depicting the history of southern Nevada. The chamber of commerce (☎ 726-3129) has a pamphlet with a walking tour of the town's old buildings.

You can stay at the *Hot Springs Motel* (☎ 726-3777), just north of the railroad tracks, for around $33, including use of hot spring spa pools. There are a few other motels, of which *Rainbow Canyon* (☎ 726-3291) is about the cheapest.

Around Caliente

A little south of town, on Hwy 317, **Rainbow Canyon** is known for the colorful cliffs on either side of the Meadow Valley wash. You can follow it for about 40 miles to Carp, or take a rough back road which reaches Hwy 93 near the Desert Wildlife Range.

East of Caliente, near the Utah Border, **Beaver Dam State Park** is well off the beaten track. There's a campground, good fishing in the reservoir, and hiking in the forests and canyons.

Panaca

This little agricultural town was founded as a Mormon colony in 1864, and was the first European settlement in southern Nevada, though uncertain boundaries placed it in Utah until 1866. Mormons were forbidden to engage in mining, but Panaca prospered supplying food to Pioche, which displayed all the sin and lawlessness that the Mormon

To Ely   To Ely
318
Timpahute Range
White River
322
320 Pioche
Cathedral Panaca
Gorge
State Park 93
319
56
Caliente
To Cedar City
375
317
93
Ash Springs Rainbow Beaver Dam
Canyon State Park
Alamo Elgin
Utah
Pahranagat
National
Wildlife
Refuge
Carp

Hwy 93

Desert
National 0   25   50 km
Wildlife
Range 0   15   30 miles

93
Mesquite
168
Muddy River
Moapa 15 To St George
UT
To Beatty Moapa River
Indian 169
Reservation
Arizona
95
Lake Mead Lake
15 National Mead
To Barstow, Recreation
CA Las Vegas Area

leaders so rightly feared in a mining town. Panaca is just east of Hwy 93, on Hwy 319. Continuing on Hwy 319 brings you to Cedar City, Utah, which is a good base for trips to nearby Zion and Bryce Canyon National Parks and Cedar Breaks National Monument. (See Lonely Planet's *Southwest USA – travel survival kit* for more information on Utah.)

Cathedral Gorge State Park On the west side of Hwy 93, just north of the Panaca turnoff, this park is another one of Nevada's little known scenic treasures, with rows of spires and buttresses like a Gothic cathedral. There are some great little hikes into narrow side canyons, and a nice campground.

Pioche
• *pop 800* • *elev 6064 feet* ☎ *702*
Highway 93 actually bypasses this town; to get there take the Castleton loop (Hwy 320), which extends from Hwy 93 north and south of Pioche.

This old silver mining town was named after François Pioche who, in 1869, established the first successful mining and ore processing operation. By 1873, Pioche was 'a synonym for murder and lawlessness throughout the state,' according to one Nevada newspaper, and 'overrun with as desperate a class of scoundrels as probably ever afflicted any mining town.' These days the town is quiet, picturesque, not excessively prettied up, and full of great stories about its wild past. The **Lincoln County Museum**, on Main St, has leaflets that tell some of the local legends and a brochure with a walking tour of the town. Exhibits include a portable dental surgery from the days when dentists made mine calls. It's open daily and deserves a donation.

Another attraction, which is a legend in itself, is the old courthouse, around the corner on Lacour St. The building was started in 1871, subject to outrageous cost increases, and financed with funny bond issues which ultimately cost the county a

Hardware stores cropped up in all mining towns as savvy entrepreneurs moved in with overpriced supplies.

million dollars. Inside the 'million-dollar courthouse' are old photos, documents, and newspaper articles, the courtroom, sheriff's office, and jailhouse. It is open daily from 10 am to 1 pm, and 2 to 5 pm.

There are a couple of motels, including the *Motel Pioche* (☎ 962-5551), 80 yards past the courthouse on Lacour St, which costs about $35 in summer. Places to eat include *Nancy's*, the *Silver Café*, and the *Grub Steak*, which is recommended.

North of Pioche
Highway 93 follows a broad valley north for about 80 miles until it joins Hwy 50, where you can go east to the Great Basin National Park, or west to Ely (see the Along Hwy 50 section in this chapter). From Ely, Hwy 93 follows other valleys up to Wells (see Along I-80). This is the easy way to travel in the Great Basin, going between the ranges, not across them. North of Wells, Hwy 93 climbs into the mountains, and crosses the Idaho border at **Jackpot**, a town that thrives by providing gambling facilities for Idaho visitors. This northern edge of Nevada is actually outside the Great Basin – the Salmon River, which starts near Jackpot, eventually flows into the Columbia River and out to the Pacific Ocean.

Glossary

AAA – The American Automobile Association, also called the 'Auto Club' (see Useful Organizations). The Automobile Club of Southern California is the local branch of the federal organization.

adobe – A traditional Spanish-Mexican building material of sun-baked bricks of mud and straw; a structure built with this type of brick.

alien – An official term for a non-US citizen, visiting or resident in the USA (as in 'resident alien,' 'illegal alien,' etc).

Amtrak – The nation's federally sponsored railroad company.

Angeleno – A resident of Los Angeles.

antojito – (Spanish) An appetizer, snack, or light meal.

Arts & Crafts – A movement of architecture and design that gained popularity in America just after the turn of the 20th century; the style emphasizes simple craftsmanship and functional design, and emerged as a reaction to the perceived shoddiness of machine-made goods; also called (American) Craftsman.

ATM – Automated teller machine, the place to find crisp $20 bills (known in various parts of the country as Tyme machines, Cashpoints, etc).

ATV – All-terrain vehicle, used for off-road transportation, recreation, and environmental destruction.

back east – To Californians, the East Coast is 'back east,' even if they've never been to the East Coast.

BLM – Bureau of Land Management, an agency of the federal Department of the Interior which controls substantial portions of public lands in the West.

blue book – A guide that lists the average prices of used cars by year, make, and model; available in most libraries.

boomtown – a town that has experienced rapid economic and population growth. Many areas experienced such a boom during the Gold Rush, then 'busted' when the gold ran out, and became ghost towns.

booster – A person who promotes the interests and growth of their town or city, usually with a view to advancing their own business interests at the same time. Historically, boosters in California attempted to attract government facilities, private investments, and especially railroads to their areas.

Camino Real – (Spanish) The Royal Road, the road that links the chain of California missions. Also known as the King's Highway, the Camino Real is distinguished by its commemorative bell-shaped green streetlamps.

CCC – Civilian Conservation Corps, a Depression-era federal program established in 1933 to employ unskilled young men, mainly on projects aimed at the conservation of US wild lands.

Chicano/Chicana – A Mexican-American man/woman.

CHP – The California Highway Patrol.

cirque – A circular depression, often containing a lake, created on a mountainside by glacial action.

CNN – Cable News Network, a cable TV station based in Atlanta, Georgia, providing continuous bulletins of US and international news.

country & western – An amalgamation of rock and folk music of the Southern and Western USA. Line dancing and the two-step are dances associated with this music.

coyote – A small wild dog, native to the central and western North American lowlands; also, a person who assists illegal immigrants to cross the border into the USA.

DEA – Drug Enforcement Agency, the federal body responsible for enforcing the nation's drug laws.

Destinet – A toll-free reservation service for national parks across the country (see

Useful Organizations in Facts about California). Previously known as MYSTIX, Destinet takes reservations up to five months in advance (seven for California state parks).

docent – A guide or attendant at a museum or gallery.

entree – The main course of a meal.
epic – (slang) The best ever.

forty-niners – Immigrants to California during the 1849 Gold Rush; also, the San Francisco pro football team.

gated community – A walled residential area accessible only through security gates, common to Beverly Hills, Palm Springs, and similar affluent neighborhoods.
GOP – Grand Old Party, nickname of the Republican Party.

HI/AYH – Hostelling International/American Youth Hostels, a term given to hostels affiliated with Hostelling International, a member group of the IYHF (International Youth Hostel Federation).
hookup – A facility at an RV camping site for connecting (hooking up) a vehicle to an electricity, water, sewer, or cable TV system.

IHOP – International House of Pancakes, a low-budget restaurant chain specializing in breakfast.
INS – Immigration & Naturalization Service, the federal body, reporting to the Department of Justice, responsible for immigration and naturalization of aliens.
IRS – Internal Revenue Service, a branch of the US Treasury Department, responsible for administering and enforcing internal revenue laws; the tax collectors.

Joshua tree – A tall, treelike type of yucca plant, common to the arid Southwest. The Joshua Tree is said to have taken its name when a group of early Mormon settlers likened its curving branches to the outstretched arms of Joshua, leading them out of the wilderness.

KOA – Kampgrounds of America, a private chain of campgrounds throughout the USA, with extensive amenities and moderate- to high-priced sites for RVs and tents.
laguna – (Spanish) lagoon.

Latino/Latina – A man/woman of Latin-American descent.
LDS – From the Church of Jesus Christ of Latter-Day Saints, the formal name of the Mormon Church.

mariachi – (Spanish) Mexican street musicians, usually elaborately dressed, playing traditional folk songs on guitars and trumpets.
marine layer – A coastal fog in Southern California, sometimes mistaken for air pollution.
morteros – Hollows in rocks used by Native Americans for grinding seeds; also called mortar holes.

NAACP – National Association for the Advancement of Colored People.
National Guard – Each state's federally supported military reserves, used most often in civil emergencies. The National Guard can be called into action either by the state's governor or by Congress, for federal service, at any time.
National Register of Historic Places – A listing of historic sites designated by the NPS, based on evidence supporting a structure's significance in the development of a community. Being listed on the National Register restricts property owners from making major structural changes to buildings, but also provides tax incentives for their preservation.
National Recreation Area – A term used to describe NPS units in areas of considerable scenic or ecological importance that have been modified by human activity, such as by major dam projects.
nevada – (Spanish) snowy; snow-covered.
NOW – National Organization for Women, strong proponents of women's issues, using education, politics, and legal action to improve the political and economic status of American women.

NPR – National Public Radio, a non-commercial, listener-supported broadcast organization that produces and distributes news, public affairs, and cultural programming via a network of loosely affiliated radio stations throughout the USA.

NPS – National Park Service, a division of the Department of the Interior which administers US national parks and monuments.

NRA – National Rifle Association, an influential lobby generally opposed to gun-control legislation of any kind.

OHV or **ORV** – An off-highway vehicle or off-road vehicle.

PBS – Public Broadcasting System, a non-commercial television network known for nature shows, British imports, and Pavarotti. The television equivalent of NPR.

pc – Politically correct; also, personal computer.

petroglyph – A work of rock art where the design is pecked, chipped, or abraded into the surface of the rock.

PGA – Professional Golfers' Association.

pictograph – A work of rock art where the design is painted on rock surface with one or more colors.

pound symbol – In the USA, # is called the pound symbol (or pound key on a telephone), not £.

PST – Pacific Standard Time, the time zone of the West Coast states and Nevada.

RV – Recreational vehicle, also known as a 'motor home.'

Santa Ana – A strong, dry, hot wind blowing from the California deserts toward the Pacific coast, usually in winter.

sierra – (Spanish) Mountain range.

skank, skanky – (slang) Sleazily unattractive.

So Cal – Southern California.

spot trip – Tour on which an outfitter carries your gear (and you, if desired) to a chosen destination and either leaves you to hike out or picks you up days or weeks later.

SSN – Social Security Number, a nine-digit code required as identification for employment and receiving social security benefits.

strip mall – a collection of businesses arranged around a parking lot, in an often-tacky, neon-lit row or 'strip,' designed to lure consumers by their proximity to one another.

USAF – United States Air Force.

USFS – United States Forest Service, a division of the Department of Agriculture which implements policies on federal forest lands on the principles of 'multiple use,' including timber cutting, wildlife management, and camping and recreation.

USGS – United States Geological Survey, an agency of the Department of the Interior responsible for, among other things, detailed topographic maps of the entire country. Widely available at outdoor-oriented businesses, USGS maps are particularly popular with hikers and backpackers.

USMC – United States Marine Corps, a branch of the armed forces which enforces US policy abroad. Though reporting to the Department of the Navy, the marines have their own ships, artillery, and aircraft, and are usually the first US forces dispatched to any foreign trouble spot.

wash – A watercourse in the desert, usually dry but subject to flash flooding.

WPA – Works Progress (later, Work Projects) Administration, a Depression-era program established under the Roosevelt administration in 1935 as part of the New Deal, to increase employment by funding public works projects. WPA projects included road and building construction, beautification of public structures (especially post offices), and the publication of a well-respected series of state and regional guidebooks.

ZIP code – A five- or nine-digit postal code introduced under the Zone Improvement Program to expedite the sorting and delivery of US mail.

Appendix – Climate Charts

Los Angeles, CA

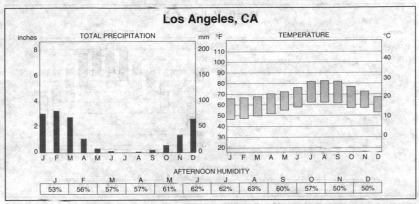

TOTAL PRECIPITATION

TEMPERATURE

AFTERNOON HUMIDITY

J	F	M	A	M	J	J	A	S	O	N	D
53%	56%	57%	57%	61%	62%	62%	63%	60%	57%	50%	50%

San Francisco, CA

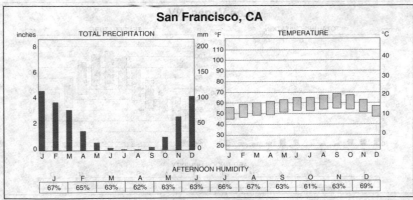

TOTAL PRECIPITATION

TEMPERATURE

AFTERNOON HUMIDITY

J	F	M	A	M	J	J	A	S	O	N	D
67%	65%	63%	62%	63%	63%	66%	67%	63%	61%	63%	69%

Yosemite, CA

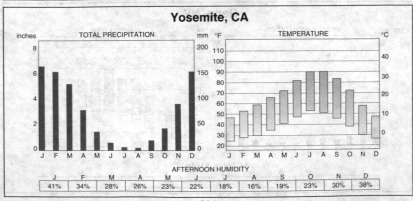

TOTAL PRECIPITATION

TEMPERATURE

AFTERNOON HUMIDITY

J	F	M	A	M	J	J	A	S	O	N	D
41%	34%	28%	26%	23%	22%	18%	16%	19%	23%	30%	38%

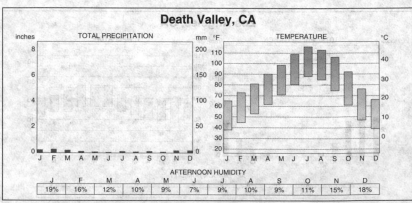

Death Valley, CA

TOTAL PRECIPITATION	TEMPERATURE

AFTERNOON HUMIDITY

J	F	M	A	M	J	J	A	S	O	N	D
19%	16%	12%	10%	9%	7%	9%	10%	9%	11%	15%	18%

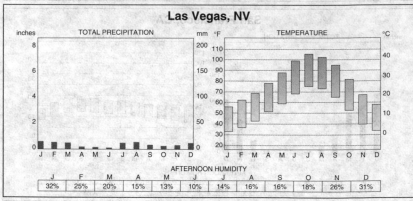

Las Vegas, NV

TOTAL PRECIPITATION	TEMPERATURE

AFTERNOON HUMIDITY

J	F	M	A	M	J	J	A	S	O	N	D
32%	25%	20%	15%	13%	10%	14%	16%	16%	18%	26%	31%

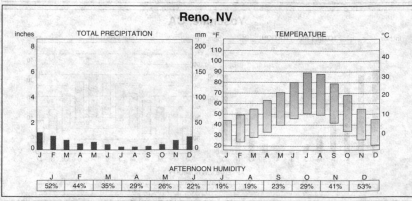

Reno, NV

TOTAL PRECIPITATION	TEMPERATURE

AFTERNOON HUMIDITY

J	F	M	A	M	J	J	A	S	O	N	D
52%	44%	35%	29%	26%	22%	19%	19%	23%	29%	41%	53%

Index

LONELY PLANET PHRASEBOOKS

Building bridges,
Breaking barriers,
Beyond babble-on

Nepali phrasebook

Ethiopian Amharic phrasebook

Latin American Spanish phrasebook

Ukrainian phrasebook

Greek phrasebook

Vietnamese phrasebook

Listen for the gems

Speak your own words

Ask your own questions.

Master of your own image

- handy pocket-sized books
- easy to understand Pronunciation chapter
- clear and comprehensive Grammar chapter
- romanisation alongside script to allow ease of pronunciation
- script throughout so users can point to phrases
- extensive vocabulary sections, words and phrases for every situation
- full of cultural information and tips for the traveller

'...vital for a real DIY spirit and attitude in language learning' – Backpacker

'the phrasebooks have good cultural backgrounders and offer solid advice for challenging situations in remote locations' – San Francisco Examiner

'...they are unbeatable for their coverage of the world's more obscure languages' – The Geographical Magazine

---

Arabic (Egyptian)
Arabic (Moroccan)
Australia
  Australian English, Aboriginal and Torres Strait languages
Baltic States
  Estonian, Latvian, Lithuanian
Bengali
Brazilian
Burmese
Cantonese
Central Asia
Central Europe
  Czech, French, German, Hungarian, Italian and Slovak
Eastern Europe
  Bulgarian, Czech, Hungarian, Polish, Romanian and Slovak
Ethiopian (Amharic)
Fijian
French
German
Greek

Hindi/Urdu
Indonesian
Italian
Japanese
Korean
Lao
Latin American Spanish
Malay
Mandarin
Mediterranean Europe
  Albanian, Croatian, Greek, Italian, Macedonian, Maltese, Serbian and Slovene
Mongolian
Nepali
Papua New Guinea
Pilipino (Tagalog)
Quechua
Russian
Scandinavian Europe
  Danish, Finnish, Icelandic, Norwegian and Swedish

South-East Asia
  Burmese, Indonesian, Khmer, Lao, Malay, Tagalog (Pilipino), Thai and Vietnamese
Spanish (Castilian)
  Basque, Catalan and Galician
Sri Lanka
Swahili
Thai
Thai Hill Tribes
Tibetan
Turkish
Ukrainian
USA
  US English, Vernacular, Native American languages and Hawaiian
Vietnamese
Western Europe
  Basque, Catalan, Dutch, French, German, Irish, Italian, Portuguese, Scottish Gaelic, Spanish (Castilian) and Welsh

---

LONELY PLANET JOURNEYS

JOURNEYS is a unique collection of travel writing – published by the company that understands travel better than anyone else. It is a series for anyone who has ever experienced – or dreamed of – the magical moment when they encountered a strange culture or saw a place for the first time. They are tales to read while you're planning a trip, while you're on the road or while you're in an armchair, in front of a fire.

JOURNEYS books catch the spirit of a place, illuminate a culture, recount a crazy adventure, or introduce a fascinating way of life. They always entertain, and always enrich the experience of travel.

'Idiosyncratic, entertainingly diverse and unexpected . . . from an international writership'
– **The Australian**

'Books which offer a closer look at the people and culture of a destination, and enrich travel experiences'
– **American Bookseller**

FULL CIRCLE
A South American Journey
Luis Sepúlveda
Translated by Chris Andrews

Full Circle invites us to accompany Chilean writer Luis Sepúlveda on 'a journey without a fixed itinerary'. Whatever his subject – brutalities suffered under Pinochet's dictatorship, sleepy tropical towns visited in exile, or the landscapes of legendary Patagonia – Sepúlveda is an unflinchingly honest yet lyrical storyteller. Extravagant characters and extraordinary situations are memorably evoked: gauchos organising a tournament of lies, a scheming heiress on the lookout for a husband, a pilot with a corpse on board his plane . . . Part autobiography, part travel memoir, *Full Circle* brings us the distinctive voice of one of South America's most compelling writers.

Luis Sepúlveda was born in Chile in 1949. Imprisoned by the Pinochet dictatorship for his socialist beliefs, he was for many years a political exile. He has written novels, short stories, plays and essays. His work has attracted many awards and has been translated into numerous languages.

'Detachment, humour and vibrant prose' – **El País**

'an absolute cracker' – **The Bookseller**

This project has been assisted by the Commonwealth Government through the Australia Council, its arts funding and advisory body.

LONELY PLANET TRAVEL ATLASES

Lonely Planet has long been famous for the number and quality of its guidebook maps. Now we've gone one step further and produced a handy companion series: Lonely Planet travel atlases – maps of a country produced in book form.

Unlike other maps, which look good but lead travellers astray, our travel atlases have been researched on the road by Lonely Planet's experienced team of writers. All details are carefully checked to ensure the atlas corresponds with the equivalent Lonely Planet guidebook.

The handy atlas format means no holes, wrinkles, torn sections or constant folding and unfolding. These atlases can survive long periods on the road, unlike cumbersome fold-out maps. The comprehensive index ensures easy reference.

- full-colour throughout
- maps researched and checked by Lonely Planet authors
- place names correspond with Lonely Planet guidebooks
  – no confusing spelling differences
- legend and travelling information in English, French, German, Japanese and Spanish
- size: 230 x 160 mm

Available now:
Chile & Easter Island • Egypt • India & Bangladesh • Israel & the Palestinian Territories •Jordan, Syria & Lebanon • Kenya • Laos • Portugal • South Africa, Lesotho & Swaziland • Thailand • Turkey • Vietnam • Zimbabwe, Botswana & Namibia

LONELY PLANET TV SERIES & VIDEOS

Lonely Planet travel guides have been brought to life on television screens around the world. Like our guides, the programmes are based on the joy of independent travel, and look honestly at some of the most exciting, picturesque and frustrating places in the world. Each show is presented by one of three travellers from Australia, England or the USA and combines an innovative mixture of video, Super-8 film, atmospheric soundscapes and original music.

Videos of each episode – containing additional footage not shown on television – are available from good book and video shops, but the availability of individual videos varies with regional screening schedules.

Video destinations include: Alaska • American Rockies • Australia – The South-East • Baja California & the Copper Canyon • Brazil • Central Asia • Chile & Easter Island • Corsica, Sicily & Sardinia – The Mediterranean Islands • East Africa (Tanzania & Zanzibar) • Ecuador & the Galapagos Islands • Greenland & Iceland • Indonesia • Israel & the Sinai Desert • Jamaica • Japan • La Ruta Maya • Morocco • New York • North India • Pacific Islands (Fiji, Solomon Islands & Vanuatu) • South India • South West China • Turkey • Vietnam • West Africa • Zimbabwe, Botswana & Namibia

The Lonely Planet TV series is produced by:
Pilot Productions
The Old Studio
18 Middle Row
London W10 5AT UK

For video availability and ordering information contact your nearest Lonely Planet office.

Music from the TV series is available on CD & cassette.

PLANET TALK

Lonely Planet's FREE quarterly newsletter

We love hearing from you and think you'd like to hear from us.

When...is the right time to see reindeer in Finland?
Where...can you hear the best palm-wine music in Ghana?
How...do you get from Asunción to Areguá by steam train?
What...is the best way to see India?

For the answer to these and many other questions read PLANET TALK.

Every issue is packed with up-to-date travel news and advice including:

- a letter from Lonely Planet co-founders Tony and Maureen Wheeler
- go behind the scenes on the road with a Lonely Planet author
- feature article on an important and topical travel issue
- a selection of recent letters from travellers
- details on forthcoming Lonely Planet promotions
- complete list of Lonely Planet products

To join our mailing list contact any Lonely Planet office.

Also available: Lonely Planet T-shirts. 100% heavyweight cotton.

LONELY PLANET ONLINE

Get the latest travel information before you leave or while you're on the road

Whether you've just begun planning your next trip, or you're chasing down specific info on currency regulations or visa requirements, check out Lonely Planet Online for up-to-the minute travel information.

As well as travel profiles of your favourite destinations (including maps and photos), you'll find current reports from our researchers and other travellers, updates on health and visas, travel advisories, and discussion of the ecological and political issues you need to be aware of as you travel.

There's also an online travellers' forum where you can share your experience of life on the road, meet travel companions and ask other travellers for their recommendations and advice. We also have plenty of links to other online sites useful to independent travellers.

And of course we have a complete and up-to-date list of all Lonely Planet travel products including guides, phrasebooks, atlases, Journeys and videos and a simple online ordering facility if you can't find the book you want elsewhere.

www.lonelyplanet.com
or
AOL keyword: lp

LONELY PLANET PRODUCTS

Lonely Planet is known worldwide for publishing practical, reliable and no-nonsense travel information in our guides and on our web site. The Lonely Planet list covers just about every accessible part of the world. Currently there are nine series: *travel guides, shoestring guides, walking guides, city guides, phrasebooks, audio packs, travel atlases, Journeys – a unique collection of travel writing and Pisces Books - diving and snorkeling guides.*

EUROPE

Amsterdam • Andalucia • Austria • Baltic States phrasebook • Berlin • Britain • Canary Islands• Central Europe on a shoestring • Central Europe phrasebook • Czech & Slovak Republics • Denmark • Dublin • Eastern Europe on a shoestring • Eastern Europe phrasebook • Estonia, Latvia & Lithuania • Finland • France • French phrasebook • Germany • German phrasebook • Greece • Greek phrasebook • Hungary • Iceland, Greenland & the Faroe Islands • Ireland • Italian phrasebook • Italy • Lisbon • London • Mediterranean Europe on a shoestring • Mediterranean Europe phrasebook • Paris • Poland • Portugal • Portugal travel atlas • Prague • Romania & Moldova • Russia, Ukraine & Belarus • Russian phrasebook • Scandinavian & Baltic Europe on a shoestring • Scandinavian Europe phrasebook • Slovenia • Spain • Spanish phrasebook • St Petersburg • Switzerland •Trekking in Spain • Ukrainian phrasebook • Vienna • Walking in Britain • Walking in Italy • Walking in Switzerland • Western Europe on a shoestring • Western Europe phrasebook

Travel Literature: The Olive Grove: Travels in Greece

NORTH AMERICA

Alaska • Backpacking in Alaska • Baja California • California & Nevada • Canada • Chicago • Deep South• Florida • Hawaii • Honolulu • Los Angeles • Mexico • Mexico City • Miami • New England • New Orleans • New York City • New York, New Jersey & Pennsylvania • Pacific Northwest USA • Rocky Mountain States • San Francisco • Seattle • Southwest USA • USA phrasebook • Washington, DC & the Capital Region

Travel Literature: Drive thru America

CENTRAL AMERICA & THE CARIBBEAN

• Bahamas and Turks & Caicos • Bermuda • Central America on a shoestring • Costa Rica • Cuba • Eastern Caribbean • Guatemala, Belize & Yucatán: La Ruta Maya • Jamaica

Travel Literature Green Dreams: Travels in Central America

SOUTH AMERICA

Argentina, Uruguay & Paraguay • Bolivia • Brazil • Brazilian phrasebook • Buenos Aires • Chile & Easter Island • Chile & Easter Island travel atlas • Colombia Ecuador & the Galápagos Islands • Latin American Spanish phrasebook • Peru • Quechua phrasebook • Rio de Janeiro • South America on a shoestring • Trekking in the Patagonian Andes • Venezuela

Travel Literature: Full Circle: A South American Journey

ISLANDS OF THE INDIAN OCEAN

Madagascar & Comoros • Maldives • Mauritius, Réunion & Seychelles

AFRICA

Africa - the South • Africa on a shoestring • Arabic (Moroccan) phrasebook • Cairo • Cape Town • Central Africa • East Africa • Egypt • Egypt travel atlas• Ethiopian (Amharic) phrasebook • The Gambia & Senegal • Kenya • Kenya travel atlas • Malawi, Mozambique & Zambia • Morocco • North Africa • South Africa, Lesotho & Swaziland • South Africa, Lesotho & Swaziland travel atlas • Swahili phrasebook • Tunisia • Trekking in East Africa • West Africa • Zimbabwe, Botswana & Namibia • Zimbabwe, Botswana & Namibia travel atlas

Travel Literature: Mali Blues • The Rainbird: A Central African Journey • Songs to an African Sunset: A Zimbabwean Story